DATE DUE

			PRINTED IN U.S.A.

Poetry Criticism

Guide to Gale Literary Criticism Series

For criticism on	Consult these Gale series
Authors now living or who died after December 31, 1959	*CONTEMPORARY LITERARY CRITICISM (CLC)*
Authors who died between 1900 and 1959	*TWENTIETH-CENTURY LITERARY CRITICISM (TCLC)*
Authors who died between 1800 and 1899	*NINETEENTH-CENTURY LITERATURE CRITICISM (NCLC)*
Authors who died between 1400 and 1799	*LITERATURE CRITICISM FROM 1400 TO 1800 (LC)* *SHAKESPEAREAN CRITICISM (SC)*
Authors who died before 1400	*CLASSICAL AND MEDIEVAL LITERATURE CRITICISM (CMLC)*
Black writers of the past two hundred years	*BLACK LITERATURE CRITICISM (BLC)*
Authors of books for children and young adults	*CHILDREN'S LITERATURE REVIEW (CLR)*
Dramatists	*DRAMA CRITICISM (DC)*
Hispanic writers of the late nineteenth and twentieth centuries	*HISPANIC LITERATURE CRITICISM (HLC)*
Native North American writers and orators of the eighteenth, nineteenth, and twentieth centuries	*NATIVE NORTH AMERICAN LITERATURE (NNAL)*
Poets	*POETRY CRITICISM (PC)*
Short story writers	*SHORT STORY CRITICISM (SSC)*
Major authors from the Renaissance to the present	*WORLD LITERATURE CRITICISM, 1500 TO THE PRESENT (WLC)*

Poetry Criticism

Excerpts from Criticism of the Works of the Most Significant and Widely Studied Poets of World Literature

VOLUME 10

Drew Kalasky
Jane Kelly Kosek
Editors

Gale Research Inc.

An International Thomson Publishing Company

I(T)P

NEW YORK • LONDON • BONN • BOSTON • DETROIT • MADRID
MELBOURNE • MEXICO CITY • PARIS • SINGAPORE • TOKYO
TORONTO • WASHINGTON • ALBANY NY • BELMONT CA • CINCINNATI OH

Library of Congress Catalog Card Number 91-118494
ISBN 0-8103-5614-7
ISSN 1052-4851

Printed in the United States of America
Published simultaneously in the United Kingdom
by Gale Research International Limited
(An affiliated company of Gale Research Inc.)
10 9 8 7 6 5 4 3 2 1

Contents

Preface vii

Acknowledgments xi

Preface

A Comprehensive Information Source on World Poetry

P *oetry Criticism (PC)* provides substantial critical excerpts and biographical information on poets throughout the world who are most frequently studied in high school and undergraduate college courses. Each *PC* entry is supplemented by biographical and bibliographical material to help guide the user to a fuller understanding of the genre and its creators. Although major poets and literary movements are covered in such Gale Literary Criticism Series as *Contemporary Literary Criticism (CLC)*, *Twentieth-Century Literary Criticism (TCLC)*, *Nineteenth-Century Literature Criticism (NCLC)*, *Literature Criticism from 1400 to 1800 (LC)*, and *Classical and Medieval Literature Criticism (CMLC)*, *PC* offers more focused attention on poetry than is possible in the broader, survey-oriented entries on writers in these Gale series. Students, teachers, librarians, and researchers will find that the generous excerpts and supplementary material provided by *PC* supply them with vital information needed to write a term paper on poetic technique, examine a poet's most prominent themes, or lead a poetry discussion group.

Coverage

In order to reflect the influence of tradition as well as innovation, poets of various nationalities, eras, and movements are represented in every volume of *PC*. Each author entry presents a historical survey of the critical response to that author's work; the length of an entry reflects the amount of critical attention that the author has received from critics writing in English and from foreign critics in translation. Since many poets have inspired a prodigious amount of critical explication, *PC* is necessarily selective, and the editors have chosen the most significant published criticism to aid readers and students in their research. In order to provide these important critical pieces, the editors will sometimes reprint essays that have appeared in previous volumes of Gale's Literary Criticism Series. Such duplication, however, never exceeds fifteen percent of a *PC* volume.

Organization

Each *PC* author entry consists of the following components:

- **Author Heading:** the name under which the author wrote appears at the beginning of the entry, followed by birth and death dates. If the author wrote consistently under a pseudonym, the pseudonym will be listed in the author heading and his or her legal name given in parentheses in the lines immediately preceding the Introduction. Uncertainty as to birth or death dates is indicated by question marks.

- **Introduction:** a biographical and critical essay introduces readers to the author and the critical discussions surrounding his or her work.

- **Author Portrait:** a photograph or illustration of the author is included when available. Most entries also feature illustrations of people and places pertinent to an author's career, as well as holographs of manuscript pages and dust jackets.

- **Principal Works:** the author's most important works are identified in a list ordered chronologically by first publication dates. The first section comprises poetry collections and book-length poems. The second section gives information on other major works by the author. For foreign authors, original foreign-language publication information is provided, as well as the best and most complete English-language editions of their works.

- **Criticism:** critical excerpts chronologically arranged in each author entry provide perspective on changes in critical evaluation over the years. All individual titles of poems and poetry collections by the author featured in the entry are printed in boldface type to enable a reader to ascertain without difficulty the works under discussion. For purposes of easy identification, the critic's name and the publication date of the essay are given at the beginning of each piece of criticism. Unsigned criticism is preceded by the title of the journal in which it originally appeared. Publication information (such as publisher names and book prices) and parenthetical numerical references (such as footnotes or page and line references to specific editions of a work) have been deleted at the editor's discretion to enable smoother reading of the text.

- **Explanatory Notes:** introductory comments preface each critical excerpt, providing several types of useful information, including: the reputation of a critic, the importance of a work of criticism, and the specific type of criticism (biographical, psychoanalytic, historical, etc.).

- **Author Commentary:** insightful comments from the authors themselves and excerpts from author interviews are included when available.

- **Bibliographical Citations:** information preceding each piece of criticism guides the interested reader to the original essay or book.

- **Further Reading:** bibliographic references accompanied by descriptive notes at the end of each entry suggest additional materials for study of the author. Boxed material following the Further Reading provides references to other biographical and critical series published by Gale.

Other Features

Cumulative Author Index: comprises all authors who have appeared in Gale's Literary Criticism Series, along with cross-references to such Gale biographical series as *Contemporary Authors* and *Dictionary of Literary Biography*. This cumulated index enables the user to locate an author within the various series.

Cumulative Nationality Index: includes all authors featured in *PC,* arranged alphabetically under their respective nationalities.

Cumulative Title Index: lists in alphabetical order all individual poems, book-length poems, and collection titles contained in the *PC* series. Titles of poetry collections and separately published poems are printed in italics, while titles of individual poems are printed in roman type with quotation marks. Each title is followed by the author's name and the volume and page number corresponding to the location of commentary on specific works. English-language translations of original foreign-language titles are cross-referenced to the foreign titles so that all references to discussion of a work are combined in one listing.

Citing *Poetry Criticism*

When writing papers, students who quote directly from any volume in the Literary Criticism Series may use the following general formats to footnote reprinted criticism. The first example pertains to material drawn from periodicals, the second to material reprinted from books:

[1]David Daiches, "W. H. Auden: The Search for a Public," *Poetry* LIV (June 1939), 148-56; excerpted and reprinted in *Poetry Criticism*, Vol. 1, ed. Robyn V. Young (Detroit: Gale Research, 1990), pp. 7-9.

[2]Pamela J. Annas, *A Disturbance in Mirrors: The Poetry of Sylvia Plath* (Greenwood Press, 1988); excerpted and reprinted in *Poetry Criticism*, Vol. 1, ed. Robyn V. Young (Detroit: Gale Research, 1990), pp. 410-14.

Comments Are Welcome

Readers who wish to suggest authors to appear in future volumes, or who have other suggestions, are cordially invited to contact the editors.

Acknowledgments

The editors wish to thank the copyright holders of the excerpted criticism included in this volume, the permissions managers of many book and magazine publishing companies for assisting us in securing reprint rights. We are also grateful to the staffs of the Detroit Public Library, the Library of Congress, the University of Detroit Mercy Library, Wayne State University Purdy/Kresge Library Complex, and the University of Michigan Libraries for making their resources available to us. Following is a list of the copyright holders who have granted us permission to reprint material in this volume of *PC.* Every effort has been made to trace copyright, but if omissions have been made, please let us know.

COPYRIGHTED EXCERPTS IN *PC*, VOLUME 10, WERE REPRINTED FROM THE FOLLOWING PERIODICALS:

The American Book Review, v. 12, March-April, 1990. © 1990 by *The American Book Review.* Reprinted by permission of the publisher.—*American Literature,* v. 42, March, 1970. Copyright © 1970 Duke University Press, Durham, NC. Reprinted by permission of the publisher.—*American Poetry,* v. 3, Spring, 1986. © 1986 by Lee Bartlett and Peter White. All rights reserved. Reprinted by permission of the publisher.—*The American Poetry Review,* v. 5, November-December, 1976 for a review of "Gathering the Tribes" by Stanley Plumly; v. 10, January-February, 1981 for "The Real and Only Sanity" by Geoffrey Gardner; v. 12, January-February, 1983 for "Towards An American Criticism: A Reading of Carolyn Forché's 'The Country between Us' " by Sharon Dubiago. Copyright © 1976, 1981, 1983 by World Poetry, Inc. All reprinted by permission of the respective authors.—*Ariel: A Review of International English Literature,* v. 1, April, 1970. Copyright © 1970 The Board of Governors, The University of Calgary. Reprinted by permission of the publisher.—*Book Forum,* v. 11, 1976 for "Tribal World of Carolyn Forché" by Eleanor Lerman. Copyright © 1976 by The Hudson River Press. Reprinted by permission of the author.—*The British Library Journal,* v. 5, Autumn, 1979 for "Innocence and Experience in the Poetry of Andrew Marvell" by George deF. Lord. Reprinted by permission of the publisher and the author.—*California Studies in Classical Antiquity,* v. 3, 1970 for "*Lascivia* vs. *ira*: Martial and Juvenal" by William S. Anderson. Reprinted by permission of the University of California Press and the author.—*The Centennial Review,* v. XIII, 1969 for "Reading Marvell's 'Garden' " by Joseph H. Summers. © 1969 by *The Centennial Review.* Reprinted by permission of the publisher and the author.—*CLIO,* v. 1, October, 1971 for "The Dialectic of History in Marvell's 'Horatian Ode' " by Thomas W. Hayes. © 1971 by Robert H. Canary and Henry Kozicki. Reprinted by permission of the author.—*The Commonweal,* v. XLII, June 22, 1945. Copyright 1945 Commonweal Publishing Co., Inc. Reprinted by permission of Commonweal Foundation.—*Comparative Literature Studies,* v. XVIII, June, 1981. Copyright © 1981 by The Pennsylvania State University. Reproduced by permission of The Pennsylvania State University Press.—*Detroit Free Press,* May 22, 1994 for "Inspired by War" by Kevin Walker. Reprinted by permission of the author.—*Early American Literature,* v. XXIII, Summer, 1988 for " 'To Finish What's Begun': Anne Bradstreet's Last Words" by Paula Kopacz; v. XXIII Fall, 1988 for "Anne Bradstreet Wrestlers with the Renaissance" by Ivy Schweitzer; v. XXIV, Spring, 1989 for " 'Then Have I...Said with David': Anne Bradstreet's Andover Manuscript Poems with the Influence of the Psalm Tradition" by Beth M. Doriani. Copyrighted, 1988, 1989, by the University of Massachusetts. All reprinted by permission of the publisher and the respective authors./v. IX, Spring, 1974. Copyrighted, 1974, by the University of Massachusetts. Reprinted by permission of the publisher.—*English Literary Renaissance,* v. 9, Winter, 1978. Copyright © 1978 by *English Literary Renaissance.* Reprinted by permission of the publisher.—*Essays in Criticism,* v. XX, October, 1970 for "Marvell's Effortless Superiority" by John Creaser. Reprinted by permission of the Editors of *Essays in Criticism* and the author.—*The Georgia Review,* v. XXXVI, Winter, 1982. Copyright, 1982, by the University of Georgia. Reprinted by permission of the publisher.—*The Hudson Review,* v. XXIII, Spring, 1970; v. XXXI, Summer, 1978. Copyright © 1970, 1978 by The Hudson Review, Inc. Both reprinted by permission of the publisher.—*The Kentucky Review,* v. VII, Summer, 1987. Copyright © 1987 by the University of Kentucky Libraries. Reprinted by permission of the publisher.—*Literature and Medicine,* v. 4, 1985. Copyright © 1985 by The Johns Hopkins University Press.

COPYRIGHTED EXCERPTS IN *PC,* VOLUME 10, WERE REPRINTED FROM THE FOLLOWING BOOKS:

PHOTOGRAPHS AND ILLUSTRATIONS APPEARING IN *PC*, VOLUME 10, WERE RECEIVED FROM THE FOLLOWING SOURCES:

Anne Bradstreet

1612(?)-1672

(Full name Anne Dudley Bradstreet) American poet and prose writer.

INTRODUCTION

Bradstreet was America's first published poet and the first woman to produce a lasting volume of poetry in the English language. Her work is considered particularly significant for its expression of passion, anger, and uncertainty within the rigid social and religious atmosphere of Puritan New England, and for the insight it provides into the lives of women from that period.

Biographical Information

Bradstreet was born in England to a Puritan family. Her father, Thomas Dudley, was steward to the Earl of Lincoln, a leading nonconformist in the religious strife of England. Because of her father's high position and the availability of the Earl's extensive library, Bradstreet's education was unusually comprehensive for a woman of her time. In 1630 she moved with her husband and her parents to the Massachusetts Bay Colony, where her husband and father served as governors of the settlement. As a New England colonist, Bradstreet encountered a life of hardship to which she was unaccustomed. In 1647 her brother-in-law returned to England, taking with him the manuscript of Bradstreet's poems. He published them without her knowledge, entitling the collection *The Tenth Muse*. The volume met with immediate success in London. Surprised by the work's reception, though unhappy with its unpolished state, Bradstreet undertook to revise the poems, some of which were lost in the fire that destroyed the Bradstreet home in 1666. Six years after her death the revisions and some new poems were published under the title *Several Poems*. Bradstreet's prose meditations and later poems did not appear in print until 1867.

Major Works

Most of Bradstreet's works may be placed into one of two distinct periods. The "public" poems that appeared in *The Tenth Muse* are structurally and thematically formal, written in the style of Renaissance poetry. The *Quaternions*, which consist of four poems, each of which are divided into four parts, treat the humours, elements, seasons, and ages of man, and are imitative of Guillaume Du Bartas's *Divine Weeks and Works*. "The Four Monarchies" is a long unfinished poem, patterned after Sir Walter Raleigh's *The History of the World*, describing what were considered the four great monarchies of civilization. The elegies contained in *The Tenth Muse* are dedications to public figures such as Queen Elizabeth I and Sir Philip Sidney. Bradstreet's later poems—described by most

scholars as her "private" poems—are less stylized in form and more personal in content. In these works, Bradstreet expressed anxiety about her health and the safety of her family, passionate love for her husband, and uncertainty over her religious devotion. The elegies "In Memory of My Dear Grandchild Elizabeth Bradstreet" and "To the Memory of My Dear Daughter in Law, Mrs. Mercy Bradstreet" are poignant meditations on death in which Bradstreet questions her religious faith. In "Some Verses Upon the Burning of Our House, July 10th, 1666," she mourned the loss of all her possessions despite the Puritan ideal positing the primacy of spiritual rewards over the pleasures of worldly goods and experiences; yet she concluded the poem with a sense of resignation and faith. As Wendy Martin has noted: "Much of [Bradstreet's] work indicates that she had a difficult time resolving the conflict she experienced between the pleasures of sensory and familial experience and the promises of heaven. As a Puritan she struggled to subdue her attachment to the world, but as

1

a woman she sometimes felt more strongly connected to her husband, children, and community than to God." Bradstreet's poems to her husband Simon contain erotic symbolism noted by many critics. Her most critically acclaimed poem, "Contemplations," evidences an appreciation of nature and solitude similar to that found in the work of the later Romantic poets.

Critical Reception

Bradstreet was praised in her own time for the formal poetry of *The Tenth Muse*, which adhered to courtly standards and thus marked her as highly talented. Afterwards, she was largely ignored by critics until the late nineteenth century, when a volume of her later poems was published for the first time. Commentators then offered little praise, viewing her poetry as a slight exception to what nineteenth-century readers perceived as the artless, repressive nature of Puritanism. In the mid-twentieth century, feminist critics took note of Bradstreet's work, recognizing the paradoxes she explored between religious doctrine and individual belief and the often blatant sexual imagery in both her poems to her husband and her poems addressing God. While Bradstreet's public poetry is now considered stilted and overly imitative, her private poetry is acclaimed for its deft use of ballad and lyric forms and its insightful exploration of complex personal issues.

PRINCIPAL WORKS

Poetry

The Tenth Muse, Lately sprung up in America 1650
Several Poems Compiled with great variety of Wit and Learning, full of Delight 1678
The Works of Anne Bradstreet in Prose and Verse (poetry and meditations) 1867
The Works of Anne Bradstreet (poetry and meditations) 1967
The Complete Works of Anne Bradstreet (poetry and meditations) 1981

CRITICISM

Elizabeth Wade White (essay date 1951)

SOURCE: "The Tenth Muse—A Tercentenary Appraisal of Anne Bradstreet," in *The William and Mary Quarterly*, Vol. VIII, No. 3, July, 1951, pp. 355-77.

[*White is the author of the biography* Anne Bradstreet: The Tenth Muse *(1971). In the following essay, she appraises Bradstreet's first book of poems on the 300th anniversary of its publication.*]

On the first day of July, 1650, there was entered in the register of the Company of Stationers of the City of London,

and six-pence duly paid for the entry, "a booke called The Tenth Muse lately sprung up in America, written by Ann Bradstreet." The book appeared in print in the same year as a modest duodecimo, bound in calf and measuring only five and one-half by three and three-quarters inches in size. Yet its two hundred and seven small pages contain a collection of poems larger in volume and more varied in subject than any previously printed work by an English woman poet. It is also the first published book of original poetry by a resident of British North America.

Anne Dudley Bradstreet was born in England in 1612. She was the daughter of Thomas and Dorothy Yorke Dudley; a few years after her birth her father accepted the position of steward to the non-conformist Earl of Lincoln. Anne's exact birthplace is not known, but her formative years were passed at the Earl's estates of Sempringham and Tattershall Castle amid the material comforts and the vigorous and independent atmosphere of intellectual, spiritual and political life of this noble family. At the age of sixteen, in 1628, she married Simon Bradstreet, a Cambridge graduate and her father's protégé, whom she loved devotedly during the forty-four years of their life together. In 1630 the Dudleys and Bradstreets emigrated to America with John Winthrop's company of founders of the Massachusetts Bay Colony. Thomas Dudley was the second governor of the colony, and he and Simon Bradstreet served throughout their lives as important leaders and public servants in the development of New England. The Bradstreets settled first at Newtown (now Cambridge), from which they moved successively to Ipswich and Andover. Although always a frail and sickly person herself, Anne Bradstreet bore eight children, all but one of whom survived her. After a life distinguished by accomplishment, richness, courage and devotion, she died on September 16, 1672, in the fine Bradstreet house in North Andover which is still standing.

To return to the book itself, the title page presents a graceful and almost complete description of the contents:

> **THE TENTH MUSE, *Lately Sprung up in America, or, Several Poems, compiled with great variety of Wit and Learning, full of delight.*** Wherein especially is contained a compleat discourse and description of The Four Elements, Constitutions, Ages of Man, Seasons of the Year. Together with an Exact Epitomie of the Four Monarchies, viz. The Assyrian, Persian, Grecian, Roman. Also a Dialogue between Old England and New, concerning the late troubles. With divers other pleasant and serious Poems. By a Gentlewoman in those parts. Printed at London for Stephen Bowtell at the signe of the Bible in Popes Head-Alley. 1650.

The "other pleasant and serious poems" are: **"To her most Honoured Father Thomas Dudley," "The Prologue,"** elegies upon Sir Philip Sidney and Queen Elizabeth, **"In honour of Du Bartas"** and **"Of the vanity of all worldly creatures."**

There is also prefatory material written by various individuals which must not be overlooked, for it casts a revealing light on the contemporary attitude toward female versifiers. Following an epistle to the reader in prose, there are eight poems, and two of the anagrams so laboredly popular in the seventeenth century on the name "Anna Bradstreate," one of which is accompanied by a rhymed couplet. Of the poems, all are simply initialed except the first, signed "N. Ward." This was contributed by the old clergyman Nathaniel Ward, who returned from New England to the mother country in 1646 to see his own book, *The Simple Cobbler of Agawam,* published in London in 1647; it merits quoting for its quaint and fatherly good-humor and, withal, pride in a young friend and neighbor of Ipswich days.

> Mercury shew'd Apollo, Bartas Book,
> Minerva this, and wisht him well to look,
> And tell uprightly which did which excell,
> He view'd and view'd, and vow'd he could not
>   tel.
> They bid him Hemisphear his mouldy nose,
> With's crackt leering glasses, for it would pose
> The best brains he had in's old pudding-pan,
> Sex weigh'd, which best, the Woman, or the
>   Man?
> He peer'd and por'd, and glar'd, and said for
>   wore,
> I'me even as wise now, as I was before:
> They both 'gan laugh, and said it was no mar'l
> The Auth'ress was a right Du Bartas Girle.
> Good sooth quoth the old Don, tell ye me so,
> I muse whither at length these girls will go;
> It half revives my chil frost-bitten blood,
> To see a Woman once, do ought that's good;
> And chode by Chaucers Boots, and Homers
>   Furrs,
> Let Men look to't, least Women wear the Spurrs.

The authors of two of the other poems in the preface have been identified as the Reverend John Woodbridge, Anne Bradstreet's brother-in-law, and his brother the Reverend Benjamin Woodbridge. The remaining poems are signed "C.B.," "R.Q.," "N.H." and "H.S."; they were presumably contributed by English Puritan poets whose identity has not so far been established. All the verses are alike in expressing gentlemanly astonishment, as well as genuine admiration, at the ability of a woman to compose so substantial a body of verse. Nathaniel Ward takes comfort, to be sure, in recognizing the strong influence exerted on Anne Bradstreet by Guillaume de Saluste du Bartas, whose elaborate writings, translated from the French by Joshua Sylvester as *Du Bartas His Divine Weekes and Workes* and published in London in 1605, are also said to have given pleasure and nourishment to John Milton. An anonymous anagramist adds the couplet:

> So Bartas like thy fine spun Poems been,
> That Bartas name will prove an epicene.

It is most interesting that these prefatory verses, offered in an age when it was not unheard-of for gentlewomen to be quite illiterate and most unusual for a woman's work to appear in print, express none of the condescension later immortalized in Dr. Johnson's observation about a woman preacher: that it is not so much a question as to whether a dog can dance well as it is surprising that it can dance at all! In other words this new poet, "lately sprung up in America," was apparently welcomed with generosity and respect by her peers.

The story of how *The Tenth Muse* came to be published is in itself a dramatic and pleasantly human one. It is told primarily in the book's epistle to the reader, by one who writes: "I fear 'twill be a shame for a Man that can speak so little, to be seen in the title-page of this Woman's Book"; yet he must, in case there be incredulity, assure the reader:

> It is the Work of a Woman, honoured, and esteemed where she lives, for her gracious demeanour, her eminent parts, her pious conversation, her courteous disposition, her exact diligence in her place, and discreet managing of her Family occasions, and more then so, these Poems are the fruit but of some few houres, curtailed from her sleep and other refreshments. . . . I fear the displeasure of no person in the publishing of these Poems but the Author, without whose knowledge, and contrary to her expectation, I have presumed to bring to publick view, what she resolved in such a manner should never see the Sun; but I found that diverse had gotten some scattered Papers, affected them well, were likely to have sent forth broken pieces, to the Author's prejudice, which I thought to prevent, as well as to pleasure those that earnestly desired the view of the whole.

The same courage of affection and conviction shown in this statement is echoed in the longest of the prefatory verses, "To my dear Sister, the Author of these Poems," where the writer's admiration is gracefully expressed:

> There needs no painting to that comely face,
> That in its native beauty hath such grace;
>
>   . . . . .
>
> If women, I with women may compare,
> Your works are solid, others weak as Air;
>
>   . . . . .
>
> What you have done, the Sun shall witness bear,
> That for a womans Work 'tis very rare;
> And if the Nine, vouchsafe the Tenth a place,
> I think they rightly may yield you that grace.

This poem, initialled "I. W.," and the epistle are undoubtedly by the same hand, that of the Reverend John Woodbridge, husband of Anne Bradstreet's sister Mercy and the first minister of Andover in Massachusetts. He sailed for England in 1647 and remained there until 1663; it is most probable that when he went he took with him the fairest existing manuscript copy of Anne Bradstreet's poems, the one prepared by her for presentation to her father, and that this was what appeared in print under his auspices as *The Tenth Muse.* A family conspiracy may here be seen at work, with the austere father, the devoted sister and the admiring brother-in-law taking upon themselves the responsibility for an act of great significance in the life of their relative.

This was in no sense a frivolous deed, for these, and the many other admirers of Anne Bradstreet's verse whose interest seemed to justify the step of publication, were serious, thrifty, self-disciplined people, who weighed every impulse primarily for its value in the sight of God. They must all have believed that their world would be better for the appearance in print, and consequent availability to more readers, of the work of one whose gracious piety and industrious intelligence they honored not only in herself but also in the poems which she had composed in the midst of a busy and often perilous life in the New England wilderness.

Let us cast a twentieth-century eye over these poems that brought pleasure and inspiration to Puritan minds of the seventeenth century. As our basic medium of intelligence and behavior is the newspaper, so that of the Puritans was the sermon. Professor Perry Miller says, in *The New England Mind*: ". . . all their writings were simply other ways of achieving the same ends they were seeking in their sermons; histories, poems or tracts were treatises on the will of God as revealed in nature, experience, history or individual lives." He goes on to conclude that for the Puritan "verse was simply a heightened form of eloquence . . . poetry existed primarily for its utility, it was foredoomed to didacticism, and because it was the most highly ornate of the arts, it was always in grave danger of overstepping proper limits and becoming pleasing for its own sake. . . . Poetry in Puritan eyes, therefore, was a species of rhetoric, a dress for great truths, a sugar for the pill. Only some two persons in seventeenth-century New England have left any evidence that they were deeply imbued with a true poetic insight . . . the Reverend Edward Taylor . . . and Anne Bradstreet."

The author of *The Tenth Muse* was not niggardly in her choice of "great truths" to wear the garment of her poetry. Her upbringing in England gave her opportunity for as wide reading as was permitted by Puritan standards. The Bible of course was the cornerstone and measuring-rod, and her own lines tell us that she read Spenser and Sidney, Sylvester's du Bartas, Speed's, Camden's, Raleigh's and Archbishop Usher's histories, and Dr. Crooke's *Description of the Body of Man*. She probably also read North's *Plutarch's Lives,* Florio's Montaigne, Chapman's Homer, Burton's *Anatomy of Melancholy,* the poems of Drayton, Browne, Wither and possibly Donne, other contemporaries who were not too anti-Puritan to be acceptable, and some Shakespeare, although plays in general were frowned upon by her people and the other dramatists were no doubt excluded. She must have been still absorbing her education, as it were, when she left England at the age of eighteen in 1630. "I changed my condition and was married," she says in her "Religious Experiences," "and came into this Country, where I found a new world and new manners, at which my heart rose. But after I was convinced it was the way of God, I submitted to it and joined to the church at Boston." Finding herself in a strange wild land, where intellectual recreation was minimized by the demands of hard labor for survival's sake, she must have felt a mental vacuum replacing the reservoir of stimulating ideas and impressions that her life in England had kept filled. So instead of looking outward and writing her observations on this unfamiliar scene with its rough and fearsome aspects, she let her homesick imagination turn inward, marshalled the images from her store of learning and dressed them in careful homespun garments, of somewhat archaic meter, to the glory of God and for the expression of an inquiring mind and sensitive, philosophical

spirit. Her intentions reveal themselves in these lines of dedication to her father, who had himself written a poem, now lost, on the four parts of the world:

> I bring my four; and four, now meanly clad
> To do their homage, unto yours, most glad:
>
> . . . . .
>
> These same are they, from whom we being have
> These are of all, the Life, the Nurse, the Grave,
> These are the hot, the cold, the moist, the dry,
> That sink, that swim, that fill, that upwards fly,
> Of these consists our bodies, Cloathes and Food,
> The World, the useful, hurtful and the good,
> Sweet harmony they keep, yet jar oft times
> Their discord may appear, by these harsh rimes.
>
> . . . . .
>
> My other four do intermixed tell
> Each others faults, and where themselves excell;
> How hot and dry contend with moist and cold,
> How Air and Earth no correspondence hold,
> And yet in equal tempers, how they 'gree,
> How divers natures make one Unity.
> Something of all (though mean) I did intend
> But fear'd you'ld judge one Bartas was my friend;
> I honour him, but dare not wear his wealth,
> My goods are true (though poor) I love no stealth;
>
> . . . . .
>
> I shall not need, mine innocence to clear,
> These ragged lines, will do't, when they appear:
> On what they are, your mild aspect I crave,
> Accept my best, my worst vouchsafe a Grave.

The device of the four-times-four allegorical personages used in the first part of *The Tenth Muse,* representing the elements, humors, ages and seasons in a stilted and highly argumentative manner, is such as to make any free poetic expression almost impossible. Yet one small passage in this first selection **"The Four Ages of Man"** does contain a beautiful, grave and compassionate poetic image, a promise of what is to be found more often in Anne Bradstreet's later poems, written when maturity and a more personal approach had freed her from the ornate du Bartian shackles.

> Childhood was cloth'd in white & green to show
> His spring was intermixed with some snow:
> Upon his head nature a Garland set
> Of Primrose, Daizy & the Violet;
> Such cold mean flowrs (as these) blossome betime
> Before the sun hath throughly warm'd the clime.

"The Four Monarchies," next among the contents, is a painful work in every sense. Though unfinished, it takes up one hundred and fourteen pages of *The Tenth Muse,* and is simply a paraphrase in rhymed couplets of the history of the ancient world as told by Raleigh and other contemporary writers. Tyrants welter in blood on almost every page; kingdoms topple and armies are destroyed, all to prove that in a world where all is vanity these pagan spectacles of greed and violence were the most vain of all.

Comparing the four monarchies to four ravening beasts, the author says:

> But yet this Lion, Bear, this Leopard, Ram,
> All trembling stand before the powerful Lamb.

Her conscious purpose in doggedly composing this long work, in which hardly a line of anything even resembling poetry appears, is clear; she wished to produce a serious moral poem, modelled on her father's work and demonstrating forcefully the degradation of the dark ages of antiquity as compared to the enlightenment, even in struggle, of the Christian world. But it is tempting to wonder why, during a period of about seventeen years in which she bore seven children, changed her dwelling twice, each time venturing deeper into unsettled country, suffered from recurring attacks of illness yet consistently managed the household of her distinguished husband, she chose so huge and ungentle a subject for creative interpretation in her leisure hours.

An examination of Anne Bradstreet's entire body of work, however, including the "Religious Experiences" and "Meditations Divine and Moral" written as spiritual legacies for her children and not published until 1867, reveals an undeniable trace of intellectual intransigence, creating conflicting thoughts which bred in turn an occasional outburst of violent expression. For example, in the "Religious Experiences," after admitting that "many times hath Satan troubled me concerning the verity of the scriptures, many times by Atheisme how I could know whether there was a God," and explaining her process of reasoning in resolving these doubts, she goes on to say: "When I have gott over this Block, then have I another putt in my way, That admitt this bee the true God whom wee worship, and that bee his word, yet why may not the Popish Religion be the right? They have the same God, the same Christ, the same word: they only interprett it one way, wee another." From these troubling speculations she reacted with a sort of self-chastising fury, as shown in these lines from **"A Dialogue between Old England and New,"** where the Puritan New England abjures her "Dear Mother":

> These are the dayes the Churches foes to crush,
> To root our Prelates head, tail, branch and rush;
> Let's bring Baals vestments out to make a fire,
> Their Mytires, Surplices, and all their Tire,
> Copes, Rotchets, Crossiers, and such trash,
> And let their Names consume, but let the flash
> Light Christendome, and all the world to see
> We hate Romes whore, with all her trumpery.
>
> . . . . .
>
> Bring forth the Beast that rul'd the World with's
> beck,
> And tear his flesh, and set your feet on's neck;
> And make his filthy Den so desolate,
> To th'stonishment of all that knew his state:
> This done with brandish'd Swords to Turky goe,
> For then what is't, but English blades dare do,
> And lay her waste for so's the sacred Doom,
> And do to Gog as thou hast done to Rome.
>
> . . . . .
>
> Then fulness of the Nations in shall flow,

And Jew and Gentile to one worship go;
Then follows dayes of happiness and rest;
Whose lot doth fall, to live therein is blest.

It seems at least possible that Anne Bradstreet, recognizing in herself the sometimes rebellious independence of mind that was thought so dangerous in a woman, and having before her as example the fate of the courageously opinionated Anne Hutchinson, either consciously or unconsciously took a skillful way out of her psychological dilemma. While conducting herself as an exemplary wife and mother, and fulfilling the duties of her social position in a manner to gain the respect of all around her, she yet devoted a considerable number of her hours of literary work to what amounted to identification of her personality with the tumult of the cruel, licentious and ungodly lives of the monarchs of antiquity. No commentator on her work has had a kind word to say for **"The Four Monarchies,"** nor is their criticism unjustified if this be considered solely as a work of poetry. But I shall venture to go a little further, and suggest that this barren exercise in rhetorical ingenuity be approached as an opportune outlet for the author's impulses of resentment against the Puritan narrowness of thinking and harshness of living, as well as a stern practice in the use of words and meter. Thus viewed, it would logically deserve credit for both the wider tranquility of spirit and the greater technical ease that manifest themselves in Anne Bradstreet's later poems.

Following the major groups of "fours" are shorter poems, three of which illustrate the author's loyalty to what she felt was best in the mother country. **"A Dialogue between Old England and New,"** written in 1642 as the Civil War in England was beginning, points up a fact of great historical interest:

> Go on brave Essex, shew whose son thou art,
> Not false to King, nor Countrey in thy heart,
> But those that hurt his people and his Crown,
> By force expell, destroy, and tread them down;
>
> . . . . .
>
> And ye brave Nobles chase away all fear,
> And to this blessed Cause closely adhere;
>
> . . . . .
>
> These, these are they I trust, with Charles our
> King,
> Out of all mists such glorious dayes will bring;
> That dazled eyes beholding much shall wonder
> At that thy setled peace, thy wealth and splen-
> dor.

Before Anne Bradstreet left England King Charles I had made prisoners of the Earl of Lincoln and his father-in-law, Lord Saye and Sele, and had set spies upon the actions of her own father Thomas Dudley because of their resistance to the enforced loans to the crown. Yet the traditional allegiance of the British subject to his monarch was strong enough to make her believe—and she must surely have reflected the feeling of many of her companions in New England—that the King himself was not so much to blame as those ardent Catholics among his advisers who sought to usurp all the powers of Parliament, in the King's name, for their own ends. Being a faithful subject as well as a Puritan, she took the attitude—shown in lines from this poem already quoted—that Popery was the root of all of England's trouble, and once that was eradicated by fire and sword peace and prosperity would prevail.

The elegies on Sir Philip Sidney and Queen Elizabeth reveal Anne Bradstreet's generous strain of hero-worship. She loved Sidney because he was a brave and romantic nobleman, possibly her relation through the Dudley family, and a writer whose *Arcadia,* which must have been anathema to the Puritan divines because of its pastoral sensuality, she has the courage to praise.

> Yet, he's a beetle head, that cann't discry
> A world of treasure, in that rubbish lye;
> And doth thy selfe, thy worke, and honour
>   wrong,
> (O brave Refiner of our Brittish Tongue;)
> That sees not learning, valour, and morality,
> Justice, friendship, and kind hospitality;
> Yea, and Divinity within thy Book.

And she honors Elizabeth for her great qualities and achievements as a monarch, but most of all for her emancipation of her sex.

> Now say, have women worth? or have they
>   none?
> Or had they some, but with our Queen is't gone?
> Nay Masculines, you have thus taxt us long,
> But she, though dead, will vindicate our wrong.
> Let such as say our Sex is void of Reason,
> Know tis a Slander now, but once was Treason.

The epitaph that ends the poem has a graceful image:

> Here sleeps The Queen, this is the Royal Bed,
> Of th' Damask Rose, sprung from the white and
>   red,
> Whose sweet perfume fills the all-filling Air:
> This Rose is wither'd, once so lovely fair.
> On neither tree did grow such Rose before,
> The greater was our gain, our loss the more.

"In Honour of Du Bartas" is an humble hymn of praise to one whom she unreservedly admired as her master and model in knowledge, wit and style. **"David's Lamentation for Saul and Jonathan"** is a paraphrase of Samuel, Chapter 2, showing real poetic feeling, and **"Of the vanity of all wordly creatures,"** the last poem in the book, echoes Ecclesiastes yet has an originality of imagery and a flowing vigor in the use of the rhymed couplets that is more noticeable than in the other poems in *The Tenth Muse*:

> Where shall I climb, sound, seek search or find
> That Summum Bonum which may stay my
>   mind?
> There is a path, no vultures eye hath seen,
> Where lions fierce, nor lions whelps have been,
> Which leads unto that living Crystal Fount,
> Who drinks thereof, the world doth nought account.

To end with the beginning, so to speak, in our examination of this little book, it remains to quote two stanzas from **"The Prologue,"** which argue eloquently this literate woman's determination to be loyal to the creative impulse

within her, and her accompanying humbleness in the appraisal of her own work.

> I am obnoxious to each carping tongue
> Who says my hand a needle better fits,
> A Poets pen all scorn I should thus wrong,
> For such despite they cast on Female wits:
> If what I do prove well, it won't advance,
> They'l say it's stol'n, or else it was by chance.

> And oh ye high flown quills that soar the Skies,
> And ever with your prey still catch your praise,
> If e're you daigne these lowly lines your eyes
> Give wholsome Parsley wreath, I ask no bayes,
> This mean and unrefined stuffe of mine
> Will make your glistring gold, but more to shine.

Book reviews were not the consumer's commodity in 1650 that they are now, so it is necessary to search a while for contemporary references to this book that appeared in England in the same year as Henry Vaughan's *Silex Scintillans.* An obscure little work which has not, to the best of my knowledge, been itself revived for many years, *An Essay to Revive the Ancient Education of Gentlewomen in Religion, Manners, Arts & Tongues,* was published anonymously in London in 1673. Its author was Mrs. Bathsua Makin, a very learned Englishwoman who had tutored the daughters of Charles I, and kept schools for young ladies of the nobility at Putney and Tottenham during the third quarter of the seventeenth century. Let us turn at once to what this writer has to say about women as poets:

> All the Instruction and Education in the World, all the pains, time and patience imaginable, can never infuse that sublime Fancy, that strong Memory, and excellent Judgment required in one that shall wear the Bayes. If Women have been good Poets, Men injure them Exceedingly, to account them giddy-headed Gossips, fit only to discourse of their Hens, Ducks, and Geese, and not by any means to be suffered to meddle with Arts and Tongues, lest by intollerable pride they should run mad.

> If I do make this appear, that Women have been good Poets, it will confirm all I have said before: for, besides natural endowments, there is required a general and universal improvement in all kinds of learning. A good Poet must know things Divine, things Natural, things Moral, things Historical, and things Artificial; together with the several terms belonging to all Faculties, to which they must allude. Good Poets must be universal Scholars, able to use a pleasing Phrase, and to express themselves with moving Eloquence.

She then speaks of the gifted women of antiquity and of foreign countries, and comes home to say: "How excellent a Poet Mrs. Broadstreet is (now in America) her works do testifie." Mrs. Makin also praises Mrs. Katherine Philips and the accomplished ladies of the nobility, but two points are significant in her mention of Anne Bradstreet. One is that the educator considered the poet an Englishwoman and therefore an English poet; "now in America" is parenthesized as incidental. Actually by the time this statement appeared in print Anne Bradstreet was in America forever, so to speak, having been laid to rest in New England earth in the early autumn of 1672. The other point is that interest in and admiration for Anne Bradstreet's writing had remained alive for over twenty years after *The Tenth Muse* was printed, although in that time no further publication of her works had appeared. This survival of recognition is also pointed out by Edward Phillips, the nephew of Milton, who noted in his *Theatrum Poetarum,* published in 1675, under the heading "Women among the Moderns Eminent for Poetry":

> Anne Bradstreet, a New England Poetess, no less in title, viz. before her Poems, printed in Old England anno 1650; then the tenth Muse Sprung up in America, the memory of which Poems, consisting chiefly of Descriptions of the Four Elements, the four Humours, the four Ages, the four Seasons, and the four Monarchies, is not yet wholly extinct.

In *The Bibliographer's Manual of English Literature,* William T. Lowndes says that the hand of Milton may be recognized in the preface and in some of the criticisms in Phillips' work; may we not therefore imagine in passing that the great poet might have seen fit to bestow a figurative "wholesome Parsley wreath" on the poems of his pioneering female contemporary? At any rate the record of three hundred years proves, I think, that Phillips had foresight as well as hindsight in remarking that the memory of this book "is not yet wholly extinct."

The second edition of Anne Bradstreet's poems appeared in Boston in 1678, with the title-page reading in part:

> ***Several Poems Compiled with great variety of Wit and Learning, full of Delight***. . . . By a Gentlewoman in New-England. The second Edition, Corrected by the Author, and enlarged by an Addition of several other Poems found amongst her Papers after her Death. Boston, printed by John Foster, 1678.

This book, the first work of belles lettres to be printed in British North America, has lately been examined by George Frisbie Whicher in an interesting monograph published in a limited edition in 1942 called *Alas All's Vanity.* The dropping of "The Tenth Muse" from the title, and the many corrections and alterations of the original text, show that once the author had recovered from the surprise and indubitable delight of having a totally unexpected printed copy of her poems put into her hands, she set about seriously to correct the faults which were all too evident to her. She must also have gone through the interesting process of changing, in her own mind, from a private amateur verse-writer, like many of her friends and associates in the colony, to a professional poet, without a peer in New England and outstanding among the few published writers of her sex in old England. However this realization came to her, it had the effect that Samuel Eliot Morison notes in his chapter on her in *Builders of the Bay Colony:*

> *The Tenth Muse* did this for Anne Bradstreet: it completely cured her of the du Bartas disease, and of writing imitative poetry. She was thirty-eight when the book came out in 1650. For the remaining twenty-two years of her life, she wrote lyrical poetry.

Since we are here primarily concerned with an examination of *The Tenth Muse* and its position in literary history, mention of Anne Bradstreet's later poems must be limited to their inclusion in the other editions of her earliest work. She was assiduous in her preparation for the further public appearance of *The Tenth Muse,* adding only five poems, but two of them her best, to the contemplated second edition and making as has been noted careful corrections of those already published. One of these poems, **"The Author to her Book,"** really demands to be quoted entire, for the fascinating light it sheds on the workings of the writer's mind. At first dismayed to see her "brat" in print, yet at the same time experiencing the extraordinary sense of fulfillment of literary parenthood, she became reconciled.

"The Author to her Book"

Thou ill-form'd offspring of my feeble brain,
Who after birth did'st by my side remain,
Till snatcht from thence by friends, less wise
      then true
Who thee abroad, expos'd to publick view,
Made thee in raggs, halting to th' press to trudg,
Where errors were not lessened (all may judg)
At thy return my blushing was not small,
My rambling brat (in print) should mother call,
I cast thee by as one unfit for light,
Thy Visage was so irksome in my sight;
Yet being mine own, at length affection would
Thy blemishes amend, if so I could:
I wash'd thy face, but more defects I saw,
And rubbing off a spot, still made a flaw.
I stretcht thy joints to make thee even feet,
Yet still thou run'st more hobling then is meet;
In better dress to trim thee was my mind,
But none save home-spun Cloth, i' th' house I
      find
In this array, 'mongst Vulgars mayst thou roam
In Criticks hands, beware thou dost not come;
And take thy way where yet thou art not known,
If for thy Father askt, say, thou hadst none:
And for thy Mother, she alas is poor,
Which caus'd her thus to send thee out of door.

The other four new poems added by the author to her second edition are: elegies to her father and mother; **"Contemplations,"** a long and beautiful poem in Spenserian stanza describing an afternoon walk through the autumn countryside and along the Merrimack River and presenting the thoughts of wonder and faith that the majesty of these surroundings brought to her mind; **"The Flesh and the Spirit,"** which Samuel Eliot Morison calls "one of the best expressions in English literature of the conflict described by St. Paul in the eighth chapter of his Epistle to the Romans." Added to these at the end of the book are thirteen poems concerning herself and her family, "found among her Papers after her Death, which she never meant should come to publick view," but which were well chosen for publication since they include five deeply moving lyrics addressed to her husband and the charming poem beginning "I had eight birds hatcht in one nest," written probably when her youngest child was six years old and her eldest twenty-five.

In this second edition also appear an ornate poem in praise of her work by John Rogers, her nephew by marriage and later President of Harvard College, and "A Funeral Elogy, upon that Pattern and Patron of Virtue, the truly pious, peerless and matchless Gentlewoman, Mrs. Anne Bradstreet, right Panaretes, Mirror of her Age, Glory of her Sex," by her young admirer the Reverend John Norton.

Thus, six years after her death, New England produced its own printing of its first recognized poet. In 1702, Cotton Mather's formidable *Magnalia Christi Americana* paid tribute to:

> Madam Ann Bradstreet . . . whose Poems, divers times Printed, have afforded a grateful Entertainment unto the Ingenious, and a Monument for her Memory beyond the Stateliest Marbles.

A third edition of her poems, reprinted with only slight changes from the second, appeared in Boston in 1758. More than one hundred years later, in 1867, John Harvard Ellis published his edition of "all the extant works of Anne Bradstreet." To her writings which had already appeared in print he added a painstaking and thorough biographical introduction and some important unpublished material—the complete contents of the little manuscript volume prepared for her children, containing "Religious Experiences and Occasional Pieces" and "Meditations Divine and Moral." Among the interesting and touching autobiographical prose entries of the "Religious Experiences" are scattered short personal and devotional lyrics which include two of her finest: **"Some verses upon the burning of our house, July 10th, 1666"** and the valedictory **"As weary pilgrim, now at rest."** The seventy-seven "Meditations," addressed to her son Simon, are short prose statements of moral fact, written with vigorous forthrightness and an appealing use of homely and familiar images, as for example:

> Corne, till it have past through the Mill and been ground to powder, is not fit for bread. God so deales with his Servants: he grindes them with greif and pain till they turn to dust, and then are they fit manchet for his Mansion.

Charles Eliot Norton contributed a rather condescending introduction to an edition of Anne Bradstreet's works published in 1897, in attractive format but with an admission by the editor that "instances of unnecessarily bad grammar" had been corrected! As is recognized now, the latter half of the nineteenth century found more to criticise than admire in the writings, particularly the poetry, of the seventeenth century, the brooding introspection and intricate imagery of which it remained for our own time to acclaim once more. The venerable historian of American literature Moses Coit Tyler, writing in the 1870's, deals kindly enough with Anne Bradstreet's more personal and spontaneous poems, but thunders at her earlier works in a way that will delight, rather than terrify, the modern student of English poetry.

> The worst lines of Anne Bradstreet . . . can be readily matched for fantastic perversion, and for the total absence of beauty, by passages from the poems of John Donne, George Herbert, Crashaw, Cleveland, Wither, Quarles, Thomas Coryat, John Taylor, and even of Herrick, Cowley and Dryden.

Indeed the sins of *The Tenth Muse* are modelled on those of a distinguished company!

The twentieth century has remembered Anne Bradstreet not only with the scholarly recognition, already mentioned, given her by Perry Miller, Samuel Eliot Morison and George Frisbie Wicher, but with a reprint of the Ellis edition of her works, published in 1932, and the inclusion of four of her poems, **"The Flesh and the Spirit," "Contemplations," "A Letter to Her Husband"** and **"As weary pilgrim, now at rest,"** in Conrad Aiken's excellent anthology, *American Poetry, 1671-1928.* And the late F. O. Matthiesen placed six of her poems at the beginning of the *Oxford Book of American Verse,* published in 1950.

Where does *The Tenth Muse* belong in the history of English literature? I wish to put forward the suggestion that it was the work of the first Englishwoman who seriously and successfully chose for her occupation the writing of poetry. For approximately four hundred years before Anne Bradstreet's poems were published, "the iron of English," as Archibald MacLeish calls it, had rung in meter from tongue and pen, yet the voices and the hands that made English poetry were almost entirely those of men. Only a handful of women, some of them shadowy figures now, are recorded as having written original verse up to the middle of the seventeenth century. To the legendary Dame Juliana Berners (sometimes confused with the anchoress Juliana of Norwich, whose beautiful *Revelations of Divine Love,* written about 1390, are in prose), has been attributed *The Book of St. Albans,* printed in 1486, which contains a treatise in verse on hunting. But it has been established that this is not an original work, but a translation of an earlier French book on hunting. Writings by the Countess of Richmond, Lady Margaret Roper (the daughter of Sir Thomas More), Henry VIII's last queen the Protestant Catherine Parr, and the ill-fated Lady Jane Grey, appeared in print between 1522 and 1575, but these all seem to have been translations or religious pieces in prose. One of Queen Catherine's ladies-in-waiting, the accomplished Anne Askew, Lady Kyme, who was mercilessly tortured and burned as a heretic in 1546, wrote an account of her own trial, published on the continent soon after her death, which includes a moving poem of faith. Mary Herbert, Countess of Pembroke, the famed "Sidney's sister, Pembroke's mother," wrote a poem in memory of her brother and a poetic "Dialogue between Two Shepherds," published in 1586 and 1602, a scholarly blank verse translation of Garnier's *Tragedy of Antonie,* printed in 1592, and, with Sidney, *The Psalmes of David translated into Divers and Sundry Kindes of Verse.* This was probably written in 1587 but was not published until 1823.

The great Elizabeth was a scholar before she was a queen. Two religious works from her pen, one a translation from Margaret of Angoulême, were published in 1548, and during her long and brilliant reign she continued to write and translate. Most of her work was in prose, but one of her poems, the vigorous "Daughter of Debate," appeared in *The Arte of English Poesie* in 1589, and this and another from a manuscript copy are reprinted in *The Oxford Book of Sixteenth-Century Verse.*

The first published volume of verse by an Englishwoman appears to exist in only one copy, and not to have been reprinted. This is Isabella Whitney's *A Sweet Nosgay, or pleasant Posye: containing a hundred and ten Phylosophicall Flowers. The Short Title Catalogue* dates this London, 1573, and lists only the example in the British Museum, which may well be the one mentioned by W. T. Lowndes in 1834 as "Probably unique. Unknown to bibliographers." Certainly no copy seems to have found its way to this country. To the same author, sister of the minor poet Geoffrey Whitney, is attributed also *The Copie of a Letter, lately written in Meeter by a younge gentilwoman to her unconstant lover.* This was printed about 1567, and has been reprinted in two collections of early English writing.

The first original poetic drama in English by a woman was probably *The Tragedie of Mariam, the Faire Queene of Jewry,* by Elizabeth Cary, Viscountess Falkland. Printed in 1613, this sombre "tragedy of blood" contains one fine poem, a chorus of six stanzas on the nobility of forgiving injuries, which Chambers' *Cyclopaedia of English Literature* reprints.

Sir Philip Sidney's niece, Lady Mary Wroath, published in 1621 *The Countess of Montgomerie's Urania,* a fantasy in prose and verse which is simply an imitation of her uncle's *Arcadia.* Rachel Speght, who may have been the daughter of the scholarly Thomas Speght, wrote two long poems which were published in 1621 in a little book of about forty pages with the title: *Mortalitie's Memorandum, with a Dreame Prefixed, imaginarie in manner, reall in matter.* From this forgotten work comes a stanza which reveals the intelligent early seventeenth-century woman's quarrel with her time:

> Both man and woman of three parts consist,
> Which Paul doth bodie, soule and spirit call:
> And from the soule three faculties arise,
> The mind, the will, the power; then wherefore shall
> A woman have her intellect in vain,
> Or not endevour knowledge to attain?

In 1630, "the noble lady Diana Primrose" offered *A Chaine of Pearle: or, a Memoriall of the peerless Graces and heroick Virtues of Queene Elizabeth, of glorious Memory.* This elegiac poem was reprinted in the *Harleian Miscellany* and in Nichols' *Progresses of Queen Elizabeth.*

Twenty years later came a voice from the wilderness, that of "the Tenth Muse, lately sprung up in America," and with this half-turn of the century and the far-reaching changes brought by the Civil War the gates of the English Parnassus seemed to open at last to women. The eccentric Duchess of Newcastle, exiled from her country by the Commonwealth but a very citizen of Utopia in the love and intellectual companionship of her husband, published her *Poems and Fancies* in 1653, and after that, with the Duke's encouragement and collaboration, produced many volumes of poems, plays and philosophical essays. Anne Collins' *Divine Songs* was also published in 1653. Katharine Philips, "the matchless Orinda," friend of Vaughan,

Cowley and Jeremy Taylor, whom Professor Douglas Bush in *English Literature in the Earlier Seventeenth Century* calls "the first real English poetess," began to be much admired soon after 1650 as the center of a literary circle where elegant and artificial Platonism was cultivated. Her poems, often reprinted in collections and anthologies, appeared in an unauthorized edition in 1664, the year of her untimely death, and in a corrected and more complete edition in 1667. Anne Finch, Countess of Winchilsea, wrote graceful and melancholy poems which were admired by her friends, among whom was Pope, but did not publish until 1713, a few years before her death.

Finally, the roaring days of the Restoration produced the first woman in England who actually made her living by her pen. She was the redoubtable Mrs. Aphra Behn, who spent her childhood in Surinam, Guiana, being the daughter of the English Governor, returned to England in 1658, served as a spy for Charles II in Antwerp, and married a London merchant. Her husband's death and her own financial difficulties forced her to become self-supporting, and this she accomplished by writing between 1671 and 1689 fifteen plays, coarse and swashbuckling comedies and dramas of contemporary life, several novels, and a body of verse containing such poems of power and beauty as the celebrated "Love in fantastic triumph sat." She was, unlike all of those mentioned before her, not in any sense a "lady," and it was by sheer uninhibited strength of character that she forged her vigorous creative talent into a weapon that won her an undisputed place in the man's world of literature.

The fact that it took so many centuries for women to gain the right to compete with men in the field of letters is examined with insight and energy by Virginia Woolf in her essay *A Room of One's Own.* She emphasizes the loneliness and frustration of women who wanted to write and cites the eccentric Duchess of Newcastle and the melancholy Countess of Winchilsea as examples of talented writers whose productions were "disfigured and deformed" by the weight of public opinion against them. She quotes a revealing contemporary comment by Dorothy Osborne, who wrote mentioning a book by the Duchess of Newcastle in a letter to Sir William Temple:

> Sure the poore woman is a little distracted, shee could never bee soe rediculous else as to venture at writeing book's and in verse too, if I should not sleep this fortnight I should not come to that.

Mrs. Woolf makes a point which provides me with a stepping-stone toward my own goal, that of demonstrating that Anne Bradstreet was the first unhampered and integrated English woman poet. Considering the obscurity of women in the sixteenth century, as its records have come to us, she says:

> Occasionally an individual woman is mentioned, an Elizabeth or a Mary, a queen or a great lady. But by no possible means could middle-class women with nothing but brains and character at their command have taken part in any one of the great movements which, brought together, constitute the historian's view of the past.

But that is exactly what Anne Bradstreet did, only about a quarter-century after the death of Queen Elizabeth. As a middle-class woman certainly equipped with brains and character, she was privileged to take part in a great movement, the opening up of the new world of North America. And in so doing she liberated herself not only as a woman and a Puritan, but also as a poet.

If Anne Bradstreet had remained in England she might, indeed, have written verse and had it published. But it seems logical to suppose that much of the passion and determination that went into what she wrote in New England would have been lacking, or largely watered down by the traditional confinements and artificial multiplicity of the kind of life she would have led in the mother country. She appears to have had no counterpart, at any rate, among the educated Puritan women of her time who remained in England, and the work of her nearest, though younger, contemporary, Katharine Philips, was marred by a super-imposed classical formalism which makes it all but unreadable today.

It would seem that a subtle but profound change took place in the attitude of the pioneering men toward the women who accompanied them into the forests of New England. During the first cruel winters when famine, disease, the lurking Indians and the inescapable cold were ever-present enemies, the men and women fought shoulder to shoulder, and when the worst battles were over the survivors looked at one another as tested human beings rather than as members of a superior and an inferior sex. The New England men were severe with their wives, as with themselves, in spiritual and moral discipline, as witness the banishment of Anne Hutchinson and the treatment of the Quakers regardless of sex. But through their very masculine dependence on their women for devotion, encouragement and shared planning and maintenance of their homes and communities, they gained a new respect for the courage and faithful endurance of the supposedly delicate creatures who had left the amenities of civilization to consecrate their talents and abilities to the making of another and better England and the building of a new generation of pioneers. It is not therefore strange that Anne Bradstreet, while discharging her obligations to her family and community without shortcoming or complaint, should have been permitted, even encouraged, by her "Dear and loving Husband" and their friends to express her creative impulse without any serious opposition. That the sound of "carping tongues" was not altogether absent from her ears Anne Bradstreet tells us herself, but after all was it not natural that somebody should carp, from sheer jealousy perhaps, at a capable wife and mother who was also clever and fortunate enough to be a successful writer?

It seems to me not accidental but logical that the first serious English poetess brought her talent to fruition in the sharp fresh air of Massachusetts rather than in the man-made atmosphere of England. Intense experience is the raw material of poetry; it was also the daily companion of the seventeenth-century New Englander. Sudden death was a commonplace; new life a necessity. Anne Bradstreet's family of eight children was unusual only in that all of them lived to grow to maturity; most parents in

those days buried more infants than their counterparts of today consider a reasonable hatching of hostages to fortune. Even in such frail bodies as Anne Bradstreet's, if they survived at all, the physical rigors of daily life bred a sort of tough resilience, and the ever-present unpredictables of this new existence kept the wits sharp and the senses constantly on the alert. And the unfailing, dauntless trust in the wisdom and goodness of God was a rock on which poetry and empire could alike be built. Samuel Eliot Morison makes this summation, in *Builders of the Bay Colony*:

> This was the strength of the pioneer woman, that she could employ every adversity to some spiritual advantage, and make good come out of evil. Anne Bradstreet was a true daughter of the Puritan breed, whose soul was made strong by faith. From the day her heart fell at beholding New England, to her last wasting illness, she had many, very many days of pain; but uttered no complaint. She was unusual, and so far as we know unique, among the men and women of the first generation, in that her character, her thoughts and her religion were expressed in poetry that has endured, and will endure.

Certainly no Englishwoman writing before Anne Bradstreet created a body of verse which has been remembered with so much respect, or has given so much quiet and moving pleasure to the generations that came after her. And, if it be granted that historically she deserves the earliest place among the women poets of England, surely no man, however jealous of his sex's poetic prerogative, could begrudge a niche in his honorable company to the woman who wrote these lines to her husband:

> How soon, my Dear, death may my steps attend,
> How soon't may be thy lot to lose thy friend
> We both are ignorant, yet love bids me
> These farewell lines to recommend to thee,
> That when that knot's unty'd that made us one,
> I may seem thine, who in effect am none.
> And if I see not half my dayes that's due,
> What nature would, God grant to yours and you;
> The many faults that well you know I have,
> Let be interr'd in my oblivion's grave;
> If any worth or virtue were in me,
> Let that live freshly in thy memory
> And when thou feel'st no grief, as I no harms,
> Yet love thy dead, who long lay in thine arms.

Ann Stanford (essay date 1966)

SOURCE: "Anne Bradstreet: Dogmatist and Rebel," in *The New England Quarterly*, Vol. XXXIX, No. 3, September, 1966, pp. 373-89.

[*Stanford was an American poet, critic, and educator whose works include* Anne Bradstreet, the Worldly Puritan: An Introduction to Her Poetry *(1974), and* Critical Essays on Anne Bradstreet *(1983; editor with Pattie Cowell). In the following essay, Stanford comments on the tensions evident in Bradstreet's poetry between her fidelity to Puritan dogmatism and her instinct to question it.*]

Commentators on America from de Toqueville on have

remarked the tensions, the simultaneous existence of opposing tendencies, within American life and literature. De Toqueville ascribed these tensions in part to the lack of mediating institutions between the individual and the state or the individual and his God. Other writers find the tensions rooted in spiritual conflicts rising out of economic developments; in the pull between the will to believe and the need to be shown; in theoretical principles, which, if consistently followed, lead to frustration in practice. The conflict shows up in literature through the individual's struggle to remain himself, to maintain his own inner values in the face of social pressure—or, as D. H. Lawrence sees it, to maintain his spiritual energy in the face of dogma—and in many works of American literature these conflicts are never brought into balance or resolved.

It is into this pattern of unresolved antitheses that much of the work of Anne Bradstreet fits. Though she occasionally resolves the conflict, it breaks out again and again. And it is this pattern of tension, which has often been demonstrated to be characteristic of later American literature, that explains much of her work as well.

When in the summer of 1630 Anne Bradstreet looked from the deck of the *Arbella* at the crude settlement of Salem, Massachusetts, it was no doubt a dismal sight compared to her own homeland—the flat, fen country of Lincolnshire, with its towns and great estates. She later told how she "came into this Country, where I found a new world and new manners, at which my heart rose," that is, her heart rebelled. "But after I was convinced it was the way of God, I submitted to it and joined to the church at Boston."

The elements of this first reaction were to be repeated again and again during Anne Bradstreet's pilgrimage through the new world. There was the rising of the heart either in dismay or rebellion and the assertion of the self against the dogma she encountered. Next, there was the need for conviction. It was only after persuasion that she could ever submit to the "way." Rebellion and a struggle for or against conviction form a pattern which runs through her writing. It is the statement of dogma and the concurrent feeling of resistance to dogma that give much of that writing the vitality we are still conscious of today.

The very fact that she wrote, that she considered herself a poet, that she continued to write in spite of criticism, indicates that she was willing to act independently in spite of the dogmatic assertions of many of her contemporaries, even those of the venerable John Winthrop. Winthrop recorded in his journal for April 13, 1645, the following comment on Anne Hopkins:

> Mr. Hopkins, the governour of Hartford upon Connecticut, came to Boston, and brought his wife with him, (a godly young woman, and of special parts,) who was fallen into a sad infirmity, the loss of her understanding and reason, which had been growing upon her divers years, by occasion of her giving herself wholly to reading and writing, and had written many books. Her husband, being very loving and tender of her, was loath to grieve her; but he saw his errour, when it was too late. For if she had attend-

ed her household affairs, and such things as belong to women, and not gone out of her way and calling to meddle in such things as are proper for men, whose minds are stronger &c. she had kept her wits, and might have improved them usefully and honourably in the place God had set her.

And Thomas Parker wrote to his sister in a public letter, published in London, 1650, "your printing of a Book, beyond the custom of your Sex, doth rankly smell."

Anne Bradstreet had already encountered such attitudes when, in 1642, she wrote in her **"Prologue"** to **"The Four Elements"**:

> I am obnoxious to each carping tongue
> Who says my hand a needle better fits,
> A Poets pen all scorn I should thus wrong,
> For such despite they cast on Female wits:
> If what I do prove well, it won't advance,
> They'l say it's stoln, or else it was by chance.

She goes on to point out that to the Greeks the Nine Muses were women and Poesy itself was "*Calliope's* own Child." But, she says, to this argument her critics reply that "the Greeks did nought, but play the fools & lye." She then makes her customary concession to current dogma:

> Let Greeks be Greeks, and women what they are
> Men have precedency and still excell,
> It is but vain unjustly to wage warre;
> Men can do best, and women know it well
> Preheminence in all and each is yours.

The pre-eminence of man over woman was for both Anglican and Puritan a God-given condition. St. Paul had asserted it, and the authority of the man, especially in the state of marriage, was the subject of much discussion among Protestant ministers. This subject was of particular theological interest because of the development of the Protestant idea of a married clergy. Anne Bradstreet had doubtless heard sermons to this effect, and perhaps had read books on domestic relations such as those of Thomas Gataker: *A Good Wife, God's Gift* (1620), and *Marriage Duties Briefly Couched Together* (1620). She was as well aware as Milton that men and women were

> Not equal, as thir sex not equal seemd;
> For contemplation hee and valour formd,
> For softness shee and sweet attractive Grace,
> Hee for God only, shee for God in him.

And she, like Eve, knew

> How beauty is excelled by manly grace
> And wisdom. [*Paradise Lost*]

Yet for Anne Bradstreet this dogma did not mean that women were not to use their wits at all. After admitting that men are superior, she asks them to "grant some small acknowledgement of ours." In other words, she would not have women confined to household affairs to the extent expected by John Winthrop.

In the following year, in her elegy on Queen Elizabeth, she stated her belief in the intellectual capacity of women much more strongly:

> Nay Masculines, you have thus taxt us long,
> But she, though dead, will vindicate our wrong.

Let such as say our Sex is void of Reason,
Know tis a Slander now, but once was Treason.

And despite the carping tongues, she kept on writing.

Two years earlier (1641) she had given evidence of a professional sense of dedication to her writing and a determination to continue with it. She said in her poem in honor of Du Bartas:

But barren I my Dasey here do bring,
A homely flour in this my latter Spring,
If Summer or my Autumn age do yield,
Flours, fruits, in Garden, Orchard, or in Field,
They shall be consecrated in my Verse,
And prostrate offered at great *Bartas* Herse.

She showed her liberalism also in the wide range of books that she thought fit to read, among them, romances. The Puritan minister Richard Baxter expressed a common view of romances when he said of his youthful reading: "I was extremely bewitched with a Love of Romances, Fables and Old Tales, which corrupted my affections and lost my time." Though Anne Bradstreet admitted that Sidney's romance *The Arcadia* was in part rubbish, she at the same time defended it by saying

But he's a Beetle-head that can't descry
A world of wealth within that rubbish lye.

However, Anne Bradstreet was careful not to make the mistake of Anne Hopkins. She did not neglect her domestic affairs. The author of the preface to her book, *The Tenth Muse,* assures the "Kind Reader" that this is the "Work of a Woman, honoured, and esteemed where she lives, for her gracious demeanour, her eminent parts, her pious conversation, her courteous disposition, her exact diligence in her place, and discreet managing of her Family occasions." Furthermore, the author assures the reader that these poems were not written during hours which should have been devoted to work, but "are the fruit but of some few houres, curtailed from her sleep and other refreshments."

Thus, because she did observe in her conduct an exact conformity to the mores of her community, Anne Bradstreet was able to continue to write though the practice of writing by women was disapproved of by many in the community and by the governor himself.

Her first book *The Tenth Muse* was published in London in 1650, the year that Thomas Parker criticized his sister for the "printing of a Book." Anne Bradstreet was protected from such criticism by the fact that the book was brought out without her knowledge, as her editor is careful to assert. Her reaction to the publication, however, was not so much annoyance at having her poems "expos'd to publick view" as it was that they were brought to public view "in raggs, halting to th' press." Her concern was with the blemishes in her work, and with the fact that the printer increased the errors. She set out to correct these flaws; the second edition, published six years after her death, states on the title page that it is "Corrected by the Author."

Thus in her determination to write and in her defense of the capability of women to reason, to contemplate, and to

read widely, she showed herself capable of taking a stand against the more conservative and dogmatic of her contemporaries. It was a quiet rebellion, carried on as an undercurrent in an atmosphere of conformity.

Further examples of this tendency toward independence carried on under the guise and beneath repeated statements of dogma occur in the case of the three early elegies and the poems she wrote to her husband. The elegies are written in the form of funeral poems for Sir Philip Sidney, Queen Elizabeth and the French poet, Du Bartas. They are modeled on similar elegies found in Joshua Sylvester work. But Sylvester concludes his elegies with a Christian apotheosis: the reader should not mourn, since the dead is with the saints in heaven. There is little of heaven in Anne Bradstreet's elegies. The apotheosis for the three characters she celebrates is not a higher Christian transformation, but fame. In such promise, she is closer to the classic poets and the Cavaliers than to the other Puritan writers. The Sidney epitaph concludes:

His praise is much, this shall suffice my pen,
That *Sidney* dy'd 'mong most renown'd of men.

The Du Bartas elegy elaborates the theme:

Thy haughty Stile and rapted wit sublime
All ages wondring at, shall never climb.
Thy sacred works are not for imitation,
But Monuments to future Admiration.
Thus *Bartas* fame shall last while starts do stand,
And whilst there's Air or Fire, or Sea or Land.

The idea of fame also permeates the elegy on Elizabeth, which begins:

Although great Queen thou now in silence lye
Yet thy loud Herald Fame doth to the sky
Thy wondrous worth proclaim in every Clime,
And so hath vow'd while there is world or time.

It continues on the note of fame and glory to the final epitaph:

Here lyes the pride of Queens, Pattern of Kings,
So blaze it Fame, here's feathers for thy wings.
Here lyes the envi'd, yet unparalled Prince,
Whose living virtues speak, (though dead long
  since)
If many worlds, as that Fantastick fram'd,
In every one be her great glory fam'd.

These poems promise a continuation of the individual life on this earth through fame. The same attitude runs through the poems to her husband and children, though the earthly fame is to be continued in a different manner. One of the interesting poems with regard to this point is that titled **"Before the Birth of one of her Children."** The poem suggests she may die, and the reader assumes she is thinking of the possibility of death in childbirth. She asks her husband to forget her faults and remember what virtues she may have had. Here, as in so many of her poems, there is a conflict between her acceptance of Puritan dogma, and her own warm personality. She states her awareness that life is brief and joys are apt to be followed by adversity. But she also says

love bids me

These farewell lines to recommend to thee,
That when that knot's unty'd that made us one,
I may seem thine, who in effect am none.

It was the Puritan belief that a marriage was dissolved at death. Marriage was for the earthly life only, and in after life any union between spirits was no longer in effect. A person must not love any earthly thing too much, and even excessive grief for a departed spouse or child was contrary to God's command, since it showed that one had too much regard for the things of this world. Anne Bradstreet voiced the Puritan view when she spoke of untying the knot "that made us one," just as she expressed it in the last line of another poem to her husband when she said, "Let's still remain but one till death divide." But she tries to get around the idea of the complete severance of death by writing lines so that "I may seem thine, who in effect am none." Despite the Puritan idea of the end of love in death, she wants to be remembered on this earth; she admits that her husband will probably marry again, as was customary, but she still hopes that

if chance to thine eyes shall bring this verse,
With some sad sighs honour my absent Herse;
And kiss this paper for thy loves dear sake.

Further, she requests that

when thou feel'st no grief, as I no harms,
Yet love thy dead, who long lay in thine arms.

A comparable passage in another of the love poems attempts to circumvent the finality of love in death at the end of **"To my Dear and Loving Husband"**:

Then while we live, in love lets so persever,
That when we live no more, we may live ever.

There are two possible interpretations of these lines: first, she may mean that they may have children, who will produce descendants, so that they may live on in their line. This is similar to the idea of some of Shakespeare's sonnets, for example. Second, it may mean that they will become famous as lovers, and live in fame. This would hardly seem to be a good Puritan idea, but the Cavalier idea of immortality through fame is not one Mistress Bradstreet would scorn.

Anne Bradstreet is also hopeful that her earthly memory will be kept green by her children. In a later poem, **"In reference to her Children"** (1658), which begins "I had eight birds hatcht in one nest," she reiterates her desire to be remembered:

When each of you shall in your nest
Among your young ones take your rest,
In chirping language, of them tell,
You had a Dam that lov'd you well,
That did what could be done for young,
And nurst you up till you were strong.

She explains this desire for remembrance on the basis that she may continue to be a good influence upon her children and their grandchildren:

And 'fore she once would let you fly,
She shew'd you joy and misery;
Taught what was good, and what was ill,
What would save life, and what would kill?

Thus gone, amongst you I may live,
And dead, yet speak, and counsel give.

But the over-all tone indicates that the remembrance itself is important to her. The desires for fame, honor, and worldly remembrance, indeed, seem to be special temptations for Anne Bradstreet. In her dialogue between **"The Flesh and the Spirit"** these are included among the temptations that Flesh sets forth:

Dost honour like? acquire the same,
As some to their immortal fame:
And trophyes to thy name erect
Which wearing time shall ne're deject.

The Spirit properly and dogmatically rejects such temptations:

Thy sinfull pleasure I doe hate,
Thy riches are to me no bait,
Thine honours doe, nor will I love;
For my ambition lyes above.
My greatest honour it shall be
When I am victor over thee.

The Spirit here has taken the proper Puritan attitude toward earthly things, but the Flesh clings to the visible. The struggle is recorded by Anne Bradstreet in prose as well as in poetry. God and his world to come are invisible, and Anne Bradstreet is reluctant to place her trust in either the actuality of God or the reality of life after death. She wrote in her notebook: "Many times hath Satan troubled me concerning the verity of the scriptures, many times by Atheisme how I could know whether there was a God; I never saw any miracles to confirm me, and those which I read of how did I know but they were feigned." These questions are not unique in Anne Bradstreet; other good Puritans such as Thomas Shepard and John Bunyan also asked them. But the elaborateness with which Anne Bradstreet formulates her answers indicates that for her too they were genuine problems. It is true that in the complete passage she does resolve her doubts through a determination to rely upon faith: "Return, O my Soul, to thy Rest, upon this Rock Christ Jesus will I build my faith." But she adds, "and, if I perish, I perish." So it takes one more assertion to close the argument: "But I know all the Powers of Hell shall never prevail against it. I know whom I have trusted . . . and that he is able to keep that I have committed to his charge."

Her distrust of death as the gateway to the supreme life is indicated more personally in an entry in the notebook for August 28, 1656:

Now I can wait, looking every day when my Saviour shall call for me. Lord graunt that while I live I may doe that service I am able in this frail Body, and bee in continuall expectation of my change, and let me never forgett thy great Love to my soul so lately expressed, when I could lye down and bequeath my Soul to thee, and Death seem'd no terrible Thing. O let me ever see Thee that Art invisible, and I shall not bee unwilling to come, tho: by so rough a Messenger.

Once more in this passage, the experience described seems to be one of conviction attempting to conquer feeling, but the final complaint of "so rough a Messenger" indicates that the delight in the future glorified state is not enough to offset earthly doubts and fear of death.

The struggle between dogma and feeling reaches its apex in the seven poems composed between 1665 and 1670, the last years of Anne Bradstreet's life. These include two personal poems and four memorial elegies upon members of her family.

These last poems present the arguments of the Flesh and the Spirit in relation to real occurrences. The Flesh argued for the visible against the invisible, and for honor, wealth, and pleasure. But what the real woman wants, rather than riches, is a home with its comforts and memories; rather than honor and pleasure, the lives of loved ones; and finally life itself. In these poems, Anne Bradstreet presents her own conflict in regard to these desires. Her feelings about her home represent the most material conflict. In 1666, when the Bradstreet home at Andover burned down, she wrote a poem about the conflagration and her own feelings. She describes her awakening to the "shreiks of dreadfull voice" and going out to watch "the flame consume" her "dwelling place." But she comforts herself with good Puritan dogma:

> And, when I could no longer look,
> I blest his Name that gave and took,
> That layd my goods now in the dust:
> Yea so it was, and so 'twas just.
> It was his own: it was not mine;
> Far be it that I should repine.

> He might of All justly bereft,
> But yet sufficient for us left.

This is an argument that Spirit might have used; the burning of the house was God's doing, and his doings should not be questioned. But she *does* question in the next three stanzas, where she lovingly goes over the contents of the house—the questioning being through feeling tone rather than statement. As she passes the ruins, she re-creates the pleasant things that had been there:

> When by the Ruines oft I past,
> My sorrowing eyes aside did cast,
> And here and there the places spye
> Where oft I sate, and long did lye.

> Here stood that Trunk, and there that chest:
> There lay that store I counted best:
> My pleasant things in ashes lye,
> And them behold no more shall I.
> Under thy roof no guest shall sitt,
> Nor at thy Table eat a bitt.

> No pleasant tale shall 'ere be told,
> Nor things recounted done of old.
> No candle 'ere shall shine in Thee,
> Nor bridegroom's voice ere heard shall bee.

In its progress the poem becomes almost another dialogue of dogma and feeling, or of Flesh and Spirit, for she chides her own heart in the manner of the Spirit:

> Then streight I 'gin my heart to chide,
> And did thy wealth on earth abide?
> Didst fix thy hope on mouldring dust,
> The arm of flesh didst make thy trust?
> Raise up thy thoughts above the skye

> That dunghill mists away may flie.

> Thou hast an house on high erect,
> Fram'd by that mighty Architect,
> With glory richly furnished,
> Stands permanent tho: this bee fled.

Despite the reasonable arguments that her goods belonged to God and whatever God does is just, there is in the poem an undercurrent of regret that the loss is not fully compensated for by the hope of treasure that lies above.

The undercurrent is even stronger in the elegies on her grandchildren. Though dogma could reason that God could take away her possessions, and though she could accept this on a rational level, even though it ran counter to her feelings, what could Spirit say when God took away her dearest relatives? The questioning extends over the last four elegies. But we must first look back to the elegy on her father written some years before. There, in contrast to the early elegies which lacked the Christian apotheosis, her aged father is seen as being among the Saints:

> Ah happy Soul, 'mongst Saints and Angels blest,
> Who after all his toyle, is now at rest.

In this elegy, there is no question of the rightness of death; her father is "timely mown," for he is "fully ripe." It is otherwise in the poems on the deaths of her grandchildren. There is in these a strong note of personal bereavement, which goes beyond the impersonal tone of earlier poems, and that of the period generally: there is an inclination to use "self-expression," in itself a move in the direction of later writers, in interpreting these deaths in their relation to herself. The first elegy is on Elizabeth who died at the age of one and a half. It is incidentally one of the finest elegies in American literature. Here she admits in keeping with dogma that her heart was set too much on one who was after all only one of God's creatures:

> Farewel dear babe, my hearts too much content,
> Farewel sweet babe, the pleasure of mine eye,
> Farewel fair flower that for a space was lent,
> Then ta'en away unto Eternity.

She concludes the stanza with a conventional question:

> Blest babe why should I once bewail thy fate,
> Or sigh the dayes so soon were terminate;
> Sith thou art setled in an Everlasting state.

This should lead into a conventional Christian apotheosis, but the problem for Anne Bradstreet is that she cannot properly, i. e. dogmatically, answer the question. She answers it by stating how she really feels instead of how she *should* feel. The reply is closer to Herrick and the Cavaliers than to most Puritan poetry:

> By nature Trees do rot when they are grown.
> And Plumbs and Apples thoroughly ripe do fall,
> And Corn and grass are in their season mown,
> And time brings down what is both strong and
>   tall.
> But plants new set to be eradicate,
> And buds new blown to have so short a date . . .

How can she end the stanza? How can she retreat from this approach to criticism of God who orders all things? Only by saying it is God's will. So she concludes, not by joy in the Christian transformation, but by a backing down from her near-criticism of the deity, and says that the taking away of this fair flower "is by his hand alone that guides nature and fate."

The elegy on the next dead grandchild is a fairly conventional one, concluding properly:

> Farewel dear child, thou ne're shall come to me,
> But yet a while, and I shall go to thee;
> Mean time my throbbing heart's chear'd up with this
> Thou with thy Saviour art in endless bliss.

But when the third grandchild, Simon, died that same year at the age of one month, she once more came closer to expressing her strong feelings:

> No sooner come, but gone, and fal'n asleep,
> Acquaintance short, yet parting caus'd us weep,
> Three flours, two scarcely blown, the last i'th 'bud,
> Cropt by th' Almighties hand . . .

Thus she lists in seemingly objective fashion what has happened. Continuing the burden of her earlier poem on Elizabeth, which implies regret that "buds new blown" should "have so short a date," these lines also imply that something is wrong. And the lines which follow convert this statement into irony, for they dwell on the goodness and power of God:

> Cropt by th' Almighties hand; yet is he good,
> With dreadful awe before him let's be mute,
> Such was his will, but why, let's not dispute,
> With humble hearts and mouths put in the dust,
> Let's say he's merciful as well as just.

Merely to state Puritan dogma about the power of God here after the ample description of what God has done is to question God's ways on the level of feeling. The words "Let's say" placed before "he's merciful as well as just" suggest doubt; the clause, "but why, let's not dispute" indicates there could be room for question. Anne Bradstreet is trying to stifle her doubt and grief by a statement of dogma. That she was aware of the irony at some level is perhaps shown by the fact that the rest of the poem is spent in a quiet settling down to a conventional and innocuous statement:

> He will return, and make up all our losses,
> And smile again, after our bitter crosses.
> Go, pretty babe, go rest with Sisters twain
> Among the blest in endless joyes remain.

Her last dated poem, the poem on the death of the mother of the children, is also conventional.

Of more interest in showing the final real outcome of the dialogue of Flesh and Spirit is the poem written in the summer of 1669, usually called **"A Pilgrim."** It was composed in the same summer as the conventional and world-weary poem on the death of her second grandchild. In it she considers the loss of the flesh itself, that is her own earthly life. Here the Flesh has already lost out; there is no internal conflict; only the inconveniences of the Flesh are considered:

> This body shall in silence sleep

> Mine eyes no more shall ever weep
>
> No fainting fits shall me assaile
> nor grinding paines my body fraile
> With cares and fears ne'r cumbred be
> Nor losses know nor sorrowes see.

There is joyous acceptance of the promise of immortality:

> What tho my flesh shall there consume
> it is the bed Christ did perfume
> And when a few yeares shall be gone
> this mortall shall be cloth'd upon
> A Corrupt Carcasse downe it lyes
> a glorious body it shall rise.
> In weaknes and dishonour sowne
> in power 'tis rais'd by Christ alone
> Then soule and body shall unite
> and of their maker have the sight
> Such lasting ioyes shall there behold
> as eare ne'r heard nor tongue e'er told
> Lord make me ready for that day
> then Come deare bridgrome Come away.

In the final analysis the spirit wins because it can outlast the flesh, and the individual submits to the loss of the flesh and the hope of the resurrection because he must. As when she first came into the country, Anne Bradstreet was always willing to submit to the inevitable during her long pilgrimage, but she did it only after using the full faculties of the soul—the imagination, the affections, and the will—and it is this clash of feeling and dogma that keeps her poetry alive. True, her tension is often resolved, and it is without the darkness, alienation, and disorder that grows out of the tension in later American writers. But Anne Bradstreet went as far as her place in a society which condemned Anne Hutchinson and Anne Hopkins would allow. And in this respect she sets the tone for a long line of American writers who would follow her, who could press farther against the limitations of society, who would express what D. H. Lawrence has called the "duplicity" of the American literary mind. These writers—men such as Cooper, Hawthorne, and Melville—according to Lawrence own "a tight mental allegiance to a morality which all their passion goes to destroy." No better description could be found for the poetry of Anne Bradstreet.

Adrienne Rich (essay date 1966)

SOURCE: "The Tensions of Anne Bradstreet," in her *On Lies, Secrets, and Silence: Selected Prose, 1966-1978,* W. W. Norton & Company, 1979, pp. 21-32.

[*Rich is a celebrated American poet and critic. In the essay below, she analyzes Bradstreet's form and themes based on biographical information about the poet.*]

1630: the expected sea-voyage with its alternations of danger and boredom, three months of close quarters and raw nerves, sickness and hysteria and salt meats; finally the wild coast of Massachusetts Bay, the blazing heat of an American June, the half-dying, famine-ridden frontier village of Salem, clinging to the edge of an incalculable landmass.

"I found a new world and new manners, at which my heart rose. But after I was convinced it was the way of God, I sub-

mitted to it and joined to the church at Boston." Sixty years later she was to write that. Other hearts had hesitated, at the first view of the same world and its manners. Anne Bradstreet's heart rose against much that lay before her, much too that had come along with her in the *Arbella*. She was eighteen, two years married, out of a civilized and humane background. Her father, Thomas Dudley, a man of education and worldly experience, had been steward to an earl; her mother, by Cotton Mather's account, "a gentlewoman whose extraction and estates were considerable." Her own education had been that of the clever girl in the cultivated seventeenth-century house: an excellent library, worldly talk, the encouragement of a literate father who loved history. Her husband was a Cambridge man, a Nonconformist minister's son. Her father, her husband, each was to serve as governor of Massachusetts; she came to the wilderness as a woman of rank.

Younger, Anne Bradstreet had struggled with a "carnall heart." Self-scrutiny, precisianism, were in any event expected of Puritan young people. But her doubts, her "sitting loose from God," were underscored by uncommon intelligence and curiosity. Once in Massachusetts, in a society coarsened by hardship and meager in consolations, any religious doubt must at times have made everything

seem dubious. Her father wrote back to England a year after their arrival:

> If there be any endued with grace . . . let them come over. . . . For others, I conceive they are not yet fitted for this business.
>
> . . . There is not a house where is not one dead, and some houses many . . . the natural causes seem to be in the want of warm lodging and good diet, to which Englishmen are habituated at home, and the sudden increase of heat which they endure that are landed here in summer . . . for those only these two last years died of fevers who landed in June or July, as those of Plymouth, who landed in winter, died of the scurvy.

To read and accept God's will, not only in the deaths of friends, but in one's own frequent illness, chronic lameness, political tension between one's father and Governor Winthrop, four changes of house in eight years, difficulty in conceiving a child, private and public anxiety and hardship, placed a peculiar burden of belief and introspection on an intellectually active, sensually quick spirit.

Seventeenth-century Puritan life was perhaps the most self-conscious ever lived in its requirements of the individual understanding: no event so trivial that it could not speak a divine message, no disappointment so heavy that it could not serve as a "correction," a disguised blessing. Faith underwent its hourly testing, the domestic mundanities were episodes in the drama; the piecemeal thought of a woman stirring a pot, clues to her "justification" in Christ. A modern consciousness looks almost enviously upon the intense light of significance under which those lives were lived out: "everything had a meaning then," we say, as if that had ever held alert and curious minds back from perverse journeys:

> When I have got over this Block, then have I another put in my way. That admitt this be the true God whom we worship, and that be his word, yet why may not the Popish religion be the right? They have the same God, the same Christ, the same word: they only interpret it one way, we another.

Thus Anne Bradstreet described in her old age, for her children, what the substance of doubt had been. And if Archbishop Laud and the Hierarchists back in England were right, what was one doing, after all, on that stretch of intemperate coast, hoarding fuel, hoarding corn, dragging one's half-sick self to the bedsides of the dying? What was the meaning of it all? One's heart rose in rebellion.

Still, she was devotedly, even passionately married, and through husband and father stood close to the vital life of the community. (Her father was a magistrate at the trial of Anne Hutchinson, the other, heretical, Anne, who threatened the foundations of the colony and "gloried" in her excommunication.) And her mind was alive. Thomas Dudley's library had passed to the New World, and the early childless years, for all their struggles with theology and primitive surroundings, left time, energy to go on reading and thinking. The Bible was the air she and everyone else breathed; but she also knew Raleigh's *History of the World,* Camden's *Annals of Queen Elizabeth, Piers*

THE TENTH MUSE
Lately fprung up in AMERICA.
OR
Severall Poems, compiled
with great variety of VVit
and Learning, full of delight.
Wherein efpecially is contained a compleat difcourfe and defcription of
The Four { Elements,
Conftitutions,
Ages of Man,
Seafons of the Year.
Together with an Exact Epitomie of
the Four Monarchies, viz.
The { Affyrian,
Perfian,
Grecian,
Roman.
Alfo a Dialogue between Old England and
New, concerning the late troubles.
With divers other pleafant and ferious Poems.
By a Gentlewoman in thofe parts.
Printed at London for *Stephen Bowtell* at the figne of the
Bible in Popes Head-Alley. 1650.

Title page of The Tenth Muse, *1650.*

Plowman, Sidney's poems; and she was deeply impressed by Joshua Sylvester's translation of Guillaume Du Bartas's *La Sepmaine du Creation.*

The Divine Weekes and Works, as this elephantine poem was called in English, was an acknowledged popular masterpiece. Du Bartas, the leading French Calvinist poet, was admired as a peer of Ronsard. Sylvester was not his only English translator: Philip Sidney among others had been moved to undertake a version. Sylvester's own poetry had been praised—in verse blurbs—by Samuel Daniel and Ben Jonson. Milton had pillaged *The Divine Weekes* in composing *Paradise Lost.* Anne Bradstreet was thus showing no provinciality of taste in her response to Du Bartas. His poem was, in fact, as one scholar has exhaustively shown, a perfect flea market of ideas, techniques, and allusions for the Puritan poet. Crammed with popular science, catalogues of diseases, gems, fauna, and flora, groaning with hypotheses on the free will of angels, or God's occupation before the First Day, quivering with excesses, laborious and fascinating as some enormous serpent winding endlessly along and forever earthbound, *The Divine Weekes* has, yet, a vitality of sheer conviction about it; one can understand its mesmeric attraction for an age unglutted by trivial or pseudomomentous information. And this poem, sublime at least in its conception, was directly concerned with the most gripping drama recognized by the seventeenth-century mind.

One thing is clear, when one actually reads Anne Bradstreet's early verse by the side of Du Bartas: however much she may have admired his "haughty Stile and rapted wit sublime," she almost never lapsed into his voice. Her admiration was in large measure that of a neophyte bluestocking for a man of wide intellectual attainments; in emulating him she emulated above all:

> Thy Art in natural Philosophy,
> Thy Saint-like mind in grave Divinity.
> Thy piercing skill in high Astronomy,
> And curious insight in Anatomy: . . .
> Thy Physick, musick and state policy . . .

She was influenced more by Du Bartas's range and his encyclopedic conception of poetry, than by his stylistic qualities. That early verse of hers, most often pedestrian, abstract, mechanical, rarely becomes elaborately baroque; at its best her style, even in these apprentice pieces, has a plain modesty and directness which owe nothing to Du Bartas. She feels herself in his shadow, constantly disclaims the ability to write like him, even if she would; but she seems further to have had reservations about mere imitation of even so stylish a model: "My goods are true (though poor) I love no stealth."

Versifying was not an exceptional pursuit in that society; poetry, if edifying in theme, was highly recommended to the Puritan reader. (A century later Cotton Mather was finding it necessary to caution the orthodox against "a Boundless and Sickly Appetite, for the Reading of Poems, which now the Rickety Nation swarms withal.") Unpublished verse manuscripts circulated in New England before the first printing press began operation. By her own admission, Anne Bradstreet began her verse-making almost accidentally:

> My subject's bare, my brain is bad,
> Or better lines you should have had:
> The first fell in so naturally,
> I knew not how to pass it by . . .

Thus ends her *Quaternion,* or four poems of four books each, written somewhere between 1630 and 1642. Her expositions of **"The Humours," "The Ages of Man," "The Seasons,"** and **"The Elements,"** and above all her long historical poem, **"The Four Monarchies,"** read like a commonplace book put into iambic couplets, the historical, scientific journal of a young woman with a taste for study. Had she stopped writing after the publication of these verses, or had she simply continued in the same vein, Anne Bradstreet would survive in the catalogues of Women's Archives, a social curiosity or at best a literary fossil. The talent exhibited in them was of a kind acceptable to her time and place, but to a later eye indistinct from masses of English verse of the period.

Anne Bradstreet was the first nondidactic American poet, the first to give an embodiment to American nature, the first in whom personal intention appears to precede Puritan dogma as an impulse to verse.

—*Adrienne Rich*

The seventeenth-century Puritan reader was not, however, in search of "new voices" in poetry. If its theme was the individual in his experience of God, the final value of a poem lay in its revelation of God and not the individual. Least of all in a woman poet would radical powers be encouraged. Intellectual intensity among women gave cause for uneasiness: the unnerving performance of Anne Hutchinson had disordered the colony in 1636, and John Winthrop wrote feelingly in 1645 of

> a godly young woman, and of special parts, who was fallen into a sad infirmity, the loss of her understanding, and reason, which had been growing upon her divers years, by occasion of her giving herself wholly to reading and writing, and written many books.

Anne Bradstreet's early work may be read, or skimmed, against this background. Apart from its technical amateurishness, it is remarkably impersonal even by Puritan standards. She was receiving indelible impressions during those years between her arrival in New England and the publication of her verses in 1650. But she appears to have written by way of escaping from the conditions of her experience, rather than as an expression of what she felt and knew. New England never enters her book except as the rather featureless speaker in a **"Dialogue Between Old and New England"**; the landscape, the emotional weather of the New World are totally absent; the natural description in her **"Four Seasons"** woodenly reproduce England, like snow-scenes on Australian Christmas cards. Theology, a subject with which her prose memoir tells us she was painfully grappling, is touched on in passing. Personal history—marriage, childbearing, death—is similarly excluded from the book which gave her her contemporary reputation. These long, rather listless pieces seem to have been composed in a last compulsive effort to stay in contact with the history, traditions, and values of her former world; nostalgia for English culture, surely, kept her scribbling at those academic pages, long after her conviction had run out. Present experience was still too raw, one sought relief from its daily impact in turning Raleigh and Camden into rhymed couplets, recalling a scenery and a culture denied by the wilderness. Yet it is arguable that the verse which gained her serious acceptance in her own time was a psychological stepping-stone to the later poems which kept her alive for us.

When, in 1650, Anne Bradstreet's brother-in-law returned to England, he carried along without her knowledge a manuscript containing the verses she had copied out for family circulation. This he had published in London under the title, *The Tenth Muse, Lately Sprung Up in America.* There was considerable plotting among friends and family to launch the book. Nathaniel Ward, the "Simple Cobbler of Agawam" and former neighbor of the Bradstreets, wrote a blurb in verse, rather avuncular and condescending. Woodbridge, the brother-in-law, himself undertook to explain in a foreword that the book

> is the Work of a Woman, honoured, and esteemed where she lives, for her gracious demeanour, her eminent parts, her pious conversation, her courteous disposition, her exact diligence in her place, and discreet managing of her Family occasions, and more than so, these Poems are but the fruit of some few houres, curtailed from her sleepe and other refreshments.

Mixed feelings entered the woman's proud and self-critical soul when the printed volume was laid, with due mystery and congratulation, in her lap. **"The Author to Her Book"** makes this abundantly clear. *She* had not given the "rambling brat" leave to stray beyond the family circle. Fond relatives, "less wise than true," had connived under her nose to spread abroad what they knew she had "resolved in such a manner should never see the Sun." The seductions of print, the first glamor of success, were paid for by the exposure of weakness, by irritation at the printer's errors which only compounded her own. Ward's jocular praise—"a right Du Bartas Girle . . . I muse whither at length these Girles would go"—surely stung the woman who wrote:

> If what I do prove well, it won't advance.
> They'l say it's stoln, or else it was by chance.

But she was a spirited woman with a strong grasp on reality; and temperament, experience, and the fact of having reached a wider audience converged at this period to give Anne Bradstreet a new assurance. Her poems were being read seriously by strangers, though not in the form she would have chosen to send them out. Her intellectual delight was no longer vulnerable to carping ("Theyl say my hand a needle better fits"); it was a symptom neither of vanity nor infirmity; she had carried on her woman's life

conscientiously while composing her book. It is probable that some tension of self-distrust was relaxed, some inner vocation confirmed, by the publication and praise of *The Tenth Muse.* But the word "vocation" must be read in a special sense. Not once in her prose memoir does she allude to her poems, or to the publication of her book; her story, as written out for her children, is the familiar Puritan drama of temptation by Satan and correction by God. She would not have defined herself, even by aspiration, as an artist. But she had crossed the line between the amateur and the artist, where private dissatisfaction begins and public approval, though gratifying, is no longer of the essence. For the poet of her time and place, poetry might be merely a means to a greater end; but the spirit in which she wrote was not that of a dilettante.

Her revisions to *The Tenth Muse* are of little aesthetic interest. Many were made on political grounds, although a reading of North's Plutarch is supposed to have prompted insertions in **"The Four Monarchies."** What followed, however, were the poems which rescue Anne Bradstreet from the Women's Archives and place her conclusively in literature. A glance at the titles of her later poems reveals to what extent a real change in her active sensibility had taken place after 1650. No more Ages of Man, no more Assyrian monarchs; but poems in response to the simple events in a woman's life: a fit of sickness; her son's departure for England; the arrival of letters from her absent husband; the burning of their Andover house; a child's or grandchild's death; a walk in the woods and fields near the Merrimac River. At moments her heart still rises, the lines give back a suppressed note of outrage:

> By nature Trees do rot when they are grown,
> And Plumbs and Apples thoroughly ripe do fall,
> And Corn and grass are in their season mown,
> And time brings down what is both strong and
>   tall.
> But plants new set to be eradicate,
> And buds new blown, to have so short a date,
> Is by his hand alone that guides nature and fate.

The delicacy and reticence of her expression at its best are seen in her poem, **"Before the Birth of One of Her Children,"** which voices woman's age-old fear of death in childbirth, in the seventeenth century a thoroughly realistic apprehension. The poem is consequently a practical document, a little testament. Neither bathos nor self-indulgence cloud the economy of these lines; they are honest, tender, and homely as a letter out of a marriage in which the lovers are also friends. The emotional interest of the poem lies in the human present and future; only in its conclusion does it gesture toward a hoped-for immortality. And the writer's pangs arise, not from dread of what lies after death, but from the thought of leaving a husband she loves and children half-reared.

> That there is a God my reason would soon tell
> me by the wondrous works that I see, the vast
> frame of the heaven and the earth, the order of
> all things, night and day, summer and winter,
> spring and autumn, the daily providing for this
> great household upon the earth, the preserving
> and directing of all to its proper end.

This theme, from her prose memoir, might be a text for

the first part of her **"Contemplations,"** the most skilled and appealing of her long poems. In its stanzas the poet wanders through a landscape of clarity and detail, exalting God's glory in nature; she becomes mindful, however, of the passing of temporal pleasure and the adversity that lies the other side of ease and sweetness. The landscape is more American than literary; it is clearly a sensuous resource and solace for the poet; but her art remains consistent in its intentions: "not to set forth myself, but the glory of God." It is of importance to bear this in mind, in any evaluation of Anne Bradstreet; it gives a peculiar poignancy to her more personal verse, and suggests an organic impulse toward economy and modesty of tone. Her several poems on recovery from illness (each with its little prose gloss recounting God's "correction" of her soul through bodily fevers and faintings) are in fact curiously impersonal as poetry; their four-foot-three-foot hymn-book meters, their sedulous meekness, their Biblical allusions, are the pure fruit of convention. Yet other occasional poems, such as **"Upon the Burning of Our House,"** which spring from a similar motif, are heightened and individualized by references to things intimately known, life-giving strokes of personal fact:

> When by the ruins oft I past
> My sorrowing eyes aside did cast,
> And here and there the places spy
> Where oft I sat and long did lie:
> Here stood that trunk, and there that chest,
> There lay that store I counted best.
> My pleasant things in ashes lie,
> And them behold no more shall I.
> Under thy roof no guest shall sit,
> Nor at thy table eat a bit.
> No pleasant tale shall e'er be told,
> Nor things recounted done of old.
> No candle e'er shall shine in thee,
> Nor bridegroom's voice e'er heard shall be.

Upon the grounds of a Puritan aesthetic either kind of poem won its merit solely through doctrinal effectiveness; and it was within a Puritan aesthetic that Anne Bradstreet aspired and wrote. What is remarkable is that so many of her verses satisfy a larger aesthetic, to the extent of being genuine, delicate minor poems.

Until Edward Taylor, in the second half of the century, these were the only poems of more than historical interest to be written in the New World. Anne Bradstreet was the first nondidactic American poet, the first to give an embodiment to American nature, the first in whom personal intention appears to precede Puritan dogma as an impulse to verse. Not that she could be construed as a Romantic writing out of her time. The web of her sensibility stretches almost invisibly within the framework of Puritan literary convention; its texture is essentially both Puritan and feminine. Compared with her great successor, Taylor, her voice is direct and touching, rather than electrifying in its tensions or highly colored in its values. Her verses have at every point a transparency which precludes the metaphysical image; her eye is on the realities before her, or on images from the Bible. Her individualism lies in her choice of material rather than in her style.

The difficulty displaced, the heroic energy diffused in merely living a life, is an incalculable quantity. It is pointless, finally, to say that Poe or Hart Crane might have survived longer or written differently had either been born under a better star or lived in more encouraging circumstances. America has from the first levied peculiarly harsh taxes on its poets—physical, social, moral, through absorption as much as through rejection. John Berryman admits that in coming to write his long poem, *Homage to Mistress Bradstreet,* "I did not choose her—somehow she chose me—one point of connection being the almost insuperable difficulty of writing high verse at all in a land that cared and cares so little for it." Still, with all stoic recognition of the common problem in each succeeding century including the last half-hour, it is worth observing that Anne Bradstreet happened to be one of the first American women, inhabiting a time and place in which heroism was a necessity of life, and men and women were fighting for survival both as individuals and as a community. To find room in that life for any mental activity which did not directly serve certain spiritual ends, was an act of great self-assertion and vitality. To have written poems, the first good poems in America, while rearing eight children, lying frequently sick, keeping house at the edge of wilderness, was to have managed a poet's range and extension within confines as severe as any American poet has confronted. If the severity of these confines left its mark on the poetry of Anne Bradstreet, it also forced into concentration and permanence a gifted energy that might, in another context, have spent itself in other, less enduring directions.

Rob Wilson on Bradstreet's depiction of the sublime:

Like latter-day American and equally Christian poets, such as William Livingston, William Cullen Bryant, Walt Whitman, Emily Dickinson, or Frederick Goddard Tuckerman, Bradstreet registers "the sublime" as a moment of pious awe before the landscape in which the poet is dislocated, undone, yet perilously uplifted into regions of spirit. The poetic result is, quite often, an elevated tone of praise and a sense, more materially speaking, of symbolic self-empowerment where the ego fits in a scene of its own self-constituted unity. The sublime, as Bradstreet early glimpsed, might have cash-value consequences if sustained through faithful labor. This scenario of *conversion,* heights and risks of ecstasy in an indigenous setting, is memorably depicted in **"Contemplations,"** a poem which suggests the emerging genre of an American sublime in its tone of "rapted wit" and master narrative of conversion.

Rob Wilson, in his American Sublime: The Genealogy of a Poetic Genre, *1991.*

Robert D. Richardson, Jr. (essay date 1967)

SOURCE: "The Puritan Poetry of Anne Bradstreet," in *Critical Essays on Anne Bradstreet,* edited by Pattie Cowell and Ann Stanford, G. K. Hall & Co., 1983, pp. 101-15.

[*Richardson is an American critic and educator. In the essay below, he examines the influence of Puritanism on Bradstreet's poetry.*]

Anne Bradstreet's poetry has been steadily reprinted, anthologized and commented upon since the seventeenth century. Yet she has been praised more often as a phenomenon than as a poet, and her poetry, when it is discussed at all, is sometimes treated in the context of Puritanism and sometimes not. John Berryman's brilliant and moving poem on Mrs. Bradstreet is, in one way, an example of the fact that it is now more common to render homage to her than it is to offer critical analysis. The present essay is an attempt to find a suitable focus for the study of her poetry as poetry. In view of the continuing and perhaps even increasing interest in Anne Bradstreet, it seems worth trying to show, in appropriate detail, that she wrote from what might be called the Puritan sensibility, that her best poetry gains rather than loses by being considered as the product of that sensibility, and that her finest work, **"Contemplations,"** is a splendid and coherent expression of what was best in New England Puritanism.

Puritanism in Massachusetts in the middle of the seventeenth century was a way of life, and its ideal is perhaps best expressed in its injunction that one must somehow live in the world without being of it. This outlook rests firmly on what Perry Miller has called "the dual contention of the Puritan synthesis," which Miller described [in *The Puritans,* 1963] as the assertion of "the fallibility of material existence and the infallibility of the spiritual, the necessity for living in a world of time and space according to the laws of that time and that place, with never once forgetting that the world will pass, be resolved back into nothingness." In practice, this meant that the Puritan was always trying to achieve a balance between this world and the next. Monastic withdrawal was out of the question; one could not safely turn one's back on this world, for the simple reason that God had made it and had found it good; yet one could not rely upon, or repose in the security of, an earthly life which was, at last, insubstantial. At their most extreme, these apparently conflicting claims on the individual produced what Edmund Morgan calls the Puritan dilemma.

> Puritanism required that a man devote his life to seeking salvation, but told him he was helpless to do anything but evil. Puritanism required that he rest his whole hope in Christ but taught him that Christ would utterly reject him unless before he was born God had foreordained his salvation. Puritanism required that man refrain from sin but told him he would sin anyhow. [*The Puritan Dilemma,* 1958]

Thus the Puritan way of life was, at worst, a series of impossible conflicts, and at best a difficult balance. Edward Taylor's extreme and contrasting moods of exaltation and despair are a rather obvious illustration of the effect of the uneasy synthesis upon one sensitive and gifted person. Samuel Sewall's well-known apostrophe to Plum Island is a momentary perception of the possible balance between this world and the next.

Anne Bradstreet also wrestled with the problem, at times rebelling, at times submitting. That she had severe doubts about her faith does not make her any the less a Puritan. In fact, according to the carefully safeguarded morphology of conversion developed by New England Puritanism, a firm and doubt-free conviction of salvation was a probable sign of damnation. As Morgan has pointed out, doubt and struggle were built into the fabric of Puritanism.

> Delusion continually threatened, because the assurance wrought by grace was easily confused with the false assurance or "security" of the unregenerate. Arthur Hildersham explained how to distinguish true from false assurance. True assurance came only after attendance on the preaching of the word, and only after a period of doubt and despair. [*Visible Saints,* 1963]

Thus it becomes possible, I think, to regard Anne Bradstreet's struggles between love of this world and reliance on the next, and the poetic expression of those struggles, not as the rebelliousness of an anti-Puritan temperament but as an attempt to achieve the Puritan ideal of living in the world without being of it.

Her early poetry tends to run to extremes; it is unable to accommodate both worlds. The earliest poem to which a date can be given is the one in ballad measure called **"Upon a fit of Sickness, Anno 1632,"** written when she was nineteen. Simple and without force, the poem expresses a reliance upon God and a routine dismissal of this world. Her point is not that tribulation or suffering compels her to turn to Christianity; it is rather an expression of contempt for this life in the medieval tradition.

> For what's this life, but care and strife?
> since first we came from womb.
> Our strength doth waste, our time doth hast
> and then we go to th' Tomb.

She turns her back on the world; it means nothing. And as her rejection of the present world is complete, her reliance upon the next reveals an almost mechanical security. The outcome is not in doubt; there is no need to hope or pray. She is simply sure of heaven.

> The race is run, the field is won
> the victory's mine I see.
> For ever know, thou envious foe
> the foyle belongs to thee.

In sharp contrast to this easy otherworldliness, the long poems in *The Tenth Muse* show a nearly unqualified worldliness. She writes of the four elements, humours, ages of man, seasons, and monarchies in a surprisingly secular way. There is no emphasis on Adam's fall, no attempt to make her subject subserve Calvinism, very little Christianity of any sort. She seems interested in contemporary knowledge about man, and she appears to have been especially attracted by the old exotic empires glittering with famous men and deeds. **"The Four Monarchies"** is, in many respects, conventional and derivative, yet it is not always predictable. In addition to the remarkable absence of Calvinism, there is the unlooked-for approbation of such figures as Nebuchadnezzar and Darius Hyspaspes. There is a quality of spectacle as well; the poem dwells on the sumptuous and the stupendous. It is climaxed by the section on Alexander the Great, by far the longest section in the poem. That Anne Bradstreet was fascinated by Alexander and not just indulging in colorless cribbing from Raleigh and Ussher is attested by the repeated references to the Macedonian conqueror in her elegy on Sir Philip Sidney. The greatest compliment she can pay Sidney is to call him another Alexander. **"The Four Monarchies"** is reminiscent of the Fall of Princes literature and it shows a concern with the great Elizabethan theme of mutability. It is a theme that was to occupy Anne Bradstreet for years; here it is given a simple secular expression. As the poem reaches the end of the third monarchy (The Grecian) it rises to a summary:

> Here ends at last the Grecian Monarchy
> Which by the Romans had its destiny;
> Thus Kings and Kingdoms, have their times,
>   and dates,
> Their standings, over-turnings, bounds, and
>   fates:
> Now up, now down now chief, and then brought
>   under,
> The Heavn's thus rule, to fil the earth with won-
>   der.

But however much she muses upon time's inconstant stay, the spectacle of the fallen ancient world does not move the poet to religious reflection. **"The Four Monarchies"** is as thoroughly caught up in this world as her earliest poem is in the other world.

Most of the other poems in the first edition of *The Tenth Muse* are similarly secular. Her poems on Sidney, DuBartas, and Elizabeth are applications of the memorializing method of **"The Four Monarchies"** to recent figures. Even **"A Dialogue between Old England and New,"** though informed by Puritan political zeal, is distinctly concerned with such things as terrestrial justice. But the final poem of the early volume, **"The Vanity of all worldly things"** swings back again to the other extreme. It is a sorrowful lament, a turning to the other world. It is on the theme and in the manner of Ecclesiastes; it is not, however, a simple rejection of the world. In rhymed couplets which are both calmer and more expressive than the early ballad meter, she painfully catalogues the vanities of life.

> If not in honour, beauty, age, nor treasure,
> Nor yet in learning, wisdome, youth nor plea-
>   sure
> Where shall I climb, sound, seek search or find
> That *summum bonum* which may stay my
>   mind?

The poem turns to God and to hopes of heaven, but only after this world has been ransacked for possibilities. The final effect is weak, however, since the earth is represented only in abstractions. But while the world is still spurned with relative ease, we do not find in this poem any simple assurance of salvation for the poet. Salvation exists—"who is possessed of [it] shall reign a king"—but she no longer finds it so easy to claim it for herself.

The poems dealt with so far suggest the extreme positions of acceptance and rejection of this world of which Anne Bradstreet was capable. The extremes are, of course, relative. They occur more often in her early work but are by no means confined to it, and they are significant mainly

in the light of her better poetry. The early poems emphasize one side or the other of the problem, but in such well known poems as **"The Flesh and the Spirit"** and **"Upon the Burning of our House,"** we see clearly the conflicting claims of earth and heaven. The form of each poem suggests a foregone conclusion, but the language and general tone of each show that there is a genuine conflict which is resolved, if at all, only with difficulty.

"The Flesh and the Spirit," though cast in the traditional debate form, is more than a routine exercise. Flesh, who speaks first, is not gross, detestable, sensual or mindless. Flesh begins with a series of carefully phrased questions which strikes at the heart of the matter.

> Sister, quoth Flesh, what liv'st thou on
> Nothing but Meditation?
> Doth Contemplation feed thee so
> Regardlessly to let earth goe?
> Can Speculation satisfy
> Notion without Reality?

The questions are designed to suggest that Spirit's beliefs are based on unprovable grounds. Meditation and contemplation are linked to mere speculation. Flesh exposes the continual doubt of the skeptical mind, the nagging fear that belief is only "notion without reality." Spirit replies, of course, but the answer is disappointing. Spirit will not condescend to argue, she simply asserts that she is right and denounces Flesh rather than answering Flesh's arguments; "Thy sinfull pleasures I doe hate / Thy riches are to be no bait." Spirit asserts that she has nourishment Flesh knows not of ("The word of life it is my meat") and by such weak rejoinders tends to validate Flesh's suspicion that it is indeed all notion without reality. The crowning irony, however, comes as Spirit describes heaven in the very material terms she has just scorned.

> My Crown not Diamonds, Pearls, and Gold
> But such as Angels heads infold.
> The City where I hope to dwell
> There's none on Earth to Parallel
> The stately Walls both high and strong
> Are made of pretious Jasper stone;
> The Gates of Pearl . . .

Spirit does not reject jewels; she merely rejects terrestrial jewels in the hope of finer ones elsewhere. The poem ends conventionally. Spirit wins. Yet the poem raises more questions than it settles, and we may fairly wonder whether Spirit deserves to win the debate.

The poem **"Upon the Burning of our House"** is, from a formal point of view, a conventional Puritan exercise in finding the hand of God behind every apparent disaster. Yet the poem moves back and forth from the human level to the divine, and it is not impossible to argue that the human level—the fear of fire, the sense of loss—is what genuinely moves the poet, while her submission to the will of God is a somewhat forced acknowledgment of an arrangement that is not really satisfactory.

> And when I could no longer look,
> I blest his Name that gave and took,
> That layd my goods now in the dust:
> Yea so it was, and so 'twas just.
> It was his own: It was not mine;

Far be it that I should repine.

These lines of submission are clipped and measured, grimly singsong: they sound forced when placed alongside the following lines which emphasize personal loss.

> Here stood that Trunk, and there that chest
> There lay that store I counted best:
> My pleasant things in ashes lye.

She makes the proper application, interpreting the event as a warning, and as an injunction to look toward the "house on high erect." But the vacillation in the poem suggests that the sense of loss outweighs, at least at times, the potential comfort promised by Puritan theology.

Whether or not these two poems are regarded as coming to a resolution, each is alive with conflict, keenly aware of the good things of this world (not just its vanities and vexations) as well as of the folly of a total or ultimate reliance on this world.

In at least one of the short poems to her husband and in the remarkable **"Contemplations,"** Anne Bradstreet reaches a state of mind which can apprehend both this world and the other, can resolve their apparently conflicting claims, and can find satisfaction in the accommodation or resolution. The poems are orthodox enough, yet they are in no sense forced or mechanical, and the poetic achievement they represent is the best indication of the depth of the poet's acceptance.

The poem to her husband beginning "If ever two were one, then surely we" is a love poem of twelve lines which, in a Shakespearean manner, considers the love from several points of view and then subsumes the whole argument in a couplet. Their love is the best of all the things of this world, more to be prized than "whole mines of gold" or "all the riches that the East doth hold." Her love, she suggests, is such that only his love can equal it, and his love for her is so great that she feels inadequate to "recompence" it fully. She therefore asks the heavens to reward him. The development of the poem is clear and logical. His love is so great that she is obliged to turn to the only thing greater than her own love in her search for something to equal his, and the concluding couplet simply expands the idea. "Then while we live, in love lets so persever, / That when we live no more, we may live ever." The union of the lovers in eternity is the outcome of their earthly love. Earthly love, the best of this world, is thus an emblem of what awaits the saved.

In this poem, this world and the next validate one another. Love is the way to heaven, and the best image of heaven is a realm of eternal love. As the poem expresses it, the transition from this world to the next involves not renunciation, not a change even, but an expansion. The poem stands in contrast to such poems as Sidney's "Leave me O Love," in which one sort of love must be rejected before another can be accepted. Anne Bradstreet's poem presents a progressive acceptance, which does not need rejection as a spur. Theology rests lightly on this poem, to be sure. It seems less than orthodox in tone, yet it is not really Arminian. The hope of heaven is only a hope. The poem is dominated by a calm sense that the best of this life must indeed be the link between it and the next. In Puritan

terms, their love is a possible evidence of justification. In personal terms, Heaven holds the only hope that love will have no date.

"Contemplations," the long poem made up of thirty-three seven line stanzas, is generally, and I think rightly, considered Anne Bradstreet's best poem. Thematically, it is permeated by a concern with time and mutability; stylistically, it is reminiscent sometimes of Shakespeare, and sometimes it anticipates Romantic poetry. **"Contemplations"** is marked by an intensity, which, unlike that of most Puritan poems, can still be felt by a reader. It is a complex poem which presents a series of reflections which are sustained and ordered, partly by the continuity of the thought, partly by an almost Romantic use of talismans or symbols. Unlike so much of Puritan poetry which records statements of faith, **"Contemplations"** records a reflective search for faith. The idea of the search is the central theme of the poem and it provides the basic structure as well. The poem may be described as a series of imaginative excursions, each of which begins in the natural world with some specific aspect of nature such as a tree or a river, which then leads the poet's mind outward into imaginative speculation or contemplation and ends eventually with a return to the poet and her present condition.

Thus it is the Puritan problem of the balance between this world and the next that actually dominates the poem and supplies its method. In section after section, the sensuous apprehension of the green world of nature leads the mind by easy and logical stages to a consideration of God and the world above the natural one. In turn, speculation about the next world leads not to statements of dogma and belief, but back to man and the natural world. In **"Contemplations,"** as in few other writings of this period, the interplay between the two worlds is so closely and carefully developed that it may be regarded as Mrs. Bradstreet's most successful expression of the Puritan ideal of living fully in the world without being of it.

The opening two stanzas start the poem off firmly in the natural world, and they set the reflective tone that characterizes the whole work. The poet begins with the recollection of a "time now past in the Autumnal Tide," a time when she was outdoors as evening was coming on. She speaks of the sun as Phoebus, and from this conventional bit of artifice goes on to emphasize the artificiality of her first impression of the scene. The trees were "richly clad," "gilded" by the sun, and "their leaves and fruits seemed painted." But this splendor, as of art, is of course the real and natural world, a "true" nature, "of green, of red, of yellow mixed hew." This vivid apprehension of the lovely natural world so moves her that, for a moment, she knows "not what to wish," but she quickly recovers and makes the observation "If so much excellence abide below, / How excellent is he that dwells on high?" This is the standard Puritan reflex. The natural world, being God's, suggests God. This connection is made several times in the poem. It would be strange if it were otherwise, of course, but the poem is remarkable, not for its unorthodox observations, but for the way it deepens and expands what is normally considered a reflex into a reasonable and persuasive conclusion. Significantly the second stanza does not stop complacently at the thought of God and his perfection, but moves back to his creation, earth.

> Sure he is goodness, wisdom, glory, light
> That hath this under world so richly dight
> More Heaven then Earth was here no winter and
>   no night.

The final line is the culmination of the first two stanzas; it is a perception of the earth and a place approaching Eden, a realm of eternal day and spring. Thus, in the opening two stanzas we are shown first the world, beautiful in terms of art, then the world lovely in its own right, then God, the maker of that world, then the world again, more beautiful now than art, resembling Eden. The rest of the poem repeats this movement, swinging back and forth, redoubling on itself, gathering force and conviction as it widens and takes more and more into account.

Each time the poet takes a fresh look at the world around her, its excellences—not its vexations—move her to think of the other world, and each time she reflects on the next world or on God, she returns to this world since it is the connection between the two that fascinates her and that gives direction to the poem. The third stanza returns to the poet and to a "stately oak," whose age and height move her to reflect on time (a theme one might claim is announced in the opening line of the poem). Even if the oak is a thousand years old, it is nothing to eternity. Again we are given the expected observation, but in an unexpected manner. Her sense of actuality, her sensuous apprehension of the world is at least as strong as her abstract sense. She does not dismiss the oak to dwell upon eternity. The oak remains, and it remains impressive. That eternity is greater merely occurs to her but does not lead her off. The oak, indeed, moves her to consider another even greater part of nature, the sun, to which stanzas four through seven are addressed.

Looking at the sun "whose beams was shaded by the leavie Tree," the poet asks "What glory's like to thee?" But in place of the ritual answer, God, she goes on, "Soul of this world, this Universes Eye. / No wonder some made thee a Deity." The lines draw attention now to the impulse to invest the world with deity, to the process by which man finds gods in nature. Far from resting on received theological truths she is speculating on the fact that nature itself, regarded for itself inevitably leads men's thoughts in certain directions. In the fifth and sixth stanzas she describes the sun and its beneficent effects, rising to an apostrophe that sounds, for a moment, almost pagan. "Hail Creature, full of sweetness beauty and delight." But at the same time that she has captured the mood of primitive sun worship, she is careful to call the sun a creature. Though addressed as a god it is not God. For there remains the question, put now in a pointed and forceful phrase, "Who gave this bright light luster unto thee?" and the acknowledgement that "admir'd ador'd for ever, be that Majesty."

Three times now, the natural world has impelled her mind, in seeking for origins and causes, to God. Yet, with a restlessness that continually brings the poem back to this world—the world in which she must live and which she cannot ignore—the eighth stanza doubles back to the poet "Silent alone, where none or saw, or heard, / In pathless paths I lead my wandering feet." Moved, lost, bewildered, she does not know how to bear witness to what she perceives. "To sing some song, my mazed Muse thought meet . . . But ah, and ah, again, my imbecility." But as nature shows the way to God, so nature prompts the poet. "I heard the merry grasshopper then sing, / The black clad cricket bear a second part." Sound breaks the silence, and if the grasshopper and the cricket can seem "to glory in their little art," why should not she?

The thought process here is close to the heart of the poem. If the poem achieves the delicate balance between the two worlds of Puritan experience, it is because Anne Bradstreet regards the natural world not as a howling wilderness but as the excellent handiwork of God, as a kind of focal point or point of intersection between this world and the other. Each time she returns to the green world she seeks not to impose something on it, but to emulate it. So in the tenth stanza, she takes a lesson from the black clad cricket and begins to apply her own art in earnest now, broadening the theme in familiar Renaissance terms to include time and imagination.

> When present times look back to ages past,
> And men in being fancy those are dead
> It makes things gone perpetually to last,
> And calls back months and years that long since
>   fled.

It is through the imagination or fancy of the living that the past exists. Partly as a way of defeating time and partly as an expression of a sense of history (as opposed to a mere knowledge of it), the poet now proceeds to do what she has just said is possible. Stanzas eleven through fifteen relive, in imaginative form, the old and basic stories of Adam and Eve, and Cain and Abel. It is important to bear in mind that the scenes which follow are not merely recounted. The poet lives in the present and the Biblical stories exist also in the present, alive in her imagination. They are all written in the present tense; "Sometimes in Eden fair, he [one who thus imagines] seems to be, / Sees glorious Adam there made Lord of all." Further, as she writes of Cain, she sees him as a baby, in Eve's lap, and describes the scene as though it lay before her.

> Here sits our Grandame in retired place
> And in her lap, her bloody Cain new born,
> The weeping Imp oft looks her in the face.

As these scenes from the past rise to her mind's eye, becoming real and present, she generalizes the experience, assuming that others, like her, think often "upon the Fathers ages." And inevitably those who are now alive compare their lives with those of the patriarchs. Not only are the lives of the present generation ten times shorter, but we continually shorten even that which we have by "living so little while we are alive." Men now seem small and foolish in comparison with men of the past. The eighteenth stanza continues this contrast as the subject broadens again to set man in the perspective of nature as well as time. The verse rises to a richness and fullness which is as reminiscent of Shakespeare as is the theme.

> When I behold the heavens as in their prime,
> And then the earth (though old) stil clad in
>   green,

The stones and trees insensible of time,
Nor age nor wrinkle on their front are seen;
If winter come and greenness then do fade
A Spring returns, and they more youthful made;
But Man grows old, lies down, remains where
 once he's laid.

The natural world is at peace with time. In the endless wheeling of the seasons, gain and loss are equalized. But, for all that nature or history can show, man is subject to loss without the consequent gain. Although man is the noblest work of creation—the argument continues in stanza nineteen—man "seems by nature and by custome curs'd," and destined for oblivion.

The above argument seems to demonstrate why the natural world is so important to this poem as the meeting place or imaginative focal point between worlds. Just as the Puritans felt that man must live in the world without being of it, so the poet finds herself surveying the natural world without being of it. While nature is in some sense at peace with time, man is not, and the poem now must turn to the only perspective that offers relief from time. To the question "Shall I then praise the heavens, the trees, the earth / Because their beauty and their strength last longer," she replies in the twentieth stanza with the promise of Christianity.

Nay, they shall darken, perish, fade and dye.
And when unmade, so ever shall they lye,
But man was made for endless immortality.

Only in ideas of God or immortality can one find an acceptable solution to the problem posed by time.

But the poem cannot come to rest yet. As if to test and retest, as if reluctant or unable to leave the natural world, the poem again doubles back on itself, coming again to the poet herself and to her walk in the woods. The promise of Eternity is all very well, but the poet cannot allow herself an easy repose in that promise. She must and does live in this world and she clearly prefers the contemplation of nature to abstract theological discussions. She now sits down by a river "under the cooling shadow of a stately Elm." She has already considered the trees, the sun and the heavens, she turns now to the river. Her first reaction, a simple one, is to think how pleasant it would be to live there by the river. She muses about the stream, how it holds its course and overcomes obstacles until it arrives at its eventual goal, the ocean. The river has direction and purpose. It runs its established course, gathering strength from its tributaries, until it empties into an ocean which is only a large version of its own element. It is, she finds, an "emblem true, of what I count the best." The river is analogous to her concept of a life which naturally and inevitably into the next life. Typically, though, she does not digress into a consideration of the next life. Rather, in allowing her imagination to play over what she can see in front of her, she is led on to consider the fishes in the river. They go where they wish, and they lead a happy life. "So nature taught, and yet you know not why / You watry folk that know not your felicity." For still another stanza, she lingers over the fish, following them in her imagination to "Neptun's glassie Hall" and through "the spacious seagreen fields," and ending by remarking on their protec-

tion, "whose armour is their scales, their spreading fins their shield." There are analogies or comparisons between the fish and men, of course, but she does not stop here to draw them out, it being perhaps obvious that while time is like the river, the carefree lives of the fish stand in sharp contrast to human life, even though men have, or can have far better armor and shields than those their own bodies provide. The comparison between the lower creatures and man is uppermost in her mind here, though it must be said that the unoriginal diction weakens this section of the poem.

In stanza twenty-six the poem redoubles on itself for the last time. Again the poet comes back to the present, to the real world which she refuses to leave however tempting a subject the other world may offer. And again it is something in nature which allows her to exist for a while in that precarious but delicate position between the two worlds of man and God.

While musing thus with contemplation fed,
And thousand fancies buzzing in my brain
The sweet-tongu'd Philomel perch't ore my
 head,
And chanted forth a most melodious strain
Which rapt me so with wonder and delight
I judged my hearing better than my sight
And wisht me wings with her a while to take my
 flight.

Again it is a sound that breaks in upon her musings, to call her back to earth, but now it is no cricket, but a bird she calls a nightingale that teases her out of thought, and for the next few stanzas her train of thought is oddly similar to the one Keats was to follow a hundred and forty years later in his "Ode to a Nightingale." The use of "Philomel" here is unfortunate, as is such diction in the preceding stanzas. Happily it is not repeated, nor does one feel that the bird is to her an abstraction.

Her first impulse is to fly away with the bird and share its happy lot. It "fears no snares," it "neither toyles nor hoards," and it "feels no sad thoughts." Its food, drink, and resting place are everywhere, and, best of all, it "Reminds not what is past, nor what's to come dost fear." Not cursed with thought, it is a part of the natural order, and its function is to sing songs before "the dawning morn." The bird leads its fellows, and together

. . . they pass their youth in summer season
Then follow thee into a better region
Where winter's never felt by that sweet airy le-
 gion.

As Keats imagined the nightingale to live forever, where no hungry generations could tread it down, so Anne Bradstreet (through an image derived perhaps from the idea of migration) sees the bird as perpetually happy. But she cannot fly away to endless summer any more than could Keats, and, like him, she is brought up short and forced to admit that whatever the nightingale's lot, human life is "subject to sorrows, losses, sickness, pain." Pressing the point, she concludes;

Nor all his losses, crosses, and vexation,
In weight, in frequency and long duration

Can make him deeply groan for that divine
    Translation.

Man without grace is worse than the nightingale in respect both to this life and the next. He does not have the bird's happiness here, nor the nightingale's "better Region." But considered from another point of view, the nightingale's life is analogous to a Christian life. The point is only implicit, yet one cannot be sure that the poem would be better if the idea were elaborated.

The poem works to a close now, reaching out in the thirty-first and thirty-second stanzas for yet another image of the human condition. This time she must have an image clearly expressive of that life that has to be lived among the perils of this world. No image from the natural world will do now, for man is apart from nature as the nightingale section has clearly shown. So at last she turns to man himself:

> The Mariner that on smooth waves doth glide
> Sings merrily, and steers his barque with ease,
> As if he had command of wind and tide.

His false security is shattered by a storm and by affliction. He is forced in the end to live more warily in this world and to acknowledge that "Only above is found all with security."

The mariner is the last major image of the poem, and it is his state that corresponds most closely to that of the poet. Like the mariner, she can live in this world only under the condition that there is a possibility of some other state which can be inferred from the natural world and which is confirmed in the Bible. The poem concludes with these lines:

> O Time the fatal wrack of mortal things
> That draws oblivions curtains over kings,
> Their sumptuous monuments, men know them
>   not,
> Their names without a Record are forgot,
> Their parts, their ports, their pomp's all laid in
>   th' dust
> Nor wit nor gold, nor buildings scape times rust;
> But he whose name is graved in the white stone
> Shall last and shine when all of these are gone.

"Contemplations" reposes at last in the hope or perhaps just in the possibility of heaven. If, in this poem, earth and earthly life were simply shrugged off and rosy hopes of heaven held out as an alternative, we could with justice dismiss the piece as altogether too easy. But what validates this poem is its intensity, its thoughtfulness, its choice of images, its complex circling movement, its weight of thought, and its continual turning back to earth until every possibility has been explored. The last stanza is a full summation. Man is at last subject to time in this world. With her eye steadily on the human theme, she runs through a Renaissance catalogue of time's ruins. Not only will earth and sun pass away, as she has considered earlier, but so will all of man's earthly accomplishments. Not history, not imagination, not poetry will at last avail. At last there is nothing but the promise held out in Revelations:

> Let him that hath an eare, heare what the Spirit
> sayeth unto the churches. To him that overcom-
> meth, will I give to eate of the Manna that is

yhid, and will give him a white stone, and in the stone a new name written, which no man knoweth saving he that receiveth it.

In the Geneva Bible that was favored by the Puritans, the white stone is thus glossed:

> Such a stone was wont to be given unto them
> that had gotten any victory or prize, in sign of
> honour, and therefore it signifieth here a token
> of God's favor and grace; also it was a sign that
> one was cleared in judgement.

The final couplet makes its point theologically no doubt, but it makes it in poetic fashion. The oak, the sun, the grasshopper, the stories of Adam and Cain, the heavens, the river, the ocean, the fish, the bird, and the mariner at sea are all talismans, each offering a starting point for the contemplative imagination. Each of these images eventually leads the mind to God, but all are temporal, and none has the quiet and final authority of the white stone, the genuine token which gives the new name hidden from all but the receiver.

"Contemplations" comes to rest in a gentle and evocative poetic reference to the selective and unknowable ways of the Puritan God. The poem is a demonstration, in the form of a recorded experience, that nature itself generates belief. In seventeenth-century New England this could only mean that the world itself leads the mind of man to acknowledge God. This search, the speculative trying of a faith, provides the fundamental structure of the poem and emphasizes steadily the idea that the much desired balance between this world and the next is best achieved by a life spent in searching rather than one spent in repose. The poetic level to which "Contemplations" rises in stanzas nine, eighteen, twenty-one, and twenty-eight is one kind of testimony to the fact that in this poem Anne Bradstreet has reached that ideal but rare state of Puritan consciousness, a carefully reasoned and emotionally convincing resolution of the problem of how to live in the world without being of it. "Contemplations" spans both worlds. It accepts both worlds, perceives their connection, and acquiesces in that connection.

Rosemary M. Laughlin (essay date 1970)

SOURCE: "Anne Bradstreet: Poet in Search of Form," in *American Literature,* Vol. 42, No. 1, March, 1970, pp. 1-17.

[*In the essay below, Laughlin discusses Bradstreet's use of varied poetic forms in* The Tenth Muse.]

It is commonly agreed by the historians and critics of colonial American literature that Anne Bradstreet's poetry of greatest merit was written after the first publication of *The Tenth Muse* in 1650. From a public poet concerned with historical events and personified abstractions she became a romantic lyricist who revealed herself as a unique and striking individual against the backdrop of her times. She emerged finally as a woman for all seasons, eminently human in her response to the experiences of life in the raw colonial world of New England. There is no picture of Anne Bradstreet but the portrait painted by her own later poems: a cultured, educated Englishwoman adapting herself to a totally strange new environment, a loving wife, a devoted mother, a questing Puritan, and a sensitive poet.

That she wrote the long quaternions and historical commemorations of **The Tenth Muse** in the first place is not surprising, however. As a young bride of eighteen straight from the household and library of the Earl of Lincoln (patron to both her father and her husband), she was overwhelmed by the rigors of the Massachusetts Bay Colony. In her memoirs to her children she wrote, "I found a new world and new manners at which my heart rose [up in protest]." It is most probable, then, that

> instead of looking outward and writing her observations on this unfamiliar scene with its rough and fearsome aspects, she let her homesick imagination turn inward, marshalled the images from her store of learning and dressed them in careful homespun garments of somewhat archaic meter, to the glory of God and for the expression of an inquiring mind and sensitive, philosophical spirit. [Elizabeth Wade White, "*The Tenth Muse:* A Tercentenary Appraisal of Anne Bradstreet," *William and Mary Quarterly,* VIII (July, 1951)]

The reasons for the subsequent turn in her poetry have been adequately investigated by various scholars and are summarized by Samuel Eliot Morison [in his *Builders of the Bay Colony,* 1930] when he says that she was "completely cured of the Du Bartas disease of writing imitative poetry" when she saw her work actually printed. Her poetic sense was immediately aware that this was, despite its occasional virtues, "a rambling brat."

The common denominator of her later poetry is evident to the most casual reader; it is the subject matter, the identification of herself and her family. But it is more than the subject matter itself that makes Anne Bradstreet a personal poet. There are also signals in the structure of her verse that are very significant in revealing her individuality. A closer reading of her poems shows changes in her versification, imagery, themes, and basic structural techniques that clearly reflect the developing attempts at personal expression. It is my purpose to trace these changes and relate them to the character of Mistress Bradstreet.

Most of the poems in **The Tenth Muse** of 1650 are long unbroken stanzas in rhymed couplets of iambic pentameter, which often become stilted and monotonous under the poet's efforts to keep rhyme and meter regular. But there is a deviation. In the prologue where Anne Bradstreet speaks for herself as a woman poet, a charming apology is carefully framed in eight stanzas of six lines that are in iambic pentameter but that rhyme alternately in the first four lines rather than in couplets. It would seem that Mistress Bradstreet intuited—if perhaps unconsciously—early in her career that the rigid form of the quaternions was not best suited for personal expression. We find her experimenting, too, in 1632 in a poem she never intended for publication: "**Upon a Fit of Sickness**" is an unbroken thirty-two line poem of iambic tetrameter alternating with iambic trimeter. Only the tetrameter lines are rhymed, with the rhymed sound changing every four lines.

The quick sprightly movement created by this form must have caught Anne Bradstreet's fancy, for she was to use it almost exclusively for the versifying of her most intense religious experiences in the 1650's. Miss Josephine K. Piercy suggests [in her *Anne Bradstreet,* 1965] that "the meditative poems of Anne Bradstreet show strong evidence that they were patterned after the Bay Psalms," but this statement must be qualified. The Bay Psalms, in the ballad form, appeared in 1640. "**Upon a Fit of Sickness**," written eight years before, shows that Mistress Bradstreet was at least not indebted to the psalms for the metric pattern; she had worked with it earlier at least once of her own accord. But the Bay Psalms undoubtedly did influence her arrangement of the verses in the four-line stanzas. It would seem likely that the association made day after day of this rhythmic pattern with the religious experiences of the Psalmist could not fail to influence the expression of her own religious feelings. The imagery of these poems (to be discussed shortly in detail) is further evidence of the Bay Psalms' influence. Concerning tone, Miss Piercy makes an important observation:

> In feeling there is one great difference between the psalms and the meditations: in the former we have the impression of a great leader and of a whole tribe for whom he is praying for deliverance from their enemies; in the latter the impression of an individual praying for deliverance from her personal distress. Both, however, have intimate contact with their God: they address Him directly and sing hymns of praise when He answers.

Almost all of Anne Bradstreet's poems that address the Lord directly are in this ballad form (or occasionally all the lines are in iambic tetrameter), be the subject petition or thanksgiving. Her problems not only were those of an inner religious nature but concerned her health, and the health and welfare of her family. Since the ballad stanza moves quickly and lends itself better to objective narration than to subjective meditation, the poems are most revealing of their author's character when read as a group and with their titles (e. g., "**Deliverance from a Fit of Fainting**," or "**For the Restoration of My Dear Husband from a Burning Ague, June 1661**"). Seen in such ways they show a persistent and remarkable faith and resignation. But her resignation was not passive. The forces of the new environment that struck her repeatedly served as a means of religious renewal; she accepted hardships with faith, yet never stopped rising against them.

Strong though the influence of the ballad stanza was on her, she came to realize its limitations as a form for personal expression. She used it for a relatively short period (the latter 1650's; I cannot find it in any poem after 1662), and during this time she did not use it exclusively. "**Upon My Son Samuel His Going for England, November 6, 1657**" is done in the long stanza of rhymed iambic tetrameter couplets, as is "**In Reference to Her Children, 23 June 1656.**" Furthermore, she began to experiment in prose.

In the last decade of her life Mistress Bradstreet devised a form that was almost perfect for the expression of feelings that were dominated by sorrow for the early deaths of her grandchildren and daughter-in-law, and by a longing to reach heaven. Two of her finest poems, **"Contemplations"** and **"In Memory of My Dear Grandchild Elizabeth Bradstreet,"** are fashioned with a variation of rime royal: the rhyme scheme is *a b a b c c c,* with the last line an alexandrine. Or perhaps this might more rightly be called the abridged Bradstreet version of the Spenserian stanza since we know Anne Bradstreet was familiar with Spenser's poetry.

At any rate, her form suited her purpose. In the memorial verses to little Elizabeth we find that the first six pentameter lines of each stanza express the brevity and mutability of all mortal things. The alexandrines effect a contrast of the eternal with the transient by referring to the "everlasting state" God grants that should more than compensate for the shortness of an earthly passage. The slow alexandrines might also suggest that resignation to God's will was a heavy thing for the poet to bear, especially since the slight irregularity of the meter produces a somewhat tortured hesitation.

In **"Contemplations"** the final hexameter line achieves much the same effect, the contrast of the immortal to the mortal; or, it simply gives the reader pause to meditate the stanza. These two poems in "Bradstreet rime royal" are examples of the poet's most mature artistry and originality.

At the same time Anne Bradstreet never completely relinquished the stanzas of iambic pentameter. The remaining memorial verses to her grandchildren and to her daughter-in-law Mercy are in such, as are some love poems to her husband; but she learned to control the meter by other devices. These poems do not ramble as did the irascible quaternions. Finally, she learned to handle iambic tetrameter successfully. In **"Verses upon the Burning of Our House, July 10th, 1666,"** she divided the poem into eight six-line stanzas, following a dramatic principle. The last poem she is known to have written, **"Longing for Heaven,"** is forty unbroken lines of tetrameter couplet.

It has been noted often enough that the quaternions of *The Tenth Muse* rambled on account of the meter and rhyme. But there is more to blame than these. The fact that the basic structure of **"The Four Monarchies"** was a historical narrative into which so many events had to be crammed, and that the Seasons, Humors, and Ages of Man were marshaling as many arguments for themselves as they could muster, explains other reasons for the weaknesses. Furthermore, as Moses Coit Tyler has pointed out [in *A History of American Literature,* 1878], "She was taught to seek for the very essence of poetry in the quirks, the puns, the contorted images, the painful ingenuities of George Herbert and Francis Quarles and especially of *The Divine Weeks and Works* of the French poet Du Bartas. In short, she was a pupil of the fantastic school of English poetry—the poetry of the later Euphuists."

The truth of Tyler's statement is easily seen in the heaps of references to ancient scientific and philosophical lore in *The Tenth Muse.* But for the expression of her own heart Anne Bradstreet saw that the same techniques would not work. What appears to be a conscious effort toward con-

trol in her formal principles can be clearly traced in the post *Muse* (1650) poems.

One way of simplifying her form was by developing her poem around a single conceit. In fact, her first reaction in poetry **("The Author to Her Book")** to *The Tenth Muse* was couched in such a way. The metaphor of motherhood is not original or striking, but it is carefully developed by one who obviously knew what motherhood involved. The work was the "ill-formed offspring of my feeble brain" that was kept hidden by her side until snatched by friends and displayed abroad in its deformity. The visage of her "rambling brat" was so "irksome" that she attempted to "amend the blemishes": "I washed thy face, but more defects I saw / And rubbing off a spot still made a flaw." This was a process she was quite familiar with in the course of raising eight children!

In the short **"To Her Father with Some Verses"** (undated, but I judge written in the later 1650's by its position in the 1768 edition where the arrangement is apparently chronological) her gratitude and love are expressed in investor's terms: She is "the principal" who ought to "yield a greater sum." She speaks of being unable to make a "part payment" for the "bond" that "remains in force" until her dying day.

For **"In Reference to Her Children, 23 June, 1659,"** Mistress Bradstreet used the conceit of a mother bird and her brood to describe her own relation with her children. In the course of the ninety-five lines it becomes overworked, perhaps; but this is understandable since she did have eight children to present. Nevertheless, the poem does not lapse into sentimentality as it might easily have done with its theme of a mother's love and moral concern for her children. Her use of the conceit is successful because it allows her a certain distance and objectivity. Her maternal farewell at the end—which could easily elicit maudlin tones—illustrates the strength of her poetic achievement here:

> Once young and pleasant, as are you,
> . . . . .
> My age I will not once lament,
> But sing, my time so near is spent.
> And from the top bough take my flight
> Into a country beyond sight,
> Where old ones instantly grow young,
> And there with seraphims set song;
> No seasons cold, nor storms they see;
> But spring lasts to eternity.

Two of her last poems show equal success in developing a single central metaphor. The first is the lament on the death of her daughter-in-law, Mercy Bradstreet. Addressing Mercy's memory, she writes:

> Ah, woe is me, to write thy funeral song,
> Who might in reason yet have lived long,
> I saw the branches lopt the tree now fall,
> I stood so nigh, it crushed me down withal;
> My bruised heart lies sobbing at the root,
> That thou, dear son, hath lost both tree and
> fruit.

The picture of the strong vital tree suddenly cut down is well chosen because Mistress Bradstreet wants to create the effect of an abrupt chopping and toppling. She does not destroy the quick shock by elaborating and straining the metaphor. She concludes simply by offering sympathies to her son.

Her final **"As Weary Pilgrim"** uses the journey metaphor, aptly, as she is indeed "By age and pains brought to decay / And my clay house mold'ring away." The poem is neatly organized as an extended simile. The first half describes the pilgrim's travails through dangers, burning suns, briars, wolves, etc., and the last half parallels her own state to this in the journey of life. It concludes with her longing for the glorious resurrection in Christ.

With one exception, her occasional poems and meditations written in the ballad stanza do not develop around a central conceit at all. She does use metaphor, but only incidentally, as, "My hungry soul He filled with good, / He in His bottle put my tears" (the latter is taken from Psalm 56:8). Almost all of these ballad stanzas are directly addressed to God or describe a previous encounter; the lack of metaphor in them either for the purpose of clarification or embellishment would seem to indicate the nature of Mrs. Bradstreet's relationship with her God. With Him she could speak as straightforward and plainly as possible and be understood. There was no need for the persuasions of rhetoric; a God who loved her would comprehend her immediately. For Anne Bradstreet He was not a God to be feared, but so loving and even human that she occasionally "bargained" with Him, as when, for example, she longed to have her husband or son return safely from abroad:

> O hear me, Lord, in this request
> As Thou before hast done,
> Bring back my husband, I beseech,
> As Thou didst once my son.
>
> So shall I celebrate Thy praise
> Ev'n while my days shall last
> And talk to my beloved one
> Of all Thy goodness past.

Once her wish is granted, she characteristically worries whether she will be able to fulfill her part of the promise:

> What shall I render to Thy name
> Or how Thy praises speak?
> My thanks how shall I testify?
> O Lord, Thou know'st I'm weak.

It is lines such as these that suggest, I am sure, the basis for Samuel Eliot Morison's observation: "As I turn the pages of Anne Bradstreet's poems, and try to project myself into her life and time, I catch the merest hint of that elfin, almost *gamin* attitude of Emily Dickinson to her God."

The simple unembellished statement directed to another is used only with the ballad stanza. In the latter part of her career Anne Bradstreet experimented with yet other organizational techniques. In a number of poems she presents a series of images or metaphors that illustrate the theme.

With a complexity that would have done credit to John Donne, she interweaves two conceits to illustrate the paradox in her feelings when her husband is gone: the loneliness of physical separation, and the spiritual union of true lovers. In **"A Letter to Her Husband, Absent upon Public Employment,"** she compares the union to that of head and heart in a body, separate yet organically connected by the neck. She then compares her loneliness to that of the earth in winter when "My Sun is gone so far in's zodiac / Whom whilst I 'joyed, nor storms, nor frost I felt, / His warmth such frigid colds did cause to melt," and begs him to "Return, return, sweet Sol, from Capricorn." She unites the two conceits in her conclusion:

> I wish my Sun may never set, but burn
> Within the Cancer of my glowing breast,
>
> . . . . .
>
> Where ever, ever stay, and go not thence,
> Till Nature's sad decree shall call thee hence;
> Flesh of thy flesh, bone of thy bone,
> I here, thou there, yet both but one.

Similarly, in **"Another Letter to My Husband"** three related metaphors are developed with perfect balance in eight lines each and then united in the concluding eight lines. The poet compares herself with (*a*) the "loving hind that (hartless) wants her deer," searching for him in the woods, (*b*) "the pensive dove all alone on withered bough" making "a deep sad groan" for the absent mate, (*c*) the mullet, "that true fish" that "launches on that shore, there for to die, / Where she her captive husband doth espy." She concludes:

> Return my dear, my joy, my only love,
> Unto thy hind, thy mullet, and thy dove,
> Who neither joys in pasture, house, nor streams,
> The substance gone, O me, these are but dreams.

The poem is exquisitely wrought and is not the only one that uses a series successfully. In the memorial verse to Elizabeth Bradstreet, she compares and contrasts the brevity of the baby's life to things in nature—trees, plums, apples, corn, grass, new plants and buds. Or, after she reflects on the imperfection of joy and bliss on earth in the memorial lines to her little granddaughter, Anne Bradstreet, she describes the baby:

> I knew she was but as a withering flower,
> That's here today, perhaps gone in an hour;
> Like as bubble, or the brittle glass,
> Or like a shadow turning as it was.

The conclusion of the poem is her resignation to the death as God's will; there are three parts to the poem, then, which turn on the images that suggest the baby's brief loveliness.

"Contemplations" reveals a series of natural images in a particular setting along the Merrimac which start a train of poetic reflections on the nature of man. The first nine stanzas are directed by the sun into an upward movement. There is a general focus on the sun-drenched autumn woodland panorama, which narrows to a single oak, leads up to the sun itself and beyond that to the Creator. The poet is inspired to "magnify" such a Creator with song, but is also aware that grasshoppers and crickets do this already. Men, like herself, can "warble forth no higher lays."

Stanzas ten through twenty focus on man in contrast to

nature. With remarkable power she creates a feeling of timelessness:

> When present times look back to ages past,
> And men in being fancy those are dead,
> It makes things gone perpetually to last,
> And calls back months and years that long since
>   fled.

She then dwells on the lives of biblical figures and draws up to the present. The conclusion she makes is that though nature perpetually renews itself, "man grows old, lies down, remains where once he's laid." She questions whether existence as a thing that endures in nature ought to be more desirable than transient human existence. The answer ends the second part of the poem:

> Nay, they shall darken, perish, fade and die,
> And when unmade, so ever shall they lie,
> But man was made for endless immortality.

In stanzas twenty-one through thirty her gaze is drawn downward by the shadow of "a stately elm" to the river. She wishes she could flow on as unrestrictedly to her heavenly destination, but she does not envy the fish in the river because they are not conscious of their bliss. Awareness had an importance and poignance for Anne Bradstreet in much the same way that it has for certain twentieth-century existentialists like Albert Camus—though for different reasons. For Anne it compensated greatly for sorrows and sufferings because it enabled her to experience the magnitudes of beauty and to know the purpose of God's ways.

Her reflection in **"Contemplations"** is distracted by the song of a bird that she fancies to be a nightingale, and in what is a remarkable prefiguration of Keats's "Ode to a Nightingale" she contrasts the carefree bliss of the warbler to the human condition that is ever "subject to sorrows, losses, sickness, pain." Yet she notes that man loves life and does not wish to die: "Nor all his losses, crosses and vexation, / . . . Can make him deeply groan for that divine translation" (stanzas twenty six through thirty).

Her concluding stanzas show that adversity's purpose is to make man realize that the pleasures he enjoys while he "saileth in this world of pleasure" are transistory. Time is "the fatal wrack of mortal things," and nothing is durable but the "white stone" God gives to His elect. Thus does reflection upon images surrounding her in nature enable Anne Bradstreet to express her strongest personal feelings on the nature of the human condition in time and eternity.

Finally, Mrs. Bradstreet's sense of the dramatic is evident in the basic operation of several of her poems. It first appears in the quaternions and is one of the strongest attractions. The spirit of argumentation that inspires each personification to convince the rest of his superiority gives a refreshing vitality to the poems. The debate between **"The Flesh and the Spirit"** is likewise dramatic. Samuel Eliot Morison has praised it highly: "Her mature poem on **'The Flesh and the Spirit'** is one of the best expressions in English literature of the conflict described by St. Paul in the eighth chapter of his Epistle to the Romans. It has a dramatic quality which can only come of personal experience."

Morison's judgment that this debate was born of personal experience is undoubtedly correct, but the association is implicit. In **"Verses upon the Burning of Our House"** the poet is explicitly speaking as Anne Bradstreet, and the dramatic structure she gives to the poem renders her situation especially sympathetic and her own character very human.

She begins by vividly recreating the "thund'ring noise / And piteous shrieks of dreadful voice. / That fearful sound of 'Fire!' and 'Fire!,' " and then her own reactions. There is clearly a struggle of her human regrets and longings with her faith and resignation in God. Her first reaction as she starts up from the burning house is to cry to God "To strengthen me in my distress / And not to leave me succorless." Even on watching "The flame consume my dwelling place . . . I blest His name that gave and took." But then the human element in her asserts itself; she mentally evokes the dear things the house had held for her, and we see that she was a woman who loved company, merriment, good food, and conversation. The lines that effect this are eloquent and bear repeating here:

> Here stood that trunk, and there that chest,
> There lay that store I counted best.
> My pleasant things in ashes lie,
> And them behold no more shall I.
> Under thy roof no guest shall sit,
> Nor at thy table eat a bit.
> No pleasant tale shall e'er be told,
> Nor things recounted done of old.
> No candle e'er shall shine in thee,
> No bridegroom's voice e'er heard shall be.
> Adieu, Adieu, all's vanity.

Her heart could not have been in the last two words. She attempts to convince herself of them in the next twenty lines, and must yet bid another goodbye, "Farewell my pelf, farewell my store." The thought of a permanent heavenly mansion "With glory richly furnished" could not entirely lift the heavy heart of Mistress Bradstreet. We feel as she must have through the reconstructed drama of her inner struggle.

The Tenth Muse is dominated by imagery that reflects young Anne Dudley's years of study with her father in the Earl of Lincoln's library and from her access to the books her father brought to America. That her education was broad is evident from the references to history, the classics, the old sciences of alchemy and medicine, to contemporary events like the untimely death of Prince Henry of Wales, the Gunpowder Plot, and the regicide of Charles, and to figures like Queen Elizabeth, Sidney, Spenser, Philip II, and Sir Walter Raleigh. But there are hints there, too, of the images and themes she would be most concerned with in her personal lyrics. In the quaternion of the Seasons, for example, there is lovely imagery of nature in the tradition of the classical pastoral. One would hardly find in autumnal New England that "The orange, lemon dangle on the tree: / The pomegranate, the fig, are ripe also," or that English nightingales "tune their lays."

The aphorisms of her prose *Meditations* written in the last part of her life as a personal legacy to her children are completely devoid of classical phrasings. In them we find biblical nature such as the green pastures of Psalm 102, the wild sea of Jonah, and the vineyards of Christ, or the yellow leaves, climbing hops, unground corn (she retains the English word for wheat), a wilderness of briars and fruitful orchards that she could well observe in Massachusetts.

The same kind of development is found in her domestic imagery. There are signs of a beginning fondness for it in **The Tenth Muse,** especially in the description of childhood from the **"Ages of Man"** quaternion, but the memorable and pungent images with the Bradstreet flavor come in a few later poems like **"Verses upon the Burning of Our House,"** and especially in the prose *Meditations*: sore fingers that disquiet the whole body, cumbersome clothes that cause a child to stumble, grinding wheat at the mill, an unswept house, devices for weaning babies, downy beds with soft pillows, honey that is too sweet and gluts the stomach, the diverse natures of children, and tender fruit that is best preserved in sugar.

There are two specific images, however, that recur again and again in Anne Bradstreet's later poetry. The first is that of the journey, and it is hardly remarkable that it should be so often used. The most critical external events of her life were marked by journeys—the great trip across the Atlantic as a bride, the frequent absences of her husband gone "on public employment," and the departure of her oldest son Samuel for England. No less than nine poems tell us of the specific journeys important to Mrs. Bradstreet, and it is not unlikely that these trips influenced her conception of the Christian life as a journey to an eternal life. (It is interesting to note that she could not have been influenced by the great allegorical journey of the seventeenth century, *Pilgrim's Progress*: it did not appear until after her death.) In three of her most significant poems life is viewed as a spiritual journey: in a 1657 ballad celebrating her coming safely through a grave crisis of body and soul, in **"Contemplations"** where she depicts men carelessly voyaging about "this world of pleasure," and in her last poem structured on that motif, **"Longing for Heaven."**

The second image shot through the poetry of her later years—except for the memorial verses to the dead where it would hardly be appropriate—is that of the sun. At first she seemed to be fascinated by it in a fashionable scientific way, but it came to symbolize the great transcending power of love. In the quaternion of the seasons "Sol" unifies the poem as it races through the zodiac. In **"A Letter to Her Husband Absent upon Public Employment"** she retains the trappings of the zodiac, but connotes sexual power, too, as she equates her beloved husband to the sun whose burning warmth she needs to make her fruitful; in **"Another"** letter to her husband, the sun is the messenger of love.

Her **"Contemplations"** are bathed in the brilliant motes of the setting sun. They gild the rich colors of the autumn leaves and cause the poet to look toward the "glistering Sun" and ponder how it is "Soul of this world, this universe's eye." She then dwells on it as the sexual lover, the bridegroom, who comes joyfully "And in the darksome womb of fruitful nature [does] dive." The sun is a great

giver of gifts: days and seasons. It is too splendid for the naked eye to gaze upon, and finally, it reflects the great glory of the Creator who gave its "bright light luster" to men. The God of such a creation can only be "admired, adored for ever." Her final statement that she cares to live in no place, no matter how beautiful, unless the sun be there is her ultimate admission of the sun's importance to her.

The significant recurring themes in Anne Bradstreet's lyrics have already been touched upon here: her poignant appreciation of the brevity and beauty of all things mortal, her strong Christian faith and resignation to the will of God, and her concerns as a wife and mother. But there is yet more to be said. It can be observed that Mistress Bradstreet was constantly questing for unity, unity in matter and spirit. Even in the dedication of **The Tenth Muse** to her father, she writes that her purpose is to show

How hot and dry contend with moist and cold,
How air and earth no correspondence hold,
And yet in equal tempers, how they 'gree
How divers natures make one unity.

The central problem of the poetic debate **"The Flesh and the Spirit"** is that of unity. Unlike Donne's "Ecstasy," this poem does not resolve the dichotomy. But though the basis of the dialogue was undoubtedly from personal experience as Morison points out, we must note that Mistress Bradstreet is not the speaker of the piece; she is only the objective narrator of an overheard argument:

In secret place where once I stood
. . . . .
I heard two sisters reason on
Things that are past and things to come.

Was she using this form, in which the Puritan concept is expressed, as a means to convince herself of the vanity of flesh? It is interesting to note that the Spirit has the longer say. Doth it protest too much, perhaps?

Finally, unity in love is the central concern in her poems to her husband. Though she is not as successful as John Donne in her analyses and resolutions, she approaches his level. In several poems the sun is the symbolic means by which unity is achieved. In the poem developed around the deer, dove, and mullet, she concludes:

Together at one tree, oh let us browse,
And like two turtles roost within one house,
And like the mullets in one river glide,
Let's still remain but one, till death divide.

In her religious poems and in the poems of resignation it is precisely her trust in an everlasting union with God that enables her to bear whatever has happened. Anne Bradstreet's poetry is pervaded by the spirit of a loving God whose mysterious ways work only unto good. Ultimate union with God and resignation to His will are desirable because He is a God of Love; her God is not Wigglesworth's God of Doom.

It is fitting, I think, to conclude by quoting the verses that express most explicitly the belief that enabled Anne Bradstreet to be fully and completely what she was and to express herself as she did:

Go worldlings to your vanities,
And heathen to your gods;

. . . . .

My God He is not like to yours
Yourselves shall judges be;
I find His love, I know His power—
A succorer of me

. . . . .

And for His sake that faithful is,
That died but now doth live,
The first and last that lives for aye,
Me lasting life shall give.

Kenneth A. Requa   (essay date 1974)

SOURCE: "Anne Bradstreet's Poetic Voices," in *Early American Literature,* Vol. IX, No. 1, Spring, 1974, pp. 3-18.

[*In the following essay, Requa contrasts Bradstreet's public and private poems, maintaining that they evidence a conflict between spiritual and earthly matters.*]

Because a New England woman of Anne Bradstreet's time could have been censured for becoming known even as a poet, John Woodbridge, the brother-in-law of Anne Bradstreet, in his Introduction to *The Tenth Muse* (1650), not only pointed out the many virtues of the author but also made clear that she wrote poetry only in her legitimately idle hours (and therefore fulfilled properly her duties) and that she did not intend to publish the poems (and therefore was properly humble). Perhaps as a result of the Introduction—and of her own discretion—Anne Bradstreet, unlike Anne Hutchinson and other women whom their contemporaries considered too bold, never was publicly criticized. But it is evident in her poetry that this minor role as public poet was a problem for her and that she never fully resolved for herself the conflict between what she considered to be her principal vocations as housewife and mother and her role as poet. How to justify the practice of versifying was an important concern, the effects of which account for the significant differences between the public and private voices in her poetry.

Perhaps as a result of her early reading of poets such as Du Bartas she had come to see the poet as a commentator on public as well as private concerns and the potential audience as at least all Englishmen, at home and in the colonies, as well as her family and herself. But the public role was for her a major problem: how could she be a historian or elegist? Such roles were not for the Puritan housewife. Her inability to comfortably fulfill these chosen public roles is evident in the self-consciousness she shows in the poems. On the other hand, the role of private poet was so analogous to her domestic vocation that she did not feel the need to speak about or to defend herself in this role.

Anne Bradstreet wrote both public and private elegies; two of them—the public elegy on Sir Philip Sidney ["**An Elegie upon that Honourable and Renowned Knight *Sir Philip Sidney,* Who Was Untimely Slaine at the Seige of Zutphon, Anno 1586**"] and the private one on her daughter-in-law Mercy Bradstreet ["**To the memory of my dear Daughter in Law, Mrs. Mercy Bradstreet**"]—provide an excellent introduction to the voices of the poet, for they

show characteristics which are typical of her most important public poems, **"The Four Monarchies"** and the dialogues, and of her other private poems. Even in the opening lines of the two poems differences are apparent. The elegy on Sidney begins:

When *England* did enjoy her Halsion dayes,
Her noble *Sidney* wore the Crown of Bayes;
As well an honour to our *British* Land,
As she that sway'd the Scepter with her hand;
Mars and *Minerva* did in one agree,
Of Arms and Arts he should a pattern be.

Anne Bradstreet recalls for her reader their common cultural heritage as Englishmen; she celebrates a national hero, with whom the reader should already be familiar. Her learned allusions to Mars and Minerva suggest that she knows and will exploit English elegaic conventions. But the elegy on Mercy begins:

And live I still to see Relations gone,
And yet survive to sound this wailing tone;
Ah, woe is me, to write thy Funeral Song,
Who might in reason yet have lived long.

Mercy is not placed in the context of citizen of "our *British* Land," but in the context of the family. Now deceased, she is mourned by her surviving "Relations." The poet will write an elegy, but it will be free from learned allusions.

The purposes for writing are different in each elegy. Throughout the elegy on Sidney, Anne Bradstreet is more concerned with praising the talents of Sidney than with mourning his death. He had been dead for more than fifty years when she first composed the poem, and so her emphasis falls on the greatness of the man, not on the event of death. In the elegy on Mercy, however, the poet says little "in honour of" the deceased and concerns herself primarily with reconciling both her son and herself to the recent death. Instead of the general lessons for the public, derived from the portrayal of a great literary and political hero, she speaks only of lessons for herself and for her son Samuel.

The public voice is imitative, the private voice original. In the elegy on Sidney, she imitates the subject-matter of other poets; she mentions Spenser, Du Bartas, and Sylvester, who before her had sung the praises of Sidney. But more important is her imitation of their method, which is most apparent throughout the elegy in her use of classical allusions. For example, Sylvester had decorated his elegy on Sidney with allusions to Apollo, Mars, Venus, Juno, and Apelles. In the elegy by Anne Bradstreet Sidney is compared to both Achilles and Hector, Philip and Alexander; he is Scipio and he surpasses all nine muses. Both subject and method thus suggest that Anne Bradstreet aspired to be like the great elegists. The private poet, however, is more modest; rather than trying to sound like other poets, she presents no more than a private statement of personal problems and personal solutions. No other poet provides a proper model for her private record of the loss of Mercy Bradstreet.

As public elegist Anne Bradstreet is more self-consciously aware of her poetry than she is as a private elegist. More than one-fifth of her elegy on Sidney concerns her fears of inadequacy as a poet. She considers herself unworthy to celebrate so great a subject: "The more I say, the more thy worth I stain, / Thy fame and praise is far beyond my strain." In the first edition, she included a comparison of her attempts at poetry to the ill-fated flight of Phaeton:

> Goodwill, did make my head-long pen to run,
> Like unwise *Phaeton* his ill guided sonne,
> Till taught to's cost, for his too hasty hand,
> He left that charge by *Phoebus* to be man'd:
> So proudly foolish I, with *Phaeton* strive,
> Fame's flaming Chariot for to drive.

In the elegy on Mercy, however, the one reference to the act of writing is not self-critical but a means for presenting her personal agony which has been caused by the death: "Ah, woe is me, to write thy Funeral Song, / Who might in reason yet have lived long." On the one hand, the death of Sidney has provided her with a motive for writing public verse and discussing her problems with versifying; on the other hand, the elegy on the death of Mercy is the result of an inner necessity to state her sorrow.

That the private poet has better control of her poetry than the public poet is noticeable in the metaphoric language. For example, in the elegy on Sidney she laments his death as follows: "Ah! in his blooming prime death pluckt this rose / E're he was ripe, his thread cut *Atropos.*" No doubt her sorrow is sincere, but her expression of it is poor: she introduces Atropos and personified death in the same cou-

plet; death "pluckt" Sidney, and, in a mixed metaphor, the fate cuts his thread "E're he was ripe." The couplet suggests that she is straining to maintain her pose as public elegist. In the elegy on Mercy, however, Anne Bradstreet develops a single symbol:

> I saw the branches lopt the Tree now fall,
> I stood so nigh, it crusht me down withal;
> My bruised heart lies sobbing at the Root,
> That thou dear Son hath lost both Tree and fruit.

The symbol of the tree (Mercy) and branches (Mercy's deceased children) is presented simply enough to be free of affectation and yet is sufficiently developed to aptly represent both the death and the effect of the death on the poet.

But more significant than her control of metaphoric language in the private elegy is her control of structure: the private elegy is a unified statement; the elegy on Sidney is not. The final lines of the latter poem are less a conclusion than an account of the poet's surrender. To explain why she quits, she invents a fiction, in which the muses demand that she desist, take away her pen, and drive her from Parnassus. She can conclude only because "Errata" helps her:

> I pensive for my fault, sate down, and then
> *Errata* through their leave, threw me my pen,
> My Poem to conclude, two lines they deign
> Which writ, she bad return't to them again;
> So *Sidneys* fame I leave to *Englands* Rolls,

The Bradstreets' house, North Andover, Massachusetts.

His bones do lie interr'd in stately *Pauls.*

Because her interpolated self-dramatization, rather than her consideration of Sidney, provides the conclusion, the structure of the poem is flawed; she stops writing but does not complete her tribute. The private elegy, however, is structured clearly in three related parts: the poet's explanation of her sorrow through the symbol of the tree; her narrative of the events of the death; and her exposition of the consolation which she and her widowed son Samuel should find in the death. The final section provides a logical conclusion to the poem; from the consideration of the death, the poet derives a lesson through which they may find comfort:

> Chear up, (dear Son) thy fainting bleeding heart,
> In him alone, that caused all this smart;
> What though thy strokes full sad & grievous be,
> He knows it is the best for thee and me.

These two elegies illustrate traits which usually are found in her other public and private poems. The public voice speaks of important subjects of which both poet and reader share an awareness, attempts to instruct the reader, imitates fashionable poetic conventions, is concerned with the public role of the poet and her poetry, and is heard in structurally flawed poems. The private voice speaks of subjects whose interest is limited to self and family, finds only private lessons in the subjects, is not self-consciously concerned with role or poetry, is free of obvious imitation and conventions but develops well both metaphoric language and structure.

"The Four Monarchies," Anne Bradstreet's chronicle of the earliest kingdoms in a poem of more than 3,000 lines, her longest work, shows best the conflict between the roles of Anne Bradstreet: she is here both historian and house-wife, the Raleigh-like master of times past and the self-conscious poet who doubts her abilities as historian-poet. For such a project as this historical poem, documents and sources would have been scarce in early America, especially for a housewife in Ipswich, but knowing well Sir Walter Raleigh's *History of the World* (1614) and hoping to speak like such a Renaissance historian, she imitates his historian's voice not only in her choice of subject and her structure but in her skeptical tone, moralization and dramatization of history. If Raleigh had questioned the dubious accounts of the past, so would she. If Raleigh had tended to moralize and if he had presented history as a drama, in which all men have their assigned roles, so would she.

Although Anne Bradstreet speaks confidently when she closely follows her exemplar in these ways, nevertheless she betrays the tension which she feels between the roles of house-wife and historian-poet through her remarks concerning her inability to cope with her chronicle and through her inability to satisfactorily complete the structure of the poem. In her first and third monarchies, the anxiety is apparent in her admission that she cannot adequately describe Babylon and Alexander's feast: "This to describe in each particular, / A structure rare I should but rudely marre"; "It far exceeds my mean abilities / To shadow forth these short felicities." Such self-deprecation could be dismissed as merely a conventional pose of modesty or an indirect means of amplification of the subject,

if her protestations did not anticipate her unconventional announcement that she will abandon her narrative. At the end of the third monarchy, she says:

> With these three Monarchyes now have I done,
> But how the fourth, their Kingdomes from them
>   won,
> And how from small beginnings it did grow,
> To fill the world with terrour and with woe;
> My tyred brain leavs to some better pen,
> This task befits not women like to men:
> For what is past, I blush, excuse to make,
> But humbly stand, some grave reproof to take;
> Pardon to crave for errours, is but vain,
> The Subject was too high, beyond my strain.

Although aware of the mediocrity of her poems, she tells the reader, she began to write again after some delay, but she soon begins to agonize anew over her poetic impotence. For her second edition, she adds a concluding apology for the imperfect work:

> To finish what's begun, was my intent,
> My thoughts and my endeavours thereto bent;
> Essays I many made but still gave out,
> The more I mus'd, the more I was in doubt:
> The subject large my mind and body weak,
> With many more discouragements did speak.

Raleigh carried out his design well into the Roman monarchy, but by the time Anne Bradstreet reached her fourth monarchy she could no longer play with ease the role of poet-historian. When her house-fire in 1666 destroyed the remainder of the manuscript on which she had begun to work, she once and for all abandoned the role of historian. In **"The Four Monarchies,"** Anne Bradstreet imitated Raleigh, so that she might sound like a historian, but her protestations reveal the poet being overwhelmed by her sense of self-limitation and the magnitude of the public role.

But Anne Bradstreet had an alternative; if she did not feel at ease as a public speaker, she could create speakers in dialogue to present her messages. This alternative posed a possible solution to the conflict of her roles as house-wife and public poet. In **"A Dialogue Between Old England and New,"** the voices indeed present a successful alternative; the two speakers are distinguished from Anne Bradstreet and from each other by tone and by insight, and the dialogue structure is an effective means both for eliciting information about the English crisis of 1642 and for presenting the solution which Anne Bradstreet considered viable.

Old England presents the information about the current crisis, but she cannot interpret the significance of the conflicts. Although limited in knowledge, she reports accurately what she knows for the benefit of her auditor. Aware of the superior powers of New England, she speaks with a respectful tone to her superior: "Oh pity me in this sad perturbation." She relies on New England to cure her illness:

> This Physick purging potion, I have taken,
> Will bring consumption, or an Ague quaking,
> Unless some Cordial, thou fetch from high,
> Which present help may ease my malady.

Another of her pleas is presented as the address of a hapless parent to her child:

> If any pity in thy heart remain,
> Or any child-like love thou dost retain,
> For my relief, do what there lyes in thee,
> And recompence that good I've done to thee.

It is no surprise in a poem by an American Puritan that Old England acknowledges New England to be the current source of truth and knowledge; Old England merely presents the earliest American Puritan's favorite theory, that, as John Winthrop had said, they were "a city upon a hill," an example for all other less-enlightened reformers.

Once Old England has finished her summary, New England's tone changes; from the role of interrogator she changes to the roles of diagnostician and prophet: "Your griefs I pity, but soon hope to see, / Out of your troubles much good fruit to be." Her prophetic voice reflects her confidence in the ripeness of the times: "These are the dayes the Churches foes to crush, / To root out Popelings head, tail, branch, and rush." She prophesies a Protestant crusade, which will move eastward, reversing the historical movement of Christianity, and will convert papistical Rome and finally even the Jews (the ultimate victory): "Then fulness of the Nations in shall flow, / And Jew and Gentile to one worship go." Although history finally proved that the religious optimism of Anne Bradstreet was ill-founded, nevertheless she created a strong, confident voice to present her vision of New England's ultimate mission to the world.

But her major dialogue, the **Quaternions,** is flawed, not so much by the created speakers as by the failure of the creating poet to provide a satisfactory structure. Bradstreet had created witty speakers who could adequately fill public roles as informative speakers, but she was unhappy with her **Quaternions.** When she herself is heard in the **Quaternions,** she is often the objective observer who introduces the speakers, provides settings and transitions yet remains apart from the discussions, but she is also the insecure poet who criticizes her own work.

In the dedication to her father, she belittles her verse and praises his *Quaternion* on the four parts of the world. She has imitated his method, she says, but has failed to produce comparable poetry; his *Quaternion* is superb, hers mediocre:

> Their worth so shines in these rich lines you
>   show
> Their paralels to finde I scarcely know
> To climbe their Climes, I have nor strength nor
>   skill.
> To mount so high requires an Eagles quill.

Her lines are "ragged," she writes with a "lowly pen," and compared to his "four Sisters," her sixteen speakers are but "meanly clad." After the final **Quaternion** she adds an apology for her poetic failings, and like the self-deprecatory conclusions of the elegy on Sidney and **"The Four Monarchies,"** this apologetic conclusion is more than conventional:

> *My Subjects bare, my Brain is bad,*

> *Or better Lines you should have had:*
> *The first fell in so nat'rally,*
> *I knew not how to pass it by;*
> *The last, though bad I could not mend,*
> *Accept therefore of what is pen'd,*
> *And all the faults that you shall spy*
> *Shall at your feet for pardon cry.*

The confession matches in part the facts of the poetry: her "Brain" is far from "bad," but she correctly has perceived the major problem of the work. The first two **Quaternions** are well-written debates, but the final two are merely orderly sets of speeches, rather than debates. Furthermore, although there are numerous cross-references between elements, humors, ages, and seasons to suggest their connections, she does not bring the **Quaternions** to any final unity. For example, she frequently speaks of them as presenting their speeches from a stage, but she fails ultimately to show why she has brought them together on this stage. Although she had created other speakers to fulfill the roles of the public poet, she was still not at ease with her public poetry.

In the second edition of her poems, Anne Bradstreet included a new poem, **"The Author to her Book,"** in which speaking of *The Tenth Muse,* her collection of public poems, she illuminates the anxieties that the public roles have caused. The book is her "offspring," her own creation, but it is also her bastard, that is, the product of illegitimate activity. The result is that the book / child is irremediably deformed. Through her witty conceit, she thus describes the unresolved tension of her public poetry: the house-wife can create public voices, but she cannot overcome her Puritan suspicion that the production of public poetry may be contrary to her principal vocations of house-wife and mother. The same kind of tension which had prevented her from successfully being an American Raleigh as well prevented her from creating an adequately finished structure for the speakers in her most ambitious dialogue.

In the private poetry, Anne Bradstreet's difficulties with poetry are not the subject; rather, for her intimate audience, she writes of her personal or family concerns and emphasizes private lessons. The poet speaks of her own illnesses (**"Upon a Fit of Sickness"**), God's favors on her behalf (**"What God is like to Him I serve?"**), personal loss (**"Upon the Burning of Our House"**), and her desire for immortality (**"As Weary Pilgrim"**). She discusses the deaths in the family, the travels of her husband and her son Samuel (**"A Letter to Her Husband," "Upon my Son Samuel his goeing for England"**), family illnesses (**"Upon my Daughter Hannah Wiggin her Recovery"**), and the growth and departure of her children (**"In Reference to Her Children"**). From the consideration of private subjects, she finds meaning for her own life (**"Contemplations"**), for her husband and herself (**"To my Dear and loving Husband"**), or for her children (**"In Reference to Her Children"**). As in her public poems, Anne Bradstreet could not escape the Puritan's inclination to write instructive verse, but the small domestic audience of the private poetry allowed her to emphasize lessons which they could share.

The domestication of subject-matter and instruction so reduces the tension between private individual and poet that it is not apparent; speaking as a private poet is so sufficiently close to her domestic vocation that she is comfortable in the private role. The lack of tension allows her to be a better poet, and throughout the private poetry she speaks with greater control than she did as a public poet. This control is apparent in her use of source-material, in her versification, and in the unity of the private poems.

Although she occasionally uses source-material, she transforms it into her own personal poetic statement. For example, in the poem **"As Loving Hind,"** Anne Bradstreet borrows from Du Bartas the "unnatural natural history" of the mullet and turtle-dove. In the *Divine Weekes* Du Bartas had said:

> O! can you see with un-relenting eyes
> The Turtle-Dove? sith, when her husband dyes,
> Dyes all her joy: for, never loves she more;
> But on dry boughs her dead Spouse deplore. . . .
> But, for her love, the *Mullet* hath no Peer
> For, if the Fisher have surpriz'd her Pheer,
> As mad with wo to shore she followeth,
> Prest to consort him both in life and death.

Anne Bradstreet tailors this material to fit her own design: the implications of death are removed from the description of the dove, so that her dove mourns not death but "the absence of her Love"; not mentioning the fisherman, she increases the emphasis placed on the two unfortunate fish. But most important is her new context; the animals are introduced to explain her love for her husband, not to provide information on nature, as Du Bartas had done.

Anne Bradstreet demonstrates a better control of the rhythms of poetry in her private verse than in her public. In the latter, the iambic pentameter couplet was her principal poetic unit. In her private verse, however, she uses not only the couplet but seven other verse forms: septets, rhyming *ababccc*; ballad stanzas; a variation of the ballad stanza in which she rhymes the trimeter lines as well as the tetrameter lines; fourteeners; tetrameter couplets; tetrameter quatrains, rhyming *abcb* or rhyming *abab*. Confident with each verse-form, she uses different forms for similar subjects: septets and couplets for elegies, ballad stanzas and tetrameter couplets for expressions of anxiety over her husband's travels.

In her private poem **"Contemplations"** Anne Bradstreet experimented with the verbal rhythms through frequent use of alliteration and assonance. Short phrases within a line are most frequent: "pathless paths," "my mazed Muse," "thousand thoughts," "first draught drinks," "stealing stream," "keeps his sheep," "that vast mansion." Sometimes, entire lines are resonant: "Each storm his state, his mind, his body break"; "Troubles from foes, from friends, from dearest, near'st Relation"; "This weather-beaten vessel wrackt with pain"; "But suddenly a storm spoiles all the sport"; "Their parts, their ports, their pomp's all laid in th'dust". In no other poem is Anne Bradstreet so careful with sound as she is in **"Contemplations."**

The poetic control, noticeable in her alliterative and assonant phrasing in **"Contemplations,"** is most apparent in

the unity of her private poems. The chief impression that the reader receives is that the poetic voice presents a coherent, unified statement of her private concerns. In some poems, the unity is the result of the consistent development of related metaphors; in others, the unity is apparent in the carefully developed structural designs.

"To Her Father with Some Verses," a statement of affection for Thomas Dudley, shows well the poet's control of metaphoric language. On one level, the poet proclaims her sense of filial obligation, but on the metaphoric level, she portrays herself as the debtor and Dudley as the creditor. Anne Bradstreet, of course, was not creating *ex nihilo* new metaphors; financial terminology is a frequent enough source of metaphors for spiritual obligations. In particular, she would have known the biblical parables in which human responsibilities to the heavenly father were presented as conflicts between debtors and their kings. Anne Bradstreet, however, has fashioned such language into her private homage. Terms employed principally for finance—*principal, sum, stock, payment*—emphasize the figurative meaning of other terms which would be more commonly employed to express filial affection—*dear, worthy,* and even *debt*. Terms associated with the Bible—*mite* and *crumbs*—as well as an echo of the Lord's Prayer—"Such is my debt, I may not say forgive"—all contribute to both the metaphoric richness and the unity of the poem. The language produces a single portrait of the poet and her father: he is the merciful creditor, like the king of a biblical parable, but she is the wasteful steward. The poem is both her admission of personal failure and her attempt to reconcile the debt. Like the biblical servant, she pleads: "Have patience with me, and I will pay thee all."

In the poem **"In Reference to Her Children,"** the metaphoric language transforms the narrative of the children's departure into a fable of a mother-bird and her chicks. Occasionally, Anne Bradstreet speaks directly of herself and the children without ornithic metaphors, but usually she manages to present the biographical detail in her figurative language: her children were "hatcht"; they are "Cocks" and "hens" who must be aware of "greedy hawks" and the "Fowlers snare"; they fly, perch, peck, and sing; and the poet speaks of her death as her final flight "Into a country beyond sight." From the consistent figurative language emerges a portrait of the poet as mother-bird. This portrayal, however, suggests more than merely her similarity to lower animals. Anne Bradstreet would have known that because in the Bible God and Christ, incomparable protectors and parents, are portrayed through ornithic metaphors, to be a protective mother was to be not only bird-like but godly. Her actions are not comparable merely to the admirable actions of a mother-bird but even to the salvific gestures of her God. The moral of her fable, addressed to her children, points toward the comparison:

> When each of you shall in your nest
> Among your young ones take your rest,
> In chirping language, oft them tell,
> You had a Dam that lov'd you well,
> That did what could be done for young,
> And nurst you up till you were strong,
> And 'fore she once would let you fly,

She shew'd you joy and misery;
Taught what was good, and what was ill,
What would save life, and what would kill.

The most carefully structured poem of Anne Bradstreet is **"As Loving Hind,"** in which her longing for Simon is illustrated by three similes. Each simile is presented in four couplets, two for the portrayal of the animal and two for the lovers. In the final four couplets of the poem, Anne Bradstreet exploits the metaphoric possibilities of her three animals to address a moving plea to Simon:

Return my Dear, my joy, my only Love,
Unto thy Hinde, thy Mullet and thy Dove,
Who neither joyes in pasture, house nor streams,
The substance gone, O me, these are but dreams.
Together at one Tree, oh let us brouze,
And like two Turtles roost within one house,
And like the mullets in one river glide,
Let's still remain but one, till death divide.

The juxtaposition of the three names, three occupations, and three actions parallels the similes of the first twenty-four lines.

Although her structural designs usually are not so rigidly parallel, yet even in the simply expressed poems of petition and thanksgiving Anne Bradstreet clearly controls the structure. The poems of petition include requests, reasons why the requests should be granted, and promises of thanksgiving. In the poem **"Upon my Son Samuel his goeing for England,"** Anne Bradstreet first reminds God that he has given Samuel to her and that Samuel, therefore, really belongs to God. If Samuel is God's, then God should protect him. After ten lines, she presents her petition: "Preserve, O Lord, from stormes and wrack, / Protect him there, and bring him back." In the final eight lines of the poem, she presents her alternative to God. If Samuel returns, she will praise God; if he does not return, she will need further assistance:

If otherwise I goe to Rest,
Thy Will bee done, for that is best;
Perswade my heart I shall him see
Forever happefy'd with Thee.

In **"Upon my dear and loving Husband his goeing into England,"** she first asks God for strength and reminds him that she is a good servant; she then asks God to protect Simon and to make his mission a success, because Simon has undertaken the mission on behalf of God's New England people; and in the final stanza she promises to praise God for granting the requests. Implicitly, she bargains with God—if God protects Simon, she and Simon will return the favor by an increase of piety:

Lord, let my eyes see once Again
Him whom thou gavest me,
That wee together may sing Praise
for ever unto Thee.

And the Remainder of oure Dayes
Shall consecrated bee,
With an engaged heart to sing
All Praises unto Thee.

For such poetic expressions of personal need Anne Brad-

street developed her own structure through which she could quickly and efficiently present her case before God.

Some of her thanksgiving poems are merely a series of stanzas in which she pours out gratitude. But most of these poems exhibit one of two basic kinds of structure. The first kind has two chief parts: a summary of favors granted and expressions of thanksgiving. In the poem **"For Deliverance from a Feaver,"** Anne Bradstreet in the first twenty-four lines narrates the tale of sickness and mentions how she prayed for succor and how God cured her. The final part is her prayer of thanksgiving:

O, Praises to my mighty God,
Praise to my Lord, I say,
Who hath redeem'd my soul from pitt:
Praises to Him for Aye!

The other kind has three parts: a narrative, a prayer of thanksgiving, and a petition for help to adequately praise God. **"On My Sons Return out of England"** begins with thanksgiving:

All Praise to him who hath now turn'd
My feares to Joyes, my sighes to song,
My Teares to smiles, my sad to glad:
He's come for whom I waited long.

The central section of the poem is the summary of divine providences on behalf of Samuel: God protected him from storms and pirates, guided him to England, cured his sickness, and brought him safely back to Massachusetts. All of these favors, the poet feels, deserve extraordinary expressions of thanksgiving. In the final stanzas, she calls on God to oversee their rendering of thanks:

O help me pay my Vowes, O Lord!
That ever I may thankfull bee,
And may putt him in mind of what
Tho'st done for him, and so for me.

In both our hearts erect a frame
Of Duty and of Thankfullness,
That all thy favours great receiv'd
Oure upright walking may express.

"As Weary Pilgrim" and **"Upon the Burning of Our House"** are meditative poems, that is, they reflect in their structure the three parts of the standard seventeenth-century meditation. These three parts corresponded to the faculties of the mind—memory, understanding, and will. In the first part of a meditation, the person would recall a scene or create an imaginary scene; in the second part, he would analyze the spiritual significance of the scene; and in the final part he would be moved to devout thoughts and prayer. Furthermore, the scenes which Anne Bradstreet explores suggest that she was familiar with another spiritual practice of her time—the use of emblems. This practice is best seen in the emblem-books of Francis Quarles, in which he presents poems to explore the spiritual significance of visual illustrations (the emblems). Anne Bradstreet may not have known his works, but her practice shows that she agreed with Quarles' general principle that creation was a collection of emblems which could be explicated in verse.

The meditative poem **"As Weary Pilgrim"** begins with the

depiction of the emblem, a pilgrim at rest, thankful that his journey has ended. Anne Bradstreet enters the mind of her pilgrim to recount the hardships through which he has passed: sun and rain, briars and thorns, wolves and wrong paths. In the second part of the poem, she analyzes her own situation. First, she contrasts the condition of the pilgrim to her own: he is at rest, but she is suffering on her pilgrimage through life and yearns for death. The thought of death introduces a second consideration: death is not eternal, she must remind herself, but merely a transitional stage, through which she will pass, so that Christ may reward her with a joyous resurrection. These personal applications of the emblem lead her to the third and final part of the poem, a prayer in which she requests divine assistance so that she may indeed reach her saintly nest: "Lord make me ready for that day / then Come, deare bridegrome Come away."

Although **"Upon the Burning of Our House"** is a more complex poem than **"As Weary Pilgrim,"** the meditative structure is apparent. In the first part of the poem, Anne Bradstreet narrates the event of the house-fire and her initial response of resignation with blind faith. The emblem in the poem is the destroyed house; what makes it a more complex emblem than the weary pilgrim is the emotional attachment which the poet has to her house. In the second part of the poem, she reflects on the now past event of the fire. Although she has said that she accepted the providence of God, she still pines over the loss and shows that she has not understood God's actions.

> My pleasant things in ashes lye,
> And them behold no more shall I.
> Under thy roof no guest shall sitt,
> Nor at thy Table eat a bitt.
> No pleasant tale shall 'ere be told,
> Nor things recounted done of old
> No Candle 'ere shall shine in Thee,
> Nor bridegroom's voice ere heard shall bee.
> In silence ever shalt thou lye;
> Adeiu, Adeiu; All's vanity.

Such a negative view of the loss is dangerously near despair. In the Geneva Bible, Anne Bradstreet could have found an explanatory note on the Preacher's reference to vanity: "He condemneth the opinions of all men that set felicitie in anie thing, but in God alone, seeing that in this world all things are as vanitie and nothing." Up to this point in the poem, she has accepted only the negative aspect without accepting the positive aspect—that God alone provides meaning. Without looking for her felicity in God, she is faced with the absurd possibility that the fire has had no meaning. But the second consideration corrects her tendency toward despair by asserting that God has had a message for her in the destruction of her home. In other words, the poet finds that the house-fire has emblematic significance: from it she can learn that only one home should have meaning for her—the heavenly mansion promised to a saintly Puritan. The final part of the poem presents the poet's pious resolve to seek before all else the kingdom of heaven:

> Ther's wealth enough, I need no more;
> Farewell my Pelf, farewell my Store.
> The world no longer let me Love,

My hopes and Treasure lyes Above.

Anne Bradstreet's melancholy reflections on her destroyed house show that the home was the center of her life. There she had been in control and had preserved order, as she believed it was her vocation to do. The poet, heard in the private poems, speaking from her center of the home, on the one hand is the more human and compassionate of the two voices in Anne Bradstreet's poetry, and on the other hand, reveals the poet more in control of the poetry. When she senses that she may be intruding into the world of public affairs—the realm of her father, husband, and in general, men, rather than women—she cannot allow herself to be at ease as public elegist, historian-poet, or even as the creator of dialogues. Our present age appears to be offering ever-expanding opportunities for the professional woman, but the environment in which Anne Bradstreet lived would cause the woman who sought fame beyond the saintly performance of household duties to become anxiously introspective and warn herself that "Men can do best, and women know it well." But Anne Bradstreet was a talented poet, who both betrays the tension of the Puritan woman undertaking public poetic roles, and shows the order and control of the private poet whose poetic concerns parallel matters which she would consider the duties and rights of her divinely assigned vocation.

Wendy Martin   (essay date 1979)

SOURCE: "Anne Bradstreet's Poetry: A Study of Subversive Piety," in *Shakespeare's Sisters: Feminist Essays on Women Poets,* edited by Sandra M. Gilbert and Susan Gubar, Indiana University Press, 1979, pp. 19-31.

[*An American critic and educator, Martin is the editor of* The American Sisterhood: Feminist Writings from Colonial Times to the Present *(1972), and a contributor to* Shakespeare's Sisters: Feminist Essays on Women Poets, *from which the following essay is excerpted. Here, she analyzes feminist themes in Bradstreet's poetry.*]

Although Anne Bradstreet was careful to observe Puritan restrictions on the feminine role in her domestic life, her feminist predilections are clearly expressed in her poetry. In *The Tenth Muse, Lately Sprung Up in America,* published in England in 1650, Bradstreet included an elegy **"In Honor of the High and Mighty Princess, Queen Elizabeth,** *Of Happy Memory,"* in which she reminds her readers of a time when the prevailing patterns of power were reversed:

> Nay Masculines, you have thus taxt us long,
> But she, though dead, will vindicate our wrong.
> Let such as say our Sex is void of Reason,
> Know tis a Slander now, but once was Treason.

By celebrating Elizabeth I's political power and personal magnetism, Bradstreet undermines the authority of the Puritan patriarchs:

> Full fraught with honour, riches and with dayes
> She set, she set, like *Titan* in his rayes.
> No more shall rise or set so glorious sun
> Untill the heavens great revolutions.

If then new things their old forms shall retain,
Eliza shall rule *Albion* once again.

This poem is a tribute to female power that is not regulated and controlled by men; the Queen in her radiant splendor is depicted as inspiring her subjects rather than chastising or correcting her constituents as do the Puritan magistrates. Bradstreet's apotheosis of Queen Elizabeth is subversive in a culture in which history is providential, that is, viewed as a means for teaching and understanding the intricate design of God's plan for man. In order to understand just how daring Bradstreet was, it is necessary to examine the fabric of the Puritan society in which she lived.

When Anne Dudley Bradstreet (1612-1672) arrived in the new world with her father Thomas Dudley and her husband Simon Bradstreet, she admitted that her "heart rose" in rebellion against the Puritan mission. She was eighteen and unhappy about being forced to leave her comfortable life in the mansion of the Earl of Lincolnshire where her father was steward. The emigration of the Dudleys and the Bradstreets from England was the result of political and religious differences between the Puritans and King Charles I, but the grievances that spurred the formation of the Massachusetts Bay Colony and the vision that brought the *Arbella* to the American shore in 1630 were not hers but belonged to the two men she loved. As John Berryman writes in his remarkable eulogy, "Homage to Mistress Bradstreet," "I come to stay with you, / and the governor, and Father, and Simon, and the huddled men."

The conviction of divine destiny that spurred the Puritans to endure the hardships of the ocean crossing was later called by Samuel Danforth "the errand into the wilderness"; but this messianic mission was grounded in economic necessity as well as in spiritual consensus. The Massachusetts Bay joint stock company, of which Thomas Dudley was a founder and Simon Bradstreet a deputy secretary, specified the legal and financial requirements of the pilgrimage, just as the enumeration of the spiritual duties of covenant theology shaped the religious destiny of the Puritan tribe.

Anne Bradstreet was dismayed by the conditions at Salem; in addition to sickness, housing was poor and food supplies uncertain. Whatever degree of pride she possessed caused her to deny her part in the tribal destiny:

> [I] came into this Country, where I found a new world and new manners, at which my heart rose. But after I was convinced it was the way of God, I submitted to it and joined the church at Boston.

This was not *her* mission—her "heart rose"—but this was an assertion of self that had to be subdued and ultimately destroyed. Her submission, as she tells us, is to join the church at Boston; that is, by joining the congregation she reconciled herself to the Puritan mission and to her fate as a sinner and a pilgrim.

According to Puritan doctrine, "the prideful monster of independence" must give way to dependence on the Divine Will. Redemption required the surrender of individual autonomy to God: paradoxically, liberty is conferred through bondage. From the age of four or five, Puritan children were drilled in the lesson that the hopeless corruption of the human race could never be undone—"in Adam's Fall / We sinned All," they read in the *New England Primer*. Anne Bradstreet's poem **"On Childhood"** emphasizes this conviction of the indelibility of original sin, and the impossibility of ever again returning to a state of primal grace and innocence: "Stained from birth with Adam's *sinfull* fact, / Thence I began to sin as soon as act."

Salvation was uncertain and could not be earned by good works; it was a gift from God, whose infinite grace and mercy was extended to the Elect. Because redemption was marked by faith not accomplishments, and salvation or election was uncertain, continual self-scrutiny and introspection were required in order to be ready for conversion: introspection was necessary in order to have a "heart prepared" to be called by God. This extraordinary uncertainty of spiritual destiny caused Puritans to scrutinize their lives for signs of salvation, for visible evidence for an invisible state. Experience was emblematic, history providential.

Ironically, suffering was a form of joy because the disaster that occasions it is a sign of God's love. In a domestic version of the fortunate fall, Anne Bradstreet writes to her children:

> Among all my experiences of God's gratious Dealings with me I have constantly observed this, that he never suffered me long to sit loose from him, but by one affliction or other hath made me look home, and search what was amiss—so usually it hath been with me that I have no sooner felt my heart out of order, but I have experienced correction for it, which most commonly hath been upon my own person, in sicknesse, weakenesse, paines, sometimes on my soul, in doubts and feeres of God's displeasure, and my sincerity toward him.

Anne Bradstreet accepted her illnesses as divine correction, and as a reminder of her moral frailty: "After some time I fell into a lingering sicknes like a consumption, together with a lamenesse, which correction I saw the Lord sent to humble and try me and doe mee good: and it was not altogether ineffectual." Elizabeth Wade White speculates [in *Anne Bradstreet, The Tenth Muse,* 1971] that Anne Bradstreet suffered recurrent illnesses due to a rheumatic heart; it is significant that Anne Bradstreet's heart-sickness was triggered whenever she was unable to sustain the tension, which was at times almost unbearable for her, between spirit and flesh, faith and doubt, renunciation and temptation, the regenerate and unregenerate, and the eternal and temporal that is the core of Puritanism.

As one of the most strenuous forms of Christianity, Puritanism is based on the central paradox that the death of the body brings the possibility of the eternal life of the spirit in union with God. The body pulls the Christian toward earth; "carnality" is Satan's lure. The body, then, becomes an arena for the battle between Satan and God. Anne Bradstreet conveys the intensity of this struggle in her poem **"The Flesh and the Spirit,"** a dialogue between two sisters about the desires of the body and the aspirations of the soul:

> "Sister," quoth Flesh, "what liv'st thou on
> Nothing but Meditation?
> Doth Contemplation feed thee so
> Regardlessly to let earth go?"

Flesh proceeds to catalogue the pleasures of this world—honor, fame, accolades, riches: "Earth hath more silver, pearls, and gold / Than eyes can see or hands can hold." Spirit retorts:

> Be still, thou unregenerate part,
> Disturb no more my settled heart,
> For I have vowed, (and so will do)
> Thee as a foe, still to pursue,
> And combat with thee and must,
> Until I see thee laid in th' dust.

Spirit berates Flesh for distracting her from God's glory with the "bait" of earthly treasures. Scorning secular honor, Spirit announces, "My greatest honor it shall be / When I am victor over thee." The tension, even enmity of body and soul in the Christian *ethos* is resolved only with the destruction of the body, "the unregenerate part," which liberates the spirit from the body's cage so that it can wear royal robes, "More glorious than the glistr'ing sun" in a place where disease and death—the infirmities of the body—do not exist.

If physical suffering was a measure of piety, Anne Bradstreet's letters, occasional poems, and poetic aphorisms are a litany of the struggling spirit: "I had a sore fitt of fainting, which lasted 2 or 3 days," she writes on July 8, 1656. On September 30, 1657, she records, "It pleased God to visit me with my old Distemper," adding, "I can no more live without correction than without food." For the Puritans, affliction is a sign of the intimate bond between God and His children, it is not an indication of cruelty. God is a stern—not a sadistic—father. On August 28, 1656, Anne Bradstreet wrote:

> . . . God doth not afflict willingly, nor take delight in grieving the children of men: he hath no benefitt by my adversity, nor is he the better for my prosperity; but he doth it for my Advantage, and that I may be a Gainer by it. And if he knows that weakness and a frail body is best to make me a vessell fit for his use. Why should I not bare it, not only willingly but joyfully.

Anne Bradstreet's faith was often severely tested and her doubt was, at times, overwhelming: ". . . sometimes I have said, Is there any faith upon the earth? And I have not known what to think." Sometimes Bradstreet's despair prevented her from sleeping:

> By night when others soundly slept,
> And had at once both ease and Rest,
> My waking eyes were open kept,
> And so to lie I found it best.

And she experienced more than one dark night of the soul:

> I have often been perplexed that I have not found that constant Joy in my Pilgrimage and refreshing which I supposed most servants of God have. . . . Yet have I many times sinkings

and droopings, and not enjoyed that felicity that sometimes I have done. But when I have been in darkness and seen no light, yet have I desired to stay myself upon the Lord.

It was expected that all pilgrims would have trials, and the afflictions that Anne Bradstreet records in her letters are part of the tradition of the testing of the soul to which both men and women were submitted. However, Cotton Mather's account of his soul's testing reveals significant differences. In his diary Mather recorded that once when he had doubts he lay prostrate on the floor lamenting his "Loathesomeness," overwhelmed "by a Flood of Tears, that ran down upon the floor . . . this Conversation with Heaven, left a sweet, a calm, a considerate, a sanctifying, an Heavenly Impression upon my Soul." John Winthrop also reported that he underwent a process of humiliation and preparation before receiving confirmation of his faith; he wrote, "the good spirit breathed upon my soule, and said that I should live." Although God's testing never ceased, permitting no rest for the Puritan conscience, Mather and Winthrop seem to have been comforted and sustained in their doubt, and they appear to have been much more certain of God's love than was Bradstreet. Her belief in God's grace was often the result of her willed resolution; her determination to resist temptation, and her self-discipline enabled her to welcome spiritual and physical affliction as God's "tender mercies."

Perhaps Anne Bradstreet's doubts about her worthiness were more intense than either Mather's or Winthrop's because she did not shape the world in which she lived. Both her father and husband were intensely involved in the governing of the church during frequent disputes about covenant theology and the fine points of church membership. Dudley was a church magistrate with Winthrop, and Bradstreet was governor of Massachusetts Bay; as pillars of the community, they were called upon to make decisions about the relationship of the church Elders—that is, the elected representatives of the church—to the congregation. Perhaps the social prominence and concrete responsibilities of these two men tended to mitigate their anxiety about salvation. Although the Puritans believed that God could be served in a variety of ways—that all callings were equal—domestic piety is less impressive than public service. Confinement to private life narrows the arena in which faith can be exercised and tested. The exhortation of Peter to "declare the wonderful deeds of him that called you out of the darkness into his marvelous light" (I Peter 2:9-10) is difficult to execute in the kitchen or nursery; it is more easily done from the pulpit or podium.

The field of service available to Anne Bradstreet was her home, her family, and her poetry. But even this internal, private landscape was treacherous, as the expulsion of Ann Hutchinson from Massachusetts Bay had demonstrated. Ann Hutchinson's efforts to participate in theological issues by holding meetings in her home proved the very real dangers of stepping beyond the boundaries of prescribed behavior. Her trial and subsequent exile demonstrated the dangers of listening too carefully to an inner voice which might be the voice of Satan and not God's at all. Both Hutchinson and Bradstreet were in a double bind: as part of the Puritan tribe, they were obliged to "go forth and make disciples of all nations" (Matthew 28:19), but the powerful intelligence of both women was not permitted public expression. It is not surprising that they found private solutions—Bradstreet in her poetry, Hutchinson in her meetings at home; however, religious politics proved to be more dangerous than writing poetry.

Anne Bradstreet's isolation from the larger community was especially acute during her husband's frequent and sometimes long absences while he was on business for the church. Her poems to Simon Bradstreet make it clear that she loved him deeply:

> If ever two were one, then surely we.
> If ever man were lov'd by wife, then thee;
> If ever wife was happy in a man,
> Compare with me ye women if you can.
> **("My Dear & Loving Husband")**

In another poem, titled **"A Letter to Her Husband, Absent Upon Public Employment,"** she asks, "How stayest thou there, whilst I at Ipswich lye?" In still another, she laments:

> Commend me to the man more lov'd than life,
> Shew him the sorrows of his widdowed wife;
> My dumpish thoughts, my groans, my brakish
>   tears
> My sobs, my longing hopes, my doubting fears,
> And if he love, how can he there abide?

She "bewail[s] my turtle true, who now is gone" and again expresses her longing for him:

> Together at one tree, oh let us brouze,
> And like two turtles roost within one house,
> And like the Mullets in one River glide,
> Let's still remain but one, till death divide.

As governor, Simon Bradstreet's duties to his constituents were time-consuming. It would have been selfish, therefore sinful, of Anne Bradstreet to claim more of his energy; to make further demands on him would mean that she was interfering with his calling by placing herself between her husband and God. Her role as wife and mother was carefully limited by Puritan custom, which defined marriage as a partnership for producing young Christians in which responsibilities were made explicit. While accepting the necessity of marriage, Puritans were concerned that conjugal love would tempt the married couple to lose sight of God, and they were warned against such idolatrous unions: "when we exceedingly delight ourselves in Husbands or Wives, or Children, [it] much benumbs and dims the light of the Spirit," warned John Cotton. Anne Bradstreet's poems reveal that she struggled with the conflict between her love for her children and husband and her devotion to God; repeatedly, she reminds herself of her duty as wife and mother to assist her family in the service of God. To love them for their own sake would indicate a dangerous attachment to this world.

There was considerable emphasis placed on the family as the basic unit of the Puritan Commonwealth. Cotton Mather asserted that "*well-ordered* families naturally produce Good Order in other *Societies*. When Families are under an *Ill Disciplined*, will feel the Error in *The First*

Concoction." The relationship of husband and wife received considerable attention; her duty was to "keep at home, educating her children, keeping and improving what is got by the industry of the man." She was to "guid the house and not guid the husband." Those husbands who failed to maintain a dominant position were censured, as John Winthrop's excoriation of Ann Hutchinson's husband demonstrates: "A man of very mild temper and weak parts, and wholly guided by his wife."

Similarly, women who stepped beyond their domestic confines through literature—by reading or writing—were considered dangerous to themselves and society. John Winthrop's journal entry for April 13, 1645, reflects the Puritan bias against intellectual women:

> [Anne Hopkins] has fallen into a sad infirmity,
> the loss of her understanding and reason, which
> had been growing upon her divers years, by oc-
> casion of her giving herself wholly to reading
> and writing, and had written many books.

Puritans expressed considerable scorn for women who wrote or published. In 1650 Thomas Parker wrote a public letter condemning his sister for publishing a book in London: "Your printing of a Book beyond the Custom of your Sex, doth rankly smell." This critical attitude toward women writers was especially difficult for Anne Bradstreet to accept because childhood training prepared her to think of herself as an intelligent and articulate person. Under her father's tutelage, she learned Greek, Latin, and Hebrew; she read Sidney, Spenser, Shakespeare, Raleigh, and Du Bartas. She also probably read Homer, Aristotle, Hesiod, Xenophon, and Pliny; and, of course, she read the Geneva Bible. In general, she was educated in the Elizabethan tradition, which valued the educated and artistic woman. It must have been extremely difficult for Anne Bradstreet to sustain her faith in her abilities as a poet in what she experienced as an alien environment. But it was probably rebellion against her harsh, punitive environment that energized her to write. Perhaps it was even a matter of writing or going mad, as John Berryman suggests:

> Versing, I shroud among the dynasties;
> Quaternion on quaternion, tireless I phrase
> anything past, dead, far,
> sacred, for a barbarous place.

It is true that there is a dogged quality in some of her longer works such as **"The Four Monarchies"** which suggests a need to persist in the creation of a large work that exceeded her desire for aesthetic expression. She wrote her quaternions relentlessly, with considerable ferocity, possibly to subdue the considerable rage she must have felt as a thinking woman in a society which had no use for her abilities.

Anne Bradstreet persisted in her poetry until she had enough material for *The Tenth Muse*, which was published in 1650 due to the efforts of her brother-in-law, Reverend John Woodbridge, who had taken her manuscript with him to London and had arranged for its publication there. The fact that Anne Bradstreet did not seek publication directly but did so by proxy has been interpreted as a sign of her modesty and piety, but this indirect approach was a practical way to circumvent the accusation of excessive ambition.

She was also careful to disclaim any interest in receiving the kind of attention given her male peers; however, more than one reader has perceived irony in these lines of her prologue: "Give Thyme or Parsley, I ask no bayes." In the preface to her volume, John Woodbridge proclaims it the

> Work of a Woman, honoured, and esteemed where she lives, for her gracious demeanor, her eminent parts, her pious conversation, her courteous disposition, her exact diligence in her place, and discreet managing of her Family occasions.

Woodbridge makes it clear that no time was taken from her family obligations to write her book: "[it is] the fruit but of some few hours, curtailed from sleep and other refreshments"; and he insists that he has "presumed to bring to publick view, which she [Bradstreet] resolved in such manner should never see the sun."

The Tenth Muse reveals Bradstreet's interest in a gynocentric universe. As we have seen, her elegy of Queen Elizabeth is a tribute to female power that is not regulated and controlled by men; the Queen eclipses the authority of the New England divines, and her regal self-assertion is a dramatic contrast to the fallen Christian woman whose only possibility for redemption lies in self-abnegation. Queen Elizabeth's royal edicts provide a healthy corrective for the passivity of the Puritan woman who was compelled to attend church meetings three times a week but forbidden to take part in the interpretation of Scripture.

In her poems **"The Four Elements"** and **"Of the Four Humours in Mans Constitution,"** Anne Bradstreet stresses the unity of life rather than the dominance of one group over another; she creates a cosmology in which the Aristotelian hierarchy gives way to an elaborate allegorical scheme that depends on cooperation rather than competition. Bradstreet creates an essentially female cosmology that marks the shift from the stratified concept of the great Chain of Being in which disruption of the orderly sequence is perceived as chaos to a world in which balance is achieved by the mutual interaction of the elements.

The four elements—earth, air, fire, and water—and the four humors—blood, choler, phlegm, and melancholy—are depicted as antagonistic sisters whose quarrels threaten to disrupt the universe. In **"The Four Elements"** each sister was so intent on achieving dominance that the turbulence in the form of floods, fires, storms, and earthquakes resulting from their wrangling threatened to destroy the cosmos. In the hierarchical world-view such disruption is the harbinger of total chaos and therefore feared. But in Bradstreet's cosmology the sisters' struggle for dominance is resolved by their collective realization that each of them plays an essential part in the functioning of the cosmos, that the interaction of the elements creates balance. The feared chaos gives way to the birth of a new world-view in which process takes precedence over product, and dominance gives way to mutuality. This need for mutuality is also recognized by the sisters representing the four humors of the body:

> Unless we agree, all falls into confusion.
> Let Sanguine with her hot hand Choler hold,
> To take her moist my moisture will be bold:
> My cold, cold melancholys hand shall clasp;
> Her dry, dry Cholers other hand shall grasp.
> Two hot, two moist, two cold, two dry here be,
> A Golden Ring, the Posey unity.

Unity based on cooperation, not order based on dominance, becomes the key to Bradstreet's view of the universe.

Unlike Cotton Mather in *Magnalia Christi Americani* or Edward Johnson in *Wonder-Working Providence of Scion's Saviour in New England,* Bradstreet did not focus her energy on providential history or on the exemplary lives of the saints. The communal destiny of the Puritan tribe did not engage her imagination; it was especially daring of her to ignore the acceptable subject of the Puritan Commonwealth because it was one of the few subjects deemed appropriate for literary efforts.

By determining her own priorities, Bradstreet risked being branded as a heretic. Ann Hutchinson had been exiled as an Antinomian for insisting on her intellectual autonomy, and Bradstreet, as a practicing poet, ran the risk of denunciation by the church elders. Bradstreet probably knew the details of Ann Hutchinson's trial and banishment. Both Simon Bradstreet, who was an assistant in the General Court, and her father, Thomas Dudley, who was deputy governor at the time of the trial, were on the board of public magistrates that convicted Hutchinson. Dudley was especially hostile to Hutchinson, accusing her of being a troublemaker from the moment she landed in Massachusetts Bay and blaming her for endangering the foundation of the church. He was, in short, one of her harshest critics. During the trial he badgered her with the subtlest distinctions in the points of theology, attempting to trick her at every turn with his legalistic definitions of difference between covenants of works and grace in order to get her to perjure herself. Surely, her father's hostility to Ann Hutchinson was not lost on Anne Bradstreet.

> **Anne Bradstreet's poems reveal that she struggled with the conflict between her love for her children and husband and her devotion to God; repeatedly, she reminds herself of her duty as wife and mother to assist her family in the service of God. To love them for their own sake would indicate a dangerous attachment to this world.**
>
> **—*Wendy Martin***

Anne Bradstreet's father died in 1653, when she was forty-one, and his death marked a transition from the rigorous public codes of the old divines to a more relaxed and private approach to faith. Although the compromises regarding church membership intensified anxiety (by creating ambiguity), at least the inner life was less subject to the scrutiny of the church Elders. Perhaps as a response to the growing liberalism of the church, in the years following her father's death Anne Bradstreet wrote poems primarily about her domestic life and private religious meditations. In 1657, three years before her death, she wrote a long letter to her "dear children" in which she enumerated her sicknesses and afflictions, which she described as evidence of God's "abundant Love to my straying soul which in prosperity is too much in love with the world." One of her major poems of this period, **"Contemplations,"** chronicled her struggle between her worldly inclinations and her longing for eternity. It is a poem of great power—lyrical, carefully crafted, sufficiently accomplished to cause some critics to speculate about its having been read by the Romantic poets. While describing the vanity of this life and her yearning for eternity, she immerses herself in sensory experience celebrating the plenitude of nature and the generative power of the elements:

> Then higher on the glistering Sun I gaz'd,
> Whose beams was shaded by the leavie Tree,
> The more I look'd, the more I grew amaz'd,
> And softly said, what glory's like to thee?
> Soul of this world, this Universes Eye,
> No wonder, some made thee a Deity:
> Had I not better known, (alas) the same had I.

Paradoxically, the more the poet longs to transcend the world, the more she feels drawn by nature's power. Her metaphor of sun as the earth's husband is suffused with eroticism:

> Thus as a Bridegroom from my Chamber rush-
> es,
> And as a strong man, joyes to run a race,
> The morn doth usher thee, with smiles & blush-
> es,
> The Earth reflects her glances in thy face.
> Birds, insects, Animals with Vegative,
> The heart from death and dulness doth revive:
> And in the darksome womb of fruitful nature
> dive.

However, the poem concludes with an acceptance of mutability and death and underscores the vanity of earthly desires. In this poem Anne Bradstreet transcends this world by experiencing and even savoring its pleasures, and her final decision to reject earthly pleasures is achieved by immersing herself in them.

Bradstreet's "Meditations Divine and Moral," written for her son Simon in 1664, convey an entirely different mood of spare practicality. Based on the *Bay Psalm Book*, these aphoristic meditations correlate domestic observations with religious analogs. In terse form they are spiritual exercises which document a pilgrim's progress:

> (VI) The finest bread hath the least bran; the purest honey, the least wax; and the sincerest Christian, the least self love.

> (XVI) The house which is not often swept, makes the cleanly inhabitant soon loath it, and the heart which is not continually purifying itself, is no fit temple for the spirit of God to dwell in.

The spareness of language, the carefully worked-out metaphors demonstrate not only discipline but a concentration on spiritual concerns characteristic of her later years.

Perhaps Anne Bradstreet's most effective poem, certainly her most frequently anthologized, is **"Verses Upon the Burning of Our House, July 10th, 1666."** Like **"Contemplations,"** this poem's power is the result of the very poignant tension between her worldly concerns as represented by her household furnishings and her spiritual aspirations:

> Here stood that Trunk, and there that chest;
> There lay that store I counted best:
> My pleasant things in ashes lye,
> And them behold no more shall I.
> Under thy roof no guest shall sit,
> Nor at thy Table eat a bit.

The poem leaves the reader with the painful impression of a woman in her mid-fifties who, having lost her domestic comforts, is left to struggle with despair at her loss, a loss which, however mitigated by faith in the greater rewards of Heaven, is very tragic: "Farewell my Pelf, farewell my Store. / The world no longer let me Love, / My hope and Treasure lyes Above."

A poem written three years later on August 31, 1669, **"Longing for Heaven,"** reveals a profound world-weariness: no longer is there a tension between earth and heaven, temporal and eternal concerns; instead there is a longing for release from physical frailty and hope for immortality.

> As weary pilgrim, now at rest,
> Hugs with delight his silent nest
> His wasted limbes, now lye full soft
> That myrie steps, have troden oft
> Blesses himself, to think upon
> His dangers past, and travailes done.

In the last months of her life Bradstreet was very sick; her son Simon Bradstreet wrote in his diary that she was "wasted to skin & bone . . . much troubled with rheum," and she had a badly ulcerated arm. She died on September 16, 1672; she was sixty years old. For most of her life she was the dutiful and loving wife of Simon Bradstreet, the devoted mother of eight children, and the resolute child of God. Her poetry reflects the tensions and conflicts of a person struggling for selfhood in a culture that was outraged by individual autonomy and that valued poetry to the extent that it praised God. Anne Bradstreet's subversive piety made her vulnerable to both her earthly and heavenly fathers, but she dared to speak out and her voice can still be heard.

Pattie Cowell (essay date 1983)

SOURCE: "The Early Distribution of Anne Bradstreet's Poems," in *Critical Essays on Anne Bradstreet,* edited by Pattie Cowell and Ann Stanford, G. K. Hall & Co., 1983, pp. 270-79.

[*In the essay below, Cowell discusses the probable distribution and availability of Bradstreet's poems from the seventeenth through the nineteenth century.*]

In her reply to the unauthorized publication of *The Tenth Muse,* Anne Bradstreet released her poems to "take thy way where yet thou art not known," directing them to roam "'mongst Vulgars" and to avoid falling "in Criticks hands." Thus sent forth, the "ill-form'd offspring of [her] feeble brain" soon found an attentive audience. They continued to attract readers throughout the eighteenth century and into the nineteenth. The documentary trail is fragmentary, but Bradstreet's wandering children have left some suggestive tracks.

Studies of the distribution of specific literary titles usually emphasize immediate connections between writer and reader. William Charvat's *The Profession of Authorship in America* reminds us of an intermediary in that relationship: "Opposite both the writer and the reader stands the whole complex organism of the book and magazine trade." When Anne Bradstreet turned her poems "out of door" to an audience beyond her family circle, neither she nor her publishers could place them directly in readers' hands. Instead the poems were given to a fledgling book trade which determined their early distribution.

The difficulties of using book trade data for tracing pre-Revolutionary editions of Bradstreet's poetry should not be minimized: potentially useful material often went unrecorded, and much that was recorded fell victim to fire, mildew, or war. In addition, available documents are frustratingly cryptic (it helps to remember that they were not kept for our benefit). Shipping invoices record, for example, the distribution of "one puncheon, one hogshead and three Bayles" of books and stationery with no clues as to the individual items. Public notices of a Boston book auction may advertise "a great Variety of Books, Chiefly printed here," including "20 Groce of Verses," but neither authors nor titles are identified. Book buying patterns are no better documented: estate inventories of private libraries frequently do not itemize. We may learn, for example, that the Reverend Thomas Bacon of Maryland owned "a parcel of old Books dissorted" but not their titles. Or that in the library of the Reverend Peter Bulkeley of Massachusetts, valued at £123 in 1659, but twenty volumes are specified by title.

We begin with a partial record, then, but one historical factor favors our inquiry into the circulation of Bradstreet's poems: they were published in London and Boston, publishing centers for their respective regions. Boston had the finest book trade organization in the North American colonies in the seventeenth century, and London's importance to the industry extends to this day. While most North American cities were cultivating primitive book trades in which printing (and sometimes binding), publishing, and selling were the function of a single individual, some Boston and London book people were specializing in a single operation. That more complex organization generated a more detailed record.

The record includes when and where Bradstreet's poems were published and, with one exception, by whom, all logical starting points for tracing their distribution:

> *The Tenth Muse Lately sprung up in America . . .* (London: Stephen Bowtell, 1650).

> *Several Poems Compiled with great variety of Wit and Learning, full of Delight . . .* (Boston: John Foster, 1678).

> *Several Poems Compiled with great Variety of Wit and Learning, full of Delight . . .* (np, 1758).

But the first important question involves neither geography nor biography: how many copies were available for distribution? No specific data on print runs survive for Bradstreet editions, but extant accounts for similar volumes allow an approximation. A painstaking search through publishing records for colonial literary titles led Lawrence C. Wroth to estimate that print runs of 300 to 500 copies were common in the early and mid-eighteenth century. Wroth's figures apply most directly to the third edition, but market factors argue that earlier print runs would have been at least as large. Publishing decisions, then as now, were based on sales potential, and Bradstreet's poetry had several pre-publication indicators of commercial viability. The prefatory verses identified seven satisfied readers (eight in the second edition); the verse conformed to contemporary tastes; the author was a woman living in the New World, a double "curiosity" which might boost sales.

These factors are further exploited in promotion campaigns for *The Tenth Muse.* Twentieth-century readers have cited the prefatory verses as evidence of the popularity of Bradstreet's work or as an attempt to excuse her for venturing outside a woman's sphere. But these testimonials also function as sales promotion. All but one of the seven poems prefacing *The Tenth Muse* are short, easily consumed in blurb-fashion by the bookshop browser. Nathaniel Ward's poem labels Bradstreet as "a right *Du Bartas* Girle," linking her with one of the more popular poets of the period. And most significantly, all but one of these commendatory verses emphasize Bradstreet's poems as curiosities from a New England woman. Neither printers nor booksellers can have missed the commercial value of such endorsements.

Though *The Tenth Muse* carried its own advertisements, book catalogs provided an additional promotional tool. The first such catalog in England had appeared in 1595, and by the eighteenth century, their use was widespread on both sides of the Atlantic. *The Tenth Muse* appears in one of the earliest of these publications, William London's *Catalogue of the Most Vendible Books in England* (London, 1658). London was a bookseller at Newcastle-upon-Tyne from 1653 until 1660, during which time he printed three such catalogs, listing thousands of titles. But the large scope of London's catalog should not minimize the importance of Bradstreet's listing: his preface emphasized that he had selected only choice and vendible items.

Even so rudimentary a sales campaign produced impressive results for *The Tenth Muse.* More than twenty years after publication, its author continued to find recognition. Bathsua Makin's *An Essay To Revive the Antient Education of Gentlewomen* (1673), for example, reminds the public "How excellent a Poet Mrs. *Broadstreet* is." Makin does not belabor the point; she seems to expect her readers to know of whom she writes. Explanatory digressions which would have been essential for a forgotten figure were unnecessary for a poet who remained in the public eye. Even Edward Phillips's less flattering *Theatrum Poetarum* (1674) finds Bradstreet's memory "not yet wholly extinct."

London published and promoted, **The Tenth Muse** found a large share of its market in England. A second edition, **Several Poems** (1678) was printed in Boston for a thriving local book trade. Before 1661 Boston had had a single bookseller, but by the 1680s there were seventeen, fifteen of whom were still in business in the 1690s. And this in a city of perhaps 7000 inhabitants. Bookshops, auctions, and travelling chapmen sold both native and imported publications at a rate suggested by Cotton Mather's diary for 1683: "There is an old Hawker, who will fill this Countrey with devout and useful Books." Though Boston booksellers had not developed such sophisticated promotional tools as the *Weekly Advertisement of Books* used by their London colleagues, nevertheless they did a brisk business in the shop and on the road.

Perhaps the most important bookseller of late seventeenth-century Boston was John Usher, wholesaler and retailer, who had taken charge of the bookselling portion of his father's mercantile business in 1669. A measure of the extent of his business is contained in shipping invoices documenting imports from London bookseller Richard Chiswell between 1682 and 1685. Usher purchased 3,421 books from Chiswell, including 81 volumes of contemporary English poetry. Sizeable as these orders were, the invoices do not include his dealing with other English booksellers or with American printers.

John Usher's activity as a wholesale distributor includes an account with Elkanah Pembroke, Boston bookseller and shopkeeper from 1689 until 1706. The account entry for January 21, 1696/7, itemizes "2 Mrs. Bradstreets poems" at 4 shillings 6. Because no other sales records for Bradstreet's poems have been located, Pembroke's account takes on special significance. Most obviously, it documents that **Several Poems** was still selling some nineteen years after publication. But a study of the entire account, covering the period from August 25, 1696, to February 6, 1696/7, discovers that Bradstreet's and Michael Wigglesworth's are the only volumes of poetry Pembroke purchased from Usher. Textbooks, books on husbandry, volumes of popular theology, almanacs, spectacles, and stationer's goods make up the bulk of the order, suggesting that Pembroke drew his patrons from among the general populace rather than the more educated classes. As a shopkeeper who sold books on the side, Pembroke would stock only such volumes as these patrons might buy.

Still more evidence of the colonial distribution of Bradstreet's poetry may be found in inventories of private libraries, at least three of which itemize Bradstreet editions. The estate inventory of almanac poet and Harvard Fellow Daniel Russell (1642-1679) of Charlestown, Massachusetts, for example, numbers Bradstreet among the poets in his surprisingly literary collection. The only volume of English verse in Edward Taylor's (c. 1644-1729) library was **Several Poems.** And a catalog of the library of minister-historian Thomas Prince (1687-1758) lists Bradstreet's second edition among his extensive holdings.

Library inventories, published references, London's book catalog, and Pembroke's accounts limit the documented distribution of Bradstreet's poetry to England and New England. Similar records for the southern and middle colonies carry no known references to either **The Tenth Muse** or **Several Poems.** By the eighteenth century, even English references disappear: Bradstreet's work made its lasting impressions on New England. But between Cotton Mather's 1702 paean to Bradstreet in the *Magnalia Christi Americana* and antiquarian James Savage's 1825 references to a Bradstreet "distinguished . . . by her literary powers," there is no documentary evidence that Americans were selling, buying, or more importantly, reading Bradstreet's poems.

They were doing all three, of course, or a third edition would not have appeared in 1758. But if we are to trace the continued circulation of Bradstreet's poems, it will be with textual rather than documentary evidence. Had there been no record of Daniel Russell's ownership of **The Tenth Muse** in the seventeenth century, for example, it might have been inferred from her apparent influence on his verses. Russell prepared *An Almanack of Coelestiall Motions for . . . 1671,* adding an eight-line eclogue for each month. Particularly for the spring and summer months, Russell's stanzas echo Bradstreet's **"The Four Seasons of the Year."** Recall these lines from Bradstreet's "summer":

> Bright *June, July* and *August* hot are mine,
> In'th first *Sol* doth in Crabbed *Cancer* shine.
> His progress to the North now's fully done,
> Then retrograde now is my burning Sun.

And then compare the end of Russell's eclogue for "June":

> Now *Sol* in's Crabbed Throne doth take his place,
> Where he performs his Longest daily Race:
> Soon after which, the dayes length 'gins to fade,
> And *Phoebus, Cancer*-like turns Retrograde.

Or consider their descriptions of birds in April. Bradstreet finds each nest-building bird "A natural Artificer compleat." Russell observes spring birds as they "By Natures Art their curious Nests do build." Similar word and image choices argue that Russell had Bradstreet's quaternion in mind as he prepared his almanac verses, textual inference corroborating available documentary evidence.

For the eighteenth century, textual inference must stand alone. The distribution of Bradstreet's poems can only be determined by locating particular readers. At least three eighteenth-century poets suggest Bradstreet's influence, among them the anonymous "tender Mother" who submitted her 31-line "Lamentation &c. On the Death of a Child" to the *New England Weekly Journal* in 1733:

> A Pritty Bird did lately please my sight,
> Ravish'd my Heart, and fill'd me with delight.
> And as it grew, at once my joy and pride,
> Belov'd by all that e're its Beauty spy'd.
> I fondly call'd it mine, nor could I bear
> A thought of loosing what I held so dear:

. . . . .

Thus while I heard, and lov'd its charming
　Tongue,
For the sweet Singer's sake admir'd the Song:
Alass, when I least dreamt of its decay,
The pleasant Bird by Death was snatch'd away.
Snatch'd, did I say, no, I recall the word,
'Twas sent for home by its most rightful LORD;
To whose bless'd Will, I must and do resign,
Since LORD, Thou tak'st but what was doubly
　thine.
'Twas thine, bless'd LORD, thy Goodness lent
　it me;
'Twas doubly thine, because giv'n back to Thee.

Reminiscent in structure and theme of Bradstreet's late elegies for children, the "Lamentation" also employs the bird conceit Bradstreet developed **"In reference to her Children."**

Though we cannot know if this "tender Mother" had Bradstreet in mind, Connecticut businessman-politician Roger Wolcott certainly did. He includes several lines which echo Bradstreet in his *Poetical Meditations* (1725). Additionally, Wolcott's private journal for 1755 contains a rough copy of Bradstreet's **"In memory of my dear grandchild Elizabeth Bradstreet,"** apparently quoted from memory on the occasion of his son's death. Lines paraphrased from Bradstreet's later poems reinforce the conclusion that Wolcott had had access to *Several Poems.*

Martha Wadsworth Brewster (1710-post 1759) may have been an equally attentive member of Bradstreet's Connecticut audience. Brewster and Bradstreet were two of only four American women to publish collections of their poetry before the Revolution. Appearing nearly eighty years apart, Bradstreet's *Several Poems* and Brewster's *Poems on divers Subjects* (1757) are organized similarly, with formal public verses near the beginning and more personal family poems in closing. Both carry a verse prologue bemoaning the special difficulties experienced by a woman poet. Though these words are Brewster's, the sentiment is not unlike Bradstreet's:

For rare it is to see a *Female Bard,*
Or that my *Sex* in *Print* have e're appear'd:
Let me improve my Talent tho' but small,
And thus it humbly wait upon you shall.

Brewster and Bradstreet share more than the frustration and ambition expressed here, however. Both write of "the four ages of man," of the path to salvation, of nature, of their relationships to their father, of love for their husbands, of the deaths of public figures, of the pain of separation from grown children, of the desire to leave written memorials for their offspring.

These broad similarities in organization and topic could be dismissed as coincidental were it not for parallel development in Brewster's "An Essay on the four Ages of Man" and Bradstreet's **"Of the four Ages of Man."** Both poets present their characters as if they are making stage entrances. In characterizing Middle Age, for example, Brewster makes the entrance dramatic:

But lo, another rising on the Stage,

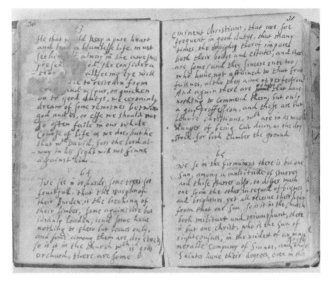

Bradstreet's autograph manuscript of "Meditations Divine and morall."

And by his Gravity 'tis Middle-age;

. . . . .

Thus Reason fully Ripe, the Judgment Keen,
Each intellectual Faculty Syrene:
His Schemes Computed, and his Goods
　Procur'd
His Seat Erected, and his Lands Manur'd;

. . . . .

But turn another Leaf, and there you'l Read
A dreadful theam, 'twill make your Hearts to
　Bleed,
To see how Tyrant Sin doth fill the Throne,
Where Righteousness should Dwell, and Reign
　alone.

Bradstreet's simpler lines have it thus:

The next came up in a much graver sort,
As one that cared for a good report,
His sword by's side, and choler in his eyes,
But neither us'd as yet, for he was wise:
Of Autumns fruits a basket on his arm,
His golden God in's purse, which was his charm.

. . . . .

Now age is more; more good you may expect,
But more mine age, the more is my defect.

In addition to their use of corresponding subject matter and quaternion form, Bradstreet and Brewster personify Middle Age with similar attributes: gravity, wisdom, material security, and spiritual poverty. Parallels can be drawn between other ages as well: the "silliness" of Childhood, the martial daring of Youth, the commanding presence of Old Age.

These correspondences should not be overemphasized, of course: both poets may simply borrow from a common poetic convention. Then, too, their poems carry differences that are the result of more than Bradstreet's superior skill.

Brewster was a product of the Great Awakening and Bradstreet of the Renaissance: Brewster is preoccupied with the next world as Bradstreet is with its mirror in this one. But even such fundamental differences do not preclude agreement with Kenneth Silverman that Brewster "consciously recaptured" Bradstreet's tone.

The colonial book trade found Bradstreet an audience, with London, Makin, Phillips, Pembroke, Mather, Russell, Taylor, Prince, Wolcott, and perhaps Brewster among its members. Distributors must have reached many others as well, for Bradstreet was still known early in the nineteenth century, though her works had been out of print for more than sixty years. James Savage's extensive notes to a new edition of John Winthrop's journal (1825-1826) recall her as a "distinguished" poet, a "credit to her education." An anonymous reviewer in the *American Quarterly Review* (1827) devoted considerable attention to the "celebrated" Anne Bradstreet, comparing her favorably with more recent poets. By the mid-nineteenth century, her poems had been included in two anthologies, James Anderson had written an extended bio-critical essay about her, and John Harvard Ellis was preparing *The Works of Anne Bradstreet* (1867). Though literary historians have used the dearth of information about Bradstreet's colonial distribution to argue that Ellis' scholarly edition renewed interest in her work, a growing body of documentary and textual evidence suggests otherwise. Ellis' fine work did not so much redirect readers to Bradstreet as climax two centuries of continued appeal. "My weak layes with me shall end," Bradstreet had written to her children in 1658, but an increasingly active book trade did not listen.

Paula Kopacz (essay date 1988)

SOURCE: " 'To Finish What's Begun': Anne Bradstreet's Last Words," in *Early American Literature,* Vol. XXIII, No. 2, Summer, 1988, pp. 175-87.

[In the following essay, Kopacz discusses Bradstreet's concern with her poems' endings.]

On a number of occasions Anne Bradstreet indicated concern about finishing her poems. In marking the hiatus after writing the first three sections of the long poem **"The Four Monarchies,"** for example, she writes, "After some days of rest, my restless heart / To finish what's begun, new thoughts impart." Three-fourths of the way finished, she found herself "restless" to get on with the job. Forced to cut short her description of the fourth monarchy, under a formal "Apology" she writes, "To finish what's begun, was my intent," and she explains the circumstances that made finishing impossible. To be sure, many critics have voiced relief that this particular poem was *not* finished. But finishing, in the sense of completing something begun, was important for Anne Bradstreet. "Perseverance, inherited and cultivated, was a strong trait in her character," wrote [Elizabeth Wade] White [in *Anne Bradstreet, The Tenth Muse,* 1971]. It was just as important to finish a poem as it was to finish her "errand into the wilderness." So she withstood the rising of her heart at first sight of New England, became "convinced it was the way of God" ("To My Dear Children"), submitted to His will and her

husband's will, gave birth to eight children, and lived to the ripe age of sixty—daughter, wife, and mother of leading magistrates of the Massachusetts Bay Colony. While other women refused to come (such as the wife of the Reverend John Wilson, who had to return to England himself to persuade her) or took one look at the glorious New World and threw themselves overboard (the wife of William Bradford), Anne Bradstreet accomplished her errand to New England. And she finished her poem on **"The Four Monarchies."**

Yet completing a poem was only part of the concern. The poem had to be concluded in an appropriate way. The critics have had much to say here. Indeed, critical evaluation of Anne Bradstreet has in some quarters depended almost exclusively on those sixteenth-century conventions of apology and seventeenth-century reaffirmations of doctrine that end so many of Bradstreet's poems. Because of these conventions and doctrinal assertions, Bradstreet's poetry was for many years regarded primarily for its historical value. *The Tenth Muse* was, after all, the first volume of poetry published by a New World author. Moses Coit Tyler and Samuel Eliot Morison, pioneers of early American literary awareness, perceived Bradstreet as a quaint historical anomaly; they seem amused that a *woman* would write the first volume of American poetry. Perhaps Bradstreet handicapped herself by frequently writing in the self-effacing, humble tone that [Jennifer R.] Waller tells us was conventional among seventeenth-century women writers. For whatever reason, the solid erudition of the poems in *The Tenth Muse* was overlooked in favor of their frankly imitative manner, and most readers have preferred the later poetry, wherein Bradstreet is said to have come into her own both as a woman and as a poet. These poems published later—poems about the deaths of family members, fear of childbirth, love poems to her husband and domestic crises such as the burning of her house—interested the cultural historians because of what they tell us about life in New England in the mid-seventeenth century. In both the early and the later poetry the literary conventions and doctrinal assertions in the poems bound Bradstreet to her culture—her English literary heritage and her New World theology.

As critical interest in Bradstreet grew, scholars clarified the literary influences and explored the religious dimension of her work. Du Bartas had been recognized as an important source for Bradstreet as early as Nathaniel Ward's commendatory verse published in *The Tenth Muse* in 1650. In addition to careful analysis of Du Bartas' influence, critics have examined the influence of Raleigh, Spenser, Sidney, and Shakespeare, as well as lesser known literary figures. At the same time, a resurgence of interest in Puritan studies made it possible to explore the play of religious themes in Bradstreet's poetry—the conflict between the visible and invisible worlds, for example, or the tension between this world and the next.

Feminist criticism brought another wave of fresh scrutiny. Some studies sought to place Bradstreet in a tradition of female writers and to acknowledge the difficulties of writing as a woman. [Cheryl] Walker points out that Bradstreet and other Puritan women were depicted even in the literature of their time as being distinctly marginal in the life of the community, historical fact to the contrary. Yet just as it was predictable that early critics, mostly men, would find Bradstreet slavishly but imperfectly trying to emulate the male writers who influenced her, it was predictable that early feminist critics would find Bradstreet rebelling both openly and covertly against her male-dominated culture. In this reading conventions cannot be praised as the ties that bind, but become thorns in the side. They must be explained—explained away, if possible. [Jane Donahue] Eberwein argues that the conventional early work amounts to an intellectual and "literary apprenticeship," preparing for the later poetry. [Eileen] Margerum complains that Bradstreet was so astute in using the literary conventions of humility that "they have been mistaken for her own feelings." [Josephine K.] Piercy finds the derivative work "an outlet for a pent-up rebellion against a new world forced upon her and against the Puritan 'pieties,' " a view that reflects White's earlier suggestion that the work was an "outlet for the author's impulses of resentment against the Puritan narrowness of thinking and harshness of living." The conventions are either deconstructed or understood ironically, as expressions of rebellion. Indeed, for [Wendy] Martin, Bradstreet's very piety itself becomes "subversive."

The issue of orthodoxy is inextricably related to Bradstreet's endings, for they seem to focus the tension that some critics see between emotion and doctrine. Whether literary or doctrinal, the endings demonstrate Bradstreet's imbedding herself within literary and religious contexts that can help her understand the world and the great questions of life that all thinking persons confront. The endings of the poems are important also because Bradstreet herself regarded them as particularly revealing. Whether exercising a religious convention or a literary one, Bradstreet was compelled by her thorough grounding in eschatalogical thinking to feel that any kind of concluding was tantamount to some final evaluation or summing up, some ultimate, transcendent meaning.

As a devout Puritan, Bradstreet believed that everything one does receives divine notice and is, given John Cotton's explanation of a "calling," a form of prayer. Therefore, writing was not an activity distinct from making meals, changing diapers, or conducting affairs of state. Even though John Woodbridge, Bradstreet's brother-in-law, assures the "Kind Reader" that her "poems are the fruit but of some few hours, curtailed from her sleep and other refreshments," writing was not an activity for one's leisure time, in a recreational sense. In separating the poetry into two distinct camps, public and private, modern historians and literary critics contend that the private poetry is more "authentic" or "genuine" than the public, but it is a distinction that Bradstreet herself would not make—all writing being equally devoted to the service of God. Bradstreet's early "public" poetry on the four elements, the humours, the ages of man, the seasons of the year, and the four monarchies is the same fabric as the "private" poetry, the work of her later years. All are forms of prayer, whether explicit or not. In defending Bradstreet's work against the charge of "pious moralizing," Piercy distinguishes between a writer's *imposing* didacticism or religion upon a reader and being thoroughly enmeshed in a religious outlook, Bradstreet is clearly the latter. Whether writing about the apparent injustice of a grandchild's death or about the history of the world, Bradstreet was mindful of her God and her mission on earth.

Given the Puritan propensity to see all activity as a form of prayer and to take spiritual stock of oneself, it should be no surprise that Bradstreet's endings show a desire to evaluate, to crystallize the meaning of an experience or thought or feeling. The endings move toward eschatological considerations sometimes explicitly, but more often, to their merit, implicitly, with a power that surpasses the cognitive implications of the words on the page. Indeed, rather than being mere conventions, literary or religious, slapped onto the end of a poem simply to mark the finish in an artistically typical or doctrinally conventional way, Bradstreet's endings often show consummate aesthetic skill in giving not only an answer to the intellectual and emotional questions raised, but also a feeling of ultimate conclusion and accomplishment. In short, Bradstreet's endings *finish* her poems and *conclude* them as well. In saying this, we need to distinguish between Bradstreet's finding peace of mind, which may or may not be achieved by an ending, and bringing a satisfactory sense of conclusion to a reader.

"The Four Monarchies" is a concluded yet unfinished work. Bradstreet never gets beyond Tarquinius Superbus in the succession of chiefs during the Roman Monarchy, the last of the four monarchies she planned to describe. And even the kings whom she does catalogue receive surprisingly short shrift compared to descriptions in the earlier monarchies. Yet despite its fragmentary nature, Bradstreet manages to convey to a reader of **"The Fourth Monarchy"** a sense of completion by using the conventional addendum of "Apology." Here the person changes from third to first, and Bradstreet explains why she could not finish the historical account: after a number of unsuccessful attempts, her papers were burned in the fire that destroyed her house. There is no attempt to blend the personal material of the "Apology" with the rest of the history, as she does in the elegy on Sidney. Yet merely explaining the reasons for not completing the work brings to the reader the satisfaction of an answered question, a sense of conclusion.

Furthermore, the final couplet deftly returns us to the history of the fourth monarchy, without the abrupt rupture that marked the move from history to personal statement earlier. In returning to the old familiar subject matter, Bradstreet gives a sense of completion even though the historical narrative is not completed in the chronological manner of the first three monarchies. Personifying her monarchies as lacking legs, Bradstreet reassures the reader that it doesn't matter, for the fourth monarchy has for "many ages been upon his knees." In the time of a couplet Bradstreet "completes" the history up to the present time ("the world *now* sees," emphasis added). The slow march of time established through the succession of kings in earlier monarchies becomes irrelevant from a different perspective, one that views the distant spanning of the centuries from a divine position. During these "many ages," durative verbs prevail (the world "sees"; the monarchy has "been" on its knees; her monarchies "lack" legs). In using these verbs of duration rather than verbs that mark percussive action, Bradstreet reinforces our sense of being so temporally distant from the monarchy that we can look back with a certain amount of cool unconcern. In fact, she tells us this is no matter ("Nor matter is't this last"), and the medial caesura emphasizes the fact. The meter conveys a tone of flat, imperial judgement. The reader senses something worthy of note, a "divine" perspective that conveys stability and permanence. In short, Bradstreet has achieved successful closure paradoxically by explaining why she could not finish and by dismissing the history she did not give us, thus making the absent present.

While it is certainly an accomplishment for Bradstreet to bring a historical narrative to successful closure without following through on the deliberate march of time set up in the poem, ending an elegy is even more difficult because the elegy dwells on a theme that itself frequently brings closure—death. Because the subject of an elegy is death, the concept of death raised at the end would not sufficiently differ from the body of the poem to bring a sense of closure, as it does with tragedy, for example. Another conventional form of closure was also denied Bradstreet in those elegies that have become most problematical—final emotional acceptance of death. Thus, elegies for both public figures and family members tested Bradstreet's skill.

The **"Elegy Upon . . . Sir Philip Sidney"** has been criticized for its ending. [Ann] Stanford, for example, says the ending is merely a long digression, so that the "faults of this poem—its lack of unity and the overworking of the lengthy digressions—overshadow its virtues." But what better way to end a poem on the death of a famous man than with a whimsical, humorous, life-giving anecdote— itself something of the spirit of the man? The poet turns to herself in bringing the poem on Sidney to conclusion. She is unable, she says, to report on Sidney's fame, and the Muses refuse to help her "Since Sidney had exhausted all their store." Furious, they take her "scribbling pen," drive her from Mount Parnassus, but allow Errata to return her pen so she can write two concluding lines. The anecdote has the effect of bringing immediacy and genuine personality to the eulogy, as well as foreshadowing a conclusion. Readers are told what to expect—exactly two more lines, so they are psychologically prepared to read those lines as an ending. And when their expectations are fulfilled, they feel the experience has been brought to a satisfactory end.

But the lines would function well in any event. The subject of Sidney's fame has been important throughout the poem; in the penultimate line Bradstreet abandons her attempt to describe this fame ("So Sidney's fame I leave to England's rolls"). "So" effectively introduces the couplet by suggesting a logical connection between everything that has preceded these lines and implying an epigrammatic finish that will follow. But even if Sidney's fame lives on, "His bones do lie interred in stately Paul's." There is no escaping the finality of mortality. The effect on the reader is that of closure, both because we have been prepared to expect it formally and because we are forced to confront the fact of physical decay. The whimsical account of the poet's being driven from Parnassus, far from being a di-

gression, brings together various themes of the poem—the difficulty of writing poetry (and to appreciate this fact enables one to better appreciate Sidney), Bradstreet's personal interest in Sidney, and the power of art to prolong "life" through fame. We laugh at Bradstreet's caricature of herself, and we accept death as the natural conclusion of life. The near rhyme of the final couplet, differing as it does from the exact rhymes that precede it, reinforces a sense of finality by duplicating that uneasy feeling we experience in contemplating death. Sidney's "bones" are a cognitive reminder of our mortality, and the slant rhyme is a sensuous reminder. Thematically and formally the poem achieves successful resolution in its ending.

The poem in honor of Du Bartas follows some of the same patterns in the ending as that for Sidney, namely the theme of fame's outliving the artist, the poet's returning to her own inability to praise adequately, and her poetic leave-taking. But this time the ending also effects a kind of frame, most noticeably because of the poet's first-person voice. In *Poetic Closure* [Barbara Herrnstein] Smith, comparing closure in poetry and painting, refers to "a point at which, without residual expectations, [the reader] can experience the structure of the work as, at once, both dynamic and whole." The frame around a painting and the framing narrative of this poem function similarly: both provide a perspective from which the audience perceives the whole. The reader thus feels the stability that is a major source of successful closure when Bradstreet returns to the first person.

Yet the ingenuity of the frame extends beyond person to subject matter: both the beginning of the poem and the ending are about finishing. Ironically, the poem begins with Bradstreet's expressing her inability to finish; indeed, the task of adequately praising Du Bartas seemed "so great" that Bradstreet "Gave o'er the work before begun withal." And thus, despite the disclaimer, she launches into a relatively lengthy poem of praise, much of which directly addresses Du Bartas. After a section on her muse, who is so amazed at Du Bartas' literary riches that he is humbled to silence, and a comparison to France's great heroes, who won fame for France only by their "heaps of wounded slain," Bradstreet returns to wonder "at the hand of heaven, / In giving one [the gifts that] would have served seven." The substitution of the third-person "one" for the expected second person of direct address subtly prepares the reader for the careful, third-person distancing from Du Bartas six lines from the end. Here, reflection on the enduring quality of Du Bartas' fame emotionally signals a leave-taking that is reinforced by the closed couplet form. Consequently, Bradstreet's return to the theme of her own inadequacy and leave-taking in the final four lines, her finishing the poem, frames the experience so a reader accepts the dynamic of continuing fame amid the finality of mortality and the conclusion of elegy. Like the circle of a frame, Bradstreet ends where she began, ending.

The word play of the final line enhances the sense of conclusion. Sounds are repeated in key words presented antithetically—"Good will, not skill." Smith notes that antithetical summaries are a conventional closure for many sixteenth-century poems. The epitaph that follows the poem exploits the convention. It flirts with polarities—birth and death, heaven and humanity, Art and Nature, dying and reviving. In the final couplet ("so Barts died; / But . . . he is revived") the passive present-tense verb counters the opposing past tense, and the reader by now almost triumphantly accepts Du Bartas' death and the conclusion of an aesthetic experience. Thus in both the frame and final antitheses Bradstreet shows herself aware of literary fashion and adept at using conventions to resolve a poem.

The third elegy on a public figure, the one for Queen Elizabeth, has achieved much critical attention because Bradstreet uses the occasion to defend women. Yet the poem also reveals the poet's skill in concluding. Repetition of the word "happy" ("happy England," "happy, happy . . . days," "happiness") builds expectation, and repetition of "she set" emphasizes the loss. In the final four lines of the poem Bradstreet plays with antithetical summaries again ("No more shall *rise* or *set* so glorious sun" and "*new* things their *old* forms shall retain," emphasis added) as she looks forward to the joy of the millennium. Her readers would have recognized the familiar device of closure and would have rejoiced in their anticipation of the millennium. Like the sun, Elizabeth has "set," but she will "rise" once more to "rule Albion once again." The conclusion works because, as in the poem on the four monarchies, Bradstreet offers at the end a totally different temporal point of view, one that makes human time, and consequently human mortality, of little consequence. In Elizabeth's ruling "once again," we have come full circle, always a positive image of closure. Not only are we reassured through the thematic, religious consolation of the millennium, but also through the reconciliation of words of opposite meaning.

While attention has been drawn to the public elegies because Bradstreet's suggestion that fame can overcome death has been seen by some critics as unusual, the private elegies have evoked the strongest disagreement. Controversy frequently centers on doctrinal assertions that appear in the final lines of the poems. The elegies written on the deaths of her grandchildren—Elizabeth, at a year and a half of age; Anne, just over three and a half; and Simon, a month and a day—show Bradstreet at her most emotional and putting her faith to its greatest test.

In the poem in memory of Elizabeth, emotional tension builds as Bradstreet reiterates "Farewell" and then questions her own discontent over this farewell: "why should I once bewail thy fate, / . . . Sith thou art settled in an everlasting state?" The second stanza is especially disconcerting; in an apparent answer to her question, Bradstreet reminds us that natural order affords decay and death only after timely growth. The next two lines focus the problem because they point out the injustice of this death: "But plants new set to be eradicate, / And buds new blown to have so short a date." The conjunction "but" clearly indicates that this death goes against natural order. The final line of the poem is the one that has caused so much debate: "Is by His hand alone that guides nature and fate," clearly attributing this untimely death to God. Murdock's reading is shared by many. He believes that Bradstreet found

herself "perilously close to writing rebelliously against God's decrees. She pulls herself up in the last line." He then asserts, "It falls flat, even metrically, because it is dictated not by real feeling but by deference to orthodox doctrine."

But instead of its failing thematically and metrically, the line closes the poem in thematically and structurally effective ways. Bradstreet deliberately vents her emotions in this poem; she was not ashamed of them, and she did not deny them. The task of the Puritan was not to repress the emotions, but to direct them. Emotions were not considered autonomous, but subject to the control of the will. Believing in faculty psychology, Bradstreet thought it her duty to restrain her emotions, to bring them in line with productive behavior. Writing a poem was just such a form of productive behavior because it was a form of prayer, and consequently an active attempt to prepare the heart. While modern sensibility sees "tension" between emotion and doctrine, the Puritan viewed them as integrally related. Consequently, the final line is not an ironic laying down of doctrine, but a fact that must be brought into line with the emotional feeling of the poem; not contradictory to emotion, but coinciding with it. Bradstreet may still feel upset about the death, but it is not accompanied by anger with God.

The poem demonstrates a number of strategies that ensure this composure. First of all, it is organized in two stanzas, the second answering the question raised by the first. A question-and-answer format structurally affords a sense of closure. The rhyme scheme of the poem is: a b a b c c c d e d e c c C. The return of familiar sound (c) in the triplet of the second stanza contributes to a sense of closure. And finally, the last line conveys the effect of closure by an additional foot. The change from iambic pentameter to hexameter adds solidity and finish. The final alexandrine comes in an assertive statement, and the last word of the poem is "fate." No devout Puritan would argue with fate. Anne Bradstreet may still regret the death of the infant; the poem cannot wipe away those feelings. But the work comes to an end that is aesthetically satisfying because it is both structurally and thematically sound. The aesthetic closure is a deliberate working toward the integration of emotional and theological stability. To oversimplify, the poem is a process, not a product. And the process is prayer.

The poem on the death of the infant Simon is the second most controversial of the private elegies. [Randall R.] Mawer finds a tone of "outrage," while Stanford finds the poem "intensely ironic" and "close to blasphemy" until the "quiet settling down" of the last four lines. Both critics suggest an orthodox ending that doesn't quite work. Yet in this poem perhaps even more than the others, the ending is an integral part of a complex web and cannot be considered distinct from what precedes it.

The entire poem juxtaposes the timely and the timeless. Consider the verbs of the opening line: "No sooner came, but gone, and fall'n asleep." The child "came" at a specific point in time; the activity could be dated. Yet he is "gone"; this verb marks a different sense of time because it reveals duration, as does the final verb of the line, "fall'n asleep."

If Bradstreet were not from the very beginning contrasting different views of time, the verbs in the line would have been parallel in form—"come" paired with "gone," or "came" paired with "left" or "went," both durative or both percussive. Yet they are not to be seen as mutually exclusive; indeed, they are quite compatible, for the devout Puritan lived constantly aware of the two levels of time—humanity's mortal time on earth and God's eternal presence.

Although the babies have been "Cropt" by God, with all the sudden abruptness the consonants imply, it is neither mere orthodox assertion nor ironic rebellion for Bradstreet to say "yet is He good." The eternal, enduring presence of His goodness is an undeniable fact, reinforced by the response of "awe" reported in the next line. Line 10, "Such was His will, but why, let's not dispute," again juxtaposes human time and God's time; "His will" is timeless, firm, while men and women are engaged in timely disputation. Although it was difficult to hold to the timely and the timeless simultaneously, the Puritan was accustomed to thinking on both temporal levels.

"Let's say He's merciful as well as just" is the most potentially explosive line of the poem, but it is only the modern reader who can read it so. "Let's say" is the imperative mood, parallel to prior exhortations in the poem—"let's be mute" and "let's not dispute," or the familiar command, "Let us pray." This hortatory accepts completely what it commands; it cannot be read as ironic or sarcastic, as Stanford suggests. Indeed, the line immediately preceding the one in question describes the Puritan posture— "With humble hearts and mouths put in the dust," hardly an attitude from which to lash out in ironic rebellion against God. In fact, it serves to remind us of divine power in creating a human being out of the dust of the earth, to which we will all return.

The final four lines effect successful closure in a number of ways. First, Bradstreet reworks the theme of coming and going with which the poem begins, but this time with millennial suggestions. God "will return" to "make up . . . our losses." Instead of the mortal coming and going of her grandchild, Bradstreet concerns herself now with the return of divinity on earth. And because she is confident of His return, she can direct the infant, "Go pretty babe, go . . . ," in marked contrast to her sense of powerlessness over the infant's departure in the first line ("No sooner came, but gone . . ."). The movement from "gone" to "go" measures the progress she has made in understanding this death over the course of the poem. The command to "go" is repeated—"go rest with sisters twain"; the author directs the child to join that timeless realm, emphasized by the durative verb "rest." We remember that in the opening line the child was "asleep"; "rest" at this point successfully closes the poem by repeating a concept, but this time with deepened meaning. That the child will successfully cross over to the world of the timeless becomes clear in the last line, for he will "Among the blest in endless joys remain." "Remain" is a durative verb, and the line preponderates with the sense of the timeless (the joys are "endless"; the child will be "Among the blest"). Even the sounds of the line are continuing

sounds—the *m* and *n* surrounding the dipthong in "remain" and the repetition of the *s/z* sound in "blest," "endless," and "joys." Thus, the ending works in this poem; it makes the poem a whole and leaves the reader in a position of stability and permanence because it so deliberately echoes the earlier, more painful view, when human time and God's time struggled against each other. The reader has come full circle with Bradstreet and is now wiser and reconciled to timeless existence.

What these "public" and "private" poems show is that Bradstreet was at all times a Puritan poet, in the fullest sense of the term. She was Puritan in her respect for the great cultural tradition she emerged from; the conventions of apology and statements of humility at the end of many poems show her attachment to this tradition and her belief that poetry was a consecrated art. She was a poet in her adept manipulation of conventions to achieve successful closure. She was a Puritan in seeing her conclusions as extremely important, in having them carry the burdens of eschatalogical implications. She was a poet in conveying these implications through ingenious concluding strategies of thematic resolution; question and answer; repetition of sounds, words, and images; in playful antitheses that strike the mind as paradoxical; and in framing narratives. She was Puritan in granting doctrine the final say. She was a poet in striving to make doctrinal statements fit the poem as a whole, in working through the process of creativity. And finally, she was a Puritan poet in seeing each poem as not so much an artifact as a prayer. After the last line was written, the success or failure of the poem would be determined by a divine judge, who would note the poem as a work in progress toward the ideal end— eternal life with God on high. The last word remains to be written.

Ivy Schweitzer (essay date 1988)

SOURCE: "Anne Bradstreet Wrestles with the Renaissance," in *Early American Literature,* Vol. XXIII, No. 3, Fall, 1988, pp. 291-312.

[*In the essay below, Schweitzer argues that Bradstreet's use of the Renaissance* topos *of humility in her public poems was subversive.*]

Anne Bradstreet was the first woman in colonial New England to raise her voice in a sustained poetic achievement. She is best known for her so-called "domestic" poetry, the lyrics and meditations she wrote later in life concerning her family, her husband, and her religious struggles. Her earlier public and formal poetry, ostensibly "male" in subject matter and style, is most often dismissed as apprentice work derivative of Elizabethan models. In other words, Bradstreet is said to have discovered her authentic, gendered voice only after her awkward attempts to write in the genres and style of formal Elizabethan poetry. Critics as diverse in their approaches as Elizabeth Wade White, Bradstreet's most thorough biographer, and Adrienne Rich, radical feminist and poet, emphasize the major shift in theme, tone, and voice from Bradstreet's public to her private poems. They contrast the frequent apologies and self-deprecation of the poems collected in the 1650 edition of *The Tenth Muse, Lately Sprung up in America* (published in London by Bradstreet's brother-in-law without her knowledge or approval) with the self-confident, unapologetic voice of the later poems and revisions published in the posthumous second edition of 1678. Kenneth A. Requa sums up this attitude in a comparison of the public and private elegies: "The public voice is imitative, the private voice original."

Eileen Margerum takes issue with this account by arguing that Bradstreet's apologies demonstrate her familiarity with prescribed seventeenth-century formulae of humility: "In the classical poetic tradition, a poem's success depended not on the validity of the poet's sentiments but on her successful use of prescribed formulae. . . . Both the classical tradition of public poetry, which [Bradstreet] learned by reading the works of her predecessors, and the Puritan narrative tradition contain formulae for humility which writers were obliged to include in their works, regardless of personal feelings" ["Anne Bradstreet's Public Poetry and the Tradition of Humility," *Early American Literature*, 1982]. Unconcerned with "personal feelings," Margerum claims that Bradstreet's use of conventional *topoi* demonstrates her self-assurance rather than self-doubt concerning classical tradition and Puritan doctrine. Most readers, she says, take Bradstreet's apologies literally and so mistake them for Bradstreet's true feelings.

In fact, as Margerum suggests, Renaissance poets routinely employed the *topos* of "affected modesty" that they learned from Greek and Latin poets, and Puritan writers followed the morphology of conversion in their personal narratives, in which an important stage was humility and self-abasement. But she, like other readers of Bradstreet, does not acknowledge that both of these traditions were androcentric, traditions whose conventions, genres, themes and foci have been determined by and for men of a specific race and class. Bradstreet was a member of that race and aspired to the privileges of that class. Although, in her early poetry, she self-consciously identified with male poetic models, she encountered the same obstacles faced by other women poets writing within a Renaissance tradition inhospitable to women writing. Her status as a colonial poet, dislocated from her native culture, further charges her relationship to the Renaissance with a particular tension. She did not spring full-blown from the rocky strand of the New World, as the title given by a well-meaning friend to her first volume of poetry suggests. The second volume strikes that misleading characterization from the first part of the original title and retains the rest, *Several Poems*. . . . However far from a court where she might seek patronage, she recognized the necessity of Renaissance poetic conventions for the fashioning of a poetic voice. As Timothy Sweet has recently pointed out [in "Gender, Genre, and Subjectivity in Anne Bradstreet's Early Elegies," *Early American Literature,* 1988] in the elegiac and epic traditions, the arena of public poetry with which we will be concerned here, a fundamental convention for the production of voice is the "specification of gender": the speaking and writing subject is always male. Bradstreet, as female, was self-conscious of the effects of sex and gender on her ability to speak and write in public, and her early poetry discloses what Sweet calls "certain effects of power" produced by conventional Renaissance assumptions of masculine subjectivity and feminine objectivity.

The daughter of a powerful public figure in Puritan New England, well-educated and steeped in the Elizabethan poetic tradition, Bradstreet was limited to imitating the poetic conventions of the literary tradition she inherited. Maria Lugones and Elizabeth Spelman, in a discussion of "feminist theory, cultural imperialism and the demand for 'the woman's voice,'" state: "Turf matters. So does the fact of who if anyone already has set up the terms of the conversation" ["Have We Got a Theory for You! Feminist Theory, Cultural Imperialism, and The Demand for 'The Woman's Voice,'" in *Women and Values: Readings in Feminist Philosophy,* ed. Marilyn Pearsell, 1986]. Bradstreet, writing in the Elizabethan idiom, is simply on someone else's turf, and the "terms of the conversation" (that is, the poetic conventions) have already been set up without reference to her experiences or interests. When used by a woman, these conventions, especially the *topos* of humility, have a different and more complex meaning than Margerum and other critics have indicated. Poets like Spenser, Sidney, and Milton, not to mention a whole host of others, could abase themselves and their talent in verse, and affect a modesty which sometimes covered an obvious arrogance (as, for example, Milton, who declares his purpose in *Paradise Lost* is to "justify the ways of God to man" and then makes his "Heavenly Muse" responsible for such an impulse). We can only speculate on the effect of this poetic convention upon the woman speaker whose very existence as a woman was defined by injunctions not merely to affect modesty, but to be "truly" humble and self-effacing in everything she did.

From the very start, Bradstreet gives voice to the fear that her male audience (including her father, who encouraged her poetry) would accuse her, not just of imitation, but of "theft," and her poems, especially the public verses, have seemed to support that charge. But our estimation of Bradstreet—and of other early women poets—changes if we see her imitation of her male literary forebears as what Luce Irigaray calls "mimicry," the deliberate, parodic, ironic, and potentially subversive repetition of the dominant discourse in which woman has no place except that of being exploited or silenced. The woman writer can, as Bradstreet does in her public poetry, enter the dominant discourse by using its conventions, which means speaking as a masculine subject. However, as Irigaray points out, this "postulate[s] a relation to the intelligible that would maintain sexual indifference" ["The Power of Discourse and the Subordination of the Feminine," in *This Sex Which Is Not One,* 1985]. That is, the female poet would always be speaking from behind a mask, in language and tropes not of her own making. The slippage inevitable in this masquerade becomes evident in the frequent disclaimers and apologies that litter Bradstreet's public poetry. Unlike those of her male precursors and contemporaries, Bradstreet's voicing of the humility *topos* discloses the dilemma of female poetic subjectivity: finding a voice in a tradition that denies women voices.

Bradstreet's recognition of this dilemma results in her deployment of an astonishing range of maneuvers most clearly recorded in a series of three elegies written during her apprentice period (1638-1642). Using the genre to thematize issues of gender politics and power, she narrates her struggles with three major figures of Renaissance literary culture: Guillaume Du Bartas, her Protestant literary precursor; Sir Philip Sidney, the ultimate "pattern" of the Renaissance man; and Queen Elizabeth, her ideal of female power. All three elegies depart from convention in bizarre passages that have mystified critics, or which they ignore. But when seen in the light of Bradstreet's struggle for poetic identity and authority as a woman writing in a male-dominated tradition, they illustrate not only the dilemma, but the remarkable success, of a colonial woman poet attempting to find her voice.

Wendy Martin has shown that "the issue of power and powerlessness is the central concern of Bradstreet's first volume of poetry" [*An American Triptych: Anne Bradstreet, Emily Dickinson, Adrienne Rich,* 1984], in which the three elegies under consideration appear. I have chosen to treat the poems out of the order in which they were composed to highlight the disturbing fantasies that begin with but go well beyond the conventional *topos* of "affected modesty." Since I am interested in Bradstreet's early reactions to Renaissance literary culture, which changed as she matured and accepted colonial life and religious dogma, I quote from the 1650 edition of *The Tenth Muse,* rather than from the standard edition, which follows the revised text of 1678.

"In Honor of Du Bartas, 1641" is Bradstreet's praise of the French Protestant poet whose *Semaines* (1578), acknowledged masterpieces of the age, were translated in 1605 by the English poet Joshua Sylvester as *Divine Weeks and Workes.* Du Bartas is remembered among Americanists chiefly as the poetic model for Bradstreet's *Quaternions,* four poems on the four elements, humors, seasons, and ages of man, which make up the bulk of *The Tenth Muse.* At the time of its publication, however, Bradstreet was figured, in several of the prefatory poems written as testimonials of a woman poet's worth by male friends and admirers, as an apprentice and replication or offshoot of the famous poet. For example, an unsigned well-wisher composed the following anagram on Bradstreet's name:

> *Anna Bradestreate.*
> Deer Neat *An Bartas.*
> So *Bartas* like thy fine spun Poems been,
> That *Bartas* name will prove an Epicene.

To find in her very name the presence of her poetic model was, for a Puritan contemporary, a divinely providential compliment. But to say that the quality of her imitation of Bartas will prove *his* name to be "an epicene" is to erase Bradstreet as an independent speaker. *Epicene* is a word from Latin grammar applied to nouns that, without changing their grammatical gender, may denote either sex. It was used in the seventeenth century "humourously" (one may read here also "demeaningly") to describe persons, their employments, characters, etc., partaking of the characteristics of both sexes. It is linked in the examples from 1604, 1633, and 1661 with "effeminate," "her-

maphroditic," and "bastard" [Oxford English Dictionary].

Aware of the prevailing attitude towards women writing and towards her own work, and in **"The Prologue"** to the *Quaternions* downright angry about it, Bradstreet first accuses the Muses of giving Du Bartas superior inspiration, then claims that her personal muse is defective, and finally blames provincial Puritan New England,

> Who sayes, my hand a needle better fits,
> A Poets Pen, all scorne, I should thus wrong;
> For such despight they cast on female wits:
> If what I doe prove well, it wo'nt advance,
> They'l say its stolne, or else, it was by chance.

Again, she foregrounds the problem for the woman poet of imitation as theft. Her concern, however, is not strictly literary; it is not a case of overzealous borrowing, but a question of woman's intellectual capacity and public visibility—a case of woman stepping out of her appointed role. Though inspired by the scope and theme of Du Bartas' ponderous poems, Bradstreet's *Quaternions* differ significantly in style and vision. Her dedication to the *Quaternions* reveals that she was also indebted for her inspiration to a poem on a similar theme written by her father and now lost. This double debt conflates the authority of biological father and literary mentor. Although she lovingly acknowledges Dudley as "Father, Guide, Instructor, too," while bristling at the comparison with Du Bartas, in both cases she casts herself as the daughter, her biological and literary fathers' creation. At the conclusion of **"The Prologue"** she accepts the "preheminence" of men and the role of daughter as one of the few means she has of speaking at all. Yet in the elegy on Du Bartas, she registers her resistance to the infantilized role by re-figuring herself, alternately, as a woman punished for the arrogance of her poetic aspirations, and as the son, seeking to inherit his rightful patrimony.

Representing herself at the opening of the poem with "ravisht eyes, and heart, with faltering tongue," silenced at the foot of Du Bartas' hearse, Bradstreet is simultaneously inspired and humbled by the figure of her precursor, who is both a literary giant and paragon of unimpeachable Protestant values. But the presence of Du Bartas ultimately paralyzes rather than enables her. She mentions a project that Du Bartas inspired but that she could not complete. Her professed failure and Du Bartas' proven success are represented in the significant terms of procreation. She recounts how reviewing his work illuminated her frozen heart with rays that, "darting upon some richer ground, / Had caused flowers, and fruits, soone to abound; / But barren I, my Daysey here doe bring, / A homely flower in this my latter spring." For Bradstreet, Du Bartas' poetic power, like sunlight on fertile ground (a metaphor for the effect of God's love upon the fruitful soul), is male. The ability to "give birth" to poetic flowers is female and ought to be hers, but she, unlike other poets described as "some richer ground," is "barren" and can yield only a "homely flower." We know from the letter she wrote "To my dear children," that she regarded her years of childlessness, like her recurring illnesses, as a "correction" sent by God "to humble and try me & doe me Good." Even the male Du

Bartas has a "pregnant brain" capable of responding to God's inseminating illumination. He is both an inspired (female) brain and an inspiring literary father. But Bradstreet, as daughter and dependent, and as the sinner who needs divine correction, cannot inspire or be inspired.

Bradstreet goes on to represent her concern with her poetic barrenness in an extended fantasy of imitation and powerlessness. She does not make use of the image of female barrenness, a condition that afflicted her in her life, but reverses the sexes and figures herself as male, expressing her wish for a power she recognized resided in maleness. She writes:

> My Muse unto a Childe, I fitly may compare,
> Who sees the riches of some famous Fayre;
> He feeds his eyes, but understanding lacks,
> To comprehend the worth of all those knacks;
> The glittering Plate, and Jewels, he admires,
> The Hats, and Fans, the Plumes, and Ladies tires,
> And thousand times his mazed minde doth wish
> Some part, at least, of that brave wealth was his;
> But seeing empty wishes nought obtaine,
> At night turnes to his Mothers cot againe,
> And tells her tales; (his full heart over-glad)
> Of all the glorious sights his eyes have had:
> But findes too soone his want of Eloquence,
> The silly Pratler speakes no word of sence;
> And seeing utterance fayle his great desires,
> Sits down in silence, deeply he admires:
> Thus weake brain'd I. . . .

We could say that the child's sense of impotence reflects Bradstreet's enforced subservience to father, husband, minister, and male God, relationships that infantilized her. Or that his ineloquence is a conventional figure for the fledgling poet's proper sense of inadequacy in the presence of her precursor. Martin speculates that Bradstreet's use of the mask of a child and her recurrent self-deprecations serve several purposes: to conceal her ambitions, solicit the approval and protection of the male figures she wrote for, and act as "a strategy to ward off attacks from hostile critics." Finally, this mask represents "a tactic traditionally used by women to conceal their socially unacceptable aggression and anger." The same can be said of Bradstreet's use of the "mask" of humility. Crucial to my argument, however, is that Bradstreet's prattling muse not only mimics the gender of her poetic precursor, but reproduces, through its desire for symbolic material objects, the prevailing cultural stereotypes that trivialized women's desires, especially the desire to write.

Further on in the homage, however, Bradstreet, without the mask of her prattling muse, is quite eloquent and adept at using literary convention and classical allusion to express her desire for poetic authority and to describe her muteness:

> A thousand thousand times my senslesse Sences,
> Movelesse, stand charm'd by thy sweet influences,
> More sencelesse then the Stones to *Amphions* Lute,
> Mine eyes are sightlesse, and my tongue is mute;
> My full astonish'd heart doth pant to break,
> Through grief it wants a faculty to speak,

> Vollies of praises could I eccho then,
> Had I an Angels voice, or *Barta's* pen,
> But wishes cann't accomplish my desire,
> Pardon, if I adore, when I admire.

The paralleling of the Angel's voice and Du Bartas' pen suggests the divine (and masculine) nature of the poetic inspiration Bradstreet is supposed to seek, but even then it would be merely the "eccho" or verbal repetition of male speech. The mythological allusion Bradstreet uses belies the power of Du Bartas' rhetoric to "move" her, and contains another veiled reference to the danger of woman's self-assertion. Amphion, to whom Du Bartas is compared, was the son of Zeus and Antiope. Upon the discovery of her liaison with the god (a rape, according to Ovid), Antiope was driven away by her angry father and later abused by her uncle and his wife, upon whom her sons took revenge. Amphion married Niobe, a mother famous for her self-assertion, which caused the death of her numerous children, and, according to some accounts, Amphion himself. Amphion became a famous musician, and in the Orphic tradition, helped build the walls of Thebes by playing ravishing music that caused the stones to move into place of their own accord. Bradstreet figures her senses as more insensible to Du Bartas' charming music than those stones. This may be hyperbolic praise of Du Bartas through self-deprecation, but it is undercut by the rhetorical strength of the passage—as Bradstreet's apologies usually are. Furthermore, it implies the ineffectuality of Du Bartas' paternalism and poetic gifts in the light of the tragic fate of daughters and mothers who transgress the bounds of paternal authority and assigned roles and depend upon the intercession of avenging sons.

It is no wonder that Bradstreet, having alluded, directly and indirectly, to the fatal flaw of femaleness for the poetic speaker, represents herself as a child and as a male, and speaks of herself in this guise in the third person. Her muse's maleness suggests a future of poetic privilege that she as a woman (daughter and mother) coveted but could never expect to inherit. At the same time, the terms of this male child's desires suggest the stereotypic desires and treatment of women, who, like little boys, were not men; and his resignation to his inadequacy suggests the internalization of patriarchal values by the woman poet. It is possible to read the ambiguous term, "some famous Fayre," as referring not just to a public exhibition but to a celebrated lady, a reading reinforced by the inclusion of "Ladies tires" in the catalogue of items the male child admires. His envy would, therefore, be envy of a woman whose femininity, defined in terms of gorgeous and, for the Puritans, illicit, outward show, is the figure of Du Bartas' rhetorical power. Through this ambiguity, Bradstreet finds a tortuous way back to her gender. The muse/child, though painfully aware of his inadequacy, unburdens himself to a listening mother, represented in the passage as the silent receptacle of his naive tales of wonder. Finally, Bradstreet effuses in the conclusion of the homage: "Thy sacred works are not for imitation, / But monuments for future admiration." This is simultaneously the highest praise she can offer and an admission that Du Bartas cannot be a model for enabling her speech as a woman. The fantasy of imitation that overtakes the heart of the homage, in which the hierarchy of power is clear, trenchantly captures Bradstreet's desire for access to knowledge and subjectivity, and her realization of the difficulties of speaking as a woman, even as she writes the poem.

This artless boy/muse stands in stark contrast to the "boy wonder" of her **"Elegie upon that Honourable and renowned Knight, Sir *Philip Sidney,* who was untimely slaine at the Seige of *Zutphon,* Anno 1586,"** composed in 1638. As "Heir to the Muses," Sidney is in their direct genealogical line, as if all nine mythological female progenitors contributed to the miraculous conception of such a poetic son. Not only does this figure at the opening of the poem suggest the "inherited" quality of poetic authority, it aligns the classical Muses with male poetic power as its placeholders, since they, as females, could not inherit or transmit it. As we will see in the conclusion of the poem, the classical Muses, as distinguished from Bradstreet's defective personal muse, are not models or sources of poetic power for Bradstreet, but the colluding guardians of literary patrimony.

The issue of inheritance, where genealogy and gender converge, is a literal as well as literary one in this poem. By attempting Sidney's praise, Bradstreet asks to be admitted to a prestigious circle of male Renaissance poets named in the poem—Du Bartas, Sylvester, and Spenser, who all attempted to praise Sidney. Like Sidney, they inhabited an England of "Halsion dayes" when his genius and Elizabeth's scepter equally brought honor to "our *British* Land." Bradstreet's nostalgia and her desire for inclusion in this past paradise surface in the plural possessive pronoun. While the reference to Elizabeth as wielder of the royal and masculine scepter makes a space for Bradstreet as the female acting out a male role, she can gain access to this literary preserve only through the freedom of her reading. This freedom, as the first part of the elegy reveals, was threatened by parochial New England Puritans, those "beetle head[s], that cann't discry / A world of treasure, in that rubbish lye" and who deemed the pleasures of Sidney's romance unfit for righteous eyes. But she boldly declares her literal and cultural inheritance of Renaissance England that honored Sidney: "Let then, none dis-allow of these my straines, / Which have the self-same blood yet in my veines." Here she invokes a distant blood relation to Sidney through the Dudley family that, relating her to one of the noble families of England, allows her to assert a literary freedom from Puritan restrictions. Though "modest Maids, and Wives, blush" upon reading Sidney, Bradstreet finds "learning, valour, and morality, / Justice, friendship, and kind hospitality; / Yea, and Divinity within thy Book."

By invoking a blood relationship to Sidney through her father, identifying with him and daring to sing his praises, Bradstreet casts herself as male, son and heir, just as her freedom to read Renaissance texts is an appropriation of culturally male privileges. Yet, her detailed defense of Sidney ends with this conventional apology: "But to say truth, thy worth I shall but staine, / Thy fame, and praise, is farre beyond my straine." How are we to read this? If we are to honor Bradstreet's "confession" and take this formulaic disclaimer as "truth," then is her obvious pride

in her kinship (both literal and literary) and her passionate defense of his (and her own) poetic freedom and religious/moral righteousness less than true?

Bradstreet cannot escape her difference from Sidney, but ironically, this admission of inadequacy furthers her identification with the dominant tradition. Her couplet alludes to Spenser's and Sylvester's confessions of their inability to praise Sidney, the latter of which she echoes closely later in the poem as she expounds upon her "errour" and presumption in writing the elegy: ". . . And makes me now with *Sylvester* confesse, / But *Sydney's* Muse, can sing his worthinesse." Tracing strains of blood and cultural inheritance, Bradstreet asserts her right to speak, which makes her an English son, but simultaneously fears that such ambition in a female will cast a blot (blood "staine") upon Sidney's reputation (which happens later in the poem in Bradstreet's confrontation with the Muses). Both her blood connection and writing, contaminated and contaminating because of her sex, are "strains," which, as the pun suggests, test her limits. She manages, however, to transform the potentially paralyzing presence of Sidney into a productive aggression against the cultural constraints on her voice while appearing suitably modest as a woman and conventionally humble as a poet.

Bradstreet's identification with Sidney as a literary son is, then, both reinforced and challenged by her mask of humility. In the next section of the poem, Bradstreet further distinguishes herself by creating a complex allusive web of myth, history, and gender. Throughout the beginning of the elegy she compares Sidney to a series of powerful male figures: Mercury, Eros, the emperor Augustus, Achilles, Hector, Scipio, Philip of Macedon, and his son, Alexander. A sharp reversal occurs when she considers the poet's attachment to Stella described in his sonnet sequence and asks, "How could that *Stella,* so confine thy will?" By way of excuse she supplies three mythological examples of similar feminine power: "But *Omphala* set *Hercules* to spin, / And *Mars* himself was ta'n by *Venus* gin; / Then wonder lesse, if warlike *Philip* yield, / When such a *Hero* shoots him out o'th' field."

This comic intertextual rationale presents a series of sexual role reversals. Hero, in mythology and in Marlowe's poem, is the beloved for whom Leander swims the Hellespont every night until he is drowned in a storm; Bradstreet puns on her name to suggest that in Sidney's war of love, Stella is the hero. Venus captivates Mars, the god of war, in her "gin" or trap. It is the same engine of illusion that, earlier in the poem, Sidney is gently chided for having constructed with his rhetoric: "Who knowes the Spels that in thy Rethorick lurks? / But some infatuate fooles soone caught therein, / Found *Cupids* Dame had never such a Gin." The story of Omphala and Hercules echoes the profemale delights and dangers to masculinity of transvestism, a motif that runs through these elegies. Omphala, queen of Lydia, bought Hercules as a slave. Ovid's *Fasti* tells how Omphala dresses a mortified Hercules in her diaphanous robes and gleefully takes on his lion's skin. This reversal causes embarrassment to Faunus, whom they have come to the woods to worship, and who tries to seduce the person dressed as Omphala.

Covering twenty-two lines that were all excised in the revised version, this complex interlude challenges the hyperbolic perfection of the Renaissance man by foregrounding woman's threatening power. The passage begins with an apostrophe to Stella, who is called a "Commet," "Star," "Meteor," "Blazer," and "sad presage" of Sidney's death. Her cosmic influence, like Queen Elizabeth's cultural influence, inverts the traditional hierarchy of male/female and replicates in the poem the Elizabethan world of power and politics in which Sidney, as courtier, royal adviser, and mercenary soldier, played a complicated role. The extended reference to Stella also foregrounds the representational nature of these relationships. Stella, after all, was Sidney's poetic creation, just as Sidney and the other historical and mythic characters are Bradstreet's. The use she makes of them subverts her own earlier rhetorical disclaimers of inadequacy. In a poem of praise she presumes to judge, excuse, and have fun at Sidney's expense. She shows women in powerful positions, exercising influence over men. She shows herself off as a canny reader of Sidney (*she* does not get caught in his gorgeous trap) who is also familiar enough with Ovid to appropriate his stories for her own proto-feminist purposes. These three points are roughly analogous. At the same time she discredits the power which gained such reversals. By comparing female wiles, symbolized by Venus' "gins" and Stella's "snares," to the rhetorical spells Sidney cast in the *Arcadia* and in which his narrator is caught in *Astrophel and Stella,* Bradstreet implicates her poetic models in this disorderly female power. She acknowledges but rejects this power, as she must, in her bid to become a literary son, for Astrophel also rejected artful "invention" and the "sugring of [his] speech" by the classical Muses for an artless plain style that would express the inward self uncontaminated by worldly discourse. Mapping out this new epistemology, Sidney's narrator invented a muse who called him "Foole," and advised him ingenuously, "Looke in thy heart and write."

The exploration of this new territory of the self must have appealed to Bradstreet as a Puritan exhorted to avoid rhetorical excess, and as a woman limited by male stereotypes to the arts of allurement. But as a woman already in a male disguise, Bradstreet needs a language to maintain that outward show. Following immediately upon the above interlude, which leaves Sidney feminized and ignominiously slain on the battlefield of love, Bradstreet tries to show "how thou fame's paths didst tread." Unaccountably, she finds herself in a labyrinth, perhaps the same intertextual maze through which she has just led the reader. This metaphorical locus of confusion suggests the feminine love "gins" and rhetorical spells in which unwitting readers and Sidney himself get caught. Presaging the "mazed minde" of the boy/muse in the homage to Du Bartas, and perhaps alluding to Sidney's "mazefull solitariness" of Sonnet 96, the labyrinth can be seen as the inward space Bradstreet represents as already contaminated by the conventions of literary rhetoric Astrophel seeks to escape. When, in this crisis, she appeals to her muse for guidance, as Astrophel did, it does not give her advice, but calls her an "ambitious fool," and recommends the idolatrous self-censorship Bradstreet articulated in the homage to Du Bartas: "Enough for me to look, and so admire." Chiding

her for her poetic aspirations, this muse advises silence rather than, in Astrophel's case, heartfelt simplicity (a simplicity Sidney as poet continually undermines). Speaking, for the woman poet, is always entangled with her labyrinthine body. As for the courtier, it is never simple.

Bradstreet next represents herself as "unwise *Phaeton*," the son of Pheobus who required that his father allow him to drive the golden chariot of the sun as proof of his divine paternity. On the surface, this is a comic allegory of the folly of grandiose aspiration, but it echoes Bradstreet's anxiety about her filial connection to the English Renaissance expressed earlier in the poem. Interestingly, she is like Phaeton in her daring and her fearful realization of what she has taken on in manning "Fame's flaming Chariot." But she is unlike the unruly son in that Apollo merely laughs at her antics, says he will "patch up what's begun," bids her drive his car, and tells her he will even "hold the Sun" for her safety, all for the "dear regard he had of Sydney's state . . . / That those that name his fame, he needs must spare." Here is the confirmation of paternity and special filial privileges Bradstreet has sought. But it is only a doting father's indulgent recognition of his favorite, and meddling, daughter. In this very recognition, Bradstreet as female and, therefore, disinherited speaker is unmasked.

Apollo promises manly aid to the poet but is displaced by the Muses in yet another reversal of tradition and sex roles. According to myth, Apollo ruled the nine, but in Bradstreet's poetic self-representation the whole fabric of the poet's conventional relationship to traditional sources of identity and authority comes unraveled. She recounts their fantastic intercession as an assault that goes far beyond the conventional *topos* of "affected modesty":

> th' muses had no will,
> To give to their detractor any quill.
> With high disdain, they said they gave no more,
> Since *Sydney* had exhausted all their store,
> That this contempt it did the more perplex,
> In being done by one of their own sex;
> They took from me, the scribling pen I had,
> I to be eas'd of such a task was glad.
> For to revenge their wrong, themselves ingage,
> And drave me from *Parnassus* in a rage,
> Not because, sweet *Sydney's* fame was not dear,
> But I had blemish'd theirs, to make 't appear[.]

Any attempt to praise Sidney, Bradstreet seems to imply here, elicits the Muses' ire. If I may hazard a paraphrase of the ambiguous fifth line, their extreme contempt for Bradstreet's overreaching is heightened by the fact of their shared sex. The perplexity would seem to be Bradstreet's, either because she has been found out to be a woman or because the Muses show so little sympathy for her plight, or so much rage for her poetic attempt. In any case, the transgressive act of woman writing cannot be tolerated. The androcentric tradition must be avenged. Bradstreet's self-styled "scribbling" "blemishes" the Muses' reputation as its virginal guardians, despite her many avowals of modesty and humility and her imitation of Sidney as the Muses' son. The elegy concludes abruptly, as "Errata" (a pun perhaps upon the name of the muse of erotic poetry, Erato, who appears here appropriately as the goddess of error) is given leave by the vengeful nine to allow Bradstreet to write two final lines, after which she must return her borrowed pen. She is left penless, symbolically castrated, exiled from a rebirth as male, and returned to the no-man's land of femaleness. However, she has managed, again, to turn an elegy to her male poetic precursor into the complex story of her own poetic plight. The consequences of putting a feminine figure at the center of previously male-centered myths are explosive, and Bradstreet quickly shuts down what she has opened up. The clearly self-punishing conclusion might just be a propitiation which reveals how far she has dared to go as a trespasser on male turf.

The world left for Bradstreet to inherit is sketched in the third elegy in the sequence, **"In Honour of that High and Mighty Princess, Queen ELIZABETH, of most happy memory"** composed in 1643. Elizabeth provides Bradstreet with a means to end her futile wrestling match with the Renaissance by transcending the rules that it set up and that define it. In the almost half century since the death of Elizabeth, Bradstreet absorbed and in the elegy reproduced the major cultural myths about this figure who stands, paradoxically, at the center of the male-dominated world Bradstreet so passionately wishes to recover. She portrays Elizabeth, through recurring references to her emblem, the mythological phoenix, giving birth to herself as the successor/son as she rises from the ashes of traditional gender roles to rule England as the virgin warrior and nurturing mother. This resurrection, finally likened to Christ's, portends a truly reborn world in which women no longer need disguises.

In transcending the restrictions placed on her sex, Elizabeth transcends the male-dominated discourses of history and poetry altogether. Unlike Sidney in whom the Muses' "nine-fold wit had been compacted," "No *Phoenix,* Pen, nor *Spencers* Poetry, / No *Speeds,* nor *Chamdens* learned History; / *Eliza's* works, wars, praise, can e're compact." While Sidney is both perpetrator and victim of his spell-binding poetic rhetoric, Elizabeth can forego words and choose, rather, to act in the public male-dominated realm: "The World's the Theatre where she did act." Elizabethan women were not allowed onto the stage, and Puritans were forbidden to attend stage plays, but Elizabeth made the world her stage, surpassing, as Bradstreet implies, even these restrictions.

The upshot of Elizabeth's actions for Bradstreet is the redemption of woman, not as an imperfect sub-species of the male, but as a sex equal, if not superior, to men: "She hath wip'd off th' aspersion of her Sex, / That women wisdome lack to play the Rex." Bradstreet's allusions to Elizabeth's public persona as a theatrical representation are curiously heretical, since the Puritans were particularly strident in their opposition to playgoing. They suggest Bradstreet's desire to flout those restrictions (as with her reading and defense of Sidney's *Arcadia*) and her awareness that Elizabeth did indeed "play" a part which was not "natural" for women.

These allusions culminate in Bradstreet's ultimate tribute to the queen: "The *Salique* Law had not in force now been, / If *France* had ever hop'd for such a Queen; / But can you Doctors now this point dispute, / She's argument enough to make you mute." Although "no printed copy of any part of Shakespeare's works is known to have existed in New England during the seventeenth century," and Bradstreet's familiarity with and use of Shakespeare is purely speculative, she seems to refer in the above passage to Act I, scene i of *Henry V,* where the learned Canterbury attempts to untangle the role of the Salic law in the succession of kings. Henry is fighting for the throne of France, but the law, revived to block his claim, forbids succession through the female. The only certainty that emerges from Canterbury's mystifying disquisition is that all entitlement passes through the female by way of mothers. Bradstreet evinced anxiety over her genealogy in the elegy on Sidney, where she contends in vain to inherit the poetic crown. By comparison, Elizabeth successfully defends her claim as the inheriting daughter/son. For the first time in this series of elegies, the men are struck mute; Elizabeth silences the learned, disputatious doctors because she is the conclusive "argument" for the right of women to assume power on the basis not of genealogy but "wisdome" to play the part of a role whose gender ascriptions are culturally, not naturally, determined. Furthermore, once she possesses her title, she refuses to pass it on by producing an heir, another flouting of assigned gender roles. Elizabeth redeems women, Bradstreet implies, as more than merely the site through which titles, and by extension discourse, pass. They can be actors in their own right, not epicenes, playing with, but not dependent upon, the characteristics of a male role.

Bradstreet's hyperbolic praise of Elizabeth as actor focuses on her acting the part of a prince—her military victories, her imperial might, and her command of heroic men. As virgin, transvestite ("Our *Amazon* i'th' Campe at *Tilberry*") and actor, Elizabeth is the daughter successfully turned son, the mimic *par excellence* not reduced merely to her imitative role. But Bradstreet also places Elizabeth in a gynolineal heritage. Following the conventional recital of her princely conquests is a long passage in which Bradstreet compares Elizabeth to historical queens and empresses: Semiramis, Tomris—"*Sythians* Queen," Dido, Cleopatra, and Zenobia. Though Elizabeth surpasses them all, this context displaces her from her historical context into the ancient world and exalts a female model of courage, strength, and leadership that contrasts sharply with the traditional passive virtues of femininity, silence, modesty, and obedience.

Such is the female no-man's land to which the self-created Elizabeth leads Bradstreet. Yet, in a moment of disturbing self-consciousness, she realizes and still mourns her exile from the male tradition in conventional terms: "Her personall perfections, who would tell, / Must dip his Pen i'th' Heliconian Well; / Which I may not, my pride doth but aspire, / To read what others write, and then admire." While she figures herself with a pen here, she is forbidden by unnamed forces from moistening it at the sacred spring of the Nine. Thus exiled to the drier margins, Bradstreet reenacts the particular form of self-censorship that appears in each elegy. Here it seems particularly insidious, for Bradstreet's obvious "pride" in the incomparable accomplishments of Elizabeth is channeled not into imita-

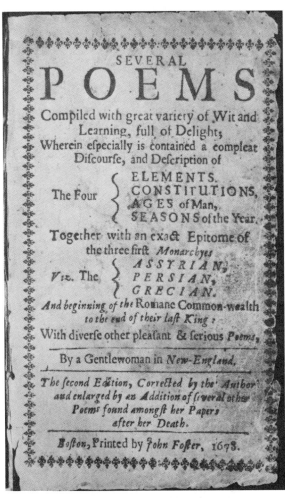

Title page of Several Poems, *1678.*

Nay Masculines, you have thus tax'd us long,
But she though dead, will vindicate our wrong.
Let such, as say our sex is void of reason,
Know 'tis a slander now, but once was treason.
But happy *England,* which had such a Queen,
O happy, happy, had those dayes still been,
But happinesse, lies in a higher sphere,
Then wonder not, *Eliza* moves not here.
Full fraught with honour, riches, and with
    dayes:
She set, she set, like *Titan* in his rayes,
No more shall rise or set such glorious Sun,
Untill the heavens great revolution:
If then new things, their old form must retain,
Eliza shall rule *Albian* once again.

In Bradstreet's world, women must endure misogyny as merely a stain upon their reputations; in Elizabeth's "halsion dayes," it was a capital offense, a crime not only against woman, but against the head of state and the state itself. She compares Elizabeth to the sun-god Titan, who threatened the Olympian powers and had to be destroyed. But implicit in this comparison, and in the imagery of setting and rising, is the image of the self-creating phoenix, the fertilizing sun, and Christ, the glorious son of God, who was to return from heaven to rule over earth for the thousand years of peace before the Last Judgment. In this "revolution," as in the civil war then raging in England, the world would be turned upside down, and Elizabeth, truly Bradstreet's "once and future Queen," would rise again to reinstitute a gynocentric renascence.

In this final vision, Bradstreet locates Elizabeth, the physical and symbolic center of the Renaissance, outside of her historical and literary context in the higher sphere of Puritan millennialism. Her rule, according to the poet, will be the return of an old "form" and the inauguration of a new, feminized content—an idea that also suggests Bradstreet's vision for her own poetry that she achieves in her later verse. Having gone through the processes of lament, critique and utopian counter-vision, she can shape Elizabethan and Puritan poetic genres to fit a less conflicted, clearly gendered poetic voice. It is significant that Bradstreet never alludes to Elizabeth as a learned woman or a poet in her own right. She realizes that Elizabeth "played" a part reserved for men, and that in doing so she, like other female figures such as Joan of Arc who don the literal or metaphorical dress of men in order to act in a male world, reinforces the traditional power accorded to maleness by implying that women can act only by appropriating male roles. However, as visible figures both inside and outside the dominant tradition, even their "mimicry" is a disruption and modification of the conventions they imitate because, as Irigaray says, "they are not simply resorbed in this function. *They also remain elsewhere*" (emphasis hers).

True, then, to her Puritanism and her female experience, Bradstreet recasts her Renaissance as a glorious gynocentrism, indefinitely deferred. In this final gesture, Bradstreet shows that she may have fought and lost the requisite oedipal wrestling match with her poetic precursors, but that the fight was on their turf. She had yet to stake out her own territory. Nevertheless, as a forerunner of other women struggling to enter (and therefore subvert)

tion of her hero's ability to act, but into the passive reading of other writers' works about the queen, presumably men. In this apology and deflection of poetic authority, Bradstreet represents herself, again, in the role of barren daughter. She pushes the conventional apology until it undoes her poetic voice. As in the previous elegies, she asks us to read her poem and to imagine simultaneously that she has not written it or is incapable of writing it. In (un)doing so, she places the reader in the double bind she has experienced as a woman poet. However, within this doubleness Bradstreet acknowledges, more directly than in the previous two elegies, the power possible for herself as a woman speaking.

For, immediately following her enactment of self-censorship, and flatly contradicting it, Bradstreet asks her male audience the ultimate question implicit in her tribute to Elizabeth: "Now say, have women worth, or have they none? / Or had they some, but with our Queen ist gone?" Her defiant answer, in the final lines of the poem, can be seen as a variation of the fantasy of imitation and power expressed in the elegies on Du Bartas and Sidney, here transformed into a triumphant prophecy that supersedes the previous fantasies of humiliation and disempowerment:

the male-dominated tradition, she fought several crucial rounds.

Beth M. Doriani   (essay date 1989)

SOURCE: " 'Then Have I . . . Said with David': Anne Bradstreet's Andover Manuscript Poems and the Influence of the Psalm Tradition," in *Early American Literature,* Vol. XXIV, No. 1, Spring, 1989, pp. 52-69.

[*In the essay below, Doriani comments on Bradstreet's use of poetic techniques borrowed from the Geneva Bible and the* Bay Psalm Book.]

"What we need to realize now," said Robert Daly in 1978 [in his *God's Altar: The World and the Flesh in Puritan Poetry*], "is that . . . Puritan orthodoxy was conducive to the production of poetry, and that Bradstreet's poetry is illuminated by an understanding of the theology which structured the experiences her poetry expressed." Daly argued that Bradstreet remained faithful to her tradition in that she celebrated the sensible world while consistently ascending to a celebration of its Creator through her contemplations of the world. But Bradstreet's orthodoxy, as it emerges in her devotional poetry, goes even beyond her attitude toward the world and poetic uses of it. What she does in her Andover Manuscript poems is not only to draw on the themes and emphases of Puritan theology but to adopt the rhetorical techniques and voice of the Psalms as the Puritans understood them. Her imitation of the Psalms—in technique, stance, and thematic patterns—indicates her ability to work comfortably within her tradition, searching for a poetic language that God would accept.

That Anne Bradstreet's poetry reflects the influence of the Psalms—the Book of Psalms as well as the *Bay Psalm Book*—has been generally acknowledged. Her indebtedness to the psalm tradition is, however, far greater than an imitation of the metrics of the *Bay Psalm Book* translations or the diction and imagery found in the Book of Psalms. The Andover Manuscript poems, written as reflections on intensely personal events in her life, show a more comprehensive reliance on the Psalm tradition than has hitherto been acknowledged. For Bradstreet, the psalter and the Puritan tradition surrounding it prove conducive to the production of poetry and provide her with a voice to imitate, the Davidic voice, as she strives to praise God even in her suffering.

The importance of the Hebrew Psalms for the New England Puritans derives from the Protestant Reformation. With Calvin and Luther's sanctioning of psalm-singing for corporate as well as private worship came the quick adoption of the psalms as the hymnody of many churches in western Christendom. Translators drew on popular secular tunes for the music of their new metrical psalms; the ballad or common meter of their renditions contrasted favorably with the unmeasured music of the Roman Catholic plain-chant. The rendering of the Psalms into vernacular poetry was a favorite pastime of poets and pastors from the Reformation through the eighteenth century. It is significant that only ten years after arriving in the New World the Massachusetts Bay Puritans produced their own psalter—the *Bay Psalm Book*—that would supersede the Pilgrims' *Ainsworth Psalter* in ease of singing and the Sternhold and Hopkins psalter in faithfulness of translation.

For the Puritans, the singing of psalms satisfied at least two priorities: their enjoyment of music and their high estimation of the language of Scripture. In the Psalms the Puritans found a catalogue of praises in a language acceptable to God. Tradition held that David, God's faithful servant, provided a model of the language of praise that God had sanctioned. Although he was admittedly human in his sinfulness, David was also regarded as a type of Christ. His composition of psalms, in their reflection of the range of human spiritual experience, opened up the channel between God and man. Thus the Psalms were important not only for joyful, corporate singing but also for serious study and meditation. The numerous metrical translations of the Psalms in the seventeenth century attest to their central place.

That David the type prefigures Christ the antitype is central to understanding the seventeenth-century view of the Psalms. In his role of suffering servant, David was seen as exemplifying Christly behavior in the struggle to overcome sin and gain redemption. In one respect, then, the Psalms were regarded as illuminations of the connection between the psalmist's situation and the struggles of the contemporary Christian. The Psalms not only gave Christians of all ages encouragement and comfort in their suffering, but also provided experiential patterns to imitate in the Christian journey towards obedient living. David was the foremost model for all pious exercise, from repentance to supplication to joyful praise. In his total dependence on God, David provided a sanctioned way of communicating with God. As a type of Christ, he provided the words suitable for imitation in the Christian struggle. Because he was human, Christians could identify with him; because he was a type of Christ, they could look to him as a guide in their own service of God.

David was a seminal figure for imitation not only in his spiritual struggles but also in his poetics. As the chief work of poetry in the Bible, the Book of Psalms itself became a model for devotional writers and poets. Luther had stressed the usefulness of the language of the Psalms in the composition of original verse. Since the age of assured inspiration had ended with the canonization of the New Testament, any devotional poet aspiring to write in a sanctioned manner had to be satisfied with imitating holy Scripture. The Psalms, then, were the essential model for sacred songs and poetry. The authors of the *Bay Psalm Book,* in justifying their metrical translations of the Psalms for worship, declared in their preface that "certainly the singing of Davids psalmes was an acceptable worship of God, not only in his owne, but in succeeding times." Further, because God Himself had sanctioned poetry by using it in the Psalms, poetry was seen as an acceptable vehicle for devotion—especially if it imitated the Psalms. Thus poetic activity had biblical justification. It is not surprising that the genres of the prayer-poem, the religious lyrical poem, and the hymn were popular in the seventeenth century: all were patterned on the models that

David had presented in the Psalms. David was viewed, then, not only as a saint but also as a sanctified artist. The psalter thus became an aesthetic guide "through its stances, its voices, and its use of the Word of artistry God accepted." It provided the best of the language of humanity in its most noble service: communication with God.

In a personal journal begun in 1656, Bradstreet's first entry is a spiritual autobiography addressed to her children; she indicates her turning to the Psalms for solace in the midst of personal affliction. In the letter "To My Dear Children," she says that, in her times of greatest affliction, "I [have] gone to searching and have said with David, 'Lord, search me and try me, see what ways of wickedness are in me, and lead me in the way everlasting.' " As the model of the faithful pilgrim, David provides the words for her as she struggles with emotional crises and physical suffering. He also provides her with a sanctified poetics. As she indicates in the letter, her intention in writing is not "to show my skill, but to declare the truth, not to set forth myself, but the glory of God." At the same time, she indicates that her immediate purpose is that her children might have the "spiritual advantage" of her experience. She follows the letter with entries about her succeeding struggles with illness and doubt, recording the entries in both poetry and prose. Reliance on the Psalms for the poetry of this notebook provides her with the means to serve the spiritual advantage of her children in the larger context of glorifying God. In providing a poetic language acceptable to God, the Psalms also provide a mode which will give her poems a lasting pedagogical importance. As the psalmist's verses teach the children of God of all times, so does her imitation of the Psalms allow her to attain a sanctified immortality for these poems intended for her children. As she writes in her letter, she has bequeathed these poems to her children so that she "may be daily in [their] remembrance" and thus teach them even after she has died, encouraging their faithfulness to and hope in God. "Make use of what I leave in love," she writes in the poem that opens her letter, "And God shall bless you from above." She shows her indebtedness to the Psalms in David's role both as faithful servant and as sanctified poet.

Certainly Bradstreet had written earlier about her personal suffering, even as early as 1632, as in **"Upon a Fit of Sickness, Anno 1632, *Aetatis Suae*, 19."** This poem, unlike the poems on "public" topics, follows the common meter of the *Bay Psalm Book,* a meter that she would adopt again in the poetry of her notebook. But the similarity of this early poem to the Psalms—or to her later psalm-like poetry—stops there. Even the metaphor with which she opens and closes the poem, the "race" of the faithful follower of Christ, is not psalmic but Pauline (as in 2 Tim. 4:7). It is not until later in her life that she experiments with a full range of psalmic techniques in her personal poetry.

As Rich points out, Bradstreet's active sensibility was decidedly changing after 1650, the year of the first edition of her *The Tenth Muse, Lately Sprung Up In America.* The titles themselves of the thirteen poems added posthumously to the second edition (1678) indicate the change. These poems show a turn to more personal subjects: her responses to illness, the anticipation of the birth of a child, her loneliness for her husband in his absence, her responses to the deaths of grandchildren. No longer would she take on such subjects as the ancient monarchies, the four humors, or Queen Elizabeth. Instead, the poems become responses to the events of a woman's life, just as the poems in her notebook are. Five of the thirteen poems bear dates congruent with those of her notebook: **"In Reference to Her Children, 23 June, 1659"** and the poems on the deaths of grandchildren Elizabeth (1665), Anne (1669), and Simon (1669), and daughter-in-law Mercy (1669). It is noteworthy that three of these poems refer to deaths that occur in the autumn of 1669; one of the poems in the Andover Manuscript is also dated August 31, 1669. Yet none of the poems not in the notebook show any significant adoption of the psalm tradition. The poems of the notebook take on a special importance as she reserves the psalmic model for them. Through these poems we get a glimpse of a deeply personal side of Bradstreet, a side in which she shows us a deep commitment to her Puritan heritage as she struggles to assume the Davidic voice.

Since childhood Bradstreet had listened to the singing of the Psalms; she had heard the Psalms in the Sternhold and Hopkins version as a young child and then in the *Bay Psalm Book* in the fifteen years preceding her first journal entry. The authors of the *Bay Psalm Book*—university-trained ministers Thomas Weld, John Eliot, and Richard Mather—wanted to replace the Sternhold and Hopkins version with renditions more faithful to the original Hebrew, even if this meant a sacrifice of poetic effect. They declare in the psalter preface that their goal was to provide the psalms in their "native purity," not to give a paraphrase or in any way vary the sense of the sacred verse. For Bradstreet, the *Bay Psalm Book* translations provided a quite close rendering of the Hebrew Psalms at the same time that they provided verse models. These, and the Geneva Bible prose versions she read and meditated upon as a faithful Puritan, give her access to the biblical poetry and the psalm tradition.

The most insistent and persistent characteristics of the *Bay Psalm Book* selections—and Bradstreet's Andover Manuscript poems—are, of course, the metrical regularity and simple rhyme schemes. All but two of Bradstreet's poems of 1656-62 are in the two most common meters of the *Bay Psalm Book*: common meter and long meter. Bradstreet uses both the open (abcb) and closed (abab) rhyme schemes of the *Bay Psalm Book*. Although she does not imitate any particular psalm, the similarity in sound to the *Bay Psalm Book* selections is striking, as Psalm 23 demonstrates:

> The Lord to mee a shepheard is,
> want therefore shall not I.
> Hee in the folds of tender-grasse,
> doth cause mee downe to lie:
> To waters calme me gently leads
> Restore my soule doth hee:
> he doth in paths of righteousnes:
> for his names sake leade mee. . . .

[Rivkah] Zim points out that, with respect to metrical psalms, metrical regularity can constrain a poet by the need either to fit his or her words to preexisting tunes, or to make the verses suitable for musical improvisation. Nevertheless, he recognizes, such metrical regularity would also have assisted a singer to read these holy songs and to sing them to brief melodies stanza by stanza. The metrical regularity and their ability to be sung would also make the verses easier to remember. Writing for an audience whom she very much wanted to edify, Bradstreet perhaps saw in the metrical psalms a form by which, in its ease of memorization, she and her lessons might be remembered.

Yet her larger purpose, as she indicates in her letter, is to glorify God. The diction and imagery found in the Psalms provide her with a sanctified poetic vocabulary. That she adopts the psalmic diction and imagery in the poems of her notebook is obvious, as in her use of the psalmic expressions of "paying vows" and "rendering praises" to God (appearing in eleven out of the fourteen Andover Manuscript poems); the biblical images of God as "light," "strength," "shelter," "shadow," and even a protective bird in His role of divine caretaker; the metaphor of God's "face" to suggest His favor; the metonomy of His rod and staff to reflect His fatherly, chastising care; and other psalmic figures. She uses such imagery to take the stance of the Davidic suffering servant. Like David, she suffers because of her own sin—and God's consequent chastisement—or because of the trials which are necessarily a part of her life, such as the loneliness she must endure in her husband's absence. In this stance as servant she voices her dependence on God by calling to Him in her afflictions or by praising Him as her help and strength. David provides a fitting model for her to emulate in her struggles with suffering and doubt. Even more strikingly, she imitates not only the psalmic diction and imagery but psalmic structural techniques as she imitates David's voice.

In her Andover Manuscript poems, Bradstreet uses interrogation, the shifting of audience, and amplification, which Fithian describes as, along with antithesis, the major rhetorical techniques used in the Psalms to express the poetic voice. As does the psalmist, Bradstreet sometimes uses the technique of interrogation to communicate her familiarity with God. This technique of direct questioning appears, for example, in Ps. 6: "My soule is also sore troubled: but Lord, how long wilt thou delay?" The psalmist often uses interrogation to call God to action. Since he enjoys a close relationship with God, he is in a position to urge God to take action, and he does so by interrogation. Likewise, Bradstreet uses interrogation in her poem **"My Soul"** when she writes, "Come Jesus quickly, Blessed Lord. / Thy face when shall I see?" More often, however, she uses the technique in the way that the psalmist uses it in Pss. 8, 27, and 89—as a sort of rhetorical device to communicate inadequacy and dependence on God. Here the direct questioning has the character of praise. Ps. 27:1 provides a good example: "The Lord is my light and my salvation, whome shall I feare? the Lord is the strength of my life, of whom shall I bee afraid?" Bradstreet uses the technique similarly in **"In Thankful Remembrance for my Dear Husband's Safe Arrival"**:

> What shall I render to Thy name
> Or how Thy praises speak?
> My thanks how shall I testify?

O Lord, Thou know'st I'm weak.

. . . . .

> What did I ask for but Thou gav'st?
> What could I more desire?

As in Ps. 8:4, she does not intend her questions to be answered; she uses interrogation to communicate her own inadequacy before a gracious and loving God. The technique also appears, used in a similar way, in the opening lines of her **"July 8, 1656"** poem: "What God is like to Him I serve? / What Saviour like to mine?" The implicit answer, of course, is "none"—thus she goes on to praise her God. Like David, she communicates her worship of God, acknowledging the magnitude of His love and care. Such worship springs from her sense of gratitude to God: He has done so much for her in removing her affliction, yet He receives so little from her, as she asserts in an early prose passage from her journal. And again, like David, she realizes that the only offering she can make is praise. Interrogation provides her a vehicle to express her gratitude and praise in an intimate way.

Imitating David's shifting of audience within the context of a single psalm allows Bradstreet to give voice to her praise of God in a full way as well as to deal with her doubts in her times of suffering. In the Psalms, David often turns from addressing God to address his own soul or a general audience. It is common to see several shifts of audience in a single psalm; David will often address God, then turn to ask his soul a question, then turn back again to God in a report of the condition of his soul, as in Ps. 42:

> As the hart brayeth for the rivers of water, so
> panteth
> my soule after thee, O God. . . .
> Why art thou cast downe, my soule, and unquiet
> within
> me? waite on God: for I will yet give thanks for
> the help of his presence.
> My God, my soule is cast downe within
> me. . . .

In the first verse, the psalmist is obviously directing his words to God. Then he turns to his soul, rebuking it for its doubt and distress; subsequently he turns his attention back to God. At times, David shifts his attention to address a general audience, as in the ninth verse of Ps. 42: "I will say unto God, which is my rocke, Why hast thou forgotten mee?"

In Bradstreet's poetry, the shifting takes on special importance in that it provides her with the opportunities both to encourage her own children—her analogue to David's audience—and to praise God directly herself. As in **"On My Son's Return,"** she urges her children on the path to obedience as she calls, in the first four lines, for "all praise to Him." Then she turns to address God herself, reviewing His faithfulness towards her in His care of her son. The shift implicitly allows her to praise God as His faithful servant as well as to remind her children—and herself—of the trustworthiness of God. In **"For Deliverance from a Fever,"** she directs most of the poem to God Himself, recounting to Him her experience with a fever and, in doing so, offering her praise to Him. The shift to a general audience occurs near the end, after line 25:

> Thou show'st to me Thy tender love,
> My heart no more might quail.
> O, praises to my mighty God,
> Praise to my Lord, I say,
> Who hath redeemed my soul from pit,
> Praises to Him for aye.

Having experienced serious illness and recovery, Bradstreet desires to remind her readers that it is God who heals, as she states in her July 8, 1656, prose entry. Thus she turns in the last quatrain to call on a general audience to give praises to God. Reminding her children of the grounds for praise—the rescue of a suffering woman from her affliction—she urges them to join in her adoration, as if teaching them how to bless God. Moreover, the technique allows her to express the fullness of her gratitude: it is as if she feels so overwhelmed with gratitude that her own individual praise is insufficient as a response to God for His goodness to her.

Bradstreet's choosing to shift between a variety of audiences instead of writing only prayers addressed to God also allows her to challenge her readers to see life's trials from a broad perspective and thereby learn the "very lesson she must force upon herself." As [Jeffrey A.] Hammond has pointed out [in " 'Make Use of What I Leave in Love': Anne Bradstreet's Didactic Self," *Religion and Literature,* 1985], the intentionally didactic nature of Bradstreet's verse is often a reflection of her efforts to identify and communicate what she saw as the real truth behind her periods of suffering and recovery—that is, that God is dealing in a fatherly way with His child. Certainly she indicates such a purpose in her letter "To My Dear Children." That her devotional poetry is "virtually a seamless blend of the confessional and the didactic" is in keeping with her shifts of audience. When she turns to address a general audience (as in **"From Another Sore Fit"**: "What shall I render to my God / For all His bounty showed to me?") she no doubt has in mind her own children, desiring to challenge them to see past their own moments of affliction, as she does, to the One who provides sustenance, strength, and loving-kindness. At the same time, the technique affords her the opportunity to give full voice to her feelings as she moves easily between audiences, prodding her soul, addressing God, or calling Jesus to return—all of which she does in **"My Soul,"** shifting four times in only twenty-eight lines. Thus her readers see her confession of her suffering, which she often perceives as chastisement from God, as in **"Deliverance from a Fit of Fainting"**: she declares that her "life as spider's webb's cut off." Yet her readers also see how thanksgiving springs from such suffering: "My feeble spirit Thou didst revive / . . . Why should I live but to Thy praise?" That the Christian expresses such thanksgiving is important to godly living, Bradstreet affirms in her July 8 prose entry. She herself "dares not pass by without remembrance" of the love God showed to her in her suffering. Such thanksgiving reflects David's model throughout the Psalms.

The psalmic technique of amplification—an addition to or expansion of a statement—also allows Bradstreet to voice her feelings about God in a way sanctioned by David. Of the three forms Fithian describes—hyperbole, *accumulatio,* and *exclamatio*—Bradstreet uses two in her Andover Manuscript poems, hyperbole and *accumulatio.* Hyperbole in the Psalms often communicates the psalmist's utter dependence on God by a graphic description of his physical condition. For example, in Ps. 31:10 the psalmist writes, "For my life is wasted with heaviness, and my yeeres with mourning: my strength faileth for my paine, and my bones are consumed." Similarly in Ps. 22 he describes his bones as being "out of joynt" and his heart as "like wax . . . molten in the middes of my bowels" as he seeks God's deliverance.

In her poems written about her periods of illness, Bradstreet also intensifies her own condition. In **"From Another Sore Fit"** she describes herself as having "wasted flesh" and as "melting" in her own sweat, before God in His grace reaches out to help her. In **"Deliverance from a Fit of Fainting"** she describes her life as a "spider's webb's cut off " to communicate her physical weakness during her sickness, and she writes that she was "though as dead" before God "mad'st [her] alive." Her self-belittling conveys the Puritan belief that deliverance is to be sought in God and not in self: she is utterly dependent on God. Moreover, that such a heartbroken speaker could call upon God for help would certainly bring consolation for her readers, as Hammond points out. Hyperbole also communicates the capacity of God to deliver His children, as in Ps. 93 where God is "more mightie" than "the noyse of many waters" and "the waves of the sea." Bradstreet similarly exalts the Lord by making hyperbolic statements: "Thy mercies, Lord, have been so great / In number numberless, / Impossible for to recount / Or any way express" (**"In Thankful Remembrance"**). Even in the midst of her trials, she knows that God will ultimately not forsake her and that in Him alone lies triumph over affliction.

Accumulatio, the amassing of detail, is Bradstreet's most frequent poetic technique, specifically in the form of Hebrew synonymous parallelism. In this technique the lines of poetry are paired, with the second of the lines repeating the basic meaning of the first while adding detail, as in Ps. 145:18-19:

> The Lord is neere unto all that call upon him:
> yea, to all that call upon him in trueth.
>
> He will fulfill the desire of them that feare him:
> he also will heare their crie, and will save them.

In each instance, the first thought is not only repeated but supplemented. Like the other psalmic techniques, the parallelism is seen in both the Geneva Bible and the *Bay Psalm Book* selections, preserved in the metrical psalms by virtue of the accuracy of the translations. In the *Bay Psalm Book,* verses eighteen and nineteen of Psalm 145 are rendered thus:

> Hee's neere to all that call on him:
> in truth that on him call.
>
> Hee satisfy will the desire
> of those that doe him feare:
> Hee will be safety unto them,
> and when they cry he'le heare.

As in the second verse of this case, the authors of the *Bay Psalm Book* often accommodate long lines of the psalms by arranging the parallelism between two pairs of lines. Bradstreet uses both forms of the parallelism. In the very first poetic entry of her notebook (**"By Night When Others Soundly Slept"**) she employs the technique, arranging the parallelism between single lines:

> By night when others soundly slept,
> And had at once both ease and rest . . .
> I sought Him whom my soul did love,
> With tears I sought Him earnestly. . . .

She too expands the content of the first line by adding detail in the second. **"From Another Sore Fit"** provides additional examples, as well as **"In My Solitary Hours,"** in which the pairings occur frequently (stanzas 1-3, 8, 10, 13). The parallelism can be found throughout Bradstreet's poetry; it appears in virtually all of the poems of her notebook. When she arranges the parallelism between two pairs of lines instead of between two single lines, she treats a two-line phrase as if it were actually a single line, as we have seen in the *Bay Psalm Book*:

> Whence fears and sorrows me beset
> Then didst Thou rid me out;
>
> When heart did faint and spirits quail,
> Thou comforts me about.
> (**"For the Restoration of My Dear Husband"**)

A two-line phrase often echoes the preceding two lines in her poetry, usually in the same stanza. Thus a line is actually paralleling the second line after it, still preserving the structure of psalmic *accumulatio*.

Bradstreet fits such paired lines into the thematic patterns found in the Psalms—the most striking similarity between Bradstreet's Andover Manuscript poems and the Psalms. In the tradition of the Psalms, the articulations of the devout person's struggle toward obedience reflect categories with distinct themes, as Fithian has noted: lament, supplication, and thanksgiving. Although elements of two categories are often combined within a single psalm (such as thanksgiving and supplication), the three kinds are arranged within quite specific structural patterns in the Psalms. The great majority of Bradstreet's Andover poems clearly expresses thanksgiving and praise, as in the Psalms. This type of psalm typically begins with an exclamation of the intention to praise, often either in an epithet or in an imperative call to worship. Next, the psalmist gives the specific grounds for praise—for example, a catalogue of dangers that God has helped the psalmist to overcome, or a list of God's activities. Often an index of God's qualities constitutes the grounds for praise. Finally, a proclamation of praise appears.

Psalm 146 exemplifies a psalm of thanksgiving. The exclamation of the intention to praise appears in the first two verses. In this Psalm both a call to worship and declaration are given in the opening: "Praise ye the Lord. Praise thou the Lord, O my soule. I will praise the Lord during my life. . . ." Next, as his grounds for praise, the psalmist describes God in terms of what He has done; this catalogue provides the major portion of the content of the Psalm. The psalmist describes God as He "Which made

heaven and earth, the sea, and all that therein is" and "Which executeth justice for the oppressed." The psalmist also describes what God does in the present, such as giving sight to the blind and "releeving the fatherless." The statement of praise appears as the last verse of the Psalm: "The Lord shall reigne for ever. . . . Praise ye the Lord."

Among Bradstreet's poems **"From Another Sore Fit"** and **"Deliverance from a Fit of Fainting"** clearly exemplify the thanksgiving theme. In each she declares her intention to praise in the first stanza by affirming God's worthiness for praise ("Worthy art Thou, O Lord, of praise," she writes in the first line of **"Deliverance from a Fit of Fainting"**). She continues in both poems with a list of the grounds for her praise by describing God's merciful acts toward her. She writes, "My plaints and groans were heard of Thee, / . . . My wasted flesh Thou didst restore," (**"From Another Sore Fit"**), similarly in lines 10-12 of **"Fit of Fainting"** she lists the reasons for her praise. Bradstreet concludes each by declaring her desire to praise: in **"Fit of Fainting"** the declaration appears in the last stanza ("Why should I live but to Thy praise?") while in **"Sore Fit"** it occupies the last four stanzas ("Thy name and praise to celebrate, / O Lord, for aye is my request. . . ."). This declaration allows her to rehearse the events of her suffering and put them into cosmic perspective, thereby affirming to herself and to her readers that, although her suffering is real, it is not ultimate. Whether she emphasizes these events or the statements of praise which follow, it is clear that such praise emerges from a strong sense of pain and suffering. The thanksgiving pattern as modeled in the Psalms gives her ample means both to recapitulate her pain and to express her gratitude to God for delivering her. Most often her thanksgiving is gratitude for removing the affliction—the "sore fit" or the "fit of fainting." Yet, as she points out in many of her prose entries, it is also gratitude for God's fatherly care, for chastising her by means of affliction to make her a "vessel fit for His use." Asserting that God "hath no benefit" by her adversity, she states that He afflicts her for her spiritual "advantage," that she may be a "gainer" by it. Moreover, she can live no more "without correction than without food." Thus she is grateful for the "mercies in His rod" (**"Sore Fit"**) and for His chiding her in her doubt (**"Fit of Fainting"**).

Among her Andover Manuscript poems Bradstreet also includes several poems of supplication, a form that allows her to affirm God's trustworthiness as she petitions Him for help. A psalm of supplication is distinguished from a lament by its mood of certainty. Although the psalmist is asking for God's help, as in the lament, he is doing so in full expectation that God will heed his call. This type of psalm typically opens with an invocation followed by a list of reasons why the psalmist expects God to respond to his cry for help. This list could be a description of what God has revealed to the psalmist about Himself in the past—either God's qualities or His saving actions—or it could be a description of the psalmist himself, of his attempts to be obedient to God as he tries to persuade God or call Him to account to be the caring father He has promised to be. In this last instance the psalmist often presents himself as the figure of a righteous man, as in Ps. 17:3: "Thou hast proved and visited mine heart in the night: thou hast tried me, and foundeth nothing. . . ." A request follows, in addition to an indication that the psalmist realizes the possibility of God's help. Sometimes the psalmist includes a promise to praise. In Psalm 71 the supplicating nature of the psalm is readily identifiable. First, the tone is that of certainty, of assurance that God will respond: "For thou art mine hope, O Lord God, even my trust from my youth," the psalmist writes. The psalm adheres to the basic structure of a psalm of supplication. The invocation occupies verses one to four ("encline thine ear unto me"), followed by a description of the Lord's graciousness, as in verses seven and nineteen, in which the psalmist points out God's trustworthiness and the "great things" He has done. The psalmist's petition is that God would deliver him, as he repeats in verses two and four and rephrases throughout the psalm (for example, "Goe not farre from mee"). He tells God of his intention to praise ("Therefore will I praise thee for thy faithfulnesse, O God, upon instrument and viole") and ends the psalm as if he had already been delivered ("they are confounded and brought unto shame, that seeke mine hurt").

Since most of the Andover Manuscript poems are thankful responses to God's graciousness, the supplication poems are few. Yet the two that do reveal such a theme—the poems about the departures of Bradstreet's son and her husband—adhere closely to the psalmic pattern of supplication. Each poem begins with an invocation, a call for God's attention:

> Thou mighty God of sea and land,
> I here resign into Thy hand. . . .
> (**"Upon My Son Samuel"**)

> O thou Most High who rulest all
> And hear'st the prayers of thine,
> O hearken, Lord, unto my suit
> And my petition sign.
> (**"Upon My Dear and Loving Husband"**)

Each continues with a description of the poet's obedience. In the poem on her son, Bradstreet concentrates on her obedience in the nurture of her son: she mentions the prayers, vows, and tears involved in raising him and her faithfulness to him as a mother. In **"Upon My Dear and Loving Husband"** she describes not only her own obedience in stanza 5—similar to the way that the "righteous man" of the Psalms does—but also her husband's (stanza 3), as if in an effort to persuade God to take care of him: "At Thy command, O Lord, he went. . . . Then let Thy promise joy his heart." She intensifies her persuasion when she calls her husband God's "servant" as a reminder to God about His responsibility to him—and her own "dear friend"—suggesting that God should take care of him because of His responsibility to Anne herself.

In both poems, as in the psalms of supplication, the speaker's request for God's help is confident. In the poem on her husband, she declares that she is commending Simon into God's "arms": she has made the initial move and trusts that God will receive her husband. She calls on God to "keep and preserve" her husband as well as herself in his absence, declaring that God is her "strength and stay" and that His "goodness never fails." In **"Upon My Son Samuel"** her request also seems confident. Again she asks God

to "preserve" and "protect" her son; she asserts her confidence in God when she declares that she has "no friend . . . like Thee to trust." Moreover, she is confident of God's favorable stance towards her son: "For sure Thy grace on him is shown."

Both poems conclude by concentrating on praise, with an indication that the poet realizes that God will help in some way. In **"Upon My Dear and Loving Husband"** Bradstreet emphasizes her intent to praise: she tells God that her and Simon's response to His safekeeping will be that they together will sing His praises. In **"Upon My Son Samuel"** she asserts that she will celebrate God's praise if Samuel returns safely, seeming to assume that he will. Almost as an afterthought she adds that she hopes that she will see him "forever happified" with God if she should die before his return. Whatever happens, it will be God's will; He will do what is best. In both poems she has an attitude of peace and confidence in God, characteristic of the psalms of supplication. She has seen God work before in her life, answering her prayers for deliverance and healing her illness and doubt. She has no reason to believe that God will not exercise His fatherly care in some way for her loved ones.

Only one "lament" poem seems to occur among Bradstreet's devotional poems; the absence of her husband is the only occasion on which she reflects in these poems a state close to depression. In this poem we see the influence of the psalmic lament as she pleads with God to comfort her in her loneliness and to return her husband to her. A psalmic lament typically involves five basic parts, as in Psalm 3. The invocation or cry for help opens the psalm ("Lord, how are mine adversaries increased? how many rise against me?"); it is followed by the complaint ("Many say to my soule, There is no helpe for him in God"). Then the psalmist voices his trust in God, reviewing God's care for him in the past ("I did call unto the Lord with my voice, and he heard mee. . ."). He follows this by petitioning God, laying his request before Him ("O Lord, arise: helpe me, my God"). These three elements following the invocation can occur in any order in a lament; sometimes they are repeated (as in Psalm 3, in which the psalmist repeats his trust in God). The lament typically concludes with a vow to praise God or with the statement of praise itself. In Psalm 3 the praise occurs in the last verse: "Salvation belongeth unto the Lord, and thy blessing is upon thy people." **"In My Solitary Hours"** is Bradstreet's single patterned psalmic lament in the Andover poems.

The invocation and complaint are combined in the first stanza. Calling on God to hear her, she tells Him to observe her "tears," "troubles," "longings," and "fears." In stanza two she asserts her trust in God: "Thou hitherto hast been my God; / . . . Through Thee I've kept my ground." She continues to express her trust in stanzas three and four, reflecting on her past close relationship with God. She even declares that God is more "beloved" to her than is her husband. Thus the foundation is laid for her petition, which occurs in stanzas five, eight, and nine: she asks God to "uphold" her, to grant her His favor, and finally to bring back her husband. She reiterates her trust in God in stanzas six and eight and concludes the poem with a vow to praise—individually and with Simon. Again she demonstrates that praise does emerge from her suffering, but this time she is in the midst of suffering and can only promise to praise. Yet though she suffers, she is still able to trust. Certainly she is a "gainer" by her adversity: like the psalmist, she has seen that, although God may hide His face, He does not desert His children. She knows that it is God to whom she must go for care, and so she lays her petitions before Him. The psalmic lament provides a fitting structure for her to voice her distress as well as her intent to praise.

By imitating David in the language, voice, stance, and thematic patterns in the poems of her notebook, Bradstreet takes on the voice of David, demonstrating her powerful identification with David: "then have I . . . said with David," she writes in her letter. In her quest for faith as well as for a poetic, David provides a model for her as both an approved servant and a sanctioned poet. As she struggles with her relationship to God, questioning His care for her periods of illness or His presence in her family's absence, she turns to David and writes psalm-like poetry. And we cannot help but hear a godly mother's desire for her children to hold fast to the faith, even after she herself has died, when she asks God

> O help Thy saints that sought Thy face
> T' return unto Thee praise
> And walk before Thee as they ought,
> In strict and upright ways
> **("In Thankful Remembrance")**

In her opening letter she remarks, "I have often been perplexed that I have not found that constant joy in my pilgrimage and refreshing which I supposed most of the servants of God have." It is in David that she finds a servant of God who knows affliction, a suffering believer with whom she can identify. Yet she has also "tasted of that hidden manna" and has had "abundance of sweetness and refreshment after affliction." This is the lesson she would have her children learn. Praise and thanksgiving can indeed emerge from pain and suffering, if one is confident in Him who returns "comfortable answers" to prayer. David's words provide sanctified poetry; his experience provides a point of identification for the suffering yet trusting Christian. And his poetic forms—both those of the Bible and the metrical translations of the *Bay Psalm Book*—provide an effective pedagogical model. Inspired and sustained by the psalms, Bradstreet is better able to voice her praise of God in a period of affliction and thereby urge her children on to greater faith.

Walter Hughes (essay date 1990)

SOURCE: " 'Meat Out of the Eater': Panic and Desire in American Puritan Poetry," in *Engendering Men: The Question of Male Feminist Criticism*, edited by Joseph A. Boone and Michael Cadden, Routledge, 1990, pp. 102-21.

[*In the following excerpt, Hughes examines the erotic undercurrents in Bradstreet's Puritan imagery.*]

Readers of seventeenth-century religious poetry have often sensed an erotic strain in the devotional meditations

---

Bradstreet's strength as a poet is more a result of her ability to exploit Puritan norms than it is of her ability to subvert them . . . [The] anger and rebellion against God expressed in Bradstreet's poems and meditations do not constitute evidence of rebellion against Puritanism, as they do for a number of her critics, but are in fact typical of the Puritan struggle for salvation.

—*Amanda Porterfield, in her* Female Piety in Puritan New England, *1992.*

---

of English poets: Herbert details his seduction by "Love" in *The Temple,* and Donne in the *Holy Sonnets* pleads with God to "ravish" him. What many readers do not know is that this theme fascinated poets on the other side of the Atlantic as well. Not only did the three major American Puritan poets—Anne Bradstreet, Michael Wigglesworth, and Edward Taylor—all make use of eroticism in their religious poetry; they brought it to a level of intensity that would surprise anyone who believes that Puritans were "puritanical" about sex. In fact, the imagery in which they embodied their relation to God would probably strike their self-styled descendents as downright pornographic . . . .

Bradstreet's writings (c. 1635-1670) confirm the assertion that Puritan religious experience was predicated upon desire. In her prose meditations, she defines the human soul as a principle of insatiability within each person:

> The eyes and ears are the inlets or doors of the soul, through which innumerable objects enter; yet is not that spacious room filled, neither doth it ever say it is enough, but like the daughters of the horseleach, cries "Give, give"; and which is most strange, the more it receives, the more empty it finds itself, and sees an impossibility ever to be filled but by Him in whom all fullness dwells.

For Bradstreet, the first step toward faith is the realization that nothing our senses present to us will satisfy the appetite that is the soul. This desire can be defined as *erotic* in that it orients itself toward a succession of "objects," in both the sense of perceptible things and that of focuses or goals. However, all material objects fail as ultimate objects of desire, because the desiring soul is so ravenous that it can consume them all without ever being filled. In short, we must search beyond sensual experience for the fulfillment of sensual desire. The closest that a Puritan could come to imagining her unknowable God was as an externalized entity corresponding to the emptiness within her, as he "in whom all fullness dwells," the only object commensurate with human desire.

In another of her prose meditations, Bradstreet uses a more specifically erotic image, that of the maternal body, to describe the process by which the individual discovers the only source that can quench her sensual thirst:

> Some children are hardly weaned; although the teat be rubbed with wormwood or mustard, they will either wipe it off, or else suck down sweet and bitter together. So it is with some Christians: let God embitter all the sweets of this life, that so they might feed upon more substantial food, yet they are so childishly sottish that they are still hugging and sucking these empty breasts, that God is forced to hedge up their way with thorns or lay affliction on their loins that so they might shake hands with the world, before it bid them farewell.

Bradstreet's conceit had a certain currency among the Puritans, who often spoke of "weaned affections" as a hallmark of sainthood; what she brings to the metaphor is the stress on the continuity of desire. The infant's appetite is not simply suppressed: it is transferred to "more substantial food." Likewise, our desire for sensual experience is not to be denied but to be redirected toward an object that can fulfill it more completely than any physical object can: God himself. Bradstreet's elaboration of the breast-feeding analogy resembles Freud's narrative of human development, in that our desire for the world and the pleasure we take in it are seen as the result of an energy that is constant throughout our lives, but constantly displaced, rechanneled, and relocated during our development. The infant in the oral stage identifies the breast as the world, but must find new means of deriving satisfaction from the interaction of its body with the world when this initial source is withdrawn. Bradstreet might be said to append another, final stage to Freud's narrative of human development, a spiritual stage in which we turn to God, not the world, for release. This ultimate reorientation of desire is the subject of Bradstreet's greatest poems.

If this is Bradstreet's great subject, the central problem posed in her poetic canon is convincing the soul that a seemingly absent God offers more "substantial" nourishment than the milk that flows from the physical world. It is not enough to dwell on the deficiencies of worldly pleasures. A greater poetic challenge lies in coaxing God through those "doors of the soul," in making him available to the senses. In other words, God must be *objectified,* that is, "made sensually perceptible" and "represented as a focus of desire," in the double sense of the word *object.* Bradstreet's primary strategy for objectifying God is to create parallels between her spiritual life and her sensual and erotic experiences.

The best example of this approach is Bradstreet's **"Letter to Her Husband, Absent upon Public Employment."** Although God is never explicitly mentioned in the poem, Bradstreet's description of her relation to her husband implicitly recalls the unity that Puritans sought to achieve with Christ:

> My head, my heart, mine eyes, my life, nay more,
> My job, my magazine of earthly store,
> If two be one, as surely thou and I.

The distinction "earthly" establishes the two levels of sig-

nificance in the poem: the temporal attachment to her husband and the spiritual commitment to God that it mirrors. These two concerns run parallel throughout, creating a kind of thematic rhyme. A Puritan reader would instantly recognize that Bradstreet's language is obliquely referring to God; the modern reader need only compare this verse to a passage from her prose meditations in which she writes, "thy maker is thy husband . . . I am a member of his Body; he, my head." Although Puritan women were expected to see their husbands as resembling God in their authority, Bradstreet does not stress this in her poem; instead, by drawing on the image of the sun, she emphasizes the ways in which her sexual relation to her husband brings her closer to God:

> I, like the earth this season, mourn in black,
> My Sun is gone so far in's zodiac,
> Whom whilst I 'joyed, nor storms, nor frost I
>   felt,
> His warmth such frigid colds did cause to melt.
> My chilled limbs now numbed lie forlorn;
> Return, return, sweet Sol, from Capricorn. . . .
> But when thou northward to me shall return,
> I wish my Sun may never set, but burn
> Within the Cancer of my glowing breast,
> The welcome house of him my dearest guest.

These lines, celebrated for their open expression of erotic longing, also have a religious analogue that readers of Puritan diaries and conversion narratives will recognize. Periods of spiritual emptiness, when God seems to have withdrawn from the writer, are conventional stages in the process of ascertaining one's salvation; longing for God when he seems to have departed is frequently noted as a promising sign of redemption. Even Bradstreet's reference to her children, the products of her sexual union with her husband/sun, supports a religious reading: "In this dead time, alas, what can I more / Than view those fruits which through thy heat I bore?" By referring to her children as the "fruits" of her marriage, she uses a word that Puritans frequently applied to the holy feelings and actions that God's grace inspired in the redeemed individual. Contemplation of these "fruits" often served the Puritan as a means of testing the reality of her redemption in times of God's withdrawal, of consoling herself when spiritually "dead." The identification of Bradstreet's relation to her husband with her relation to God is a theme uniquely suited to poetic expression, which allows her to speak of both with the same words; God is immanent in her sexual experience just as he is implicit in her language and imagery.

In a poem called **"Contemplations,"** Bradstreet again invokes the trinity of sun, lover, and God:

> Thou as a bridegroom from thy chamber rushes,
> And as a strong man, joys to run a race;
> The morn doth usher thee with smiles and
>   blushes;
> The Earth reflects her glances in thy face.
> Birds, insects, animals with vegative,
> Thy heat from death and dullness doth revive,
> And in the darksome womb of nature dive.

The simile of the eager bridegroom points in two directions: it refers to the sun, as in Psalm 19, but also to Christ, as in the typological reading of Canticles. This poetic association imitates the process by which God becomes available to the poet's senses, and then becomes the object of her desire. Her sensual enjoyment of the sun's light and warmth leads her to the image of the sun arousing and fertilizing the female earth as a male lover; this in turn leads to thoughts of the Creator who is the source of all life.

By paralleling her erotic yearning for her husband with the earth's seasonal response to the sun's movement through the zodiac, Bradstreet combines the personal and the cosmic, the vast and the intimate in a way that ultimately gains her poetic access to God. The intermittent presence and absence of the sun, Simon Bradstreet, and God himself all serve to heighten and direct the poet's longing. Bradstreet does not believe complete fulfillment to be possible in this life; but the foretastes of it she experiences in nature and sexuality help her to orient her desiring soul toward God. These experiences are transitional, leading her through earthly pleasure to a knowledge of the divine.

FURTHER READING

Bibliography

Sckeick, William J., and Doggett, JoElla. "Anne Bradstreet." In their *Seventeenth-Century American Poetry: A Reference Guide*, pp. 34-54. Boston: G. K. Hall & Co., 1977.
    Covers Bradstreet criticism from 1844 to 1975.

Stanford, Ann. "Anne Bradstreet: An Annotated Checklist." *Early American Literature* 3, No. 3 (Winter 1968-1969): 217-28.
    Provides a brief sketch of highlights in Bradstreet criticism as well as an annotated bibliography of works by and about Bradstreet.

Biography

White, Elizabeth Wade. *Anne Bradstreet: The Tenth Muse.* New York: Oxford University Press, 1971, 410 p.
    Critical biography of Bradstreet.

Criticism

Aldridge, A. Owen. "Anne Bradstreet: Some Thoughts on the *Tenth Muse.*" In his *Early American Literature: A Comparatist Approach*, pp. 25-52. Princeton, N.J.: Princeton University Press, 1982.
    Considers the possible influence of *The Tenth Muse* on the work of the later seventeenth-century Spanish woman poet Sor Juana Inés de la Cruz.

Cowell, Pattie, and Stanford, Ann, eds. *Critical Essays on Anne Bradstreet.* Boston: G. K. Hall & Co., 1983, 286 p.
    Includes Colonial, nineteenth-century, and twentieth-century responses to Bradstreet's works.

Eberwein, Jane Donahue. "The 'Unrefined Ore' of Anne Bradstreet's *Quaternions.*" *Early American Literature* IX, No. 1 (Spring 1974): 19-26.
    Asserts that Bradstreet's early "public" poetry contrib-

uted significantly to the development of the more highly regarded poetic style of her later poetry.

————. "Civil War and Bradstreet's 'Monarchies.'" *Early American Literature* XXVI, No. 2 (Fall 1991): 119-44.
    Argues that in "The Four Monarchies" Bradstreet was addressing the Civil War in England and the threatened dissolution of the English monarchy.

Hildebrand, Anne. "Anne Bradstreet's *Quaternions* and 'Contemplations'." *Early American Literature* VIII, No. 2 (Fall 1973): 117-25.
    Challenges readings of the *Quaternions* and "Contemplations" that place the two at opposite ends of Bradstreet's poetic style, asserting that the poems are linked by "a Renaissance view of the world which had more to do with classical and medieval tradition than with foreshadowing the Romantics."

Keeble, Neil H. "Anne Bradstreet: The First Colonial Poet." *Literary Half-Yearly* 13, No. 1 (January 1972): 13-28.
    Overview of Bradstreet's themes and her place in American poetry.

Maragou, Helena. "The Portrait of Alexander the Great in Anne Bradstreet's 'The Third Monarchy'." *Early American Literature* XXIII, No. 1 (Spring 1988): 70-81.
    Contends that "Bradstreet's depiction of Alexander the Great is at odds with the Puritan dogma that subordinates the worldly desires for power, fame, and honor to higher spiritual and moral values."

Martin, Wendy. "Anne Bradstreet: 'As Weary Pilgrim.'" In her *An American Triptych: Anne Bradstreet, Emily Dickinson, Adrienne Rich,* pp. 15-76. Chapel Hill: The University of North Carolina Press, 1984.
    Presents an historical and biographical portrait of Bradstreet as a poet, focusing particularly on the significance of her Puritanism, creative aspirations, roles as a mother and wife, and the harsh living conditions of seventeenth-century America.

Piercy, Josephine K. *Anne Bradstreet.* New York: Twayne Publishers, 1965, 144 p.
    Profile of Bradstreet's life and critical perspectives on her works.

Porterfield, Amanda. "Anne Hutchinson, Anne Bradstreet, and the Importance of Women in Puritan Culture." In her *Female Piety in Puritan New England: The Emergence of Religious Humanism,* pp. 80-115. New York: Oxford University Press, 1992.
    Examines the influence of such atypical women as Hutchinson and Bradstreet on New England Puritan law, theology, and culture.

Stanford, Ann. *Anne Bradstreet: The Worldly Puritan, an Introduction to Her Poetry.* New York: Burt Franklin & Co., 1974, 170 p.
    Analyzes Bradstreet's poetry, arguing that her "entire canon represents the struggle between the visible and the invisible worlds." Stanford also includes a chronology of Bradstreet's works, a list of books with which she was acquainted, and a selected bibliography of works about her.

Sweet, Timothy. "Gender, Genre, and Subjectivity in Anne Bradstreet's Early Elegies." *Early American Literature* XXIII, No. 2 (Fall 1988): 152-74.

Argues that Bradstreet's early public elegies succeed because they attempt to reform the discursive conventions of elegiac poetry.

Waller, Jennifer R. " 'My Hand a Needle Better Fits': Anne Bradstreet and Women Poets in the Renaissance." *Dalhousie Review* 54, No. 3 (Autumn 1974): 436-50.

Places Bradstreet in the tradition of Renaissance women poets.

Wilson, Rob. " 'Enrapted Senses': Anne Bradstreet's 'Contemplations'." In his *American Sublime: The Genealogy of a Poetic Genre*, pp. 67-93. Madison, Wis.: University of Wisconsin Press, 1991.

Discusses Bradstreet's place in the history of the American poetic sublime, asserting that "Poems like 'Contemplations' created representative landscapes and scenarios of selfhood that, however threatened or deprived, helped the community of such sublimity fitfully to answer, 'Yes'."

Additional coverage of Bradstreet's life and career is available in the following sources published by Gale Research: *Concise Dictionary of American Literary Biography, 1640-1865*; *DISCovering Authors*; *Dictionary of Literary Biography*, Vol. 24; and *Literature Criticism from 1400 to 1800*, Vol. 4.

Hayden Carruth

1921-

American poet, critic, novelist, and editor.

INTRODUCTION

Carruth is a well-respected and prolific author whose poetry is frequently autobiographical, varied in mood and form, and noted for its unadorned and precise language. Often addressing such themes as the fragility of life, the fine line between sanity and madness, and the importance of social responsibility, Carruth has called his philosophy of poetry a "radical secular existentialism." Carruth's criticism, which is collected in such volumes as *Working Papers* (1982) and *Effluences from the Sacred Cave* (1983), is recognized for its directness and tolerance, while *The Voice That Is Great within Us* (1970), a poetry anthology edited by Carruth, is frequently used in university literature courses and is considered one of the best representations of contemporary American poetry.

Biographical Information

Carruth was born to Gorton Veeder Carruth, a newspaper editor, and Margery Barrow Carruth in Waterbury, Connecticut. He received a B.A. from the University of North Carolina at Chapel Hill in 1943 and earned an M.A. from the University of Chicago in 1947. During World War II, Carruth served for two years in the United States Army Air Corps, advancing ultimately to the rank of staff sergeant. He worked as editor of *Poetry* magazine from 1949 to 1950, associate editor of the University of Chicago Press from 1950 to 1951, and project administrator for New York's Intercultural Publications from 1952 to 1953. In 1953 Carruth suffered an emotional breakdown and was admitted to Bloomingdale, the psychiatric branch of New York Hospital in White Plains, New York. He kept journals and wrote poetry while hospitalized; these writings were encouraged by his doctors as a means of therapy but his condition worsened and he underwent electroconvulsive therapy. Carruth later acted as consulting editor of the *Hudson Review* and poetry editor of *Harper's*, and served on the faculties of the University of Vermont and Syracuse University. He has won numerous literary awards, including the 1968 Morton Dauwen Zabel Prize, Guggenheim Foundation fellowships in 1965 and 1979, a senior fellowship from the National Endowment for the Arts in 1988, and the 1990 Ruth Lilly Poetry Prize.

Major Works

Carruth has published more than twenty-five volumes of poetry, some of which are single poems divided into sections. His long poem *The Bloomingdale Papers* (1975) was composed during his 1953 hospitalization and chronicles his experiences as a patient, including the endless routines,

the isolation, and the howls and suffering of the patients. Carruth's poetic form, subject matter, and tone vary widely, even within a single collection, but he is almost entirely consistent in maintaining the importance of subject over poetic form. For example, in *The Bloomingdale Papers*, Carruth asserted: "I am a poet / whereby I mean no boast. / I want to / say simply, I am a poet, not a good one, / whereby neither do I mean any abasement. / Poetry is profuse and multinominal / the latency of action." In *For You* (1970) Carruth collects five of his previously published but revised long poems, beginning with "The Asylum," which treats the irony of the word "asylum" and is marked by stark, striking imagery, and an apparent rejection of meaning. In "Journey to a Known World" and "North Winter," the second and third poems in *For You*, he forms a connection between the speaker and elements of the natural world, and in "Contra Mortem" Carruth focuses upon a Vermont village and its inhabitants. In "My Father's Face," the final poem in *For You*, he departs from the contained, imagistic approach of the first four poems and gives voice to his distress over the loss of a parent. Considered by many to be one of Carruth's best poetry collections, *Brothers, I Loved You All* (1978) treats a variety of subjects and themes, including the madness inherent in society and the importance of the natural world in confirming thoughts and emotions. Carruth has commented: "By evolving into a state of self-consciousness, we [human beings] have separated ourselves from the other animals and the plants and from the very earth itself, from the whole universe. So there's a kind of fear and terror involved in living close to nature. My poems, I think, exist in a state of tension between the love of natural beauty and the fear of natural meaninglessness or absurdity." *The Sleeping Beauty* (1982), another highly respected poetry collection, consists of 124 intricately rhymed stanzas and addresses attitudes about women and love.

Critical Reception

Many critics have praised Carruth's honesty, integrity, and directness of approach in both his poetry and his literary criticism. He has been noted for his ability to elicit intense emotional reaction through a variety of poetic forms and for spare, tightly controlled language to treat common subjects. Nevertheless, some critics have characterized Carruth's use of plain language in his poetry as rigid and didactic, and fault his poetry for lacking insight. Several commentators have noted that the quality of Carruth's verse tends to be uneven, but contend that Carruth captures basic human thoughts and emotions and expresses them in a sincere and unassuming manner. Alastair Reid has commented: "[Carruth's] poems have a sureness to them, a flair and variety. . . . His work teems with the struggle to live and to make sense, and his poems carve out a kind of grace for us."

PRINCIPAL WORKS

Poetry

The Crow and the Heart, 1946-1949   1959
Journey to a Known Place   1961
The Norfolk Poems: 1 June to 1 September 1961   1962
North Winter   1964
Nothing for Tigers: Poems, 1959-1964   1965
Contra Mortem   1967
The Clay Hill Anthology   1970
*For You   1970
From Snow and Rock, from Chaos: Poems, 1965-1972   1973
Dark World   1974
The Bloomingdale Papers   1975
Loneliness: An Outburst of Hexasyllables   1976
Brothers, I Loved You All: Poems, 1969-1977   1978
Almanach du Printemps Vivarois   1979
The Mythology of Darkness and Light   1982
The Sleeping Beauty   1982
If You Call This Cry a Song   1983
Asphalt Georgics   1985
Lighter Than Air Craft   1985
The Oldest Killed Lake in North America   1985
Mother   1986
The Selected Poetry of Hayden Carruth   1986
Sonnets   1989

Tell Me Again How the White Heron Rises and Flies across the Nacreous River at Twilight toward the Distant Islands   1989
Collected Shorter Poems, 1946-1991   1992
Collected Longer Poems   1993

Other Major Works

Appendix A   (novel)   1963
After "The Stranger": Imaginary Dialogues with Camus   (essays)   1964
The Voice That Is Great within Us: American Poetry of the Twentieth Century   [editor]   (poetry anthology)   1970
Working Papers: Selected Essays and Reviews   (criticism)   1982
Effluences from the Sacred Cave: More Selected Essays and Reviews   (criticism)   1983
Sitting In: Selected Writings on Jazz, Blues, and Related Topics   (essays and poetry)   1986
Suicides and Jazzers   (criticism)   1992

*This volume contains revised versions of the previously published long poems "The Asylum" (first appeared in *The Crow and the Heart*), "Journey to a Known Place," "North Winter," "Contra Mortem," and "My Father's Face."

CRITICISM

Geoffrey Gardner   (essay date 1981)

SOURCE: "The Real and Only Sanity," in *The American Poetry Review,* Vol. 10, No. 1, January-February, 1981, pp. 19-22.

[*Gardner is an American editor, translator, and critic. In the following review, he surveys Carruth's early works, concluding that* Brothers, I Loved You All *is the most accomplished.*]

We live in the way of such a constantly drenching flood of new poetry—those of us who try to keep up with it at all—and so much of it "good," that I worry our responses grow soggy, and we fail to recognize what is more than good. Hayden Carruth's new book, ***Brothers, I Loved You All (Poems 1969-1977)****,* is at every step at least a shade beyond all the current categories of praise, categories for coping with the last ten years' welter of poetry. And I find myself frightened that its arrival will go unnoticed and unremarked.

I don't mean to suggest that Carruth is, in any sense, unknown or his work neglected beyond what it would be fitting to expect for a poet who has always chosen to make his stand just aside from any of the presently conflicting mainstreams. In fact, since the late forties, Carruth has been active as an editor for many well known literary periodicals and publishers, written much telling criticism and been a tough and omnivorous reviewer of new poetry. ***Brothers, I Loved You All*** is the thirteenth book of his poetry to appear since *The Crow and the Heart,* his first, was published in 1959.

The Crow and the Heart. The title suggests much of the intention of Carruth's earlier work: to discover correspondences—both figures and "reasons"—in the outward social and natural world for the inward collapse and slow regeneration Carruth knew intimately in his struggles with alcohol and mental illness. The effort was to restore equilibrium to the soul, clarity to vision, through a passionate command of language. There is a Lear-like words-against-the-storm quality underlying much of Carruth's early poetry. It can be felt most forcefully in "Asylum," a sequence of thirteen "sonnets" each of fifteen lines, the long poem, *Journey to a Known Place,* and some of the longer pieces in his second collection, *Nothing For Tigers.* It's a pervasive quality, given more in the aggregate than in any of the parts, but perhaps these lines from "Asylum" will serve to illustrate the point:

> We lived. An aftersilence fell
> Like a wave flooding the plains of hell,
> For what word matters? Pity? Shame? The roots
> Try my breast-cage, my bone
> Gleams in the rot. I hear you, sir, cahoots
> Calling from many a dolmen stone,
> *Murther, murther!* Come on then, jacket me,
> A flawed mind's falling. Look, the petals blown
> On an idle wind, far, far out to sea!

But—alas! —often as not, the passionate effort fails and Carruth's command of language and vision falters.

I won't be the first to say Carruth's early work is cumbered by archaisms, forced inversions, sometimes futile extravagances of vocabulary and a tendency of images and metaphors to reify into a top heavy symbolism. My sense of it is that despite all his great effort to the contrary Carruth too often could not restrain his impulse to make an asylum of language itself, a protective shell of poetry against the assaults of both his outward and inward worlds. But the courage of these poems can't be faulted. From the earliest and against great odds, Carruth made many attempts at many kinds of poems, many forms, contending qualities of diction and texture. My feeling is that through all the jumble of his early work, Carruth was seeking to discover in love, sources for the lineaments of a theodicy, a position that could be maintained in the teeth of his experience of a vainly chaotic world. If the struggle of contending voices and attitudes often ends in poems that don't quite succeed, it remains that the struggle itself is moving for its truthfulness and intensity. And this all the more so, if we allow ourselves to realize that there is nothing about them of what we still hear forlornly called "confessionals," and they all were written before Bedlam became a literary fad. Carruth uniformly refuses to glorify his crazies. They are pain and pain alone. What glory there is—and there are sparks of it everywhere through these early poems—he keeps for the regenerative stirrings against the storm of pain and isolation.

In *Brothers, I Loved You All,* suddenly reflecting on "reading myself, old poems, their inside truth that was / (is is!) crucial," Carruth says:

> . . . complexities,

> modes, names, manners, words laden
> with terror. What true voice? Where? Humiliat-
>   ed in throes
> of vacillation, roundhead to cavalier to ivy
>   league to smartass—
> Never who I was. Say it plain . . .

I don't think we need be any harsher about the early work than that.

How to find the medium of the "true voice"? How to discover "who I was," who I am? By the early sixties these obsessive questions were rife among fortyish and formerly baroque poets, especially those of "the eastern establishment" and the colleges and their followers. The result was a widespread abandonment of the metaphysical manner and set forms in favor of a more extreme imagism, a seemingly more colloquial diction and syntax, and the adoption of either free or irregular versification—all sometimes telling, but all more often than not, for my eye and ear, clumsy and halting. The materials of the turn were personal biography and history, gossip, some routinely puerile speculations on the nature of "Self" and world, and quasi-surreal renderings of one's waking nightmares. All this became the foundation of much of the poetry that surrounds us still. That Carruth was never a whole-hearted participant in the earlier habits of these poets is clear enough, especially when one considers his very different and wholly unique response to similar promptings.

By 1963, Carruth was living pretty much in reclusion in the farm and hill country of northern Vermont. Life in that part of the world is still, for many if not most, a pattern of necessity and borderline poverty. The better part of Carruth's living was being got through various country labor and literary shit-work. By the same date, Carruth in some detail had worked out for himself in his prose—most thoroughly in his book of arguments with Camus, *After the Stranger*—a philosophical position we could jargonize as Kantian-existentialism.

Also in 1963, gathering all these elements for poetry, Carruth wrote *North Winter.* It's a long poem in fifty-seven fairly brief, mostly "imagistic" sections and an "Afterword." Superficially the poem describes the advent and experience of winter and the first signs of thaw. The poems are without regular meter and rhyme, and the diction and syntax are stripped down considerably from Carruth's earlier practice, but still full of variety, subtle music and occasional complexity. But what really sets *North Winter* off from the work of the other poets I've mentioned is Carruth's total rejection at *his* turning point of their materials. The pronoun "I" never occurs in *North Winter.* The surface of the poem is all outward awareness, from merest perception to deepest reflection. It's as if Carruth had felt compelled to risk the consequences of his own Kantianism: if the very having of experience presupposes equal contributions of both self and world, why not try as rigorously as possible to render experience in its own terms without any explicit reference back to an apprehending consciousness? Why might that not disclose "who I am" and provide the medium of the "true voice"? And the risk succeeds! Carruth's abjuring of "I" yields anything but a cold "objectivism." *North Winter* is, in fact, one of the most intensely personal and intimate poems written by an American in those years. Once more the effect is a product of the whole work, and quotation of parts won't do it justice. Still, there's nothing like trying:

26

Pale dawnlight spooks the mist
and the valley glimmers and
higher behind this mountain
whitely rises a farther peak
in remote majesty a presence
silent and unknown and gone
by noon.

This is more than mere imagism and far more musical than the habitual aural flatness of most imagists.

52

Small things
hardest to believe
redpoll snatching
drops from an icicle.

Less a scene than a reflection of considerable depth. Or better, the reflection is given immediately in the rendering of scene and object. The poem is an act of contemplation.

As a whole, the fifty-seven sections of *North Winter* accrue to a powerful sense of winter and world as indifference and hazard. At the same time, both winter and world are full of events and beings of great fundamental beauty, worthy of celebration and capable of rousing compassion. The long **"Afterword,"** really a kind of coda written in long lines of fuller intensity and music, is a vision of Peary and Henson at the pole. It is Carruth at his fullest Lear-like pitch, raging against the disorder of things. Here "north is nothing" and chaos, all instruments reading zero or gone haywire. But the vision

. . . flowers in a
glance wakening compassion and mercy and
lovingkindness . . .

where north is also "deliverance emancipation." Carruth has seen the worst and survived it and yet found much to praise. He walks straight through *North Winter* without the least clumsiness or halting.

Three years later Carruth wrote *Contra Mortem,* following a similar discipline. But here the environment is denser and more varied, more full of other people. In this poem the world is altogether a warmer place and Carruth more at home in it, though his unflinching regard for what is ultimately, and perhaps pervasively, absurd and cruel in it hasn't altered. *Contra Mortem* is a sequence of thirty poems, each written in fifteen lines as in **"Asylum."** Except for final periods ending poems or pairs of poems, the work is without punctuation. Rhyme and meter are fundamentally regular but highly idiosyncratic and very much to the background as a matrix against which the complex but headlong syntax is laid. And these characteristics of the poem make for a tone at least as intimate as that of *North Winter* and no less passionate. But passion here is handled so that the overall feeling of the poem, in its parts and as a whole, is a subtle modulation from the ecstatic to the hermetic and back.

"The Woman," "The Child," "The Trees," "The Village," "The Moon," "The Stone," "The Water," "The Being as Memory," "The Being as Moment," "The Being as Prevision," "The Ecstasy": the titles of the separate poems indicate Carruth's intention to celebrate the elements of a common world, to recombine them in their natural order and lay open the meanings of their mutual dependence. As in *North Winter* the first person pronoun is suppressed, functioning only directly as voice and eye and ordering mind in contemplation. Finally, in the very last poem, **"The Wheel of Being II,"** the first person breaks through to the surface as "we." And while this "we" refers first to poets, it also includes anyone given—however occasionally—to song, for "Such figures if they succeed are beautiful / because for a moment we brighten in a blaze of rhymes." But every poem is only approximate and fails and must "give way to other poems" constantly. It is only in this constant cycle of revisions that any art can succeed, can approach the transcendence of

our small song done in the faith
of lovers who endlessly change heart for heart
as the gift of being . . .

And the final words of *Contra Mortem* half invite, half exhort the exclusion of everything trivial and trivializing. "Come let us sing against death." Far from a distracting personal obsession, the death Carruth means is universal fact, the binding condition of everything connected to the living. And the ramifications of that "against" are as varied as you will let them be.

These long poems are as near to full realization as they could be and bear the marks of urgency and grace that belong only to necessary acts. But they are also important because their discipline seems to have dissolved for Carruth the iron boundary standing for so many poets—solipsist and objectivist alike—between self and world. This discipline granted Carruth the gift of that true spontaneity which is the ability to refuse alienation for the sake of a life and power of vision wedded by necessity to the world. A condition of that necessity, and a proof of it, is that these long poems also released from Carruth a constant flow of shorter poems of great force and variety.

What is most striking about Carruth's shorter poems, collected in part in two later books, *From Snow and Rock, From Chaos* and *Dark World,* is the way in which over and over again they habitually acknowledge their own presence in a world beyond literature and narrowly literary concerns. It is a world of mortality, love, parental care, poverty and communal collapse, work and seasonal changes. Often it is also a world of calamity near to despair. These poems, mostly written in free lines of exquisite skill and control, are the efflorescence of a life lived "in a kind of rural twilight" by a man who for all his learning and literary accomplishment has passed perhaps near to half his hours in non-literary work, frequently as a peer of farmers and other country laborers.

These are all poems very much of their place, and most of them wear the stamp of actual Vermont speech, some blatantly in passages approaching narrative, most as a more subtle undertone. Vermont suits Carruth. It is after all a country of stone quarries and granitic geological records, where rock seems anything but permanent. It's also a place where winter lasts half the year, and preparing for it takes up the other half. Snow in Vermont is nothing like the transitory thing it may seem to others elsewhere. Where else could "chaos" so truthfully be placed in apposition to "snow" and "rock"? Certainly there is nothing hayseed about this record of rural life, and these poems are far from idyllic or pastoral. Carruth is not in the least tempted to sentimentality about country life. He's too seasoned and knows it is often a life of care and pain, sometimes of great risk and always of small return, especially small monetary return. But what these poems also recognize is that it can be a life of value and nobility in the midst of difficult facts and chaos. This is a harsh knowledge to bear because it's also plain that these are habits of life and livelihood which are being killed off, leaving no inheritors.

> Mr. Washer is gone, and in any useful sense
> his virtues are gone with him.

It is to this "dark world" that Carruth has lost his heart. And in these poems compassion is not just a promise but a redeeming fact, including the fact that compassion itself can be pain:

> . . . I write
> (in the grey end of every night)
>
> myself, who holds in translucent hands
> everyone's lost light.

But there is also humor in these poems, not just funny lines—though there are those too—but the greater humor, the saving ability at times to glimpse all of striving life *sub species aeternitatis.* And at the center there is this which is grace:

> what saves the undoubted collapse
> of the driven day and the year
> is my coming all at once
> when she is done in or footsore
> or down asleep in the field
> or telling a song to a child
>
> coming and seeing her move
> in some particular way
> that makes me to fall in love
> all over with human beauty
> the beauty I can't believe
> right here where I live.

And so, at last, I come to **Brothers, I Loved You All.** I think it's Carruth's best book to date. Certainly it's the richest for the scope of its materials and the overwhelming mastery of its huge variety of forms and styles. It's also that rarest of things, not just a collection of poems, but a whole book, and in that lies its greatest excellence. Not every poem here is equally a gem. But taken all together in its sequence and unity, **Brothers, I Loved You All** gives full reign of expression to the whole experience of a poet of deep imagination and clear intelligence. And it insists powerfully on the utter continuity of life—in its widest range—and art. Reading a book like this, I sometimes become furious that for years and years and years, longer than I can remember, our poetry has been read by virtually no one but poets and college students and their teachers.

More than twenty-five years ago, in his Harvard lectures,

The Estate of Poetry, Edwin Muir, speaking in surpassingly assured and gentle tones, tried to understand this gap between poetry and its audience as a function of poetry's loss of contact with its popular origins: song, ballads, myths and the world of primary creatures and happenings. Muir was trying to encourage the return of poetry to a common language, however heightened, and the refounding of our view of poets as—whatever else they might be—public people with public responsibilities. We all know very well what stands between and what such an attitude is up against. Wordsworth's formulation of it is quickest and, perhaps, still best, provided we magnify for ourselves its intensity to make up for all that's passed in the nearly two hundred years since he wrote it:

> The most effective . . . causes are the great national events which are daily taking place, and the increasing accumulation of men in cities, where the uniformity of their occupations produces a craving for extraordinary incident, which the rapid communication of intelligence hourly gratifies.

All I'll add to Wordsworth's list is a reminder of the all but unavoidable and dinning presence in our lives of the centralized "mass media," the debasement of our language by public men whose perpetual lies are the outward sign of the futility of their acts and institutions, and the endless styles of academic criticism that have disturbed communication by twisting all the arts, and especially poems, back in on themselves, often with the gleeful consent of artists hungry for acknowledgment. But the last three decades have also brought a revival in poetry of what *is* urgent, common, primary and public. And some of our best poets—Rexroth, Levertov, Kinnell, Ginsberg, Snyder, Berry and Paul Goodman, to name just an obvious few—have long been writing as if in response to Muir's quiet challenge or in recognition of the universal situation behind it. It is important that not one of these people writes at all like another. It is also within this frame of reference that Carruth's work, especially **Brothers, I Loved You All,** needs to be read.

There is a saying of Herakleitos that "eyes are better informers than ears." I for one doubt the truth of it. But certainly many, if not most, poets now working write as if it were so. We've grown accustomed in our poetry to exhaustless chains of images that follow too quick, and often too arbitrarily, on one another, so that we lose ourselves and can't take them in. And this image spinning, more often than not, is set in a syntax and to a music that are lax and unaffecting and frequently deadening. What we get from much of our poetry is very little more than a momentary *petit frisson,* clothing mere remarks about the world and our lives in it. For the reader, they are hearsay. And that, perhaps, is what Herakleitos meant by his dictum: only what we know directly can inform us; what we have by hearsay leaves us cold.

Reading Carruth's new book, I've thought often of Herakleitos. Not because there's anything oracular or esoteric about these poems—far from it!—but in part because in them "the vision is cold chaos." One phase of this world is endless, ungraspable flux and change. But even endless change is not necessarily betrayal. For Carruth, the chaotic world of destructive flux is also the very body of value, at times beautiful and encouraging of fidelity and love. How can this be? Herakleitos also says that embedded in flux, as its principle and meaning, there is the Logos which

> . . . is eternal
> but men have not heard it
> and men have heard it and not understood.

I've got no idea what Carruth thinks of Herakleitos or whether he even reads the fragments or has taken them into account. In any event, there is a more than fortuitous coincidence between Herakleitos' feel for the nature of things and Carruth's.

But what matters most is that Carruth measures his experience in the world with an ear that is as responsive as his eye is discriminating and acute. And his ear also listens to what the poems say, measuring and shaping them so that they can come across to us as far more than hearsay. Over and over in the lyrical philosophic and elegiac poems that fill more than a third of ***Brothers, I Loved You All,*** it is something heard—often as a voice—that starts a poem or becomes the hinge point or resolution of a poem: "The oven door creaks / in the night in the silent / house, like all old things." ". . . the earth too cried out for justice, / justice!" "The brook talks. The night listens." And there are human voices as well: a Pueblo woman, applying fresh mud to the wall of her adobe house, the voice of a black urban guerrilla come over the mountains from the city to Carruth's imagining ear. Frequently his ear picks out and names what cannot be heard as when, writing an elegy on the proliferation of dead animal elegies in our times, he ends by saying:

> . . . I don't know
> if the animals are capable of reproach.
> But clearly they do not bother to say good-bye.

But let me give a larger example. In **"The Joy and Agony of Improvisation,"** Carruth and his wife have listened to the wind in the pines as though "in the midst of voices in some / obscure contention." Then later the wind changes, and Carruth wakes to hear:

> . . . how the voices
> have turned to song. Hear
> it rising, rising, then breaking, then
> rising again, and breaking again. Oh, something
> is unutterable, the song cannot reach it.
> Yet we know it, know what we cannot
> hear—out on the night's great circle,
> the circle of consciousness with its far rim al-
>   ways
> hidden, there where suffering and joy
> meet and combine,
> the inexpressible. How the song is striving
> and how beautifully failing—the measure
> of beauty, beyond plentitude,
> never but always enough . . .
> . . . it is the gathering of our love
> into all love, into that suffering and joy.

How close this is to the ungraspable Logos! But there are other times when Carruth manages to hear its music and directly translates it, as when he gives us this "little song"

of the wind high in the trees and its whispered meaning, while he sits at a fire in the forest with his son:

> Sweet Bo I know thee
> thou art ten
> and knowest now thy father is
> five times more again
> and more
> and most gone out of rhymes
> sweet Bo
> for thou dost know me
>
> And thou old spruce above us
> many are they of comrade and kin
> who love us
> so that their loving proveth
> everything
> although their way hath not
> the same compassion
> as thy nonloving.

I have passed many hours under similar trees across the Connecticut River just into New Hampshire, not seventy miles from Carruth's forest, and that *is* the song the wind makes in them. And when I'm lucky, it does intimate something very much like that.

By talking so long about Carruth's ultimate sense of the order of things, I hope I haven't given the impression that these poems are abstractly philosophical or cold. On the contrary, they are all poems about very daily affairs: things seen and heard, the loneliness of missing friends absent or dead, the alternations of love for and estrangement from those present, the experiences of a man frequently alone with the non-human which all too often bears the damaging marks of careless human intrusion. Courage, human fidelity and love and their failures, loyalty to the nonhuman—these are the obvious subjects Carruth writes about in these poems. But the underlying drama of what passes and what abides, of what is hidden and what is revealed is never very far from their surface. They are also exemplary of what Carruth says he learned to hear in the music of "that beautiful hot old man Sidney Bechet": "that tone, phrasing, and free play / of feeling mean more than originality." In all their variegation and intensity, these lyrics have much in common with the "wavering music" of the loon's song which occurs in the first of them as though it "came from inside the long wilderness / of my life" and "seemed / the real and only sanity to me."

If these lyrics were all of this book, it would be worth reading and reading again. But there's far more. Carruth's long poem, **"Vermont"** was one of the very few bicentennial poems to come from a poet of serious intention. I also think it is the best. Surely, for all its gravity, it is the funniest.

> We need a new crop, something that will grow
> on hillsides, and on granite hillsides at that . . .
> My own idea that I've been working on
> is a neat machine that will exactly crack
> butternuts so the meat will come out whole.
> Oh, there's a market for them. Rose Marie
> knows eighteen recipes. But cracking them
> the butternuts, that is, though Rose Marie's
> handwriting can be pretty near as hard—
> takes hammer and anvil, and generally it means

bloody fingers and nutshells in your cookies
and a visit to the dentist. Who needs that?
Well, all I need is *half* a hundred grand.
That's all; no more. Think what the state would
    save . . .
Then what? Easy. I'd make all Butternut Moun-
    tain
one huge farm and then hire half the town
at harvest time, which would just nicely fill
that slack, fidgety season after the cider
has been put down to work and everyone
is sitting around uptight, waiting to test it.

"**Vermont**" is both a parody and expansion of Frost's "New Hampshire." Carruth's faultless ear allows him the assumption of a Yankee—more specifically Vermont—speech that is wholly authentic and natural to him, wholly assimilated to his own voice. To my taste, the exquisite skill with which the vernacular rhythms and inflections are laid against the blank verse far outdoes Frost at his best. "**Vermont**" is an investigation of the history, prehistory and character—both human and natural—of its place. It also serves as a detailed study in the grim and absurd relations of Americans to nature, place, speech, poetry and each other. The poem moves along on a progression of epithets. Vermont is "a land of passage" whose people are "passing on" and whose (official) business, quite regardless of people, is business above all. The special virtue of the Vermonter is "curiosity" which Carruth also insists was the virtue shared by "those two old enemies," Frost and Pound, who "had more between them, I expect, than either / would have been willing to allow." By character the Vermonter is "a-son-of-a-bitch" who takes "the directest way in everything but speech." Politically he is a "Republican" which (here) is to say an "anarchist" and a "forlorn believer," traveling by himself "or with a dog" through "Vermont's protracted gloom / our end-of-winter desolation." At its core the poem is an overwhelming protest against grinding poverty and the destruction of farming and native character that are the consequences of development and tourism, the famous ski slopes and poster pictures of quaint barns that in fact are going irrevocably all to hell. Carruth comes to the politics of all this with a vengeance and avoids absolutely anything like the foolishness of Frost's persona of official public sage.

"**Vermont**" is Carruth's conscious extension of his characteristic attitudes and poetic practice to regional materials of political and historical urgency. Not that he's "applied" any of it to the subject, it's rather that in "**Vermont**" he's hit on a form and style that have allowed him to advance his habitual equipment to meet new materials and give them shape. He does something similar in four other longish poems that follow "**Vermont.**" How to describe them? I don't know anything else quite like them. At the least they are character portraits of particular Vermonters, written with an extreme compulsion to render the native speech as accurately as possible. But more than that, two of them, "**Johnny Spain's White Heifer**" and "**Lady,**" are really masterful short stories in which only the most essential details are given and under the greatest possible compression. The other two, "**John Dryden**" and "**Marshall Washer,**" are more like short novels in their scope, though the method of selection and intense compression is the

same. All four are attempts to show the effects on individual souls of life in a difficult region, especially as it has come to be under the extraordinarily corrosive influence of an overpowering economic and industrial style that explicitly takes everything small and direct for its victim. Taken together the four poems are also a masterpiece of human sympathy.

I won't quote from these poems. Each is too much of a piece with itself, and quotation would be a violation. Three are full of a weirdly hilarious gravity. The fourth, "**Marshall Washer**" is just utterly grave. They all bear strong public witness against the wastes and shames of our culture that are destroying human value with a will in a world where values are already hard enough to maintain, in a universe where they are always difficult to discover. Carruth does not express much anger in these poems. Yet one feels that an enormous energy of rage has forced them to be.

What is most outstanding in these poems is Carruth's uncanny fidelity to the speech of the people in them. It's not just that he's gotten it all down so accurately, or even that it comes up off the page at you as it does. Rather it's that through all the accuracy and life of this talk one can still hear so clearly Carruth's own voice as pedal point. That, I take it, is the embodiment of compassion. It's a kind of unawares participation, and it can't be chosen. Carruth knows this.

> . . . but have you noticed
> I can't talk *about* him without talking *like* him?
> That's my trouble. Somehow I always seem
> to turn into the other guy . . .

What's the "trouble"? The trouble is that if one refuses nostalgia and the picturesque and at the same time acknowledges that the chances for amelioration and reform—especially in any direct way through poems—is at best a forlorn hope, then compassion itself becomes a heavy burden.

How then to continue honestly to resist? What are the sources, if any, of hope or, at least, endurance? What are the springs of joy? These are the questions Carruth faces in "**Paragraphs,**" the most ambitious piece of work in the book, and for me the most successful and the most moving. In "**Paragraphs,**" with magnificent energy and compactness, Carruth gathers all the elements of his previous concerns and allows them their fullest scope. Once more the poem focuses on the difficulty and destructiveness of oblivious natural forces and the superadded destruction of human exploitation. The poem begins in Vermont, the scene again of the ravages of development, the intrusion of "the national mean taking over. Or / the mean nationals." It ends at a jazz recording session in New York, February 12th, 1944. In between, woven with these events, are scenes and episodes of a vast range: Siva on Kailas, Dante, the partition of Verdun, Thoreau at Walden Pond, the Ulster Troubles, Puerto Rico, Vietnam, even a long, splendid and dead accurate direct quotation from Bakunin on the meaning of liberty, perhaps the very best piece of writing ever to come from that particular pen. And again it is Carruth's uncannily faithful ear that extends to the most remote of these sections and unifies the whole.

In its general outlines, **"Paragraphs"** owes much to the methods of Pound. It is true to Pound's ideals of clarity and hardness of detail and the avoidance of sentimentality. But Carruth's language itself, its cadences and feeling, owe nothing to Pound. Unlike so much Pound-inspired work, this is no imitation. And even though the poem combines and intercuts immediate events and historical and cultural concerns, public questions and personal attitudes in a manner close to *The Cantos,* there are none of Pound's fragmentary loose ends or lapses of coherence.

There is anguish here and horror and enraged accusation. But there are also long moments of contemplative power. In paragraph 11 there is a kind of ritual communion, a catalog of the names of jazz musicians, ending "Brothers I loved you all." And there is this intimation of love itself:

> It was the custom of my tribe to be silent
> to think the song inwardly, tune and word
> so beautiful they could be only heard
> in quietness . . .
> . . . and always we were alone.
> Yet sometimes two
> heard it, two separately together. It could come
> nearby in the shadow of a pine bough
> on the snow, or high in the orchestral lights,
> or may be (this was our miracle) it would have
>   no
> intermediary—
>   a suddenness,
>   indivisible, unvoiced.

All these are the sources of joy and persistence. And at last, at that recording session there is the transcendence of an art which does not close in on itself, which never leaves the world, but starts there and returns the world to us and us to it—purified, enlivened and both whole again.

> . . . for they had come
>
>   28
>
> high above themselves. Above everything, flux,
>   ooze,
> loss, need, shame, improbability / the awfulness
> of gut-wrong, sex-wrack, horse & booze,
> the whole goddamn mess,
> *And* Gabler said "We'll press it" *and* it was
> "Bottom Blues"
> BOTTOM BLUES five men knowing it well
>   blacks
> & jews
> yet music, music   high
> in the celebration of fear, strange joy
> of pain: blown out, beaten out
> a moment ecstatic
> in the history
> of creative mind and heart / not singular, not the
>   rarity
> we think, but real and a glory
> our human shining, shekinah . . .
>   Ah
>   holy spirit, ninefold
> I druther've bin a-settin there, supernumerary
> cockroach i' th' corner, a-listenin, a-listenin . . .
> than be the Prazedint ov the Wuurld.

There again are the sources and the song that is "the real and only sanity."

I've heard that Carruth is working on a new long poem. We've got much to look forward to.

Hayden Carruth on modern literature:

I think there are many reasons for poets and artists in general to be depressed these days. . . . They have to do with a lot . . . [of] things that are going on in our civilization. They have to do with the whole evolution of the sociology of literature during the last fifty years. Things have changed; they've turned completely around. I don't know if I can say it briefly but I'll try. When I was young and starting to write poetry seriously and to investigate the resources of modern poetry, as we called it then, we still felt beleaguered; modern poetry was still considered outrageous by most of the people in the publishing business and in the reading audience at large. We still spoke in terms of the true artists and the philistines. We felt that if we could get enough people to read T. S. Eliot and Wallace Stevens and e e cummings and William Carlos Williams and other great poets of that period, then something good would happen in American civilization. We felt a genuine vocation, a calling, to try and make this happen. And we succeeded. Today thousands of people are going to colleges and attending workshops and taking courses in twentieth-century literature. Eliot and Stevens are very well known, very well read; and American civilization has sunk steadily, progressively, further and further down until most of the sensible people are in a state of despair. It's pretty obvious that good writing doesn't really have very much impact on social events or national events of any kind. We hope that it has individual impact, that readers here and there are made better in some way by reading our work. But it's a hope; we have no proof.

Hayden Carruth, in an interview with Contemporary Authors New Revision Series, *Volume 4, Gale Research, 1981.*

Herbert Leibowitz   (essay date 1983)

SOURCE: A review of *Sleeping Beauty,* in *The New York Times Book Review,* August 21, 1983, pp. 12, 23.

[*Leibowitz is an American educator and critic, and has served as editor of the magazine* Parnassus: Poetry in Review. *In the following review of* The Sleeping Beauty, *he praises the "classic order and restraint" of Carruth's style as well as the poet's treatment of love.*]

Hayden Carruth's **Sleeping Beauty** is a complex sequence of 15-line rhymed lyrics that conducts an impassioned inquiry into the spirit of romance. The fairy tale "The Briar Rose" by the Grimm brothers serves well as the narrative spine of the poem. A poet-prince embarks on an arduous quest for a princess who is sleeping in a thorn hedge and waiting for the kiss that will awaken her from a trance that is a simulacrum of death. Mr. Carruth's wife, Rose Marie Dorn, the *Dornroschen* (brier rose) to whom the poem is an offering of reconciliation, is a mature woman, though the memory of her as a slender girl of 17 also haunts the poet. Along his meandering ("northfaring") route, the shy petitioner, contrite for transgressions against his lady, does not encounter the monsters and wizards, the damsels in distress and evil knights, of medieval romance; his adventures are internal and hallucinatory. As if he were an actor in a condensed allegory, he slips into the protean figures of a dreamer's fantasies, all of whose names begin with the letter H: poets (Homer, Hesiod, Hölderlin), philosophers (Heraclitus, Hegel), political leaders (Hannibal, Herod, Hitler), literary figures (Hamlet, Harlequin, Heathcliff), social types (Husband, Householder) and others.

Like traditional cycles of love sonnets, *The Sleeping Beauty* explores love's disordering emotions and the poet's sometimes neighborly, sometimes uneasy commerce with nothingness, as the amplitude of love shrinks to "a space in a boneyard." The retrospective analysis parallels the course of the poet's relations with his wife. For Mr. Carruth, romance, which thrives in the chill landscape of New England as it did in ancient Greece and the sultry climate of Languedoc, is an imperishable myth with two heads, one benign, the other destructive. Enchanted, the lover experiences the "pure euphoria / Of idealization," an access of power that leaves him paradoxically selfless and whole and that he identifies with the feminine aspect of himself. The woman is at once the desirable, mysterious other and a partner in a "fierce heretical love."

But that harmony is precarious, shadowed by the fury of romance (what Mr. Carruth calls its "lurid sunstreakings"), in which the self, unbalanced by its will to power and domination, becomes a marauder, raping, exploiting, enslaving and murdering. The lovers' sexual passion is a force that can fuse them together or consume them. And the aggressive, feral temper of love is not a purely private concern but has its counterpart in the body politic. Digging in the rubble of history, Mr. Carruth broods morosely that love and death are joined like Siamese twins. The apocalyptic fires that reduced cities like Hiroshima and Dresden to charred ruins and the slaughter of innocents are testimony to the unspeakable brutalities of the human mind. Yet, almost prayerfully, he clings to a slim hope that love, the "flower / Of Consciousness," can survive such repeated violation:

> He was a soldier, he was a madman, he was a
>   hermit
> Always in deprivation, always in love.
> The cast-out seraph within him yearns
> For the unattainable, to give,
> To give and give: to the wounded, imprisoned,
>   poor,
> And ever to women, the captive people. What
>   for?
> He asked and asked. No death delayed,
> Not one lover was left undismayed
> In her ego torture. Love solves nothing. He ma-
>   tured
> In despondency, the old deep
> Melancholia. But again what for?
>   The abhorred
> Stars in their slow explosion creep

> Through the sky, mindless, and the mindless
>   moon
> Is a loveliness that mocks him.
>   Mind is sleep,
> Dream, evolutionary error,
> bound for extinction soon.

Each sentence measures a militant generosity thwarted by painful isolation. Only the poet's song can conquer imperfect love's mutability and embody "mind's power / To outlast the mind."

What holds *The Sleeping Beauty* together is its "echo of coincidental voices" and a commodious structure that allows the cerebral, aging Chevalier of the Rose to ponder ideas about politics, ecology, eros and identity. It is as if the emissaries of romance had gathered under the roof of the poem in urgent conclave. During night vigils the poet talks aloud to himself about "spiritual / Outreaching and inreaching." Then he chats with Amos, the ghost of a humorous Vermont seer whose crusty vernacular gives the poem an earthy realism. Like his Old Testament namesake, Amos denounces the "takers," the speculators and developers who (in biblical language) "swallow up the needy" and the gentry who buy farm property as tax shelters. Amos is wry and sage:

> Some ways
> It don't work so good, like nature herself, like
> A hen partridge setting six weeks on a clutch of
>   eggs
> Ain't even fertile. But look now.

At the end, snatches of blues and jazz riffs, the "huge boozy flame / Of the miserloos and the careless joys," lighten the grave moods that memory and nightmarish history stir up.

One current orthodoxy in American poetry banishes ideas as alien and abstractions as pedestrian. Never one to follow fashion, Mr. Carruth is enamored of ideas, and like the jazzman Ben Webster, whose music "Was oneness, the abstract made personal in a tone," he trusts the cumulative eloquence of mingling elevated and plain speech. Even at their most rhapsodic, his poems maintain a classic order and restraint.

The Sleeping Beauty weeps, bleeds, exalts and moves in slow, swaying, "beautiful helical rhythms." Its emotional range owes much to the sonnet, that unappeasable ghost treading the formal rooms of all recent American poetic sequences. Mr. Carruth sums up the integrity of his long career and of *The Sleeping Beauty:*

> One knows one has gone
> As into a mirror that contains an ever so slightly
> Distorted image,
>
> Or perhaps from dreamt objectivity to the forth-
>   rightly
> Seen—subjective, brilliant, undamaged.
>
> The poem moves alone now, but without loneli-
>   ness.
>
> Self has been left among the objects that fash-
>   ioned it.

> Action and knowledge are one, free, far in the
> depths of consciousness.

J. D. McClatchy　(essay date 1984)

SOURCE: A review of *If You Call This Cry a Song,* in *The New York Times Book Review,* January 22, 1984, p. 12.

[*McClatchy is an American poet, educator, editor, and critic. In the following review of* If You Call This Cry a Song, *he questions Carruth's technical skills and faults the collection's organization.*]

Coming so soon after the appearance of his major work, **The Sleeping Beauty** (1982), Hayden Carruth's new book, [**If You Call This Cry a Song**], will seem a disappointment. But then, this book is not new. The poems gathered here, written between 1964 and 1979, had been "mislaid among accumulations of other paper or were intentionally omitted from the books they might have gone into because there wasn't room." Some poems would be best forgotten, even by their author. The instinct to retrieve them is always tender but not necessarily good.

If Mr. Carruth had dated or ordered the poems, they might have helped sharpen the profile of his career. Instead, the book is helter-skelter—good poems and bad, occasional and sturdy prayers, epistles, Imagist lyrics, jeremiads, rural character sketches and translations.

Among these scraps from the cutting room floor are poems that remind one of qualities found in Mr. Carruth's better work. One is his moral canniness. **"On Being Asked to Write a Poem Against the War in Vietnam"** recalls *that* poem and others he had written against earlier wars:

> and not one
> breath was restored
> to one
>
> shattered throat
> mans womans or childs
> not one not
>
> one
> but death went on and on
> never looking aside
>
> except now and then like a child
> with a furtive half-smile
> to make sure I was noticing.

Mr. Carruth writes hauntingly about loneliness, as when:

> the high murmur
> in tree crowns, far
> and near, tells human
> loneliness something
> about itself.

Perhaps it would be better to say that conscience and loneliness conspire to make his true theme—isolation. It is a great theme, and it cracks apart many of his poems, whose technical resources are insufficient to contain it. If isolation is his ground note, there is a harmony line as well, the lure of "remembered song." Jazz, blues, Provencal plaints—their rhythms pulse in his memory and his poems.

Eclecticism has always been Mr. Carruth's motto. In one poem he celebrates a neighbor's rock garden—"no design, just swatches of color, bold / rough splashes." But in them is the thought "to bring art / to nature." The same could be said of this book—of its troubled sympathies, its formal allegiances, its

> reparation, such as the poor
> might make, whose sorrow
> had been done here.

R. W. Flint　(essay date 1985)

SOURCE: A review of *Asphalt Georgics,* in *The New York Times Book Review,* July 14, 1985, p. 15.

[*In the following review, Flint offers a laudatory appraisal of* Asphalt Georgics.]

Our standards for verse naturalism have risen sky-high since Edgar Lee Masters wrote *Spoon River Anthology.* Our fiction, in its mostly unconfessed but entirely licit commerce with poetry, is chiefly responsible. The baggier monster has been secretly feeding on the less baggy. But poets are poets, and Hayden Carruth has always had a special gift for demotic speech—the talk of streets, bars, barnyards, jam sessions, lunch counters. A devoutly private man of the widest reading and cultivation, equally at home with the jazz musician Sidney Bechet and Alexander Pope, he has a first-class ear. It's a principled alertness, closely tied to what he likes to call anarchism but which those less metaphysically inclined might want to call a radically intelligent populism with strong country coloring. In many of his earlier poems, written in Vermont, he ventriloquized friends and neighbors with rare force and eloquence.

Even when a teaching opportunity in Syracuse took him from the strenuous, not invariably blissful life of Johnson, Vt., he could hardly be expected to confine himself to the conversation of students and faculty. **Asphalt Georgics** is brilliant proof of that. The highway strip culture he currently explores is not confined to upstate New York. Some of these 14 poems may have been years in the making. In any case the mixture here is as broad as the author's ripened, gentled, deeply relishing craft and experience would lead one to expect. Some poems sizzle with rage at the universal plastic nothingness of mallsville; they writhe with the psychic unease and fantasies of escape the strip can be assumed to generate even in those who love or are resigned to it. But anger is not the dominant note. Mr. Carruth's people are incited to great feats of compensation. Gallantly they improvise, imprecate, experiment, drench their greaseburgers in dream sauce and generally make do, bent but far from broken. Theirs is a syncretic dialect in which an uncle is known as "unk," one takes a "dekko" (look) at someone else, one says "What's the diff?", doughnuts are "sinkers" and coffee a "hunk of java, heavy on the moo-moo."

All in all, **Asphalt Georgics** might be described as a dead-serious diversion, executed with an almost Chinese self-discipline. The stanza employed is a half-rhymed quatrain in which syllables are strictly counted, and rhymes are often achieved by word breaks and sometimes by assonance so faint as to exist only for the eye. Such formal control is standard for this poet when he is especially moved by his occasions. But the quatrains of this sequence are far less demanding than the 15-liners developed in his *Sleeping Beauty* and other long poems. They allow him the widest freedom of stress and accent and appear to cast emulative glances at the satires of Horace. For all their moral fervor and ecological and political timeliness, they have an engaging holiday flair, as if someone were to visit Disneyland determined to take exactly x number of steps, each exactly y inches long, and hope meanwhile to pass for an ordinary tourist. Is this the "classic and earthy elegance" his publisher proclaims? Certainly, but something more. It's excellent sport.

Lillian Feder   (essay date 1985)

SOURCE: "Poetry from the Asylum: Hayden Carruth's *The Bloomingdale Papers*," in *Literature and Medicine,* Vol. 4, 1985, pp. 112-27.

[*An American educator and critic, Feder is the author of* Madness in Literature *(1980). In the following essay, she illustrates how Carruth's struggle for identity and selfhood while writing* The Bloomingdale Papers *contributed greatly to his growth as a poet.*]

Poems about confinement in a mental asylum, whether by an established poet or an amateur, have certain common features. Inevitably, such writers feel themselves imprisoned, although there are times when the asylum also seems a haven; and in their limited physical environment, they use what they have—the atmosphere and routine, the doctors, other patients, the treatment, and the symptoms and effects of their illness—as materials for self-exploration in poetry. Despite such similarities, there is no characteristic asylum poetry. Even when writing is clearly an act of survival, it is a product of a poet's individual personality and talent interpreting the world he or she has internalized when all defenses outside the walls of the asylum have failed. Many poets have written about their experiences in mental institutions, but no one has conveyed the physical and emotional "actuality" as vividly as has Hayden Carruth in *The Bloomingdale Papers.* The struggle against psychic dissolution is a common subject of modern poetry, but *The Bloomingdale Papers* is unusual in its explicit treatment of writing as an effort toward self-restitution. In fact, the poem discloses processes of selfhood and creation that are closely related and sometimes indistinguishable. For this reason alone it deserves attention, which surprisingly it has not received, from literary critics, psychologists, and psychiatrists. It is now more than thirty years since Carruth wrote *The Bloomingdale Papers*; but, as I will demonstrate in this essay, a study of his later poetry indicates that his apprehension of his psychic experience in the very act of writing this early poem remains fundamental to his entire development as a major contemporary American poet.

In his **"Explanation and Apology, Twenty Years After,"** which serves as an introduction to *The Bloomingdale Papers,* Carruth describes the circumstances under which the poem was written and tells why he agreed to its publication in 1975. Near the end of the summer of 1953, having suffered a breakdown after years of mental illness, he entered the White Plains Psychiatric Division of New York Hospital, known as Bloomingdale. After a few months of what seemed ineffectual treatment and no perceptible change in his condition, Carruth took the suggestion of one of his doctors that he "write something that might be helpful to him and his colleagues in their consideration of [his] case", the result being "the poem, or sequence of poems, in this book". *The Bloomingdale Papers* deals with only the first period of his confinement. In January 1954, still at the institution, Carruth had another breakdown. "Thereafter," he says, "I wrote no more". He does not say exactly how long he remained at Bloomingdale after having been subjected to electroshock treatments for the second breakdown, but does refer to "many months" of playing solitaire at the institution.

After leaving Bloomingdale, Carruth says, he "apparently" revised excerpts from the poem which "were included in [his] first book, *The Crow and the Heart* (1959)". He attributes his vagueness about revising these portions and his lapse of memory regarding the poem as a whole to the effects of the electroshock therapy. Years later, when the editors at the University of Georgia Press, who had been shown a copy by his friend Albert Christ-Janer, offered to publish it, his "first inclination was to burn it". Although critical of the diction, the "tight-lipped psychopathic compression", he nonetheless agreed to publication partly because friends urged him to do so and partly because of the nature of the poem itself. His explication of this second motive suggests that he had reasons other than a doctor's suggestion for writing this poem and elucidates some of its basic qualities. His comments are worth quoting at length:

> . . . I have the impression from reading the whole poem that in spite of the bad writing—in some sense even because of it—the total effect is what it should be, the truth of a spirit caged and struggling. Readers should remember that for people in certain crises of disintegrating personality the act of writing, or of making any utterance, is a self-assertion entailing risks literally tantamount to death, so that every word must be forced out willfully and then controlled with rigid, disguising care. This is the emotional matrix of the poem.

The Bloomingdale Papers is written in a variety of stanzaic patterns and meters as well as in brief sections of prose. There are narrative, elegiac, and lyrical parts, sections in couplets, blank and free verse, prose dialogues and descriptions, and a list of the "inmates," their professions, and illnesses. These shifts in form and style express abrupt alternations in the speaker's moods, perceptions, and concerns. Moving backward and forward in time, he uses the asylum as a microcosm of longings, conflicts, alienation, compromises, and despair, an internalization of the world he left behind. Yet these disparate elements do compose a single poem because they are all intrinsic to the poet's struggle to reconstitute his self, successive stages of an effort to integrate unconscious and conscious processes in relation to reality, a concept he attempts to define throughout *The Bloomingdale Papers.* Thus, poetic creation and self-creation become one—processes that involve perception, cognition, love, memory, dream, guilt, and the very terror of being overwhelmed by unconscious fears and impulses and thus of losing even the fragmented sense of selfhood he still retains.

The act of writing induces continual revision of the psychic history it explores. The poet's attempts to achieve a measure of tranquillity in his "narrowed world" by identifying himself with external nature are shattered by associations his own images produce. Beginning his poem in November, Carruth describes the "wintertime realities" as "thin". In an effort to comprehend his presence in a mental hospital, he views its grounds as his particular scene of the general "withdrawing time, / Time for the turning in and inward". Observing the wind driving the last leaves from the trees, the grass "dry and frayed," the "colorless" light outside his barred window, for a moment he conceives of his own and his fellow patients' confinement as part of this natural inward movement, like the hibernation of bears in winter: "Prison grows warm and *is* the real asylum". But retreat into this association with nature only intensifies "the murmurs that so insidiously / Lurk in a sounding skull". Soon anxiety, terror, and despair, like the continuous activity of insects working their destruction, break through the apparent peace of winter hibernation.

Before long the "nest of consciousness is loosed, . . . / And the bird is dead among the dancing worms". The images of the bird and the worm within the mind recur many times in this poem, signifying the poet's struggle to assert his identity together with the risk involved—the conviction of physical and moral corruption that threatens to destroy him. In this passage, still dwelling on the meanings of retreat, Carruth emphasizes the worm, a familiar image of obsession with evil that unites him with his fellow patients. For them, as for him, the worm is no "fancy." Its "captives, sick and sore", they have internalized its cultural history.

In so doing, they have taken an ambiguous role. Unable to adapt to the normal demands of everyday society, they have become the keepers of its hidden terrors. Remote from this world with their consciousness of evil, the patients seem to be inhabitants of a "monastery" in which concentration on their illness is a form of religious devotion:

> No one reads our meanings with an eye
> So ready as ours to mark an obelus.

Carruth's corrections to the typescript of "At Least."

Like monks, studying an ancient manuscript and marking its doubtful passages, they interpret their own "failed hope," their "sickening faith," as if these were written words, seeking out and noting what is spurious. Acting out their compulsions, reflecting "each other's terror" in their eyes, recognizing evil in their "veins," these patients, whom Carruth calls "my friends," have "an insight of the real world". It is their manuscript along with his own that he both writes and "reads" in this poem, noting its revelations and omissions in his painful, conflicted effort to interpret the "reality"—a term he uses repeatedly—in which the self he struggles to reconstitute could not survive.

The atmosphere of the asylum and its grounds, the weather, the commonplace events of daily life are all materials for this manuscript of exploration. Recalling earlier days of his confinement in October when the weather was still mild, he tells of a way he devised to treat his illness by lying in the grass in the sun to relax and induce memories of "Sorrow and melancholy," which brought serenity. The subject of a sonnet, this phase of his self-examination is structured to allay anger and appease guilt. As a result,

> The fears
> Fall, if for just an hour, all away,
> And the old essential person reappears.
> Sorrow can shape us better than dismay.

There is relief in imagining the forgiveness of "old friends and lovers" and, more important, in forgiving "the self this sorrow still recovers". But this effort to restore the self in the tranquillity of forgiveness ends with the carefully structured sonnet that emerges from such "sentiment." The lines that follow question its authenticity in free verse that mocks sorrow as the "flattery of regrets," since it cannot transform the "reality" that created the self and continues to exist as intrinsic to its very processes:

> All the rudenesses,
> The steep blows that have been done
> And are now ever and ever Hayden, . . .

"Reality," compounded of panic, hate, fear, and guilt, all conflicting with and overcoming love, emerges in daydreams and memories. It breaks through the "hours of nothingness," the avoidance of "the shock of being" that life in the asylum induces. The inadequacy of his sonnet discloses the delusions of October, forcing the poet to face the "pain" that "cut a vivid course / Through these as through all days," and he returns to the reality of the asylum.

His descriptions of the other patients, the conversations he records, and his implicit approval of their touching, sometimes comic, resistance to institutional despotism convey his involvement with and compassion for them, but also a need to stand apart, to make his own sad and ironic commentary on their complaints as well as their accommodations to the routines of confinement. He is able to empathize with the nurses and attendants when they "preserve themselves against" the despair they can neither comprehend nor alleviate by arguing and complaining as a homeopathic protection. Only the doctors seem remote; having dismissed their diagnosis of his illness—"Anxiety

psychoneurosis / (Chronic and acute)"—as "meaningless, / Even in clinical usage", Carruth tries to create his own case history by examining memories of life in "Mongolia," his term for the world outside, in connection with his present pain and isolation. First he lists the physical and psychological manifestations of his seizures of panic, which occur in seemingly innocuous circumstances. The result is a bare, precise description of loss of control over body and mind, the desperate need to flee and the overwhelming terror of psychic dissolution: the "Fear of fear".

In contrast, his attempt to explain the cause of these symptoms results in mere generalizations, the mind's evasions of its very efforts at self-exploration. Taking his clue from William James, Carruth attributes his panic to an extremely sharp perception of "almost hidden things" and an awareness of "evil" that quickens his knowledge of "nature's rapacities." Conscious that "it is more and less / Than that," that his illness can be traced "down the fathering / Years as through a labyrinth," that his obsession with evil, the "demon," the "worm," cannot be omitted from the "dreadful design" which constitutes his being, he nonetheless depersonalizes this knowledge. In a long passage that would seem simplistic were it not so obviously a need to avoid what is too painful in detail, he rationalizes the father-son relationship as a perennially difficult one. Furthermore, neither here nor anywhere else in the poem does he account for his preoccupation with evil either in religious or psychological terms. Only when he returns to the seizures of panic, which he experiences as both a source and an act of self-knowledge, does he reveal a connection between these speculations and his individual conflict and suffering.

Recalling the first of these seizures, he emphasizes the "separateness" it produced. Utterly alone in his terror of dissolution, he could not cry out even to "friends, lovers, / Blood relations." But, as he recreates this episode in the asylum, he is aware that others have also experienced this type of "self-knowledge . . . / our murdering rush, / The brain's explosion". Association with those who have also endured the disintegration of the self allows him to confront and include in *The Bloomingdale Papers* a graphic account of such an occurrence in a poem he wrote three years before which, he now says, he "deceptively" labeled a "recitative." In this poem the complex operations of memory disclose the relationship between his need to find comfort in and identification with external nature and the panic that its "rapacities" induce.

The epigraph to this poem consists of three lines from a tale in Ovid's *Metamorphoses* in which the fury Tisiphone drives Ino and Athamas mad. The lines Carruth quotes tell of the means she uses: poisons, hallucinations, forgetfulness, crimes, tears, and the mad love of slaughter. This epigraph too, he says, is deceptive, since it implies a greater knowledge of Latin than he had, a judgment that seems unduly harsh. However limited his familiarity with Latin, his use of the lines from Ovid discloses more authentic feeling than he seems to realize, for it suggests his need to break through the aloneness he feels in his panic, which occurs with the suddenness and force of an invasion by hostile forces, by associating it with an ancient tradition in which madness is externalized in myth.

The scene of the poem is a peaceful lakeshore on a lovely April day in Chicago, where the speaker hoped to evoke memories of his childhood joy in nature. But soon, without warning, "oceanic memory in the mind," dissolving the barriers between the poet and the outside world, produced in this loss of autonomy not the expected bliss of union with all creation but "terrors unknown before." What he calls "memory's accident" unleashes hostile feelings which he obviously projects on external nature invading his being: "the unsaid pains / Gossiped like an elm of frightened birds"; his "nerves were wings"; his "memory" became "rains" that "hissed in the mind's quick fires." These sounds are a language of memory, evoking even deeper ones that would seem to be their source:

> What thuds against the hollow ears!
> A cry to murder is a trumpet call,
> The boy's voice crying down the fathering years.

The phrase "down the fathering years" in this poem written three years before Carruth's confinement in the asylum is more revealing in its context than is his later use of it in the passage discussed above. The "cry to murder" emerging from those years in the context of idealized nature turned hostile suggests his displacement of childhood murderous wishes on the natural processes of disintegration and death while he consciously identified himself with nature's productivity and freedom, particularly the flight and song of the bird. The other "voice" which he had repressed now returns to destroy the very defenses he had used throughout his youth in forming his image of himself. When this image is shattered even as he seeks to restore it in "sweet rememberances" of external nature, his hold on reality dissolves in panic, and the one identity left to him is with a sick gull, whose "rotten flesh" conveys his own feelings of helplessness and corruption as he watches it fall to the fish below.

Defending the poem three years later in the asylum, Carruth describes it as a part of himself, a hard initiation into mysteries only those afflicted with madness can know. Addressing friends who refused to take the episode seriously, and probably the doctors in the institution as well, he asks:

> Tell me, what
> Do you know of Pillicock-hill
> Anyway? Has it occurred
> To your eminences
> That the grips of lunes are not
> Fit emprize for pavid
> Imaginations? We, we are
> The ones hardened and rudely
> Enriched by these trials,
> For all our weaknesses that you
> Delight on, and, it may be,
> Made braver, forced to endure.

If the experience and the poem, which he views as one, are unacceptable by rational standards, they unite him with those who have come to know processes of mind and body that challenge the validity of this sole norm. Chief of these is memory, cherished as an essential process of selfhood and recognized now as also its potential annihilator. Un-

conscious memories, he realizes, break through past repressions and denials to determine present observations, perceptions, and feelings, transforming symbols long imbued with hope into omens of destruction which fuse past and present. Thus, his identification with the bird, his symbol of love and song, the essence of self-fulfillment for the poet, has long concealed the unacknowledged guilt of boyhood and the terror of extinction. Violence, sickness, and death, inherent in human as in external nature, inhabit the gull; "the loathsome birds" and the dead bird "among the dancing worms" at the beginning of *The Bloomingdale Papers*; and the blackbird later on. However painful, this is nonetheless the poet's "fourteenth way," added to Wallace Stevens's thirteen, of looking at a blackbird, which "plummets down, / Severing the snowy world with his death-fall". Accepting this "way" of knowing himself, with all its risks, means exploring these symbols which have escaped his control and which represent both the limits and possibilities of his life and art. The bird recurs again, trapped and maimed, but it is still the "I" who "Expectantly and fearfully" sings.

> In *The Bloomingdale Papers*, poetic creation and self-creation become one— processes that involve perception, cognition, love, memory, dream, guilt, and the very terror of being overwhelmed by unconscious fears and impulses and thus of losing even the fragmented sense of selfhood he still retains.
>
> —*Lillian Feder*

The allusion to Pillicock-hill in the poem written three years before is one of several to *King Lear* in *The Bloomingdale Papers,* where Edgar and Lear are evoked as prototypes that unite the literary and actual history of madness as a form of self-revelation. Carruth uses a passage from the sixty-ninth Psalm to develop the meaning of this tragic understanding. In his continuous effort to come to terms with reality, at one stage he questions the seemingly needless complexities he has himself imposed, trying to dismiss the "world of fears and dreams." But then he hears "an ancient wail of blood":

> Save me, O God; for the waters are come in unto
>   my soul.
> I sink in deep mire, where there is no standing:
> I am come into deep waters, where the floods
>   overflow me.
>
> · · · · ·
>
> Let not the waterflood overflow me, neither
>   let the deep swallow me up,
>   and let not the pit
>   shut her mouth upon me.

This perennial song, a "lisping of the sea that lies within," is a revelation and warning of how fragile are the boundaries that separate human beings from the psychic flood of dissolution:

> Anciently the psalmist mourned that sea
> For all of us; his drowning heart called out
> For all of us; and we still hear the call,
> A misery that rises in our throats.

Identifying himself with "all of us" who have lived from time immemorial threatened by unconscious guilt and fear and with the psalmist who sang of such dangers symbolized in external nature, the poet approaches this "new reality" as a field of "exploration. / New knowledge" that will now determine his perception of himself and the world, and thus his use of language:

> Reality will never be safe again,
> Nor any image made to a fixed design.

But, all too aware of the vulnerability to destruction denied but ever present in what passes for the reality of daily life for most human beings, he turns from "the way of the world" and even from "the fearfulness of love".

Although early in *The Bloomingdale Papers,* in a defense of himself as a poet, Carruth mentions his associations of love with panic and elsewhere in the first part of the poem refers briefly to memories of love, only in the last third does he explore this central experience of his life. He begins with an imagined trial on New Year's Day, explicitly stating that "his love is what we try". Written in heroic couplets, this section of the poem mocks its own efforts at imposing order on the most turbulent of emotions. The defendant is "self-arraigned," "self-confessed," "his own accusor," but his crime is "unknown". All that emerges from this mock-trial is the association of love with undefined guilt and the impossibility of any resolution of his conflict through reason and order. The trial leads only to memories of the loss of love and the continual pain of each attempt to regain it.

Implicit in the poet's recollections of a boyhood love, a marriage, divorce, and a second marriage are the conviction that only in love is self-realization possible and a simultaneous acceptance of solitude as his one means of survival. Each effort toward self-fulfillment is inevitably connected with loss of the beloved and of the self invested in this love. Although Carruth ultimately renounces love as inextricably bound to guilt and panic—"the sea within"— he clings to memories of love as a potential form of knowledge, which has survived all losses. One of the most important symbols of this knowledge is his first beloved, Marjorie Marie St. Pierre, idealized in the stone for which she is named. In a long passage, Carruth meditates on the stone as a symbol of perfection: it signifies balance, faithfulness, the absolute realization of its essential components. As artist and lover, the speaker is the shaper of the stone, but at the same time, his "image"—"my stone, my girl"—also "makes . . . and shapes" him. This comprehension of fearless surrender of the self in love is an ideal, the stone, that remains with him even in despair. In a later section of the poem that deals bitterly with his divorce, he states it more explicitly as a hope:

> Let love flow back and lift
> My being with the rest

> Where self becomes the gift
> I give to be possessed.
> Thence, selfless but unspent,
> Let me achieve content.

But *The Bloomingdale Papers* ends with an acknowledgment of the difference between the "gist / Of love" that exists between the poet and his daughter, whom he hardly knows, and the actuality, the hurt he cannot help inflicting on himself and those he most cares for. He is resigned to the knowledge his own explorations have produced: that the self he has so painfully tried to recover is too fragile to risk the surrender that love demands.

Carruth wrote other poems about his stay at Bloomingdale, among them the sequence **"The Asylum."** *The Bloomingdale Papers,* he says, "was the generator of them all". But the importance of this poem lies not only in its illumination of specific references to the asylum in his later poetry. It is clear that Carruth's experience of poetic creation as a mode and test of the self, which emerges in the revelations, the evasions, and the very fragmented structure of *The Bloomingdale Papers,* remains the dominant motif of the body of his work. In his later poetry, he returns again and again to the challenge he renounced at the end of *The Bloomingdale Papers*: his drive to unify the processes of selfhood, loving, and creation in his life and art. Throughout his career, Carruth has continued to rely on the major images and symbols of *The Bloomingdale Papers* to express this personal and aesthetic goal, which has determined the basic character of his poetry.

In **"The Asylum,"** a sequence of thirteen sonnets that he wrote in 1957, Carruth's aim, he says, was "to condense and give firmer objective structure to [the] materials from the hospital". Here, his attempt to view his own breakdown and effort to reconstitute a self in relation to myth and history results in a vagueness, perhaps intentional, about his own psychological experience as well as the historical events to which he refers. As in *The Bloomingdale Papers,* he uses external nature symbolically. The wind occurs in each poem of the sequence as memory associating his own aspirations and defeats with the history of human efforts to build cities and nations and their inevitable devastation by violence and war. The wind, continuous and unrelenting in its threat of destruction, merges the personal and historical past with the speaker's present struggle to maintain a sense of his own identity:

> For it is a curious blast,
> Both full and faint, as if my ears were dinned
> By pulses not my own, but past.
> Dusk, and the Troy fires wink below our hill.
> And here we came to search the self at last,
> And here the long wind comes, and comes to
>   kill.

The quest for asylum in "this nation" and on "the whole earth," where "mankind" seeks "refuge," leads to the conclusion that "ultimately asylum is the soul," the occasional discovery of "Our tiny irreducible selves". In this sequence, Carruth's attempt to extend the meaning of mental breakdown and confinement in a hospital to history and culture is less successful than is his confrontation with the "irreducible" conditions of selfhood: the acceptance of himself as a "small particular death", who seeks asylum from the very mortality he struggles to acknowledge.

The intrinsic connection between selfhood, the consciousness of death, and poetic creation is developed with increasing subtlety and conviction in Carruth's later poetry. In the volume *For You* (1970), in which **"The Asylum"** is reprinted, the long poem **"Contra Mortem"** concludes with the explicit statement: "Come let us sing against death". It is an ancient and continuous theme of poetry, but Carruth's conviction here and in other poems carries with it his particular experience of "nothing," the dissolution of the self, on which his knowledge of this "great determining reality" is founded.

In Carruth's later poetry his acceptance of nothingness as a challenge intensifies his drive to assert the creative power of his own and all individual life in opposition to the essential meaninglessness of existence. His continued use of the central images of *The Bloomingdale Papers*—the stone, the bird, the worm—which often refer directly or obliquely to their functions in that poem, reflects his mature understanding that reality is neither an ideal nor a threat but a changing concept of nature and history created by human action, reason, and imagination.

The stone, in a poem of that name which appeared in *For You,* remains a symbol of perennial security and recurrence, linking past with present in nature as in human life. But in **"Essay on Stone,"** a later poem, Carruth explores the connection between earlier and present meanings of the stone in his life and work:

> Once I wrote a poem about
> making love to stone
> and a whole book in which the protagonist,
> who was myself, carried a stone with him
> everywhere he went. I still like
> that poem and that book, . . .

The stone defies his disbelief in "absolutes": "It is / the abyss inverted, the abyss made visible." This thought, he says, might have pleased him "Years ago when I wrote that other poem," but now, as he stands on a "great rock" in Vermont, watching the snow fall "as into our own abyss," the stone, the unyielding symbol of that reality he once sought so fearfully, is an ever-present reminder of his own vulnerability: he is middle-aged, struggling to survive the long Vermont winters, and he has just fallen in the snow. Unhurt but "shaken," he asks himself whether it is "consoling / to know I might have fallen / into the abyss," but the stone, which he loves, affirming that possibility by its very presence, offers no consolation. As in the past he allied himself with Shakespeare and the biblical psalmist in facing the perennial chaos within, so now he joins with Heine in acknowledging the components of reality that signify the inevitable void. The poem is as stark in its beauty as the stone and the North Sea, which these poets, "unconsoled," celebrate.

Carruth refers to *The Bloomingdale Papers* in **"Paragraphs,"** another recent poem in which his evaluation of its language is a study of the self that produced it. First he acknowledges its lasting meaning for him:

> Reading myself, old poems, their inside truth
> that was (is, is!) crucial, . . .

Then, he goes on to face the past in a series of questions:

>   Was it shameful
> to be insane, or so grotesque
> to wrench lucidity out of nowhere? . . .

Seeking his "true voice" in this poetry and appalled by the poses he took, the affectations of his language, he now tries to understand what then he could only evade:

> Dear mother, dead father, what burlesque
> of feeling phonied us, that made you make me
> hate myself?

His method of using rhetorical questions whose implicit answers convey the conflict that raised them is reminiscent of a passage in *The Bloomingdale Papers,* quoted above, in which he defends the earlier poem included in that volume. Still searching, but now using the directness and precision of his language to probe his formative years, Carruth reveals how painfully he has examined and lived with the "truth" disclosed obliquely in words chosen to conceal it. His inner voice now speaks to the past without sarcasm or anger, in fact, with pity and affection for the parents who could not comprehend the hurt they inflicted.

Carruth's absorption in external nature and his identification with its processes remain essential to his self-exploration. In the poems written after *The Bloomingdale Papers,* his focus is the hills, soil, land, air, and climate of Vermont, where he has lived for many years. In his poem **"Vermont,"** employing a technique he had first used in *The Bloomingdale Papers,* he explores the connotations of the literal meaning of its name, "green mountain." Then, recalling having heard the name pronounced with the accent on its first syllable, he divides it into "Verm" and "ont," "the Worm of Being." The worm here is an imposition of the human on nature; the "depravity" he detects is "mostly new" in contrast with the "beauty" which is "mostly old." Carruth's identification with Vermont's perennial features—even its "protracted gloom"—is part of his ongoing existence, the challenge of self-creation:

> From this we make ourselves,
> remake ourselves each moment, stronger,
> harder,
> with our own beauty. Yes, our great green
> mountain
> is the worm of being, long and irregular,
> twined lengthwise through our state, our place,
> our now.

The awareness of "depravity," the worm, is no longer the threat to the self that it signified in *The Bloomingdale Papers*; on the contrary, it is an integral part of the process of being.

Another part, and perhaps the most important, is the paradoxical realization of selfhood in surrender to the beloved who both receives and shapes his creation. Having imagined and renounced the possibility of such a union in *The Bloomingdale Papers,* he celebrates his renewed struggle to achieve it in later poems to and about Rose Marie Dorn, his second wife, including his most recent volume, *The Sleeping Beauty* (1982). In this poem, once again using the literal meaning of a name—in this case, Dornröschen—as a central symbol, he depicts her as the "Princess / Of the Briar Rose," who lies asleep, waiting for the prince to awaken her with a kiss. The poem is a modern romance, in which the speaker takes various roles in the dreams of his beloved. These personae, whose names all begin with the letter "H," are derived from literature, history, and daily life in society, their characters and deeds merging with the individual aspirations, disappointments, and achievements of the poet. Including figures as disparate as Homer, Hitler, Hölderlin, and Husband, these dreams express various aspects of the conflict between love and death inherent in human nature, history, and society.

The Sleeping Beauty, like *The Bloomingdale Papers* and "The Asylum," is a sequence of poems beginning with the cold grayness of a November day that seemed like "no season". But out of this nothingness comes the "grace" of a "plume," the sign of the bird, the pen, the song that is to redeem the speaker even as he incorporates the limits of mortality and participates emotionally in the errors and crimes of history. As the sleeping beauty dreams the poet in his various forms, he is her "maker / Whom [she] made." He comes to her as "Hero," as "History," as "Ego in all its radiance." His sword is transformed into song; bearing death, he converts it to love.

This realization of the self in love and creation is the continuous dream, an ongoing struggle which engages and reconstitutes the past. It is also part of daily experience; for example, an automobile accident on a snow-covered road late at night leaves the speaker with no recourse but to "Crawl upward through the dark". The next poem of the sequence develops this act as a symbol of the inner struggle to reach beyond nothingness, beyond even identity, history, and love in "the poem crawling upward through the dark".

As so often in Carruth's poetry, memories of the period of his mental breakdown remain part of this continuous process. In this sequence, the asylum is even given a name beginning with "H," the "Hatch," which connects the "torture" of electroshock, the "abyss" into which it threw him, his dissociation and fear, and the question "Why?" that he kept asking in vain with the dreams that forge his being as a creator and extend his questions to history and culture.

Such questions, which trouble the sleeping princess and the speaker as well, have to do with unconscious forces in history; love and death. Painfully acknowledging the suppression and murder that inevitably result from revolution, the poet, middle-aged "yet still the boy-anarchist" demands of the past and present heroes:

> Why could you not have let love be? And why
> Was loving never enough?

The question he poses to political and social leaders returns to haunt his own history: "No love without hurt?" The fear that dominated *The Bloomingdale Papers* has become a knowledge and acceptance of love as inextricably bound to the "bitterness" of death. But he still seeks "another way"; addressing the princess, he says, "We must

sing / Our passion," a love "Without distortion, yet still this wondrous thing". The song is to redeem love even from death.

At the end of *The Sleeping Beauty,* the beloved emerges as the woman Rose Marie and the speaker as himself:

> The work is done.
> My name is Hayden and I have made this song.

Separating himself from the poem, he says that it "moves alone now, but without loneliness". An independent entity exceeding the scope of any individual life, it is also "an act of self-creation." This process so fearfully approached in *The Bloomingdale Papers* is the major subject and formal principle of Carruth's later poetry:

> Self has been left among the objects that fashioned it.
> Action and knowledge are one, free, far in the depths of consciousness.

M. L. Rosenthal   (essay date 1986)

SOURCE: A review of *The Selected Poetry of Hayden Carruth,* in *The New York Times Book Review,* May 11, 1986, p. 17.

[*Rosenthal is a well-known American poet, editor, critic, and scholar of British and American poetry. In the following review, he praises the wide range of themes, perspectives, and poetic styles in* The Selected Poetry of Hayden Carruth.]

Hayden Carruth, author of a score of volumes of poetry, now offers a very welcome selection [in *The Selected Poetry of Hayden Carruth*]. Uncompromising and very often dour or bitter, his poems are full of private twists and torques, yet sharply expressive for the rest of us too. Their range is wide. They can be minutely and delicately attentive, as in these lines from **"The Poet"**:

> He hears
> the woodmouse scream—
> so small a sound
> in the great darkness
>
> entering his pain.

And they can repossess the trauma of unresolved horror and anger, as in the opening poem, **"On a Certain Engagement South of Seoul"**:

> When I was nineteen, once, the surprising tears
> Stood in my eyes and stung me, for I saw
> A soldier in a newsreel clutch his ears
>
> To hold his face together. Those that paw
> The public's bones to eat the public's heart
> Said far too much, of course. . . .

Mr. Carruth's poems send out currents of communion to all of us from his intimately personal realm of reverie and emotion, even when the predicaments out of which they speak are most particularly his own. **"Lines Written in an Asylum,"** a quietly desperate poem (Mr. Carruth is a lover of Thoreau overtaken by the general condition), has to do with a time of breakdown and irrevocable separation from a loved woman. The poet calls the helpless "ravage of the will" attendant upon all this "the incontinence of loss"—a condition "Where all becoming only seems / A false, impossible return / To a world I labor to unlearn." Much of the book is in this key.

"I Tell You for Several Years of My Madness I Heard the Voice of Lilith Singing in the Trees of Chicago" makes a visionary leap away from trapped expression of such a dark, immediate kind. It uses the same pressures of loss and guilt to project itself into an imagined alternative sensibility, that of Lilith, the primal woman, who here sings of the ages-long betrayal and violation of the life-bearing, nourishing female energy in all earthly existence. Like the major tone of Mr. Carruth's other poems, hers in this song fuses the sense of defeat with something like a final affirmation with a dying breath:

> A woman's bone is bright as the tree of the olive
>   in sunlight:
> a woman's flesh is beat down like the unripe
>   fruit:
> a woman's death lies gleaming and twisted like
>   a torn-out root in the early morning dew.
>
> Therefore the awakened bird cries once in the
>   night:
> therefore the sweet fire sings when it reaches the
>   knot:
> therefore, o therefore Lilith her cry, and Lilith
>   her curse and her detestation, and again I
>   sing: *therefore*.

The poem is a strange triumph of incantatory transcendence, strange partly because it has Mr. Carruth's own idiosyncratic stamp despite so many echoes in it. One hears the Bible, Christopher Smart, Blake, Whitman, Yeats and even Ted Hughes, at one point or another. Yet the music is after all Mr. Carruth's own fierce, desolate creation.

In this selection from a quarter-century of publication (1959-83), Mr. Carruth reveals another gift again and again. He is able to lose himself in a transport of intense absorption in concrete reality. He does this in his splendid poem **"The Ravine,"** finding all mortality embodied in a bit of landscape that at first seems dull enough: "Stones, brown tufted grass, but no water, / it is dry to the bottom." Thus the beginning, but continued observation spots "A seedy eye / of orange hawkweed," a ring-necked snake, a dead young woodcock and a "bumbling" mink in the ravine; and the landscape's changing appearance in other seasons is then remembered, and its possible future changes envisioned. What troubles the poet is that he cannot rest content with literal reality at hand, that he sees "not things but relationships of things, / quick changes and slow. These are my sorrow." His gift—and poetically it is surely one—is, to him, a tormenting obsession with mutability that dominates "the sequences of my mind" without clarifying anything: "I wonder what they mean. Every day, / day after day, I wonder what they mean."

But still, he does well enough with "things." Just look at the start of **"The Cows at Night"**:

> The moon was like a full cup tonight,
> too heavy, and sank in the mist
> soon after dark, leaving for light

> faint stars and the silver leaves
> of milkweed beside the road,
> gleaming before my car.

Then the piece becomes an altogether lovely poem as Mr. Carruth describes coming upon a herd of cows lying in a pasture "in that great darkness." The mystery of his sudden confrontation with their "sad / and beautiful faces in the dark" ("like girls very long ago") almost leads him into sentimentality but doesn't—the sign of one type of true lyric poem.

Perhaps I have overstressed Mr. Carruth's poetry of psychic pain. He has other dimensions. The gaily awefilled closing poem, **"Moon-Set,"** ends: "And on my slow / snowshoes I danced and skipped / gravely down the meadow." And there's the calm acceptance (and rich affirmation within it) of loss in the beautifully self-consolatory **"Anima."** In addition, Mr. Carruth has a rough-and-ready side, full of persiflage, tough-guy defiance and roistering volatility. He showed it early on, in the ironic, restrainedly randy **"Notes From Robin Hill Cottage."** But he lets go far more in later poems connected with his love of jazz, such as **"Who Cares, Long as It's B-Flat,"** a fairly hip, flip elegy for remembered musicians: "Floyd O'Brien, Teagardens Charlie & Jack / where are the snowbirds of yesteryear?"

Finally, there are hard-bitten New England monologues and related pieces—a little too close to Frost's manner but grittier and angrier—and an interesting, though loosely strung and uneven, series called **"Paragraphs,"** a number of which have a similarly harsh, knowledgeable Yankee localism. (Other "paragraphs" touch on a variety of concerns—political, historical, musical, self-analytical; at times they resemble Berryman's "dream songs" and Lowell's "sonnets.") Despite his versatility, however, elegy is Mr. Carruth's dominant mode. He mourns lost loves, lost friends, lost pride, lost American glories of pride and integrity and innocence (though he has questions to raise about brutalities even before the days of napalm). His elegy for Paul Goodman, **"In Memoriam,"** is a small masterpiece: an unrhetorical, image-centered expression of affection. Of living American poets, indeed, Mr. Carruth has now become our elegist par excellence.

Carruth's poetry is grounded and simple: It flickers with a frail, durable tenderness, often addressing loneliness and the dread engendered by lifelong mental instability with dignity. . . .

—*Clayton Eshleman, in* The Los Angeles Times Book Review, *June 3, 1984.*

David Weiss   (essay date 1990)

SOURCE: "The Incorrigible Dirigible," in *The Southern*

Review, Louisiana State University, Vol. 26, No. 2, April, 1990, pp. 466-69.

[*In the following review, Weiss characterizes the poems in* Tell Me Again How the White Heron Rises and Flies across the Nacreous River at Twilight toward the Distant Islands *as "ungainly, temperamental, prosy, anecdotal, discursive, yet 'lighter than air'," and asserts: "Only the helium of the poet's intelligence holds them impossibly up."*]

"The pure poem," writes Robert Penn Warren in a recently republished essay, "tries to be pure by excluding, more or less rigidly, certain elements which might qualify or contradict its original impulse. . . . [P]ure poems want to be, and desperately, all of a piece." Warren sides with impurity, conflict, complication, contradiction, with, in a New Critical catchword, irony. He does so, he says, because experience is compounded of all these. And while it is partly true that this concept of the "impure" poem is now associated with a baroque and involuted poetry, its axis of distinctions seems more valuable than the formal/free verse debate of recent years. It allows us to see, for example, that the poems of Robert Bly, Robert Creeley, and Richard Wilbur have much in common, although each aims for a different sort of purity in the making of the lyric.

Hayden Carruth grew up in the poetic cultural milieu of Warren's essay, which first appeared in 1943. He has pushed the notion of impurity, by which I mean heterogeneous inclusiveness, further than almost anyone, and with his new book, *Tell me Again How the White Heron Rises and Flies Across the Nacreous River at Twilight Toward the Distant Islands,* he pushes it into a realm of rare freedom which brings to mind the late W. C. Williams of "Asphodel, That Greeny Flower," "The Sparrow," and "The Ivy Crown." There's a great and eccentric mastery here which chooses at almost every turn to be recalcitrant and unpoetic. Carruth, whose formal talents are staggering, has chosen to write poems that resemble, to borrow from the title of the opening poem, "incorrigible dirigibles." This is, indeed, an apt figure for these new poems: they are ungainly, temperamental, prosy, anecdotal, discursive, yet "lighter than air." Only the helium of the poet's intelligence holds them impossibly up. Only in C. K. Williams's *Flesh and Blood,* which renovates the sonnet, can I think of another recent attempt to push out the walls of the house of poetry, to "unscrew the doors from their jambs!" as Whitman in a moment of hysterical afflatus put it. Others, of course, like the Language poets, following Stevens, have tried to push the walls in, or, to remove the pejorative from that metaphor, to discover unsuspected rooms within. Pushing outward toward prose, Carruth is involved in a renewal—of the essay-poem, Ovid's and Pope's, using a long, yet measured line. One feels this renewal frequently in the book—as in this passage, for example, from **"The Impossible Indispensability of the *Ars Poetica"*:**

> No, what I have been trying to say
> For all the years of my awakening
> Is that neither of the quaint immemorial views
>   of poetry
> is adequate for us.
> A poem is not an expression, nor is it an object.

Yet it somewhat partakes of both. What a poem is
Is never to be known, for which I have learned
    to be grateful. But the aspect in which I see
    my own
Is as the act of love. The poem is a gift, a bestowal.
The poem is for us what instinct is for animals,
    a continuing and chiefly unthought corroboration of essence.

For Carruth a poem is always an act, "an act of love"; its instinctual "corroboration of essence" occurs in that act. A poem, he says further on, "has almost the quality of disappearance / In its cage of visibility. It disperses among the words. It is a fluidity, a vapor, of love." These poems all put themselves under a great self-applied pressure to become poems, to turn the lead of their unlikely material and language into helium and become "lighter than air." We feel in these poems the finite self lift out of the "mind-forged manacles" of its circumstances to experience, often painfully, its more unbounded and fuller being.

Another way to think about the act of renewal that poetry requires is through the start of W. C. Williams's own *ars poetica,* "The Ivy Crown": "The whole process is a lie, / unless, / crowned by excess, / it break forcefully, / one way or another, / from its confinement—/ or find a deeper well." That "deeper well," however, may be what separates the modernist from the postmodern temper—that need to make the disparate and disjointed, the dissonant and fragmented, cohere. Carruth's "deeper well" was dug in *The Sleeping Beauty.* Here Carruth admits into his poems an excess of the seemingly "unpoetic," not in order to salvage or transform it but to make it yield, to overcome it. The most despairing of poets about our culture's poisonous decay, Carruth nevertheless makes us feel most fully the effort to establish in the humanly diminished world a place where the self in its wholeness can be. Where for Whitman the structure of American democracy itself expressed and embodied that place, for Carruth it's the jam session. His vision, from the final essay in *Sitting In,* is worth quoting:

> I don't know what a poet's dreams are worth—
> maybe not much. But I dream continually of a
> great session where race, or more properly
> speaking ethnicity, has no significance at all,
> where "culture" is irrelevant, where every performer and listener participates freely and equally in the bodily and spiritually wrenching, exhilarating, purging experience of jazz-in-itself.

The poems in this collection also have this ambition: to escape from the isolation of singularity, to find freedom most fully realized in community, in communion—making love, discoursing with Ovid, listening to wild geese or to a jazz singer on the radio he hasn't heard in years.

> You, a black woman singing a white Tin Pan
>   Alley tune in Sweden about my home back in
>   Vermont,
> And I in Syracuse, where the jasmine has no
>   scent—
> feelings and values scattering as the death-
>   colored leaves scatter on this windy day.
> Maxine, I cling to you, I am your spectral lover,

both of us crumbling now, but our soul-dust
    mingling nevertheless
in the endless communion of song, and I hope,
    I believe,
that you have striven, as I have
beyond the brute moments of nostalgia,
into the timelessness of music,
and that you have someone with you, as I have
    Cindy.

("Letter to Maxine Sullivan")

Often isolation is not overcome, but alienation is. What overcomes alienation for the reader is the presence not of persona but of a person—by turns wry, cranky, enraptured, angry, admiring, explanatory, prosaic, disturbed, playful, pedantic, tormented, struggling against the forces of diminishment inside and outside the self in search of a just and, to use another New Critical catchphrase, hard-earned expression of their transcendence.

The jazz improvisation, like the "incorrigible dirigible," brings all elements and sounds into a harmony, consonant or dissonant, giving to being a true form. In the crucible of his medium, the improvisor makes his materials cohere, or serve a purpose beyond themselves. There's great richness in ruin, fragments, detritus, which are our "dump" as Stevens called the stuff of our civilization, yet unavoidably there is also a wish, particularly in a poet so formally at ease as Carruth, to have as one's inheritance an unbroken tradition, and a refined, allusive language. **"Of Distress Being Humiliated by the Classical Chinese Poets"** contains this admiration of purity:

Masters, the mock orange is blooming in Syra-
    cuse without scent, having been bred by pa-
    tient horticulturists
To make this greater display at the expense of
    fragrance.
But I miss the jasmine of my back-country
    home.
Your language has no tenses, which is why your
    poems can never be translated whole into En-
    glish;
Your minds are the minds of men who feel and
    imagine without time.
The serenity of the present, the repose of my eyes
    in the cool whiteness of sterile flowers.
Even now the headsman with his great curved
    blade and rank odor is stalking the byways for
    some of you.
When everything happens at once, no conflicts
    can occur.
Reality is an impasse. Tell me again
How the white heron rises from among the reeds
    and flies forever across the nacreous river at
    twilight
Toward the distant islands.

This is among the least "impure" of the poems in this volume, yet its impurity expresses Carruth's modernist suspicions, and our own, about pure poetry, about the trouble with Byzantium, about our necessary allegiance to incompleteness and imperfection. By these means, it is Carruth's implicit contention, do we find our freedom.

Ben Howard   (essay date 1990)

SOURCE: A review of *Tell Me Again How the White Heron Rises and Flies across the Nacreous River at Twilight toward the Distant Islands,* in *Poetry,* Vol. CLVI, No. 6, September, 1990, pp. 345-48.

[*Howard is an American poet, educator, and critic. In the following review of* Tell Me Again How the White Heron Rises and Flies across the Nacreous River at Twilight toward the Distant Islands, *he extols Carruth's blending of disparate images and ideas.*]

In his celebrated essay on the metaphysical poets, T. S. Eliot contended that the mind of the poet amalgamates the ideas of Spinoza with the sound of the typewriter and the smell of cooking. Some years later (in his *Modern Poetry*), Louis MacNeice cast a cool eye on Eliot's pronouncement, observing that Eliot's "famous obscurity" stemmed, in part, from his narrow conception of poetry. "I suspect," wrote MacNeice, "that Eliot is bound to be a rather esoteric poet because . . . he really is more interested in ideas on the one hand and sense-impressions on the other—Spinoza and smells—than in concrete life or the concrete human being."

I am reminded of Eliot's comment in reading Hayden Carruth's [*Tell Me Again How the White Heron Rises and Flies Across the Nacreous River at Twilight Toward the Distant Islands*], where the ideas of Heidegger, Schopenhauer, Leibniz, Ruskin, William James, and others mingle with the smells of coffee and cigarettes, and where the poet's considerable erudition undergirds his finely observed impressions of the natural world. Unlike Eliot, however, Carruth is very much interested in concrete life, be it the joys of the flesh or the miseries of living in Syracuse, New York:

Freedom is not to be proved but is rather a pos-
    tulate
of action. Thus excellent Berdyaev,
who has meant much to me,
although I must shake my head and make a face
when he undertakes to explain
the Holy Ghost. We are unbelievers,
which may be (I regularly
think it is) our misfortune. But we are still
existentialist lovers.
Strange Soren Kierkegaard of Hamlet's prov-
    ince
would approve of us in our unchurchly dark
devotions. In Syracuse the rain falls every day,
the faces of the burghers of Edgehill Road
are as bland as marshmallows and as puffy.

As this poem continues, a general idea of freedom encounters the specific environs of a sunless city, and the world of impersonal ideas is brought into accord with the poet's most intimate acts:

To live here, to love here,
as Jack our friend the Gilbert would say,
sighing, smiling,
requires an extraordinary knowledge of free-
    dom,
unhistorical and reinvented by us here in every
act, as when I brought to you for a love token

the plastic sack of just sprouted lilies-of-the-
    valley
to plant around the steps of our arched doorway.
That was phenomenon, not poetry, not symbol,
    the act
without a proof, freedom-in-love.
                    "Poem Catching Up With An Idea"

MacNeice would, I suspect, have approved of this lucid
amalgam, in which the ideas of a Christian existentialist
illuminate the concrete life of the poet and his lover.

Most of the poems in Carruth's collection—his twenty-
third—perform feats of this kind, whether their subject is
language, erotic love, metaphysics, faith, jazz, aging, mortality, or urban desolation. **"Of Distress Being Humiliated by the Classical Chinese Poets"** explores contrasts between the "minds of men who feel and imagine without
time" and the advanced technology of the Western world,
where the mock orange is bred "to make [a] greater display at the expense of fragrance." **"Ovid, Old Buddy, I
Would Discourse with You a While"** draws parallels between the Roman poet's exile in Tomis and Carruth's in
rain-drenched Syracuse. And the final poem, a wrenching,
seven-part sequence in memory of the poet's mother, integrates linguistic, historical, and biographical materials
with a son's experience of anguish, juxtaposing reflections
on language ("The Indo-European root *pha,* suggesting
light and clarity, surfaces in *phenomenon,* the thing that
appears, / And also in the Greek for "I say," *phemi,*
thence in *phonation, verb, word . . .*") with horrified impressions of physical decay ("How your pallid, brown-
spotted, wrinkled, half-paralyzed countenance gri-
maced"). The result is not discord but heightened perception—a congruence of sensuous immediacy and intellectual detachment.

For the bulk of these explorations Carruth has adopted a
fluid, expansive, half-prosaic line which, by turns, calls to
mind Whitman, Robinson Jeffers, and C. K. Williams:

    Now I remember Lucinda de Ciella who drank
        a pony of Strega every morning before break-
        fast
    And was sober and beautiful for ninety years, I
        remember her saying how peaceful
    Were the Atlantic crossings by dirigible in the
        1930's when her husband was Ecuadorian am-
        bassador to Bruxelles.
                        "The Incorrigible Dirigible"

He has also employed a richly variegated diction, encompassing American slang ("I just blew fourteen thou . . ."),
colloquial lingos ("Oh, Ammons rolled the octaves
slow"), and arcane vocabularies drawn from science and
philosophy ("Such a magnificent, polychronogeneous
idea"; "unable to conceive any *suppositum* of your predicament"). In the best of these poems, the exact word and
the long line converge, balancing intellectual austerity and
rhythmic abandon:

    For once I will risk the word *zephyr,* which is
        right and which reminds me of *sapphire,*
    And I realize that beneath all these colors lay an
        undertone of blue, the gentle sky as it curls
    Below the penumbra of vision.
                **"A Post-Impressionist Susurration
                    For The First Of November, 1983"**

Not all of Carruth's conjunctions are so pleasing. At
weaker moments, his abstract language drifts into impre-
cision ("Reality is an impasse"), or his scholarly diction
turns pedantic, or the weight of reflection overburdens its
occasion:

    Loving Cindy, on the other hand, is an exercise,
        so-called,
    in metaphysics while the mind is perfectly
        aware,
    For sex would be merely an objective conduct,
        an addiction, without the intellect to discover
        the meanings
    Implicitly always in it.
            "Survival As Tao, Beginning At 5:00 A.M."

But at their finer moments, these poems reflect the melancholy wisdom and the spiritual freedom of a poet who no
longer writes for self-advancement ("Now I write poems
to be read once and forgotten, / Or not to be read at all"),
and who expresses, in the fluent rhythms of his lines, his
heart's most urgent longings:

                    Tell me again
    How the white heron rises from among the reeds
        and flies forever across the nacreous river at
        twilight
    Toward the distant islands.
                **"Of Distress Being Humiliated By The
                    Classical Chinese Poets"**

Ted Solotaroff (essay date 1992)

SOURCE: "One of Us," in *The Nation,* New York, Vol.
55, No. 16, November 16, 1992, pp. 600-05.

[*Solotaroff is an American educator, editor, and critic. In
the following positive review of* Collected Shorter Poems,
1946-1991, *he provides an overview of Carruth's career.*]

In his literary career, Hayden Carruth has been as resourceful and steadfast as the Vermont hill farmers he
lived among for many years. He is a people's poet, readily
understood, a tribune of our common humanity, welfare
and plight. Carruth is also a poet's poet, a virtuoso of form
from the sonnet to free verse, from medieval metrics to
jazz ones. I'm abbreviating: At least half his twenty-three
collections have tended to put aside or recast the molds
of their predecessors.

Carruth has also been, to my mind, the most catholic, reliable and socially relevant critic of poetry we have had in
an age of burgeoning tendencies, collapsing standards and
a general withdrawal of poets from the public to the private sector of consciousness. Further, he has worked as
much in the American grain as any figure of his generation, and his anthology, *The Voice That Is Great Within
Us,* is the best presentation of its poetry that I know of.

But although Carruth's career has been of inestimable
value, his reputation has remained marginal. This is partly
because his varied *oeuvre* eludes the trends and schools
that fix reputations; the spare directness of his work does
not have the aura of big-time postmodern poetry and no
doubt turns off the Blooms and Vendlers and other influ-

ential interpreters and promoters. Nor has he been part of the circuit of readings and conferences, the gossiping and networking that the Poetry Establishment uses to constitute membership and keep score. So the MacArthurs and the poetry chairs, the slots at the American Academy of Arts and Letters and Library of Congress, have passed him by. As with some other notable poets of his generation, the quality crunch in trade publishing has relegated most of his recent work to the small presses. His broad, deep river of criticism has been channeled into small, dispersed reservoirs (*Working Papers,* University of Georgia; *Effluences From the Sacred Caves: More Selected Essays and Reviews,* University of Michigan; *Sitting In: Selected Writings on Jazz, Blues and Related Topics,* University of Iowa). As he would say, "Well, it's a goddam shame." (As I write this I learn that [*Collected Shorter Poems, 1946-1991*] has been selected as a finalist for a National Book Award. *Esperons.*)

Of course, not even seminal writers are promised justice in their lifetime, and there are other reasons why Carruth's career has unfolded in a kind of counter-famous way, from the center to the periphery, from riches to rags. When he was in his late 20s he became the editor of *Poetry* magazine, still the journal of record in the decade after World War II, and a few years after that, he was editing books published by New Directions, which was then at the height of its importance. He was also writing and publishing the kind of culturally ambitious and accomplished poetry that enabled him to win a prominent place among the New Poets, i. e., the generation that came after the modern masters:

> Fortunate land, that Egypt, where
> From time to time the phoenix comes
> And wheels among the temple domes,
> A golden circle in the air, . . .

And so on in its measured, skillful, magisterially nostalgic, Yeatsian way. There are similar traces and echoes of Pound and Williams in the early Carruth of *The Crow and the Heart* (1959). The difficulty is not that the poems in his first collection are derivative, though some are; it is that most of them stand so resolutely apart from the times and man who wrote them that they seem not only autonomous but virtually anonymous, psychologically unsigned. From this kind of practice some art can come but not much reality. I'm thinking not just of **"Cappadocian Song," "The Buddhist Painter Prepares to Paint,"** etc., which are remarkably sensitive transcultural experiments, but of poems like **"Lines Written in an Asylum"** and **"On a Certain Engagement South of Seoul,"** in which the smooth texture and decorum of the poetry work like a scrim over the terror of madness and battle they seek to render. Like most of us in that daunting literary time, Carruth was more sure of the force of his literary values of complexity, order and detachment than he was of the force of his own experience, more aware of his place in the literary community than he was of it in the world.

Well, that was to change, as it had to. In Carruth's case as in some notable others—those of Robert Lowell, John Berryman, Delmore Schwartz, Sylvia Plath, Theodore Roethke, Anne Sexton, Randall Jarrell—he cracked up and was institutionalized. Much has been said and written about the seeming contagion of madness among many of the best poets of the postwar generation, and I have little to add to it, except what I can infer about Carruth from his poetry and prose. Perhaps it is glib to say that the house had to be leveled so that the new road could go through, but that is what I think happened to him. His illness, which was to last in a modified form for the next twenty years and forced him to live an isolated and mostly impoverished life in rural Vermont, must have made the fashion he had first adopted of the autonomous poem and the poet whose identity consists mostly in its refinement seem either like occupational therapy or a terrible joke.

The change is immediately apparent in the difference between **"Lines Written in an Asylum,"** which ends:

> The mind is hapless, torn by dreams
> Where all becoming only seems
> A false, impossible return
> To a world I labor to unlearn.

and **"Ontological Episode of the Asylum,"** written a few years later:

> Many of us in there would have given all
> (But we had nothing) for one small razor blade
> Or seventy grains of the comforting amytal.

In the first lines the poet's suffering has left his persona intact. His mind may be hapless but you wouldn't know it from the firm control of the beat or the thought. In the fashion of the time, he presents his predicament in a tightly wound paradox, but there is little current going through its circuit. In the later poem about the same experience, the persona has lost its gentle airs and graces and been reduced to its membership in the company of the suicidal; the language is nakedly direct in its anguish; the rhyme is as bluntly functional as the overdose. In short, the poetry has become genuinely personal: The language and the experience are inseparable, the one liberating the other from the merely conceptual and rhetorical, the incompletely felt, the secondhand. The poetry has also become real and serious because it changes and indelibly marks our consciousness of its subject.

The poem continues:

> So I went down in the attitude of prayer,
> Yes, to my knees on the cold floor of my cell
> Humped in a corner, a bird with a broken wing,
> And asked and asked as fervently and well
> As I could guess to do for light in the mists
> Of death, until I learned God doesn't care.
> Not only that, he doesn't care at all,
> One way or the other. That is why he exists.

After such knowledge, what detachment? In finding his own voice for his own life—spare, plain, unliterary speech that is even willing to risk cliché because the pain of the lines reactualizes the image of the bird—Carruth also began speaking for his age. One of the reasons that the reign of the autonomous poem came into question is that the idea of art as a higher life, a supreme reality, not unlike the religious one, was hard and dangerous to maintain in an era that was trying to fathom Auschwitz, Hiroshima, the gulag, the cold war. His growing antipathy for this irrealist art became one of the central themes of Carruth's criticism as well as the agent of change in his poetry: Henceforth he tended to praise and practice poetry that accepted the responsibility of immersing itself in the life of its time.

Under the influence of Eliot, Pound, Tate, et al., there had been a marriage of poetry and faith as part of the conservation of high culture against the vulgarity of the age. However, as the supreme reality became that of the frail human figure in a field of lethal and dehumanizing forces, the only recourse for many writers was that of existential engagement by which one accepted the responsibility of creating his or her own freedom, fortifying his or her own selfhood. This of course had a profound effect across the board, from Abstract Expressionism to crisis theology, but it was particularly felt by poets, some later than others, who had been lulled into a kind of spiritual fellow-traveling with their mentors. Lowell's recusancy not only from Catholicism but from the elegance of his first two collections and his re-emergence in *Life Studies* (1959) as an inmate of his life and times in poems like "Memories of West Street and Lepke" is a similar example of the acceptance that is taking place in the rock-bottom paradox of the final lines of Carruth's poem.

In 1963, writing against the self-complete poem, Carruth put the position for topical moral realism about as well as it's ever been put. If it reminds you of Thoreau and Twain as well as Williams, you'll see what I mean in saying that Carruth is one of the hewers of the American grain:

> such self-completeness is only the dream-product of a deeply divisive mania. The truth is that things and ideas and poems are realities among many realities, conformable to the general laws, not opposable in any useful sense. But reality (whatever it is) is intractable, and usually ugly and boring as well, with the result that some people will always try to escape it by one means or another. You can't blame the poets more than the rest. Beyond this, reality consists of Right and Wrong; and since Wrong is by nature always immanent if not ascendant, Right is continually tempted into sanctimony and unction (to say nothing of bigotry), and the effort to resist these temptations is difficult and tedious—another reason for escaping. It is all a misfortune, the whole business, so great a misfortune that people lately have taken to calling it an absurdity. God knows it is absurd. But putting a name on it cannot extricate man from reality, or relieve him, as long as he is alive from the necessity of thinking about it, of having ideas about it.

Carruth's prescription of existential rather than artistic autonomy was one that he had to take himself. His illness, which left a residue of agoraphobia so that he could not teach or give readings, took him away from "the social machine" of poetry from which he'd made his living. He saw that poets were getting by better than before, "provided that they teach, recite, perform, expound, exhibit—in short that they tickle the institutional vanity of the age." He believed that this new version of "the scrimmage of appetites behind the hedges of privilege," in Delmore

Schwartz's phrase, had destroyed the life and much of the work of his friend. In his tribute to Schwartz, he wrote: "I wish that somehow he had gone away when he was about twenty-five, had gone out West perhaps, to live on the desert or in the mountains. He wouldn't have liked it, he was too much a city boy. But if he had been forced to stay until he learned to like it, until he learned to recognize the strength he possessed within himself . . .''

These words were written in 1967. By then Carruth had been living for years on a small farm in Johnson, Vermont, where he supported himself, his wife and son mainly by reviewing books of poetry. During this period I thought he had the hardest life of any well-known writer. But he had also found the strength within that enabled him to be creative in his piece of the real world. Revitalized and stirred by his love for his family, by his attentiveness to the intense phenomenology produced by rock and soil, cows and loons, and by making a place for himself in a community where hardship and usefulness were taken for granted, he also found his master theme. Here is a poem from the early seventies, titled **"The Ravine"**:

> Stones, brown tufted grass, but no water,
> it is dry to the bottom. A seedy eye
> of orange hawkweed blinks in sunlight
> stupidly, a mink bumbles away,
> a ringnecked snake among stones lifts its head
> like a spark, a dead young woodcock—
> long dead, the mink will not touch it—
> sprawls in the hatchment of its soft plumage
> and clutches emptiness with drawn talons.
> This is the ravine today . . .

One notes immediately the all-but-total reliance now upon a hard, clear, natural language that draws heavily upon its Anglo-Saxon origins. Similarly, the steadiness of vision is here not a contrivance of tone but an outcropping of character. Carruth sees the hawkweed, the mink, the snake, the dead young woodcock evenly, holding the subject through its physical mutations: the barely and fully sentient, the harsh and the gentle, the quick and the dead, the hardy and the futile. The figurative language—*spark, bumbles, hatchment*—is so nearfetched that it seems to have its own literalness. This evenness and terseness of vision creates a texture as expectant as a new spiderweb. It looks simple but takes great moral concentration and imaginative strength as well as verbal and syntactical resourcefulness to spin it. Carruth's handling of genuine experience has become like his neighbor Marshall Washer's handling of an ax: "rolling the post / under his foot in the grass: quick strokes and there / is a ringed groove one inch across . . ."

After commenting quickly on the seasonal changes he has seen in the ravine, the geological ones he envisions, Carruth continues:

> . . . These are what I remember and foresee.
> These are what I see here every day,
> not things but relationships of things,
> quick changes and slow. These are my sorrow,
> for unlike my bright admonitory friends
> I see relationships, I do not see things.
> These, such as they are, every day, every
> unique day, the first in time and the last,

are my thoughts, the sequences of my mind.
I wonder what they mean. Every day,
day after day, I wonder what they mean.

The allusion to William Carlos Williams's famous dictum, "No ideas but in things," is not an allusion to him—his tutelary spirit joins Carruth's in the first stanza—but to Williams's "bright admonitory" followers for whom writing poetry is a discrete activity rather than an endless quest for lived meaning. He indicates something of what he means by "relationships" in his essay on Muriel Rukeyser, in which he speaks of lyric poetry as a form of prayer which in a secular age requires an absolute honesty. "Suppose, in the straits of reason and experience, you must deny the supernatural but assert the ultranatural, those extreme susceptivities of consciousness which govern our spiritual and moral lives." In poem after poem in Carruth's middle period there is an ongoing struggle of those extreme susceptivities for the absolutely honest, affirming relationships that can be wrested from "the conspiracy of the natural and the human."

One finds them structuring and empowering a poem like **"August First,"** in which a weary and tattered moth, a drying-up brook and a burgeoning geranium plant growing from a 19-cent seedling present themselves to a poet who quietly tells us he is down to nothing, and then the force of the flower begins to assert itself. Brooding on the relatedness of things, Carruth creates a naturalism of the spirit, and the poems in *From Snow and Rock, From Chaos* (1973), *Dark World* (1974) and culminating in *Brothers, I Loved You All* (1978) form something like an anarchist's bible. There is the missing great elm in the meadow in **"Once and Again"** that evokes Carruth's love of England, a place that he has never seen, and the God "who does not exist"—to believe in whom is "a heroism of faith, much needed in these times." The poem rises in the trumpet of Hopkins, with a New England mute, as it returns to nature:

> . . . To discover and to hold, to
>   resurrect
> an idea for its own sake. Ah my heart,
>   how you quicken in unrecognized
>   energy
> as hard little pellets of snow come
>   stinging, driven on the gray wind.

The deep-down relatedness of things continued to conduct Carruth through his green pastures and his valleys of the shadow. It informs his love poems to Rose Marie, a refugee of the Nazi occupation:

> Liebe, our light rekindled
> in this remoteness from the other land,
> in this dark of the blue mountain where
>   only
> the winds gather
>   is what we are for the time that we are
>   what we know for the time that we
>   know
> How gravely and sweetly the poor
> touch in the dark.

Or again, he draws upon it to summon and mourn the spirit of Paul Goodman. Reading his friend's "sweet and bitter" poems, Carruth suddenly feels the heat of a chunk of beech blazing up in the woodstove of his cabin; he dampens it with a shovel of snow and then goes outside and sees a plume of steam rising "straightly" from the stovepipe: a simple perfect eulogy for another spiritual naturalist. His trust in his sense of relationships when it is absolutely honest enables him to bring off a poem as risky as **"Emergency Haying"**: Hanging onto the side of a haywagon in a cruciform position, his side pierced by kidney pain, Carruth rides in from a brutal day in the fields. This leads to thoughts about forced labor under the Nazis and sugar barons that rise to a furious prophetic note struck in the name of a rehumanized Christ. "My eyes / sting with sweat and loveliness. And who / is the Christ now, who / if not I? . . . woe to you, watch out / you sons of bitches who would drive men and women / to the fields where they can only die."

In the 1980s, being able by then to teach, Carruth was at Syracuse University, where he became a poet of the outskirts—the ruined lakes and fast-food strips, the uprooted values and fading chances of the local blue collars. His work, like his life, had its ups and downs. Whose didn't, in that low decade that was the antithesis of art and spirit? His major work became mostly his love poetry: the greatly ambitious *The Sleeping Beauty* of 1982 (the one book of his I edited), which invokes the troubadour tradition of male feminism and gives it various historical, erotic and ecological settings for both good and evil; also his collection *Sonnets* (1989), which wittily, tenderly, acutely records the arrows to the heart of a late-in-life love affair and which also rejuvenates and tempers the sonnet form. The other three collections of the past ten years seem to me uneven. Perhaps goaded by neglect (particularly of *The Sleeping Beauty,* which I felt he regarded as his masterpiece), he said at one point that from then on he'd write in the way he damn well pleased; but this has sometimes unsprung his structure and line and taken some of the finish off his texture, i. e., his sense of significance. A number of the character studies and narratives of bar and diner life around Liverpool, New York, don't have as much moral and emotional resonance as their earlier Vermont "cowshit farmer" counterparts: the indomitably capable and doomed Marshall Washer; the morally androgynous "Lady" who both farms and nurses in the state hospital; the aphasic Marvin McCabe, the pathos of whose life becomes so eloquent in Carruth's liberation of his near-strangled voice and feelings. Carruth's gift of empathic intelligence and natural language seems to be too readily proffered in the life-story poems in *Asphalt Georgics* and *The Oldest Killed Lake in North America* (both 1985). Also, the depressed element that he could earlier manage to hold in solution with his other extreme susceptivities of consciousness tends to precipitate out into the bitter sediment of the Septic Tank poems and others.

We can infer from Carruth's recent essay on suicide that there were some terrible years in which any poem he could manage to finish was a gift and its publication a confirmation. I can wish he had done more winnowing in selecting from the recent collections and the new poems. But part of the purpose and justice of the spacious *Collected Shorter Poems* is to allow a poet as exacting and undervalued as Carruth generally has been to receive a full hearing, as well as to commemorate his continuing efforts to reconstitute himself. That the Copper Canyon Press people, who are otherwise to be congratulated for producing such an ample, handsome and affordable book, have scrambled the Table of Contents seems like a final reminder of the grimly mixed and contingent conditions of this career and quest.

Carruth says somewhere that his father, the editor of a socialist newspaper, once told him never to take a job that wasn't socially useful. Well, if there is a social use for poetry, this is the man whose poetry and criticism have embodied and husbanded it. As he said of William Carlos Williams, Carruth has been, more than any other poet of our time, "one of us, committed to our life, our reality, our enigma."

FURTHER READING

Criticism

Davison, Peter. "Poets of Exile and Isolation." *The Washington Post Book World* XVI, No. 15 (13 April 1986): 6-7.
    Lauds Carruth's compassion and treatment of the human condition in *The Selected Poetry of Hayden Carruth*.

Flint, R. W. "The Odyssey of Hayden Carruth." *Parnassus: Poetry in Review* 11, No. 1 (Spring-Summer 1983): 17-32.
    Surveys *The Sleeping Beauty* and *Working Papers*, and

asserts that Carruth is "a writer so well endowed with character, courage, stamina, honesty, and independence as to make whatever styles he has adopted or adapted peculiarly his own."

McClatchy, J. D. "Labyrinth and Clue." *The Nation* 236, No. 5 (5 February 1983): 148-51.
    Brief positive assessment of *The Sleeping Beauty* in which McClatchy comments: "Carruth has fashioned a rich, complex poem on a human scale."

Oliver, Mary. "Gathering Light." *The Kenyon Review* VIII, No. 3 (Summer 1986): 129-35.
    Responds positively to *Asphalt Georgics*, asserting: "In a time when the poems of many poets are frighteningly similar in style, it is salutory and important to find work that strikes out in a different direction."

Shaw, Robert B. Review of *The Selected Poetry of Hayden Carruth*, by Hayden Carruth. *Poetry* CXLIX, No. 2 (November 1986): 98-100.
    Mixed review of *The Selected Poetry of Hayden Carruth* in which Shaw remarks: "Warts and all, this is a collection animated by a seriousness of purpose, a vocational commitment which few poets nowadays can match."

Swiss, Thomas. " 'I Have Made This Song': Hayden Carruth's Poetry and Criticism." *The Sewanee Review* XCIII, No. 1 (Winter 1985): 149-57.
    Surveys several of Carruth's collections of poetry and criticism, and lauds the author for his technical skill and his earnest and straightforward approach to writing both poetry and criticism.

Additional coverage of Carruth's life and career is contained in the following sources published by Gale Research: *Contemporary Authors*, Vols. 9-12 (rev. ed.), 126; *Contemporary Authors New Revision Series*, Vols. 4, 38; *Contemporary Literary Criticism*, Vols. 4, 7, 10, 18; *Dictionary of Literary Biography*, Vol. 5; *Major 20th-Century Writers*; and *Something about the Author*, Vol. 47.

Paul Celan

1920-1970

(Born Paul Antschel) Romanian-born poet, essayist, and translator.

INTRODUCTION

Celan is regarded as among the most important poets to emerge from Europe after World War II and, with Rainer Maria Rilke, is widely considered the finest German lyric poet of the twentieth century. Often described as obscure and hermetic, his inventive poetry reveals the influences of symbolism, Expressionism, Surrealism, and Hasidic mysticism, and is deeply concerned with the Jewish experience of the Holocaust. Rika Lesser commented: "Celan's language—peculiar, idiosyncratic, transformational, at times almost incomprehensible—seems the only one capable of absorbing and expressing a world changed by the Holocaust. His language and poetry issue from the urgent need to communicate, to speak the truth that lies in deeply ambiguous metaphors."

Biographical Information

Celan was born in Czernowitz, the capital of the Romanian province of Bukovina, to German-speaking Jewish parents. As a youth, he became proficient in several languages, including Hebrew and French. After beginning premedical studies in France, Celan returned home prior to the outbreak of World War II and witnessed the Soviet occupation of his hometown. His parents were captured and died shortly after the German invasion of Czernowitz in 1941, and Celan himself was interned for eighteen months in a Nazi labor camp. The anguish and grief Celan experienced during this period informed his verse throughout his career. In 1944, for example, he wrote "Todesfuge" ("Death Fugue"), a lyric piece which has been lauded by some critics as one of the most powerful holocaust poems ever written. Celan left Czernowitz in 1945 for Bucharest, where he joined a circle of surrealist artists, befriended leading Romanian writers, and worked as a reader and translator for a publishing house. Following a brief period in Vienna, where he associated with a group of avant-garde artists, Celan settled in Paris and began studies in German philology and literature. He received his *Licence des Lettres* in 1950, and in 1952 he married the graphic artist Gisèle de Lestrange, with whom he had a son in 1955. In 1959 Celan became a professor of German Language and Literature at L'École Normale Superieure, a position he held until his death. Celan committed suicide in 1970 by drowning himself in the Seine River.

Major Works

Characterized by rhythmical repetition and surrealistic imagery, Celan's first two poetry collections, *Der Sand aus*

den Urnen (1948) and *Mohn und Gedächtnis* (1952), combine paradox, negation, and intricate word association to convey the psychological trauma suffered by survivors of Nazi atrocities. With his next volume, *Von Schwelle zu Schwelle* (1955), Celan became increasingly concerned with the nature of poetic language—a theme which distinguished his poetry throughout his career. In *Sprachgitter* (1959), for example, he employed ruptured syntax, unusual diction, enigmatic imagery, and condensed lines to address the inability of language to genuinely convey profound misery. The persecution and suffering that Jews have endured throughout history is the subject of *Die Niemandsrose* (1963), which presents a negative theology—a study of God in terms of what He is not—derived from Jewish and Christian mysticism. The longer lines and rhyme in this collection are reminiscent of the comparatively traditional style of his early volume *Mohn und Gedächtnis*. In *Atemwende* (1967) Celan turned from Jewish subject matter to focus again on the nature of poetic language. His last three volumes, *Fadensonnen* (1968), *Lichtzwang* (1970), and *Schneepart* (1971), are progressively cryptic and fragmented, qualities some critics interpret as reflecting the poet's search for new ways to express the ineffable horrors of the Holocaust. Many of Celan's poems have been translated and published in such collections as *Selected Poems* (1972), *Paul Celan: Poems* (1980), and *Last Poems* (1986).

Critical Reception

Celan has been praised by many critics for virtually inventing a new poetic language to describe an unspeakable episode in history. The difficulty of interpreting and translating his cryptic poetry has been the subject of extensive discussion, with many critics concluding that the obscurity of his verse is a necessary product of its mysticism and varied literary, theological, and linguistic allusions. Commenting on *Last Poems*, Reginald Gibbons stated: "[These poems] are not joyful, nor erotic, nor often textured with either the reality of the physical world or that of social relations or politics; they are therefore not very 'accessible.' . . . They offer not a revelation of their meaning but rather a containment of it—as if protecting it." Some critics, however, have disputed the critical emphasis on the esoteric nature of Celan's poetry, arguing that his writings are informed by social and historical reality rather than personal concerns. J. M. Cameron, for example, commented: "From the collection *die Niemandsrose* to his death in 1970 Celan's poetry becomes more fragmentary and obscure. It is often sharply beautiful, but it has seemed to some critics to have sense only in relation to a private world. . . . [Celan's obscurity] is rather the sign of an attempt to work into his poetry, in his own idiom, material that belongs to the harsh public world. He is not—he protested he was not—a hermetic poet."

PRINCIPAL WORKS

Poetry

Der Sand aus den Urnen   1948
Mohn und Gedächtnis   1952
Von Schwelle zu Schwelle   1955
Gedichte: Eine Auswahl   1959
Sprachgitter   1959
Die Niemandsrose   1963
Gedichte   1966
Atemwende   1967
Ausgewählte Gedichte: Zwei Reden   1968
Fadensonnen   1968
Ausgewählte Gedichte   1970
Lichtzwang   1970
Schneepart   1971
Speech-grille, and Selected Poems   1971
Nineteen Poems   1972
Selected Poems   1972
Gedichte: In zwei Bänden. 2 vols.   1975
Zeitgehöft: Späte Gedichte aus dem Nachlaß   1976
Paul Celan: Poems 1980; also published as *Poems of Paul Celan* [revised and enlarged edition],   1988
Gesammelte Werke in fünf Bänden. 5 vols.   1983
Todesfuge   1984
Gedichte: 1938-1944   1985

65 Poems   1985
Last Poems   1986
Das Frühwerk   1987

Other Major Works

Edgar Jené und der Traum vom Traume [*Edgar Jené and the Dream of the Dream*]   (essays)   1948
Der meridian: Rede anläßlich der Verleihung des Georg-Büchner-Preises, Darmstadt, am 22. Oktober 1960 ["The Meridian" published in *Paul Celan: Prose Writings and Selected Poems*, 1977 and *Collected Prose*, 1987]   (essay)   1961
Paul Celan: Prose Writings and Selected Poems   (prose and poetry)   1977
Collected Prose   (essays and dialogues)   1987

CRITICISM

Michael Hamburger   (essay date 1979)

SOURCE: An introduction, in *Poems of Paul Celan*, translated by Michael Hamburger, Persea Books, 1980, pp. 17-32.

[*Hamburger is a German-born English poet, translator, and critic who is recognized as an outstanding interpreter of German poetry for English readers. His translations in* Poems of Paul Celan *are highly praised. In the following excerpt from his introduction to this work, he offers an analysis of Celan's use of language and explains his approach to translating several major poems by Celan.*]

From whatever direction we approach it—as plain readers of poetry, as critics or literary historians, as biographers or sociologists, or as translators—Paul Celan's work confronts us with difficulty and paradox. The more we try to concentrate on the poem itself, on its mode of utterance, which includes both theme and manner, the more we are made aware that difficulty and paradox are of its essence. As for "placing" his work within the body of German imaginative literature after 1945, or against the larger background of international modernism, all we can be certain of at this point is that it occupies a prominent, isolated, and anomalous position. With Nelly Sachs this German poet, born of a Jewish family in Romania, shared an obvious pre-occupation with the mass killings he had physically survived but could never recover from; and a not so obvious immersion in Jewish history and religious—especially mystical—tradition. Yet, apart from their differences in poetic practice, Nelly Sachs had been a German poet before persecution turned her into a Jewish one. Like other assimilated German Jews, she had to look for her Jewish roots—with the help of Gentile friends, as it happened. Celan, too, had written juvenile poems in German before he was marked for life by the events of the war years—a facsimile edition of Celan's holograph collection of such poems written between 1938 and 1944 was published in 1985—but the inception of his characteristic work dates from the news of his mother's violent death, reported to him in the winter of 1943.

Paul Celan spent his formative years in a Jewish community that had recently ceased to be within the frontiers of the Austrian Empire; and most of his productive years were spent in France. His poetic affinities were French, Romanian, Russian and English, as well as German and Austrian. Among his German-language contemporaries, those closest to him in sensibility and manner—though that is not saying much—were Johannes Bobrowski, a resident in East Berlin with distinctly Christian allegiances, and the West German poet Ernst Meister. Like them, Celan can be seen as continuing a line of development in German poetry that runs from Klopstock and Hölderlin in the eighteenth century to the later Rilke and Georg Trakl, at a time when the dominant trends in both Germanys were adverse to that line. Bobrowski is on record as disliking and rejecting Celan's later work; but he included two poems of Celan's middle years in the anthology of his favourite German poems he compiled for his own use, with no obligation or reason, therefore, to make it representative. (This anthology was published posthumously in 1985 as *Meine liebsten Gedichte.*) The affinity, as far as it goes, could be real even if neither Bobrowski nor Meister had acknowledged it. Yet it offers no significant point of entry into Celan's work. Literary scholars are still in the process of tracing Celan's imagery to the books he read, the life he led, the places he visited, of unravelling his complex concerns and uncovering the sources of many seemingly cryptic allusions in his poems. . . .

Much of Celan's later poetry can be intuitively grasped, but not rendered in another language, without as much knowledge as possible of his sources; and any help a translator can get from scholars makes it that much more penetrable. Yet it is as a translator, too, that I insist on the essential difficulty and paradox of his poetry. These can be illumined, but not resolved or dissolved, by scholarly research. It is the difficulty and the paradox that demand a special attention to every word in his texts, and this attention is something other than what is normally meant by "understanding". I am by no means sure that I have "understood" even those of his poems—a small proportion of his output—which I have been able to translate over the years; but every time I return to his poems, with or without the help offered by their interpreters, this or that poem, left untranslated before, suddenly becomes translatable. This has to do with the precision and reliability of Celan's later work. Despite the "darkness" that belongs to it, necessarily and genetically, despite the characteristic leaps and bounds of his poems, their haltingness and their silences, nothing in them is slapdash or vague, nothing is meaningless, nothing has been left to chance or to merely emotive gestures. What makes them difficult is the terrain itself—a terrain in which milk is black, death is the all-encompassing reality—not the nature of its charting.

Paul Antschel—then Ancel, then Celan, an anagram adopted in 1947, when his first poems appeared in a Romanian periodical—was born at Czernowitz (now Chernovtsy) in Bukovina on 23 November 1920. After his schooling there, he paid his first visit to France in 1938 as a medical student at Tours, but returned to his home town in the following year to study Romance languages and literatures. In June 1940 Czernowitz was occupied by Soviet troops, but Celan was able to continue his studies until 1941, when German and Romanian forces occupied the region and the Jews were herded into a ghetto. At this period he learned Russian and began to translate poems by Yesenin. In the summer of 1942 his parents were deported to an internment camp in Transnistria, where his father died of typhus and his mother was murdered later by a shot in the neck. Paul Celan managed to escape arrest until conscripted for labour service in Southern Moldavia, where he worked on road building. On a short leave to Czernowitz he stayed with his grandfather, then with the parents of his friend Edith Horowitz. In February 1944 the Romanian labour camp was dissolved, and Celan returned to Bukovina, which had been re-occupied by the Soviets and annexed to the Ukraine. For a time he is reported to have worked as a "field surgeon" in a psychiatric unit. Then he took up his studies again until April 1945, when he left the Soviet Union for Bucharest, working as a publisher's reader and translator of Russian texts into Romanian. (It was then that he adopted the spelling "Ancel" for his surname.) In December 1947 he succeeded in leaving Romania illegally for Vienna, but stayed there only until July of the following year. After the publication in Austria of his first book of poems, *Der Sand aus den Urnen,* which he withdrew because of the many misprints it contained, he settled in Paris, where he took up the study of German literature. In 1950 he obtained his "Licence" and became a lecturer in German literature at the École Normale Supérieure. After his marriage in 1952 to the graphic artist Gisèle Lestrange—who contributed etchings to several limited editions of poems by Celan—Paris remained his home until his suicide by drowning in the Seine in April 1970, at the age of forty-nine. The death in infancy of their first son, François, is commemorated in a poem included [in *Poems of Paul Celan*]. Celan's second son, Eric, survived his father.

Most of the poems in the rejected first collection, *Der Sand aus den Urnen,* were reprinted in *Mohn und Gedächtnis,* which appeared in West Germany in 1952 and won him immediate recognition, confirmed by an invitation to read at the annual gathering of the "Gruppe 47" in the same year. Celan's next collection *Von Schwelle zu Schwelle* followed in 1955. Between 1957 and 1967, Celan received a number of prizes, including the prestigious Georg Büchner Prize (awarded by the German Academy for Language and Literature, Darmstadt) in 1960. A speech delivered by Celan on that occasion, "Der Meridian", [published in *Collected Prose*], is one of the very few prose pieces he published and his nearest approach, in terms hardly less idiosyncratic than the practice on which it comments, to a manifesto of his aims as a poet.

With the publication of *Sprachgitter* (1959) and *Die Niemandsrose* (1963), Celan's work moved into a second phase. These two central collections marked the height of his undisputed acclaim in the German-speaking world. For reasons that have to do not only with his subsequent development but with the almost exclusively political and social interests that became predominant in West German literature in the later sixties and early seventies, fewer and fewer of his readers and critics were prepared to follow him into what they regarded as the increasingly private world of his later poetry. His next books, *Atemwende* and *Fadensonnen,* had a mixed reception; and so did his three posthumous collections, *Lichtzwang, Schneepart* and *Zeitgehöft.*

Throughout his working life Celan was also active as a translator. His many translations from the French included poetry by Rimbaud, Valéry, Apollinaire, Michaux, Char, André du Bouchet, and Jean Daive. From the English he translated sonnets by Shakespeare and poems by Emily Dickinson and Marianne Moore; from the Russian, selections of poems by Blok, Yesenin, and Mandelstam. During his stay in Bucharest he had produced translations into Romanian of Russian prose works.

These basic facts of Celan's life—. . . very few biographical documents have been released for publication—may indicate something of the anomaly and extremity of his position as a poet. What the facts do not reveal, and his productivity may seem to belie, is that the loss of his parents and his early experience of persecution left indelible scars. Throughout his later years, he suffered acute crises and breakdowns that affected both his personal and his professional life. One such crisis occurred soon after his emergence as a poet, when Claire Goll, the widow of the Franco-German poet Yvan Goll, with whom Celan had become personally acquainted in 1949, accused Celan of having plagiarized Goll's work. Since Celan's early poems linked up with both German Expressionism and French Surrealism, movements with which Goll had been associated, certain stylistic features were bound to be common to the two poets. If Celan had not been predisposed towards paranoia, the foolish and protracted public controversies that ensued could not have hurt him; as it was, Claire Goll's maniacal accusations, renewed even after Celan's death and right up to her own, obsessed and unbalanced him. I recall a meeting with Celan when he was similarly obsessed with the "treachery" of one of his publishers, who had decided to reissue the poems of a ballad-writer popular during the Nazi régime. Towards the end of his life, the crises became more violent and more disruptive.

Paul Celan had no wish to be a confessional poet, except in so far as all poets are confessional, because they must be true to their own experience. Even in the early **"Death Fugue"**, his most famous and most widely anthologized poem, the personal anguish was transposed into distancing imagery and a musical structure so incompatible with reportage that a kind of "terrible beauty" is wrested from the ugly theme. Realists and literalists among Celan's critics were to object to his "aestheticizing" of the death camps. Yet the power and pathos of the poem arises from the extreme tension between its grossly impure material and its pure form. The impossibility of writing poems after Auschwitz, let alone about Auschwitz, has become a critical commonplace. Celan knew that even he could not hope to do so directly, realistically, but only by an art of contrast and allusion that celebrates beauty and energy while commemorating their destruction. Though he turned against his **"Death Fugue"** in later years, refusing permission to have it reprinted in more anthologies, that was because he had refined his art in the meantime to a point

where the early poem seemed too direct, too explicit. Meanwhile, he had also found a place for ugliness in his poems—but in poems that were judged to be private and "hermetic". Yet the anguish, the darkness, the shadow of death are present in all his work, early and late, including the most high-spirited and sensuous.

The aspiration towards a pure or "absolute" poetry was pervasive in France after Mallarmé, among poets of almost every school, and it was not necessarily thought to be incompatible with political or moral commitments. Like Paul Eluard and René Char, of the French poets to whom Celan felt close, Celan resisted the constraint to sacrifice the freedom of his art to an "engagement" outside or beyond it. Celan's religious, ethical, or political commitments could become explicit at times, as in his poem in memory of Eluard, but more often they had to remain implicit. At his most difficult, most elliptic and paradoxical, he insisted that he was not a hermetic poet but one out to communicate, describing his poems as "ways of a voice to a receptive you", a "desperate dialogue", and "a sort of homecoming". Another way of putting it is that his poetry never ceased to be rooted in experience, extreme experience that could not be enacted in any manner less difficult than his. The hiatuses, the silences, the dislocations of normal usage belong to what he had to say and to the effort of saying it.

If Celan had set out to write hermetic poems, his work would be less difficult than it is, because it would not require us to make the kind of sense of it that we know it can yield. That is why his earlier verse, though purer, is less difficult than the later. Any reader familiar with the kind of poetry whose progression is one of imagery rather than argument will know how to read the earlier poems, whose diction, too, is closer to established conventions. From *Sprachgitter* onwards the images grow sparser, more idiosyncratic, and more laden with conflict, the syntax more broken, the message at once more urgent and more reticent. The available resources of language and prosody become inadequate. Celan begins to coin new words, especially compound words, and to divide other words into their component syllables, each of which acquires a new weight. The process of condensation and dislocation is carried farther in the subsequent collections. Both verse lines and whole poems tend to be shorter and shorter.

One exception, the longer poem, **"The Straitening"**, both records and exemplifies the change. Its German title, **"Engführung"**, is a technical term for a device employed in the composition of fugues. Its counterpart in English usage would have been the Italian word *stretto,* "an artifice by which the subject and answer are, as it were, bound closer together, by being made to overlap" . . . This title recalls the precedent of Celan's earlier **"Death Fugue"**, and a comparison between the two poems shows just how daring, cryptic, and spare Celan's manner had become in the interjacent thirteen years. Although the form of the later poem is an even closer approximation to fugal composition with words—an impossibility, of course, because words cannot be counterpointed if they are to remain intelligible—[in *Poems of Paul Celan*] I decided not to use the technical term for the title. (The French translation by Jean Daive, which was authorized by Celan, does use the technical term, *Strette*.) A German reader of the original text not versed in specialized musical terminology would take the title more literally as a "narrowing down" or "reduction"; and since this wider, more general and more revealing connotation would not be conveyed by the strictly musical term, I looked for an English word that would at least suggest it. Ambiguity, in any case, occurs throughout the poem; and since Celan took every word as literally as possible, often breaking it down etymologically in the manner of Heidegger, one of his reasons for choosing the German word must have been that it characterized not only the structure of his poem but its theme as well, the development that drove Celan himself into his narrowest bounds and his utmost intensity.

The later poems included in my selection are those not rendered totally untranslatable by polysemy—to use an ugly neologism more accurate than "ambiguity"—play on words, or a degree of uncertainty as to what the poem is about that would have made translation little more than guesswork. It was a question not of whether I could catch this allusion or that—many must have escaped me even in poems that I did translate—but whether I could respond to the gesture of the poem as a whole. If the gesture of the poem came home to me, the oddities of diction and usage, including the ambiguities, could usually be conveyed in English, with certain modifications due to the different characters of the two languages. German, for instance, lends itself to the formation of compound words in a way that English does not. German verbs, too, can be given new directions, new functions, by combining them freely with prepositions like "in", "through", "into", "around", "after",—a freedom by which the later Rilke had profited as greatly as Celan did after him. German also permits nouns to be preceded by complete clauses that qualify them, a peculiarity of the language that was especially congenial to Celan when the movement of his poem had come to be governed by breath units rather than metrical or syntactical units:

> Und du:
> du, du, du
> mein täglich wahr—und wahrer—
> geschundenes Später
> der Rosen—:

where the German capitalization of nouns helps to bring out that the adverb "später" has been turned into a noun. This had to be transposed as follows:

> And you:
> you, you, you
> my later of roses
> daily worn true and
> more true—:

A structurally faithful rendering would have demanded:

> And you:
> you, you, you
> my daily true—and truer—
> worn later
> of (the) roses—:

with the additional substitution of a stronger word than

"worn" to convey the sense of abuse and maltreatment contained in the German word "geschunden".

Those lines are from a poem of Celan's middle period. More puzzling innovations abound in the later collections, as in this short poem, **"Once"**:

> ONCE
> I heard him,
> he was washing the world,
> unseen, nightlong,
> real.
>
> One and Infinite,
> annihilated,
> ied.
>
> Light was. Salvation.

The German word corresponding to "ied" is "ichten". Since it comes after "vernichtet" (annihilated) it could be the infinitive of a verb that is the positive counterpart of "annihilate", and that is how it was construed by a reviewer for *The Times Literary Supplement,* who translated it as "ihilate". This new verb would not be more far-fetched than other neologisms of Celan's, since in the Middle High German, which he knew, there was a positive "iht" (ought) corresponding to the negative "niht" (nought). My authority for "ied" is Paul Celan himself. When I last met him, in April 1968, he was convinced that I was the author of the anonymous *TLS* review and would not accept my repeated denial. He explained that "ichten" was formed from the personal pronoun "ich", so that it was the third person plural of the imperfect tense of a verb "ichen", (to i).

An equally ambiguous word formation occurs in the poem **"Etched away"**, but Celan did not comment on the translation offered by the same reviewer of *Atemwende.* I refer to

> . . . das hundert-
> züngige Mein-
> gedicht, das Genicht.

rendered there as

> . . . the hundred-
> tongued my-
> poem, the noem.

"Mein-gedicht" could indeed mean "my-poem", but it could also mean "false poem" or "pseudo-poem", by analogy with the German word "Meineid", a false oath. Probably Celan had both senses in mind when he coined the word. In this case translation had to resolve the ambiguity, and after much pondering I decided in favour of "pseudo-poem", although "Meineid" is the only modern German word that retains this sense of "mein". Paul Celan was a learned poet with an outstandingly rich vocabulary derived more from reading than from practice in the vernacular—inevitably, considering how little time he spent in German-speaking countries. The retention of that root in a single modern word is the kind of thing that would have struck and intrigued him no less than the ambiguity of "my" and "false" in that syllable.

Celan's interest in Yiddish usage also brought him up

against the medieval roots of the German language. Like other twentieth-century poets, such as W. H. Auden or Francis Ponge, he must have been fascinated by dictionaries, especially etymological ones. What is certain is that he both loved and mistrusted words to a degree that has to do with his anomalous position as a poet born in a German-speaking enclave that had been destroyed by the Germans. His German could not and must not be the German of the destroyers. That is one reason why he had to make a new language for himself, a language at once probing and groping, critical and innovative; and why the richer his verbal and formal resources grew, the more strictly he confined them to the orbit of his most urgent concerns.

These permitted no separation of Celan's personal experience from the larger implications it held for him, no convenient division into a private and public *persona.* That is why a full documentation of Celan's life is needed for the elucidation of many of his later poems—and why he was perfectly right to insist that he was not a hermetic poet. ("Ganz und gar nicht hermetisch"—"absolutely not hermetic"—are his words in the copy of **Die Niemandsrose** he inscribed for me.) An interpretation of a late poem of Celan's by the distinguished critic Peter Szondi—who was close to Celan and followed him into suicide soon after writing the essay in question, "Eden", in 1971—unlocks the imagery of that poem only by virtue of knowing what Celan saw, read, and talked about on his visit to Berlin in December 1967. The poem **"Du liegst"** from **Schneepart** combines allusions to the murder of Karl Liebknecht and Rosa Luxemburg, and the throwing of Rosa Luxemburg's corpse into the Landwehrkanal—a political theme, that is—with details of Christmas street scenes that had struck Celan during his visit. Szondi's elucidation of the double or triple meanings of the operative words in that poem might have enabled me to translate it, but not to make those meanings accessible to English-language readers without notes; and one link in the triple rhyme of the poem—"Schweden-Eden-jeden"—could not be reproduced in English. So I chose not to translate the poem.

Another late poem, included here, makes a more public and explicit connection between historical events separated by nearly two millennia. It is **"Think of It"**, from **Fadensonnen.** The poem not only associates, but fuses, the last attempt of the Jews to hold out against the Romans at Massada in 70 A.D., which ended with the suicide of those besieged in the fortress there, with the Prussian concentration camp at Börgermoor, whose inmates composed the song known as the "Börgermoor-Lied". This song gave them a sense of group identity, in the teeth of group extermination, and was finally adopted even by the German guards at the camp. Celan's poem, then, celebrates the only kind of victory—a moral one—available to the defenders of Massada and the inmates of Börgermoor; and it was characteristic of him to do so not by comparing and explaining the two events but by presenting them as a dual event, in his own, most intimately personal, terms. Celan chose not to help his readers by providing clues to any of his poems in the form of notes. Very few of his German readers, for instance, could possibly be expected to know that Mapesbury Road—the title of another late poem—is a street in north-west London where Celan used to visit

a surviving relative, his father's sister, who is addressed in the poem.

To understand the poem **"Todtnauberg"** (from **Lichtzwang**) we have to know that its title is the name of the place where Martin Heidegger lived; and that Celan found it possible to maintain an intense intellectual relationship with Heidegger despite the philosopher's notorious record of public support for the Hitler régime, and Heidegger's adamant refusal, right up to his death, to take back one word he had spoken or written in praise of the régime. Celan's poem enacts his hope that Heidegger might, after all, speak the word that would acknowledge the survivor's wound—an act of atonement, if not of healing, since Celan's wound could not be healed. As ever, the enactment is an indirect, symbolic one, conveyed in images of the well, the wild flowers, and the book. The plant whose English name is "eyebright" or "euphrasy" is called "Augentrost" (literally "eyecomfort") in German; and the significance of eyes and seeing in Celan's poetry needs no comment. The flower's name alone gives the botanical reality—and Celan had been a keen practical botanist since his early youth—its full poetic charge. (In medieval times the plant was used to cure diseases of the eye.) The book of the poem is Heidegger's visitors' book, with entries going back to the period in question between the two men. Celan's entry in the book is an intimation of his hope, but for which he could not have inscribed the book at all. As ever, too, each tiniest detail in the poem is meaningful, though the meaning is one that lies in the complex and subtle interactions between literal data and their symbolic extension.

Literalists could object that in one of Celan's last poems, **"Die Posaunenstelle"**, I have mistranslated "Posaune" ("trombone") as "trumpet". Again it is a matter not of literal rendering but of interpretation. An interpretation of this poem by Bernhard Böschenstein has shown that it alludes to the "seven angels which had the seven trumpets" in Revelations 8. In the Lutheran German Bible those trumpets are trombones, but the allusion—cryptic enough, as it is—would be totally obscured by a literal rendering in English. For the same reason Celan's "Fackel" ("torch") in that poem is rendered as "lamp": "And the third angel sounded, and there fell a great star from heaven, burning as it were a lamp, and it fell upon the third part of the rivers, and upon the fountains of waters"—where Luther's version has a torch instead of a lamp. These allusions are crucial. Amongst other things they mark the apocalyptic extremities that Celan's negative theology had reached, and the extent to which his preoccupations bore on Christian, as well as Jewish, tradition. Even here the negation—the "lacuna" or "time hole"—is not absolute. There is a suggestion that the emptiness can and must be filled.

Negation is a strikingly recurrent feature not only of Celan's new word formations but of his later poetry in general. The seemingly negative theology of his great poem **"Psalm"** has been shown to have antecedents in both Jewish and Christian mysticism, and Celan is known to have been well versed in both. Less explicitly than in **"Psalm"**, something of this theology is prefigured even in very early poems, as is the related dialectic of light and darkness that runs through all of Celan's work. Celan's religion—and there can be no doubt as to his profoundly religious sensibility, whatever he may have believed or not believed—had to come to grips with the experience of being God-forsaken. Negation and blasphemy were the means by which Celan could be true to that experience and yet maintain the kind of intimate dialogue with God characteristic of Jewish devotion.

At the same time negation and paradox served him as a basic stylistic principle, as expounded in the early poem **"Speak, You Also"**. In that poem he exhorts himself to "keep yes and no unsplit", to admit enough darkness into his poems, because "he speaks truly who speaks the shade." With its dialectic of light and dark, life and death, this poem anticipates the whole of Celan's subsequent development, as well as linking the formal aspects of that development—the reduction carried farther from book to book—with the inner necessity from which they arose: "Thinner you grow, less knowable, finer." This applies to the poems as much as to the poet; and so does the star image, towards the end of the poem, that stands for the urge towards transcendence and resolution of paradox present in Celan's work right up to the posthumous collections.

One thing sets Paul Celan's work apart from that of most of his German coevals: he had hardly any use for realism of a kind that merely imitates and reproduces, for what Northrop Frye has called "the low mimetic". Direct social comment is not to be found in his work, though it became increasingly realistic in a different sense—the widening of its vocabulary to include twentieth-century phenomena and technologies. From *Die Niemandsrose* onwards, invective becomes prominent in Celan's poems, though the invective is as rich in cryptic allusions and intricate wordplay as every other mode that he employed. He was realistic, too, in doing full justice to "the foul rag-and-bone shop of the heart". Yet he was never satisfied with mere reportage. As a very short late poem attests, he found Brecht's poetry of social and political comment too "explicit". One reason is that he wanted poetry to be open to the unexpected, the unpredictable, the unpredeterminable. His poems were "messages in a bottle", as he said, which might or might not be picked up. That element of risk was as necessary to them as the need to communicate. On the few occasions when he spoke about poetry in public he spoke of it as a process, a groping forward, a search. Paradoxically, once more, he spoke of its practice, and the practice of any art, as a driving of the practitioner into the "inmost recess of himself", his narrowest place, and as a "setting free". It is this peculiarity I had in mind when choosing not to translate his title **"Engführung"** as "Stretto".

No feature of Celan's later poems is more characteristic of their openness and mysteriousness than their unidentified personal pronouns, the "you" that can be the woman addressed in a love poem or an alter ego or a deity or only the amorphous, unknowable "other" to whom all Celan's poems make their way; the "he", "she", or "they" that enters a poem without any introduction or identification. Many of these persons may have no existence or signifi-

cance outside the poem. It is the poem that creates them or discovers them. A reader can either relate himself to them through his own experience and imagination or he can not, in which case the "message in the bottle" has not reached him. If it does reach him it will tell him something of which he was not aware before reading it. That is the distinction of poetry like Celan's, poetry always close to the unutterable because it has passed through it and come out on the other side.

Such poetry demands a special kind of attention and perhaps a special kind of faith in the authenticity of what it enacts. Without the same attention and faith it could not have been written, for the risk is shared by writer and reader. Speaking about poetry, Celan quoted this definition by Malebranche: "Attention is the natural prayer of the soul." I neither know nor consider it my business to know what Celan believed. It is this quality of attention in his poems that points to a religious sensibility. The more we read his poems, the more his kind of attention proves to be the only adequate response to them.

John Felstiner   (essay date 1987)

SOURCE: " '*Ziv,* That Light': Translation and Tradition in Paul Celan," in *The Craft of Translation,* edited by John Biguenet and Rainer Schulte, The University of Chicago Press, 1989, pp. 93-116.

[*In the essay excerpted below, which originated as a presentation to the Stanford Humanities Center narrative theory seminar and was first published in the Spring 1987 issue of* New Literary History, *Felstiner closely examines Celan's use of language in several poems, noting the influence of the poet's multilingualism.*]

Recently a letter of Paul Celan's from 1954 came to light, in which he admitted "shame and sadness" at having to abandon the project of translating Rilke and Gide's French correspondence into German. [See "Three letters," in *Sulfur,* Vol. 11, 1984]. Celan had wanted to begin "only after reading and re-reading Rilke's German letters," he said. But "this language can't simply be translated, it must be *translocated*" (*ubersetzt . . . ubergesetzt*). "I have hesitated for an unpardonably long time," Celan said, "translating and retranslating—with the unfortunate result that my doubts increased with each attempt." He hoped this correspondence would find its way into hands that have "no need to page endlessly through Rilke's German works before deciding to use this word or that; hands that can replace a semicolon with a period without hesitation."

Considering that Celan, with his wife Gisèle Lestrange, an artist, was living off such commissions at the time in Paris, and badly needed the money (shortly afterwards he did two novels by Simenon), his scruples over Rilke speak all the more tellingly. They presume for translation an exhaustive sense of the entire oeuvre combined with a painstaking intimacy, all subject to the trials of revision and open at the same time to the venture of "translocation."

If Rilke's French letters daunted him in the early fifties—as well they might, since he would be translating them into

Rilke's own language—Celan still went on to do remarkable, often brilliant work in the art of translation: Valéry's *La Jeune Parque,* Rimbaud, Char, Supervielle, Michaux, along with a dozen other French poets, and Shakespeare, Dickinson, Frost, as well as Aleksandr Blok, Sergei Esenin, and Osip Mandelshtam. Paul Celan never expressed himself fully or programmatically on the question of translation. But he once said about Mandelshtam, the Russian-Jewish poet hounded to death in 1938 whose poems he translated as those of a blood brother and alter ego: "I consider translating Mandelshtam to be as important a task as my own verses." [Quoted in a letter (1975) from E. M. Rais to Gleb Struve, in Victor Terras and Karl S. Weimar, "Mandelstamm and Celan: A Postscript," *Germano-Slavica* 2, 5 (Spring 1978): 367.] Since Celan's own verses cost—and always almost gained—him everything, that remark about Mandelshtam could turn into a thoroughgoing mission for translation.

Translating Celan—translating any poet, in fact—appropriates all the resources of interpretive criticism. Even more than that: in translating, as in parody, critical and creative activity converge. The fullest reading of a poem gets realized moment by moment in the writing of a poem. So translation presents not merely a paradigm but the utmost case of engaged literary interpretation.

Paul Celan's own poems themselves often take on the largest tasks of translation, thereby enhancing his translator's task. A single lyric may carry one tongue or text across to another, may gestate within itself the epitome of a tradition, may reach from some certain past toward an uncertain yet open future. And while eight or nine foreign languages crop up in Celan's writing, in no way does he bring about a startling renascence of the word so much as when, amid or after the German verses of a poem, he breaks into Hebrew utterance. [See John Felstiner, "Mother Tongue, Holy Tongue: On Translating and Not Translating Paul Celan," *Comparative Literature* 38, 2 (Spring 1986): 113-36.] Admittedly, that break would seem to raise twofold the generic question of translation. For if lyric verse in the mother tongue, especially verse as idiosyncratic as Celan's, resists the assimilative process of translation, then Hebrew should create a double strangeness, doubly resistant, doubly inalienable.

Yet doesn't the holy tongue specifically belong everywhere, at any time, its persistent identity making translation impossible, even uncalled for? Take for instance **"Du sei wie du"** (**"You be like you"**); composed just before Celan's brief but intensive 1969 visit to Israel:

Du sei wie du, immer.

Stant vp Jherosalem inde erheyff dich

Auch wer das Band zerschnitt zu dir hin,

inde wirt
erluchtet

Knupfte es neu, in der Gehugnis,

Schlammbrocken schluckt ich, im Turm,

Sprache, Finster-Lisene,

kumi
ori

You be like you, ever.

Ryse vp Ierosalem and
rowse thyselfe

The very one who slashed the bond unto you,

and becum
yllumyned

knotted it new, in memoraunce,

spills of mire I swallowed, inside the tower,

speech, dark-buttress,

kumi
ori.

Celan's poem migrates back and forth between modern and medieval German, the medieval being Meister Eckhart's vernacular—*Stant vp Jherosalem . . . inde wirt erluchtet*—for Saint Jerome's Vulgate of Isaiah 60:1, *Surge, illuminare, Jerusalem.* [See Felstiner, "Translating Paul Celan's 'Du sei wie du,' " *Prooftexts* 3, 1 (1983): 91-108.] Then this poem closes by converting to the original Hebrew, the prophet's *kumi ori* ("Arise, shine").

Merely to write in German means carrying on a tradition; for Celan to write Meister Eckhart into his own verse practically seals that tradition. But then he takes the miniature biography of **"Du sei wie du"**—someone who slashed his bond to Jerusalem has renewed it in exile, through memory and speech—and makes this story issue in biblical Hebrew. Such a trope leaves the poem slightly but significantly at odds with the given tradition and turned toward the imperative of another tradition. Celan's German listeners may possibly recognize those Hebrew imperatives, *kumi ori.* More likely they may not.

Still, the mother tongue was what he had. For Celan, his parents murdered and the Austrian-Jewish community and culture of Bukovina destroyed by Nazi Germany, to go on writing in German after 1945 meant paradoxically holding on to the thread of life. "Within reach, close and not lost," he later said, *nah und unverloren,* "there remained in the midst of the losses this one thing: language. This, the language, was not lost but remained, yes, in spite of everything" [Celan's 1958 speech on receiving the Bremen Prize]. Yet this language, Celan insisted, had "passed through the thousand darknesses of deathbringing speech." Toward the end of the war someone asked him why he did not begin writing in Rumanian, the majority language he had learned at school, or in French, which he knew quite well. "Only in the mother tongue can one speak his own truth," Celan explained, "in a foreign tongue the poet lies." Some years later he was questioned by a Viennese bookseller in Paris about bilingualness. "I do not believe in bilingualness in poetry," he replied. "Poetry—that is, the fateful uniqueness of language" [**Gesammelte Werke**, Vol. 3]. So this cleaving to the *Muttersprache* makes his recourse to Hebrew in certain poems all the more pointed, and all the more fateful.

Franz Rosenzweig, in a 1921 letter to Gershom Scholem

about why he has reluctantly translated the Hebrew Grace after Meals, speaks of his German-Jewish "predicament" in terms of the need for translation. "As long as we speak German," Rosenzweig says, "we cannot avoid this path that again and again leads us out of what is alien and into our own" [letter to Gershom Scholem, 10 March 1921, in Franz Rosenzweig, *Briefe und Tagebucher* 2 (1918-29), ed. Rachel Rosenzweig and Edith Rosenzweig Scheinmann]. Paul Celan's **"Du sei wie du,"** within the compass of eleven lines, leads from "what is alien and into our own," from the choking mire of exile into earshot of Isaiah's messianic call, *kumi ori*. Whereas the medieval German stands in a vernacular tradition and thus calls for an English equivalent, those italics distinguishing *kumi ori* obviate the need to translate. The Hebrew (and how many were left in Germany to recognize Isaiah's words, which also occur in the Sabbath hymn "Lekha dodi," summoning Israel to arise and shine?) —the Hebrew stands as if at the beginning and the end of time, at the Babylonian exile and the ultimate return to Zion, at once archaic and messianic.

Not many of Celan's lyrics come to rest with so clear a voice. More often he will speak as in **"Psalm"** [*Gesammelte Werke,* Vol. 1] about

> our corona red
> from the purple-word we sang
> over, O over
> the thorn.

"That which happened," as Celan referred to the destruction of European Jewry, now prevents anything like the gratifying immediacy of lyric speech. No word can get to us except by way of suffering and death: we sing "over, O over/the thorn."

To feel the force of translation in its fullest sense, I want to read quite slowly and consider translating an even shorter lyric than **"Du sei wie du"**—namely, the twenty-three words disposed over ten lines beginning **"Nah, im Aortenbogen"** (1967; [*Gesammelte Werke,* Vol. 2]):

> NAH, IM AORTENBOGEN,
> im Hellblut:
> das Hellwort.
>
> Mutter Rahel
> weint nicht mehr.
> Rubergetragen
> alles Geweinte.
>
> Still, in den Kranzarterien,
> unumschnurt:
> Ziw, jenes Licht.
>
> CLOSE, IN THE AORTIC ARCH,
> in the bright blood:
> the bright word.
>
> Mother Rachel
> weeps no more.
> Carried across,
> all that was wept.
>
> Quiet, in the coronary arteries,
> unconstricted:
> *Ziv,* that light.

Nah, "close" in space or time, not distant, not long to await: the poem opens here and now on a single syllable, an adjective with no noun or verb modifying the poise of the word. In a way, this initial syllable countervails everything previous, everything about us that until now has not been "nigh"—everything distant, displaced, sundered, estranged.

To unfold Paul Celan's poem word by word, or say, moment by moment, means releasing it into the dimension of time and thus into a way of fulfillment. Yet before this poem moves on from its first moment, *Nah,* it harks back (in my ears, at least) to something Celan had written ten years before, a poem he called **"Tenebrae"** (1957; [*Gesammelte Werke,* Vol. 1]), which began,

> Nah sind wir, Herr,
> nahe und greifbar.
>
> Close by, Lord, we are
> close and claspable.

Having subscribed to the rubric of Tenebrae, that sacred office darkening into Christ's Passion, Celan's poem then exposes another passion:

> Clasped already, Lord,
> clawed into each other as though
> each of our bodies were
> your body, Lord.

Not Golgotha now but the gas chamber—human being so broken that it throws down divinity:

> Pray, Lord,
> pray to us,
> we are close,

wir sind nah. "Warped," says the speaker, we went "To the water through" and found "It was blood, it was / what you shed, Lord."

Possibly the desperate irony marking Christ's blood here in **"Tenebrae"** can be heard giving way to "bright blood" and a "bright word" in the later poem, **"Nah, im Aortenbogen."** There is no doubt that in **"Tenebrae,"** in its opening lines themselves—"Nah sind wir, Herr, nahe und greifbar"—Celan was summoning a far earlier voice, Friedrich Holderlin and the opening of "Patmos":

> Nah ist
> Und schwer zu fassen der Gott.
> Wo aber Gefahr ist, wachst
> Das Rettende auch.
>
> Close by
> and hard to grasp is the God.
> Yet where danger is, grows
> What rescues as well.

After this, Holderlin's hymn makes its way from Saint John, Christ, and the disciples, to divine scripture, and finally to God the Father's solicitude for "German song." So, what made Holderlin a tremendous presiding spirit for Paul Celan also made him an impossible exemplar. No saving grace of a God "close by and hard to grasp" was to fall upon those "close and claspable" Jews "clawed into each other" at Sobibor, Chelmno, Maidanek, Treblinka, and Auschwitz.

One would have to trace Germany's Christian-Jewish history as refracted in romantic through expressionist poetry in order to spark the distance between "Patmos" and "Tenebrae," between *Nah* spoken by Holderlin and eventually by Celan. "In the beginning was the Word, and the Word was with God, and the Word was God. . . . In him was life, and the life was the light of men" (John 1:1-4). By the time this dispensation has descended two millennia to a Central European boy who in 1934, just after becoming Bar Mitzvah, told his aunt recently emigrated to Palestine: "Why, as for antisemitism in our school, I could write a 300-page opus about it"; by the time *das Wort* has descended from John through Luther to Holderlin and then has "passed through its own answerlessnesses," as Celan put it, "passed through a frightful muting, passed through the thousand darknesses of deathbringing speech" [*Gesammelte Werke,* Vol. 3]—by this time God's life- and light-bringing Word sounds barely audible and asks the keenest ear. . . .

James Rolleston (essay date 1987)

SOURCE: "Double Time, Double Language: Benn, Celan, Enzensberger," in *Narratives of Ecstasy: Romantic Temporality in Modern German Poetry,* Wayne State University Press, 1987, pp. 133-74.

[*Rolleston is an English-born American critic who specializes in comparative literature. In the following excerpt from his analysis of Celan's poetry, he focuses on the concepts of time and history.*]

Celan's strategy is to freeze history, to stop time; the opening of time that his poems project is always also an effort to reenter the frozen moment. With the passing years this retrospective journey becomes ever more formidable, the poetic narration that of a sealed and inaccessible history. Indeed, in one sense his words can never reach their goal, must always shatter before the unique darkness of Auschwitz. As Meinecke puts it [in her *Wort und Name bei Paul Celan*]: "The more the word endeavors to approach the origin, the more opaque it becomes." In this perspective Celan's texts condemn themselves to falling short, to speaking when only silence is adequate; their is the eloquence of knowing their own failure.

But Celan himself, in his Büchner Prize speech, does not talk of failure. For him the potentiality of a historical poetic narrative is always immanent; the journey into the unique historical moment and out again, the attainment of that point where the poem can not only speak the unimaginable to the world, but can reconstitute a "self," can peak the simplicities of "I" and "thou": "But there are also at the same time paths, among so many other paths, on which language achieves its voice, there are encounters, paths from a voice to a recipient Thou, creatural paths, perhaps sketches for existence, sending the self ahead of itself to its own being, on a quest for itself . . . a kind of journey home" [*Ausgewählte Gedichte*]. The very image of a journey is paradoxical if neither beginning nor end can be more than "sketches." Nevertheless Celan retains the Romantic imagery of homecoming, of the identity of inner and outer journeys. Overcoming the denial of Auschwitz,

finding the language for its silence, is the ultimate challenge to the narrative imagination. It remains feasible because, although the uniqueness of Auschwitz is absolute ("the wholly other," in Celan's own phrase), it is not outside the world. The Western tradition has culminated in this horror and so there are myriad points of contact, both through imagistic analogy (the famous perversion of mystical longing in Celan's **"Death Fugue"**) and through total antithesis, between the event itself and the complexities and contradictions of the tradition. The death camps are silent, but not mute.

Brutal animality, colorless bureaucracy, staggering nihilistic dreams—the complexity of Western experience is concentrated in Auschwitz, but as antiexperience, as silence. Thus, Celan's sense of this event as definitive, his own historical unfreedom, is what liberates his poetic urgency. He is always speaking this finality, he lacks all distance from it, he cannot select and juxtapose his material as Benn does: the more the world's time and language accumulate on top of the unique event, apparently weakening its impact, the harder it becomes to hear the authentic silence. Yet the goal of Celan's temporal poetics, his quest for "sketches for existence," remains binding: the narration of the end of time as the only possible beginning.

That is not to say that all his poems are "about" Auschwitz: **"The Syllable Pain"** clearly does not thematize the camps directly. But the event has converted the entire tradition into a binding repertoire; and whatever motif Celan draws from that repertoire, the poetics of speaking an ending is always at the text's center. All themes are transformed by the silence, their vehicle a language from which it can never be absent. Celan's insistence on this limit gives his texts an analytic fascination with sound and etymology that is never pedantic, an associative freedom that is never arbitrary. His poems also have a unique ability to release contingent narrative out of sheer verbal elan (**"Die Silbe Schmerz"** is very much a case in point); but the spontaneity of such movements always provokes a counterrhythm, the renewed stirring of the one story that puts all others in question, the story that subverts all potential history.

Textual hints in **"Die Silbe Schmerz"** suggest that the poem is conceived in part as a "refutation" ("Widerruf") of a well-known modern "story," the journey into the death realm in Rilke's Tenth Duino Elegy. The clear connection is made early in the poem with the word "deathless" which Rilke uses as the brand name of a beer that people drink to distract themselves from the fact of death. Celan then subtly reinforces the reference in line 12 through the word "behind" ("dahinter") a term stressed by Rilke immediately after mentioning the beer: "right in back of the billboard, right behind it, is reality." Verbal links are of course not in themselves significant. What Rilke offers in his poem is a kind of negative theology, a solemn celebration of images of passivity, melancholy, and nonlife. Although the word "suffering" ("Leid") is used frequently, there is no sense at all that dying involves pain; rather, it is viewed as the only avenue to "reality." It is not difficult to read such a poem as a kind of consolation in advance for the death camps, a picture of death as a place complete with a hierarchy of characters, landmarks, and ritual gestures. To say that is to say nothing whatever about Rilke's intention, but only about the historical function of his language.

Celan's title, then, acquires a polemical resonance. With its reduction of language to the syllable, experience to pain, its insistence on the primal and irreducible, the title demystifies any tendency to view death as a realm. It also denotes an impossibility: pain is precisely what cannot become language. But it is an impossibility that must be explored; if it is to become authentic, language must be doubled, confronted at every stage with the fact that it is language, always at one remove from the originating pain.

Celan has written the opposite of a death journey, namely a creation poem, as his Genesis-like landscape and language emphasize, an allegory of whatever possibilities for a new beginning are imaginable. And since all such imagining is inherently linguistic, the poem circles around its own language, putting in question its own emancipatory gestures. If a rhetorical space opened between the non-language of pain and the imperative confidence of "Let there be" ("Es sei"), the poem would collapse. Initially all gaps are filled with echoes from the silent "chaos," the rupture of history that both demands a new creation poem and renders it paradoxical. Certainly Celan has rendered such suggestive phrases as "wordless voices," "numbers," and "the uncountable," so abstract that no thematic connections to the camps need be made. But my point is that such connections are, by definition, never absent, and that if the reader allows them to echo in his consciousness, certain "obscurities" in the text will become less obscure. Thus the disembodied, uncannily well-ordered quality of Celan's primal chaos connotes a landscape after Auschwitz: speaking is continuous, the metamorphosis from the material into the immaterial and back again is an incessant process. Yet the emergence into individuality, or even into identifiable species (as in Genesis), never takes place. The multiplication of "thou" and the quantification of "self" in the opening lines ensure that this landscape cancels all alternative perspectives. "I" and "thou" still exist—human speaking is impossible without them—but they no longer signify subject and object, creator and created.

Dietlind Meinecke comments on the interplay of the personal pronouns in this poem and the way in which the concept of identity is not so much abandoned as redefined: "Where anonymity can no longer be broken open, the poem must come to rest by the pure being of identity as such." This identity is "pure" in the sense of being generated by the poem itself; but both its premise and its articulation are historical. The ease with which this unique configuration is "given" to the speaker, as well as its Protean variety and continuity, suggests the special problem posed by this history: the poetic self cannot embark on a journey, for the end of all journeys immediately surrounds him. The orientation of inherited language toward hierarchies, quests, and varieties of singular experience is obsolete. In this sense the reference to Rilke constitutes a necessary antithesis, a starting point. In the context of Auschwitz "deathless" means not a Rilkean critique of human superficiality, but a systematic denial of both death and life. The

victims neither live nor die, their "death" is nothing but a dissolution. They become "empty forms."

Yet it is these "Leerformen" that inaugurate the narrative. Again unlike Rilke, Celan moves not toward lament ("Klage,") but toward a kind of allegorical remoteness, a linguistic completion of the tradition's systematic self-destruction. These first two sections of the poem have tremendous energy, as the multiplying verbs close all the gaps, complete all the circles. The landscape is essentially horizontal ("around," "before and behind"), the space of nonexperience endowed with purely verbal life. Its movement includes "everything"; all the temporal strands of the tradition have become pure spatial repetition ("repeatable matter," "Wiederholbares" is Meinecke's term).

In the second section however the circle begins to become a vortex. As prefigured in the title, the fundamental division in human consciousness between the exclusively abstract and the exclusively organic enters the poem. Numbers are projected by the system of "Leerformen," which strives to impose its circular rhythm on them ("greater . . . smaller"). But numbers are incorrigibly linear, they keep suggesting a story, even history. The abstractions become more intense more explicit ("the uncountable," "the Never"). But the verbs move in the opposite direction toward the organic, the generative: "woven into . . . overripened . . . transformed backward and forward . . . burgeoning." This section unites the beginning and ending of time in an allegory of symmetry and completion. But such intensification instigates life at the center of abstraction, in the numbers themselves; they are rounded off, then begin to run riot.

We may detect here an explicit reference to [the German poet] Novalis's fascination with mathematical symbols and his sense that the system life of mathematics, in its purity, offers the closest possible analogy to the primary structure of the absolute: "Everything real that is created from nothing, like for example numbers and abstract expressions, has a wondrous relationship with things of another world—with infinite series of strange combinations and linkages, with, as it were, a self-contained mathematical and abstract world, with a poetic, mathematical, and abstract world." Celan is offering precisely that perspective on history that for Novalis remained within the realm of theory: history completed, rounded off, all time zones coalescing into a single oscillation. Moreover, Novalis's cosmology cements the links between the language of numbers and the poem's opening scenery of "Ich" and "Du," the language of self-realization: "Self-consciousness in the larger sense is a task, an ideal—it would be that condition in which linear time would cease to pass, a timeless, forever constant condition."

Out of the heart of his allegory of completion, of time become empty but systematic space, Celan has extracted the possibility of a new event. It is of course also impossible: "burgeoning never." But poetic language, however negative, is both linear and visionary: differentiated time has been reshaped into the potentiality of narrative. The circle has become a vortex, the perspective of infinite flatness is yielding to the vertical. And the monochrome texture implicit in the term "deathless" is being replaced by the sharp antitheses that endow life's contingent sequences with the possibility of meaning: a "lot" ("Los") including death, but not paralyzed by it.

With a masterly transition from the "Never" to "The forgotten," and maintaining the rhythm of oscillating completion ("sank and swam"), Celan directs the energy of the first two sections upward (and downward) into a reopened time zone. The generative force of forgetting . . . operates here on the largest possible scale. What is wholly forgotten can be wholly remembered. Things "to be forgotten" have escaped the obliterating closure of "deathless." And thus the "empty forms" are now "earth parts, heart parts"; they sink, they resurface.

In the presence of fragments, in the struggle with a newly imagined water there is the possibility of an originating human event: the disintegrative rhythm points now not toward the regularity of the void but toward the most ancient narratives of adventure, toward Sinbad and Odysseus. From the repertoire of the Western tradition, now opening in its singularities rather than its collective collapse, Columbus emerges: he *is* "the time." He also embodies the antithesis that is to dominate the poem, blending devout Catholic concentration on the Virgin with a resolute individualistic assault on the elements. At this point the verb "murdered" seems merely a strong image. The Virgin's "timelessness" is immediately qualified by her association with deeply temporal, even fragile, qualities as "mother flower": the purgatory of "deathless" is wrenched open in both directions. And in "All was unleashed," at the poem's approximate center, the reversal of the centripetal motion in section 1 is fueled by the cumulative energy of all the earlier verbs: the entire Western tradition is bursting out onto this one voyage.

In the fourth section the singular moment of creation is evoked as in essence a colonization, a transformation into narrative uniqueness of the spatial repetitions of the opening. Thus, the sequence "faded, lost its leaves . . . bloomed massively" simultaneously expands the organic imagery of section 2 and accelerates it into a single cosmic moment: *"One* world ocean." This "blooming" of the nominally sterile ocean is presented as a toweringly vertical event and also as intensely visual, with extreme light contrasts: "into the day, in the black light." The defining quality of the opening sections has been abstraction, refusal of the visual, as well as plurality and horizontal recurrence. The many smoothly linked verbs are transformed in effect into the single emphatic "bloomed," which is then echoed by "awoke." This blooming is indeed a resurrection (the "death," the "losing leaves" of the medieval world's compass is its prerequisite), and the images then cluster to confirm it. The meaning of Columbus's voyage is not so much that the medieval world ended, as that it was reborn in a new and vital form.

Celan conveys this vitality by filling his singular event with a series of "trinities," ritual groupings of medieval images, which the context renders specific, functional, full of future. Again the contrast is with the "empty forms": this historical moment is not empty but teeming. Yet it teems with delicacy: the "Weltmeer" has produced a most fragile resurrection. The children are perhaps a "refuta-

Edgar Jené's lithograph "Sie flüchten." In Edgar Jené und der Traum vom Traume *Celan discussed Jené's art and poetic theory.*

tion" of Rilke's "young dead, in the initial state of timeless indifference." However alchemically imagined, the children of this text are the opposite of timeless, they are awakening to the world, not withdrawing from it. Two aspects of the trinity of precious stones seem relevant. Albertus Magnus assigns a curative quality to each of them: jasper drives away fever, agate reveals the presence of poison, amethyst protects against drunkenness. A sealed-off, protected humanness is evoked. Moreover, jasper and amethyst have significant functions as, respectively, the first and last (twelfth) precious stones garnishing the foundation of the city of God (Revelation 21: 19-20). Columbus's tempestuous voyage has resurrected this ultimate and wholly static ancient vision, a vision based explicity on purification and exclusion: "there was no more sea" (verse 1); "there shall be no night there" (verse 25).

Even as the structure of trinity sequences conveys synthesis, the poem's fundamental antithesis (between horizontal closure and vertical dynamism, deathly space and resurrected time) breaks into the open, as the counter-trinity of "peoples, tribes, and kinsmen" expresses the rush of energy, the indiscriminate colonization generated by Columbus's voyage. This section is dominated by the wave rhythm of the "Weltmeer," the stillness in the trough and the crashing breaker. The paradox of creation, of the narration of a new time zone, is the paradox of the poem's title: language alone releases the extremes of life (animals lack "syllables"), but it also functions as a system in which extremes can meet and the purely physical ("pain") can become a link in a newly conceptualized chain of being.

But this poem imagines the paradox through to its conclusion, imagines the death of the unique event generated by its own act of creative rupture. The climactic "Let there be" is isolated textually, but only textually. It is "blind" in the sense that Columbus himself was blind, bringing realities into being of which his late-medieval mind could have absolutely no conception. And immediately it is firmly attached ("wove itself") to the ambiguous intricacies of subsequent Western history. The moment of the poem is not the original voyage of Columbus, but the re-emergence of that voyage in language at a time when the tradition, at the source of which the voyage stands, seemed finally extinguished. Such a moment is both singular in history and language—and multiple, in that it opens Columbus's violent purity to everything that followed. It is "one knot" and "thou-sand knots." It crystallizes Columbus's unique role in our mythology, establishing the liberating image of the New World at the center of Western consciousness. And it constitutes Columbus's story in a quite new way, both compressing its outline toward abstraction and bringing some thoroughly defamiliarized details of ship and sea into extreme close-up. This Columbus is a mythological skeleton, his original historical flesh eaten away by the unholy alliance of complacent forgetting and barbaric perversion of the adventurous spirit.

The language of poetry can convey such doubleness directly, but only by doubling itself without reservation, by narrating its own structure as language. The final section of the poem attempts the task, culminating in a kind of stammering, an openness both tentative and slightly sinister, decisive only in its refutation of the closure with which the poem began. The formidable difficulties of this ending fall into two specific areas: what is the resonance of this intensely vertical imagery, ranging from the stars down through the rigging on Columbus's ship into the depths? And what are "marten stars"? Some things can be said through an immanent reading: the imagery concentrates a multiplicity of concrete detail (details that expressly multiply themselves into the thousands) into its linguistic-temporal oneness. Thus, the open, potentially dissolving movement of the "deciphering" of "Let there be" remains bound by innumerable knots into an interpretive narration that can never end. The poem's language thematizes itself to the point of "becoming" the ship's ropes. But it also tells us that its aspiration toward such identity, toward becoming the historical moment, means that it must dissolve itself into the "world-ocean" of subsequent events, resisting the temptation of unitary creative gestures, prefigured in the opening lines. The poem's difficulty derives from the refusal of its own solutions, the refusal to say . . . "Everything is said."

And so the reader is following the poem's own rhythm if he looks outside it for the illumination of its central enigmas. In two poems of Celan's subsequent collection, *Atemwende* (1967), we encounter seascapes that can be seen as meditations on the concluding section of **"Die Silbe Schmerz"**:

> Es scheren die Buchstaben aus,
> die letzten
> traumdichten Kähne—
> jeder mit einem
> Teil des noch
> zu versenkenden Zeichens
> im
> geierkralligen Schlepptau.
>
> ("Flutender")

> The letters cut themselves loose,
> the last
> boats thick with dreams—

> each with a
> part of the still to be
> submerged sign
> in the
> vulture-clawed towline.
>
> ("Flooding")

> ein Wahndock,
> Schwimmend, davor
> abweltweiss die
> Buchstaben der
> Grosskräne einen
> Unnamen schreiben, an dem
> klettert sie hoch, zum Todessprung, die
> Laufkatze Leben,
> den baggern die sinn—
> gierigen Sätze nach Mitternacht aus,
> nach ihm
> wirft die neptunische Sünde ihr korn—
> schnapsfarbenes Schleppseil. . . .
>
> ("Hafen")

> mirage of a dock,
> swimming, before it
> the unearthly white
> letters of the
> great cranes
> write a cipher, on which
> it clambers up, ready for the death leap,
> life's crane crab,
> the cipher is dredged out after midnight
> by the sentences hungry for meaning,
> after it
> Neptune's sin throws its
> rye-colored towrope.
>
> ("Harbor")

What this imagery has in common is a powerfully vertical dimension, with movement both upward and downward, and a concretely imagined coincidence of impossibles, words, climbing creatures, and the sea. The rope is the unifying factor, and its power to link land, sea, and air in the functionality of the human voyage endows it with an animistic, slightly savage quality ("serpent-headed," "vulture-clawed"). In each passage Celan evokes the binding of words, of human creativity, into the rope—which, embodying the prehistoric discovery of how to generate strength from the binding of slender reeds, is perhaps to be seen as a human miracle analogous to that of language, its toughness resisting the sea as imaginative language resists silence. The difference, in **"Die Silbe Schmerz,"** lies in the function of the words: here they are specific, identified as the creative formula "Let there be," whereas in the later poems they are obscure, slipping into the subverbal realm of "signs" or "ciphers," and provoking the longing of everything alive to grasp and consume them. In **"Die Silbe Schmerz"** the problem is in the very transparency and energy of the "Es sei." The world is galvanized, but which of its many dreams, dark or light, should it set about realizing? Certainly the ambivalence of the final lines seems total: the persistent struggle to "spell" the formula means that it is not lost, but also that it cannot be realized, that human understanding is never adequate to transform the vision of creation into a functioning, humane language.

For interpreting the enigmatic image of "marten stars,"

the poem's link to Rilke's Tenth Elegy offers a hint. Evoking the stars above the "grief land" ("Leidland"), Rilke mentions "the Staff" and "the Burning Book" (suggestive in the context of Celan's dismantling of his key—untranslatable—term, "buchstabieren"), and then:

> pure as in the palm
> of a blessed hand the clearly gleaming "M"
> that signifies Mothers.

Such imagery may seem remote from the actuality of the "marten," an unpleasant variety of weasel, of whom *Grimms Wörterbuch* says: "The marten's name may have been derived by the Germans from murdering, since it strangles and murders everything." But earlier in Celan's text precisely this juxtaposition occurs:

> The mother-
> flower,
> murdered . . .

From the poem's title onward Celan has been projecting ways of making fruitful the paradox of purity and violence, the impossible truth of a history that cannot be rendered accessible through interpretive narration. The urgency of this contingent narrative does not seal language in, but drives it into ever more extreme contradiction. And in fact the etymology of "Marder," according to Kluge [in *Etymologisches Wörterbuch*], suggests that the word itself embodies the central paradox. It is connected with the Lithuanian word "marti," meaning bride, and with other words denoting a young woman, and is in fact a taboo word used for community protection: "Name of the weasel that people fear and want to avoid attracting by the use of its true name." This primitive use of a word is by no means foreign to Celan's intention: by linking the feared yet linguistically masked creature to the image of remote stars actualized in the abyss, the poet has given new potency to his rope/language in the very act of sealing in this enigmatic fusion of purity and violence ("Marder" occurs nowhere else in Celan).

The procedure may seem esoteric, but so was Columbus's original project; his driving of history toward a new "Let there be" pressed an entire tradition of illusions and rituals into a not-yet-imaginable generative moment. The poem suggests that the very creatures struggling to decipher history's text contain that text in their etymological being. Moreover it is language itself that can resist history's collapse into reductive uniformity. In the density of myth and etymology opposites coexist, maintaining the perpetual possibility of new narratives.

The key words at the beginning and end of this text, "deathless" and "marten stars," compel the reader to look toward other texts. This is entirely consonant with Celan's view of the poem as always "under way," to be actively embedded in history. In a sense we should speak of a tripling rather than a doubling of time and language by Celan. His disruptive force is directed against a destruction of history itself, which has already taken place and can never be masked; his colonization of that desolate completion opens the way not toward any new version of personal identity (we have seen how fragments, "heart parts," are all man has and all he now needs), but toward

a vision of the ambiguity and incompleteness of all such colonizations. The poem's language reflects upon itself, but its self-sealing is also a self-opening. Its esoteric images confront the silence of the past with the noise of the escapist present. The poem makes no sense at all as a self-contained aesthetic object. It exists exclusively as a stimulus to dialogue between a past and a future that seem to have collapsed definitively into the machine of the present: the exhilaration of its emergent contingency is inseparable from its implicit historical narrative, which simultaneously closes and opens an endlessly festering event.

Saul Myers (essay date 1987)

SOURCE: "The Way Through the Human-Shaped Snow: Paul Celan's Job," in *Studies in Twentieth Century Literature*, Vol. 11, No. 2, Spring, 1987, pp. 213-28.

[*In the following essay, Myers analyzes several of Celan's later poems.*]

To read Paul Celan's later poems is to travel with them, often to get lost with them, as they speed in a restless search for a place. Each poem traces a solitary trajectory through the most uninhabitable landscapes, only staying long enough in any one no-man's-land to sketch the insufficiency as well as the danger of tarrying. Each poem seems born of an initial implosion, a highly charged vacuum that draws it and the "Du" it addresses in quest of common terrain. Such poems demand a special kind of reading, a reading *unterwegs;* for it is only in response to a summons from elsewhere and on the way to this elsewhere that such poems constitute themselves on the page.

"Weggebeizt" presents special problems for the translator and interpreter; it draws not only upon word-roots from *Mittel-*and *Alt-hochdeutsch,* but also upon very specific passages in the *Book of Job.* The reader must be prepared to enter into an encounter with one of the most problematic and mysterious wisdom books of the Hebrew Bible. The following reading of "Weggebeizt" will show how Celan's volatile, synthetic German veers close to *Job,* so close in fact that some of Celan's astonishing neologisms are cryptic translations and glosses of the Hebrew.

> *WEGGEBEIZT vom*
> *Strahlenwind deiner Sprache*
> *das bunte Gerede des An-*
> *erlebten—das hundert-*
> *züngige Mein-*
> *gedicht, das Genicht.*
>
> *Aus-*
> *gewirbelt,*
> *frei*
> *der Weg durch den menschen-*
> *gestaltigen Schnee,*
> *den Büsserschnee, zu*
> *den gastlichen*
> *Gletscherstuben und-tischen.*
>
> *Tief*
> *in der Zeitenschrunde,*
> *beim*
> *Wabeneis*
> *wartet, ein Atemkristall,*

dein unumstössliches
Zeugnis.

TRIED OUT from the
beaming wind of your language
the various talk of lifted experience, the hundred-
tongued forsworn-
poem, the noem.

Whirled
out,
free
the way through the human-
shaped snow,
the pilgrim snow, to
the hospitable
glacier-rooms and-tables.

Deep
in the time-crevasse,
by the
honeycomb-ice
there waits, a crystal of breath,
your incontrovertible
witness.

WEGGEBEIZT vom: etched away, searched out, tried out
from.

One is loath to separate the component parts of the opening word. One wants, at first, only to marvel at the surgical
precision with which the poet stitched it together. To differentiate finely compressed layers of meaning without
breaking the skin, as it were, that unites them, is the accomplishment of a very delicate hand. [In **Paul Celan:**
Poems] Michael Hamburger saw fit to translate *Wegge-*
beizt according to the modern senses of the elements. *Weg*
he took in its prefix form, meaning "away" or "off." *Ge-*
beizt he rendered along the somewhat chemical lines as
"etched," though "corroded" or "cauterized" were also
possibilities. If, however, *Weg* is taken as a noun (*Atem-*
wende contains many such noun/participle *Zusammen-*
setzungen), then *Weggebeizt* would carry the sense of a
path or way having been made, etched through something.
There are also older senses of *beizen* that haunt the meaning of *Weggebeizt*: in *Mittelhochdeutsch beizen,* meant "to
hunt" (as with falcons) and further back in the history of
the language, *beizen* was the *Althochdeutsch* word for "to
try," "put to a test."

When the modern uses, stressing pain and the biting action of acid, are combined with the older ones, stressing
the searching out of a way, the synthetic meaning becomes
clearer: a way is being *assayed* or *tried.* This metallurgic
metaphor for the juridical trial of someone has a key place
in the *Book of Job.* We read it in Job's self-justificatory
plea for a fair hearing from God (23:10):

> But he knoweth the way that I take, when he
> hath tried me I shall come forth as gold. My foot
> hath held his steps, his way have I kept and not
> declined. Neither have I gone back from the
> commandment of his lips, I have esteemed the
> words of his mouth more than my necessary
> food.

The Hebrew word *bochan* means in this passage "to try,

search out thoroughly, to prove." The same root appears
in the noun form *bochon,* "an assayer, one who tries met-
als." Not only does Job yearn for a fair hearing before God
in this passage, but he also affirms his unwavering commitment to God's way, an attestation of innocence that recurs
throughout Job's speeches and which culminates in the
Reinigungseid that summons God's speech out of the
whirlwind. But where Job uses these words as figurative
extensions of his argument with God, Celan has turned
the trying of the way into an actual event. Celan is taking
Job at his word.

Strahlenwind deiner Sprache: the beaming wind of your
language.

As careful readers of Celan, we must be sure to respect the
systematic ambiguities that the poet presses into his
words. For example, the passive introduction of *Strahlen-*
wind as the object of the preposition *vom* forbids us to construe it merely as the agent of *wegbeizen;* that is only one
reading. *Strahlenwind deiner Sprache* can also be read as
that which is undergoing, or better, has undergone the
process of *wegbeizen;* out of this process something has
been tried out.

No one at all familiar with biblical idiom can mistake its
presence in *Strahlenwind deiner Sprache.* Of all the references to wind as divine speech, spirit, and intention, the
mention of it in *Job* is especially important for understanding Celan's poem. Just as the *Strahlenwind* passes through
negating forms of utterance in this stanza, so in the *Book*
of Job do we find wind figures absolutely positive in one
context and absolutely negative in others. The positive
sense is, of course, wind as God's breath in action. The Hebrew word *ruach* denotes this pneumal manifestation of
God, but it is also used to designate something of no value,
a vain thing of naught. "Do you imagine to reprove words
and speeches of one that is desperate," says Job (6:26) to
his would-be comforters, "words which are as wind." And
Job replies to Eliphaz (16:13) with a wind figure intended
to deprive his words of substance: "Shall vain words have
an end"; this line translates more literally to "shall words
of wind have an end." The same sense of the emptiness of
wind appears in Job's lament (7:7), "O remember that my
life is wind."

Both Hans-Georg Gadamer and Peter Horst Neumann
have read *Strahlenwind deiner Sprache* as a sort of absolute language, one which, according to Gadamer [in *Wer-*
bin Ich und wer bist Da?], has the quality of "die Reinheit
und strahlende Helligkeit, die wahre Geistigkeit der Sprache, die nicht nachgemachte und nachempfundene Aus-
sagen vortäuscht, sondern alle solchen entlarvt." Neumann surmises that "Eine solche Sprache, welche Bun-
theit und schönen Schein *jeder anderen* auszulöschen ver-
möchte, könnte die Sprache Gottes sein" [in *Zur Lyrik*
Paul Celans]. What we have said concerning the double
nature of "wind-speech" in *Job,* its unification of the pneumal and the vain elements in a single word, casts doubt
upon simple emphasis of the absolute positive sense of
Strahlenwind deiner Sprache; and what we have discerned
in the syntax of *Weggebeizt vom,* leads us to suspect that
Strahlenwind is not merely the agent of the trying, searching out process, but perhaps more emphatically that out

of which or from which something else is etched. This relative reflexivity has a further implication for the rest of this first strophe: it implies that God too is Job's witness as Job is his witness. In other words, Job's trial is also God's trial. As Martin Buber put it [in *The Dimensions of Job*], Job appeals from God to God. A more radical formulation would be that Job appeals from God against God—an ethical irony hardly foreign to Paul Celan.

das bunte Gerede des An-erlebten—

the various talk of lifted experience,

In 11:12 Zophar reduces Job's argument to vain words:

Should not this multitude of words be answered?
Should a man full of talk be justified?

This last line was translated by Luther as "Muss langes Gerede ohne Antwort bleiben?" This charge of speaking vain, foolish words without knowledge is leveled at Job repeatedly by his pious friends, and is the charge that he brings against himself in the dramatic about-face, the "repentant" speeches following his meeting God out of the whirlwind. But just as before the empty words of Job and God's absolute word were both expressed by the same wind-stream, so here it would be rash to read *das bunte Gerede des An-erlebten* only negatively. The word-break *An-erlebten* shows rather, that a transformation is taking place. Separation and unification—the primary logical operations—are brought by Celan into a single contorted *topos*. The more the *Strahlenwind* comes into contact with the multitude of vain words the more it searches through them and tries to cut itself away. It is as if the *Strahlenwind* were looking for a counterpart of itself in the profane *Gerede*. I have translated *das bunte Gerede* as "the various talk" because the archaic senses of various, "prevaricating, inconstant," akin to the Latin *varus*—"bent and crooked"—suggest both the physical and moral transformations undergone in a twisting path of speech.

An-erlebten is a difficult neologism to interpret. There is in German a sub-class of "an"-prefixed verbs, all of which express a rote-like internalization of something which is not, in the first and last instance, one's own. *Anerzogen, angelernt* and *angelesen* signify knowledge acquired by such routinized activities as imitation and repetition. *An-erlebten* would then be a paradoxical conflation of second-hand experience (what is not one's own) with *erlebten*, experience that is one's own. It is as if the *Strahlenwind deiner Sprache* cut closer to the speaker's experience than his own words do. "Your language" becomes, paradoxically, what is most "my own." This is fully in keeping with Job's last speech, when he says that before he had known only what others had told him, but now he knows God first hand. In 30:23, before confronting God, Job anticipates the whirlwind speech of God, but characterizes it as the source of his travail:

Thou liftest me up to the wind, thou causest me to ride upon it and dissolvest my substance. . . .

We shall return to this pivotal passage. For now it is sufficient to justify the translation of *An-erlebten* as "lifted experience," the word "lift" with its Old English sense of

"air," has the contemporary meaning "to take from or steal." Thus "lifted ex-perience" conserves the tension between first and second-hand experience while at the same time it offers the sense of something being dissolved into air. Interestingly, the English word "experience" is derived from "experiri"—to try—so that all the while, like the transformation of *Anerlebten* into *erlebten*, Job's insistence on a true hearing and witness is retained—even amidst his mortal dissolution in the wind.

das hundert-
zūngige Mein-
gedicht, das Genicht.

the hundred-
tongued forsworn-
poem, the noem.

A turbulent motion of unsparing negation and a searching, singling-out process take the shape of violent hybrid forms of speech. "Hundred-tongued" must surely conjure the image of Satan, the Adversary in God's court, whose crafty tongue it was that first challenged God to test Job. The line break between *hundert* and *zūngige* performs a cutting away and condensing action that has the effect of a silencing. D. Meinecke and Michael Hamburger [in ***Paul Celan***] have pointed out the affinity between *Meingedicht* and "Meineid"—a false oath; the *Mittelhochdeutsch* "Mein" carrying the sense of "false," "deceitful," or "fraudulent," hence "forsworn-poem."

As we must by now have come to expect, there are passages in Job to which Celan's lines refer, and, as we shall see, at one point Celan literally translates a word from the Hebrew.

As we already remarked, Job's friends repeatedly charge him with speaking in vain; at times this takes the form of an accusation of uttering false testimony, as in 15:5:

For thy mouth uttereth thine iniquity and thou choosest the tongue of the crafty. Thine own mouth condemneth thee and not I; yea thine own lips testify against thee.

Passages like this one are important to our reading of Celan's lines because here "true witness" and "false witness" are conflated. Only a searching through of the ways of speech could etch the one out of and away from the other. The line break between *Mein* and *gedicht* seems to implicate the poem itself in this turbulent twisting of the ways.

Still in 24:25 we find the solitary Job maintaining the veracity of his testimony:

And if it be not so now, who will make me a liar and bring my words to naught?

This is part of the *Reinigungseid* that Job speaks not so much to his friends, but as a direct challenge to God, for he has accused God of letting evil go unpunished in the world and of indifference to mortal suffering. If God were to prove Job wrong and overturn the truth of his testimony then he would have to show that he does deal justly and that he is not indifferent to the suffering of the innocent. But this is *not*, of course, how God argues in the *Book of Job*. When he does finally answer Job, it is the fact, the event, of contact with divine speech that leads Job to re-pent of his claim to having spoken truly, not God's argument *per se*. In and of itself God's concluding answer to Job is no argument against him.

So concerned with the letter of Job's rhetoric was Celan that he chose to translate a very unusual word from the Hebrew. In fact, Celan's *Genicht* renders a word into German that only appears once in the whole Bible. Ordinarily, *ahl* is used as an adverb of negation like "nicht." Just this once however, in 24:25 *ahl* is used as a substantive, meaning "nothing" or "naught." In like manner, the last word of Celan's strophe is a substantivized adverb of negation. In the context of the poem, the act of bringing Job's words ("my words") to naught is actually carried out. *Genicht* is at one and the same time a kind of utterance and the effect of silencing that utterance.

The windy nothing of *das Genicht* is counterposed to the *Strahlenwind deiner Sprache*. But unlike Gadamer and others, we ought to refrain from evaluating these two poles in terms of true and false, positive and negative. For in the trial of Job a person reduced to the mere breath in his nostrils may bear testimony that is true. Even reduced to wind Job's oath may stand (27:3-4):

> As long as there is still breath in me and the spir-it (*ruach*) of God is in my nostrils: my lips will not speak falsehood, and my tongue will not utter deceit.

> *Aus-*
> *gewirbelt*

> Whirled [whirlwinded]
> out

Where the first strophe dwelt upon the violent conflation of true and false ways of speech even in the process of separating them, the second records an ultimate break. The setting of *aus* by itself, severed off from the verb, emphasizes a centrifugal motion outwards. Some residuum has been salvaged from out of the multitude of vain words and out of the purge of the previous stanza. God speaks out of the whirlwind storm in *Job*, and here again Celan constructs his active and continuous metaphor by taking a biblical figure and re-casting it: to speak out of the whirlwind becomes the same as wresting something out of it. We have made it a point in this commentary that, unlike most of the other readers who have stressed *Strahlenwind deiner Sprache* as an absolute language of truth, the *Strahlenwind* is involved (in the Miltonic sense of this word) in the negative and false forms of speech that it etches its way through. No surer sign of this involvement can be seen than the difference between a "strahlen" motion and a "wirbeln" motion. The latter has a twisting, turbulent movement that the former does not have. Perhaps it is this change in manner and direction of the wind of *deiner Sprache* that gives us an *Atemwende*.

> *frei*
> *der Weg durch den menschen-*
> *gestaltigen Schnee*

> free
> the way through the human-
> shaped snow

This strophe has, as a whole, the character of a clearing, the winning of a direction. *Aus, frei, der Weg durch* are encapsulations of the wandering motif in *Exodus*. At no point in the *Book of Job*, though, does God announce himself as the liberator of Israel. Shadai is recognized as an all-powerful creator God, who is "just" in an abstract and transcendent way, but a far cry from the God of *Exodus* who hears the lament of the slaves in Egypt, delivers them, and leads them through the wilderness. It cannot be stated strongly enough that the transformations of the first stanza are not just undergone by the mortal side of the God/man relation—God too has been searched and tested. On the other side, the solitary fate of Job has become fused to the collective one of Israel. Unlike the redemptive act in *Exodus*, the way is not made through a desert wilderness here, but through a snow wilderness. These silent shrouds of snow and ice, bereft of all but the faintest traces of life, number high in Celan's poems, early and late. All speech dies down in these windswept ice-scapes; and yet there is a mute receptivity about the snow that muffles the spoken word. Reading Celan's single-word lines here, one is reminded of the hush amidst mountain snow that Webern's sacred music evokes.

The line-break between *menschen* and *gestaltigen* displaces the object of *durch* from "human" to "human-shaped snow." This shift suggests that in passing through the human form, the wind takes on the contour, the image, of the human without being identified with it. And like an etching process there is a dissolving of a substance (the human) and the creation of an image that bears the shape, in the way that snow takes the shape of the thing that it covers. It should not come as a surprise that these very cold images should follow the "hot" ones of the first stanza. There is a technical form of wind action known as "wind etching," also called "wind frosting," that sand particles carried by winds perform on stone and mineral surfaces. In Celan's poem it is not sand that is carried by the wind (though this is hinted at later by the formation of an *Atemkristall*), rather it is the dissolved substance of the human.

To what end, though, is this mortal dissolution carried out? Returning to the whole verse of 30:23 we read Job's anticipation of death:

> Thou liftest me up to the wind, thou causest me to ride upon it and dissolvest my substance. For I know thou wilst bring me to death and to the house appointed for all living.

For comparison's sake, it might be instructive to counterpose Job's yearning for death, his anticipation of God's wind piloting him to Sheol, with Gadamer's rather aestheticized view of this journey in Celan's poem:

> Es führt die Höhenwanderung im winterlich unbetretenen Gebirge zu einer gastlichen Stätte. Wo man fern genug von den Aktualitäten des menschlichen Treibens ist, ist man dem Ziel nahe, dem Ziel, das das wahre Wort ist.

If Celan's poem is a re-rendering of *Job*, as we have been reading it, then the goal of the journey would be one of the most *menschlich* of all—death, especially yearned for by the suffering Job. As we shall see, in Celan's careful re-reading and re-writing, Job *is granted his wish.*

> *den Büsserschnee, zu*
> *den gastlichen*
> *Gletscherstuben und-tischen.*
>
> the pilgrim-snow, to
> the hospitable
> glacier-rooms and -tables.

Original language of the kind forged by Celan always presents the translator with difficult choices: if he chooses to highlight one sense of a word, often he must place in the background other semantic resonances of perhaps equal importance. Michael Hamburger's "penitents' snow" for *Büsserschnee,* while keeping to the lexical sense of *Büsser,* loses the active sense of the snow taking the shape of the wind-swept person wandering through it; this is largely because Hamburger turned *Büsserschnee* into a possessive compound. "Pilgrim snow" is an attempt to render this active re-shaping.

It would have taken some familiarity with the Hebrew original of "house appointed for all living," which Celan could easily have managed since crypto-translation of Hebrew terms abound in **Atemwende,** to know that the Hebrew *bayit moaid,* house or meet-house, has the idiosyncracy of referring both to an appointed place and to an appointed time, and it is used in other biblical contexts to refer to gatherings and festal assemblies. Celan's hospitable rooms and tables give us the sense that this glacial meeting place *expects* its pilgrim visitor to come at the appointed hour. This idea of Job's finding a haven in Sheol, the biblical Hades, is expressed earlier in 14:13:

> O that you would hide me in Sheol,
> conceal me till your anger pass,
> Then set me a time and remember me.

Marvin Pope points out that "Job here gropes toward the idea of an afterlife. If only God would grant him asylum in the netherworld, safe from the wrath which now besets him, and then appoint him a time for a new and sympathetic hearing, he would be willing to wait and even endure the present evil." The only problem with our Jobian interpretation of this part of Celan's poem is that Celan locates the house of all living in a glacier-world, a land we associate with the rare air of the mountains, with the hoarfrost of heaven, rather than the netherworld. [In an endnote, the critic adds: There exists a folk etymology for *büssen,* in which it takes on the meaning, "to care by magical incantation."]

We have already mentioned that Celan's poem enacts the trial of Job in a different way than the original, the most critical difference being that Celan has interpreted the ironic or otherwise rhetorical challenges of both Job and God as real events. There is thus a hint of Celan's strange, spellbound glacier world in God's famous snow and ice imagery:

> Hast thou entered into the treasures [stores] of
> snow and hail which I have reserved against the
> time of trouble?

Celan's *gastlichen Gletscherstuben und-tischen* fuses to-gether the house of all living and a place in God's dominion that God ironically holds out as being inaccessible to Job.

From Christian and Jewish sources we hear tell of a banquet that is set for the end of days when the redeemed are to gather with the messiah and with their long-dead ancestors. It is impossible to read of the hospitable rooms and tables without hearing the New Testament "my mansion is of many rooms." And it is equally impossible to read these lines without recalling the Chasidic legends of the Passover *seder* prepared from time immemorial and all ready to begin, but for the delayed arrival of a mysterious guest, whose place is still empty at table.

> *Tief*
> *in der Zeitenschrunde,*
> *beim*
> *Wabeneis*
>
> Deep
> in the time-crevasse,
> by the
> honeycomb-ice

God's dramatic answer to Job (38:18) contains the following in its barrage of rhetorical questions:

> Hast thou walked in search of the depth? Out of
> whose womb came the ice? and the hoary frost
> of heaven, who hath gendered it? The waters are
> hid as with a stone and the face of the deep is fro-
> zen.

At one level, God's counter-challenge to Job is no answer at all: the rhetorical questions merely overwhelm the small mortal in an ironical *ad hominem*: "who are you to bother me about the justice of your suffering; were you there when I created the universe? Do you know the secrets hid in the hoarfrost of heaven?" Here again, the secret places God holds out as transcendent, which mortal Job can never know, are recast by Celan as within Job's reach, meant for him precisely. To the question "hast thou walked in search of the depth?" the poem anticipates just such a search. To the forbidding question "hast thou entered into the treasure stores of heaven?" the poem expects just such an entrance.

Celan's version of God's speech purges it of its rhetorical function while, at the same time, it draws a kind of redemptive significance from the figures themselves. By taking it literally, Celan translates figurative language into a first order reality instead of leaving it a second order representation. One should be careful about labeling this kind of literalism a symbolism. It is more accurate to call it an antisymbolism or even a reverse symbolism, because it treates the material of representation as a reality in itself. Previous studies have variously pointed to a kabbalist influence in Celan's scrupulous attention to the literal. It should be well noted, however, that the literal breakdown of words in scripture and the reconstruction of meaning from out of this literalism is no monopoly of the mystics in Judaism; this treatment of scripture was a strong feature of rabbinic commentary on the bible. Even the staunch rationalist Maimonides used this procedure of ideation through literal breakdown of Hebrew terms—he just pointed this method toward rationalist instead of theosophical ends. Celan is thus in keeping with this peculiarity of Jewish speculation: his literalism is poised to interrogate the word-secrets of the Torah.

It is, then, very unenlightening to pluck the strand of mysticism from Celan's poem without considering the biblical fabric into which it is woven. Interpretations of **"Weggebeizt"** under headings like "Mystische Paradoxie" actually understate the powerful interrogation of scripture that courses through this poem and so many others—one may speak of the *midrashic* element of Celan's poetry as well as the mystical element.

Zeitenschrunde is a synthetic word with affinities to other time terms in Celan's later poetry. (Compare, for instance, with *Zeitloch* in **"Die Posaunenstelle"** from the **Zeitgehöft** collection.) Time is imaged as a passageway through a liminal zone both at the end and outside of time. Time appears in the form of a *lacuna* that is an entrance-way as well as an exit. By making that which is at the limit of time reside in its very deepest depths, Celan gives a temporal dimension to the mysterious depth of which God speaks in *Job.*

Though not itself the goal of the search, *Wabeneis* pulsates with an expectation of arrival; it connotes a translucent preserve, a womb of ice, where there is preserved, as cold as it may be, something as warm as milk and honey. If it were possible to speak of warmth at the heart of arctic cold, of a truly hyperborean poetics, surely the place where it can be found is in Paul Celan's work. In this suspension between time and the timeless, a heavenly search and an earthly pilgrimage are to meet, each expecting the other.

> *wartet, ein Atemkristall,*

> there waits, a crystal of breath,

"Out of whose womb came the ice? and the hoary frost of heaven, who hath gendered it? . . . [T]he face of the deep is frozen." Since this contains an allusion to the secret of creation, Celan has placed the life-engendering *ruach* in the depth of the time-crevasse. From the dialectical searching of the way that we have traced in the previous stanzas, which brought about a tried unity between the wind-speech of God and the dissolved life of Job, there is no way to tell whether the *Atemkristall* is Job's or God's exhalation. But we may recall Job's desperate wish that he be hidden in Sheol until God's anger passes, there to wait for a new hearing; and we may recall also how Celan has translated this wish into an ice-bound refuge, one we associate with the ice and hoarfrost of heaven. Further evidence for Celan's having drawn *Atemkristall* out of the Hebrew is the fact that *kerach,* the word used for ice in Job, like the Greek κρυσταλλο, is also used to mean (glass) crystal.

There is a desperate expectation-horizon in the conclusion of **"Weggebeizt."** *Wartet* is like a pedal point announcing and waiting for an imminent resolution. All hinges on a Genesis that has still yet to be: the real Genesis that comes at the end. The actual point of contact, of arrival, is left hanging between "now" and "at any moment."

> *dein unumstössliches*
> *Zeugnis*

> your incontrovertible
> witness.

The final stress on the witness that cannot be overturned, whose testimony is incontrovertible, has a Hebrew antecedent. The Hebrew word for witness *ayd* is related to a root meaning "reiterating, emphatically affirming." This root is probably kin to the temporal adverb *ode,* which expresses continuance and perpetuity through time. It is not absent from *Job,* nor is it likely that traditional as well as modern interpretations of Job's *Zeugnis* were missed by Paul Celan. In 16:10-22 there is a very famous invocation of the witness:

> O Earth, cover not thou my blood, and let my
> cry have no place. Also now behold, my witness
> is in heaven and my record is on high. . . . O
> that one might plead for a man with God as a
> man pleadeth for his neighbor.

Rabbinic lore, certainly well established by Maimonides's time, ascribes the role of witness to an interceding angel in God's "court" who gives testimony on behalf of the person who is brought to trial by God. On the other hand, Martin Buber concludes his essay on *Job* [published in *The Dimensions of Job*] with the double or bi-polar nature of the witness in *Job:* "and in all his revolt [Job] was God's witness on earth; as God was his witness in heaven." The bi-polar interpretation is much in keeping with the ambiguous grammar of *dein unumstössliches Zeugnis,* which, unlike *deiner Sprache,* cannot be a property of *Du,* but rather refers to an other who witnesses *for Du.* This reading also accords nicely with our emphasis on the *Strahlenwind deiner Sprache* as both agent and object of the turbulent trying of the ways of speech. There is an irony here that cuts to the central problem of the *Book of Job*: that Job may have been a truer witness for God than God himself, appealing as Job does from God against and to God.

It is the poem that has taken Job's cry and God's words and turned them in a purge against themselves. In this trying of the way of speech, the wind-blast of the omnipotent Shadai is turned and etched into the breath of a finite creature.

A one-way retrospective reading of **"Weggebeizt,"** from the poem back to its biblical source, would relegate it to a kind of dependence on the source, a dependence that would cloud the integrity of the poem. There is always the danger of *over-mediation* in the reading and interpretation of Celan's later poetry which misses the astonishing event of the poetic utterance itself. **"Weggebeizt"** underscores the problematic relations between an immediate original language and its subsequent transformations, between source, destination, and end-point. Celan set his German in a painful process of deformation in order to bring it into contact with the language of Job: the result is a poem that gives the effect of being charged and coursed by a sacred language. Taking the direction traced by our reading *unterwegs,* we can see the language of *Job* as the source of the *Strahlenwind* and of the poem. But if we view the source from the vantage of its destination we must also say that the source becomes hidden once it is expressed in the ray or beam, that the source, even, ceases to be once the ray twists into and through the turbulent *Wirbelwind*-motion. We can know the source, finally, only through contact with its manifestations. In this way the source disappears, search as we may for it in the *Strahlenwind deiner Sprache.*

Lesley Chamberlain   (essay date 1988)

SOURCE: " 'Into Your Narrowest Being': The Poetry of Paul Celan," in *P. N. Review,* Vol. 14, No. 6, 1988, pp. 32-4.

[*Chamberlain is an English journalist, critic, and lecturer in Russian and German languages who has written several books on Eastern Europe. In the following essay, she asserts that Celan's poetry is informed by "extreme negativity" and "personal grief"—emotions that are often expressed through images of nature and death in his poems.*]

Celan's poetry presents difficulties for the English reader at once linguistic, cultural and spiritual. He was marked ineradicably by the deaths of his parents in a Nazi extermination camp and his senses seem to work fitfully in the scores of poems written in tribute. They suddenly fasten on an object, spurt into life, exaggerate its proportions, only to name the place of that object in a world beyond healing. His language throws out words in unpredictable rhythms, becomes obsessed with certain sounds and colours, then denies them. The lyrical heart broken, the troubled senses try by perceiving patterns and analogies to build beyond it. Celan's experience of the wasteland is more personal and more self-destructive than Eliot's, not so much a doubting of culture but a declaration of a seismic fault in the possibility of living.

Celan writes out of a loss of faith in death. To describe what it is to dwell in the human space without this prospect of grace and ultimate companionship is his bleakest vision. Men exist virtually beyond solace, when nothing is loved or hated or possessed in memory which is not devastated into random fragments.

Extreme negativity produces in Celan an hallucinatory after-hope, resembling Sartrean nausea, of a return to nature. Viewing dehumanization as a change of substance, he plays with endless metamorphoses, creating a new mythology out of unnatural death. Shocked feeling becomes aqueous matter and the heart and the head become stones. **'Dark eye in September'** for instance begins (my translation): Stone bonnet age. And the locks of pain / flow round the earth's face more luxuriously'. In that poem an eye is alone and arguing when it catches sight of 'the slim itinerant figure of feeling'. Then the poet switches into the second person and the argument is forestalled as both feeling and the ability to see it are destroyed: 'You plunge your sword into the wet of its eye.' Another poem, **'The Stone from the Sea'**, speaks of the white heart of 'our' world having rolled away, leaving 'us' to spin the reddish wool of dreams. The heart is a stone from the depths of the sea with 'hair' and a memory of mussels and waves. From these tortured surreal dreams it is as if Celan is recovering his mother's transubstantiated remains from the earth or the seabed, or, as in **'Aspen Tree'** from within the substance of the rain.

The metamorphosed landscape only faintly recalls the familiar earth. Colours once drawn from nature come on the other side of death from the laboratory of chemical analysis and reconstruction. The greens and blues of the forest and the browns and golds of a mother's hair, having lost their emotional meaning, have seemingly been put under a microscope to be verified and classified and their relationship with other natural phenomena established. The eye chronically shocked no longer sees with feeling but inhabits a new realm, in which it is itself a visible object, a hangover from a past emotional life, a bluish thing, related to the rain and the sea. In the ghostly, mournfully erotic **'Chanson of a Lady in the Shade'** two eyes are petrified into a jewel on a ring. 'He wears them like shards of sapphire and lust', the lady sings. In **'Night'** included in the 1959 collection, two petrified human eyes which in life had the physiological capacity to exchange glances now in eternity audibly collide in a moment before dawn. 'Heart-grey puddles' on the flagstones are 'two mouthsfull of silence' in the poem **'Language Mesh'**.

It is a particular combination of history, personal grief and a sense of the crisis of language they have engendered, which allows Celan's poetry to resist comparison in any language. He is at once painter, pained man, and chronicler of grief. As fascinated by colour as by words, he finds both receding from his grasp *in extremis.*

One experience of Celan's which seems essential to understanding his idiom was a unique year of happiness he enjoyed as a medical student in France in 1938, at the age of eighteen.

The medical experience gave him a language in which to analyse the difference between living and dead tissue dispassionately, which helped stabilize, at least on the page, his revolted vision of his parents' asphyxiation. With a pathologist's and a physiologist's vision he set about the metamorphosis of his unhappiness and the device created a bridge between the human body and the human language. He wrote often in terms which related as much to the hurt organism as to the disabled word.

Grief does not interfere with the working of the elements, with plant cycles, or with the properties of oxygen or the functions of the blood. By recalling their certainty Celan can achieve a vision of the first signs of life struggling to start anew, such as we might imagine after the nuclear destruction of the planet, and such as Celan experienced in the years he chose to remain living after the Holocaust.

It is not a generous vision. The rebuilt emotional landscape of his poetry can resemble a microscopic slide. Likewise the position of his poetry in the surrounding silence resembles that of one living cell pinpointed in a blank mass. But the vision is of necessity strange. He declared in a speech in 1960, on being awarded the Büchner, prize, that poetry was perhaps 'congenitally dark'.

In several of Celan's poems there is a crossing-over, a point at which the order of the familiar world is reversed into a new, similar but absurd order. In this sense Celan's work seems to be a vast chiasmus. The rhetorical figure establishes an order of words; the other side of a dividing line that order is reversed. This scheme built into Celan's poetry charts the relationship of organic to inorganic, blood to stone, eye to water, humanity to its bodily fate, meaning to senselessness, language to babble, as each phenomenon passes through the point of death into its dehumanized complement.

It is a particular combination of history, personal grief and a sense of the crisis of language they have engendered, which allows Celan's poetry to resist comparison in any language. He is at once painter, pained man, and chronicler of grief.

—*Lesley Chamberlain*

The idea of the chiasmus helps us understand Celan's simultaneous exploration of the death of the body and the death of language. The dual crisis is contained in the very idea of the *Sprachgitter,* for which the English translation 'language mesh' can only be provisional. The word *Gitter* suggests language is both imprisoned, fenced in behind bars, and that it might through itself create a lattice or a series of crossings-over, of meaning. It suggests both involuntary confinement and voluntary building. The poetry often amplifies this theme, even when the word *Gitter* is absent. **'Crowned Out'** from **Die Niemandsrose,** for instance, opens with these lines about weaving the stuff of painful memory:

> Crowned out,
> spewed out into night.
>
> Under what
> stars! So much
> grey-beaten heart-hammer silver. And
> Berenice's head of hair, here too.—I plaited.
> I unplaited,
> I plait, unplait.
> I plait.

By analogy the mesh suggests one of the body's key healing processes, the clotting of the blood. Human tissue heals itself by spinning sticky fibres which enmesh themselves, catching up platelets of hard blood in the spaces. Celan, the ex-medical student, speaks often of wounds and scars and scabs, and scab formation gave him a scheme for all potential healing. In those positive moments Celan seems to have believed that healing was possible.

The closest Celan came to spelling out the philosophy of the absurd the chiasmic scheme implies was in his prose, a scant collection of forced but important utterings, invaluable as accessories to the poems. (Now translated by Rosmarie Waldrop [in] *Selected Prose.*) A speech after he received the Büchner prize in 1960 picked up the traditional German comparison between man and puppet. Though death made us believe we were puppets of fate

there would always be voices to declare the absurdity of the human predicament as a triumph. Poetry, driven to extremes, taking metaphors to the last degree of absurdity, and tending towards silence, belonged among those voices. Going beyond Celan's own immediate references we can compare his outlook with that expressed in Kleist's classic essay 'On the Puppet Theatre' (1811). Kleist wrote of the impetus towards artistic creation out of humanity's disasters, using an image recalling Celan's in the last stanza of **'Aspen Tree'**:

> Failures . . . are inevitable, since we have eaten from the tree of knowledge. Yet Paradise is locked and bolted and the Cherub is behind us; we must make a journey around the world, and see if perhaps somewhere it is open from behind.

His description of art as reconstituted nature also recalls the chiasmus in Celan:

> We see that in the organic world, as reflection becomes weaker and more obscure, grace emerges all the more gloriously and commandingly. Just as the intersection of two lines, on one side of a point, suddenly comes out on the other side after passing through infinity, or the image in a concave mirror, after it has moved away into infinity, suddenly reappears right in front of us; so it happens too that when the mind has as it were passed through something infinite, grace reappears; so that at the same time it is most purely manifest in that human form which either has no consciousness or infinite consciousness, i. e. in the puppet or in the God.

Celan's petrified hearts and the blinded 'slim itinerant figure of feeling', however they are evaluated, belong in this realm of puppets, as does his imagined reconstruction of his parents' deaths.

In *Shoah,* Claude Lanzmann's film about the extermination camps, the German guards referred to their prisoners, even before they fell like rag dolls out of the gas chambers, as *Figuren* (figures, puppets).

Yet Celan insisted for many years on trying to recall nature back from the realm beyond, an impulse which is also well documented in his prose. He spoke in 1958 of the poet 'being in the open air':

> . . . not only my own efforts, but also those of other lyric poets of the younger generation . . . are the efforts of those with stars above their heads, the achievements of men; they are the efforts of those who are also tentless in this previously unrealised sense and thereby most strangely in the open air; the efforts of those who with their existence go and seek out language, sore with exposure to reality and seeking reality.

Celan's negativity thus gathers positive momentum. The Büchner speech expresses a fundamental, metaphysically charged, even erotic desire to communicate: For the poem is not outside time. Certainly it stakes a claim to eternity, it tries to grasp something beyond time, but by passing through it, not over and above it.

The poem can be, since it is a manifestation of language and therefore in essence dialogue, a message in a bottle, sent off in the belief—albeit not always a very strong hope—that it might sometime and somewhere be washed up onto land, perhaps onto land of the heart. In this way poems are on the move: they are aiming to get somewhere.

Robert Pinsky   (essay date 1989)

SOURCE: "The Language Net," in *The New Republic,* Vol. 201, No. 5, July 31, 1989, pp. 36-9.

[*Pinsky is an American poet and critic. In the following review, he discusses the difficulty of accurately translating Celan's highly inventive poetry and praises the sensitivity of Michael Hamburger's translation in* Poems of Paul Celan.]

In the writing of Paul Celan, even we readers who can hear poetry only dimly in German can sense the greatness of his invention: the cadences of a music titled against music's complacency; words punished for their plausibility by being reinvented and fused together and broken apart; syntax chopped and stretched to crack and expose its crust of dead rhetoric. Language in general, perhaps German in particular, is associated by Celan not with light but with darkness, ice and snow. In one poem, truth makes its unlikely appearance among mankind in the midst of our "*Metapherngestöber,*" a neologism translated by the English poet Michael Hamburger [in *Poems of Paul Celan*] as "flurrying metaphors." The term suggests an obliterating, aimless, and smothering proliferation of things that stand for other things a storm that covers all in its cold, blank drifts.

This idea of language against itself is a 20th-century commonplace, but Celan, a victim of Nazism writing in German, gives it the full emotional pertinence of the century's history. His work and his life of exile, ending in 1970 with his suicide in Paris at the age of 49, seem a defining outgrowth of that history. Celan's late work is justly known as "difficult," but its difficulty has the authority of its material. A Romanian Jew whose parents were murdered in the notorious work camps of Transnistria, Celan chose to write his poems in German, and after the war he chose to live in Paris. Thus, a person of many European cultures and languages, but also of none, Celan was historically situated so as to witness Europe's great spasm of self-destruction, and to re-create that massive unmaking in his poems.

Elliptical, rhythmically hypnotic, each word obdurate and inward as a geode, these poems embody the conviction that the truth of what has been broken and torn must be told only with a jagged grace. German was the language of his parents, Romanian and Hebrew the languages of his schools, French the language of his adult daily life. From English Celan translated poems by Shakespeare, Dickinson, Frost, and from Russian Mandelstam and Blok. The act of translation that most determines his writing is the translation from the world of the living to the world of the dead.

Caught in the language-net (*Sprachgitter,* in the title of one of his volumes) or metaphor-storm, the living can lose all touch with the dead. Celan's imaginative pilgrimage to the world of the slaughtered seems to be couched in a discovered language of destruction:

> Augen, Weltblind, im Sterbegeklüft: Ich komm,
> Hartwuchs im Herzen.
> Ich komm.
>
> Mondspiegel Stailwand. Hinab.
> (Atemgeflecktes Geleucht. Strichweise Blut.
> Wölkende Seele, noch einmal gestalnah.
> Zehnfingerschatten—verklammert.)
>
> Augen weltblind.
> Augen im Sterbegeklüft,
> Augen Augen:
>
> Das Schneebett unter uns beiden, das Schneebett.
> Kristall um Kristall,
> zeittief gegittert, wir fallen,
> wir fallen und liegen und fallen.
>
> Und fallen:
> Wir waren. Wir sind.
> Wir sind ein Fleisch mit der Nacht.
> In den Gängen, den Gängen.
>
> ("Schneebett")

Comparison of the original and the translation of this one poem can stand both for the virtues of the translator's achievement and for translation's necessary, severe limitations. Michael Hamburger has earned our gratitude for rendering these poems in a reasonably inventive English that has the tact to gesture toward the impossibility of his task. (The present volume [*Poems of Celan*] is a revised and expanded version of Hamburger's *Paul Celan: Poems,* which appeared in 1980 and has had a great impact on American poets.) Since Celan's implosions and distortions, his oblique puns and his violent exaggerations of German's compound words, can be neither rendered nor ignored, Hamburger can only indicate them, as if with a gesture.

Such salvaging and rendering from language to language is a specialized case of the difficulty of making poems, the difficulty of creating a presence that is not a version of something else, but an actual emotional reality in language. Frost said that poetry is what is lost in translation; but like translation, poetry itself pursues what has been lost. Both translation and metaphor put one thing in the place of another. George Steiner (Celan's advocate) suggests in *After Babel* the identity of poetic composition and translation. If perfect translation is impossible, translation itself is inevitable, part of the ongoing process of culture moving through time. Everything we say, according to Steiner, is a kind of translation.

There is all the more reason, then, to read Celan's poems in at least two languages at once, and to absorb as best one can their peculiar defiance of translation. Here is Hamburger's version of the first three stanzas of the poem I have quoted:

> Eyes, world-blind, in the fissure of dying; I come,
> callous growth in my heart.

I come.

Moon-mirror rock-face. Down.
(Shine spotted with breath. Blood in streaks.
Soul forming clouds, close to the true
shape once more.
Ten-finger shadow, clamped.)

Eyes world-blind,
eyes in the fissure of dying,
eyes:

                              ("Snow-bed")

The first three terms—*Augen, weltblind, Sterbegeklüft*—launch a journey to the dead, a process embodied by the broken off substantives of the second stanza. Then, in a good example of the term "untranslatable," *Augen, weltblind, Sterbegeklüft* return again in the third stanza, but transmuted. How can English evoke that syntactical repetition, which brings the poet himself closer to those three terms of death, as in a macabre version of Keats's "already with thee"?

Celan's imaginative pilgrimage to the world of the slaughtered seems to be couched in a discovered language of destruction.

—*Robert Pinsky*

A translator in the manner of Ezra Pound might try for cognate English terms like "deathcleft" for Hamburger's "in the fissure of dying." But "Hard-waxed" for "*Hartwuchs*" would sound like car polish, while the syllable "*wuchs*" indicates a waxing as in the growth of the moon, the "*Mond*" of "*Mondspiegel Steilwand*." So in the two collided syllables "*Hartwuchs,*" the hard-spot that has formed on the human heart—a heart wart—is associated with the hard rockwall of the reflective moonmirror, with its breath-flecked light that seems to condense again the cloudy souls of the exterminated and long-buried, now nearly formed anew: *gestaltnah*—"gestalt-nigh," to form another impossible English cognate. Somewhere between such inventions or the pseudo-Hopkins "death-cleft" (or "deathchasm"?) and "breath-flecked" (*Atemgeflecktes*) on one side, and Hamburger's discrete solutions on the other side ("shine spotted with breath," "close to the true shape once more") lies the extraordinary, tormented verbal music I can only imagine and half-sense. It is the music of a death embrace, living imagination and irrefutable death clamped together like the jammed syllables of "ten-fingershadow—full clamped."

After that stanza of horrific nouns, the opening words come back as subjective rather than objective: the eyes, world-blind, that are addressed by the poet in the first line become those of the poet, or merged with his, in the third stanza. The epic theme of the Journey to the Underground governs the arc of all Celan's language. Here in the Snow-bed that arc is completed with terrible thoroughness. "I

come," the poet tells the dead in the first line, but by the third stanza, with the adjective following the noun, as in English "eyes open"; now he not merely comes but arrives, eyes open and eyes world-blind, his eyes in the staring binary repetition of the line "*Augen Augen*" as purely and merely eyes as the unblinking eyes of the frozen dead. The double noun, each half modifying the other—these eyes are not seeing eyes or brown eyes or blue eyes, but eye eyes: not eyes awake or eyes open or eyes sleeping, but entirely eyes eyes—executes its grim tautological joke. In "*Augen Augen*" one thing does not stand for another: here where a equals a the metaphor-flurry is still.

And indeed, the rest of the poem is made mainly of binary repetitions:

The snow-bed under us both, the snow-bed,
Crystal on crystal,
meshed deep as time, we fall,
we fall and lie there and fall.

And fall.
We were. We are.
We are one flesh with the night.
In the passages, passages.

The journey to the dead is a great falling and lying down and falling, like the coming apart of sentences and distinctions: eye-eye and crystal on crystal, an interwoven mesh or network of negations, "meshed deep as time," as Hamburger's English has it. But the weave of "*zeittief gegitter*" has a jammed, explosive eloquence, as if we could say something like "timedeep engridded." "*Gegittert*" recalls that the book in which **"Snow-Bed"** appeared was titled after a poem called **"Sprachgitter"**. **"Languagemesh,"** the trapping and supporting grid of crosses that entangles life, the metaphor-flurry as a binding trellis. The force of that net or latticework, connecting everything with the sticky web of words, finds its counterforce and its representation in Celan's laconic repacking of language into painfully overfreighted fragments.

And yet this overpacking is characteristically yoked with the echo of a grammar textbook: "*Wir waren. Wir sind.*" We were, we are: the symmetry and relentlessness of a language lesson. The tyrannical entropy of everything boiling down to one thing, eye eyes, crystal on crystal, devolves into the poem's final line: "*Inden Gängen, den Gängen.*" "In the passages, passages." But also, in German, the ways, the ways of going and the ways of walking, and also the works, as in the movements of watches, so not only the corridors of Night and the passages of Night's flesh, but also Night's gears and its gaits and its wellsprings.

In short, the words of the poem seem to hover in the land of the dead, partly by using traditional aspects of poetic language with a kind of destructive, ranging terseness, so that repetitions, figures of sound, and images seem ready to collapse into a furious silence. That is the genius of Celan, and in translation the fury and unmaking recede, while a more ordinary poetry of construction takes the foreground.

At the age of 23, immediately after the war Celan wrote the **"Todesfuge"** (**"Deathfugue"**). John Felstiner has described the remarkable career of this poem (TNR, "The

Biography of a Poem," April 2, 1984). It became a central part of the German school canon, much anthologized and translated and quoted ("Black milk of daybreak we drink it at sundown . . ."), an essential work in Holocaust literature and—in short—one of those great works that are pressed by the weight of attention toward the shape of a chestnut. The honoring integument of anthology and pedagogy seemed to muffle, nearly to deride, the poem's rejection of poetry's euphony, a rejection that in the poet's work became more stringent and sardonic. (For whatever reason, Celan began refusing permission to reprint the poem in anthologies.) From a great poet of explicit rhetoric, Celan became a great anti-rhetorical poet, with a moral strictness that makes mere "experiment" seem frivolous, and mere literal translation seem tepid. Language undoes itself best, these poems suggest, in the original.

None understands this situation better than Hamburger, a gifted poet and resourceful translator. In the reprinted version of his 1979 introduction, Hamburger speaks of the "process of reception" by which poems by Celan over repeated readings and over many years "became accessible." The magnitude and humility of this work are a great gift to us readers who with Hamburger's guidance pick our way through the German on the facing page.

That halting labor is itself a reflection of the work of Celan's poems, an effort to pick out the truth from among the swirling flurry or network of mere representations, the interstices where *this* is oriented by *that*. In his Jewish family in a now lost region of Romania, German was his mother tongue, and the language in which the order was given to shoot his mother in the head when she became too weak to work. Steiner has said that only Primo Levi and Celan among survivors have found language adequate to that period. Celan's resource appears to be something like a disassembly of language's network of expectation, a commensurate destruction and mastery. In the phrase from **"Todesfuge"** "Death is a master from Germany," the poet's word *Meister* surely conveys some sense not only of "boss" but also of the prowess in art we indicate in English by the Italian borrowing "maestro," and in "masterpiece."

Death is a maestro from Germany, in these austere German poems, and in the **"Todesfuge"**: *süsser*, "play more sweetly," he calls out to the musicians as the forced labor digs the graves. That dramatic scene, in the later poems, becomes transformed into an inward drama. Michael Hamburger helps us perceive that drama, a contest like the more explicit **"Todesfuge"** of music and torment, labor and despair, the accursed and the articulated, sweetness and breaking.

J. M. Cameron (essay date 1990)

SOURCE: "Poet of the Great Massacre," in *The New York Review of Books*, Vol. XXXVI, Nos. 21 & 22, January 18, 1990, pp. 3-4.

[*Cameron is an English-born critic, essayist, nonfiction writer, and professor of philosophy. In the following review of* Poems of Paul Celan, *he argues that despite the obscurity of much of his verse, Celan should not be regarded as a hermetic poet but rather as "a public poet, a writer concerned with the great events of the time."*]

The character of Paul Celan's work raises the question how far poetry can be—is—a central human activity in our time. Even when Milton played with the thought of writing a poem "doctrinal to a nation," at first having in mind an Arthuriad, such a project, in a lively form, was scarcely possible. Milton had in mind Homer and Virgil. Homer was certainly doctrinal to a nation, a principal source of moral and theological ideas current in Hellenic culture, and this was the ground for Plato's attack upon his poems—they taught false doctrines and offered bad examples. Virgil was not the shaper of a culture but rather the celebrant of a certain moment in the history of the Roman republic. His real triumph was in the Middle Ages, when he is taken to be a prophet, or a magician, and in the early modern period:

> his single words and phrases, his pathetic half-lines, giving utterance, as the voice of Nature herself, to that pain and weariness, yet hope of better things, which is the experience of her children in every time.

What the poet's role may now be is obscure. With the rise of industrial society and the drying up of oral culture we are overcome with doubts over the significance of poetry. We hesitate to make big statements, even though we may be confident that poetry in its manifold shapes is still an important part of our culture, that within the great secular shifts in the outlook on the world the poets are still nibbling at their pens and bringing themselves to write. But we cannot now think of the poets as their publics thought of Byron and Wordsworth. The direct relation Byron and Wordsworth had to their own time seems no longer possible today.

Everything that comes within the Modernist movement employs modes of discourse and sequences of images that are oblique; such poetry is on the whole inaccessible to many readers and perhaps to all readers unprovided with some kind of commentary.

This transformation of poetry is linked with stylistic changes in other arts as well. In successive periods poets have felt unable to write "in the old way," just as other artists could no longer paint or compose in the old way, and have cast about for new styles, new voices. The old styles and voices persist, sometimes without great change, as in Philip Larkin's work, more often as elements in a new way of speaking. Milton and Pope are thus present in Wordsworth's *The Prelude*. Sometimes the old voices are used for particular purposes, as when in *Don Juan* Byron uses the voices of Dryden and Pope in a satirical, mocking way. Sometimes, the use of the old is startling. It startles me to find Skelton's voice in Yeats; and this goes with the use of quotation, as in *The Waste Land* and the *Four Quartets*; the effect is arresting just because it starts up against the background of a new kind of discourse. Some wish to argue that more is involved, more than I have so far suggested, in the dislocations of syntax, the fracturing of common uses, the breaking of ordinary semantic connections, that begins with Mallarmé and Rimbaud; and they fly to the terminology of linguistics, and see the received link between signifier and signified as having been broken, sometimes through a felt pressure to diversify the poetry and escape banality and stock responses, sometimes because what the poet has directly in mind is unassimilable to the older poetic modes. This last consideration is, as we shall see, decisive for Paul Celan's work, and especially for his later work.

Much of his poetry, and this is plain in his earlier work, is "about" the great massacre of the Jews in the death camps of the Third Reich. (I prefer, with others, not to use the term "holocaust"; a holocaust is traditionally a burnt offering to the God of Israel, and even those who on account of the massacres wish to repudiate the God of Abraham, Isaac, and Jacob don't—I think—want to use "holocaust" with such savage irony.)

There are in Celan's poetry two other presences: the Russian poet Mandelstam, done to death by Stalin; and—this shakes the mind—the philosopher and Nazi Martin Heidegger, to whose disintegrative pressure on the German language Celan is manifestly indebted, and to whom—or rather to whose house—Celan consecrates a poem.

Little of Celan's poetry, then, can be thought to be self-referential or hermetic. Most of the poetry is obscure, some of it grievously so. But however oblique may be Celan's manner of proceeding, and however much he takes on this manner because he feels the moral force of Theodor Adorno's saying that it is impossible to write poems about—or after—Auschwitz, the obscurity can always in principle be dissipated by a commentary. The poems are "messages," as he himself insisted, like messages in bottles cast into the ocean. Some of the bottles may be lost; if they are not lost it is a matter of chance which person gets hold of a particular message. The message, when it is taken out of the bottle, turns out not to be the polished aphorism of a mandarin but a Delphic pronouncement, portentous, teasing, mysterious, beautiful. (This insight, along with much else, I owe to George Steiner.) The poems are messages, then, but not directed to an elected public and are in a form of discourse that doesn't readily yield up its meaning.

His most famous poem, often translated and much commented on, anthologized, a subject of study in German schoolrooms, is **"Todesfuge," "Death Fugue"** in Michael Hamburger's translation. It is one of the least Delphic, most available, of the poems. The phrases with which it begins transfix us:

> Schwarze Milch der Frühe wir trinken sie
>   abends
> wir trinken sie mittags und morgens
> wir trinken sie nachts
> wir trinken und trinken
>
> Black milk of daybreak we drink it at sundown
> we drink it at noon in the morning
> we drink it at night
> we drink and we drink it . . .

This is incantatory and provokes a recognizably poetic response in us, and the rest of the poem, painful as it would be if it were a matter of direct reporting, a direct account of the reduction of human beings to ash and smoke,

doesn't travel too far from the obscenity of the death camp and the incident that is one of the occasions of the poem. The commandant of the camp impressed gypsy musicians into a band and ordered them to play the tango and other dance measures to accompany the processions of victims to the ovens. Of course, in the end the musicians themselves perished, presumably in silence. Later Celan seems to have distanced himself from this poem, in part because it was used in the immense scholastic discussions of German guilt, in part because he found it too direct in its references to the bitter realities.

In his introduction to the poems Hamburger suggests that we should compare **"Todesfuge,"** with the later **"Engführung" ("The Straitening")**; we shall see, he urges, "how daring, cryptic, and spare Celan's manner has become" in the thirteen years since **"Todesfuge,"** Without a knowledge of the poet's life, dates, and situation it would be a rare and penetrating reader who would be able to guess at the poem's ultimate reference. It is plain from this late section that the extremes of human horror provide the ground of the poem.

> In der Eulenflucht, beim
> versteinerten Aussatz
> bei
> unsern geflohenen Händen, in
> der jüngsten Verwerfung,
> überm
> Kugelfang an
> der verschutteten Mauer:
>
> At owl's flight, near
> the petrified scabs,
> near
> our fled hands, in
> the latest rejection,
> above
> the rifle-range near
> the buried wall.

In **"Todesfuge,"** there is a fair amount of more or less explicit material; here in **"Engführung"** the material is deliberately hidden, as though he is constructing a deep parable and choosing not to provide a key. "He that hath ears to hear, let him hear."

From the collection *Die Niemandsrose* (1963) to his death in 1970 Celan's poetry becomes more fragmentary and obscure. It is often sharply beautiful, but it has seemed to some critics to have sense only in relation to a private world. His last years seem to have been unhappy and he had severe paranoid episodes. Paranoid beliefs are rarely quite groundless, and there was something right in his feeling that the world was ranged against him. In particular, quite unjustified charges that he had plagiarized the work of Yvan Goll troubled him severely. One who was not predisposed to have a paranoid vision of the world would have shrugged it off, finding the accusation preposterous. All the same, the dense obscurity is not, at least for the most part, a sign of mental derangement; it is rather the sign of an attempt to work into his poetry, in his own idiom, material that belongs to the harsh public world. He is not—he protested he was not—a hermetic poet.

Many themes, alongside the dominant theme of the great

> **Despite the difficulties his work offers the reader, Celan is a public poet, a writer concerned with the great events of the time.**
>
> —*J. M. Cameron*

massacre, are present in the later poems. There are some exquisite love poems; and there is much that is religious, a wrestling with the deepest and most troubling problems in Judaism and Christianity. He stands within the tradition of Meister Eckhart and the later developments of "negative" theology. He is far removed indeed from the optimistic theodicy of Leibniz and from German liberal theology, Jewish or Christian.

I choose for comment, using Hamburger's translations, some of the more accessible poems. First, **"Tenebrae"**:

> We are near, Lord,
> near and at hand.
>
> Handled already, Lord,
> clawed and clawing as though
> the body of each of us were
> your body, Lord.
>
> Pray, Lord,
> pray to us,
> we are near.
>
> Wind-awry we went there,
> went there to bend
> over hollow and ditch.
>
> To be watered we went there, Lord.
>
> It was blood, it was
> what you shed, Lord.
>
> It gleamed.
>
> It cast your image into our eyes,
> Lord.
> Our eyes and our mouths are so
> open and empty, Lord.
>
> We have drunk, Lord.
>
> The blood and the image that was in
> the blood, Lord.
>
> Pray, Lord.
> We are near.

Almost certainly the title refers to the Holy Week—the week devoted to the contemplation of Christ's Passion—office of Tenebrae (ironically, abandoned in the recent liturgical reform). The Eucharistic imagery is plain; the body and blood of the suffering Christ, and what goes with the savage eating—clawing—of the spiritually famished, are central images in the poem. (The reference is also, I take it, to the Passover meal.) The great inversion—we feel it like a blow—is that the relation between the Lord and those who are participants in the rite (not a ritual act but the actual bloody processes of living and dying in the camps) is the reverse of the traditional relation; the Lord is comforted, reassured that we are near; he is asked to pray to *us;* and there is a dreadful ambiguity about "It was blood, it was what you shed, Lord."

A very different poem strikes me as full of charm, soberly beautiful.

> Led home into oblivion
> the sociable talk of
> our slow eyes.
>
> Led home, syllable after syllable,
>   shared
> out among the dayblind dice, for
>   which
> the playing hand reaches out, large,
>   awakening.
>
> And the too much of my speaking:
> heaped up round the little
> crystal dressed in the style of your
>   silence.
>
>   ("Below")

In German the last three lines are:

> Und das Zuviel meiner Rede:
> angelagert dem kleinen
> Kristall in der Tracht deines
> Schweigens.

But it is the poetry of indictment, the expression of what might without absurdity be called God's dereliction that remains with us. A short poem linked to **"Tenebrae"** is:

> I heard him,
> he was washing the world,
> unseen, nightlong,
> real.
>
> One and Infinite,
> annihilated,
> ied.
>
> Light was, Salvation.
>
> ("annihilated, / ied" is the translator's rendering
>   of *vernichtet, / chten.*)

The supreme expression of the poetry of indictment is undoubtedly **"Psalm."**

> No one moulds us again out of
>   earth and clay,
> no one conjures our dust.
> No one.
>
> Praised be your name, no one.
> For your sake
> we shall flower.
> Towards
> you.
>
> A nothing
> we were, are, shall
> remain, flowering:
> the nothing—, the
> no one's rose.
>
> With
> our pistil soul-bright,
> with our stamen heaven-ravaged,

our corolla red
with the crimson word which we
   sang
over, O over
the thorn.

Celan stands within the tradition of Hölderlin and Rilke and it seems the common judgment of competent critics that his achievement is not less than theirs. Despite the difficulties his work offers the reader, he is a public poet, a writer concerned with the great events of the time. He stands in the same relation to the world of the massacres as does the author of *Lear* to the cruelty, poverty, and madness of his time. And just as in *Lear* the horror is not diminished or tempered, so in Celan's work the death camps and what went on within them are not made less terrible. But we have also to say, though the analysis of this isn't clear, that in each case the effect of the poetry is that we do in a mysterious way come to a new understanding of the horror, though not, emphatically not, through our being reconciled to it. On the contrary, it is the poetry that keeps the crust of familiarity from forming.

Michael Hamburger's translation is a great achievement. Any translation is an arduous business; but to translate Celan is uncommonly arduous. It is not the job of the translator to make what is obscure clear but to give us an equivalent obscurity. I once heard a man say that a certain modern translation of Paul Celan's letters made them understandable for the first time. I thought this a dubious compliment and a misconception of what a good translation is for. Celan's being a polyglot, with Romanian, French, Yiddish, Hebrew, English (he himself made a remarkable translation into German of Shakespeare's sonnets) under and sometimes on the surface of the poetry, presents the translator with peculiar difficulties. So far as I can judge, Hamburger has come close to overcoming them. It is a memorable volume and will influence our moral outlook and the practice of poetry for a long time to come.

Paul Oppenheimer   (essay date 1990)

SOURCE: "Language Mesh," in *The American Book Review* Vol. 12, No. 1, March-April, 1990, pp. 17, 29.

[*Below, Oppenheimer offers a positive review of* Poems of Paul Celan, *discussing Celan's approach to "making poetry from terror, horror, and speechlessness."*]

Paul Celan's poetry presents an exquisite imagination wrapped in an unspeakable pain. The pain is literally unspeakable. That is Celan's theme. The language, whether Celan's German or a translator's English, is inadequate to the pain. To express it approximately, he must pummel and reconstitute grammar, combine and recombine words, often eliminate information and facts, and allow ordinary acts and objects to assume extraordinary dimensions, as symbols of the most enormous and ineffable excruciation.

The challenge of this sort of problem—of making poetry from terror, horror, and speechlessness—and Celan's often interesting solutions to it, his exquisite phrases, are

a source of his recent posthumous celebrity. His obviously tormented life is another source, though one that, to judge from Michael Hamburger's introduction to this volume of translations, Celan himself would have dismissed. Celan saw himself, according to Hamburger, as aspiring to write "pure" poetry, along with a great many other poets in France after Mallarmé. "Pure" poetry, even in the dismal shadow of the Second World War, in the Paris of the early fifties, was not viewed as unfriendly to political and social issues. The terrors of the concentration camp, the horror of a mother shot to death, genocide, and the death of a young son were not incompatible with writing a poetry that could simultaneously respond to these events and stand on its own as poetry, that would be something more than an outraged letter to a friend or a tortured entry in a diary. The enduring question is whether and how well Celan succeeded.

His very life seems to have been a kind of surrealistic roller coaster, with many details, especially of the final years (he committed suicide in 1970), apparently not yet made public. He was born in Czernowitz, in Bukovina, in 1920, as Paul Antschel. His name changes—first to Ancel, then to Celan, an anagram adopted after the publication of his first poems in Romania in 1947—may or may not offer clues to what often seems a chameleon existence and a chameleon art. Adaptations of the life and of the work, a constant restructuring, took place against a background of violence and changes of nationality and language. An obsession with language, one that came to exclude most forms of empiricism, seems to have been the natural result. Certainly his circumstances were not congenial to the writing of a stable, or even formal, poetry, *à la* Yeats, in which a system of values might easily have emerged. Shuttled between Czernowitz and Southern Moldavia under the German occupation, starting in 1942, Celan escaped both arrest and the mass murder of other Jews, the genocide that claimed the lives of his parents. How he survived is not made clear by Hamburger's introduction, but by 1945 Celan had arrived in Budapest. He next turned up, illegally, in Vienna, and then in Paris (which he had visited at the age of eighteen to study German literature), and where he married a French graphic artist in 1952. His major work dates from this period. Invited to read at the

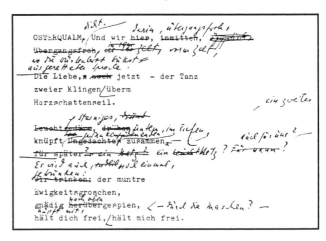

Manuscript of "Osterqualm."

annual meeting of the famous *Gruppe 47* in West Germany, also in 1952, Celan won wide recognition and subsequently a number of German literary prizes. The bitterness of youth, amply attested to in his poems, became the tormented achievement of maturity.

The present bilingual volume substantially adds to the collections of Celan's poems that Michael Hamburger published in 1972 and 1980. Readers of Celan should also be aware of *65 Poems,* translated by Brian Lynch and Peter Jankowsky and *Last Poems,* translated by Katharine Washburn and Margret Guillemin along with work by Joachim Neugroschel and Rosmarie Waldrop, which complement Hamburger's choices. Celan's complete poetry runs to more than 760 pages, much of which remains untranslated, with some poems still uncollected. The 163 poems offered here, from Celan's nine volumes of poetry, including posthumous ones, are nonetheless representative of a poet regarded by many as the most important writing in German since the Second World War, of his difficulty and fascination.

The difficulty is easily described, while the fascination in various ways baffles description. Celan writes an almost exclusively literary German, as one might expect from someone who never lived in Germany and who lived only briefly in Austria. His poetry abounds with a deliberately shattered syntax, a testament to the influence of French Symbolist and modernist poets such as Valéry. It also abounds with new compounds, invented words. Too much can be made of the tolerance of German for this sort of thing. While German is linguistically congenial to compounding, as is (to a lesser extent) English, the actual value of the new words lies, as it must, in their meanings, or in a context that illuminates them. Often Celan's new compounds are interesting in themselves, as in **"Psalm,"** in which *Niemandsrose* ("No one's rose") and *Nichtsrose* ("Nothingrose") supply a shape for spiritual emptiness and express a barren spiritual yearning: "A nothing / we were, are, shall / remain, flowering: / the nothing—, the / no one's rose." Often the compounds seem quite meaningless, as in the untitled poem that begins with the bizarre *Eingejännert:* "Januaried / into the thorn-covered / rock recess. (Get drunk / and call it / Paris.)" The extreme awkwardness of "Januaried" is hardly relieved by the obvious question, never dealt with in the poem, why not "Februaried" or "Marched"?

One is in fact marched through a steady stream of such words in reading Celan's poems, and there is no escaping their frequent lumpiness. For every *Niemandsrose* there is a *nachzustotternde,* as in "World to be stuttered by heart." Hamburger has in general done a remarkable job of translating these peculiar, and often inexplicable, combinations, in which it seems questionable whether missing data from the poet's life would do much to resolve the linguistic murkiness.

The fascination of the poetry remains. It echoes with Büchner (on whom Celan published an essay) as well as Baudelaire and Hölderlin. It is the fascination of walking through a museum of agonies. It is the fascination of hell without purgatory or any hint of a heaven beyond life itself: "I hear that they call life / our only refuge." The encounters with others-lovers, poets such as Nelly Sachs, Heidegger—are dark, skewering, perilous: "Your hand full of hours, you came to me—and I said: / Your hair is not brown. / So you lifted it lightly on to the scales of grief; it weighed more than I. . . ." The voice here, confident and transforming, is that of a true and potentially major poet. The "hand full of hours" sketches a dimension beyond the visible and sets it to a public music. The "Black milk of daybreak," in the intensely moving **"Death Fugue,"** an ode to Jewish concentration camp victims, nets the slippery dimensions of horror in what Celan calls his *Sprachgitter,* or "language mesh."

The grim accuracy of Celan's "language mesh," in a number of his poems, exposes the nonsense of Theodor Adorno's famous dictum that poetry is impossible after Auschwitz. In fact the dictum reduces evil to melodrama. Applied to poets other than Celan, it becomes a poor apology for the mediocrity of a good deal of poetry, in which incompetence is excused on grounds of the supposedly ineffable nature of horror. Celan himself, moreover, is most successful, as in the grisly "I hear that the axe has flowered," when he is clearest, when he is most syntactically sound. The unspeakable finds its terrible metaphors. The poet understands that the point is not to be adequate to his horrors but to be adequate to his language. The result, in these cases, and in their frequently fine translations by Michael Hamburger, is the creation of a new refuge from horror, of another refuge beyond life, of powerful poetry.

David McDuff   (essay date 1990)

SOURCE: A review of *Poems of Paul Celan,* in *Stand Magazine,* Vol. 31, No. 3, Summer, 1990, pp. 14-15.

[*Below, McDuff offers a positive review of* Poems of Paul Celan.]

The German-Jewish-Romanian poet Paul Celan, born Antschel (his name is an anagram of the Romanian form 'Ancel'), did not experience the concentration camps at first hand, but when he was twenty-two his parents were deported to one—there his father died of typhus and his mother was murdered with a shot in the back of the neck. The scars left by this terrible loss and the persecutions that attended it remained with Celan throughout his life—he too committed suicide, in 1970, and as in the case of Levi, writing and language seem to have been the principal means of his defiance against a uniquely intolerable manifestation of evil. Yet where Levi could have recourse to the Italian language and literary tradition in order to find a medium for his 'saying of the unsayable', Celan had to use the language of his oppressors in order to write the poetry of after Auschwitz. The version of the German language he finally chose was one hyperconscious of itself, strongly marked by the influence of Yiddish yet filled with echoes of classical German poetry and lent a strange and distanced resonance by being filtered through a negation of classicism. The result is very nearly untranslatable. While the poems of Celan's first collection *Mohn und Gedächtnis,* which contains the famous **"Todesfuge"** (**"Death Fugue"**), are in some respects close to the Expressionist and Surrealist traditions in style, form and content, and may therefore be slightly easier to render into a foreign language, those of the later collections (which include *Sprachgitter, Die Niemandsrose,* and the Heideggerian *Lichtzwang*) are almost entirely bound up in the nature and fabric of the German linguistic medium, and defy the translator's efforts. The problem is mainly that Celan's German conducts a debate with itself, a debate that stems from the poet's urgent desire to establish the literal truth of the world, to de-mystify and demythologize it, spanning the literal sense and the metaphoric suggestions of certain words, many of which possess a tension that has no direct counterpart in English: thus, for example, the strange quality of the line

> Wir spielten Karten, ich verlor die Augensterne
>
> **('Erinnerung an Frankreich')**

where 'Augensterne' are 'pupils' but also 'apples of the eye', is lost, as is the weirdness, in a later poem, of a coining such as 'Zwienacht' (literally 'twi-night', patterned after 'twilight'). Michael Hamburger, who deserves the greatest possible credit for his often ingenious attempts to overcome such difficulties [in *Poems of Paul Celan*] is inevitably stuck in this instance with 'twinight', which looks like a misprint. While for the reason outlined it cannot be said that the present volume succeeds all the way in presenting the true essence of Celan to an English-speaking reader with no German, Hamburger's often fluently impressive versions can, if read in conjunction with the facing German text, provide a searching interpretation of the original. . . .

Amy Colin   (essay date 1991)

SOURCE: "Resonances of the Night," in *Paul Celan: Holograms of Darkness,* Indiana University Press, 1991, pp. 53-74.

[*In the following excerpt, Colin analyzes Celan's poetic techniques and the political, historical, and literary influences evident in his early poetry.*]

Paul Celan's early poetry strikes the reader through its multiplicity of themes, ranging from love encounters and linguistic play to Jewish suffering. Similar to the texts of other Bukovinian poets, Celan's poems play with different modes of writing: some allude to *Minnedichtung* and German ballads, others to Rilke's and Trakl's poetry or to Roumanian folklore; biblical images, metaphors from the New Testament, and a nihilistic view of the world often clash in these early verses. While his texts display thematic and stylistic diversity, they share an interest in problems of language.

Though a poet's literary beginning sheds light on his later work and helps others understand his poetic development, there is no *critical* edition of Celan's early poetry. Some of the verses Celan wrote in Czernowitz were published in various literary journals such as *Der Plan* (1948) and in his first collection of poems, *Der Sand aus den Urnen* (1948); others appeared as *Gedichte 1938-1944* (1985). Yet for a long time many of them existed only in manuscript form, scattered among the private collections of his

friends. The recently published complete collection of Celan's early texts—*Das Frühwerk* (1989)—is no substitute for a critical and annotated edition, because it does not include the different versions of poems and comprehensive commentaries on their sources, history, and genesis.

In contrast to Celan's late, enigmatic work, which often resists interpretation, his early poetry appears so accessible that some critics try to reduce its meaning to preconceived frames of reference, such as biographical or literary allusions. In her book *Antschel Paul—Paul Celan,* Wiedemann-Wolf includes a detailed discussion of the few available studies of Celan's early poetry and shows how critics, including Stiehler and Chalfen take their own psychological or biographical speculations for the poem's ultimate function and sense. Wiedemann-Wolf's book presents a researched overview of various poetic devices and themes in Celan's early texts and analyzes some of these in detail. Most critics have assumed that Celan's *Von Schwelle zu Schwelle* (1955) includes his earliest reflections on linguistic problems, but Wiedemann-Wolf's *Bestandsaufnahme* reveals self-reflective elements inherent in such early Holocaust poems as the **"Todesfuge."** Wiedemann-Wolf views Celan's use of diverse literary traditions as a manifestation of his growing concern for poetic language. According to her, Celan's love and flower poems, written prior to the **"Death Fugue,"** anticipate some poetic devices of the later works but do not reflect poetological ideas, for they do not thematize them. Since words such as *Name* and *Wort* rarely appear in these early texts, she argues: "Antschel reflektiert zwar noch kaum explizit die Funktion des dichterischen Wortes . . ." (Antschel hardly reflects upon the function of the poetic word explicitly . . .).

But poetic language is by its very nature self-reflective. In his later poetry Celan succeeds in making words vibrate so as to uncover their literariness. In contrast, his early poems do not yet attain such an innovative mode of writing. Still, as textual analysis shows, his concern with linguistic problems is already apparent in the playful verses and love poems he wrote prior to 1944. Moreover, Celan's poetic ideas disclose themselves not merely in response to literary traditions (as Wiedemann-Wolf assumes) but throughout his early poems, in subtle allusions to the inadequacy of poetic language, as well as in his untiring quest for new means of poetic expression.

The war and the Holocaust did not prevent Celan from continuing his literary endeavors. In the midst of the ongoing deportations, Celan studied Rilke, Apollinaire, Blok, and Esenin, while hiding in the apartments of various friends. He translated some of Shakespeare's sonnets into German at that time, in an attempt to compete with Kraus's and George's renditions. During those months, he also created his first German adaptations of poems by Eluard, Housman, Verlaine, and Yeats. Not only in the ghetto, but also during the months in the Roumanian labor detachment, he continued to write poetry. As for many Bukovinian writers, literature became for Celan the crucial means of intellectual survival. The experiences of the Holocaust, the persecutions of the Bukovinian Jews, and the death of his parents in Transnistria left their imprint upon his early poems.

Like Bukovinian poets of his time, including his mentor Margul-Sperber, Celan believed that poetry created a world unto itself, detached from a reality overshadowed by the war. In April of 1943, while working in the Roumanian labor detachment, Celan composed several neo-Romantic love poems—**"Tulpen," "Rosenschimmer," "Windröschen,"** and **"Von diesen Stauden"**—for his friend Ruth. Celan's note from the labor camp, [an unpublished letter to Roth Kraft dated 16 April 1943], conveys his feeling of joy as well as pride at having succeeded in writing these poems in such somber surroundings: "In einer Landschaft, der auch die allergeringste Blume fehlt, kann ich diese Gedichte schreiben" (I could write these poems in a setting where there is not even a single flower). He likewise expresses confidence and satisfaction with the progress he has made: "meine Gedichte sind reifer geworden und schöner . . ." (my poems have become more mature and more beautiful . . .).

Celan's **"Tulpen"** appeared in the volume *Gedichte 1938-1944.* The different version cited here has not been published elsewhere.

> Tulpen, ein stummes Gestirn
> von Schwermut und süsser Gewalt,
> liess ich, dein Herz zu entwirrn:
> findet ihr Leben dich bald?
> Was in den Kelchen geheim
> ein Staubblatt mit Schimmer befiel,
> schwört den unsäglichen Reim
> für deinen wehen Gespiel.
>
> Sind es die Tulpen heut, sieh,
> die herrschen im Dämmergemach,
> hegst du ein Dunkles noch wie
> einst, als ich Rotdorn dir brach?
>
> Tulips, a silent constellation
> of heavy heartedness and sweet violence
> I left, to unravel your heart:
> Will their life find you soon?
>
> That which overcame a stamen with a shimmer
> in the calyxes privately
> swears the unspeakable rhyme
> for your wounded playmate
>
> Look: is it the tulips today
> that reign in the growing dimness of the room,
> do you foster a darkness still as
> when I cut red hawthorn for you, once?

The artistic structure of Celan's **"Tulpen"** recalls Stefan George's elaborate verse. Similar to them, Celan's three-stanza poem consists of long sentences whose interpolated appositions and relative clauses conceal the connections between subject, object, and verb. Each stanza is one sentence, and the recurrent enjambments heighten the flow of speech. As Celan's statements gradually transform themselves into questions, they enhance the intricacy of the text and suggest the idea of a linguistic unity. Only the poem's dactylic meter and the repetition of close, front, rounded vowels (*u, o*) lend these lines a grave tone, attuning the reader to their themes.

Here, Celan imbues the poem's almost classical form with romantic images of flowers, love, and a feeling of sorrow. As silent constellations of "Schwermut und süsser Gewalt," the tulips suggest a symbolist idea of metaphors as the flowers of language, and assume the speaker's sadness and melancholy. Since their function is to decipher the beloved's heart, they become a means of both cognition and communication. But as the subsequent line reveals, these messengers have not fulfilled their task, and the final question—"finder ihr Leben dich bald?"—implies a doubt about, rather than a belief in, their adequacy.

Through the image of stamens on which a glimmer falls, lines 5 to 6 lend to the strongly erotic image of pollination an impression of secrecy: "Was in den Kelchen geheim." These verses evoke an oath in unutterable rhymes and an unspoken wish for a language beyond words that may mediate between the speaker and his beloved: "schwört den unsäglichen Reim / für deinen wehen Gespiel."

The contrast between tulips and other messengers further develops this motif: "Rotdorn," whose color and thorns may stand for passion and suffering, reminds the speaker of past disharmony. In the published version of the poem, Celan writes: "hegst du ein Dunkel noch, wie / einst, als ich Rotdorn dir brach?" The interpolated comma ("noch, wie") and the substantivization of the adjective "dunkel" to "Dunkel," rather than "Dunkles," interrupt the melody of the line, enacting the moment of disruption. As the poem's concluding verse suggests, Celan questions the metaphors' commensurability with their task. Although tulips have become the speaker's new messengers, the poet—in "hegst du ein Dunkles noch wie / einst, als ich Rotdorn dir brach?" —still doubts whether they will accomplish the decipherment of the beloved's heart and the mediation between the speaker and "You."

Since Celan's romantic and symbolist images point to the inadequacy of metaphor as a cognitive device and as a means of poetic expression, they undo the harmonic unity evoked by the poem's classical form. In light of these connotations, the poet as "wehe(r) Gespiel" may suffer not only because of his unfulfilled love, but also because of his play with tropes, which makes him aware of their insufficiency. The differences between the published and unpublished version are significant. In the unpublished version, Celan uses the image of "silent constellations" for "shining constellations" (*leuchtend Gestirn*), thus emphasizing the linguistic ideas of his poem. As silent and even secret codes, the tulips bring to mind Hugo von Hofmannsthal's *The Lord Chandos Letter* (*Ein Brief*), which pleads for a language beyond words as the only still-adequate means of expression. The poem's unpublished version also stresses the discrepancy between its classicist form and its romantic images, because—in contrast to the published version—it does not disrupt the flow of speech in the concluding line. Such slight changes in Celan's diction point to his increasing awareness of the fissures inherent in poetic language. They also exhibit Celan's growing ability to play with words as a means of uncovering the incongruities between the poem's form and its themes.

Many of Celan's early love poems, which speak of the "You" as the mother or the sister, evoke a rather peaceful relationship between "You" and "I." In contrast, **"Tulpen"** shows the beloved to be a source of suffering—a destabilizing force. The speaker's unsuccessful attempt to establish a harmonious relationship with his beloved parallels the endeavor to come to terms with language. In fact, the poem suggests that it is the unsettling love for the "You," rather than a response to war and violence, that inspires the poet's quest for another, more adequate poetic idiom.

Celan's doubts about metaphors and the subversive elements inherent in his poem signal a difference between the Bukovinian confidence in words and Celan's own view of poetic language. These doubts show that Celan, unlike his compatriots, remained receptive to the disruptive aspects of romantic poetry, which had deeply influenced avant-garde writings. In contrast to the Bukovinian poets, he was much more interested in the language crisis of such fin de siècle Austrian authors as Hofmannsthal than in Kraus's attempts to revive trite phrases and traditional poetic devices.

Celan's earlier **"Weiss sind die Tulpen"** conveys another difference between his own romantic thought and the ideas of other Bukovinian poets. A version of the poem appeared in *Gedichte 1938-1944,* and Ruth Kraft placed it in the period July/August 1941; a second version (marked "23 Mai 1942") is one of the few early poems which Celan dated himself. The text cited here is this latter version.

> Weiss sind die Tulpen; neige dich über mich.
> Die Nacht tauscht Wind für fächelnde Hände
> ein.
>
> Sag:
>
> es werden die Falter schwärmen?
>
> Sag:
>
> mein Mund wird der einzige Kelch sein?
> Und du schliesst dein Aug vor dem rötlichen
> Schimmer—
>
> Sag?
>
> Denn diesmal—fühlst du?—lässt dich mein
> Arm nicht mehr in die Welt . . .
>
> Weiss sind die Tulpen; neige dich über mich!
> **"(Liebeslied)"**

> White, the tulips; bend over me.
> The night trades wind for fluttering hands.
>
> Say:
>
> will the butterflies swarm?
>
> Say:
>
> My mouth is to be the only cup?
> And you shut your eye on the reddish shim-
> mer—
>
> Say?
>
> For, this time—do you feel it?—my arm is no
> longer letting you into the world . . .
>
> White, the tulips; bend over me!
> **"(Lovesong.)"**

Critics such as Wiedemann-Wolf have already pointed to the remarkable innovative structure of the poem, which—unlike other early texts—no longer uses rhyme and a regular meter, but engages in sound interplay. Through the contrast between one-word and two-line stanzas, Celan integrates the blank space into the poem's form, recalling a stylistic device often used by French Symbolists to illustrate silence. The poem's imagery reflects its formal composition. Celan's **"(Liebeslied.)"** deploys metaphors of love and flowers in a remarkable way: the opening lines create a dreamlike atmosphere where erotic allusions merge with the image of the night exchanging wind for fanning hands. Gradually, almost unnoticeably, the text introduces the speaker's questions to a beloved. But the speaker not only poses questions; he also provides the answers to his persistent "Sag," subverting the idea of a dialogue. As the "I" implies—and even dictates—the answers of his partner and anticipates his beloved's feelings, the text evokes an ultimate unity between these lovers. The line "mein Mund wird der einzige Kelch sein?" associates the speaker's mouth with the calyx of a flower, conveying his wish for truthfulness and a harmonious relation. In "fühlst du?—lässt dich mein Arm nicht mehr in die Welt . . . ," the speaker reveals that "I" and "You" now reside within a realm that belongs to the world no longer.

The differences between the two versions are slight, but significant. In the opening line, Celan had originally written: "Weiss sind die Tulpen: neige dich über mich", in the later version Celan replaced the colon after "Tulpen" with a semicolon, perhaps he realized that the second part of the line neither explains nor details the initial image, but rather introduces a new metaphor of love. Initially line 6 did not contain a verb, but "wird" (see later version) is, in fact, necessary in order to emphasize the flow of speech. In line 7, the poem replaced the conventional "rosigem Schimmer?" with "rötlichem Schimmer—" which suggests the color of lips, and a dash for a question mark at the end of this line evokes the image of the "I" closely observing his beloved. The first version of this poem had no title. According to Wiedemann-Wolf, the parentheses in the title of the second version—**"(Liebeslied.)"**—signal the stylistic difference between Celan's text and a *Lied* in the German romantic tradition. But the parentheses may also signify that love is not the poem's major theme and that these lines participate only marginally in the tradition referred to in their name.

In the wake of Theodor W. Adorno's theories, some critics might be inclined to interpret poems such as **"(Liebeslied.)"** as a political act: the poet's withdrawal into poetic language is ultimately his protest against violence and war. But Celan's text contains other connotations as well. It recalls the romantic idea that "I" and "You" constitute themselves within language. The image of the speaker discloses itself through his speaking to an "other," and the beloved is created through and exists only within "I's" monologue. The interplay between "I" and "You" thus enables the poem to come into being. Celan's nationalist Bukovinian contemporaries used these concepts from German Romanticism to argue that the national identity of their people manifests itself in their native tongue and folk poetry. In contrast to these poets, Celan subverts the link between poetic language and its referents. As his verse "lässt dich mein Arm nicht mehr in die Welt . . ." implies, "I" and "You" inhabit a poetic sphere that is entirely detached from the "outside world."

Like most other German poets of Jewish descent from the Bukovina, Celan turns poetic language into a home and a refuge for lovers attempting to evade reality. Yet his poem also varies from the German-Jewish tradition of his homeland because of Celan's strong interest in more fundamental linguistic problems and phenomena. Celan's concept of the "You" as an idea inherent in the speech of the "I" even anticipates basic thoughts in "The Meridian," which explicitly treats the interaction between "I," "You," and poetic speech: "Das Gedicht will zu einem Anderen . . . es spricht sich ihm zu. . . . Erst im Raum dieses Gesprächs konstituiert sich das Angesprochene. . . ." (The poem intends another, needs this other, needs an opposite. It goes toward it, bespeaks it . . . Only the space of this conversation can establish what is addressed.) In light of these connotations, the image of the tulips in Celan's love song appears as a symbol for his play with tropes, which come to generate the poem. A comparison of the two versions of this poem reveals not only Celan's stylistic progress but also his growing awareness of the potential implications in the images he uses. Metaphors such as "mein Mund wird der einzige Kelch sein?" —which bring to mind his later enigmatic image "Trink / aus meinem Mund" (Drink / from my mouth) [in **"Das angebrochene Jahr"**]—testify to the innovative dimensions of his early work.

Celan's awareness of rhetorical devices and linguistic questions is also evident in his earlier **"Dein Schimmer,"** written in 1940.

Dein Schimmer, dein Schimmer
naht nimmer, naht nimmer . .

Dein Schweigen, dein Schweigen
trieft von den Zweigen.

Dass Krähen, dass Krähen
staunen und spähen.

Dann eifern die raschen
nach Tränen zu haschen.

Doch viele, doch viele
sterben beim Spiele.

Dein Schimmer, dein Schimmer
naht nimmer, naht nimmer . . .

Your shimmer, your shimmer
never nears, never nears . .

Your silence, your silence
drips from the branches.
So that crows, that crows
wonder and watch.

The quick ones then hurry
to snatch after tears.

But many, but many
die in the gamble.

Your shimmer, your shimmer
never nears, never nears . . .

The poem strikes the reader through its interplay of sounds, recalling not only the writing of Russian Symbolists, but also children's rhymes and magic spells. As Celan omits or adds a letter, he transforms a combination of repeated sounds into new words: *n* for an *sch* in "Schimmer" generates "nimmer"; a *z* for a *sch* alters "Schweigen" into "Zweigen"; *sp* instead of *kr* in "Krähen," creates the term "spähen"; and an interplay of the two consonants *r* and *h* reveals a phonetic kinship between "raschen" and "haschen." In stanzas 3 and 4, configurations of three phonemes—*sta* and *trä* in "staunen" and "Tränen"— attest to the variety within the repetitions. Since one sound cluster triggers the next, it is their sequence rather than semantic necessity that determines the choice of words and images. By unsettling the apparent thematic linkage, Celan makes language vibrate and free itself from usual semantic structures.

At first glance, the phonetic interplay appears to move beyond meaning, but a closer analysis reveals its direction and sense. The poem opens with absence: "Dein Schimmer . . . naht nimmer" draws on the colloquial German expression "keinen Schimmer haben," pointing to a lack of ideas or clues, and evokes the distance of the "You" from the speaker. In the subsequent verses, absence and negation manifest themselves in silence, which is associated here with raindrops falling off the tree branches ("dein Schweigen / trieft von den Zweigen."). These heterogeneous metaphors converge in a powerful image of death: the raindrops turn into tears snatched by the crows that die while playing with them. The poem ends as it began, assuming a circular structure: "Dein Schimmer, dein Schimmer / naht nimmer, naht nimmer . . ." As in **"(Liebeslied.),"** the *absence présente* of the "You," here a symbol for the missing traditional thematic bond between words, generates an interplay of tropes and images.

"Dein Schimmer" is not Celan's only early poem to play with phonetic and semantic elements to destabilize a familiar verbal coherence and to undermine customary modes of reading. His **"Zauberspruch"** (1940), **"Dämmerung"** (1940), and **"Mein Karren knarrt nicht mehr"** (spring 1941), [all from *Gedichte 1938-1944*], also engage in similar childlike linguistic experiments. In **"Mein Karren knarrt nicht mehr,"** Celan uncovers potential meanings by expanding "Herbstzeitlose" (meadow-saffron), the name of a flower, into an unusual image: "Die Zeitlose holt / Atem für tausend Herbste. . . ." In the concluding verse of this poem, "Das Herz der Espe / setzt aus" (the heart of the asp / ceases to be), the acoustic play on sibilants, rather than semantic principles, determines the choice of words and thus the creation of an image. These early poems anticipate aspects of Celan's later linguistic experiments in **"Grosses Geburtstagsblaublau mit Reimzeug und Assonanz"** and **"Abzählreime"** (1962) and his use of paronomasia in late, somber poems such as **"Huhediblu,"** where the interplay of phonemes turns words into "wordweeds" and "wordaxes"—"als Beikraut, als Beiwort, als Beilwort" [*Gesammelte Werke*]. In contrast to his later poems on the Holocaust, **"Dein Schim-**

mer" (like his **"Abzählreime"** from the early sixties), works with the theme of death, not as an expression of a tragic personal experience but as a trope that elucidates a playing with words and their acoustic components. Still, both types of poem exhibit Celan's dissatisfaction with traditional poetic devices and his quest for new means of poetic expression. In this respect, these entirely different poems represent two aspects of the same phenomenon. Celan's verbal experiments in his early and late poetry mark yet another difference between his own work and Bukovinian poetry, which rejected such language games.

When Celan wrote his poems **"Dein Schimmer," "Zauberspruch,"** and **"Dämmerung,"** he had already acquired a comprehensive knowledge of French Surrealism in Tours (1938) and had already read Breton, Eluard, and Aragon. Yet his early texts reveal that, despite his fascination with the avantgarde, he had not yet succeeded in transforming his poetic language according to their linguistic ideas. His early texts, however, signal the direction in which his poetry was to evolve.

In response to the Holocaust and the experience of the war, some of Celan's early poems—such as his **"Ballade von der erloschenen Welt,"** written in Czernowitz around 1942—use linguistic play to undo familiar notions of the transcendent.

> Der Sand. Der Sand.
> Vor die Zelte, die zahllosen Zelte
> trägt der Sand scin Geflüster.
> "Ich bin das Meer. Ich bin der Mond.
> Lasst mich ein."
>
> "Nacht", murmeln die Zelte.
> "Sei Nacht."
>
> Da rücken die Speere heran:
> "Wir sind es.
> Und das eiserne Blau des Morgens.
> Lasst uns die Schwingen alle
> durchbohren.". . .
>
> Da regen,
> da regen sich bange die Arme der Krieger:
> "Uns gaben die gottlosen Engel recht—
> und Fremde häufen hier Finsternis?
> Wir dringen ein.["]
>
> (Doch was,
> doch wer ist im Gezelt?)
>
> Ein atmendes Antlitz
> hängt sich hell vor die Zelte:
> "Regengrünes Geschick
> bin ich.
> Und ich bin das Gras.
> Ich wehe.
> Und ich wehe hinein."
>
> (Doch was,
> doch wer ist im Gezelt?)
>
> Versanken sie alle?
> Der Sand? die Speere?
> Die Arme der Krieger? das atmende Antlitz?
>
> Versanken, versanken sie?
>
> Die stammelnden Seelen der Neger ringsum

> tanzten rundum und drangen ein:
> die Schatten fanden sie, die Schatten
> von Keinem.
>
> Zersprengt ist der Seelenreigen.
> **("Ballade von der erloschenen Welt")**

> The sand. The sand.
> Before the tents, the tents without number
> the sand carries its whisper.
> "I am the sea. I am the moon.
> Let me in."
>
> "Night," murmur the tents.
> "Be night."
>
> The spears approach:
> "We are the ones.
> And the iron blue of the morning.
> Allow us to pierce through all
> pinions." . . .
>
> In fear then
> the arms of the warriors move, they move:
> "The godless angels granted us right—
> and strangers heap up darkness here?
> We will press in."
>
> (But what,
> but who is in the tents?)
>
> A breathing face
> hangs bright before the tents:
> "I am
> raingreen fortune.
> And I am the grass.
> I drift.
> And I drift inside."
>
> (But what,
> but who is in the tents?)
>
> Did they all sink?
> The sand? the spears?
> The warriors' arms? the breathing face?
>
> Did they sink, did they sink?
>
> The stammering souls of the Blacks all around
> danced in circles around and pressed in:
> the shadows, they found the shadows
> of No One.
>
> Exploded, the soul's roundelay.
> **("Ballad of the World Extinct")**

Like **"Dein Schimmer,"** this ballad orchestrates diverse clusters of sounds. One phoneme configuration engages the other, and their interplay determines the acoustic structure of each stanza. In the opening lines, the sibilants *s* and *z* (in "Sand," "Zelte," and "zahllosen") dominate the linguistic interaction; they are counteracted by alliterations of *m* and *n* (lines 6-7) and repetitions of *r* (lines 8-16). The subsequent lines work with prolonged vowels *e* and *i,* while the concluding two stanzas imbue the initial configuration of sibilants with the consonant *r.* This interweaving of sounds lends the text a melody which unsettles the narrative tone of traditional ballads.

Celan's poem, a dramatic scene in which different voices are contrasted with one another, derives its unusual character from the personification of objects, such as the sand, the spears, the tents, and the arms of the warriors. It recalls fables and ballads by the Bukovinian Yiddish writers Manger and Steinbarg, texts in which objects become the protagonists.

In the opening lines, a narrator's voice confronts the reader with the vision of a world devoid of life. Sand covers up the earth; of our entire civilization nothing is left but tents, the shelter of the Bedouins and of the Jews who once wandered through the desert after leaving Egypt. Winds carry the sand's whisper: one with the sea and the moon, the sand forces its way into the tents—tents which call, however, for the night, and thus perhaps for suffering and death. Gradually other voices resonate in the somber scenario: the spears—whose metallic sheen resembles the color of the morning—seek to break through "all wings," perhaps the wings of an angel guarding the entrance to the "inner world." But the arms of the warriors question the right of others to cause evil ("und Fremde häufen hier Finsternis?") and claim that the "godless angels" justify their actions alone. The unusual image of the "gottlose(n) Engel" hints at their deceptive holiness and at God's absence.

In a series of questions that interrupt the narration—"(Doch was, / doch wer ist im Gezelt?)"—the voice of a commentator urges the reader to reflect upon why these forces seek entrance into the tents. But instead of providing answers, the subsequent lines heighten the suspense: they mention yet another entity that seeks to penetrate the tents; this is a breathing face identified here with both nature and fate, "Regengrünes Geschick." In the next line the poem finally signals a denouement: though the indicative in "Wir dringen ein" and "Ich wehe. / Und ich wehe hinein" implies that the forces may have succeeded in intruding into the tents, the final question "Versanken sie alle?" suggests their destruction, anticipating the surprising end: the souls of Black people who perform a round dance, perhaps a *Todesreigen,* intrude into the tents; they discover nothing but "die Schatten / von Keinem," and, as a result, the souls disperse: "Zersprengt ist der Seelenreigen."

Such an ending leaves room for speculation, compelling readers to explore the multiple potential meanings of images such as the tents. In his late texts, Celan often associates tents with the world itself: his commentary *Edgar Jené and the Dream about the Dream* (1948) compares the world devastated by the war with a "Blutzelt" (tent of blood), and his *Bremen Speech* (1958) characterizes man's *Dasein* as "zeltlos" (unsheltered), meaning here a lack of protection and the absence of "God." Celan's early ballad seems to anticipate these later images by conveying the vision of a world after an exodus, after an atomic war, when there is nothing left of humankind but its shadows.

Yet the poem's self-reflective moments lend these lines another meaning. By juxtaposing the tents with forces residing outside the tents, the text evokes a contrast between an inside and an outside realm. Since the intrusion into the tents is linked to images of the world's extinction, the poem ultimately breaks down the inside/outside polarity that it evokes. Moreover, the enigmatic image "die Schatten / von Keinem," describing the tent's inside, conveys

a paradox: the nonexistence of a person, "Keinem," presupposes here the existence of a shadow. To "intrude" into the tents thus ultimately means to discover the paradox inherent in such cognitive models as inside/outside.

Rainer Maria Rilke, in "Am Rande der Nacht," used an interplay of sounds and antithetical images to first evoke and then undo the idea of a synthesis of the poem and the universe, of an "inside" and an "outside." Under the impact of violence and war, Paul Celan takes up Rilke's poetic devices as a means of conveying his disbelief in a transcendent force that may protect human life from destruction. The non-existence of a world's "inside"—whether a divine spirit or an inner sense—becomes a conceptual frame for his poem **"Legende,"** also written around 1942:

> Nach dem rostigen Rätsel der Erde
> komm Bruder forsch mit mir mit hellem Spaten-
> stich.
> Ich fand nichts. Du findest nichts.
> Doch die Erde splittert dabei.
>
> For the rusty riddle of the earth,
> come, brother, search with me with bright spade
> cut.
> I found nothing. You found nothing.
> But the earth splits with our work.

The poem searches for the secrets, and perhaps for a meaning in the world. But the speaker does not find anything; his search ends in nothingness and the destruction of the earth. The "rusting riddle of the earth" is nothing but a myth. Celan's early **"Ballade vom Auszug der drei"**—also written during the war—characterizes the entire universe and eternity as empty: "In die leere Ewigkeit ziehn wir mit schwelenden Fackeln" (Into empty eternity we draw ourselves with flickering torches) say the three fictional characters of the poem, which evokes the total annihilation of their and Celan's homeland. Again, the play with phonemes and use of paronomasia become the poet's means of unsettling universal concepts and beliefs such as the idea of a sheltered human existence.

Celan's early artistic endeavors also consciously relate themselves to his political engagement of that time, an engagement which—as Marlies Janz has shown [in *Vom Engagement, absoluter*]—deeply marks his later poetry as well. In fact, Celan's literary aspirations were to a certain extent a direct result of his political activities.

As a high-school student, Celan joined the illegal Communist youth organization in the Bukovina, braving the severe Roumanian reprisals against all Communist activities. Together with his friends, Celan studied Karl Marx, Gustav Landauer, Rosa Luxemburg, Peter Kropotkin, Mikhail Bakunin, Werner Sombart, and even the economist Karl Kautsky; they illegally brought out a leftist pamphlet, *Elevul Rosu* (The Red Student), and distributed it among students and workers. These leaflets included not only Celan's translations into Roumanian of passages from Marxist writings, but also essays by some of his friends on the situation of the working class. . . .

After the show trials and after reading André Gide's *Retouche du "Retour de l'U.R.S.S."* (*Afterthoughts: A Sequel* to "*Back from the U.S.S.R.*") (1937), Celan turned away from Soviet Communism, but he remained an attentive observer of political events. Celan's **"Fackelzug,"** probably written during the war, illustrates the relationship between the author's political engagement and his growing awareness of potential connotations inherent in poetic images and rhetorical devices.

> Kamerad, die Fackel heb
> und den Fuss setz stramm.
> Ferne ist nur Drahtgeweb.
> Und die Erde Schlamm.
>
> Kamerad, die Fackel schwing,
> meine Fackel raucht.
> Deine Seele ist ein Ding,
> das jetzt Feuer braucht.
>
> Kamerad, die Fackel senk,—
> und verlösche sie.
> Wie das Leben ist bedenk.
> Und das Sterben wie.
>
> ("Fackelzug")

> Comrade, raise the torch
> and stand at attention.
> Distance is but woven wire
> and the earth slime.
>
> Comrade, swing the torch
> my torch is smoking.
> Your soul is a thing
> that now needs fire.
>
> Comrade, lower the torch
> and put it out.
> Consider what life is.
> And what death.
>
> ("Torch Procession")

The poem's regular, accelerated rhythm recalls a military song. Through the iambic meter, alternating rhyme, and parallelisms, Celan enhances both the poem's emphatic tone and its structural symmetry, which appears even in the recurrence of indented lines. In the last stanza, however, the reversals ("Wie das Leben ist, bedenk. / Und das Sterben wie.") counteract the poem's repetitive aspects, signaling a change in the poetic mood.

The title, **"Fackelzug,"** evokes the procession of torches often used in Nazi demonstrations and thus attunes the reader to the subsequent images of violence. Such a traditional Nazi term as "Kamerad" and the military commands "die Fackel heb / und den Fuss setz stramm" reveal that the opening lines are written not only in the style, but also from the perspective, of Nazi war propaganda. The subsequent prosaic observations, devoid of any sorrow or regret, typify the attitude of comrades during World War II. For them the earth is nothing but mud, the horizon a wire netting, and the world a trench. Even the soul is a *thing,* that is, an object to be used or misused according to need and necessity.

But in the second stanza, the speaker contrasts the appeal to start the battle with the image of a burned-down torch, a symbol of the waning of the fighting spirit. In the same emphatic tone as appears in the opening lines, he urges the comrade to lower, to extinguish his torch and thus to put an end to violence. The poem closes compelling a "You" to reflect upon the value of life and the consequences of war: "Wie das Leben ist, bedenk. / Und das Sterben wie."

The poem's employment of idioms of Nazi war propaganda urging comrades first to fight and then to recognize the significance of life and peace, shows that Celan was well aware of the writer's capacity to manipulate language. Celan's **"Fackelzug"** consciously uses the comrades' military language to make them rethink the outcome of their violence. Although the poet was politically active, his text propagates no particular ideological view, but protests violence independent of its political justification. Like other European authors, including Kraus and some of Celan's Bukovinian contemporaries, he attacks the society of his time for misusing poetic language to drive people into war.

The interaction between Celan's political engagement and his artistic creativity also manifests inself in his **"Chanson Juive,"** which was later entitled **"An den Wassern Babels"** and was probably written during the war.

> Wieder an dunkelnden Teichen
> murmelst du, Weide, gram.
> Weh oder wundersam
> keinem zu gleichen?
>
> Den deine Kralle zaust,
> sucht sich in Sünden.
> Wendet sich von deinem Zünden
> flammende Faust.
>
> Kehr mit grausem Getös
> ein in kauernde Hütten.
> Komm unser Blut verschütten.
> Den Lehm erlös.
>
> ("Chanson Juive")

> Again at darkening pools
> You murmur, willow, grieving.
> Wounded or wondrous
> Equal to none?
>
> The one whom your claw clutches
> seeks himself in sins.
> Turns away from your enflaming,
> flaming fist.
>
> Come with hideous roar
> into cowering huts.
> Come spill our blood.
> Redeem the clay . . .
>
> ("Chanson Juive")

Despite the title's explicit allusion to Judaism, **"Chanson Juive"** follows the German stanza tradition of a "Lied." The poem's musicality expresses itself through the alternation of close, front, rounded vowels, and open, back, unrounded vowels (*u, e, ei*), as well as through the sibilants *s* and *z* that accompany the diphthongs *ei* and *au*. As in the texts of Russian Symbolists, the poem's melody is attuned to the imagery: in the opening lines, the willow motif evokes suffering and death, and the image of the darkening pools intensifies the poem's somber tone, which is counteracted only by the play of sounds in "Weh oder wundersam." The stanza emphasizes that the murmur of the willow has been heard before, and inquires into the nature of that which resembles the mourning tree.

In the second stanza, the sibilants *z* and *s* signal violence and aggression. Yet the *f* in "flammende Faust" prolongs the emphatic articulation of the stanza, anticipating the nearly hesitant attitude of the ending line. The willow, characterized by tugging claws, metamorphoses into a figure of punishment that forces self-recognition in a past of sins, "Den deine Kralle zaust / sucht sich in Sünden." The speakers address themselves to this threatening force, requesting its intrusion into their homes and spilling their blood. In the concluding line, this gruesome death wish becomes an appeal for redemption, "den Lehm erlös."

Similar to **"Chanson Juive,"** the second title of the poem, **"An den Wassern Babels"**—alluding to Psalm 137, **"By the Waters of Babylon"**—also sets the metaphors of violence and aggression in the context of Jewish suffering. As a burning fist and punishing force, the "You" assumes characteristics of the Jewish God, YHWH. The "fire" in "brennnende Faust" is a recurrent biblical metaphor of God (Gen. 19:24, 22:7; Ex. 3:2, 32:20, 40:38). Time and again, the Hebrew Bible characterizes YHWH as entering the "tents" of the Jews (Ex. 40:38, for example), proving His power or punishing their sins. These images also recur in the poem's concluding lines, "Kehr mit grausem Getös / ein in kauernde Hütten. / Komm unser Blut verschütten."

As the second title and the biblical allusions imply, Jewish songs from the time of the Babylonian captivity come to life in Celan's "Lied." The willow's murmur, a symbol of these songs, can be heard in the present time; ultimately, such images reveal that Celan identifies the fate of Jews in the death camps with their persecution in antiquity. The speakers plead for their own destruction, as death appears the only possible escape from their captivity and persecution. Bitter irony resonates in these lines: God offers His chosen people nothing but violence and death. Such an ironic tone underlying the melody of the concluding stanza ultimately questions the Jewish ideas that the poem seems to evoke. It points to Celan's doubt in the Jewish belief that God punishes only those whom he really loves and that past sins brought about the Holocaust.

The differences between the two versions of the poem illustrate Celan's quest for greater linguistic precision. Thus Celan in the later version **"An den Wassern Babels"** writes: "Weh oder wundersam: / Keinem zu gleichen?" The colon after wundersam" marks a halt; it emphasizes the poem's rhythm, drawing the reader's attention to the subsequent "Keinem zu gleichen?" Moreover, by capitalizing "Keinem," Celan stresses its significance in this context. In stanza three Celan includes a direct address to both the willow and YHWH—this is the "Du" so characteristic of his later poetry: "Kehr du mit grausem Getös / ein in kauernde Hütten." In addition, the later version ends in an ellipsis implying silence or perhaps "a turning of our breath."

The poem's themes and second title were a source of inspiration for Celan's friend Weissglas, who wrote his "Babylonische Klage" many years after Celan wrote **"Chanson Juive."** Though Celan's poem and Weissglas's text share some thematic affinities, their style and thoughts vary considerably. In contrast to Celan, Weissglas does not disguise his motifs through an intricate interplay of sounds and images, but presents them rather explicitly. Moreover, as the interpretation of Weissglas's verses exposed, the poet internalizes prejudices against his people, while Celan protests Jewish acceptance of anti-Semitism. These substantial differences between the two poems show that Weissglas "learned" as much from Celan as Celan supposedly learned from him.

In contrast to **"Chanson Juive,"** which places Jewish suffering in a broad historical context, Celan's poem **"Dornenkranz"** evokes a tragic and personal experience, the deportation and death of his mother. As a poetic expression of a biographical event, this poem creates a space of interaction between reality, poetry, and poetics:

> Lass von dem Purpur.
>
> Die Nacht
> hämmert den Herzschlag der Stunde zurecht:
> die Zeiger, zwei Speere,
> bohrt sie dir brennend ins Aug.
>
> Die Blutspur dunkelt und winkt nicht.
>
> Dein Abend,
> der Seen entschleiertes Antlitz,
> sank ins spärliche Schilf;
> der Engel besiegte Heerschar
> löscht ihn mit ihrem Schritt.
>
> Im Wald
> schnitzen die Messer der Winde
> in die Eschen dein zierliches Bild.
> Mit dem Nachtwind birg mich in deinen Armen.
> An die eschenen Brüste zünd ich dir Sterne zum
>   Abschied.
>
> Bleibe nicht. Blüh nicht mehr.
>
> Es ging das Schneelicht aus. Allein sind alle Ent-
>   blössten . . .
>
> Ich ritt in die Nacht; ich kehre nicht um.
>   **("Dornenkranz")**

> Let go the purple.
>
> The night
> hammers the hour's heartbeat into place
> the clock hands, two spear points,
> it bores burning into your eyes.
>
> The trace of blood darkens and ceases to sign.
>
> Your evening
> unveiled face of the seas
> sank into sparse reed;
> the angels' heavenly host, conquered,
> extinguishes it with its stride.
>
> In the forest
> the knives of the winds carve
> in the ash trees your delicate image;
> take me with the night wind into your arms.
> At ashen breasts I light you stars goodbye.
>
> Don't stay. Bloom no more.
>
> The snow-light went out. All the naked are
>   alone . . .

I rode into the night, I will not return.

("Crown of Thorns")

The poem plays with heterogeneous traditions, combining allusions to the New Testament with expressionist metaphors for violence ("Die Blutspur dunkelt") and romantic motifs with images recalling Rilke's poetry. The "crown of thorns," a metaphor for Christ's suffering, sheds light on the poem's seemingly unrelated opening line: "Lass von dem Purpur." "Purpur" evokes the scarlet cloak—a symbol of power and splendor—in which the Roman soldiers wrapped Christ to mock him (Matt. 27:28). In such a context, line I is an appeal to detach one's self from the world of power and beauty when confronted with death. As the color of the dusk and of blood, "Purpur" anticipates the subsequent description of the night. Like the Roman soldiers with their spears (Matt. 26:47), the night bores its hands into the eyes of the "You," causing eternal darkness (line 5). The verb "dunkeln" fuses the previous night-metaphor with the image of a blood trace ("Blutspur"), the evidence of the crime.

Stanza 3 speaks of the wind carving the image of the "You" into ash trees and of the speaker's wish to be concealed in the arms of the "You." In Germanic myth, the ash tree is the center of the world and symbolizes eternal life, and the carving of an image into such a tree of life appears as a means of preserving the memory of a "You." Yet the Middle High German word *asch* from which *Esche* derives, denotes not only ash trees but also ashes, the telling residue of destruction. As a species of olive tree, the "ash tree" may stand for the olive garden, where the Roman soldiers captured Christ. The text's hidden connotations recall Rainer Maria Rilke's "Der Ölbaum-Garten," one of Celan's favorite poems, which also speaks of Christ's isolation and loneliness.

Lines 14 to 16 introduce a decisive thematic change. Words such as "Brüste" and "zierlich" as well as the maternal embrace in "birg mich in deinen Armen" suggest that the death and suffering motifs refer to a woman rather than to Christ. Moreover, Celan here fuses the image of the extinguished light, with the idea of barrenness and deprivation, turning them into powerful metaphors for the bodies of murdered Jews that were thrown naked into mass graves.

In the last lines, Celan presents a new theme. The speaker suddenly exhorts himself not to stay any longer: "Bleib nicht. Blüh nicht mehr." His/her wish to ride into the night and never to return resonates with pain and suffering: "Ich ritt in die Nacht; ich kehre nicht um."

These unusual images referring to Christ, to a woman, and to the speaker himself resist interpretation. Yet in another of Celan's early poems that displays strong similarities to **"Dornenkranz,"** similar metaphors recur:

> Es fällt nun, Mutter, Schnee in der Ukraine:
> des Heilands Kranz aus tausend Körnchen
>   Kummer. .
> von meinen Tränen hier erreicht dich keine;
> von frühern Winken nur ein stolzer stummer. .

> There falls now, Mother, snow in the Ukraine:
> the Saviour's crown of thousand grains of
>   grief . . .
> from my tears here, none will reach you
> from past winks, a proud, a silent one alone. .

"Es fällt nun, Mutter, Schnee in der Ukraine," later entitled **"Winter"** [in *Gedichte 1938-1944*], associates the falling snow with maternal suffering, death, and with Christ's passion. In the unpublished version, Celan replaced the phrase "Empfang den Kranz" with "Heiland," the synonym for Christ the Savior, thus stressing the relation between the mother's and Christ's fates. These lines work with the same set of motifs as "Dornenkranz"—deprivation, barrenness, redemption: "erlöst das Linde und entblösst das Scharfe?" (the gentle, does it redeem and the cutting, does it strip naked?). In the last lines of **"Winter,"** Celan anchors the speaker's reflections in his wish to follow the mother into a realm of darkness and death: "Was wär es, Mutter: Wachstum oder Wunde— / versänk ich mit im Schneewehn der Ukraine? . ."

Through the connotations and allusions that invisibly link stanzas and lines and give silence a crucial part in the structure of the poem, **"Dornenkranz"** suggests the identification of the mother's suffering in a death camp with Christ's passion and the speaker's desire to share their fate.

In his painting "Crucifixion" (1943), Chagall used the image of the crucified Jesus as a symbol for the Jews who died in pogroms. Chaim Potok's *My Name is Asher Lev* (1972) works with a similar theme. In this book, the protagonist sees his mother leaning against the crossed window bars in her fearful wait for his return and imagines her crucified: the Orthodox father considers such a thought unforgivable blasphemy. For a German writer or poet of Jewish descent, this comparison is novel and points in Celan's case to his secular education.

Through the fusion of such diverse stylistic devices and motifs, Celan's **"Dornenkranz"** ultimately enacts its title, a "crown (or rather a wreath) of thorns." The wreath metaphor implies linkage and rupture, interweaving and separation. As a linguistic *Geflecht* (wreath, netting), Celan's poem anticipates his later basic concept of poetry as a *Sprachgitter* (speech-grille). Critics have associated Celan's term *Sprachgitter* with a multiplicity of often disparate meanings, ranging from a cloister window with a grating, and a metaphor for a divine realm or for a prison, to a barrier of linguistic expression and a symbol of the impossibility of communication. As Alfred Kelletat has pointed out, the term *Sprachgitter* suggests not only separation but also an inextricable link, because *Gitter* derives from the Indo-European verb *godh,* meaning "unite, bind tightly." In contrast to most scholars, Jean Bollack, in his essay "Paul Celan sur la langue: Le poème *Sprachgitter* et ses interprétations," relates this key term of Celan's poetry to poetic language itself and points out that it evokes the texture of Celan's poem **"Sprachgitter,"** in which a poetic idiom quests for its own space, by "composing, decomposing and recomposing itself . . . , by being trapped within and at the same time transgressing its own contradictions in search of its own space."

Although Celan's **"Sprachgitter"** became a focal point of diverse readings, scholars have not realized the crucial relationship between this poetic concept and Celan's early work. In the sense of "linkage," **"Sprachgitter"** continues **"Dornenkranz"** and other early poems which draw together elements from different literatures and cultural traditions. As a separation of motifs, **"Sprachgitter"** further advances subversive tendencies already apparent in the texts Celan wrote in Czernowitz. Ultimately, Celan's **"Sprachgitter"** enacts a characteristic of his cultural background, the simultaneity of receptivity to and the barriers between multilingual cultural traditions.

"Dornenkranz," with its image of the speaker's ride into the darkness and into a realm of death, anticipates yet another key motif of Celan's later work: the movement of the "I" and the poem toward an "Other." As Celan writes in "The Meridian,"

> Das Gedicht . . . ist einsam und unterwegs. Wer es schreibt, bleibt ihm mitgegeben. . . .
>
> Das Gedicht will zu einem Andern, es braucht dieses Andere, es braucht ein Gegenüber. Es sucht es auf, es spricht sich ihm zu.
>
> Jedes Ding, jeder Mensch ist dem Gedicht, das auf das Andere zuhält, eine Gestalt dieses Anderen.
>
> The poem . . . is lonely and *en route*. Its author stays with it. . . .
>
> The poem intends another, needs this other, needs an opposite. It goes toward it, bespeaks it.
>
> For the poem, everything and everybody is a figure of this other toward which it is heading.

Though these reflections on the nature of poetic language are much more intricate then Celan's early poetic ideas, **"Dornenkranz,"** along with many early texts written in Czernowitz, laid the foundation for Celan's later poetic development.

FURTHER READING

Biography

Cassian, Nina. " 'We Will Be Back and Up to Drown at Home': Notes on Paul Celan." *Parnassus: Poetry in Review* 15, No. 1 (1988): 108-29.

    Cassian, a former friend and translator of Celan, relates episodes in the poet's life and career.

Chalfen, Israel. *Paul Celan: A Biography of His Youth.* Translated by Maximilian Bleyleben. New York: Persea Books, 1991, 214 p.

    Biography of Celan with an introduction by John Felstiner. Felstiner comments: "Chalfen has assembled a firsthand account [of Celan's life] from numerous interviews, memoirs, and other documentary sources."

Criticism

Gibbons, Reginald. Review of *Last Poems*, by Paul Celan. *TriQuarterly* 67 (Fall 1986): 172-76.

    Offers a positive assessment of *Last Poems*.

Glenn, Jerry. Review of *Gesammelte Werke*, by Paul Celan. *The German Quarterly* 58, No. 4 (Fall 1985): 634-35.

    Positive review of *Gesammelte Werke*.

Huppert, Hugo. " 'In the Prayer-Mill's Rattling': A Visit with Paul Celan." *Acts: A Journal of New Writing*, Nos. 8-9 (1988): 156-62.

    Includes Celan's commentary on the "abstract" qualities of his verse and concludes with a discussion of Celan's last poems and his suicide.

Steiner, George. "North of the Future." *The New Yorker* LXV, No. 28 (28 August 1989): 93-6.

    Provides a laudatory assessment of *Poems of Paul Celan*, commenting on Celan's literary and theological influences and his use of experimental language to describe inhumanity, mystery, and sorrow.

Young, David. "Recent Poetry in Translation." *The Antioch Review* 45, No. 1 (Winter 1987): 90-7.

    Questions the value of Celan's poetry but nevertheless concludes that *Last Poems* "deserves a wide readership."

Additional coverage of Celan's life and career is contained in the following sources published by Gale Research: *Contemporary Authors*, Vols. 85-88; *Contemporary Authors New Revision Series*, Vol. 33; *Contemporary Literary Criticism*, Vols. 10, 19, 53, 82; *Dictionary of Literary Biography*, Vol. 69; and *Major 20th-Century Writers*.

Carolyn Forché

1950-

(Full name Carolyn Louise Forché) American poet, journalist, editor, and translator.

INTRODUCTION

Chiefly regarded as a political poet, Forché is best known for *The Country between Us* (1982), which graphically documents the horrors inflicted upon the Salvadoran people during the Civil War of the late 1970s. Reacting against critics who fault her inclusion of partisan themes, Forché has asserted: "All poetry is both pure and engaged, in the sense that it is made of language, but it is also art. Any theory which takes one half of the social-esthetic dynamic and accentuates it too much results in a breakdown. Stress of purity generates a feeble estheticism that fails, in its beauty, to communicate. On the other hand, propagandistic hack-work has no independent life as poetry. What matters is not whether a poem is political, but the quality of its engagement."

Biographical Information

Born in Detroit, Michigan, Forché was raised in its neighboring suburbs and attended Catholic schools. She developed an interest in literature at age nine when her mother gave her a poetry anthology to read and suggested that she try writing a poem. Forché has commented that writing then became "an escape. Writing and daydreaming. Writing was simply the reverie that I recorded, and I wrote volumes of diaries and journals. Then, when I wasn't writing, when I was doing housework or whatever, I kept some sort of little voice running in my mind. I told myself narratives, and I made a parallel life to my own. It was completely imaginary, and most of the time everything would take place a hundred years earlier on the same spot where I was. I suspected, when I was young, that this was madness, but I couldn't give it up." Forché attended Michigan State University and later earned an M.F.A. from Bowling Green State University. After the publication of her prizewinning debut collection, *Gathering the Tribes* (1976), she traveled to Spain where she lived with exiled Salvadoran poet Claribel Alegría and, in translating Alegría's poetry into English, learned of the Salvadoran Civil War. Upon her return to the United States, she was visited by Leonel Gómez Vides, Alegría's cousin and an activist in El Salvador who encouraged Forché to witness the situation in Central America. Forché journeyed to El Salvador in 1978 in an attempt to document the war. Fearing for her life, she left the country in 1980 at the urging of her friend Archbishop Oscar Romero—two weeks before he was assassinated. A staunch critic of United States military support of the Salvadoran government's repressive forces, Forché wrote of her experiences in various journals and,

eventually, in *The Country between Us*. Forché continues to remain politically active: she has served on various committees studying the situation in Central America; she has worked for Amnesty International and the Western chapter of the International Association of Poets, Playwrights, Editors, Essayists and Novelists (PEN); and she has been employed as a foreign news correspondent in Beirut, Lebanon.

Major Works

The largely autobiographical *Gathering the Tribes*, which won the 1975 Yale Series of Younger Poets Award, has been praised for its focus on community, kinship, memory, ritual, and sexuality. The long poem "Burning the Tomato Worms," for example, concerns Forché's sexual awakening, her relationship with her Slovak grandmother, and her grandmother's upbringing. *The Country between Us*, for which Forché earned the 1981 Lamont Selection of the Academy of American Poets, established her reputation as a political poet. The collection is divided into three sections: "In Salvador, 1978-1980," "Reunion," and

"Ourselves or Nothing." The first details the horrifying events Forché witnessed in Central America and her eventual return to the United States. In the prose poem "The Colonel," for instance, she focuses on El Salvador's totalitarian regime and the mutilation inflicted on political prisoners. The second and third sections of the book continue to emphasize the importance of memory and witness, but additionally stress the importance of interpersonal relationships as a means of achieving peace and communion. Comprised of a single poem, the third section is dedicated to Holocaust scholar Terrence des Pres and is often considered representative of Forché's poetics and political beliefs. The piece concludes: "There is a cyclone fence between / ourselves and the slaughter and behind it / we hover in a calm protected world like / netted fish, exactly like netted fish. / It is either the beginning or the end / of the world, and the choice is ourselves / or nothing." Focusing, in part, on the acts of genocide that have occurred in Latin America and the inhumanity of the Holocaust and Hiroshima, Forché's book-length poem, *The Angel of History* (1994), is similarly concerned with war, human misery, remembrance, and survival.

Critical Reception

Forché has been the recipient of numerous awards and fellowships yet her work has often been faulted for what some critics consider its overt polemics. Some scholars, however, argue that all poetry can be interpreted as a political message on some level and note that Forché's work signals the need for new schools of criticism and poetics that deliberately emphasize the political arena. Sharon Doubiago has asserted: "[This] poet, this extraordinary woman has already gone further than most ever will in trying to authenticate her voice, immersing herself and her language in the 'real' and very dangerous world. She has used her verbal training like a guerilla uses intimate knowledge of the land, taking the aesthetic jammed into her as a young working class woman gone to college and jamming it right back into the real, the political. This is a poetry of terrible witness, the strains of our villainies on the language and ethical constructs undoubtedly show. Thus the phrase 'the country between us.' "

PRINCIPAL WORKS

Poetry

Gathering the Tribes   1976
The Country between Us   1982
Against Forgetting: Twentieth-Century Poetry of Witness
   [editor]   1993
The Angel of History   1994

CRITICISM

Stanley Kunitz   (essay date 1976)

SOURCE: A foreword to *Gathering the Tribes* by Carolyn Forché, Yale University Press, 1976, pp. xi-xv.

[*An American poet, editor, essayist, translator, and journalist, Kunitz won a Pulitzer Prize in 1959 for his* Selected Poems, 1928-1958 *(1958). In the following essay, taken from the preface to Forché's* Gathering the Tribes, *he offers a thematic and stylistic analysis of the collection.*]

Kinship is the theme that preoccupies Carolyn Forché. Although she belongs to a generation that is reputed to be rootless and disaffiliated, you would never guess it from reading her poems [collected here in **Gathering the Tribes**]. Her imagination, animated by a generous life-force, is at once passionate and tribal. Narrative is her preferred mode, leavened by meditation. She remembers her childhood in rural Michigan, evokes her Slovak ancestors, immerses herself in the American Indian culture of the Southwest, explores the mysteries of flesh, tries to understand the bonds of family, race, and sex. In the course of her adventures she dares to confront, as a sentient being, the overwhelming questions by which reason itself is confounded: Who am I? Why am I here? Where am I going?

In **"Burning the Tomato Worms,"** a central poem, the narrative focuses on Anna, "heavy sweatered winter woman" seen "in horse-breath weather." She was the poet's paternal grandmother, who spoke a Slovak of the Russian-Czech borderlands and who, with her Old World lore and old wives' tales, profoundly influenced the poet's childhood.

> Anna's hands were like wheat rolls
> Shelling snow peas, Anna's hands
> Are both dead, they were Uzbek,
> Uzbek hands known for weaving fine rugs
>
> Eat Bread and Salt and Speak the Truth

Here as elsewhere the local color is vivid and unforced. But the poem is not to be construed as an exercise in sentimentality or ethnic nostalgia: it is woven of two strands, one commemorating a beloved person and place, the other recounting a girl's sexual initiation. The burning of the tomato worms can be read as a ritual of purification. Everywhere in these pages ritual and litany are close at hand. Even the act of bread making, a recurrent image, assumes a ceremonial aspect.

Love of people, love of place. Carolyn Forché's poems give an illusion of artlessness because they spring from the simplest and deepest human feelings, from an earthling's awareness of the systemic pulse of creation. The poems tell us she is at home anyplace under the stars, wherever there are fields or mountains, lakes or rivers, persons who stir her atavistic bond-sense. In **"Song Coming Toward Us"** she writes:

> I am spirit entering
> the stomach of the stones.
>
> Bowls of clay and water sing,

set on the fires to dry.
The mountain moves
like the spirit of southeast morning.

You walk where drums are buried.
Feel their skins tapping all night.
Snow flutes swell ahead of your life.
Listen to yourself.

She listens. At Justin Morrill College, an experimental residential branch of Michigan State University, where five
years ago the earliest parts of *Gathering the Tribes* were
conceived, she began her avid consumption of languages.
Now she studies Russian, Spanish, Serbo-Croatian,
French and Tewa (Pueblo Indian), listening beyond grammar for the secret texts. She acknowledges a primal sense
of the power of words. The power to "make words"—in
the mouth, in the heart, on the page—is the same to her
as to give substance. Aiming at wholeness, strength, and
clarity, she works at language as if it were a lump of clay
or dough in her hands. In her search for poetry, in her effort to understand it, she has bent over the potter's wheel,
climbed mountain ranges, ventured into the Mojave Desert. And she has sought out teachers. Among her teachers she lists her grandmother Anna, who died in 1968
("Grandma, come back, I forgot / How much lard for
these rolls"); her father, Michael Sidlosky, a tool and die
maker, and her mother, Louise, who bore seven children
before going to college, from which she graduated the
same year as Carolyn, her eldest daughter; Teles Goodmorning of the Taos pueblo ("His voice scoops a swarm
of coals, / dust rising from it"); Rosita of the same pueblo
("Her laugh is a music / from the time of Christ"); and
Lama Kalu Rimpoche (an unknown and humble, very old
man encountered in the mountains of New Mexico).

The places dearest to her include the south Michigan
heartland where she was raised, Truchas and the Pueblo
village of Taos in New Mexico, the Washington coast, and
the Okanogan region of southern British Columbia. Anna,
Alfansa, Teles Goodmorning, the dulcimer maker, Rosita,
Jacynthe, the child born in the Okanogan, the monks of
the mountain abbey, and Joey, a first love, who went off
to study for the priesthood, are all characters clearly
drawn from life and attached to specific locations. One
might say that they are embodiments of the reality of their
settings.

If I am right in supposing that **"Year at Mudstraw,"**
"Taking Off My Clothes," and **"Kalaloch"** are among the
last poems written for this book, it would appear that Forché is moving toward a tauter line, packed with incisive
detail, and a firmer dramatic structure than is evident in
her earlier narratives. **"Taking Off My Clothes"** begins

I take off my shirt, I show you.
I shaved the hair out under my arms.
I roll up my pants, I scraped off the hair
on my legs with a knife, getting white.

My hair is the color of chopped maples.
My eyes dark as beans cooked in the south.
(Coal fields in the moon on torn-up hills)

I have little doubt that the poem in *Gathering the Tribes*
that will be most discussed, quoted, and anthologized is

"Kalaloch" (pronounced ka-lā'-lok), an almost faultlessly
controlled erotic narrative of 101 lines. In its boldness and
innocence and tender, sensuous delight it may very well
prove to be the outstanding Sapphic poem of an era. Here
is its concluding section:

Flies crawled us,
Jacynthe crawled.
With her palms she
spread my calves, she
moved my heels from each other.
A woman's mouth is
not different, sand moved
wild beneath me, her long
hair wiped my legs, with women
there is sucking, the water
slops our bodies. We come
clean, our clits beat like
twins to the loons rising up.

We are awake.
Snails sprinkle our gulps.
Fish die in our grips, there is
sand in the anus of dancing.
Tatoosh Island
hardens in the distance.
We see its empty stones
sticking out of the sea again.
Jacynthe holds tinder
under fire to cook the night's wood.

If we had men I would make
milk in me simply. She is
quiet. *I like that you*
cover your teeth.

Stanley Plumly   (essay date 1976)

SOURCE: A review of *Gathering the Tribes*, in *The Amer-*
ican Poetry Review, Vol. 5, No. 6, November-December,
1976, p. 45.

[*Plumly is an American poet, critic, and editor. In the fol-*
lowing, he provides a thematic and stylistic examination of
Gathering the Tribes.]

Carolyn Forché's hold on her material [in *Gathering the*
Tribes] is ingratiating if sometimes tenuous. One wants
the ambitions of her poems to be realized even when they
fail, just as one wants the author herself to emerge even
when she refuses to appear. The tribes being gathered here
are all local—that is, relative to the poet, whether by
blood, as with her Slovak ancestry, or by spirit, as with her
Indian "fathers." The locales of her poems, the territories,
range from her native Michigan to her adopted New Mexico. The total theme involves the initiation rites of innocence—rituals of conversion to experience. A growth
story, a kind of Bildungsroman of consciousness-raising.
What is finally learned involves the two-way perception of
the spiritual in the carnal, the carnal in the spiritual. Forché is safest in shorter forms. . . . In longer, more self-
demanding forms, the poet is forced farther and farther
away from her own center of gravity and the confidence
of her rhythms. This dilution is particularly in evidence
in the central, "Indian" section of the book. The poems
of a full page or more too often become awkward, un-

focused, and pushed at the reader. The fault is certainly not in Forché's ability with texture—she is especially adept with image, detail, naming, and a complement of languages. What is typically missing, in poems as technically different as **"Ha Chi Je Na I Am Coming"** and **"Alfansa,"** is the clear organizing presence of the speaking voice—or what in fiction is called the narrator. This is another kind of matter altogether from the speaking parts Forché is fond of using, just as the characters are to be distinguished from the storyteller. Forché's signaling device for her "tongues" is italics, but one is hard pressed in several poems (including those mentioned above) to differentiate between speaking part and speaker. The problem seems to lie in Forché's attempt to emulate the ritualistic speech of the territory—whether it be Taos or Tonasket—while reducing her own impulse toward a personal, identifiable rhetoric. She in effect substitutes the language of the tribe for her own. And it becomes much more the language of conversion. . . . Forché creates a shadow voice, one that renders, records, and reports, but never from the center, always at one remove. She either respects or fears her adopted material too much. That is why the first and last sections of her book are superior—familiarity has bred sufficient contempt. The first part deals with her native Slovak heritage, notably Forché's paternal grandmother, Anna, in a poem entitled **"Burning the Tomato Worms."** Here the speaking parts work beautifully. . . . [They do so because] the poet is in primary, not secondary, territory. One's grandmother can have more to offer one's emotional past than one's guru. In the last and best part of her collection, Forché deals with her real, and future, subject, sexual identity. None of the poems here wanders from its source. The power of each begins and ends in the unmitigated voice of the poet, that arbitrating presence that seeks to establish a one-to-one relationship with sensual (all five and country senses seeing) experience, male and female, sky and earth. The rhetoric is hard without being brittle, the narrative sure of itself without being type-cast. **"Kalaloch"** is one poem in particular in which the rhythm of the natural world is realized in counterpart to the carnality of the human . . . in the language of the experience.

Eleanor Lerman   (essay date 1976)

SOURCE: "Tribal World of Carolyn Forché," in *Book Forum*, Vol. II, No. 3, 1976, pp. 396-99.

[*Lerman is an American poet. In the mixed review below, she discusses the thematic and technical aspects of* Gathering the Tribes.]

On first reading Carolyn Forché's *Gathering the Tribes* my impression was that the book seemed to be a dissertation on the need for tribal togetherness, the necessity of exploring one's heritage—both the inherited and adopted—in order to integrate the ancestral past into the ongoing process of an individual life. There is much here to reinforce that impression: two thirds of the book deals with the poet's two heritages: first, that of the Slavic grandparents whose culture and memories obviously permeated her childhood, and second, that of the Southwestern American Indians, whose society, based on the passing down of knowledge and customs from generation to generation,

she has come to know quite well. One quickly understands why the poet sees parallels in two such seemingly divergent races of people; both are based on closely knit family groups that are in turn bound to other family groups by the harshness and isolation of their environment, both have intimate and respectful relationships with the land that nourishes them, and both—having been uprooted by changing times and superseded by an American culture that demands absorption or annihilation—are in decay. That decay is no more eloquently expressed than in the poem **"Las Truchas"** in which Forché describes an Indian village:

> Adobe walls crack, rot in Las Truchas.
> Sometimes a child in a doorway
> or dog stretched on the road
> Always a quiet place.
> Wooden wheelbarrows rest up against
> boarded windows
> Not yet Semana Santa
> when people of Truchas and Mora
> will fill them with human bones
> and walk with blood-stained eyes
> in the mountains where Pecos water
> flows among cork-barked fir
> and foxtail grows dwarfed, gnarled.

It was this poem that led me to a rereading of the first two sections of the book and so to a different, admittedly more personal, perception of Forché's work: the tribes may indeed be gathered to teach each other about the ancient and honored beliefs and occupations, about the harvesting and building, and the preparation of food, but this gathering will be, perhaps, the last.

The poems seem to me to be more a mourning than a celebration, and from that deep sorrow at the ending of a way of life comes a further insight: that within the tribes, even when they flourished, there were always the stirrings of individual alienation. The shared rituals of the tribe, the physical closeness of living together may bring some sense of belonging, but there is always the moment when one feels one's own heart and mind pulling away to experience the terrible awareness of being a single soul trapped within the unreachable confines of the body, subject to fears that can be assuaged by no one, needing the answers to questions that no one can—or will—give. Forché expresses this in the poem **"Burning the Tomato Worm"**:

> *I want to ask you why I live*
> And we go back apart across the field
> *Why am I here and will have to feel the way*
> I die
> It was all over my face
> Grandma flipped kolacy rolls
> Dunked her hands in bowls of water
> Looked at me
> Wrung the rags into the stoop
> Kept it from me
> Whatever she saw

Therefore we understand that the tribal experience, no matter how much we yearn for it, must be accepted as having its limitations. The tribal campfires may indeed burn all around us (I am borrowing an image from Forché's poem **"Skin Canoes"**), but ultimately, it is our own fire that we end up staring into, and it is with whatever we see there that we must bargain for our own life or death.

It is in the third section of the book, "The Place That Is Feared I Inhabit" that this aloneness is dealt with on a one to one basis. I find this a very ordered and logical progression, as if the poet is in the process of distilling the individual experience down to its basic essence: first, as part of a community, then within that community as part of a lover relationship, and then even within that lover relationship as a single self that, finally, can be neither vanquished nor saved by another. In the poem **"Taking Off My Clothes,"** Forché says:

> In the night I come to you and it seems a shame
> to waste my deepest shudders on a wall of a man
>
> You recognize strangers,
> think you lived through destruction.
> You can't explain this night, my face, your
>   memory
>
> You want to know what I know?
> Your own hands are lying.

Your own hands are lying. The hands of love often do, no matter how well intentioned they seem. And be they the myriad hands of the tribe working in unison to teach and assist, or just the two hands of a lover trying to reach across the darkness to find their twins, there is always the knowledge, within the individual, that those hands, no matter how tightly gripped, will soon have to be let go again, and that is the lie our tribes and our lovers force us to experience: they tell us that we can hold on forever, and yet we have learned that we cannot.

If there is fault to be found with Forché's work, it is a fault that she shares with many contemporary poets: her line is too often stilted, and the words sometimes stumble over each other; she is so eager for us to hear what she has to say that she tends to neglect the form she is using to speak with. Our language can be a lovely and rhythmic one, but we need poetry to remind us of this because so much of what we read in the course of our daily lives is simply facts or stories related to impart information or directions: bare words giving us the bare news. Therefore, I think that more than ever now, it is left to the poet to preserve the idea that the skillful and loving use of language can be just as important—if not sometimes more so—as the subjects of which language speaks. It is, after all, the way we use language that gives, to the tale told, its beauty, its terror, or its comedy, and the poet, who sits and listens to the way one word sounds when it's fitted against another, should constantly be aware of this and should make the reader aware of it too. Forché seems still to be learning about these qualities of language, still to be listening for the rhythms. I'm hopeful that her future work will bring us a poet who understands and hears more clearly, and that is something to look forward to.

Wendy Knox (essay date 1976)

SOURCE: "Relatedness and Ritual," in *Moons and Lion Tailes*, Vol. 2, No. 2, 1976, pp. 79-85.

[*In the review below, Knox offers a favorable assessment of* Gathering the Tribes.]

In **Gathering the Tribes**, Carolyn Forché gives us voices of people around her. . . . Her mode is generally narrative, slowly spinning out revelation by means of direct references to scenes, people, and natural objects with which she is familiar. Each poem seems to have an exact location drawn for us, and she often moves into a poem by describing the room, geography, or central character objectively. . . .

She also writes with a certain slow descriptiveness and a simple statement that seem very native in character. Wood, sounds, bread, smells, birds, water, aspens, and owls—all seem to speak for her, *through* her, in a way. She has only to mention them, and they evoke other sounds and smells—pine, dust, adobe, or wool. She seems to play the learner in many encounters, the young shaman gathering her trade.

The theme of prophecy or learning from some other person, most often female, recurs throughout the book. These clearly rooted characters: her grandmother, the dulcimer-maker, the old Indian Teles Goodmorning, Alfansa, Rosita, Jacynthe in **"Kalaloch"** (which, [Stanley] Kunitz says in his introduction [to the book], "may very well prove to be the outstanding Sapphic poem of an era," and I agree), all these characters seem to be living examples of some natural principle, extensions of the earth itself and the places in which they live. She comes to these people openly . . . and is rewarded with signs at once simple and mysterious. . . .

A close look at [the] stanzas from **"Mientras Dura Vida, Sobra el Tiempo"** brings out two distinct characteristics of Forché's language, one brilliant, one troublesome. First is her tough, almost Hopkins-like use of onomatopoetic speech, alliteration, and rhythms. Her use of plosive consonants cuts edges sharp and deep. In her poem about butchering, **"From Memory,"** the *s, p, b, l,* and hard *c* and *k* sounds seem hardly placed by chance but support her feeling and tone. . . .

This "consonant ethic" may come from her Slavic background, as well as from her skill as a linguist. She studies Russian, Spanish, Serbo-Croatian, French and Tewa (Pueblo Indian) and seems to take rhythms and flows from them all. The drawback of this skill, however, is the inclusion of many foreign words that puzzle or distract. In some poems, one can derive that a *fogon* is a stove or fireplace from the context, but often words and clusters like *ma-he-yo, alfansa, mokva,* and *dusha* trip the reader mid-thought, prompting futile backtracking and speculation. If the thought is worth expressing in another language, I'd appreciate some minor glossary or explication to help non-linguists out. This applies to particularly significant acts, rituals, or symbols of native culture not ordinarily recognizable or easily deduced.

Forché's plunges into what Kunitz calls "her atavistic bond-sense" remain nonetheless invigorating, a recurrence of power much needed in an over-individualized and disconnected era. When her human shamans are silent, the woods, moose, water, rituals of bread-making, dishwashing, child-feeding, and lovemaking provide a continuity of wordless places in an all-too-verbal and chaotic world. . . .

[In Forché's poetry there is] some of the "nearsightedness" of women's point of view, returning us to mundane miracles we've almost forgotten. The violent beauty of sexuality, the mysterious comforts of memory and known people and places, the terrifying and awesome fecundity and regularity of plants, animals, and natural forces—we turn to these when the glitter of controlled efficiency and voyeuristic titillations runs dry. This world of the earth and the body can be brutal and chaotic, but it is a root from which great power and meaning flows. Dillard, Rukeyser, Kinnell, Lifshin, Muske, Forché—all these poets seem to be digging in the first gardens and prairies since Whitman to bear real fruit without "chemical" additives, simple and *from* the earth without being simplistic or dull, without leaning on the earth, body, or myth to do their magic *for* them. It's rather sad that a return to the human seems so shocking and courageous to us now.

Forché on metaphor and extreme events:

Events of extremity render metaphor problematic. . . . Certain images resist metaphor. Ashes, smoke, crematoria—none of these are symbolic, because of the overwhelming nature of their actuality and historical significance, and the demand that evidence not be manipulated so as to be lost. Neruda wrote, "The blood of the children ran in the streets like the blood of the children." These things are not comparable to anything. There is nothing to be gained by any comparison. There's only loss.

Carolyn Forché, in an interview with K. K. Roeder, in The San Francisco Review of Books, *August-October 1993.*

Peter Stitt (essay date 1982)

SOURCE: "A Remarkable Diversity," in *The Georgia Review,* Vol. XXXVI, No. 4, Winter, 1982, pp. 911-22.

[*An American critic and educator, Stitt has served as editor of several literary journals, including the* Carolina Quarterly *and the* Gettysburg Review. *In the excerpt below, he offers a mixed assessment of* The Country between Us, *praising its emotional content but faulting its egotistical stance.*]

Carolyn Forché's **The Country Between Us** turns out to be not precisely the book it appears, not quite the one promised on the jacket, where her subject is announced unequivocally to be El Salvador, and where she is heralded as the poet who replaces Pablo Neruda in singing "the beauty, sufferings, fears and dreams" of Latin America. The first section is indeed political, and the focus is certainly upon El Salvador. **"Return"** chronicles a conversation between the poet and a friend, who defines for her and us what happens in these poems: "Go try on / Americans your long, dull story / of corruption," she says, "but better

to give / them what they want." What that is is considerably more sensational, as this same character explains: "So you've come to understand why / men and women of good will read / torture reports with fascination."

These early poems in the book are deeply affecting, as they record, often in lines of great beauty, horrible suffering. **"The Memory of Elena"** captures the fear that some remembrances can bring even to situations that ought to be entirely pleasant; the speaker and another friend are at lunch:

> As she talks, the hollow
> clopping of a horse, the sound
> of bones touched together.
> The *paella* comes, a bed of rice
> and *camarones,* fingers and shells,
> the lips of those whose lips
> have been removed, mussels
> the soft blue of a leg socket.

Many other poems carry similar burdens, some presented in even more graphic detail. And yet the reader gradually becomes aware that this material is not the real and ultimate subject of the book. At the end of **"Return"** the friend shines an entirely different light upon the speaker of these poems; "Your problem," she says, "is":

> that you were born to an island of greed
> and grace where you have this sense
> of yourself as apart from others. It is
> not your right to feel powerless. Better
> people than you were powerless.
> You have not returned to your country,
> but to a life you never left.

It is an important passage; up to this point in the book we are beginning to form an unflattering portrait of the speaker as a privileged visitor to a land of pain, one who needn't suffer herself, but can make saleable poems out of the suffering of others. The words of **"The Colonel"** as he pours out his bag of human ears upon the table cut two ways: "Something for your poetry, no?"

But the above lines show that Forché is as aware of the ambiguity of her position as we are; she is also well aware of her "powerlessness" and her distance, as an American, from the kind of suffering she records. In fact, it turns out that the "country" of the title is not El Salvador after all, but America, the land that gives us our ambiguous privileges. Our lives are insulated from the harsh political realities of places like Poland, Hungary, Latin America, and thus America itself becomes "the country between us." What the first section may establish most strongly of all is that sense of powerlessness, the horrifying realization that an outsider, even one with a deep sense of commitment, cannot do anything either to relieve the suffering she sees or to change the political climate that causes it.

Thus the book turns from active political involvement to another, paler but more realistic, solution—the speaker will extend her sympathy, her love, her artistry to these people. There are poems celebrating many characters, people whose lives have been deprived, ruined, destroyed through political oppression; characters like Anna, Maya, José Rudolfo Viera, Camillo Torres, Victor Jara. Love as a subject, in fact, increases as the book goes along, down to the final, moving love poem, **"Ourselves or Nothing,"** which celebrates the speaker's lover, a man who suffered for years writing a long and feeling work on the holocaust. The poem, and the book, ends:

> There is a cyclone fence between
> ourselves and the slaughter and behind it
> we hover in a calm protected world like
> netted fish, exactly like netted fish.
> It is either the beginning or the end
> of the world, and the choice is ourselves
> or nothing.

There is ultimately a strong sense of disillusionment with politics expressed in these poems; all of the chronicled political activity here has led precisely to nothing, *nada*, death for thousands of good people. Love, on the other hand, is a beginning, a look toward the future, the only thing we may have that can carry us forward. And that is what the book finally is about.

All of this is attractive and affecting, a powerful and moving pattern for a book of poems to have. What undercuts this strength and makes the book finally an uneven performance is a relentless egotism that washes over the reader in waves of increasing magnitude. The jacket is indicative of this spirit; it offers on the front a large photograph of the author, as though it were an album cover. And there are passages in the political poems that are embarrassingly self-absorbed, like these lines from **"Return"**:

> Josephine, I tell you
> I have not rested, not since I drove
> those streets with a gun in my lap,
> not since all manner of speaking has
> failed and the remnant of my life
> continues onward. I go mad, for example,
> in the Safeway, at the many heads
> of lettuce, papayas and sugar, pineapples
> and coffee, especially the coffee.

This is a bit self-indulgent, to say the least, in a poem which chronicles "a labor leader" who was "cut to pieces and buried." The writing is also unconvincing—the "for example" rather makes us doubt the "I go mad" that precedes it. Equally unconvincing is the poem **"Selective Service,"** which is spoken to younger people by a member of the Vietnam generation. When the current crop of collegians was still studying fractions in grammar school, Forché and her friends were at the barricades: "We'll tell you / about fractions. Half of us are dead or quiet / or lost. Let them speak for themselves / We lie down in the fields and leave behind / the corpses of angels." The attempt is to gain status by overstating (rather vastly) the actual case; however black the moral stain of Vietnam on America, it did not take quite this toll.

It may be this quality of egotism that accounts for some of the uncharacteristic bad writing in the volume, as when Forché, in **"Reunion,"** recounts: "How my breasts feel, years / later, the tongues swishing / in my dress, some yours, some / left by other men." Generally, though, her touch and judgment are much better, as in the lines which begin **"Departure"**: "We take it with us, the cry / of a train slicing a field / leaving its stiff suture, a distant / tenderness as when rails slip / behind us and our windows /

touch the field." Forché is often on the verge of overwriting, but this extremism also accounts for some of her best effects. *The Country Between Us* is a moving book, more complicated and intelligent than one is at first led to believe. To compare her to Neruda is hyperbolic, but Forché is a talented and powerful writer.

Katha Pollitt   (essay date 1982)

SOURCE: "Poems on Public Subjects," in *The Nation*, New York, Vol. 234, No. 18, May 8, 1982, pp. 562-64.

[*An American poet and critic, Pollitt won a National Book Critics Circle Award for her first poetry collection,* Antarctic Traveller *(1982). In the following review, she faults Forché's focus on the self and lack of "verbal energy" in* The Country between Us. *For a response to Pollitt's remarks, see Sharon Doubiago's essay dated 1983.*]

Why is so little good political poetry written in America today? The very phrase "political poetry" conjures up visions of smudgy sectarian newspapers where verses with titles like "Death to All Fascists" appear next to letters signed "A Brother in Detroit." And yet, it wasn't so long ago that poets wrote about the major issues of the day as a matter of course. Subjects like Italian (or Greek or Polish) independence, slavery and the plight of the industrial poor were as much a staple of nineteenth-century verse as were the deaths of beautiful girls. Our own century offers Pound, Auden and his circle, and Lowell. Among poets working now, however, only a few treat the sorts of events and issues one reads about in the newspapers or demonstrates about in the streets, and I think it's significant that those who do—Bly, Levertov, Rich, Ginsberg—are middle-aged. For most young poets, I suspect, the prospect that a poem might address the election of Ronald Reagan, the arms race or the organizing of office workers must seem both comical and insulting. Many would quarrel with the whole notion of thinking of poems in terms of what they are "about."

The problem is not that poets are apolitical. It's that they have inherited a literary form so diminished and so privatized that many things lie outside its purview. If the prototypical magazine poem of 1910 was a sonnet to Eleonora Duse adorned with allusions to nightingales, Greek gods and the poet's fainting heart, ours is a free-verse elegy on the isolation of the self, set on a campus in the Middle West and decorated with references to snow, light, angels and the poet's nostalgia for his childhood. Ours is a poetry, in other words, of wistful longings, of failed connections, of inevitable personal loss, expressed in a set of poetic strategies that suit such themes—a lax syntax and simplified vocabulary that disclaim intellectual pretension, and ethereal, numinous images that testify to the poet's sensibility. There is little place in this sort of poetry for politics, for whatever its repercussions in the realm of private feeling, politics is fundamentally a public affair.

Carolyn Forché's [*The Country Between Us*] is interesting both because Forché is a talented poet—her first book, *Gathering the Tribes*, was a Yale Younger Poets selection—and because it tackles the political subject matter I am arguing is so uncongenial to young poets. The first section, dedicated to the memory of Oscar Romero, the murdered archbishop of San Salvador, is set in El Salvador, where Forché lived for two years and worked as a journalist. Other poems are addressed to old friends from the working-class Detroit neighborhood of Forché's childhood: one has become a steelworker haunted by memories of Vietnam: another, with whom Forché had shared adolescent dreams of travel and romance, lives with her husband and kids in a trailer. Elsewhere in the poems we meet a jailed Czech dissident, the wife of a "disappeared" Argentine and Terrence Des Pres, author of *The Survivor,* a study of the death camps. This is strong stuff, and the excited response *The Country Between Us* has already provoked shows, I think, how eager people are for poetry that acknowledges the grim political realities of our time.

At their best, Forché's poems have the immediacy of war correspondence, postcards from the volcano of twentieth-century barbarism:

> A boy soldier in the bone-hot sun works his knife
> To peel the face from a dead man
>
> and hang it from the branch of a tree
> flowering with such faces.
> ("**Because One is Always Forgotten**")

. . . . .

> a labor leader was cut to pieces and buried.
> Tell them how his friends found
> the soldiers and made them dig up
> and ask forgiveness of the corpse, once
> it was assembled on the ground like a man.
> ("**Return**")

Testicles are "crushed like eggs," rats are introduced into vaginas, José waves his bloody stumps in the air, Lil Milagro is raped and forced to defecate in public. "There is nothing one man will not do to another," Forché tells us. So shocking are the incidents reported here—so automatic is our horror at a mere list of places where atrocities have occurred ("Belsen, Dachau, Saigon, Phnom Penh")—that one feels almost guilty discussing these poems as poems, as though by doing so one were saying that style and tone and diction mattered more than bloody stumps and murdered peasants and the Holocaust.

This unease, though, should not have arisen in the first place, and it points to an underlying problem: the incongruity between Forché's themes and her poetic strategies. Forché's topics could not be more urgent, more extreme or more public, and at least one of her stated intentions is to make us look at them squarely. And yet, she uses a language designed for quite other purposes, the misty "poetic" language of the isolated, private self. She gives us bloody stumps, but she also gives us snow, light and angels. You have to read "**The Island**" several times, for instance, to get past the exotic tropical scenery, the white dresses, the "seven different shawls of wind," the mist that is like bread and so forth, and realize that this is a poem of homage to Claribel Alegria, a heroic woman whom Forché would like to resemble, and that Claribel is telling Forché not to give up hope for El Salvador. At least, I think that's what it's about.

In other poems, a man manufactures bullets in "the spray

of stars that is / a steel mill"; a political prisoner sees people as "those cold / globes of breath that shape / themselves into bodies"; the coffin of a Salvadoran martyr is seen "rocking into the ground like a boat or a cradle." The trouble is, if her images are to bear the burdens Forché places on them and move us in the way she wants, a steel mill can't be a lovely play of light, or bodies dreamlike apparitions, or death either a calm voyage or the sleep of a baby. They have to be real.

When Forché speaks plainly, she can be very good indeed. "**The Expatriate**" is a clever satire on a young American left-wing poet whose idea of solidarity with the Third World is to move to Turkey and sleep with women who speak no English. "It would be good if you could wind up / in prison and so write your prison poems," says Forché ironically, and we know she's got his number:

> You have been in Turkey a year now.
> What have you found? Your letters
> describe the boring ritual of tea,
> the pittance you are paid to teach
> English, the bribery required for so much
> as a postage stamp. Twenty-year-old poet,
> Hikmet did not ask to be Hikmet.

Equally memorable is "**The Colonel**," an account of dinner at the home of a right-wing Salvadoran officer, who, after the wine and the rack of lamb, dumps his collection of human ears on the table: "Something for your poetry, no?" The precise, observed details—the bored daughter filing her nails, the American cop show on TV, the parrot in the corner and the gold bell for the maid—work together to make a single impression, and the colonel himself, with his unpredictable swings between domestic boredom and jaunty brutality, is a vivid character, as Claribel Alegria is not. Interestingly, in view of what I've been saying about Forché's poetics, "**The Colonel**" is written in prose.

Perhaps what I miss in this collection is simply verbal energy. The poems, especially the longer ones, do tend to blur in the mind. Forché insists more than once on the transforming power of what she has seen, on the gulf it has created between herself and those who have seen less and dared less:

> And when I speak with American men
> there is some absence of recognition:
> their constant Scotch and fine white
> hands, many hours of business, penises
> hardened by motor inns and a faint
> resemblance to their wives. I cannot
> keep going.
> ("**The Return**")

But how can we grasp the power of this transforming vision when it is expressed in lackluster assertions ("I cannot keep going") and facile caricatures of "American men" as adulterous Babbitts?

Whether or not one admires Forché for stressing the intensity of her responses to the sufferings of others—many readers, I should point out, do not share my discomfort with this emphasis—the intensity is vitiated by the inadequate means by which it is conveyed. It is embarrassing to read that Forché goes "mad, for example, / in the Safeway, at the many heads / of lettuce, papayas and sugar, pineapples / and coffee, especially the coffee." It trivializes torture to present it in terms of lunch:

> The *paella* comes, a bed of rice
> and *camarones,* fingers and shells,
> the lips of those whose lips
> have been removed, mussels
> the soft blue of a leg socket.
>
> ("In Memory of Elena")

It is wildly histrionic—and slanderous, too—to accuse politically moderate human-rights activists of deriving masturbatory pleasure from torture reports:

> they cup their own parts
> with their bedsheets and move
> themselves
> slowly, imagining bracelets
> affixing
> their wrists to a wall
>
> ("The Return")

Does Forché think we read her poems as pornography?

It is not enough—this too may be a minority opinion—to dedicate one's poetry to the defeat of the torturers, to swear that

> I will live
> and living cry out until my voice is
> gone
> to its hollow of earth, where with our
> hands and by the lives we have
> chosen
> we will dig deep into our deaths.
>
> ("Message")

The boldness of the promise is undermined by the commonplace rhetoric ("hollow of earth" for "grave") and woolly syntax (the hands and lives dig into our deaths *after* the voice is dead?).

On the other hand, to make such a promise is not nothing, either. If poetry is to be more than a genteel and minor art form, it needs to encompass the material Forché presents. Much credit, then, belongs to Forché for her brave and impassioned attempt to make a place in her poems for starving children and bullet factories, for torturers and victims, for Margarita with her plastique bombs and José with his bloody stumps. What she needs now is language and imagery equal to her subjects and her convictions. The mists and angels of contemporary magazine verse are beneath her: she *has* seen too much, she has too much to say. Of how many poets today, I wonder, could that be said?

Judith Gleason   (essay date 1982)

SOURCE: "The Lesson of Bread," in *Parnassus: Poetry in Review,* Vol. 10, No. 1, 1982, pp. 9-21.

[*Gleason is an American novelist, poet, and author of children's books. In the following essay on* The Country between Us, *she applauds Forché's focus on the Salvadoran civil war and the need for community.*]

Is the country between us a medieval sword laid down between sleeping lovers on a soft pine forest floor like a steely

> When [*The Country between Us*] came out, I was working in a men's prison in Juneau, Alaska. *Columns* had come out, the book was being read much more widely than the usual book of poetry in the United States. There was this great flaring controversy about politics and poetry. I was being called upon to answer why I had become a "political poet." I hadn't been aware of how far I had come from my own culture.
>
> —*Carolyn Forché, in an interview with Husayn Al-Kurdi, in* The Bloomsbury Review, *July-August 1993.*

oath of obdurate sublimation? Is it a country you would have to visit in order to be where I now am on the other side of the frontier? (Until you understand the horror, the horror, the cold chills, the sweat and oil, all that I saw, that I went through, we'll never be able to communicate with each other again.) Or, is it by any chance a country we implicitly share—roads groping from your flesh to my flesh? Or perhaps our territory . . . both . . . and . . . the sacramental conjunction of bread?

Whatever, between *us.* It is not only the lyric plurality of the pronoun that is important here, where two or three are gathered together, but its objective case—implying a sort of paralysis of the communal will, a screen (like that between the living and the dead) through which we (whoever we are) would have to burst with enormous energy in order to come out into the nominative light of existential affirmation. And were we fully to become it, whatever country (including the pun embedded there) formerly kept us apart would contain us whole, all of us, leaven of a deeper plenitude than want could possibly be aware of.

If we want to think in cosmo-biological terms we have to import them, from Africa or elsewhere. For it is a paradox of Roman Catholic thought (Western culture's home remedy for the mind-body split) that spiritual value is accepted as incarnate, only thence in this form to be regarded with suspicion, dichotomized, trans-substantiated before being implanted in the good earth all over again. But if we can't plant our feet as surely on the ground of Being as the Africans can, our hands need not idly wait for that devastating paradox to resolve itself. And so it is that poets from Catholic traditions tend to massage the imagination, substantiate, gash and gild things, knead them; and so it is that Catholic priests of Latin America, having identified the hungry and the oppressed with the body of Christ, have vigorously espoused the cause of social justice, thereby spiritualizing revolution.

At this particular moment in history the country between us happens to have an incredibly suggestive name: El Salvador, where these bones and this flesh (as Aquinas said)—that body, hers, his—are being continuously broken and blood shed beyond the power of the outraged earth to absorb it. El Salvador, that is, where masses are hourly said over massacred fragments of our common humanity.

> Those who commit themselves to the poor have to be open to the same destiny as the poor; and in El Salvador we already know the destiny of the poor: to disappear, to be captured, to be tortured, to reappear as corpses.

The man who said these words out loud above a whisper, who lived to be himself the language of truth incarnate, was shot saying mass on March 24, 1980. It is to him, Monsignor Oscar Romero, that Carolyn Forché dedicates the first section of [*The Country between Us*], her second book. A section of her life for the first time publicly located in time and space: "In Salvador, 1978—80," she calls it.

Here it was, documenting my own case against the Death Squads (knowing full well that we all carry them within us) and the complicity of U.S. military aid, that I made first acquaintance with the work of Carolyn Forché. In a looseleaf collection of writings called *Women and War in El Salvador* appeared her strong description of a few hours of grim, hectic life shared with a woman doctor in a rural hospital, together with three incisive, probing poems. [The critic adds in a footnote: "The collection was put together by the Women's International Resource Exchange, 2700 Broadway, New York, New York 10025."] Of the photographs accompanying her article Carolyn Forché said, "It is perhaps impossible to translate one reality into another. Photographs do not give off the smell of pain, oil, human waste. Yet the words alone lacked a context."

Habeas corpus. Bodily presence, however transmitted to us, is, I would argue, all we need. Well, we have it now, that contact, those of us who are in the habit of looking elsewhere than in the establishment press or to commercial movie houses and television channels for images of what's going on in the world. Never has the dismemberment of a population been so stunningly documented in film and stills published in the dissident press and in special publications prepared by solidarity groups, coalitions in the public interest, and religious task forces. And many of these talented, committed cameramen have been shot down in the act, as Oscar Romero predicted, or have piecemeal disappeared: most recently, on the eve of the Salvadorian "elections" (March 28, 1982) four Dutch journalists, one of whom, Han ter Lag, wrote a prescient "last letter" to his fiancée, a missive whose very format shows him on the way out.

> Today we filmed the suffering of the people, and I have been crying in my bed for hours. . . . It is terrible what's happening here. . . .
>
> Think of the people here. It is a duty for all of us.
>
> Think of these people.
>
> Just believe me.
>
> Han.

Things are speeding up. How quickly the private becomes public! Less than two months after he was shot, only two days ago (May 22, 1982), Han's letter reached all of us on the concerned list [of COALITION for a New Foreign and Military Policy]. We waited decades to hear how Akmatova waited outside Leningrad Prison for months during the Yezhov terror. Carolyn Forché's poems from El Salvador reach us while events duplicate to those she describes are still taking place. It's not as though we were waiting for faded or blurred records of ignominious naked genocide to be salvaged from history and released like a nightmarish family album. The film these days is smuggled out, processed, and wired almost immediately. Those maimed, violated bodies seem to be falling and decomposing before our very eyes, severed heads of youths falling, as it were, on our breakfast plates. With words alone Carolyn Forché brilliantly records such characteristic dismemberment:

> . . . José lying
> on the flat bed truck, waving his stumps
> in your face, his hands cut off by his
> captors and thrown to the many acres
> of cotton, lost, still, and holding
> the last few lumps of leached earth.
> Tell them of José in his last few hours
> and later how, many months later,
> a labor leader was cut to pieces and buried.
> Tell them how his friends found
> the soldiers and made them dig him up
> and ask forgiveness of the corpse, once
> it was assembled again on the ground
> like a man. . . .
>
> ("**Return**")

For to be whole is to be all that we can be, entire selves, complete human beings. But this isn't the way things are any more.

> . . . . The colonel returned with a sack used to bring groceries home. He spilled many human ears on the table. They were like dried peach halves. There is no other way to say this. He took one of them in his hands, shook it in our faces, dropped it into a water glass. It came alive there. I am tired of fooling around he said. As for the rights of anyone, tell your people they can go fuck themselves. He swept the ears to the floor with his arm and held the last of his wine in the air. Something for your poetry, no? he said. Some of the ears on the floor caught this scrap of his voice. Some of the ears on the floor were pressed to the ground. (**"The Colonel"**)

Ah, were they to hear the vengeful chants of the Furies, long since silenced by that Athenian "father's daughter" on behalf of the male political establishment . . . !

In *The Birth of Tragedy* Nietzsche asks us to imagine Dionysos as virtually present, "visible for every eye," in the embodied character of the tragic hero within the "transfiguring frame" provided by the chorus of concerned citizens as votaries. Unlike photos or film footage the words of the poet abstract us from the event at the same time that they fix it on the inner retina. Within the frame provided by the poet's moral vision we see doubly, make a mental as well as a visceral connection. Oscar

Romero's words were those which first materialized Dionysos in El Salvador for me, before he himself became the tragic exemplar of his own speech. The words of Carolyn Forché inevitably create a different sort of aperture through which to view El Salvador, a perspective through which we must look, a voice we cannot ignore precisely because though courageous, she is not a Latin American saint. In Conradian terms she is "one of us."

So we, academic guardians of the ancient texts, have lived to see the myth of Orpheus, of Dionysos, of Osiris happening before our very eyes over and over again, for real. A sacred chill runs down the spine. What is the meaning? A deep taboo having to do with the integrity of the flesh has been violated. All these dismembered divinities in antiquity were supposed to be sacred manifestations of the agricultural cycle—stopped in its tracks now, it would seem. Everything torn limb from limb with no hope of regeneration. And, as the subjective corollary of this: endless disintegrative suffering, blighted personal relationships, with no assurance of personal growth therefrom or renewal. What is the meaning, what the cure? Should it be cause for wonder, then, that we sit before the frame frozen with empathetic dread? That we sleep with a sword of political chastity drawn between ourselves and the Salvadorian people?

Some don't. On April 27, 1982, John David Anderson, a U.S. citizen fighting with the revolutionaries in the province of Morazan, was killed during an army offensive there. Originally come to El Salvador as a tourist, Anderson witnessed a massacre in the capital city.

> I remember going back to the hotel and writing a poem for that child dead in the street. But that wasn't enough. . . . I read a lot. But later that week I began to think, reading isn't enough, so I moved to Mejicanos (a working class suburb) to make direct contact with the reality. . . . Eventually I decided to join a collective of neighborhood militia. [From an interview published in the *Guardian* (26 May 1982)]

Enough was everything. Anderson's fate. In Carolyn Forché's poem of **"Return,"** the device of an interlocutor enables the poet to be bitterly hard on herself:

> Better people than you were powerless.
> You have not returned to your country
> but to a life you never left.

She had to return to tell us. As she herself puts it of someone else in reversed context: "Hikmet did not choose to be Hikmet" (**"Expatriot"**).

The poem of herself in dialogue with an elder (but, I would argue, not necessarily wiser) woman, raises a host of fascinating moral questions. The real problem, her elder argues, has to do with money (American dollars in particular), with political corruption, with an Augean stable of social, economic, and sanitary problems which no one can take arresting photos of, printed discussion of which no one wants to plough through. To envisage the years of hard, patient work it would take to set things to rights down there is tiresome, whereas

> men and women of good will read

torture reports with fascination

Ah, so we do, *hypocrites lecteurs, frères et soeurs,* but why? And if all a gifted well-meaning poet can do is provide us with violent metonyms for the bodily equivalent of the tortured inter-subjective world, does this mean she must feel her work can come to no human good? Or may not this verbal work of hers indicate within its own texture of act and image a possible road of return from an alienation further from the gods, the earth, and each other than we supposed human beings have ever known? And were this so, then those tortured, dismembered bodies (which fascinate because they tell us something we can't see or don't want to face about the violence in ourselves) will not have suffered in vain?

An important variant of the Dionysian *pathos* which is beginning to surface among those of us concerned with healing arts is the Shamanic. Indeed, what the poet bears witness to "In Salvador, 1978-80" might be compared to a Shamanic voyage of dismemberment, a process with imaginative agony undergone in order to remake one's self whole for the benefit of others. As the traditional Shaman's dramatic passion is re-enacted in the enabling-space of his "theatre," a magic circle centered in his body-mind, those present not only benefit from his charismatic power (through suffering hard won) but also vicariously (as in tragic drama) go through his motions. Souls stolen by demons of various sorts are brought back into their proper bodies. Order and form are given to otherwise seemingly inchoate and disintegrative forces at large in the universe as in the uninitiated and undisciplined human soul. That El Salvador was not Carolyn Forché's first journey of this sort, a bleak poem called **"City Walk-Up, Winter 1969"** is sufficient testimony. We know that country too, a place characterized by absence of ordinary, living time:

> A previous month is pinned to the wall where
> days are numbered differently and described by
> the photograph of a dead season. . . .
> We do not rid ourselves of these things
> even when we are cured of personal silence
> when for no reason one morning
> we begin to hear the noise of the world again.

Madness in small doses. A natural homeopath, the poet. Contained within the enabling format of her poems "In Salvador" are metonyms of violence which are the very substance of cure. In **"Return"** the severed hand clutches the soil. And so, as a last resort, must we. In **"San Onofre,"** the last step before the frontier dividing us from a Latin America where hands are tied together and disappearance probable, Carolyn Forché sees "children patting the mud." A reassuring image rooted in most childhoods, in this poet's life-work it has a special resonance. For behind Carolyn Forché as a child stands the grandmother baking bread, stands Anna, heroine of her first volume [*Gathering the Tribes*] and of that **"Endurance"** with which the second section of the present collection begins. "There is nothing one man will not do to another," concludes the visitor to a Salvadorian prison. By implication, then, may our cure come from the observation of women? And the final couplet of one of those devastating ballads of dismemberment reads:

The heart is the toughest part of the body
Tenderness is in the hands.
            ("Because One is Always Forgotten")

The bread-maker's hands are strong, rhythmic, and respectful of the "otherness" of an increasingly lively substance whose consistency is subtly programmed by an experienced human intelligence. No cookbook can tell you how. It's a process you have to develop a feel for. When an overly sticky dough invades the hands—helpless dismay, a taste of what it would be like to be passively trapped by a tar baby. At the other extreme, matter rears its stiff upper lip and retreats into that friable, clod-like obstinacy which we so often defensively project upon the world in other contexts. In the destructive element immerse? No! Rather up to the elbows in the glutinous, the albuminous! Look into what straits Conrad's advice has led us! The bread-maker discloses the recipe for a different type of heroism.

    Grandma, come back, I forgot
    How much lard for these rolls . . .

Already in this first poem of her first volume Carolyn Forché establishes the eucharistic parameters of her moral world. It is an intentionality which offers itself willingly, and with a ready dexterity. To what? Ah, often to that which is on the way out, or walled up, to a vital ingredient in life that's missing.

    I'll tell you I don't remember any kind of bread
    Your wavy loaves of flesh
    Stink through my sleep
    The stars on your silk robes
                ("The Morning Baking")

Anna is the peasant ancestress, Queen of the poet's Revelations, whose hands—primary metonym of a working connectedness to the world—are imagined to be of that self-same material they manipulate.

    Anna's hands were like wheat rolls
    Shelling snow peas, Anna's hands . . .
            ("Burning the Tomato Worms")

Years later, visiting Belgrade, the poet is haunted by visions of Anna:

    . . . hard yellow beans in her lap
    her babushka of white summer cotton,
    her eyes the hard pits of her past.
    . . . Peeling her hands
    with a paring knife, *saying in your country
    you have nothing . . .*

The hands of the ancestress have vegetatively rooted themselves in the old country from whose bourn the young traveller must return to make something come of nothing. Hamlet too was fat. And Anna always of great age and a prophetess:

    . . . Each word was the husk
    of a vegetable tossed to the street
    or a mountain rounded by trains
    with cargoes of sheep dung and grief.
                        ("Endurance")

What is Anna, through the poet as medium, trying to tell us, if we would only shut up and listen? Is it about love?

Whatever it is we have to be patient, for, as the poet continually cautions, it takes a long time for voices to reach each other, to percolate through the loam of the country between us. Meanwhile, one readies the ingredients for lovemaking. . . .

    I'd roll off my hands and let the wind come dust
    me, shape my pillow into Joey's chest and sleep.
    I work the dough between my fists, pull it back
    toward me, punch it then dust it with flour
    again.
        ("This is their Fault," *Gathering the Tribes*)

. . . . .

    These are my breasts, your eyelids
    on my throat. *are you hungry?*
            ("Taproot," *Gathering the Tribes*)

. . . . .

    . . . take our clothes
    in our fingers and open
    ourselves to their hands.
                ("Poem for Maya")

. . . . .

    . . . the tongues swishing
    in my dress, some yours, some
    left by other men.
                    ("Reunion")

As if preparing a meal of herself, in poem after poem the poet is seen peeling her potatoes, unbuttoning her blouse, taking off her clothes. But what should be the prelude to a shaping, mutually self-constituting experience so often turns out to be its opposite—the libidinal corollary in our country of being subjected to Salvadorian dismemberment. The hands of the jailors down there efface what they touch. Their iron weapons but bestow the *coup de grâce*. And a lover's hands may lie because his heart is cold. For a while, the poet finds hope in a woman's mouth, which is "not different," and being akin is more than kind, but in the end it is "the stranger" with whom she would share that scrap of bread which is our transubstantiated "nothing."

The words of Carolyn Forché inevitably create a different sort of aperture through which to view El Salvador, a perspective through which we must look, a voice we cannot ignore precisely because though courageous, she is not a Latin American saint. In Conradian terms she is "one of us."

—*Judith Gleason*

Hers not the hand which seizes the part of fire, hers not the chameleon self which feeds on air, nor does she dive for safety into the depths of water. Carolyn Forché's erotic landscape is horizontal, its contours shaped by the intimacy (or the denial) of touch. It requires time and the vastness of the southwest to unfold itself:

> . . . The creator smoothed over the valley. The man and woman were quiet and their thoughts passed between them. These were of the substance of motionless wind, awake to the quiet, quiet within the hungry space of their presence.
> **("The Place That Is Feared I Inhabit,"**
> ***Gathering the Tribes*)**

But modern life reduces it to the size of a window box, to the space between rushing railway cars, to the confines of a hastily rented room (the same in every city).

> . . . how much tenderness we could
> wedge between a stairwell
> and a police lock . . .
> **("Reunion")**

What landlord is responsible for such a *lebensraum* of lock-up/bolt-out?

In the long poem **"Ourselves or Nothing,"** which concludes *The Country Between Us,* Carolyn Forché gives us the portrait of a present-day Faust working night after night in a "ruined house" going after "that which is lost," a minute reconstruction of the ravages of the Holocaust, of the last hours of those who

> . . . *turned to face the worst*
> *straight-on, without sentiment or hope*
> *simply to keep watch over life . . .*

But ironically, though this driven researcher's words, italicized, ring out strong and true, they come from beyond the pale, from beyond the bourn of that other country from which ghosts, moistening their dried lips with blood, speak to us. What the italicized voice on the page lacks is a body. The poet in memory walks through that house, impatiently smoking, her nightdress characteristically open, but the advocate of self-healing time, of didactic, politically committed poetry upon the slopes of *Parnassus* doesn't even notice her. What is the meaning?

> It is either the beginning or the end
> of the world, and the choice is ourselves
> or nothing.

Concludes that poem.

Upon clay tablets in the third millenium B.C. was inscribed the story of a Sumerian goddess, Inanna, splendid in love and battle, who decided to sojourn a while in the underworld. At each of the seven gates she was stripped of one of her garments. "Crouched and stripped bare" she was judged, after which she was killed and her corpse hung on a peg like a hunk of rotting meat. Thus nailed down in the darkest recess of horror, a new spirit was fertilized within her and slowly, sprinkled with the food and water of life, Inanna revived, returned to the upperworld and sought out her lover, Dumuzi, that he might undergo the sacrificial journey of replacement. True, history has cordoned us off from the slaughter "In Salvador," but not from its inner equivalent. Which is what these wonderful poems consistently give us. And surely the choice of ourselves requires not only engaging from our side of the "cyclone fence" in the battle, whatever the outcome (as

Krishna admonished Arjuna), but also in behalf of love the undertaking of a series of journeys—some as far as the country of the dark goddess, or, closer to home, into the gingerbread house once more with a liberated understanding of its still fearsome oven.

Sharon Doubiago   (essay date 1983)

SOURCE: "Towards an American Criticism: A Reading of Carolyn Forché's *The Country between Us,*" in *The American Poetry Review,* Vol. 12, No. 1, January-February, 1983, pp. 35-9.

[*Doubiago is an American poet, fiction writer, essayist, and educator. In the essay below, in part a response to Katha Pollitt's negative review of* The Country between Us *(see Pollitt's essay dated 1982), Doubiago offers praise for* The Country between Us *and argues that the thematic focus of the volume and the critical controversy surrounding it demonstrate the need for a new criticism and poetics based on politics.*]

The Spring '82 publication of *The Country Between Us* by Carolyn Forché has stirred the old cauldron, painstakingly labeled in our culture, "political poetry." The book has already made literary history, winning the di Castagnola and Lamont prizes, going into its second printing in six weeks, with reviews in *Time* and *People Magazine* and other non-literary "main-stream" publications. As one poet put it, *The Country Between Us* is close to becoming, unlike any poetry book of our times, a bestseller. In a culture noted for its disdain of poetry, and, among its poets, a disdain (in regards to subject matter) of the political, this is a phenomenon that cannot be readily dismissed.

The label "political" is a confused and confusing one, symptomatic, I think, of the current state of literary criticism, of our severe cultural biases and conditionings that prevent genuine critical and creative thought. The rigidity of the label, yet the sloppy way it is regularly used, reveals the cultural paucity in and from which our poets work, a paucity of political and social understanding and intellectual maturity. Current criticism, fed by the same aesthetics from which much contemporary poetry evolves, is grounded in old language, concepts, constructs, wornout clichés and provincialisms, and most obviously, the politics of the *status quo.* This is ironic, *in the least,* since criticism perpetuates itself on the myth of being thought, not programming. It is quite maddening—though typical of the many contradictions and tragic wastes of our lives—to read criticism in the pursuit of real thought and to find instead only standard and predictable reaction. There is not much thinking going on, just vast and mindless processing. A case in point is Katha Pollitt's review in *The Nation* (May 8, 1982) of Forché's book, a review I would like to use here to discuss both *The Country Between Us* and the current state of criticism. We need, I think, a new criticism just as we need a new poetic ethic.

Pollitt's review begins with the question "Why is so little good political poetry written in America today? The very phrase 'political poetry' conjures up visions of smudgy sectarian newspapers where verses with titles like 'Death to All Fascists' appear next to letters signed 'A Brother in Detroit.' " Then she makes an interesting point, the main and most valuable point, I believe, of her review. "Among poets working now . . . only a few treat the sorts of events and issues one reads about in newspapers or demonstrates about in the streets, and I think it significant that those who do—Bly, Levertov, Rich, Ginsberg—are middle-aged. . . . The problem is not that poets are apolitical. It's that they have inherited a literary form so diminished and so privatized that many things lie outside its purview. . . ." She describes our "prototypical magazine poem" as "a free verse elegy on the isolation of the self, set on a campus in the Middle West and decorated with references to snow, light, angels and the poet's nostalgia for his childhood. Ours is a poetry, in other words, of wistful longings, of failed connections, of inevitable personal loss, expressed in a set of poetic strategies that suit such themes—a lax syntax and simplified vocabulary that disclaim intellectual pretension, and ethereal numinous images that testify to the poet's sensibility."

It is against this brilliantly perceptive description of contemporary poetry's dominant aesthetic that Pollitt then discusses *The Country Between Us*. But in doing so I think she misses a great point of the book. Forché's book is not a book of "political poetry," at least not in the way that concept is normally held. As Forché herself has said,

> My poetry is no more political than that of a poet who is celebrating an afternoon as the sun sets in the Mediterranean. It's foolish to say because you're talking about poor people, or because your poetry celebrates or gives witness to the plight of the poor, that it's political. That is the perception of the right. The *status quo* never views itself as political, so it's only others, others in opposition or in striking contrast, who are viewed as political.

And she has said it the other way: " 'Political poetry' often means the poetry of protest, accused of polemical didacticism, and not the poetry which implicitly celebrates politically acceptable values. . . . There is no such thing as a non-political poetry."

Neither is *The Country Between Us* essentially about El Salvador, as it is being lauded, and I suspect, as in Pollitt's case, mis-read. Pollitt's difficulty with the book lies in what she sees as "the incongruity between Forché's themes and her poetic strategies. Forché's topics could not be more urgent, more extreme or more public. . . . And yet she uses a language designed for quite other purposes, the misty 'poetic' language of the isolated, private self." What Pollitt doesn't understand is that *The Country Between Us* is precisely *about* this incongruity, it is the subject matter, *the country between us,* it is the story told: a poet's struggle with the "diminished" and "privatized" poetic ethic Pollitt describes, the struggle with, and out of, the "isolation of the self." The book is a poetry of witness, a narrative, the story of a Northamerican woman in search of her self and her country, any country it seems—for *"in your country / you have nothing"* (**"Endurance"**)—that she can honorably claim and survive in. Chronologically, **"City Walk-Up, Winter 1969"** is the first poem of this story (though **"Joseph"** and **"As Children Together"** describe conditions of her childhood, and there is a reference

in **"Photograph of My Room"** to "the bundle of army letters / . . . sent from Southeast Asia / during '67")—the story of a devastated twenty-year-old woman confronting insanity, i. e., adulthood in the culturally impoverished, crazed, warmongering United States of 1969. "The shelled daylight that followed her / everywhere." The poet wanders continuously, by train across Europe, across the Midwest. Poems are entitled **"Departure," "Return," "Reunion," "For The Stranger," "Expatriate," "Letter From Prague," "Message," "The Visitor," "On Returning To Detroit."** The terrain covered is incredible; if added to the list of Northamerican places of Forché's first book, even more so. "I left Belgrade for Frankfurt last / summer, Frankfurt for New York, / New York for the Roanoke Valley / . . . to this Cape," where the fir tree *outside* her window is "like / a woman who has lived too much. / *Piskata, hold your tongue,* she says. / *I am trying to tell you something"* (**"Endurance"**). The poet is a woman who has "nothing." And she will give it to us (**"For The Stranger"**). This is the "correct" stance of the Northamerican poet. But this is a poet who is not satisfied with "nothing," with the "isolation of the self," who struggles to hear what is being said to her outside the window, who journeys to find more, for herself and for us. (For what is the poet if not a bringer of gifts to the reader. This admission is also missing in much contemporary poetry, the poem often pretending, in its obscurity and attitude, contempt for the reader.) The tone is of great sorrow, of world weariness, but not of the resignation so typical of her contemporaries. *"Half of us are dead or quiet / or lost"* (**"Selective Service"**). She keeps moving/searching rather than give in to despair and insanity. "I searched in Belgrade for some holy / face" (**"Endurance"**). She is committed to finding the larger world, for despite its barbarisms—and our cultural cynicism—she loves the world and its things. She is a sensualist, a lover. She collects images and precise, observed details in this narrative, the journal she brings back to us as poems, in this "world-walking," to quote Rukeyser, as a sort of armor against its cruelties, to remind us of its beauties and goodness, to find, stubbornly, like a lover, redemption for and in the Beloved, to find the path though it eludes her every time. "Go after that which is lost" (**"Ourselves or Nothing"**). **"Because One Is Always Forgotten."** This is the dangerous task of Psyche as she wanders to collect and sort the impossibly fine seeds and shining sheep's wool; it is the task of Isis wandering the land to collect the mutilated parts of her lover, her people. Forché carries her own past with her. "I have kept everything / you whispered to me then," (**"Reunion"**). "We do not rid ourselves of these things / even when we are cured of personal silence / when for no reason one morning / we begin to hear the noise of the world again," (**"City Walk-Up, Winter 1969"**) just as she insists on finding the dead who have "no belongings" (**"Photograph of My Room"**). This collecting of images in order to love the world, this restoration of the things of earth, this bringing of gifts to the reader, this digging up and "asking forgiveness of the corpse, once / it is assembled again on the ground / like a man" (**"Return"**) creates a highly taut, perhaps strange sensuousness (strange not in terms of our reality, but in terms, perhaps, of our poetry) and is at the heart of Pollitt's criticism that

Forché's language is too beautiful for what she describes, too "misty" for "political poetry." On the contrary, I think this language is an innate part of this poet's psyche and search, documented also in her first book—and note the title—*Gathering the Tribes.*

That she ends up in El Salvador is testament to the depth and seriousness of her commitment to find the "real" world. "One day two men knocked on my door in San Diego," Forché recently shared in a Minneapolis workshop, "The Poetry of Witness." "They had driven in an old truck up from Salvador." They came because she is a Northamerican poet, translator of the poetry of one of the men's aunt, Claribel Alegria. In other words they sought her out *as a poet*. "It was thought important that a few Northamericans, particularly writers, be sensitized to Salvador prior to any military conflict. They spent the next seventy-two hours in my kitchen explaining the situation of Salvador. They wanted me to go back with them." In other words she was drafted for this work, drafted as a poet, more obviously, as a human rights worker. A lesser person or, rather, a different person would not have gone, would have clung to her already successful Midwestern poetry and identity. "My poet friends were unanimously opposed to my decision to go to Salvador. They said my poetry would suffer."

She was instructed and trained ("a moral and political education") about El Salvador in order to return to this country to instruct us Northamericans. Her task, she makes clear in all her work, is as witness, as writer. "I am not a guerrilla. I see now that I am most effective as a writer, as an artist, as someone who serves as witness." In Salvador, she describes herself as a "daydreamer." "They would take me down a street and ask me what I saw. What I saw was hardly what was there. So they would take me back down it again. And again, until I *saw* and could remember long enough to report it." They took her from coffee plantations to poverty-ridden villages where starving children stared at her with worms in their eyes, to the elegant homes of the military and American foreign service bureaucrats, to a field hospital where she worked along side a Salvadorean woman doctor who performed caesareans without anesthesia.

> Document it, they said, "go back and tell them what you've seen." They did not tell me what to say or how to say it. They just took me to the places to see for myself. But over and over I found I had been trained *not* to see, and to quickly forget what I had seen. They knew this about me, since I am a Northamerican. I came out of Ahuachapan prison and a mile down the road vomited for what I had seen. In that moment I wanted to be comforted, maybe taken to the Regency for a drink. Instead they said, Okay, now. You pay attention. This is what oppression feels like. Now you have begun to learn something. When you go back to the States, what you do with this is up to you.

Repeatedly she asked herself and her "educators" *why me?* She is after all *just a poet*. Why indeed? This question is essential to the larger story of *The Country Between Us* and to Pollitt's criticism. Forché says she never had any intention of writing Salvadorean poems, "not even a single one. I knew nothing of political journalism but was willing to learn—it seemed, at the time, an acceptable way for a poet to make a living." She says she intended to keep her art and her politics in two separate compartments. "There was something in me that believed the terrible, I think subliminal, message in the literary world, especially among poets, that politics are not poetry. But every time I would be tired and wanting so much just to write a poem—go back to my love, poetry—then it would start. It would be about my friends, it would be taking place . . . *there*." Is not the answer to the question, "why me? I'm just a poet" *because* she is a poet and the book, in part at least, a message to us poets isolated by our literary institutions, our MFA programs where we learn how to write: i. e., how not to be political? As everyone knows poetry *matters* in Latin America; it is the voice, or one of them, of the people. Were Forché's Salvadorean educators ignorant of the impoverished status of poets in the States, or is this book not, in fact, a message to us about the only path our culture grandly opens to poets: that city walk-up in dead of winter where personal redemption from our corrupt and evil country is silence, insanity, suicide.

I am taking liberties. The book, in our tradition at least, must stand on its own. Hints of the turmoil and sense of inadequacy of being "just a poet" in witness to such a place and ordeal *are* strewn throughout the poems—that is, the story continues, even in Salvador, of the Northamerican wanderer seeking her work, her words, her world. **"The Colonel,"** the most oft-quoted and reprinted poem of the book is, interestingly, set in prose and the witness breaks down midpoint when the Colonel spills a sack of human ears onto the dinner table: "There is no other way to say this." Who is it that is breaking down here? Not the witness, but the poet with the burden of her U.S. aesthetics. Who is she apologizing to? First and foremost, to us, her fellow poets (or is it to her teachers and critics who will disapprove?). The opening lines of the piece are also addressed to us, I think. "What you have heard is true. I was in his house," as if a poet should not have been, as if to answer her poet friends who warned her about this. The ears "are like dried peach halves," the poet's only simile here and one I think that undeniably authenticates her experience. *We* need this simile, for how many of us have had the experience? It brings the ears alive for us, just as the one dropped in the glass of water by the Colonel "came alive." And even he addresses the poet's "problem" as he performs his heinous act. "Something for your poetry, no?"

And again, this is the tension, the underlying story of **"Return."** The poem is self-satire, framed in Josephine's impatience with the poet who has returned to this country and is having a hard time adjusting. "So you know now," Josephine says over and over in the ironic tone of "so what?" The poet uses herself as foil against which Josephine lists atrocities while saying "Go try on Americans your long, dull story / of corruption, but better to give them what they want": the stories and images of sexual torture and humiliation, and for us poets, the imagistic (voyeuristic?) convention in which we have been trained. Pollitt misses this point, calls it "wildly histrionic—and slanderous, too—to accuse politically moderate human-rights activists of deriving masturbatory pleasure from torture reports." This is simply naive, the terrible naivety of one who is without experience, overly isolated, perhaps, in the self. Josephine knows the long dull story won't get our attention, nor will a poetry of direct statement, more strident, perhaps, and of less beautiful language. "Your problem . . . is that you were born to an island of greed / and grace where you have this sense of yourself as apart from others": precisely the ethic of Northamerican poetry. But "it is not your right to feel powerless. Better / people than you were powerless."

The extraordinary success of the book is not for its politics, nor simply, for its poetry. It is for the synthesis of these two phenomena. We hunger for this synthesis. Still, the book is poetry, first and foremost. I would argue that Forché's beautiful language vivifies the fact of torture rather than trivializes it, as Pollitt charges. "She gives us bloody stumps but she also gives us snow, light and angels." "We need the force of beauty," Michael Daley says, "to show the force of horror." I for one suspect that "angels and light" are more present in torture chambers than in most places, and the beautiful, simple things of life that appear in all of Forché's poems, the baskets of fruit, eggs and wine, etc., most numinous under great stress. Besides, Forché's angels are the snow angels of our childhoods, the terrible "corpses of angels" we've left behind (**"Selective Service"**). Pollitt says "it is embarrassing to read that Forché goes 'mad / for example / in the Safeway,' " that "she visualizes torture in terms of lunch." On the contrary I believe this is a common experience among politically aware people and the reference succeeds most in its universalness. It is embarrassing that Pollitt is embarrassed. "Who is it that *can* eat?" Daley asks, "without visualizing the torture victims? There'll be no change until none of us can eat without seeing them." And I am reminded of what another U.S./Salvadorean reporter has said:

> People need information—for example if you don't know that you have an unconscious, a subconscious, and an ego, or you've never heard the psyche described in terms other than your spirit or your mind, you have much less control over yourself, your behaviour and your growth than you do if you know. . . . The main thing that is really hard for people here to understand, even though it's the most obvious, is poverty, and what poverty really is. . . . Everybody thinks, *stop laying a guilt trip on us.* That's why I say one has to know one's psyche and how it works; for instance, where your reactions come from when you hear certain words. Is this person saying there's poverty because they're attacking me and saying I'm to blame? Is this person saying there's poverty thinking, oh but I don't know what poverty is, I can never know what poverty is, why are they talking to me about poverty? (Central America Split: The Partisan Reporter, by Stephen Kessler, *The Santa Cruz Express,* April 15, 1981)

I think we are witness here to an aspect of Pollitt's psyche that she herself is unaware of, the one that is a part of the collective Northamerican psyche that insists on a "nonpolitical" poetry.

And, finally, Pollitt cannot admire Forché "for stressing the intensity of her response for the sufferings of others," though earlier in her review she has perceived the unfortunate poetic rule that "whatever its repercussions in the realm of private feeling, politics is fundamentally a public affair." The critic reveals again here that she does not understand what this book is about and her aesthetic is identical to the aesthetic she so adequately identifies and finds wanting. Her own critical practice trails her understanding (which is, interestingly, the fault she finds in Forche). Political witness, contemporary experience, and direct statement that reveals "intellectual pretension," and I might add, love, passion and commitment, are taboo in our "official" poetry.

For me, Forché's book is "political"—to try here to understand, to perhaps even claim the word—in that it is the female voice in many ways of my generation, representative of a vast number of women who are living outside of, and have been for some time now, the lives we were programmed for, the lives of our mothers. This is a poetic voice from which we have not heard much yet. The powerful, revolutionary female voice of our generation, besides that of popular music, has been the inestimably important lesbian-separatist one. (The majority of other well-published women poets write from the conservative, domestic stance Pollitt describes.) Forché is clearly a nonseparatist feminist, the one we are familiar with in our music, though strangely, not our poetry: very female, erotic, sexual, mobile, independent, exploratory, nondomestic, childless (a nagging awareness in the book typical of the many still childless women who came to puberty with the advent of the Pill). "In what time do we live that it is too late / to have children?" [**"Selective Service"**]), a woman traveling alone, the hunter rather than the hunted, a very lonely *caminante*—but not a loner and not a separatist. The voice is that of the female veteran of the Viet Nam War—the central event, as John Froines once said, of the second half of the Twentieth Century—if not of the actual Asian battlefield, veteran then of the destruction of a whole generation's inherited values, ruins as clear and as profound in their reverberations as those of the well documented cultural ruins of World War I. (Forché is in fact the ex-wife of a Viet Nam veteran.) *The Country Between Us* is political also, I think, in its American-ness. That she is a Northamerican is a fact, a reality never forgotten or dismissed in her travels, in her work, and never, never trivialized. We are not used to this and therefore I sense we are deeply moved, and not *just* to the customary anger and self-loathing. There is something wonderful here about being American. Her language, for instance: taut, raw, stretched, becoming new, always becoming something else than it was, of a directness, plainness, and personalness that so often turns toward the surreal, or the American, or, to use a veteran, near forgotten word of our generation now well into mid-adulthood, the psychedelic. There is also something political and revolutionary in her use of literature's most ancient and traditional form, the narrative. I suspect it is a natural form or process for one so deeply rooted in and in many ways faithful to "non-literary" people. But this female narration creates an incredible mix of traditional and non-traditional values, typical of the concepts and forces with which we have had to struggle. Her stories, the story, so easy to follow, indeed, so seductive, allows her to speak to us of things we (of *all* persuasions) might not otherwise listen to, *"in the voice / of a woman singing to a man / who could make her do anything."* (**"Reunion"**). *"I am a childless poet,"* she cries to her dead Slovak grandmother, Anna, *"I have not painted an egg, made prayers / or finished my Easter duty in years"* (**"Endurance"**). One of the most obvious revolutionary demands of our time is the one of learning the self, to know, see, hear, and then to follow the line of one's own story, utilizing the vast wealth of human knowledge—psychological, sociological, anthropological, ecological, economical, physical, metaphysical, etc.—accumulated in the past century, rather than following the storyline that the State, the old culture demands. Forché's deeply personal account, while revealing the tremendous psychic toll these explorations and role-changes have taken, becomes another call, a suggestion at least, to every reader to find and follow her or his true story. This is very revolutionary—as the State knows, very threatening to its hold on the people. In the Salvadorian narratives, Forché speaks directly and personally out of a tragic story that does not get resolved, but needs, desperately, urgently, *now,* to be resolved. It is a story we are all a part of, responsible for, one that depends on us, for we are its resolution, whatever we decide, or don't decide, to do. For none of us are really childless, of course. There are the generations coming up behind us, our true daughters and sons, and still, there are our brothers and sisters, and even still our parents who have been deeply affected by what we have seen and done, all of us in true need of this voice, our voice, a rather common, near universal voice, but still so rare, still new in our poetry, that most conservative, and therefore, most enduring, art form.

The critic is the puritan in North America, Meridel Le Sueur has said and that is why, as unlike in any other country, the critic here is more powerful than the artist. Why is it that critics never acknowledge the very large and essential issue of their "personal taste"? They pronounce a work as "bad" (Calvin Bedient, *The Nation,* May 22) without defining their terms. They use expressions like Pollitt's "at their best" (in terms of what?), "you have to read the poem several times" to understand it (who does? Is this a command, or a confession?), "though the poem be flawed" (by what and whose standards? This is Ferlinghetti on Jack Hirschman), "the poems tend to blur in the mind" (whose mind? How much courage does it take to say "my mind"?), "when she speaks plainly she can be very good indeed"—*this is taste!* And yes, the language of the puritan. Judgments are rarely framed as expressions of the individual but as some Godly Absolute. Why do we allow this? For a profession that lauds itself for logic, rationality, clear and impartial thinking, and in our collective homage to it has extraordinary power over our lives—our most private lives, I might add, i. e., what we read, enjoy, what we think and feel—its standards and usages are outrageously "lax," to use Pollitt's word, indeed laughable, if not immoral. ("The critic must be counted right up there with the military and FBI for lives destroyed" Le Sueur). Pollitt demands that Forché be more stringent in her language, less poetic, but does not have to, in the sacrosanct tradition of *her* form, account for the very real fact that if the poems were written less in the aesthetic we have been taught is poetry, if written without the degree of refinement so cherished in our schools, if publishable at all, would have ended up in the "smudgy sectarian newspapers" she relegates political poetry to. Harper and Row would not have published the book, it would not have been awarded the prestigious Lamont Prize, Pollitt would not have reviewed the book in *The Nation,* we would not be reading it, particularly we poets, and the Salvadorians who invested time and training in Forché, sent her back to this country to write, that they may speak to us through her—those other Americans who seek any and all ways to find their story onto the northern part of their continent, into our lunches as well as into our poetry, would have failed in their mission. These are political realities, of course, the "outside factors" not allowed into our reviews. The book must stand on its own. And it is time, for the danger is very great, that we begin to examine the politically acceptable values we do permit, indeed, insist on, in our "objective" "non-political" aesthetics.

And, of course, there has been great political poetry written in the past ten to fifteen years by the "younger generation," and by those other great poets, the mature, incorruptable and persistent ones still not recognized by their own generations, their own country. To not understand this is to display still further naiveté about literary politics. What Pollitt is referring to when she asks "Why is so little good political poetry written in America today?" is not the state of the art, but the state of publishers, educators, critics and readers. *The State.* By "good" she is referring to the "taste" of authorities, of academia and government. By "written" she means published. And obviously, "published" does not mean those "smudgy sectarian newspapers" where in fact much fine poetry *is* being published. And by "America" she means North America. Pollitt is speaking politically, from the aesthetic that a work is flawed that has the potential of altering the society's *status quo,* from the aesthetic of our government-funded literary establishment and NYC presses owned by the oil corporations, from the aesthetic of an elite culture that feeds off of, but does not want to be reminded in its poetry of where its clothes, its food, its coffee and liquor, its oil, dope, sugar and stimulants are produced, the aesthetic that a "good" poem is not political. And this is why we are such a precious lot, we poets, practitioners of "a genteel and minor art form," as Pollitt fears, and why we do not have readers, in contrast, for instance, with poets of Latin America, who have large followings, the political scene giving their work impetus, validity, excitement. Poetry *matters* in Latin America. Here, our voices, our power has been taken from us, leaving us "confined / to a window," (**"City Walk-Up"**) probably the most prominent image of contemporary poetry, so that at best we are impotent voyeurs of a barbaric and stupid world. But, someday, it *must* happen. We will understand that we are not Europe. We will know our geography, our American hemisphere, our fellow Americans. When that happens we will have, along with, *at last,* the New World, a valid poetry.

There is a cyclone fence between
ourselves and the slaughter and
behind it
we hover in a calm protected world
like
netted fish, exactly like netted fish.
It is either the beginning or the end
of the world, and the choice is
ourselves
or nothing.

                              ("Ourselves or Nothing")

Again, in light of Pollitt's criticism, *The Country Between Us* is the work of a late-twentieth-century-educated-and-trained Midwest poet. The work does contain many of the characteristics and values Pollitt describes of our contemporary literary form. Forché is working within the current "tradition," except perhaps for subject matter. And perhaps it is that subject matter—in both of her books—along with her wonderfully wild sensuous energy, her commitment to the present rather than the past, her subliminal ethic of action, that causes her always to transcend the static, "fascist" form. How true her language is to the "real" voice and the land and experience from which she comes is a question perhaps time will help to answer (though time is not necessarily free of the coercion of culture). But this poet, this extraordinary woman has already gone further than most ever will in trying to authenticate her voice, immersing herself and her language in the "real" and very dangerous world. She has used her verbal training like a guerrilla uses intimate knowledge of the land, taking the aesthetic jammed into her as a young working class woman gone to college and jamming it right back into the real, the political. This is a poetry of terrible witness, the strains of our villainies on the language and ethical constructs undoubtedly show. Thus the phrase, "the country between us." The strain, the gap, the "other voice that calls" her creates an extraordinary beauty and courage, moves her toward an old "avant-garde" (still, avant-garde) Northamerican tradition—Whitman, Pound, Olson, H.D., Levertov, Rukeyser, Le Sueur, Duncan, Hirschman, McGrath, Di Prima, and how many lost, unpublished? —of the work as process rather than as static *thing*. Perhaps the real point is our language has still not found its true story. Our language, *still,* the King's English. Male and of Europe's Court.

Carolyn Forché   (lecture date 1984)

SOURCE: "A Lesson in Commitment," in *TriQuarterly*, No. 65, Winter, 1986, pp. 30, 32-8.

[*In the following lecture, originally delivered at a November 1984 Symposium entitled "The Writer in Our World," Forché discusses the events that led to her travels in El Salvador, her aims as a poet, and the relationship between poetry and politics.*]

I would like to begin with a little story about how I came to go to El Salvador in the first place, to provide a context for the statement that I would like to read. I traveled in 1977 to Spain to translate the poetry of a Salvadoran woman poet living in exile there. Her name was Claribel Alegría. I was doing translation because, following the completion of the book, *Gathering the Tribes*, I suddenly couldn't write any more poems. I suffered from what writers call a "block" and I, of course, despaired and thought that it was permanent and so I became a translator. I went to Spain because I had tried to translate the poetry of Claribel Alegría alone, in California, at my kitchen table. I was very naive. And so I appealed to Claribel's daughter, who advised me to come to Spain for the summer and if I had problems with the poetry I could ask "Mummy" and "Mummy" would tell me what I should put in her poems. "Mummy" was fond of an English which would say something like—she would say to me, "Why don't you use 'rolling hills' here?"

And I said, "Well, that's very nice but everyone else has already thought of it, also." That was the kind of problem one encountered translating the poem with the poet at one's side.

There I met a number of Latin American writers, some well-known, some not so well-known, because Claribel holds a kind of "salon" in Deya, Majorca, for any writer who has had to go into exile from any part of Latin America and has chosen to relocate in Europe. Claribel's home is a kind of way station. So, while there, I spent the summer listening to their stories of conditions in Latin America and beginning my education.

I returned to San Diego, California, in the fall and began teaching again and working for Amnesty International. I felt, however, after a while, that writing letters for Amnesty International was, for me, not quite enough and I felt vaguely depressed and compelled to do something more—I didn't know quite what—about what I had learned in that summer. And, on into fall, the stacks of letters and literature about human rights violations in Central America grew on my table. One day, while I was grading freshman compositions, a white Hiace van pulled into my driveway. It was covered with dust and had El Salvador license plates. I went to the door, looked out and I didn't recognize the man getting out of the van, but there were two little girls with him so I relaxed. I felt, "Well, it can't be too bad. There are two little girls there." He had a very large roll of white butcher paper and a fistful of number-two pencils. And he walked up to my front door and said, "You are Carolyn Forché, and I am Leonel Gomez [Vides]." I thought for a moment and then I remembered the name. I had heard it in Spain that summer from Claribel. This was Claribel's nephew, the crazy one who slept with his motorcycle outside on the ground "like a woman," they said, which was a very odd thing, odder than the fact that he had given land away to the peasants in the countryside and was living in some kind of shack. I was worried; maybe this was him, maybe this was not, so I ran up to my room for the snapshots I had taken of the family in Spain and I said, "If you are Leonel Gomez, I want you to tell me who the people are in these pictures." I made him identify the relatives, the cousins, the babies, and he did a good job. He looked at me and said, "That was pretty good, a good test, that you find out who I am." So, I let him in and he said, "Clear this junk off the table. We have work to do." I defended my junk, my literature about human rights and my student composition papers, but I cleared it, and he told me to make some coffee; we had work to do. And then he started to cover the kitchen table with shelf paper, taping it at the corners with some tape. And he sat down and he said, "O.K., how much do you know about Central American military dictatorship?"

And I said, "Nothing."

And he said, "Good, you know that you know nothing. Now, this is a good beginning."

So he spent seventy-two hours drawing cartoons on the shelf paper—and diagrams and charts and graphs. Everything he explained to me, he drew a picture of as he spoke. And he began with a structure of the Salvadoran military and he drew the coffee plantations and the American embassy. Then he brought salt and pepper shakers over to the table, and spoons and various other household objects. And he called the salt shaker this "colonel" and he called the pepper shaker that "colonel" and this spoon was the American ambassador. And so on and so forth. And he arranged them all in a scenario, as he called it, and then he said, "All right, you are this colonel and this happens and that happens and that happens, what are you going to do?" And then he said, "Think like a colonel." So I had to answer his questions, one after the other, for seventy-two hours. He sent the little girls out in my backyard to play with the twenty-three rabbits that were the offspring of the three Easter bunnies my creative writing students had given me that spring. And so we didn't see much of them, and we put them to sleep from time to time, but he would not sleep and he would not eat. He would only talk, and he kept saying he didn't have much time. And at the end of the seventy-two hours, he said to me, "All right now, you have a Ph. D. in El Salvador studies." He said, "I have some questions for you. Do you want to do something for the rest of humanity?"

Now what would *you* say if someone asked you that? There's only one answer. So I said, "Yes."

And he said, "Would you like to do something for the people of Central America?"

A little more specific. And I said, "Yes."

And he said, "You have a Guggenheim."

And I said, "Yes."

And he said, "That means you can do pretty much anything you want, right?"

And I said, "Yes." I had received one and, of course, my friends had advised me that, since I was a poet, I should go to Paris and write poetry or, at least, New England, to become a real poet. This was my plan, but I couldn't choose, yet, where I was going to go.

And so he said, "All right, I think you should come to El Salvador. Because," he said, "you can just come and learn about the country. If you want to translate Central American poetry, you have to know more." And then he said, "Also, do you want to write poetry about yourself the rest of your life?"

And I said, "You've read my poetry?"

And he said, "Yes."

So I said, "No, well, no, I don't think so, now that you put it that way. It was something that I hadn't really thought of before."

So he said, "Listen to me, Forché. In three to five years, my country is going to be the beginning of your country's next Vietnam. Did you understand Vietnam when it was going on?"

I said, "No."

Well, Mr. Gomez had touched a nerve, because I had been married to a man who fought in Vietnam and who suffered from what they now call "Post-Vietnam Syndrome," and so for many years I had had an interest in Vietnam and read everything I could get my hands on because I thought there was some way that if I knew enough about Vietnam, I would understand what had happened to my husband. And so Mr. Gomez said, "Would you like to see it from the beginning? From inside, close?"

And I thought, "He's crazy. He must be crazy. El Salvador is the size of my small fingernail on the largest map I can find. It can't be possible."

And he said, "Look. Forty nuns have been put into exile. Two priests have been killed and the government has killed one American. There will be more American deaths." He said, "If you want to come, arrive in January, and we will take you anywhere you want to go in the country. You can sleep with various friends that we have, and stay in houses. You can work in a hospital if you want, or in an orphanage. You can do whatever you want and, as a journalist, you can interview the high-ranking officers of the military and of your own embassy."

I said, "I am not a journalist. I am a poet."

He said, "Same thing."

I said, "No, it isn't the same thing. I don't know anything about journalism."

He said, "You'll learn."

I said, "What do you want in exchange?"

And he said, "In three to five years, when the war begins, maybe you will want to be in the United States so that you can explain what is happening to the Americans."

I said, "I think you have the wrong person. I'm a poet."
I said, "Americans don't listen to poets."

He said, "Well, change that." He said, "We want a poet. This is important."

So I thought about it and after he left I asked everyone if I should go or not. And everyone said, "No." They all said, "You don't know this guy. You don't know anything about El Salvador. And your Spanish is lousy. You have to go to Paris and write poetry." Everyone said that and so I went.

And when I got to the country, I was taken to Benihana of Tokyo on the first night. San Salvador. I sat there with a little dinner party that Leonel had arranged in my honor. It was three young men who were later, quite a few years later, to become guerillas, two Embassy staff members, one Peace Corps volunteer; and several other Salvadorans whom I never saw again. Men and women. And we were sitting around, having those Benihana shrimps that they fry on a hot grill, and listening to koto music. And he said, "You are in Saigon and it is 1959. Now I am going to show you everything."

Well, this was the way I was educated. I stayed two years, off and on, back and forth: Guatemala, El Salvador, the United States, and, finally, I left on March 16, 1980. I had to leave the country—I was unable to stay, even though I had wanted to stay, especially to return that summer. And so, out of that kind of feeling one has for one's friends, and loneliness, and isolation, and some kind of impulse that is not explained by personal reasons, I began to write some poems, and some of them were about El Salvador, and they were included in a book called *The Country Between Us.* I am going to read a statement now, about this issue that we are addressing: poetry and politics, now that you know how I came to be a "political poet":

I find it somewhat difficult to address the controversy concerning the issue of poetry and politics in the United States. I hadn't realized until the publication of my second book of poems in early 1982 that certain subjects were considered inappropriate for poetry in America, or beyond the grasp of American poets, who, after all, were not affected by politics, as were the poets of Eastern Europe, Latin America, Asia, Africa and the Middle East. It became clear that this objection to the political wasn't limited to explicitly polemical work, slogans, chants and the flat, predictable poetry of those who would submit art to ideology, but was extended to include the impassioned voices of witness, those whose diction departed from the acceptable mode, those who left the safety of self-contemplation to imagine and address the larger world. In my own case, the poems of *The Country Between Us* were considered political, it seems, because seven of them were written in El Salvador, a country associated, in American minds, with political turmoil, and more to the point, with a controversial American policy of support to a government deemed responsible for the systematized slaughter of its political opponents. Those who welcomed my book felt obliged to defend or celebrate its political stance, which, nevertheless, remained somewhat elusive. This is perhaps because I am most compelled by moral and ethical questions, the aesthetic nature of morality, and the moral aspect of aesthetics, but almost never was concerned, explicitly, with politics in the narrow sense of the term. This is not to disparage poets who would define themselves that way, but rather to point out the strangeness of the response to *The Country Between Us,* by both those who praised and those who condemned the book.

Before it was written, I had been unable to write for two years, a condition I attributed to the untimely death of my muse. When I left for El Salvador in early 1978, I considered that I might perhaps be leaving poetry forever, but I would take the opportunity of a Guggenheim grant to spend one year in Central America. My reasons for going there were personal, having to do indirectly with my decade-long interest in the Vietnam War, which I have ex-

plained to you. The poetry which came of my time there was written out of a private grief and a dark vision of historical repetition to which I could not reconcile myself. I approached the page, as I always have, in the wakeful reverie of impassioned remembrance, this time with more sadness than joy, but never with the intention to persuade, inspire, or define the war which could not be stopped and was to become the most significant influence upon my life and the education of my heart. The poems were written out of desperation and, for eighteen months, they were kept silent in a drawer. I had been told not to publish the manuscript for the reason that it was political, and that perhaps the work I had done was best considered a private release of emotion necessary to my recovery from the circumstances illuminated in the poems.

The poet, Margaret Atwood, discovered this reluctance and enabled the work to find a publisher. I was taken aback by the response but, fortunately, had already embarked on a four-year journey around the United States, in which I spoke continually and to whoever would listen about the tragedy of Central America and what I then perceived as the blindness of U.S. policy there. During those four years, I was generously given other opportunities to further my education in the twentieth-century human condition, so was able to travel and work in Northern Ireland, the Israeli-occupied territories of the West Bank and Gaza Strip, Guatemala and Lebanon, with pilgrimages to Yed Vashem, Hiroshima and Nagasaki. I have not been, thus far, equal to this journey, and so have lost, perhaps—and God help me, temporarily—the agility to wander within myself in that region of focused reverie which might yield another poem. I am now capable of the reverie again, but I seem no longer able to focus my imagination to the exclusion of all that haunts and distracts me. No single voice lifts pure from the cacophony of voices and each image is one of horror, with no single image burned more deeply than others and all seeming to be fragments of a vague and larger horror that has something to do with my sense that we are, as a species, now careening toward our complete destruction with ever-greater velocity and that our survival is by no means assured except by the drastic steps we have not yet begun to take. Sometimes, forgive me, but I imagine that I don't have enough time to finish another book of poems and so I am restless each time I sit before the paper thinking it might perhaps be more useful in a particular moment to do something else. I ask to be forgiven if in my current state of mind I am unfairly devaluing poetry. In preparation for this conference I questioned my Columbia University students, and those involved in the Writers' Community Workshops, regarding contemporary American poetry and the relationship between poetry and politics; they spoke of sensing a certain emptiness in American work and lamented the lack of intensity and passion so evident in the poetry of other parts of the world. One student referred to Joseph Brodsky's suggestion that each word or image used well in a poem would reveal its relation to every other in the poem and in the world. But to achieve that, countered another, one must write as if one believes in an integrated universe. Yes, he tells them, and adds to this his faith in the shapeliness of the imagination. He gives them the poetry of Zbigniew Herbert and they embrace even the palest

English versions of his impassioned witness; seemingly starved for something they vaguely define as substance. During a particularly wistful classroom discussion at Columbia last week, a student praised recent efforts by American poets to confront the threat of thermonuclear war. In this, one ventured, perhaps only in this, do we share the fate of the world. The consensus on that afternoon was that perhaps it was impossible to reflect the twentieth-century human condition from a position of relative privilege and protection, except in the matter of apocalyptic annihilation. I don't know. To return to my personal case, in a sense, now, I am free of concerns about critical responses to my poems. If I continue to write about El Salvador, I am a poet of limited range, a topical poet. If I permit myself to write from experiences in other places, as for example, those in Beirut last winter, where I worked as a radio correspondent for National Public Radio, I might be considered an opportunist and a dilettante. If I abandon these subjects altogether, I would be guilty of failing to endure as the poet I was praised for having become. Or I might, lamentably, be praised for having converted to a higher aesthetic. Therefore, it doesn't matter what sort of poems I write next, and this is a happy condition. I don't have answers for many of the questions regarding the apparent self-censorship of American literary artists. I am amazed at the extent to which issues which I view as essentially moral and ethical are treated as if they are merely political in the narrowest sense: imprisonment for matters of conscience, torture, the slaughter of civilian noncombatants in time of war, the introduction of first-strike weapons under cover of defense, sexism, racism and the poisoning of common water and air supplies by private interests, are examples of these. I am hoping to learn more about the relationship between literary art and the world from my colleagues. It seems that during the four years of travel in the United States, addressing American audiences interested in poetry and peace, I have become somewhat myopic with regard to the sensibility of my countrymen—I was mistaking the sentiments of small groups for the common wisdom of the whole. After this last election (1984), it is simply no longer possible for me to nurture the same intuitive faith in the wisdom of my countrymen. It is perhaps, however, dangerous for me to believe that one writes in exile even in one's own country, and perhaps especially there.

John Mann   (essay date 1986)

SOURCE: "Carolyn Forché: Poetry and Survival," in *American Poetry*, Vol. 3, No. 3, Spring, 1986, pp. 51-69.

[*In the essay below, Mann examines thematic, structural, and stylistic features of* The Country between Us, *arguing that Forché's poetry of witness "becomes in the reading of the book an exemplar for our collective response" to the horrors of the twentieth century.*]

Ezra Pound now seems, at the remove of sixty years, among the most acute interpreters of our century's disastrous second decade. Pound's achievement was to recognize, amidst the painful hollowness of his own most cherished illusions, larger and more dangerous self-deceptions in western civilization. Thus *Hugh Selwyn Mauberley* in-

> **Forché's images have a way of crisping and elegizing moments—she stamps them as precisely as one writes a single word on a field of snow. Added to the beauty of the singular image is the mystery of what she leaves out—images minus the story, the logical connections. So the reader is left with a movement of pictures more like music than it is like prose.**
>
> **—*Nancy L. McCann, in her review of* The Country between Us, *in* The Christian Century, *27 October 1982.***

terrupts its literary story of Pound's years in London to put us "eye-deep in hell," and the trench warfare of the World War would present the archetype for the mass destruction and inhumanity of the twentieth century. Short, syncopated lines chronicled modern war's obliteration of the old world in the shredding of bodies and the creation of a new world that somehow had to be faced by survivors of mass death ("There died a myriad"). Looking at the ruins, Pound concluded that civilization itself had experienced a kind of suicide, with "young blood" spilling itself in unimaginable amounts "For an old bitch gone in the teeth, / For a botched civilization." Modern history, in turn, has been the unraveling spool of nightmare, and twentieth-century writing has become the literature of survival. As Carolyn Forché put it in the concluding poem of *The Country Between Us*: Ponder recent history and "all the mass graves of the century's dead / will open into your early waking hours."

Forché had already created a sensation among poets by describing her experience in war-torn El Salvador [in her "El Salvador: An Aide Memoire"] and calling for "a poetry of witness" more accountable than ever before to "the twentieth century human condition." *The Country Between Us,* Forché's second volume of poetry, has reached a surprisingly large audience, and apart from the book's topical interest, one can sense in its powerful impact on readers and hearers an important argument for poetry. Initial commentary on the book evokes an old fear, the New Critics' fear of the corrupting influence of politics on the purity of the poem's language. Actually, Forche's book goes beyond the question "Can a good poem be political?" to some far more significant and fearful ones: Is poetry adequate to a century of holocaust? Can an intensely personal language and vision of things suffice? Can poetry help us? (*Are* we still human? some have asked.) *The Country Between Us* possesses one of the severest orderings of poems of any collection in recent memory, and an examination of its three-part structure will help us ponder some of these questions. The book embodies the process by which Forché became a survivor who somehow found the courage and honesty to make of the atrocities she witnessed the test and education of her moral will. Her personal transformation becomes in the reading of the book an exemplar for our collective response. Above all, the book will suggest what a poetry of witness might involve in a time such as ours. *The Country Between Us* enacts with intense drama and sensuous immediacy the agony of human survival in an age of mass death, and as such it is the compelling story for our century's ninth decade.

Nothing could have prepared the winner of the Yale Series of Younger Poets prize (awarded for her first book, *Gathering the Tribes,* in 1976) for what she found when she journeyed to El Salvador in 1978. She describes herself in a recent interview in [the 14 April 1983 issue of] *Rolling Stone* as a midwesterner with working-class roots teaching and writing in San Diego when, in 1977, Leonel Gómez Vides appeared at her door. A translator of Claribel Alegría's poems, and a worker for Amnesty International, Forché was perhaps ready to accept Gómez's invitation to visit and learn about his small country (on maps, the size of a chestnut); but her recollection of agreeing to go now strikes her as absurdly naive: "I thought I would be the lady in white working in the orphanage for one year who pats the little bottoms! I pictured myself that way, rather heroically." Instead, what she found in several journeys to El Salvador between 1978 and 1980 was twentieth-century reality. The eight poems in Part I of *The Country Between Us* bear the title "In Salvador, 1978-1980." They represent an immersion (really a kind of baptism) for the poet—what quickly would become a political education, but more importantly a moral education as well. As she recalled later, "A young writer, politically unaffiliated, ideologically vague, I was to be blessed with the rarity of a moral and political education—what at times would seem an unbearable immersion, what eventually would become a focussed obsession. It would change my life and work, propel me toward engagement, test my endurance and find it wanting, and prevent me from ever viewing myself or my country again through precisely the same fog of unwitting connivance." This immersion ultimately issued in an outcry and a transformation.

Although many describe *The Country Between Us* as "Forché's book on El Salvador," the poems in Part I—the one part wholly devoted to Latin America—account for only eight of the twenty-two poems in the book. Additionally, four of the eight (**"San Onofre, California," "The Island," "The Memory of Elena,"** and **"Return"**) are spoken from other places—Mallorca and California in the United States. Her El Salvador journeys score all eight poems, however, reaching back to the first poem (dated 1977) and forward to the one dated 1980-81 and her return to the U.S. It is as if the fact of El Salvador inevitably altered even her memories of her past, making them all seem preparation, and touched all her future. The first three poems, especially, dramatize the quality of the poet's preparation—who prepared her for El Salvador, and when, and why. They show the poet listening to others and suggest a remarkable quality of *The Country Between Us*: it is a book of voices speaking, or silenced, or attempting to speak, and many of them are not the poet's own. Listening to others, one concludes, is a preliminary obligation of the poet who would survive by being witness. Then must come seeing.

Thus in her first poem, **"San Onofre, California"**, whose title places us in a small coastal village near San Diego, the poet (in imagination) ranges much farther down the neck of North America—"We have come far south," to Mexico and beyond—in order to listen. She tries to explain "why we feel / it is enough to listen"; later, in a crucial inner turning in the book, she will have to convince herself that she must speak or write poems, and that the utterance will be enough. Here the sensuous plunge into the atmosphere of Latin America yields immediately to its defining fact: "the street in the very place / where someone disappeared." We would rather listen "to the wind jostling lemons / to dogs ticking across the terraces," than to the cries of the disappeared, and in a brilliant inversion that captures the precise lack of our "Northamerican" awareness, the poet leaves us "knowing that while birds and warmer weather / are forever moving north, / the cries of those who vanish / might take years to get here." Do these cries, most often in this book unheard, issue from Salvador, or from any one of a dozen other places in the region or the world? The poet does not say, but the insistent repetition of "we" or one of its variants ("our," "us"), not "I" or "mine," suggests our complicity—a suggestion that will become before the end of her book the poet's chief integrity. San Onofre provides a first listening post for what is not yet known, but strongly sensed.

We hear and see more explicitly in the next two poems, **"The Island"** and **"The Memory of Elena."** These are still preparation for the poet's Salvador journey (note the dates, before 1978), and they recollect a crucial stage in her education: her stay on the island of Mallorca in 1977 with Salvadorean poet Claribel Alegría, whose poems she had begun to translate. Forché remembers of that time [in "El Salvador: An Aide Memoire"],

> I was busy with Claribel's poems, and with the horrific accounts of the survivors of repressive Latin American regimes. Claribel's home was frequented by these wounded; writers who had been tortured and imprisoned, who had lost husbands, wives and closest friends. In the afternoon more than once I joined Claribel in her silent vigil near the window until the mail came, her "difficult time of day," alone in a chair in the perfect light of thick-walled Mallorquin windows. These were her afternoons of despair, and they haunted me. In those hours I first learned of El Salvador, not from the springs of her nostalgia for "the fraternity of dipping a tortilla into a common pot of beans and meat," but from the source of its pervasive brutality.

Listening and talking to Claribel Alegría in **"The Island,"** Forché senses her own inevitable difference as an American: "Although José Martì has said / we have lived our lives in the heart / of the beast, I have never heard / its pounding. When I have seen / an animal, I have never reached / for a knife. It is like / Americans to say it is only a bear / looking for something to eat / in the garbage." This essential difference between American and Salvadorean is only the first version of "the country between us," the yawning gulf, mirrored in the title of this poem, between human beings on the same planet. When Alegría says "I can't / help you," she means the lessons of moral understanding which Forché must learn herself by seeing, by living. The word "nothing" recurs twice, as if to show what is to come: Forché's book repeats that word so often, and in so many different contexts, that it becomes a litany of a nihilism greatly feared and barely avoided. Alegría's despairing question echoes the end of **"San Onofre, California"**: "Carolina, do you know how long it takes / any one voice to reach another?"

Voices, cries, and survivors' memories continue to haunt the poet in **"The Memory of Elena."** For the woman Forché meets here—the title is double, the memory both Forché's and this Argentine exile's—talking is remembering, and both are so agonizing that the poem ends in "this particular silence." Forché and Elena lunch on *paella* on beautiful Mallorca, they gather flowers, they count "the dark tongues of bells" when memory invades: a husband shot down beside Elena in Buenos Aires three years ago. Forché crafts her imagery of mouth, teeth, tongue, throat, and bells into memory's dialogue between voice and silence, and these will be compelling obsessions in the remainder of *The Country Between Us.* Most powerful is the sudden horror of dismemberment in the third stanza, as fingers tear apart *paella* that becomes "the lips of those whose lips / have been removed, mussels / the soft blue of a leg socket. / This is not *paella,* this is what / has become of those who remained / in Buenos Aires."

Having heard the testimony of Latin American survivors, we plunge with the poet into the horror of El Salvador in 1978, 1979, and 1980. Traveling with her guides and mentors, perfecting her education, growing into a witness, she retrieved three of these experiments in completed wholes as poems. **"The Visitor," "The Colonel,"** and **"Because One Is Always Forgotten"** provide a distillation, pared down with powerful discipline, of what Forché saw. Each involves dismemberment, spiritual or physical; each generates the anguish of individual ruin; yet each engages twentieth-century collective experience. **"The Visitor"** is most powerful because the shortest: we enter a prison to see "Francisco," who feels "his wife's breath / slipping into his cell each night while he / imagines his hand to be hers." This is the first reference of many in this book to hands disembodied, sundered from their loved ones, wrenched out of appropriate human contexts. At the end of **"The Visitor"**—really the poet herself, standing in this prison—Forché learns a central lesson of El Salvador: "There is nothing one man will not do to another."

In the prose poem **"The Colonel"** torture and literal dismemberment spill out into the open with a sackful of dried human ears dumped on a dinner table. Like the poet straining to hear the voices crying out in this book, these dismembered ears too can listen: "Some of the ears on the floor caught this scrap of his voice." Even the dismembered body parts of the tortured victims become witnesses, ironically recalling Hannah Arendt's comment [in her 1963 *Eichmann in Jerusalem: A Report on the Banality of Evil*] that there are no "holes of oblivion" large enough to bury all the victims of torture and mass murder: One man will remain alive to tell the story. These ears are dead; they do not talk; yet they seem to come alive to listen with the poet.

This single poem, widely noticed, has done more than any other to tell Forché's story of El Salvador. The spectacle of a ruling Colonel spilling a bag of severed human ears onto a table focuses Forché's perceptions in the eight poems of "In Salvador" on one of her primary themes: the violation of the human body. This man so outrages our sensibilities that we tend to miss the significance of his question to the poet, "Something for your poetry, no?" The Colonel is another of Forché's teachers, forcing her to listen and to see. Unbearably menacing in their evocation of linked violence and wealth, the details of this poem constellate quickly to suggest a festering sickness.

The third poem of this group closes the "In Salvador" section of the book with another landscape of mutilation and individual ruin. Forché dedicates **"Because One Is Always Forgotten"** to the memory of José Rudolfo Viera, director of the Salvadorean land reform agency, who was murdered—along with Michael Hammer and Mark Pearlman, two American labor officials—by an anonymous assassination squad in 1981. This event, rendered in six couplets, becomes the summarizing poem for her Salvador experience. Even Viera's death has made her learn, as the poet returns to the collective pronoun of the first of the eight Salvador poems: "When Viera was buried we knew it had to come to an end, / his coffin rocking into the ground like a boat or a cradle." The echo of Whitman's "Out of the Cradle Endlessly Rocking" seems deliberate and ironic, since the knowledge of death Forché gains here remains final, not transforming. Images of horror and dismemberment pile up so rapidly that they become an unfathomable mystery: a "boy soldier in the bone-hot sun" uses his knife to peel a face from a dead man to hang in a tree "flowering with such faces." Viera's death—one good man dead among many—and the robbing of the dead of even their last poor mark of identity, together teach the final lesson of El Salvador: "The heart is the toughest part of the body. / Tenderness is in the hands." In a world where mutilation has become a daily occurrence, one can no longer afford to sentimentalize: Caring comes not from the heart or its pretty sentiments (in this poem the heart is a dark chamber imprisoning every bestial impulse). Caring shows itself only in hands attached to unmutilated bodies—not "tied together" like the hands in **"San Onofre, California,"** not grown incapable of merest acts of kindness. Given the horrors Forché witnessed and recorded in these three poems, it is not surprising that on her final trip to the airport to leave the country, when she and her guide drove over the entrails of a corpse lying in the road, she records this response: "My friend looked at me. *Just another dead man,* he said. And by then it had become true for me as well; the unthinkable, the sense of death within life before death." The first stage of her education now complete, henceforth she must live as a survivor.

Before dealing with the burden of this knowledge—the real subject of *The Country Between Us*—Forché had literally to learn to *see* the things her poems describe. Once driving past Salvadorean cotton fields, she saw only the rows, the dust, and the hot sun, and failed to see the emaciated women and children huddled between the rows, cowering under plastic sheets which did not protect them from

> The Visitor
>
> In Spanish you he (?) whisper
> There is no time left.
> It is the sound of scythes
> arching in wheat, / the ache
> of some field song in Salvador. /
>
> The wind along the prison, cautious
> as Francisco's hands on the inside
> Touching the walls as he walks
> It is his wife's breath
> slipping into his cell / each night
> as he imagines his hand / to be hers
>
> space → It is a small country. /
> There is nothing one man
> will not do to another.
>
>   Carolyn Forché

Rough draft of Forche's "The Visitor."

planes spraying pesticides. "I saw the thing endlessly and aesthetically; I saw it in a certain special way. So I had to be *taught* to look and to remember and to think about what I was seeing." A poet of witness must learn to see, even among the various silences and concealments all these poems record, and to see clearly.

The moral cost of this seeing, however, is very great. "Feel this," the poet's guide tells her after taking her into Ahuachapan prison, an experience that caused Forché to vomit. "This is what oppression feels like. Now you have begun to learn something. When you get back to the States, what you do with this is up to you." The knowledge of "death within life before death" could extinguish response. It nearly did in her case, as the final two poems in Part I—"Return" and "Message"—make clear.

"Message," the seventh poem in Part I, is agonized outcry. Here the poet bids goodbye to friends left behind in El Salvador—to "Pedro," "Margarita," "Leonel." The poet's despair seems complete: Terror, mutilation, and tyranny will prevail. For the poet, nothing remains but a lone voice that (like the ones in the first poem) no one will hear, and the silence of the grave ("my voice is gone / to its hollow of earth," "we will dig deep into our deaths").

In a deliberate foreshadowing of her book's final poem, **"Ourselves or Nothing,"** she can only ask to "link hands, link arms" in the hereafter, where "we will not know each other / or ourselves, where we will be a various / darkness among ideas that amounted / to nothing, among men who amounted / to nothing." "Nothing" is doubled; ideas and men are waste. The last lines—"where we lived / in the hour farthest from God"—might be read as a gloss on a whole century's experience of terror.

In **"Return,"** Forché extends the outcry and deepens its problematical import. Back in the U.S., she meets another dispenser of wisdom—"Josephine," a woman in her fifties—who takes over and narrates much of the poem.

[In his "War as Parable and War as Fact: Herbert and Forché," *The American Poetry Review* 12, No. 1 (January-February 1983)] Larry Levis rightly finds it "a mature and brilliant act when Forché relinquishes her poem and allows Josephine to speak, when the poet becomes a listener as well as a speaker," but we have seen the poet as listener and learner from the very first poem of this section. **"Return"** chronicles Forché's painful return to the U.S., carrying her knowledge of death and mutilation ("What one man will do to another"), but also describes her confrontation with America itself. Images of American riches, materialism, greedy uncaring, and myopia coexist with even more desperate stories of Latin American torture and death. Forché and Josephine alternate long verse paragraphs. Paragraphs one and three capture Forché's mental and moral dislocation on her return. Josephine, in paragraphs two and four, ignores the poet's anguish, concentrating instead on the lessons to be learned. Josephine ends the poem by admonishing Forché that her problem is not that her hands are "tied," not Forché's frustration, her inability to help her friends left behind. Instead, Josephine attacks Forché's sense of apartness, as poet and American: "It is / that you were born to an island of greed / and grace where you have this sense / of yourself as apart from others. It is / not your right to feel powerless. Better / people than you were powerless. / You have not returned to your country, / but to a life you never left." The "country" is America, in the second gloss Forché offers for *The Country Between Us.* Josephine implies that only an examination of her thus far unexamined life in America will allow the poet to bear the burden of her moral education in El Salvador, and it is precisely the "life you never left" that Part II ("Reunion") will analyze. This task will involve even greater burdens of memory, through which the poet as survivor will struggle not only to listen and to see, but to speak.

Of her eight "In Salvador, 1978-80" pieces, Forché has said that "I wrote the poems when I got home, mostly out of despair." Only three of her journalistic dispatches got printed: "Upheaval in El Salvador—Stories of Three Women," in *Ms* (January 1980); "The Road to Reaction in El Salvador," in *The Nation* (June 14, 1980); and "El Salvador: The Next Vietnam?" in *The Progressive* (February 1981). Forché noted, "I tried not to write about El Salvador in poetry, because I thought it might be better to do so in journalistic articles. But I couldn't—the poems just came." Beyond sheer despair, the agony and powerlessness to change anything **"Return"** records, she faced other problems. First stood the material itself, horrifying in the extreme. How can anyone talk or write about children starving in thousands, or men and women mutilated before and after death? What Goya could depict the fountains of blood loosed in the twentieth century? Moreover, [as Forché notes in her "El Salvador: An Aide Memoire"], "there is the problem of metaphor which moved [Pablo] Neruda to write: 'the blood of the children / flowed out onto the streets / like / . . . the blood of the children.' There is the problem of poeticizing horror. . . ." Dare a poet falsify herself or her material by transforming ultimate horror to metaphor? (All eight of the "In Salvador" poems include metaphors, but they are spare and revealing—"the moon" swinging "bare on its black cord," starving children "strung together" as if in a paper chain, "the branch of a tree / flowering" with severed faces. These metaphors are human pain and mutilation—existence in El Salvador—made concrete and they testify to the growing moral vision of the poet.) The material places impossible moral and aesthetic demands on the poet.

But the poet faced an even greater danger: the possibility that she might respond to her material with silence. This the Cavafy epigraph to Part II of her book makes clear:

"An obstacle was often there / To silence me when I began to speak." More than any editor's censorship, she had most to fear the self-censorship which lurks in all these poems as the ultimate response to horror. We have heard voices in each of the poems thus far, and have observed silence as a particular danger in the three poems preliminary to the Salvador jouneys. Bells have "their tongues cut out / for this particular silence" at the grave of Elena's husband. Silence and speech—their different and compelling attractions and guilts—remain in obsessive counterpoint a central agenda of *The Country Between Us.* Forché's voice in **"Message"** pitches very close to the scream which is silence—a comprehensible response when men and women experience "the hour farthest from God." Who would listen, after all? Forché's poem for Viera's grieving mother—**"Because One Is Always Forgotten"**—defines despair as disappearance, vanishing, the silent cries of the lost drifting north in **"San Onofre, California."**

Yet the poems wrote themselves, and despair was to some extent overcome in the act of the poet speaking. Terrence Des Pres's *The Survivor,* a study of holocaust victims who lived, suggests how and why silence must be broken. Des Pres writes:

> Silence, in its primal aspect, is a consequence of terror, of a dissolution of self and world that, once known, can never be fully dispelled. But in retrospect it becomes something else. Silence constitutes the realm of the dead. It is the palpable substance of those millions murdered, the world no longer present, that intimate absence—of God, of man, of love—by which the survivor is haunted. In the survivor's voice the dead's own scream is active. . . . This is a primary source of the will to bear witness: the survivor allows the dead their voice; he makes the silence heard.

"The conflict between silence and the scream" of anguish, says Des Pres, constitutes in survivors "a battle between death and life" (*The Survivor*). Forché immersed herself unknowingly in a kind of holocaust in El Salvador; and in her "In Salvador" poems Milton's "darkness visible" becomes silence palpable. Yet, for her as for the protagonists of Elie Wiesel's novels, "the pressure of the scream persists" and they "desire a silence they cannot keep" (*The Survivor*). The poems record the battle between death and life played out in Forché's sensibility, all but extinguished in El Salvador. The poems wrote themselves, she said, and thus spoke for the dead. They are the voice for those who cannot speak: for the lost ones, the "disappeared"; for Elena's husband; for Francisco, whispering in his prison; for the ears severed from voiceless heads; for the woman huddled under a tarp in a cotton field, futilely covering her children; for Pedro, Margarita, Leonel, and José Rudolfo Viera. They speak for ("In Salvador" is in memory of) Archbishop Oscar Romero, shot while saying mass in a hospital for incurables two weeks after Forché left the country in 1980. These poems remain the only tenderness the poet's hands can offer the voiceless dead, and they reveal the survivor's passion to tell, to witness.

Thus the silence everywhere in *The Country Between Us,* barely avoided and painfully transcended, makes abundantly clear the special struggle to speak which is the unfortunate burden of any twentieth-century poet. Had Forché stopped with the handful of Salvador poems, we would still be grateful to be made to see these things. In a crucial act of choice, however, she extended her understanding of the poet as survivor and witness to the deeper silences of her own past. She chose to confront what Josephine in **"Return"** had described as "a life you never left": She had to discover the connection between what she saw in El Salvador and what she experienced in her own life. Poetry grows from the deepest experiences of the whole sensibility. It gathers the resources of the whole self. This is why Forché could not stop with simple observation of what she had witnessed in El Salvador; she had to integrate those observations with what she herself had lived. Learning to see, learning to speak hence must involve memory as well. The thirteen poems of Part II ("Reunion," suggesting the wedding of past and present) dramatize memory as a process of painful confrontation, and the importance of this section to the whole book lies not just in the number of the poems, but in the striking illumination they give to the poet's Salvador experiences, to her moral growth, and to twentieth-century history. They provide the title phrase and a way to read it (in **"Joseph"**) and a series of parallels that make one woman's personal history a searing walk through a century in which "there is no path" ("Caminante, no hay camino," the epigraph from Antonio Machado). In their strong dialectic between withdrawal from and return to responsibility, these poems reach for moral vision.

Forché has spoken [in her *Rolling Stone* interview] of what the poems in "Reunion" confirm about her own past: "I had very difficult, sad times in my early adulthood, and I thought, 'Well, I'm not responsible for what happened to me, but I *am* responsible for my responses. So I have to respond well or else I'll become deranged or whatever.' Then, midway through my twenties, it occurred to me that I was also responsible for what happened to me, that I had a certain amount of choice, and that the ways in which I tended could determine events." Thus arose her urge to translate Salvadorean poet Claribel Alegría and then discover the reality behind Alegría's poems. Yet a poet who would remember encounters an unexpected difficulty: memory itself has been corrupted, even poisoned by a century that makes atrocity and genocide routine. Remembering, the essential human act, the working realm of any poet, now falters, and each poet must exert great courage to examine the past. (Milan Kundera entitles his brilliant recent novel *The Book of Laughter and Forgetting*.) For Forché, the need to remember grows apace with the need to speak the silence of the dead in El Salvador.

"Reunion" drives the poet back to times in her early twenties and before. Here we can feel the poet more personally than we could in the listening ear of "In Salvador." The poems focus on wandering, loss, exile, broken communication. We see the concern for roots that animated Forché's first book, *Gathering the Tribes,* but now her people are curiously disembodied, rootless. The defining imagery of hands, voices, tongues, and above all silence—a kind of failed communication—continues, underscored by the now-familiar reiteration of nothingness. The poems show the development into the poet's own past of the moral perceptions acquired in El Salvador. What occurs is a complex measuring or reassessment of private experience: through a stunning fusion, "Reunion" becomes the memory of those times when Forché played out at twenty what she would only come to understand in El Salvador at thirty.

The first memory in **"Endurance"** recounts a journey to Belgrade, where the poet confronts the spirit of her dead grandmother Anna, who had been a controlling presence and teacher in her first book. The poet hears Anna saying *"in your country / you have nothing."* America, a rich "island of greed / and grace" in **"Return,"** for Anna is the spiritually impoverished "country between us." Forché's travels multiply surrealistically until Anna's voice ends the poem: *"Piskata, hold your tongue, she says. / I am trying to tell you something."* Memory's voice, could the poet but understand it, might offer through Anna some sustaining vision of reality, or wisdom. Yet the next three poems carry the poet back to things far less positive. **"Expatriate"** portrays a young, would-be poet and revolutionary as an obscene poseur. **"Letter from Prague, 1968-78"** presents a nameless Czech, imprisoned now for ten years. He is a man deprived of voice, echoing merely the death of all the human impulses of that brief Prague spring: "To touch myself now, there is nothing." In **"Departure"** we board a train where "the dead are awake and so reach / for each other"; a disembodied hand lights cigarettes of a man and a woman who asks "if the dead hold / their mouths in their hands like this / to know what is left of them."

Forché walks the death-in-life landscape of loss in the remainder of the poems in "Reunion." Her memories, however, do not begin to constellate in moral perceptions until she returns to two crucial experiences: the war in Vietnam and her childhood in Detroit. **"Photograph of My Room"** follows a Walker Evans photograph to portray defining objects of the poet's life: "china cups" from Serbia; Anna's quilts, frayed after her death; a pouch of *"pesetas, dinar, francs"*; notebooks collecting erotic encounters and self-told "lies" of "Paris," "Salvador," and "Granada"; a bullet "spooned from the flesh / of a friend"; and a "black cheese crock" containing ashes and bone. Especially these dead things from the past include the memory of Vietnam, which in the remainder of "Reunion" will loom preeminent: "The bundle of army letters / were sent from Southeast Asia / during '67, kept near a bottle / of vodka drained by a woman / in that same year who wanted / only to sleep; the fatigues / were his, it is she / whom I now least resemble." The room "belonged / to someone already dead, someone / who has no belongings."

Memory next returns the poet to the Detroit of her girlhood (**"On Returning to Detroit"**) and a childhood friend on the eve of adulthood (**"As Children Together"**). The passengers coming by train into Detroit in the first poem are old and broken, like the doomed ethnic neighborhoods they inhabit. One woman "has so rubbed her bright grey eyes / during grief that all she has seen can be seen in them." Forché imagines her blasted memories: "the century, of which twenty years are left, / several wars, a fire of black potatoes." The poet's friend Victoria, in **"As Children Together,"** does not find Forché's dream "that there might / be a way to get out." Instead, Victoria lives in a trailer with a husband destroyed by Vietnam, and Forché closes with yet another example of a voice speaking to silence. "If you read this poem, write to me. / I have been to Paris since we parted." Forché has escaped Victoria's life, but memory weighs her down with ambiguity and guilt.

Increasingly, in Part II, Forché's remembered characters seem broken on the rack of history. The legacy of Vietnam reasserts itself to make of memory a kind of waste land. **"Joseph,"** in one of the central poems of the book, returns from Vietnam to a broken, empty life. When he calls the poet, his voice runs on lapsed wires "scalloping the cold length / of the country between us." Yet, the poet writes, "It is another voice that calls me / after all this time. / It has nothing to say to you, Joseph." The literal and emotional distance between them (is Joseph a brother?) gives the aching, personal dimension to the title of Forché's book. No voice can cross this distance.

There follow three poems of sexual encounter, each in some way reduced or corrupted by the war. **"Selective Service"** depicts the "rituals of coffee, or airports, regret," the "shot glasses," and "the black and white collapse of hours" lying between a man and a woman shriveled or silenced by Vietnam. The romantic encounter on a train in **"For the Stranger"** links a man and a woman who can barely tell each other their names: "We have, each of us, nothing. / We will give it to each other." And in **"Reunion,"** a Billie Holiday record—again, a disembodied voice of pain from "a woman already dead for three / decades"—reminds the poet of an affair gone wrong in frantic travels through many cities and many hotel fire escapes. Memory evokes sexual battlescars like war wounds.

Two poems remain in Part II to force the poet's moral perceptions into her past. **"City Walk-Up, Winter 1969"**— the most powerful poem in this section—demonstrates the withering effect of Vietnam, of recent history on personal life, and Forché's imagery suggests especially strong connections with her El Salvador material. Memory recalls a ruinous time: alienated, nearly insane, the poet "at twenty" lives in a condemned house, wears "three winter coats from Goodwill," writes "names on walls," "steals bread," and is "aware / of her hands." From Jerzy Kosinski's young Polish survivor in *The Painted Bird,* she learns to carry a can enclosing a small fire for heat and light. Kosinski's novel remains one of the incandescent postwar studies of survival; already at twenty, Forché has begun to ponder the moral consequences of surviving. She endures a kind of implosion in memory as her decaying rooms and life fall claustrophobically back on themselves. She keeps "a footing on the slick silence / of the hysterical deaf," and the images suggest the peculiar combination of noise and mendacity that made the Vietnam years nightmarish. Although Forché notes that "when I tell of my life / now it is not this version," her ending unmistakably stamps these memories as an inheritance that all her travels cannot shed: "We do not rid ourselves of these things / even when we are cured of personal silence / when for

no reason one morning / we begin to hear the noise of the world again." These lines—arguably, the most important in the book—make clear the obligation to speak that the Salvador poems witnessed, but they also suggest that a poet's voice can be easily extinguished by contemporary history, that a survivor poet must come back from the dead.

As if to complete her excursion into personal memory, Forché offers **"Poem for Maya,"** set in the Mallorquin days just prior to her immersion in El Salvador. So suspending her life on the brink of the horror wisely concludes "Reunion": we see the poet innocent of the moral knowledge of El Salvador, but feel prepared for what is to come. The poet and her friend eat bread dipped in oil, open their rooms to "almonds, olives, and wind" in days "when we did not yet know what we were." They stand at their window whispering "*yes,* there on the intricate / balconies of breath, overlooking / the rest of our lives." The fine, summarizing integrity of the poet's memory concludes by reminding us of the moral education that must be acquired, of the survivor to come, and of the witness who would not be denied her speech. Suspended on the lip of that balcony, she will fall into experiences that are searing and, in the twentieth century, inevitably collective.

In a recent negative review of *The Country Between Us* [appearing in *Sulfur* 6 (1983)], Eliot Weinberger places Forché's poems in "the genre of revolutionary tourism" and suggests that she blurs "the line between participation and observation" to make us "believe that the suffering of El Salvador is Forché's own suffering." The result, Weinberger concludes, is "the liberal side of colonialism." The difficulty here is, in part, the special character of the poet as witness: Either one believes the report of that sensibility from its immersion in twentieth-century horror or one does not. More importantly, Weinberger's criticism—at bottom, a charge that Forché is insufficiently political, insufficiently engaged—misses the point that in El Salvador Forché encountered a story that *had* to be told, and could only be told in personal terms. This moral imperative shaped the book as a record of the transformation in the poet's sensibility, such that all of her experiences, present and past, had to be reevaluated. Arguing against the perceived separation between the personal and the political in poetry, Forché recently wrote [in "Sensibility and Responsibility," in *The Writer and Human Rights,* 1983] that

> my work in El Salvador made the profoundest difference in my poetry, precisely because it was not poetic. It did not confirm my preconceptions. The transformation occurred in my sensibility; it was my life that was changed and hence my poetry. . . . To locate a poem in an area associated with political turmoil does not in itself render the poem in the narrow sense political. In the larger sense, to write at all in the face of atrocity is in itself a political act.

Because she was not herself born in El Salvador, Weinberger would have Forché keep silent.

Speaking in an interview [with *Rolling Stone*] of the difference between her first and second books, Forché turned to a related aspect of her own voice: "The voice in my first book doesn't know what it thinks, it doesn't make any judgments. All it can do is perceive and describe and use language to make some sort of recreation of moments of time. But I noticed that the person in the second book makes an utterance. . . . It was a little haunting to realize that some sort of maturation had occurred unconsciously." We have seen in Parts I and II of *The Country Between Us* how a poet who would encounter twentieth-century history and survive to be a witness must struggle first to listen, then to see clearly, and then to speak. The quality of that "utterance," so dependent upon the poet's moral education, her gifts for understanding experience and mining memory, is of intense interest. In Part III—the single long poem **"Ourselves or Nothing"**—the poet risks "utterance" through a final excursion into personal memory which quickly becomes the collective memory of the century. The poem narrates two stories simultaneously. The first is the story of a book called *The Survivor,* written by Terrence Des Pres, the friend to whom Forché dedicates the poem. The second is the larger story of Forché's memory of twentieth-century history, an act of recovery that will be her poetry of witness. *The Survivor* (published in 1976)—the most compelling and beautifully written of recent books on the holocaust—studies the memoirs of victims of the Nazis and of Stalinist terror to try to discover how some managed to survive. Des Pres also ponders the survivors' call to bear witness to those horrors in countless narratives, and the significance of the survivor to the human race at large. In Forché's poem, Des Pres's book provides the text for all the murderous impulses of contemporary inhumanity, and Des Pres's writing of it represents a personal triumph over despair and near-suicide. Accordingly, we can see in the double narrative strong analogues to her own experience in El Salvador. **"Ourselves or Nothing"** shows Forché's effort to come to terms with the grief her El Salvador experience brought her, if not to transcend that grief. Its burning hope is that the survivor's act of bearing witness through memory will become a collective act, fusing with the voice of humankind. **"Ourselves or Nothing"** offers a vision of a twentieth century that confirms Des Pres's remark in *The Survivor* that "when men and women are forced to endure terrible things at the hands of others—whenever, that is, extremity involves moral issues—the need to remember becomes a general response. . . . survival and bearing witness become reciprocal acts" (*The Survivor*).

"Ourselves or Nothing" begins as do almost all the poems in *The Country Between Us*—as an effort of memory that painfully calls back lost events to illuminate present imprisoning terrors. Reversing the southward movement of the first poem, **"San Onofre, California"**—or perhaps paralleling the cries of the vanished in that poem struggling to move northward—Forché remembers watching Des Pres "north" in December, seven years ago, struggling with his book in a "ruined house" in upstate New York. (Recall the "attic ribs" of the **"City Walk-Up, Winter 1969,"** and all the wrecked houses so suggestive of the ruined habitations of the spirit of the characters in this book.) Forché's images converge upon the tension of Des Pres's struggle with the holocaust material, a fearful immersion that drives him near suicide.

Suddenly, in a characteristic switch in her poem's narrative, Forché turns from Des Pres's research to her own consciousness and her discoveries of our twentieth-century collective memories: "Go after that which is lost / and all the mass graves of the century's dead / will open into your early waking hours: / Belsen, Dachau, Saigon, Phnom Penh / and the one meaning Bridge of Ravens, / Sao Paulo, Armagh, Calcutta, Salvador, / although these are not the same." The significance of twentieth-century history may indeed lie in "the mass graves," and interestingly Forché goes beyond Belsen and Dachau to include Vietnam and Cambodia, Northern Ireland, and archetypes of mass starvation and misery in Brazil and India. We are back to the insurmountable problem of how to describe atrocity, genocide, holocaust: one way is simply to utter the names, if not of the countless nameless victims, then of the places hallowed by horror. The impulse is to utter the names *so that they will not be lost,* as the names of the two million children killed by the Nazis were lost. Yet Forché cannot even utter Ravensbrück, the name of the infamous Nazi camp for women, but must translate, and the very mention of Theresienstadt carries the adult Forché into one central meaning of the holocaust: "the dark wormy heart of the human desire to die."

At this point Forché introduces the first of several direct quotations from *The Survivor,* letting Des Pres's voice speak out of terror, nihilism, and despair, but also dramatizing "that act of contrition for despair" which the book became for him. Des Pres's voice provides another teacher for Forché: *"Vast numbers of men and women died, you wrote / because they did not have time, the blessing / of sheer time, to recover."* This quotation from the chapter of *The Survivor* entitled "Nightmare and Waking" speaks to the reality of the camps that survivors somehow had to face down. We hear Des Pres whispering "finish this or die." Slowly, the survivor's consummate passion to witness becomes Des Pres's own affirmation of life (from "Nightmare and Waking"): *"They turned to face the worst / straight-on, without sentiment or hope, / simply to keep watch over life."* Obviously, for both Des Pres and Forché, the survivors here become models.

Immersed in the winter memory of those nights with the despairing writer, Forché recalls a specific night with Des Pres, walking his "rooms with my / nightdress open" as he works through his darkness. (This is one of many moments in *The Country Between Us* when sexual communion will not suffice to deal with contemporary reality, suggesting a profound change for the poet of powerful but innocent sexuality in *Gathering the Tribes.*) On her waking, she finds Des Pres gone, but talismanic sayings remain behind in his notes: *"recalcitrance"*—which came to describe the survivors' "stubborn refusal to be completely shaped by their environment"; and *"you will die and live / under the name of someone / who has actually died"*—which describes the adoption by one survivor, Alexander Donat, of the name of a man who accidentally died in his place (*The Survivor*), but also the sense of responsibility felt by Des Pres and Forché herself to speak for the dead. **"Ourselves or Nothing"** graphically dramatizes the developing of the survivor-poet as witness in the transformation of the poem's voice from "I" to "We," and Forché closes the poem with her retrieval of knowledge from the voices of the dead in *The Survivor* and *The Country Between Us*: imagining mass graves, standing as she once did at Garcìa Lorca's grave in Spain, the repeated admonition to "go after that which is lost" becomes the essential act of memory in the twentieth century. Her final moral choice—**"Ourselves or Nothing,"** rendered in the language of the apocalypse—makes clear that this act of witness and recovery remains an alternative to collective suicide. The "cyclone fence between / ourselves and the slaughter" provides yet another gloss on her book's title, and may stand as the summarizing image for all those failed moments of communication, those illusions and self-deceptions (we are caught "like netted fish," soon to be eaten ourselves) which prevent the voices of the disappeared from reaching our ears. *The Country Between Us* does not attempt to explain mass evil in the twentieth century, but the title may well remind us of Hannah Arendt's hypothesis (about Adolf Eichmann) of ultimate human separation—we commit atrocity out of an "almost total inability ever to look at anything from the other fellow's point of view."

Human separation points to a profound collapse of value, according to Terrence Des Pres. In an analysis which gave Forché the title of her final poem, he finds in the slaughter of the last seventy years a crisis of civilization:

> At the heart of our problem is that nihilism which was all along the destiny of Western culture: a nihilism either unacknowledged even as the bombs fall or else, as with Hitler or Stalin, demonically proclaimed as the new salvation. And it was inevitable; for when mythic structures collapse and symbolism fails, the choice is ourselves or nothing. Nietzsche was the great prophet of this development, and he foresaw the choice we would face. 'What is dawning,' he wrote in 1886, 'is the opposition of the world we revere and the world we live and are. So we can abolish either our reverence or ourselves.' So far we have preferred to abolish ourselves, and how easy it has been. Amid high cant and pieties obscenely cynical, whole cities and peoples are wiped out. The value of life has been reduced to zero, to excrement. (*The Survivor*)

For Des Pres, then, the survivor sounds a warning to humanity against self-imposed extinction. However one regards his philosophical analysis, Des Pres is surely right about our age when he declares that

> modern history has created the survivor as a moral type. His or her special task, moreover, has become indispensable. When terrorism and mass murder prevail, there will be no sources of concrete information unless men and women survive. Conscience is not awakened by hearsay or surmise. Care for life beyond ourselves is born of personal knowledge, of the compassion which comes from knowing the fate of actual lives. In an age of total propaganda, furthermore, there is no way past falsehood and confusion, save in the testimony of eyewitnesses. (*The Survivor*)

Speaking again of the work of one Latin American eyewitness, Claribel Alegría, Carolyn Forché wrote that her

"poems are testimonies to the value of a single human memory, political in the sense that there is no life apart from our common destiny." Forché's great distinction in *The Country Between Us* is to have become "globally aware of human fragility and mutual dependencies" through fidelity to personal experience. She has somehow grasped—lived—how private experience inexorably becomes collective and public in the twentieth century. To the will to bear witness she has added a powerful impulse to communion. Thus, her "utterance"—won through careful listening to the voices of the lost, through clear sight, even of atrocity's numberless victims, through speech that retrieves and overcomes the despair of memory and is not silenced—becomes vision. That such has occurred in a poet so young (thirty-four at this writing) may indicate a gathering cultural response to the analyses of our civilization Ezra Pound made after staring into the trenches of Flanders. Questioning on nearly every page the ability of poetry even to talk to others, *The Country Between Us* nonetheless offers the voice of the poet as witness and the body of the poet as survivor, paradoxically affirming poetry as still the most intimate and communal of our arts. It may well be, as Galway Kinnell said recently, that there can be but one subject for poetry now: the relationship of human beings to the life of the planet.

Carolyn Forché with David Montenegro (interview date 1988)

SOURCE: An interview in *The American Poetry Review*, Vol. 17, No. 6, November-December, 1988, pp. 35-40.

[*In the interview below, Forché discusses* The Angel of History, *her upbringing and family, her experiences abroad, and stylistic and thematic concerns of her poetry.*]

[Montenegro]: *What happens to language when it is used to describe—even almost photographically—brutalities that are terrible to describe? What kind of weight does this place on language? Does this change language?*

[Forché]: An unbearable weight. Odysseas Elytis, whose work I have been recently studying, cautions poets not to attempt to compete with events, nor endure their experiences once in life and a second time in art. I doubt that we "use" language other than "to describe," but I have found it very difficult to transform such events as those to which you refer, and I'm not certain I've done so to the degree I would wish possible. It isn't enough simply to *recount,* in the linear sense of legal discourse, because the work must also be somehow *redemptive,* and the narrative re-structured. I now believe that to write of conditions of extremity is the most difficult. Well, no. To write *out* of conditions of extremity is the most difficult. Paul Celan, in his "Geschichter Fügue" might be one of the few who have found a way. But that way isn't found except by passing through unendurable pain, as is apparent in his work.

Does language, then, reach a boundary where it can't cross over into certain areas of experience and come back whole?

It's interesting, the idea of boundaries. If you view language as a means of reporting and recording, then, yes, there are boundaries everywhere. If language itself is a force which has created our consciousness, which *is* capable of generating a world, then there are no boundaries.

Again, turning to the work of Paul Celan, what happened with language? *Within* Paul Celan, what happened? It emerged broken, fragmented, possible, suggestive, in agony. That is why his language is to be trusted. He is never facile. The boundary that I perceive has to do with one's intentions. As one moves farther from events, they become more apparently complex. And it becomes impossible to say *one* thing, which would not only be reductive, but exclusive, and would therefore create a notion of privilege within the poem.

The other difficulty is with the position of the speaker, with the creation of the fictional, first-person voice which then attempts to speak about things. Very often this voice is most especially speaking of its own sensitivity, and positing a "self" to be regarded. That might be an inappropriate act, if the self derives its authority from its privilege over the "other," whether this be the privilege of knowledge or experience, and whether the "other" be the implied reader or the one to whom the poem is addressed. That is not to say that witness mustn't be borne, that testimony mustn't be attempted. Within the poem, or the language, or the text, it is possible to question this voice, or to permit a dialogue of selves, or at least to render the artifice apparent. Lately I've had difficulty with the first-person, lyric, narrative, free-verse poem. I began by questioning the idea of closure, which almost always implies linearity, and then to contemplate the idea of resolution, and this has provoked a revolutionary change in my thinking, and in my own work. In my new work I have been attempting to rupture that voice, and to critique it from within in order to expose its artifice.

For five years I wrote fragments and notes which I kept in a binder. The binder grew to two or three reams of paper. I hadn't a poem. I thought with some amusement that I'd been abandoned by the Muse, who suspected me of infidelity because I had spent too much time doing other work. But I *had* written every day, and I did have these reams of paper. There's a proverb: "Whatever keeps you from doing your work has become your work." I looked at this material and realized that it constituted the beginning of my new work. I wasn't writing the poem I had written in the past, and the only leap I needed to make was to acknowledge that fact. So I'm attempting to honor and continue this new form, rather than dismissing page after page as mere notes toward "the poem."

To write out of extremity is to incise, with language, that same wound, to open it again, and, with utterance, to inscribe the consciousness. This inscription restructures the consciousness of the poet.

—*Carolyn Forché*

There is another proverb: "When the student is ready, the teacher will come." I began to discover other poets and thinkers who were of great help to me. I read the work of Jacques Joubert, translated by Paul Auster. Then I rediscovered Evan S. Connell, his *Notes in a Bottle Found on a Beach in Carmel,* and then his *Points for a Compass Rose* and finally, *St. Augustine's Pigeon.* I began to read Jean-Francois Lyotard and Walter Benjamin, then the works of René Char. I've also been translating, with William Kulik, the *Selected Poems* of Robert Desnos. One work has led me to another and another. I feel that I've broken through something, and there is new territory, and there are new guides. That's what seems to have happened.

Are you talking about **The Angel of History?**

Yes. Well, that's a tentative title. The work shows no sign of coming to a last page. It's already one hundred and fifty pages long. It's composed of sequences. I wouldn't say that there are individual poems. The title comes from Walter Benjamin, from his work *Illuminations*:

> This is how one pictures the angel of history. His face is turned toward the past. Where we perceive a chain of events, he sees one single catastrophe, which keeps piling wreckage and hurls it in front of his feet. The angel would like to stay, awaken the dead, and make whole what has been smashed. But a storm is blowing in from paradise. It has got caught in his wings with such a violence that the angel can no longer close them. The storm irresistibly propels him into the future, to which his back is turned, while the pile of debris before him grows skyward.

I began the new work on April 4th of last year, and within a few days it was coming of itself. There were six voices. One of them was an interrogator, or a simple questioner. And one of them I recognized as a woman who had shared a hospital room with me in the Hôtel-Dieu in Paris two years ago. We were together for a week. She was a German Jew who had spent the war years hiding in barns in Europe, making her way farm to farm. The first night when I was brought into the hospital, I was very depressed, particularly at having to leave my husband and newborn son. I was given a room with Elie. She was awake in the middle of the night, sitting at the edge of her bed, peeling her skin from her body. She had acute eczema. She turned to me and asked, "And *what* are you?" She didn't say: Who are you? or What is your name? So I answered, "I am a poet." And she responded "I am also a poet." We talked all night, and all the next day and next. Her voice may have entered this work. Some of the other voices I am uncertain of—one seems to be the voice of the poetry itself, and not a human being.

I'm immersed in this work completely. I've been working daily in Provincetown, in two separate residences, both facing the bay. When I leave this place, my voice and the voices of the others also depart. So the condition of the work is such that it has to be completed here, I think, where it began.

If events occur in the work, they are perceived from their

periphery. The events are not central. The work is "about" history, time, and perception, more than about lives or occurrences.

Yours is often a poetry of conversation with friends and relatives, present or absent. It seems that the conversations are almost a means of survival. What is making them happen?

Dislocation. When I was very young, I was deeply affected by Czeslaw Milosz's *The Captive Mind* and, in particular, by the assertion that: "If a thing exists in one place, it will exist everywhere." In this passage, he describes a village in which everyone is going about their business—going to work, pedaling bicycles, with baguettes and newspapers and so on. Everyone is very preoccupied with the day's activities in the day's beginning. And the village is bombed. The next day in the rubble someone is trying to find a spare potato buried in the ruins. And so this provokes from Milosz a discussion about assumptions having to do with the "natural" order of things.

I began in childhood to be very disturbed by that idea. I was first aware of it in 1955, when *Life* magazine published an essay of the first photographs documenting the liberation of the camps by the Allies. I took this magazine to my mother, and I asked her to explain the photographs. There was one taken before the liberation, in which two soldiers were beating a woman with a chain. I asked my mother why they were doing this, and she answered, "Because they are Nazis." I asked her what Nazis were, and she decided that I was too young for an answer. She took the magazine away and hid it from me, because she thought I was too young for such photographs. But I found it, and put it between the mattresses, and took it out at different times in my childhood.

My grandmother, Anna, had often spoken of this kind of dislocation. She talked of coming to this country, of things that occurred in Europe before she came, of her father who was turned away at Ellis Island because of a sore on his leg. She never saw him again. When I was nineteen, I married—But it's difficult for me to talk about this. I've always harbored a dark sense that the world is at risk.

*The word nothing appears relatively often in your poetry. For instance, in **"The Island"** or in **"Ourselves or Nothing."***

It's dangerous to try to explain some of these things because I doubt that I really know what they mean. I'm not making excuses. I remember reading a transcript of Josef Brodsky's trial in the Soviet Union, and I remember him saying, when asked where his poetry came from, that he thought it came from God. I have the usual difficulties with God, but I would say that I felt very sympathetic to his answer in that context.

Remembrance plays a large part in your work. In a sense, your poetry is a rosary of names, as you said of Claribel Alegria's poetry. Memory; is it loss, an obstacle? Is it a source, nourishment?

Terrence Des Pres, in his book *The Survivor: An Anatomy of Life in the Death Camps,* spoke of survivors as men and women who simply kept watch over life. Memory must be kept alive; those who perish at the hands of others must

not be forgotten. I'm not sure anymore if holding the memory before the eye, before consciousness, is in itself redemptive, but this work of incessant reminding seems to arise from the exigencies of conscience. In my own life, the memory of certain of those who have died remains in very few hands. I can't let go of that work if I am of that number.

You grew up outside of Detroit?

My first five years were spent in Detroit, then my father worked in Dearborn and we lived in Farmington township. My aunts and uncles remained in Detroit.

The city has changed dramatically since I was there. Its appearance has changed. The underlying reality hasn't—the extreme poverty, the racial segregation, racism and violence. Since the demise of the automobile industry, things have gotten worse. I went back a few years ago and drove around alone, not realizing that this was no longer a wise thing to do. Perhaps because of my naiveté or my stupidity, I had no problems. But sections of Detroit reminded me, physically, of Beirut.

How does that make you feel?

As if I were always on my way to Beirut, from the beginning. It was strange, and very sad. On the other hand, for me Beirut was one of the most beautiful cities in the world, even in ruins. The most passionate and intense and vital of cities.

From Detroit, a very industrial city, to San Salvador, to Beirut to Johannesburg to Paris and the other cities you've been to—how does this all fit together?

I don't think you are speaking about geography now, as much as about the matter of socio-economics. I was born in Detroit, and was the eldest of seven children. My father was a tool-and-die maker and my mother a mother. Had it not been for President Johnson's "Great Society" programs, and my father's labor and willingness, and my mother's interest and encouragement, I would never have gone to a university. I wouldn't have imagined it possible. None of my friends, no one I grew up with and knew well, went to a university. All of my brothers and sisters later attended. I went to the only possible school, the very large state school, and became lost there in the beginning, until a few professors read my work and took me under wing. They gave me the kind of attention usually given as a matter of course to students in smaller, more elite schools. I'm deeply grateful to them.

When I look at photographs of my younger self, I want to tell her—and she does seem often someone other than myself—not to worry, that she would one day travel, and understand more about life, and perhaps even something about that horrifying photographic essay in *Life.*

I was very sad as a child. It was a sadness of the soul, and had nothing to do with my upbringing. I return to Detroit once or twice a year if I can. And every time I go back, I'm in a familiar world again, but farther from that world. When ***The Country Between Us*** became the Lamont Selection, my mother baked a cake and decorated it with flowers, and wrote in icing "Happy Lamont," and lit a candle, and my family sang the birthday song.

My childhood friends are poorer now than they were when we were growing up. They've suffered terribly this past decade, and it isn't getting better. We're talking about something very painful. It isn't possible to understand why I'm here in Provincetown in this rented house by the sea writing poetry, while they are there, working and suffering.

Does poetry feel, in some ways, superfluous or like a luxury?

No, no, never. Never a luxury. I didn't mean that. I meant that I have the luxury to think and write, yes, but poetry is a necessity. It has been written and spoken by those who work and suffer, as well as by those who live in rented houses on the sea even for brief periods of their lives. If it is true that language creates consciousness, then the self is constituted in language. Poetry is a necessity, not a commodity, a necessity. The only danger is that this "self" will be constituted in a hegemonic discourse—

But it is poetry's great good fortune that it could never be commodified in this culture.

So it won't be corrupted or used?

It seems difficult to corrupt something that has no value, as value is consigned by the culture.

Does our culture's valuation of the poet and poetry, though, reflect its sense of people, since poetry often is people speaking more openly than usual?

Do you mean does the lack of value given to poetry reflect upon the lack of value given to person?

Yes.

Probably it has to do with a lack of understanding of the human being. If someone wants to understand what a human being is, they should spend time with a corpse—the corpse of someone they knew—it is then less possible to make a mistake about what a human being is. This culture does not value the human body.

Is there a type of numbness in our culture? In your poem "Return" you mention an absence of recognition.

It isn't numbness. It's ignorance. I used to believe more firmly in goodwill. I now suspect that goodwill is more precious and more rare than I'd previously supposed. I think that Americans want to be considered "good." There is an inherent sense of true morality in the American culture, almost inversely proportional to its manifestation. But it is there.

The source of this morality is historical, and nearly always accompanied by the desire to occult American complicity in crimes against conscience.

For non-native Americans, America is a nation of exiles in search of a homeland, and now that this need for homeland has become interiorized, and is experienced as interior exile, the homeland sought has become figurative.

Last week, during the Summit, I was reading the English translations of the poetry of Yunna Moritz before audi-

---

> Poetry has been written and spoken by those who work and suffer, as well as by those who live in rented houses on the sea even for brief periods of their lives. If it is true that language creates consciousness, then the self is constituted in language. Poetry is a necessity, not a commodity, a necessity.
>
> —*Carolyn Forché*

---

ences in New York and Washington. Yunna Moritz was travelling as part of a PEN-sponsored delegation of Soviet writers visiting the United States. After one of these readings, some of us were talking about the Russian idea that anyone who leaves the Motherland, for whatever reason, is a traitor. And the retort, of course, was that we were a country of such traitors, a people who, by that definition, are descended from traitors or are traitors themselves. I exclude from this definition those brought here by force. This might be considered in any discussion having to do with the national character.

The Vietnam War casts a shadow in some way over your work.

Over my life.

What is that shadow?

That of my first husband, and that of my childhood friend, Joseph. The two. We grew up together. Joseph was three years older but we were quite close. He left for Vietnam when I was sixteen, and had, some point in his tour of duty, refused to do anymore fighting, and was put into a stockade. He wrote letters to me from the stockade. His life when he returned from Vietnam was very harsh, with moments of respite which he spent in a Trappist monastery. When I was nineteen, I married a man deeply scarred by the war. Many of the boys in my class in school—we were a class of eighty-seven students—who had gone through grades one through twelve together—many went to Vietnam. A few died. Others were injured. The boy who kept pigeons returned a heroin addict.

During our high school years, we were supportive of the war. We were fooled. We felt deeply patriotic, and we believed that the boys were dying for something worth fighting for, and were to be supported. We were emotional and sentimental about ourselves and the war.

When I went to the university, I discovered for the first time the other view, and I became, as a result of what had happened to my husband, very active in the anti-war movement, committed to non-violent resistance. Because of my class background (or, some would say, despite it), I was uncomfortable with extreme radicalism. I suffered no estrangement from my parents, and wasn't at ease with those who had. I didn't trust anyone who had the luxury of jeopardizing their education, an option I didn't perceive for myself.

Michael Herr says that Vietnam is what we had instead of happy childhoods. I think the war marked my generation, and I would define that generation as anyone, man or woman, who reached conscription age during America's involvement in Southeast Asia. No one of that generation was untouched by the war.

Sometimes, in the course of speaking about Central America, the subject of Vietnam is raised by a member of an audience. I have asked them how many people died in Vietnam. The hands go up one by one, and finally the answer is given that more than 57,000 died. The question was not how many North American soldiers, but how many people? More than two million. It isn't a trick, something to shame or fool an audience, but simply a means of reminding ourselves of what is easily forgotten here.

I suppose every writer is more marked by what happened in the earliest years. And for me, those years include the war. I don't know that I'll ever be able to write directly about it, or certainly not until I'm older, which might be the reason why relatively little poetry has been written out of Vietnam. Bruce Weigl's work is a notable and fine exception. He is a veteran. Perhaps it takes longer for those who didn't fight—

Our writing reflects our concerns. Our consciousness, our sensibility is *in* the text. When something is missing, we note the omission. The war, for many of us, is missing.

Can we talk a moment about violent imagery? Is there a danger in the gratuitous use of such imagery by people who have not been at risk? Can it become a sort of counterfeit poetic currency applied to language to add a supposed intensity?

Perhaps, but I would feel reluctant to suggest such a caveat, if by implication we are valuing the human imagination any less. It might be possible to counterfeit such experience, but never successfully, and there might be a danger, too, in relying upon the intensity of a grotesque image to compensate for a lack of intensity in the work, but then we would be speaking of falsification, distortion, and the poet's failure to honor the language or the subject.

The danger has more to do, I think, with assumptions the poet makes about the experience, and his or her ability to achieve empathetic imagination, which is never easy. Inherently dramatic material presents difficulties for the poet, and challenges the poet's ability to mediate, or transform, the experience through the work. It is to this difficulty that Elytis refers, I think, when he speaks of the uselessness of competing with events.

It's said that Americans are inured to images of violence, but I don't think this has been caused by an inundation of images of *true* violence. We've been numbed by counterfeit images of violence, and by our own insensitivity, our own inability to react. We've made of violence an abstraction. If we truly perceived the pain of a particular image—and let's refer to a photographic image now, rather than a poetic one—such pain as is apparent in a photograph of a maimed victim of a Salvadoran death squad would be too excruciating, if truly perceived, to contemplate or regard.

In situations of extremity, rather than our becoming numb to pain, the pain worsens, and lessens our ability to endure. Each death seems more difficult than the last, and each inflicts its wound on the survivor, who remains tender from that wound when the next is inflicted, when the next loss is suffered.

To write out of such extremity is to incise, with language, that same wound, to open it again, and, with utterance, to inscribe the consciousness. This inscription re-structures the consciousness of the poet.

What has happened in America has less to do with violence itself than with the way such images of violence are read, and with the desire to abstract the violence, as a means of anesthetization. As Americans, we cling, however precariously, to the myth of our staunch individualism. We are inclined to view ourselves as apart from others. Perhaps we do this because we are haunted by the past, by the occulted memory of the founding genocide. If it were true that we imagined ourselves as connected to others, as part of a larger human body, it would no longer be true that we would suffer the lack of feeling in ourselves which we now describe as the condition of being inured to images of violence.

I've read poetry that fails in its attempt to speak for the suffering of others. But it might have been the attempt itself which was wrongly thought, and the work was then doomed from the beginning. It's a question of where you position yourself with regard to others. Grace Paley suggests that we write, and then take out all the lies. Sometimes it's difficult to recognize them. The lie, for example, of our own moral superiority.

Do you think there is any kind of censorship operating in this country?

No, not in the strictest sense.

Of neglect or omission?

In that sense yes, of neglect *and* omission. And the censorship of crude self-interest, which has to do with the idea of what poetry is, not poetry, but publishable poetry, grantable poetry. Such calculation engenders mediocrity.

There is evidence of a measure of self-censorship in the cyclical uproar about the question of the relationship between poetry and politics, which wouldn't even be taken seriously in any other country.

El Salvador and South Africa; the differences in the political situations are obvious. You've been in both countries. Were there any particular differences or similarities that struck you while in South Africa?

I was in each place under different circumstances. I went to El Salvador in 1978 on January 4th at the invitation of a member of Claribel Alegría's family, who believed that it would benefit me to spend the period of my Guggenheim grant in Central America. This was before the period that is known in this country as the war. I didn't journey to a dangerous El Salvador, but to a Salvador in silence, the silence of misery. Death squad activity was just beginning. While there, I was in contact with Michael McClintock, then of Amnesty International's International Secretariat in London. We corresponded as Amnesty began to study the situation in El Salvador regarding human rights. I was a correspondent. Later, I worked with the woman who was then the voice of Monsignor Romero's radio station YSAX. We collected information and provided that information to various human rights organizations by various means. I made several trips to Guatemala, and returned to the United States from time to time. I left El Salvador for the last time on March 16, 1980. I've spoken elsewhere more extensively about this.

When my husband was assigned to return to Lebanon as photographic correspondent for *Time,* I accompanied him, having already experienced waiting here for his return. During that period, I was often unable to reach him by phone, and on one occasion was told by an international operator that his hotel had been shelled. When contact with the hotel management was established, I was informed that his room had been among those destroyed, and it wasn't until several hours later that I learned he had taken refuge in the basement during the shelling and was alive. I didn't want to re-live those hours. When he told me he was going back, I said "not without me." I got a job with National Public Radio's *All Things Considered* program, through Noah Adams, and was assigned to broadcast from Lebanon via satellite to NPR, which I did.

In South Africa, I was a housewife, and wouldn't have received my visa otherwise. I was pregnant, and accompanied by my husband, who was a credentialed member of the foreign press. I've written previously in *The American Poetry Review* about my activities there. I had determined that my task would be to record everything I saw, to make a document, and to assist my husband with the documentary work of preserving photographs and testimony which would never reach the public through mass media, but would remain available through alternative media groups.

My experiences were in great part determined by these various contexts. I don't want to make facile comparisons between the political situations of Central America and Lebanon and South Africa. I will say that in none of these countries was the United States perceived as a friend of the common people, the people whom I met, the working people. That condition unites my experience in these countries: Americans were not perceived as friends, and to be an American in that context is very instructive. My personal conditions usually had nothing to do with nationality—so I am speaking more about lessons regarding the perception of my country as a nation state.

In El Salvador and in South Africa, you have seen the often painful effects of history and politics on people's lives. How has this affected your life?

History and politics affects everyone's life, everywhere, always. Any difficulties I've experienced have been relatively minor. There is no comparison between the experience of an outsider (such as I was) and the experience of someone whose own country is under seige or who is engaged in a struggle against injustice.

I wouldn't say that I am unaffected, however. In the context of my life here in the United States, I would say that it's true for both my husband and myself that there have

been periods quite painful for us, in which we've found re-assimilation difficult. We sometimes experience dislocation.

Experiences of extremity are not necessarily assimilated over time. In 1981, while attending a human rights conference for writers which was held in Canada, I had the occasion to talk with Jacobo Timerman. My experiences of El Salvador were still very fresh. I walked out into a hallway during a cocktail reception, and found Jacobo Timerman alone. We walked a little. He said, "It's rather difficult for me to attend these things sometimes." And then, "My terror is that, even after twenty years, it might not be possible to forget." He explained that he did not mean by "forget" to relegate his experience to oblivion, but to be able to live in certain moments, *as if* he had never endured that particular pain.

For my husband and myself, the most difficult period was in South Africa. If it weren't for the threat of abduction, we would rather have returned to Beirut. We would rather have been shelled again, would rather have stayed in West Beirut, even again through the attacks of the American battleship USS *New Jersey,* than bear the psychological terror of South Africa, even as whites. What we felt there was absolute, and, for us, unendurable, because we didn't have the psychological stamina for it. We're in awe of those who have been conditioned to endure such a horror and still preserve their humanity.

When we left South Africa to give birth to our son in Europe, rather than on South Africa's soil, our plan had originally been to return there. We'd committed ourselves to two years of work, but I would say that we weren't unhappy when our applications for visa renewals were denied by the South African government. It wasn't as if we weren't expecting the denial. We were half-expecting it. But we were relieved to receive it. We'd become parents, and we were at a crossroads ourselves. We decided against further subjecting ourselves to conditions of war voluntarily, as we had done for several years. My husband had been a *war* photographer for twelve years. He'd lived through the war in Nicaragua against Somoza, then was in El Salvador until 1982, then in Beirut until 1984, and then in South Africa until 1986. In the profession of war photography there are two ways out: death or early retirement. Most don't retire. My husband had come perilously close to death on many occasions, and we felt within ourselves this new responsibility, not only to our baby and each other, but to the work which we imagined we had to do. And so we believed that, because we were older, and war photography is a profession for young men and women who believe in their immortality, that he might not be as equipped for it, as agile, as lucky as he'd been in the past.

Also, he had lost his sense of immortality, which is in itself a kind of shield.

I should add that I am not, by nature, a courageous person, and was always afraid, and my fear manifested itself in different ways.

One or two more questions. Would you mind talking a moment about Terrence Des Pres and about your friendship with him over the years?

It hasn't been a month since he died. He was one of my dearest and oldest friends. He was my mentor, my brother, my confidant and, more than once, my defender. Although he himself was not a Jew, he so deeply entered the body of survival testimony in his work on the Holocaust that I imagine when he died there were six million souls to receive him.

We began our correspondence in 1976. I had contracted viral meningitis, and his book was among the few I read during convalescence. Later we became friends, and he guided my work for eleven years. He also guided my life and thought in a very particular and special way.

In 1979 and 1980, during one of my trips home from El Salvador, we visited each other. He'd been having difficulty after completing the book, and was casting about for something which might so move him that he could commit himself to it fully. I had a box of poetry books in the trunk of my car. Nazim Hikmet was there. We read "On Living" together, and moved from book to book, most of them contemporary poets in translation. Terrence was very deeply moved by the poems, and so began his next long work. The book, *Praises and Dispraises,* was completed before his death, and will be published by Viking Press in August [1988]. The subject of the work is the relation between poetry and the political, and it is a deeply intelligent work.

I will miss him much more than I could ever say. He was the only person with whom I was always in contact, during my time in El Salvador and beyond it. If I want to know now what I was feeling in those years, I have only to go to his fireproof safe in upstate New York and read the letters he preserved for me.

He was morally brilliant, and luminously intelligent. Among his friends he is irreplaceable.

*In your poem, **"Selective Service,"** you write, "In what time do we live that it is too late / to have children?" You now have a son. How has having a child changed your life?*

For Harry, I think, it was the beginning of his self-preservation. In many ways, the beginning of a new life. It was his way of saying no to the evil he had seen. For me, it was the fulfillment of a long desire. I think that the idea that it is "too late to have children" was an intellectualization, substituting for an explanation for my refusal of that desire, whether because of the circumstances of my life or my own self-absorption. Sean Christophe's arrival in our lives profoundly changes us, and is the most wonderful thing that has ever happened to us.

He may not have a full human life, if the earth, if *we* do not protect his generation. Our decision to be receptive to his conception had nothing to do with any assurance we felt about human survival. But our children must also desire to be with us—I'm already speaking as if there were two of them, and there isn't second yet—that is how much I hope.

Leonora Smith   (essay date 1993)

SOURCE: "Carolyn Forche: Poet of Witness," in *Still the Frame Holds: Essays on Women Poets and Writers,* edited by Sheila Roberts, The Borgo Press, 1993, pp. 15-28.

[*In the excerpt below, Smith examines Forché's ability to balance political, personal, and aesthetic concerns in her poetry.*]

Is a political poetry *possible?* In "On the Edge of Darkness: What is Political Poetry" [from her 1981 *Light Up the Cave*] Denise Levertov answers a resounding yes, tracing the tradition for such poetry, of which her work is a continuation, and examining the still common romantic view of the poet as isolated, estranged from action and community, a view which raises these widespread suspicions of poetry and political action's mutual exclusivity. In western medieval life, art and religion functioned together, inseparable; today, the moral and aesthetic have not only separated, but are often set against each other as if they are, by nature, diametrically opposed. Yet despite this pervasive skepticism about the possibility of a poetry that is both morally and aesthetically successful, Carolyn Forche, whose first book, *Gathering the Tribes* won the Yale Younger Poets Award, was awarded the Lamont Prize for her second, *The Country Between Us* which the *New York Times Book Review* called "mainly political poetry," giving her two-thirds of a literary triple crown. Forche's work—as the work of Levertov, Adrienne Rich, and others (among first-world white poets) of various political particulars—gives clear evidence that political poetry is not only possible, but is being pursued in the United States by women with grace, vigor, and moral concern.

Stanley Kunitz says [in "Poet and State" in *A Kind of Order, a Kind of Folly,* 1975] that the "revolutionary is concerned with changing others; the poet is concerned with changing himself." But if there is one clear problem for all poets in our time, it is the reconciliation of such opposites—the interior and the exterior, the impulse and the craft, the personal and the public, the active and the passive—what Jung calls, in the psychological realm, integration. Levertov says [in "The Poet in the Word" in *The Poet in the World,* 1973] "Poetry is necessary to a whole man, and that poetry cannot be divided from the rest of life is necessary to *it*. Both life and poetry fade, wilt, shrink, and then they are divorced."

Any poetry in our time exists in the context of tradition, no longer of received, replicable forms but of less explicit, shifting aesthetic principles; whatever "school," poetry relies on a personal, authentic voice for which no amount of sheer technique or skill, no simple manipulations of the language, no control of form can substitute. Yet this voice must find its own tenor in the context of the prevailing poetic, which, Forche says in "An Aide Memoire," "limits the range of our work and determines the boundaries of what might be said." The demand for "authenticity," despite its moral ring, is not a direct judgment of the poet's forms of life, but the life as it is objectified in the poem itself—the underlying motion of the life. So the problem of the contemporary poet is not simply one of language or psychology or morality, but all of these engaged in the work "*to do all that one can* in any given instance" [Levertov, "Origins of a Poem," *The Poet in the World*]. For poets with pervasive political concerns, politics is *de-*

manded as a subject, else what poetry remains is limited, truncated, psychologically lopsided.

Yet the suspicions of overtly political subjects, and other elements of the contemporary literary aesthetic—a poetry which follows and reveals the motion of the poet's mind as it is cast over concrete and particular objects and events, a poetry with the ring of personality, the quality of an individually distinctive spoken English—also creates some special problems for the poet whose consciousness is politicized.

Each subject a poet chooses—or is chosen by—has built-in pitfalls, natural failings of excess: the domestic into so many pots and pans, the "personal" into solipsistic self-indulgence (what Howard Nemerov called recently "our measly selves"), the dream-like into plain fogginess, the life of mind into self-conscious mental somersaults. Political content tends toward polemic and abstraction. Forche says, in the previously mentioned essay, that there is "no such thing as non-political poetry"; by this I take her to mean that all of us, poets as well as plumbers, live in political contexts which shape not only our external circumstances and forms of life but also the forms of consciousness that emerge from the life in whatever activities we engage. When this consciousness is explicit and direct in a poem, it presses toward abstraction. The central feature of poetry we identify with the word "political" is its direct confrontation with distributions of power, that is, who exercises power over whom and what use is made of it; our response to such poetry is based in platonic, shared notions of the way this power *ought* to be distributed—"justice." So all political poetry works from collective abstractions, shared visions—or visions the poet believes should be shared, that "something can yet / be salvaged upon the Earth" [Levertov, "On the 32nd Anniversary of the Bombing of Hiroshima and Nagasaki"]. Yet our poetry, our dominant aesthetic, resists abstraction. Kipling could use "Motherland" with some feeling such langague is for us at once too abstract and too polemical—and downright *ah shucks* embarrassing. A political poem must tread a delicate path, using the language of poetry without, as Forche puts it, "prettifying;" it must "engage our aesthetic response just as one with whose content—spring, love, death, a rainbow—we can have no argument" [Levertov, "What Is Political Poetry?"].

. . . . .

The sense of intelligence, of balance and engagement with humankind that illuminates Levertov's work, pervades Carolyn Forche's *The Country Between Us.* On the jacket of this book, of which about a third is directly concerned with her experiences in El Salvador, and all of which is explicitly political, Levertov says:

> Here's a poet who's doing what I want to do, what I want to see all of us poets doing in this time without any close parallels or precedents in history: she is creating poems in which there is no seam between personal and political, lyrical and engaged. And she's doing it magnificently, with intelligence and musicality, with passion and precision.

This "seamlessness," the mutual transformation of life by art and art by life, is evident in *Gathering the Tribes,* where the political content takes the form of a pervasive humanism, a rudimentary political vision developing from the memories of her Slovak ancestors, and with the Southwestern Indians with whom she lived: in all, an identification with the dispossessed. In **"What It Cost,"** she describes how

> We ate the chunks bobbing in the soup,
> everyone thinking it excrement, . . .
>
> how the children ate flesh
> pulled from the pyres.
> Mothers wrapped dead babies
> in blankets and carried them.

The "we" here does not *literally* include Forche, but the poem creates a sufficient sense of her identity with the refugees from Kiev, whom I assume to be her ancestors, for us to accept her voice as one that carries the voices of these suffering others—the source of the moral vision carried in *The Country Between Us.*

It was Forche's poetry that drew her into an active political life, and not the reverse. On Mallorca, translating the poems of Claribel Alegria, an exile from El Salvador, she met survivors of repressive Latin American regimes, some physically maimed, many with their lives ruined by abuses of political power—epitomized by people like Elena, who was ambushed with her husband after celebrating their anniversary, he now dead, she now mutilated:

> In Buenos Aires only three
> years ago, it was the last time his hand
> slipped into her dress, with pearls
> cooling her throat and bells like
> these, chipping at the night—
>
> As she talks, the hollow
> clopping of a horse, the sound
> of bones touched together.
> The *paella* comes, a bed of rice
>
> and *camarones,* finger and shells,
> the lips of those whose lips
> have been removed, mussels
> the soft blue of a leg socket.
>
> This is not *paella,* this is what
> has become of those who remained
> in Buenos Aires. This is the ring
> of a rifle report on the stones,
> her hand over her mouth,
> her husband falling against her.
>   **("The Memory of Elena")**

She joins Claribel in her silent afternoons, "her difficult time of the day." Claribel wears a white dress, and Forche says,

> Tiny mirrors have been stitched
> to it—when I look for myself
> in her, I see the same face
> over and over . . .

and

> When I talk to her
> I know what I will be saying
> twenty years from now
>   **("The Island")**

Forche's experiences with Claribel persuaded her to accept an invitation to El Salvador, against the advice of friends who felt political action would harm her work. In El Salvador, she had what she describes in ["El Salvador: An Aide Memoire," *American Poetry Review* (July-August 1981)] as a "moral and political education" which would

> . . . change my life and work, propel me toward engagement, test my endurance and find it wanting, and prevent me from ever viewing myself or my country again through precisely the same fog of unwitting connivance.

She became a literal witness for Amnesty International, as she saw men who were locked for a year in cages a meter square:

> José lying
> on the flat bed truck, waving his stumps
> in your face, his hands cut off by his
> captors and thrown to the many acres
> of cotton, lost, still, and holding
> the last few clumps of leeched earth
> ("**Return**")

She says "It is my feeling that the twentieth-century human condition demands a poetry of witness." Despite her recognition of the problems inherent in such a poetry, the "impulse to witness confronted the prevailing poetic; at the same time it seemed clear that eulogy and censure were no longer possible and that Enzensberger is correct in stating 'The poem expresses in exemplary fashion that it is not at the disposal of politics.' I decided to follow my impulse to write narratives of witness and confrontation, to disallow obscurity and conventions which might prettify that which I wished to document."

The position of witness is a difficult one; the poet can slip into a gratuitous appropriation of others' suffering, a "poetization of horror," a kind of ghoulish colonialism of anguish, or slip into what Levertov identifies in "What Is Political Poetry?" as a common misconception of partisan poets, "that the subject matter carries so strong an emotive charge in itself that it is unnecessary to remember poetry's roots in song, magic, and the high craft that makes itself felt as exhilarating beauty even when the content voices rage or utters a grim warning." Forche's prose poem, "**The Colonel**" is a masterful instance of her handling of highly charged subject matter, where what craft is used cannot afford to be seen at the risk of turning the reader's moral repugnance and horror from the subject to the poem itself. At the colonel's home, "We had dinner, rack of lamb, good wine, a gold bell was on the table for calling the maid." Then the dinner is taken away, a commercial comes on the "cop show" on the TV.

> There was some talk then of how difficult it had become to govern. The parrot said hello on the terrace. The colonel told it to shut up, and pushed himself from the table. My friend said to me with his eyes: say nothing. The colonel returned with a sack used to bring groceries home. He spilled many human ears on the table. They were like dried peach halves. There is no other way to say this. He took one of them in his hands, shook it in our faces, dropped it into a water glass. It came alive there. I am tired of fooling around he said. As for the rights of anyone, tell your people they can go fuck themselves. He swept the ears to the floor with his arm and held the last of his wine in the air. Something for your poetry, no? he said. Some of the ears on the floor caught this scrap of his voice. Some of the ears on the floor were pressed to the ground.
> —May 1978

"Almost a *poème trouvé*," Forche says. "I had only to pare down the memory and render it whole, unlined, and precisely as recollection would have it."

This "paring down" is the essence of her poetry: the sparse but perfectly selected detail, structured by the demands of narrative; the restrained use of metaphor; rhythms with prose-like constructions of plain speech underlaid with a sheer music; a voice that reproduces on the page her spoken voice, which I can only describe as enormously sweet, with an exotic undertone that comes from the slight turn of her constructions ("There was some talk then. . . ."), as if, somewhere beneath the poem, another language is moving. It is the flow of narrative from this voice that gives her poems the physical, sensual sense of life that makes us attend to subject matter we may otherwise refuse to hear, and at the same time, affirms life, takes enormous pleasure in the sheer physicality of human being. The internalization of the suffering to which she is witness is not appropriation; it surfaces at the skin to disturb the natural flow of this sensuality.

In "**Return**," she chronicles what she has seen,

> the razor
> the live wire
> dry ice and concrete

this is what Americans want, not

> the long
> dull story of corruption.

To Josephine Crum, to whom the poem is dedicated, she says,

> I tell you
> I have not rested
>
> I go mad, for example,
> in the Safeway, at the many heads
> of lettuce, papayas and sugar, pineapples
> and coffee, especially the coffee.
> And when I speak with American men,
> there is some absence of recognition:
> their constant Scotch and fine white
> hands, many hours of business, penises
> hardened by motor inns and a faint
> resemblance to their wives.

Josephine replies:

> people
> who rescue physicists, lawyers and poets
> lie in their beds at night with reports
> of mice introduced into women, of men
> whose testicles are crushed like eggs.

That they cup their own parts
with their bedsheets and move themselves
slowly, imagining bracelets affixing
their wrists to a wall where the naked
are pinned, where the naked are tied open
and left to the hands of those who erase
what they touch. We are all erased
by them, and no longer resemble decent
men. We no longer have the hearts,
the strength, the lives of women.

The external corruption invades all of us, so that we

. . . no longer resemble decent
men. We no longer have the hearts,
the strength, the lives of women.

These mutilations, these perversions of sexuality, stand in
contrast to the spontaneous flow of female physicalness in
the earlier poem **"Kalaloch,"** which Stanley Kunitz says
in his introduction to *Gathering the Tribes,* "in its boldness and innocence and tender, sensuous delight it may
well prove to be the outstanding Sapphic poem of an era."
The horrors Forche witnesses are persuasively internalized, not only in the poet's body, but in our own, where
they emerge in such distortions. Levertov raises the question of how we can respond to the sheer amount of destruction in the world, when:

We've been used
to the daily recitation of death's
multiplication tables: we don't notice
the quantum leap: eighty-seven thousand
killed outright by a single bomb,
fifty-one thousand missing or injured.

("On the 32nd Anniversary of the
Bombing of Hiroshima and Nagasaki")

Forche's poems move this horror into the mind through
their sensuality, truncations, misdirections. In **"Letter
from Prague, 1968-78,"** Carolyn takes the voice of a
young Czech jailed at eighteen for an improvident toast
made to a Russian soldier, "*viva / Dubcek / viva svoboda,
viva / socialisme.*" At 18, "still / in prison having bowls
of paste / for breakfast," he says:

I could have
fallen in love. There were
plenty of women in the streets
calling *roses, roses*; I should
have given them money, taken
their petals to a room where
I might have dropped to a bed,
my eyes tongued open at morning.
To touch myself now, there is nothing.

The inner self in Forche's poetry surfaces and meets the
world where all of us meet it—at the skin, a more persuasive friction than any simply intellectual motion of mind
could create. **"For a Stranger"** recounts, like **"Kalaloch,"**
a chance meeting, this time on a train with

few clues to where
we are: the baled wheat scattered
everywhere like missing coffins.
The distant yellow kitchen lights
wiped with oil.

Each time the train slows, she steps to the platform.

Each time I find you
again between the cars, holding out
a scrap of bread for me, something
hot to drink, until there are
no more cities and you pull me
toward you, sliding your hands
into my coat, telling me
your name over and over, hurrying
your mouth into mine.
We have, each of us, nothing.
We will give it to each other.

The images are physical, bodily. In **"Reunion"** she remembers

My fingernails, pecks of light
on your thighs. . . .

How my breasts feel, years
later, the tongues swishing
in my dress, some yours, some
left by other men. . . .

How much tenderness we could
wedge between a stairwell
and a police lock.

It is this tenderness that offers some healing force, a possibility of redemption, and this tenderness is a property of
Forche's voice, perfectly suited to already explosive content which would be grossly sensationalized by a more
forceful diction (as, for example, Plath or Hughes), using
for emphasis repetition ("like netted fish / exactly like netted fish") (**"Ourselves or Nothing"**), or direct address
("they were like dried peach halves. There is no other way
to say this") rather than verbal force.

In the poem **"As Children Together,"** less overtly political
than the others discussed here, she remembers her childhood friend, Victoria, ashamed of her house:

its round tins of surplus flour,
chipped beef and white beans,
relief checks. . . .

I am going to have it, you said.
Flowers wrapped in paper from carts
in Montreal, a plane lifting out
of Detroit, a satin bed, a table
cluttered with bottles of scent.

So standing in a platter of ice
outside a Catholic dance hall
you took their collars
in your fine chilled hands
and lied your way to adulthood.

But the servicemen who took her breasts in their hands,
gave her the "silk tassels of their graduation," offer no escape.

They say you have children, a trailer
in the snow near our town,
and the husband you found as a girl
returned from the Far East broken
cursing holy blood at the table
where nightly a pile of white shavings
is paid from the edge of his knife.

If you read this poem, write to me.
I have been to Paris since we parted.

These last lines, their compression, their sweetness, their force of surprise, demonstrate Forche's consummate skill with narrative, and it is the combination of this narrative with voice that carries the political weight of her content—her role as witness. Such a poetry requires a totally persuasive veracity, a plain believable recounting of the tale. In the United States, the political situation in El Salvador has been largely unknown; and if known, in Forche's view, known incorrectly. So the tale must be, before anything, told.

Forche's poetic inclination to narrative is evident in the earlier *Gathering the Tribes.* "Alfonso" is the story of a life, beginning with specific geographically-rooted detail—a setting:

> Alfonso strings Chemayo's chilies
> like sacred hearts, tongues of fire tied together,

and moving through the life—

> as a child her father roamed San Mateo;

nine short lines later

> . . . she was eighty, her neck
> swelled, lack of salt.

Forche's poetry has the compressed emotion, the music, the attention to language of a lyric, yet often the poem's structure resembles the testimony of a witness in a court of law. First a physical description, a pinning detail, testifying to presence, the time, the place, then the unfolding of suspenses, the hush developing as we wait to hear what happens next. **"Memory of Elena," "Letter from Prague," "The Colonel," "Departure,"** all function very much as stories. Yet standing as they do between lyric and narrative, they require an absolutely sure hand, a restraint in the selection of events that make the tales, the whole story in a few lines:

> Here is the name
> of a friend who will take you in,
> the paper of a man who vanished,
> the one you will become when
> the man you have been disappears
>   **("Departure")**

Yet the poems do not end simply with the final event; they require the openness of those last luminous lines of **"As Children Together,"** or of the final poem in *The Country Between Us,* which intertwines the separate tales of Forche's political experience with Terrence Des Pres' life in the years he worked writing *The Survivor,* accounts of death camp experiences:

> There is a cyclone fence between
> ourselves and the slaughter and behind it
> we hover in a calm protected world like
> netted fish, exactly like netted fish.
> It is either the beginning or the end
> of the world, and the choice is ourselves
> or nothing.

Denise Levertov, in *Light Up the Cave,* quotes Goethe: "In order to *do* something, one has to *be* something." She goes on to say that "the internal and external work, the self-directed or introspective and the publically directed or extroverted, must be concurrent, or at least rhythmically alternating."

The integration—mind and body, interior and exterior, politics and poetry; lyric and narrative poems that "speak for themselves, obstinate as always," as Forche describes it in her *APR* essay—is a lesson in the poetry of total engagement that expands, for all of us, the shape of the possible.

Publishers Weekly (essay date 1994)

SOURCE: A review of *The Angel of History,* in *Publishers Weekly,* Vol. 241, No. 5, January 31, 1994, pp. 77-8.

[*Here, the critic offers a favorable review of* The Angel of History.]

Though Forché's (*The Country Between Us*) previous books have been groundbreaking works of political and moral depth, this new volume may be the most remarkable. Ambitious and authentic, *The Angel of History* is an overarching book-length poem, composed in numbered sections, that invokes the horror of contemporary times in a mode reminiscent of Eliot's *The Waste Land.* Much as Eliot's poem refracted WW I, the vacuity of culture and the fragmentation of modern life, Forché considers the Holocaust, Hiroshima and genocide in Latin America—the dismal past that predicates the chaotic present. Her vehicle is the Angel of History, who confronts human cruelty and misery but can do no more than record them, as explained by Walter Benjamin in an epigraph: "The angel would like to stay, awaken the dead, and make whole what has been smashed. But . . . the storm irresistibly propels him into the future to which his back is turned, while the pile of debris before him grows skyward." Though the poetry is powerful, it is not always easily understandable; one must follow the Angel through serpentine lines, a disjointed and oblique nightmare whispered by an indeterminate narrator, and a splintered pastiche that borrows apocalyptic phrases from Elie Wiesel, Kafka, Canetti, Trakl, Char and Valery. But the journey ventured is well worth the occasional wrong turn: Forché has not only created poetry of consummate beauty, but has borne witness to the wounds of our collective history, fulfilling the conviction that "surely all art is the result of one's having been in danger, of having gone through an experience all the way to the end."

Kevin Walker   (essay date 1994)

SOURCE: "Inspired by War," in *Detroit Free Press,* Section G, May 22, 1994, p. 8.

[*In the following review, Walker favorably assesses* The Angel of History, *briefly comparing it to* The Country between Us *and noting Forché's focus on World War II, survival, and remembrance.*]

Carolyn Forche's second book, *The Country Between Us,* became one of the most talked-about books of poetry of the 1980s. The heart of it is a group of poems about the war in El Salvador. Forche wrote with haunting precision about the cruelty of that war and the questions of conscience it should have raised for all Americans.

In *The Angel of History*, Forche again bears witness to the shattering of lives. But her technique has evolved magnificently. In her 1981 work, she transformed suffering into the musical, unifying shape of the lyric poem. In *The Angel of History*, she has done something more challenging.

This book-length poem is as fragmented as a bombed-out house or a shattered mirror. But each puzzling fragment is exquisite, and the whole possesses a unity that defies easy understanding.

The Angel of History is a meditation on destruction, survival and memory. What the characters who float in and out of it like ghosts have in common is that their lives have been shaped irrevocably by the events of World War II. Forche gives voice to survivors whose loved ones are all dead; to child victims who left behind only their names; to the countless human beings who were killed or ruined by events beyond their control and beyond their comprehension.

Like most of Forche's subject matter, this is grim territory. But *The Angel of History* is not a harrowing book, so much as an inspiring one. Forche has found a way of examining the unbearable that neither diminishes the terror nor drives the reader away.

The key to her success is the poem's unique blend of lucidity and elusiveness. Unwinding as it does in fragments of stories, wisps of personality, snapshots of landscapes, the poem resists the reader's desire to get a grip on it. It slips by like time itself. Left behind is the memory of wreckage, miraculously intertwined with the memory of beauty.

In one passage, a survivor of Hiroshima stands in a restored ornamental garden in that city, considering her life and that of fellow survivors:

> We have not, all these years, felt
> what you call happiness,

> But at times, with good fortune, we
> experience something close,
> As our life resembles life, and this
> garden the garden.
> And in the silence surrounding
> what happened to us
> it is the bell to awaken God that
> we've heard ringing.

This entire book is as bright, as serene, and as tender as those lines. *The Angel of History* achieves what Forche hopes for when she writes,

> And so we revolt against silence
> with a bit of speaking.
> The page is a charred field where
> the dead would have written
> *We went on.*

FURTHER READING

Criticism

Lapinski, Ann Marie. "The Education of a Poet: El Salvador Sojourn Gives Life to Her Art." *Chicago Tribune*, No. 347 (13 December 1982): Section 3: 1-3.

> Feature article in which Forché discusses her experiences in El Salvador and the composition, publication, and reception of the poems collected in *The Country between Us.*

Russell, Sue. "The Workings of Chance and Memory." *The Women's Review of Books* XI, Nos. 10-11 (July 1994): 31.

> Laudatory review discussing Forché's global focus, narrative stance, use of language, and emphasis on history in *The Angel of History.*

Additional coverage of Forché's life and career is contained in the following sources published by Gale Research: *Contemporary Authors*, **Vols. 109, 117;** *Contemporary Literary Criticism*, **Vols. 25, 83; and** *Dictionary of Literary Biography*, **Vol. 5.**

Guido Gozzano

1883-1916

Italian poet, short story writer, and fabulist.

INTRODUCTION

Known for his detailed narration of events, descriptions of place, and frequent borrowings from other poets' works, Gozzano is aligned with the early twentieth-century Italian literary movement known as *crepuscolarismo*, or twilight, because of the melancholic tone, autumnal themes and colors, and imagery of death in his verse. Reacting against the poetics of the Romantic period, Gozzano sought to use an even bolder language and less restricted formal verse. Noting his pivotal role in the transition in Italy to Modernism from Romanticism as exemplified in the work of the prominent writer Gabriele D'Annunzio, Nobel laureate Eugenio Montale described Gozzano as "the first poet of the twentieth century who succeeded . . . in 'crossing D'Annunzio' in order to get to a territory of his own, just as, on a larger scale, Baudelaire had had to cross Hugo in order to lay the foundations of a new poetry."

Biographical Information

Gozzano was born in Turin to an upper-middle-class family. During his third year of university studies in 1902 in Savigliano, he was introduced to the works of German philosopher Friedrich Nietzsche and poet Gabriele D'Annunzio. While in Savigliano, Gozzano—influenced by Nietzsche's condemnation of religion—denounced his Catholicism for atheism. In 1903 he entered the law school at the University of Turin, although, preferring the literature courses taught by professors Luigi Einaudi and renowned poet Auturo Graf, he subsequently abandoned the study of law. Gozzano published his first poem, "Il castello d'aglie," in a local daily in 1904. While at the university, he developed tuberculosis, a malady that was to shape the theme and content of his work as well as his character. The first collection of poetry, *La via del rifugio* (*The Road to Shelter*), was published in 1907 to favorable reviews. During work on the second collection of lyrics, *I colloqui: liriche di Guido Gozzano* (1911; *The Colloquies: Lyrics of Guido Gozzano*), Gozzano returned to his former Christian beliefs, and in a 1910 letter to the editor of *Il momento*, Gozzano expressed his disillusionment with current popular scientific and philosophical trends, stating: "But today no one denies the spirit anymore . . . And so there is a trembling new idealism, a need for faith." In February, 1912, he embarked on a trip to India and returned in May to compile a new prose narration and the letters he produced while abroad. This collection was published posthumously under the title *Verso la cuna del mondo, lettere dall'India (1912-1913)* (1917; *Towards the Cradle of the World*). Turin's burgeoning silent film indus-

try fascinated Gozzano and he devoted himself to experimenting with the medium, producing a film based upon an extended poem on butterflies and another on the life of St. Francis of Assisi, which was never completed. After suffering another bout of tuberculosis, Gozzano died in Turin at the age of 32.

Major Works

The poems in Gozzano's collection, *The Road to Shelter*, are thematically linked by their reflective mood and evocations of the natural world, signifying the influence of French poets Francis Jammes and Sully Prudhomme, whom he emulated. In the title lyric, Gozzano provides a description of his niece and nephew chasing, capturing, and torturing a butterfly, a symbolic summation of Gozzano's philosophy on suffering and the meaning of life at that point in his career. In "L'analfabeta" ("The Illiterate") Gozzano confronts the ethical dilemma of his propensity to imitate other poets. One of his most lyrical poems, "L'amica di nonna Speranza" ("The Girlfriend of Grandmother Speranza"), is a narrative recalling his grandmother's youth in Piedmonte in the 1850s. In "The Girlfriend of Grandmother Speranza," "Le due strade," and "Il responso," Gozzano's images of young women represent Gozzano's feelings about the ephemeral nature of romantic love, a common theme in his works. Describing his next collection of poetry, *The Colloquies,* as "a kind of synthesis of my first youth, a pale reflection of my inner drama. The poems . . . will be united by a fine cyclical thread," Gozzano divided the work into three sections entitled "Il giovenile errore" ("Youthful Indiscretions"), "Alle soglie" ("At the Threshold"), and "Il reduce" ("The Veteran"). These poems contain several autobiographical lyrics such as his masterpiece, "Totò Merùmeni," in which Gozzano expresses his decision to abandon his following of Nietzsche; his disdain for the "rhetoricians" Giovanni Pascoli, D'Annunzio, and Giosuè Carducci; and his refusal to follow traditional poetics.

Critical Reception

The most controversial aspect of Gozzano's poetry is his borrowings from—if not plagiarism—of past and contemporary Italian and French masters such as Dante, Petrarch, Bernardin de Saint-Pierre, and the more modern D'Annunzio, Pascoli, Francis Jammes, and Émile Zola. While some critics have praised Gozzano's talent for imitation, others view it as detrimental to his work. Although *The Road to Shelter* received an overwhelmingly positive reception, *The Colloquies* did not. One critic stated that Gozzano repeated the themes in *The Colloquies* from *The Road to Shelter* for the sake of maintaining the good reputation he had previously earned. Federigo Tozzi in a 1913 review of *The Colloquies* stated: "We don't know if there is anything more ridiculously presumptuous than [Gozzano's] verse." Other commentators refer to his poetry as artificial, while poet Aldo Palazzeschi disparaged Gozzano's "bourgeois banality." Erasmo Gerato stated that Gozzano's lengthy panegyric on six subspecies of butterflies, "Le farfalle" ("Butterflies"), deserves critical reevaluation, while Montale noted the poem's stylistic inferiority to the previous *Colloquies.*

PRINCIPAL WORKS

Poetry

La via del rifugio [*The Road to Shelter*] 1907
I colloqui: liriche di Guido Gozzano [*The Colloquies: Lyrics of Guido Gozzano*] 1911
Verso la cuna del mondo, lettere dall'India (1912-1913) [*Towards the Cradle of the World*] (poetry and prose) 1917
Opere, di Guido Gozzano. 5 vols. 1934-1937
Opere (poetry and prose) 1948; revised and reprinted as *Poesie e prose,* 1953 and 1956
Poesie e prose (poetry and prose) 1961; revised edition 1966
I colloqui e prose (poetry and prose) 1974
Colloquies and Selected Poems of Guido Gozzano 1981
Poesie 1983

Un natale a Ceylon e altri racconti indiani (poetry and prose) 1984
Guido Gozzano: The Colloquies and Selected Letters (poetry and letters) 1987

Other Major Works

I tre talismani (fables) 1914
La principessa si sposa (fables) 1917
L'altare del passato [*The Altar of the Past*] (short stories) 1918
L'ultima traccia (short stories) 1919
La fiaccola dei desideri: Fiabe (fables) 1951
Lettere d'amore di Guido Gozzano e Amalia Guglielminetti (letters) 1951
Fiabe (fables) 1961
I sandali della diva: Tutte le novelle (short stories) 1983

CRITICISM

Ruth Shepard Phelps (essay date 1924)

SOURCE: "Guido Gozzano's Book of Youth," in *Italian Silhouettes,* Alfred A. Knopf, 1924, pp. 67-78.

[*In the following essay, Phelps describes Gozzano's poetry as an evocation of his youth and romanticization of a past era.*]

It might be an interesting speculation in minor aesthetics to determine what distance of time is required to make a past epoch picturesque. It is arguable that it takes just four generations. We know that the fashions of the immediately preceding generation are nearly always odious, whether in clothing or house-decoration, in philanthropy or poetry; and this means that our grandfather's day is almost as bad as our father's, since we grow up with the latter's disparagements in our ears. But throw it back one generation further, and impatience and derision give way to sentiment; we find our great-grandmother charming, whether she wear hoops or Empire high-waists, basques or even balloon sleeves—though this last is harder to believe, since these are not great-grandmother's as yet. Her furniture and her ideas are as acceptable as her styles; what was lamentable to her children has become, to her great-grandchildren, quaint. Absolving difference, which she does not live to see!

But we may live long enough to see rehabilitated the generation that preceded our own; our grandchildren will be its fourth generation, they will find all its ways adorable, and as they begin to say so in artistic verse and prose, they will teach us a valuable lesson in the relativity of taste. People in middle life can already see their grandfather's generation putting on a literary halo in the verse of the newest poets, and the newest poets may look to see their children read Tennyson and Matthew Arnold, and relegate painted furniture once more to the attic.

It is the same with centuries; your only tolerable century is the one before last. The eighteenth held in elegant contempt the wild rich seventeenth which the nineteenth steeped itself in; the nineteenth, which loved efflorescence and spontaneity, detested the chill formalities of the Age of Reason, and could endure nothing about the eighteenth except the fact that it blew up in the French Revolution and the Romantic Movement. Now the twentieth feels as it does feel about the Victorian era, and designs Adam rooms and writes *Jennifer Lorn.*

In the pages of the *Yellow Book,* Max Beerbohm, by a *tour de force* of his imagination, once described the year 1880 in the language of the fourth generation, investing the fads and follies of that period with the charm of an elder day. He hung a curtain of words, impalpable as the modern stage-manager's gauze, between his reader and the Jersey Lily, between his reader and "blue china . . . and the poet Swinburne," and with the artificial distance they took on the atmosphere of romance. Just so, if we live to be old enough, the youngest poet will give us back our youth, seen through the glamorous atmosphere of the past. A little out of focus it will look, though, for what was natural and matter-of-course to us, the only right and simple thing, will be "periodic" to him. We shall not quite like that.

Italians who were young in 1848, and who lived to be old—like the Emperor Francis Joseph, who had his own memories of the *Quarantotto* from his side of the shield—had the strange and rather beguiling experience of seeing their lost youth through the eyes of a sentimentalizing posterity, when Guido Gozzano, a poet who certainly had little sentiment left for his own times, published his **Colloquies** in 1911. He was twenty-five before he had finished them, as he tells us in several poems as carefully dated as certain of Petrarch's sonnets, and the book is a veritable book of youth. He sees most things through the golden haze of literary association, as youth does. The name Carlotta on the back of an old photograph sets him dreaming of Foscolo and "Jacopo Ortis"; he heads a group of his poems with a phrase of Petrarch's, *il giovenile errore;* the moon seen above a village *campanile* translates into Italian for his imagination Musset's huge romantic dotted "i"; a love-affair with a little maidservant beguiles his fastidiousness because he can fancy himself to be living a tale out of the *Decameron;* provincial Turin, where he grew up, is glorified for him as soon as he recollects the narrow-minded Recanati where Leopardi lived his tragic childhood; the hour of sunset there reminds him of Massimo d'Azeglio's *Ricordi,* and he regrets that he was born too late for the *Risorgimento.*

But while he borrows thus the robes of poesy to deck out his own life, he returns good measure by throwing a veil of poetic association over a time and place that had not yet begun to seem romantic—the Turin of 1850. That period has been reflected in so many memoirs of persons still living, or living not long since, that it seems very recent background to any but the latest comer. For Guido Gozzano it wears the tender grace of a day that is dead.

An old photograph-album with her name in it, dated 1848, evokes his great-grandmother's *salotto* hung with crimson damask, with its bust of Alfieri, its views of Venice executed in mosaics, its faded daguerreotypes and water-colours, its great chandelier hung with prisms like a Christmas-tree, its little boxes made of shells with "Remember" on their covers, its marble fruit under a glass bell—

> The nice old things in execrable taste

—and peoples it for his imagination with his great-grandmother's refined guests making fashionable talk about the soprano of La Scala who was growing too fat for *Ernani,* of the new operatic success, *Rigoletto,* of Radetzsky and the Armistice and the ugly but *simpatico* visage of the young King Charles Albert, of Mazzini, and the *salon* of the Countess Maffei. There are people living who may have been taken as children into that drawing-room, to be politely petted and kissed, and to catch the well-bred undertones of that talk, but seen through Guido Gozzano's young eyes it is all as remote as an eighteenth-century vignette.

Still, the book of his youth is not given wholly to resuscitating the past, he does not live only through literature, though he suffers from that psychic malady of the literary artist which makes him often seem to himself like two men, one who lives and one who watches his double live. The *blasé* young poet has had many loves to recount by the time he is twenty-five, though none that went deep. He is still seeking the real love, the great love, and deploring his own incapacity for emotion. There is a moment when he seems to feel something more real, in a sympathetic inclination for the country maiden Felicita, who welcomes him modestly every day to her father's ancient villa in the hill-town where he is sojourning for his health—a villa where the *marchesa's* ghost is sometimes seen to walk, and "which wears a garment of growing corn waist-high about it, like a seventeenth-century lady masquerading as a peasant girl"; but his mocking literary self is on the watch to warn him, as he says farewell, that if he takes it too seriously he will be cutting a figure like a lover in one of Prati's ballads—

> The man of other days, the Young Romantic,
> Which I am not and but pretend to be.

Yet he has something of the Young Romantic in him for all that, this young gentleman in his early twenties who sees himself as cold, intellectual and inaccessible, beset with loving women whom he does not love, yet holding to a belief in Love itself, with a capital letter. To be so blasé, so selfconscious, so fearful of a bit of sentiment, is to be engagingly youthful.

But love and literature are part of every young poet's life, and while Guido Gozzano reveals them through the glaring clear white glass of his twentieth-century temperament, with that touch of acridity characteristic of present-day youth, he is most interesting when he describes those aspects of his life which he shares with no other. When he said good-bye to Felicita that day, and watched his double,

> *Qui me ressemblait comme un frère,*

playing the romantic lover, it was on the eve of departure for some soft climate—Morocco, or the islands of the South Atlantic—which should heal his ailing lungs; and he gets some very striking effects out of this experience, with his belief that there is no difference between the language of poetry and the language of conversation, and that everything is matter for verse—*tout ce qu'il y a dans la nature est dans l'art.* It is "new" poetry, realistic poetry, the poetry of "actuality" in both the French and the English senses; it seeks not to produce beauty, but to report the facts. Yet the facts, when worked into the patterns of rhyme and metre, take on a beauty they would not have in prose. They get the distance upon them needed to make them "compose," as when we step back to see an impressionist picture across a width of museum floor.

"On The Threshold"

I

My heart, little lad full of mirth, whose laughter
    breaks even through tears,
My heart, but an urchin in years, so happy to
    live on this earth,

Shut close in your niche softly napping, you
    hear, I am sure, on strange mission,
Someone at your door who keeps tapping and
    tapping?—It is the physician.

He taps me in rhythmic notation; he holds, I
    know not on what quest,
To the front and the back of my chest, machin-
    ery of auscultation.

Now what does he hear, the old faker? They al-
    most would move me to laughter,
His airs of a skilful wiseacre, were it not for the
    bill to come after.

"I catch a slight whisper away on the apex—not
    much, just a clue,"
And with his ridiculous crayon he draws a small
    circle of blue.

"High feeding, no more versifying, no more of
    your 'white nights' passed waking,
No more cigarettes, no love-making—some cli-
    mate that's drier, less trying,

San Remo perhaps, or Rapallo—no depression,
    take things with a laugh.
Then, if you permit, we shall follow our search
    with the radiograph."

II

O heart, do you not perhaps mark, O heart—and
    with what perturbation!
Through your house so well shuttered and dark
    there flashes an illumination?

There flows through my thorax a fluid, through
    all its parts, lower and higher,
And painlessly shown, darker-hued against a
    bright background of fire,

My bones and my organs it weaves—as lightning
    will paint on the night
A skeleton woodland of light—in patterns of
    branches and leaves.

And what does he see, the old faker? They al-
    most would move me to laughter,
His airs of a skilful wiseacre, were it not for the
    bill to come after.

III

My heart, little lad full of mirth, whose laughter
    breaks even through tears,
My heart, but an urchin in years, so happy to
    live on this earth,

O heart, my suspicion is keen (for your sake
    alone I spend breath
In grieving), there draws nigh that Queen whom
    mortals denominate Death. . . .

A Lady with no shape or form, a Lady in noth-
    ingness dressed,
Wherever her cold fingers rest, she touches
    things but to transform.

You'll feel, heart, well-being throughout, a light
    load, without pain or care,
You'll waken quite altered without—in name
    and in face and in hair.

You'll waken *in corpore sano,* to feel yourself dif-
    ferent, unmembered,
The colloquies no more remembered you held
    with that *guidogozzano.* . . .

He came back cured, as he believed, from his ultimate island, and settled quietly in a remote villa, "with a sick mother, a white-haired great-aunt, and a demented uncle," his only other companions being puss, a hoarse-voiced jay, and a Barbary ape named Makakita. As he says in his vigorous *martelliano* verses, the fourteen-syllabled lines with marked caesura, of which this is a rude imitation:

With its neglected garden, its vast saloons, its
    fine
Seventeenth-century balconies, the vine-hung
    villa looks
As though it had been taken from certain poems
    of mine,
It looks the typical villa out of the story-books.

The villa, sad, is thinking, thinking of better
    days,
Gay groups beneath the trees there, yonder, cen-
    turies old,
Resplendent banquets served in great dining-
    halls ablaze,
Balls in the ball-room, stripped now of spoils the
    dealers sold.

But where in other days the Ansaldis used to
    come,
Rattazzis, Casa Oddone, d'Azeglios, it is said,
There stops to-day a motor, panting, with throb-
    bing hum,
And bearded foreign folk lift the knocker's Gor-
    gon head. . . .

Here, in his hermitage,

A veteran from the fields of Love and Death,
Two lovely things which both have lied to him,

he worked in his laboratory and wrote verses. A true young modern, it is science which can console him for the disappointments of love and religion, and for his reprieve from death.

Ah! Nature is not blind and deaf and mute;

I question flint and lichen, and I hear
Her speak her purposes, benign and clear.
Born of herself, herself is absolute,
The only truth that has no norm to suit:
Before her face I have to drop my sneer.

Indeed he took his poet's note-book into the laboratory with him sometimes, and experimented a little with scientific poetry; crystals, chrysalids and retorts intrude strangely here and there upon amorous reminiscence.

At the end of his book, still living a companioned hermit in his villa, Guido Gozzano was still twenty-five. He looked over the brink of his youth into the gulf of increasing age, to discern "thirty, turbid with moribund instincts," "forty, terrifying age of the defeated," then old age, and decided not to let this dismal procession of the years fly the banner of poesy. Himself will close youth's manuscript:

"The Colloquies"

I

"The Colloquies."—Restored now, lithe and tanned,
He takes his verses, files them, makes them chime,
Poises his manuscript upon his hand.

—This trivial game of syllable and rhyme:
Is this the whole here of my youth's short lease?
Is this all there is left of fleeting time?

Better be silent now, better to cease,
While still my garden-wall with flowers is hung,
Now before envy learns to hold her peace.

Better to stop half-way, while still I'm young,
Now while the world to my unskilful Muse,
As to the songstress singing her first song,

Its friendly right hand will not yet refuse.

II

Unlike the actress getting on in years,
My Muse shall never smirk or ape young ways,
Derided by the crowd which sneering hears.

But like that lovely Countess of old days,
The Castiglione, shut within her walls,
My Muse grown mute, still young, shall cease her lays,
And disappear before her beauty falls—
Like her who sealed her doors, still in her prime,
To live a prisoner in her own halls,
Among her faded stuffs, alone with Time,
Mirrorless, friendless, waiting her last day,
Hiding from court and people, like a crime,

The last humiliation of decay.

III

I wish my image ever to remain,
As in a portrait, twenty-one or -two.
My friends, you shall not see me on the wane,

Bent with the years, shaking, forlorn of hue.
But keeping mute, I still shall seem that youth,
A trifle hare-brained, who was dear to you. . . .

Needless precaution! By the time Guido Gozzano reached the dreaded thirties, it was not only on his not young instincts that death had set the seal. The vanquished forties he did not even approach. Before he died in 1916, he had written several other books—fables, short stories, travel sketches—but his self-denying ordinance against more verses was never violated.

Ernest Hatch Wilkins   (essay date 1954)

SOURCE: "Writers of the Twentieth Century," in *A History of Italian Literature,* Cambridge, Mass.: Harvard University Press, 1954, pp. 478-95.

[In the excerpt below, Wilkins discusses Gozzano as a "Twilight poet."]

The mood prevalent among the most characteristic younger [Italian] poets of the early twentieth century was one of desolation. They had lost faith in life; their world was a world without compelling values and without dependable reality; and they lacked the energy to attempt renovation. The literary influences they felt most strongly were those of recent French poetry. Carducci's enthusiasms, D'Annunzio's rhetorical flamboyance, and Pascoli's sense of mission were alike repugnant to them: in Pascoli, however, they found a humility they could share—a humility that dealt with humble themes, in verse that was unpretentious, yet patiently woven of musical and mood-conveying sounds. The critic G. A. Borgese, contrasting them with their more radiant predecessors, called them *i crepuscolari,* "the twilight poets," and the name has found a general acceptance.

Guido Gozzano is perplexed, but not distressed by his perplexity; conscious of a limiting fate, but resigned to an acceptance that is without probing or rebellion; and aware of a suffering humanity, but content, not without sympathy, to observe the persons and the experiences that come most immediately within his ken.

—*Ernest H. Wilkins*

The Piedmontese Guido Gozzano (1883-1916) is the most restful interpreter of the twilight mood. His verse, limited in extent, is limpid, musical, and of a refined artistry. He is perplexed, but not distressed by his perplexity; conscious of a limiting fate, but resigned to an acceptance that is without probing or rebellion; and aware of a suffering humanity, but content, not without sympathy, to observe the persons and the experiences that come most immediately within his ken. He writes by preference, and often with much charm, of simple folk and of simple things: of children and of the people of Piedmontese hills and valleys, or of the knicknacks of an old parlor. Of himself he writes, as lying in a clover field and lulled by a children's ring-around song he wakes from semi-consciousness:

> Ma dunque esisto! O strano!
> vive tra il Tutto e il Niente
> questa cosa vivente
> detta guidogozzano!—

> But then I do exist! How strange! 'twixt All and Nothing there lives this living thing called "gui-dogozzano."

His longest and most memorable poem, **"La signorina Felicita,"** is a unique and very personal idyll, yearningly nostalgic and yet completely modern.

Eugenio Montale   (essay date 1960)

SOURCE: An introduction to *The Man I Pretend to Be: The Colloquies and Selected Poems of Guido Gozzano,* edited and translated by Michael Palma, Princeton University Press, 1981, pp. xvii-xxv.

[*Considered one of the greatest Italian poets of the twentieth century, Montale received the Nobel Prize for Literature in 1975. He began his career as a poet of landscape, but under the influence of the works of Paul Valéry and the French Symbolists he broke away from the staid conventions of Italian poetry in the 1920s to produce richly symbolic, often cryptic verse. In the following essay, originally published in 1960 as the introduction to a collection of Gozzano's poetry,* Le poesie, *Montale analyzes Gozzano's stylistic devices in* The Colloquies *and* Butterflies, *classifying his artistic temperament as Parnassian.*]

Why was Gozzano so readily greeted, on his arrival, with such exceptional recognition from the critics? Was there any validity in proclaiming him chronologically the last (but not the least) of our classics? If one reflects that, in a certain sense, every author is a classic who has mastered and perfected material that isn't his own, then one must frankly acknowledge that there was a validity to the judgment. One who aided in *The Colloquies'* success records that Gozzano "came into the public eye" in a way that is since no longer the case with poets—familiarly, with his hands in his pockets. Thus he seems to belong completely to a time before that much-lamented and hypothetical gulf that is supposed to divide the public from serious writers. Gozzano was immediately read and understood by the readers of D'Annunzio and Pascoli and the minor poets of the "Treves type," who were all more or less followers of D'Annunzio and Pascoli. And he was understood the way he wanted to be: his drama, his "croaking ghost wrapped in a fantasy," was taken very seriously, leaving to a few subtle initiates (Serra more than any other) the work of distinguishing between his real art and the theatrical cleverness of his "fiction."

And yet the fact that there was a distinction immediately tells us something. Gozzano fit into the public taste without arousing suspicion because he worked a sort of reduction upon the poetry that had come before him. He presented a new species of poetry, that poetry of *faux-exprès,* of semitones and harmonies in gray, that poetry truly not heroic but *en pantoufles* that the French, Belgian, and Flemish post-symbolists had already been experimenting with for so many years (Calcaterra has given a complete list of these poets); and much more than Orsini, Graf (the later Graf), Gianelli, and the others who were beating that path, he stayed close to the verbal impasto of the *Poema paradisiaco,* of the sounds and accents of D'Annunzio at his most crepuscular (*avant lettre*).

There's been much discussion about whether Gozzano was the first to import into Italy the poetics of "good things in terrible taste," the "bourgeois" paraphernalia of the new poetry; and it doesn't really seem that the early Govoni, Moretti, Giorgieri Contri and others were waiting to take the hint from him. But it's a pointless discussion. Gozzano underwent many influences: he was a D'Annunzian at twenty, and much later as well; he beseeched God in verse to deliver him from the lues of D'Annunzianism; he read those foreign poets who could best free him from that peril, but he was the only one of the poets of his time who knew how to give us his complete portrait in a brief collection of lyrics. In this way he was saved from his D'Annunzianism, or if you prefer, his incurable aestheticism. If he had tried to follow the premises of his new poetics to the end, if he had tried to give us, as others tried, a poetry of *grisailles,* Verlainish, spent, attenuated, he would no longer be remembered, not because of the incoherence of the enterprise but because of the instrumental difficulties he would have encountered (the same difficulties which, from Betteloni to Graf 's undervalued *Rhymes of the Forest,* have encumbered every attempt, in Italy, at a poetry that would be humble and vernacular in a bourgeois way). Gozzano, however, had the shrewdness to be incoherent and to stop halfway. I don't even think that it was shrewdness; it was instinct. There was a verbal experiment in the air—plastic, lively, and new—that had found in D'Annunzio its supreme craftsman, and that, stripped down, led D'Annunzio into the liveliest parts of his *Alcione.* Gozzano didn't push himself as far forward as *Alcione,* he stopped at the *Poema paradisiaco,* and he wrapped the bric-a-brac of the good things in terrible taste in a sumptuously *négligé* cloak. He was, verbally, a rich pauper or a poor rich man. He reduced D'Annunzio as Debussy had reduced Wagner, but without ever arriving at results that we could call Debussy-like.

The poetry of Gozzano belongs to the climate that scholars of late eighteenth-century Italian theater call "verist," a climate that is for the most part of nondecadent origins. I realize that the step from this verism to decadent aestheticism is a short one and that both veins can be readily discovered in the same author (Albert Samain, the Puccini who leaps from *La Bohème* to *Turandot,* the Gozzano who goes from **"Signorina Felicita"** to **"Paul and Virginia"**), but it seems to me certain that in Gozzano's case the romantic-bourgeois-verist strain remained the most fruitful. Gozzano reduced the Italian poetry of his time to its lowest common denominator, and here once again the comparison with Puccini becomes irresistible. When we read *The Colloquies* with a fresh mind, we have to recognize that this poetry is neither the richest nor the newest of those years, but it is the most "secure." It's a small thing, perhaps, this poetry; but one can never doubt that it exists; whereas this doubt continually assails us when we reread D'Annunzio and Pascoli, who were so much more authentically lyrical than Gozzano.

Infallible in his choice of words (the first one to give off sparks by striking the aulic against the prosaic), the later Gozzano had the instinct and the good fortune to know he ought to remain what he was: a provincial aesthete, deeply Parnassian, a young and ill Piedmontese, D'Annunzian, bourgeois, but indeed Piedmontese and indeed bourgeois in his own way. I say that he had the good fortune because I doubt his intentions in this regard. The poem on **Butterflies,** to which he then turned his attention, shows clearly enough that after **The Colloquies** Guido Gozzano was exhausted. Even if he had discovered any new horizons, I doubt whether he could have found a fit instrument in himself to turn them into poetry. His most beautiful poems (and they are many) sing, but they don't sing lyrically like the best poems of D'Annunzio and Pascoli, and even more than they sing, they recount, they describe, they comment. And I believe that by now, at the distance of forty years, we can see clearly that when Gozzano wrote **The Colloquies** he instinctively grasped the unique position that was his; and that he was capable of this realization because, unlike those other poets who had influenced him (Graf included), he was born to be an exceptional storyteller or prose writer in verse.

And yet always a poet, we agree; and on this point a few words of explanation are necessary. Among Gozzano's critics, Gargiulo more than any other sensed the poet's prosaic base, but he forced his insight into deductions that seem to me unjustified, finally coming to maintain that Gozzano's major work was his prose (**Towards the Cradle of the World** and a few of the stories in *The Altar of the Past*). The truth appears otherwise to me. If one admits, as few admit, that in comparison with the Tasso of *Jerusalem,* the epic Ariosto is above all a supreme prose writer and storyteller in verse, then one ought to concede that Gozzano was, in his own time and within his own limits, the Ariosto of decadentistic themes that were not his own but that came together in him. It was his inclination to give form and artistic value to the material of others, and his classicism, his relative antimodernity is all here. I wouldn't, however, wish to create a misunderstanding: a verse that is "also" prose is the dream of all modern poets from Browning on, a dream that finds its possibilities in that integrity of style that makes Dante and Shakespeare the newest and most current of poets.

Now, Gozzano's poetry is not of this nature; it is a Parnassian poetry, and all Parnassian poets (I don't see any exceptions) are above all prose writers in verse. It's their way of making poetry, a perfectly acceptable way, and to understand this is to comprehend Gozzano, not to diminish him. Even D'Annunzio, Pascoli, and the early Rilke were not totally "modern" (that is, they were partly alien to the Browning-Baudelaire "junction" that is the source of all modern poetry), but their verse often sings at a depth at which Gozzano's verse never sang. Gozzano's verse is functional, narrative, a verse that fills and sustains the stanza and in which it is extremely difficult to detect any padding or to find those leaps and descents, that unevenness, that bathos, that are so common in grand lyrics. And

yet there is a moment in rereading Gozzano when he seems to be all padding. From certain of his poems he cut entire stanzas without any damage, and there are other cuts that one could make; many of his stanzas could be repositioned without any damage, and others could emigrate from one poem to another without troubling us in the least. This seems to contradict what I said earlier, that Gozzano's verse is a functional verse; but in reality it doesn't. Altering his verses might produce a better or a different functionality, but it wouldn't destroy their basic character. Infusing a strong charge of auto-irony into the material of the *Poema paradisiaco,* Gozzano had the sense to keep his formal innovations to a minimum. He stopped where he did because another solution would have been premature, at least for him. He based his poetry on the collision, or "shock," of a psychologically poor, threadbare material, apparently fit only for minor tones, with a verbal substance that was rich, joyous, and very pleased with itself. This "shock" animates the brief psychological romance of Gozzano's that remains and in all likelihood will remain his true book.

Gozzano remained more of an artist than any other poet of his time; and he seems to have done so deliberately to exhume a distinction used, not always clearly, by De Sanctis, one that ought to be used with extreme caution in aesthetic discussions, since it can be the source of a great deal of misunderstanding. [In a footnote the editor, Michael Palma, states: "The distinction that Montale would seem to have in mind is the one between the idea of a work of art and its manifestation; De Sanctis maintained that the true value of a work of art proceeds from the quality of its presentation, not the quality of its conception. Similarly, in judging the finished work of art, the critic must distinguish between its artistic value and any other value— moral, historical, philosophical—that it may possess."]

An insertion of simple and direct "bourgeois" truth (his Piedmontese truth, in short) into that world of the *Paradisiaco,* where at certain moments we can still make out the stirring of Pre-Raphaelite figures, images of a late literary romanticism, and a slight lowering of the D'Annunzian tone: here is Gozzano, and here is his slight and firm originality, that, born as it was between 1906 and 1911, ought to have found itself very quickly short of material.

Reread the poem **"The Road to Shelter"** (which gives its title to the book and which was reworked from an earlier lyric, **"The Convalescent"**), and you will realize that after that work—unsatisfying but nevertheless layered, rich, and promising—Gozzano embarked on increasingly limited investigations. His most secure poems (**"The Two Roads," "Grandmother Speranza's Friend," "Turin," "A Wintry Scene," "A Woman Resurrected"**) have the perfection of a miniature, of an old engraving. It's a miracle that they don't descend into stereotypes. More complex and more digressive, **"Signorina Felicita"** reveals even in its metrics (which bring up to date the six-line stanza, that halved octave dear to comic poets) its essential character, that of a tale in verse; and it remains in the end Gozzano's most typical poem, though perhaps not his most balanced. Here, and even better in others of his poems, he develops through hints his catalogue of true women:

An illustration for Gozzano's poem "Il richiamo" ("The Call"), published in Lettura, June, 1909.

She listened quietly,
her hands held at the sides
of her firm chin, her eyes
fixed earnestly on me

under her lashes' sweep, . . .

. . . . .

I saw the delicate
nostrils, I knew again
the expert lips, and then
the little teeth that bit, . . .

("**A Woman Resurrected**")

. . . brunette vivacious iridescent

fearless in her cravat and upright collar, her
  brown
hair flowing freely down from under her jockey
  cap.

("**The Two Roads**")

"Stay!" And she held my arm against her side,
the live links of her fingers eagerly
twining with mine. "If you love me, stay with
  me!"

("**A Wintry Scene**")

This catalogue of true women extends from Totò Merùmeni's serving maid, drawn with Liotard's brush, to the
modern horse-women on bicycles whose ghosts we have
just called up, firmer than the best figures of Boldini. And
in comparison with these women, the more fully drawn
figures of Felicita and Carlotta are immersed in a certain
sickly-sweet mannerism.

In "**Absence**," you'll find a more lyrical Gozzano at last,
but one who more closely resembles the other "harmonists

in gray and in silence" of the beginning of the twentieth
century:

A kiss. And she's gone. She's away
down there, where the path can't be seen
in the deep woods, still making its way
like a long corridor through the green.

. . . . .

The pool is resplendent. And stilled
are the frogs. But there flashes a spear
of blue ember, bright emerald
lightning: the kingfisher's here . . .

Here and elsewhere one senses how great a need Gozzano
had to narrate an action, to weave a fable, even if that need
alone was not enough to save him. The colonial rococo
scenography, the style of eighteenth-century sylvan *folie*
couldn't totally save the exercise of "**Paul and Virginia.**"
And one finds confirmation of Gozzano's inability to sustain a discarnate lyrical afflatus in nearly all of the blank
verse of **Butterflies,** slack as blank verse always is when
used by poets of a Parnassian temperament. One finds it
also in the last part of "**Cocotte,**" which contains some of
his emptiest verses:

Come! It will be as if you took my hand
and brought me to the child that I was then.
The boy will talk to the Lady once again.
We'll rise together from time's distant land.

The Colloquies, then, don't lack stuffing; parts of the
scheme that Gozzano outlined couldn't be filled in, suffused with the color of poetry. And only from a total renewal of his physical and moral life, after a lapse of years,
could a new Gozzano have emerged, a Gozzano recon-

ciled to God (so Calcaterra speculates, and not without justification). In what language could he have expressed his new sentiments? Certainly not that of *The Colloquies.* I say this, parenthetically, because converts, as a rule, are bad writers. It is nonetheless certain that Gozzano the consummate artist would have always distrusted those "good sentiments that make for wretched literature"— because he was literary all the way to the ends of his hair.

That he was such a one, rich with good culture, of restless but not illicit ambitions, is shown by those letters of his to Guglielminetti that for the reader of *The Colloquies* complete his image. These letters don't add anything to Gozzano's reputation, but on the other hand, they don't take anything away from it, as has been claimed. There Gozzano appears as he was: a gentlemanly boy, amateurish, sensual, not timid and certainly not at all introverted; a poet, in this sense, who was barely romantic and barely a "poet." A concrete, matter-of-fact temperament, with all the good qualities of a provincial bourgeois intellectual. Cultured, intrinsically cultured even if unexceptional in his reading, a first-rate judge of his own limits, naturally D'Annunzian, even more naturally disgusted by D'Annunzianism, he was the first poet of the twentieth century who succeeded (as was necessary then, and as it probably continued to be even after him) in "crossing D'Annunzio" in order to get to a territory of his own, just as, on a larger scale, Baudelaire had had to cross Hugo in order to lay the foundations of a new poetry. Gozzano's results were certainly more modest: an album of old engravings that will remain for the early twentieth century what Aloysius Bertrand's *Gaspard de la Nuit* remains for early nineteenth-century France, with so much less mystery, modesty, and magic, and so much more of our warm Italian blood. A limited and authentic book, totally incomprehensible to those modern intellectuals who are ashamed of Puccini and prefer *Falstaff* to *Il Trovatore* (but the only music that they love in their hearts is black music). And in this sense, yes—and not because he inlaid his verses with classical citations and loved his "trade" of poet—the last of our classics, or if you prefer, the next-to-last, the third-to-last . . .

Just as a good Persian carpet isn't left without a defect, I would like to leave some empty space in the Pantheon of poets, a few empty easy chairs, just in case two or three post-Gozzano lyricists might one day be thought worthy of occupying them. To see Guido again in his present whereabouts, to talk with him of Turin, to evoke once more those walks through the Valentino, those fine dinners at Molinari's and the Cambio (my memories of 1918, but Guido was already dead and I had never seen him), to hear the sound of his voice, with a Piedmontese accent, no doubt—what a temptation for a poet-man who even in the here-after would want to find himself among men and not mannequins!

I'm not talking about myself, you understand. It may be that the chairs will never be filled.

> **Erasmo Gabriele Gerato on Gozzano's imitation of other poets:**
>
> It is our postulation that Gozzano had a remarkable poetic ingenuity and prowess. His keen, vivid, inventive imagination coupled with a most sincere and uniquely sensitive personality, made him a truly remarkable writer at the turn of this century. Gozzano possessed an uncanny power of mental recollection that he so often employed in his behalf when imitating other's poetic contributions, or creating his very own. We are convinced that his uniquely superior power of recollection, imitation and recreation of pre-existing literary works is at the primary base of his falling short of ever reaching the stature of a major or innovative writer. If one were to scan the existing literary criticism on Gozzano, one would be impressed by the substantial amount that his critics have dedicated to "Gozzano-the imitator."
>
> *Erasmo Gabriele Gerato, in his* Guido Gustavo Gozzano: A Literary Interpretation, *1983.*

J. G. Nichols   (essay date 1987)

SOURCE: An introduction to *Guido Gozzano: The Colloquies and Selected Letters,* edited and translated by J. G. Nichols, Carcanet, 1987, pp. 7-18.

[*Nichols is an English educator, poet, and critic. In the following excerpt, he asserts that Gozzano's poetry evinces both traditional and modernist qualities.*]

In 1907, with the publication of *The way of refuge* (*La via del rifugio*), Guido Gozzano strolled into prominence (in Montale's admiring phrase) "in a friendly way, with his hands in his pockets". Four years later a second volume of poems, *The colloquies* (*I colloqui*), increased his reputation. Today several good editions of his poems are in print, and the critical work grows steadily. He wrote much fascinating prose, and indeed much verse that he never published in book form; but today it is *The colloquies* which receive, quite rightly, the most, the most appreciative, attention.

In England he is still virtually unknown. A reader coming to *The colloquies* for the first time, and noticing that more than half of Gozzano's short life was lived in the last century, may well wonder where his work belongs. With the second half of the nineteenth century, dominated poetically by Carducci? Or with the modernists of this century? When he has finished the poems the reader is likely to be left still wondering.

There are obvious traditional qualities. The poems are discursive and expansive. Gozzano works, not by a rapid succession of stabs at meaning, or by a piling-up of images with no apparent connection, but very simply and straightforwardly, in a rather leisurely way. Syntax, so far from being fractured, is not even bruised. In poem after poem the theme is announced:

> Sadness, sweet thing, you used to be the friend,

not long since, of the boy just back from
school . . .
> ("The ultimate infidelity")

I, once upon a time, was Paul. The name
Virginia stirs me still . . .
> ("Paul and Virginia")

How often in bright lands among bright flowers,
on shipboard, near the rigging, have my dreams
been only of your snows and sombre limes . . .
> ("Turin")

Then the theme is developed at what is often, for a modern
poem, quite some length. Finally the poem is rounded off
neatly:

> Oh, honestly I don't know what's more sad than
> never to be sad again.
>> ("The ultimate infidelity")

> Have mercy, lovers! Hear
> my prayer! Mercy on this ironical
> desert of mine where such chimeras are!
>> ("Paul and Virginia")

> *No point in getting roused . . . I do agree,*
> my   wise   Gianduia,   Piedmont's
> puppet-clown! . . .
>> ("Turin")

Much of the poetry is quite clearly narrative. This includes
the very best poems—**"Paul and Virginia"** and especially
"La signorina Felicita"—and it is significant that these
two best poems are also the longest. Another narrative,
"Wintry", might even have been written, although with
some loss of elan, in prose as an old-fashioned short story,
one with a shock O. Henry ending.

With this expansiveness, this willingness to explain, goes
a remarkable clarity, and clarity is not the most striking
feature of modernist poetry, in Italy or anywhere else. The
references and allusions Gozzano makes are far from esoteric: he clearly expects his reader not only to catch them,
but to catch them without feeling particularly clever. Even
those which might cause some difficulty to an English
reader are not hermetic: an Italian reader would usually
have no problem. To take a few examples: the epigraph to
the first section of *The colloquies,* "The youthful error",
is very familiar to Italians as a quotation from the first sonnet of Petrarch's *Canzoniere;* Bernardin de Saint-Pierre's
Paul et Virginie, on which **"Paul and Virginia"** is based,
is the book "which made all the world weep"; then "Jacopo's fate, so sad, in Foscolo's tender book", which is
mentioned in **"The friend of Grandmother Speranza"**, alludes to the famous *Last letters of Jacopo Ortis,* a work
which performed the same service, or disservice, for Italian youth at the turn of the eighteenth and nineteenth centuries as, a quarter of a century before, had been performed for a whole European generation by another work
mentioned more than once in the same poem—*The sorrows of young Werther.* Even when Gozzano refers to people only by their first names, it is not in order to be evasive
or oblique, but only to show a rather insouciant familiarity. The "Giacomo" mentioned in **"Turin"** is Leopardi, and
Gozzano makes the matter more than clear by quoting, within inverted commas, from two of Leopardi's

poems. In the second poem entitled **"The colloquies"**, the
one which concludes the volume, "Artur" is certainly
more obscure than anything so far, but his identification
with Schopenhauer is helped by the collocation with
"Friedrich" who cannot be anyone else but Friedrich
Nietzsche, who is not only mentioned, but also used as a
rhyme-word, several other times in *The colloquies.* Even
"Makakita, his one friend" of **"In the survivor's home"**—
who might at first seem to be as exotically elusive as Eliot's
Pipit, Hakagawa, or Mr Silvero—has been introduced to
us in an earlier poem as "an ape called Makakita": Totò
Merùmeni has some strange friends, it is true, but we do
know who they are. There is something reassuring about
such a sphere of reference, and the reader never feels that
he is trying, and failing perhaps, to break into a social circle which would prefer to exclude him.

Something else which distinguishes Gozzano from modernist poets is his faithfulness to traditional verse-forms.
This must have been the result of a conscious decision; it
cannot have been simply that the option of free verse did
not occur to him: he had read much French poetry in irregular verse, and other Italian poets of his time were experimenting with it, including the great d'Annunzio. Why
then did Gozzano make such a decision? Would it not
seem to be the obvious thing to loosen the verse up in keeping with his choice of a humdrum, domestic subject matter? Perhaps, but for the moment we may notice that his
insistence on writing of little, ordinary things is matched
by his insistence on the poem as a highly-wrought artefact.
Quite alien to Gozzano are both the sentiment and the
looseness of form in Sergio Corazzini's famous cry:

> Why do you call me a poet?
> I am not a poet.
> I am only a little lad who is weeping.
> ("Desolation of the poor sentimental poet",
>   1906)

Gozzano was made, not only of sterner, but more meticulous stuff.

Like many another poet, Gozzano has suffered the misfortune of having a label pasted over his contents. The fact
that he shares the label with, among others, Corazzini
should make us suspicious of its accuracy. Gozzano is
often included among the "crepuscolari" (twilight poets).
The term was first used by G.A. Borgese in 1910 with reference to Gozzano's friend, Marino Moretti. In the way
in which it is often used now, and in what is probably its
most obvious significance, this term has little bearing on
the hard, clear outlines of Gozzano's poetry; but in its
original intention there is some insight. Borgese compared
the history of Italian poetry to a day, of which the second
half of the nineteenth century was the twilight, the decline,
the decadence. To see Gozzano as in some sense an epi-
gone is not to misread him, and indeed he went to considerable trouble to stress his own dependence on what had
gone before. Certainly Borgese's label puts him firmly in
the nineteenth century.

And yet, and yet . . . When we know that a card-carrying
modernist like Eugenio Montale has praised Gozzano
(and praised him by implication as his own predecessor)
then we know that we must think again. . . .

Even if [the reader] admits the justice of what has so far been suggested, he may be unable to get out of his head his first impression that Gozzano is very reminiscent of the early T.S. Eliot. Parallels can easily be adduced:

> I'm twenty-five now! Yesterday I wasn't.
> Now I am old. My youth, now it has gone,
> leaves me the present of not being present.

and

> I grow old . . . I grow old . . .
> I shall wear the bottoms of my trousers rolled.

The epigraph to the first section of *The colloquies,* "The youthful error", is used for a purpose that Eliot also often had in mind—to contrast the heroic or sublime connotations of the quotation sharply with the mundane matter of the poem. In Gozzano's epigraph Petrarch is brought to mind, to contrast his passionate love of twenty-one years with the inability of Gozzano's protagonist even to love at all. The date which Felicita writes upon the wall, *"September the thirtieth, nineteen-o-seven",* may easily remind us of the dates which Petrarch included in his poems in order to stress the duration of his love for Laura. Apart from that, the incident in Gozzano is immediately qualified by the bathos of

> I didn't smile. Deep down inside I even
> enjoy romantic gestures straight from school.

And that is very like Eliot's

> I smile, of course,
> And go on drinking tea.

Eliot and Gozzano had not read each other, and there is no question of direct influence. What we have is an interesting manifestation of the Zeitgeist: Gozzano is clearly seen to resemble in important ways the poet who introduced modernism into England.

As again with Eliot, we cannot discuss Gozzano for long without mentioning his irony. Its most obvious function is to guard against sentimentality, or at least qualify the sentimentality once it appears:

> A lunar kiss, where clouds are brightening up,
> such as was à la mode some seventy
> years back!

It also has a wider function, in that it distances the speaker from what he is describing, and so underlines his half-humorous, wholly sad, detachment from the life around him:

> But now the Storm is rising on the sea,
> a very beautiful and stylised storm
> as shown in ancient paintings of the Flood.

Most important of all, the irony often consists in a sense, diffused throughout *The colloquies,* that everything is open to mockery:

> Towards nine or so there would assemble there,
> for cards, the entire illustrious faculty
> of local statesmen, viz. the Notary
> Public, the Doctor, and the honoured Mayor;
> but—since I was an absentminded player—
> those gentlemen did not think much of me . . .

> I found things were much pleasanter and cleaner
> among the brightly-coloured crockery . . .

Modernist poetry in England began with Imagism, and it has continued with images and still more images: the concrete is approved, the abstract frowned upon. The same tendencies are noticeable in Italian poetry. For all the value of Gozzano's discursiveness—and it is worth pointing out that, whatever the current fashion or our personal likes and dislikes, language has to move continually between both the concrete and the abstract, simply because that is how the human mind works—his least successful passages are those where abstract explanation is predominant, his most successful those which consist of sharp, usually visual, images.

> Look at your friends. How they already place
> their diverse faith in diverse schools of thought.
> Not you. You sneer. Now what does your grimace
> offer the anguished soul? What goal? What butt?
> The Homeland? God? Humanity? Words that
> the rhetoricians have made nauseous! . . .

That passage not only suggests the crisis of language and belief that lies behind modernist poetry, but—in its lack of particularity—it illustrates the very faults that modernists try to avoid. Gozzano is most successful when he allows the abstract meaning to emerge of its own accord from the concrete particulars, when he does not have to drag it out by the scruff of its neck. We remember all the "good things in the worst of taste" mentioned so lovingly and so memorably at the beginning of **"The friend of Grandmother Speranza"** and, among so many other instances, we remember the descriptions of the Vill'Amarena in **"La signorina Felicita"**:

> Sad uninhabited fine edifice!
> Big-bellied gratings rust away and writhe!
> Silence and stealth of rooms! Nothing alive!
> An odour of the past pervades the house!
> An odour of abandoned emptiness!
> Legends are fading on the architrave!

Gozzano frequently works, in what seems to be an authentic modernist way, by a piling-up of disparate images:

> Echoes prolong each footstep as it goes
> among such odds and ends of time gone by,
> and the Marchesa with the Grecian nose,
> high-waisted, seen beneath a pagan sky
> one bare foot in her hand, takes her repose
> umbrageous in a grot of Arcady.

> About her, smiling in her Grecian dress
> and Grecian dream, who came to die of hunger,
> there lay a tattered and promiscuous race:
> some furniture, some oil lamps, the odd hamper,
> mattresses, rats' nests, crockery: the lumber
> that since it is rejected charms my Muse!

Here, however, there is a qualification to be made. We never see in Gozzano the true "musée imaginaire" of modern art with

> every clime and age
> Jumbled together

for these images do not merely come together in the poet's

mind: they are quite naturally and realistically found together in an attic, whatever they may suggest also or sym-
bolise.

> *What's glory in an attic room alas?*

So it is quite possible—and in surveys of the history of
modern Italian poetry almost inevitable—to see Gozzano
as a poet who tried to be a modernist and almost succeeded. Yet that judgement may obscure a more important fact. It is not just the nineteenth-century expansiveness we admire, nor just the twentieth-century irony and
image-making, but rather the fact that they are found together under the same roof: and this is only one of many
contrasts.

The poems show, not so much shock-tactics, as a total
strategy of shock and contrast. There is a contrast between
the stylised expression, insistently literary and in the strictest of verse-forms, and the domestic and humdrum nature of the content. This is particularly obvious where the
contrast between life and art is itself the subject:

> What blessed spells of idleness, at noon
> in the ancestral park where some slight trace
> still lingered of the epoch that had gone!
> The Seasons—armless, broken-nosed, of course,
> knee-deep in dung and grapeskins—nonetheless
> looked over leeks and lettuce in disdain.

There is a related contrast between the past and the present—the present seen through the literary and artistic
spectacles of the past, the past seen with the loving but
judging eyes of the present. The movement most typical
of a Gozzano poem—found in **"Paul and Virginia", "La
signorina Felicita",** and **"The friend of Grandmother
Speranza"**—is from the present to the past and then back
again to the present. Characters in the poems are often
sharply contrasted: a poet-lawyer and a simple country
girl; a middle-aged woman and one who is scarcely more
than a child; an innocent little boy and a cocotte. This
constant use of glaring contrasts is the main reason why
I hesitate to describe Gozzano as a "crepuscolare": of no
poet could it less helpfully be said that

> A common greyness silvers everything,—
> All in a twilight . . .

In his poetry nothing is ever simply itself but always at the
same time something else:

> Then came the time for parting; truly bitter
> that parting from another century:
> ladies in crinolines, each hair in order,
>
> leaned out of gardens that appeal to me
> and, sobbing very loudly, waved goodbye
> to diligences making for the border . . .

The poet sees the present in terms of the past, he uses the
present to project himself into the past, and—most important—he sees present and past together in all their disparity.

In *The colloquies* the past is bound to send continual
shock-waves through the present, since the poems are full
of echoes of previous poets, particularly Dante and Petrarch. There is nothing accidental about this: Gozzano

kept notebooks in which he entered the passages he intended to use. He does not try to disguise his borrowings—he flaunts them. Where it is possible that an Italian
might not catch the echo, then Gozzano uses inverted
commas:

> Midnight was striking loud and long and high
> through that dear region which I do not name.
> I saw the moon above the bell-tower gleam
> out "like a dot upon a massive i".

De Musset is hardly an obscure poet, but Gozzano is taking no chances. Then the allusion may not always be specific, but it is always made obvious that there is an allusion:

> I wandered all around with my regret . . .
> and lingered by the cemetery-gate
> as people do in books of poetry.

How can we define the effect of this? It is as though the
protagonist of the poems, wandering through life with little but literature to guide him (and perhaps rather too
much of that), is again and again surprised to find that life
really is like literature: his map was right after all. Such
passages give us a pleasing gentle shock, for what we have
is a reversal of the usual process by which literature is
praised for being like life. Gozzano had, in Italian translation, read Oscar Wilde's "The Decay of Lying":

> At twilight nature becomes a wonderfully sug-
>   gestive
> effect, and is not without loveliness, though
> perhaps its chief use is to illustrate quotations
> from the poets.

In both writers, with humour predominating in Wilde and
sadness and alienation in Gozzano, there is a shrewd point
behind the dandyish affectation: to our perception, if not
in objective reality, nature does, as Wilde insists, imitate
art:

> Where, if not from the Impressionists, do we get
> those wonderful brown fogs that come creeping
>   down
> our streets, blurring the gas-lamps and changing
> the houses into monstrous shadows? . . . The
>   extraordinary
> change that has taken place in the climate of
>   London
> during the last ten years is entirely due to a
> particular school of Art.

The world of Gozzano's art is a solid and substantial one.
This is largely because, while the constituents of this world
often clash with each other, they do not fight to a finish.
Nothing is there simply to be denigrated, but to enhance
something else and in its turn to be enhanced. In the
Vill'Amarena we see, above an architrave,

> the flying Daphne as the god draws near
> transmuted into laurel, green for ever . . .

Then in the drawing-room we see

> tucked inside a looking-glass la Belle
> Otero on a postcard . . .

Both images are striking; but more striking than either
separately is their collocation.

The man I never am, but feign to be!

What is the relation between Gozzano and the protagonist of his poems? The question is bound to arise, whatever artistic distortion we allow for, simply because the two clearly have so much in common. Against a background familiar to Gozzano—the famous park in Turin, the Valentino, for instance, or the Canavese with the town of Ivrea and the River Dora—we see a protagonist who is a poet, and a tubercular one too, with an interest in insects, especially butterflies, and seen sometimes with a woman reminiscent of Amalia Guglielminetti to whom so many of the letters are addressed. . . .

The poems show, not so much shock-tactics, as a total strategy of shock and contrast. There is a contrast between the stylised expression, insistently literary and in the strictest of verse-forms, and the domestic and humdrum nature of the content. This is particularly obvious where the contrast between life and art is itself the subject.

—J. G. Nichols

An autobiographical approach to the poems can at times be misleading or reductive. We have to allow for a certain licence, as when the protagonist (as in **"La signorina Felicita"**) is a lawyer, while Gozzano himself never managed to qualify. Then there seems no doubt, for instance, that the "almighty youngster, square-shouldered, broad of chest" of **"Survival of the fittest"** is Guido's younger brother, Renato, and the speaker of the poem, who is dying, is readily identifiable with Guido himself. However, the poem is quite clear without any such information, and its significance is wider than such a narrow reading might suggest.

What matters most is that Gozzano is so often at pains both to identify his protagonist with himself and at the same time distinguish his protagonist from himself: with his usual engaging frankness, he tells us that a kind of alter ego is involved. That is why his irony and detachment are so thorough-going: they are not merely stylistic features but symptoms of the deepest psychology of the poems: "I have to smile to see myself alive." The detachment is such that the poems sometimes move between the first person and the third:

These *Colloquies* . . . Now sound of body and
    mind,
he groups his verses and he alters them,
weighing the manuscript with even hand.

—A bit of fun with syllables and rhyme:
is this what stays of my so fleeting spring?
Is it all really here, my youthful prime?

*The villa appears to be taken from certain verses
    of mine*

Il Meleto, the villa where Gozzano spent so much of his time and which was one of the sources for the Vill'Amarena, has of recent years been carefully restored, furnished with relics of the poet, and opened to visitors. It is easy to see how the poetry could inspire such a proceeding; but it would be a mistake to read the poetry merely (or mainly) in order to gain a picture of life in Turin and its environs in the early years of this century along with a realistic portrait of its inhabitants. No, *The colloquies* form their own world, a world of words which—while they must, as words always must, refer to matters outside themselves—also refer continually, and very interestingly, to each other.

The opening poem of the book not only has the same title as the book, but also has the book for its theme, as does the concluding poem, which repeats the title once more; the protagonist of **"In the survivor's home"** is identified with Totò Merùmeni; lines from **"In the survivor's home"** are used as the epigraph to the first poem of the book, and referred to again at the end of **"Banquet"**; **"Paul and Virginia"** quotes itself for epigraph; and we could go on and on. The result is such an artistic coherence that—whatever Gozzano was "really" like—he has achieved his aim:

As for my image, I want it to stay
twenty, as in a portrait, never altered . . .

He has made himself like one of his favourite old prints:

The silent poet hardly glances up,
happy to find himself in such a group
with all the sadness of an old engraving.

This self-consciousness, self-obsession, self-quotation may at times be rather precious: one can see the force of Amalia Guglielminetti's shrewd comment on **"Paul and Virginia"**: " . . . that poem is written with the most subtle artistry, which scholars will certainly enjoy; but it is a virtuoso performance, and it has the coldness of mere virtuosity." One can see the force of this and still believe that **"Paul and Virginia"** is the best of the poems after **"La signorina Felicita"**. To those who argue that poetry's prime function is to communicate experience of life one can reply that literature and art are a part of life, and—in these poems—the ostentatious literariness and artiness of the protagonist are an important, and attractive, feature of the portrait of him which the book as a whole presents:

But now the Storm is rising on the sea,
a very beautiful and stylised storm
as shown in ancient paintings of the Flood.

Memories are important in *The colloquies.* Often the things remembered are themselves reminiscent of something else, so that the reader—who, after all, is now as distant in time from Gozzano as he was from Carlotta or Speranza or Massimo d'Azeglio—feels he is being moved further and further into the past:

You seemed a lady weeping, in some frantic
lyric of Prati's, someone on his way
to undiscovered isles in the Atlantic . . .

To balance Amalia Guglielminetti's strictures on **"Paul and Virginia"** it may be pointed out that nostalgia—the attraction of what is either temporally or spatially out of reach—is at the heart of Gozzano's poetry, and nostalgia always has a wide appeal.

Peter Hainsworth   (essay date 1991)

SOURCE: "Gozzano's Voices: A Reading of 'Totò Merùmeni'," in *The Modern Language Review,* Vol. 86, Part 4, October, 1991, pp. 852-66.

[*In the following essay, Hainsworth explicates "Totò Merùmeni," particularly focusing on Gozzano's borrowings from other poets.*]

If, instead of restricting ourselves to *I colloqui* and to various texts that are consonant with it (some of the uncollected poems, parts of *La via del rifugio,* parts of *Le farfalle,* some novelle), we look at the writings of Guido Gozzano as a whole, we are as likely to be struck by their heterogeneity as by features which they have in common. Gozzano is not always playful or ironic: witness the letters or, in a different way, *Verso la cuna del mondo.* Indeed, sometimes he is Christian: witness his last work, the film script on the life of St Francis, or, to go back to the years before *I colloqui,* the essay of 1905 on spirituality, [collected in *Poesie e prose,* edited by Alberto de Marchi, 1961], 'Il misticismo moderno e la rievocazione del passato'. And of course within the three canonical collections, the stylistic and thematic disparity between *I colloqui* and *Le farfalle* is blatant, and not to be explained as a progression from one stage of life and writing to another (as the concluding poems of *I colloqui* might be taken to suggest), since it has now been clearly established that Gozzano was working on both collections at the same time. Some of *Le farfalle* come later, but the overlaps are at least as extensive.

Up to a point there is nothing particularly remarkable in all of this. Almost all of Gozzano's work belongs to the last ten years of his life. It would be a blinkered view which did not allow for contradiction or diversity within that quite short span of time, or for the recurrence of what had apparently been rejected or surpassed at an earlier moment. At the same time it is remarkable how Gozzano shapes the image of himself in different ways in different works, how he changes the voice with which he speaks. We can readily identify a quest on his part for authentic self-expression and self-definition. But what is more noticeable is how he consciously works on partial self-realization, elaborating each one almost as a separate whole, though, in his more finished literary enterprises, often including allusions to what has been omitted. Partly because the objectification of the self is so intense, there is little sense of experimentation in his work but rather of authorial control and construction at every stage. If, when we pass to his most important poetry, this aspect of his work leads us to take too literally Montale's characterization of him [in *Gozzano dopo trent'anni,* 1951] as 'l' ultimo dei nostri classici' and imagine Gozzano the artist finding or creating a kind of Olympian detachment in the individual artefact, whether poem or story, it is also hard not to be aware of an aura of provisionality, of uncertainty. Any one voice is less something that seems natural at that particular moment or in that particular context than a composite in which the writer identifies and simultaneously disavows himself.

In this process of self-creation and self-denial other figurations of the self inevitably have their part to play. The Gozzano projected in *I colloqui* has written *La via del rifugio* and will write *Le farfalle.* But, though he acknowledges it less, he is also a reader and a user of other poets, who enter his own work as alternately disturbing and helpful forces in the struggle to self-definition. As his notebooks demonstrate, Gozzano (the author) was a committed collector of other men's flowers, many of which were then incorporated, often in recognizable form, in his own verse. Quite how extensive these 'borrowings' are is only now coming to be acknowledged and thoroughly charted. What is perhaps less recognized is how they are integral to the poems in which they appear, a weaving into their very fabric of the issue of self-expression. Far from being pointers to imaginative inadequacy, the appropriation of others' words proves to be the necessary means to authentic selfhood, albeit in the key of irony. When Gozzano speaks directly in his own voice (the letters are the signal example) the risk is cliché, the falling prey to the trivialized formulae belonging to everyone and to no one. When he takes hold of the words of others and reworks them in ways that acknowledge difference and similarity, then the abyss of inauthenticity is avoided if not transcended. How difficult it is to take the further step and pass beyond irony by appropriating others' words is demonstrated by substantial parts of *La farfalle,* in which the combination of Dante and Maeterlinck on the one hand and the rejection for the most part of the thematic of the self leads not to a new poetic vitality but to inertia.

The perspective on Gozzano which I have just sketched out owes a great deal to recent studies of his work without having been formulated in these terms in any of them. What follows is an attempt to justify it and to explore it further through an examination of **'Totò Merùmeni'**. This is the poem which introduces the third section, **'Il reduce'**, of *I colloqui.* It is a poem which has been regularly discussed in broad terms in studies of Gozzano, but it seems to me that it merits more detailed attention, partly in view of its general implications but also because of its particular importance within the collection. . . .

I colloqui was published in February 1911. **'Totò Merùmeni'** was probably one of the later poems to be written. Though it is unlikely, it is conceivable that it goes back to 1908, when Gozzano was twenty-five, as he presents himself as being throughout the collection, and as he states explicitly is the age of Totò. The poem was published twice in reviews, oddly enough after the collection appeared, first together with **'Verso la fede'** (= **'Pioggia d'agosto'**) in *La Tribuna* of 22 February 1911, and then with **'Le non godute'** in *La rivista ligure* of April 1911. In the latter it was dated 20 October 1910. Whilst it seems extremely unlikely that the poem was written in one day, it seems probable that it was composed, or at least completed, about that time, in view of the related letter to the editor of *Il momento* to which I shall turn shortly.

At all events, in a fairly banal sense, Totò and Guido are one and the same. After a misspent youth Totò, the twenty-five-year-old poet, has returned to the decaying family villa in the countryside, where he lives with his infirm and aged relatives, filling his time with trivial pastimes and pleasures, writing a few poems, meditating on his own life and on life in general, and looking forward to something more positive occurring before he dies. Without expecting a detailed correspondence, we can find enough of Guido in all of this—the Guido who had written and published *La via del rifugio* and was still writing, who was spending long periods at the family villa at Agliè, whose mother was indeed suffering from the illness that would eventually kill her. Letters of 1908 and thereabouts show something like the same state of mind, most noticeably a letter to Amalia Guglielminetti of 30 March 1908 [collected in *Poesie e Prose*, edited by Alberto de Marchi], in which he stresses his emotional aridity, his inability to feel real love, and yet also the strength of his sensuality. But the really striking parallel is with the letter, dated 22 October 1910, that is, two days after the date given for the poem in *La rivista ligure*, a letter which Guido wrote in reply to a questionnaire sent out from *Il momento* to various writers. The letter takes its start from *I colloqui,* which Gozzano sees as having a distinct autobiographical aspect. 'La raccolta adunerà il men peggio delle mie liriche edite e inedite e sarà come una sintesi della mia prima giovinezza, un riflesso pallido del mio dramma interiore' [*Poesie e prose*]. Gozzano then identifies the three sections into which the collection is divided. Of the third he writes:

> III—Il Reduce: 'reduce dall'Amore e dalla Morte, gli hanno mentito le due cose belle' e rifletterà l'animo di chi superato ogni guaio fisico e morale, si rassegna alla vita sorridendo.

The quotation is from '**In casa del sopravissuto**', a poem closely connected with '**Totò Merùmeni**'. But the phrasing and the state of mind of the second part of the sentence corresponds more specifically to the last section of the latter. The correspondences continue; a little later Gozzano writes:

> Io ho fatto—come ho saputo—i versi: ora che li sto adunando posso forse notare nel loro insieme una tendenza che mi compensa delle mie fatiche e mi consola: l'ascensione dalla tristezza sensuale all'idealismo più sereno.

> Oggi credo nello spirito, sento, intendo in me la vita dello spirito. Da quella troppo bene accolta 'Via del Rifugio', peccante qua e là di ingenuo materialismo, la mia fede si è elevata in questi 'Colloqui' a speculazioni più pure e più consolanti.

In fact it is hard to see this new-found spirituality in the collection as a whole, except as a project in some of the poems of '**Il reduce**'. But there is a clear connexion with '**Totò Merùmeni**', being clearly echoed here ('Chiuso in sè stesso, medita, s'accresce, esplora, intende / la vita dello Spirito che non intese prima').

All the same there is a difference of emphasis and tone. The letter goes on to sketch out a spiritual rebirth in much more positive and general terms than those used in the conclusion of the poem. Positivism has been transcended, and so too have the philosophers, who in its wake denied the force of the spirit. As in the poem, Nietzsche is mentioned by name, but, assuming that the discredited reading 'desidera' is not to be restored in place of 'derideva' in line 30, in much more dismissive terms:

> Lo stesso Nietzsche, lo stesso Schopenhauer—cito due fra i più gloriosi banditori della materia e dell'istinto—non s'avvidero che, negandolo, esaltavano lo spirito. L'idealità balza dal canto stesso di chi la rinnega e chi la rinnega è come uno che canti e che si prema gli orecchi per non udire la propria voce.

The letter ends with a Christian affirmation which it would be difficult to find in the poem or, indeed, anywhere else in *I colloqui*:

> Ultimo punto: la necessità della moralizzazione cristiana. Credo fermamente anche in questo, ma non so distinguere morale e cristianesimo. La vera morale non può non coincidere in tutto con l'insegnamento del Cristo.

So the figure of Totò Merùmeni has correspondences with the life of Guido Gozzano. We might say it has its basis in his experience and in his state of mind at what was probably its time of composition. At the same time it is clear that there are differences of a substantial nature. The self of the poem has been shaped in a way that largely conforms with *I colloqui* as a whole and in particular with the rest of the concluding section. The same persona, caught between rueful retrospection and anticipation of a change of spiritual direction, reappears in various poems, the positives being particularly accented in '**Pioggia d'agosto**'. With some poems there are more precise parallels. For instance, '**Un'altra risorta**', amongst various verbal and thematic echoes, depicts the family situation in almost the same words: 'Vivo in campagna, con una prozia, / la madre inferma ed uno zio demente', and '**In casa del sopravissuto**' fills out the picture of the monkey, Makakita, who in '**Totò Merùmeni**' is little more than a name. The poem is thus closely bound up with the section which it introduces. All the same, in some ways it is unique, even if it looks forward and simultaneously (in its allusions to spiritual renewal) marks something of a break with the two preceding sections. Ironic detachment from representations of the self is, of course, the keynote of *I colloqui* as a whole. But in all the poems, except for '**Totò Merùmeni**' and '**In casa del sopravissuto**', Gozzano none the less writes of himself in the first person. In '**Totò**' he uses, for the most part, a third-person persona, to which he gives a name which he does not use elsewhere. From this point of view the poem is the extreme example of detachment from the self in the entire collection, a *ne plus ultra* from which the poems that follow recoil.

The name is, of course, not randomly chosen. Indeed, encapsulated in it is a procedure which in various different guises runs through the whole poem. The source is not so much Terence as Baudelaire's 'L'Héautontimorouménos', which Gozzano has deformed in a grotesque or perhaps childish way. What is suggested in this deformation is an allusion to Baudelaire's poem, indicating simultaneously comparison and contrast. This is borne out by the poem as a whole. Totò suffers from the same excessive self-awareness and its resultant aridity as does Baudelaire. But he is obviously no tragic or Romantic hero. Baudelaire writes of his irony as if it were damnation ('Ne suis-je pas un faux accord, / Dans la divine symphonie, / Grâce à la vorace Ironie / Qui me secoue et qui me mord?') and concludes his poem with a grandly melodramatic paradox: 'Je suis de mon coeur le vampire, /—Un de ces grands abandonnés / Au rire éternel condamnés, / Et qui ne peuvent le plus sourire!' Gozzano is much more low-key and much more ironic in his actual tone. But the most notable difference is in the ending. Totò smiles ('sorride') and looks forward to something better. So Baudelaire (and with him the figure of the Romantic hero damned to impotent mirth or its lack, canonically represented in Italian by the Leopardi of the concluding lines of 'Aspasia': 'E conforto e vendetta è che su l'erba / Qui neghittoso immobile giacendo, / Il mar la terra e il ciel miro e sorrido') is evoked and simultaneously denied. Totò Merùmeni is and is not 'L'Héauton-timorouménos', just as he is and is not Guido Gozzano.

This is the general pattern at its simplest. In the course of the poem Gozzano alludes, with varying degrees of explicitness, to a succession of other texts. With the one important exception of Petrarch (or a part of Petrarch), all these texts evoke figurations of the self which are both comparable and different as far as his own self is concerned. They become thus the measure by which the self is assessed and the means by which it defines itself, as well as the means of reaching out beyond the individual self of Gozzano into the larger discourse of the self in poetry in both its absolute and its historical dimensions. Inevitably the other texts have both benign and threatening aspects. They may allow the self of the author to come into focus, may support it in some way against the perils of ostensibly direct statement, but they also threaten to absorb, to subordinate, to deny the very birth of the self which they were evoked to assist. Baudelaire and the Romantic Tradition can be relatively easily managed: it is what has happened since Baudelaire that is more difficult to handle.

For Gozzano the visionary and absolutist path of Rimbaud and Mallarmé is irrelevant. The poets who matter (who, to use a dangerously bland term, are most congenial to him) are those who are usually roughly grouped together as the second generation of symbolists: Francis Jammes, Sully Prudhomme, Francis Vielé-Griffin, and others, whose work he first came to know through the anthology of Van Bever and Léautaud, *Poètes d'aujourd'hui,* first published in 1900. Of these the most important for him was undoubtedly Jammes (1868-1938), whose first collection, *De l'angélus de l'aube à l'angélus du soir,* had appeared in 1898 and whose popularity was at its height in the first decade or so of the twentieth century. Gozzano never discusses or refers explicitly to Jammes (or any other of these poets), though his notebooks contain a quite remarkable number of echoes or adaptations of particular lines. For the late twentieth-century reader of European poetry Jammes may be little more than a name. For Gozzano's contemporaries he was a definite presence, so much so that it could be suggested that Gozzano was a Piedmontese version of the poet of Orthez. Whilst most readers dis-

agreed from the very beginning, undoubtedly Gozzano drew heavily on Jammes and in a way which he found impossible to acknowledge, for the persona and manner of Jammes were all too close to his own manner and persona in *I colloqui.* Jammes may touch sentimental or *faux-naif* chords which Gozzano eschews, may be different in other ways (he is more overtly Catholic, more pastoral, more verbose), but the similarities are equally noticeable. Most important is a general feature: the concern to combine prosaic content and diction with (more or less) regular poetic forms. But there is also the ironic detachment from the self which Jammes displays in spite of his religious sensibility, his eroticism, his nostalgia for childhood and for other pasts which have been lost, his sense of a local habitation, of names that evoke a whole provincial world of which he is part and yet from which he has been separated. Obviously not all of the Gozzano of *I colloqui* is here, and the emphases are in any case frequently different, but there are enough points of contact for us to recognize how powerful an attraction the French poet exercised. We may surmise that in one way the results were patently beneficial: Jammisme was a means of escape from d'Annunzianism. At the same time it exposed Gozzano to all the risks I discussed in the previous paragraph, with no doubt the added dimension of sacrificing the independence of the Italian tradition to French dominance: in this specific instance, to dominance by a manner which may have had justifiable appeal, but which could not be accounted great poetry by the standards to which late nineteenth-century Italian poetry habitually aspired.

'Totò Merùmeni' not only strikes a Jammiste note, and mimics phrases from various Jammes poems, but also, unlike any other poem by Gozzano, takes one particular poem by Jammes as its principal subtext, with some noteworthy contamination from another. The poem in question is 'Il s'occupe' from *De l'angélus.* Its thirty-five more or less imperfectly rhymed and calculatedly prosaic alexandrines portray a lawyer who has returned home to the gloomy and decaying family house in the country, after compromising adventures in Paris. There he fills his time looking after his land in a bored and inefficient sort of way. He helps out illiterate peasants: 'Parfois on lui porte un acte notarié, / un paysan, pour savoir comment être payé'. He has an empty affair with the maid: 'Il nettoie son fusil et couche avec la bonne'. But basically his life has no meaning: hence the conclusion, which furnishes Gozzano with his conclusion too: 'Il vit ainsi doucement, sans savoir pourquoi. / Il est né un jour. Un autre jour il mourra'.

Gozzano's 'Un giorno è nato. Un giorno morirà' is his most striking appropriation from Jammes in the whole poem. All the same Totò Merùmeni is obviously not a lawyer, not least in beginning to understand in the final section of the poem where the lawyer does not, though it may be that the impulse to the comic name comes from the lines 'Que c'est triste, que c'est triste, / ce temps où on se nommait Evariste'. Other texts have interfered. One of the most important is 'Jean de Noarrieu', a long narrative poem, which appeared in the 1902 collection, *Le triomphe de la vie,* which itself reads like an outgrowth of 'Il s'occupe'. Jean is a thirty-year-old wastrel who has withdrawn into the country after squandering his fortune. He now lives alone in his large house, except for his pretty seventeen-year-old servant, Lucy, with whom he sleeps. The narrative development is different (the girl is eventually married off and the poem ends with Jean looking for a replacement), but here is the specific origin of the cook-and-master situation of Gozzano's poem. Indeed, the same phrasing is used: Lucy 'le baise à la bouche', just as the girl 'lo bacia in bocca'.

If these two poems provide substantial underpinning, other more scattered echoes are also discernible. The 'villa triste' of the opening owes something to the evocation of the 'vieille maison triste' of 'J'ai été' (*De l'angélus*). The list of Piedmontese families who used to come on visits in better days parallels a similar list in 'Il y a par là' (*De l'angélus*). ('On annonçait les Perceval, le Demonville, / qui arrivait, dans les voitures, de la ville'). This poem also opens with the image of an abandoned house in which the flowers run riot, which is compared, moreover, to the poet's heart in a way that corresponds to Section IV of **'Totò Merùmeni'**, though the actual image of the burnt-out house is more Baudelairian than Jammiste. Totò's cook is 'fresca come una prugna': in his 'Prière pour avoir une femme simple' (in *Le deuil des primevères* of 1900), Jammes had prayed that 'que sa chair soit plus lisse et plus tiède et dorée / que la prune qui dort au declin de l'été'. Jammes even has a poem expressing an ambiguous attitude towards Nietzsche, 'Il m'ont dit' (*Le deuil des primevères*), in which, as Gozzano does in lines 30-31 of **'Totò Merùmeni'**, he has the name in rhyming position, though, noticeably enough, his rhyme is very imperfect (Nietzsche/m'ennuie) compared to Gozzano's (Nietzsche/dice). There is one other imperfect rhyme in **'Totò Merùmeni'** (Ansaldo/sobbalzando). But generally in this poem as elsewhere, Gozzano regularizes his rhymes and his metre where, no doubt as part of his anti-poetic stance, Jammes is happy to be loosely assonantal and metrically irregular.

As this last point suggests, Gozzano is not Jammes, just as Totò Merùmeni is not the lawyer of 'Il s'occupe' or Jean de Noarrieu. Rather, in these two poems Gozzano saw a way in which to represent himself from the outside, quite unlike Jammes, who does not represent himself directly in either poem (though in fact in Jean de Noarrieu he has created a figure with some autobiographical features). As for the more specific appropriations, Gozzano here is following his common practice of incorporating elements scattered throughout the source texts into one single discourse. In the case of Jammes the source texts retain their identity to a surprising degree. At the other extreme is Petrarch, whose presence, at least as far as the most notable appropriations are concerned, is much more submerged.

Just as Gozzano copied out line after line of the French poets in his notebooks, so he made collections of lines of Petrarch and Dante, working in the case of Petrarch from the Carducci—Ferrari edition which he acquired in 1908. In the case of **'Totò Merùmeni'** the work-book published by Rocca in 1977 contains drafts, in more or less their final form, though not in their final order, of stanzas from Parts III, IV, and V of the poem, immediately followed by some

lines from the *Canzoniere*. These in turn are followed after line 17 by lines which are not by Petrarch, though they are Petrarchan in tone, and then by what will become the rhymes of lines 53 and 55 of the poem, with the opening of line 56.

> ond'io gridai con carta e con inchiostro
> so ben io che a voler chiuder in versi
> sia la mia vita ch'è celata altrui
> ma, mentre che parlo, il Tempo fugge
> —dopo i perduti giorni, dopo le notti
> —vaneggiando spese
> —perché la vita è breve
> una dolcezza inusitata e nuova
> —si chiusamente
> il sempre sospirar nulla rileva
> Dei passati miei danni piango e rido
> del presente mi godo e meglio aspetto
> nè del vulgo mi cale nè di fortuna
> Io per me sono un'ombra
> e vivo e il viver più non m'è molesto
>
> Sono per me come persone
> fu la sua vita un fuggire continuo
> vedo gli amici
> vicende—rima
> intende la vita dello spirito

What is remarkable is that the lines from Petrarch, taken together, seem to represent the state of mind represented in the last section of the poem. But it is even more remarkable to see how many of Petrarch's words, phrases, and cadences have actually been incorporated, with greater or lesser adjustments, into the final version of these lines. Line 4 = line 58 ('perché il Tempo—mentre ch'io parlo! va'): line 7 = line 57 ('Perché la voce è poca'): line 12 = line 59 ('e meglio aspetta'): line 15 = line 60 ('E vive'). And another line copied out on a different but nearby page ('E così riste standomi in disparte') provides one further phrase, 'in disparte' of line 59.

Gozzano's manner of composition here is that of the most consummate Petrarchist of the Cinquecento. Direct expression is completely disallowed: instead there is intarsio, mosaic, interestingly enough with phrases which in themselves are mostly not striking and which certainly do not reveal themselves readily as Petrarchan to the reader who has not been alerted to them. Yet as I have already indicated, Petrarch is not the only presence in these last lines. There is also Baudelaire (or Baudelaire and Leopardi) and Jammes. Indeed, the conclusion of the poem is almost entirely composite: 'Totò opra in disparte (Petrarch), sorride (Baudelaire/Leopardi), e meglio aspetta. (Petrarch) / E vive. (Petrarch) Un giorno è nato. Un giorno morirà' (Jammes).

We shall gain a better understanding of what is at stake in the last few lines of the poem if we see them in their formal and thematic relation to the struggle for self-articulation and self-definition which has occupied the poem from its very beginning. In this complex process, which occurs with varying degrees of overlap and mutual contamination, Baudelaire, Petrarch, and Jammes are probably the most important external voices, but they are by no means alone, as the opening of the poem shows.

The first voice to be evoked is that of the earlier Gozzano.

The 'certi versi miei' are not so much generic as an allusion to **'I sonetti del ritorno'** in **La via del rifugio,** which are concerned with a similarly decayed paternal home, with lines such as 'delle panciute grate secentiste / il cemento si sgretola', or 'O casa fra l'agreste e il gentilizio / coronata di glicini leggiadre'. These sonnets, like **'Totò Merùmeni',** are also concerned with loss as well as with return. But if Gozzano suggests an identity between the author of those sonnets and his present self, he also suggests difference. The villa is now a *topos:* it is the 'villa-tipo, del Libro di Lettura'. It has lost its poetic vitality: the old Gozzano does not function poetically any more. But the 'I' who is speaking now is left undefined, except as being different from what he was.

The remainder of Part I amplifies and develops these initial negatives. The sonnets already had a Jammiste tone and Gozzano now makes the Jammisme here more explicit, though the nostalgia of the second and third stanzas has a slight air of poetic falsication, thanks to the personification of the 'villa triste'. The authenticity is in fact no greater than it had been initially. But then the voice of Jammes is rudely counteracted by modernity in the shape of the 'automobile' of line 11. A brutal realism is fleetingly evoked, though it is simultaneously overlaid: the car becomes a mechanical beast ('fremendo e sobbalzando') in the manner of early Futurist or d'Annunzian representations, the d'Annunzian aura being accentuated in the following line. The 'villosi forestieri' may be either hairy (this is the sense in which Gozzano uses the word of his *farfalle*) or, as is Sanguineti's *lectio facilior,* clad in furs. Either way they are threateningly exotic, as is the liberty knocker in the shape of a Gorgon (an equally unusual sense for 'gorgòne') on which they beat. Whatever the precise sense of line 12 (and it is the most metaphorical and most obscure in the whole poem), the distaste is evident. Linguistic glamour is not the answer either.

But leave the glamour outside, enter the gloom of what is no longer a villa but a cross between a cloister and a barracks, and we meet emptiness, silence, decay. The name, Totò Merùmeni, which is now introduced, may be a grotesque childish deformation, but any humour that the name may connote is immediately subverted. Deformation is represented in veristic vein, without metaphorical overlay or personification of the inanimate, in the raddled humanity of the three figures: the mother, the great-aunt, and the uncle. This, the culmination of the section, is the denial of 'poesia': the opening of the door has revealed a 'prosa' of isolation, illness, madness, senescence.

Part II is a reworking of Part I, with variations and inversions: there is also a change of key from the bleakly pessimistic to the ruefully reflective, a playful note also creeping in through the prominent repetitions of words and phrases as well as through the imagery with which the section ends. The first stanza may or may not echo specifically de Musset's title *Memoires d'un enfant du siècle* or the figure of Egaeus in Poe's story 'Berenice', which Gozzano had read in Baudelaire's translation. The important thing is that Totò is presented as a topical figure, the decadent young poet of countless late nineteenth-century novels and poems, a stereotype corresponding to the 'villa-tipo'

of the opening, and on the face of it one that is equally unpromising for any future development.

Just as now, in contrast with the greater part of the opening section, the poem has shifted from personified objects to an explicitly human dimension, so now it elucidates some of its literary points of reference. The first is Petrarch, with an explicit citing of *Rerum vulgarium fragmenta* 360, where Love is made to say of Petrarch: 'Questi in sua prima età fu dato a l'arte di vender parolette, anzi menzogne.' The actual mention of Petrarch's name is, of course, self-deflating: Gozzano or Totò is not Petrarch, and the question of whether he can say that he has somehow a special Petrarch that he has made his own is at this stage quite open: the more so, because, if we probe a little, we can find other names emerging. Some of them jostle behind this very phrase, 'il suo Petrarca!', which again goes back to **'I sonetti del ritorno'**: in 3, line 9, referring to his grandfather's favourite authors, Gozzano had had the line 'il *tuo* Manzoni . . . Prati . . . Metastasio'. A past self and a whole past tradition are in the air but at this point in an ungraspable way, as is indicated by the transition in the remaining two lines of the stanza to a rather grandiloquent representation of Totò as Dante. Like the impossibly great *fons et origo,* Totò has chosen exile, and now thinks back on his misdemeanours, which he characterizes in a phrase ('che sarà bello tacere') that echoes *Inferno,* 4.104, 'parlando cose che 'l tacere è bello'. This line relates to Dante's conversation with 'la bella scuola': what hope has Totò or Gozzano of anything of the kind?

The temporary solution to the impasse is a return to the present and the more recent past for a characterization of Totò in more humble, but largely negative terms. 'Non è cattivo' in line 25, and repeated in the identical position in lines 27 and 29, returns once again to the apparently superseded world of **La via del rifugio,** this time to the fourth section of **'Un rimorso'** 'Avevo un cattivo sorriso: / eppure non sono cattivo, // non sono cattivo, se qui / mi piange nel cuore disfatto / la voce: ("Che male t'ho fatto / o Guido per farmi così? ").' With this reversion comes the reversion to the Jammes of 'Il s'occupe': the mode of the opening section is, it seems, only to be repeated. Totò is inoffensive but weak: so, too, poetically speaking, is Gozzano. The weakness is now made ironically explicit. All that he can do is name Nietzsche in Jammiste fashion and (as he has already briefly done with the words of Petrarch a little earlier) cite his words directly, the quotation being from the chapter 'On Those who are Sublime' in Book II of *Also sprach Zarathrustra* ('Verily I have often laughed at the weaklings who thought themselves good because they had no claws'). The poetic art is limited to translation, to fitting into Italian rhyme the difficult German name in a way that surpasses Jammes.

There is a small advance here. Things are now out in the open. The last stanza looks back to the corresponding stanza of Part I with this in mind. Totò again has three companions, but they are now animals, not humans, and he plays with them outside the decaying house. Threat has been removed. Instead of horrors there is childishness, escape, a homely circus, though the full significance of Makakita as an image of lost exotic innocence will be decipherable only from **'In casa del sopravissuto'**. But, notably enough, two of the animals allude indirectly to poetic failure: the raucous jay and the ape may be carnivalesque in a small way, but they suggest anything but purity of song or originality.

Parts III and IV parallel each other as Parts I and II had done. Both reiterate the negative movements which have already occurred, but they also attempt to transform the negatives into positives, though it is only in Part IV that the transformation is tentatively carried through in what seems to be preparation for the conclusion to the whole poem.

Part III begins with more retrospection of the kind found at the beginning of the poem. This time the subject and the idiom regard the failure of d'Annunzian dreams of love. Again the present is Jammiste. In the image of the young cook and the comparison of her freshness to the freshness of a 'prugna' in the cool of the morning (both taken from Jammes), the poem strikes a note of natural sensual pleasure and vitality for the first and only time. But the positive is fleeting, illusory. Totò is passive; he is said to possess her. In fact it is more as if she possesses him, just as Gozzano has allowed himself to be, once again, possessed by the poetry of the French writer. The section ends on a note of distaste for the degrading pleasure which is being indulged.

Just as Part III opened by looking back to Part I, so Part IV looks back to the opening of Part II. This is the most Baudelairian moment of the poem, Totò being described here in ways that recall the persona not only of 'L'Héautontimorouménos' but also of the *Spleen* poems. But it is only by confronting and making explicit the fundamental aridity of the self that a more convincing positive can be made to emerge. The comparison of the self to a house may owe something to Jammes, but it is more important here that it is made plain that it *is* a comparison, in contrast to the image of the pseudo-poetic and highly Jammiste 'villa triste' of the opening, in which the human and the animate were elided. Here they have been analysed in a way that corresponds to the 'analisi' practised by Totò himself. And from this destructive analysis growth is made to come. Where the natural sensuality of Part III had been corroded, because it was, fundamentally, unnatural, here destruction is the necessary prelude to the emergence of flowers whose colour and vitality is unquestioned. There is an air of Baudelairian perversion to the gladioli which emerge from the burnt-out ruins, but the final result is an assertion of the poetic being achieved. Gozzano has continued in the analytic form of the simile in lines 49-50. Now in lines 51-52 he synthesizes through metaphor and yet makes plain what the metaphor refers to: the flowers are the poems (this poem?) which he is writing. What is worn out, inert, is being made to speak, if in that insubstantial way.

So we arrive at Part V. Discursively its two stanzas elaborate on the last line of Part IV, and transpose its poetic implications into a more spiritual key. Totò writes poetry, and he also continues his investigations, now seen as enriching, not destructive. With this comes the exit from the Baudelairian and Jammiste impasse: he is content, he

smiles, he is hopeful and alive. But the work of poetic renewal is also extended. There is, first and foremost, a solution to the problems raised in Part II. There the difference between Totò and Petrarch had been highlighted. Here, as I argued above, Petrarch (or a part of Petrarch) has been assimilated. Gozzano has now found 'il suo Petrarca'. Then various negatives from the first section are also recast in a positive light. The 'chiostro' had already dimly anticipated the tone of the conclusion. Other correspondences are more precise. The villa 'pensa migliori giorni', that is, in the past; Totò 'meglio aspetta' in the future. The 'villa triste' itself has been transmuted into the 'tristi vicende' which can now be assumed to be in the past where they belong (the syllable 'vi' is a powerful formal and semantic motif in the poem as a whole). The 'sala da pranzo immensa' has grown into 'l'arte prediletta / immensa'. And the 'vive' which opens line 15 now opens the last line, with quite different connotations: from living death Totò Merùmeni (the full name making here its second and final appearance, here preceding 'vive' where in Part I it followed) has passed to a much more positive attitude to life, although the opening into his world ('si schiude cautamente / la porta') has become closure again ('Chiuso in sé stesso'). Whilst obviously this must inevitably happen again at the end of a poem, now the closure conceals active exploration and enquiry.

At the same time a question-mark hovers over this apparent resolution of the difficulties which the poem has raised. In his letter to *Il momento* Gozzano states what he says here and amplify the positives without a trace of irony. Here an ironic tone remains. Just as at the beginning he had separated himself as author of 'certi versi miei' from Totò, so he performs a similar separation at the end in the phrase 'mentre ch'io parlo'. Obviously the return to the opening, like the transmutations of other elements of Part I just mentioned, serves also to round the poem off in a formal sense. But there is also suggested an infringement of the wholeness which seemed to have been achieved: Totò is, as he has really been throughout the poem, an objectified version of the self, a form in which Gozzano can only partly speak because he also speaks of him, as well as in him.

All these tensions come together in the last line, to which I can now return. In some way, even on a fairly simple reading, it is a deflating line after the renewal which has been so strongly stressed in these two concluding stanza, as if Gozzano is not so much confronting the spiritual implications of a recognition of the passage of time as falling prey once again to a sense of the futility of life. Poetically the line marks a final return to the risks and terrors which have inhabited so much of it. From one point of view a synthesis has been achieved in this section. Much as Petrarch himself drew on a diversity of other texts in fragmentary form and harmonized them to produce his own voice, so Gozzano seems to have brought together his various fragments in a distinctive unity. But it is remarkable how Gozzano has chosen to clinch his poem with a line juxtaposing a phrase from Petrarch with a *sententia* from Jammes. The phrase from Petrarch may be perfectly assimilated, but the debt to Jammes is patent. In a dramatic acknowledgement of difference and conflict, the repressed, the name which could never be mentioned openly, has been allowed to return with a vengeance. The others (or the Other) with whom the poem has tussled throughout can, it seems, be only managed, not superseded. The move to the positive, as we perhaps have suspected since its first appearance in the penultimate section, has something willed to it. It remains a project, not something achieved. It appears that it is only in the projection of false voices, whose falseness is always recognized, that Gozzano can speak.

'Totò Merùmeni' is probably Gozzano's most troubled and complex poem: certainly it is more troubled and complex than the other poems of **'Il reduce'** which derive from it and which expand on its themes and procedures, returning frequently to Petrarch, though overall not sensing the problem of Jammes with anything like the same intensity. At the same time, it conceals its troubles behind formal control and perspicuousness of diction and imagery and, indeed, gives to its troubles to the very end a shaping role in its economy. In this respect it differs from a much better-known poem with which it is in other ways comparable, 'The Love Song of J. Alfred Prufrock', which was written only a few years later and which might be connected historically with Gozzano through Laforgue, to whom both he and Eliot were drawn. The very form and structure of Eliot's poem emphasize the discord and unease of his similarly grotesquely-named persona. But with Eliot (at least in this poem) there has been a decisive shift into a modernist aesthetic. Gozzano is more thoroughly ambiguous on every front, hovering between 'prosa' and 'poesia', between self-assertion and passivity, between classicism and expressionism, in every instance refusing to be caught in one of the opposing categories. That refusal (and the whole tenor of my analysis) may suggest that Gozzano is not, and cannot be, a 'strong' poet in the Bloomian sense, that he is to be kept firmly among the 'minori' where he has always been. Yet in this poem, if nowhere else to the same degree, he faces the issue of poetic weakness with outstanding constancy and in the very act of rejection of the solution which the poem projects shows himself stronger poetically than his own comments in his letter to *Il momento* allow. Self-affirmation can be weak. In the Italian tradition it is commonly, to use Eliot's famous phrase from a later poem than 'Prufrock', the 'familiar compound ghost' which has spoken from strength. Gozzano makes it speak again, whilst recognizing in the very act of articulation its fragility and otherness.

One further question remains. It may well seem that the reading of **'Totò Merùmeni'** which I have carried out is not warranted by the text as we read it in anthologies or in most published edition. Most readers will not, I think, have felt that the poem is 'difficult' or 'problematic'. It seems to me that its clarity is illusory. Individual parts of the poem may be lucid, but it is hard to find a coherence or rationale to its movement, as if something has been omitted, as perhaps the frequent use of dots at line-ends

suggests. To try to fill in those spaces may cancel some of that vagueness which may be thought necessary for poetic effects to occur. But the intelligence and the critical awareness which are apparent in the poem even on a fairly cursory reading of the bare text, propel us to look further, and the explicit references to at least some of the authors I have mentioned point us in certain directions. At all events, one set of problems remains: given that we can identify some at least of the echoes of other texts in the poem, given that we have Gozzano's notes, we can hardly help asking ourselves how this additional information affects our interpretation of the poem. What is known cannot be unknown and to relegate this information to some limbo of poetic archaeology is to attempt a repression which is bound to fail. What is discussed when we attempt to integrate it into our reading of the poem may ultimately be hypothetical, but it establishes and justifies connexions, makes sense, albeit a provisional one, of what is dispersed and inchoate, and increases (though it may not exhaust) our comprehension of that group of texts which for us is Guido Gozzano.

FURTHER READING

Biography

"A Return to Guido Gozzano: An Italian Poet Rediscovered." *Italy: Documents and Notes* XVII, No. 1 (January-February 1968): 55-60.

Sketch of Gozzano's life.

Criticism

Gerato, Erasmo Gabriele. *Guido Gustavo Gozzano: A Literary Interpretation.* Potomac, Md.: Studia Humanitatis, 1983, 132 p.

Brief biography and explications of Gozzano's major poetical works.

Montale, Eugenio. "Two Artists of Yesteryear." In his *The Second Life of Art: Selected Essays of Eugenio Montale*, edited and translated by Jonathan Galassi, pp. 234-38. New York: Ecco Press, 1982.

Notes affinities between Gozzano and Italian operatic composer Giacomo Puccini, stating that they shared "extraordinary plasticity . . . which allowed them to draw the lyrical from material that for others was only secondhand goods, small-time romanticism, folklore, and gossip."

Nims, John F. "Guido Gozzano (1883-1916)." In *The Poem Itself*, edited by Stanley Burnshaw, pp. 292-95. Cleveland: World Publishing Co., 1962.

Line-for-line translation and critical analysis of "Totò Merùmeni."

Additional coverage of Gozzano's life and career is contained in the following source published by Gale Research: *Dictionary of Literary Biography*, Vol. 114.

Ishikawa Takuboku

1886(?)-1912

(Born Ishikawa Hajime; also wrote under pseudonym of Ishikawa Hakuhin) Japanese poet, novelist, short story writer, essayist, and critic.

INTRODUCTION

Takuboku is acknowledged to be one of the most significant poets in modern Japanese literature. His most famous works fuse tanka form, a classic Japanese verse structure consisting of five lines and thirty-one syllables, with intellectual and autobiographical subject matter that was not previously considered acceptable for such a traditional poetic form. For this innovation and his variations on the tanka form, Takuboku is credited with revitalizing Japanese poetry and strongly influencing the work of many twentieth-century Japanese poets.

Biographical Information

Takuboku was born in rural northern Japan, the only son of a Zen priest who broke his vows and secretly married. Although his parents were quite poor, they were committed to providing Takuboku with the finest education they could afford. As a young student, Takuboku showed intellectual and literary ability. His aspirations to become a poet grew particularly strong in his adolescence and never subsided. As an apprentice poet, Takuboku greatly admired the works of Tekkan Yosano and the Romantic school to which Yosano belonged. He persistently submitted poems to Yosano's literary journal, *Myojo*, but met with no success. Finally in 1902 *Myojo* accepted one of Takuboku's poems for publication. With renewed confidence and conviction in his future as a poet, Takuboku quit school and moved to Tokyo, where he could study under Yosano. In 1905 he published his first volume of poetry, *Akogare* (*Longing*). In 1906 Takuboku's father disappeared after being dismissed from the Hōtoko Temple for misuse of temple funds, and to his son fell the responsibility of supporting the family. Takuboku left Tokyo and accepted a teaching position in a small village, but his meager income could not adequately provide for his wife, child, mother, and ailing older sister. They all lived close to starvation and steadily declined in health. Unable to cope with these pressures, Takuboku left his teaching post after one year and traveled around Japan, during which time he worked at a variety of jobs, mostly with newspapers and print shops, and continued to send money back to his family. As his life became increasingly filled with poverty and hardship, Takuboku came to believe that poetry, if it was to have lasting meaning and truth, must confront and include these less sublime facts of life. During the last two years of his life, he continued to work when circumstances and his health permitted. Over a span of approximately eighteen months his newborn child died, his

wife contracted tuberculosis, and he was operated on for a severe case of peritonitis. His aged and ailing mother nursed the family until she too collapsed and died of tuberculosis. Takuboku's last collection of poems, *Kanashiki gangu* (1912; *Sad Toys*), reached publication one week before he died of tuberculosis and was cremated in a pauper's funeral.

Major Works

Longing primarily comprises longer lyrical poems written in the "shintai-shi" ("new style"), a form derived from the well-established Western models of poetry found in an 1882 anthology that had considerable impact on Japanese writers of the day. The poems in *Longing* have a restrained but musical language and a romantic belief in heightened individualism and spiritual awareness. In *Ichiaku no suna* (1910; *A Handful of Sand*), which contains a type of poetry that Takuboku believed more earnest and vital than the shintai-shi verse he had previously written, he used the verbally spare and precise tanka form to describe the everyday events and impressions that he had come to believe are essential subjects for poetry. *A Handful of Sand* combines the pathos of life in the modern world with the formal simplicity of classic Japanese poetry—which heretofore was largely devoted to pastoral subject matter. *Sad Toys*, which mixes colloquial language with classical form, exhibits Takuboku's growing social and political awareness. In 1909 he had written a serialized essay entitled "Poems to Eat" that summarized his emerging conceptions of the highest intentions of poetry. In Takuboku's own words, true poetry is "poems written without putting any distance from actual life. They are not delicacies or dainty dishes, but food indispensable for us in our daily meals."

Critical Reception

Longing received enthusiastic praise but contained little of the fierce individual voice that Takuboku expressed in his subsequent volumes. *A Handful of Sand* is considered highly original, as Shio Sakanishi remarked in the introduction to this work: "Lifting it from anarchy and stiltedness, [Takuboku] again restored poetry to the human heart, extended its scope, and made language his willing servant." Critics feel that in *Sad Toys* Takuboku achieved the artistic and socialistic goals he had sought to attain, introducing unprecedented personalism and passion to Japanese poetry while removing verse from its elitist pedestal to be distributed to the masses.

PRINCIPAL WORKS

Poetry

Akogare [*Longing*] 1905
Ichiaku no suna [*A Handful of Sand*] 1910
Yobuko to kuchibue [*Whistles and Whistling*] 1911
Kanashiki gangu [*Sad Toys*] 1912
The Poetry of Ishikawa Takuboku 1959

Other Major Works

Chōei [*The Shadow of a Bird*] (novel) 1908
Rōmaji nikki [*Romaji Diary*] (diary) 1909
Jidai heisoku no genjo [*The Status of a Stagnant Age*] (criticism) 1910
Poems to Eat (essays) 1966

CRITICISM

Shio Sakanishi (essay date 1934)

SOURCE: An introduction to *A Handful of Sand* by Takuboku Ishikawa, translated by Shio Sakanishi, Marshall Jones Company, 1934, pp. 1-17.

[*In the following excerpt, Sakanishi discusses Takuboku's prominence in modern Japanese poetry, praising the dramatic quality of his verse and his success in restoring simplicity and fluidity to Japanese poetry.*]

In the development of modern Japanese poetry, Takuboku Ishikawa occupies a place apart. Born in the transitional period when the stilted diction and theme of poetry were no longer sufficient to express a new spirit and the new experiences of men, and acknowledging Tekkan Yosano as his literary master, Takuboku, nevertheless, remained outside the straight line of development that had its starting point in Tekkan. In a brief space of nine years, he lived through the three stages—romantic, naturalistic, and socialistic—which the remaining literary world took the next twenty-five years to experience. Therefore, though a product of his age, he was not of his age, and it was only after his death that the full significance of his work came to be fully appreciated . . . .

The volume entitled *Ichiaku no suna* (*A Handful of Sand*) contained 551 poems. . . . The volume caused a stir in the literary world because of its extreme simplicity of diction and unconventional subject matter. Therefore those who had been nourished on the set notion of what poetry should be raised their hands in horror and denounced it most emphatically. On the other hand, among those who had been frightened away from Japanese poetry because of its classical formalism or who had never had any particular interest in it, his work was welcomed with joy. Takuboku's direct expression as well as the freshness of his verse delighted them. Indeed, with the publication of the **Handful of Sand**, Takuboku humanized Japanese poetry; he took it out of the hands of a select few and gave it to the masses. . . .

In the minds of those who loved Takuboku's poetry the thought of what his genius actually achieved and the pathos of the unfulfilled promise of his life are ever present. Even with no advance of artistic power, but merely with the wider experience and greater independence which are the gifts of time rather than of genius, he might have attained his high ideal. At the age of twenty-five in spite of an uninspiring environment, hostile criticism, and the haunting presence of starvation and illness, he had produced work mature in thought and execution and full of human significance. His subsequent works are further marked by great objective power and dramatic skill.

There is no doubt that Takuboku is one of the great poets of the modern period, but the significance of his poetry in the history of Japanese literature is even greater than its intrinsic value. He recreated Japanese prosody, giving it back the simplicity and the fluidity that it had lost centuries ago. In the early part of the tenth century Ki no Tsurayuki, distinguished courtier and poet, wrote: "The heart of men is the seed whence springs our native poetry and the countless leaves of language." In the course of its development, however, Japanese poetry departed from its original spirit, and fostering tricks and phrases of its own, became in itself a seed. Lifting it from anarchy and stiltedness, Takuboku again restored poetry to the human heart, extended its scope, and made language his willing servant. He saw no reason why the language of poetry had to be different from that of every day life.

Simplicity of expression is complemented in his poetry by simplicity of content. We may call Takuboku a poet of the simpler human experiences. He does not complicate or subtilise the world of the senses by those higher activities of the human spirit which go to create the landscape of Priest Saigyo or of Shelley. In the maturing process which intervenes before the birth of a poem, he does not analyse deeply or reconstruct what he has seen or felt. As he once wrote to a friend, his poems are often no more than entries in a diary, unpremeditated outgrowths of the moment and the event. Only through his genius these spontaneous records of the passing moment acquired glowing intensity and lasting human significance. This achievement of freedom and simplicity within the framework of traditional form was his contribution to Japanese poetry.

The most outstanding characteristic of his poetry, however, is its dramatic quality. Japanese poetry has been known for its brevity and suggestiveness, but Takuboku was able to present a five-act play in the brief space of thirty-one syllables. . . . Indeed, perhaps his greatest ambition was to write a drama. Early in 1905 he had in fact started a play, *Death's Victory,* and advance notice of it was printed in his first volume of poems. How far he might have realized his ambition it is difficult to conjecture. Genius for dramatic writing is seldom developed early, but judging from his poems, Takuboku seems to have possessed it to an eminent degree. . . .

To Takuboku the world of reality was profoundly dissatisfying, and he sought an escape in poetry in which to express his yearning for a fuller life and the good things his spirit and senses lacked. Yet his poems are fully charged with reality. The charm of his native village, the bleak shores of the northern island, the poverty, the disease, the birth and the dying, the friends he made, the women he loved, the ambition that fretted like a hair shirt—all find their place in the simple structure of his poems. Indeed, of all his writings, his poetry is the most autobiographical. Yet he protested at being called a poet, and it is an irony of fate that to-day Takuboku is considered one of the most significant poets of the Meiji period which closed with his death in 1912. . . .

Carl Sesar   (essay date 1966)

SOURCE: An introduction to *Takuboku: Poems to Eat,* translated by Carl Sesar, Kodansha International Ltd., 1966, pp. 13-18.

[*In the following essay, Sesar remarks on Takuboku's conception of poetry.*]

Ishikawa Takuboku's first book of poetry, *Akogare* (*Longing*), was published in 1905 when Takuboku was nineteen. It was a collection of poems in the so-called "new-style," that is, poems of varying length in free verse after the example of European poetry. Ueda Bin, the well-known poet and translator from the French, wrote the preface, and Yosano Tekkan, *tanka* poet and editor of *Myōjō,* one of the leading poetry magazines of the day, added a postface to the collection. *Akogare* attracted immediate public and critical attention for its startling imagery and outspokenness, and on the merits of this collection Takuboku gained a certain measure of recognition as a rising young poet.

The writing of "new-style" poetry had begun nearly a

quarter of a century earlier with the publication in 1882 of the *Shintaishishō* ("An Anthology of New Style Poetry"). The appearance of this anthology reflected the general trend of the times in Japan of adopting Western ideas and methods in Japan's drive toward modernization. The editors of the *Shintaishishō* were hoping to create a new poetry capable of expressing the temper of a modern Japan with new thoughts and ideas that could not be contained in the short, traditional *tanka* and *haiku* forms. The early experiments were on the whole crude, but by Takuboku's time the "new style" had been well established in Japan and had improved considerably in artistic quality. Takuboku, in imitation of his immediate predecessors, had proved himself to be quite skilled in this style. In spite of this, and for crucial reasons of his own, Takuboku finally went back to the shorter *tanka* form, devoting himself almost exclusively at the height of his powers to the writing of *tanka,* and it is on the quality of these short poems that his fame as a poet rests.

Takuboku had been writing *tanka* long before the publication of *Akogare.* In fact, his first major success in breaking into print occurred in 1903 when several of them appeared in the magazine *Myōjō.* Not long afterward he came under the influence of Yosano Tekkan and his wife, Akiko, both *tanka* practitioners and leaders of the Romantic *Myōjō* school, but in later years, with the perfection of his own individual style, he broke away from that group.

Takuboku's views on poetry are contained in an article he wrote in 1910, called "Poems to Eat." About the title, he explains:

> I got the idea for the title "Poems to Eat" from a beer advertisement I often saw in the streetcar. I mean by it poems that are down to earth, poems with feelings unremoved from real life. Not delicacies, not a feast, but poems that taste like our daily meals; poems then, that are *necessities* to us.

Takuboku discusses his reasons for abandoning the "new-style" poetry in favor of the *tanka.* Reviewing his early poems, Takuboku remarks:

> The poems I wrote then, as everybody knows, except for a certain visionary and youthful ring, and later on, some feeble religious content, were nothing more than a surrender to hackneyed sentiments. To get to the point of putting my real feelings into a poem was a very long and complicated process. Say I saw a tree about six feet high standing in an empty lot with the sun shining on it. If I were in any way moved by it, I'd end up by turning the empty lot into a vast wilderness, the tree into a mighty tree, the sun into either the rising sun or the setting sun and, if that weren't bad enough, I turned myself into some poet or wanderer contemplating the scene. Had I just left myself an unhappy young man, the feeling would have been all wrong for the exalted tone of the poem I'd written and I could never be satisfied with it.

As for what makes a poet, or a poem, he says:

> Somewhere along the line I was jolted out of my childish infatuation with such high-powered

words as "poet" . . . I deny the existence of any special quality to a poet. It's all right for others to call someone who writes poems a poet, but he cannot think of himself as such. Maybe it's improper of me to say so, but that kind of thinking will corrupt his poetry—it's all quite unnecessary. The qualifications of a poet are three: he must be a human being, first, second, and last. He must be a man having no more or less than the qualities any ordinary person possesses . . .

A poem should be a strict report of events taking place in one's emotional life (for the want of some better term)—a straightforward diary. This means it has to be fragmentary, it can't have unity or coherence.

The qualifications of a poet are three: he must be a human being, first, second, and last. He must be a man having no more or less than the qualities any ordinary person possesses.

—Ishikawa Takuboku

Takuboku's rejection of the notion that poetry belongs to a special realm or that poetic experience is in some way exalted marks the turning point in his development as a poet. He says that a poem should in fact be just the very opposite, the setting down of impressions that may seem trivial and fragmentary, and which usually are ignored or even held in contempt for their lack of unity or import. But, Takuboku insists, it is precisely such impressions which hold in them the germ of poetry. They are swift and, by their immediacy, truer. The *tanka,* then, was the perfect form for this kind of poetry.

> People say the *tanka* is too short to work with. But I think that is precisely its advantage. Isn't it so? A small poem, that doesn't take time, is best—it's practical. It's the best thing that ever happened to the Japanese, having this *tanka* form!

The quality most striking in Takuboku's poems is their overwhelming personalism. Takuboku is the subject of every poem he writes—even in what seems to be a detached scene or picture one is always aware of Takuboku's presence. His poems in this respect actually resemble diary entries, each poem marking a single emotional event. Ultimately, like most diarists, Takuboku becomes his own audience, writing poems to keep a lasting record for himself of impressions that might otherwise be irrevocably lost.

Written in simple, direct language, Takuboku's short poems have a frankness and sudden power unprecedented in Japanese poetry. They are the work of an original, modern poet who wrote out of new depths of personal experience with relentless fidelity.

In effect, Takuboku discovered in the *tanka* inherent qual-

ities that had gone stale, buried in the language and feelings of an earlier age. By giving the *tanka* new language and feeling Takuboku succeeded in restoring the form to what it had always been, the perfect vehicle for capturing the swift, direct pulse of emotion.

Sanford Goldstein and Seishi Shinoda   (essay date 1977)

SOURCE: An introduction to *Sad Toys* by Takuboku Ishikawa, translated by Sanford Goldstein and Seishi Shinoda, Purdue University Press, 1977, pp. 1-42.

[*In the following excerpt, Goldstein and Shinoda examine the tanka poems in* Sad Toys *and discuss Takuboku's conception of tanka both as a poetic form and as a mode of autobiography.*]

In "Various Kinds of Tanka," an article Takuboku Ishikawa serialized in the Tokyo *Asahi* newspaper from December 10 to December 20, 1910, he pointed out that tanka poets ought to be free to use more than the traditional thirty-one-syllable rhythm of 5-7-5-7-7. Even the content of tanka need not be limited, Takuboku insisted, and he urged poets to disregard "the arbitrary restrictions which dictate that some subjects are not fit for tanka and will not make one." Modern readers may be surprised when Takuboku, in this context of defining tanka, suddenly lapsed into the nihilistic frame of mind so deeply rooted in him: "What can I do with those many things which really inconvenience me and pain me? Nothing. No, I cannot continue my existence unless I live a miserable double life, submitting with resignation and servility to these inconveniences. Though I try to justify myself, I cannot help but admit I have become a victim of the present family, class, and capitalist systems and the system of trading in knowledge." It was in this mood of pessimism and defeat that Takuboku turned his gaze from the clock at which he had been staring "to a doll thrown down like a corpse on the *tatami* mats. Tanka are my sad toys," he concluded.

Were Takuboku's tanka merely "toys" he played with in times of misery and sadness? Or did he feel his tanka were "toys" because they had no social value? An examination of Takuboku's life provides a kind of synecdoche on the eternal struggle of the artist in society, and while *Sad Toys* contains penetrating moments into that sad life, these poems go beyond it to provide tanka with a much greater range than it had in its twelve-hundred-year history. Along with the famous Akiko Yosano (1878-1942), Takuboku became a supreme tanka-reformer. The words *sad* and *toy,* contradictory and clever and yet edged with pathos—that of a child who cries over his toys—contain on closer scrutiny a much deeper significance when viewed in the light of Takuboku's diaries, letters, and articles.

We ought to keep in mind the fact that Takuboku did not give his second and last tanka collection the title *Sad Toys* (*Kanashiki Gangu,* 1912). His friend Aika Toki had wanted to call the posthumous volume *After "A Handful of Sand": From the End of November 1910,* but the publisher wisely refused because readers might have easily confused it with Takuboku's earlier collection. Toki finally selected the title from the memorable last line in the *Asahi* article.

The poet died on April 13, 1912, and his last days were described in Toki's postscript to **Sad Toys**: "Several days before Takuboku's death," wrote Toki, "he asked me to find a publisher for his book of poems as he was penniless. Immediately I went to Tōundō's and persuaded them, though with some difficulty." With the twenty-yen payment in his pocket, Toki hurried to Takuboku's home. Despite the emaciation in the poet's face and body due to the final stages of tuberculosis, Takuboku's eyes revealed his excitement on hearing the news. He felt he had to polish some of the poems, and he also wanted to arrange the series, but only after he recovered from his illness. However, Toki informed his friend that the publisher insisted on having the manuscript at once. Surprised, Takuboku waited a moment in silence before asking his wife, Setsuko, to fetch what he called his "dismal-looking" notebook. It was medium-sized with gray flock-paper covers. This notebook Takuboku entrusted to his friend with the words, " 'From now on I must look to you for help.' "

Poverty, illness, and tanka permeate many of the twenty-six years of Takuboku's life, and like the contradictory manifestations moderns are bombarded with, this triumvirate represents Takuboku's fall and greatness. His own definition of tanka in "Poems to Eat," an article serialized in the Tokyo *Mainichi* newspaper from November 30 to December 7, 1909, was that "Poetry must not be what is usually called poetry. It must be an exact report, an honest diary, of the changes in a man's emotional life." Takuboku loaded his poems with events from his own personal history. The detailed biographical aspects of that life, like the I-novel which forms so much a part of Japanese literature, cannot be ignored. In an I-novel, the author-hero exploits with a fair degree of accuracy the details of his own life. Takuboku's life is tanka, his tanka his life. . . .

What is there in Takuboku that breaks the heart yet bears along with this fragile feeling a strength that cannot crumble into sentimentality? The slippery wire Takuboku walked along remained taut. That fragile yet taut line was of course tanka. We must ascertain Takuboku's view of tanka, his sad toys; many of the 194 tanka in this posthumous volume serve as examples of the evolution of an idea of tanka that was to radically modernize it and lift it from the mechanical reliance on technique that had brought tanka to its last dying gasp in the Meiji period.

In our *Tangled Hair: Selected Tanka from "Midaregami" by Akiko Yosano,* we noted how Akiko and her husband, Tekkan, had removed tanka from the stranglehold of history and mere technicality. The earlier court poets had made the *Kokinshū,* Japan's second oldest anthology (completed 905), their sacred book:

> . . . as time passed, many words and phrases were totally incomprehensible to the mass of readers. Those families versed in the art of tanka capitalized on the inscrutable expressions in these poems and monopolized the field. The prestige of the poetry families was heightened; moreover, the financial rewards were great. For hundreds of years the heirs of these families were initiated into the well-guarded techniques of the art. As a matter of course, poets and their poems were conservative in the extreme.

In 1871 what later became the Imperial Poetry Bureau was established under the Ministry of the Imperial Household, the commissioners of the bureau descendants of these very court poets and their disciples. The commissioners were rigid formalists absorbed in preserving tradition yet quite deficient in creative energy. Until the end of the second decade of the Meiji era . . . , poets were completely dominated by the Poetry Bureau School, or, as it was later called, the Old School. The poets of the Old School were removed from the dynamic life of Meiji as it experienced the impact of Westernization. Their poems, deficient in real feeling, were concerned only with the beauty of nature. Suddenly aware of the rapidly progressing materialism of the new age, the Old School poets began to feel something of its impact and tried to adapt their art to the new era. But inadequate in talent and sensibility, they were unable to keep pace with the times, even though they introduced into tanka the telegraph and the railroad. Their newness never went beyond mere subject matter.

Early in his career Takuboku met Akiko Yosano and her husband, Tekkan. The young Takuboku soon saw the limitations in Tekkan's work; he liked Akiko's much more and admired her talent. But he felt he was going beyond their direction as he continued to create tanka as diary, the record of a man's life, a tanka without restriction of subject, its form open to certain kinds of change. That is to say, we feel Takuboku was carrying tanka to its very outermost limit before it broke down into prose. Takuboku's tanka still remain poetic, obviously, but it is a poetry almost lapsing into prose, into the commonplace; and perhaps the more prosaic and commonplace the subject, the more Takuboku would have called it "his" kind of tanka.

In letters, diary entries, and articles, Takuboku probed his attitude toward tanka. What was this poetic form and who were the people who composed it? In his early days he had difficulty in deciding what the content and the mood of the poem ought to be. "Once," he tells us in his article "Poems to Eat" as he continues along this line,

> I used to write "poems." It was for a few years from the age of seventeen or eighteen. At that time there was nothing for me but poetry. My mind, which was yearning after some indescribable thing from morning to night, could find an outlet to some extent only by making poems. And I had absolutely nothing except that mind. —As everyone knows, poetry in those days contained only conventional feelings besides fantasy, crude music, and a feeble religious element or something equivalent to it. Reflecting on my attitude toward poetry at that time, I want to say this: a very complicated process was needed to turn actual feelings into poetry. Suppose, for instance, one derived a certain sentiment from looking at a sapling about three meters tall growing on a small plot lit up by the sun: he had to make the vacant plot a wilderness, the sapling a towering tree, the sun the rising or setting sun, and he had to make himself a poet, a traveler, or a young man in sorrow. Otherwise, the sentiment was not suited to the poetry of those days, and he himself was not satisfied.

With this early attitude that poems ought to emerge from the "inspiration" of the "poet," Takuboku discovered he could not write poems when he felt "inspired," but only "when I was in a mood in which I despised myself or when I was driven by some practical circumstance, such as nearing a deadline. I wrote many poems at the end of every month, for then I found myself in circumstance which made me despite myself." He came, he continues in "Poems to Eat," to reject such words as *poet* and *genius,* and when he recalled those youthful days in which he had written "poems," the regret at no longer being able to turned to sorrow and then to self-scorn. Forced to make a living, Takuboku became a stranger to poetry:

> From my home to Hakodate, from there to Sapporo, then farther on to Kushiro—in that way I wandered from place to place in search of a livelihood. Before I knew it, I had become a stranger to poetry. When I met someone who said he had read my old poems and who talked about the bygone days, I had the same kind of unpleasant feeling one has when a friend who had once indulged in dissipation with him talks about an old flame. The actual experience of life caused a change in me. When a kind old politician who took me to the office of a newspaper in Kushiro introduced me to someone by saying, "He is a poet of the new school," I felt in his goodwill the greatest contempt I had experienced till then.

What revived Takuboku's interest in poetry and other forms of literature was the naturalist movement in addition to his own boredom in thinking of literature as fantasy (that is, removed from reality). His own tormented grasp of the reality of his own life caused him to further accept the spirit of the new naturalism at work in Meiji Japan. He did not object to the attempt to bring into poetry words from everyday life, yet he drew a line—and this is extremely important in the evolution of his own tanka: "Naturally poetry is subject to a certain formal restriction. When poetry is completely liberated, it must become prose."

For this reason Takuboku's later tanka, especially those in **Sad Toys,** are more often than not a mixture of colloquial and formal diction, though even in this last volume many are formal in tone. When he came to Tokyo after living in Hakodate, "that colonial town in the north, where the crude realities of life were left unveiled," he often said he too would write colloquial poems in the new style, but his words were simply for those hard-liners who regarded the form of tanka as fixed, cemented in the techniques of history and tradition. In Tokyo, where the difficult life he lived is so movingly described in his *Romaji Diary,* he apparently wrote four or five hundred tanka during that year, the pleasure from them "somewhat like that which a husband beaten in a marital quarrel derives from scolding or teasing his child without reason." His boardinghouse life, which sometimes hurled him toward the pit of suicide, made him appreciate more fully the spirit behind the new naturalism and the new poetry, the name he gave to the latter being "poems to eat": "The name means poems made with both feet upon the ground. It means

poems written without putting any distance from actual life. They are not delicacies or dainty dishes, but food indispensable for us in our daily meal. To define poetry in this way may be to pull it down from its established position, but to me it means to make poetry, which has added nothing to or detracted nothing from actual life, into something that cannot be dispensed with."

> **Poetry must not be what is usually called poetry. It must be an exact report, an honest diary, of the changes in a man's emotional life. Accordingly, it must be fragmentary; it must not have organization.**
>
> *—Ishikawa Takuboku*

Poetry had become for Takuboku as indispensable as food. In this context, of course, his tanka had to be much more than mere toys. He hacked off the outer protective shell that had made the genre into something curious and rare for the elite few, and he turned it into something to be seized by the very teeth, all moments of life available to it. And this meant that the rarefied name "poet" had to be eliminated: ". . . I deny the existence of a special kind of man called poet. It is quite right that others should call a man who writes poems a poet, but the man should not think himself a poet. My way of putting this may be improper, but if he thinks himself a poet, his poems will degenerate; that is, they will become something needless to us. First of all, a poet must be a man. Second, he must be a man. Third, he must be a man. Moreover, he must possess all that the common man possesses." Nor must the content of poetry be "poetic" in the refined connotation of its earlier meanings:

> . . . to say that poetry is the purest of arts is tantamount to saying that distilled water is the purest water. It may serve as an explanation of quality, but it cannot be a criterion in deciding its value or necessity. Future poets should not say such a thing. At the same time they should firmly decline preferential treatment given to poetry and the poet. Like everything else, all literature is in a sense a means or a method to us and to our life. To regard poetry as something high and noble is a kind of idolatry.

> Poetry must not be what is usually called poetry. It must be an exact report, an honest diary, of the changes in a man's emotional life. Accordingly, it must be fragmentary; it must not have organization. (Poetry with organization, i. e., philosophy in literature, is the novel deductively and the drama inductively. The relationship between them and poetry is what exists between a daily balance of accounts and a monthly or yearly settlement.) The poet must never have preoccupation like the priest looking for material for a sermon or a whore looking for a certain kind of man.

In "Various Kinds of Tanka," Takuboku introduces a letter written by an unhappy schoolteacher living in some out-of-the-way village in which the writer describes his boring life in a community he feels is without taste, declaring he will do his utmost in studying tanka and will contribute at least one tanka a day to the *Asahi.* Takuboku considers his correspondent a fool "to think writing tanka is something great." At the same time, however, Takuboku feels a kind of envy toward this man who is free from the pain of self-scrutiny. Takuboku continues: "From the fact that he said he would do his utmost in the study of tanka in spite of his unsatisfactory circumstances . . . I found that he was a man who had never seriously thought how pitiable he was or why, though he called himself 'pitiable'. . . ."

The schoolmaster, Takuboku discovered, continued to send daily contributions to the tanka column Takuboku was in charge of. The poet found himself perversely waiting for the mail to see how long the man would "be able to continue his meaningless effort." The writer did continue to send an "enormous" number of tanka which Takuboku judged as "no more than mere representations in thirty-one syllables of natural features suited to poetry. There was hardly one good enough to print." What Takuboku concluded was that the man's poems might truly become poems by a living person if the writer squarely faced the fact of his own "pitiable" quality and "unflinchingly thought through how pitiable he was and why."

At the end of the article Takuboku reflects on the "reality" of tanka:

> Smoking a cigarette and resting one elbow on my desk, I was idly looking at the hands of the clock, my eyes tired from writing. And I thought the following: When anything begins to inconvenience us, we had better attempt to boldly reconstruct it so as to remove the inconvenience. It is only right that we should do this. We do not live for others but for ourselves. Take, for instance, the tanka. We have already been feeling it is somewhat inconvenient to write a tanka in a single line. So we should write it in two lines or three according to its rhythm. Some may criticize us by saying this will destroy the rhythm of tanka itself. No matter. If the conventional rhythm has ceased to suit our mood, why hesitate to change it? If the limitation of thirty-one syllables is felt inconvenient, we should freely use lines with extra syllables. As for the content, we should sing about anything, disregarding the arbitrary restrictions which dictate that some subjects are not fit for tanka and will not make one. If only we do these things, tanka will not die as long as man holds dear the momentary impressions which flash across his mind, disappearing a moment later during his busy life. The thirty-one syllables may become forty-one or even fifty-one, yet tanka will live and we will be able to satisfy our love for the fleeting moments of life.
>
> Thinking thus, I remained motionless while the second-hand of the clock completed a circuit. Then I felt my mind getting more and more somber. What I now feel inconvenient is not merely

writing tanka in a single line. Nevertheless, what I can freely change now or will be able to change in the future are only the positions of the clock, the inkstone case, and the ink-pot on my desk, and, besides these, tanka. They are all matters of little importance. What can I do with those many things which really inconvenience me and pain me? Nothing. No, I cannot continue my existence unless I live a miserable double life, submitting with resignation and servility to these inconveniences. Though I try to justify myself, I cannot help but admit I have become a victim of the present family, class, and capitalist systems and the system of trading in knowledge.

> From the clock I turned my gaze to a doll thrown down like a corpse on the *tatami* mats. Tanka are my sad toys.

It seems that Takuboku had to find some means of justifying his life as a writer of tanka, for the words of the novelist Futabatei Shimei (pen name of Tatsunosuke Hasegawa, 1864-1909) that a man cannot devote his life to literature had considerable impact on the young poet, though Futabatei himself could not break away from his craft. Takuboku tried stories and socialism, but in neither could he succeed. And yet even as he was successful as a young tanka poet, it almost seems as if he was fighting this talent in himself. "The Glass Window," an article published by Takuboku in June 1910, a year after the cessation of his *Romaji Diary,* sharply explores this contradictory tendency. Takuboku begins the article by claiming there is nothing interesting left in the world. He has discovered that even the cigarettes he incessantly smokes have become less appealing. His walks outside are directionless, and on his return home he carries only "dissatisfaction in [his] mind . . . . It was as if [he] didn't know what to do with [his] life." As he reviews the past, he once more notes his contempt for poets or literary men:

> Three years passed. Five years passed. Before I knew it, I had ceased to have sympathy for men younger than I who wanted to become poets or literary men, titles the sound of which had once thrilled me. Before I knew their personalities by seeing them or considered their literary endowments, I found myself feeling pity and contempt and at times distaste for them. As to those people living in the countryside who do nothing but pass their time writing poems and yet have such strong pride as cannot be imagined by outsiders and who write me vague, enigmatic letters—I sometimes felt that the world would become a much cleaner place if I dug a big hole and buried them all.

He felt the gap between the Philistines and the literati or the gap between the actual world and the life in literature itself. He notes in this article the rise of naturalism as a movement to bring literature closer to actual life, yet Takuboku concludes that naturalism could not fully bridge the gap between the two. Perhaps Takuboku meant that inevitably naturalism could not remain a literary movement, for the gap that must remain between the created form and life as it is actually lived is one "which even an operation by the most ingenious surgeon could not suture." Takuboku claims that it is only by this gap that literature can preserve its territorial integrity forever (should that line be crossed literature could not call itself such). Nevertheless, Takuboku could not help pointing to the deep sorrow men who create literature must feel because of this gap. And still he had to admit he was most content when he was busily at work at his desk completing one piece of work after another:

> When I am too busy, I sometimes feel dizzy. At such moments I scold myself by saying to myself, "How can you lose your head because of this?" and I concentrate my attention, which is apt to be distracted, on my work. Though the work may be uninteresting, I have no other desire and no dissatisfaction. My brain, eyes, and hands work in combination so efficiently I myself am surprised. It is so pleasant. I think to myself, "I want to be busier, much busier."
>
> After a while the work is completed, and with a sigh of relief I have a smoke. I become aware of a healthy hunger. I feel as if I were still seeing myself working hard. Again I think, "I wish I had been busier!"
>
> I have various hopes: I want money, want to read books, want to obtain fame, go on a trip, live in a society which suits me. I have many more additional desires, but all of them put together cannot replace the joy of being immersed in work, forgetting all desire, all gain.

Innumerable times as he returned home by streetcar, he thought: "I wish I could work all my life from morning to night without even time to speak or think, and then die a sudden death." Yet these thoughts, too, like tanka, were only moments of the floating world:

> But sometimes a quite different feeling suddenly occurs to me. I feel as if I have once more begun to experience the throbbing pain of a wound I had forgotten. I cannot control the feeling, nor can I divert my attention from it.
>
> I feel as if the world which had been bright were growing dark rapidly. Things which gave me pleasure cease to do so; things with which I was contented cause dissatisfaction in me; things I need not be angry with make me angry. There is nothing I see or hear that does not increase unpleasantness. I want to go to the mountains, I want to go to the sea, I want to go to a place where no one knows me, I want to be lost among people who speak a language I don't understand at all. It is at such moments that I laugh to my heart's content at the unbounded ugliness, at the unbounded pitiableness, of this being called myself.

Despite these contradictions Takuboku could not after all abandon tanka. His article "A Dialogue between an Egoist and His Friend" further explores this ambivalence toward tanka. As the egoist Takuboku had said, tanka would die out, but this event would not occur for many years because the form would continue to exist in the same way a man is said to have lived long when he becomes an octogenarian. Only when the Japanese language was unified would it become possible for tanka to die, and the Japanese language would unify itself only when the confusion existing

in its mixture of colloquial and formal in its written forms was eliminated. As for other aspects of tanka structure, Takuboku repeated his belief that tanka itself might contain more than the traditional thirty-one syllables and need not be patterned in the traditional one or two lines. In fact, he claimed that because each tanka is different in tone, each might have different line divisions. In one of the most revealing sections of this dialogue, Takuboku (speaker A) notes the convenience of tanka, its length, its capturing of moments, its preciousness in allowing preservation of the fleeting and momentary and ephemeral:

> A. Yes. Each second is one which never comes back in our life. I hold it dear. I don't want to let it pass without doing anything for it. To express that moment, tanka, which is short and takes not much time to compose, is most convenient. Yes, it is convenient indeed. It is one of the few good fortunes we Japanese enjoy that we have a poetic form called tanka. (Pause) I compose tanka because I love life. I make tanka because I love myself better than anything else. (Pause) Yet tanka will die. I won't theorize, but it will collapse from the inside. Still, it will not die for a long time. I wish it would die as soon as possible, but it will not, not for a long time to come.

As if to heighten the contradiction, Takuboku once more expresses his desire not to compose tanka:

> A. Honestly speaking, I don't want to let myself make such a thing as tanka.
>
> B. What do you mean? You are a tanka poet after all. Why not? Do your best.
>
> A. I love myself far deeper than to let myself compose tanka.
>
> B. I don't understand you.
>
> A. Don't you? (Pause) But it becomes rather foolish when expressed in words.
>
> B. Do you mean that you cannot devote yourself to such a trifling thing as tanka?
>
> A. I have never intended to devote my whole life to tanka. (Pause) What can I devote my life to? (Pause) I love myself, but I don't trust myself very much.

These attitudes toward tanka may best be summarized in a letter Takuboku wrote to Fukashi Segawa, a medical student at the time and a former schoolmate at Morioka Middle School (letter dated January 9, 1911):

> First of all, I want to write about the fact that we have both changed in the same way. You said you had drifted farther and farther from poetry, and the same is true with me. The tanka I am now writing are different from those I wrote in the old days. You have ceased to write poetry, and I have become unable to—I have become unable to write such poems as I did in the old days and as the young still do today, just as I can no longer repeat the love affairs I had in the old days. Not that I don't feel any nostalgia for those bygone days when I was happy dallying with my

own sentiments. . . . But I cannot repeat such foolish efforts again.

The tanka I am writing nowadays have hardly any raison d'être—I know that quite well. It makes little difference, so to speak, whether I make them or not. I don't know whether you keep a diary or not, but now I am writing tanka as if I were writing a diary. Perhaps there are well-written diaries and badly written ones, but the value of a diary does not vary according to the writer's skill. A diary is of value only to the writer, and the value is quite irrelevant to the outsider. "I felt so and so" or "I thought so and so"—this is all that my tanka purport now. They have no other meaning, none above that.

Therefore, it makes no difference whether I compose them or not. When I say this, I am not just theorizing. In fact, I don't mind at all if I don't feel like making any tanka for days or even months. I remain quite indifferent. But because I am obliged to lead a dissatisfied daily life, it often becomes imperative to seek the proof of my existence by becoming conscious of my *self* at each moment. At such times I make tanka; I console myself a little by turning the self at each moment into words and reading them. Accordingly, the day in which I make tanka is an unhappy day for me. It is a day I spent purposelessly, a day in which I could not obtain any satisfaction except by finding my real "self" at each moment. You see, even though I write tanka now, I want to become a man who has no need to write any.

You wrote you understood me. And I believe it. From what I have written above, I believe you must have grasped my attitude toward tanka. But there is one circumstance which causes me sorrow. My tanka have a meaning quite different from the tanka of other people. Nevertheless, because I write tanka people regard me as a tanka-poet, and I myself sometimes feel like one. Whenever others treat me as a tanka-poet, a certain rebellious spirit is engendered in me. I cry inwardly, "I'm not such a special curiosity, but a man, an independent man worthy of the name." And yet, a moment later, I sometimes feel proud by comparing my tanka with those of others. I have hardly any respect or sympathy for the life of a man who lives to make tanka. I regard it as crippled and hollow. So I am well aware that it is meaningless to compare my tanka with his. I also think that it is to debase myself to make such comparisons. Yet I often do; sometimes I am impressed by his work, and sometimes I feel proud of mine. This is what makes me sad, and it reveals my weakness at the same time. This weakness induces me to promise I will write a given number of tanka by a fixed date.

In Takuboku's first collection of tanka, *A Handful of Sand,* 551 poems had been included; yet in *Sad Toys,* posthumously published from the notebook in which the poet kept his tanka (the first two in the volume added by his friend Toki from a slip of paper found later), there were only 194. Illness, poverty, the demands of his job as proof-reader, his attempt at writing stories, and the pursuit of socialism provide some explanation for the smaller number of tanka; yet these very conditions, painful as they were, lent themselves to the creation of "sad toys." Is it not possible to speculate that Takuboku made greater demands than ever on tanka that pared life down to the essentials of a "self" he was perpetually trying to find? We have seen how Takuboku spent a triumphant three days in his earlier career in which he had set down at least 246 tanka during that short interval. In the slightly less than seventeen months remaining in his life after the publication of *Handful,* he probably demanded more from each tanka so that he was much more critical of each effort. He saw the moments slipping by, each moment in itself containing infinite possibilities for the creation of tanka:

a family at a time of discontent:

> Husband's mind on travel!
> The wife scolding, the child in tears!
> O this table in the morning!

an appreciation of the most trivial:

> How precious the winter morning!
> Soft against my face,
> Steam from the hot water in this bowl . . .

a moment of emptiness bordering on nihilism:

> As if these hands, these feet, were scattered—
> O this sluggish waking!
> This sad waking!

the sudden isolation of midnight:

> Awakened at midnight
> And wondering if Fate rode me—
> O the heaviness of this quilt!

the image of one's hands:

> These poor thin hands
> Without power
> To grasp and grasp hard!

a crisis of intense concentration to keep oneself from raging:

> On this day in which my wife behaves
> Like a woman unleashed,
> I gaze at these dahlias . . .

Takuboku felt the necessity of preserving the most ephemeral element in man's life, the individual moment, whether that moment was high or low, bright or dark, inspiring or frustrating, and he set for himself a task no other tanka poet before him had undertaken—that of extending tanka's range, of revising its form and content, of blending the unique mixture of colloquial and formal which adds so much to the complexity of the Japanese language. He carried his tanka to a point where the poem was almost destroyed because it came so close to breaking down into prose. At times he wished tanka might collapse, and he felt that it would at some future day, but he refused to allow himself to be the one to make that disastrous move. He called his tanka "sad toys," but even toys so easily broken can become precious and indispensable, for his tanka were also "poems to eat." Takuboku gave to the Everyman in each of us moments we can immediately recognize and value as commonplace, real, honest, compassionate, unflinching, and human.

Satoru Tsuchiya (essay date 1979)

SOURCE: A review of *Sad Toys* in *World Literature Today,* Vol. 53, No. 1, Winter, 1979, p. 184.

[*In the review below, Tsuchiya discusses the social context in which Takuboku wrote and notes innovative qualities of his poetry.*]

The modernization in Japan commenced with the Meiji Era (1868-1912). Having broken free from the feudal system of the Tokugawa shogunate, the Japanese in the early Meiji Era were full of spirit and were stirred with the excitement of awakening thoughts of individual liberty and civil rights. In due course the literature of the time began to glorify the emancipation of self and to show romantic tendencies, as seen in the works of Tōson Shimazaki, Tōkoku Kitamura and Akiko Yasano. The whole atmosphere began to change, however, in the middle of the era. Due to the unbalanced distribution of capital and exploitation by the capitalists and landowners, the discontent of the poor, of laborers and tenants began to grow. Moreover, the influence of European socialism became increasingly stronger. But the socialist movements were severely oppressed, as seen typically in the case of the Taigyaku (Treason) Incident in 1910. Thus the hope and enthusiasm of the earlier era was gradually overtaken by despair. Takuboku Ishikawa is a poet who lived through this period of turmoil and transition, submerging himself in such social misery. It is because of this that Takuboku has received admiration as a national poet.

Sad Toys, first published posthumously in 1912, is a collection of 194 tanka poems. As Takuboku himself said, "I am writing tanka as if I were writing a diary"; this book is a record of his life, a life in isolation and poverty. By writing down each momentary scene of his hard life in the form of tanka, he must have tried to find release from the

heavy pressure of society and the patriarchal family structure peculiar to Japan, as well as from his illness (he died of tuberculosis). In this sense, tanka were sad toys for him, alienated as he was from the affluent society. . . .

It is also worthy of note that Takuboku has challenged the traditional style of thirty-one-syllable rhythm (5-7-5-7-7) by dividing it into three lines and using colloquial language, for which he stands as one of the forerunners of the revolutionary movement in the form of the tanka.

Yukihito Hijiya (essay date 1979)

SOURCE: *Ishikawa Takuboku,* Twayne Publishers, 1979, 205 p.

[*Hijiya is a Japanese professor of English literature and the author of* Ishikawa Tauboku, *the most comprehensive study in English of Takuboku's life and works. In the following excerpt, he examines the style and themes of Takuboku's tanka poems from* A Handful of Sand *and* Sad Toys.]

Takuboku's literary reputation rests first and last upon his tanka. It was through tanka written while still a student at Morioka Middle School that he was initiated into the literary world. But the tanka of his school days, though they demonstrated dexterity in imitating the Romantic school of tanka, particularly the style of Yosano Akiko, lacked originality. As might be expected of a fledgling poet the subjects he dealt with were conventional and the language, heavily dependent on traditional poetic diction, is rather affected. Takuboku's tanka composed before 1908, in short, have little literary value—as Akiko's husband, Tekkan, immediately saw. The works that have made Takuboku famous as a revolutionary poet of unique style are the tanka written between 1908 and 1911, those which were published in ***A Handful of Sand*** and ***Sad Toys***. . . .

Takuboku's unique style did not come from a vacuum. It is the product of intense discipline as a writer in every literary genre except the drama. During his nearly five-year period (1903-1908) of training as an essayist, a poet and a novelist, the basic groundwork necessary for the creation of his tanka was laid. His keen observation of every detail of his life, his inborn gift for descriptive writing and his honesty in dealing with his inner life, all qualities essential for creating the kind of tanka he wrote, were developed in this five-year span.

In early April of 1910, in an attempt to have his first collection of tanka published, Takuboku carefully selected 255 out of some 400 of his recent compositions. Although the first publisher he approached turned him down, the second, Nishimura Yōkichi, himself a tanka poet who was personally interested in Takuboku, accepted the manuscript. When an agreement between them was reached in October of the same year, the number of tanka to be included had increased to about 400. It is significant that Takuboku selected tanka for the collection only from among those written between June 23, 1908, and August 4, 1910. Takuboku's selection is a natural consequence of the change in his poetic sensibility about which he had in "From Yumi-chō" remarked. The hackneyed Romantic

---

Donald Keene on Takuboku's attitude toward his skills as a poet:

Takuboku's diaries, though they provide splendid testimony to his growth as a human being, are surprisingly uninformative about his career as a writer. Early in life, he sometimes expressed joy at being a poet. "Ah, when I have thought that I was born to be a poet, I have felt such heartfelt joy that it has made me weep." But he never wrote in his diary (though he did elsewhere) why he chose to write tanka rather than more modern forms of poetry. He seems to have taken his poetic gifts for granted and rarely expressed surprise or pleasure when his tanka were printed in poetry magazines.

Donald Keene, in "The Diaries of Ishikawa Takuboku," in Japan Quarterly, *October-December 1989.*

---

sentiment of his early tanka was incompatible with his present down-to-earth tastes. It is apparent that Takuboku was aware that in the tanka composed in 1908 he had begun to develop a style of his own, one most suited to his poetic sensibility.

The title Takuboku first proposed for the collection was *After Work,* a title indicative of his attitude toward tanka, and all the tanka were written as one-line poems. But immediately after the manuscript was accepted for publication, Takuboku removed for further revision thirty to forty tanka and added seventy to eighty more. Then, obviously inspired by Toki Aika's *Tears and Laughter* (1910), a collection of tanka written in *rōmaji* and in three-line verse form, Takuboku divided each of his tanka into three lines and changed the title to *A Handful of Sand.* In the meantime, when Takuboku's infant son, born on October 4, died only twenty-three days after birth, the bereaved father added eight pieces in memory of the boy. The total number of tanka in *A Handful of Sand* in its final form reached 551, eighty-three percent of them written in 1910.

The collection is comprised of five sections, each having a title put by Takuboku himself. The title of each section and the number of tanka in it are as follows: "Love Songs to Myself," 151; "Smoke" (1), 47; "Smoke" (2), 54; "The Good Feel of the Autumn Wind," 51; "Unforgettable People" (1), 111; "Unforgettable People" (2), 22; and "When I Pull Off My Glove," 115. From the standpoint of its subject matter and the number of tanka it contained, the first section was obviously to Takuboku the most important part of the collection.

The tanka included in "Love Songs to Myself" give us an account of this "self" in its struggle with hardship. Takuboku sings of poverty and of family life made difficult by privation, of the frustration of his ambitions, of despair and of loneliness. The songs are a journal of his everyday life kept with sincerity and candor. Consideration of these problems could have made the poet complacent with self-pity, and the tanka could have been no more than a toy to play with to comfort himself. Takuboku, however, overcame the temptation to self-indulge, and instead used the tanka as a means of mental discipline through which he learned how to objectify and govern his powerful emotions.

The subjects Takuboku treats are those such as arouse strong passions, yet the reader is struck by the plain language and simple style of his poetry. This simplicity leaves an impression that the tanka have been composed effortlessly; ironically, it is precisely because of this naturalness of style that critics have given little attention to the evaluation of Takuboku as an artist. This unaffected simplicity, however, is the result of a conscious effort to elevate his private powerful emotions into art. Such poignant feelings as loneliness and despair are crystallized when transformed into tanka. Through the tanka the reader can enter a carefully designed world and catch a glimpse of Takuboku in the latter's endeavor to preserve human dignity in the midst of the wretchedness of life. This is not to say that all the poems in *A Handful of Sand* display masterful artistic control, but there is ample evidence of Takuboku's accomplishment as an artist. . . .

The second section of *A Handful of Sand* is divided into two parts, "Smoke" (1) and (2), dealing respectively with Takuboku's nostalgia for his childhood and for his childhood home. The subject has offered him an opportunity to objectify himself, and as a result the tone of the section is on the whole much lighter and livelier than that of the first section examined above, as represented by the following tanka:

> ameuri no charumera kikeba
> ushinaishi
> osanaki kokoro hiroeru gotoshi

> with the candy seller's flute
> returns
> my lost childhood

Takuboku's imagination flows freely as his memories of the past momentarily emancipate him from morbid preoccupation with himself and his present unhappiness. The memories of childhood, now too soon lost, are to the heart of Takuboku in the arid desert of his adult life in the city an oasis, so to speak. . . .

Forty-four of the fifty tanka that comprise the third section of *A Handful of Sand* were written in 1908, and the majority of them deal specifically with autumn, as the title of the section indicates. It should be noted that 1908 was the year when Takuboku suddenly resumed writing tanka, not yet conscious of the possible development of a style and content of his own. In short, it was Takuboku's second apprenticeship in tanka composition, the first being in his middle school days at Morioka. Simplicity of language and ease of style demonstrate increased masterly, yet the scope of the tanka is limited in that he follows the convention of waka poets whose major interest lay in objective description of the world of nature. A few examples will suffice to show Takaboku's imitations of the conventional style:

> matsu no kaze
> yo hiru hibikinu
> hito towanu yama no hokora no
> ishi-uma no mimi ni

> the wind in the pines
> day and night
> whistles in the ears
> of the stone horse
> at the mountain shrine
> no man visits

> . . .

> mizutamari
> kureyuku sora to kurenai no
> himo o ukabenu
> akisame no nochi

> in the puddle
> the sunset sky and a crimson
> spider's web floating
> after an autumn rain

> . . .

> hatahata to kibi no ha nareru
> furusato no nokiba natsukashi
> akikaze fukeba

I can hear the flapping
of the corn stalks
under the eaves of
my old home
when the autumn wind blows

. . .

honoka naru kuchiki no kaori
soga naka no take no kaori ni
aki yaya fukashi

in the gentle scent
of the decayed tree
the fragrance of mushrooms
deeper into autumn

. . .

shigure furu gotoki oto shite
kozutainu
hito ni yoku nishi mori no
sarudomo

like the sound of rain falling
they fly from tree to tree
the forest monkeys
resembling people

Suppressing his personal feelings, the poet evokes the detached impersonal loneliness of the season, a sensation powerful enough to make the reader oblivious to the poet's presence.

The danger of too closely following the convention of waka is, of course, that the work tends to be contrived, especially when the poet attempts to sing about an imaginary poetic situation. A good example illustrating the case in point is:

ao ni suku
kanashimi no tama ni
makurashite
matsu no hibiki o
yomosugara kiku

transparent blue
jewel of sadness for a pillow
I hear the soughing of the
pines all night

The subject is trite, the language affected and spontaneity of feeling absent. Another example of affected convention is:

ametsuchi ni
waga kanashimi to gekkō
amaneki aki no yo to narerikeri

in heaven and earth
my grief and the moonlight
everywhere in the autumn night

However, the fact that Takuboku in 1911 selected these tanka for publication in spite of their demerits indicates that he could perceive in them early buds of the flowering of his own style. Even among the tanka of conventional style and subject matter, one can discern the touch of Takuboku's individuality. The following example, for instance, clearly shows Takuboku moving toward his own style: that is, a subjective portrayal of nature:

aki no sora kakuryō to shite
kage mo nashi
amarini sabishi
karasu nado tobe

the autumn sky desolate
and empty
too lonely
crow or something, fly

After describing in the first seventeen syllables the forlorn scene of the autumn sky, he unhesitatingly pours out his personal reaction. In other words, in the last half of the poem he transfers the emphasis of the tanka from an external to an internal loneliness. The violent expression of feelings in the second half damages the poetic quality of the tanka, yet the abruptness of the shift in perspective all the more intensifies the sense of loneliness within, which is contrasted with that of the vast autumn sky. The loneliness the tanka deals with is of the kind felt by an individual awakened to the question of his identity. The poet has been driven to consciousness of self by the awareness of his isolation from nature, a consciousness brought about by the impersonal atmosphere nature has created. It is this awareness of isolation which makes him cry out. This declaration of his loneliness functions therefore as a reaffirmation of his existence under the vast impersonal expanse of the autumn sky; and his call for a crow to fly is not for the sake of the sky but for himself, out of desire for fellowship with another living thing. The juxtaposition of the impersonal loneliness of the outside world and the loneliness the poet feels within him enlarges the scope of the poem: the division between man and nature is irreconcilable. . . .

The individuals Takuboku sings about in the section of "Unforgettable People" represent the wide variety of people he was acquainted with. No other tanka poet wrote so extensively about his own circle of friends and acquaintances as did Takuboku. This concentration on individuals is a valuable development of an additional possibility of the tanka. The majority of the people sung about are those Takuboku came to know while he was in Hokkaido; his status as a newcomer there and the frequent separations from his family must have intensified for him relations with people in his immediate environment. At any rate, the people who were especially significant to him are immortalized in Takuboku's tanka.

Takuboku divided this section into two parts. In the first he included tanka about a variety of people in no special order and put in some tanka on nature as well. The second part, on the other hand, concentrates on only one individual [a school teacher named Tachibana Chieko that Takuboku came to know in June, 1907]. . . .

The last section of *A Handful of Sand* is a miscellaneous assortment of tanka, the tone of which is aptly set forth in the first tanka, from which the title is taken:

tebukuro o nugu te futo yamu
nani yaramu
kokoro kasumeshi
omoide no ari

I pull off my glove and chance

to pause
there's something
a memory flitting through
my heart

On the whole the poetic quality of the tanka here is inferior to that of the previous sections. . . .

In addition to themes already dealt with in the first four sections of *A Handful of Sand,* Takuboku included in this last section tanka inspired by two unforgettable experiences of 1910. The first event, the High Treason Incident, was of course too large a subject to be covered in tanka. What Takuboku did condense into tanka were sketches of himself with a book that had been banned by the government, and a chance meeting with the author of the same book:

akagami no hyōshi tezureshi
kokkin no
fumi o kōri no soko ni
sagasu hi

the banned book with
the worn red cover
the day I searched for it
in the bottom of the trunk

. . .

urukoto o sashitomerareshi
hon no chosha ni
michi nite aeru aki no asa kana

the autumn morning I met
on the street
the author of the book
whose sale had been banned

The original version of the first tanka was:

akagami no hyōshi tezureshi
kokkin no sho yomi fukeri
natsu no yo o nezu

absorbed in reading
the banned book with worn out
red covers
the sleepless autumn night

The original contains a sense of excitement aroused by the poet's violating the law in secret, yet the static description lacks the intensity and thrill that the published form brings out. Takuboku gave more life to the poem by creating in the last fourteen syllables a dramatic situation of almost fearful anticipation by bringing the spotlight to bear on the man searching for the outlawed book.

Another event of major significance for Takuboku was, of course, the birth and death of his son. On October 4, 1910, Takuboku became the father of a son, an event celebrated by the following tanka: "jūgatsu no asa no kūki ni atarashiku iki suisomeshi akanbo no ari" ("in the air of an October morning an infant newly began to breathe"). But his joy was not to last long. On October 27:

yoru osoku
tsutome-saki yori kaerikite
ima shinishi chō ko o
dakeru kana

late at night
returning from work
to hold the just-dead child

. . .

futamikoe
imawa no kiwa ni kasuka ni mo
nakishi to yū ni
namida sasowaru

two or three faint cries
just before he died
hearing this brought tears

. . .

mashiro naru daikon no ne no
koyuru koro
umarete
yagate shinishi ko no ari

the white *daikon* grows fat
a child was born
and died

. . .

osoaki no kūki o
sanshaku shihō bakari
suite waga ko no shini-
yukishi kana

the late autumn air of
one small room
breathing only this
my child has gone

. . .

shinishi ko no
mune ni chūsha no hari o sasu
isha no temoto ni
atsumaru kokoro

the heart concentrated
on the physician's hand
putting the injection in
the dead child's chest

. . .

soko shirenu nazo ni mukaite
arugotoshi
shiji no hitai ni
matamo te o yaru

as though facing
a fathomless riddle
on the dead child's forehead
again I place my hand

. . .

kanashimi no tsuyoku itaranu
sabishisa yo
waga ko no karada
hiete yukedomo

how lonely
to feel no grief
though my child's body
grows cold

. . .

kanashiku mo
yo akuru made wa nokori-inu
iki kireshi ko no hada no
nukumori

pathetic
the body of the child
without breath
warm till daybreak

There is no trace of sentimentality nor outburst of sorrow over the death of the short-lived baby. Takuboku simply describes the situation in as much detail as the thirty-one syllables permit. In fact, the simplicity of language and realism of description are what made it possible for him to put his personal grief under control, completely refined without a touch of pretense or exaggeration. This simplicity, however, the most eloquent expression of his sorrow as a father who has lost his first and only son, arouses all the more sympathy in the minds of those who read these lines. The boy's funeral was paid for by the money advanced by the publisher of *A Handful of Sand.*

Sad Toys was published on June 20, 1912, about two months after Takuboku's death. The title of the book was chosen by Toki from the last words of "Various Things about Poetry," one of the two essays included in the volume. The collection contains 194 tanka, all written between the end of November, 1910, and August 21, 1911.

The tone of *Sad Toys* is reminiscent of that of the section "Love Songs to Myself " in *A Handful of Sand,* but with an added intensity and desperation, as evident in the two opening tanka of the collection:

ikisureba,
mune no uchi nite naru oto ari.
kogarashi yori mo
sabishiki sono oto!

when I take a breath,
there's a rattle in my chest,
more desolate than
a cold blast!

. . .

me tozuredo,
kokoro ni ukabu nani mo nashi.
sabishikumo, mata, me o
akeru kana.

I close my eyes in meditation,
in my heart there is nothing.
from loneliness I
open them again.

The intensity of feeling, whether of loneliness or despair, comes from the fact that Takuboku composed many of the tanka from his sickbed. His perception has become more realistic, centering on the details of his everyday life. Consequently, he no longer yearns much for the past, focusing instead on the time and place of his present life. Takuboku's final years were indeed ones of struggle, both physically and mentally.

Significantly, however, the intensity of feeling of *Sad Toys* is moderated by discipline of style. In order to heighten the effect of the words, Takuboku made two distinct stylis-

tic innovations in these later tanka. First, for the use of simile, prominent in *A Handful of Sand,* Takuboku has substituted the use of various forms of punctuation. Takuboku had discovered that punctuation functions as effectively as simile in enlarging the poetic dimension of the tanka form. He uses punctuation, therefore, for a specific purpose and makes it an integral part of the tanka. Secondly, in *Sad Toys* Takuboku makes full use of the various possible arrangements of the thirty-one syllables of the tanka. While following most of the time the basic 5-7-5-7-7 syllabification Takuboku freely arranges it in three lines, ignoring the particular rhythm the division of the 5-7-5-7-7 syllabification usually creates. More than rhythm Takuboku places stress on the meaning of a tanka. Along with Takuboku's mastery of the three-line verse form, his flexibility in syllabification contributed to making his tanka close to free verse in the western style. Takuboku's conscious efforts, then, following the publication of *A Handful of Sand,* to bring about innovations in the tanka led to the discovery of a form and style most suited to his particular sensitivity and personality. This development, the result of strict discipline on his part, had the secondary effect of helping make the pain of his daily life more bearable.

> **Along with Takuboku's mastery of the three-line verse form, his flexibility in syllabification contributed to making his tanka close to free verse in the western style.**
>
> **—Yukihito Hijiya**

One might say that in *Sad Toys* stylistic restraint is used as a protective shield against the encroachment of despair. In *Sad Toys,* therefore, more so than in *A Handful of Sand,* Takuboku comes forth as an accomplished artist of modern tanka, master of the style by which he could integrate form and content. Takuboku's originality lies in this development of his own unique style, which in turn gave new life to his treatment of the now old subject, the private world of his inner feelings.

Let us here examine some examples of Takuboku's new poetic development. Takuboku uses, for instance, exclamation marks to reveal the feelings of the characters presented in a situation:

tabi o omou otto no kokoro!
shikari, naku, tsuma-ko no
kokoro!
asa no shokutaku!

husband's heart thinking
of a trip!
scolding, crying, hearts of
wife and child!
the breakfast table!

The function of exclamation points in this tanka is twofold. One is to make the reader visualize the situation at the breakfast table: the husband, longing for a moment of freedom, watching unconcernedly while his wife scolds their child; the other is to distinguish the kind and degree of sadness felt by the three individuals. That Takuboku can portray a scene of which he himself is a part with such detached objectivity is an indication of his maturation as a poet.

Two examples of the use of exclamation points for a different effect are:

> kyō mo mata sake nomeru kana!
> sake nomeba
> mune no mukatsuku kuse o
> shiritsutsu.

> I drink sake again today!
> knowing I'll be upset
> if I drink.

. . .

> yamite areba kokoro mo
> yowaruramu!
> samazama no
> nakitaki koto ga mune ni
> atsumaru.

> in sickness the heart, too,
> becomes weak!
> all kinds of sadness
> collect in my chest.

The first tanka was written before Takuboku became ill and the second after. In both cases various kinds of emotions felt by the poet are conveyed by the exclamation points. In the last two lines following the punctuation mark the poet gives the reason for his pause, and the exclamation point intensifies the sense of self-disgust implied in the last two lines. The punctuation in Takuboku's tanka calls on the reader to exercise his own imagination, thereby bringing him into the world of the poem, to feel what the poet feels and to grasp intuitively the message hinted at by the punctuation. Other tanka in which exclamation points are used for a similar effect are:

> te mo ashi mo hanare-banare ni
> aru gotoki
> monouki nezame!
> kanashiki nezame!

> a fatigue like feet and hands
> fallen off
> melancholy awakening!
> sad awakening!

. . .

> jitto shite,
> mikan no tsuyu ni somaritaru
> tsume o mitsumuru
> kokoro motonasa!

> the wretched heart
> of one staring fixedly
> at juice-stained
> fingernails.

. . .

> kamisama to giron shite
> nakishi—
> ano yume yo!
> yokka bakari mo mae no
> asa narishi.

> arguing with God and crying—
> that dream!
> in the morning four days
> ago.

. . .

> me samashite sugu no
> kokoro yo!
> toshiyori no iede no kiji nimo
> namida idetari.

> just wakened with a clear,
> pure heart!
> can't stop crying at the news
> of an old man who ran away
> from home.

Another mark of punctuation which Takuboku uses to fill a gap between what is said and what is not said is the dash:

> ie o dete gochō bakari wa,
> yō no aru hito no gotoku ni
> aruite mitaredo—

> leaving the house,
> like one on an errand,
> walked about five blocks—

. . .

> atarashiki asu no kitaru o
> shinzu to yū
> jibun no kotoba ni
> uso wa nakeredo—

> when I say
> I believe a new day is coming
> I am not lying—

. . .

> warau nimo waraware-zariki—
> nagai koto sagashita naifu no
> te no naka ni arishi ni.

> no laughing matter—
> the knife I searched for
> all that time
> was in my hand.

In these tanka what is left unsaid, indicated by dashes, is what the poet wishes most to stress. The silence created by these dashes intensifies the sense of the frustration, anxiety and anger by which the sensitive poet is incessantly tormented.

The dash is also used for creating a different kind of effect:

> omou koto nusumi-kikaruru
> gotoku nite,
> tsuto mune o hikinu—
> chōshinki yori.

> as if my thoughts were
> being overheard,
> suddenly pulled my chest

back—
from the stethoscope.

. . .

unmei no kite noreru ka to
utagainu—
futon no omoki yowa no
nezame ni.

wondered if my fate
had jumped up on my bed—
wakened up by the
heavy quilt.

. . .

atarashiki sarado no iro no
ureshisa ni,
hashi toriagete mi wa
mitsuredomo—

delighted with the fresh
lettuce leaves
I pick up my chopsticks,
but I cannot eat—

. . .

mō uso o iwaji to omoiki—
sore wa kesa—
ima mata hitotsu uso o
ieru kana.

I'll tell no more lies—
that was this morning—
now I've already told
another one.

. . .

aru hi, futo, yamai o wasure,
ushi no naku mane o
shiteminu,—
tsuma-ko no rusu ni.

one day, momentarily forgetting
sickness,
I tried mooing like a cow,—
while my wife and child
were out.

In each of the above examples, by using a dash Takuboku has created a dramatic situation with activity. The first tanka, for example, shows the poet pulling himself back from a doctor's stethoscope as if to protect his secret thoughts from being overheard. In the pause produced by the dash, the reader can feel the poet's fear, hope and curiosity, focused all at once on the stethoscope. Similarly, in the second tanka one can immediately visualize the poet in the middle of the night trying to move the quilted bed cover to ease his feeling of oppression. The dashes function as stage directions in a dramatic piece, enabling the reader to follow the movements of the poet's heart. A similar use of a dash can be seen in another tanka:

yogoretaru te o miru—
chōdo
konogoro no jibun no kokoro ni
mukau ga gotoshi.

my dirty hands—

looking at them is like
looking at my heart.

In this poem, the best example of Takuboku's purposeful manipulation of the tanka syllabication, the dash spotlights the poet looking at his soiled hands, which he, Macbeth-like, sees as symbolic of the state of his heart.

Of all punctuation marks the most frequently used is the comma:

bon'yari to shita kanashimi ga,
yo to nareba,
nedai no ue ni sotto
kite noru.

a vague sadness,
when night falls,
comes and jumps upon my bed.

The commas, which indicate a pause after one action before another follows, at the end of the first and the second lines enable the reader to understand sadness through the concrete visual image of a pet (presumably a cat) creeping silently into a room at night and jumping gently onto the bed. Thus through the use of commas along with the image of a tamed pet, Takuboku has created a serene tone, which shows that he has come to terms with sorrow, embracing it with calm resolution. Even sadness, which has been a constant tormentor of his life, has become a friendly visitor to a heart now accustomed to it.

To quote some other tanka well controlled by commas:

aonuri no seto no hibachi ni
yorikakari,
me toji, me o ake,
toki o oshimeri.

leaning on the blue china
hibachi,
closed my eyes, opened them
again,
just to kill time.

. . .

suppori to futon o kaburi,
ashi o chijime,
shita no dashite minu, dare ni
tomo nashini.

pull the quilt clear over
my head,
pull up my legs,
stick out my tongue,
at nobody.

. . .

ko o shikareba,
naite, neirinu.
kuchi sukoshi akeshi negao ni
sawarite miru kana.

scolded, in tears the child
fell asleep,
with her mouth half open.
I touched her sleeping face.

. . .

yamai iezu,
shinazu,
higoto ni kokoro nomi kewashiku
nareru nana-yatsuki kana.

not getting well,
not dying,
a heart growing daily
more bitter.

. . .

nanigoto ka ima ware
tsubuyakeri.
kaku omoi,
me o uchitsuburi, ei o ajiwau.

muttered something just now.
so thinking,
closed my eyes, to enjoy
being drunk.

. . .

arano yuku kisha no gotoku ni,
kono nayami,
tokidoki ware no kokoro o tōru.

like a train through
a wasteland,
this suffering at times,
runs across my heart.

. . .

yamite shigatsu—
sono ma nimo, nao, meni miete,
waga ko no setake nobishi
kanashimi.

four months since I fell ill—
during that time, I can see
my daughter's grown
that much.

The period is another punctuation mark with which Takuboku achieves unity between the form and the content of a tanka. Let us look at the following:

tonomo niwa hanetsuku
oto su.
warau koe su.
kyonen no shōgatsu ni kaereru
gotoshi.

outdoors the sound of
the shuttlecock.
laughing voices.
like returning to last
year's New Year.

. . .

nan to naku,
kotoshi wa yoi koto
arugotoshi.
ganjitsu no asa, harete
kaze nashi.

there's the feeling somehow,
this will be a good year.
the New Year morning,
bright and calm.

In the first example by using a period at the end of each line Takuboku shows himself becoming aware of the sounds from out of doors as he lies indoors confined to his bed. They are the typical sounds of New Year's Day, sounds of the shuttlecock and of laughter. He lets them sink into his consciousness one by one, his moments of reflection indicated by the periods. The last line brings the two sounds together and combines them with the poet's recollections of New Year's Days of the past, when he, too, was participating in the games and the laughter. In the second piece, the period at the end of the second line emphasizes the poet's sentiment: he is convinced (or perhaps wants very much to be convinced) that something good will happen this year. In the last line he describes the beautiful clear day with no wind, surely a harbinger of good fortune, which has brought him to this conclusion.

A period by separating two parts of a tanka may also serve to heighten a sense of alienation:

hito ga mina
onaji hōgaku ni muite yuku.
sore o yoko yori
mite iru kokoro.

everybody's
going in the same direction.
the heart of one who
watches from the side.

The periods used in this tanka point up the emotional distance between the poet and others by creating a sensation of steady movement in the first sentence and a feeling of marking time in the second. The sense of movement is produced by the uninterrupted flow of the first two lines: the people are all going in the same direction unimpeded by someone moving in an opposite direction just as the lines describing them are unimpeded by punctuation. The sentence ends with a verb ("*yuku*"—"go"), making the reader's last impression of the people one of movement. The period effectively separates this active society from the solitary world of the poet who stands on the sidelines, watching these people going their own way. The noun ending of the last line ("*kokoro*"—"heart") emphasizes the static feeling.

Finally let us look at an example in which Takuboku uses a comma, a period and a question mark:

kono shigonen,
sora o aogu to yū koto ga
ichido mo nakariki.
kō mo narumono ka?

these four or five years,
I haven't once looked up
at the sky.
could this really have
happened?

The comma carries the feeling of a downward look and forces a pause as if a person is moving slowly, thoughtfully. The period brings the poem to a complete stop: the poet is stunned to realize how preoccupied he has been. In the last line a question has already been indicated by the particle "*ka*"; the addition of a question mark stresses the poet's incredulity that he has developed such a pattern of life.

Takuboku conducts one further experiment with method. He gives a direct quotation of a statement made to him and his own reaction to it:

> "Ishikawa wa fubin na yatsu da."
> toki ni kō jibun de iite,
> kanashimite miru.

> "Ishikawa is a pitiful fellow."
> sometimes saying this to
> myself,
> I make myself sad.

                    . . .

> sonnaraba inochi ga hoshiku-
> nai no ka to,
> isha ni iwarete,
> damarishi kokoro!

> then you really don't want
> to live?
> scolded by my physician,
> my heart gave no answer!

                    . . .

> mō omae no shintei o yoku
> mitodoketa to,
> yume ni haha kite
> naite yukishi kana.

> I know what you're thinking.
> in a dream my mother appeared
> and weeping went away.

                    . . .

> jitto shite nete irasshai to
> kodomo ni demo yū ga gotoku ni
> isha no yū hi kana.

> now just be quiet and rest.
> as though talking to a child
> the day the physician said that.

In the first tanka the speaker is the poet's own superego; the other tanka quote his mother or his physician. In every instance, however, the poet is faced with an authority figure, someone passing judgment on him or in some other way treating him as a child. It is this pointing up of his imagined shortcomings which evokes his own internal reaction. This miniature dialogue makes the tanka as dramatic as the short form will allow. The use of direct quotations creates living people in an actual situation, thus bringing a new realism to the tanka form, a legacy perhaps of Takuboku's early apprenticeship in novel writing.

As was observed at the beginning of this section, many of Takuboku's last tanka, written from a sickbed, were more than ever concerned with the details of his present life, fast slipping away from him. Of all of his everyday worries Takuboku's parents were always among his chief concerns; they appear again in the tanka of *Sad Toys.*

Takuboku's father had become a drifter like his son after he failed to regain his position at Hōtoku Temple at Shibutami. When Takuboku moved in August into a house after leaving the hospital in the spring of 1911, Ittei joined his son's household:

> kanashiki wa waga chichi!
> kyō mo shimbun o yomi akite,
> niwa ni koari to asoberi.

> my pitiful father!
> today again bored with
> reading the newspaper,
> he plays with the ants
> in the garden.

The son's verse vividly catches the tragedy of the father's life. A man in the prime of life, formerly a person held in high respect in his community, deprived of position, esteem and livelihood, is now passing his days to no purpose dependent on an invalid son.

Takuboku's mother seems torn between determined hope and frustration:

> cha made tachite,
> waga heifuku o inoritamau
> haha no kyō mata nanika
> ikareru.

> even giving up her
> favorite tea,
> to pray for my recovery
> what is Mother angry about
> today?

Giving up the tea she is so fond of is for her a form of abstinence or fasting as she prays for her son's recovery. Her faith and patience, however, are wearing thin as her prayers seem to fall on deaf ears. The disruption of her own household, long separations from her husband, the illness of her son and lack of compatibility with her daughter-in-law, aggravated by poverty and privation and her own poor health, all contribute to her frequent outbursts of temper.

Takuboku, now a parent himself, can empathize with his parent's expectations of him. He realizes that as the only son he was the recipient of special favors and the focus of special hopes. Even their present misfortune is of course due to their overindulgence of their son. Takuboku, now confined to bed, can only feel remorse at his inability to help them, a feeling mingled, no doubt, with guilt over the single-minded pursuit of his own ideals:

> tada hitori no
> otoko no ko naru ware wa
> kaku sodateri.
> fubo mo kanashikaruramu.

> to have their only son
> turn out like this.
> my parents must surely be
> grieving.

From the standpoint of subject matter one particular area of concentration in *Sad Toys* is the world of a sick person. Some of the pieces have already been cited; here we see others which catch feelings of hopelessness, loneliness and the suppressed yet ever present fear of death, written while Takuboku was in the hospital:

> fukuretaru hara o nadetsutsu,

byōin no nedai ni, hitori,
kanashimite ari.

stroking my swollen stomach,
in the hospital bed, alone,
in sorrow.

. . .

doa oshite hitoashi dereba,
byōnin no me ni hatemonaki
nagarōka kana.

push the door open and step
out,
to the eyes of the sick person
the long corridor seems endless.

. . .

mayonaka ni futo me ga samete,
wake mo naku nakitaku narite,
futon o kabureru.

awaking in the middle of
the night,
for no reason wanting to cry,
pull the quilt over my head.

. . .

hanashi kakete
henji no naki ni
yoku mireba,
naite itariki, tonari no kanja.

no reply
then I notice he is crying,
the patient in the next bed.

. . .

yoru osoku doko yara no
heya no sawagashiki wa
hito ya shinitaramu to,
iki o hisomuru.

late at night, from somewhere
a stir
has someone died, maybe?
I hold my breath.

In the monotonous daily routine details take on an added
significance:

myaku o toru kangofu no te no,
atatakaki hi ari,
tsumetaku kataki hi mo ari.

the hand of the nurse
checking pulses,
some days warm,
some days hard and cold.

. . .

myaku o toru te no furui koso
kanashikere—
isha ni shikarare
wakaki kangofu!

the trembling of the hand
that checks my pulse
has a special sadness—

the young nurse scolded by
the physician!

Yet the stay in the hospital has had some good effects as
well on Takuboku's feelings. The separation from his family and respite from the cares of their daily life has called
forth more positive feelings for them:

byōin ni kite,
tsuma ya ko o itsukushimu
makoto no ware ni
kaerikeru kana.

in the hospital,
love my wife and child
I've found myself again.

As we have seen in both **A Handful of Sand** and **Sad Toys**
Takuboku made of his tanka a poetic journal of his private
life, recorded in thirty-one syllable entries. This personal-
ization of the tanka was a marked break with tradition, the
significance of which cannot be overemphasized. From the
time of the *Man'yōshū,* which was compiled in the middle
of the eighth century, the traditional subject matter of
tanka had been the world of nature. Furthermore, Takuboku's break with traditional subject matter led also to a
break with traditional form. Tanka convention called for
the poet to produce a regular phrasal sequence in a syllab-
ic count of 5-7-5-7-7 while achieving a perfect unity between the sound of the words and the image they create.
It was generally felt that writing the thirty-one syllables
in one single line was the most effective way to accomplish
this. In his employment of the three-line form, Takuboku
liberated himself from the restraints of the long tanka tradition and opened the way for further modifications. As
Odagiri Hideo points out:

> Rather than the traditional unity in meter and
> rhythm, Takuboku has moved toward a form
> and style that correspond to the content, the
> meaning of a tanka. While preserving the basic
> form of the tanka, and while maintaining the
> method of creating the intended unified effect
> by combining imagery and the sound of
> words . . . , by organization a tanka in three
> lines he tried to develop a new possibility in the
> tanka. Takuboku did not abandon the basic tra-
> ditional frame of the tanka in which the poet
> condenses the reality of humanity into thirty-
> one syllables . . . ; he merely expanded its origi-
> nality, and made of the tanka a poetic expression
> most appropriate for the description of truthful
> experience of humanity. By using three lines for
> the tanka, Takuboku has brought the tanka
> closer to poetry, which has flexibility in form ac-
> cording to its content. [Quoted by Iwaki Yuki-
> nori in *Collected Works of Ishikawa Takuboku*]

The world of Takuboku's tanka is that of his actual life
brought into sharp focus. It is the private world of one individual, but the personal feelings of that individual transformed into art of lasting value. In this sense, one can say
that it is the most personal tanka that possess universal
quality. Takuboku drew his tanka from the deepest levels
of his emotional experience, the most human experience
of all.

Yukinori Iwaki   (essay date 1981)

SOURCE: "An American Collection of Western Poems and the Early Career of Ishikawa Takuboku," in *Comparative Literature Studies,* Vol. XVIII, No. 2, June, 1981, pp. 104-13.

[*In the following essay, Iwaki discusses the poems and translations in Takuboku's notebook,* Ebb and Flow, *and the influence of English and American poetry on Takuboku's early writings.*]

Ishikawa Takuboku (1886-1912) was a poet who lived and wrote at the end of the Meiji period. Although he died young, at the age of 27, he was a rare genius. His main works consist of just one uncompleted collection of poems, *Yobuko to Kuchibue,* and two collections of *tanka,* *Ichiaku no Suna* and *Kanashiki Gangu.* However, he left an eternal mark on the history of the modern *tanka* by the new form of expression which he used in the above two collections of *tanka,* (that is, writing *tanka* in three verses) and by his unique works whose subjects are closely connected to life.

His poems have been appreciated and recited by many who have had difficult times in their youth in the midst of the harsh events of Japanese history since the Taisho period. The poignancy of the failures in his youth and the passionate spirit of his poetry, with which he challenged the irrationality of society, gained an eternal life for his poetry by appealing to the naive and sensitive souls of young people. His first complete works were published by Shinchosha in 1919. The last ones were published by Chikuma Shobo in 1968. They have been published six times from 1919 to 1968. This tells us that he was one of the greatest poets, one who has been loved by many Japanese people for the last half century.

His real name was Ishikawa Hajime. He was born in Hinoto Village in Minami—Iwate District in I wate Prefecture on February 20, 1886. According to another report, his birthday is October 27, 1885. His father, Ishikawa Ittei, was a curate of Jōkō Temple of the Sōtō Sect in this village. His mother, Katsu, was a younger sister of Ittei's master, Katsuhara Taigetsu. In the spring of 1887, Takuboku's father became a curate of Hōtoku Temple in Shibutami Village in Kita—Iwate District, and his family moved there. This is the village Takuboku called his home town and loved all his life.

In 1898, when Takuboku was thirteen years old, he entered Morioka High School of Iwate Prefecture with a high score in the entrance examination; he was the tenth highest out of 128 students who passed the examination. However, as he advanced in school, he indulged himself in literature and love, neglecting his studies. Consequently, he left high school on October 27, 1902, just a half year before graduation, and went up to Tokyo with the intention of taking up a literary career. But this trial failed, and he returned home to take care of himself because he was defeated and sick.

Although Takuboku was very talented, unfortunately he did not complete a formal education. This ruined his whole life. For without a formal education he found that, even with his talent, it was impossible to be freed from a miserable fate and to climb up in society, leaving the hardships of life. Indeed, the pathway he took was not easy after he left Morioka High School. In the spring of 1905, his father, Ittei, was dismissed from the position of curate Hōtoku Temple by the Affairs Office of the Sōtō Sect because he failed to pay fees to the sect. This marked a turning point in Takuboku's life. After that his wandering life began: he moved from Morioka to Shibutami and from Shibutami to Hokkaido.

In April of 1908, Takuboku left Hokkaido and went to Tokyo to start a literary career. The only way to succeed in this society for one who was gifted in literature and yet who did not have formal education was to go up to Tokyo, to write novels, and to become a popular writer. This is why Takuboku longed for a literary life in Tokyo with an almost excessive enthusiasm while he was in Hokkaido, why he abandoned the life of a journalist in Kushiro, and why he went to Tokyo even though he had to leave his family behind in Hakodate. He tried to grasp this only chance by himself. However, in spite of his hope and his efforts, his literary life in Tokyo turned out to be a failure.

On March 1, 1909, Takuboku obtained employment as a proofreader at Tokyo Asahi Press. He called his family from Hakodate to Tokyo and rented a room on the second floor of a barber shop, Kinotoko, in Yumi-chō in Hongō. His desperation in these days is expressed in one of his poems:

> Today all my friends seemed better off than I
> Flowers I bought to bring home
> With my wife I enjoy them

His three-verse *tanka,* which were created out of his bitter life, inspired the circle of poets of his time. He was also elected to be a judge of "Asahi Kadan" (Asahi Poets Circle) through the favor of the city editor of Asahi Press, Shibukawa Ryujiro. However, he had never attained the glory of a writer, as he had intended, and the bitter life of a failure was his destiny. Toward the end of his life he wrote a poem:

> Although I have worked
> Although I have worked, my life still does not
>   become easier
> I look hard at my hands

Thus, although he suffered from poverty and solitude, he never lost his hope; he confronted the oppressive reality of the time seriously and tried to view the future of mankind. After the case of high treason of June 1910, he approached socialism by responding to the writings of Kōtoku Shūsui and Kropotkin. The fact that he drew a socialistic image of Japan's future is explained by this shift in his thought. His collections of tanka, *Ichiaku no Suna* [*One Handful of Sand*] (1910) and *Kanashiki Gangu* [*Sad Toys*] (1912), his collection of poems, *Yobuko to Kuchibue* [*Whistles and Whistling*] (1911), and his criticism, *Jidai Heisoku no Genjo* [*The Status of a Stagnant Age*] (1910) are all representative works of Takuboku's literature and were created from his thought and life in Tokyo in the later period of his life when he was influenced by the new thoughts as mentioned above. They eloquently describe for us Takuboku's life flaring up to fight with his misfortune, to work faithfully as a man of letters, and to try to grasp the future of Japan correctly.

Takuboku's poems eloquently describe for us Takuboku's life flaring up to fight with his misfortune, to work faithfully as a man of letters, and to try to grasp the future of Japan correctly.

—*Yukinori Iwaki*

On April 13, 1912, Takuboku's stormy and unfortunate life ended in a rented house in 74 Hisakata-chō in Ko-ishikawa in Tokyo. He died from tuberculosis.

Takuboku joined the "Myōjō" group of poetry with the publication of "**Shūchō,**" five poems, in the magazine *Myōjō* in December 1903 and of "**Mori no Omoide**" in *Myōjō* in January 1904. This was also the first time for him to use the name Takuboku. He was encouraged by the praise from his friends and from Yosano Tekkan. Henceforth, he began the career of a poet. It did not take very long for the new poet to publish his first completed collection of poems, *Akogare,* which was published by Odajima Book Company in Tokyo in May 1905.

However, this turning point in his career has not been fully explained. The existing biographies claim that his letter of January 1, 1904 to Anezaki Chōfū explains his motivation for writing poems. In this letter Takuboku wrote:

In the beginning of last November, when my sickness was losing its strength, I thought of writing poetry, by which I had been fascinated all my life. Just by chance, a new style flashed in my mind. Since then I have been composing quite earnestly. This became a sort of secret pleasure for me.

However, this letter is too general and vague to explain what happened in his mind during this turning point in his career. The newly discovered notebook, *Ebb and Flow,* not only shows the influence of poems in English on his writings but also helps us to understand this hidden period.

After his failure in Tokyo in the fall of 1902, Takuboku returned to his home in Shibutami. There, as he took care of his health, and as he tried to return to the literary life, he began to study the German composer, Richard Wagner, and he wrote a series of articles entitled, "The Ideas of Wagner," for the newspaper, *Iwate Nippō.* At the same time, he read various literary journals such as *Myōjō* and *Taiyō.*

The articles on Wagner, however, were a failure. He could not complete the series, and his articles did not draw any special attention. He needed some new inspiration. It seems that around this time, the summer of 1903, he obtained an American collection of poems, *Surf and Wave:*

The Sea as Sung by Poets. Why and how he came across this collection is not clear. It might be a mere coincidence, however, that Nonohito (Saitō Shinsaku) published a very inspiring article about the sea, "Umi to Jinsei" ["The Sea and Life"]. Because Takuboku was reading all sorts of literary magazines at this time and also because the author, Nonohito, was the younger brother of Takayama Chogyū, whom Takuboku admired, it is very possible that Takuboku read this article, and this might have been the reason why he obtained the collection of the poems of the sea. Here is a quotation from the article:

The man who suffers, the man who smiles, the man who admires beauty, the man who is in love, how could they not love the sea? The sea is a portrait of life. I love the sea. Ah, I love the sea! . . . Indeed the sea has been the same since ancient times. Smiles and anxiety, indeed all the feelings and thoughts of life are still flowing with the current.

Ebb and Flow was discovered in the Hakodate City Library. It consists of English poems in Takuboku's handwriting and of his own writings, mainly poems. The notebook shows his reaction to these poems in English and the development of his writing from the fall of 1903 to the next spring.

This Western-style notebook is 20 cm. wide and 21 cm. long, with 108 pages. A doubled, brown velvet paper is attached as a cover, since the original cover has been damaged and lost. A single sheet of the same paper is pasted inside of both front and back covers as the inside cover pages. The title is written down clearly on the top of the first page. The notebook is divided into two parts. The first half, pages 1-56, is filled with poems in English. The second half of the notebook begins from the back of the book and runs to the middle, from pages 108-57, and it contains his own writings. Following is a list of the poems in English which he copied:

"The Waves" by Bayard Taylor; "Dover Beach" by Matthew Arnold; "A Reflection at Sea" by Thomas Moore; "The Sailing of the 'Swallow' " by Swinburne; "Chrysaor" by Longfellow; "The Voice and the Peak" by Tennyson; "To the Ocean" by Thomas Hood; "On the Sea" by Keats; "Is My Lover on the Sea?" by Bryan Waller Procter; "Vineta" by Wilhelm Müller; "By the Seaside" by Wordsworth; "The 'Three Bells' " by Whittier; "God Bless the Ships" Anonymous; "A Tune on the Water" by Francesco Redi; "Sailing Beyond Seas" by Jean Ingelow; "The Waters are Rising and Flowing" by George Macdonald; "The Ocean" by Charles Tennyson Turner; "Song" by Heine; "To—" and From "Clytemnestra" by A. Owen Meredith; "Sonnet" by Robert Southey; "Listening to Music" by Richard Watson Gilder; "By the Seaside" by James Drummond Burns; "Music in the Air" by George William Curtis; From "Each and All" by Emerson; "Hopes and Waves" by Ludwig Uhland; From "Don Juan" by Byron; "Faces on the Wall (Storm and Calm)" Robert Buchanan; From *King Richard III* by Shakespeare; "Song" by Arthur Hugh Clough; "Sleep at Sea" by Christina Rosetti; "The Tides" by

Longfellow; "Rafe's Chasm, Cape Ann (September 28, 1882)" by Elizabeth Stuart Phelps; "Funeral at Sea" by Robert Southey; "A Wet Sheet and a Flowing Sea" by Allan Cunningham; "The Sea-Limits" by Dante Gabriel Rosetti; "Voices of the Sea" Anonymous; "The Ocean" by James Montgomery; "The Sea" by Brian Waller Procter; "Break, Break, Break" by Tennyson; "Oh, Had We Some Bright Little Isle of Our Own!" by Thomas Moore.

The first poem, "The Waves," is copied just beneath the title of the notebook on the first page. Actually, Takuboku copied only the first eight lines of this poem, which consists of five stanzas. There are big circles in pencil on the left side of the titles of nine poems; "Dover Beach," "A Reflection at Sea," "Vineta," "By the Seaside," "The Ocean," "Each and All," "Faces on the Wall (Storm and Calm)," "The Sea-Limits," and "Break, Break, Break." This probably means that Takuboku was impressed by these poems.

Takuboku's own writings start from page 108 at the back of the book and continue toward the middle, to page 57. There are twelve poems, one essay, one *tanka,* and eight fragments. The "Essay on Contemporary Novels," which is on page 108, is an unfinished essay of literary criticism. Since the place and his name are added between the title and the main text, it might have been written for some newspaper. However, it was never published. Following is a list of some of his own poems in the order in which they appear:

> "Tama yo Shizume" ["Soul, Be Calm"]; "Yūbe no Umi" ["Evening Sea"]; "Mori no Omoide" ["Memories of the Forest"]; "Mori no Michi" ["A Forest Path"]; "Omoide" ["Reminiscence"]; "Inochi no Fune" ["The Boat of Life"]; "Shiberia no Uta" ["Song of Siberia"]; "Kokyo" ["Solitude"]; "Nishikigizuka" ["The Commemorative Mound of the Decorated Tree"]; "Tsurugaibashi" ["Tsurugai Bridge"]; "Gekishi: Chimmoku no Koe" ["Dramatic Poem: Voice of Silence"]; "Kita no Umi" ["The Northern Sea"].

It is not certain from where he took the title of the notebook, *Ebb and Flow,* but in *Surf and Wave,* there is a poem entitled "Ebb and Flow," by an American novelist and journalist, George William Curtis, although Takuboku did not copy this poem in his notebook. This poem compares man's life with the ebb and flow of the ocean tide. Also, in "Dover Beach," by Matthew Arnold, there are the lines: "and it brought / Into his mind the turbid ebb and flow / of human misery." In any case, he intended to convey his reflections on his own life in this phrase.

The date of *Ebb and Flow* cannot be pinpointed either. On January 15, 1904, Takuboku presented his *Surf and Wave* to his friend, Kanaya Shugen. In a letter of August 26, 1903, he quoted Uhland's "Hopes and Waves" from *Surf and Wave.* Takuboku must have possessed the book by then. We can assume that he was copying English poems from the beginning of fall 1903 to January 1904. On the other hand, we can say that most of his poems were written from the beginning of December 1903 to early spring

of 1904. The "Essay on Contemporary Novels" was probably written early in December 1903, and **"Tama yo Shizume"** ["Soul, Be Calm"] was composed on December 3, 1903, and most of the other works were composed by January 1904. Furthermore, the letter heading on page 75, "Tetsuro, Tetsuro, Kawamura 530 11th St. Oakland," corresponds to the mention of "writing a long letter to Mr. Tetsuro Kawamura in Oakland, California, U.S.A." in Takuboku's diary entry of February 8, 1904. Thus, *Ebb and Flow* seems to have been completed from the beginning of fall 1903 to the early spring of 1904.

Surf and Wave: The Sea as Sung by Poets was edited by Anna L. Ward and was published by Thomas Y. Crowell in 1883. She collected songs and poems about the sea from Europe and America and published them in English. There are five chapters in the book: "Sea-Breezes," "Waves of the Deep," "Sea-spray," "Surf-edges," and "Ocean-soundings." Three hundred and fifty-two poems are included in this collection. The contributors include such well-known authors as Dickens, George Eliot, Sir Walter Scott, Shelley, Matthew Arnold, Tennyson, Wilde, Swift, Poe, Wordsworth, Byron, and Emerson.

After close examination of a microfilm copy of *Surf and Wave* the following facts were confirmed: all the poems in English in *Ebb and Flow* are from this book. Takuboku chose them from all the chapters: six from Chapter 1, six from Chapter 2, seven from Chapter 3, twelve from Chapter 4 and ten from Chapter 5. Takuboku's arrangement of the titles, main texts, names of authors and also of the translators is exactly the same as in the book, and even the decorative lines used to separate poems from one another are also imitated by Takuboku.

Surf and Wave, the source of the forty—one poems in English which Takuboku copied in *Ebb and Flow,* was not found for a long while, even after *Ebb and Flow* had been discovered. Later, however, with the help of Professor Unosuke Shimizu and Mr. Hitoshi Fukai of Waseda University Library, one copy of *Surf and Wave* was found in Waseda University Library.

When we compare the poems of *Surf and Wave, Ebb and Flow,* and *Akogare [Longing],* we note a number of similarities. First, Matthew Arnold's "Dover Beach" and **"Kita no Umi" [The Northern Sea]** from *Ebb and Flow* should be compared. "Dover Beach" is well known in Japan, and it has been translated into Japanese many times. However, since in Takuboku's time there was no translation available, Takuboku must have read the poem in English. He seems to have been profoundly moved by the fresh poetic sentiments of the poem. **"Kita no Umi"** was written down in the space above "Dover Beach" in *Ebb and Flow.* Here is a translation of Takuboku's poem:

> On the white sand reflecting the moonlight
> The sea draws gently
> Blooms like flowers along the long coast
> Draws a blue and lonesome line
> Traces eternity intermittently
> Beats the rhythm of the cold waves to an ancient
>   melody
> The moon of the seventh night

The moon sobbing and setting into the dreadful
   ocean
The sea draws and embraces me
Rolls me up and will never let me go, the Northern Sea

Arnold and Takuboku may have been looking at different seas, but their poems share a similarity in tone and imagery.

Next, let us examine "Vineta" in *Surf and Wave* and **"Shizumeru Kane" ["The Sunken Bell"]** in *Akogare.* "Vineta," which appears on pages 12-13 of *Ebb and Flow,* was written by the German poet, Wilhelm Müller (1794-1827) and was translated by Samuel W. Duffield. The title is the name of a legendary city (Wendenstadt in the original). It is said that this city existed on the Baltic coast, that it was inhabited by Wendens and Vikings in the 8th and 9th centuries, that it flourished with trade and then sank under the water because of an extraordinary change in the earth in the 10th century. In this poem, Wilhelm Müller expressed his sense of loss and wonder at the Vineta legend.

Takuboku seems to have been fascinated by this poem. He not only marked a big circle in front of the title, but he also copied a couple of the first lines of the poem on page 103, among his own poems in *Ebb and Flow.* He even gave a Japanese title to "Vineta"—"Umi ni Sasaguru Uta" [A Song Offered to the Sea].

Takuboku's long poem **"Shizumeru Kane" ["The Sunken Bell"]** is obviously written under the influence of "Vineta." This poem was first published in the magazine *Jidai Shichō* and later included in *Akogare* as the opening poem. This is a long poem for Takuboku, and it is known that Takuboku spent thirty-five days to compose it. Following is a translation of the poem:

"The Sunken Bell"

I

From the dreamy and misty chaos, the dawn separated the darkness as earth and the light as heaven. On returning high to the throne of the heavens, [God] in the purple cloud in which seven treasures bloom, the wagon of "time" under the eave with hanging and swinging decorations, instructed the eternal, gigantic bell to exhort toward life and law, as a witness to eternal life, [and he] threw it into the ocean. God ruled from high in the blue heavens. Time has passed, spring has come eight hundred, thousands of times. How many glories have flourished and disappeared? However, without aging, over the earth day and night, echoing the endless sound (a miracle?) from the bottom of the ancient ocean, the "secret" sound, the sunken bell tolls.

II

In the morning and in the evening, and even in the deep breath of nights, in the midst of the day storm, although there is nobody to strike the bell, the great bell tolls ceaselessly. Is it the voice of the heart of nature? Eternal "sleep"? Or the "wakening" of the infinite life? Faintly, cheerfully, reverberating into the clouds, the high tide overflow, sighing an invitation to tragic love. In the color of small shells, in the whispering of dead leaves, plentifully filled, the soundless echo of love.

To the grieving mind, for the lips of the thirsty spirit, it gives the beads of light of the crystal water. And it sends heavenly music to those who adore the blue flower in the holy land among the fragrant clouds. The Messiah, the voice of the sunken bell—Ah! You toll to tell us the sacred secret?

III

Once your voice touches the heartstrings, hundreds of people on the earth go beyond the limit of human powers. Like the exultation of Pegasus, they make a cry of love. Looking at the free spirit, the beaming light of the spirit shines in their eyes, and they look forward to the infinite and advance history in the golden light. Carved names are rusted, every where, on this hill, on this gravestone—I look up at the memento of this lesson.

Trailing the torn skirt over the dark earth, ah! be heard now, telling of orders given from heaven. The voice of light drifting from the ancient abysses—Filled with light, do I resemble God? Sky, leave the earth! Or heaven, descend and in this world erect the throne of the poet, filled with lotus flowers.

(March 19, 1904)

Takuboku handles this theme of the eternal sounds of a sunken bell and creates a dense poetic sentiment. Not only does the situation of the poem resemble that of "Vineta," but the images are very likely borrowed from "Vineta." For example, "gōsho" from "long ago," "ōgane" from "bell," "naru" from "chiming," "unazoko" from "the sea's deep, deep unfathomed distance," "ai" from "love" and "fukami" from "abysses." These similarities suggest that Takuboku's **"The Sunken Bell"** was modeled on "Vineta."

Besides **"The Sunken Bell,"** Takuboku wrote three other poems about bells. They are **"Akatsuki no Kane" ["The Morning Bell"]**, **"Kure no Kane" ["The Twilight Bell"]**, and **"Yūbe no Kane" ["The Evening Bell"]**. They were all published in the magazine *Myōjō* in April 1904 and later included in *Akogare.* These poems were composed three days before he completed **"The Sunken Bell."** They have the same theme as **"The Sunken Bell,"** and are naturally related to "Vineta." One line in **"Kure no Kane"** is, "In the evening, when the ruin of 'the eternal capital was told." This line contains a similar image to one in the second stanza of "Vineta," "In the bosom of the ocean, hidden / Far beneath, these ruins still remain."

After comparing *Surf and Wave, Ebb and Flow,* and *Akogare,* we can conclude that at the beginning of his career as a poet, Takuboku was strongly inspired and influenced by this American collection of poems of the sea. Actually, there are not many poems of the sea in *Akogare.* They are: **"Shizumeru Kane" ["The Sunken Bell"]** (March 19, 1904); **"Shiraha no Toribune" ["The Boat of the White**

Feather Bird"] (early November 1903); **"Gakusei"** ["**The Musical Voice"**] (November 30, 1903); **"Umi no Ikari"** ["**The Anger of the Sea"**] (December 1, 1903); **"Ariso"** ["**The Reefy Coast"**] (December 3, 1903); **"Yūbe no Umi"** ["**The Evening Sea"**] (December 5, 1903); and **"Inochi no Fune"** ["**The Boat of Life"**] (January 12, 1904). However, his poems of the sea are, as the dates show, the earliest works among his poems, and this fact confirms again that *Surf and Wave* was influential, especially in Takuboku's early career. Among these poems, **"Ariso,"** **"Yūbe no Umi,"** and **"Inochi no Fune"** are found in *Ebb and Flow.*

Hitherto, the argument on the influences on Takuboku's *Akogare* has been limited to contemporary and preceding poets, such as Susukida Kyūkin, Kambara Ariake, Shimazaki Tōson, Ueda Bin, Yosano Tekkan, Tsuchii Bansui, and so on. However, their influence seems to have come afterward. That is, as the newly discovered *Ebb and Flow* makes clear, these poems about the sea in English must have been a significant influence and inspiration for Takuboku to begin his career as a poet of the "Myōjō" group. In fact, we might say that only after Takuboku was inspired by these poems was he able to react to and accept the poems of the Japanese romantic group and thus to develop his poetic sense. Then, for the first time, he could leave these poems in English in order to establish his unique world of poems of youth, *Akogare.*

Therefore, a closer examination of the relationships among *Surf and Wave, Ebb and Flow* and *Akogare* is necessary in order to understand the meaning of *Akogare* in Takuboku's career.

Makoto Ueda   (essay date 1983)

SOURCE: "Ishikawa Takuboku," in *Modern Japanese Poets and the Nature of Literature,* Stanford University Press, 1983, pp. 95-136.

[*Ueda is an educator and scholar specializing in Japanese literature. In the following excerpt, he discusses Takuboku's development as a poet, focusing especially on his experimentation with the tanka form.*]

Since his death, Ishikawa Takuboku . . . has gained great fame as a poet, attracting many followers and admirers in succeeding generations. More books and articles have probably been written about him than about any other modern poet. His popularity, however, seems to depend less on his poetry than on the life that produced it. Takuboku's poems—many of them tanka—often sound trite or sentimental, or seem facile, when they are read as autonomous works of art. More appealing are the diaries that he kept intermittently from 1902 on, which honestly trace the vicissitudes of his restless mind. His life was a dramatic one, sprinkled with incidents that seem stranger than fiction. He had many failings: it is easy to accuse him of being irresponsible, overdependent, self-indulgent, emotionally unstable, or given to self-aggrandizement. Yet he was also brilliant, dynamic, and unremittingly honest with himself. He had explosive passions and a penchant for action, and seldom hesitated to do what he believed to be right. Seen against such a biographical background, his poems begin to breathe. They are a vital part of his life rather than inde-

pendent works of art. For a tanka poet, the distance between life and art is usually short; for Takuboku, it hardly existed at all . . . .

Takuboku published his first book of verse, entitled *Longing,* in 1905. It included 77 poems, all written in the shi form, their images and idioms much like those of the leading poets of the day, including Yosano Akiko, for whom the young Takuboku had great respect. The reactions of contemporary reviewers were mixed. Some praised the poems' youthful exuberance, flamboyant vocabulary, and precocious artistry; others condemned their pedantry, imitativeness, and self-indulgence. Today the collection is largely neglected, having been eclipsed by Takuboku's highly esteemed later volumes of verse: nevertheless, the book is a valuable document, for a number of its poems reveal Takuboku's early view of poetry in varying degree . . . .

Takuboku was not able to sustain for very long the idealistic view of poetry he developed in his youth. Just before the publication of *Longing,* his father was excommunicated by the hierarchy of his Zen sect on the charge of failing to pay dues levied on his temple. The elder Ishikawa, an outcast priest at age 46, had no prospect of employment, and suddenly responsibility for supporting the family fell onto the shoulders of his only son. Another dependent was added when Takuboku's daughter Kyōko was born in 1906. The long and bitter struggle for survival that ensued not only changed Takuboku's life but affected his idea of poetry . . . .

Takuboku's changing attitude toward literature was suggested in various writings at this time. In his diary entry for January 29, 1907, for example, he expressed disillusion with his former ideals:

> Poems written by the New Poetry Society and other schools of poets neither interest me nor impress me these days. I keep wondering what the reason could be. . . . Could it be because my heart has become rough and prosaic? More likely it is because poetry has plummeted from heaven to earth in my mind, because it has transformed itself from a melodious recitation in an auditorium to a chat in a shabby little room. I think of prose fiction day after day. I really must write a story.

A comment Takuboku made in 1908 reveals the poet's parallel fall into experience and sets out the specific realities he had come to consider the most appropriate material for poetry. In an essay called "A Branch on the Desk," he observed that every person initially believes in his own capabilities, but when some painful experience forces him to realize his limitations, he concedes his defeat by nature and mutters to himself, "Whatever will be will be." Takuboku continued:

> However, nothing could sound as disgraceful as these words to a person who has had a profound confidence in himself and has prided himself on his dignity as an individual. Often, therefore, these words turn into a desperate wailing. Yet at other times, when a person carefully reconsiders them, he may conclude that defeat by nature is

really a process by which to make that undefeatable power his own.

Although here Takuboku did not mention literature, he was talking about basic attitudes toward life that he thought should be the concern of all thinkers, including poets and novelists. According to him, these attitudes result in two types of literature. One is the "desperate wailing" of a person who has empirically learned human limitations; the other is a revelation of nature's forces, which, although intimidating, may benefit a person who can identify with them. The first mode is more lyrical, the second more naturalistic; both feature a man defeated by external forces. The proud poet confident in his extraordinary sensitivity is gone.

These two views of literature are embodied in **A Handful of Sand.** although the poems in that volume, being tanka, show the lyrical mode more clearly than the naturalistic . . . .

Takuboku's lyrical wailing can also be observed in some of his shi. Although his production in this genre markedly decreased after the publication of **Longing,** he did continue to write shi and planned to publish a collection in 1908. The short proem he wrote for this abortive collection expresses his new view of poetry, and can serve as a preface to all the lyrics he wrote after **Longing**:

> Sing out, when an everlasting struggle
> makes your tired joints ache,
> when a bitter grief almost overwhelms you,
> when your ailing child is on the verge of death,
> when you see your mother's image in a beggar,
> or when you are helplessly bored with your love.
> Gaze at the wordless sky
> and sing out, when those times arrive,
> O my starving friends!

Takuboku's poems were the outcries of a man suffering from the sorrow of life in this world. . . .

The dark days of Takuboku's last years brought another significant change in his attitude toward poetry. Part of this can be viewed as a transference of his naturalistic impulse from prose fiction to verse: having failed as a novelist, he tried to do in poetry what he could not do in prose. His new stance is expressed in the essay "Various Kinds of Poetry," written in 1910. There he remarked, tongue in cheek, that he envied a poet who did not possess "a mind that must scrutinize everything he does or says or contemplates throughout the very process of his doing or saying or contemplating, a mind that must challenge every problem squarely and reach its inmost core, or a mind that every day discovers many irrationalities and contradictions in himself and in the world, each discovery in turn intensifying further the irrationalities and contradictions in his life." Takuboku clearly wanted to become a poet who *did* have such a mind, one who scrutinized the forces operating in himself and in society. This is the type of naturalism he wanted to attain in his prose fiction, except that it places more emphasis on the mind of the writer himself. It is a more subjective, personal naturalism.

The same attitude can be detected in the most celebrated of Takuboku's critical writings, "Poems to Eat," a short

autobiographical essay published in 1909 that traces his growth as a poet. Its opening section is filled with negative rhetoric, vehemently rejecting the stance of Takuboku's younger days. He describes his early poetry as made of fantasies, childish music, a tiny intermingling of religious (or pseudoreligious) elements, and stereotyped sensibility. He then reveals how he became disillusioned with poetry during his days of struggle in Hokkaido [the northernmost main island of Japan]. The latter part of the essay is an exposition of his newly discovered poetic, whose essence can be seen in the excerpts below. At this stage in his life, Takuboku defined the poet as follows:

> A true poet must be as resolute as a statesman in reforming himself and in putting his philosophy into practice. He must be as singleminded as a businessman in giving a focus to his life. He must be as clearheaded as a scientist, and as straightforward as a primitive. He must have all these qualities and thereby make a calm, honest report on the changes of his psyche as they happen from one moment to the next, describing them without a word of adornment or falsehood.

In a corollary to the first definition, he defined poetry:

> Poetry must not be the so-called poetry. It must be a detailed report of changes that take place in a man's emotional life (I cannot think of a better word); it must be an honest diary. Hence, it must be fragmentary—it must not have unity. (Poetry with unity, namely philosophical literature, will turn into prose fiction when it takes an inductive form; into drama when it takes a deductive form. True poetry is related to fiction and drama in the same way daily reports of receipts and disbursements are related to a monthly or yearly balance sheet of accounts.) Furthermore, unlike a minister gathering material for his sermon or a streetwalker looking for a certain kind of man, a poet must never have a preconceived purpose.

The essay concludes with an appeal to his fellow poets, urging them not to be too imitative of Western poetry but to look intently at their own lives. . . .

In a sense, "Poems to Eat" expresses an idea of poetry to which Takuboku had unconsciously subscribed from the beginning, for if the essay's central thesis is an equation of poem and diary, he had been a diarist all along. Even as a teenage poet who gazed longingly at the sky, he sang about himself rather than about the sky. He was a diarist in the literal sense from an early age, too: his earliest surviving diary dates to the autumn of 1902, when he was sixteen; his last ends on February 20, 1912, a few weeks before his death. The surviving diaries cover much of the intervening ten years, the entire span of his literary career. The most moving of them all is known as *The Rōmaji Diary,* a diary of 1909 written in romanized Japanese because Takuboku did not want his wife and others to read the private thoughts he set down there. Clearly superior to any of his works in prose fiction, it provides ironic testimony that he was temperamentally less suited to be the novelist he wished to become than to be an author of diaries, which he wished to hide.

The Rōmaji Diary is a fine work of literature because it

gives "a detailed report of changes that take place in a man's emotional life," the very quality Takuboku sought in poetry. It and the other diaries are sprinkled with poems, both tanka and shi, expressing the kind of psychological changes that cannot well be expressed in prose. . . .

One weakness inherent in this theory of composition is that the poem sometimes becomes so much a part of the author's diary that it loses its appeal to readers unfamiliar with the details of his life. To the poet, all his autobiographical poems are valuable because they are directly related to his personal life; however, unless they embody an experience rooted in universal human reality, they lose the means of relating themselves to readers. Unfortunately, some of Takuboku's later poems fall into this category: they have a measure of appeal to those who are thoroughly familiar with his biography, but they mean little to others. The fault lies less with the poems themselves than with Takuboku's poetic, his equation of poem and diary.

Takuboku himself was aware of this weakness. In a letter to a friend he once said: "At present I write tanka almost exclusively in the same frame of mind as I would have when keeping a diary. I suppose there are well- and ill-written diaries, depending upon the author's literary craftsmanship. But the merit of a diary should have nothing to do with the author's skill in writing. Indeed, a diary is valuable to no one but its author." Here Takuboku concedes that poetry is valuable to no one but the poet, that the value of poetry is entirely personal.

Such an admission implies a devaluation of poetry in relation to all other human activities. Takuboku recognized this. In an essay written in 1910, he compared a man of letters to a planner without the ability, opportunity, or financial resources to carry out his plans. He even compared literary composition to masturbation. . . . Ultimately, literature seemed too passive to him. He had learned from bitter experience how ineffectual it was in the real world, and he wanted to be more active, to become part of a force that directly participated in changing society.

Given such a pragmatic view of literature, it seemed that the only way poetry could play a positive role was by becoming overtly ideological in the service of a political movement. When poetry incites the masses to social reform, it can be said to have made a positive contribution to actual change. Takuboku's view of poetry seems to have been moving in this direction in his last years, especially after he became attracted to socialism in around 1910. . . .

The poems with socialist overtones, however, are only a small portion of Takuboku's later poetry. Of the 194 tanka that constitute *Sad Toys,* no more than a dozen overtly suggest his leftist beliefs. At least two reasons may explain this scarcity. One has to do with the nature of Takuboku's socialist beliefs. His socialism was more personal than political or philosophical, and therein lay its weakness, as well as its strength. It was an empirical belief deduced from a series of tragic experiences in actual life. When he discovered that no matter how hard he worked he was un-

able to support his family, he had to conclude that something was wrong with the existing capitalist society. On the other hand, he was not a systematic thinker who could, after sustained thought, arrive at a series of possible solutions for current social problems. Nor was he a political activist who could, through some drastic action, incite fellow workers to social reform if not to revolution. Socialism was a general direction in which his personal frustrations found an outlet. His belief in it was utterly sincere, but tended to be more emotional than ideological, more anarchist than Marxist.

That fact leads to the second possible explanation of why Takuboku did not write more political poems. He knew that poetry was of secondary value, that it was "masturbation"; yet he had to continue writing it because he had feelings too intense to contain. His dilemma was that of the poet who comes to hold a contemptuous view of poetry. . . . His unhappiness with being a poet sometimes made him take a sadistic attitude toward poetry. In fact, his abusive use of poetry began when he failed to become a successful novelist. He told of his changing attitude then: "A husband who has lost a quarrel with his wife sometimes finds pleasure in giving a bad time to his child. I discovered that kind of pleasure in willfully abusing the tanka form." The same attitude is suggested in another of his metaphors for tanka, "sad toys." For Takuboku, poems became toys to which he would return whenever he was frustrated by his struggles in adult life; he could take out his frustrations on his toys.

Takuboku's last poetry collection, to which his friends posthumously gave the title *Sad Toys,* contains numerous tanka showing that attitude—so numerous, indeed, as to overshadow his leftist poems almost completely. . . . Takuboku, who wanted to reach a state of mind where he had no need to write poetry, never succeeded in that attempt. He was aware of his failure, and as a result a mixture of self-pity and self-contempt underlies his lyricism. He ended as a masochistic lyricist, a poet who tortured both himself and his form.

In conclusion, throughout his short and eventful career Takuboku consistently wanted to depict in his poetry fluid inner reality, the changes that occurred within his mind. Never greatly interested in external nature, he always sang of himself, depicting a vision of the self that constantly changed. At first he conceived of himself as a divine messenger from heaven, and accordingly he described the joys, hopes, and ecstasies of being a poet, the ethereal landscapes that were his inner reality at the time. Frustrations in his outer life quickly changed those landscapes, however. He came to see more shadows than sunlight, and subsequently he began to sing of the things that cast the darkest shadows. But singing did not remove the shadows, and he became increasingly aware of the powerlessness of poetry. He made an effort to restore its strength by absorbing the destructive energy of a revolutionary. Yet basically he remained a man of longing. Just as he longed to reach the far-off land of the Creator in his younger days, so he dreamed of a proletarian paradise that was to come after a wholesale destruction of the existing social order. When he tired of dreaming, he vented his impatience with himself by writing self-depreciating poems, or pitied his circumstances and wrote sentimental poems, or did a mixture of the two. He was a diarist in verse who was at times too dreamy, at times too wide awake. His poetry is a record of both those occasions, and as such it is intensely personal, honest, and alive.

FURTHER READING

Criticism

Iwaki Yukinori. "Ishikawa Takuboku and the Early Russian Revolutionary Movement." *Comparative Literature Studies* 22, No. 1 (Spring 1985): 34-42.

> Examines the reaction to Peter Kropotkin's *Memoirs of a Revolutionist* expressed in Takuboku's *Sad Toys* and *Whistles and Whistling.*

———. "Biography and Modern Japanese Literature: Ishikawa Takuboku." In *Aesthetics and the Literature of Ideas: Essays in Honor of A. Owen Aldridge,* edited by François Jost and Melvin J. Friedman, pp. 225-232. Newark: University of Delaware Press, 1990.

> States the aims and value of the biographical study of a literary figure and outlines the preliminary investigation done by Yukinori for his *Thirty Years of Research on Takuboku.*

Additional coverage of Takuboku's life and career is contained in the following sources published by Gale Research: *Contemporary Authors,* Vol. 113; and *Twentieth-Century Literary Criticism,* Vol. 15.

Martial

c. 40-c. 104

(Full name Marcus Valerius Martialis) Roman epigrammatist.

INTRODUCTION

Called the "father of the modern epigram" by Harold Edgeworth Butler, Martial is widely considered to be the greatest epigrammatist of all times. In Rome he transformed the passionate and lyrical Greek epigram into satirical and pointed verse. His more than 1,500 epigrams are noted as clear, simple, and realistic portraits of Roman life and established the archetype of the modern epigram.

Biographical Information

Martial was born a Roman citizen on March 1, a date which is believed to be the source of the poet's name, c. 40, in Bilbilis, Spain. His parents used their means to give Martial a proper literary education. Around the year 64, Martial moved to Rome, and more than fifteen years later he published his first book, *Liber Spectaculorum.* In Rome he befriended other literary figures, including the scholar Pliny the Younger, the rhetorician Quintilian, and the satirist Juvenal. He also found wealthy patrons, such as the Seneca family—whose friendship became a liability when they were later found guilty of conspiring to kill the Roman emperor Nero. Typically, Rome's patron system called for writers to be obsequious to supporters through often undeserved flattery in their works and tireless attendance of daily receptions and dinner parties. For their efforts, authors would receive money, gifts, and—as in Martial's case (though it is generally presumed that he never married or fathered children)—political and economic benefits usually bestowed on men with a certain number of offspring. Martial was also given the advantages of a knight during Titus and Domitian's reigns despite a paltry amount of military service. During his early association with the Senecas, Martial had become friends with the poet Lucan, and in the mid 80s, Lucan's widow bequeathed to Martial a home outside of Rome, which he used as a retreat from the outrageous lifestyle in the city. Upon retirement, Martial returned to Spain. A patroness provided him with a dwelling where he lived his last years until his death in c. 104.

Major Works

Influenced by the subjects and themes of other prominent Roman poets such as Catullus, Horace, and Ovid, Martial depicted many facets of Roman life in his epigrams at a time when morals, government operations, and religious thinking were degenerating. His epigrams, which vary from 1 to 51 lines in length, portray intriguing characterizations of all classes and discuss both light-hearted and

A page from a 15th-century Italian edition of Martial's epigrams.

serious topics. *Liber Spectaculorum,* for which he received many honors, was written on the occasion of the emperor Titus's dedication of the Colosseum. A few years later Martial produced *Xenia* and *Apophoreta.* The former celebrates the Saturnalia, a riotous festival honoring Saturn, and the latter was produced as a gift for social occasions. Considered his best achievements, subsequent collections were published in twelve volumes, simply titled Books I-XII. Even though epigrams were a fashionable form of verse during Martial's time, not many examples besides Martial's have survived.

Critical Reception

Some scholars have described Martial's best epigrams as perfect representations of the genre. His poignant verse has been praised for its directness and sharp-witted endings. However, his work has also been charged with being offensive and sycophantic. Though these accusations may be valid, most critics defend Martial's work as a sign of his times; Rome, during this period, upheld patronage and found amusement in vulgarities. Kirby Flower Smith concluded, "The world of Rome was an open book before [Martial]. He read the text, fathomed its import, and wrote his commentary upon it in brilliant and telling phrase, and in a literary form of which he was undoubtedly the master."

PRINCIPAL ENGLISH TRANSLATIONS

Martial's Epigrams: Translations and Imitations (translated by A. L. Francis and H. F. Tatum) 1924
Martial: The Twelve Books of Epigrams (translated by J. A. Pott and F. A. Wright) 1924
Selected Epigrams (translated by Rolfe Humphries) 1963
Poems after Martial (translated by Philip Murray) 1967
Sixty Poems of Martial: In Translation (translated by Dudley Fitts) 1967
Selected Epigrams (translated by Ralph Marcellino) 1968
Epigrams of Martial (translated by Palmer Bovie) 1970
Selected Epigrams of Martial (translated by Donald Goertz) 1971
After Martial (translated by Peter Porter) 1972
The Epigrams of Martial (translated by James Michie) 1972

CRITICISM

Harold Edgeworth Butler (essay date 1909)

SOURCE: "Martial," in *Post-Augustan Poetry: From Seneca to Juvenal,* 1909. Reprint by Books for Libraries Press, 1969, pp. 251-86.

[*In the following essay, Butler reviews various themes in Martial's epigrams, noting the mundane subjects and scarcity of emotion in his verse.*]

In Martial we have a poet who devoted himself to the one class of poetry which, apart from satire, the conditions of the Silver Age were qualified to produce in any real excellence—the epigram. In a period when rhetorical smartness and point were the predominant features of literature, the epigram was almost certain to flourish. But Roman poets in general, and Martial in particular, gave a character to the epigram which has clung to it ever since, and has actually changed the significance of the word itself.

In the best days of the Greek epigram the prime consider-

ation was not that a poem should be pointed, but that it should be what is summed up in the untranslatable French epithet *lapidaire*; that is to say, it should possess the conciseness, finish, and relevance required for an inscription on a monument. Its range was wide; it might express the lover's passion, the mourner's grief, the artist's skill, the cynic's laughter, the satirist's scorn. It was all poetry in miniature. Point is not wanting, but its chief characteristics are delicacy and charm. [J. W. Mackail, in an introduction to *Greek Anthology,* opined,] 'No good epigram sacrifices its finer poetical substance to the desire of making a point, and none of the best depend on having a point at all.' Transplanted to the soil of Italy the epigram changes. The less poetic Roman, with his coarse tastes, his brutality, his tendency to satire, his appreciation of the incisive, wrought it to his own use. In his hands it loses most of its sensuous and lyrical elements and makes up for the loss by the cultivation of point. Above all, it becomes the instrument of satire, stinging like a wasp where the satirist pure and simple uses the deadlier weapons of the bludgeon and the rapier.

The epigram must have been exceedingly plentiful from the very dawn of the movement which was to make Rome a city of *belles-lettres.* It is the plaything of the dilettante *littérateur,* so plentiful under the empire. Apart from the work of Martial, curiously few epigrams have come down to us; nevertheless, in the vast majority of the very limited number we possess the same Roman characteristics may be traced. In the non-lyrical epigrams of Catullus, in the shorter poems of the *Appendix Vergiliana,* there is the same vigour, the same coarse humour, the same pungency that find their best expression in Martial. Even in the epigrams attributed to Seneca in the *Anthologia Latina,* something of this may be observed, though for the most part they lack the personal note and leave the impression of mere juggling with words. It is in this last respect, the attention to point, that they show most affinity with Martial. Only the epigrams in the same collection attributed to Petronius seem to preserve something of the Greek spirit of beauty untainted by the hard, unlovely, incisive spirit of Rome.

Martial was destined to fix the type of the epigram for the future. For pure poetry he had small gifts. He was endowed with a warm heart, a real love for simplicity of life and for the beauties of nature. But he had no lyrical enthusiasm, and was incapable of genuine passion. He entered heartwhole on all his amatory adventures, and left them with indifference. Even the cynical profligacy of Ovid shows more capacity for true love. At their best Martial's erotic epigrams attain to a certain shallow prettiness, for the most part they do not rise above the pornographic. And even though he shows a real capacity for friendship, he also reveals an infinite capacity for cringing or impudent vulgarity in his relations with those who were merely patrons or acquaintances. His needy circumstances led him, as we shall see, to continual expressions of a peevish mendicancy, while the artificiality and pettiness of the life in which he moved induced an excessive triviality and narrowness of outlook.

He makes no great struggle after originality. The slight-ness of his themes and of his *genre* relieved him of that necessity. Some of his prettiest poems are mere variations on some of the most famous lyrics of Catullus. He pilfers whole lines from Ovid. Phrase after phrase suggests something that has gone before. But his plagiarism is effected with such perfect frankness and such perfect art, that it might well be pardoned, even if Martial had greater claims to be taken seriously. As it is, his freedom in borrowing need scarcely be taken into account in the consideration of our verdict. At the worst his crime is no more than petty larceny. With all his faults, he has gifts such as few poets have possessed, a perfect facility and a perfect finish. Alone of poets of the period he rarely gives the impression of labouring a point. Compared with Martial, Seneca and Lucan, Statius and Juvenal are, at their worst, stylistic acrobats. But Martial, however silly or offensive, however complicated or prosaic his theme, handles his material with supreme ease. His points may often not be worth making; they could not be better made. Moreover, he has a perfect ear; his music may be trivial, but within its narrow limits it is faultless. He knows what is required of him and he knows his own powers. He knows that his range is limited, that his sphere is comparatively humble, but he is proud to excel in it. He has the artist's self-respect without his vanity.

His themes are manifold. He might have said, with even greater truth than Juvenal, 'quidquid agunt homines, nostri est farrago libelli.' He does not go beneath the surface, but almost every aspect of the kaleidoscopic world of Rome receives his attention at one time or another. His attitude is, on the whole, satirical, though his satire is not inspired by deep or sincere indignation. He is too easy in his morals and too good-humoured by temperament. He is often insulting, but there is scarcely a line that breathes fierce resentment, while his almost unparalleled obscenity precludes the intrusion of any genuine earnestness of moral scorn in a very large number of his satiric epigrams. On these points he shall speak for himself; he makes no exacting claims.

'I hope,' he says in the preface to his first book,

> that I have exercised such restraint in my writings that no one who is possessed of the least self-respect may have cause to complain of them. My jests are never outrageous, even when directed against persons of the meanest consideration. My practice in this respect is very different from that of early writers, who abused persons without veiling their invective under a pseudonym. Nay more, their victims were men of the highest renown. My *jeux d'esprit* have no *arrières-pensées,* and I hope that no one will put an evil interpretation on them, nor rewrite my epigrams by infusing his own malignance into his reading of them. It is a scandalous injustice to exercise such ingenuity on what another has written. I would offer some excuse for the freedom and frankness of my language—which is, after all, the language of epigram—if I were setting any new precedent. But all epigrammatists, Catullus, Marsus, Pedo, Gaetulicus, have availed themselves of this licence of speech. But if any one wishes to acquire notoriety by prudish severity, and refuses to permit me to write after the good

Roman fashion in so much as a single page of my work, he may stop short at the preface, or even at the title. Epigrams are written for such persons as derive pleasure from the games at the Feast of Flowers. Cato should not enter my theatre, but if he does enter it, let him be content to look on at the sport which I provide. I think I shall be justified in closing my preface with an epigram

TO CATO

Once more the merry feast of Flora's come,
With wanton jest to split the sides of Rome;
Yet come you, prince of prudes, to view the show.
Why come you? merely to be shocked and go?

He reasserts the kindliness of his heart and the excellence of his intentions elsewhere:

> hunc servare modum nostri novere libelli;
> parcere personis, dicere de vitiis (x. 33).

[For in my verses 'tis my constant care
To lash the vices, but the persons spare.]

Malignant critics *had* exercised their ingenuity in the manner which he deprecated. Worse still, libellous verse had been falsely circulated as his:

> quid prodest, cupiant cum quidam nostra videri
> si qua Lycambeo sanguine tela madent,
> vipereumque vomant nostro sub nomine virus
> qui Phoebi radios ferre diemque negant? (vii. 12. 5).

[But what doesn't avail,
If in bloodfetching lines others do rail,
And vomit viperous poison in my name,
Such as the sun themselves to own do shame?]

In this respect his defence of himself is just. When he writes in a vein of invective his victim is never mentioned by name. And we cannot assert in any given case that his pseudonyms mask a real person. He may do no more than satirize a vice embodied and typified in an imaginary personality.

He is equally concerned to defend himself against the obvious charges of prurience and immorality:

> innocuos censura potest permittere lusus:
> lasciva est nobis pagina, vita proba (i. 4. 7).

[Let not these harmless sports your censure taste!
My lines are wanton, but my life is chaste.]

This is no real defence, and even though we need not take Martial at his word, when he accuses himself of the foulest vices, there is not the slightest reason to suppose that chastity was one of his virtues. In Juvenal's case we have reason to believe that, whatever his weaknesses, he was a man of genuinely high ideals. Martial at his best shows himself a man capable of fine feeling, but he gives no evidence of moral earnestness or strength of character. On the other hand, to give him his due, we must remember the standard of his age. Although he is lavish with the vilest obscenities, and has no scruples about accusing acquaintances of every variety of unnatural vice, it must be pointed out that such accusations were regarded at Rome as mere matter for laughter. The traditions of the old *Fescennina locutio* survived, and with the decay of private morality its obscenity increased. Caesar's veterans could sing ribald verses unrebuked at their general's triumph, verses unquotably obscene and casting the foulest aspersions on the character of one whom they worshipped almost as a god. Caesar could invite Catullus to dine in spite of the fact that such accusations formed the matter of his lampoons. Catullus could insert similar charges against the bridegroom for whom he was writing an *epithalamium*. The writing of Priapeia was regarded as a reputable diversion. Martial's defence of his obscenities is therefore in all probability sincere, and may have approved itself to many reputable persons of his day. It was a defence that had already been made in very similar language by Ovid and Catullus, and Martial was not the last to make it. But the fact that Martial felt it necessary to defend himself shows that a body of public opinion—even if not large or representative—did exist which refused to condone this fashionable lubricity. Extenuating circumstances may be urged in Martial's defence, but even to have conformed to the standard of his day is sufficient condemnation; and it is hard to resist the suspicion that he fell below it. His obscenities, though couched in the most easy and pointed language, have rarely even the grace—if grace it be—of wit; they are puerile in conception and infinitely disgusting.

It is pleasant to turn to the better side of Martial's character. No writer has ever given more charming expression to his affection for his friends. It is for Decianus and Julius Martialis that he keeps the warmest place in his heart. In poems like the following there is no doubting the sincerity of his feeling or questioning the perfection of its expression:

> si quis erit raros inter numerandus amicos,
> quales prisca fides famaque novit anus,
> si quis Cecropiae madidus Latiaeque Minervae
> artibus et vera simplicitate bonus,
> si quis erit recti custos, mirator honesti,
> et nihil arcano qui roget ore deos,
> si quis erit magnae subnixus robore mentis:
> dispeream si non hic Decianus erit (i. 39).

> [Is there a man whose friendship rare
> With antique friendship may compare;
> In learning steeped, both old and new,
> Yet unpedantic, simple, true;
> Whose soul, ingenuous and upright,
> Ne'er formed a wish that shunned the light,
> Whose sense is sound? If such there be,
> My Decianus, thou art he.]

Even more charming, if less intense, is the exhortation to Julius Martialis to live while he may, ere the long night come that knows no waking:

> o mihi post nullos, Iuli, memorande sodales,
> si quid longa fides canaque iura valent,
> bis iam paene tibi consul tricensimus instat,
> et numerat paucos vix tua vita dies.
> non bene distuleris videas quae posse negari,
> et solum hoc ducas, quod fuit, esse tuum.
> exspectant curaeque catenatique labores:
> gaudia non remanent, sed fugitiva volant.
> haec utraque manu complexuque adsere toto:

> saepe fluunt imo sic quoque lapsa sinu.
> non est, crede mihi, sapientis dicere 'vivam'.
> sera nimis vita est crastina: vive hodie (i. 15).

> [Friend of my heart—and none of all the band
> Has to that name older or better right:
> Julius, thy sixtieth winter is at hand,
> Far-spent is now life's day and near the night.
> Delay not what thou would'st recall too late;
> That which is past, that only call thine own:
> Cares without end and tribulations wait,
> Joy tarrieth not, but scarcely come, is flown.
> Then grasp it quickly firmly to thy heart,—
> Though firmly grasped, too oft it slips away;—
> To talk of living is not wisdom's part:
> To-morrow is too late: live thou to-day!]

Best of all is the retrospect of the long friendship which has united him to Julius. It is as frank as it is touching:

> triginta mihi quattuorque messes
> tecum, si memini, fuere, Iuli.
> quarum dulcia mixta sunt amaris
> sed iucunda tamen fuere plura;
> et si calculus omnis huc et illuc
> diversus bicolorque digeratur,
> vincet candida turba nigriorem.
> si vitare voles acerba quaedam
> et tristes animi cavere morsus,
> nulli te facias nimis sodalem:
> gaudebis minus et minus dolebis
> (xii. 34).

> [My friend, since thou and I first met,
> This is the thirty-fourth December;
> Some things there are we'd fain forget,
> More that 'tis pleasant to remember.
> Let for each pain a black ball stand,
> For every pleasure past a white one,
> And thou wilt find, when all are scanned,
> The major part will be the bright one.
> He who would heartache never know,
> He who serene composure treasures,
> Must friendship's chequered bliss forego;
> Who has no pain hath fewer pleasures.]

He does not pour the treasure of his heart at his friend's feet, as Persius does in his burning tribute to Cornutus. He has no treasure of great price to pour. But it is only natural that in the poems addressed to his friends we should find the statement of his ideals of life:

> vitam quae faciunt beatiorem,
> iucundissime Martialis, haec sunt:
> res non parta labore sed relicta;
> non ingratus ager, focus perennis;
> lis numquam, toga rara, mens quieta;
> vires ingenuae, salubre corpus;
> prudens simplicitas, pares amici;
> convictus facilis, sine arte mensa;
> nox non ebria sed soluta curis.
> non tristis torus et tamen pudicus;
> somnus qui faciat breves tenebras:
> quod sis esse velis nihilque malis;
> summum nec metuas diem nec optes (x 47).

> [What makes a happy life, dear friend,
> If thou would'st briefly learn, attend—
> An income left, not earned by toil;
> Some acres of a kindly soil;

The pot unfailing on the fire;
No lawsuits; seldom town attire;
Health; strength with grace; a peaceful mind;
Shrewdness with honesty combined;
Plain living; equal friends and free;
Evenings of temperate gaiety;
A wife discreet, yet blythe and bright;
Sound slumber, that lends wings to night.
With all thy heart embrace thy lot,
Wish not for death and fear it not.]

This exquisite echo of the Horatian 'beatus ille qui procul negotiis' sets forth no very lofty ideal. It is frankly, though restrainedly, hedonistic. But it depicts a life that is full of charm and free from evil. Martial, in his heart of hearts, hates the Rome that he depicts so vividly. Rome with its noise, its expense, its bustling snobbery, its triviality, and its vice, where he and his friend Julius waste their days:

> nunc vivit necuter sibi, bonosque
> soles effugere atque abire sentit,
> qui nobis pereunt et imputantur
> (v. 20. 11).

> [Dead to our better selves we see
> The golden hours take flight,
> Still scored against us as they flee.
> Then haste to live aright.]

He longs to escape from the world of the professional lounger and the parasite to an ampler air, where he can breathe freely and find rest. He is no philosopher, but it is at times a relief to get away from the rarified atmosphere and the sense of strain that permeates so much of the aspirations towards virtue in this strange age of contradictions.

Martial at last found the ease and quiet that his soul desired in his Spanish home:

> hic pigri colimus labore dulci
> Boterdum Plateamque (Celtiberis
> haec sunt nomina crassiora terris):
> ingenti fruor inproboque somno
> quem nec tertia saepe rumpit hora,
> et totum mihi nunc repono quidquid
> ter denos vigilaveram per annos.
> ignota est toga, sed datur petenti
> rupta proxima vestis a cathedra.
> surgentem focus excipit superba
> vicini strue cultus iliceti,
>
> .   .   .   .   .   .
> sic me vivere, sic iuvat perire.
> (xii. 18. 10).

> [Busy but pleas'd and idly taking pains,
> Here Lewes Downs I till and Ringmer plains,
> Names that to each South Saxon well are
>   known,
> Though they sound harsh to powdered beaux in
>   town.
> None can enjoy a sounder sleep than mine;
> I often do not wake till after nine;
> And midnight hours with interest repay
> For years in town diversions thrown away.
> Stranger to finery, myself I dress
> In the first coat from an old broken press.
> My fire, as soon as I am up, I see
> Bright with the ruins of some neighbouring tree.

.   .   .   .   .   .
Such is my life, a life of liberty;
So would I wish to live and so to die.]

Martial has a genuine love for the country. Born at a time when detailed descriptions of the charms of scenery had become fashionable, and the cultivated landscape at least found many painters, he succeeds far better than any of his contemporaries in conveying to the reader his sense of the beauties which his eyes beheld. That sense is limited, but exquisite. It does not go deep; there is nothing of the almost mystical background that Vergil at times suggests; there is nothing of the feeling of the open air and the wild life that is sometimes wafted to us in the sensuous verse of Theocritus. But Martial sees what he sees clearly, and he describes it perfectly. Compare his work with the affected prettiness of Pliny's description of the source of the Clitumnus or with the more sensuous, but over-elaborate, craftsmanship of Statius in the *Silvae*. Martial is incomparably their superior. He speaks a more human language, and has a far clearer vision. Both Statius and Martial described villas by the sea. . . . [Statius described] the villa of Pollius at Sorrento; Martial shall speak in his turn:

> o temperatae dulce Formiae litus,
> vos, cum severi fugit oppidum Martis
> et inquietas fessus exuit curas,
> Apollinaris omnibus locis praefert.
>
> .   .   .   .   .   .
> hic summa leni stringitur Thetis vento:
> nec languet aequor, viva sed quies ponti
> pictam phaselon adiuvante fert aura,
> sicut puellae non amantis aestatem
> mota salubre purpura venit frigus.
> nec saeta longo quaerit in mari praedam,
> sed a cubili lectuloque iactatam
> spectatus alte lineam trahit piscis.
>
> .   .   .   .   .   .
> frui sed istis quando, Roma, permittis?
> quot Formianos imputat dies annus
> negotiosis rebus urbis haerenti?
> o ianitores vilicique felices!
> dominis parantur ista, serviunt vobis (x. 30).

> [O strand of Formiae, sweet with genial air,
> Who art Apollinaris' chosen home
> When, taking flight from his task-mistress
>   Rome,
> The tired man doffs his load of troubling care.
>
> .   .   .   .   .   .
> Here the sea's bosom quivers in the wind;
> 'Tis no dead calm, but sweet serenity,
> Which bears the painted boat before the breeze,
> As though some maid at pains the heat to ban,
> Should waft a genial zephyr with her fan.
> No fisher needs to buffet the high seas,
> But whiles from bed or couch his line he casts,
> May see his captive in the toils below.
>
> .   .   .   .   .   .
> But, niggard Rome, thou giv'st how grudgingly!
> What the year's tale of days at Formiae
> For him who tied by work in town must stay!
> Stewards and lacqueys, happy your employ,
> Your lords prepare enjoyment, you enjoy.]

These are surely the most beautiful *scazons* in the Latin tongue; the metre limps no more; a master-hand has wrought it to exquisite melody; the quiet undulation of the sea, the yacht's easy gliding over its surface, live before us in its music. Even more delicate is the homelier description of the gardens of Julius Martialis on the slopes of the Janiculum. It is animated by the sincerity that never fails Martial when he writes to his friend:

> Iuli iugera pauca Martialis
> hortis Hesperidum beatiora
> longo Ianiculi iugo recumbunt:
> lati collibus imminent recessus
> et planus modico tumore vertex
> caelo perfruitur sereniore
> et curvas nebula tegente valles
> solus luce nitet peculiari:
> puris leniter admoventur astris
> celsae culmina delicata villae.
> hinc septem dominos videre montes
> et totam licet aestimare Romam,
> Albanos quoque Tusculosque colles
> et quodcumque iacet sub urbe frigus (iv. 64).

> [Martial's few acres, e'en more blest
> Than those famed gardens of the West,
> Lie on Janiculum's long crest;
> Above the slopes wide reaches hang recessed.
> The level, gently swelling crown
> Breathes air from purer heavens blown;
> When mists the hollow valleys drown
> 'Tis radiant with a light that's all its own.
> The clear stars almost seem to lie
> On the wrought roof that's built so high;
> The seven hills stand in majesty,
> And Rome is summed in one wide sweep of eye.
> Tusculan, Alban hills unfold,
> Each nook which holds its store of cold.]

Such a picture is unsurpassed in any language. Statius, with all his brilliance, never came near such perfect success; he lacks sincerity; he can juggle with words against any one, but he never learned their truest and noblest use.

There are many other themes beside landscape painting in which the *Silvae* of Statius challenge comparison with the epigrams of Martial. Both use the same servile flattery to the emperor, both celebrate the same patrons, both console their noble friends for the loss of relatives, or favourite slaves; both write *propemptica*. Even in the most trivial of these poems, those addressed to the emperor, Statius is easily surpassed by his humbler rival. His inferiority lies largely in the fact that he is more ambitious. He wrote on a larger scale. When the infinitely trivial is a theme for verse, the epigrammatist has the advantage of the author of the more lengthy *Silvae*. Perfect neatness vanquishes dexterous elaboration. Moreover, if taste can be said to enter into such poems at all, Martial errs less grossly. Even Domitian—one might conjecture—may have felt that Statius' flattery was 'laid on with a trowel'. Martial may have used the same instrument, but had the art to conceal it. There are even occasions where his flattery ceases to revolt the reader, and where we forget the object of the flattery. In a poem describing the suicide of a certain Festus he succeeds in combining the dignity of a funeral *laudatio* with the subtlest and most graceful flattery of the *princeps*:

> indignas premeret pestis cum tabida fauces,
> inque suos voltus serperet atra lues,
> siccis ipse genis flentes hortatus amicos

> decrevit Stygios Festus adire lacus.

> nec tamen obscuro pia polluit ora veneno
> aut torsit lenta tristia fata fame,
> Sanctam Romana vitam sed morte peregit
> dimisitque animam nobiliore via.
> hanc mortem fatis magni praeferre Catonis
> fama potest; huius Caesar amicus erat (i. 78).

> [When the dire quinsy choked his guiltless breath,
> And o'er his face the blackening venom stole,
> Festus disdained to wait a lingering death,
> Cheered his sad friends and freed his dauntless soul.
> No meagre famine's slowly-wasting force,
> Nor hemlock's gradual chillness he endured,
> But like a Roman chose the nobler course,
> And by one blow his liberty secured.
> His death was nobler far than Cato's end,
> For Caesar to the last was Festus' friend.]

The unctuous dexterity of Statius never achieved such a master-stroke.

So, too, in laments for the dead, the superior brevity and simplicity of Martial bear the palm away. Both poets bewailed the death of Glaucias, the child favourite of Atedius Melior. . . . Martial's poems on the subject, though not quite among his best, yet ring truer than the verse of Statius. And Martial's epitaphs and epicedia at their best have in their slight way an almost unique charm. We must go to the best work of the Greek Anthology to surpass the epitaph on Erotion (v. 34):

> hanc tibi, Fronto pater, genetrix Flaccilla, puellam
> oscula commendo deliciasque meas,
> parvola ne nigras horrescat Erotion umbras
> oraque Tartarei prodigiosa canis.
> inpletura fuit sextae modo frigora brumae,
> vixisset totidem ni minus illa dies.
> inter tam veteres ludat lasciva patronos
> et nomen blaeso garriat ore meum.
> mollia non rigidus caespes tegat ossa nec illi,
> terra, gravis fueris: non fuit illa tibi.

> [Fronto, and you, Flaccilla, to you, my father and mother,
> Here I commend this child, once my delight and my pet,
> So may the darkling shades and deep-mouthed baying of hellhound
> Touch not with horror of dread little Erotion dear.
> Now was her sixth year ending, and melting the snows of the winter,
> Only a brief six days lacked to the tale of the years.
> Young, amid dull old age, let her wanton and frolic and gambol,
> Babble of me that was, tenderly lisping my name.
> Soft were her tiny bones, then soft be the sod that enshrouds her,
> Gentle thy touch, mother Earth, gently she rested on thee!]

Another poem on a like theme shows a different and more fantastic, but scarcely less pleasing vein (v. 37):

puella senibus dulcior mihi cycnis,
agna Galaesi mollior Phalantini,
concha Lucrini delicatior stagni,
cui nec lapillos praeferas Erythraeos
nec modo politum pecudis Indicae dentem
nivesque primas liliumque non tactum;
quae crine vicit Baetici gregis vellus
Rhenique nodos aureamque nitellam;
fragravit ore quod rosarium Paesti,
quod Atticarum prima mella cerarum,
quod sucinorum rapta de manu gleba;
cui conparatus indecens erat pavo,
inamabilis sciurus et frequens phoenix,
adhuc recenti tepet Erotion busto,
quam pessimorum lex amara fatorum
sexta peregit hieme, nec tamen tota,
nostros amores gaudiumque lususque.

[Little maiden sweeter far to me
Than the swans are with their vaunted snows,
Maid more tender than the lambkins be
Where Galaesus by Phalantus flows;
Daintier than the daintiest shells that lie
By the ripples of the Lucrine wave;
Choicer than new-polished ivory
That the herds in Indian jungles gave;
Choicer than Erythrae's marbles white,
Snows new-fallen, lilies yet unsoiled:
Softer were your tresses and more bright
Than the locks by German maidens coiled:
Than the finest fleeces Baetis shows,
Than the dormouse with her golden hue:
Lips more fragrant than the Paestan rose,
Than the Attic bees' first honey-dew,
Or an amber ball, new-pressed and warm;
Paled the peacock's sheen in your compare;
E'en the winsome squirrel lost his charm,
And the Phoenix seemed no longer rare.
Scarce Erotion's ashes yet are cold;
Greedily grim fate ordained to smite
E'er her sixth brief winter had grown old—
Little love, my bliss, my heart's delight.]

Through all the playful affectations of the lines we get the portrait of a fairy-like child, light-footed as the squirrel, golden-haired and fair as ivory or lilies. Martial was a child-lover before he was a man of letters.

Martial was destined to fix the type of the epigram for the future. For pure poetry he had small gifts. He was endowed with a warm heart, a real love for simplicity of life and for the beauties of nature. But he had no lyrical enthusiasm, and was incapable of genuine passion.

—*Harold Edgeworth Butler*

Beautiful as these little poems are, there is in Martial little trace of feeling for the sorrows of humanity in general. He can feel for his intimate friends, and his tears are ready to flow for his patron's sorrows. But the general impression given by his poetry is that of a certain hardness and lack of feeling, of a limited sympathy, and an unemotional temperament. It is a relief to come upon a poem such as that in which he describes a father's poignant anguish for the loss of his son (ix. 74):

effigiem tantum pueri pictura Camoni
servat, et infantis parva figura manet.
florentes nulla signavit imagine voltus,
dum timet ora pius muta videre pater.

[Here as in happy infancy he smiled
Behold Camonus—painted as a child;
For on his face as seen in manhood's days
His sorrowing father would not dare to gaze.]

or to find a sudden outbreak of sympathy with the sorrows of the slave (iii. 21):

proscriptum famulus servavit fronte notata,
non fuit haec domini vita sed invidia.

[When scarred with cruel brand, the slave
Snatched from the murderer's hand
His proscript lord, not life he gave
His tyrant, but the brand.]

Of the *gravitas* or dignity of character specially associated with Rome he shows equally few traces. His outlook on life is not sufficiently serious, he shows little interest in Rome of the past, and has nothing of the retrospective note so prominent in Lucan, Juvenal, or Tacitus; he lives in and for the present. He writes, it is true, of the famous suicide of Arria and Caecina Paetus, of the death of Portia the wife of Brutus, of the bravery of Mucius Scaevola. But in none of these poems does he give us of his best. They lack, if not sincerity, at least enthusiasm; emotion is sacrificed to point. He is out of sympathy with Stoicism, and the suicide doctrinaire does not interest him. 'Live while you may' is his motto, 'and make the best of circumstances.' It is possible to live a reasonably virtuous life without going to the lengths of Thrasea:

quod magni Thraseae consummatique Catonis
dogmata sic sequeris salvus ut esse velis,
pectore nec nudo strictos incurris in enses,
quod fecisse velim te, Deciane, facis.
nolo virum facili redimit qui sanguine famam;
hunc volo, laudari qui sine morte potest (i. 8).

[That you, like Thrasea or Cato, great,
Pursue their maxims, but decline their fate;
Nor rashly point the dagger to your heart;
More to my wish you act a Roman's part.
I like not him who fame by death retrieves,
Give me the man who merits praise and lives.]

The sentiment is full of common sense, but it is undeniably unheroic. Martial is not quixotic, and refuses to treat life more seriously than is necessary. Our complaint against him is that he scarcely takes it seriously enough. It would be unjust to demand a deep fund of earnestness from a professed epigrammatist dowered with a gift of humour and a turn for satire. But it is doing Martial no injustice to style him the laureate of triviality. For his satire is neither genial nor earnest. His kindly temper led him to avoid direct personalities, but his invective is directed against vice, not primarily because it is wicked, but rather because it is grotesque or not *comme il faut.* His humour, too, though often sparkling enough, is more often strained and most often filthy. Many of his epigrams were not worth writing, by whatever standard they be judged. The point is hard to illustrate, since a large proportion of his inferior work is fatuously obscene. But the following may be taken at random from two books:

> Eutrapelus tonsor dum circuit ora Luperci
> expingitque genas, altera barba subit (vii. 83).

> [Eutrapelus the barber works so slow,
> That while he shaves, the beard anew does
> grow.]

> invitas ad aprum, ponis mihi, Gallice, porcum.
> hybrida sum, si das, Gallice, verba mihi (viii. 22).

> [You invite me to partake of a wild boar, you set
> before me a home-grown pig. I'm half-boar,
> half-pig, if you can cheat me thus.]

> pars maxillarum tonsa est tibi, pars tibi rasa est,
> pars volsa est. unum quis putet esse caput? (viii. 47).

> [Part of your jaws is shaven, part clipped, part
> has the hair pulled out. Who'd think you'd
> only one head?]

> tres habuit dentes, pariter quos expuit omnes,
> ad tumulum Picens dum sedet ipse suum;
> collegitque sinu fragmenta novissima laxi
> oris et adgesta contumulavit humo.
> ossa licet quondam defuncti non legat heres:
> hoc sibi iam Picens praestitit officium (viii. 57).

> [Picens had three teeth, which he spat out alto-
> gether while he was sitting at the spot he had
> chosen for his tomb. He gathered in his robe
> the last fragments of his loose jaw and interred
> them in a heap of earth. His heir need not
> gather his bones when he is dead, Picens has
> performed that office for himself.]

> summa Palatini poteras aequare Colossi,
> si fieres brevior, Claudia, sesquipede (viii. 60).

> [Had you been eighteen inches shorter, Claudia,
> you would have been as tall as the Colossus on
> the Palatine.]

> tanti non erat esse te disertum (xii. 43).

> ['Twas scarce worth while to be thus eloquent.]

There is much also which, without being precisely point-less or silly, is too petty and mean to be tolerable to modern taste. Most noticeable in this respect are the epigrams in which Martial solicits the liberality of his patrons. The amazing relations existing at this period between patron and client had worked a painful revolution in the manners and tone of society, a revolution which meant scarcely less than the pauperization of the middle class. The old sacred and almost feudal tie uniting client and patron had long since disappeared, and had been replaced by relations of a professional and commercial character. Wealth was concentrated in comparatively few hands, and with the decrease of the number of the patrons the throng of clients proportionately increased. The crowd of clients bustling

to the early morning *salutatio* of the *patronus,* and strug-gling with one another for the *sportula* is familiar to us in the pages of Juvenal and receives fresh and equally vivid illustration from Martial. The worst results of these un-natural relations were a general loss of independence of character and a lamentable growth of bad manners and cynical snobbery. The patron, owing to the increasingly heavy demands upon his purse, naturally tended to be-come close-fisted and stingy, the needy client too often was grasping and discontented. The patron, if he asked his cli-ent to dine, would regale him with food and drink of a coarser and inferior quality to that with which he himself was served. The client, on the other hand, could not be trusted to behave himself; he would steal the table fittings, make outrageous demands on his patron, and employ every act of servile and cringing flattery to improve his po-sition. The poor poet was in a sense doubly dependent. He would stand in the ordinary relation of *cliens* to a *patronus,* and would be dependent also for his livelihood on the generosity of his literary patrons. For, in spite of the comparative facilities for the publication and circula-tion of books, he could make little by the public sale of his works, and living at Rome was abnormally expensive. The worst feature of all was that such a life of servile depen-dence was not clearly felt to be degrading. It was disliked for its hardship, annoyance, and monotony, but the client too often seems to have regarded it as beneath his dignity to attempt to escape from it by industry and manly inde-pendence.

As a result of these conditions, we find the pages of Mar-tial full of allusions to the miserable life of the client. His skill does not fail him, but the theme is ugly and the histor-ical interest necessarily predominates over the literary, though the reader's patience is at times rewarded with shrewd observations on human nature, as, for instance, the bitter expression of the truth that 'To him that hath shall be given'—

> semper pauper eris, si pauper es, Aemiliane;
> dantur opes nullis nunc nisi divitibus (v. 81);

> [Poor once and poor for ever, Nat, I fear,
> None but the rich get place and pension here.]

or the even more incisive

> pauper videri Cinna vult: et est pauper (viii. 19).

But we soon weary of the continual reference to dinners and parasites, to the snobbery and indifference of the rich, to the tricks of toadyism on the part of needy client or leg-acy hunter. It is a mean world, and the wit and raillery of Martial cannot make it palatable. Without a moral back-ground, such as is provided by the indignation of Juvenal, the picture soon palls, and the reader sickens. Most un-pleasing of all are the epigrams where Martial himself speaks as client in a language of mingled impertinence and servility. His flattery of the emperor we may pass by. It was no doubt interested, but it was universal, and Mar-tial's flattery is more dexterous without being either more or less offensive than that of his contemporaries. His rela-tions towards less exalted patrons cannot be thus easily condoned. He feels no shame in begging, nor in abusing those who will not give or whose gifts are not sufficient for his needs. His purse is empty; he must sell the gifts that Regulus has given him. Will Regulus buy?

> aera domi non sunt, superest hoc, Regule, solum
> ut tua vendamus munera: numquid emis? (vii. 16).

> [I have no money, Regulus, at home. Only one
>   thing is left to do—sell the gifts you gave me.
>   Will you buy?]

Stella has given him some tiles to roof his house; he would like a cloak as well:

> cum pluvias madidumque Iovem perferre negaret
> et rudis hibernis villa nataret aquis,
> plurima, quae posset subitos effundere nimbos,
> muneribus venit tegula missa tuis.
> horridus ecce sonat Boreae stridore December:
> Stella, tegis villam, non tegis agricolam (vii. 36).

> [When my crased house heaven's showers could
>   not sustain,
> But flooded with vast deluges of rain,
> Thou shingles, Stella, seasonably didst send,
> Which from the impetuous storms did me de-
>   fend:
> Now fierce loud-sounding Boreas rocks doth
>   cleave,
> Dost clothe the farm, and farmer naked leave?]

This is not the way a gentleman thanks a friend, nor can modern taste appreciate at its antique value abuse such as—

> primum est ut praestes, si quid te, Cinna, rogabo;
> illud deinde sequens ut cito, Cinna, neges.
> diligo praestantem; non odi, Cinna, negantem:
> sed tu nec praestas nec cito, Cinna, negas (vii. 43).

> [The kindest thing of all is to comply:
> The next kind thing is quickly to deny.
> I love performance nor denial hate:
> Your 'Shall I, shall I?' is the cursed state.]

The poet's poverty is no real excuse for this petulant mendicancy. He had refused to adopt a profession, though professional employment would assuredly have left him time for writing, and no one would have complained if his output had been somewhat smaller. Instead, he chose a life which involved moving in society, and was necessarily expensive. We can hardly attribute his choice merely to the love of his art. If he must beg, he might have done so with better taste and some show of finer feeling. Macaulay's criticism is just: 'I can make large allowance for the difference of manners; but it can never have been *comme il faut* in any age or nation for a man of note—an accomplished man—a man living with the great—to be constantly asking for money, clothes, and dainties, and to pursue with volleys of abuse those who would give him nothing.'

In spite, however, of the obscenity, meanness, and exaggerated triviality of much of his work, there have been few poets who could turn a prettier compliment, make a neater jest, or enshrine the trivial in a more exquisite setting. Take the beautifully finished poem to Flaccus in the eighth book (56), wherein Martial complains that times have altered since Vergil's day. 'Now there are no patrons and consequently no poets'—

> ergo ego Vergilius, si munera Maecenatis
> des mihi? Vergilius non ero, Marsus ero.

> [Shall I then be a Vergil, if you give me such gifts
>   as Maecenas gave? No, I shall not be a Vergil,
>   but a Marsus.]

Here, at least, Martial shows that he could complain of his poverty with decency, and speak of himself and his work with becoming modesty. Or take a poem of a different type, an indirect plea for the recall of an exile (viii. 32):

> aera per tacitum delapsa sedentis in ipsos
> fluxit Aratullae blanda columba sinus.
> luserat hoc casus, nisi inobservata maneret
> permissaque sibi nollet abire fuga.
> si meliora piae fas est sperare sorori
> et dominum mundi flectere vota valent,
> haec a Sardois tibi forsitan exulis oris,
> fratre reversuro, nuntia venit avis.

> [A gentle dove glided down through the silent
>   air and settled even in
> Aratulla's bosom as she was sitting. This might
>   have seemed but the sport
> of chance had it not rested there, though unde-
>   tained, and refused to
> part even when flight was free. If it is granted to
>   the loving sister to hope
> for better things, and if prayers can move the
>   lord of the world, this bird
> perchance has come to thee from Sardinia's
>   shore of exile to announce
> the speedy return of thy brother.]

Nothing could be more conventional, nothing more perfect in form, more full of music, more delicate in expression. The same felicity is shown in his epigrams on curiosities of art or nature, a fashionable and, it must be confessed, an easy theme. Fish carved by Phidias' hand, a lizard cast by Mentor, a fly enclosed in amber, are all given immortality:

> artis Phidiacae toreuma clarum
> pisces aspicis: adde aquam, natabunt (iii. 35).

> [These fishes Phidias wrought: with life by him
> They are endowed: add water and they swim.]

> inserta phialae Mentoris manu ducta
> lacerta vivit et timetur argentum (iii. 41).

> [That lizard on the goblet makes thee start.
> Fear not: it lives only by Mentor's art.]

> et latet et lucet Phaethontide condita gutta,
> ut videatur apis nectare clusa suo.
> dignum tantorum pretium tulit illa laborum:
> credibile est ipsam sic voluisse mori (iv. 32).

> [Here shines a bee closed in an amber tomb,
> As if interred in her own honey-comb.
> A fit reward fate to her labours gave;
> No other death would she have wished to have.]

Always at home in describing the trifling amenities of life, he is at his best equally successful in dealing with its trifling follies. An acquaintance has given his cook the absurd name of Mistyllos in allusion to the Homeric phrase μιστυλλον τ' αρα ταλλα. Martial's comment is inimitable:

> si tibi Mistyllos cocus, Aemiliane, vocatur,
> dicatur quare non Taratalla mihi? (i. 50).

He complains of the wine given him at a dinner-party with a finished whimsicality:

> potavi modo consulare vinum.
> quaeris quam vetus atque liberale?
> Prisco consule conditum: sed ipse
> qui ponebat erat, Severe, consul (vii. 79).

> [I have just drunk some consular wine. How old,
> you ask, and how generous? It was bottled in
> Priscus' consulship: and he who set it before
> me was the consul himself.]

Polycharmus has returned Caietanus his IOU's. 'Little good will that do you, and Caietanus will not even be grateful':

> quod Caietano reddis, Polycharme, tabellas,
> milia te centum num tribuisse putas?
> "debuit haec" inquis. tibi habe, Polycharme, tabellas
> et Caietano milia crede duo (viii. 37).

> [In giving back Caietanus his IOU's, Polycharmus, do you think you are giving him 100,000
> sesterces? 'He owed me that sum,' you say.
> Keep the IOU's and lend him two thousand
> more!]

Chloe, the murderess of her seven husbands, erects monuments to their memory, and inscribes *fecit Chloe* on the tombstones:

> inscripsit tumulis septem scelerata virorum
> 'se fecisse' Chloe. quid pote simplicius? (ix. 15).

> [On her seven husbands' tombs she doth impress
> 'This Chloe did.' What more can she confess?]

Vacerra admires the old poets only. What shall Martial do?

> miraris veteres, Vacerra, solos
> nec laudas nisi mortuos poetas.
> ignoscas petimus, Vacerra: tanti
> non est, ut placeam tibi, perire (viii. 69).

> [Vacerra lauds no living poet's lays,
> But for departed genius keeps his praise.
> I, alas, live, nor deem it worth my while
> To die that I may win Vacerra's smile.]

All this is very slight, *merae nugae*; but even if the humour be not of the first water, it will compare well with the humour of epigrams of any age. Martial knows he is not a great poet. He knows, too, that his work is uneven:

> iactat inaequalem Matho me fecisse libellum:
> si verum est, laudat carmina nostra Matho.
> aequales scribit libros Calvinus et Vmber:
> aequalis liber est, Cretice, qui malus est (vii. 90).

> [Matho makes game of my unequal verse;
> If it's unequal it might well be worse.

> Calvinus, Umber, write on one dead level,
> The book that's got no up and down's the devil!]

If there are thirty good epigrams in a book, he is satisfied (vii. 81). His defence hardly answers the question, 'Why publish so many?' but should at least mollify our judgement. Few poets read better in selections than Martial, and of few poets does selection give so inadequate an idea. For few poets of his undoubted genius have left such a large bulk of work which, in spite of its formal perfection, is morally repulsive or, from the purely literary standpoint, uninteresting. But he is an important figure in the history of literature, for he is the father of the modern epigram. Alone of Silver Latin poets is he a perfect stylist. He has the gift of *felicitas* to the full, but it is not *curiosa*. Inferior to Horace in all other points, he has greater spontaneity. And he is free from the faults of his age. He is no *virtuoso*, eaten up with self-conscious vanity; he attempts no impossible feats of language; he is clear, and uses his mythological and geographical knowledge neatly and picturesquely; but he makes no display of obscure learning. 'I would please schoolmasters,' he says, 'but not *qua* schoolmasters' (x. 21. 5). So, too, he complains of his own education:

> at me litterulas stulti docuere parentes:
> quid cum grammaticis rhetoribusque mihi? (ix.
> 73. 7).

> [My learning only proves my father fool!
> Why would he send me to a grammar school?]

As a result, perhaps, of this lack of sympathy with the education of his day, we find that, while he knows and admires the great poets of the past, and can flatter the rich poetasters of the present, his bent is curiously unliterary. He gives us practically no literary criticism. It is with the surface qualities of life that he is concerned, with its pleasures and its follies, guilty or innocent. He has a marvellously quick and clear power of observation, and of vivid presentation. He is in this sense above all others the poet of his age. He either does not see or chooses to ignore many of the best and most interesting features of his time, but the picture which he presents, for all its incompleteness, is wider and more varied than any other. We both hate him and read him for the sake of the world he depicts. [In the introduction to *Select Epigrams of Martial*, R. T. Bridge and E. D. C. Lake commented,] 'Ugliness is always bad art, and Martial often failed as a poet from his choice of subject.' There are comparatively few of his poems which we read for their own sake. Remarkable as these few poems are, the main attraction of Martial is to be found not in his wit or finish, so much as in the vividness with which he has portrayed the life of the brilliant yet corrupt society in which his lot was cast. It lives before us in all its splendour and in all its squalor. The court, with its atmosphere of grovelling flattery, its gross vices veiled and tricked out in the garb of respectability; the wealthy official class, with their villas, their favourites, their circle of dependants, men of culture, wit, and urbanity, through all which runs, strangely intermingled, a vein of extreme coarseness, vulgarity, and meanness; the lounger and the reciter, the diner-out and the legacy-hunter; the clients struggling to win their patrons' favour and to rise in the social scale, enduring the hardships and discomfort of a sordid life unillumined by lofty ideals or strength of will, a life that under cold northern skies would have been intolerable; the freedman and the slave, with all the riff-raff that support a parasitic existence on the vices of the upper classes; the noise and bustle of Rome, its sleepless nights, its cheerless tenements, its noisy streets, loud with the sound of traffic or of revelry; the shows in the theatre, the races in the circus, the interchange of presents at the Saturnalia; the pleasant life in the country villa, the simplicity of rural Italy, the sights and sounds of the park and the farm-yard; and dimly seen beyond all, the provinces, a great ocean which absorbs from time to time the rulers of Rome and the leaders of society, and from which come faint and confused echoes of frontier wars; all are there. It is a great pageant lacking order and coherence, a scene that shifts continually, but never lacks brilliance of detail and sharply defined presentment. Martial was the child of the age; it gave him his strength and his weakness. If we hate him or despise him, it is because he is the faithful representative of the life of his times; his gifts we cannot question. He practised a form of poetry that at its best is not exalted, and must, even more than other branches of art, be conditioned by social circumstance. Within its limited sphere Martial stands, not faultless, but yet supreme.

Gaston Boissier on the proper approach to appreciating Martial's epigrams:

[The] true method for finding pleasure in [Martial's] study is to put yourself back in his time, to pass with him for a moment into his life and that of the people with whom he associated. It was a wealthy society, restricted and select; he is very careful to tell us that he does not address himself to everybody: 'Others write for the multitude; for my part I only aim at pleasing the few'; he wishes to divert men of taste, men of wit accustomed to light conversation, who are not startled at a risky story, who pardon a piece of foolery, if it be but neatly put. His book seems to deserve another fate than that of being solemnly stored in a library cheek by jowl with works of philosophy and science, and from time to time being consulted by persons of a serious turn of mind. As it is compact in form, of agreeable aspect and quite portable, it can be carried under the toga and taken out and read under the porticoes or carried to those dinner-parties where a good company is assembled. Towards the end of the repast, when the guests are tired of talking charioteers and horses, or retailing the scandal of the day, they will pass to Martial's latest epigrams and regale themselves therewith.

Gaston Boissier in "The Poet Martial," in his Tacitus, and Other Roman Studies, *translated by W. G. Hutchison, 1906.*

Kirby Flower Smith   (essay date 1918)

SOURCE: "Martial, the Epigrammatist," in *Martial, The*

Epigrammatist, and Other Essays, The Johns Hopkins Press, 1920, pp. 1-36.

[*In the essay below, originally published in 1918 in* The Sewanee Review, *Smith offers insight into Martial's character and poetry through discussion of his life and times.*]

About twenty miles to the west of Saragossa, in that part of Spain now known as Aragon, there was in the first century after Christ a small country town which has since disappeared from the map. It was known as Bilbilis. The name is obviously un-Roman, and, as a matter of fact, the place was no doubt a Celtiberian fortress as far back as the days when the Phoenician adventurers swept the seas and Rome herself was nothing but a small village on the bank of the Tiber. As befitted its origin, Bilbilis was perched high up on the edge of beetling cliffs—*acutis Pendentem scopulis,* as the Christian poet Paulinus of Nola described it. At the foot of the precipice ran the small but bustling stream of the Salo, the water of which was supposed to impart a sovereign temper to steel. For that reason the principal industry of the town was the manufacture of hardware—for the most part, weapons of war.

The inhabitants of the district were an amalgamation, more or less complete, of Roman settlers, generally military veterans, with the descendants of those Celtiberian troopers who, two hundred and fifty years before, had harried Italy from the Po to the Sicilian Straits, and had done no small part in rendering the name of "Hannibal the Dread" a useful adjunct of nursery discipline until late in the Empire. The average denizen of Bilbilis still took an un-Roman delight in hunting and fishing, his inky locks were disposed to be stiff and rebellious after the manner of his forbears; but those stormy days had long since passed away, the power of Rome was supreme, and the profound peace of distance and obscurity had reigned for generations in this remote corner of the world, where, perhaps, the only sound that interfered with the stillness of nature was the tinkling of anvils in the armories near by.

The fame of such a place, if it ever becomes famous at all, is usually due to accident. Such was the fortune of Bilbilis. The renown of this little village rests entirely upon a single event—a strictly family matter—which took place there on the first of March in the year 39 or 40 of the Christian era. On that day Flaccilla presented her husband, Valerius Fronto, with a son. The boy was called Marcus Valerius, and to commemorate the month in which he was born the cognomen was added of Martialis. He was destined to become the greatest of Roman epigrammatists—indeed, if we may believe Lessing, the greatest epigrammatist the world has ever produced.

Martial's parents belonged to the old Celtiberian stock, and were distinctly well-to-do for that neighborhood. He describes their house as plain and unconventional, but overflowing with rustic cheer. This home and the country round about, its forests of oak, its echoing gorges, its lonely mountain tarns, its icy streams and springs, its snow-capped sierras, to all of which the poet reverts again and again, were the setting of an unusually healthful and happy childhood, the golden memory of which never left him. After more than thirty years in the world's Capital he could still recite all the local industries of Bilbilis with the characteristic pride of a small-townsman. He was as proud of his Celtiberian strain as any Virginian could be of the blood of Pocahontas. He even loved to dwell upon the old barbarian place-names of his native land, those oddly uncouth words which, like our own 'Walla-Wallas' and 'Popocatepetls,' are the lonely monuments of an elder race rising here and there in the midst of a newer civilization.

It was only such surroundings as these that could have given Martial that fund of buoyancy and nerve-force, that strength and poise of mind and body, which amid the deadly routine of his long years in Rome was destined to keep him alive and human. Indeed, it would be hard to say how far the man's unerring yet sympathetic vision of the realities of life, how far his ability to steer clear of the various literary and social illusions, insincerities and artificialities so characteristic of his time—in short, how far his most striking qualities as a man and as an author were fostered and strengthened by this close contact with genuine nature and with the simple honest folk among whom his early life was passed.

But although Bilbilis was remote from Rome, it was not remote from cultivation. At that time Spain was in the zenith of her influence at the Capital and of her prosperous activity at home. Martial's province of Hispania Tarraconensis supported some of the finest schools in the Empire, and his parents saw to it that their son received the best education available. "Which was utter folly on their part," he remarks in an epigram written nearly forty years later; "What have I gained by consorting with professors of literature and oratory in these days when an ex-shoemaker can become a millionaire?"

One ought not to take an epigrammatist too seriously; and at all events when the youth of twenty-three set out for Rome to seek his fortune he was undoubtedly filled with energy and enthusiasm. And few young provincials ever began a career in the great city under more favorable conditions or with fairer hopes for the future. In his position all depended on patronage. Here Martial was peculiarly fortunate. He could number among his patrons the great Spanish house of the Annaei, at that time represented by the three brothers, Seneca the philosopher, Junius Gallio, who as proconsul of Achaea presided at the trial of Paul the apostle at Corinth, and lastly, Annaeus Mela, father of Lucan the poet. Still another patron was Cn. Calpurnius, head of the famous patrician house of the Pisones.

But at the very hour of Martial's arrival the shadow of imminent disaster had already fallen upon these men. In April, 65, the tragic discovery of the Pisonian Conspiracy swept away not only all Martial's friends, but also many others among the best and greatest of the State. It was clearly a stunning blow to the young man just from the Provinces. His friends were gone, new friends had to be made, and his Spanish blood was no longer a passport.

The next fifteen years were among the most eventful in Roman history. They contained the spectacular death of Nero, and with it the end of Caesar's line, the awful year of the three emperors, and the accession of the Flavian

house. But so far as the life of Martial is concerned, this period is a complete blank. It may or may not be significant that he himself makes no reference to it. Nevertheless, we know that our keen-eyed, quick-witted looker-on from the Spanish country-side was acquiring every day a perception of the sights and humors of the great Capital, and that he was rapidly losing his illusions, if he ever had any; in short, that he was laying the foundation of his future career. In fact, we know that he actually made some essays in the department of epigram which years afterward, much to the poet's dismay, were republished as a speculation by Pollius Quintianus, an enterprising Macmillan of Domitian's time.

For us, however, the first appearance of Martial as an author was in the year 80, when Titus dedicated the Coliseum with a brilliant series of games and entertainments. The so-called *Liber Spectaculorum* which now stands at the head of our modern editions was originally written by Martial for that occasion and addressed to the Emperor. Most of the epigrams in this collection are pot-boilers; but they brought their author to the notice of the Court, and such was in reality their principal object.

Two honors came to the poet as a result. One was the *ius trium liberorum,* that is to say, the special privileges granted by law to any Roman citizen who was the father of three children. The value of it to Martial was the fact that he was henceforth exempt from that law of Augustus which forced a bachelor into matrimony whether he liked it or not. The second honor was a titular position as a *tribunus militum,* by virtue of which the poet was raised to the rank of a Roman Knight. The principal advantage of it to Martial appears to have been the fact that whenever he attended the theatre he now had the privilege of a seat in the first rows back of the orchestra. He never received any more substantial recognition than this from either Vespasian or Titus. Both emperors encouraged literature. But, unfortunately, Vespasian had a close fist, and Titus a short life.

The so-called *Xenia* and *Apophoreta* were published four or five years later by Martial's bookseller Tryphon. They afterwards formed an appendix to the *édition définitive,* and are now numbered as Books 13 and 14. Xenia were presents given to guests during the Saturnalia. Apophoreta were the presents given to the guests at dinner parties, and, as the name implies, were intended to be taken home. It was usual to accompany these Christmas presents, Xenia, and these dinner souvenirs, Apophoreta, by a verse or two. The two books of Martial supply the verses for appropriate presents on such occasions. It will be seen that they were designed to meet the wants of those who were not adepts in the polite art of turning a distich. Like the obituary poetry of the Baltimore *Sun,* these distichs of Martial could be kept on hand, and dealt out as needed. The fact that he ever bored himself with composing them suggests that one of his recurrent attacks of poverty was upon him. Indeed, as he himself says to his reader, "The Xenia in this slim little booklet can be bought for four nummi. You may have 'omnis turba,' the whole gang of them, for twenty cents. Is that too much? Well, Tryphon can afford to knock off fifty per cent. He would be making money at it even then. You can present these distichs to your guests instead of a gift—'si tibi tam rarus quam mihi nummus erit,' if pennies are as far apart with you as they are with me."

But a better time was now at hand. Books 1 and 2 appeared in 86, and from that time he published at the rate of about one book a year until his return to Spain. Book 12 appeared in 102, three years from that date. Shortly after came the poet's death, and then a second edition of Book 12, which is the one we now possess.

During the fifteen years that followed the publication of Book 1, Martial was one of the best-known men in the Empire. "The other day, Rufus," he says in one of his epigrams, "a certain man looked me all over with the thoroughness of one who intended to buy me for a slave or train me for the prize-ring. After he had gazed at me and had even felt of me for some time, 'Can it be,' he cried, 'that you really are that famous Martial whose jests and lively sallies are known to everyone who does not possess a downright Dutchman's ear?' I smiled a little, and with a slight nod admitted that I was the person whom he had named. 'Why then do you wear such bad cloaks?' 'Because,' I replied, 'I am such a bad poet' " (vi, 82).

At the time his third book was published Martial had retired to Forum Corneli in Cisalpine Gaul. "If any one asks you," he says, "why I went, tell him I was worn out with my empty round of duty calls at the houses of the great. If you are asked when I am coming back, you may say that I was a poet when I left, I shall return when I have learned how to play the guitar" (iii, 4).

With the single exception of this one visit, which was not as long as he had expected, thirty-five continuous years of Martial's life were spent in Rome. Even summer resorts were not to his liking. Among other things they were beyond the depth of his purse. He tried it once at Baiae (I, 59). "The baths," he says, "are excellent. But man cannot live on the baths alone. My one dole a day [35 cents from his patron] was mere starvation down there. I prefer the suburbs with regular meals and the natatorium."

At the time his first book was published the poet had rooms in the third story of a house which faced the laurels in front of Agrippa's portico on the west side of the Quirinal. After 94, during the days when he was best off, he had a small house of his own near the temple of Quirinus. In spite of his various ups and downs he managed to keep his little country place at Nomentum until he finally left Rome. It was dry and unproductive. He once asked Domitian for permission to tap the aqueduct which ran near by, but was refused. Domitian liked his poetry, and once invited him to dinner, but it is somewhat to the poet's credit that he never received any substantial recognition from Domitian. Of course Martial's country place was expensive. Those who have watched the steady rise in prices during the last few years will not fail to see the point of the following epigram (viii, 61):

> Charinus pines with envy, bursts with spite;
> He weeps; he raves; indeed, the rumor goes.
> When once he finds a branch of proper height,
> He means to hang himself and end his woes.

> Because my epigrams are said and sung
> From Thebes to Britain, Cadiz to Cathay?
> Because my book fares sumptuously among
> The thousand nations neath the Roman sway?

> Oh no. My country place just out of town,
> The span of mules I own—Dame Rumor saith
> These be the things that cast Charinus down,
> These be the things that make him dream of death.

> What curse invoked repays such envy best?
> Severus, what's your judgment of the case?
> My own in just nine words may be expressed:
> I wish him this: my mules, my country place.

Martial, however, spent his summers there, and as he himself tells us, it was at all times of the year his frequent haven of refuge from the bores and the noisy streets of Rome.

With his universal fame and his numerous patrons he must have had a very comfortable income for several years. His references to his poverty are, no doubt, often exaggerated. The most of us are not in the habit of underestimating our poverty. Moreover, we must remember that poverty had always been, and still is, a traditional theme of the epigram. When Catullus, for instance, who owned a yacht and a country place, tells us that "his purse is full of cobwebs," we do not take him too seriously. Poverty, however, is comparative; and doubtless Martial often found it something of a struggle to make both ends meet. Rome in the first century was quite as expensive as New York in the twentieth century. Martial also had many rich friends. But, above all, he was one of those men who are constitutionally unable to save anything. When he finally decided to return to Spain, the younger Pliny, to whom he had once written a very pretty little poem, sent him his travelling expenses. It was characteristic of Martial that after thirty-five years of hard work in Rome he really needed the money.

This was in 98. The assisted death of Domitian had occurred in 96. His successor, the aged Nerva, a former patron of Martial's, had just passed away and the formal accession of Trajan had closed another volume of Roman history. It was the volume to which the best of the poet's life belonged. The Empire had had her last fling under Domitian. But she was already near the period of wrinkles and lithia tablets, and now she entered upon her *âge dévot* under the care of such family physicians as Trajan and Hadrian, and of such family chaplains as Juvenal and Tacitus. At this juncture Martial was somewhat in the position of a playwright under the Commonwealth, or of a 'regular' after one of our political cyclones. He may have made one or two faint attempts to swing into line. But his heart was not in it. The times had changed, and it is not easy to begin life anew at sixty. Moreover, the splendid vitality which had made him Martial had been sorely taxed. It is worth noting that the boredom of calls, the noisy streets, the inability to sleep, and those other inconveniences of urban life to which the third satire of Juvenal is devoted are, in Martial's case, confined for the most part to the last two or three books. For example, when he was asked by one of his rich friends why he retired so frequently to his country place, Martial replies in his own characteristic fashion (xii, 57):

> There is no place in Rome where a poor man can either think or rest. One cannot live for bakers' mills before daylight, schoolmasters at daylight, and brass foundries all day long. Here an idle money-changer rattles his pile of copper coins on his dirty counter, there a beater of Spanish gold belabors his stone with his polished mallet, the fanatic gang of Bellona's priests never cease from shouting, nor the clamorous sailor as he carries a piece of the ship upon which he says he was wrecked, nor the little Jew whose mother has taught him to beg, nor the blear-eyed vendor of matches. Many indeed are the murderers of sleep. 'Tis all well enough for you, Sparsus, in your palace, your *rus in urbe,* your country place within the city walls. But as for me, I am roused anon by the laughter of the passing throng. All Rome is at my bedroom door.

The baker's mill has yielded to the trolley car, the priests of Bellona to the Salvation Army, but the description has lost none of its force—especially for those who have ever had the opportunity to compare the rural stillness of London at eight in the morning with that insane clatter which in every Latin town begins promptly at dawn and never lets up until well into the small hours of the following night.

But strongest of all, perhaps, was that longing for the old Spanish countryside which had always haunted him. Years before when his friend and countryman Quintilian was urging him to practise law—the profession for which his education had fitted him—Martial's characteristic reply had been: "No, let me really live while I may. No one is ever too soon in getting about it. What are wealth and station, if we must put off living until we acquire them? I am not ambitious. Give me—'tis all I ask—

> A homely house, with ease the rule of life,
> A natural lawn, a spring not far away,
> A well-fed slave, a not too learnèd wife,
> Sound sleep by night, and never a quarrel by
>   day."

We may be sure that more than one memory of his boyhood home was suggested to Martial in these lines. Indeed, I suspect that the "not too learned wife," like the ideal helpmeet of many another incorrigible old bachelor, was, in reality, a replica of his mother. However that may be, Martial found friends and patrons in Bilbilis who made rest and retirement possible. Notable among them were Terentius Priscus and, especially, the lady Marcella, who gave him a small place upon which he was enabled to live as he had desired.

Several epigrams in Book 12 show that, at first, he thoroughly enjoyed the change. But if he had cherished the illusion—as he actually appears to have done—that he would continue to enjoy it, he was soon to be undeceived. The golden memories of the past can always glorify the gray realities of the present; but the horizon of youth is not the horizon of age, and the dial-hand of Time will not turn backward.

Martial's awakening is seen in his preface to Book 12. The hurry, bustle, and activity of the city had wearied him; but he had been in the midst of it for a generation and, after all, it was his life. Above all, he missed the intellectual stimulus of the great Capital, the libraries, the theatres, the social gatherings, the cultivated reading public. Epigram was the work of his life, and the possibilities of Bilbilis for epigram were soon exhausted. Moreover, he had little in common with the average denizen of Bilbilis. And it is easy to guess how the average denizen of Bilbilis looked upon Martial. Indeed, the poet himself complains of the "municipalium robigo dentium," as he calls it, "the backbiting that goes on in a country town." "What I get," he says, "is envy, not genuine criticism—and in a little insignificant place one or two disagreeable people are a host. In the face of that sort of thing I find it hard to keep in a good humor every day." "Marcella," he acknowledges in another place (xii, 21), "is the only one who can give me back the city again." It is not surprising, therefore, to find that in this last book of Martial's very few of the epigrams suggest Bilbilis. Most of them hark back to the home and the scenes of his prime.

In a poem written on his fifty-seventh birthday (x, 24) he had expressed the hope of living until seventy-five. With the constitution and the temperament which nature appears to have given him he was justified in believing that he might live even longer than that. But it was not to be. The long tension and the high pressure of a metropolitan existence so like our own, the sudden relief from it in the afternoon of his day, the cessation of the paramount interests and occupations of a lifetime—all these things are peculiarily trying to the physique. It is not surprising, therefore, to learn that Martial died soon after the publication, in 102, of his last book. He was barely sixty-four.

I know of no ancient writer whose personal character has been more bitterly assailed by modern critics of a certain class. I know of few who have deserved it so little. We may say, at once, that all Martial's faults are on the surface. Otherwise, many of his critics never would have discerned them at all. The just and sympathetic appreciation of an ancient author demands a much larger background of knowledge and experience than seems to be generally supposed. It is, of course, obvious that, first of all, before attempting to criticize an author one ought to read his entire works with care and understanding. In the case of a man like Martial, one must also be thoroughly acquainted with all of the conditions of his life and times; one must know all about the history of the antique epigram as a department, one must be able to realize the peculiarities of the Latin temperament as such, and make due allowance for them.

For example, most prominent and most widely circulated—indeed, with many persons, the only association with the name of Martial—is the charge that both in subject and in language his epigrams are offensive to modern taste. To a certain extent this is true. We should add, however, that Martial himself cannot be held responsible for it. The conventional tradition of the epigram demanded that a certain portion of one's work should be of this character. That in Martial's case the peculiarity is more the result of this convention than of individual taste, is shown by the fact that it does not run through his entire text. On the contrary, it is confined to certain epigrams, and those epigrams do not represent his best and most characteristic work. Lastly, the proportion of these objectionable epigrams is by no means as large as the majority of people appear to suppose. The text of Martial contains 1555 epigrams. The Delphin edition of 1660 excluded 150 of this number. The standards of another age and a different nationality would probably exclude about 50 more. All told, hardly a seventh of the total. This leaves more than 1200 little poems into which anyone may dip without hesitation, and on this residuum Martial can easily support his claim to be called one of the wittiest, one of the most amusing, and at the same time one of the most instructive, writers in any period of the world's history.

Martial's flattery of Domitian is a charge easily disposed of. Flattery of the reigning emperor has been the rule since Augustus. By this time it was almost as conventional as our titles of nobility. What do these mean when we interpret them literally? Moreover, Martial is outdone not only by his predecessors but, which is more to the point, by his graver contemporaries, Statius and Quintilian. Still more to his credit is the fact that he did not revile the memory of Domitian after his death. Finally, we must remember that Martial was a Spaniard and a provincial. Why should he care about Domitian's vices or virtues, or about his moral fitness or unfitness to be a Roman emperor?

The third and, on the face of it, the most serious charge against Martial is his relation to his patrons. To state the matter baldly as well as briefly, it is Martial's idea that his patrons owe him a living, and if he has reason to think that they are forgetting it, he does not hesitate to refresh their memories. For instance, he frequently reminds his readers in general, and his patrons in particular, that a poet is a person who needs money. Again, he makes pointed reference to the depleted condition of his wardrobe. Once, he reminds Stella that unless he is moved to send him some new tiles, the farmhouse at Nomentum will have to go on leaking as before.

Now all this is unpleasant to us, but we must not forget that, as a matter of fact, Martial's patrons actually did owe him a living. Such were the habits and standards of his time, the accepted and unavoidable conditions of his life. That life was the life of a brilliant provincial who came to the city without an independent fortune and chose literature as his profession. Nowadays, the most of us are familiar with the idea that an author is entitled to a share in the success of his book, that he draws his income for literary work from that source. But this idea was not generally entertained until the nineteenth century; and our recent experience with the law of international copyright shows that the idea is still rudimentary in many minds. In antiquity, therefore, unless an author possessed independent means, his only alternative was patronage; and until 1800 patronage was the general rule of literature.

The relation of client to patron was an ancient and honorable institution in Roman society. There was nothing to criticize in the relation of Vergil and Horace to Maecenas and Augustus. And at the time of his death Vergil possessed not less than half a million in our money. But whatever Vergil was worth, the bald fact remains that practically all of it was acquired by gift. It was only through the generosity of a patron that a poor author could secure the leisure for literary composition. In return, he undertook to immortalize his patron in his works. He also attended him in public from time to time, he went to his regular morning receptions, and if his patron invited him to dinner, he made himself agreeable. In short, he made every return in his power for the favors he had received or hoped to receive.

It will easily be seen that this relation—like the fee to the waiter—was peculiarly liable to abuse. The pages of Martial, Pliny, and Juvenal show how much it had deteriorated by the time of Domitian. Both sides were to blame. Prices were outrageous, and wealth the standard of life. The rich were largely the descendants of dishonest nobodies, and with habits, tastes, and views to match; the poor had lost their pride, their independence, their spur of ambition. Each class despised the other, and each class was justified in it. Both Juvenal and Martial tell us that men of birth and education, men of high official position, even men with fortunes of their own, were not ashamed to take the *sportula* (originally the basket of food for the day, now the dole of money) given to those who had made the regular morning call. One is reminded of the retainers of a noble house in the Middle Ages, or of the poor courtiers under the old régime in France and England.

Not pleasant, this custom; but it existed, and Martial in paying court to a patron was only following the universal rule of his time. He had the further justification of necessity, and it is also clear that he made all the return for it in his power. Indeed, it was characteristic of the man, and, all things considered, rather to his credit, that he insisted upon the business aspect of it, and refused to pretend that it was anything else. So far, therefore, from severely criticizing Martial's relation to his patrons, it seems to me that in a situation which he could not avoid, and for which he was not responsible, he showed himself a better man than most of his contemporaries would have done under the same conditions.

It was a hard, uncertain, Bohemian sort of life in many respects. But to a certain degree Martial was himself a genuine Bohemian. The type is excessively rare in the annals of Roman literature. The one other striking example whom I now recall is that brilliant old reprobate Furius Bibaculus. Martial's combination of improvidence and gaiety is distinctly Bohemian. He also seems to have had the peculiarly attractive personality by which that temperament is sometimes accompanied. At any rate, his epigrams show not only that he knew everybody in Rome who was worth knowing, but that few men as great as he have at the same time been so universally liked by their contemporaries. Some of Martial's best epigrams are to his friends. In one of his last poems (xii, 34)—it is addressed to Julius Martialis, whom he had known and loved for four-and-thirty years—the poet closes by saying: "If you would avoid many griefs, and escape many a heartache, then make of no one too dear a friend. You will have less joy, but you will also have less sorrow." This can only be the observation of a man who has had real friends, and has really loved them.

Another attractive side of his nature was his evident devotion to little children. I content myself with a single illustration. This is his epitaph for Erotion, a little girl belonging to his household who died at the age of six. Martial, who was then a man of nearly fifty, was deeply affected by the loss of his little favorite. The poem, which is one of three devoted to her memory, recommends the child to the care of his own parents, who had long been dead—a touchingly naïve conception quite in harmony with antique methods of thought, but inspired with a simple and homely tenderness for which there are few parallels in the annals of literature (v, 34):

> Dear father and dear mother: Let me crave
> Your loving kindness there beyond the grave
> For my Erotion, the pretty maid
> Who bears these lines. Don't let her be afraid!
> She's such a little lassie—only six—
> To toddle down that pathway to the Styx
> All by herself! Black shadows haunt those
>   steeps,
> And Cerberus the Dread who never sleeps.
> May she be comforted, and may she play
> About you merry as the livelong day,
> And in her childish prattle often tell
> Of that old master whom she loved so well.
> Oh earth, bear lightly on her! 'Tis her due;
> The little girl so lightly bore on you.

Lines like these help us to understand why under continual provocation he could still be patient with a fussy, dictatorial, old slave who was utterly unable to realize that the boy he had spanked forty or fifty years before had now arrived at years of discretion.

The only contemporary reference to Martial which has happened to survive is found in the passage of Pliny to which I have already alluded. He describes the poet whom he knew as "acutus, ingenious, acer"—clear-sighted, clever, shrewd. And, truly, as a keen observer of men and things, Martial has rarely been equalled. The world of Rome was an open book before him. He read the text, fathomed its import, and wrote his commentary upon it in brilliant and telling phrases, and in a literary form of which he was undoubtedly the master.

But, after all, the mainspring of Martial's character and career, the real secret of his abiding greatness as an epigrammatist, is found as soon as we learn that he possessed the quality which Pliny calls *candor*. *Candor* means frankness, genuineness, sincerity. It was one of the highest tributes to character that a Roman could pay.

Here we have, according to Pliny's showing, a man who was witty, yet kindly, who was clear-sighted, yet tolerant, who was shrewd, yet sincere. This is the character of one who is never blind to the true proportion of things. And, as a matter of fact, a sense of proportion, a conception of the realities as applied to life, conduct, thought, art, literature, style, everything, is the leading trait of Martial's character, the universal solvent of his career and genius. All is expressed in Μηδεν αγαν—*nil nimis*—"avoid extremes," that phrase so characteristic of antiquity, the

summary of its wisdom and experience, its most valuable contribution to the conduct of life.

So it was that in spite of his surroundings and associations Martial remained simple, genuine, and unaffected to the end. In an age of unutterable impurity he had no vices. In an age of cant, pedantry, affectation, and shams of every sort and description, he was still true to himself. In an age as notable for exaggeration as is our own, Martial knows that strength does not lie in superlatives. He tells us again and again in his own characteristic fashion that the secret of happiness has not been discovered by the voluptuary, nor the secret of virtue by the ascetic. The present is quite good enough for him; to live it heartily and naturally as it comes, to find out what he is best fitted to do, and then to do it—this is the sum of his philosophy. It is true enough that most friendship is mere feigning. But there are real friends. Let us, therefore, bind them to us with bonds of steel. It is true that life is hard and bitter. But we have to live it. Let us, therefore, find the sunshine while we can. In v, 58, he says (Cowley's translation):

> To-morrow you will live, you always cry.
> In what far country does this 'morrow' lie,
> That 'tis so mighty long ere it arrive?
> Beyond the Indies does this 'morrow' live?
>
> 'Tis so far-fetched, this 'morrow,' that I fear,
> 'Twill be both very old and very dear.
> "To-morrow I will live," the fool does say;
> To-day itself 's too late—the wise lived yesterday.

The sentiment is as characteristic of antiquity as it is of Martial. Not very elevated, perhaps, but Martial is not a reformer. Like most men of the world he is generally indifferent on the subject of other people's vices. He is not an enthusiast, for he has no illusions. Nor is he a man of lofty ideals. But he is natural and sensible as he is witty and brilliant. Therefore he was in harmony with his own days, and would have been equally in harmony with ours. For if Martial seems so intensely modern, it is not because he has advanced beyond his own time. It is because he is universal. Martial is a cosmopolitan poet and, with the single exception of Menander, the most pronounced example of the type in all classical antiquity.

The prose preface to Martial's first book indicates very clearly some of his views with regard to the sphere and character of the epigram. It also illustrates the man. "I trust," he says,

> that the attitude I have maintained in these books of mine is such that no reasonable man can complain of them. They never make their fun at the expense of real people, even of the humblest station—a thing quite absent from the old epigrammatists. Those men not only attacked and vilified people by their real names, but also attacked people of consequence. I do not care to buy fame at such a price. My witticisms contain no innuendoes. I want no malicious commentators who will undertake to re-write my epigrams for me. It is unfair to be subtle in another man's book. For my free plainness of speech, that is, for the language of the epigram, I should apologize if the example were

mine. But so Catullus writes, so Marsus, so Pedo, so Gaetulicus—so everyone who is read through. Still, if there is anyone so painfully Puritanical that in his eyes it is unholy to speak plain Latin in a book, he would better content himself with the preface or, better still, with the title. Epigrams are written for those who attend Flora's entertainments. Cato should not come into my theatre. But if he does come in, let him take his seat and look on with the rest.

Perhaps I ought to add, by way of explanation, that the theatrical performances regularly given at the spring festival of the Floralia were proverbial for their gaiety and license. Once upon a time, the younger Cato, a proverb of Stoic virtue and gravity, went into the theatre during this festival, but finding that his presence put a damper on the occasion, he walked out again. The Stoics of the Empire were never weary of repeating this anecdote of their patron saint. We might expect a man of Martial's temperament to detect the essential ostentation of such a performance. Witness the closing words of his preface:

> Pray tell me, when you knew 'twas Flora's holiday,
> With all the license, all the sport expected then,
> Why, Cato, came you stalking in to see the play?
> Or was it that you might go stalking out again?

So, too, referring to the theatrical way in which the contemporary Stoics preached and practised their favorite doctrine of suicide, Martial says (i, 8, 5–6): "I care nothing for a man who buys fame with his blood—'tis no task to let blood. Give me the man who can deserve praise without dying for it." That the ostentatiousness of the proceeding was the cause of his criticism, is shown by the fact that he yields to none in his admiration of real heroism where real heroism is needed. Ostentation in vice is quite as repellent to him. "Tucca," he says, "is not satisfied to be a glutton, he must have the reputation of it."

All this goes back to his doctrine of *Nil nimis*—temperance in the real meaning of the word. Neither virtue nor happiness is compatible with excess of any sort. Writing to his friend Julius Martialis, he says (x, 47, translated by Fanshawe):

> The things that make a life to please,
> Sweetest Martial, they are these:
> Estate inherited, not got;
> A thankful field, hearth always hot;
> City seldom, lawsuits never;
> Equal friends, agreeing ever;
> Health of body, peace of mind;
> Sleeps that till the morning bind;
> Wise simplicity, plain fare;
> Not drunken nights, yet loos'd from care;
> A sober, not a sullen spouse;
> Clean strength, not such as his that plows;
> Wish only what thou art, to be;
> Death neither wish, nor fear to see.

It is extremely difficult to reproduce the exquisite poise and simplicity of Martial's style and thought. No one knew better than he how hard it was to write good epigrams. "Some of your tetrastichs," he says to one Sabellus (vii, 85), "are not so bad, a few of your distichs are well

done. I congratulate you—but I am not overpowered. To write one good epigram is easy, to write a bookful is another matter." To those who insisted that no epigram should exceed the length of a distich, his characteristic reply was (viii, 29): "If a man confines himself to distichs, his object, I suppose, is to please by brevity. But, pray tell me, what does their brevity amount to, when there is a whole bookful of them?"

Everyone knows his famous judgment of his own work (i, 16):

> Sunt bona, sunt quaedam mediocria, sunt mala plura
> Quae legis hic: aliter non fit, Avite, liber.

> Good, fair, and bad
> May here be had.
> That's no surprise!
> 'Twere vain to look
> For any book
> That's otherwise.

So good a criticism of books in general, and of books of epigrams in particular, that one might almost be excused for overlooking the fact that Martial himself is really an exception to his own rule. At any rate, no one has written so many epigrams, and at the same time has contrived to produce so many good epigrams. It is clear that he was one of those rarest of men who have resolution enough to throw their bad work into the waste-basket.

So far as they illustrate the life of contemporary Rome, many of Martial's themes are also to be found in the letters of that literary Bostonian of antiquity, the Younger Pliny. They are, likewise, the same which Juvenal worked into his satires twenty years after—when Domitian was safely dead. Each of these three has pictured the situation from his own point of view. It was Martial who really saw it. So far as that situation applies to our own life, much has always been familiar, some has grown familiar during the last decade, and the remainder will probably come home to us with the advancing years of the twentieth century.

A marked feature of this age was the feverish production of literature. One may say without exaggeration that it was really the fashion to write books. In fact, the situation politically and socially was such that for an ambitious Roman of birth and education, literature was one of the few avenues to fame which was still open. No wonder Juvenal and Martial believed that neither literature nor learning was a paying investment. "There are quite too many persons of quality in the business," says Martial in one place, "and who ever knew an author who was interested in other people's books?" "Of course (x, 9), one may become famous through one's books. I myself, for example, am well known all over the Empire—almost as well known, I may say, as Andraemon, the race-horse!"

But although literature may bring fame, it never brings a large income. "I understand, Lupus," he says in another epigram (v, 56), "that you are debating on the best training for your son. My advice is, avoid all professors of literature and oratory. The boy should have nothing to do with the works of Vergil or Cicero. Let him leave old Professor Tutilius to his own glory. If he makes verses, disown the poet. If he wants to follow an occupation that will pay, let him learn the guitar or the flute. If he proves to be dull, make an auctioneer of him or an architect."

The business of an auctioneer was despised, but it was proverbially lucrative. Hence the point of the following epigram (vi, 8):

> Two praetors, seven advocates,
> Four tribunes and ten laureates—
> Such was the formidable band
> Of suitors for a maiden's hand.
> All twenty-three approached her sire,
> All twenty-three breathed their desire.
> Father dismissed that deputation
> Without a moment's hesitation,
> And straight bestowed his daughter dear
> On Eulogus, the auctioneer.

Of course, we hear a great deal about the deadly *recitatio* and all its attendant horrors, such as the amateur poet, the Admirable Crichton in literature, etc., etc. The ostensible and legitimate object of the *recitatio* was to allow an author to read his work to his friends and get their criticisms of it. But this unfortunate invention of Vergil's friend Asinius Pollio had become literally pestiferous by the time of Domitian, and more especially for its inordinate length and intolerable frequency. Martial speaks in all seriousness of the entire days which politeness or policy often obliged him to waste on these things. Pliny attended them religiously. But Pliny performed all the functions of his life religiously. Moreover, Pliny was himself an author. He was, therefore, as Horace said, an 'auditor et ultor'—in a position to get even now and then by giving a reading himself.

Martial is only too well acquainted with all the types. Here is Maximus (iii, 18) who begins his reading by saying that he has a bad cold. "Why then do you recite?" inquires Martial solicitously.

I know of no ancient writer whose personal character has been more bitterly assailed by modern critics than Martial. I know of few who have deserved it so little.

—*Kirby Flower Smith*

"Gallicus," he says in another epigram (viii, 76), "you always say, 'tell me the exact truth about my poetry and my oratory. There is nothing which I would rather hear.' Well, Gallicus, listen then to the great truth of all. It is this: Gallicus, you do not like to hear the truth."

"Mamercus," he says (ii, 88), "you wish to be considered a poet, and yet you never recite. Be anything you like, Mamercus, provided you don't recite!"

Of course, the reader often gave a dinner to his hearers. But in Martial's opinion such dinners are quite too dear at the price. In iii, 45, he observes:

They say the Sun god turned backward that he might flee from the dinner of Thyestes. I don't know whether that is true or not. But I do know, Ligurinus, that I flee from yours. I don't deny that your dinners are sumptuous, and that the food you furnish is superb. But absolutely nothing pleases me so long as you recite. You need not set turbot and mullet before me; I don't care for mushrooms, I have no desire for oysters. Just be still.

The most important and characteristic feature of Roman social life was the dinner party. Martial accepted the invitations of his patrons as a matter of course; and it is inconceivable that a man of such unrivalled wit and social qualities could have failed to be in constant demand elsewhere. Between the two, he probably saw as much, if not more, of this side of life than any other man of his time. No wonder he did not live to be seventy-five, in spite of his temperate habits!

Nothing has been added to Roman experience in the methods of giving a dinner. Singing, for example, music, vaudeville, and the like, which some of our wealthy contemporaries are just beginning to discover, were already old when Martial began his career. His own opinion is (ix, 77) that "the best kind of a dinner is the dinner at which no flute-player is present." Doubtless there are some in these days who will agree with him.

But of all the persons one met at these large entertainments the best known and the most frequently mentioned is the professional diner-out, the 'dinner-hunter.' One of Juvenal's best satires is devoted to this character. But not even Juvenal can surpass Martial's observation of this specific type of 'dead-beat.' "Some of these people carry off as much food as they can conceal in their napkins. The next day they either eat it themselves or sell it to someone else. They try to make you believe that they don't care to dine out, but this is false. Others, on the contrary, swear that they never dine at home, and this is true—for two reasons."

But the Nemesis of the dinner-hunter is the stingy host. The stingy host has many ways of displaying his really remarkable ingenuity. He can blend good and bad wines, he can give a different wine to his guests from that which he drinks himself—though he sometimes tries to conceal it by giving them poor wine in good bottles. He can allow his guests the privilege of watching him eat mushrooms. Or if he does give them something good, he may give them so little of it as to be merely an appetizer. Such, for example, is Mancinus, who set out one poor, little, unprotected boar for no less than sixty hungry men. Or the stingy host never invites a man except when he knows that he has a previous engagement. Again, he furnishes handsome decorations at the expense of the dinner, or he gives a poor dinner and tries to excuse himself by abusing the cook. You will observe, however, that these persons are only niggardly with other people. In their own pleasures they are extravagant enough.

The strangest type, however, are those who are too stingy to do anything even for themselves. A curious anomaly, the miser. Here is Calenus, for example. Calenus never became stingy at all until he had inherited a fortune and could afford to be generous. The twin brother of the miser is the spendthrift, and they are both alike in their inability to realize the value of money.

One of the most tedious duties of a client was the necessity of presenting himself at the daily receptions of his patrons. These took place regularly at daylight. On the whole, it was the heaviest burden of Martial's life in Rome. He often complained that his literary work was sadly interfered with by this duty. And there is no real affection in it, he says. Some patrons, for instance, insist upon having all their titles. Nor is there much profit in it. The only ones who get anything are the rich, or those persons who know too much about their patron. And as for the sportula, it is so small and so poor that foreign competition for it is quite discouraged. For example, there was my countryman Tuccius (iii, 14):

> Poor Tuccius, quite starved at home,
> To seek his fortune here in Rome
> Came all the way from Spain.
> But when he reached the city gate,
> He heard about the dole—and straight
> Went posting back again.

No one knows better than Martial all the possible varieties of the genus Millionaire. The type which we have recently named "the migratory rich" is nothing new to him, and his comment is, that "a man who lives everywhere lives nowhere." He knows the sort who cherish a high temper, "because it is cheaper to fly into a passion than it is to give." Another one gives, but he never ceases to remind you of the fact. He knows the wealthy invalid and recommends, free of charge, one dose of real poverty. Nor does he fail to observe the rich upstart who is forever trying to steal a Knight's seat in the theatre, or who attempts to get into society by changing a too significant name. Mus is a small matter—as Horace says, "ridiculus mus." But observe what a difference it makes between Cinnamus, the ex-slave, and Cinna, the patrician.

Martial devotes more than one caustic epigram to that large class in Rome who lived beyond their means— "ambitiosa paupertate," as his friend Juvenal puts it— eking out what they lack by all sorts of shifts and hypocrisies, the mere counterfeit presentment of wealth in an age of high prices and vulgar ostentation. Most hopeless of all is the semi-respectable person, too indolent to work, too self-indulgent to be independent.

> You say you desire to be free (ii, 53). You lie, Maximus, you do not desire it. But if you should desire it, this is the way. Give up dining out. Be content with *vin ordinaire.* Learn to smile at dyspeptic Cinna's golden dinner service. Be satisfied with a toga like mine. Submit to lower your head when you enter your house. If you have such strength of mind as this, you may live more free than the Parthian king.

Nor are the fortune-hunters forgotten (ii, 65): "Why are you so sad?" says Martial to his acquaintance Saleianus. "Why, indeed? I have just buried my wife." "Oh great crime of Destiny!" Martial cries with exaggerated sympathy, "Oh heavy chance! To think that Secundilla is dead—

and so wealthy too—she left you a million sesterces, didn't she? My broken-hearted friend, I cannot tell you how much I regret that this has happened to you."

No new observations have been made on the various professions since Martial's day, and surely no classical scholar would venture to guess how long it has been since anything new has been contributed to the theme of lovely woman.

"Diaulus (i, 30) began as a doctor. Then he became an undertaker. Really, a distinction without a difference. In either case he laid us out."

"In the evening Andragoras supped gaily with me. In the morning he was found dead. He must have dreamed that he saw Dr. Hermocrates!" (vi, 53).

"The artist (i, 102) who painted your Venus must have intended to flatter Minerva." The point of this criticism is seen as soon as we recollect that the only time Minerva ever contended in a beauty-show was on that memorable occasion when Paris was umpire and gave the prize to Venus. Perhaps Martial was justified in his suspicion that if the severe and unapproachable goddess of wisdom was sufficiently human to enter such a contest, she was also sufficiently human to enjoy seeing her victorious rival so dreadfully caricatured by the artist.

"All of Fabulla's friends (viii, 79) among the women are old and ugly to the last degree. Fabulla thoroughly understands the value of background."

To Catulla, fascinating but false, Martial says (viii, 53):

> So very fair! And yet so very common?
> Would you were plainer, or a better woman!

Which is really far superior to Congreve's famous song which ends:

> Would thou couldst make of me a saint,
> Or I of thee a sinner!

Many of Martial's best epigrams may be grouped under the head of character sketches. So many of these men are quite as familiar to us as they were to him eighteen centuries ago.

Here is Cinna (i, 89) who takes you aside with a great air of mystery to tell you that "it is a warm day."

Here is Laurus (ii, 64) who all his life has been intending to do something great, but has never been able to decide what it shall be.

We all know Naevolus (iv, 83). Naevolus is never polite or affable except when he is in trouble. On the other hand, we also know Postumus (ii, 67). Postumus is the painfully civil person. If he saw you from a merry-go-round, he would say "how do you do?" every time he passed.

And which one of us has failed to meet Tucca (xii, 94), the Admirable Crichton, the Jack-of-all-trades, the man who knows it all? Tucca always reminds me of the Welsh Giant in my old copy of Jack the Giant-killer. Whenever you have done anything, he at once lets you know that "Hur can do that hursel."

Poor Tom Moore, among his titled friends, finds his proto-type in Philomusus (vii, 76), of whom Martial says:

Delectas, Philomuse, non amaris,—

"You divert them, Philomusus; you are not an object of their regard."

Another type is represented by Linus (vii, 95). Linus is the affectionate person with a long beard and a cold nose who never misses the chance of kissing you on a winter's day. "Pray put it off," Martial cries, "put it off, until April!" These kissers, these 'basiatores,' as he calls them, were the poet's *bête noire*. "You cannot escape them," he com-plains (xi, 98), "you meet them all the time and every-where. I might return from Spain; but the thought of the 'basiatores' gives me pause."

One other familiar type in Rome was also the poet's espe-cial dislike. This was the 'bellus homo'—the pretty man, the beau.

"Pray tell me," he inquires of Cotilus in iii, 63, "what is a 'bellus homo' anyhow?" "A bellus homo," Cotilus re-plies,

> is one who curls his locks and lays them all in place; who always smells of balm, forever smells of cinnamon; who hums the gay ditties of the Nile and the dance music of Cadiz; who throws his smooth arms in various attitudes; who idles the whole day long among the chairs of the la-dies, and is always whispering in someone's ear; who reads little billets-doux from this quarter and from that, and writes them in return; who avoids ruffling his dress by contact with his neighbor's sleeve; he knows with whom every-body is in love; he flutters from entertainment to entertainment; he can give you to the uttermost degree every ancestor of the latest race horse.

"That, then, is a bellus homo? In that case, Cotilus, a bel-lus homo is a monstrously trifling affair."

Sextus the money-lender (ii, 44) hates to say no, but has no intention of saying yes:

> Whenever he observes me purchasing
> A slave, a cloak, or any such like thing,
> Sextus the usurer—a man, you know,
> Who's been my friend for twenty years or so—
> In fear that I may ask him for a loan,
> Thus whispers, to himself, but in a tone
> Such as he knows I cannot choose but hear:
> "I owe Secundus twenty thousand clear,
> I owe Philetus thirty thousand more,
> And then there's Phoebus—that's another
>   four—
> Besides, there's interest due on each amount,
> And not one farthing on my bank account!"
> Oh stratagem profound of my old friend!
> 'Tis hard refusing when you're asked to lend;
> But to refuse before you're asked displays
> Inventive genius worthy of the bays!

Of a fascinating but moody friend Martial says (xii, 47, translated by Addison):

> In all thy humours whether grave or mellow
> Thou'rt such a touchy, testy, pleasant fellow,

> Hast so much wit and mirth and spleen about
>   thee,
> There is no living with thee or without thee.

It is high time, however, for me to bring this imperfect sketch of Martial and his work to a close. I have said noth-ing of the history, form, and style of the antique epigram. One should be well acquainted with them in order really to understand and appreciate Martial. I have also said nothing of his supreme position in the later history of his department. His influence on the English poets is a large chapter by itself. So, too, a few of his happy phrases still linger in cultivated speech. But, so far as I know, only one of his epigrams, as such, has penetrated our popular con-sciousness. This is i, 32:

> Non amo te, Sabidi, nec possum dicere quare:
> Hoc tantum possum dicere, non amo te.

An epigram which through a lawless Oxford undergradu-ate of the seventeenth century is responsible for the pro-verbial jingle:

> I do not love thee, Doctor Fell,
> The reason why I cannot tell;
> But this I know, and know full well,
> I do not love thee, Doctor Fell.

I have also said nothing of Martial's occasional tender-ness, of his frequent touches of real poetry, and of many other important matters. I trust, however, that I have suc-ceeded in giving some idea of the scope and character of his genius.

Not altogether a pleasant period, those evil days of Domi-tian. It is always saddening to watch the long senescence of a great nation. But after dwelling in the gloom of Taci-tus, after being dazzled by the lightning of Juvenal's rheto-ric, it is well for us that we can see that age in the broad sunlight of Martial's genius, that we can use the keen and penetrating yet just and kindly eyes of one who saw it as it really was. And bad as it may have been, there was at least a large reading public which was highly cultivated, and the great traditions of literary form and style were still intact. Patronage was unpleasant enough, but I fancy that one could find authors in this age who would prefer the slavery of patronage to slavery to the modern descendant of Scott's "Gentle Reader."

However that may be, the genius of Martial was the genius of one who knew how to write for time, and time has justi-fied his methods. As he himself said, "his page has the true relish of human life." And in its essentials human life is unchangeable. Thus it was that the first and last great poet whom the Provinces gave to the literature of Imperial Rome could also take his place among the few who have written for all men and for all time.

Keith Preston   (essay date 1920)

SOURCE: "Martial and Formal Literary Criticism," in *Classical Philology*, Vol. XV, No. 4, October, 1920, pp. 340-52.

[*In the following essay, Preston studies Martial's epigrams as literary criticism.*]

What constitutes real literary criticism is always debatable, in the case of Martial as much perhaps as anywhere. Martial does not give us the masses of criticism that we find in Horace, nor are his critical ideas systematized as Horace's are. No doubt this is what is meant by Mr. H. E. Butler when he says in his essay on Martial [in *Post-Augustan Poetry from Seneca to Juvenal,* 1909], "He gives us practically no literary criticism." But Martial, at first sight not a bookish poet, has a surprising amount of informal literary comment and reflection. Along certain lines he imitated largely, and imitation is at least the softer side of criticism. His imitations, collected in special studies and swallowed, if not bolted, in Friedlander's commentary, are a field in themselves. In specific references to Greek and Latin writers as well as to theories of composition Martial also richly repays sifting. On contemporaries he is as uncritical as Pliny; both, for slightly different reasons, must be subject to heavy discount. But on the elder writers, and on writing in general, Martial's views have interest and value, especially for comparison with Quintilian, Tacitus, and Pliny. Not only did these three have forensic interests to which their criticism was in some degree adapted, but they represented, much more directly than Martial could, one phase at least of the cultivated or school tradition of the age. Martial, as but slightly interested in oratory, and professedly popular in his appeal, might be expected to supply an independent, if not insurgent, critical position. How far he does so is what we wish to determine.

The archaist movement was making itself felt in Martial's time. [In his *Institutio Oratoria*] Quintilian, as a moderate Ciceronian, posts himself midway between Horace and the professional "lovers of Lucilius," but he prefers the work of Horace in satire. Martial exceeds Quintilian or even Horace in his opposition to the archaists and their chief fetish. Adopting Horace's comparison of the muddy torrent, to which Quintilian had filed a mild objection, Martial condemns the early satirist for his bumpy style, cascading over rocks. He takes pains to submit his lemma, xi. 90. 1-4:

> Carmina nulla probas molli quae limite currunt,
> Sed quae per salebras altaque saxa cadunt,
> et tibi Maeonio quoque carmine maius habetur,
> "Lucili columella hic situst Metrophanes."
> [Martial, *Epigrammaton libri,* edited by
> Ludwig Friedlander]

Lucilius is, however, the representative of satire (Martial xii. 94. 7). In the cited epigram, flinging out a tag of Ennius, *terrai frugiferai,* Martial fleers at the cult of Ennius, to which Quintilian accords respect without adherence. Ennius is contrasted unfavorably with Vergil (Mart. v. 10. 7). On Accius and Pacuvius, two more totems of the archaists, Martial is frankly spiteful,

> Accius et quidquid Pacuviusque vomunt.

To these, Quintilian allows perfunctory praise, excusing blemishes of form as the fault of their times. An interesting feature of Martial's criticism of the archaists is his associating with the antiquaries in literature those who affected a similar taste in architecture:

> Hi sunt invidiae nimirum, Regule, mores,

> praeferat antiquos semper ut illa novis.
> sic veterem ingrati Pompei quaerimus umbram,
> sic laudant Catuli vilia templa senes.

In this case as elsewhere when Martial reflects on old fogies a compliment to Domitian is implied. How far old-fashioned tastes in art went with political intransigence is an interesting question. In general Martial seems opposed to the ancients as a smooth joiner of verses would naturally despise a clumsy craftsman. With this reasoned prejudice blends the usual anger of moderns against such critics as demand the seasoned classic, a feeling which comes out very well in the pert epigram to Vacerra who "liked his poets high," Mart. viii. 69.

Not far from the archaists, and in some cases identical, stood the obscurantists or over-learned poets, with whom Martial had nothing in common. Quintilian, who was no pedant, sneers civilly at this class. *Virium tamen Attio plus tribuitur; Pacuvium videri doctiorem, qui esse docti affectant, volunt.* Martial x. 21, attacks a gentleman who prefers Cinna to Vergil and whose works require a corps of grammarians, nay, Apollo himself, to interpret them. Mere learning, he says, can save no poem from oblivion:

> nescioquid plus est, quod donat saecula chartis:
> victurus genium debet habere liber.

Hoping he may chance to please the grammarians, Martial notwithstanding aims to win his public without benefit of grammarians:

> mea carmina, Sexte,
> grammaticis placeant, ut sine grammaticis.

Sotadean juggling, echo verses, trick stuff of any kind, Martial sensibly pronounces trivial. Even the *Attis* of Catullus with its galliambics, a brilliant *tour de force (luculentus),* so Martial concedes to general opinion, has no message for him:

> Turpe est difficiles habere nugas
> Et stultus labor est ineptiarum.

Much erudition was at this time going into various mythological confections, such as the star myths, Καταστερισμοιν, done into flowing elegiacs by Pliny's young friend Calpurnius Piso, *eruditam sane luculentamque materiam,* as Pliny remarks, with many other encomiums. Such things as this, along with the parlor epic and the closet drama, Martial condemns alike for bombast, and for the deadly staleness of the themes. They are the lucubrations of long-faced dullards and the bane of school children (viii. 3. 15-18). The man who would be completely dead to the world of reality is urged to bury himself in the *Aetia* of Callimachus (Mart. x. 4. 11-12). Listing repeatedly the stock epic and tragic themes, Martial pronounces them a waste of time and paper. Whether any of this vehemence was aimed at Statius, whom Martial does not directly mention, has been much and uselessly discussed. Certainly Martial does not admire the *genre.* Mythology serves him mostly as a kind of shorthand, by the Ovidian system. Orestes and Pylades suggest friendship, Hecuba and Andromache, sorrow, Nestor, Priam, Pelias, or Hecuba, age, and so through a wide range of types. Few obscure myths find reference in the epigrams, though Martial seems particularly well primed on the myths of Hercules, in whose cult Domitian had a peculiar interest. In tributes, dedications, bread-and-butter poetry generally, Martial falls into myth easily and with his eyes open. For his compliments to Domitian it made by far the best vehicle. In estimating the element of flattery in Martial, one should consider the coin in which he renders payment to Caesar. As the coin of compliment, mythological comparisons were as cheap as Russian rubles. Quintilian flatters quite as grossly and with a clumsier touch. Despite his contempt for stale erudition and for anything resembling pedantry, Martial respects learning. The epithet *doctus* on his lips seems sincerely though vaguely complimentary. He covets this quality in his own work, courts learned criticism, and affects dread of the grammarian Probus iii. 2. 12. His deferential address to Quintilian has perhaps little value as evidence. More informing are his mentions of the Attic tradition; Attic charm and Attic salt are frequently on Martial's lips. He flares up at a pretender to Atticism, vi. 64. 16 ff.

> Sed tibi plus mentis, tibi cor limante Minerva
> acrius et tenues finxerunt pectus Athenae.
> Ne valeam etc.

Mention of particular writers and types of writing is exceedingly common in Martial but often quite perfunctory. On the Greek side, his provincial education left him well enough read in Homer to play with Homeric tags, as in i. 45 and i. 50 and to allude intelligently. Homer he couples with Vergil, and Vergil with Silius Italicus. Archilochus comes in with the conventional reference to the sensitive and high-strung Lycambes (Mart. vii. 12. 6). Sappho, whom Quintilian ignores, presumably on moral grounds, Martial calls *amatrix,* comparing Lesbian morals unfavorably with those of the chaste Theophila. If Sappho could have had lessons from the poetess Sulpicia she would have been more learned and less experienced (Mart. x. 35. 15-16). Of Greek tragedians, Martial mentions only Sophocles. Martial, like Quintilian, rates Menander high, making him, not incompatibly, share a distich with Ovid. A neat play on the comic rule of three actors occurs (Mart. vi. 6). Callimachus, otherwise the "limbo of learned poets," is first among the Greeks in epigram, but the comparison to Martial's friend Brutianus does not flatter the Greek (Mart. iv. 23. 4-5). Excepting for his knowledge of Homer, a few imitations of the late Greek epigrammatist Lucillius, and a propensity for feeble punning on Greek proper names, Martial's information on Greek letters might have come at second hand.

On the Latin side, we have seen that Martial, rating form even before content, rejects the older poets as far down as Catullus, who was, along with Domitius Marsus, Martial's avowed model and master. His epithets for Catullus are *doctus, tenuis, argutus, lepidus,* and *tener.* His imitations and references go mostly to the shorter poems of Catullus, especially to his hendecasyllabics, which are certainly straightforward and unassuming. In slighting the more ambitious work of Catullus, Martial is like Quintilian, who passes judgment on Catullus only as an iambic poet, commending his *acerbitas* (Institutio Oratoria), and Pliny, who quotes Catullus [in his Epistulae] in defense of epigrammatic license. Martial defends his own drastic

vein by the same precedent. The deftness of Catullus shows in several details of Martial's technique. For example, the type of epigram which consists of a piling up of comparisons, sometimes agreeable, and sometimes, as in ix. 57, quite the reverse, seems a direct legacy from Catullus. Martial and his contemporaries admired the "pet" poems of Catullus extravagantly. The Lesbia cycle also delighted Martial, but real passion was foreign to his experience. Lesbia, says Martial, inspired Catullus; love made the elegists and Vergil; give me a Corinna or an Alexis, and neither Ovid nor Vergil will have cause to scorn me. Compare, however, Mart. viii. 55. (56) and xi. 3. 7-10, where the fatal lack is leisure and a patron like Maecenas.

To Martial, as to others of his age, Vergil was unique, above criticism. His appropriate epithets are *sacer, cothurnatus.* The *Aeneid* is often referred to, and quoted, Mart. viii. 55 (56). 19 and xiv. 185. 1; for a reference to the *Ecologues* cf. viii. 55 (56). 17-18. We are indebted to Martial for a testimony on the *Culex* with a suggestion of criticism viii. 55 (56). 20:

> Qui modo vix Culicem fleverat ore rudi

cf. also xiv. 185, where the *Culex* is recommended as light verse for after-dinner consumption. That technique of citation which coupled the elegiac poets regularly with their amorous inspirations, Martial extends to Vergil, persistently associating him with the boy Alexis. Vergil could have shone first in any field of poetry (Mart. viii. 18. 5-8).

To Martial, as to Quintilian, Horace is the type of Latin lyric poetry (Mart. xii. 94. 5), *fila lyrae movi Calabris exculta Camenis.* Reminiscences, not confined to the odes, are fairly common, including some of Martial's few touches of parody, where Fever mounts behind the horseman, bathes beside the bather, and trenches on the trencher man (because there is no verbal handle this reminiscence seems to have slipped the commentators). Martial's odd impression that Horace was a Calabrian, is one of several blunders in literary history. This one may go back to a blurred recollection of Horace, *Odes* ii. 6. 9-16.

A much more lively personal interest on Martial's part seems indicated for Domitius Marsus and the elegiac group. Marsus was Martial's master no less than Catullus, and his debt to the former was undoubtedly large. Had Martial found a Maecenas, he would not have been a Vergil but a Marsus (viii. 55 [56]. 21-22). He modestly deprecates comparison with Marsus and Catullus (ii. 71. 3). Marsus, along with Catullus, Pedo, and Gaetulicus, supplies sanction for calling a spade a spade (Mart. i. pref. 12). Martial, consistently enough, slights Marsus' epic, the *Amazonis.* As for Marsus' elegies, Martial lets us know that they were addressed to a pronounced brunette, *fusca Melaenis.* The epigrams, *Cicuta,* seem to have inspired Martial's regard for Marsus. Tibullus, as we have seen, Martial rates high, agreeing in this with Quintilian, x. 1. 93, who calls him first in elegy, *tersus atque elegans.* References to Gallus, and to Propertius, *lascivus,* and *facundus* are not particularly significant. Much more to Martial's liking was Ovid, all of whose works he seems to have read and assimilated. Metrical dexterity, smooth and polished phrasing, and verbal prettiness were his chief lines of imitation. Ovid's excesses in rhetoric he sensibly avoids, but the whimsical way with myths which is so pleasant in Ovid appealed to Martial.

The poets so far considered include those who did most to influence Martial's style. He approves also the vogue of Persius, as does Quintilian. Both comments remark the fact that Persius was a "one book" wonder. On Lucan, Martial seems to recognize and differ from the academic verdict. Quintilian, praising Lucan's rhetoric, declares him a model for orators rather than poets. Martial, calls Lucan *unicus,* citing also (xiv. 194), the "best seller" argument for his poetical preeminence:

> Sunt quidam qui me dicunt non esse poetam:
> Sed qui me vendit bibliopola putat.

Of course Martial had personal grounds for a kindness toward Lucan. A clear allusion to formal criticism comes in Martial's distich for a copy of Sallust, xiv. 191:

> Hic erit, ut perhibent doctorum corda virorum,
> primus Romana Crispus in historia.

Cf. Quint. *Institutio Oratoria* x. 1. 32. The series of little book mottoes in Martial's *Apophoreta* xiv. 183-96 might be called the beginning of book advertising and tabloid reviewing.

Coming now to epigram, a field in which Martial's critical views deserve peculiar respect, we may first consider the status of the type as Martial found it. Epigram was one variety, not too clearly defined, of that brief occasional verse, *lusus, nugae, ineptiae,* the vogue of which Pliny amply attests. Pliny defines the *genre: Fas est et carmine remitti, non dico continuo et longo (id enim perfici nisi in otio non potest) sed hoc arguto et brevi, quod apte quantas libet occupationes distinguit. Lusus vocantur.* Collections of such verse went under a variety of titles, as Pliny notes when considering a title for his own collection; Pliny iv. 14. 9-10: *Proinde sive epigrammata sive idyllia sive eclogas sive, ut multi, poematia seu quod aliud vocare malueris licebit voces, ego tantum hendecasyllabos praesto.* Pliny chose to call his poems "Hendecasyllabics" because "this title is bound by no law but that of meter." Sentius Augurinus, Pliny iv. 27, entitled a similar collection *poematia.* The content was as various as the titles. A lively play of shifting emotions was desirable (cf. Pliny iv. 14. 3; iv. 27. 1). The honorific element was large. For example, the estimable Capito, Pliny i. 17, besides collecting portraits of distinguished republicans, wrote verse in praise of great men, quite possibly to go with the portraits.

Epigram, then, was one name for a short poem on almost any subject. Neither Pliny nor Martial pays much attention to Greek epigram, though both mention the epigrams of Callimachus and contemporary imitations. Pliny, in discussing his hendecasyllabics, and Martial, on his epigrams, stress Roman tradition and Roman examples. According to this tradition epigram was characterized by *sal Romanum,* which differed from Attic salt chiefly by a superior crudity. More specifically, Latin epigram had developed license of tone and theme, *lascivia, petulantia,* sharpness and asperity, *amaritudo, acerbitas, bilis,* and a brutal directness of language, *simplicitas.* Both Martial and Pliny eagerly defend these qualities, on much the

same sanction. Pliny, as an orator, cites mainly those statesmen and orators who had composed epigrams in odd moments. He admits that by giving a public reading of his verses he had perhaps gone farther than his precedents. Martial cites mainly poets in his own defense. Catullus, Gaetulicus, Lucan, and the Emperor Augustus are cited by both. The matter of definite personalities in epigram was treated similarly by Pliny and Martial. Though Pliny has nothing to say of his own practice we can hardly suspect him of hurting anyone's feelings, and his theory comes out in comment on the plays of Vergilius Romanus. Martial abstained from definite personalities, following the procedure which had long been a convention for satire:

> Hunc servare modum nostri novere libelli,
> parcere personis, dicere de vitiis.

Yet Martial abhorred the saccharine type of epigram, vii. 25:

> Dulcia cum tantum scribas epigrammata semper
> et cerussata candidiora cute,
> nullaque mica salis nec amari fellis in illis
> gutta sit, O demens, vis tamen illa legi!
> Nec cibus ipse iuvat morsu fraudatus aceti,
> nec grata est facies cui gelasinus abest.
> Infanti melimela dato fatuasque mariscas:
> nam mihi, quae novit pungere, Chia sapit.

Martial was himself criticized for saccharine tendencies, probably in his flattering epigrams:

> Si quid lene mei dicunt et dulce libelli,
> si quid honorificum pagina blanda sonat,
> hoc tu pingue putas

Martial makes no very satisfactory defense. It is worth recalling that Pliny also was criticized for puffing his friends.

We have been at some pains to compare the light verse of Pliny and Martial, not that Pliny's hendecasyllabics were probably worth their salt, but for evidence on the convention of Roman epigram. It appears that epigram was a popular medium, saddled firmly with certain conventions of crudity, which required constant apology, and held lightly or rather not handled at all by the higher critical opinion. Pliny made some effort to assert the dignity of epigram; cf. his comment on Martial, Pliny iii. 21, and ix. 25. 2. *Incipio enim ex hoc genere studiorum non solum oblectationem verum etiam gloriam petere post iudicium tuum.* Martial seems rather hopeless of critical approval for his medium. In addition to the conventions already noted we might add a convention of meter. Martial himself regarded hendecasyllabics and elegiacs as his principal meters. But he makes exceptions and finds precedent for them:

> "Hexametris epigramma facis" scio dicere Tuc-
>   cam.
> Tucca, solet fieri, denique, Tucca, licet.

The convention of brevity in epigram was clearly recognized and when Martial exceeds average length he meets criticism by citing precedents.

"Sed tamen hoc longum est." Solet hoc quoque, Tucca, licetque: Marsus and Pedo, says he, often wrote one epigram to fill two pages. Curiously enough, Martial does not

seem conscious of originality in that insistence upon point which is the peculiar virtue of his epigrams. He is annoyed with the spoiled reader who demands nothing but point. All point and no padding is hard on the artist, Mart. x. 59:

> Non opus est nobis nimium lectore guloso;
> hunc volo, non fiat qui sine pane satur.

This epigram asserts that body is necessary to explain and develop the subject, *lemma;* it also insists on the intrinsic merit of this exegesis. Martial speaks as a lecturer who suspects that his audience wants nothing but the slides. He sneers at the popular demand for distichs, nothing but distichs. On the other hand, belittled by a critic because of his brevity, Martial hotly defends his *genre,* comparing the miniature in plastic art:

> Nos facimus Bruti puerum, nos Langona vivum:
> tu magnus luteum, Gaure, Giganta facis.

With so much that was conventional in his literary creed, Martial was and felt himself to be original in some very important respects. The choice of live subjects was his first tenet:

> Vivida cum poscas epigrammata, mortua ponis
> lemmata. Qui fieri, Caeciliane, potest?

The colors of life must be in his work, viii. 3. 19-22:

> At tu Romano lepidos sale tinge libellos:
> adgnoscat mores vita legatque suos.
> Angusta cantare licet videaris avena,
> dum tua multorum vincat avena tubas'.

Cf. also x. 4. 9-12,

> non hic Centauros, non Gorgonas Harpyiasque
> invenies: hominem pagina nostra sapit.
> Sed non vis, Mamurra, tuos cognoscere mores
> nec te scire: legas Aetia Callimachi.

Martial appreciates to the full the essentially personal nature of epigram, "I can see why tragedy or comedy should carry a letter of introduction, for they may not speak for themselves: epigrams need no herald and are pleased to hail you with their own saucy tongue." Martial's book expresses him better than a picture (vii. 84. 6). In all of this we have a code of realism, modernism, and personal expression perhaps unique in Martial's time. By no means all his epigrams fit the creed, as he was the first to recognize, vii. 81:

> Triginta toto mala sunt epigrammata libro.
> Si totidem bona sunt, Lause, bonus liber est.

Martial does not subscribe to Quintilian's doctrine of *aequalitas:*

> Iactat inaequalem Matho me fecisse libellum:
> si verum est, laudat carmina nostra Matho.
> Aequales scribit libros Calvinus et Umber:
> aequalis liber est, Cretice, qui malus est.

As the seamy side of Martial's modernism may be urged his insistence on popularity, his use of booksellers' arguments, and his admission that *mime* had influenced his technique. The aims that Martial ascribes to the harlequin Latinus are essentially his own. But on the whole Martial represents an entirely wholesome reaction against a stagnant literary age. Despite this reaction he shows himself docile as regards literary tradition and amenable to the best critical opinion.

J. Wight Duff on Martial's strength and weakness as an epigrammatist:

Martial is at his best where he is most himself—where he adheres to the theme of humanity which he recognized as his own. When he has beasts of the arena or an imperial *dominus et deus* for his subject he is tempted into artificiality. Here the quest for variety of style makes a display of skill that over-reveals itself. But humanity he can depict, disdain, loathe, pity with a convincing truth which brings into play simple style and fitting metres used with consummate mastery. This realism and his literary genius for reserving to the end the point or sting in many of his most celebrated epigrams are, amidst all his manysidedness, the sure pillars of his fame.

J. Wight Duff, "Varied Strains in Martial," in Classical and Mediaeval Studies in Honor of Edward Kennard Rand, *edited by Leslie Webber Jones, 1938.*

T. K. Whipple   (essay date 1925)

SOURCE: "Martial," in *Martial and the English Epigram from Sir Thomas Wyatt to Ben Jonson,* The University of California Press, 1925, pp. 285-99.

[*Below, Whipple comments on Martial's depiction of Roman life in his poems and studies the style and structure of Martial's epigrams.*]

No author was ever more completely the product of his environment than Martial. Both in the material which he treats and in his attitude toward it, he is representative of Rome in the latter half of the first century after Christ. The same statement holds true of the form in which he casts his epigrams; it is the natural result of the rhetorical training of the time.

In the first place, his subject-matter is limited only by Rome as Martial knew the city, under Nero and Domitian. He has left us a remarkably detailed picture of his surroundings. He occupied a most advantageous position from which to view the life of the imperial capital. He himself was evidently poor and lived in bohemian fashion on his doles as client and the gifts he could obtain with his verses. However lacking in dignity and manliness this manner of life may have been, it at least brought him into contact with all sorts and classes of people. As a client and as a distinguished poet, he had the acquaintance of the aristocracy and the literary cliques; whereas his hand-to-mouth way of living made him see much of the poorer class and especially of those who like himself were dependent upon the caprices of the rich.

The vivid picture he gives us shows Roman life as brilliant on one side as it is squalid on the other. His laudatory epigrams, addressed for the most part to the Emperor Domitian and to members of the imperial court, show to what lengths flattery can go without discomposing its object, and how the resources of the most highly developed literary art may lend themselves to heightening the effect of fulsomeness. The flattery which Martial addresses to the favorite slaves and freedmen of those in power sheds some light on the state of society in which could flourish the cliques and intrigues that centered about the emperor. On the other hand, when he addresses his friends and acquaintances, most of whom seem to have been more prosperous than himself, we see the best side of contemporary life; for his friends were men of culture with philosophic and literary interests, many of them authors in their own right, connoisseurs of art, and the like. When to one of these friends Martial sends an invitation to dinner, or congratulations on marriage, or a gift accompanied by an epigram, we see him at his most likable; for he is at his best in dealing with the theme of friendship, which seems to have been the deepest and most sincere emotion he experienced.

The second class of his epigrams—the gnomic or reflective—are usually addressed to these friends. His moralizings aspire to no elevation; he professes an epicureanism even less exalted and less attractive than Horace's. *Carpe diem*—eat, drink, and be merry—is the burden of his advice: to have as good a time as possible, without worrying about anything more remote than the pleasure offered by the present moment. His real point of view is mildly cynical, strictly speaking, rather than epicurean, though neither harsh nor bitter. He sums the matter up in the well-known **"Vitam quae faciunt beatiorem,"** in which he wishes for a modest income, health, peace and quiet, and a farm. He seldom presents himself so pleasingly.

The taste for country life indicated in the epigram just mentioned is one of Martial's outstanding characteristics. Many of his epigrams are concerned with rural Italy—with the life on the country estate of the rich city man, that is, rather than with the life of the real farmer or the peasant. Martial has all the enthusiasm for the country usually shown by dwellers in large cities, not the less sincere because called forth by the glamor of distance and contrast. These epigrams usually take the form of epistles to his friends, and are closely allied to those of the preceding type, the reflective. Martial is entirely free from the pastoral convention. In his writing we see the real Italian countryside, not an ideal land of shepherds and their loves.

Martial wrote a number of epitaphs. A few of these are satirical, but for the most part they display to perfection that vein of sentiment and pathos, often half-playful, in which he excelled. Many of the best are on children, chiefly young slaves, or on animal pets. Others are composed for the benefit of his friends. Closely akin to these, but more conventional and of less merit, are his mere *jeux d'esprit*, concerning his friends' pets, or dealing cleverly with objects of art or natural curiosities, such as the bee enclosed in amber.

Friendship, pathos, sentiment, mark the height to which Martial rises in poetic feeling; when dealing with love he is at his worst. To be sure, most of the epigrams which re-

late to that theme have to do with other people's love affairs and treat them satirically. But those in which he talks of his own amatory concerns are devoid of passion, with the possible exception of a few addressed to favorite slaves. It would scarcely be going too far to say that love, as an inspiration to poetry, is absent from Martial's work.

Finally we arrive at his epigrams which depict more specifically the city life of ancient Rome. Most of these, but by no means all, are satiric. Favorite themes with Martial are the spectacles in the arena, food and drink, and presents. He asks for gifts, he—less often—returns thanks for them, he writes verses to accompany those he gives his friends. He sends verses as an excuse for not calling in person on his patrons. Many of his epigrams are no more than detailed descriptions of dinners, which often include invitations to his friends to dine with him. In describing the spectacles, he finds occasion to flatter the emperor who provided them.

Generally, however, he sees in the life about him occasion for amusement, for contempt, once in a while for disgust. The vast majority of his epigrams are satiric. Especially he attacks all the forms of hypocrisy and pretence to which such a society as he knew gives birth. The poor who pretend to wealth, the lowborn who pretend to high station, the old men and women who pretend to youth, the dissolute who pretend to rugged virtue—all provide him with material for his jests. The literary life in which he took part also furnishes him with a fertile field, and he attacks poetasters, bad reciters, and plagiarists. But in truth the objects of his satire are as varied as the life of the metropolis. Sycophants, dinner-seekers, newsmongers, social upstarts, gourmands, sots, dandies, misers, bad lawyers and doctors, courtesans, legacy-hunters—he lampoons them all. In terms of unrivaled obscenity he describes the debauchery and vice of the time. We see the streets of the capital with their contrasts, their extreme luxury and extreme poverty, their dirt and noise; we go to the baths; we wait for hours in the great man's antechamber to be presented with the price of a dinner. All this is depicted without moral indignation; Martial fell in with the spirit of the age, and it is to this fact that we owe the extraordinary vividness of the picture he has drawn of Rome in the days of Domitian.

There has been a tendency to underestimate the variety in Martial's work. It has become common to refer to the satiric pointed epigram as the "Roman" or the "Martial" type. For this reason the wide range and the varied treatment both of material and of form in the *Epigrammata* need to be emphasized. And yet there is of course some excuse for the over-insistence on Martial's satire. Certainly as a class his satiric verses are more amusing and have therefore won more popularity than his others. The point I make is only that this portion of his work must not be allowed to obscure the rest, that we must not forget his epitaphs, his praises of country life, his reflective verse, his eulogies.

In form, likewise, Martial exhibits a considerable variety. His epigrams range in length from a single verse to fifty lines and more. Many of them an English reader would not call epigrams at all. They might with equal propriety be termed epistles, epodes, short satires. Some of them differ only in meter from certain odes of Horace. A few fail to terminate in a "point." Yet the author apparently regarded them all as epigrams, although even in his own time there seem to have been demurrers on this point. I emphasize Martial's variety because much has been said of the restricting influence which he has exerted upon the modern epigram.

That this restriction has been associated with his influence will not be denied. The reason lies in the fact that with him the pointed epigram is the rule, the unpointed the exception. In giving an account of the form of his epigrams, we shall therefore confine ourselves to this, the representative and preponderating type.

In the form of Martial's epigrams, the first thing to note is the structure. On the basis of structure, most of his work may be divided into two groups: those epigrams which consist merely of exposition and conclusion; and those which contain also a transition from the one to the other.

In the first group, exposition and conclusion usually take one of the three following forms: statement and comment; statement and question; question and answer. The simplest type of epigram is that in which the exposition consists of a mere statement in the third person, the conclusion containing the poet's comment. An illustration is III 21:

> Proscriptum famulus servavit fronte notatus.
> Non fuit haec domini vita, sed invidia.

This type, however, is rare in Martial; more frequently the statement is in the second person, or is an indirect quotation:

> Bellus homo et magnus vis idem, Cotta, videri:
> sed qui bellus homo est, Cotta, pusillus homo
>   est. (I 9)

> Dicis formonsam, dicis te, Bassa, puellam.
> istud quae non est dicere, Bassa, solet. (V 45)

Instead of comment, the conclusion may take the form of a question:

> Iurat capillos esse, quos emit, suos
> Fabulla: numquid [ergo], Paule, peierat? (VI 12)

Or the exposition, instead of statement, may take the form of question, the conclusion containing the answer, or some comment, perhaps in the form of another question:

> Quid mihi reddat ager quaeris, Line, Nomen-
>   tanus?
> Hoc mihi reddit ager: te Line, non video. (II 38)

> Abscisa servom quid figis, Pontice, lingua?
> nescis tu populum, quod tacet ille, loqui? (II 82)

The preceding illustrate the simplest type of epigram; much more numerous are those which contain also a third element, a transition from the exposition to the conclusion. In III 15, for instance:

> Plus credit nemo tota quam Cordus in urbe.
> 'Cum sit tam pauper, quomodo?' Caecus amat—

we have one of Martial's favorite methods of constructing

an epigram: by a statement in the exposition, a transitional question, and an answer in the conclusion. Sometimes he develops a little dialogue out of this form:

> Petit Gemellus nuptias Maronillae
> et cupit et instat et precatur et donat.
> Adeone pulchra est? Immo foedius nil est.
> Quid ergo in illa petitur et placet? Tussit. (I 10)

Another form to which he is partial is a combination of question, answer, and comment:

> Esse quid hoc dicam quod olent tua basia mur-
>   ram
> quodque tibi est numquam non alienus odor?
> hoc mihi suspectum est, quod oles bene, Pos-
>   tume, semper:
> Postume, non bene olet qui bene semper olet. (II
>   12)

Martial's favorite ways of opening an epigram, then, are with a statement in the second person, a question, an indirect quotation. He uses habitually some form of direct address. In addition to the varieties already mentioned, he employs apostrophe, exhortation, exclamation: "I, felix rosa" (VII 89); "Sili, Castalidum decus sororum" (IV 14); "Barbara pyramidum sileat miracula Memphis" (Spec. 1); "Quantus, io, Latias mundi concentus ad aras" (VIII 4).

Occasionally he will develop one of the three simple elements of exposition, transition, and conclusion to a considerable length. One of his methods of doing this has already been mentioned: his use of several questions and answers so as to produce a short dialogue. Another of his methods is enumeration, of details or of specific instances. An example is III 63:

> Cotile, bellus homo es: dicunt hoc, Cotile, multi.
> audio: sed quid sit, dic mihi, bellus homo?
> 'Bellus homo est, flexos qui digerit ordine crines,
> balsama qui semper, cinnama semper olet;
> cantica qui Nili, qui Gaditana susurrat,
> qui movet in varios bracchia volso modos, *etc.*

Much like the preceding are those epigrams which he develops by a series of comparisons, such as II 43 or VIII 33. But the simple epigrams are more numerous and more typical of Martial than the developed, which remain after all the exception, not the rule.

A thorough classification of Martial's ways of making a point is perhaps impossible. Only an indication of some of the more frequent will be attempted here. A great many of his epigrams depend for their point upon surprising or startling the reader. This surprise is effected by several means. Sometimes what the poet says is in itself startling, because of its apparent impossibility or its incongruity, as in the conclusion of Spec. 11:

> deprendat vacuo venator in aere praedam,
> si captare feras aucupis arte placet.

The same device appears in II 78, although here it is used with an ironical implication:

> Aestivo serves ubi piscem tempore, quaeris?
> In thermis serva, Caeciliane, tuis.

More often, however, the surprise is less in what Martial

says than in the way he says it. He likes to work up a suspense or deliberately to mislead the reader, so that the solution of the difficulty, when it comes, is contrary to the reader's expectation. This device, technically known as paraprosdokia, is used with signal effect in VI 51:

> Quod convivaris sine me tam saepe, Luperce,
> inveni noceam qua ratione tibi.
> irascor: licet usque voces mittasque rogesque—
> 'Quid facies?' inquit. Quid faciam? veniam.

Other and not dissimilar means of securing this effect are antithesis, paradox, oxymoron, and hyperbole. Antithesis gives point to the conclusion of II 68:

> servom si potes, Ole, non habere,
> et regem potes, Ole, non habere.

Paradox is one of Martial's favorite figures; in XII 46 we find it combined with oxymoron:

> Difficilis facilis, iucundus acerbus es idem:
> nec tecum possum vivere nec sine te.

The whole point of III 35,

> Artis Phidiacae toreuma clarum
> pisces aspicis: adde aquam, natabunt—

depends upon mere hyperbole; more often, however, we find the hyperbole combined with some other figure. In III 25 it is combined with an ambiguity, a play upon the two kinds of frigidity:

> Si temperari balneum cupis fervens,
> Faustine, quod vix Iulianus intraret,
> roga lavetur rhetorem Sabineium.
> Neronianas is refrigerat thermas.

Furthermore, even plainer than in the preceding is the ironical implication of the hyperbole in VI 53:

> Lotus nobiscum est, hilaris cenavit, et idem
> inventus mane est mortuus Andragoras.
> Tam subitae mortis causam, Faustine, requiris?
> In somnis medicum viderat Hermocraten.

Irony, in fact, is one of Martial's most frequent satirical weapons. It rarely takes the form of downright sarcasm; he does not often say the opposite of what he means. Rather, he deals in innuendo, he damns by implication. Straightforward, bludgeoning abuse is not his line; even if his satire sounds far from over-delicate or subtle to modern ears, it yet involves a certain indirection. In VII 59, for instance,

> Non cenat sine apro noster, Tite, Caecilianus.
> bellum convivam Caecilianus habet—

or in VI 24,

> Nil lascivius est Charisiano:
> Saturnalibus ambulat togatus—

although no doubt the point is obvious enough, still the method employed is not direct statement. We have already seen how the same effect is sometimes secured by means of a surprising incongruity or an hyperbole. Another device which Martial often uses for ironical effect is ambiguity. See, for instance, the ironical *double entendre* in the close of IV 33:

> Plena laboratis habeas cum scrinia libris,
> emittis quare, Sosibiane, nihil?
> 'Edent heredes' inquis 'mea carmina.' Quando?
> tempus erat iam te, Sosibiane, legi.

Sometimes by a question at the end he will import an ironical equivocation into what has preceded, as in IX 15, or in VI 12 (quoted above) on Fabulla's hair. Or by his final statement he will give a new satiric sense to what before was dubious or obscure, as in I 10 (quoted above) by the final word 'Tussit.'

Martial's use of parallelism and repetition and also his use of question and answer, of quotation direct and indirect, of the first and second persons, of dialogue, of exclamation and apostrophe, impart to his style an emphasis, a liveliness and animation, which are among its most conspicuous characteristics.

—T. K. Whipple

Word play furnishes the point of many of Martial's epigrams. Sometimes he plays with the meaning, sometimes with the sound, of a word. In III 15, although the point is in the unexpected resolution of a difficulty, it depends upon the double meaning of *credit:*

> Plus credit nemo tota quam Cordus in urbe.
> 'Cum sit tam pauper, quomodo?' Caecus amat.

The twofold sense of *nil* gives point to III 61:

> Esse nihil dicis quidquid petis, inprobe Cinna:
> si nil, Cinna, petis, nil tibi, Cinna, nego.

The point of such epigrams as these, depending as they do altogether upon meaning, is not lost in translation. When, however, Martial plays with sound, the point is lost in translation. The pun in IX 21 or in III 34, which depends upon the similarity of the name Chione to the Greek word for snow, is an illustration:

> Digna tuo cur sis indignaque nomine, dicam.
> Frigida es et nigra es: non es et es Chione.

Perhaps the most extreme case in Martial of playing with sound is I 100:

> Mammas atque tatas habet Afra, sed ipsa tatarum
> dici et mammarum maxima mamma potest.

But mere sound play is not habitual with Martial; it is scarcely, indeed, common enough to be called characteristic of him.

Martial employs two other devices for securing point. One of them is his manner of ending an epigram with an implied comparison or analogy, as in the following:

> Muneribus cupiat si quis contendere tecum,
> audeat hic etiam, Castrice, carminibus.

> nos tenues in utroque sumus vincique parati:
> inde sopor nobis et placet alta quies.
> Tam mala cur igitur dederim tibi carmina,
>   quaeris?
> Alcinoo nullum poma dedisse putas? (VII 42)

Finally, Martial makes very large use of aphoristic material. One of his most frequent ways of concluding an epigram is with a pithy generalization: "hunc volo, laudari qui sine morte potest"; "qui bellus homo est, Cotta, pusillus homo est"; "sera nimis vita est crastina: vive hodie"; "ille dolet vere qui sine teste dolet."

Besides the structure of Martial's epigrams, and besides his methods of introducing, developing, and concluding an epigram, there are other features of his style which must be noted. Most important of these are the parallelism and the balance which so pervade all Martial's work as to constitute an outstanding feature of his style. Especially in those epigrams which he develops by an enumeration of details or instances or by a series of comparisons, he makes use of parallelism for the sake of clearness and emphasis. He is particularly fond of putting a balanced antithesis in chiastic order, as in the familiar line, "Lasciva est nobis pagina, vita proba." Usually the parallelism is strengthened by the repetition of words or phrases. Martial uses every conceivable species of repetition. He repeats the same words at the beginning of consecutive clauses, or at the end of them:

> Hermes Martia saeculi voluptas,
> Hermes omnibus eruditus armis,
> Hermes et gladiator et magister, etc.
> (V 24)

> Appellat rigida tristis me voce Secundus:
> audis et nescis, Baccara, quid sit opus.
> pensio te coram petitur clareque palamque:
> audis et nescis, Baccara, quid sit opus.
> esse queror gelidasque mihi tritasque lacernas:
> audis et nescis, Baccara, quid sit opus. (VII 92,
>   vv.3–8)

> Primum est ut praestes, si quid te, Cinna, roga-
>   bo;
> illud deinde sequens ut cito, Cinna, neges.
> diligo praestantem; non odi, Cinna, negantem:
> sed tu nec praestas nec cito, Cinna, negas. (VII
>   43)

The repetition at the end of clauses is usually, as in the preceding, varied by the use of different forms and constructions. Sometimes Martial combines these two types of repetition, as in the first two lines of XII 79:

> Donavi tibi multa quae rogasti;
> donavi tibi plura quam rogasti.

Again, Martial uses the first words of one clause as the last of the next, or the last of one as the first of the next; he even does both:

> Pauper videri Cinna vult; et est pauper. (VIII
>   19)

> Cogit me Titus actitare causas
> et dicit mihi saepe 'Magna res est.'
> Res magna est, Tite, quam facit colonus. (I 17)

> κοινα φιλων haec sunt, haec sunt tua, Can-
>   dide, κοινα.
> (II 43, v. 1)

Finally, as an illustration of the lengths to which repetition can be carried, IX 97 may be cited:

> Rumpitur invidia quidam, carissime Iuli,
> quod me Roma legit, rumpitur invidia.
> rumpitur invidia quod turba semper in omni
> monstramur digito, rumpitur invidia.
> rumpitur invidia tribuit quod Caesar uterque
> ius mihi natorum, rumpitur invidia, etc.

He uses the same words, but in opposite relations—that is, with a reversal of the thought:

> Insequeris, fugio; fugis, insequor; haec mens est:
> velle tuum nolo, Dindyme, nolle volo. (V 83)

Martial's method of fitting the structure of his epigrams and the devices of parallelism and repetition just enumerated into the structure of his verse is also noteworthy. He commonly ends exposition, transition, and conclusion at the end of a line, often in his shorter pieces allotting to each element a couplet or a single verse. Frequently he begins with a couplet of exposition, makes the transition in a line, and devotes the final verse to making the point; or he opens with two couplets of rhetorical questions and gives over the final couplet to the conclusion. Again, he likes to save his point until the final word of the last line, especially when it is intended to surprise the reader. In that case, all save the final word will usually be filled with a transitional question. The same strictness of form is exhibited in his treatment of parallelism and repetition; he arranges to have the repeated words at the beginning or the end of lines, or at least in the same metrical position in succeeding lines. He is especially given to introducing the name of the victim of his satire in line after line in this fashion, so as to produce a sneering effect.

In form as in substance Martial's work is typical of his age. He lived at a time when the art of rhetoric was as highly developed as it has ever been, and when, moreover, it constituted the chief—almost the only—subject of education. The natural result is seen in his masterly control of devices for heightening the effect and point of his epigrams, for upon them he lavishes all the resources of the most elaborate rhetoric. His brilliance, his polish and vivacity, are in large measure due to his use of parallelism and repetition. Both these devices and also his use of question and answer, of quotation direct and indirect, of the first and second persons, of dialogue, of exclamation and apostrophe, impart to his style an emphasis, a liveliness and animation, which are among its most conspicuous characteristics. With all that terseness and concision which is essential to the successful epigram and which is in none more evident than in Martial's, he has managed to secure a colloquial ease which makes his way of writing as unconstrained as a casual conversation. This quality too is the result of his way of constructing and developing his epigrams.

It is therefore in large measure due to the devices which we have been discussing that his epigrams have attained their effect of reality and individuality, that in reading them we seem to be overhearing the talk of two real men.

In many if not most of his epigrams he speaks in the first person; he addresses some one by name, and refers to a common acquaintance. When he begins, "Do you see that fellow yonder, Decianus, that needs a haircut?" we seem to be present at the gossip of the baths or the porticos. It is thus that Martial contrives to give the air of writing about, and to, definite and actual people.

Both his manner and his matter are calculated to render as clear to us as possible the world he lived in. He draws his material from the ordinary life and the everyday interests of himself and his acquaintances, and he treats it, though in the most finished style and with the most finished art, yet without imagination and without emotion. We see both the author and the age through the least distorting of mediums. And this quality is the quality of the time: in fresher, less sophisticated, and more imaginative periods there is no demand for this microscopic realism, for these *minutiae* of common life and this mirror-like verisimilitude.

Martial's spiritual quality, or rather his lack of it, is also significant. For all his sentimental pathos and his genuine expression of friendship, he is wanting in poetic feeling and imagination. Superficial both in feeling and in vision, he was above all observant and easy-going, but easy-going without benevolence, even without good nature. He makes no pretense to that earnestness which most satirists affect if they do not feel. Although sharp and clever, quick of eye and of wit, a finished workman and complete master of his medium, he gives at best an accurate rendering of the outside of a society which even in its brilliance was frivolous and squalid.

If we ask ourselves, then, when we may expect to find Martial influencing modern literature, we need be at no loss for an answer: in an age which appreciates his literary skill, which is interested in his subject-matter, and which sympathizes with his spirit. An age which exalts Martial, we may be sure, is a disillusioned and skeptical, a sophisticated and cynical age; it holds up realism as the end of art, for it understands and has faith in only the concrete and the immediate. Martial cannot appeal to an imaginative and idealistic age which trusts enthusiasm and generous aspiration, which cherishes high hopes and thinks more of the possibilities of human life than of the spotted actuality.

William S. Anderson   (essay date 1970)

SOURCE: "*Lascivia* vs. *ira*: Martial and Juvenal," in *Essays on Roman Satire*, Princeton University Press, 1982, pp. 362-95.

[*An American educator and critic specializing in classical literature, Anderson is the author of* Pompey, His Friends, and the Literature of the 1st Century B.C. *(1963) and* Anger in Juvenal and Seneca *(1964). In the following excerpt, which was originally published in 1970 in* California Studies in Classical Antiquity, *he contrasts the sportive epigrams of Martial to the angry satires of Juvenal, but notes the influence of Martial on his younger contemporary.*]

Sandwiched between two lighthearted epigrams on the dubious physical attractions of a Galla and a Chloe, there appear in Martial's Third Book the following four elegiac lines:

> empta domus fuerat tibi, Tongiliane, ducentis:
> abstulit hanc nimium casus in urbe frequens.
> conlatum est deciens. rogo, non potes ipse videri
> incendisse tuam, Tongiliane, domum? (3.52)

Martial has so contrived his development that each line begins with a crucial verb, each marking an important stage in the total situation, and the final one driving home the witty point. The first couplet establishes the situation in general terms: the cost of the house, then its total destruction (cause unspecified). To correct the impression of disaster, however, to make sure that we grasp Martial's attitude and correctly view the character of Tongilianus, the second couplet reports the huge profit made from the fire because of public contributions (again, cause undefined), then ever so politely raises the question of arson. What might have been mistaken for sympathy in the first couplet has changed to ridicule, while Tongilianus has been transformed from a pitiable victim to a criminal. The careful placing of *domus* close to the start of line 1 and *domum* at the end of line 4; the alliterative use of personal pronoun *tibi* and possessive *tuam* with vocative *Tongiliane* respectively in 1 and 4; the variation between the structure of the first couplet (one clause in each line) and of the second (one clause in a half-line, the next expanding to a line and a half); the use of three verbs to express the various nuances of Martial's suspicions in 3 and 4—these are some of the principal artistic devices employed to enhance this witty epigram. The incident with which it plays was no doubt one of the common scandals of the day, somewhat analogous to cases of arson today when a man sets fire to his house or factory in order to collect fraudulently on insurance. And Martial has treated this arson with the naughty laughter which is so typical of him.

Twenty to twenty-five years after the appearance of Martial's epigram, Juvenal published Satire 3, in which there occurs a sequence remarkably like that of those four elegiac lines.

> si magna Asturici cecidit domus, horrida mater,
> pullati proceres, differt vadimonia praetor.
> tum gemimus casus urbis, tunc odimus ignem.
> ardet adhuc, et iam accurrit qui marmora donet,
> conferat impensas; hic nuda et candida signa,
> hic aliquid praeclarum Euphranoris et Polycliti,
> haec Asianorum vetera ornamenta deorum,
> hic libros dabit et forulos mediamque Minervam,
> hic modium argenti. meliora ac plura reponit
> Persicus orborum lautissimus et merito iam
> suspectus tamquam ipse suas incenderit aedes.
>   (3. 212–222)

Juvenal has devoted eleven lines to his development, which he presents as a number of related scenes leading up to the same point as Martial's. Instead of talking to the arsonist, the speaker addresses the audience. Thus, he does not inquire or report the price of the mansion, but focuses on the disaster to the building and the immediate public outcry that it provokes. The first three lines, it might be said, represent an elaboration of the single line in which Martial recorded and affected to deplore the total destruction of Tongilianus' house. Martial's equally terse and generalized report of contributions is also amplified here by a list of six contributors and donations, five of which are organized by means of anaphora with the initial demonstrative. After devoting a full line in 217, 218, and 219 to three contributors, Juvenal rapidly closes the list after the first half of 220. Then he starts to develop his point on the arson. First of all, what may have been somewhat puzzling in Martial, namely, why people should contribute so heavily to a victim of fire, receives explanation from Juvenal: his arsonist Persicus is one of the richest men in Rome and has no immediate heirs; hence, people are contributing so as to earn a profitable place in his will. Then, with the conjunction *et* followed by *merito* and a monosyllable, Juvenal deliberately creates a harsh ending to the hexameter of 221 and a jerky beginning of the enjambment into 222. Instead of the mockingly polite construction of three verbs employed by Martial, Juvenal cleverly exploits the line division to hold us in suspense as to what Persicus has "deservedly" accomplished, before placing *suspectus* in its prominent position at the beginning of 222. Martial's naughty question becomes a statement, and the satirist voices a decisive bias about the popular scandal: it has a likely basis in fact.

Martial and Juvenal have worked with the same kind of scandalous incident and built towards the same witty point, though Juvenal has gone at the situation with greater amplitude than Martial. Taken in isolation, too, this Juvenalian scene might appear to be using its wit in the same amused and amusing way as that of the epigram. Suppose we knew Juvenal's poetry only through this excerpt, found in some anthology of the tenth century: could we accurately assess its tone? Might we not be tempted to believe, especially after seeing the parallel in Martial, that the speaker of these lines was not seriously engaged with the criminal behavior of Persicus, but, like Martial, intent on the manipulation of words and details so as to extract from the well-told anecdote the maximum amount of wit for the audience's pleasure? The problem which I have set myself forms part of the larger traditional problem involving Martial and Juvenal. For years, scholars have inquired into the connections between epigrammatist and satirist, in an attempt not only to define but also to explain them. I shall briefly review this scholarship, then proceed to the particular problem involving Martial and Juvenal which seems to have the most contemporary importance for us. I may put it this way: to what extent does Juvenal accept, along with the material, the basic method of Martial; to what extent is his wit a clever variation on Martial's? In terms of my title ["*Lascivia* vs. *ira:* Martial and Juvenal"], to what extent can we regard Juvenal's announced mood of *indignatio* and *ira* as an instrument of a dominant wit that closely parallels the integrated witty mood of *lascivia* proclaimed by Martial?

In reviewing the main facts about the relationship of Juvenal and Martial and the theories erected on these facts, we may classify the facts as biographical and literary. Evidence can be drawn from the life and times of the two poets and (as has been done at the beginning of this [essay]) from common material in their poetry. To begin in conventional manner with the biographical facts of the

older poet, Martial, born in Spain about A.D. 40, came to Rome in the early sixties, hoping perhaps to gain advancement through the other Spaniards who had acquired influence at the court of Nero, for example, Seneca and the family of Lucan. Although the Pisonian Conspiracy ended that particular hope, Martial remained in Rome nearly thirty-five years, at first forced to struggle for survival, then gradually establishing himself as a clever poet who merited patronage, whose epigrams deserved not only to be recited in Rome but also to be published and read all over the empire. He produced a slight volume to mark the inauguration of the Colosseum in 80, when Titus ruled; his major works, however, twelve books of Epigrams, appeared more or less year by year after 85, all but the last during the reign of Domitian. Success came to him, then, when he was about 45. Having been conditioned by early years in Spain, by the chaos of Nero's last years, and by the decade of Vespasian's sound rule, Martial flourished under the Flavian brothers, as Rome somewhat relaxed from the necessarily austere ways of their father.

Juvenal arrived in Rome during those years when Martial first began to enjoy fame. Born about 60 and raised, it appears, in the Italian town of Aquinum, he proceeded to Rome at approximately the same period as his contemporaries Tacitus and Pliny, though with entirely different hopes. They immediately entered upon the political career to which their background and influence entitled them; both progressed steadily and had reached high positions during the reign of Domitian while Juvenal remained insignificant. Since we hear nothing of Juvenal's political career, indeed virtually nothing at all of his experience, we assume that his background and influence (not his innate talent) were negligible. He apparently settled for a literary career, first perhaps as a teacher of rhetoric, then later as a more or less independent poet under the patronage of various men of wealth. Martial counted Juvenal as a friend by 92, for in Book 7 published that year, he mentioned him twice. Exactly when Juvenal began to develop his satiric talents and write the Satires we now possess, is uncertain. Most of the earliest poems, it is generally agreed, were written during the reign of Trajan; and Book I does not seem to have been published before 110. Since Martial had by then been dead five years and since Juvenal avoids giving specific details about himself and his friends, we should not be surprised to find no reference to Martial by name in the Satires. Assuming that Juvenal, like Martial, remained in Rome during the eighties and nineties—I find the evidence for Juvenal's exile at this time or any time unconvincing—we may conclude that both were involved contemporaneously, if not alike, for about fifteen years in the literary activities of the city, Juvenal as a tyro, Martial as an established figure. Martial left Rome in 98 and returned to his native Spain, from which he addressed to Juvenal a last epigram. Juvenal's success, which came under Trajan and Hadrian, sprang from conditions considerably different from Martial's.

Though twenty years younger than Martial, then, Juvenal did know him during the nineties and shared the literary scene in Rome with him at a significant period of his own poetic development. So much for the biographical facts linking the two. Now for the facts provided by the poems.

In Juvenal's earliest Book of Five Satires, four out of five have basic themes that appear frequently as the material of Martial's epigrams; and the single exception, Satire 4, uses as the partial occasion of its drama an oversize turbot (*rhombus*), which is also a topos in Martial. Satire 6, large enough to qualify by itself as Book II, surveys women's sexual proclivities; nobody needs to be reminded that Martial and his audience enjoyed the same subject. Book III, consisting of three Satires, was published probably early in the reign of Hadrian, some twenty years after Juvenal had last seen Martial. Nevertheless, Satire 7 describes the plight of poets and other practitioners of verbal arts in Rome, and Satire 9 toys with the world of male homosexuals: both topics occur over and over again in Martial. Finally, Satires 11 and 12 and the description of old age in Satire 10, all from Book IV, and to a lesser extent parts of Satires 13 and 14 in Book V show continued preoccupation with material common to Martial. In short, there can be little doubt that between A.D. 110 and 130 Juvenal used topics and themes which had earlier won wide favor in the epigrams published by Martial between 85 and 101. It is a significant exercise to go systematically through Juvenal's Satires, especially the earlier ones, and point out line by line, passage by passage, what he shared with the epigrams of his Spanish friend.

We have a combination of biographical and literary facts: the two poets were both in Rome and knew each other fairly well, and after Martial's death Juvenal wrote poems which repeatedly parallel in significant detail the epigrams of Martial. How can we interpret these facts so as to illuminate the relationship between the two? Modern preoccupation with this problem received major stimulus from ["The Life and Poems of Juvenal," in *Journal of Philology* 16] published in 1888 by Henry Nettleship, who, while assessing Juvenal's achievement in general, took time to put forth a provocative explanation for the links between Martial and Juvenal, Epigrams and Satires. According to him, Martial and Juvenal worked side by side in Rome during the nineties, but independently of each other, each drawing upon a common store of literary material then available in the city. And to make his thesis more plausible, Nettleship argued that the major portions of the Satires of Book I were composed, like the Epigrams, in the nineties.

Most scholars have rejected Nettleship's dating of the early Satires as well as his view of Juvenal's originality or independence. Thus, J.D. Duff, in [*D. Iunii Iuvenalis Saturae XIV*] which was first published in 1898, wrote: "The resemblance [between the two poets' themes] will not seem more than can be accounted for, if we believe that Juvenal, having already a thorough knowledge of Martial's epigrams, began to direct his satires against the same period and persons whom Martial had already riddled with his lighter artillery." That same year, Harry Wilson printed his significant paper [in *American Journal of Philology* 19 (1898)], which he had read in 1897 to the American Philological Association, on "The Literary Influence of Martial upon Juvenal." The title alone indicates that he stood with Duff against Nettleship on the question of independence. Studying the mechanics of Martial's influence rigorously, Wilson argued that Juvenal used the typical techniques of *imitatio* normal for Latin poets; he knew Martial by heart, but did not simply copy him word for word. He either reused Martial's ideas in different words or used Martial's words in an altered context, to create Satires that were substantially different from the Epigrams.

The meticulous argument of Wilson and the general likelihood of his and Duff's assumptions that the older, successful poet influenced, but did not totally dominate, the younger have continued to prevail. There are, however, some questions which they did not face. Duff, for example, in stating that Juvenal dealt with the same period and persons as Martial, did not go on to explain the effect intended or achieved. What did the people and events of the eighties and nineties mean to Juvenal and his audience twenty to thirty years later? What was the point of being indignant over the dead past when Martial had treated it with his charming *lascivia*? By substituting heavy artillery for light (to keep Duff's image), was Juvenal moving farther away from reality or closer to the feelings of his audience? Wilson, too, left unexplained the fundamental literary connection between Juvenal's artful variations on Martial's wording and what he regarded as the evident difference between their respective styles and poetic purposes. If, as he wrote, "the high moral purpose and seriousness of the former [Juvenal] stand in sharp antithesis to the mocking triviality of the latter [Martial]," one wonders about the range of Juvenal's *imitatio*. Assuming that we can distinguish the "high moral purpose" in the account of Persicus' arson from the "mocking triviality" of Tongilianus' arson in Martial, can we also say that this is a function of *imitatio*? Was Juvenal doing anything like Horace who used Lucretian language to comment on epic enthusiasm and on Epicurean exaggerations? That is, did Juvenal allude to the whole context of Martial and subtly differentiate his own attitude on all levels, or was he merely playing with Martial's words and, from quite another perspective, aiming at a moral purpose and seriousness to which the borrowings from Martial had no relevance?

Granted, then, that Juvenal did make use of Martial, both his words and his epigrammatic situations, the question remains: what was the extent of this use; what was its effect with the audience? It is not really an adequate answer to respond that Martial was a kind of satirist and so Juvenal drew from him what was naturally "satiric," for satire is so amorphous in form and manner (even without Martial) that turning Martial, for the purposes of argument, into a satirist says very little about how he might be utilized by Juvenal. In theory it would be possible to argue that, because Juvenal regards Roman society with the dissatisfied eye of a wretched client and the literary situation in Rome with the unhappiness of a poet struggling for recognition, and because Martial earlier exhibited similar attitudes, Juvenal adopted his attitude from Martial. In fact, the shared viewpoints serve scholars rather to document the relative continuity of Roman conditions and the basis of the two poets' friendship: Juvenal is supposed to have felt the situation as personally as Martial.

In more recent years, two scholars have offered more comprehensive answers to the problem of this relationship, directing attention as much to *how* the borrowings were made as to *what* was borrowed. Gilbert Highet, while discussing the broad tradition from which Juvenal drew, commented [in *Juvenal the Satirist,* 1954] on Martial's part in it as follows: "So many of Juvenal's jokes and satiric ideas and proper names and turns of phrase are adapted from Martial that the epigrams of Martial were clearly one of the chief influences that trained him to be a satirist. What he did was to take Martial's keen perception, his disillusioned but witty sense of contrast, his trick of epigram, and his peculiar blend of suave poetry and vulgar colloquialism, to clean them up, to give them a moral purpose, and to build them into poems of major length." This seems promising, especially because it does not exploit the invidious contrast between Martial's "triviality" and Juvenal's "high seriousness," but gives full credit to the artistry of the Epigrams. Highet represents Juvenal as a skillful poet who engages himself creatively with the art of Martial at every level and extracts from it material to which he can give new shape and life. Unfortunately, in his analysis of the individual Satires, Highet did not attempt to work out this view of a Juvenal trained by Martial. His emphasis upon the satirist as an unhappy, hypersensitive person who has experienced profound personal suffering and upon the passionate personal truth of the Satires obscures any concern with the creative poet who saw merits in and exploited Martial's obvious assets.

It was in patent disagreement with Highet's emphasis that in 1962 H. A. Mason published his influential essay [in *Arion* 1, No. 1] entitled: "Is Juvenal a Classic?" In order to deny the crucial assumption of Highet and other biographical critics that Juvenal's Satires tell us the truth about himself and his period, Mason resorted to Martial. As he explained this tactic, "the key to Juvenal's art lies in the study of Martial. The two poets appeal to the same taste and presuppose the same habits in their listening and reading public." Later, by way of conclusion, he imaginatively elaborated what he believed Juvenal presupposed in his public, wording it cleverly as if the satirist were making prefatory remarks to an edition of the Satires:

> Dear readers, you have enjoyed Martial; now come and see whether I cannot give extra point to his favorite topics by setting them, as it were, to a different tune: the declaimer's mode. But I assume you understand what Martial was doing when he confined his poems to the conventional jokes of polite society. You will know then that to enjoy us you must both suspend and apply your critical and moral sense. We are not called on in our art to give you *all* the facts (you know them as well as we) or to assume all the moral attitudes (we are not moral censors) but to take those that allow the maximum witty play of the mind. Prepare yourselves, therefore, dear readers, to find in my poems all the butts of Martial's epigrams, and in particular, the comically obscene situations you enjoy so much in the mime. You will see from my rewritings of Martial that I have my own notes, particularly the sarcastic and the mock-tragic and epic, and that by fitting my sections together I can exhibit more attitudes to the same episode than you will find in any one of his epigrams.

Mason offers the most detailed literary explanation of Martial's influence known to me, and he extends the range of this influence farther than any other interpreter: not only has Juvenal used his predecessor with great creativity but he also agrees with the basic attitude of Martial. In both poets wit is the main device for achieving effects: the essential manner of both is witty. So the answer to the question in Mason's title would be: Juvenal is a classic of wit. Accordingly, "he was more interested in literature than social conditions and . . . he lacks any consistent standpoint or moral coherence. Indeed his whole art consists in opportunism and the surprise effects obtainable from deliberate inconsistency." Whereas earlier commentators plunged into problems because they insisted on the basic difference in attitude and technique of Juvenal even when he was using Martial, Mason has eliminated that problem by insisting on the identity of the two poets' subjects, witty manners, and audiences. Juvenal has become Martial set to a slightly different tune.

There can be no question that Mason has at last properly emphasized one of the most important elements of Juvenal's art and most cleverly employed Martial to demonstrate his thesis. Wit *is* important in the Satires. However, in order to win his argument, he has claimed too much. He has, I believe, tended to overstress wit at the expense of other important factors of Juvenalian art and to force Juvenal too harshly into the mould of Martial. Aside from the fact that Juvenal himself had different origins from Martial and a personality of his own, it is evident that the eras of Trajan and Hadrian differed markedly from that of Domitian, and it seems dubious to posit an audience for Juvenal equipped with the "same taste" as Martial's. To limit one's attention, as Mason does, to verbal opportunism or manipulation of the Latin language is risky. To defend these limits by asserting that there is no sustained theme of significance in Juvenal's Satires, no engagement with genuine moral issues is to provoke a protest from those who read Juvenal otherwise. Martial may provide "the key to Juvenal's art" in a way quite different from what Mason believes: his work happens to be the most conveniently available to show how much Juvenal reshaped his literary heritage to fit his own purposes. In the remainder of this [essay], I shall criticize Mason's thesis more fully, particularly by reference to Satire 3 and other Satires of Book I, in the hope of estimating more satisfactorily the function of Juvenalian wit and of defining its relation to the announced mood of indignation that characterizes the earlier Satires.

Now that I have sketched out the lines of controversy, I return to the passage of Satire 3 with which I began. I had posed the problem of the tone behind Juvenal's wit and suggested that, taken in isolation, the passage about the arsonist-profiteer might possibly be interpreted like the parallel epigram of Martial, as a cleverly reported joke of Roman society. That would be Mason's view of the passage and the entire Satire; he would add only that Juvenal's tune differed and that the satirist was able to accumulate more attitudes around the episode by reason of his broader scope. Nevertheless, according to Mason, Juvenal's audience responded here, as they were meant, primarily to the joke; all other effects in the passage are subordinate to that.

When we study this arson narrative in relation to its context, I believe, it becomes evident that Juvenal has drastically altered Martial (assuming that he did work here under some influence of Martial). Above all, he has shaped what was supposed to be only a joke so that it no longer is an end in itself, but has become subordinate to what must be called larger thematic purposes. First of all, take the matter of names. Martial called his arsonist Tongilianus. We can be sure that the name did not identify anyone, because Martial has fabricated this odd name. Since the name possesses no automatic connotations, the narrative determines the identity of the arsonist. Probably Martial's audience was expected to substitute for this fantastic name the name of a real Roman or wealthy alien resident to whom scandal attributed arson. Calling him Tongilianus, Martial caught the alliteration and supported the lighthearted purposes of his wit. Juvenal, on the other hand, offers two names: Asturicus (212) and Persicus (221). These names are meaningful in themselves: we are to think of remote Asturia in Spain and of Persia in the East, and then we imagine the nobility and wealth that could be won by Romans in these exotic spots. We are not expected to play drawing-room games and guess the identity of Juvenal's arsonists: the names identify them as Romans from distinguished families.

Second, Juvenal has totally altered the narrative occasion and thereby changed our attitude toward the arsonist. Martial pictures himself, the irreverent Spaniard, striking up a conversation with Tongilianus, affecting to be sympathetic as the latter reports on his fire, then naughtily raising the question of arson at the end. In Satire 3, the speaker who recounts the episode is Umbricius, a character especially created by Juvenal for the poem. He is not talking with the arsonist but with us, and he could never affect sympathy or amusement over this arson. Thus, the narrative has no real surprise, as Martial's does; it builds steadily toward its climax. For Umbricius, Asturicus and Persicus represent villains to whom he points with anger as he addresses each of us in the second person singular. The reasons for this anger, which are obvious from the fuller context (soon to be discussed) may be summarized in this way: he is a victim of the Rome which allows a distinguished Roman like Persicus to profit, not be executed, as a result of his criminal arson. The altered point of view and altered form of dialogue in turn decisively shape the wit here deployed.

Finally, Martial's totally independent joke, told for itself, has been subordinated by Juvenal to a larger context and thematic purposes. This case of arson is introduced in 212 in a conditional clause, to produce an antithesis to an actual instance of accidental fire, when the apartment of a poor man named Cordus was burned and all its miserable contents consumed. The list of people who react with horror at Asturicus' plight corresponds ironically to a heavily emphasized nobody (*nemo* in anaphora 211) who answered Cordus' need. The list of precious things contributed by "friends" to Asturicus corresponds to the list of diminutive, pathetically cherished possessions of Cordus which the fire destroyed. Whereas Umbricius summarizes Persicus' situation by saying that he recovered more and better things than he had before his planned fire, his pa-

thetic summary of Cordus' plight dwells on the "nothing" he really possessed to begin with, all of which paltry "nothing" was lost without chance of replacement (*nil* rhetorically repeated 208–209). The antithesis rather than the verbal manipulation of the arson anecdote determines the ultimate effect of Juvenal's wit here. Cordus, the innocent, pathetic victim of a fire over which he had no control, decisively qualifies our attitude toward Persicus, profiteer from his act of arson. We can now conclude that Juvenal did not amplify Martial's anecdote with his lists of people sympathetic to Asturicus and of donors and donations merely to enhance his narrative with vivid details and so increase the final point. The expansions serve the antithesis, which in turn functions to express a pervasive theme about the injustice and un-Roman degeneracy controlling Rome. I think I can safely claim Martial never portrays a poor man as genuinely pathetic, never allows his audience to engage its emotions with problems of Roman justice.

Juvenal places the two contrasting stories about Cordus and the arsonists in a larger context that begins with Umbricius' question in 190:

> quis timet aut timuit gelida Praeneste ruinam?

Beside Praeneste, Umbricius names three other charming towns of Latium or Southern Etruria, which implicitly offer pleasant, secure if humble homes in contrast with the Roman apartments that constantly threaten collapse. The contrast is worked out by a description of us (*nos urbem colimus* 193ff) fearfully sleeping when *ruina* is imminent. Then, the subject turns to fires, another aspect of urban residential danger, and "your" plight, anyone of "you" in the audience, as Umbricius suggests that outside Rome no fires occur at night, no sudden scares. He pictures "you" trapped on the top floor of a highly combustible apartment as fire races up the flimsy structure: "you" are doomed, it appears, when he suddenly abandons the desperate scene to describe Cordus' troubles. Plainly, though, "you" and Cordus are alike victims of fire in contrast with the arsonists, except that "you" will not survive, whereas Cordus did escape with nothing and became a beggar. Having closed the antithesis with what now we would call savage wit about profitable arson, Umbricius returns to "you." He offers "you" a fine home—a place of safety from that menacing fire—for the price you now pay annually for your dark Roman garret, away from Rome in three typical towns of Latium. These three towns obviously balance the four names in 190ff. And the paragraph closes with an elaboration of the attractions of rusticity, both charming and witty, as "you" are invited to entertain the vision of a small plot of land which you yourself work, at last the master of something you can count on, if only a lone lizard. "You" seem to have a choice between death in Rome and secure life in the country, between losing your few possessions in Rome (where arsonists profit) or enjoying them undisturbed elsewhere, between victimization in Rome and honorable rustic independence. How can "you" hesitate? Umbricius, the angry speaker, is now about to abandon this corrupt city, and the whole trend of this paragraph is to persuade "you" to follow his example.

Juvenal, then, has re-worked the naughty wit of Martial's light epigram to voice anger and serve the needs of a thematic antithesis. And this revised joke about arson is not the only wit in the passage to be so shaped. Umbricius starts with hyperbole: *nos urbem colimus tenui tibicine fultam;* note the alliteration used to enhance the wit. The closest analogy to this—and not very close at that—Mayor found in witty Ovid, who described a modest farm house "standing by means of a prop" (*stantem tibicine villam, Fast.* 4.695). To give substance to his exaggeration, Umbricius goes on to describe how the agents of apartment owners criminally conceal the structural faults in a building, then "urge renters to sleep soundly in the face of imminent collapse" (*securos pendente iubet dormire ruina* 196). Sound sleep, used paradoxically here, might well remind Juvenal's audience of the way Horace idealized the condition of the simple countryman in terms of easy, peaceful slumber. When the fire starts in "your" apartment, "you" learn of it by the shouts and bustle of "your" downstairs neighbor Ucalegon. In this instance, the wit inheres in the phrasing of the Latin and the choice of the name, which echo a passage from [Virgil's] *Aeneid* 2. Aeneas had a next-door neighbor in Troy, whose house was already afire when Aeneas awoke from his last sleep in his home, then rushed out to fight. The modern Ucalegon is an impoverished "son of Troy," and his neighbor, the modern Aeneas, is "you" in your garret, about to be burned unheroically to a cinder. Martial commonly uses metonymy with names of mythical heroes, but you would never find him using the trope in this thematic manner, to underline the degeneracy of Rome from the noble ideals of the *Aeneid.*

Umbricius shifts to Cordus, characterizing his few possessions by diminutives. "Cordus owned a bed that was too short for little Procula" (who was apparently a dwarf, 203). An old bookcase contained his tiny Greek texts (206); illiterate mice gnawed on the divine poetry of Greece (207): *et divina opici rodebant carmina mures.* With this witty hexameter, shaped as a Golden Line, Juvenal concludes his detailed list of Cordus' belongings. The mice and poetry, illiteracy and divinity, all linked by the pungent verb, establish the clever paradox, which contains both pathos and humor. While Cordus loses his precious diminutive library, Asturicus will be gaining one, expensive tomes plus bookshelves and ornamental busts. Umbricius then epitomizes Cordus' condition with a witty sequence on the word *nil / nihil.* Nothing was what Cordus really owned, and yet he lost all that nothing: the key word begins and ends the sentence. To make sure we react here in a way different from Martial's audience, Juvenal adds the adjective *infelix* and makes Cordus "poor, pathetic." He does what Vergil and Ovid frequently did to direct sympathy. Martial uses *infelix* to characterize people who cause unhappiness, not suffer it. Thus, in the Epigrams, only an ungenerous patron, an unfaithful wife, and a lion that has killed two children can be called *infelix.*

After reworking Martial's epigram on arson, Umbricius returns nastily to "you" and starts: "If you can tear yourself away from the Circus" (*si potes avelli circensibus* 223), then goes on to offer "you" a pleasant home in a country town. The implication here, as on the other occasions

when Juvenal uses this common motif, is that most Romans let themselves be lulled by the exciting spectacles of the Circus and Colosseum into quiescence about the indignities they were suffering. Umbricius' attitude suggests a man of moral integrity: we find it exhibited by Cicero earlier and near Juvenal's time by Pliny. Martial, on the other hand, wrote epigrams expressing in witty terms marvel and delight with the shows in the Colosseum. Umbricius resorts to wit to give a prejudiced picture of the garret "you" rent in Rome: *tenebras conducis.* Martial, as commentators note, describes an ill-lit public bath in terms of *tenebrae,* without, however, aiming at or achieving this typical Juvenalian pathos. In the country, "you" can raise vegetables in your little garden, an idyllic scene which Umbricius punctuates wittily with a relative clause neatly worked into a complete hexameter: *unde epulum possis centum dare Pythagoreis.* Again, we are dealing with a joke that does not belong to Martial's repertoire and is not employed in Martial's manner. Juvenal also attaches pathos to the same joke in 15.173. Horace and Ovid handle differently the familiar jibe at the Pythagoreans and their foolish beans. Finally, Umbricius brings the paragraph to a close on the hyperbolical note of "becoming master of a lone lizard." Commentators cite analogues in both Martial and Pliny for this figure of speech, but I dare say that a formula existed, learned in school, for this kind of expression. What counts here is not the verbal parallel, but the special thematic way in which Juvenal uses the figure to support Umbricius' jaundiced view of Rome as a place where one securely owns nothing so long as one is afflicted with *paupertas.*

We may now pause to draw some conclusions about how Juvenal uses wit in this section of Satire 3, before extending our analysis to other passages.

1. Juvenal obviously knew Martial's epigrams well, prized their wit and used it.

2. Juvenal also drew his wit from many other sources in his extensive literary tradition, not only from witty writers of earlier times such as Horace and Ovid, but also dead-serious epic poets like Vergil.

3. Wit saturates this passage: every two or three lines exhibit an example.

4. Juvenal uses a number of methods to introduce wit: (a) he brings a development to a neat close in a single hexameter, often in the form of a relative clause or some surprising descriptive detail; (b) he punctuates with hyperbole or paradox; (c) he focuses attention on a single word in metonymy or a single resonant name; (d) he manipulates a telling word like *nil / nihil.*

5. Not only does each instance of wit enliven its lines, but it also serves the thematic purpose of the larger context.

6. The versatility of Juvenal's wit in respect of sources and mechanism, together with its crucial thematic functions, gives it a tone very remote from Martial's: it is either utterly angry or a blend of anger and humor, but never the naughty, basically tolerant *lascivia* which Martial rightly assigned to his *nugae.*

It seems to me that these conclusions place us somewhere between the positions occupied by Mason and Highet. Mason, conducting a polemical argument, tried to answer those like Highet who stress Juvenal's truth and moral sincerity, so he emphasized the factor of wit and depicted Juvenal as "a supreme manipulator of the Latin language." This manipulator, according to him, negates the business of truth and moral fervor. However, his view of Juvenal's artistry is so confined as to be half-damning, for Mason feels obliged to deny the satirist any systematic themes and to insist on opportunism as Juvenal's dominant poetic strategy. Such a conception may, I think, arise from overemphasis of Martial's relevance. Although Mason rightly points out the common use of wit by Juvenal and Martial and frequently of the same witty situations, it does not follow that, because Martial's brief epigrams cannot develop themes and must limit themselves to mere verbal manipulation, Juvenal's broader scope must be similarly confined and represented as Martial set "to a different tune." . . .

[Juvenal's] Satire 9 deals with a type familiar in Martial, and it gives him a name that occurs five times in Martial. We are introduced to one of those interesting "professionals" who hires himself out as both adulterer and satisfier of male homosexual desires. Naevolus' current employer requires his ambidextrous services for himself and for his wife. To open the Satire, Juvenal uses a method reminiscent of Martial. Having bumped into Naevolus on the street (*occurras* 2), the satirist solicitously asks what is wrong, why Naevolus looks so badly. For about 25 lines he elaborates with seeming concern on his "friend's" condition, and only after this clever build-up does he surprise us by revealing the source of Naevolus' income: he is notorious throughout Rome as both *moechus* and *cinaedus*. This is precisely the tone of affected concern punctured by cynical realism that we met in the Tongilianus epigram and that can be found in numerous poems of Martial. Juvenal maintains that same tone of nonreproving realism to the end of the Satire, letting Naevolus dominate the conversation and voice his complaint in detail. I hardly need to note that Naevolus bears little resemblance to Umbricius of Satire 3, and the satirist's mockery in Satire 9 differs radically from his sympathy in the earlier Satire. But it is interesting and important to recognize that in Book I Juvenal does not touch such a versatile character as the *moechus-cinaedus,* ideal for a Martial-like display of wit as it would be. When he encounters an adulterer or a homosexual in Book I, he exchanges no words of solicitous concern with them; the mere sight of them and the awareness of what they are sends him into paroxysms of rage. This is clear from Satire 1 where, claiming that what justifies his indignant satire is the variety of depraved people he meets in his beloved Rome, he cites as illustration the professional gigolo who ministers to the lust of rich hags, the husband who connives like a pander with the adulterer of his wife, the man who seduces his own daughter-in-law, and the adolescent who sets out on his affairs sporting his juvenile robe (*praetextatus adulter* 78), already corrupted.

Adultery is among the vices that stimulate indignation in Satire 1. Although Juvenal's vignettes are phrased cleverly and memorably, it is plain that he is not joking, like Martial, about the gigolo, husband-abetted adulterer, father-in-law, or juvenile adulterer. He leaves to Satire 6 more elaborate and lurid scenes that feature the adulteress, but his mood of indignation is essentially the same. In Satire 2, he vents his rage on homosexuals without clouding the issue or attenuating the picture of corruption by amusingly combining *cinaedus* with *moechus*. Again, he expects us to picture him meeting people on the street, not conversing with them but erupting in anger as he realizes what they represent for Rome. "What Roman street," he asks, "is not crowded with perverts masquerading as strict moralists?" (*quis enim non vicus abundat tristibus obscenis?* 2.8–9). Even worse, as he strolls through the Forum and other public places, he must listen to these people orating piously against female adultery; for these are not just average perverts: they come from distinguished families and so exercise influence in Roman politics as Senators and Censors. Juvenal attacks them in two phases in Satire 2. First, he roars at the crypto-homosexuals who pose as Puritans; then, having stripped off their disguise, he pours his wrath on various homosexual acts which presumably are practised in secret by these same people, members of the "gay set" in Rome.

Martial treats these topics, as we would expect, with clever good humor. A favorite homosexual-joke in Rome exploited the unmistakable meaning of the verb *nubere:* to put on the marriage veil for another, that is, to marry. It must properly describe the act of a woman, a bride. Martial uses this topos in two epigrams published more than ten years apart, in each case to play with a situation that Juvenal in Satire 2 presents as outrageous. The first provides a useful contrast to the opening of the Satire:

> aspicis incomptis illum, Deciane, capillis,
> cuius et ipse times triste supercilium,
> qui loquitur Curios adsertoresque Camillos?
> nolito fronti credere: nupsit heri. (1.24)

Martial points out to a companion a shaggy, severe-looking moralist who is apparently orating, denouncing contemporary corruption and citing the great virtuous Roman examples of the early Republic. The three lines of build-up are then suddenly broken by the surprise of 4: the "moralist" was married yesterday, to another man! Our amusement is not disturbed by complicated feelings about the pervert, for Martial has not identified his class.

Now compare the opening of Satire 2:

> ultra Sauromatas fugere hinc libet et glacialem
> Oceanum, quotiens aliquid de moribus audent
> qui Curios simulant et Bacchanalia vivunt . . .
> frontis nulla fides; quis enim non vicus abundat
> tristibus obscenis? castigas turpia, cum sis
> inter Socraticos notissima fossa cinaedos? (1–3,
> 8–10)

Juvenal is indignant from the first line, ready to leave Rome in disgust for the remotest spot beyond the limits of the Roman Empire, and he makes no witty surprise of his reason. Line 3 is memorable and frequently cited, but it is significantly different from Martial's line 3 and elicits a quite different response from the audience. Martial has a "moralist" talking of two virtuous old patriotic types, and this line forms part of his deceptive build-up to the surprise of line 4. Juvenal epitomizes in his two phrases, each occupying half the line, the outrageous paradox that provokes his indignation: people are pretending to be virtuous according to ancient Curio, but in fact living perversely. The same paradox is repeated neatly in *tristibus obscenis* and *Socraticos cinaedos.* Juvenal brands the pretense from the start, and he indicates, by the phrase about posing as a Curio, as well as by subsequent details, that he is dealing exclusively with the Roman upper classes, whose perversion gravely affects the whole character of Rome.

Martial's second epigram starts from the surprise use of *nupsit,* develops the scene of marriage, then proceeds to an unexpected final question.

> barbatus rigido nupsit Callistratus Afro
> hac qua lege viro nubere virgo solet.
> praeluxere faces, velarunt flammea vultus,
> nec tua defuerunt verba, Talasse, tibi.
> dos etiam dicta est. nondum tibi, Roma, videtur
> hoc satis? expectas numquid ut et pariat? (12.42)

Martial constructs his first line brilliantly: the pair of initial adjectives, which imply that we have to do with a bearded moralist and a stern Catonian personality, are startlingly related by the verb, upon which follow the pair of identifying names. Callistratus, who has grown a beard so as to masquerade as a Cynic, has married Afer, a man as seemingly stern as the proverbial *rigidi Catones* of Martial 10.19.21. It has been a Roman ceremony, even though Callistratus has hardly been the usual *virgo.* So Martial apostrophizes Rome and asks her what she is waiting for, for Callistratus to have a baby? There is, I believe, some impatience behind the question, but the incredible hyperbole manipulated into the final word shows that Martial's emphasis is, as usual, on the joke. Callistratus appears a few epigrams earlier, also as a pervert, upon whom Martial comments with his typical cool amusement, without the slightest impatience. Furthermore, in choosing a Greek name for Callistratus, Martial has weakened the force of the appeal to Rome: she is not being asked to punish one of her degenerate children, but to drive out a foreigner who is polluting the scene. Afer, who has a Roman name, receives little emphasis, and furthermore he plays the less disgraceful role in this marriage.

Juvenal breaks the elements of this epigram of Martial into two dramatic sequences involving "marriages" between males. In the first, he gives a detailed description of the marriage-ceremony, then angrily apostrophizes Mars without using the special joke of Martial; in the second, he first listens to someone else eagerly represent the occasion as one of the "society weddings" of the season, then angrily denounces such corruption, consoling himself with the thought that at least children cannot be born from such unnatural unions. Juvenal's point is totally different from Martial's and entirely consistent with his stance in Satires 1 and 3 as an indignant Roman: Rome has become unmanned, and its once-heroic families now produce effeminates. The "bride" in 117ff is now not a Greek Callistratus but a Roman Gracchus, scion of one

of Rome's most distinguished families. The groom, a nameless trumpeter, probably a Greek or Easterner, further establishes the disgraceful qualities of this "marriage." And it is not by chance that Juvenal apostrophizes Mars. As he constructs the scene, the bridal attire of Gracchus forms a sharp antithesis to the military setting of the ceremonies in honor of Mars in which he participated as a Salian priest. So how can Mars ignore the disgrace? In disgust, he tells Mars to quit his own Campus Martius, for, if he permits this marriage, then he is no longer the warlike Roman Mars.

The second marriage involves no names, but every indication suggests that the "bride" again is a "man of distinction." The first three lines are organized as a rapid conversation which conceals its point until the end, and we might well see in them some of the successful touches of Martial.

> 'officium cras
> primo sole mihi peragendum in valle Quirini.'
> quae causa officii? 'quid quaeris? nubit amicus
> nec multos adhibet.' (132–135)

Somebody starts talking to Juvenal about the important *officium* which he just *must* perform the very first thing in the morning. It sounds important, cast as it is in the traditional Roman terms of public responsibility. So Juvenal inquires about the *officium.* The social butterfly replies without the slightest shame that he has been invited to an exclusive wedding where a male friend will be the "bride." That ends the Martial-like sequence. Note the difference, however: the shocking point is placed in the mouth of a despicable member of the "gay set"; it is not the amused observation of the satirist. As a result, Juvenal is free to comment, and the remainder of the passage consists of savage denunciation, in typical Juvenalian manner, of this perversion that threatens Rome itself. Instead of producing the incredible fantasy of Martial to end his scene, he consoles himself with the thought that at least these vile marriages can produce no offspring, no matter how much a Gracchus wishes to hold his/her "husband." Thus, Satire 2 establishes the typical tactics of Juvenal's angry wit, whereas Satire 9 (which Mason wrongly employed to define the standard of Juvenalian wit) reflects a later stage in Juvenal's development, when he was moderating his indignant manner and experimenting with the cynical humor of Martial. . . .

To conclude, wit is a vital element of Juvenalian satire, but it stands in a different relation to Juvenal's purposes than wit does to Martial's goals. In Martial, wit and *lascivia* operate in full agreement with each other; the verbal manipulation and the manner that Martial repeatedly professes have identical effects. The audience performs no complicated process when it hears or reads the Epigrams, for Martial does quite brilliantly exactly what he says he does. Mason assumes that the wit of Juvenalian satire constantly undermines the announced mood of the speaker, who is quite apparently laughing at himself and literary seriousness; that would mean that individual passages in the Satires would operate generally in the manner of separate epigrams of Martial, the sudden final surprise dispelling an initially affected seriousness. His argument, however, as I have attempted to show, over-simplifies and hence falsifies the art of Juvenal. It tends to imply that wit is supreme in the Satires, that indignation is secondary, in fact, meretricious. If we read carefully the early Satires, the only ones which in fact proclaim *indignatio* or *ira* as their mood, and if we study the wit in context for its thematic and dramatic relevance, we discover that wit and anger operate, at the primary level, in full agreement with each other. That is, they produce a dramatically credible impression of a violently angry man who cannot distinguish between facts and his own extravagant reactions to them. However, this same angry wit functions at a second level with the audience, which can and must draw the distinctions that are not made in the Satires. Whereas Martial inclines us to like his witty picture of Rome, Juvenal inclines us by his extravagance to reject the distorted interpretation of what he claims is the real Rome. We enjoy the angry Satires, accordingly, by opposition to their wild anger; we treat Umbricius and the satirist who rage in the early Satires as dramatic characters whose indignation is part of the drama, not a requisite part of our response to the facts.

The contrast between the wit of Martial and Juvenal can be epitomized in their treatments of Rome's moralistic tradition. In the introduction to Book I of the Epigrams, Martial assumes an attitude that he maintains throughout Book XII. His poems are *ioci,* written with *lascivia verborum,* designed for an audience that enjoys the lusty humor of the Floralia. Therefore, he forbids Cato to enter his "theatre" in his conventional moral rôle; he may enter only as a "spectator," that is, prepared to enjoy himself. The short poem that concludes this Preface repeats the same ideas: where *licentia* is the mood, *Cato severus* has no place. Book XI announces a similar program in two poems. It rejects the severe brow of Cato and proclaims the wild deeds of the Saturnalian mood; it also dismisses Cato's wife from its audience, because it intends to be naughtier than all other books (*nequior omnibus libellis* 11.15.4). Book X has another variation: stiff Cato will be allowed to read the epigrams only if he has drunk well. For the poems of Martial, then, morality is ostensibly irrelevant. By contrast, Juvenal's indignation insists that morality is crucially relevant. The satirist repeatedly appeals to the venerable moralistic tradition of Rome, laments that it has fallen into disuse, and himself voices the anger of one who is out of touch with his own times. But whereas he takes himself seriously and denounces Roman vice with honest passion, the audience judges him to be a largely comic figure, full of irrelevancy. He is, in a sense, a Cato born 250 years too late. Thinking that his wit expresses the extreme extent of vice, he in fact rather exposes his own ridiculous extremism. Nevertheless, correcting or laughing *at* moral extremism is not totally negating morality. Whereas Martial allows us to reject Cato and relax in witty amorality, laughing *with* him, Juvenal obliges us to achieve our amusement by adjusting to our moral awareness the extravagance of his Catonian speaker. The more complex operation of Juvenal's wit demands a more complex, less passive response from us in the audience.

FURTHER READING

Biography

Bellinger, A. R. "Martial: The Suburbanite." *Classical Philology* XXIII, No. 6 (March 1928): 425-35.
  Portrays Martial's ambivalence towards the grandeur and frenetic urban lifestyle characteristic of Rome.

Hawes, Adeline Belle. "A Spanish Poet in Rome." In her *Citizens of Long Ago: Essays on Life and Letters in the Roman Empire*, pp. 91-110. New York: Oxford University Press, 1934.
  Offers an overview of Martial's life and poetry.

Criticism

Allen, Walter, Jr.; Beveridge, Martha J.; Downes, William J.; Fincher, Hugh M., III; Gold, Barbara Kirk; Kopff, E. Christian; Simms, Lawrence J.; and Walsh, Lois H. "Martial: Knight, Publisher, and Poet." *The Classical Journal* 65, No. 1 (October 1969): 345-57.
  Strives for a more complete understanding of Martial's career as a poet by discussing his social standing, the initial publication of his works, and the earnestness with which he viewed his poetry.

Carrington, A. G. *Aspects of Martial's Epigrams.* Eton and Windsor, England: The Shakespeare Head Press, 1960, 125 p.
  Looks at Martial's work through details about his life, his character, and early Roman history.

Chaney, Virginia M. "Women, According to Martial." *The Classical Bulletin* 48, No. 2 (December 1971): 21-5.
  Inspects women's roles in Martial's epigrams.

Downs, Robert B. "Creator of the Epigram." In his *Famous Books: Ancient and Medieval*, pp. 217-20. New York: Barnes & Noble, Inc., 1964.
  Capsule of Martial's career, describing the pinnacle of his writing.

Duff, J. Wight. "Martial—The Epigram as Satire." In his *Roman Satire: Its Outlook on Social Life*, pp. 126-46. 1936. Reprint. Hamden, Conn.: Archon Books, 1964.
  Examines the use of satire in Martial's epigrams, concluding: "With the world of contemporary Rome for the object of his satire, he departs constantly from any Greek or Latin models he employs."

——. "Martial and Minor Flavian Poetry." In his *A Literary History of Rome in the Silver Age: From Tiberius to Hadrian,* third edition, edited by A. M. Duff, pp. 397-422. London: Ernest Benn Limited, 1964.
  Discusses the autobiographical elements and the realism found in Martial's poetry. Duff explains, "[Martial's] personality is reflected in his themes, and is inseparable from the things he described and the men he loved or hated."

Marino, Peter A. "Woman: Poorly Inferior or Richly Superior?" *The Classical Bulletin* 48, No. 2 (December 1971): 17-21.
  Depicts the relationship between ancient Roman men and women through Martial's epigrams.

Mendell, Clarence W. "Martial and the Satiric Epigram." *Classical Philology* XVII, No. 1 (January 1922): 1-20.

Focuses on the history of the epigram, comparing Greek and Roman influences. Mendell includes discussion on early Roman philosophies and various literary figures, including Martial, Horace, Catullus, and Pliny the Younger.

Nixon, Paul. *Martial and Modern Epigram.* New York: Longmans, Green and Co., 1927, 208 p.
  Describes the magnitude of Martial's influence on literature. Nixon comments: "The day of his direct influence upon much of the world's writing perhaps is done, but, be that as it may, the stamp already borne by so many of the things we prize in modern literature, MADE IN ROME, might often, very often, show the added words, BY MARTIAL."

Andrew Marvell

1621-1678

English poet and satirist.

INTRODUCTION

One of the last of the seventeenth-century metaphysical poets, Marvell is noted for his intellectual, allusive poetry, rich in metaphor and conceit. His work incorporates many of the elements associated with the metaphysical school: the tension of opposing values, metaphorical complexities, logical and linguistic subtleties, and unexpected twists of thought and argument. The poems generally thought to be his best, such as "To His Coy Mistress" and "The Garden," are characterized by an ambiguous complexity and a thematic irresolution which critics believe both define his talent and account for his appeal.

Biographical Information

The son of an Anglican clergyman and his wife, Marvell was born in Winestead-in-Holderness, Yorkshire. He received his early education at nearby Hull Grammar School, and later attended Trinity College at Cambridge University, where he earned his bachelor's degree in 1638 or 1639. For a period of four years in the next decade, he traveled in Europe, evidently employed as a tutor. By the early 1650s he was living at Nunappleton in Yorkshire, where he was tutor to the daughter of Sir Thomas Fairfax, retired commander-in-chief of the Commonwealth Army under Oliver Cromwell; it was during his stay at Nunappleton that Marvell wrote most of the lyric poems which now form the basis of his literary reputation. In 1657 he was appointed Assistant Latin Secretary to the Council of State through the influence of his friend John Milton. Two years later Marvell was elected Member of Parliament for Hull; from this point on he ceased to write lyric poetry, concentrating instead on political satire and polemics in prose. Marvell lived during a tumultuous period of British history. Although he did not actively participate in the Civil War, which broke out in 1642 while he was traveling in Europe, Marvell was deeply affected by the bitter fighting between the Royalists and Parliamentarians and later by Charles I's execution and Cromwell's assumption of the Protectorate. A dedicated, conscientious statesman, Marvell channelled all his energy and talent into his political career, serving in Parliament until his death. Although it has often been rumored that he was fatally poisoned by his political enemies, it is now generally accepted that he died of an accidental overdose of medicinal opiates.

Major Works

Marvell is the author of several very well-known verses. In perhaps his most famous poem, "To His Coy Mistress," the narrator importunes a woman to abandon her con-

cerns for her honor and become his lover, arguing that the transience of life and the inevitability of death necessitate their immediate enjoyment of sensual pleasure. Complicating the message of the poem, however, narrative irony and multivalent imagery undermine the apparent argument of the narrator. "An Horatian Ode," ostensibly a paean to Cromwell's military and political victories, includes a moving and sympathetic description of Charles I's execution that commentators have found inconsistent with the general impetus of the piece. In "The Garden," Marvell explores an individual's journey toward spiritual bliss; however, the validity of the narrator's pastoral garden retreat as a refuge from earthly cares and passions is compromised by Marvell's sensuous description of the garden itself, which critics have often remarked is couched in undeniably sexual language and imagery. "The Nymph Complaining for the Death of Her Faun" relates the story of a nymph whose pet fawn, given to her by a lover who has since proved unfaithful, has been killed by "wanton troopers." Narrated by the grieving nymph, the poem is unquestionably about loss and suffering, but beyond that there is no critical agreement.

Critical Reception

The history of critical assessment of Marvell's work is one of shifting focuses and sharp reversals. During his lifetime and the subsequent century, Marvell was known primarily for his political career; he was lauded as an upright, incorrigible statesman, his name becoming synonymous with disinterested patriotism. His poetry, when it was considered at all, was judged to be clever but of secondary importance. With the nineteenth century, critical opinion began to shift: critics of Marvell, though few in number, assigned his poetry a greater importance, while his prose works suffered a corresponding decline in popularity. In the twentieth century, Marvell's lyric poetry has come to be seen in an entirely new light, largely due to an essay of 1921 in which T. S. Eliot emphasized Marvell's metaphysical wit. Since being allied with the metaphysical school, Marvell has been viewed as a much more complex and rewarding poet. Critics contend that the thematic ambiguity of his poetry is indicative of his recognition of the potentials and possibilities of both sides of an issue. Many commentators have attributed Marvell's elusiveness not only to his characteristic thematic irresolution, but also to a deliberate ambiguity of style and language. Twentieth-century scholars have especially emphasized Marvell's adroit use of complex imagery and allegory, as well as his myriad allusive references, all of which tend to augment the difficulties of interpretation characteristic of his poetry. This complexity, critics believe, heightens the dramatic tension inherent in his ambiguous use of style, tone, and mood. Also noted as contributing to the general elusiveness of Marvell's meaning is his language play—puns, ambiguous syntax, and a complicated and frequently quite unexpected use of imagery, often imbuing a poem with a meaning directly contrary to that explicitly stated.

PRINCIPAL WORKS

Poetry

The First Anniversary of the Government under His Highness the Lord Protector 1655
Miscellaneous Poems 1681
The Complete Works in Verse and Prose of Andrew Marvell. 4 vols. (poetry and satire) 1872-75
The Poems and Letters of Andrew Marvell. 2 vols. (poetry and letters) 1927

Other Major Works

The Rehearsall Transpros'd (satire) 1672
The Rehearsall Transpros'd: The Second Part (satire) 1673
An Account of the Growth of Popery and Arbitrary Government in England (satire) 1677

CRITICISM

T. S. Eliot   (essay date 1921)

SOURCE: "Andrew Marvell," in *Selected Essays,* Harcourt Brace Jovanovich, Inc., 1950, pp. 251-63.

[*Perhaps the most influential poet and critic of the first half of the twentieth century, Eliot is closely identified with many of the qualities denoted by the term Modernism: experimentation, formal complexity, artistic and intellectual eclecticism, and a classicist view of the artist working at an emotional distance from his or her creation. The following essay, originally published on the occasion of the tercentenary of Marvell's birth, was pivotal in the revival of critical interest in Marvell's poetry. Here Eliot examines the nature of Marvell's wit.*]

The tercentenary of the former member for Hull deserves not only the celebration proposed by that favoured borough, but a little serious reflection upon his writing. That is an act of piety, which is very different from the resurrection of a deceased reputation. Marvell has stood high for some years; his best poems are not very many, and not only must be well known, from the *Golden Treasury* and the *Oxford Book of English Verse,* but must also have been enjoyed by numerous readers. His grave needs neither rose nor rue nor laurel; there is no imaginary justice to be done; we may think about him, if there be need for thinking, for our own benefit, not his. To bring the poet back to life—the great, the perennial, task of criticism—is in this case to squeeze the drops of the essence of two or three poems; even confining ourselves to these, we may find some precious liquor unknown to the present age. Not to determine rank, but to isolate this quality, is the critical labour. The fact that of all Marvell's verse, which is itself not a great quantity, the really valuable part consists of a very few poems indicates that the unknown quality of which we speak is probably a literary rather than a personal quality; or, more truly, that it is a quality of a civilization, of a traditional habit of life. A poet like Donne, or like Baudelaire or Laforgue, may almost be considered the inventor of an attitude, a system of feeling or of morals. Donne is difficult to analyse: what appears at one time a curious personal point of view may at another time appear rather the precise concentration of a kind of feeling diffused in the air about him. Donne and his shroud, the shroud and his motive for wearing it, are inseparable, but they are not the same thing. The seventeenth century sometimes seems for more than a moment to gather up and to digest into its art all the experience of the human mind which (from the same point of view) the later centuries seem to have been partly engaged in repudiating. But Donne would have been an individual at any time and place; Marvell's best verse is the product of European, that is to say Latin, culture.

Out of that high style developed from Marlowe through Jonson (for Shakespeare does not lend himself to these genealogies) the seventeenth century separated two qualities: wit and magniloquence. Neither is as simple or as apprehensible as its name seems to imply, and the two are not in practice antithetical; both are conscious and cultivated, and the mind which cultivates one may cultivate the other. The actual poetry, of Marvell, of Cowley, of Milton, and of others, is a blend in varying proportions. And we must be on guard not to employ the terms with too wide a comprehension; for like the other fluid terms with which literary criticism deals, the meaning alters with the age, and for precision we must rely to some degree upon the literacy and good taste of the reader. The wit of the Caroline poets is not the wit of Shakespeare, and it is not the wit of Dryden, the great master of contempt, or of Pope, the great master of hatred, or of Swift, the great master of disgust. What is meant is some quality which is common to the songs in *Comus* and Cowley's Anacreontics and Marvell's **"Horatian Ode."** It is more than a technical accomplishment, or the vocabulary and syntax of an epoch; it is, what we have designated tentatively as wit, a tough reasonableness beneath the slight lyric grace. You cannot find it in Shelley or Keats or Wordsworth; you cannot find more than an echo of it in Landor; still less in Tennyson or Browning; and among contemporaries Mr. Yeats is an Irishman and Mr. Hardy is a modern Englishman—that is to say, Mr. Hardy is without it and Mr. Yeats is outside of the tradition altogether. On the other hand, as it certainly exists in Lafontaine, there is a large part of it in Gautier. And of the magniloquence, the deliberate exploitation of the possibilities of magnificence in language which Milton used and abused, there is also use and even abuse in the poetry of Baudelaire.

Wit is not a quality that we are accustomed to associate with "Puritan" literature, with Milton or with Marvell. But if so, we are at fault partly in our conception of wit and partly in our generalizations about the Puritans. And if the wit of Dryden or of Pope is not the only kind of wit in the language, the rest is not merely a little merriment or a little levity or a little impropriety or a little epigram. And, on the other hand, the sense in which a man like Marvell is a "Puritan" is restricted. The persons who opposed Charles I and the persons who supported the Commonwealth were not all of the flock of Zeal-of-the-land Busy or the United Grand Junction Ebenezer Temperance Association. Many of them were gentlemen of the time who merely believed, with considerable show of reason, that government by a Parliament of gentlemen was better than government by a Stuart; though they were, to that extent, Liberal Practitioners, they could hardly foresee the tea-meeting and the Dissidence of Dissent. Being men of education and culture, even of travel, some of them were exposed to that spirit of the age which was coming to be the French spirit of the age. This spirit, curiously enough, was quite opposed to the tendencies latent or the forces active in Puritanism; the contest does great damage to the poetry of Milton; Marvell, an active servant of the public, but a lukewarm partisan, and a poet on a smaller scale, is far less injured by it. His line on the statue of Charles II, "It is such a King as no chisel can mend," may be set off against his criticism of the Great Rebellion: "Men . . . ought and might have trusted the King." Marvell, therefore, more a man of the century than a Puritan, speaks more clearly and unequivocally with the voice of his literary age than does Milton.

This voice speaks out uncommonly strong in the **"Coy Mistress."** The theme is one of the great traditional commonplaces of European literature. It is the theme of "O mistress mine," of "Gather ye rosebuds," of "Go, lovely rose"; it is in the savage austerity of Lucretius and the intense levity of Catullus. Where the wit of Marvell renews the theme is in the variety and order of the images. In the first of the three paragraphs Marvell plays with a fancy which begins by pleasing and leads to astonishment.

> Had we but world enough and time,
> This coyness, lady, were no crime,
> . . . I would
> Love you ten years before the Flood,
> And you should, if you please, refuse
> Till the conversion of the Jews;
> My vegetable love should grow
> Vaster than empires and more slow. . . .

We notice the high speed, the succession of concentrated images, each magnifying the original fancy. When this process has been carried to the end and summed up, the poem turns suddenly with that surprise which has been one of the most important means of poetic effect since Homer:

> But at my back I always hear
> Time's wingèd chariot hurrying near,
> And yonder all before us lie
> Deserts of vast eternity.

A whole civilization resides in these lines:

> Pallida Mors aequo pulsat pede pauperum tabernas,
> Regumque turris. . . .

And not only Horace but Catullus himself:

> Nobis, cum semel occidit brevis lux,
> Nox est perpetua una dormienda.

The verse of Marvell has not the grand reverberation of Catullus's Latin; but the image of Marvell is certainly more comprehensive and penetrates greater depths than Horace's.

A modern poet, had he reached the height, would very likely have closed on this moral reflection. But the three strophes of Marvell's poem have something like a syllogistic relation to each other. After a close approach to the mood of Donne,

> then worms shall try
> That long-preserved virginity . . .
> The grave's a fine and private place,
> But none, I think, do there embrace,

the conclusion,

> Let us roll all our strength and all
> Our sweetness up into one ball,
> And tear our pleasures with rough strife,
> Thorough the iron gates of life.

It will hardly be denied that this poem contains wit; but it may not be evident that this wit forms the crescendo and diminuendo of a scale of great imaginative power. The wit is not only combined with, but fused into, the imagination. We can easily recognize a witty fancy in the successive images ("my *vegetable* love," "till the conversion of the Jews"), but this fancy is not indulged, as it sometimes is by Cowley or Cleveland, for its own sake. It is structural decoration of a serious idea. In this it is superior to the fancy of "L'Allegro," "Il Penseroso," or the lighter and less successful poems of Keats. In fact, this alliance of levity and seriousness (by which the seriousness is intensified) is a characteristic of the sort of wit we are trying to identify. It is found in

> Le squelette était invisible
> Au temps heureux de l'art païen!

of Gautier, and in the *dandysme* of Baudelaire and Laforgue. It is in the poem of Catullus which has been quoted, and in the variation by Ben Jonson:

> Cannot we deceive the eyes
> Of a few poor household spies?
> 'Tis no sin love's fruits to steal,
> But that sweet sin to reveal,
> To be taken, to be seen,
> These have sins accounted been.

It is in Propertius and Ovid. It is a quality of a sophisticated literature; a quality which expands in English literature just at the moment before the English mind altered; it is not a quality which we should expect Puritanism to encourage. When we come to Gray and Collins, the sophistication remains only in the language, and has disappeared from the feeling. Gray and Collins were masters, but they had lost that hold on human values, that firm grasp of human experience, which is a formidable achievement of the Elizabethan and Jacobean poets. This wisdom, cynical perhaps but untired (in Shakespeare, a terrifying clairvoyance), leads toward, and is only completed by, the religious comprehension; it leads to the point of the *Ainsi tout leur a craqué dans la main* of Bouvard and Pécuchet.

The difference between imagination and fancy, in view of this poetry of wit, is a very narrow one. Obviously, an image which is immediately and unintentionally ridiculous is merely a fancy. In the poem **"Upon Appleton House,"** Marvell falls in with one of these undesirable images, describing the attitude of the house toward its master:

> Yet thus the leaden house does sweat,
> And scarce endures the master great;
> But, where he comes, the swelling hall
> Stirs, and the square grows spherical;

which, whatever its intention, is more absurd than it was intended to be. Marvell also falls into the even commoner error of images which are over-developed or distracting; which support nothing but their own misshapen bodies:

> And now the salmon-fishers moist
> Their leathern boats begin to hoist;
> And, like Antipodes in shoes,
> Have shod their heads in their canoes.

Of this sort of image a choice collection may be found in Johnson's *Life of Cowley*. But the images in the **"Coy Mistress"** are not only witty, but satisfy the elucidation of Imagination given by Coleridge:

> This power . . . reveals itself in the balance or

reconcilement of opposite or discordant qualities: of sameness, with difference; of the general, with the concrete; the idea with the image; the individual with the representative; the sense of novelty and freshness with old and familiar objects; a more than usual state of emotion with more than usual order; judgment ever awake and steady self-possession with enthusiasm and feeling profound or vehement. . . .

Coleridge's statement applies also to the following verses, which are selected because of their similarity, and because they illustrate the marked caesura which Marvell often introduces in a short line:

> The tawny mowers enter next,
> Who seem like Israelites to be
> Walking on foot through a green sea . . .

> And now the meadows fresher dyed,
> Whose grass, with moister colour dashed,
> Seems as green silks but newly washed . . .

> He hangs in shades the orange bright,
> Like golden lamps in a green night . . .

> Annihilating all that's made
> To a green thought in a green shade . . .

> Had it lived long, it would have been
> Lilies without, roses within.

The whole poem, from which the last of these quotations is drawn (**"The Nymph and the Fawn"**), is built upon a very slight foundation, and we can imagine what some of our modern practitioners of slight themes would have made of it. But we need not descend to an invidious contemporaneity to point the difference. Here are six lines from **"The Nymph and the Fawn"**:

> I have a garden of my own,
> But so with roses overgrown
> And lilies, that you would it guess
> To be a little wilderness;
> And all the spring-time of the year
> It only loved to be there.

And here are five lines from "The Nymph's Song to Hylas" in the *Life and Death of Jason*, by William Morris:

> I know a little garden close
> Set thick with lily and red rose.
> Where I would wander if I might
> From dewy dawn to dewy night,
> And have one with me wandering.

So far the resemblance is more striking than the difference, although we might just notice the vagueness of allusion in the last line to some indefinite person, form, or phantom, compared with the more explicit reference of emotion to object which we should expect from Marvell. But in the latter part of the poem Morris divaricates widely:

> Yet tottering as I am, and weak,
> Still have I left a little breath
> To seek within the jaws of death
> An entrance to that happy place;
> To seek the unforgotten face
> Once seen, once kissed, once reft from me
> Anigh the murmuring of the sea.

Here the resemblance, if there is any, is to the latter part of **"The Coy Mistress."** As for the difference, it could not be more pronounced. The effect of Morris's charming poem depends upon the mistiness of the feeling and the vagueness of its object; the effect of Marvell's upon its bright, hard precision. And this precision is not due to the fact that Marvell is concerned with cruder or simpler or more carnal emotions. The emotion of Morris is not more refined or more spiritual; it is merely more vague: if any one doubts whether the more refined or spiritual emotion can be precise, he should study the treatment of the varieties of discarnate emotion in the *Paradiso*. A curious result of the comparison of Morris's poem with Marvell's is that the former, though it appears to be more serious, is found to be the slighter; and Marvell's **"Nymph and the Fawn,"** appearing more slight, is the more serious.

> So weeps the wounded balsam; so
> The holy frankincense doth flow;
> The brotherless Heliades
> Melt in such amber tears as these.

These verses have the suggestiveness of true poetry; and the verses of Morris, which are nothing if not an attempt to suggest, really suggest nothing; and we are inclined to infer that the suggestiveness is the aura around a bright clear centre, that you cannot have the aura alone. The day-dreamy feeling of Morris is essentially a slight thing; Marvell takes a slight affair, the feeling of a girl for her pet, and gives it a connexion with that inexhaustible and terrible nebula of emotion which surrounds all our exact and practical passions and mingles with them. Again, Marvell does this in a poem which, because of its formal pastoral machinery, may appear a trifling object:

> CLORINDA. Near this, a fountain's liquid bell
> Tinkles within the concave shell.
>
> DAMON. Might a soul bathe there and be clean,
> Or slake its drought?

where we find that a metaphor has suddenly rapt us to the image of spiritual purgation. There is here the element of *surprise,* as when Villon says:

> Nécessité faict gens mesprendre
> Et faim saillir le loup des boys,

the surprise which Poe considered of the highest importance, and also the restraint and quietness of tone which make the surprise possible. And in the verses of Marvell which have been quoted there is the making the familiar strange, and the strange familiar, which Coleridge attributed to good poetry.

The effort to construct a dream-world, which alters English poetry so greatly in the nineteenth century, a dream-world utterly different from the visionary realties of the *Vita Nuova* or of the poetry of Dante's contemporaries, is a problem of which various explanations may no doubt be found; in any case, the result makes a poet of the nineteenth century, of the same size as Marvell, a more trivial and less serious figure. Marvell is no greater personality than William Morris, but he had something much more solid behind him: he had the vast and penetrating influence of Ben Jonson. Jonson never wrote anything purer than Marvell's **"Horatian Ode"**; this ode has that same quality of wit which was diffused over the whole Elizabethan product and concentrated in the work of Jonson. And, as was said before, this wit which pervades the poetry of Marvell is more Latin, more refined, than anything that succeeded it. The great danger, as well as the great interest and excitement, of English prose and verse, compared with French, is that it permits and justifies an exaggeration of particular qualities to the exclusion of others. Dryden was great in wit, as Milton in magniloquence; but the former, by isolating this quality and making it by itself into great poetry, and the latter, by coming to dispense with it altogether, may perhaps have injured the language. In Dryden wit becomes almost fun, and thereby loses some contact with reality; becomes pure fun, which French wit almost never is.

> The midwife placed her hand on his thick skull,
> With this prophetic blessing: Be thou dull . . .
>
> A numerous host of dreaming saints succeed,
> Of the true old enthusiastic breed.

This is audacious and splendid; it belongs to satire besides which Marvell's Satires are random babbling, but it is perhaps as exaggerated as:

> Oft he seems to hide his face,
> But unexpectedly returns,
> And to his faithful champion hath in place
> Bore witness gloriously; whence Gaza mourns
> And all that band them to resist
> His uncontrollable intent.

How oddly the sharp Dantesque phrase "whence Gaza mourns" springs out from the brilliant contortions of Milton's sentence!

> Who from his private gardens, where
> He lived reservèd and austere,
> (As if his highest plot
> To plant the bergamot)
>
> Could by industrious valour climb
> To ruin the great work of Time,
> And cast the kingdoms old
> Into another mold;
>
> . . . . .
>
> The Pict no shelter now shall find
> Within his parti-coloured mind,
> But, from this valour sad,
> Shrink underneath the plaid:

There is here an equipoise, a balance and proportion of tones, which, while it cannot raise Marvell to the level of Dryden or Milton, extorts an approval which these poets do not receive from us, and bestows a pleasure at least different in kind from any they can often give. It is what makes Marvell a classic; or classic in a sense in which Gray and Collins are not; for the latter, with all their accredited purity, are comparatively poor in shades of feeling to contrast and unite.

We are baffled in the attempt to translate the quality indicated by the dim and antiquated term wit into the equally unsatisfactory nomenclature of our own time. Even Cowley is only able to define it by negatives:

Comely in thousand shapes appears;
Yonder we saw it plain; and here 'tis now,
Like spirits in a place, we know not how.

It has passed out of our critical coinage altogether, and no new term has been struck to replace it; the quality seldom exists, and is never recognized.

In a true piece of Wit all things must be
Yet all things there agree;
As in the Ark, join'd without force or strife,
All creatures dwelt, all creatures that had life.

Or as the primitive forms of all
(If we compare great things with small)
Which, without discord or confusion, lie
In that strange mirror of the Deity.

So far Cowley has spoken well. But if we are to attempt even no more than Cowley, we, placed in a retrospective attitude, must risk much more than anxious generalizations. With our eye still on Marvell, we can say that wit is not erudition; it is sometimes stifled by erudition, as in much of Milton. It is not cynicism, though it has a kind of toughness which may be confused with cynicism by the tender-minded. It is confused with erudition because it belongs to an educated mind, rich in generations of experience; and it is confused with cynicism because it implies a constant inspection and criticism of experience. It involves, probably, a recognition, implicit in the expression of every experience, of other kinds of experience which are possible, which we find as clearly in the greatest as in poets like Marvell. Such a general statement may seem to take us a long way from **"The Nymph and the Fawn,"** or even from the **"Horatian Ode"**; but it is perhaps justified by the desire to account for that precise taste of Marvell's which finds for him the proper degree of seriousness for every subject which he treats. His errors of taste, when he trespasses, are not sins against this virtue; they are conceits, distended metaphors and similes, but they never consist in taking a subject too seriously or too lightly. This virtue of wit is not a peculiar quality of minor poets, or of the minor poets of one age or of one school; it is an intellectual quality which perhaps only becomes noticeable by itself, in the work of lesser poets. Furthermore, it is absent from the work of Wordsworth, Shelley, and Keats, on whose poetry nineteenth-century criticism has unconsciously been based. To the best of their poetry wit is irrelevant:

Art thou pale for weariness
Of climbing heaven and gazing on the earth,
Wandering companionless
Among the stars that have a different birth,
And ever changing, like a joyless eye,
That finds no object worth its constancy?

We should find it difficult to draw any useful comparison between these lines of Shelley and anything by Marvell. But later poets, who would have been the better for Marvell's quality, were without it; even Browning seems oddly immature, in some way, beside Marvell. And nowadays we find occasionally good irony, or satire, which lack wit's internal equilibrium, because their voices are essentially protests against some outside sentimentality or stupidity; or we find serious poets who are afraid of acquiring wit, lest they lose intensity. The quality which Marvell had,

this modest and certainly impersonal virtue—whether we call it wit or reason, or even urbanity—we have patently failed to define. By whatever name we call it, and however we define that name, it is something precious and needed and apparently extinct; it is what should preserve the reputation of Marvell. *C'était une belle âme, comme on ne fait plus à Londres.*

Christopher Hill   (essay date 1946)

SOURCE: "Andrew Marvell and the Good Old Cause," in *Mainstream,* Vol. 12, No. 1, January, 1959, pp. 1-27.

[*Hill is recognized as Great Britain's foremost historian of the English Revolution (1640-1660). In the following essay, which was originally published in 1946 in* Modern Quarterly, *he contends that Marvell's best poetry reflects the internal conflict and debate experienced by him as a result of contemporary sociopolitical upheaval during the English Revolution.*]

The purpose of this [essay] is to consider the poetry of Andrew Marvell in relation to the age in which he lived. Marvell wrote a good deal of political satire, which is of considerable interest to the historian, but has little poetic value; his greatest poems (except the **"Horatian Ode upon Cromwel's return from Ireland"**) have no direct reference to the political and social revolution of the seventeenth century. Yet this revolution transformed the lives of Englishmen; it faced them with intellectual and moral decisions which it was difficult to evade. I believe that if we study Marvell with a knowledge of the political background of his life we can discover in the great lyrics new complexities which will increase our appreciation of those very sensitive and civilized poems.

Marvell was born near Hull in 1621, his father being a clergyman of the Church of England—the only existing Church in those days before toleration for Dissent had been won. Andrew described his father as "a conformist to the established rites of the Church of England, though none of the most over-running or eager in them." Marvell went to Cambridge, then much the more Puritan of the two universities, and remained there until 1640. He then travelled on the Continent for four or five years, during which period the Civil War between Charles I and his Parliament broke out. Most of Marvell's friends at this time seem to have been aristocratic young cavaliers of the type he was likely to meet in Continental salons; and when he returned to England his own sympathies were apparently royalist. But we have no real evidence for his activities, and little for his views, until 1650, the year after the execution of Charles I. Then he wrote the **"Horatian Ode upon Cromwel's return from Ireland,"** from which it is clear that he was prepared to accept the triumphant revolution. In the following year he became tutor to Mary Fairfax, daughter of the famous general who had led the Parliamentary armies to victory. This suggests that he was already accepted as a sound parliamentarian. The period in Yorkshire with the Fairfaxes and the years immediately following seem to have been those in which his greatest poetry was written.

In his early thirties Marvell emerged as a more active supporter of the new Government. In 1653 he was personally recommended by no less a person than Milton as his assistant in the secretaryship for foreign tongues. Marvell failed to get this post then, becoming tutor to a ward of Oliver Cromwell instead. But in 1657 Marvell became Milton's colleague in the Latin secretaryship. Like Pepys, he was one of the new type of civilian middle-class official who came into their own after the Civil War, during the soberer years of the Protectorate. In 1658 Marvell was elected M.P. for Hull, for which he continued to serve in successive parliaments until his death in 1678. His correspondence shows him to have been an indefatigable defender of the interests of his constituency. But his main activity was as a pamphleteer for the parliamentary opposition to Charles II's governments and as a stalwart defender of religious liberty and freedom of thought, the struggle for which had originally attracted Milton and no doubt Marvell to the parliamentary side.

Despite his early royalist phase, then, Marvell became decidedly a partisan of the cause of Parliament: he was intimate with its noblest figures. He was not only the protégé of Milton, but also the friend of Harrington, shrewdest of the parliamentarian political thinkers, and of Baxter, most resolute of Nonconformist martyrs. Marvell accepted the revolution only in his late twenties; he was no juvenile or light-hearted enthusiast. But he remained stalwart to the "good old cause" in the dark days after 1660, his partisanship becoming increasingly open as the power of reaction grew. He ran great risks in attacking the cynical extravagance of the King, the brutalities of the advocates of religious persecution, and the treacherous activities of the pro-French party at court.

For the purposes of this [essay], I am going to assume what I believe to be the irresistible conclusions of modern research, that the conflicts of the interregnum were something far more like a "class struggle" than orthodox Whig accounts allow; and that there is some connection between puritanism and the "spirit of capitalism." The struggle was a continuation of that which had begun in the sixteenth century: a new competitive system, based on production for the market, with its new standards of conduct, its new morality of effort and self-discipline (Puritanism) was impinging on a static, loosely organized hierarchical society, based on the nearly self-sufficient village community and corporate town, with its traditional loyalties, its communal life and worship, its freedom from the bondage of the market. The battles of the Civil War were fought between the retainers of great lords (Newcastle's white coats) and Montrose's Highlanders, on the one hand, and on the other the New Model Army of the career open to the talents, financed by a new national tax levied by Parliament and by the loans of the merchants of London. Two civilizations were at war.

Marvell, as we have seen, came to be unreservedly on the parliamentary side in this struggle. His oft-quoted remark about the Civil War, "The Cause was too good to have been fought for," does not mean at all what those who cite it out of its context usually appear to think—that Marvell was disavowing "the good old cause." He meant, on the contrary, that the war *should* not have been fought be-

cause it *need* not have been fought, because the victory of Parliament was inevitable, war or no war. Here Marvell is following the historical and political theory of his friend Harrington, the author of *Oceana,* who argued that government must follow the balance of property. During the century before 1640 the bourgeoisie and the progressive section of the gentry had been buying up the landed estates of the King and the old aristocracy had gathered the bulk of the property of the kingdom into their hands. It was therefore inevitable, thought Harrington and Marvell, that political power must follow. "To come to Civil Laws, if they stand one way and the balance [of property] another, it is the case of a Government which of necessity must be new modelled; wherefore your lawyers advising you upon the like occasion to fit your Government to their laws are no more to be regarded than your tailor if he should desire you to fit your body to his doublet. . . . A monarchy divested of its nobility has no refuge under heaven but an army. Wherefore the dissolution of this Government [the Stuart would-be absolute monarchy] caused the war, not the war the dissolution of this Government." That is why Marvell, "upon considering all," thought that the cause of religion and of liberty was "too good to have been fought for." "The King himself," he continued—with pardonable exaggeration if we recollect that he was writing under Charles II's censorship—"being of so accurate and piercing a judgment, would soon have felt where it stuck. For men may spare their pains when Nature is at work, and the world will not go the faster for our driving. Even as our present Majesty's happy restoration did itself come, all things else happen in their best and proper time, without any need of officiousness."

"The war was begun in our streets before the King or Parliament had any armies," wrote [Richard Baxter in *A Holy Commonwealth,* 1659], another of Marvell's friends, in whose defense some of his greatest pamphlets were later to be written. As the tension within society became more acute, so a new type of lyric arose, charged with the most intense feeling of the age. These lyrics, unlike the Elizabethan, were no longer intended to be sung: they had lost their social function, and existed only to resolve the conflict within the poet's mind. The poet has become an isolated individual in a divided society, and his own mind is divided too: we find this internal conflict in poets so dissimilar as Marvell's early friend Lovelace, Crashaw and Vaughan.

The whole point of the conceit, indeed, from Donne to Traherne (precisely the revolutionary period) is that it lays incompatibles side by side, that it unites the apparently unrelated and indeed the logically contradictory, that it obtains its effects by forcing things different in kind on to the same plane of reference. In this broad sense we may speak of the lyric of conflict, whose characteristics are an awareness in the poet's mind of the new and troubling (especially the new scientific discoveries) as well as the old and familiar, and an effort to fit them into a common scheme—first by the violent and forced juxtaposition of Donne, then by the unresolved conflict of the later metaphysicals; until finally, after the victory of the new political and intellectual forces, we get a new type of poetry drawing on new philosophical assumptions, and disturbed by none of the doubts which have tormented the sensitive since the days of Shakespeare. The tortured conceit gives way to the neatly balanced rhymed couplet. This new equilibrium satisfied poets less and less in the second half of the century but was not finally upset until the fresh social and political crisis of the French Revolution—and Wordsworth.

Marvell's poetry is shot through with consciousness of a conflict between subjective and objective, between the idea and the reality, which it is perhaps not too far-fetched to link up (very indirectly, of course) with the social and political problems of his time.

—Christopher Hill

The existence of a conflict of some sort in Marvell is apparent from the most careless reading of his poems. At the risk of alienating some of my readers by an excessively crude and oversimplified statement, I wish to say briefly and dogmatically what I think may have underlain this conflict, and then to try to prove and illustrate this thesis. The suggestion is that Marvell's poetry is shot through with consciousness of a conflict between subjective and objective, between the idea and the reality, which it is perhaps not too far-fetched to link up (very indirectly, of course) with the social and political problems of his time. This conflict takes many forms, but we can trace a repeated pattern, a related series of symbols, which suggests that fundamentally all the conflicts are inter-related, and that this "double heart" (Marvell's phrase) is as much the product of a sensitive mind in a divided society as is Day Lewis's "divided heart." That of course is one reason why Marvell and the other "metaphysical" poets have so attracted our generation.

One of Marvell's qualities which is most sympathetic to us is his humor, his refusal to take his agonies too seriously. This is in itself one of the aspects of the "double heart," Marvell's ability to see both sides; but it also shows his attempt to come to terms with and to control the contradictions between his desires and the world he has to live in, his ideals and the brutal realities of the civil war. Humor is for Marvell one way of bearing the unbearable: it is a sign of his enviable maturity, besides which Waller, Cowley, Dryden and the other ex-royalist and future royalist panegyrists of Cromwell look so shabby. The opening lines of the **"Horatian Ode"** perfectly illustrate this aspect of Marvell's manner:

> The forward Youth that would appear
> Must now forsake his *Muses* dear.

Less than three years after writing these lines Marvell offered his services to the parliamentary cause, which he was never to desert in the remaining twenty-five years of his life. The light touch, the self-mockery, the hatred of the

portentous which are obvious in these lines should not obscure for us the genuine doubts and struggles, conflicts and despairs, which had preceded Marvell's acceptance of the position which he here states with an irony made possible only by deep conviction. Marvell has come through when he has gained this tone.

But I propose to defer consideration of the **"Horatian Ode"** until after we have looked at some of the lyrics, in which the political approach is less obvious. Let us begin with **"The Definition of Love,"** for here the points can be made merely by quotation:

> My Love is of a birth as rare
> As 'tis for object strange and high:
> It was begotten by despair
> Upon Impossibility.
>
> Magnanimous Despair alone
> Could show me so divine a thing,
> Where feeble Hope could ne'er have flown
> But vainly flapt its Tinsel Wing.
>
> And yet I quickly might arrive
> Where my extended Soul is fixt,
> But Fate does Iron wedges drive,
> And alwaies crouds it self betwixt. . . .
>
> And therefore her Decrees of Steel
> Us as the distant Poles have plac'd,
> (Though Loves whole World on us doth wheel)
> Not by themselves to be embrac'd. . . .
>
> As Lines so Loves *oblique* may well
> Themselves in every Angle greet:
> But ours so truly *Paralel*,
> Though infinite can never meet.
>
> Therefore the Love which us doth bind,
> But Fate so enviously debarrs,
> Is the Conjunction of the Mind,
> And Opposition of the Stars.

This is a very sophisticated poem, playing about with newly fashionable geometrical theories. The main point, obviously, is the one that I have already suggested as typical of Marvell—the conflict between Love and Fate, desire and possibility. Fate "defines" Love in both senses of the word—it both limits it and expresses its full significance. But the poem is far more than a clever conceit. The image in lines 11 and 12 is perfect for the age of Civil War. Fate is symbolized by the products of one of the industries which were transforming rural Britain, by the conventional symbol for warlike arms; and it "crowds itself betwixt" with irresistible force: here Fate is thought of as a tumultuous multitude of human individuals, as well as abstract military and industrial processes. Nor is fate merely an external force. [As M. C. Bradbrook and M. G. Lloyd Thomas have said in *Andrew Marvell*], "Material Fate and spiritual Love, though apparently in complete opposition, are in reality two aspects of the same situation."

> Magnanimous Despair alone
> Could show me so divine a thing.

If "the Stars" were not so completely opposed, the love could not reach such heroic stature.

The individual exposed to and triumphing over and

through the buffetings of Fate is the theme of the bombastic rhodomontade of **"The Unfortunate Lover"**:

> See how he nak'd and fierce does stand,
> Cuffing the Thunder with one hand;
> While with the other be does lock,
> And grapple, with the stubborn Rock: . . .

> This is the only *Banneret*
> That ever Love created yet:
> Who though, by the Malignant Starrs,
> Forced to live in Storms and Warrs:
> Yet dying leaves a Perfume here,
> And Musick within every Ear:
> And he in Story only rules,
> In a Field *Sable* a Lover *Gules.*

Marvell too had been forced "by the Malignant Starrs" to "live in Storms and Warrs"; his finest music was wrung out of him, I suggest, in the grapple with a stubborn world.

Let us examine some of the other poems with these symbols and our main thesis in mind.

The titles of many speak for themselves: **"A Dialogue Between the Resolved Soul, and Created Pleasure," "A Dialogue Between the Soul and Body."** In the first of these the conflict is between a militantly puritan soul, conscious of its mission, its calling, its arduous pilgrimage to heaven, on the one hand, and the distracting and illusory pleasures of the senses and of idleness on the other. In the second poem the conflict is more subtle:

> SOUL—O who shall, from this Dungeon, raise
> A Soul inslav'd so many wayes?
> With bolts of Bones, that fetter'd stands
> In Feet; and manacled in Hands.
> Here blinded with an Eye; and there
> Deaf with the drumming of an Ear.
> A Soul hung up, as t'were, in Chains
> Of Nerves, and Arteries, and Veins.
> Tortur'd, besides each other part,
> In a vain Head, and double Heart. . . .

> BODY—But Physick yet could never reach
> The Maladies Thou me dost teach;
> Whom first the Cramp of Hope does Tear:
> And then the Palsie Shakes of Fear.
> The Pestilence of Love does heat:
> Or Hatred's hidden Ulcer eat.
> Joy's cheerful Madness does perplex:
> Or Sorrow's other Madness vex.
> Which Knowledge forces me to know;
> And Memory will not forgoe.
> What but a Soul could have the wit
> To build me up for Sin so fit?
> So Architects do square and hew,
> Green Trees that in the Forest grew.

Here the antithesis is not just between soul and body, for the soul may betray the body as well as the body the soul: it is a complex, four-handed conflict, which blends the familiar themes of puritan asceticism against sensual pleasure with action against rest. (The symbolism of the last two lines is a favorite of Marvell's: the loss of certain natural qualities that the civilizing process makes inevitable. There seems, as will be shown later, to be a direct connection between this symbolism and the more obvious conflict of the Civil War.) The point is that Marvell's sympathies

are here less decisively on one side than they were in the **"Dialogue Between the Resolved Soul and Created Pleasure,"** where the moral issue was clear: here opposite concepts are jostling in Marvell's mind. (He is indeed one of the few parliamentarian writers—if we except Winstanley on the extreme left—who frankly enjoys and praises the pleasures of the body.)

The same complexity occurs in **"Upon Appleton House"**:

> As first our *Flesh* corrupt within
> Tempts impotent and bashful *Sin.*

This is not just good against evil, but evil that is also good against good that is also evil. In these complicated problems and relationships there are no easy solutions or evasions:

> To what cool Cave shall I descend,
> Or to what gelid Fountain bend?
> Alas! I look for Ease in vain,
> When Remedies themselves complain,

cried Damon the Mower. The Soul lamented to the Body that it was—

> Constrain'd not only to indure
> Diseases, but, whats worse, the Cure.

Again, in complex form, though with a different solution, conflict pervades **"To His Coy Mistress."** It is no longer soul against body, but the sensual pleasures up against the hard facts of an uncongenial world in which effort is demanded. The moral is not "Gather ye rosebuds while ye may." It is—

> Let us roll all our Strength, and all
> Our sweetness, up into one Ball:

> And tear our Pleasures with rough strife,
> Thorough the Iron gates of Life.
> Thus, though we cannot make our Sun
> Stand still, yet we will make him run.

That, as has been well said, is a Puritan rather than a libertine conclusion: the sensual pleasures are put into a subordinate place:

> Had we but World enough, and Time,
> This coyness Lady were no crime.

But as we have neither world nor time enough, coyness *is* a crime. The gates of life are iron, time's winged chariot is hurrying near—

> And yonder all before us lye
> Desarts of vast Eternity.

This strikes a note we shall find repeated. The individual and his desires come up against the outer world, life and time. The mock-serious moral of that flippant and very un-Puritan poem, **"Daphnis and Chloe,"** is the obverse of that of **"To his Coy Mistress"**; it is better to forego a pleasure than to be casual or half-hearted about it—

> Gentler times for Love are ment
> Who for parting pleasure strain
> Gather Roses in the rain,
> Wet themselves and spoil their Sent.

In the **"Coy Mistress"** mere epicureanism is *rejected* for a more rigorous coming to terms with reality. Again it is the old laxity and ease of the *rentier* ruling class at grips with the new effort, asceticism, concentration of puritanism and commercialism. And again iron symbolizes the harshness and impersonality of this world which we *must* accept.

The Mower, whose iron scythe cuts down himself as well as the grass, the innocent as well as the guilty, is a favorite symbol with Marvell. He appears in **"The Mower against Gardens," "Damon the Mower," "The Mower to the Glo-Worms," "The Mower's Song,"** and **"Upon Appleton House."** The theme of **"The Mower against Gardens"** is one which frequently recurs: it contrasts natural and artificial cultivation, the coarse toil and sweat of the mowers is set against the leisured sophistication, the luxury products of the garden. "Luxurious Man," the Mower says

> —First enclos'd within the Gardens square
> A dead and standing pool of Air:
> And a more luscious Earth for them did knead,
> Which stupifi'd them while it fed.
> The Pink grew then as double as his
>   Mind. . . .
> 'Tis all enforc'd; the Fountain and the Grot;
> While the sweet Fields do lye forgot.

And over all this ostentatious opulence the Mower stands brooding like Fate, confident in his power:

> The *Gods* themselves with us do dwell.

But the nostalgia for a simpler pre-commercial age is qualified by an irony of humorous over-statement which shows that Marvell was arguing a case in which he did not wholly believe:

> And *Fauns* and *Faryes* do the Meadows till,
> More by their presence then their skill.

(There is the same semi-serious regret in **"The Nymph complaining for the death of her Faun"**; see below).

The formal garden, as something essential to any gentleman's mansion, was relatively new in seventeenth-century England. There was still something exotically luxurious about it. "God Almighty first planted a garden," but they began to become common in England as a result of the Tudor peace, of the internal order and security which allowed manor houses to replace baronial castles and created the conditions in which lesser gentry, yeomen and merchants were able to prosper. In *The Faerie Queene* the garden is a symbol of the sheltered and opulent life of courtly society: Spenser follows in this the tradition of the mediaeval allegory of love. Bacon writes his essay to tell the very wealthy how a garden should be laid out. Stuart gardens, as the Mower has already told us, were still very formal: they were "the greatest refreshment to the spirit of man," as Bacon put it, *because* of their contrast with rude Nature in the unenclosed waste outside. It is thus easy to see how the garden became a symbol of security, property, ease, repose and escape: it was shut off from the commons, the open fields, the sweaty vulgar outside, from the Mower. For other seventeenth-century poets as well as Marvell and Milton the garden is normally Eden rather than Gethsemane.

If we take the garden as Marvell's equivalent of the ivory tower, the mere title of **"The Mower against Gardens"** is a political tract in itself. It is Fate, the historic process which lowers over these artificial and walled-off paradises, as Milton's Satan broods over the Garden of Eden.

The Mower is always a portentous figure:

> Sharp like his Sythe his Sorrow was,
> And wither'd like his Hopes the Grass.
>   [**"Damon the Mower"**]

When he is lost he is guided by glow-worms—

> —Country, Comets, that portend
> No War, nor Princes funeral,
> Shining unto no higher end
> Then to presage the Grasses fall.
>   [**"The Mower to the Glo-Worms"**]

War and the death of kings are never very far away, even if they only point a contrast. In this poem and in **"The Mower's Song"** the Mower is overcome by the power of love: Juliana—

> What I do to the Grass, does to my Thoughts
>   and Me.

(cf. the Fate and Love motive in **"The Definition of Love"** and **"The Unfortunate Lover"**). But in **"Upon Appleton House,"** as we shall shortly see, the Mower is directly related to the blind forces of the Civil War.

The garden had its deep attractions for Marvell in the years before he plunged into public life. For he had his escapism, of which the opening of **"The Garden"** is typical:

> How vainly men themselves amaze
> To win the Palm, the Oke, or Bayes;
> And their uncessant Labours see
> Crown'd from some single Herb or Tree.
> Whose short and narrow verged Shade
> Does prudently their Toyles upbraid;
> While all Flow'rs and all Trees do close
> To weave the Garlands of repose.

But even here the poet is tripped up: "Insnar'd with flow'rs, I fall on Grass." The calm and peace are transient, an interlude: "*Temporis O suaves lapsus!*" says the Latin version. The garden is a place of temporary repose and refreshment, not a permanent haven. The mind seeks an intenser satisfaction than the merely physical pleasures of the garden: it

> —Creates, transcending these,
> Far other Worlds, and other Seas.

The soul looks forward to further activity even while the body is at rest:

> Casting the Bodies Vest aside,
> My Soul into the boughs does glide:
> There like a Bird it sits, and sings,
> Then whets, and combs its silver Wings;
> And, till prepar'd for longer flight,
> Waves in its Plumes the various Light.

Whilst the soul thus anticipates eternity, the garden itself recalls Paradise before the Fall. But the ambiguous phrase "Garden-state" hints at England, and the terms of the comparison remind us that Marvell's garden is in and of this world:

> —'Twas beyond a Mortal's share
> To wander solitary there.

"Society is all but rude"; yet it needs impinge remorselessly upon the ideal world of escape, prevent it being final. Already in the second verse Marvell had doubted whether quiet and innocence were to be found at all on earth. The poem began by mocking at the vanity of human effort; in the last verse "th' industrious Bee" is introduced, who—lest we should have missed the significance of the adjective—"computes his time as well as we." The garden clock, for all its fragrance, reminds us of "Times winged Chariot." We cannot think ourselves out of time any more than we can escape from fallen humanity.

"The Nymph complaining for the death of her Faun" pictures a garden-Eden shattered by violence from without: the violence of soldiers:

> The wanton Troopers riding by
> Have shot my Faun and it will dye

Marvell plays with the idea later to be elaborated in the **"Horatian Ode,"** of the innocent victim sacrificially redeeming the users of violence, but here rejects it:

> Though they should wash their guilty hands
> In this warm life-blood, which doth part
> From thine, and wound me to the Heart,
> Yet could they not be clean: their Stain
> Is dy'd in such a Purple Grain.
> There is not such another in
> The World, to offer for their Sin.

There is no easy redemption. But the tone of the complaint is curious: "Ev'n Beasts must be with justice slain." The Faun symbolizes an escape, and is not uncritically regarded:

> Thenceforth I set my self to play
> My solitary time away,
> With this: and very well content,
> Could so mine idle Life have spent. . . .
> Had it liv'd long, I do not know
> Whether it too might have done so
> As *Sylvio* did: his Gifts might be
> Perhaps as false or more than be

As always in Marvell, the conflict is far from simple: he cannot wholly praise "a fugitive and cloistered virtue."

In **"The Coronet,"** the poet seeks "through every Garden, every Mead" for flowers to crown his Saviour (flowers "that once adorn'd my Shepherdesses head"). But—

> Alas I find the Serpent old
> That, twining in his speckled breast,
> About the flow'rs disguis'd does fold,
> With wreaths of Fame and Interest.

And the conclusion is—

> —Let these wither, so that he may die,
> Though set with Skill and chosen out with Care.

The garden is not enough.

In **"Upon Appleton House,"** Marvell's longest poem, all this symbolism becomes specific. The house has been a nunnery, which had come to the Fairfax family in the rough-and-tumble of the Reformation. In the poem the retirement, the cultured and indeed opulent ease of the nunnery is frankly opposed to the claims of a Protestant and commercial civilization. The words which Marvell writes of the earlier Fairfax who acquired the Church lands clearly presage the dilemma of the Fairfaxes, father and son, when they had to take sides in the Civil War:

> What should he do? He would respect
> Religion, but not Right neglect.

The elder Fairfax built his family mansion and his fortune on the site of the nunnery; the younger Fairfax took up arms in the name of liberty against the Lord's Anointed.

In the poem England before the Civil War is depicted as a garden, in which Fairfax—

> —did with his utmost Skill
> *Ambition* weed, but *Conscience* till.

(That other great parliamentary general, Oliver Cromwell, as we shall see when we come to analyze the **"Horatian Ode,"** left "his private Gardens, where He liv'd reserved and austere," at the call of duty in the Civil War.)

Fairfax's garden (or England) is clearly linked up with the Garden of Eden (stanzas XLI-XLIII), concluding:

> What luckless Apple did we tast,
> To make us Mortal, and The Wast?

The symbolism of the Mower, who blindly massacres all that he meets in "the Abbyss . . . of that unfathomable Grass," is repeated in stanzas XLVII-LIII, and the reference to the Civil War is again explicit:

> The Mower now commands the Field; . . .
> A Camp of Battail newly fought:
> Where, as the Meads with Hay, the Plain
> Lyes quilted ore with Bodies slain:
> The Women that with forks it fling,
> Do represent the Pillaging

War is no respecter of persons, cuts down the innocent and unconcerned together with the guilty:

> Unhappy Birds! what does it boot
> To build below the Grasses Root;
> Where Lowness is unsafe as Hight,
> And Chance o'retakes what scapeth spight? . . .
>
> Or sooner hatch or higher build. . . .
>
> —What below the Sith increast
> Is pincht yet nearer by the Beast.

Escapism brings no neutrality: the forces shaping our lives can neither be controlled nor evaded. This reintroduces Marvell's other theme of the need for equalizing desire and opportunity, the conflict brought to a crisis by the brutal external force of the Mower. Thus Marvell's key ideas are linked in one symbol, suggesting the possibility that all his poems really deal with a single complex of problems.

In **"Upon Appleton House"** there is humorously ironical escapism again (stanzas LXXI-LXXXI). The whole passage is of the greatest interest as evidence of Marvell's "double heart." On a careless reading the picture is one of ideal happiness, a Garden-of-Eden life, an escape particularly, from war:

> How safe, methinks, and strong, behind
> These Trees have I incamp'd my Mind;
> Where Beauty, aiming at the Heart,
> Bends in some Tree its useless Dart;
> And where the World no certain Shot
> Can make, or me it toucheth not.
> But I on it securely play,
> And gaul its Horsemen all the Day.

But again Marvell makes continual digs at his own dream world:

> Strange Prophecies my Phancy weaves. . . .
>
> I in this light *Mosaick* read.
> Thrice happy he who, not mistook,
> Hath read in *Natures mystick Book.*

(The heavy emphasis its position gives to "not mistook" can hardly be entirely without significance.)

> Thus I, easie *Philosopher,*
> Among the *Birds* and *Trees* confer. . . .
>
> The Oak-Leaves me embroyder all,
> Between which Caterpillars crawl;
> And Ivy, with familiar trails,
> Me licks, and clasps, and curles, and bales.
> Under this *antick Cope* I move
> Like some great *Prelate of the Grove.*

"Easie" prepares us for incomplete acceptance, and the political note would strike for contemporaries the requisite undertone of disapproved in the last lines quoted, even without the hint of "Caterpillars." A bishop and his vestments could not but call up reactions of hostility in a good parliamentarian (cf. "Safe from the Storms, and Prelat's rage" in **"Bermudas"**).

There is a snare hinted in the very placidity of this garden-world, in the attractions of its philosophy:

> And where I Language want, my Signs
> The Bird upon the Bough divines:
> And more attentive there doth sit
> Than if She were with Lime-twigs knit.

(Cf. **"The Garden"** and the passage about the falconer in the **"Horatian Ode,"** quoted below.) For all its fair seeming, this Eden does not really satisfy the poet:

> —Languishing with ease, I toss
> On Pallets swoln of Velvet Moss;
> While the Wind, cooling through the Boughs,
> Flatters with Air my panting Brows.

("In this time," Hobbes wrote in 1651, "that men call not onely for Peace, but also for Truth," flattery was not enough.) Chains are not less because men cling to them, nor are half-truths truths because sincerely held:

> Bind me ye *Woodbines* in your 'twines,
> Curle me about ye gadding *Vines,*
> And Oh so close your Circles lace.
> That I may never leave this Place:
> But, lest your Fetters prove too weak,

> Ere I your Silken Bondage break,
> Do you, *O Brambles,* chain me too,
> And courteous *Briars* nail me through.

The idyllic scene suddenly suggests the Crucifixion. And the succeeding stanzas show that escapism is not in fact Marvell's ultimate ideal. It is not the highest wisdom to discover "I was but an inverted Tree." For now Mary Fairfax enters. Whatever she symbolizes (and it is clear from stanza LXXXXI that she is associated with Puritan "Goodness" as well as Fairfaxian "Discipline"), there can be no doubt of the condemnation of "loose Nature" (cf. "easie Philosopher") in the lines describing her advent:

> See how loose Nature, in respect
> To her, it self doth recollect;
> And every thing so whisht and fine,
> Starts forth with to its *Bonnie Mine* . . .
>
> But by her *Flames,* in Heaven try'd,
> *Nature* is wholly *vitrifi'd.*
> 'Tis *She* that to these Gardens gave
> That wondrous Beauty which they have
> *She* streightness on the Woods bestows; . . .
>
> *She* yet more Pure, Sweet, Streight, and Fair,
> Then Gardens, Woods, Meads, Rivers are . . .
>
> For *She,* to higher Beauties rais'd,
> Disdains to be for lesser prais'd.
> *She* counts her Beauty to converse
> In all the Languages as *hers.*

Her wisdom subsumes and includes the wisdom of the garden, just as her discipline and morals reduce its luxuriance to order.

> Go now fond Sex that on your Face
> Do all your useless Study place,
> Nor once at Vice your Brows dare knit
> Lest the smooth Forehead wrinkled sit:
> Yet your own Face shall at you grin,
> Thorough the Black-bag of your Skin;
> When *knowledge* only could have fill'd
> And *Virtue* all those *Furrows* till'd.

The new standards and discipline transmute the old cosmos by putting it into its place, and a higher reality emerges:

> 'Tis not, what once it was, the *World;*
> But a rude heap together burl'd;
> All negligently overthrown,
> Gulfes, Deserts, Precipices, Stone.
> Your lesser *World* contains the same,
> But in more decent Order tame;
> *You Heaven's Center, Nature's Lap,*
> *And Paradice's only Map.*

(cf. **"Clorinda and Damon"**—

> DAMON—   These once had been enticing
>   things,
> *Clorinda,* Pastures, Caves, and Springs.
> CLORINDA—And what late change?
> DAMON— The other day
> *Pan* met me. . . .)

In many of the poems Marvell is concerned to show the mutual indispensability of apparent opposites. He says of Fairfax in **"The Hill and Grove at Bill-borow"**—

> Therefore to your obscurer Seats
> From his own Brightness he retreats:
> Nor he the Hills without the Groves,
> Nor Height but with Retirement loves.

In **"Bermudas"** the vision of the prefect haven (which is also an idealized England) is set between two quatrains which remind us unobtrusively of the difficulty of getting there.

The conflict in the poet's own mind between the attractions of an impossible life of communing with Nature and easy evasion of reality, and the necessity of coming to terms with the world, is shown in its most interesting from in the **"Horatian Ode upon Cromwel's return from Ireland."** This poem was probably written before the great lyrics, before Marvell entered the Fairfax household, but it is convenient to consider it here since to some extent it sums up the argument by its direct political reference.

> The forward Youth that would appear
> Must now forsake his *Muses* dear,
> Nor in the Shadows sing
> His numbers languishing . . .
> 'Tis Madness to resist or blame
> The force of angry Heavens flame:
> And, if we would speak true,
> Much to the Man is due,
> Who, from his private Gardens, where
> He liv'd reserved and austere,
> As if his highest plot
> To plant the Bergamot,
> Could by industrious Valour climbe
> To ruine the Great Work of Time,
> And cast the Kingdome old
> Into another Mold.
> Though Justice against Fate complain,
> And plead the antient Rights in vain:
> But those do hold or break
> As Men are strong or weak.

The poet is clearly arguing with himself rather than with Cromwell; and note the garden symbol again. Then there comes the famous passage in which the parliamentarian Marvell shows his sympathy for the old-world virtues of the executed Charles I, consoling himself with the vision of new life through sacrificial death:

> A bleeding Head where they begun,
> Did fright the Architects to run;
> And yet in that the *State*
> Foresaw it's happy Fate.

Again Marvell takes up the struggle with himself, and hints back at the lost ideals of the Garden in a passage where the needs of the State are again shown as triumphing over the private interests of the individual:

> So when the Falcon high
> Falls heavy from the Sky,
> She, having kill'd, no more does search,
> But on the next green Bow to pearch;
> Where, when he first does lure,
> The Falckner has her sure.

(The falconer is England, the State; but he is also Fate, the reality which has to be accepted, the historical process.) Marvell concludes reasonably on the side of action, the impossibility of neutrality:

> But thou the Wars and Fortunes Son
> March indefatigably on;
> And for the last effect
> Still keep thy Sword erect:
> Besides the force it has to fright
> The Spirits of the shady Night,
> The same *Arts* that did *gain*
> A *Pow'r* must it *maintain*.

("Shady," it will be observed, continues the symbolism; cf. "Shadows" in line 3.)

Critics have frequently commented on the rather left-handed compliment to Cromwell in this poem: his use of force and fraud is indeed a little openly praised. I suggest that this is part of Marvell's own internal struggle, and is evidence of his desire to be honest with himself. The artist in him dislikes the unpleasant actions which alone can "cast the Kingdome old into another Mold"; but like his master, Milton, Marvell has come to realize that the immortal garland is to be run for not without dust and heat. He has come down from the ivory tower into the arena.

In so far as Marvell is thinking of Cromwell at all, he is not treating him as an individual: the general is for the poet the personification of the revolution, the victory of the parliamentary cause over the King.

> Nature that hateth emptiness,
> Allows of penetration less:
> And therefore must make room
> Where greater Spirits come.

Cromwell draws his greatness from the events of which he has been the instrument—a view of history with which the Protector would have agreed and which Milton assumes in *Samson Agonistes*. For Marvell the revolution is "the force of angry Heavens flame," ruining "the great Work of Time," something real which must be accepted or rejected, which cannot be wished away nor even excluded from the garden. "'Tis Madness to resist or blame" an elemental power of this kind. "The world will not go the faster for our driving," but it will also not go the slower for our regrets. Wisdom is "To make their Destiny their *Choice*" (**"Upon Appleton House,"** line 744). In the **"Horatian Ode"** Marvell is clearly aware of a fusion of opposites, a synthesis at a higher level: the life of the community demands the death of the individual, rest is obtainable only through and by means of effort, eternal vigilance is the price of liberty, freedom is the knowledge of necessity.

But this paradox, this dialectical thought, recurs throughout Marvell's poems. The soul, in **"On a Drop of Dew"**—

> Does, in its pure and circling thoughts, express
> The greater Heaven in an Heaven less. . . .
> Moving but on a point below,
> It all about does upwards bend. . . .
> Congeal'd on Earth: but does, dissolving, run
> Into the glories of th' Almighty Sun.

It is also in **"Ametas and Thestylis making Hay-Ropes,"** ironically as in the **"Coy Mistress"** seriously. The solution of the conflict may not be the victory of either side, but a fusion of aspects of both from which something new emerges. We find the synthesis again in **"Eyes and Tears"**:

> How wisely Nature did decree,

With the same Eyes to weep and see!
That, having view'd the object vain,
They might be ready to complain. . . .

I have through every Garden been,
Amongst the Red, the White, the Green;

And yet, from all the flow'rs I saw,
No Honey, but these tears could draw. . . .

Thus let your Streams o'erflow your Springs,
Till Eyes and Tears be the same things:
And each the other's difference bears;
These weeping Eyes, those seeing Tears.

The suggestion then is that all Marvell's problems are inter-connected. They are the problems of an individual in an age of revolutionary change. I do not think the following lines from **"The Fair Singer"** were intended to be taken at more than their surface value (though one never knows with Marvell); but they could be interpreted as a perfect allegory of the influence of society on the individual:

I could have fled from One but singly fair:
My dis-intangled Soul it self might save,
Breaking the curled trammels of her hair.
But how should I avoid to be her Slave,
Whose subtile Art invisibly can wreath
My Fetters of the very Air I breath?

Soul and body, Love and Fate, illusion and reality, escape or action—all the poems in the last analysis deal with the adjustment of individual conduct to external conditions and forces. Marvell's life and his poetry form a single whole. I would also suggest that the resolution of the conflict revealed in the lyrics is almost exactly parallel to the resolution of the political conflict revealed in the political poems: the individual soul never can disentangle itself from society, never can save itself in isolation; "the very Air I breath" even in the remotest garden comes from outside. Since we cannot escape we must submit.

The resolution of the conflict revealed in Marvell's lyrics is almost exactly parallel to the resolution of the political conflict revealed in the political poems: the individual soul never can disentangle itself from society, never can save itself in isolation.

—Christopher Hill

The significance of this solution of his own crisis for Marvell is shown by the number of times he recurs to it. The moral of **"The First Anniversary of the Government under O. C."** is exactly the same as that of the **"Horatian Ode"**:

For all delight of Life thou then didst lose,
When to Command, thou didst thyself Depose;
Resigning up thy Privacy so dear,
To turn the headstrong Peoples Charioteer;

For to be *Cromwell* was a greater thing
Then ought below, or yet above a King:
Therefore thou didst thy Self depress,
Yielding to Rule, because it made thee Less.

The subordination of self to political purposes which he believed to be right: that is the lesson Marvell had taught himself once he found that he could not escape from the disagreeable realities of the world. It was not only Cromwell

—Whom Nature all for Peace had made,
But angry Heaven unto War had sway'd.
["A poem upon the Death of O. C."]

Like so many other parliamentarians, Marvell had been pushed reluctantly to approve of revolution and regicide since otherwise "religion and liberty" could not be secured. Here again the wise and virtuous man "makes his destiny his choice."

Far different Motives yet, engag'd them thus,
Necessity did them, but Choice did us.
["On Blake's Victory over the Spaniards"]

Marvell was a true Cromwellian, truer perhaps than Milton, who could not accept the new tactics of the restoration. For Marvell, as we have seen, the restoration illustrated the point that "things happen . . . without any need of officiousness." He had Cromwell's carelessness of forms of government, provided the root of the matter were secure. Yet Marvell has Milton's sense—a conception surely born of the agonies and triumphs and sufferings of the revolution? —of good through evil, of the impossibility of good without evil, of the meaninglessness of rejecting good because of concomitant evil. It was from the rind of one apple tasted in a garden that the knowledge of good and evil came into the world. Tearing our pleasures "with rough strife Thorough the Iron gates of Life" makes them greater, not less.

Thus, though we cannot make our Sun
Stand still, yet we will make him run.

That is the final triumph over circumstance. The highest praise of Cromwell was that he

—As the Angel of our Commonweal,
Troubling the Waters, yearly mak'st them Heal.
["The First Anniversary"]

Or as Endymion, who wanted the moon, said to Cynthia:

Though I so high may not pretend,
It is the same so you descend.
["Marriage of Lord Fauconberg and Lady Mary Cromwell"]

By the time of **"The First Anniversary"** and **"On Blake's Victory over the Spaniards,"** all Marvell's problems are solved: and the great poetry ceases. Marvell became a public servant, and his experiences in writing compact business prose helped him, with Pepys and Dryden, to contribute a fresh element of conciseness and clarity to English prose style. Though the restoration was to bring new complications, the inward assurance Marvell had so hardly won in the fifties was never lost. The poet became a pamphleteer as soon as he saw some of the returned cavaliers try to set the clock back to before 1640, trying to interfere with liberty of thought. With a purity of style reminiscent of Pascal, Marvell laughed down the enemies of religious toleration. The irreligious fashionable world enjoyed his polished and sophisticated wit no less than Paris had enjoyed the *Lettres Provinciales* in which Pascal had exposed the Jesuits. It is no part of my purpose to discuss Marvell's admirable prose, but it is perhaps worth recording the judgment of Miss Bradbrook and Miss Lloyd Thomas that its wit and ridicule are based on "a security of unquestioned and untroubled belief which gives him a standard by which he can relate the different levels of feeling, with their intensity." That is what we should have expected from our study of the poems.

This security, this stability in his political principles, this poised maturity and urbanity, are Marvell's peculiar strength: and they were won in the conflicts of the early fifties to which the great lyrics testify. In a lengthy simile in **"The First Anniversary,"** primitive man, terrified by the setting of the sun and the shadows, continues to look for light in the west, and is beginning to despair—

> When streight the Sun behind him he descry'd,
> Smiling serenely from the further side.

That is the dialectic of life and change as Marvell came to know it.

John Press   (essay date 1958)

SOURCE: *Andrew Marvell,* Longmans, Green & Co., 1958, 42 p.

[*Press is an English poet and critic who has published monographs on such poets as Marvell, Robert Herrick, Louis MacNeice, and John Betjeman. In the following excerpt, he surveys Marvell's verse, grouping his poems according to theme and tone.*]

We cannot date more than a handful of Marvell's poems with any precision and since even the most learned critics disagree about their order of composition it may be more helpful to group them roughly according to theme and tone, even if in doing so we are obliged to make certain assumptions about their chronological order. Bearing in mind our ignorance of dates, we may suggest the following crude and tentative grouping:

(I) Verse tributes to Villiers, Hastings and Lovelace; elegant and witty poems on love and on women, such as **"Mourning," "Eyes and Tears," "The Match," "The Fair Singer," "Daphnis and Chloe," "The Gallery," "The Unfortunate Lover"**; love poems in the pastoral convention, such as **"Ametas and Thestylis making Hay-Ropes," "Clorinda and Damon," "A Dialogue between Thyrsis and Dorinda."**

(II) Poems of retreat, contemplation and solitude, including those in which appear the Mower and Juliana; the finest poems in this group are **"The Garden"** and **"Upon Appleton House."**

(III) Poems of Marvell's full maturity on themes of love and death. **"To His Coy Mistress"** and **"The Definition of Love"** are the outstanding

poems in this group, to which we may add **"The Picture of Little T.C. in a Prospect of Flowers"** and possibly **"The Nymph complaining for the death of her Faun."**

(IV) Philosophical and religious poems, strongly tinged with a Puritan renunciation of worldly vanity. The outstanding poems in this group are **"On a Drop of Dew," "A Dialogue Between the Resolved Soul, and Created Pleasure," "A Dialogue between the Soul and Body,"** and **"The Coronet."**

(V) Poems celebrating Oliver Cromwell and the Protectorate, notably **"An Horatian Ode," "The First Anniversary of the Government under O.C.," "A Poem upon the Death of O.C.," "The Character of Holland," "On the Victory obtained by Blake"** and **"Bermudas."**

(VI) Satires of the reign of Charles II, to which may be added **"Fleckno, an English Priest at Rome,"** whose date of composition is unknown.

The early poems of Marvell are occasionally spoiled by a conscious self-indulgence in witty but frigid conceits, yet even in these slight, elegant lyrics one notices the assurance of the poet's control and the delicacy of his touch. In **"Mourning,"** for example, the poem moves through a succession of faintly cynical reflections upon Chlora's tears, rises to the beautiful penultimate stanza about the Indian slaves diving for pearls and ends with a gravely ironical judgment by the poet:

> I yet my silent Judgment keep,
> Disputing not what they believe:
> But sure as oft as Women weep,
> It is to be suppos'd they grieve.

The gradation of tone is managed with even more subtlety in **"Daphnis and Chloe,"** where the lover resists the importunities of his mistress who, too late, is bent upon giving herself to him at the very moment of parting. He breaks away from her in anguish, and then suddenly Marvell reverts to a cool speculation about masculine inconstancy and feminine coyness in the game of love:

> At these words away he broke;
> As who long has praying ly'n,
> To his Heads-man makes the Sign,
> And receives the parting stroke.
>
> But hence Virgins all beware.
> Last night he with *Phlogis* slept;
> This night for *Dorinda* kept;
> And but rid to take the Air.
>
> Yet he does himself excuse;
> Nor indeed without a Cause.
> For, according to the Lawes,
> Why did *Chloe* once refuse?

The pastoral poems also occasionally take an unexpected twist, for though Ametas and Thestylis end their duel of wits in the traditional country manner:

> Then let's both lay by our Rope,
> And go kiss within the Hay

Clorinda and Damon turn from love to sing the praise of

Pan, and Thyrsis and Dorinda prepare wine steeped in poppies that they may more speedily find Elizium.

Marvell's retreat into the solitude of Appleton House seems to have inspired poetry of a deeper, more reflective nature than any he had composed hitherto. The poems in which the Mower and Juliana appear, though they are partly love poems, and partly poems about the country-side, contain some darker and more serious undertones. Death is present and with his scythe mimics the destruction wrought upon the grass by the mower and upon the mower by Juliana:

> For *Juliana* comes, and She
> What I do to the Grass, does to my Thoughts
>   and Me.

Marvell reflects also upon man's relationship with Nature, and upon the way in which his ordering of the countryside is both a perfecting and yet a perversion of Nature:

> His green *Seraglio* has its Eunuchs too;
> Lest any Tyrant him out-doe.
> And in the Cherry he does Nature vex,
> To procreate without a Sex.

The world of nature held for Marvell a profound moral and spiritual import. Unlike Randolph and the French libertine poets, who used the garden as a symbol to inculcate a naturalist glorification of sensual indulgence, Marvell depicts it as the *hortus conclusus,* the enclosed garden of *The Song of Songs,* where the withdrawn and solitary intellect may pass beyond the senses and contemplate the Divine. We need not pause to investigate the precise debt (if any) that Marvell owed to Bonaventura, Hugh of St. Victor, Richard of St. Victor, Plotinus, Lipsius or the Divine Casimire. Such refinements of scholarship may serve to strengthen our understanding of **"The Garden"** and **"Upon Appleton House"**; but our first task must be to respond, by an exercise of imaginative sympathy, to the images and symbols which he employs in these poems of contemplative ecstasy.

"Upon Appleton House," for all its brilliance and variety, has seemed to many readers a muddled and uneven poem, because in it Marvell is trying to counterpoint a number of complex and diverse themes. He desires to pay a courtly, reasoned compliment to the Fairfaxes, and in the process to convey his admiration of the secure, harmonious life which a country house guarantees. This leads him to survey the history of the house, in the course of which he attacks the Catholic technique of sensual sublimation, contrasting it with the Puritan ideal personified in Mary Fairfax, a child soon to be become a woman. Fairfax's retirement from politics is lamented, because he might have saved England from the desolation which threatens it, the notion of England as a garden inspiring Marvell to a characteristically poignant, yet witty, stanza:

> Oh Thou, that dear and happy Isle
> The Garden of the World ere while,
> Thou *Paradise* of four Seas,
> Which *Heaven* planted us to please,
> But, to exclude the World, did guard
> With watry if not flaming Sword;
> What luckless Apple did we tast,
> To make us Mortal, and The Wast?

Marvell then passes to the central portion of the poem, his retreat into the countryside surrounding the house. The precise and loving description of the creatures thronging the woods, meadows and pools; an evocation of nature's teeming, elaborate richness; the play of a shimmering wit upon the objects of the poet's contemplation; a quaint humour, a steady piety and a soaring ecstasy are entwined by Marvell in this poem with a consummate artifice. He draws from the sight of the birds, insects, trees and plants the certainty reserved for those who find a pattern behind the fluctuations of the visible world, and rejoices in the strength that comes from rural solitude:

> Already I begin to call
> In their most learned Original:
> And where I Language want, my Signs
> The Bird upon the Bough divines;
> And more attentive there doth sit
> Then if She were with Lime-twigs Knit.
> No Leaf does tremble in the Wind
> Which I returning cannot find.
> Out of these scatter'd *Sibyls* Leaves
> Strange *Prophecies* my Phancy weaves:
> And in one History consumes,
> Like *Mexique Paintings,* all the *Plumes.*
> What *Rome, Greece, Palestine,* ere said
> I in this light *Mosaick* read.
> Thrice happy he who, not mistook,
> Hath read in *Natures mystick Book.* . . .
>
> How safe, methinks, and strong, behind
> These Trees have I incamp'd my Mind;
> Where Beauty, aiming at the Heart,
> Bends in some Tree its useless Dart;
> And where the World no certain shot
> Can make, or me it toucheth not.
> But I on it securely play,
> And gaul its Horsemen all the Day.

There follow stanzas that combine a formal compliment to Mary Fairfax with a description of nightfall:

> The modest *Halcyon* comes in sight
> Flying betwixt the Day and Night;
> And such a horror calm and dumb,
> *Admiring Nature* does benum.
>
> The viscous Air, wheres' ere She fly,
> Follows and sucks her Azure dy;
> The gellying Stream compacts below,
> If it might fix her shadow so;
> The stupid Fishes hang, as plain
> As *Flies* in *Chrystal* overt'ane;
> And Men the silent *Scene* assist,
> Charm'd with the *Saphir-winged Mist.*
>
> *Maria* such, and so doth hush
> The World, and through the *Ev'ning* rush.

After the praise of Mary Fairfax is concluded, this brilliant poem draws to its close with the conceit about the salmon-fishers, and with a final couplet that reinforces our sense of having traversed a world of rich sensual experience, now subject to the dark:

> Let's in: for the dark *Hemisphere*
> Does now like one of them appear.

"The Garden," though it is shorter and less widely-ranging than **"Upon Appleton House,"** is at once the most sensuous and the most philosophical of all Marvell's poems. Its concealed puns, tantalizing ambiguities and metaphysical complexity have, in recent years, given rise to many learned commentaries. Scholars have minutely investigated the sources and the precise connotation of the images which Marvell employs with such certainty and lyrical resonance—the bird waving its plumes, the melon, the garden itself; while the single word green (a favourite word of Marvell's) has been interpreted by reference to Renaissance colour-symbolism, hermetic speculation and mediaeval neo-Platonism, though in this context it is almost certainly meant to conjure up associations of freshness and innocence. Yet for all the latent word-play and subtle undertones which mould and colour the poem, its central theme is clearly defined.

After deprecating human ambition, Marvell launches into the praise of woodland solitude, contrasting the green of plants and trees with the emblematic colours of female beauty, white and red:

> No white nor red was ever seen
> So am'rous as this lovely green.

Even the god's pursuit of Daphne and Syrinx has as its true end their metamorphosis into laurel and reed.

Then follow three stanzas, which bring together the poem's leading motifs:

> What wond'rous Life in this I lead?
> Ripe Apples drop about my head;
> The Luscious Clusters of the Vine
> Upon my Mouth do crush their Wine;
> The Nectaren, and curious Peach,
> Into my hands themselves do reach;
> Stumbling on Melons, as I pass,
> Insnar'd with Flow'rs, I fall on Grass.
>
> Mean while the Mind, from pleasure less,
> Withdraws into its happiness;
> The Mind, that Ocean where each kind
> Does streight its own resemblance find;
> Yet it creates, transcending these,
> For other Worlds, and other Seas;
> Annihilating all that's made
> To a green Thought in a green Shade.
>
> Here at the Fountains sliding foot,
> Or at some Fruit-trees mossy root,
> Casting the Bodies Vest aside,
> My Soul into the boughs does glide:
> There like a Bird it sits, and sings,
> Then whets, and combs its silver Wings;
> And, till prepar'd for longer flight,
> Waves in its Plumes the various Light.

In this paradisal Garden, Woman being absent, even the Fall is innocent, as the contemplative soul prepares for its flight towards God.

Finally, after the rapt vision of these stanzas, Marvell returns again to the garden where Woman is excluded but where the industrious bee, symbol of social order, computes Time which is itself dependent on the living flowers woven into that sophisticated invention of man, the floral sundial:

> How well the skilful Gardner drew

> Of flow'rs and herbes this Dial new;
> Where from above the milder Sun
> Does through a fragrant Zodiack run;
> And, as it works, th' industrious Bee
> Computes its time as well as we.
> How could such sweet and wholsome Hours
> Be reckon'd but with herbs and flow'rs!

Less brilliant and ingenious than **"Upon Appleton House," "The Garden"** has a sustained piety and gravity, a perfectly controlled sensuous melody and a profound yet delicate wit that Marvell never surpassed. If indeed it was the last poem he wrote before quitting the Fairfax household for the 'uncessant labours' of public life, it was a worthy farewell.

"To His Coy Mistress" celebrates with passionate conviction the power and the ardour of physical desire. Yet even here Marvell's customary wit and intellectual control do not desert him, the poem unfolding with the rigorous exactitude of a mediaeval syllogism.

—John Press

Although Marvell insisted that there was no place for Woman in the Garden, he wrote two love-poems of the highest quality, one of which celebrates with passionate conviction the power and the ardour of physical desire. Yet even in **"To His Coy Mistress,"** Marvell's customary wit and intellectual control do not desert him, the poem unfolding with the rigorous exactitude of a mediaeval syllogism. It opens with a quiet, conversational remark:

> Had we but World enough, and Time,
> This coyness Lady were no crime.

In a series of extravagant conceits the lover assures his mistress that he would prolong his love-making indefinitely,

> And you should if you please refuse
> Till the Conversion of the *Jews*

which, according to ancient tradition, would take place immediately before the end of the world. Then follows the second movement of the poem which, though logically inevitable, achieves a poetic surprise by its swift change of tone:

> But at my back I alwaies hear
> Times winged Charriot hurrying near:
> And yonder all before us lye
> Desarts of vast Eternity.
> Thy Beauty shall no more be found;
> Nor, in thy marble Vault, shall sound
> My eccohing Song: then Worms shall try
> That long preserv'd Virginity:
> And your quaint Honour turn to dust;
> And into ashes all my Lust.
> The Grave's a fine and private place,

But none I think do there embrace.

Finally, the lover demands that he and his mistress should enjoy what John Donne calls 'the right true end of love'; yet despite the uncompromising sexuality of the lines quoted above and of the imagery in the poem's concluding lines, Marvell has invested the old classical commonplace of *carpe diem* with an intensity and a nobility that seem to affirm the triumph of love over time, in the teeth of the evidence:

> Let us roll all our Strength, and all
> Our sweetness, up into one Ball:
> And tear our Pleasures with rough strife,
> Thorough the Iron gates of Life.
> Thus, though we cannot make our Sun
> Stand still, yet we will make him run.

"The Definition of Love," though far less sensuous than **"To His Coy Mistress,"** conveys with equal force the longing of two lovers to be united:

> And yet I quickly might arrive
> Where my extended Soul is fixt,
> But Fate does Iron wedges drive,
> And alwaies crouds it self betwixt.

By means of geometrical and astronomical images Marvell develops the paradox that the lovers' separation is a proof of their spiritual correspondence, and a guarantee of their spiritual union:

> As Lines so Loves *oblique* may well
> Themselves in every Angle greet:
> But ours so truly *Paralel,*
> Though infinite can never meet.
> Therefore the Love which us doth bind,
> But Fate so enviously debarrs,
> Is the Conjunction of the Mind,
> And Opposition of the Stars.

"The Picture of little T.C. in a Prospect of Flowers," differing as it does in theme and tone from the love-poems, reminds us that fate and death shatter the most innocent dreams of youthful love. Little T.C., 'this Darling of the Gods', plays among the flowers, courted by Nature, aware only of life. In the third stanza Marvell introduces the image of the shade:

> Let me be laid,
> Where I may see thy Glories from some shade

as though to prepare us for the sudden turn of the poem in the final stanza, where the shadow of death falls upon this Arcady:

> But O young beauty of the Woods,
> Whom Nature courts with fruits and flow'rs,
> Gather the Flow'rs, but spare the Buds;
> Lest *Flora* angry at thy crime,
> To Kill her Infants in their prime,
> Do quickly make th' Example Yours;
> And, ere we see,
> Nip in the blossome all our hopes and Thee

There is still much controversy about the significance of **"The Nymph complaining for the death of her Faun."** To regard it as the lament of an Anglican for his stricken Church or as a conscious allegory of the Church's love for Christ crucified borders on the improbable: this is not to deny that there are in it unmistakeable references to *The Song of Songs* or that Marvell allowed these symbolic overtones to deepen the poem's imaginative richness and to enlarge its range. Overtly and primarily, it remains the lament of a young girl for her fawn, given to her by a faithless lover. The rhythm, the diction and the imagery are so dramatically appropriate that many readers will be content to accept the poem at its face value or, if they feel compelled to probe for a hidden meaning, may find in it a lamentation for love destroyed, not by time, fate or death, but by the sinful inconstancy of man.

Marvell, though a sensual and a religious man, did not, like Crashaw, explore the relation between divine and erotic love, for such a procedure would have been repugnant to his fastidious temperament even if it had not run counter to his doctrinal beliefs. He was indeed acutely aware of the conflicts between the warring impulses within himself, two of his dialogues being variations on this theme. In one of them, **"A Dialogue Between the Resolved Soul, and Created Pleasure,"** the soul wins the battle a shade too easily, the Chorus celebrating the victory with an operatic flourish:

> Triumph, triumph, victorious Soul;
> The World has not one Pleasure more:
> The rest does lie beyond the Pole,
> And is thine everlasting Store.

The scales are poised more evenly in **"A Dialogue between the Soul and Body,"** which opens with the complaint of the soul:

> O who shall, from this Dungeon, raise
> A Soul inslav'd so many wayes?
> With bolts of Bones, that fetter'd stands
> In Feet; and manacled in Hands.
> Here blinded with an Eye; and there
> Deaf with the drumming of an Ear.

Yet the body, which rebels against the even more insidious tyranny of the soul, is granted the last word:

> What but a Soul could have the wit
> To build me up for Sin so fit?
> So Architects do square and hew,
> Green Trees that in the Forest grew.

A recent commentator on this poem [A. Birrell, "Marvell's 'A Dialogue between the Soul and Body,'" *Downside Review,* No. 232 (1955)] has challenged the conventional view that it is deeply rooted in Christian theology, accusing Marvell of a 'deliberate indifferentism' to the problems of existence. There can be no disputing the fact that in the most moving of all his religious poems Marvell unequivocally renounces the subtlest lures of the world, sacrificing even the long-cherished illusion that his poems are garlands woven for Christ's head, and acknowledging that the Serpent lies hidden there. **"The Coronet"** invites comparison with George Herbert's "The Collar" in the exactitude with which its fluctuating rhythm mirrors the twists and turns of the recalcitrant spirit, in the harmonious progression of its imagery, and in the unaffected humility and grace of the poet's final surrender to God:

> But thou who only could'st the Serpent tame,
> Either his slipp'ry Knots at once untie,

And disintangle all his winding Snare:
Or shatter too with him my curious frame
And let these wither, so that he may die,
Though set with Skill, and chosen out with Care.
That they, while Thou on both their Spoils dost
     tread,
May crown thy Feet, that could not crown thy
     Head.

"An Horatian Ode upon Cromwel's Return from Ireland," presumably written in the early summer of 1650, was one of the three Cromwell poems which have been cancelled by the printer in all but two surviving copies of the 1681 *Miscellaneous Poems.* This alone casts grave doubt upon the modern supposition that it is a Royalist poem, though the mere fact that reputable scholars can put forward this hypothesis is a tribute to the extraordinary balance which Marvell preserved in the greatest of his political verses.

In 1672 Marvell wrote, of the Civil Wars:

> I think the cause was too good to have been fought for. . . . For men may spare their pains where nature is at work, and the world will not go the faster for our driving. Even as his present Majestie's happy Restoration did it self, so all things else happen in their best and proper time, without any need of our officiousness.

A similar recognition of historical necessity informs the "Ode," enabling Marvell to pay tribute to Charles I's serene courage upon the scaffold, and yet to acknowledge that his blood had to flow before a new order could be created out of chaotic violence:

> *He* nothing common did or mean
> Upon that memorable Scene:
> But with his keener Eye
> The Axes edge did try:
> Nor call'd the *Gods* with vulgar spight
> To vindicate his helpless Right,
> But bow'd his comely Head,
> Down as upon a Bed.
> This was that memorable Hour
> Which first assur'd the forced Pow'r.
> So when they did design
> The *Capitols* first Line,
> A bleeding Head where they begun,
> Did fright the Architects to run;
> And yet in that the *State*
> Foresaw it's happy Fate.

Marvell speaks of Cromwell with a kind of horrified awe, as if he were a destructive aspect of Nature, like three-forked lighting:

> Then burning through the Air he went,
> And Pallaces and Temples rent.

So, in Marvell's eyes, all the unscrupulous, destructive acts of Cromwell—the trapping of Charles at Carisbrooke, the massacre of the Irish, the coming subjugation of the Scots—are justified, because he is the product of fate:

> But thou the Wars and Fortunes Son
> March indefatigably on

and because, like a falcon, he still remains obedient to England the falconer.

The puns, ironies and ambiguities which give this **"Ode"** its peculiar tension cease to be puzzling once we understand how deeply all are imbued with Marvell's exultant sense of religious destiny that finds so perfect an expression in the weighty grandeur of the poem's metre and language.

Of the remaining poems written during the Commonwealth only **"Bermudas"** recaptures the impassioned vision of a divinely ordered society living in harmony with itself. The other two Cromwell poems, for all their energy and formal splendour, reveal a sense of strain, even of desperation, as if Marvell were aware that between England and chaos there stood only Cromwell, depicted as a cross between a Hebrew warrior-statesman and a Neo-Platonic mythological hero. By 1658 Marvell is moving away from the beautifully poised assurance of the earlier poems to the reiterated bludgeoning violence of the post-Restoration satires.

It is possible to argue that the satires do not represent a sad decline in Marvell's genius: but once we have allowed that they possess the rollicking vigour of good street ballads and a certain rough effectiveness we have said almost all there is to be said in their favour. The lines on young Douglas's death, and the set-piece on the vision of England which appears to Charles II (both in **"The Last Instructions to a Painter"**) glow with something of Marvell's former ardour:

> Like a glad Lover, the fierce Flames he meets,
> And tries his first embraces in their Sheets.
> His shape exact, which the bright flames infold,
> Like the Sun's Statue stands of burnish'd Gold.
> Round the transparent Fire about him glows,
> As the clear Amber on the Bee does close:
> And, as on Angels Heads their Glories shine,
> His burning Locks adorn his Face Divine.
>
> Paint last the King, and a dead shade of Night,
> Only dispers'd by a weak Tapers light;
> And those bright gleams that dart along and
>   glare
> From his clear Eyes, yet these too dark with
>   Care.
> There, as in the calm horrour all alone,
> He wakes and Muses of th' uneasie Throne:
> Raise up a sudden Shape with Virgins Face,
> Though ill agree her Posture, Hour, or Place:
> Naked as born, and her round Arms behind,
> With her own Tresses interwove and twin'd:
> Her mouth lock't up, a blind before her Eyes,
> Yet from beneath the Veil her blushes rise;
> And silent tears her secret anguish speak,
> Her heart throbs, and with very shame would
>   break.

More typical of the satires are the following passages, one taken from **"The Statue in Stocks-Market,"** describing Sir Robert Viner's statue of Charles II, and one from **"A Dialogue between the Two Horses"**:

> But Sir Robert affirms we do him much wrong;
> For the graver's at work to reform him thus
>   long.

275

But alas! he will never arrive at his end,
For 'tis such a king as no chisel can mend. . . .

More Tolerable are the Lion Kings Slaughters
Than the Goats making whores of our wives and
    our Daughters.
The Debauch'd and the Bloody since they
    Equally Gall us,
I had rather Bare Nero than Sardanapaulus.

The satires are, like *The Rehearsal Transpros'd,* larded
with crude jokes about vomiting, the bodily functions and
venereal disease; and spiced with wild accusations of secret crimes and unnatural vice. Unlike Dryden and Pope,
who are equally obscene but who contrive by sheer energy
and artifice to transcend their dirtiness, Marvell all too frequently gets stuck in his own filth. The fact seems to be
that as he grew older Marvell, for reasons which we can
only conjecture, suffered an emotional or even a physiological coarsening which betrays itself in the very rhythms
of his later poetry.

Yet Marvell himself may have believed the price worth
paying in order to safeguard the liberties of England. All
the poems published in his life-time sprang from a desire
to celebrate a public occasion, pay tribute to a friend, or
attack a specific evil, the later satires conforming precisely
to Marvell's conception of the poet's task as defined in
"Tom May's Death":

When the Sword glitters ore the Judges head,
And fear has Coward Churchmen silenced,
Then is the Poets time, 'tis then he drawes,
And single fights forsaken Vertues cause.
He, when the wheel of Empire, whirleth back,
And though the World's disjointed Axel crack,
Sings still of ancient Rights and better Times,
Seeks wretched good, arraigns successful
    Crimes.

Marvell's lonely and perilous opposition to Charles II's
government matches in faith and courage the defiant gesture of the Cavalier Sir Robert Shirley, whose epitaph in
Staunton Harold church records that:

in the year 1653, when all things sacred were
throughout the nation either demollisht or pro-
faned, Sir Robert Shirley baronet founded this
church, whose singular praise it is to have done
the best things in the worst times, and hoped
them in the most calamitous.

Even if it is true that Marvell's place in English literature
is secure only because he wrote a handful of lyrics which
display an intuitive moral and aesthetic certainty as rare
as the perfection of their phrasing, to concentrate on them
alone would be to distort Marvell's true image. The dusty
political and religious causes for which he laboured in the
last twenty years of his life, although to us they may seem
not worth the devotion he gave them, were to Marvell of
supreme importance. Had he cared less passionately for
things other than poetry his verse might have lacked the
urgency, the gravity and the resolute dignity that lend it
so fine a distinction. Little as we may concern ourselves
with the quarrels of seventeenth-century Englishmen, and
with the part which Marvell played in them, we shall find
that a lively sympathy for the aspirations of the puritan

and the patriot will help us to understand more fully the
achievement and the stature of the poet.

**Frank Kermode on the pedantic quality of recent
Marvell scholarship:**

After a lapse of a dozen or more years I have been looking at the reports of the learned on Marvell's poetry, and
I cannot believe that I am alone in my dismay at their
treason. The trouble . . . had begun before. One was accustomed to being told to look for the key of **"The Garden"** in Plotinus or in Bonaventura. History of ideas is
a slippery discipline. . . . [And now] everybody seems
even clumsier, less aware of the tact required, and of the
uselessness of specially got-up learning as an instrument
to investigate "a quality of civilisation.". . .

Scholarship is not barren of itself, but in relation to the
kind of programme it ought to have, the kind implied in
Eliot's essay [on Marvell]. It needs this humane justification, and it needs a sense of the civilised probabilities.
Further, it needs an habitually suspicious attitude to
one's scholarly self-regard. . . .

Marvell's Hobbesian opponent Parker disliked the poetic habit of relating metaphor and allegory to reality.
"These schemes do not express the nature of things but
only their similitudes and resemblances," he complained. But who, in fact, "puts us off with nothing but
rampant metaphors and pompous allegories"? Marvell
only rarely; his modern interpreters, who do not share
his power to control the figures by means of a civil poetic, constantly.

*Frank Kermode, in "Marvell Transprosed," in
Encounter XXVII, No. 5 (November 1966).*

Joseph J. Moldenhauer   (essay date 1968)

SOURCE: "The Voices of Seduction in 'To His Coy Mistress': A Rhetorical Analysis," in *Texas Studies in Literature and Language,* Vol. X, No. 1, Spring, 1968, pp. 189-
206.

[*Moldenhauer is a German-born American educator and
critic. In the following essay, he explicates Marvell's "To
His Coy Mistress."*]

Obedient to the neoclassical aesthetic which ruled his age,
Andrew Marvell strove for excellence within established
forms rather than trying to devise unique forms of his
own. Like Herrick, Ben Jonson, and Campion, like Milton
and the Shakespeare of the sonnets, Marvell was derivative. He held imitation to be no vice; he chose a proven
type and exploited it with a professionalism rarely surpassed even in a century and a land as amply provided
with verse craftsmen as his. Under a discipline so willingly
assumed, Marvell's imagination flourished, producing superb and enduring examples of the verse types he attempted: of the emblem poem in **"On a Drop of Dew"**; of the
allegorical debate in **"A Dialogue between the Resolved**

Soul and Created Pleasure"; of the devotional meditation in "The Coronet"; of the philosophical elegy in "The Nymph Complaining for the Death of Her Fawn"; of the metaphysical lyric, following Donne, in "The Definition of Love" and "The Garden"; of the pastoral love lament in the four "Mower" poems; of the commendatory verse portrait in "The Picture of Little T. C."; and of the ode in "An Horatian Ode upon Cromwell's Return from Ireland." Like Jonson's and Herrick's best poems, these by Marvell are conspicuous for their grace, their poise and balance, their architectural firmness of structure, their precision of language, and their sure command of tone.

When he undertook to write a *carpe diem* lyric in "To His Coy Mistress," Marvell was working once more within a stylized form, one of the favorite types in the Renaissance lyric catalogue. Again he endowed the familiar model with his own special sensibility, composing what for many readers is the most vital English instance of the *carpe diem* poem. We can return to it often, with undiminished enthusiasm—drawn not by symbolic intricacy, though it contains two or three extraordinary conceits, nor by philosophical depth, though it lends an unusual seriousness to its theme—but drawn rather by its immediacy and concreteness, its sheer dynamism of statement within a controlled structure.

The *carpe diem* poem, whose label comes from a line of Horace and whose archetype for Renaissance poets was a lyric by Catullus, addresses the conflict of beauty and sensual desire on the one hand and the destructive force of time on the other. Its theme is the fleeting nature of life's joys; its counsel, overt or implied, is Horace's "seize the present," or, in the language of Herrick's "To the Virgins,"

> Gather ye Rose-buds while ye may,
> Old Time is still a flying.

It takes rise from that most pervasive and aesthetically viable of all Renaissance preoccupations, man's thralldom to time, the limitations of mortality upon his senses, his pleasures, his aspirations, his intellectual and creative capacities. Over the exuberance of Elizabethan and seventeenth-century poetry the pall of death continually hovers, and the lyrics of the age would supply a handbook of strategies for the circumvention of decay. The birth of an heir, the preservative balm of memory, the refuge of Christian resignation or Platonic ecstasy—these are some solutions which the poets offer. Another is the artist's ability to immortalize this world's values by means of his verse. Shakespeare's nineteenth and fifty-fifth sonnets, for example, employ this stratagem for the frustration of "Devouring Time," as does Michael Drayton's "How Many Paltry, Foolish, Painted Things." In such poems the speaker's praise of the merits of the beloved is coupled with a celebration of his own poetic gift, through which he can eternize those merits as a "pattern" for future men and women.

The *carpe diem* lyric proposes a more direct and immediate, if also more temporary, solution to the overwhelming problem. Whether subdued or gamesome in tone, it appeals to the young and beautiful to make time their own for a while, to indulge in the "harmless folly" of sensual

enjoyment. Ordinarily, as in "To His Coy Mistress" and Herrick's "Corinna's Going A-Maying," the poem imitates an express invitation to love, a suitor's immodest proposal to his lady. Such works are both sharply dramatic and vitally rhetorical; to analyze their style and structure is, in effect, to analyze a persuasive appeal.

Before turning to the text of "To His Coy Mistress," [from *The Poems and Letters of Andrew Marvell,* edited by H. M. Margoliouth (1927) deriving from *Miscellaneous Poems by Andrew Marvell* (1681)], I would declare certain of my critical presuppositions, even at the risk of rehearsing commonplaces. If "rhetoric" is taken to mean "verbal embellishment" or "decorative writing," all literature is necessarily rhetorical. But the narrower and commoner definition, "persuasive discourse," is also applicable. When we speak of the rhetoric of a poem in this sense, we do not imply that its author steps forth and confronts us, man to man, to engage in instruction or special pleading. Rather, we refer to a persuasive effort within the poem's hypothetical situation, and we attribute this effort not to the author as a biographer would regard him, but to the *persona,* the personality he has devised as the speaker of his work. The persona is technically distinguishable from the author (the human agent, "doing and suffering") even in didactic poetry. And when an author creates two or more speakers for a dialogue poem or a play, none of the voices of the work will be his own, however much one of them may serve as spokesman for his values.

Confining the discussion to univocal poems, we understand, moreover, that the speaker's rhetoric is directed toward another literary personage. Though silent, the *addressee* of the poetic situation is more or less definable. Between him and the audience proper there exists an imaginative distance similar in kind to that which separates the author from the speaker. To be sure, many poems address a "generalized audience." It would seem that epics, for instance, speak to us directly. Yet in reading such works, are we not invited or required to put on a "generalized" identity distinct from our particular selves? The univocal poem appeals at the very least to some abstraction of ourselves. Insofar as we obey this summons we are made over into that sort of addressee which the poet has designed. The addressee is more objectively realized as a "character" in dramatic monologues, verse prayers, and love poems. Here the poet's authority in creating the addressee is obvious; in the former case it is less conspicuous but equally significant. Like the reader of a devotional lyric or a love poem, the reader of the epic enjoys a measure of detachment. This distance between the actual audience and the addressee of a poem was of sufficient importance to John Stuart Mill that he made it central to his conception of poetry. Defining literary discourse by contrast to overt persuasion, Mill wrote, "eloquence is *heard*; poetry is *overheard*."

Implied throughout these reflections is an analogy between poems—however lyrical or "personal"—and dramas. This relationship has been examined by John Crowe Ransom, who observes [in *The World's Body,* 1938] that while the two are not generically identical, poetry "maintains faithfully certain dramatic features. The poet does not speak in his own but in an assumed character, and not in the actual but in an assumed situation." Poems are "little dramas, exhibiting actions in complete settings." Tension is the grand prerequisite of drama, and in stage plays (as in dialogue poems) the conflicting interests are assigned to separate personae. Only slightly less dramatic are those numerous poems (including **"To His Coy Mistress"**) in which the presence of a particular addressee, with particular interests and motives, is assumed in the very mode of address. The dramatic view may be extended even to the meditative poem. Though the speaker here muses in solitude, addressing himself alone, the tensions among the themes, images, and structural units of the lyric comprise the dramatic agon of the work. Standing for various motives or attitudes in the speaker, they serve as so many "voices," so many "characters," in the poem.

Analysis of **"To His Coy Mistress"** need not begin with this refinement of the dramatistic approach, however useful it may prove at last, for the poem presents a distinct dramatic and rhetorical situation. Its central agon pits the speaker's desire for erotic fulfillment against the hesitancy of his lady. Within its dramatic confines the language of the poem is a mimesis of persuasion or (in a variation upon Mill's aphorism) "rhetoric overheard". . . .

Rhetorical analysis of the poem requires first an adequate conception of the persona, his lady, and the circumstances which evoke his argument or appeal. The speaker's urbanity is at once apparent. No newcomer to love, no apprentice to the craft of wooing, he exhibits a sophistication born of long experience. He must therefore be envisaged, I think, as a man of mature years—neither youthfully sentimental and self-indulgent about love, nor so exhausted by age that he can summon no energy for the present endeavor. His eloquence, his wit, and his concern for the logic of his argument place him among the educated, while his self-assurance and poise are the attributes of a courtier. A virile, attractive figure, he seems quite as impatient of delay as that persona of Suckling's, who exclaims,

> Out upon it! I have loved
> Three whole days together.

Marvell's speaker, however, enjoys a finer gift of self-control and a more flexible wit.

Though the lady of the poem is given no active verbal role, we derive an image of her through her suitor's statements and implications. She is by no means his concubine: to take "Mistress" in its derogatory modern sense would be to reduce the poem to nonsense. We learn, of course, that she has preserved her virginity; but even if this information were not given, the speaker's rhetoric would lack an intelligible motivation were the lady his accomplished lover. "Mistress" here carries its older meaning of sweetheart or beloved—the woman who commands one's affections. Like her distant literary grandame, the Laura of Petrarch's sonnets, and like the numberless ladies of the courtly love tradition since Petrarch, the mistress in Marvell's poem is both fair and cruel. Proud of her beauty, she not only relishes but *expects* her lover's praise. Her coyness, her reluctance to yield to his advances, has about it an air of deliberate display which again recalls the disdainful women of earlier lyrics, who demand that their suitors prove their worthiness by interminable gestures of adoration and patient fidelity. Her social position is no lower than the speaker's; if she were, say, the innkeeper's daughter, his eloquence would be gratuitous. She is probably younger than he, and somewhat less sophisticated—though worldly enough, it would appear, to appreciate his wit.

Like Donne's "The Canonization," **"To His Coy Mistress"** implies a remark by the addressee, before the poem proper, to which the speaker's language constitutes a response. In the former lyric the addressee is a practical man who has advised the persona that love is wasting his time and substance. In **"To His Coy Mistress"** the lady's assumed remark is something on this order: "Not yet; we have time. Court me further, and keep saying beautiful things." Her suitor's response, accordingly, discusses their courtship and love under the categories of those "Iron gates" of life—the mortal limitations, specified in the opening line, of space and time. The structure of his statement is neatly tripartite, each strophe or verse paragraph possessing its own distinctive grammar, imagery, and tone or quality of voice and each serving a precise logical function in the *carpe diem* argument. Structurally, the poem resembles a syllogism of which the first section is a suppositional premise and the second a premise of refutation. The concluding third part, in the light of these premises, has all the authority of a necessary deduction.

In the opening section, the speaker presents the vision of a courtship wholly free from the restraints of space and time—a condition in which the lady's reluctance, far from being objectionable, takes on positive value, since it provides the continual occasion for praise. All history becomes the lovers' own: they "*have*" time in their power as their wooing extends backward into the remote past—ten years before the Flood—and forward into the unimaginable future—till the conversion of the Jews. It is an idyllic, almost a paradisic, vision: like the unfallen first parents, the lovers enjoy eternal life, and the world is their moist and pleasant garden. Images of water and of leisurely growth are conspicuous in this section, as the lady is imagined in a setting appropriate to her beauty and social rank—the exotic banks of the Ganges—while the speaker, with stylized, painless melancholy, laments her coyness by the shores of the chilly Humber. The grandeur and power of the antique world are further evoked by the image of the speaker's love growing "Vaster then Empires, and more slow." With the magnanimity of an ancient monarch, he pours forth his treasures and bestows them on his queen. As well as gathering rubies in their realms, she receives from him the richer gift, the higher "state" or ceremonial tribute, of a flattery protracted through centuries, millennia, ages. Within the terms of this vision, then, the opening section is a stupendous act of homage to the lady's charms.

But the vision is at all times undercut by reminders of its unreality. First and most importantly, the grammar of the section is subjunctive, and every verb conforms to the mood of the opening condition: "*Had we but* World enough, and Time." Behind any optative or conditional statement lurks the rejoinder that what it expresses might not, or cannot, be true to fact. Each image of delight and each gesture of flattery in the first paragraph contains its own refutation, as the persona makes the subjunctive mood his grammatical instrument of irony. The development of the section, furthermore, can be described as a progressive joke or a *reductio ad absurdum* of the notion that there is "World enough, and Time." Each of the pleasant situations the speaker envisages is more unlikely than its predecessor. The first, "We would sit down, and think which way / To walk, and pass our long Loves Day," seems plausible; and "long . . . Day," as the first elaboration upon "enough," does not arouse disbelief. But that the speaker and his lady should be found, in the next three lines, at opposite ends of the earth is distinctly improbable. The two ensuing couplets propose an impossibility, taking the condition beyond the realm of fact, and taking the vision of extended courtship far beyond all human reality. From this point onward the ludicrous dominates—both in the image of the suitor's "vegetable Love" (of which more will be said presently) and in the hyperbolic sequence of time units from "An hundred years" through "An Age at least." These lines, 13 through 18, may remind us of Bergson's definition of the comic predicament: "something mechanical encrusted on the living" [*Laughter: An Essay on the Meaning of the Comic,* translated by C. Brereton and F. Rothwell]. Devoid of spontaneity, devoid almost of will, the machine-like speaker will turn out huge quantities of praise.

Behind the ironic mask his point is, of course, that time and space do not suffice for the kind of wooing which the lady expects and which the courtly love conventions prescribe. The opening section parodies several of these formulas: the inventory of the lady's matchless features, the requirement upon her suitor to offer her an almost religious admiration, and the indefinite suspension of the physical act. I would by no means suggest that Marvell was the first or only writer to ridicule courtly conventions. The stereotypes and the whole system of love-Platonism which underlay them had been fair game for ironic poets throughout the high Renaissance. Shakespeare's 130th sonnet—to glance at but one English instance—mocks the standard similes for women's charms:

> My mistress' eyes are nothing like the sun;
> Coral is far more red than her lips' red;
> If snow be white, why then her breasts are dun;
> If hairs be wires, black wires grow on her head.
> I have seen roses damask'd, red and white,
> But no such roses see I in her cheeks;
> And in some perfumes is there more delight
> Than in the breath that from my mistress reeks.
> I love to hear her speak, yet well I know
> That music hath a far more pleasing sound;
> I grant I never saw a goddess go;
> My mistress, when she walks, treads on the
>   ground:
> And yet, by heaven, I think my love as rare
> As any she beli'd with false compare.

Like Shakespeare's speaker, the suitor of **"To His Coy Mistress"** exposes the inadequacy and insincerity of the conventional modes of praise. His emphasis upon the mechanical character of his flatteries demonstrates to his mistress that such gestures are at best a hollow and passionless routine.

These major ironies are supported by a number of lesser ones in the imagery of Section I. "Ten years before the Flood" and "Till the Conversion of the *Jews*" serve most directly to describe an enormous tract of time for the pleasures of wooing; but both of these termini suggest the death of the world. If the waters of the Ganges are timeless, mystical, and romantic, those of Noah's flood imply human fallibility and catastrophic punishment. As for the conversion of the Jews, it was supposed that this would take place just before the final destruction of earth. Equivocal implications are likewise to be found in the phrase, "My vegetable Love." According to an Aristotelian distinction, popular in Renaissance science, man's nature was compounded of three elements or "spirits," which linked him—for he was a microcosm or little world—with the macrocosm or universe. He shared the highest of these elements, the *rational,* with God and the angels. The intermediate element, called the *sensitive* spirit, he held in common with the beasts: it provided him with sensation, mobility, and will. The last of the three was the *vegetative* spirit, the principle of simple life and growth, which he shared with the plants. A "vegetable Love" is not, then, merely a love which grows slowly: it is a *rudimentary* love, something less than human and even less than bestial. Inevitably, too, the phrase "My vegetable Love" evokes a visual image, the absurd picture of a gigantic plant—a squash vine, say—spreading itself over the earth in green imitation of Alexander's conquests. The final irony of Section I lies in its last word, "rate," by which the persona calls attention once more to the mechanical, statistical nature of the praise he would bestow upon his mistress. In addition, the commercial meaning of the term dehumanizes the lady, transforming her organic features into things—rare commodities on the market—which command, it seems, an excessive price.

Low over this strophe hangs an air of artifice and unreality which cannot be attributed entirely to the supposition contrary to fact. Everything in these lines seems remote, dreamlike, somehow drugged. The cadences are slow and regular; the images lethargic or static. The timeless world of the vision is motionless as well: the lovers do not walk but "think which way / To walk" as they *sit down* to plan their leisurely courtship, and they simply *appear* by the Ganges and the Humber. The speaker's vegetable love grows imperceptibly. In the itemized flattery of lines 13-18, the rate of progression slows down to less than a snail's pace. Thus, while the main rhetorical function of Section I is to refute its own vision, to show that the lovers are *not* free in space and time, the speaker also reveals that even in imagination, immunity from human restraints would be intolerable.

If in the opening verse paragraph the speaker's voice is jocular or teasingly ironic, with an undertone of pessimism, in the second it is essentially somber, though tempered by macabre humor. The transitional term "but" signals a shift in logic and rhetoric, and the suitor's argument turns from hypothesis to fact, from a wish-fulfillment dream of freedom to an authentic nightmare of mortal constraint.

The dominant verbal mood is now indicative rather than subjunctive, and the tense is future rather than indefinite. The prospect the speaker offers in this strophe *will* come to pass if the lady persists in her coyness.

The world he projects in this portion of the argument is at once the antithesis and the echo of the idyllic suppositional vision. There he examined time as a function and servitor of love; here he considers love *sub specie temporis,* love as a function of time and of time's instrument, death. Both worlds, it should be noted, are equally static and enervated; but the immobility which reigns in the second vision differs significantly from the suspended animation in the first. The stillness now results from time's authority over the lovers, rather than the reverse. Pleasure and perpetual life are superseded by pain and a quite different version of timelessness, the "vast Eternity" of oblivion in death. No longer does the speaker pretend that he and his mistress "have" time; he now acknowledges how fatally time possesses *them*:

> But at my back I alwaies hear
> Times winged Charriot hurrying near:
> And yonder all before us lye
> Desarts of vast Eternity.

"Times winged Charriot" most immediately designates the mythological car of Apollo, the sun god, which measures off the passage of the days; but in this context it suggests, further, the armored vehicle of some ancient lord of war. The imagery of imperial conquest, associated earlier with the speaker himself, is now attached to time—the speaker becoming, by contrast, a helpless and hunted wretch. Time, in this metaphysical symbol, looms as a pursuer so terrible and merciless that his victim dares not turn to face him. Barbaric time behind them and emptiness ahead, the lovers can flee in no direction. Though eternity is "vast," vaster yet than the empire of love, their lot will be enforced confinement as time and tomb alike close in. There will indeed be endless space and time, the speaker suggests, but not for *them* to rule over, to enjoy in courtship, or even to understand.

Unlike the hospitable and watery vistas of Section I, the landscape of the future is parched, sterile, and desolate. The faculties of sensual delight are reduced to "dust" and "ashes"; and in the "Desarts of vast Eternity" no refuge can be seen. The rich rubies of the earlier vision are succeeded by pale memorial marble; and the languid image of a vegetable love gives way not only to the sterility of the inorganic desert and dust, but also to the animal rapacity of the charioteer and the hungry grave-worms. The rhythms of the antistrophe, ponderous as a knell, are even slower than those in Section I. "Desarts of vast Eternity," its most important line with respect to cadence, begins with a solemn trochaic thud, proceeds, in seventeenth-century pronunciation, through the three-fold repetition of the long *a* sound on alternating syllables, and comes at last to the full stop of a period.

Both visions presuppose that the mistress will continue to withhold her favors; and in the second, the suitor declares outright that no courtship can take place in the grave. In developing this theme, however, he portrays a ghastly *equivalent* of love in death—a version of Eros so shocking as to constitute the most powerful of arguments against coyness and "quaint Honour." We might summarize the major irony of Section I as the denial, through conditional grammar, hyperbolic progression, equivocal allusion, and comic imagery, of the timeless condition and the lavish praise to which that strophe is devoted. In Section II, on the contrary, the speaker's irony resides in his *affirmation,* through metaphor, of a morbid species of love, at the same time as he declares love impossible in that none-too-distant future. Even as he asserts that his "ecchoing Song" will not be heard in the lady's tomb, he creates the very image he excludes. Together with the lady, we hear a futile lyric resounding from the pallid walls. Death becomes, in the images of the antistrophe, a seducer who will not be refused, taking the place of the unsuccessful speaker; and death as a lover is to the last degree unflattering and crude. In that "fine and private place," the grave as love-nest, death clasps the now wholly defenseless and unresisting mistress: "Worms shall try / That long preserv'd Virginity." The grim image of deflowerment is echoed in the next line, "And your quaint Honour turn to dust," where the persona puns on "quaint." "Honour," in seventeenth-century diction as today, refers to woman's chastity and good reputation for the same virtue. "Quaint" has more numerous meanings in this context: "peculiar," "prim," "fastidious," "ingenious," and "artful" or "cunningly designed." Most interestingly, "quaint" is an old vulgarism denoting, in the Elizabethan John Florio's definition, "a woman's privities." To paraphrase, then: long preserved or defended in life, and however well preserved or embalmed in the tomb, the mistress's celebrated maidenhead is not proof against worms. The curious and pretentious honor associated with her "quaint," and the "quaint" itself, will yet be reduced to insubstantial dust.

The pun on "quaint" amplifies a bawdy overtone in "Vault." Trained Latinist that he was, Marvell would have been at least as sensitive to the word's possibilities as was Shakespeare, who wrote in *Henry the Fifth* of "caves and womby vaultages of France" (II, iv, 124). The anatomical meaning of "vault," "one or another of certain concave structures or surfaces normally facing downward," was used as early as 1549, while the denotation of drain or sewer (and thus, by extension, privy) is even older. "Vault" as a verb had been first applied to sexual congress well before Marvell's day: the *OED* illustration, "Whiles he is vaulting variable ramps (prostitutes)," is taken from *Cymbeline,* I, vi, 134. "Vaulting-house" was a common seventeenth-century synonym for "brothel." The connection between the architectural reference and the anatomical and erotic senses goes beyond parallels of shape and motion: the Latin word for arch or vaulted chamber was *fornix,* from which "fornicate" derives. In a transferred sense *fornix* also designated a brothel, while the English adjectives "fornicate" and "fornicated" have been employed since the sixteenth century for vault-shaped structures. Milton exploited this association in *The Reason of Church-Government,* where he punned, "[she] gives up her body to a mercenary whordom under those fornicated arches which she cals Gods house" (Columbia ed., III, 268). Although "vault" refers to the womb or vagina in none of the instances recorded in the *OED,* it would appear that Marvell has concealed such a reference, either metaphorical or punning, in **"To His Coy Mistress"**: he could draw upon both the current vulgar meanings of "vaulting" and the subtle etymological and semantic links between "vault," *fornix,* "fornication," "brothel," "sewer," and "privy" (cf. "private place," line 31). The context of the term permits the interpretation of an "ecchoing Song" in the "marble Vault" as another obscene parody, in death, of the sexual consummation which the lady presently denies her suitor.

Sexual innuendo had played a minor role in the opening vision, as the speaker pledged himself to devote "thirty thousand" years to adoring the "rest" of his mistress's charms—gazing, that is, upon what lies below eyes, forehead, and breasts. In the second section, erotic *double-entendre* and the incongruous prospect of death as seduction are the major resources of irony. And common to the innuendo in both sections is the idea of abnormal love: in the first, voyeurism, or the substitution of visual for all other forms of gratification; in the second, necrophilism, or the substitution of a dead for a living partner. More specifically yet, these implied perversions are both, like the ruling atmosphere of parts I and II of the argument, characterized by an unwholesome passivity.

It has been objected on historical and philosophical grounds that Hegel's dialectic formula of thesis-antithesis-synthesis does not accurately label the structure of **"To His Coy Mistress."** Perhaps the special kind of syllogism Marvell's persona employs is named in scholastic philosophy; but the critics have not, to my knowledge, discovered its proper descriptive label. I see no hazard in using the term "dialectic" for the relationship of the three parts of this poem, particularly of the first with the second, or in describing the third as a "synthesis" of the oppositions which precede. In so doing I assign no particular philosophical meanings to the words, but construe them in a logical and rhetorical sense only.

The opening word of Section III, "Now," establishes the present as the speaker's temporal reference, and the next word, "therefore," signals a necessary synthesis or resolution of conflict. We note at once the shift of verbs into the present tense, and the change of mood into the imperative, the true modality of *carpe diem.* This grammatical transformation has a clear psychological purpose in the suitor's argument, insofar as the present tense affords release from the dreamlike conditional of the first strophe and the terrifying future of the second. Two trances are broken, two unhealthy visions of inactivity are dispelled, as the speaker adopts the imperative mood for his statements. The imperative present verbs at last depict the lovers as *agents* in the realm of possibility. Having advised his mistress of what they *would do* under wildly impossible conditions, and what *will be done to them* in the future, he now tells her what they *can do* in a realistic present—or, to be more precise, he exhorts that they do these things. Any imperative implies that what it enjoins can be accomplished. Though each of the first two visions contains its own ironic antitheses, and though the second section directly counters the first, lines 1 through 32 are fundamentally absolutist in outlook. Section III can be seen as the grand qualification of all dogmatism in the foregoing debate. It is the "comic

corrective," [as Kenneth Burke might say—see his *Attitudes Toward History,* 1961], for the pessimism of the second strophe as well as for the idealism of the first.

Another grammatical feature worth noting is the predominance, in the final strophe, of the first person plural pronouns "us," "our," and "we." Almost every action in the earlier visions is performed by or upon the lovers singly, and the unilateral character of those acts reinforces the impression of their aberrancy, their inappropriateness to normal love. Now, actions are dually performed. The separate "I" and "thou" unite as one compound agent under one name, and their grammatical union corresponds to the sexual communion which this section demands.

The voice of Section III, like its grammar, is active and urgent. This strophe is pre-eminently one of dynamic images and of vigorous, kinetic verbs—"sport us," "devour," "roll," "tear," "make," "run." After the suspended animation of the preceding visions, the impression of motion and life is overwhelming. The poem's movement may be said to duplicate the rhythm of sexual intercourse: its first two paragraphs, in which the gamesomeness of wit and the pleasure of verbal display are combined with the pain of sinister meanings, defer almost intolerably the emotional climax which occurs in the final fourteen lines, yet lead to it inevitably. In any event, that strategic delay through thirty-two lines gives rhetorical force to the full-voiced *carpe diem* of the last strophe, just as, from the rational standpoint, the materials of Sections I and II must wait upon Section III for their synthesis. The solution to the conflict of sensual desire and mortal limitation which the speaker now overtly proposes is this: frankly acknowledging their subjection to space and time, the lovers can achieve temporary triumph, brief freedom, through a sexual consummation which makes them, for a while, oblivious to the burdens and fully sensitive to the advantages of their humanity.

Many of the images of freshness, fertility, and power which characterize this section of the argument are reversals or transposed echoes of earlier imagery. The moist, timeless dream gardens of the initial vision are now plausibly realized in the "youthful hew" which rests on the mistress's skin "like morning dew." ("Lew," or warmth, the other common emendation of the text at this point, supports the impression of a moist flush almost as well as "dew" and anticipates the "instant Fires" of line 36; but the rarity and regional quality of "lew" seem inconsistent with the diction of **"To His Coy Mistress."**) Similarly, "transpires" and "pore" reflect the "vegetable Love" of the first section, but without the earlier connotations of involuntary growth. Now, the succulent figure is endowed with urgency and active passion; the lady's *"willing* Soul" emits "instant Fires" as rational, sensitive, and vegetative spirits are equally aroused. No longer seen as a series of separate "charms"—eyes, forehead, breasts, *et cetera*—or as a moldering corpse, the mistress is presented as vibrantly alive and organically integral. If "the Conversion of the *Jews*" suggested a world in flames, and if the image of cold ashes depicted a love gone dead for want of fuel, the "instant Fires" of passion here create as they consume; from that sexual dying the speaker and his lady can rise again repeatedly, phoenix-fashion, as do Donne's lovers in "The Canonization."

I indicated earlier that the *carpe diem* poem differs markedly from many of the great love lyrics of the Renaissance in its advocacy of a physical, rather than an aesthetic, solution to the problem of time. In **"To His Coy Mistress"** art is not only subordinated to spontaneous nature; it is shown as a hindrance and a delusion. The pseudo life of the opening vision, including its superficially "natural" images of water and vegetation, is conceived, we will remember, in conventional literary terms: all is artificial, false, and stylized. Far from "immortalizing" physical beauty, the speaker's extended praise and his song ("complaint") at the Humber's banks, together with the rest of the initial supposition, are an unsatisfactory verbal surrogate for reality. His overt refutation of this fictive world in the second verse paragraph incorporates a disclaimer of the poet's ability to preserve his lady's charms: "Thy Beauty shall no more be found; / Nor, in thy marble Vault, shall sound / My ecchoing Song." It is small wonder, then, that references to poetry are absent from the final strophe, where physical life prevails.

Images of animal rapacity, used so startlingly before to describe time's fatal power over the lovers, appear again in the third verse paragraph, but in lines 37 through 40 the original relation is inverted. Time's "slow-chapt pow'r," the force of his slowly grinding jaws or beak, recalls the brutal charioteer, his viceroy death, and, more concretely yet, the things that feed on corpses. Instead of submitting helplessly to time's maw, the lovers can themselves become carnivorous creatures, "am'rous birds of prey," who "devour," in their brief present, the devourers of the future. By "sporting" themselves, taking their pleasure, they "eat up their time," as the colloquialism has it, and they feed ferociously. In this reversal of the image, as in the representation of sex as an affectionate "strife" and the seeming contradiction of the last couplet, the speaker employs a strategy of paradox not unlike Donne's "Death, thou shalt die."

The figure of the ball, in lines 41-42, is interesting on several counts. It looks back to Apollo's chariot and anticipates the sun reference in the last couplet; but further, it names the microcosm, the *sphere* of autonomous space and time, which the lovers can become through passion, and which they could not attain to in the earlier visions. A specifically erotic innuendo, furthermore, is harbored in the metaphor of the ball, though unlike the *double-entendres* of the earlier sections it is in no wise aberrant. The speaker offers it without a leer; the rolling ball suggests the lovers, literally conjoined, exerting "all their strength" and sharing "all their sweetness" in the sexual act. By implication, then, the "Iron gates of Life" through which they "tear" their pleasures are the lady's maidenhead, as well as the restraints of space and time. Earlier, her "quaint Honour" had been associated with the cold, resistant walls of the marble vault, impenetrable by the speaker; only the grave-worm, awful proxy for the human phallus, could gain entrance and reduce the maidenhead to dust. Though the "woman's privities" are now represented by an even more inflexible image, the iron portals cannot resist the lovers' efforts.

The paradox in the concluding couplet admits of a simple resolution: though the suitor and his mistress are powerless to stop the passage of time, their acts of passion, absorbing all thought and energy, figuratively "make" time pass swiftly. Free from anxiety about time's progress as they devour their brief days in pleasure, the lovers are, for all practical purposes, time's tyrants. In a once-familiar joke, an angry father, reprimanding his insolent son, tells him to stand up in his presence. Lolling in an easy chair, the youth refuses to comply. "Sit down, then," shouts the father, "I *will* be obeyed!" The last two lines of **"To His Coy Mistress"** comprise a similar jest. Let us recall that the first strophe was developed as an incremental or hyperbolic joke, ending with the punch line, "Nor would I love at lower rate." Section II, with its grotesque coupling of sex and death, might be described as a sick joke, aptly culminating in the sardonic lines, "The Grave's a fine and private place, / But none I think do there embrace." The wit of the last verse paragraph is bawdy, its punch line a paradox in which the lovers cannot be losers. While sex as a stratagem for overcoming time may be a fraud, it is a necessary and comforting illusion, endorsed by the mind and body alike.

Tempted to paradoxes of my own, I will assert that the vitality and uniqueness of **"To His Coy Mistress"** arise from its formal discipline and underlying conventionality; and that for all its seriousness it is a comic poem, while for all its levity it is deeply serious. To account for the permanent value of **"To His Coy Mistress"** I think we should look to its aesthetic autonomy and distance. Neither the familiarity of the *carpe diem* materials nor the richness of Marvell's verbal patterning would give the poem special recommendation outside their controlling dramatic context. The gestures which make up this "little drama," this action complete in itself, are audibly rhetorical; every statement, every image, every turn of wit, is purposive. Measured against even so lively a *carpe diem* lyric as Herrick's "Corinna," **"To His Coy Mistress"** impresses us as a singularly tight-knit and cleanly structured argument. And although we are not licensed to speculate about the lady's response, for the curtain descends with the speaker's final word, we will doubtless acknowledge the power of his appeal. The argument is so framed as to allow no reasonable alternative but erotic union. By persuasive no less than by poetic criteria, **"To His Coy Mistress"** stands the unchallenged masterpiece among lyrics of seduction.

Joseph H. Summers   (essay date 1969)

SOURCE: "Reading Marvell's 'Garden,'" in *The Centennial Review*, Vol. XIII, 1969, pp. 18-37.

[An American educator and critic, Summers is the editor of Andrew Marvell: Selected Poems *(1961) and* George Herbert: Selected Poetry *(1967) and the author of* George Herbert: His Religion and Art *(1954) and* The Heirs of Donne and Jonson *(1970). In the following essay, he interprets "The Garden," offering a tempered view of the paradise described in the poem.]*

Some years ago I heard Professor Helen Gardner casually remark that she hoped no one would write another essay on either *Measure for Measure* or Marvell's **"The Garden."** At the time I knew exactly what she meant, and I felt sympathetic. There have been so many studies and "readings," scholarly and critical, of those and a few other works in English and American literature that it begins to seem that most teachers of English are busy reading and writing about the same few texts. Already compendiums of commentaries on our sacred texts are beginning to compare, in bulk at least with the medieval scholastics' commentaries on their sacred texts. For someone who merely happens to like the modern works and wishes to understand more about them, the effect is often of too many voices talking at once in a large room with a bad echo: we simply can no longer hear them.

But despite my understanding and sympathy, I also felt guilty when Professor Gardner made her remark, for I knew at the time that I, too, intended to get my own reading of **"The Garden"** down on paper some day. My lame excuse (aside, of course, from the fact that, like every other writer on the subject, I think I have at last discovered the "true reading") is the faint hope that my account of **"The Garden"** may cast a little light on ways in which certain other currently favorite literary works might be rescued from their conversion into objects of deep and dazzling darkness.

In so far as we know, Charles Lamb, Emerson and Poe were among the earliest enthusiastic readers of Marvell's poem, and that bit of knowledge seems significant. Discovered by the Romantics, admitted to the pantheon of Romantic and Victorian poetry (and compared to Shelley) by Palgrave in 1861, **"The Garden"** is still usually read as a Romantic poem. The usual procedure seems to be roughly as follows: The reader responds intensely to those three stanzas, v through vii, which describe ecstatic fulfillment. Having responded, he then leaps intuitively to the certainty that those stanzas *are* the poem, and that they are profound and serious in every way. (After all, the sensitive and intelligent reader responded to them, didn't he?) The reader assumes that no "true poet" could possibly create such sensuous and evocative stanzas except as the expression of his highest ideals, or primary imagination, or, perhaps, "true self." (Of the English Romantics, I believe only Byron would have seriously doubted such a formulation—but Byron is not particularly influential these days.) Certain of his central response or "truth," the reader usually either ignores the rest of the poem or else attempts to work it out on the assumption that the whole should be as serious and profound as he thinks stanzas v through vii are.

Certain other modern tendencies should probably be distinguished from the Romantic. Most important is the assumption that complexity is always preferable to simplicity in good poetry—or even, the more complex the better. Related to that assumption but distinguishable from it is the notion that a poem may justly be valued in direct proportion to the quantity of intellectual and literary history which it can be demonstrated to contain. Even stranger are the notions that tradition is always a good thing; that

a "traditional" reading is always to be accepted in preference to an "untraditional"; and that, where more than one tradition must be recognized, the older or more orthodox tradition must be the predominant one in a good poem. Since nearly everyone agrees that **"The Garden"** is a good poem, a number of readers, often sensitive and intelligent ones, have expended an enormous amount of ingenuity in attempts to demonstrate its enormous complexity in language and attitude and both its complexity and orthodoxy in philosophical and theological doctrine.

Dryden, who may have been taking a smack at George Herbert when he wrote about poets who "torture one poor word ten thousand ways," could hardly, I believe, have anticipated William Empson's reading of Marvell's **"Garden."** But Empson's subtleties are more than equalled by the readers who have found key "sources" of, or analogues to, the poem's central "meaning" or "doctrine" in an extraordinarily impressive range of figures and writings: Buddha and The Canticles and the Mass, Plato and Plotinus and "Hermes Trismegistus," St. Paul and the Kabbala, St. Bonaventura and St. Thomas Aquinas, Hugh of St. Victor and the *Ancrene Riwle,* Ficino and Leone Ebreo, Henry More and John Smith, Spinoza, Blake and Keats, Alfred North Whitehead and John Dewey. No one would deny that most of these contain profundities or that many provide either images of or patterns for the good life—or dreams of perfection. One could even suggest that plausible analogies can be discovered (or constructed) between the profound writings associated with these names and stanzas v through vii of **"The Garden"**—if we take those stanzas in isolation. If one admits all this and still persists in the conviction that the learned analogies have usually proved misleading about the poem as a whole, one should at least try to determine how the readers have gone wrong.

I think the first mistake (to repeat) is to interpret the poem by means of the three magic stanzas instead of reading those stanzas within the context of the poem. Close to it, both in error and frequency, is the tendency for a reader to develop an elaborate interpretation of the poem with little or no consideration of the probabilities that the same man could have written the reader's poem and Marvell's other poetry and prose. Of course it is theoretically possible for a poet to write a poem utterly unlike his other work, *sui generis* in ideas and values and language; but to assume lightly that any one poem is such a work seems to me extremely dangerous. The problems differ with different poets, and this is not the place to go into them in detail. But, although I shall not be very obviously concerned here with Marvell's other poems, I do think it is generally a good idea to have read most of a writer's work before one starts writing about individual poems, and to keep as much of that work in mind as one possibly can in readiness for those occasions in which one passage may provide a helpful gloss upon another. I believe, for example, that anyone who has read carefully Marvell's prose as well as his other poems would be unlikely to interpret **"The Garden"** as the systematic mystical meditation of a Roman Catholic religious.

A third error may be the oddest and most debilitating of all. In a critical age when the word "tone" has been used incessantly and when "wit" has become a term of almost unmitigated praise, few readers have bothered to evaluate—or even to notice—the wit of **"The Garden."** The possibility that the sounds and rhythms of the poem might help one to determine the degrees of seriousness of specific passages has very often been ignored. The lines of **"The Garden"** have frequently been read as if they were spoken by a preacher or formal philosopher or a nineteenth-century poet instead of by an oddly individual speaker within a seventeenth-century poem.

Frank Kermode's essay, "The Argument of Marvell's 'Garden' " [in *Essays in Criticism* II (1952)], and the final chapter of J. B. Leishman's *The Art of Marvell's Poetry* (1966) are exceptions to most of what I have said: both Kermode and Leishman considered the poem as a whole, both knew Marvell's other works and both got most of the jokes. (Only my differences with some of their conclusions make me think I still have something to say.) Anyone who has read their essays—or even merely read much in Renaissance literature—must realize that the seventeenth-century literary woods were full of gardens. There was Eden, of course, and the mystical gardens of the Canticles and of the Virgin. More important than the Virgin's for most English Protestants were the secular gardens of "retired life," some of Horatian or more or less neostoic design; and those gardens could easily blend into very real gardens (such as that of Lord Fairfax at Nun Appleton, Yorkshire), which could, in turn, represent the temporary or permanent places of retirement and pleasure for an active and distinguished man—or for, say, his daughter's tutor, who had not chosen to fight in the English Civil War. And there were other gardens—"*libertin*," "naturalist," "Epicurean" or what-have-you—which were symbols for sensuous and even sensual fulfillment, often with a lady present and willing and "unnatural" concepts such as honor banished. Each of these gardens could be considered, seriously or playfully, a "paradise," lost or found, but on differing occasions, and by different men. It is hardly safe to assume that Marvell was ignorant or unconscious of any of these (it seems to have been his delight to write on subjects and in genres which possessed multiple and often contradictory literary traditions); it is even less safe to assume that *his* "garden" is adequately represented by any one of the traditional types: for Marvell's **"Garden"** is a poem rather than a place or a "type," and what the poem is and does is what we wish to discover.

With **"The Garden,"** as with most other seventeenth-century poems, it is helpful to pay some attention to the poem's shape and the way the "argument" is organized. If we look at the shape of Marvell's English poem, we notice that those famous stanzas v-vii that celebrate the ecstasies which define "What wond'rous life in this I lead"—stanzas that are certainly central to the poem if not equivalent to it—are framed by stanzas which are witty distortions, first, of classical myth, and then, of the biblical account of Eden. With such obvious symmetry, one might expect more. But the poem begins with three introductory stanzas which claim that the garden contains a truer fame, quiet, innocence and amorousness than the world outside; and it ends with only one: that concerning the gardener, the floral sundial and the industrious bee. With a poet who

cared so much about formal elements as Marvell did, one might ask, why? And for our reading of the poem it is more important to ask, how does the formal imbalance work? If the poem succeeds formally, one might expect that stanza ix alone truly concludes it in a manner somehow related to the way that stanzas i through iii begin it. (The formal problem may be considered an exaggerated analogy to the usual problem of the Italian sonnet: how do those last six lines "answer" or complete or transform, "balance" or overbalance—at any rate, *conclude*—those first eight?)

"Hortus," Marvell's Latin poem which seems to be an earlier version of the English one, is organized in a different fashion, but substantiates the impression that the beginning and the ending of **"The Garden"** were conceived in relationship to each other. Moreover, both poems begin with the rejection of the worlds of ambitious action, urban life and passionate love, and celebrate a supposed entrance into an entirely new life within the garden. (In **"Hortus"** the speaker calls himself a "new citizen" and prays that the "Leafy citizens" may accept him "in the flowery kingdom.") Both poems end with almost identical lines concerning time and certain precious hours. Any satisfactory reading of **"The Garden"** should attempt to account for the relationship between the beginning and the end.

While I believe, of course, that my hints concerning formal problems are of major importance for the poem, I cannot expect to convince sceptics unless I can demonstrate their relevance in a reading of the poem which more or less convincingly accounts for the way it works and moves. It is not enough with seventeenth-century poems, I think, to develop erudite and plausible "historical meanings" or to elaborate diagrams and "spatial forms" unless we can show how the reader is supposed to acquire his knowledge or experience of those constructions as he reads the poems, line by line and stanza by stanza. For the seventeenth-century poems we care most about really do move—not at all like "Chinese jars in their stillness," but openly in rhetorical shifts, changing assumptions, resolutions lost or modified. Their "meanings" cannot be defined by any abstract statement partly because they often concern precisely the process of change from one position to another.

Let us turn to the poem:

> How vainly men themselves amaze
> To win the palm, the oak, or bays;
> And their uncessant labors see
> Crowned from some single herb or tree:
> Whose short and narrow vergèd shade
> Does prudently their toils upbraid;
> While all flowers and all trees do close
> To weave the garlands of repose.

Although I have met few bright students, knowing in the intricacies of modern criticism, who have even smiled at those lines, I find their self-conscious false naïveté very funny. The speaker looks at the incredible labors which men undergo for "the palm, the oak, or bays" and pretends he thinks that all they want are those "crowns," each made from the leaves of only one tree, as shades from the sun—the physical symbols for a doubtful utilitarian purpose rather than the recognition of victory and triumph that the symbols signify. (It is as if one thought the only possible reason anyone could wish to win the Davis cup would be to drink out of it.) But the symbols themselves, short-lived and not really offering much protection from the sun, offer prudent reproof to such toils. And if one merely *rests* in the most pleasant place—a garden—*all* flowers and *all* trees "close" to weave much handsomer, richer and more efficient garlands. For readers who live in a society with different status symbols and who are not continually reminded of Renaissance notions concerning mortal and immortal fame, the extravagance and the joke may be less obvious than for a seventeenth-century reader, but we can still recognize both.

In one of his earliest poems, Marvell had had fun with the famous lines on Fame in *Lycidas*: he had expressed the "frail ambition," "The last distemper of the sober brain," that there had been a witness to assure future ages how he endured his "martyrdom" when Fleckno recited his hideous verses. But there Marvell presented himself as the gallant man of common sense who had read Donne's Satires and was busy exposing another monstrous aberration. Milton's original lines are more to the point here: Why shouldn't a shepherd "sport with Amaryllis in the shade" instead of "with uncessant care" (Marvell may have remembered Milton's use of "uncessant") tending the "shepherd's trade" and strictly meditating "the thankless Muse"? The answer is clear:

> Fame is the spur that the clear spirit doth raise
> (That last infirmity of noble mind)
> To scorn delights, and live laborious days. . . .

Even though death may intervene before the great work is completed, Phoebus assures the poet that true fame will be granted by "all-judging Jove"—in just proportion, manifestly, to the tended trade and meditated Muse. Although the desire for fame may be an "infirmity," what it is the spur to is the "clear spirit" which creates and acts—and is rewarded. Marvell begins **"The Garden"** with an extravagant dismissal of all efforts for fame. Instead of being raised, the spirit is advised to relax and give up any attempt for military, civil or poetic distinction: the whole duty of man here seems summarized in that climactic word, *repose*. The outrageous suavity and the calculated rationality (notice "prudently") of the lines invite us to smile and warn us of extravagances to come. The poem is going to claim *everything* for a life of infinite leisure in the garden; but the ways in which it makes its claims reveal the urbanity of the poet who created this fictional voice, his recognition of values beyond those which he pretends to dismiss and those which he pretends exhaust all the pleasant and virtuous possibilities of human life.

The exclamatory apostrophe to Quiet and Innocence of stanza ii has a pseudo-operatic quality of sudden discovery:

> Fair Quiet, have I found thee here,
> And Innocence, thy sister dear!
> Mistaken long, I sought you then
> In busy companies of men.
> Your sacred plants, if here below,
> Only among the plants will grow.

> Society is all but rude,
> To this delicious solitude.

Yet if these lines stood alone, we should probably have to take them simply and seriously. After all the theme is hoary: true quiet and innocence do not exist in great places but in the simple life. Our suspicions have, however, already been aroused by stanza i, and they are sustained. This, too, is extravagant. The simple life was usually, in secular literature at least, considered a life in a landscape with *some* figures, the villa or the village away from the centers of power and ambition or the retreat with the mistress, but not the anchorite's totally divorced from human contact. (And the anchorites, we might remember, usually took a cell in the desert or a pillar, not a pleasant garden, as a place of retirement.) Reading these lines one may come to wonder whether it is really so remarkable that it should be quiet if no one at all is present to make noise. And is it surprising to discover that one may be relatively "innocent" if one sees no other human beings at all, either to be corrupted by or to harm? The virtue of this "innocence" is so fugitive that it would find a cloister crowded.

The latent incongruities explode with the final couplet of the stanza:

> Society is all but rude,
> To this delicious solitude.

The marvelously dancing rhythm, the temporal fall of the rhymes with the meanings of "rude" and "solitude," the delicate mock-precision of "all but" and the lovely misuse of "delicious" (perhaps a reminiscence of Crashaw) are the very embodiment of the wit. If one thinks at all about the relationships between "rude" and "polished," between "society" and life outside of society, one can paraphrase what the lines actually say in a number of ways which, unwittingly, make the absurdity obvious: society is almost rustic in comparison to rusticity; the state which polishes is almost rough in comparison to the state of roughness; civilization is almost barbaric in comparison to no civilization. That we may think, in certain times and places and moods, that each paraphrase contains more than a bit of truth in addition to its absurdity is all to the point. Marvell's own phrasing assures us that the speaker must have received the highest possible polish from society before he could formulate the couplet; and he (or the author) knows it. Never has civilization been rejected in a more elegantly civilized fashion. The wit reminds us strongly of values which are beyond the gift of Quiet and Innocence and which were never learned in a garden.

In the third stanza the speaker rejects the beauty of human female figures for the superior "amorousness" of the trees:

> No white nor red was ever seen
> So am'rous as this lovely green.

The second stanza, with its "delicious solitude," has given us fair warning that this is to be no ordinary "naturalistic" garden of sensuous delight as the lover and his mistress return to nature. But we can hardly have anticipated, I believe, such a bold claim for the total fulfillment of man's amorous nature without the ladies. The speaker "proves" that the trees are capable of inspiring his passion by his comment on the ordinary lovers who carve their mistresses' names in the bark of the trees:

> Fond lovers, cruel as their flame,
> Cut in these trees their mistress' name.
> Little, alas, they know, or heed,
> How far these beauties hers exceed!
> Fair Trees! wheres'e'er your barks I wound,
> No name shall but your own be found.

It takes a very solemn reader indeed not to smile at the figure of the man so in love with the trees that, to express that love, he carves "Plane," "Cypress," "Poplar" and "Elm" on the corresponding love-objects. (**"Hortus"** spells it out: precisely those names will be substituted for Naera, Chloe, Faustina and Corynna.) One horridly surrealist analogy would be a mad lover who carved his mistress's name on his mistress. Almost equally mad is the sentimental botanist with many loves, satisfied in the homage of the carved labels, since no other words could equal the grandeur or the erotic passion of the names themselves.

Stanza iv, continuing the eroticism, turns to the gods and goddesses:

> When we have run our passion's heat,
> Love hither makes his best retreat.
> The gods, that mortal beauty chase,
> Still in a tree did end their race:
> Apollo hunted Daphne so,
> Only that she might laurel grow;
> And Pan did after Syrinx speed,
> Not as a nymph, but for a reed.

Of course Marvell knew the moralizations of the myths. Of course he knew that, although the speaker had supposedly rejected the "laurel" in the "bays" of stanza i as something actively to be striven for, *we* in large part value Apollo for the laurel and Pan for the reed. And the idea that the garden is the "best retreat" of Love after the "heat" and the "race" of passion is neat and plausible. (The puns on "heat" and "race," like all of Marvell's best ones, seem inevitable and without strain.) But the extravagance of the word "Still" assures us that we have not abandoned the realm of conscious and playful exaggeration: "The gods, that mortal beauty chase, / *Still* in a tree did end their race." Many of the gods did—and **"Hortus"** adds Jupiter and Mars to Apollo and Pan—but not all the gods, and not all of the "races." And the same sort of exaggeration is present in that word "Only": "Apollo hunted Daphne so, / *Only* that she might laurel grow." It is one thing to claim, as **"Hortus"** does at one point, that the gods rejoice when the tyrant Love loses his heat and that, although experienced in all the nymphs and goddesses, "Each one achieves his desires better now in a tree." It is quite another (and a complete reversal of the myth) to say that all that Apollo ever wanted from Daphne was that she turn to laurel. And that goat-footed Pan sought Syrinx "Not as a nymph, but for a reed," is even more delightfully absurd. As he has done consistently thus far in the poem, Marvell gets some of his wittiest effects from blandly pretending either to identify a symbol with the thing symbolized or one element of a myth or situation with the clusters of meanings which are truly involved.

It is in stanzas v through vii that the speaker describes in

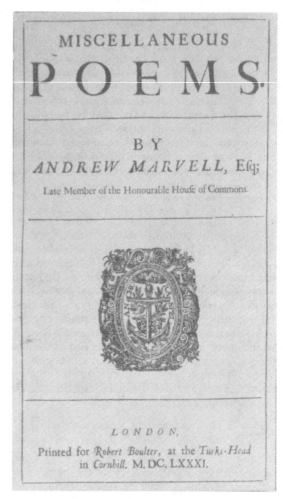

Title page of Miscellaneous Poems, *1681.*

detail the absolute fulfillment within the garden which up until then he has merely claimed to exist:

> What wond'rous life in this I lead!
> Ripe apples drop about my head;
> The luscious clusters of the vine
> Upon my mouth do crush their wine;
> The nectarine, and curious peach,
> Into my hands themselves do reach;
> Stumbling on melons, as I pass,
> Ensnared with flowers, I fall on grass.
>
> Meanwhile the mind, from pleasure less,
> Withdraws into its happiness:
> The mind, that ocean where each kind
> Does straight its own resemblance find;
> Yet it creates, transcending these,
> Far other worlds; and other seas;
> Annihilating all that's made
> To a green thought in a green shade.
>
> Here at the fountain's sliding foot,
> Or at some fruit-tree's mossy root,
> Casting the body's vest aside,
> My soul into the boughs does glide:
> There like a bird it sits, and sings,
> Then whets, and combs its silver wings;
> And, till prepared for longer flight,

Waves in its plumes the various light.

We should certainly be grateful here for all the useful learning and special knowledge that we can get. But we must make sure that the learning is truly relevant and that it will help us to read these stanzas instead of distracting us from them. It may be interesting to know that the Greek root of *melon* means "apple" and that the roots of the words for other English fruits here may also mean "apple" in other languages; but if we get too many apples in stanza v we may miss the more important point that for this ecstasy the pleasantly aggressive fruits systematically overwhelm differing parts of the man's body (head, mouth, hands, legs and feet) without any wilful or even masculine behavior on his part. And although "Stumbling," "Ensnared" and "fall" may make us think of sin and Adam's fall in another Garden, we should recognize that the chief points of the stanza are that this is *not* Eden and this is not sinful: *this* "fall" is pleasant and innocent, on grass rather than into sin, a truly "wond'rous" ecstatic fulfillment of the body without overt sexuality. That is why the speaker prefers the trees to the mistresses and the gods now prefer their trees or reeds to their former loves.

Similarly, I think we would do well to forget the "ambiguities" which have been found in "Meanwhile the mind, from pleasure less, / Withdraws into its happiness." It seems obvious that the ecstasies are in an ascending order (reversing the descent from the crowns and garlands to the loves of the opening stanzas), and that the most important thing the lines mean is that the mind withdraws from the lesser pleasure of the body to experience its own separate and greater pleasure in its ecstasy of knowledge and creative thought. If the structure of the poem counts for anything, the lines cannot possibly mean that the mind is "reduced" or "lessened" by pleasure, for the entire movement is towards the extravagant claim that each aspect of man enjoys its highest pleasure in the garden.

The single most important thing of all to notice about the three stanzas is, I believe, that they neatly divide man's being, not into the difficult but conventional body and soul, but into a more divisive body, mind and soul. Their mischievously witty claim is that the completely separable perfect pleasures of body, mind and soul can be experienced here on earth, simultaneously and without strain— and, according to the poem through stanza vi, supposedly without end. Had Marvell wished chiefly for credibility, had he intended his readers seriously to consider these stanzas the expression of the highest possible "Garden-state," embodying a paradisiacal perfection outside of time and human measure, he would, I think, have handled that claim quite differently. If, like Milton in his description of Eden, he had wished to emphasize that all the aspects of man were truly fulfilled in paradise, he would have shown the union, not the separation, of body, mind and soul; or he might, like innumerable other writers in their serious or playful descriptions of "perfection" and ecstatic fulfillment, have emphasized one sort—sensuous, mental or spiritual—as truly "transcending," surpassing and including, the other forms. In those cases, however, we have other poems: serious descriptions of unfallen man or serious or playful descriptions of the "perfections" to be sought in the libertine paradise or in the mental para-

dises of knowledge and creativity or in the spiritual paradises of song and mystical illumination. But **"The Garden"** is claiming *all.* By that very extravagance and by the strict compartmentalization of the three ecstasies, Marvell dramatizes precisely the strains which the poem's surface claims do not exist, and he places the heaviest possible burden on the speaker's simple acquiescence: *while* the body, "Ensnared with flowers," has fallen on the grass, the mind is "Annihilating all that's made / To a green thought in a green shade"; and at the same or similar moment, "Casting the body's vest aside," the soul glides into the boughs:

> There like a bird it sits, and sings,
> Then whets, and combs its silver wings;
> And, till prepared for longer flight,
> Waves in its plumes the various light.

It is within stanza vii that time first enters significantly into the life of the garden; until then, apart from the witty emphasis on the simultaneity of the ecstasies, time has been merely part of that world of action, ambition, society and passion from which "we" have retreated, we had thought, forever. But here, as it "sits, and sings" and "Waves in its plumes the various light" of this world, the soul knowingly awaits the time when it is prepared for the "longer flight" into the unvarying light of eternity. That very modification of the absoluteness of the former claims—the recognition that there is a flight longer than any the soul can know in the garden—gives a reality and poignance to the stanza beyond anything we have met so far. It is at this moment that the poem nearly becomes something like the "serious" poem that many readers assume it to be throughout. The longing for fulfillment, which has been just beneath the surface even if we "know" that all the divisions of man's nature cannot experience complete and eternal ecstasy on earth, must be recognized openly here. But this note is touched only for a moment.

Stanza viii, with its witty reversal of Genesis ii. 18 ("And the Lord God said, It is not good that the man should be alone; I will make him an help meet for him") returns us to the world of laughter, paradox, mortality and measure:

> Such was that happy Garden-state,
> While man there walked without a mate:
> After a place so pure, and sweet,
> What other help could yet be meet!
> But 'twas beyond a mortal's share
> To wander solitary there:
> Two paradises 'twere in one
> To live in Paradise alone.

St. Ambrose and St. Jerome may have literally believed that man would have been happier without a mate, but, despite all the misogynist literature of the ancient and medieval and Renaissance worlds, such a belief was never central nor widely held by poets. This particular poem, moreover, was written neither by nor for a St. Jerome. More to the point are the play on "mate" and "meet" and the self-consciously blasphemous reversal of the biblical accounts both of the creation of woman and the loss of Eden. The implications are inescapable: that the chief cause for the loss of Paradise was the creation of woman rather than sin; and that, simply by returning to the garden, solitary man can recover the state of innocence. These extravagances, along with the dancing movement of the couplets in which they are conveyed, assure us that, whatever the speaker's sexual condition or private beliefs, he is not seriously proposing for our approbation the notion of Adam as the happy hermaphrodite. The gaiety and the reminder of the biblical account of Paradise provide a comic perspective on some assumptions that may underlie the seductive ecstasies that have gone before: the notions that heterosexual relations are "unnatural," and that no more than one man should ever have existed. Whatever the opinions of individual theologians and philosophers, most readers of poetry eventually see limitations in notions of "perfection" based on such assumptions.

Stanza viii goes so far that it almost undercuts all the claims which have been made for the garden. It may seem for a moment that the perception of any values whatsoever for the solitary and contemplative life within the place of ordered natural beauty is a delusion, that the "real" life of man can only be found in the worlds of public action, social colloquy and the pursuit of love. But the concluding stanza modifies that extravagance, too. It is, once again, with the introduction of time that we touch a wider reality:

> How well the skillful gard'ner drew
> Of flowers and herbs this dial new;
> Where from above the milder sun
> Does through a fragrant zodiac run;
> And, as it works, th' industrious bee
> Computes its time as well as we.
> How could such sweet and wholesome hours
> Be reckoned but with herbs and flowers!

Since the first stanza began with "How vainly," it is proper that the final stanza should begin with "How well." But what is done so well is not the retreat from all action to solitary contemplation but the "skillful" construction by the gardener of a dial which measures time. Here for the first time since those pursuing gods in stanza iv do we see a figure in human shape that moves purposefully; for the first time since stanza i do we hear of anything that labors or works: the gardener has "drawn" the dial; the sun "runs" through a "fragment zodiac"; the "industrious bee" "Computes its time" "as it works." And we, too, are invited to the mild labor of "computing" or "reckoning" "sweet and wholesome hours" with an objectivity and a sense of multiple possibilities which we could not possibly have summoned at the moments of ecstatic fulfillment that seemed eternal. The dial implies not only time, but the vicissitudes of times; it measures for us only our pleasant hours of retreat within the garden when the sun runs through the "fragrant zodiac," neither those of cloud or night within the solitary life nor those of the less "mild" sun of the world of action beyond the garden. And the herbs and flowers are proper for reckoning our sunny hours within the garden not only because they are "sweet and wholesome," but also because the grass withers and the flowers fade. (The phrase *brevibus plantis* of **"Hortus,"** l. 50, encourages me to believe that I am not reading into the poem meanings which Marvell did not intend to be there.) The final stanza truly balances and "answers" those three introductory stanzas as well as concludes the

entire poem in its summary of our experiences within the garden: they have been in time, not in eternity; and however pleasant, they are only an evanescent part of the life that we value, and a smaller part still of the life that we live.

I hope that no one will think I have created a "Marvell's **'Garden'** for tired business men"—although perhaps Lord Fairfax was, according to elevated seventeenth-century standards, something of a "tired businessman." I am more nearly intimidated by the thought of a modest reader who considers my reading overly elaborate and may wish to remark, "I just thought Marvell was a man who liked gardens." But whatever the criticisms, and however inferior in profound philosophical and religious meanings my reading may be, I am convinced that it comes close to the poem that Marvell actually wrote. I believe that in **"The Garden"** Marvell was trying to do something other than to express or dramatize eternal philosophical or religious choices, and I also believe that he was doing more than expressing personal taste in horticulture. Of course the poem recognizes the absurdities and the losses associated with the mindless pursuit of the active life: no literate poet in the mid-seventeenth century could have been unaware of them. But more immediately important for the poem, I think, were the extravagant claims for the retired life which were made, with more or less seriousness, by devotees of pastoral poetry, neo-stoic gentlemen, mystical contemplatives and libertines alike, in an age which had experienced and remembered the dangers and horrors of civil war: the claims that one mode of the retired life exhausted all the "real," the valuable possibilities of human life. By pretending to accept precisely such claims and by pushing them to their ultimately absurd limits, Marvell wrote a poem which is both one of the wittiest of the age and which contains one of the age's most moving accounts of the dream of absolute fulfillment. But the end of the poem is inevitable: the gentle and eminently civilized recognition that retirement to a garden may provide truly sweet and wholesome hours—and a marvelous occasion for a poem—but not a way of life.

K. W. Gransden   (essay date 1970)

SOURCE: "Time, Guilt, and Pleasure: A Note on Marvell's Nostalgia," in *Ariel: A Review of International English Literature,* Vol. 1, No. 2, April, 1970, pp. 83-97.

[*In the following essay, Gransden asserts that Marvell's poetry addresses the theme of humankind's biblical fall from grace.*]

Marvell, like other seventeenth-century poets, notably Herbert, shows a profound nostalgia for the lost Elizabethan order, and for the art in which this was embodied. This nostalgia must be linked with another, no less profound: for paradise and for childhood—the 'golden daies' of little T.C. in a prospect of flowers. The 'golden daies' are man's racial, national and individual past. Both Marvell and Herbert are alienated from their own world and seek to regress to a lost, idealized order. Their obsession with Time, while it should be related to Spenser's, is more personal, and may indeed be described as romantic, as in Herbert's 'Life':

But Time did beckon to the flow'rs, and they
By noon most cunningly did steal away
And withered in my hand . . .

and in Marvell's **'The Picture of Little T.C. in a Prospect of Flowers'**:

And roses of their thorns disarm;
But most procure
That violets may a longer age endure.

Herbert's sacred parody of Sidney's rejection of artificiality in writing about love is more than a literary nostalgia: it is social, moral and psychological. And if Herbert's sense of alienation may be defined by allusion to Sidney, Marvell's may be approached by allusion to Jonson, whose poetry commands a deep sense of man's 'community', of man being joined to God and nature by the 'golden chaine' of love, as in his 'Epode' (*Forrest,* XI):

A forme more fresh then are the Eden bowers
And lasting, as her flowers.

(II.57-8)

Jonson's 'Penshurst' offers a paradigm of man, God and nature in ideal harmony. Marvell alludes to the opening of this poem (with its Sidneian rejection of foreign artifice) in the opening of **'Appleton House'**. Again, the nostalgia is both moral and patriotic. For Jonson, the Sidney estate offered a sense of moral and historical continuity, and embodied a non-repressive, essentially abundant order, like that of Eden. The fruits of the earth offer themselves freely and voluntarily, as in Virgil's second *Georgic*: but the myth is now Christianized: 'every child may reach', for of such is the kingdom of heaven. In **'Appleton House'**, and in **'The Garden'**, the fruits also offer themselves freely and abundantly. This occurs again in **'Bermudas'**:

He makes the Figs our mouths to meet;
And throws the Melons at our feet.

So, too, in Herbert's 'Man', the herbs 'gladly cure our flesh'; the whole of nature still conspires to make man rich and happy:

Nothing we see, but means our good;
As our delight, or as our treasure:
The whole is either our cupboard of food
Or cabinet of pleasure.

The great moments in **'The Garden'** and **'Appleton House'** are those in which the poet dramatizes his attempt to regress behind the unsatisfied ego:

And now to the Abbyss I pass
Of that unfathomable Grass,
Where men like Grashoppers appear,
But Grashoppers are Gyants there:
They in their squeking Laugh, contemn
Us as we walk more low then them.
And from the Precipices tall
Of the green spir's, to us do call.

To see Men through this Meadow Dive,
We wonder how they rise alive.
As, under Water, none does know
Whether he fall through it or go.

But as the Marriners that sound,
And show upon their Lead the Ground,

They bring up Flow'rs so to be seen,
And prove they've at the Bottom been.

(XLVII-XLVIII)

In the first line of the above passage, 'pass' is a kind of pun: it is both literary and psychological, the next item in the poem as catalogue, and the moment in which the poet experiments in losing his identity. Regression may be self-indulgent, and Marvell's poetry is often self-indulgent, but it also corresponds to a profound psychic need. The sense of tiredness and release is also important. One finds it in Herbert too, notably in 'The Pulley', which describes man's sense of restless alienation since losing the riches of Paradise (through the classical myth of Pandora's box). God here allows for the Fall by withholding from man the gift of rest (the idea comes from Augustine) so that man will ultimately regress through weariness not through goodness.

In **'The Garden'**, Marvell describes the regressive act in terms of the body, the mind and the soul. The body falls into the grass, exhausted with the strain of life. The mind withdraws into creative meditation. The soul glides into the tree in eager anticipation of the ultimate regression of death. But the tree refocuses our attention on the tree of knowledge (from which it has never been allowed to stray for long). 'We must eat again of the tree in order to fall back into the state of innocence' [quoted from von Kleist by H. Marcuse, *Eros and Civilisation,* 1956]. In Marvell the most sophisticated of all pleasures is the recreation of the Fall. Even the paradise of the Bermudas allows for this:

But Apples plants of such a price,
No Tree could ever bear them twice.

It is typical of Marvell to express the Fall in economic terms. The price of the re-entry into innocence is the price we paid for experience, and are still paying.

Man's presumptuousness in reaching to the tree of knowledge induces a compensating humility, expressed in the gaiety and laughter of nature in the **'Appleton House'** stanzas. Man's sense that the grass must have been greener before the Fall induces an envious nostalgia, producing in the imagination a cycle of pleasurable relief, followed by guilt and dissatisfaction. Milton pointed out that there was something ridiculous in the Fall; and the act of regression in **'The Garden'** is slightly absurd, as the lines about stumbling on melons show.

Man's relationship with the natural order has been disturbed. In the **'Horation Ode'** Marvell recognized the inevitability of Cromwell: nature abhors a vacuum, and the confrontation between strong Cromwell and weak Charles re-dramatizes that between Bolingbroke and Richard and places the nostalgia historically. Justice 'pleads the ancient rights in vain', for the ruined order is that of Time itself, a fracturing of the continuum of history. Yet the word 'ruin' is also *ruina*, the Fall, as in **'The Mower's Song'**:

And Flow'rs and Grass and I and all
Will in one common Ruine fall.

Cromwell's 'highest plot' was originally to 'plant the Bergamot', and the pun on 'plot' associates gardening with revolution (the bergamot was a newly introduced variety). But even gardening was only a wholly innocent activity before the Fall, so that Cromwell was really preparing himself. (Eve started the Fall by criticizing prelapsarian gardening.) In **'Appleton House'** garden imagery parodies military: 'and all the Garrisons were flowers' (see stanzas XLII, XLIII). And when Cromwell came out of his retreat to ruin the great work of Time

> And cast the Kingdome old
> Into another Mold

the word 'mold' continues the punning association with gardening (cf. **'The First Anniversarie of the Government under O.C.'**, l. 160).

So ruined work of Time in both the England of the past and man himself, created in a timeless world from which he contrived his own inevitable expulsion and to which he has ever since, in fantasy, sought re-entry. The paradise he lost, when he fell into the world of Time and history, was God's world, in which there is no work, only play. This world re-appears briefly for us in the world of childhood. But after childhood man works, he becomes acquisitive, to try to accumulate his lost wealth, to consume time. In Marvell's **'Garden'** there is no competitiveness 'to win the Palm, the Oke or Bayes'. The imagery of **'Appleton House'** is all of retreat into safety and sanctuary, into the womb (hence the meadows are like water), into the protection of nature, an anti-social act:

> How safe, methinks, and strong, behind
> These Trees have I incamp'd my Mind
> . . . Where the World no certain Shot
> Can make, or me it toucheth not.
>
> (LXXVI)

Again, there is military imagery. Alienated man is besieged. And it is not only the protection of nature that is sought, but also that of God. Marvell compares entering the wood to entering a sanctuary, a 'green yet growing Ark' (see LXI). If he is not yet back to the Fall here, he is at least back to the Flood, seeking the innocence of Noah who had divine approval, and also seeking a lost sense of sharing creation with the rest of God's creatures: 'and where all creatures might have shares', as they did both in Eden and in the Ark. But there is a sense in which *this* Ark is superior to the mythical one, for Marvell does not have to violate nature, as Noah did, by cutting down the trees. Art and the imagination create images of lost innocence more perfect than those of which they are a paradigm. Man is not only Adam the destroyer but God the creator. In the **'Dialogue Between the Soul and Body'** the body has the last word:

> What but a Soul could have the wit
> To build me up for Sin so fit?
> So Architects do square and hew
> Green Trees that in the Forest grew.

Man has dragged innocent nature after him under the rule of time.

In **'The Garden'** the race for power, sex and success is a race against time: Marvell actually uses the image of running, as at the end of **'To his Coy Mistress'**. From this world we retreat into a superior world of pleasure, that of

contemplation (Aristotle's *summum bonum*): the contemplation of our own lost innocence. The recreation of the Fall in the poem is not Milton's heroic act of daring, of baroque energy released in (and into) the world of time once and for all. It is rather a self-indulgent, languid, autoerotic act, a game which can be played over and over again; a return home, not a setting out. There is an almost sexual pleasure in moving through the poem, back behind the Ovidian metamorphoses (here used almost Miltonically) to that moment of sensuality on which all human experience pivots. The mind that creates 'far other worlds and other seas' imitates the creativity of God as an act of pure play, the filling of the vacuum in space-time, as in **'The Nymph Complaining for the Death of her Faun'**

> Thenceforth I set myself to play
> My solitary time away.
>
> (ll.37-8)

The creative mind 'annihilates all that's made' because it is deliberately destroying the 'great work of time', and re-enacting the pure pleasure of primal creation. It is important that the poem ends by saying that time in the garden can as well be computed by the industrious bee as by man. The bee does not distinguish between 'work' and 'play': there is only the single natural activity.

In the **'Dialogue between the Resolved Soul and Created Pleasure'** the soul's victory is presented as the ultimate and most sophisticated pleasure: that which God enjoys. There is no pleasure so exquisite as the prolonged resisting of pleasure. When the Soul answers Pleasure's siren-song about music with the words:

> Had I but any time to lose,
> On this I would it all dispose.
> Cease Tempter. None can chain a mind
> Whom this sweet Chordage cannot bind.

we are reminded of 'Had we but world enough and time' in the **'Coy Mistress'**. But there is never enough time, as a result of Adam's guilt; just as (in another sense) there is always too much. In paradise before the Fall, man could spend or pass time without ever losing any. Paradise lost is time lost as well as time gained.

The soul also speaks as Christ spoke to Satan. The pun on 'Chordage' associates music (of all the secular arts, the one most closely determined by, and through, time) with the binding of Christ for the Passion (the attempt to imprison God in Time), and this hint offers a characteristic *frisson*, as in **'Appleton House'**, where the poet asks masochistically for bondage from flowers in order to be held back from the enactment of the Fall:

> Bind me ye Woodbines in your 'twines,
> Curle me about ye gadding vines,
> And Oh so close your Circles lace
> That I may never leave this Place;
> But, lest your Fetters prove too weak,
> Ere I your silken bondage break,
> Do you, O Brambles, chain me too,
> And courteous Briars, nail me through.
>
> (LXXVII)

The poet seeks immunity from Time through imprisonment in the prelapsarian womb. But at the same time he wants to experience Christ's passion without being its guilty cause: he wants the atonement without the Fall. This may seem pure sophistication, but I see it as a brilliant attempt to find an image to express that obsessional guilt which determines the whole structure of man's psychic being. In Adam man suffers and is guilty; in Christ man suffers, and is innocent.

In this **'Dialogue'** the soul has no time to lose, just as the ego has no time to lose in the **'Coy Mistress'**. The possibilities of time are infinite (all guilt is the result of having to choose) but time itself is not. Thus from the same premise we may reach different conclusions: either 'as there is so little time, let us not waste it on sensuality'; or, 'as there is so little time, let us make love quickly'. The mind cannot be chained precisely because it is able to envisage alternatives of this kind. At the end of the **'Coy Mistress'** the proposition put forward is an attempt to escape from the power of time: let us

> Rather at once our Time devour
> Than languish in his slow-chapt pow'r.

In **'Appleton House'** the poet speaks of 'languishing at ease' as in **'The Garden'**. The act of nostalgic regression can free us from the choice presented by Time—the choice being either to master it or be mastered by it. But either alternative involves admitting to a damaged relationship with the natural world. The tempo of human experience itself changed when the apple was eaten. Eve 'hasted' (*Paradise Lost*, VII, 555) to tell Adam of her first taste of human experience. The coy mistress feigns innocence: the time-devouring ego demands the satisfactions of experience. Adam after the Fall, like Marvell's Cromwell, 'does both act and know.'

The temptation offered to the soul by pleasure, like that offered to the coy mistress, involves faking the phenomena of temporality:

> Hark how Musick then prepares
> For thy stay these charming Aires;
> Which the posting Winds recall
> And suspend the Rivers Fall.

But no Fall can really be suspended. Art interferes with and confuses nature as in Spenser's Bower of Bliss. In offering a delusion of victory over time, the lover in the **'Coy Mistress'** is really conceding time's victory. And in the triumphal chorus which follows pleasure's temptation of the soul through art, Marvell again alludes to Spenser in his use of military imagery to describe the traditional conflict of reason and affection: but now the conqueror uses the language of the defeated.

> Earth cannot shew so brave a Sight
> As when a Single Soul does fence
> The Batteries of alluring Sense,
> And Heaven views it with delight . . .

Compare Spenser's *Faerie Queene*, II. iv. 34:

> For when they (affections) once to perfect
>   strength do grow,
> Strong warres they make, and cruel battry bend
> Gainst fort of Reason . . .

But what is striking about Marvell's lines is not the con-

ventional military imagery but the fact that the defeat of sensuality is described in sensual language. The voyeurism of 'Earth cannot shew so brave a sight' (with its anticipation of Wordsworth) is the pleasure taken by God in just *looking* at Creation, in *Paradise Lost*:

> how it shewd
> In prospect from his Throne, how good, how
>   fair,
> Answering his great Idea.
>
>   (VII, 555)

This brings me to Marvell's love-poetry. His allusions to Sidneian Petrarchism are both wittily ironical and nostalgic (cf. **'The Definition of Love'**). Herbert criticized (in 'Jordan I') the allegorizing fantasies of Elizabethan erotic pastoral with its enchanted groves, purling streams and 'sense at two removes'. In the eighth song from Sidney's *Astrophel and Stella* ('In a grove most rich of shade') the pastoral setting increases the poignancy of the impossible syndrome of repression and frustration in which the lovers have placed themselves. Donne resolved this Petrarchan dialogue in 'The Ecstasie' by using neoplatonic transcendentalism. Donne's poem leads on to Edward Herbert's great 'Ode upon a Question Moved, Whether Love Should Continue for ever?' Lord Herbert, like his brother, and like Marvell, is obsessed with the connection between sex and time. He looks forward, in tone as in metre, to the domesticated transcendentalism of Tennyson. He shares with Tennyson, and with Marvell, an obsession with 'sense':

> And shall our Love, so far behind
> That low and dying appetite,
> And which so chaste desires unite,
> Not hold in an eternal bond?
>
> Is it, because we should decline,
> And wholly from our thoughts exclude
> Objects that may the sense delude
> And study only the divine? . . .
>
> For if no use of sense remain
> When bodies once this life forsake,
> Or they could no delight partake,
> Why should they ever rise again?

In **'Daphnis and Chloe'** Marvell returns with nostalgic irony to the Sidneian erotic dialogue. The poem's imagery wittily links the lover's refusal with the first guilty act of love which followed the Fall:

> But I will not now begin
> Such a Debt unto my Foe;
> Nor to my Departure owe
> What my Presence could not win.
>
> . . . Farewell therefore all the Fruit
> Which I could from love receive . . .

Daphnis refuses to enter the cycle of debt and guilt inaugurated by Eve. But the point of the poem is to reveal that Daphnis is getting sexual satisfaction elsewhere, so that the speech to Chloe is a rhetorical game. The entire structure of the Petrarchan 'protestation' becomes absurd. Chloe's refusal makes the poem and also 'justifies' Daphnis's double standard of sexual duplicity. The poem explores modes of fallen sexuality: virginity and promiscuity are extremes of a lost 'norm'. Sex can only be discussed in terms of a conventional guilt-inducing propaganda, as contemporary writing on the subject amply demonstrates. We are frustrated if we repress, guilty if we consummate; sexually, we cannot win. Marvell's poem ironically brings out the schizophrenia implicit in the Sidneian attitude.

The connection between sex and time is characteristically expressed in Jonson's 'To Celia', which begins as an imitation of the fifth poem of Catullus ('Vivamus, mea Lesbia . . .'):

> Come, my Celia, let us prove
> While we may, the sports of love . . .

Marvell alludes to this text in the **'Coy Mistress'**, but in the Catullus–Jonson version the mistress is not being coy, merely careful. Since she was another man's wife social pressures existed as well as psychic ones. Jonson's poem, indeed, continues in a manner closer to the Ovidian first elegy of Donne:

> Cannot we delude the eyes
> Of a few poor household spyes
> Or his easier eares beguile . . .

Worrying about one's virginity is not the same as worrying about one's husband; the social situation is different. But the two can be related: in both cases the woman is concerned (I use the economic term deliberately) with the choice between 'saving' herself and giving herself. Coyness is a kind of sadism, and the characteristic relationship between lover and mistress in Sidney's or Spenser's love-sonnets is a sado-masochistic one. The poet is obliged to live on an image or an idea, to sublimate into a world of idealized fantasy which tries to create a compensating illusion of timelessness.

'To his Coy Mistress' is an ironic address (almost a game) in three parts. The first two explore a hypothesis which is rejected as unacceptable, leaving us in the final section with an inescapable paradox which we started out by dismissing. It is a favourite structure of both Donne and Herbert.

The first section makes a series of nostalgic jokes about Petrarchism: extravagant rhetoric, 'complaints', gestures, separations. There is even a parody of the traditional 'catalogue of the mistress' delights' like the one to Philoclea in Sidney's *Arcadia*, Bk. II, ch. II. The lines

> My vegetable Love should grow
> Vaster then Empires, and more slow

recall the pastoral eroticism of Virgil's last eclogue in which the rejected lover carves his mistress' name on trees (thereby misusing nature like the lovers in **'The Garden'**) and makes a joke about it

> crescent illae [sc. arbores] crescetis, amores. (*Eclogue* X, 54)

But the 'vast empires' also represent a lost traditional order. The traditional tempo of love is no longer valid. Nor is the traditional price or contract. The famous line 'Nor would I love at lower rate' associates sex with time-as-value: it implies love at cut-price, which is what Daphnis settles for. But the nostalgia within the irony also sug-

gests a bargain wrung from the seemingly reluctant heart, as in Herbert's 'The Pearl': in that poem, having rejected the worlds of learning, honour and pleasure the poet recognizes

> At what rate and price I have thy love.

Time is the enemy of lasting gratification, a fact of fallen nature which Spenser admits in the garden of Adonis in *Faerie Queene,* III.vi. Marvell too sees time as the dominant factor in man's psyche:

> But at my back I alwaies hear
> Times winged charriot hurrying near

Time is here personified visually as an allegorical image out of Petrarch's *trionfi,* but for the poet it is invisible. The visual image clashes with the aural because time exists both outside and inside the vault of our individual consciousness: the ambivalence is terrifying, which is why the poet does not turn round, and the aural image prepares for the later image of the poet's song echoing inaudibly in the vault of death (an aural equivalent of the paradox about the flower that wastes its sweetness on the desert air).

Time's victory having been logically established, the last section can begin 'Now therefore . . .' The hypothesis having been eliminated, there remains only one way. The violence of the ending reflects the social and political violence of the **'Horatian Ode'**. In the modern age, sexuality too must be violent and be expressed in terms of man's acquisitive instinct (cf. the recent novel by Kingsley Amis, *I Want It Now*). The imagery becomes military (as in **'Daphnis and Chloe'** with its reference to sieges). The round ball is both a cannonball and the world. This prepares us for the astronomical joke at the end

> Thus, though we cannot make our Sun
> Stand still, yet we will make him run.

This is Donneian: though we cannot make the sun stand still as it did in the Old Testament (an allusion back to the Flood and the Jews in the first section) love can work psychological miracles: 'we can eclipse and cloud him with a wink'. We can also make the sun run in the sense in which restless Cromwell

> through adventrous War
> Urged his active Star

Time that was experimentally slowed down in the first section of the poem is now speeded up, to the guilt-ridden tempo of the acquisitive society. Sexuality is expressed in the language of man the consumer: 'and now . . . our Time devour'. The association of sexual guilt with eating again takes us back to the Fall. The last section of the **'Coy Mistress'** is spoken by Adam to Eve after eating the fruit. 'Now let us play,' says Milton's Adam, in a deluded parody of the God he thinks he has become: 'they their *fill* of Love and Loves *disport* / Took largely, of their mutual guilt the seal' (*Paradise Lost,* IX, 853). Thus Marvell describes sex in terms of play, consumption (of time) and violence. 'Sport' ironically concedes the sense of desperate urgency engendered by the Fall. The iron gates are man's exit from the golden world.

In his garden-poetry Marvell seeks to prolong indefinitely the exquisite sensations of retreat into Eden

> That I may never leave this place

Before Eve came, Adam contemplated nature narcissistically: it was his mirror, as it was God's. And Eve herself awoke into narcissistic self-contemplation: pure pleasure. But this was not the goal of man and woman: they had to seek elsewhere for a world to love. 'Imparadised in one another's arms' Adam and Eve experienced something God had not experienced: and it led to the Fall. In Marvell's Mower poems Juliana expresses the link between sexual guilt and the expulsion from Eden:

> For she my Mind hath so displac'd
> That I shall never find my home.

'Home' is the double paradise of contemplative solitude:

> Two Paradises twere in one
> To live in Paradise alone.

Guilt works retrospectively, so that this happiness is seen as having been 'too good to last'. Before Juliana dispossessed him the Mower, like Adam in *Paradise Lost*, VIII, looked upon the world of nature with delight:

> My Mind was once the true survey
> Of all these Medows fresh and gay,
> And in the greenness of the Grass
> Did see its Hopes as in a Glass.

Juliana is Eve, the sexual instrument of the Fall. The Mower now becomes subservient to her will: she does to him what he does to the grass. He cuts it down to make hay. Before he was dispossessed, his mowing was the 'pleasant task' of *Paradise Lost,* IX:

> For not to irksome toil but to delight
> He made us . . .
>
> (IX, 242)

But hay also means work and profit. When the Mower competes with the shepherd, we are reminded of rival lovers in a Virgilian pastoral contest, but the competitiveness is expressed in economic terms: 'I am richer far in hay' refers to the economy of Adam (naturally richer). The sun dries the Mower's sweat in **'Damon The Mower'** as it dries the sweat of the newly-awakened Adam in *Paradise Lost*:

> Soft on the flourie herb I found me laid
> In balmie sweat, which with his Beames the sun
> Soon dried . . .
>
> (VIII, 254-5)

But the hay is not only nature's original cycle; it is also a dance, image of the lost gaity between man and nature; and the kiss in the hay, 'country pleasures'. The love of Juliana leads to guilt, work and death. Mowing becomes a matter of the time-profit ratio ('make hay while the sun shines'). Work becomes repressive sublimation. The scythe (pun on sighs) becomes blunt. Man begins to lose the long battle with Time. The grass that once represented hope for the future now represents grief for the past.

When the Mower mows himself he visits on himself the curse of Adam: man . . . 'shall soon be cut down like the grass.' The thistles that now appear in the meadow are guilt-symbols, and guilt, like Time, is cumulative. In **'The Mower Against Gardens'** Marvell describes how man, after the Fall, seduced nature. The idea in that poem that a single tulip is worth a whole meadow illustrates the corrupt value-structure created by the acquisitive instinct. And man's experiments on nature are perversions: the 'forbidden mixtures' are the repetition throughout the fallen world of the original act in the garden of Eden. The garden in the poem is a 'seraglio': the fields outside the garden are nature as she was before the Fall. Marvell's language here again recalls Jonson's:

> Where willing Nature does to all dispence
> A wild and fragrant innocence.

The hectic tempo at the end of the **'Coy Mistress'** must be associated with the feverish activity of the love-sick Mower. Mowing, formerly a symbol of man's harmony with nature, now becomes a sublimation-symbol: having 'made his pile', having turned time and energy into work and profit, the Mower destroys himself. What passes for an accident, a clumsiness with the scythe, becomes both self-castration and racial suicide, the wish to destroy man: cf. 'depopulating all the ground', or, in the words of Eve when proposing suicide to Adam in *Paradise Lost,* 'destruction with destruction to destroy' (X, 1006).

Marvell's apprehension of the guilt in pleasure is one of the most striking and persistent features of his work. And it is closely associated with his sense of Time: Time as the price man pays for the Fall, and the process by which he expiates his guilt through history. The quicker it passes, the quicker the unpayable debt may perhaps be discharged. Even the doctrine of the *felix culpa* involves a further burden of guilt, for the death of God: 'the son of man shall be made as grass.' In **'The Coronet'** the poet seeks 'with garlands to redress that wrong' (the crown of thorns) but in the flowers he picks, the Serpent 'disguised does fold / with wreaths of Fame and *Interest*'. The characteristic economic pun emphasizes the corruptness of all human motivation. In his images of a violent consumer-sexuality, too, Marvell describes the sickness of the human psyche. This is why his poetry is so extraordinarily modern in its range and direction, while remaining firmly rooted in the literary tradition of Spenser, Sidney, Donne and Jonson.

John Creaser   (essay date 1970)

SOURCE: "Marvell's Effortless Superiority," in *Essays in Criticism*, Vol. XX, No. 4, October, 1970, pp. 403-23.

[*In the following essay, Creaser attributes Marvell's greatness as a poet to the "witty poise" and—more importantly—transcending equanimity expressed in his verse.*]

The sense of alarm and dismay at what the academic industry is fabricating out of Andrew Marvell's poetry is becoming acute. Frank Kermode, in an appalled account of 'some weeks of desperate reading', has written:

> After a lapse of a dozen or more years I have been looking at the reports of the learned on Marvell's poetry, and I cannot believe that I am alone in my dismay at their treason. . . . One

was accustomed to being told to look for the key of **'The Garden'** in Plotinus or in Bonaventura. . . . And now, in the third and terribly numerous generation everybody seems even clumsier, less aware of the tact required, and of the uselessness of specially got-up learning as an instrument to investigate 'a quality of civilisation'. (*Encounter,* November, 1966)

He quotes a critic who calls **'To his Coy Mistress'**

a testament of faith in which Marvell at once rejects the materialism and determinism of Hobbes, spiritualises the Deism of Lord Herbert of Cherbury, and cements the union of faith and reason which the Cambridge Platonists thought they had found implied in Descartes. . . .

This, says Professor Kermode, is 'the most ridiculous single observation' which he encountered, but 'it is not at all uncharacteristic'. More recently, John Carey has deftly and decisively surveyed the uncomprehending ingenuities of the 'literature' on Marvell [in *Andrew Marvell: A Critical Anthology,* edited by John Carey, 1969], and his analysis, despite its *brio,* deepens the sense of dismay.

Of course, some scholars have illuminated the margins of the poems, and thanks to the late J. B. Leishman and others Marvell's next editor will have some valuable new commentary to assimilate. There have also been some enlightening critical discussions of the poems since T. S. Eliot's classic essay ['Andrew Marvell' (1921), reprinted in *Selected Essays,* 1951], which is now almost 50 years old. But on the whole the books and journals are clogged either with trivial displays of irrelevant erudition or with crude paraphrases of Eliot, and in both flabby thinking and pretentiously obscure writing tend to masquerade as profundity.

Perhaps Eliot is partly responsible; his few pages placing Marvell in a European tradition of wit and 'intense levity' are sometimes cryptic as well as suggestive. However, the incomprehension of this almost universally praised essay is much more an object lesson in how literary insights are not achieved once and for all, but have to be re-created for each generation and re-experienced by each competent reader.

Eliot's central point was that Marvell's 'intense' levity involved an 'alliance of levity and seriousness (by which the seriousness is intensified)', and 'a tough reasonableness beneath the slight lyric grace'—and 'probably, a recognition, implicit in the expression of every experience, of other kinds of experience which are possible'. The emphasis in these comments on gravity ('the *seriousness* is intensified'; 'the *slight* lyric grace'), and with it Eliot's disparagement—mistaken, I think—of two burlesque stanzas from **'Upon Appleton House'** have perhaps encouraged the undue solemnity of Marvell's commentators. Nevertheless, it is from these insights of Eliot's that intelligent appreciation must still begin. The questions to be asked afresh are: How is this alliance of levity and seriousness brought about? What, precisely, is a tough reasonableness? How are these implicit experiences to be recognised? How is it—to juxtapose two more quotations—that Marvell always finds 'the proper degree of seriousness' for his

subject, while he 'takes a slight affair, the feeling of a girl for her pet, and gives it a connexion with that inexhaustible and terrible nebula of emotion which surrounds all our exact and practical passions and mingles with them'?

When Eliot, quoting three quatrains from **'An Horatian Ode'**, referred to their having 'an equipoise, a balance and proportion of tones', he isolated one of the qualities of Marvell's 'reasonableness'. The presence or absence of this witty poise, weighing the possible attitudes of an intelligent mind against one another, is one criterion of success or otherwise in the verse. Without it the writing is liable to dwindle into lampoon or flattery; the poems' power to convince depends upon the presence of reservations.

The literary parallels for **'An Horatian Ode'** include the Roman plays and mature histories of Shakespeare; indeed, as Patrick Cruttwell has pointed out [in *The Shakespearian Moment,* 1954], the balance of insights is close to that of *Richard II.* Both turn on the 'woeful pageant' (*Richard II,* IV. v. 351) of a sympathetic 'Royal Actor' deposed by an efficient politician. Marvell's principal interest, of course, is in the Bolingbroke figure, but there is a similar juxtaposition of an ineffective king who is a superb actor with a forceful man of action who, from somewhat ambivalent motives, violates traditional sanctions and values. On the other hand, the eulogistic **'First Anniversary'** often reads as a convert's recantation of the **'Ode'**, while the earlier **'Fleckno'** is an example of the mere lampoon, rightly called by Kermode 'a nasty young-bladish poem attacking the poet Flecknoe for being hungry, Catholic, poor, and the inhabitant of a small apartment'. Marvell is determined to find anything about Flecknoe laughable, just as in the Protectorate poems he is determined to find anything about Cromwell laudable.

Witty poise, however, is not the sole criterion of major quality in the poems. **'A Dialogue between the Resolved'**, **'Soul and Created Pleasure'**, **'The Fair Singer'**, and **'Ametas and Thestylis making Hay-Ropes'** are all charming in their intelligent and witty finesse, but they are minor when compared to the finest and most unmistakably Marvellian poems (by which I mean principally the Mower quartet, **'The Garden'**, **'The Nymph complaining for the death of her Faun'**, **'To his Coy Mistress'**, **'An Horatian Ode'**, **'Upon Appleton House'**, **'The Definition of Love'**, and **'The Picture of little T.C.'**). What these also contain—and this is the other criterion of excellence in the verse—is some intimation of the inescapable causes of dread implicit in the myth of the Fall. The *Genesis* story represents the onset of what must weigh on the adult consciousness: 'death . . . and all our woe', or in modern idiom, mortality and alienation. The poems' creation of vulnerable because paradisal states of being reflects man's deeply unsettling awareness that death is inevitable and that an idyllic condition of innocence and wholeness is unattainable. A secure harmony within man and between him and his fellows and his universe is only imaginable.

Yet for all this, the poems are gay. This raises the crucial preliminary questions which T. S. Eliot ignored: Why doesn't Marvell's levity undermine his seriousness? Considering the pervasiveness of the Fall within the verse, and considering the vast social upheaval through which Marvell lived, are the balance and poise for which he has been so much praised in fact a limitation? Are they perhaps complacent evasions of human involvement and irresponsible triflings with the causes of our dread?

An answer can be best approached through a discussion of **'Damon the Mower'**, as this poem seems to me an extreme example of Marvell's characteristic strategy. The scant comment hitherto elicited by **'Damon'**, although it is one of the most enchanting short poems in the language, also makes it especially worth analysis. Its problems are more those of subtlety in what is implied than of obscurity in what is stated.

In the first place, there is a typically pervasive implication in **'Damon'** of the Fall, death and destruction, which becomes explicit in the final couplet:

> 'Tis death alone that this must do:
> For Death thou art a Mower too.

As July's sun scorches the meadow, so Juliana's eyes burn up the mower; she also maddens Sirius, the Dog-star that makes dogs mad, and she overheats the sun itself. Juliana's 'burning' of the meadow, Damon's imitation of death as he 'depopulates' the ground, and the mowing down of the mower himself add further strands of destruction. In the opening lines of Damon's song the silenced grasshoppers seek out the *shades*. Only the serpent, which has kept within the shades, glitters as if revitalised amid the scorched earth. This reminds us that Damon is 'With love of Juliana *stung*' (my italics)—the woman and the serpent more than once have similar roles in Marvell's lost paradises. When Damon gives her 'the harmless Snake . . . / Disarmed of its teeth and sting' the plaintive innuendo of the gift is obvious. Damon is now a post-lapsarian worker:

> But now I all the day complain,
> Joyning my Labour to my Pain;

(cf. *Genesis* iii. 19), and though he can delight in the 'deathless' fairies, he is distinct from them.

In this setting of death stands—and falls—the absurdly Narcissistic and complacent mower. He is confident of his good looks, his fine voice, his high repute in the mowing world, and he is assured of personal attention by all creation, from flowers to the sun. The mower, a pastoral *parvenu*, treats the ancient figure of the 'piping Shepherd' with contempt, and—as if it mattered—is confident in the ability of his scythe to uncover more ground than his rival's sheep can cover up. His calm assumption of the inferiority of wool to hay ('the golden fleece') is typical of his self-satisfaction.

He is a laughable figure, belittled by all the reverberations around him. Yet he arouses an intense affection, and the solicitous admiration we reserve for children and the childlike. His self-absorption is complemented by a touching innocence, so that even his gifts' innuendoes (that Juliana might be better without her sting, her inflexibility and her sourness) are guileless and themselves disarmed of teeth and sting. The detail of his fancy, even when self-glorifying, is as charming as it is innocent: the long tongue of the sun licks off his sweat; his face reflected in his scythe resembles the sun within a crescent moon (a development at once fanciful and particular of a pastoral commonplace).

Damon secures our sympathy because he is so vulnerable—so open both to the darts of love and the glances of his own scythe—and our admiration because he is so resilient. Love's devastations liberate his fancy; the pain and indignity of mowing down himself are turned with magnificent absurdity into what is in effect an insult to death. Death becomes his colleague and a mere medicine for the pains of love, as Clowns-all-heal is for cuts. Damon, his innocence intact, is superbly free from the fear of mortality and talks of death as one might now of a sleeping pill.

Damon therefore is a sort of Don Quixote. He has the comic and narrow nobility of an intense but simple consciousness, which through its independence defeats the destructive power of anything it happens to undervalue. For him death is 'disarmed of its teeth and sting' because Juliana's sting is so much the more potent. Grave, where is thy victory?

The core of Marvell's achievement here is that he is mocking death by giving it such a charmingly absurd colleague, and it is possible from this insight to begin a generalisation about the art of the finer poems. These poems are the mind's declaration of independence from the Fall and the causes of dread which weigh on the human consciousness. The sense of death's inevitability concentrates the mind wonderfully. Marvell maintains lucidity without dwindling into self-pity, without luxuriating in the grandeur of his anguish, without any tremors of anxiety. He can be associated with the kind of scaffold and deathbed humour represented, for example, by Sir Thomas More mounting to the block ('I pray you, master Lieutenant, see me safe up, and my coming down let me shift for my self'), or by Charles II ('He had been, he said, an unconscionable time dying; but he hoped that they would excuse it'), or by Oscar Wilde dying in poverty ('I suppose that I shall have to die beyond my means'). The impeccable demeanour of Marvell's own Charles I is a version of this (**'An Horatian Ode'** 53-64).

Presumably Marvell had no special reason to think when writing that he was about to die (we must turn to a Ralegh or Chidiock Tichborne for that). But the causes of dread assimilated into his verse are lasting, even though not always urgent, and his humour is a demonstration parallel to those of More and the others that, whatever the suffering, the mind is in command and the spirit indomitable.

It is from this perspective that we should view Marvell's delicate manners and poise. His achievement is that out of deep fears and frustrations he creates exquisite works of joy. The poems are acts of urbane and imperturbable defiance, affirmations of the mind's effortless superiority heightened by the virtuoso's ease of poetic detailing. Damon's pastoral absurdity belittles his colleague's death, and more generally such threatening forces are belittled by their setting, even though their power is acknowledged. Death, be not proud.

Marvell's serenity is not a callous cheerfulness, therefore, but the equanimity of courage. The levity *is* the serious-

> Marvell's achievement is that out of deep fears and frustrations he creates exquisite works of joy. The poems are acts of urbane and imperturbable defiance, affirmations of the mind's effortless superiority heightened by the virtuoso's ease of poetic detailing.
>
> —*John Creaser*

ness. Marvell does not inexplicably connect slight affairs with Eliot's 'inexhaustible and terrible nebula of emotion', he yokes them by insolence together. He does not merely leave implicit 'other kinds of experience which are possible', he commands their presence. Poems which lack the 'gaiety transfiguring all that dread', such as **'On a Drop of Dew'**, are less deeply serious through their very seriousness.

Because the insult to what is inevitable is made as nearly explicit as the effortless superiority allows, **'Damon the Mower'** represents, as I have said, an extreme form of Marvellian strategy. To demonstrate fully his other versions of serene defiance would require several essays, and here I shall merely sketch out some possibilities. However, **'The Mower to the Glo-Worms'** calls for close attention, as it is among the most subtle short poems written before Blake and has not had much relevant criticism.

> Ye living Lamps, by whose dear light
> The Nightingale does sit so late,
> And studying all the Summer-night,
> Her matchless Songs does meditate;
>
> Ye Country Comets, that portend
> No War, nor Prince's funeral,
> Shining unto no higher end
> Then to presage the Grasses fall;
>
> Ye Glo-worms, whose officious Flame
> To wandring Mowers shows the way,
> That in the Night have lost their aim,
> And after foolish Fires do stray;
>
> Your courteous Lights in vain you wast,
> Since *Juliana* here is come,
> For She my Mind hath so displac'd
> That I shall never find my home.

The primary level of this exquisite address is not difficult to trace. The Mower views the glow-worms affectionately because they help mowers and the nightingale, and because their appearance portends no disaster worse than hay-making. However, this help is useless to him, as the arrival of Juliana has so disturbed him that he will never find his way home.

This is obviously inadequate for the poetic experience, inadequate, for example, if one considers the confidence of the poem's movement, its falling into one perfectly turned sentence. The poise of the three parallel addresses to the glow-worms is the more marked because Marvell rarely

carries over his sentences from stanza to stanza. There does not seem to be much displacement of the mind here.

Browning in his dramatic monologues aims at a self-sufficient speaker rather than a persona for himself. In Marvell's dramatic lyrics, one is aware of a larger consciousness enclosing the naïve and innocent speaker (especially in **'Damon the Mower'** with its introductory stanza). Here (in **'to the Glo-Worms'**) the bewildered rustic of the displaced mind is penetrated by an amused sophisticate, who makes fun of the Mower's world. From this perspective it is comic that the nightingale seems merely to sit and study by the light of the glow-worms, rather complacently thinking of her 'matchless Songs'. The glow-worms are trivial compared to the grave portents of a comet; they are 'officious', not only zealous but unduly forward in proffering their so limited services; that their lights are termed 'court-eous' merely indicates how rustic they are. I am reminded of the elder Hamlet's farewell:

> The glow-worm shows the matin to be near,
> And 'gins to pale his *uneffectual* fire.
> (I. 5. 89, my italics)

The teasing is not without affection; the glow-worms are doing what they can, although clearly it is not much. They can guide mowers who stray after 'foolish Fires', but they are helpless against the 'unusual Heats' raised by Juliana.

On the other hand, if one allows 'meditate' the meaning 'to practise or cultivate the art of poetry', which it has in Virgil and which is imitated in Milton's 1645 collection (echoed several times by Marvell), then the so-kindly-aided nightingale is less passive. More significantly, in the middle stanzas the glow-worms seem to have a more than literal function. Stanza iii seems an analogue of moral guidance, and to presage the fall of the grass is not necessarily trivial, because the grass is associated in Marvell's 'green' poems with hope (**'Damon the Mower'**, 8; **'The Mower's Song'**, 4), and because Isaiah xl. 6—'All flesh is grass'—pervades the poems. The fall of the grass thus brings to mind the Fall of man.

The close of the poem carries these hints further (they are no more than hints). The resonance of the word 'home' is not accounted for by the literal meaning that the Mower will never find where he lives. Clearly the common associations of security, peace and rest are appropriate. The obvious metaphorical meaning of the grave, the 'long home' of *Ecclesiastes* xii. 5, is excluded by the word 'never', but the related and common metaphorical meaning of the afterlife, of man's heavenly home from which earthly life is an exile, may well be relevant. *Hebrews* xiii. 14 ('For here have we no continuing city, but we seek one to come') and 2 *Corinthians* v are among the biblical sources for this, and there are many contemporary parallels.

Another possible overtone is suggested by the proverb, 'The lover is not where he lives, but where he loves'. This is echoed frequently in the writing of the period, for example by Florio: 'Nay where my love is, there my heart is, not lodging where it liveth, but where it loveth'. Hence the beloved can be imagined as the lover's 'home', his true resting place—home is where the heart is—and this underlies passages such as:

My heart to her but as guest-wise sojourned
And now to Helen is it home returned,
There to remain.
            (*A Midsummer Night's Dream*, III. 2. 171-3)

The mower will never know the content of this 'home'.

The poem seems therefore to present in comic miniature an analogue of various disruptive and alienating experiences. Love so dominates the lover's mind that he will never find peace and rest. It has so unbalanced his mind that he will sacrifice the life to come for it. And it so displaces his mind that it has removed him from the paradisal world of the pastoral idyll, where all live in content and co-operation, where the glow-worm aids nightingale and mower alike. In short, he has 'fallen'.

It is, however, a genial and even a fortunate fall. Whatever the sophisticate behind the rustic may think, the Mower rejects the guidance of the glow-worms and their 'dear light' courteously. Because Juliana, however unresponsive she may be, is now his 'home', the centre and goal of his affections, he seems no longer to care for either his comforting earthly or his continuing spiritual 'homes'.

What makes this brief lyric the epitome of Marvell's writings is not alone the surprising complexity of suggestion which can be teased out of it, but rather the confidence and gaiety with which the suggestions are handled. Just as death is mocked by its association with Damon and by his *insouciance* before death, so the disruptive experience implied here is mocked by its amusing projection on so tiny a scale.

Although trapped in body, the Lady tells Comus: 'Thou canst not touch the freedom of my mind', and this freedom is manifest at least as much by Marvell's weaving witty variations on the threat as it is by the Lady's fervent indignation.

A similar strategy of wit underlies the other, rather less remarkable, Mower poems. The four poems—in the order of the 1681 folio, as it happens—present a progressive awareness of the Fall, of the breaking of the primal sympathy between man and nature. In **'The Mower against Gardens'**, and in **'Damon'**, nature's benignant co-operation is assumed (rather more fully in the first poem); in **'to the Glo-Worms'** it still exists, but is ineffective; in **'The Mower's Song'** nature flourishes while the mower pines. This alienation is accompanied by an inner alienation (the displaced mind of 'my Thoughts and Me'). In **'The Mower's Song'**, by concluding this process with such a slight affair and by associating it with the horrors of some universal destruction, of 'one common Ruine', Marvell again makes fun of the sources of pain. The gay poignancy of **'against Gardens'** comes from the pervasive realisation of the Fall and the channelling of this through a naïvely one-sided speaker.

Similarly, the basis of [the power of **'The Garden'** is] its presentation of a state which triumphantly neutralises major consequences of the Fall: mortality, labour, the displaced mind. The significance of the poem lies not in any arcane meaning that can be strained out of it, but in the liberation of mind communicated by the poet, whose 'erected wit' delivers its green world, its paradise regained.

The reservations and intelligent complexities which critics have so often discussed overwhelm any suspicion of mere escapism.

I am not trying to impose one pattern onto these greater poems. **'The Nymph complaining'**, for example, is clearly a partial exception. Here the mind's metamorphosing and creative powers tend rather to establish than to transcend human sorrow. The Nymph is something of an Ophelia; she has learned that 'there's tricks i' the' world', and 'thought and affliction . . . she turns to favour and to prettiness'. She is, however, an Ophelia not bereft of sanity, for all her loose hold on reality. She does not quite forget that the loved creature is only a beast, and she hovers affectingly between 'thou' and 'it' in her speech; she retains the common sense to 'bespeak' a grave. The Nymph is also something of a Damon; both are delicately, solemnly self-dramatising, both are creative in sorrow, both offhand about their own deaths, and both the innocent victim of more immediate sorrow. But the Nymph pathetically lacks Damon's resilience; life seems so empty without her faun that she imagines there is nothing for her to do but to die. However unreal this determination may be, however slight she may seem by comparison with her biblical and mythological allusions, she is so vulnerable and so open to abuse that her grief must be sympathised with.

It may perhaps still be objected that the argument so far has given the poet the benefit of some doubt, and that his witty and effortless superiority is able to hold dread at bay because so little dread is felt. The citing of **'The Nymph'** is relevant here because in this poem Marvell very movingly *creates* the sense of sorrow. An even clearer example is the middle paragraph of **'To His Coy Mistress'**, which communicates a *frisson* as grimly humorous as anything in Donne. Here, for a few lines, Marvell belongs not so much to the tradition of gaiety on the scaffold which I have already mentioned, as to one of sardonic mastery, that of St. Lawrence's bitter joke while being grilled over the flames—*assum est, versa et manduca*—or of Archbishop Laud, about to be beheaded, speaking of the Red Sea he was to cross. The outer paragraphs of **'To His Coy Mistress'**, however, are in Marvell's more characteristic vein of the liberated mind neutralising the fear; the two modes are adjacent.

                    . . . . .

Marvell's fascination with the creative possibilities of the mind,

        The Mind, that Ocean where each kind
        Does streight its own resemblance find;
        Yet it creates, transcending these,
        Far other Worlds, and other Seas,

sometimes exists independent of the transfiguring of dread and the elegantly insulting defence. T. S. Eliot's emphasis on 'tough reasonableness' has hindered adequate recognition of Marvell's deep and complementary joy in unreason and fantasy. This fantasy is not, moreover, wish-fulfilment and self-glorification, but enchantment at the bizarre or mysterious creations and mutations possible within the mind's eye.

It is not surprising, therefore, that some critics have failed to deal relevantly, which is to say tactfully, with **'Upon Appleton House'**, the clearest expression of high-fantastical exuberance ('Exuberance is Beauty'). Some sternly ignore the lightness of tone and discipline Marvell's political and spiritual hints into solemn parades. The value of this tendency may be gauged by the recurrent desire to identify the corncrake of line 395 with Charles I, on the grounds of the bird's death, its association with royalty, and its killer's dread. Such wishful thinking overlooks these facts: that this Charles is killed by chance, is about to be eaten, is of lowly station, is survived by his lamenting parents, and—curiouser and curiouser—that this Charles is a young female.

Other critics have been influenced by Eliot's description of stanza VII as 'immediately and unintentionally ridiculous' and as 'merely a fancy', and by his belief that the 'leathern boats' image of the final stanza is distracting and supports nothing but its own misshapen body. They sense the lightness of tone, and find it irresponsible. The most telling voice here is that of Robin Grove, yet the basis of his powerful critique is that the poem fails to validate an inquiry into philosophical speculations which it 'seems to undertake'. He adds:

> Marvell appears intent on the intimation of a subtle and ambiguous speculative position, but instead we prize the witty swiftness of intelligence and the startling images that are cleverly given an air of mock-seriousness. [Grove, in *Andrew Marvell: A Critical Anthology*, edited by John Carey, 1969]

His 'seems' and 'appears' foist onto the poem a failure which is not there, for it is not serious in any ambitious way.

Both groups of critics, variously aware that **'Appleton House'** is substantial in more than length, are after a more earnest and a more rigorously organised poem than is there, and the groups invent it or are disappointed, according to the nature of their critical insight. **'Appleton House'** has a clear narrative thread and it is easy to trace a general coherence by relating the paradisal retreat of the estate to the false innocence and withdrawal of the nuns and to the fallen paradise that is England. The poem is not formless, but it is informal and capacious. It is by an *'easie Philosopher'* (561) and is in no ordered way philosophical or even thematically subtle. It would be absurd to try to find significant cross-reference between the *'Fairfacian Oak'* (740) and the tainted and 'hollow Oak' of stanza LXIX. We are not invited to dwell on the contradictory ways in which stanzas IV, X, XXXVI *et seq.* and LXXXVII express the apparently central concern of art and nature, and, for example, to attempt a reconciliation by seeing Maria as representative of nature and Fairfax of art (and hence nature the daughter of art . . .). Because 'The World when first created sure / Was such a Table rase and pure' (445-6), are we to imagine the whole of the estate, *'Paradice's only Map'* (768), as perfectly flat? Marvell is dealing out conventional emblems and ideas as they suit his play of wit.

Why then does the poem matter? We may begin an answer with the full title: **'Upon Appleton House, to my Lord Fairfax'**. It is a country-house and estate poem dedicated to the lord of the house by a resident there, and it is nourished by a warm and assured familiarity with the family and the setting. The sense of familiarity, which can make it almost a private poem, emerges from many details. Stanzas IX and X, for example, echo and perhaps gently burlesque the solemn piety of Fairfax's own poem, 'Upon the New-built House att Apleton'. In stanza LXXXIX Maria is praised for a fluency in languages for which the poet, as her tutor, must have been partly responsible, and, like little T.C., she is often praised teasingly in hyperboles of affectionate excess. Marvell's confident affection also enables him to imply in passing that the retired Fairfax still has more to devote himself to than his estate.

But Marvell's main intent is the celebration of that estate. He takes delight in familiar routine—a walk in the garden and grounds, mowing, fishing—and through the intervention of the creative (though not here 'transcending') mind turns what is keenly observed into something rich and strange. Bees and flowers lead to the proliferating fancy of this:

> Then in some Flow'rs beloved Hut
> Each Bee as Sentinel is shut;
> And sleeps so too: but, if once stir'd,
> She runs you through, nor askes *the Word*.
> (317-20)

Detail extends into more witty detail; the impression is of a mind brilliantly at play, delighting in its own powers. All the metamorphoses and abrupt shifts of perspective are not, however, a gallimaufry of Clevelandisms. Marvell's delight in what his mind can make of the estate, and his delight in the estate for itself, intensify one another. The description of it is internally coherent and harmonises with the known facts. The ground-plan of accuracy emphasises Marvell's powers of re-creation; he is not merely imagining in a void. Furthermore, the frequent and alert self-mockery (as in stanza LXXIV) prevents the far-fetched wit from seeming a cocky and indulgent cleverness.

In a curious and crucial way, **'Appleton House'** anticipates *Tristram Shandy*. At the heart of that novel—for all the oddities of form, narrator and characters—lies a celebration of the ordinary and the everyday. The work is more than a supremely clever anti-novel because of its basis in common domestic fidelities and vexations, however flat out the hobby-horses may be ridden. The eccentric methods of narration enable Sterne to dwell with more detail on minor domestic affairs than a conventional storyteller would dare or care to, and the everyday is revitalised and enriched because it is seen so exactly and affectionately by a narrator of volatile intelligence. While **'Appleton House'** is clearly less focused on the inhabitants than on house and estate, these are valued because of the inhabitants. And because the house and estate are delighted in by a mind of Marvell's idiosyncratic and unsycophantic intelligence, the reader's sense of the worth of the everyday is deepened.

It may now be possible to see more justly the stanzas disparaged by Eliot. He cites first:

> Yet thus the leaden House does sweat,
> And scarce indures the *Master* great:
> But where he comes the swelling Hall
> Stirs, and the *Square* grows *Spherical*;
>
> (49-52)

commenting that this, 'whatever its intention, is more absurd than it was intended to be'. It certainly is, as Eliot has substituted 'leaden' for 'laden' and imported irrelevant associations of molten metal. The unusual and meticulous run-on into the fourth line, emphasised by the pause after 'Stirs', enacts the swelling of the house, and this deftness should indicate that the poet knows what he is about. The ostensible theme here is to praise the 'sober Frame' (line 1) of the house and the associated virtues of order and humility, and in the opening stanzas Marvell advances the conventional proposition that man's dwellings should not be pretentiously large but proportioned to the inhabitants, for 'No Creature loves an empty space' (15). Just before the offending passage he comes closest to an apparently straight-forward acceptance of this:

> *Humility* alone designs
> Those short but admirable Lines, . . .
> These *holy Mathematicks* can
> In ev'ry Figure equal Man.
>
> (41-8)

As C. R. Markham records [in *A Life of the Great Lord Markham*, 1870] the central part of the house was surmounted by a cupola. In the 'laden House' stanza Marvell gently mocks his conventional theme—that in these 'dwarfish Confines' (38) here 'ev'ry Thing does answer Use' (62)—by demonstrating a necessity for such a prominent and hardly man-sized feature. The lowly hall cannot contain the great figure of Lord Fairfax and 'clownishly ascends' (60) into the cupola, which then becomes properly functional. The need for such a sophistical treatment of moral stature as if it were physical teasingly qualifies the conventionally celebrated humility of Fairfax's retired life. Marvell's smiling praise implies that the house is, after all, far from a 'Bee-like Cell' (40), and, like stanza XLIV, that Fairfax is rather out of his element. The stanza's extreme absurdity is its very point; there is no sycophantic excess.

The final stanza seems to me among the most delightful and, through its placing, most moving written by Marvell:

> But now the *Salmon-Fisher's* moist
> Their *Leathern Boats* begin to hoist;
> And, like *Antipodes* in Shoes,
> Have shod their Heads in their *Canoos*.
> How *Tortoise* like, but not so slow,
> These rational *Amphibii* go?
> Let's in: for the dark *Hemisphere*
> Does now like one of them appear.

Read as a conceit illuminating a situation (like the oblique and parallel lines of **'The Definition of Love'**) this is, of course, ridiculously far-fetched. Dr. Johnson would not have thought it worth the carriage. But the poem has been more concerned with the witty variations of the imagination on what is precisely known than with the attainment of precision. This final stanza is so extremely far-fetched because it *is* the final stanza, a coda epitomising the poem's methods as well as reminding us of the everyday activity

of the estate after the episode praising the 'genius' of the place.

Just as the wit is a recapitulation of procedure, so the detail of the stanza recapitulates earlier episodes. The reference to the salmon-fishers draws the alert mind (and this is not an indulgent but an alert stanza, conscious of its absurdity) back to the floods of stanza LIX *et seq.*, where '*Salmons* trespassing are found' (479), and to the fishing of stanza LXXXI, Marvell's final activity in his delicious solitude before the appearance of Maria. The leathern boats recall the boats of line 436 and imply the presence of the river which flows through the central episodes, 'the only Snake' (632) in this restored Eden, and the cause of many typical metamorphoses. The tortoise occurs in the second stanza, exemplifying the theme of order and humility. The phrase 'but not so slow', coming as it does before a reference to the darkening sky, brings lines 463-4 back to mind:

> They (the cattle) feed so wide, so slowly move,
> As *Constellations* do above.

The Antipodes, as topsy-turvy as their name suggests, echo stanza LXXI:

> Or turn me but, and you shall see
> I was but an inverted Tree,

the ancient notion of man-as-heavenly-plant treated with smiling literalism. 'Rational *Amphibii*' in two words suggests the fluctuations of the poet and other actors as perceived by the creative mind—now mowers on land, now sinking through a green sea, now merging into bird and tree (LXXI) or into river. Nightfall, with the ending of the day's activity, is obviously a fitting moment to end, as the tour of the estate has lasted throughout a day (lines 289, 369, 388, 465, 625, 651). 'Let's in' returns us to the country house which has been the occasion of the poem.

It would be idle to attempt to find thematic relevance for these echoes. The poem, as I have argued, is moving through its very lack of such stringency. The informality is expressive, for it adds to the sense of ease and intimacy and delighted relaxation which the '*easie Philosopher*' communicates. The stanza is effective because it is a fanciful but concentrated recapitulation of a series of fanciful re-creations. Eliot's influential disapproval is irrelevant.

However, it is important that Marvell's affectionate play is at times deepened by his characteristic resonance. Stanza XLVII, for example, the finest in the poem, is a joyously bizarre transfiguring of Hell. It brings to mind the *Apocalypse*, especially the opening verses of chapter 9, where locusts arise from the abyss commanded to hurt not 'the grass of the earth' but men who do not bear the seal of God. More generally, there are numerous hints of the Fall and of England's 'Fall', of which the Civil Wars were the consequence. Marvell is aware of the claims of the outer world, and stanza LXXVII implies that he will leave Appleton, just as stanza XLIV implies that Fairfax still has wider responsibilities. But the estate is deeply and movingly delighted in as an enclave of Paradise within the fallen land, where the beneficent river is 'the only Snake', and (as in Denham's praise of the Thames in 'Cooper's Hill')

No unexpected inundations spoyl
The mowers hopes.

(175-6)

Here warfare is enacted only by flowers and mowers—that the Nun Appleton tenantry had fought under and sometimes alongside Fairfax throughout the actual Civil Wars makes this poignantly relevant. Such transmutation of fallen and all too familiar strife into, on the one hand, the joyous and sociable activity of the mowers ('And now the careless Victors play, / Dancing the Triumphs of the Hay') and, on the other, into the charming fancy of flower and bee is once more Marvell consummately refusing to be overwhelmed, once more insulting by imperturbability.

Rosalie L. Colie (essay date 1970)

SOURCE: "Love Poems" and "*Carpe Diem* Poems," in *"My Ecchoing Song": Andrew Marvell's Poetry of Criticism,* Princeton University Press, 1970, pp. 43-56.

[*Colie was an American educator, historian, and poet. In the following excerpt, she studies Marvell's love poetry.*]

In a period so productive of brilliant love poetry, Marvell's love poems are remarkable for their coolness and self-sufficiency. From his love poetry, critics have often been tempted to derive a given poet's attitude to love and psychological involvement generally, and Marvell has not been spared diagnosis from his poems. Precisely because of the detachment of his love lyrics, readers have come to various conclusions about the poet's nature—that he was frigid, impotent, homosexual, capable only of "vegetable" love (whatever that may be). Actually, there is no more need to interpret Marvell's love poetry as autobiographical than so to interpret Herrick's or Donne's or (perhaps the best comparison) Crashaw's. In Marvell's case, the temptation to autobiographize his love poetry is particularly tactless, since the open directives he gives us in that poetry are so clearly to traditions of literary expression, not to immediate experiences. As in his pastorals, Marvell practiced here also in the conventions he received; his love poetry touches on most of the current themes and styles, and, again as in his pastoral poetry, in the lyrics of love too he seems to question and to test most of them. In **"The Fair Singer,"** for instance, the poet plays with petrarchan language, as he sings of his total enslavement to a lady blessed with both a pretty face and a sweet voice. Many different and thoroughly familiar amatory hyperboles are brought together in this little poem: the notion that there is a battle between lady and lover; that the battle is sweet for its very fierceness; that love, though like a battle, is also like harmony in music; that both battle and harmony have their correspondences in cosmic warfare and in cosmic harmony. All these notions, traditional in love poetry, are so intricately intertwined and so trickily played off against one another, that they are difficult to take seriously, the more so because the setting is so clearly just a musical party. The point of this poem is the poet's dexterity with familiar idioms. The extravagance of the developed "petrarchan" rhetoric is here made so intellectually melodious that the silliness of the "curled trammels of her hair," the "Fetters" made of air, or the airs of the lady's breath

and her song, seem somehow natural, in so thoroughly and frankly artificial an environment. The lady's voice controls the air, is like the wind; her eyes are like the sun: against an army so favored, how can mere man hope to contend?

Not only are there many concepts in the poem, but conventional conceits are pushed to extremes as well. By their sheer accumulation, the extravagant clichés point to their own nonsense. Against this nonsense-quality, though, something else tugs in another direction, toward composure and sanity. The regular metrics and beautifully counterpoised phrases of

Love did compose so sweet an Enemy,
In whom both Beauties to my death agree,
Joyning themselves in fatal Harmony;

manage to contain and to prolong the image and its meanings. What can this poet not get away with? From curls of hair, which from contemporary usage we expect to signalize wanton irregularity, he manages to move in quite another direction, to cosmic harmony, blending and contrasting the elements in the figures to stress their sweet traditionalism and their literal foolishness.

Quite clearly, the speaker's heart in this poem is left untouched. What concerns him is the nature of the amatory clichés: what can he do with them to make the poem, not the condition of love, interesting? Indeed, it is just the lyricism of the untouched heart that strikes us so strongly in this verse; the poet seems to speak in love's conventional language in order to show its inadequacies, its silliness as applied to an emotion either too stereotyped (as in **"The Fair Singer"**) or too uncontrolled (as in **"The unfortunate Lover,"** discussed below). One might group with **"The Fair Singer"** such poems as **"The Match"** and **"The Gallery,"** in which the beloved seems a construct, not a woman, set up for the poet's display of the school-figures of love.

In **"The Definition of Love,"** a poem ostensibly about passion thwarted—the same theme, so differently treated, as in **"The unfortunate Lover"**—the poet appears to have stretched the possibilities of a love lyric to the utmost: this definition of love is in fact a definition of not-love. A poem called a "definition" may be expected to be intellectual, or intellectually constructed; this poem is surely that. It has an extraordinarily tight logic and consistent argument, rare in any poetry, but the poet's intellectualism lay even more in his poem's plan than in its strategy. Once more, in this poem Marvell has turned a recognized genre on its head, by the simple means of reconsidering and reinterpreting its title. The ordinary "definition" pattern, by which a series of bracketing partial answers to a question offer some approximation of definition, has been abandoned for quite another sort of definition, taken from an entirely different vocabulary, that of Euclidian geometry. As Mr. Hyman's able analysis of the poem has demonstrated, the logic has to be carefully worked out by readers—and, to be successful, had to have been worked out long beforehand by the poet. The "Iron wedges," the "Decrees of Steel," the "Poles," the sphere and the planisphere, the oblique and the parallel lines all maintain their consistency in sequence and in logic, to give an appearance of explanation to the situation in which poet and lady find themselves. What is that situation? Theoretically, an emotional one, the conventions of which are as scrupulously criticized as other conventions are in such poems as **"Mourning"** and **"The Nymph complaining"**: this poem is about star-crossed love, with none of the resignation or the hope, for instance, of Donne's great valedictions. The lover in this poem is quite content to be separated from his beloved; his geometrical demonstration and his proof of irrevocable parting seem to please him by their implacable logic. Whatever emotion this poem bears comes not from the poet's grief at his situation's hopelessness, but from his satisfaction in having solved his problem intellectually, in having his geometry come out right. In stanza VII, he plays on the geometrical notion of osculation, rather than on the passionate fact of kissing:

> As Lines so Loves *oblique* may well
> Themselves in every Angle greet:
> But ours so truly *Paralel*,
> Though infinite can never meet.

Even the geometry flattens out, as the solid figures become plane. There is a beautiful appropriateness to the last stanza too: certainly the metaphysical bluestocking who could understand this lover's poem is best bound to him by "the Conjunction of the Mind."

In these poems, the lover is a cool customer, deliberately distancing himself from the prickly irritations and irrationalities generally attendant upon unhappy love. Though so different in tone, language, and narrative from these poems, **"Daphnis and Chloe"** has some affinity with **"The Definition of Love,"** in the detachment of the speaker's conclusions about the psychology of love. Chloe loses Daphnis, it seems, because she is coy:

> . . . she neither knew t'enjoy,
> Nor yet let her Lover go.

That is, the thwarted Daphnis has come to the end of his rope and resolves to leave his unyielding lady. At this point, we are on his side; but so, it turns out, is Chloe. Shocked by the possibility of losing Daphnis, she lets down all her conventional defenses, to permit him anything—but by that time, it seems, Daphnis is far too intent on acting his part to take account of her offer of total surrender. For all his passionate utterance, he too turns out to be a very cool customer, enjoying the drama he creates far more than he cares for the girl. At first, his misery seems real enough, even if a little overstated:

> His disorder'd Locks he tare;
> And with rouling Eyes did glare,
> And his cruel Fate forswear.

"Dead," "shrieks," "distracted," "wretched," "torture," "condemned Wight"—Daphnis is torn on the rack of his gothick emotions. We can sympathize, until we realize that in these emotions his pleasure lies. Naturally, he finds his ranting delicious, far too pleasurable to be cut short, or to resolve practically in relation to the girl. He deliberately protracts his suffering valediction, as coy in protesting his love's agony as Chloe had ever been in preserving her virtue. To put it at its plainest, Daphnis does not love the girl—and, if the tenses of the poem can be trusted, he

never had loved her. Refusing to be won over by her love for him, he turns out to be much chillier than poor cozened Chloe, coy by convention only:

> Why should I enrich my Fate?
> 'Tis a Vanity to wear,
> For my Executioner,
> Jewels of so high a rate.
> Rather I away will pine
> In a manly stubbornness
> Than be fatted up express
> For the *Canibal* to dine.

Such language might suggest that Daphnis has come to his senses, but that is by no means the case. He is simply using "love" as his excuse for emotional self-indulgence. He enjoys his own part as chief actor in the scene staged; and though Chloe tries to make some part in it for herself, he consistently upstages her in his determination to act out his part. Daphnis maintains his integrity, all right, but it is the integrity of histrionics rather than of a "self":

> Joy will not with Sorrow weave,
> Nor will I this Grief pollute.

"Pollute"! One must grant to professional emotionalists their rights to live in perpetual crisis, however disruptive the crises may be of other people's peace and quiet; Daphnis is indeed a familiar psychological type. But such people do not, or cannot, love: their satisfactions come from the climactic display of their passions, and their release comes not from the unions of love but from the lonely pressures of their dramatic drives. Daphnis exists to criticize not only the extravagant gestures of lovers, but also the use of "love" as a screen for other kinds of self-indulgence and self-expression, regardless of social cost.

The poem makes no bones of its morality: had it ended at the twenty-fifth stanza—

> At these words away he broke;
> As who long has praying ly'n,
> To his Heads-man makes the Sign,
> And receives the parting stroke.

—we would have had a commentary on the imaginary, fantastic, unreal, beautifully private nature of renunciation, with all its selfishness gentled in its sentimentality. Daphnis might then have been the male counterpart of the complaining Nymph, who after all does no one any harm; or he might have been another renouncing lover, in a different style, like the speaker in **"The Definition of Love,"** proud of his iron control over his behavior. But the poem does not end with the twenty-fifth stanza, with the dramatics of Daphnis and the revealed concealments of Chloe. Rather, the poet mercilessly undercuts his chief character, to show him at last a crude sensualist. Chloe's refusal has, in a way, lasted just long enough to justify Daphnis' systematic promiscuity with the other nymphs in the neighborhood:

> But hence Virgins all beware.
> Last night he with *Phlogis* slept;
> This night for *Dorinda* kept;
> And but rid to take the Air.
>
> Yet he doth himself excuse;

In the last line, there is a wealth of observation of real life: pastoral convention does not yield young men like this one. By allowing Daphnis his "cause" for sleeping around, the poet comments on the brutality underlying the conventional relations of lovers:

> Nor indeed without a Cause.
> For, according to the Lawes,
> Why did *Chloe* once refuse?

One of the ironies in this poem is entirely literary: its title. Those original pastoral lovers, so gentle with one another, so devoted through all difficulty and trial, are the exact opposite of these unfeeling creatures, quite out of tune with one another and with their pastoral environment. Like **"The Definition of Love,"** which undercuts the conventions of passionate love lyric, this poem stretches the pastoral, that sentimental mode, quite out of shape. Really, this poem is emotionally anti-pastoral and anti-love. The ranting lover is an unfeeling calculator, a sensualist denying sentimental rights to anyone else. This love lyric turns out to be about quite different emotions masked under the name of love.

Daphnis has some kinship with the hero of **"The unfortunate Lover,"** a poem very difficult to explicate, which also deals with the psychological impasses, the self-frustrations of an unfortunate lover. The first stanza begins with a picture of happy lovers unharmed by their passion, the beautiful picture smudged by the stanza's first word:

> Alas, how pleasant are their dayes
> With whom the Infant Love yet playes!
> Sorted by pairs, they still are seen
> By Fountains cool, and Shadows green.

The tonal interloper, "Alas," ushers in, in the fifth line, its reliable "but":

> But soon these Flames do lose their light,
> Like Meteors of a Summers night:
> Nor can they to that Region climb,
> To make impression upon Time.

About another exhibitionist and compulsive lover, this poem is, however, written from quite a different point of view, that of an almost material figure who sympathetically tries to understand and explain the passionateless and unsuccess of the lover, who raves, like Daphnis, but has not Daphnis' capacity to resolve his dilemma in brutality. The lover's emblematized birth was of course unfortunate: he was born in a storm characteristic of his nature and his behavior in later life:

> The Sea lent him these bitter Tears
> Which at his Eyes he alwaies bears.
> And from the Winds the Sighs he bore,
> Which through his surging Breast do roar.
> No Day he saw but that which breaks,
> Through frighted Clouds in forked streaks.
> While round the ratling Thunder hurl'd,
> As at the Fun'ral of the World.

The image-structure is clear enough, the familiar likening of human temperament to the elements of the physical universe, winds turned to sighs, rain to tears, thunder to groans and cries. But the correspondence-pattern in this poem is also stretched beyond conventional limits, to bring the convention to obvious absurdity. The incredible, emblematic, mysterious nature of this poem's figures flaunts the conceitedness of the hyperbolical notion in the first place, comments on the clichés of this particular hyperbolical style—but it does not merely reduce to absurdity an over-used set of psychological clichés; it leaves us wondering, also, about the problems of compulsive behavior. This language, though so deliberately stilted and deformed, has the advantage of matching the poor lover's spiritual tumult. His quality as unfortunate resides in his having been born into his temperament. This gloomy Promethean figure characteristically overreacts, struggling against his life with the froward stubbornness of a King Lear:

> . . . he, betwixt the Flames and Waves,
> Like *Ajax*, the mad Tempest braves.

The ridiculousness of this poem does not lie wholly in the sad but inevitable foolishness of the lover; it lies as well in making a lover like this the inhabitant of a lyric poem. This man was born to tragedy, not lyric; like Daphnis, his real occupation is not in being a lover, but in being something else—in his case, an unfortunate. He must be self-frustrated, even before he can fix on an object of desire. Furthermore, like Daphnis, he loves his own role:

> See how he nak'd and fierce does stand,
> Cuffing the Thunder with one hand;
> While with the other he does lock,
> And grapple, with the stubborn Rock:
> From which he with each Wave rebounds,
> Torn into Flames, and ragg'd with Wounds.
> And all he saies, a Lover drest
> In his own Blood doth relish best.

His own quibble turns him into food; his appetite feeds on himself. The speakers in **"The Definition of Love"** and **"The Nymph complaining"** certainly "relish" their conditions, too, and enjoy their own sense of deprivation; they too stage their emotions to suit their temperaments. But what they do with taste and tact, delicacy and grace, this lover does at the top of his voice, farcically exaggerating gesture and word. Indeed, the controlling "voice" in **"The Definition of Love"** is very like the anonymous speaker of **"The unfortunate Lover,"** who seems by understanding the hysterical subject to distance him, even from his own passions; who seems to accept the Lover's violence without judging his personality or requiring him to alter his behavior in any way. Unlike the desperate Chloe or the hypersensitive Nymph, the cool voice speaking **"The unfortunate Lover"** is an art critic, enjoying the lover's turning into a heraldic pattern, ending the din, ending the story. Dying, the Lover is far prettier, to say nothing of more manageable than when alive. He

> . . . dying leaves a Perfume here,
> And Musick within every Ear:
> And he in Story only rules,
> In a Field *Sable* a Lover *Gules*.

On the face of it, Marvell's love poetry also seems to rule in story rather than in anything like real life. The kind of amatory fiction the poet deals in is neither lyrical nor dramatic, though cast in those modes; it is critical. No lover could of course linger with Chloe; before long all the nymphs of the environment will have had enough of Daphnis, as he of Chloe. No lady could get a word in edgewise with the unfortunate Lover. Really, no lady exists, in effect, in **"The Definition of Love"**: the lady is so abstracted by the predestining geometry that she relinquishes all claim to flesh and blood. These poems are not about love between persons, with its overwhelming intensities, its painful misunderstandings, and its peaceful satisfactions and boredoms. They are about the literary languages of love, about poses struck by lovers, about love as an excuse for emotional and poetical play. They are studies in feelings masked, disguised, concealed, repressed; they consider emotions detached from situations and from personality. They are about behavior loosed from its normal emotional sources. As such, these poems comment not only on the language poets are assigned to "express" their conventional and their real notions, but on the social and psychological states to which such languages are assumed to correspond. Therefore they reach out to say something not in their mandate, or in the mandate of lyric poetry—they say something definite about love itself. To be real, it cannot be like this; the conventions by which love is expressed, like the psychomachic conventions of the Body-Soul dialogue, must be revised to bring love's language into line with psychological actuality. Such ironic comments on literary love as these say something important about life as well—that lovers who fit such patterns are mutilated human beings. . . .

> Marvell's love poems are about the literary languages of love, about poses struck by lovers, about love as an excuse for emotional and poetical play. They are studies in feelings masked, disguised, concealed, repressed; they consider emotions detached from situations and from personality.

—*Rosalie L. Colie*

In **"Young Love"** and **"The Picture of little T.C. in a Prospect of Flowers,"** the poet offers slant-examples of *carpe diem, carpe florem,* different comments on the theme of the young budding girl. **"Young Love"** owes most to an epigram in The Greek Anthology (V. iii) and to Horace, I, xxiii, and II, v, all involving the seduction of a "green" girl, a girl by convention too young for sexuality; an older and experienced man plucks this "bud," both the girl and her virginity. In Marvell's first stanza, the speaker makes clear how experienced he is, as he takes his customary care to fool the *senex,* the girl's defending father:

> Come little Infant, Love me now,
> While thine unsuspected years
> Clear thine aged Fathers brow
> From cold Jealousie and Fears.

The speaker reinforces a radical contrast between innocence and experience, between love and lust, as he permits his persuasion to turn on the oldest of *carpe diem* arguments, an appeal to the girl on the basis of her own transience:

> Now then love me: time may take
> Thee before thy time away:

She is likened to a sacrifice of lambs and kids; he assures her that if love is a good thing, then to "antedate" love, to enter into its initiations early, will simply be to enrich her yet more. What the speaker says is conventional enough; that he says it to so young a girl gives the poem its peculiar twist. This speaker is an honest sensualist, quite aware of what he is doing. His love is lust; the "plucking," that seems so delightful between young lovers of equal age, is simply self-indulgence at a child's expense. In **"Little T.C."** the same situation prevails, in that an older man observes a young girl, like the child in **"Young Love,"** "too green / Yet for Lust," and (it seems) for love too. She is a figure in the pastoral scene, herself *carpens,* picking the flowers of transience all about her, but a flower-element herself as well, in the "prospect of flowers."

These two poems demonstrate something quite interesting and, once one has grasped the problem, quite obvious: that *carpe diem* is a fundamental element of the pastoral love code as well as of the sensualist's code. We can tell a virtuous shepherd from Comus, or an innocent from an experienced lover, not by what each says, since each uses the same language, but by the context in which he says it. In **"Little T.C.,"** the speaker remarkably "cleans" the poem of any suggestion of the girl's, or his own present, sexuality; as the poet in **"Upon Appleton House"** sees an unblemished sexual future for Maria, so does the poet foresee no wantonness in T.C.'s future:

> Who can foretel for what high cause
> This Darling of the Gods was born!
> Yet this is She whose chaster Laws
> The wanton Love shall one day fear,
> And, under her command severe,
> See his Bow broke and Ensigns torn.
> Happy, who can
> Appease this virtuous Enemy of Man!

The speaker here, then, is the exact opposite of the speaker in **"Young Love"**; here, entirely without prurience, he watches a mode of *carpe diem* appearing emblematically before him. He himself is not tempted, denies temptation, retires from competitive *carpere*: as he images T.C.'s future triumphs over love, he himself becomes steadily more passive, watching the child, as the poet watches Maria in the Nunappleton evening go about her business. T.C. is not free from danger, but this speaker is on her side against what threatens her. Though he warns her that she will be plucked in the end, like all things, he advises the same self-control in her that he asks of Nature on her behalf; there is certainly real love for the little girl in this poem, but as opposed to **"Young Love,"** a protective rather than a predatory love. Like Horace, Marvell writes one poem of seduction, another of renunciation of too-young love.

In **"Ametas and Thestylis"** the sexual theme is presented in yet another way, this time as entirely without consequences, emotional or social. Here, sexuality is for once simple, and simply treated, with neither the sidelong libertinism of **"Young Love"** nor the protectiveness, of girl and self, of **"Little T.C."** The only odd note in this dialogue is that Thestylis insists on the transience of her relation to Ametas, consenting to "kiss within the Hay" not because all youth is transient and must be seized before it is gone, but because Ametas promises her that their relation shall not build into a complicated future. Her reasons for "coyness," then, are just the opposite to the received reasons; she extracts from her lover the promise of infidelity. These two are guileless naturalists, not sophisticated libertines like the speaker in **"Young Love."** Their love is designed for and from psychological uninvolvement, accepted by the two as an equal experience, an equal irresponsibility. Theirs is "plucking" at its most agreeable, and its most natural.

"To his Coy Mistress" is obviously Marvell's most remarkable poem of *carpe diem,* his most remarkable love poem in any form. The speaker speaks out of a desire that may be transitory; he promises nothing beyond an experience of shared joy. This poem plucks the day, laying immense stress on the day itself, a point in all time; it promises nothing beyond that day except the night of endless sleep to which all mortals must go down. Further, there is no shred of flower imagery in the poem. Rosebuds are not gathered; the lady does not put on her foliage, is never seen in a prospect of flowers—rather, surrealistically, she stands against a background of desert sand stretching to infinity. The implications of *carpe diem* are explored in the poem; the lady, and by implication all love, are threatened by time; the speaker is as aware of his imminent death as he is of hers. Whereas most poems on this theme tend to intensify the poet's desire at the expense of other aspects of life, this poem prolongs fulfilment, stretches out the courtship to make more intense its short, powerful consummation.

Further, the poem examines its own official premises, following their implications to their logical conclusions. Time threatens love, so the poet takes a long look at all time and all space, made "endless" in the literary hyperbole of compliment. *Adunata* serve to praise this lady, imaginatively seen in a prospect of all time and space, her beauties measured off against slices of time. The secondary sense of love as "value" is explored and set forth; love is accounted for and appraised, in the commercial sense— and, as usual, Marvell has managed to literalize the concept in an idiom proper to the environments of the poem, the customary overpraise of lovers looking for physical love. The Ganges, so romantic and exotic, alternates with the Humber, the local stream; the scriptural-historical Flood alternates with the never-never conversion of the Jews. The millennium, "the last Age," shows the lady's heart, concealed till then—and yet, and yet, all that compliment turns into "worms" trying, as the poet hopes to try before them, the lady's "long preserv'd Virginity." Preoccupation with the flesh in life suggests the career of the flesh after death.

The time which all *carpe diem* poems exploit is here extended to eternity, and eternity is spatially presented ("Desarts of vast Eternity"). *Nox una perpetua dormienda* is made actual in an intensely imagined, intimate tomb

scene, to frighten the living lady into taking comfort in her lover's arms. The elements are purely literary, but the poet's psychology is sound. This poem shows how to accomplish a seduction, to pluck love's day, made bright against the dark night of death. And, to stress that it is *day* that is to be plucked, the lover and his lady challenge the sun itself, hastening their day by loving proudly and professionally. In this poem, unlike so many of Marvell's other love poems, passion and criticism seem to support one another: for all the poem's acute examination of its own sources, it finds new resources to affirm the intense experience of life that love can be. The speaker, for once, is committed to an act and to affirming that act. This poem . . . [shows] some of the expansions possible of a hackneyed theme, which the poet transforms into one of the most imaginative of all formal persuasives to love.

J. P. Kenyon on the overly academic character of modern criticism on Marvell:

Anyone reading [recent book-length studies of Marvell] must conclude that "Marvell studies" are in an inextricable muddle, and that a great deal of intellectual effort is being expended to very little effect. . . .

[In his 1921 essay on Marvell, T. S. Eliot] set a style for the minute examination of Marvell's verse. This has produced a drastic upwards revaluation, though it is now possible to argue that if Marvell had produced more he would merit less attention. Certainly if we knew more about him his poems would not have to be squeezed so drastically to extract the last lingering inference. . . .

In 1971 Pierre Legouis remarked crushingly of **"Upon Appleton House"**: "Several allegorical interpretations of this poem have been offered, to my mind quite unnecessarily; they are more or less incompatible with one another and at some points palpably impossible. The composition of the poem, in spite of recent ingenious apologies, still seems to me loose, and the tone chatty, except at rare moments of exultation." Yet the "ingenious apologists" still ply their trade. . . . I am afraid I regard it as a self-sustaining industry, in that its only consumers are other academics, whose main purpose is to gain doctorates, secure appointments and confirm tenure. Given the subjectivity and impalpability of so much literary work, Marvell is not the only victim, but our ignorance of his life and character makes him particularly vulnerable. No final interpretation is possible, yet one tormented explication succeeds another, apparently to infinity.

J. P. Kenyon, in his "In Pursuit of Marvell," in The Times Literary Supplement, *17 November 1978.*

Thomas W. Hayes (essay date 1971)

SOURCE: "The Dialectic of History in Marvell's *Horatian Ode,*" in *CLIO,* Vol. 1, No. 1, October, 1971, pp. 26-36.

[*In the following essay, Hayes offers an interpretation of*

"An Horatian Ode upon Cromwel's Return from Ireland," focusing on Marvell's representation of providential and historical forces underlying Cromwell's rise to power.]

"An Horatian Ode upon Cromwel's Return from Ireland"

was written during the latter part of 1650, at a time when Marvell was serving as tutor to Mary Fairfax, daughter of the recently resigned General of the Parliamentary forces. Fairfax was opposed to the King's execution and resigned his commission rather than engage in the campaign against the Scotts. Marvell apparently felt compelled to assert his independence of mind. In so doing he wrote one of the most controversial poems in English literary history. Embodying the results of the Civil Wars, the poem assesses the role of the individual in history through its focus upon the conflict between the apocalyptic intervention of "fate" and the harsh complexities of secular life where imperfect human "justice" attempts to form a more perfect society. The poem's motivation springs from a dialectical conflict between two ideas of historical change; revolutionary upheaval (represented by Cromwell and "fate") is in opposition to the incremental tradition (represented by Charles and "justice").

Cromwell destroys traditional values and undermines long established institutions in fulfilling the leader's role innovatively; furthermore, he is allied with providential authority through "fate," not by divine right. In the poem "justice" and "fate" are finally reconciled as a result of Cromwell's actions in saving the state. This dialectical pattern of the historical process, central to Marvell's understanding of the situation, leads to the conclusion that Cromwell combines his internal will with external circumstances to accomplish great works. This process is expressed in the poem in an attempt to trace out the internal connection between human will, secular justice, and what was known as "natural law."

In dealing with the Civil Wars and the King's execution Marvell's **"Ode"** shows how the interaction between socio-political forces and individual initiative influences historical change. Marvell's accommodation to Cromwell was gradual and cautious. Marvell remained abroad during much of the Civil War era, as did his model, Horace, at the time of the Roman civil conflict. Evidently during the Civil War period Marvell did not share the more extreme republican views of his friend John Milton, who nevertheless wrote a letter recommending Marvell for a government post in February 1653. Although Marvell left Fairfax in 1653 to become tutor of Cromwell's ward, William Dutton, it was not until four years later that he was appointed Latin Secretary and thus became a formal member of Cromwell's administration. Even though Marvell became Cromwell's unofficial poet laureate his other poems on the Lord Protector, **"The First Anniversary of the Government Under His Highness The Lord Protector"** (1655) and **"A Poem upon the Death of His late Highnesse the Lord Protector"** (1658), do not simply try to make political commitment into an object of contemplative pleasure, to carve a comfortable situation out of unfortunate circumstances. Like the **"Horatian Ode"** they combine restraint and respect and show a realistic awareness of political conditions as well as optimistic belief in the future.

Marvell did not welcome the socio-political upheaval associated with civil dissension, but he was not one of those who wanted law and order at any cost. To him, the socio-political world, just as the world of nature, was, from time to time, subject to violent upheavals. Natural law corresponded to divine law, and since cataclysms occurred in the heavens and in nature—comets, falling stars, floods, earthquakes—revolutions in accordance with providential purposes could also take place in the socio-political world. For in submitting to reason and nature man acknowledged God and his unknown purposes; in this way man could achieve a clearsighted view of the causal scheme of the universe. No mechanistic determinist, Marvell did not deny man's free will or the possibility of contingency in nature or society; God could perform miracles or cause "accidental" events to take place not conforming to natural law. He was not subject to "fate," but man was. According to the Neo-Stoic Justus Lipsius, whose ideas on the relationship between providential and secular causation were influential in England at this time, God's providence ensured true liberty and prevented chaos. The temporal equivalent of providence, natural law, governed the created world; if man wished to follow heaven's wishes he had merely to follow nature, that is, to submit to providence. This did not, of course, deny free will; the fact that God, in His wisdom, had foreknowledge of every event did not jeopardize man's freedom. According to Lipsius, "to deny any part of God's foreknowledge is to deny His providence, the grossest impiety and a thing unthinkable." As Herschel Baker notes, following Lipsius, "the Neo-Stoics could urge the utmost liberty for man's conscience and conduct precisely because they could not conceive of freedom without law. And the law which no man could break was that providence or destiny which determined the course of all things in nature" (*Image of Man: A Study of the Idea of Human Dignity in Classical Antiquity, the Middle Ages, and the Renaissance*, 1947).

In Marvell's **"Ode"** "fate" is indicative of a generalized concept of divine guidance overseeing events. Although this guidance is not specifically identified with the deity, indications of a divine power overseeing events discloses an inner law running throughout history. The source of Cromwell's unassailable power is conveyed through the terms "fate" and "fortune." Cromwell acts as a heavenly directed scourge:

> And, like the three-fork'd Lightning, first
> Breaking the Clouds where it was nurst,
> Did thorough his own Side
> His fiery way divide.
>
> (ll. 13-16)

Thus he is allied, by the simile, with natural forces, yet he acts upon his own initiative.

> For 'tis all one to Courage high
> The Emulous or Enemy;
> And with such to inclose
> Is more then to oppose.
> Then Burning through the Air he went,
> And Pallaces and Temples rent:

And *Caesars* head at last
Did through his Laurels blast.
'Tis Madness to resist or blame
The force of angry Heavens flame.

(ll. 17-26)

Cromwell is the willing agent of a cosmological cataclysm; his power results from a combination of external and internal necessities. He seizes opportunities and is seized by them. He burns, he rends, he blasts, he ruins, he casts, and, having shown how much was due to forces, events, and circumstances with which Cromwell had no previous connection, Marvell insists that "Much to the Man is due" (l. 28), who, with "industrious Valour" (l. 33), casts the kingdom into a new mold. But much also is due to the circumstances, the occasions offered by them, the opportunities he grasped, his seizing the day, and particularly the combination and accord of Cromwell and an external power designated as "angry Heavens flame," aiding him in speeding up historical processes. Cromwell "does both act and know" (l. 76), but he does so by relating his own will to heaven's.

The historical process operating behind the Civil Wars is described allegorically in one of the poem's strongest sections:

Though Justice against Fate complain,
And plead the antient Rights in vain:
But those do hold or break
As Men are strong or weak.
Nature that hateth emptiness,
Allows of penetration less:
And therefore must make room
Where greater Spirits come.

(ll. 37-44)

"Justice" and "Fate" here represent a dialectical union of opposites. "Justice" symbolizes the "antient Rights" of the past and the laws handed down from generation to generation, in other words, the English tradition of king, lords, and commons through which the constitution is made and enforced; "Fate" is an active bond between man, the future, and heaven—the most powerful force in history. "Fate" is infinite; it is an open-ended force of which Cromwell has become the instrument. History is a process of many individual wills interacting and conflicting for various reasons, and from their conflict emerges an historical event no one human being willed, an event conforming to providence, or "fate." In this sense "fate" is more decisive than human volition.

The theatrical staging of the King's beheading extends this dialectical opposition between Cromwell's fateful actions and Charles' passive obedience. The King's execution is deliberately objectified through pageantry. It becomes a cathartic act purging the audience of pity and fear:

That thence the *Royal Actor* born
The *Tragick Scaffold* might adorn,
While round the armed Bands
Did clap their bloody hands.

(ll. 53-56)

The royal tragedian complies with the act; he plays his role in the historical drama according to the script. But neither Charles' tragedy nor Cromwell's triumph allows

them the role of hero; they are both part of a process of development.

The **"Ode"** describes the most significant historical act of the era, an act that brought together in one moment the social, political, and religious consequences of the revolution. The destruction of "the great Work of Time" (l. 34), as well as the prospect of a new governing order, presents a frightening aspect to those "Architects" unwilling or unable to accept radical change as part of the nature of things:

So when they did design
The *Capitols* first Line,
A bleeding Head where they begun,
Did fright the Architects to run;
And yet in that the *State*
Foresaw its happy Fate.

(ll. 67-72)

"Fate" here alludes to the struggle between it and "Justice" in line 37. Charles played his part, and his death symbolizes the displacement of one government by another. Yet respect for Charles is shown in the poem because in the struggle between "Justice" and "Fate" the difficulties, at first, outweigh the favorable conditions and so constitute the principal aspect of the conflict; immediately after the King's execution the future of the Commonwealth was uncertain. But, as the poem indicates, the seeds of a favorable new situation are contained within the death of the old. Charles' execution is a dramatic reenactment of the killing of the divine king archetype, reborn triumphantly in a new vision of the future.

At the opening of the **"Ode"** Cromwell leaves his "private Gardens" (l. 29), where he "liv'd reserved and austere" (l. 30), in order to assume his role, in alliance with cosmic forces, as one of the main figures in the revolution. He undergoes a transformation from the man of contemplation to the man of action, and his personal transformation is mirrored in the world around him. The Civil Wars and the destruction and suffering accompanying them are not just the signs of a transition from one stage of history to another; they constitute the transition itself. The catastrophes of civil dissension and social chaos are finally tolerable because they offer the potentiality of making a better world.

The dialectical conflict which exists between the garden and the world of strife outside provides another example of how unified opposites are the theoretical core of Marvell's view of the historical process. The enclosed garden is traditionally a microcosm, a Garden of Eden, a representation of England itself, and a reflection of the ideal world of nature, past and future. Again, conventionally, the real world and the heavens were related by the natural and heavenly correspondences and formed a comprehensive picture of the causal pattern of the universe. The chain of causes reaching from divine providence to the influence of the stars ("fate," "fortune," or "destiny"), to the natural world ("necessity"), to man himself, has its focal point in the garden, a *locus standi* from which the poet views the world and Cromwell emerges. "The forward Youth that would appear" (l. 1) is both Cromwell and the poet himself; both are transformed by the historical process from men of quiet repose to men who "both act and know."

When history enters directly into Marvell's poetry and begins to influence its development, the pattern of dialectical thinking provides a basis for arriving at decisions in accordance with the moral precepts discovered in self-conscious reflection. The logic of the truths learned in the garden becomes a correlative of the poet's reflection on historical events. The tension between imaginative appearance and material reality expands to include the historical conflict between what "is" and what "ought to be," and the internal contradictions of the poet's personal garden world are understood in terms of the process of history-man in his struggle with nature and society. Metaphysical reality becomes historical reality. To know *means* to act; to act *means* to know.

Cromwell is goaded by the external pressure of civil strife and guided by an internal necessity to confront the world of practical activity. The poem shows destructive deeds bringing about constructive consequences when the principle of constant change ("mutability") is accepted. But in this case the moral sanction usually accorded a hero is deliberately ambivalent. If providence, in the form of "angry Heavens flame," had, for some reason, directed and decreed the downfall of the monarchy, the obvious injustice of usurpation could not be pardoned. The situation could no longer be justified by simply applying the traditional *Mirror for Magistrates* formula of seeing virtue rewarded and vice punished; the convenient pattern of sinful acts followed by just retribution was inapplicable. The context in which Marvel stresses the providential formula as a causational motive takes into account the necessary separation of God's purposes and man's actions. History could no longer be used as a bludgeon to justify the maintenance of existing authority based on mere tradition. Change itself is morally neutral; the means does not justify the end, but the end is taken into account in judging means. Since God's purposes were not always clear to man, "fortune" would make guilty whomever she chose. And beyond the fortunes of individual men lay the destiny of the state, and this, in the last analysis, was more important than the justification of individual acts.

In Marvell's **"Ode"** Charles' death symbolizes the transformation from one stage of history to another, consequently the results of Cromwell's actions are stressed. His may be an usurping power, the poem indicates, but the consequences of his power change the nature of the state. Charles' execution was a terrible act, yet it provided the opportunity for the state to foresee "its happy Fate." And it gave Cromwell the chance to cast the old kingdom into a mold in which the House of Commons possessed more authority:

> He to the *Commons Feet* presents
> A *Kingdome,* for his first years rents:
> And, what he may, forbears
> His Fame to make it theirs:
> And has his Sword and Spoyls ungirt,
> To lay them at the *Publick's* skirt.
>
> (ll. 85-90)

Cromwell the private gardener becomes Cromwell the public man of action because he accepts the goals and ideals represented by the garden at the beginning of the poem and applies them for the public good. Near the end of the poem Cromwell is urged to remain committed to the life of action; he cannot return to the garden after the wars without endangering the stability of his hard won achievements.

According to Ruth Nevo, Marvell shows the "beginning of a dialectical determinism which, through a new analysis of the nature and function of the republican leader, of authority vested not alone in personal power but in a collective public body can reconcile the hero's personal significance and value with his historical instrumentality" [*The Dial of Virtue: A Study of Poems on Affairs of State in the Seventeenth Century,* 1963]. For those who accepted the revolutionary government, patriotism rested to a large extent in the new idea of a nation as a parliamentary republic, and the economic well-being of the interests that saw themselves as that nation's representatives was more important than any individual ruler's personal glory. Reflecting consolidation of the economic and political power of townsmen, yeomen, freeholders and middling men, plus some gentry, against the nobility, most of the gentry, their tenants, and the poor and depicting the destruction of absolute monarchy, the **"Horatian Ode"** presents the goals, values, and aspirations of middle-class hegemony:

> What may not them our *Isle* presume
> While Victory his Crest does plume;
> What may not others fear,
> If thus he crown each Year!
> A *Caesar* he ere long to *Gaul,*
>
> To *Italy* an *Hannibal,*
> And to all States not free
> Shall *Clymacterick* be.
>
> (ll. 97-104)

Launched on this imperialistic course, Cromwell is warned to keep his "Sword erect" (l. 116). History is forever mutable, and Marvell expresses some concern over whether Cromwell will persist in the revolutionary program. Immediately after the aristocracy has been defeated the former ruling class still possesses dangerous strength, and there is the possibility of a counter-revolution or of the revolutionary government adopting the ideas and methods of the aristocracy; therefore:

> The same *Arts* that did *gain*
> A *Pow'r* must it *maintain.*
>
> (ll. 119-120)

Violence can contribute to the shattering of the existing state, but it is an unacceptable means of enforcing governmental authority. The questions of the legitimate rights of the head of state, the extent of governmental control over the individual, and the right of government to demand allegiance from its constituents, are ones that Marvell carefully weighted throughout his career as a Member of Parliament from 1659 to his death in 1678. In a frequently quoted passage from *The Rehearsal Transpros'd* (1672-1673), Marvell expressed his mature reflections on the Civil Wars. As in the **"Ode,"** his thoughts are set forth dialectically:

Whether it be a war of religion or of liberty, is not worth the labour to inquire. Whichsoever was at the top, the other was at the bottom; but upon considering all, I think the cause was too good to have been fought for. Men ought to have trusted God; they ought and might have trusted the King with that whole matter. 'The arms of the Church are prayers and tears;' the arms of the subjects are patience and petitions.

The yoking together of paired opposites: religion-liberty, top-bottom, God-King, Church-subjects, prayers and tears-patience and petitions, leads to the paradoxical conclusion, prepared for in the **"Ode,"** that however good the cause, the deeds were bad. In answer to the charge that he had helped animate the people to rebellion Marvell considered the examples of Caligula and Nero as oppressive tyrants and indicated that magistrates are but tools of the state under which they serve. Ultimately even the legitimacy of the prince is no assurance of correct action: "for some Usurpers, because of the tenderness of their title, have thought fit to carry with the greatest clemency and equality to the people, and to make very good and wholsome laws for the publick."

Acting as a heavenly conqueror, savior, and scourge, traditionally derived from biblical analogies, Cromwell operates outside recognized monarchical rights, and although his motives are sincere his actions are disruptive. Yet the poet's duty is not to prosecute or punish successful crimes; his task is to mark them for all to see and judge. The poet is not a legislator in regard to historical events but a moral witness. This view is implicit in Marvell's discussion of the "several families of Necessities" in *The Rehearsal Transpros'd* where he stated his causational rationale and suggested that the vagaries of "fate" were something God not only permits but acquiesces in through natural processes:

> God has hitherto, instead of an eternal Spring, a standing serenity, and perpetual sunshine, subjected mankind to the dismal influence of comets from above, to thunder, and lightning, and tempests from the middle region, and from the lower surface to the raging of the seas and the tottering of earthquakes, beside all other the innumerable calamities to which humane life is exposed, He has in like manner distinguish'd the government of the world by the intermitting seasons of discord, war, and publick disturbance. Neither has he so order'd it only (as men endeavor to express it) by meer permission, but sometimes out of complacency. For though it may happen that both the parties may be guilty of War, as both of Schisme, yet there are many cases in which War is just, and few, however, where there is not more justice on one side than the other.

The linked analogy of the world of nature and the world of government provides the conclusive element in understanding Marvell's dialectical pattern of the historical process.

Applied to the **"Ode,"** the antithetical elements, "Justice" and "Fate," are transformed by the inherent qualities of "Nature," the laws of the natural world. Natural law both abhors a vacuum and disallows two objects to occupy the same space simultaneously. The assumed correspondence between natural law and human law, between nature and society, aids in the resolution of the conflict between "Justice" and "Fate" because natural law is an extension of divine law but is accessible to man. It is an internal rather than an external cause. The "antient Rights" must give way, "make room," for "The force of angry Heavens flame" because Cromwell operates in league with natural forces. A conflict exists between "the great Work of Time" (l. 34), that is the legal constitution, which is slow and phlegmatic, and Cromwell's "industrious Valour" (l. 33), which, by speeding time, destroys it. Since Cromwell is allied with heavenly power he is representative of the "greater Spirits" triumphing through "Nature." Cromwell's power is morally ambivalent because he destroys and creates, yet he is master of time and speeds the dynamics of change. The abstract syllogism Justice-Fate-Nature corresponds concretely and specifically to the syllogism Charles-Cromwell-State as a dialectical pattern of the historical conflict. The unity of opposites is a fundamental law of nature, of society, and of thought.

In the **"Ode"** a dialectical transformation takes place. Cromwell, who had earlier been identified with "Fate" against "Justice," is finally called "just" (l. 79). He exhibits, in other words, the same quality that earlier described the conflict between him and Charles. He therefore negates the negation. In the revolutionary situation each of the two contradictory aspects transforms itself into its opposite; Charles suffers his "fate" at the hands of the "just" Cromwell. With Charles' legal execution the previous contradiction has been stood on its head; the revolution is accomplished.

Through dialectics Marvell accommodated Cromwell to a framework that traditionally saw the self-willed man as the image of Satan, the Machiavellian monster, or usurper of order. The Royalist, James Scudamore, called Marvell "a notable English Italo-Machiavellian" (sic) [quoted in Pierre Legouis's *Andrew Marvell: Poet, Puritan, Patriot*, revised edition, 1968]. And Marvell's friend James Harrington adapted many of Machiavelli's ideas in his *Common-wealth of Oceana* (1656), but whether or not Marvell had read Machiavelli or considered his ideas with more than conventional opprobrium is largely irrelevant. As Felix Raab has shown, [in *The English Face of Machiavelli: A Changing Interpretation, 1500-1700*, 1964], many of Machiavelli's ideas were intellectual commonplaces in the seventeenth century. Marvell retained the conventional teleological Augustinian conception of history as an extension of God's will. But, more significantly, as Machiavelli and Bacon had done, he telescoped the humanistic and providential views in an awareness of the realistic and secular ideas of historical causation and thus arrived at a more specific recognition of man's responsibility for the conditions of his existence.

In the **"Horatian Ode"** an ideal past is negated by a harsh present reality, and the poet strives to unify these opposites in the idealized future. The best guarantee of that future was that, in Marvell's words, "the 'common people' in all places partake so much of sense and nature, that, could they be imagined and contrived to be irrational, yet they would ferment and tumultuate at the last for their own preservation. Yet neither do they want the use of reason, and perhaps their aggregated judgement discerns most truly the errours of government, forasmuch as they are the first, to be sure, that smart under them.''

Philip Larkin   (essay date 1978)

SOURCE: ''The Changing Face of Andrew Marvell,'' in *Required Writing: Miscellaneous Pieces 1955-1982*, Farrar, Straus and Giroux, Inc., 1983, pp. 245-53.

[*One of England's most popular and acclaimed poets of the post–World War II era, Larkin was offered but declined the position of poet laureate. In the following essay, which was originally published in* English Literary Renaissance *to commemorate the tercentenary of Marvell's death, Larkin comments on the evolution of Marvell's literary reputation and finds much twentieth-century Marvell criticism pedantic and mundane.*]

The celebration in 1921 of the tercentenary of Andrew Marvell's birth evoked an unexpected tribute: an essay on his work and position in English literature by T. S. Eliot. At that time Eliot was far from being the authoritative figure he later became; *Prufrock* (1917) and *The Sacred Wood* (1920) had sounded a new baffling voice, and even this sober reassessment of a familiar author could be seen as part of a campaign of subversion. He was not, he said, trying to heighten Marvell's reputation, simply to isolate his individual quality, but since by the end of his essay he had contrived to suggest that this was something that was lacking in Shelley, Wordsworth, Keats, Morris, Browning, Yeats, Hardy, and several others, it is not surprising that Marvell's standing began to alter nevertheless.

At the end of the nineteenth century the common view of Marvell as a poet was that of an author still half entangled in the artificial traditions of Cleveland and Donne on the one hand, and the political upheavals of his time on the other, but who none the less achieved a number of charming and exquisite poems in the pastoral tradition about gardens and mowers, presumably ascribable to a period spent as a tutor in the household of Lord Fairfax at Nun Appleton in Yorkshire. His political poems, furthermore, and especially **'An Horatian Ode upon Cromwell's Return from Ireland'**, represented the best of Puritan tradition, that could still find room for a magnanimous nod to Charles I. In the *Cambridge History of English Literature* (1910-16) Marvell is respectfully handled by the Reverend John Brown DD, who classes him with 'Herrick, Lovelace and Wither, rather than with Waller, Sedley, Dorset or Rochester', and sees **'The Garden'** as having both the classical spirit of Horace's Epodes and the imaginative intensity of Shelley's 'Ode to the West Wind'. The monumental 11th edition of the *Encyclopaedia Britannica* (1910-11) (although terming him 'a great Puritan poet' and mentioning 'his exquisite "garden poetry"') plainly warms to him as a 'humorist and as a great "parliament man"', giving the greater part of its space to an account of him in these roles. The general impression is of a public figure whose poems were only one of his many claims to our attention.

Eliot's view of Marvell, in a seminal essay that was reprinted in the memorial volume published for the City of

Kingston-upon-Hull in 1922, was very different. Conceding right away that 'his best poems are not very many', he nevertheless sees him as an altogether larger poet than Herrick, Lovelace and Wither. 'Marvell's best verse is the product of European, that is to say Latin, culture,' and Eliot finds in it a kind of distillation of an age's mental completeness that can be most simply labelled 'wit': a tough reasonableness beneath lyric grace, an alliance of levity and seriousness found in Gautier, Baudelaire and Laforgue, Catullus, Propertius and Ovid:

> I would
> Love you ten years before the Flood:
> And you should if you please refuse
> Till the Conversion of the *Jews*.
> My vegetable Love should grow
> Vaster than Empires, and more slow.

Marvell (Eliot goes on to claim) possesses the ability to make the familiar strange, and the strange familiar, attaining a brightness and clarity that of itself carries a poetic suggestiveness. He contrasts Marvell's **'The Nymph and the Fawn'** with a poem by William Morris, finding Morris misty and vague, Marvell hard and precise in a way that gives his slight theme 'that inexhaustible and terrible nebula of emotion which surrounds all our exact and practical passions'. And he quotes:

> So weeps the wounded Balsome: so
> The holy Frankincense doth flow.
> The brotherless *Heliades*
> Melt in such Amber Tears as these.

Although one may not feel that these lines quite justify Eliot's magnificent description of them, one suspects in fact that his account of Marvell's quality is to some extent a description of his own, or what he would like his own to be. His essay, after all, was one of a number designed to draw attention to the seventeenth century (that seems 'to gather up and to digest into its art all the experience of the human mind'), for this was the period from which many aspects of his own verse derive as well as his Anglicanism and royalism, and the four lines quoted have just that easy assumption of common erudition that Eliot himself had begun to patent. The reference to 'European culture' (one must never forget that Eliot, and for that matter Pound, was American) reinforces this conclusion. In another essay he made it clear that Marvell shared with his contemporaries 'a mechanism of sensibility which could devour any kind of experience'—a mechanism we have, alas, lost. But that is another story.

Eliot's growing influence, supported at first by Pound and then by Leavis, was enough to bring Marvell to the attention of the young critics, and in the space of a remarkably few years he became one of the favourite subjects on their dissecting tables. It would, no doubt, be a gross oversimplification to say that twentieth-century criticism has been motivated by a desire to demonstrate that what looks simple is in fact complicated, that what seems to have one meaning has in fact three or four, and that works of literature are good in proportion to how far they can be shown to exhibit this, but it is impossible to read far in contemporary Marvell studies without believing that it has a sufficiency of truth. Here, for instance, is J. V. Cunningham, in *Tradition and Poetic Structure,* picking up Eliot's praise of the phrase 'vegetable love':

> [His readers] envisage some monstrous and expanding cabbage, but they do so in mere ignorance. *Vegetable* is no vegetable but an abstract and philosophical term, known as such to every educated man of Marvell's day. Its context is the doctrine of the three souls: the rational, which in man subsumes the other two; the sensitive, which men and animals have in common and which is the principle of motion and perception; and, finally, the lowest of the three, the vegetable soul, which is the only one that plants possess, and which is the principle of generation and corruption, of augmentation and decay. Marvell says, then, my love, denied the exercise of sense, but possessing the power of augmentation, will increase 'Vaster than empires.'

Possibly. Another reader might simply think that 'vegetable' was a good adjective for something that grows slowly. In *Some Versions of Pastoral* William Empson is equally illuminating on Marvell's second most famous couplet:

> Annihilating all that's made
> To a green thought in a green shade.

> . . . either contemplating everything or shutting everything out. This combines the idea of the conscious mind, including everything because understanding it, and that of the unconscious animal nature, including everything because in harmony with it. Evidently the object of such a fundamental contradiction (seen in the etymology: turning all *ad nihil,* to nothing, and *to* a thought) is to deny its reality; the point is not that these two are essentially different but that they must cease to be different so far as either is to be known. So far as he has achieved his state of ecstasy he combines them, he is 'neither conscious nor not conscious', like the seventh Buddhist state of enlightenment. This gives its point, I think, to the other ambiguity, clear from the context, as to whether *all* considered was *made* in the mind of the author or the Creator; to so peculiarly 'creative' a knower there is little difference between the two.

Possibly again. And again another reader might simply think the lines a good description of the mind of someone half-asleep under the summer trees in a garden. Certainly critic quarrelled with critic on what could or should be read into Marvell's lines: Leavis with Bateson, Douglas Bush with Cleanth Brooks, Pierre Legouis with William Empson, Frank Kermode with Milton Klonsky. The whole situation was summarized by Brooks with an irony as devastating as it was unintentional: 'Marvell was too good a poet to resolve the ambiguity.'

Whether true or not, much of modern Marvell criticism has a curiously inhibiting effect on one's ability to read the poems, just as a description of a chair in terms of whizzing molecules would make one afraid to sit down on it. But whatever its excesses, it is Marvell who has provoked them, and not Herrick or Lovelace or Wither: there must be something in his work to call them forth. Possibly it is a kind of overloading:

> **Much of modern Marvell criticism has a curiously inhibiting effect on one's ability to read the poems, just as a description of a chair in terms of whizzing molecules would make one afraid to sit down on it.**
>
> **—*Philip Larkin***

> What wond'rous Life is this I lead!
> Ripe Apples drop about my head;
> The Lucious Clusters of the Vine
> Upon my Mouth do crush their Wine;
> The Nectaren, and curious Peach,
> Into my hands themselves do reach;
> Stumbling on Melons, as I pass,
> Insnar'd with Flow'rs, I fall on Grass.

—the paradisal lushness of the garden is made so overwhelming, with a hint of menace in the independently acting fruit, and a touch of the ludicrous in the Hulot-like figure of the speaker (conked on the head with apples, hit in the face by a bunch of grapes, and finally sprawling full length over a melon), that the reader cannot be blamed for seeking an interpretation over and above the poem's face value: that it is the Garden of Eden, for instance, replete with Apple and Fall, or that Marvell is really saying, What a life of sin and temptation I lead! The ingenuity that sees **'The Nymph and her Fawn'** as an allegory of the Crucifixion, or a lamentation for lost virginity, while perhaps less understandable, arises from the same cause: an excess in the poem of manner over matter. The quality of Marvell's verse is such that the reader cannot believe that it relates only to a garden, or a pastoral conceit about a girl and her pet; there must be something else, and the reader—the academic reader—is determined to find it. The only one of the major poems where matter approximates to manner is **'To His Coy Mistress',** and it is significant that no one so far has propounded a political or theological explanation of it.

Such convolutions seem all the more remarkable when we consider that for some hundred and fifty years after his death Marvell was hardly thought of as a poet at all: Johnson, for instance, a century later, did not include him in his *Lives of the Poets.* The manner of his works' survival is as extraordinary. None of the poems for which Marvell is known today was published during his lifetime: no manuscripts have survived, either holographs or copies. Possibly the Fairfax family had seen some of the Nun Appleton poems (if they really were written there), possibly the coy mistress (if she really existed) had read her ode, possibly the encomia upon Cromwell had reached their subject's austere eyes—possibly, but there is no evidence. On his death in 1678 his housekeeper, Mary Palmer, put together such pieces as she could find as did not seem treasonable and published them as *Miscellaneous Poems* in 1681, signing the preface Mary Marvell. Whether or not she had any claim to this title is one more uncertainty. Some eight years later his satiric poems (for in the latter part of his life Marvell had become a keen critic of Charles

II and his court) were published in a volume called *Poems on Affairs of State,* and this was reprinted several times in the next quarter of a century, in contrast to *Miscellaneous Poems,* which was never reprinted.

It seems impossible that a poem such as 'To His Coy Mistress' should not, once printed, become widely celebrated, but again we see an age finding its own image in Marvell and no more. The eighteenth century, like the Restoration, was an age of satire, and Marvell survived as a political figure, a Commonwealth patriot who had made much dangerous fun of the restored monarchy and its public men. His prose polemic, *The Rehearsal Transpros'd* (1672), a reply to *Discourse of Ecclesiastical Polity* by Samuel Parker, was declared by Burnet to be with its successor 'the wittiest books that have appeared in this age', and Charles II is reputed to have read them 'over and over again'. Swift, in his Apology for *A Tale of a Tub* (1704), wrote 'We still read Marvell's Answer to Parker with Pleasure,' even though the substance of their quarrel had long since been forgotten. Those willing to test the truth of these recommendations are welcome to try. As a verse satirist Marvell was clearly effective in the context of his age, but he does not transcend it, as Dryden (whom he sometimes resembles) so manifestly does. The characters and events of which he writes are not preserved in the amber of poetry, or even rhetoric (as in 'An Horatian Ode'); they are roughly handled in coffee-house vernacular:

> But fresh as from the *Mint,* the *Courtiers* fine
> Salute them, smiling at their vain design;
> And *Turner* gay up to his Pearch doth march
> With Face new bleacht, smoothen'd and stiff
>   with starch;
> Tells them he at *Whitehall* had took a turn,
> And for three days, thence moves them to adjourn.
> Not so, quoth *Tomkins*; and straight drew his
>   Tongue,
> Trusty as Steel, that always ready hung;
> And so, proceeding in this motion warm,
> Th' army soon rais'd, he doth as soon disarm.

Few of the satires attributed to Marvell are certainly his, but this was the kind of poem he was writing in his later years. An American critic, anxious to make some sense of the change, suggests that, having brought his own particular brand of lyricism to perfection, Marvell was looking for fresh styles to conquer, but this is not convincing. Not the least of Marvell's claims to distinction is that he is the only substantial English poet to have been a Member of Parliament for eighteen years, and there is nothing more probable than that irritation with public affairs should become the mainspring for his verse.

Curiously enough, he was an exceptionally efficient Member of Parliament. Elected to represent Kingston-upon-Hull in 1660, he wrote every few days—whenever the post went—to the officers of that city to report what was happening at Westminster. Mostly he wrote of maritime business or other matters that concerned them (such as 'the cutting of Hull from Hezle' or the duties on spirits and tobacco), but he did not ignore national events, or even gossip ('at two a clock some persons reported to be of great

quality . . . set upon the Watch & killd a poore Beadle'). Between two and three hundred of these letters are preserved in the Guildhall at Hull, and are exceptionally valuable in that they provide a record of parliamentary business at a time when public reporting of it was prohibited. The city in its turn was grateful, and sent him presents of ale and salmon from the Humber. Not much is known of Marvell, and this unexpected well-documented glimpse of him as a conscientious public servant is attractive. Poets are not normally thought of as either efficient or conscientious.

Even Marvell's reputation as a satirist, however, died with his subject-matter, and a profound disregard ensued. When interest in him began to stir again (thanks to a large extent to two essays by Charles Lamb), his name was slow to get clear of his old associations; Leigh Hunt thought that he 'wrote a great deal better in prose than verse.' But FitzGerald provides a fascinating reminiscence of Tennyson in the Forties reciting 'But at my back I always hear/Time's winged chariot hurrying near,' with the characteristic comment, '*That* strikes me as sublime, I can hardly tell why.' It was Tennyson who persuaded Palgrave to include at least 'An Horatian Ode' in *The Golden Treasury* (Palgrave also added 'The Bermudas' and 'The Garden'), but his growing fame is evidenced by the appearance of Grosart's edition in 1872. 'A most rich and nervous poet,' Gerard Manley Hopkins called him, providing yet another instance of Marvell's work seeming something 'where each kind/Does streight its own resemblance find,' and by this time we are within sight of the remarkable celebrations at Hull in 1921. Anyone reading their official record may smile at the decorated tram cars and the Lord Mayor's designation of the poet as 'the biggest and cheapest advertisement' Hull had ever had, but their sheer comprehensiveness—the mass meeting of schools, the Holy Trinity service, the Grammar School's wreath, the luncheon, the public meeting in the Guildhall, and above all the involvement of so many leading citizens and representatives—and even more their evident sincerity—confers great credit on a sometimes maligned city.

It is clear that during the three hundred years since his death Marvell's reputation has taken pretty well every turn it could. If his readers and critics are agreed on anything, it is his extraordinary diversity and the numerous contradictions exhibited by his work and what we know of his character. He was in fact a most ambivalent figure. His poetic manner extends from Elizabethan to Augustan, from metaphysical to classical; its subjects nature versus order, Charles I versus Cromwell, the spirit versus the senses; nor is one ever quite sure how serious he is. He seems to have been equally at home under King or Protector and to have taken easily to the devious ways of practical politics. It has never been possible to say what kind of man he was: according to his eighteenth-century editor, Thompson, 'he had no wife, and his gallantries were not known.' He was variously accused of impotence, homosexuality, and 'frenchified manners', and while such charges were common in the scurrilous pamphleteering of the day, his poem 'The Definition of Love' might bear such an interpretation as well as many another. John Aubrey reports that he was a private drinker ('he kept bottles of wine at his lodgeing, and many times he would drinke liberally by himselfe to refresh his spirits'); oddly enough, Bishop Hensley Henson picked this up at the meeting in the Hull Guildhall, saying it would be nasty if it were true, and also commented that 'the notion of a man writing intensely bitter things about his contemporaries, however much they deserved it, passing them about in manuscript and himself moving unsuspected and unconfessing among them, is unattractive. There is an element in Marvell of aloofness which has not yet been cleared up.' Nor has it. But if we ask how Marvell is regarded today, as compared with 1921 or any other time, we must acknowledge that the question has been made harder to answer by the formidable Marvell industry that has grown up in the last half-century. Certainly it has promoted his reputation far beyond those of Herrick, Lovelace and Wither among what might be called professional readers, but its growth has been in the esoteric areas of Neoplatonic symbolism, linguistic philosophy, and the history of inner literary conventions. Marvell has become the poet of enigma, of concealed meaning, of alternative explanation, of ambiguous attitude, and as such has been found a rich quarry for interpreters. On the other hand, he has not come to be thought more perceptive of human experience, or more sensitive to its pathos, or a better celebrant of its variety. For the general reader his achievement is still the witty tender elegance that informs perhaps half a dozen of his best-known pieces.

Every poet's reputation fades in so far as his language becomes unfamiliar, his assumptions outmoded, and his subject-matter historical, and despite the iron lung of academic English teaching Marvell is no exception. We no longer make much of adulatory poems, whether of national heroes or owners of big houses; the teasing of conceits, whether literary or scientific, strikes us as frigid; conventions such as pastoral now seem wan substitutes for imagination. What still compels attention to Marvell's work is the ease with which he manages the fundamental paradox of verse—the conflict of natural word usage with metre and rhyme—and marries it either to hallucinatory images within his own unique conventions or to sudden sincerities that are as convincing in our age as in his.

> But at my back I alwaies hear
> Times winged Charriot hurrying near:
> And yonder all before us lye
> Desarts of vast Eternity.
> Thy Beauty shall no more be found;
> Nor, in thy marble Vault, shall sound
> My ecchoing Song: then Worms shall try
> That long preserv'd Virginity:
> And your quaint Honour turn to dust;
> And into ashes all my Lust.
> The Grave's a fine and private place,
> But none I think do there embrace.

The sentiment is a familiar one; it has been said before, and will no doubt be said again. It will never be said better.

George deF. Lord (essay date 1979)

SOURCE: "Innocence and Experience in the Poetry of

Andrew Marvell," in *The British Library Journal*, Vol. 5, No. 2, Autumn, 1979, pp. 129-44.

[*An American educator and critic who specializes in seventeenth-century English literature, Lord is the editor of* Andrew Marvell: Complete Poetry *(1968) and* Andrew Marvell: A Collection of Modern Essays *(1968). In the following essay, he contends that Marvell's best poems combine contrasting views and opposing ideological positions to create a balanced perspective.*]

Andrew Marvell is the most enigmatic of English writers. Aubrey tells us that he was merry and cherry-cheeked, but that he would not drink in company, keeping, nevertheless, some bottles of wine in his lodgings 'to refresh his spirits and exalt his muse'. Nearly all the poems on which his fame depends were not published until after his death, and, if they circulated in manuscript during his lifetime, they made nothing like the impression that Donne's *Songs and Sonnets* did. Even when they were published posthumously in 1681, Marvell's poetry met, as far as we can tell, with indifference. The fact that so many extant copies of the folio lack the portrait suggests that interest in Marvell was confined to the political figure and not the poet.

Marvell's lyrics are as nearly anonymous as lyric poetry can be, despite their imaginative and intellectual brilliance. I get no sense in Marvell of that debonair ostentation of personality found in Donne, or the intimate meditative voice of Herbert, or the naughty whimsicality of Herrick, or the suave courtliness of Carew. Even in the political poems there is scarcely a trace of that social tone which Dryden was making a *sine qua non* of the genre. Oddly enough, the closest Marvell comes to an expression of personal feeling is in his formal tributes to Cromwell: **'The First Anniversary'** and **'Upon the Death of the Lord Protector'**. The solicitude and grief which they express may, indeed, correspond to the indignation that fuels his post-Restoration satires in verse and prose.

I suggest then an anomaly: that Marvell's lyrics are impersonal and that personal feelings come out only when he is engaged in vital public matters, and from this I would draw the conclusion that Marvell was the least egotistical of poets and one of the most passionately patriotic. For him, as well as for Dryden, the British constitution was the Ark, which is death to touch, however differently they may have construed constitutional fundamentals.

Like many others whom Marvell has fascinated, I have tried over the years to make connections between the superlative lyric poet, the diplomat, the associate of Fairfax and Cromwell, the friend and defender of Milton, the Foreign Office Secretary, the indefatigable M.P. sometimes rebuked for disorderly behavior in the House, the clandestine agent of a pro-Dutch fifth column, the often boisterous, not to say obscene, satirist, and the beleaguered defender of Britain's freedom. I have even tried to trace an evolutionary process from the lyrics to the poems on affairs of state, from retirement to action, but I must confess that what I took for process may simply have been a change of occupation.

Faced with Marvell's anonymousness and his extraordinary career, I am struck with two salient aspects of his character: his versatility (sometimes construed wrongly as inconstancy) and his devotion to truth. His versatility was exemplified by the splendid Marvell exhibition in the British Library; his devotion to truth, as I shall try to show, entails a profound and sensitive awareness of the claims of the ideal and the possible, of innocence and experience.

Even the most casual reader of English poetry is likely to remember two poems by Marvell: **'To his Coy Mistress'** and **'The Garden'**. Among the best-known lyrics of the seventeenth century—certainly the most intensively criticized and interpreted in our era—these two poems are the best of their kinds. **'To his Coy Mistress'** is the outstanding poem dealing with the persuasion to love; **'The Garden'** is pre-eminent among a host of poems exploring the delights of rural retirement and contemplation. While one celebrates disengagement from the pressures of the moment, the other proposes the most intense surrender to them imaginable.

Marvell's achievement in these two contrasting modes raises an obvious but important question: is there any significant connection between the pastoral evocation of asexual, vegetable tranquillity and the urgent invitation to engage in a moment of sexual ecstasy? Faced with contrary positions such as, 'Two Paradises 'twere in one / To live in Paradise alone' and

> Let us roll all our Strength, and all
> Our sweetness, up into one Ball:
> And tear our Pleasures with rough strife,
> Thorough the Iron gates of Life.

must we conclude that Marvell, like the Milton of *L'Allegro* and *Il Penseroso,* was exhibiting his skill at writing on either side of a question?

If we look at them side by side, each poem develops its argument in a way antithetical to the other. **'The Garden'** begins with a rejection of the hectic temporal pace of the world:

> How vainly men themselves amaze
> To win the Palm, the Oke, or Bayes;
> And their uncessant Labours see
> Crown'd from some single Herb or Tree, . . .
> While all Flow'rs and all Trees do close
> To weave the Garland of repose.

It proceeds, through hyperbolic celebrations of vegetable love, to a serene of the soul's ecstasy:

> Here at the Fountains sliding foot,
> Or at some Fruit-tree's mossy root,
> Casting the Bodies Vest aside,
> My Soul into the boughs does glide:
> There like a Bird it sits, and sings,
> Then whets, and combs its silver Wings;
> And, till prepar'd for longer flight,
> Waves in its Plumes the various Light.

Conversely, the lover in **'To his Coy Mistress'** begins by imagining an infinitude of time and space in which he might conduct his courtship at just such a leisurely pace:

> Had we but World enough, and Time,
> This coyness Lady were no crime.
> We would sit down, and think which way
> To walk, and pass our long Loves Day.

> Thou by the *Indian Ganges* side
> Should'st Rubies find: I by the Tide
> Of *Humber* would complain. I would
> Love you ten years before the Flood:
> And you should, if you please, refuse
> Till the Conversion of the *Jews.*
> My vegetable Love should grow
> Vaster than Empires, and more slow.

Such 'World enough, and Time' can exist, however, only in fantasy. In fact, all the lovers can anticipate at the end of their brief lives is 'Deserts of vast Eternity'. Better, then, to seize the moment and make up by intensity for the imagined extension in time and space which mortality denies them:

> Thus, though we cannot make our Sun
> Stand still, yet we will make him run.

The predatory and incontinent lovers at the end of the poem embody the single-minded concentration on the satisfactions of the moment that resembles the 'uncessant Labours' of the worldings in **'The Garden'**.

Both poems, then, confront unbridled human aspirations with temporal realities in pursuit of a qualified fulfilment. In both the innocence (or *naïveté*) of unlimited hope is corrected by the severely limited view of experience. Both poems lead us through a process by which the vanity of human wishes is exposed to the facts of mortal life.

If there is a common theme running through the best of Marvell's lyric poems it is the reconciliation of the opposing claims of innocence and experience. The eye of innocence is single, a virtue to be sure, but also a shortcoming. Experience, on the other hand, is afflicted by ambiguity, something close to the 'vain Head, and double Heart' of **'A Dialogue between the Soul and Body'**. Innocence produces the unison and melody of **'Bermudas'**, experience the harmony of discords celebrated in **'Musicks Empire'**. Innocence is often satisfied with its condition, even to the point of sounding a little smug, like the Resolved Soul rejecting the temptations of Created Pleasure:

> A Soul that knowes not to presume
> Is Heaven's and its own perfume.

Experience, on the other hand, is restless and dissatisfied, like the Body in **'A Dialogue between the Soul and Body'**:

> What but a Soul could have the wit
> To build me up for Sin so fit?

The contentment of innocence derives from self-containment, like the Soul in **'On a Drop of Dew'**, which

> Round in its self incloses:
> And in its little Globes Extent,
> Frames as it can its native Element.

Experience, however, is riven by inner conflict, like the speaker in **'The Coronet',** who is dismayed to find, intertwined in the garland he has woven for his Saviour, 'wreaths of Fame and Interest'.

If the contending claims of innocence and experience are found at the heart of Marvell's best poems, we scarcely need to be reminded that the issues are fundamental to the human condition, however divertingly they may sometimes be treated. Nor need we be reminded, thanks to Cleanth Brooks, that wit can be compatible with high seriousness. What is at stake in Marvell is the need to harmonize the idealism of innocence with the awareness of reality characteristic of experience.

What is at stake in Marvell is the need to harmonize the idealism of innocence with the awareness of reality characteristic of experience.

—*George deF. Lord*

The more intense and discriminating the dialectic of thought and feeling on both sides, the more intense the reader's response. With this in mind we can dismiss from our discussion a handful of poems which fail to develop much dialectical intensity, those celebrating a more or less tranquil innocence, such as **'A Dialogue, between the Resolved Soul, and Created Pleasure'**, **'On a Drop of Dew'**, and **'Bermudas',** and such cynical, *libertin* poems as **'Thyrsis and Dorinda'** and **'Mourning'.**

Assuming that Marvell's most interesting poems are those which combine the most exquisite balance between contending forces with the maximum of imaginative power, we might first consider poems where the balance of power is relatively uneven.

One such is **'The Coronet'**, Marvell's most Herbert-like poem, which explores the labyrinthine divarications of the will as it seeks to contrive a tribute to the divine only to discover that the proffered coronet is a hopeless tangle of vanity and self-interest. Deliverance can come only through a self-annihilating submission to Christ:

> But thou who only could'st the Serpent tame,
> Either his slipp'ry knots at once untie,
> And disintangle all his winding Snare:
> Or shatter too with him my curious frame:

When inextricable confusion of motives confronts the absolute of redeeming Grace there is no contest, and yet the poem remains as a brilliant memorial to its creation and rejection.

More painful is the dilemma in **'Upon Appleton House'**, where, in a quest for lost Paradise, Marvell, at first sight, appears to undergo the contemplative retirement of **'The Garden'**:

> But I, retiring from the Flood,
> Take Sanctuary in the Wood;
> And, while it lasts, my self imbark
> In this yet green, yet growing Ark;

Yet the nature in which he seeks lost innocence is disturbingly ambiguous. There is an oak 'tainted' by the '*Traitor-Worm*, within it bred', and the security he hopes to find suggests a labyrinthine enthralment:

> The Oak-Leaves me embroyder all,

> Between which Caterpillars crawl:
> And Ivy, with familiar trails,
> Me licks, and clasps, and curles, and hales.

In pursuing an ecstatic liberation of the spirit, as in **'The Garden'**, he seems to have consigned himself to a hedonistic bondage touched with masochism:

> Bind me ye *Woodbines* in your twines,
> Curle me about ye gadding *Vines,*
> And Oh so close your Circles lace,
> That I may never leave this Place:
> But, lest your Fetters prove too weak,
> Ere I your Silken Bondage break,
> Do you, *O Brambles,* chain me too,
> And courteous *Briars* nail me through.

Clearly this is a travesty of contemplative retirement, with solipsism masquerading as spiritual reflection and narcissism disguised as self-discovery. The situation is reflected in the description of the flooded River Wharfe, which runs through the meadows below Appleton House:

> . . . a *Chrystal Mirrour* slick;
> Where all things gaze themselves, and doubt
> If they be in it or without.
> And for his shade which therein shines,
> *Narcissus* like, the *Sun* too pines.

Having projected its egotism on the sun, the infatuated ego returns to contemplating its own histrionics:

> Oh what a Pleasure 'tis to hedge
> My Temples here with heavy sedge;
> Abandoning my lazy Side,
> Stretcht as a Bank unto the Tide;

Abandoned to the idleness of a piscatory eclogue, 'While at my Lines the Fishes twang!', Marvell is disconcerted by the advent of the young Maria Fairfax, heir to Appleton House and its genius loci. Her untainted innocence has the power to put an end to the dizzying metamorphoses we have witnessed, for

> But by her *Flames,* in *Heaven* try'd,
> *Nature* is wholly *vitrifi'd.*

Maria's eye is single, she can distinguish 'within' and 'without' and restore her tutor's power of discrimination. In celebrating her dedication to a public career in service to 'some universal good', Marvell may also have been bidding farewell to the private and self-reflective themes with which his lyric poems had been concerned. With subject and object, 'within' and 'without' restored to their proper places, the poem seem to arrive at a point of view that sees a loss of innocence in a retirement too long protracted at a time when public responsibilities beckon. The usual association of innocence with retirement and experience with involvement in affairs is now reversed, and the poet seems to be anticipating the commitment to public service from which he never turned back. For the remainder of his life, as a Foreign Secretary under Cromwell, as M.P. for Hull, as secretary to the Earl of Carlyle on a mission to Moscow, and as political pamphleteer and satirist, he was to compile the record as a patriot which, for two and a half centuries, overshadowed his achievement as a lyric poet.

From the perspective of **'Upon Appleton House'** with its resolution of the claims of retirement and involvement in favour of the latter, we can look back on a group of pastoral poems where the conflict of innocence and experience seems to result in a deadlock. Marvell's 'mower' poems are recognized as a sort of subspecies of pastoral, with the mower taking the place of the traditional shepherd. The substitution of a mower for a shepherd may seem an insignificant one unless we see that the pastoral innocence of the shepherd gives way to a more qualified innocence in the mower. The shepherd, at least according to the convention, pursues the most passive of occupations, but the mower is active and aggressive, and the fact that he cuts down the grass, that ubiquitous green emblem of hope in Marvell, makes him a more complicated figure in the pastoral landscape. He may be more complex, but he is also naïve:

> My Mind was once the true survey
> Of all these Medows fresh and gay;
> And in the greenness of the Grass
> Did see its Hopes as in a Glass;
> When *Juliana* came, and She
> What I do to the Grass, does to my Thoughts
>   and Me.

The haunting refrain, in which the mower associates his occupation with Juliana's devastation of his hopes, implies a link between loss of innocence and the mower's task. The blessed leisure of the pastoral shepherd has given way to the cursed labour of fallen man. Of this connection the mower is clearly unaware: he can only juxtapose what he does to the grass and what Juliana does to him.

In **'Damon the Mower'** the transformation from innocence to experience is made more explicit:

> Heark how the Mower *Damon* Sung,
> With love of *Juliana* stung!
> While ev'ry thing did seem to paint
> The Scene more fit for his complaint.
> Like her fair Eyes the day was fair;
> But scorching like his am'rous Care.
> Sharp like his Sythe his Sorrow was,
> And wither'd like his Hopes the Grass.

In the grass withered like Damon's hopes Marvell has modified the pastoral convention. Exiled from a fictional world devoted to idyllic love, the mower is baffled by unrequited passion, while Juliana, a figment of that world, is conditioned by its conventions to respond only to the overtures of shepherds. Marvell's mower, who has blundered into the pastoral world, is thus the victim of generic specialization. Presumably, Juliana cannot even hear his song. She is on another wavelength, as it were.

Doomed to an isolation unwittingly created by his occupation, Damon can only direct his frustrated passion at 'Depopulating all the Ground'. Unrequited love drives him to genocide, but that brings no relief, and his passion is finally and inevitably turned upon himself:

> The edged Stele by careless chance
> Did into his own Ankle glance;
> And there among the Grass fell down,
> By his own Sythe, the Mower mown.

In Marvell's vegetable world those who live by the scythe perish by the scythe, as Damon realizes in a final epiphany:

> Only for him no Cure is found,
> Whom *Julianas* Eyes do wound.
> 'Tis death alone that this must do:
> For Death thou art a Mower too.

In **'The Mower to the Glo-Worms'** Damon moves a little further along the line from innocence to experience. He begins by evoking poignantly an earlier state in which he seemed to live in harmony with nature and ends with a recognition of the hopeless disorientation and alienation which Juliana has brought into his life:

> i
>
> Ye living Lamps, by whose dear light
> The Nightingale does sit so late,
> And studying all the Summer-night,
> Her matchless Songs does meditate;
>
> ii
>
> Ye Country Comets, that portend
> No War, nor Princes funeral,
> Shining unto no higher end
> Than to presage the Grasses fall;
>
> iii
>
> Ye Glo-worms, whose officious Flame
> To wandring Mowers shows the way,
> That in the Night have lost their aim,
> And after foolish Fires do stray;
>
> iv
>
> Your courteous Lights in vain you waste,
> Since *Juliana* here is come,
> For She my Mind hath so displac'd
> That I shall never find my home.

As a solitary reaper in a pastoral world Damon has no choice but to submit to his homelessness.

Given the narrow limits of the genre and the limited awareness of the naïve mower, these poems strike a delicate balance between the poles of innocence and experience.

A quite different treatment of the same themes is to be found in **'The Nymph Complaining for the Death of her Faun'**. Unlike the terse Damon, the Nymph responds to the withering of her hopes with a flood of mannerist conceits reminiscent of Crashaw. This poem won the heart of Edgar Allan Poe: 'How truthful an air of deep lamentation hangs here upon every gentle syllable! It pervades all. It comes over the sweet melody of the words, over the gentleness and grace which we fancy in the little maiden herself, even over the half-playful, half-petulant air with which she lingers on the beauties and good qualities of her favorite—like the cool shadow of a summer cloud over a bed of lilies and violets'. This fatuous rhapsody, which appeared in the *Southern Literary Messenger* for August 1836, may suggest some reasons why Marvell's poetry had to wait so long for proper appreciation. Certainly, if **'The Nymph Complaining'** were as Poe saw it, it would never have received the extensive and distinguished attention that later critics have given it. Poe failed to see that the naïve effusions of the little maiden are qualified both by her own hyperboles and by Marvell's sympathetic but also ironic awareness of the implications of her reaction to the events she deplores. A critic who construes the poem as an allegory of the Crucifixion also misses the qualifications of irony. No doubt, as others have suggested, the poem does allude to the Song of Songs and to Ascanius's slaying of Sylvia's faun in *Aeneid* vii, but it is to be understood in its own terms. It is essential to keep in mind that it presents the emotional, intellectual, and imaginative *process* by which the innocent nymph tries to deal with a devastating experience. *Process* is affirmed in the title, which is not **'The Nymph's Complaint'** but **'The Nymph's Complaining'.** Unlike Marvell's other poems of loss of innocence, where the point of view is retrospective, this elegy—in the opening and closing sections, at any rate—moves in time with the nymph's experience of the faun's dying:

> O help! O help! I see it faint:
> And dye as calmely as a Saint.
> See how it weeps. The Tears do come
> Sad, slowly dropping like a Gumme.
> So weeps the wounded Balsome: so
> The holy Frankincense doth flow.
> The brotherless *Heliades*
> Melt in such Amber Tears as these.

The slow movement of the verse is part of another process of transformation, in the course of which tears and drops of blood, like gum and frankincense, are gradually congealed into the immobility of art, represented by the statues of faun and nymph which the nymph finally imagines at the end of the poem. In addition to this retardation of process we find a growing aesthetic distance between the event and the nymph's response to it in her elegantly learned reference to Phaeton's sisters as 'The brotherless *Heliades*'. The nymph is not as naïve as she makes herself out to be, and there is even a suggestion in this transformation of personal experience into myth, that she derives some pleasure from her skill as artist. The poem implies then that the price of art is the loss of innocence, or at least the gaining of a wider awareness.

Marvell is the least sentimental of English poets. His awareness, in Eliot's famous phrase, 'involves, probably, a recognition, implicit in the expression of every experience, of other kinds of experience which are possible'. A striking appreciation of this quality is found in Hemingway's allusion to Marvell in *A Farewell to Arms* (1929). On the eve of his departure for what turns out to be the rout of the allied forces at Caporetto, Lt. Henry and Catherine Barclay are spending the night at a hotel in Milan:

> The waiter came and took away the things. After a while we were very still and we could hear the rain. Down below on the street a motor car honked.
>
> 'But at my back I always hear
> Times winged chariot hurrying near.'
>
> I said.
>
> 'I know the poem' Catherine said. 'It's by Marvell. But it's about a girl who wouldn't live with a man.'

The sound of the horn evidently sets the train of association going in Lt. Henry's memory, but the unmentioned link is the allusion in *The Waste Land* to 'The sound of horns and motors, which shall bring / Sweeney to Mrs. Porter in the spring'. In quoting Marvell's famous couplet while suppressing Eliot's desolate version of it Hemingway's young officer brilliantly exemplifies the ironic complexity of response in Marvell which Eliot had identified in his essay. The innocence of Hemingway's lovers is thus disturbingly qualified by two voices of experience, that of Marvell's lover and that of Eliot's Tiresias.

Unlike Hemingway, Marvell never pursues the dialectic of innocence and experience to a tragic conclusion. Instead, he usually brings the conflict to some sort of resolution or, at least, to some kind of existential adjustment. Where neither of the parties concerned is capable of concessions there may be a painful but comic deadlock, as in **'A Dialogue between the Soul and Body'.** Here neither party is capable of recognizing any kind of experience but its own, and the result is utter incompatibility between two balanced sets of paradoxes:

> O Who shall, from this Dungeon, raise
> A Soul enslav'd so many wayes?
> With bolts of Bones, that fetter'd stands
> In Feet; and manacled in Hands.
> Here blinded with an Eye; and there
> Deaf with the drumming of an Ear.
> A Soul hung up, as 'twere, in Chains
> Of Nerves, and Arteries, and Veins.
> Tortur'd, besides each other part,
> In a vain Head, and double Heart.
>
> O who shall me deliver whole,
> From bonds of this Tyrannic Soul?
> Which, stretcht upright, impales me so,
> That mine own Precipice I go;
> And warms and moves this needless Frame:
> (A Fever could but do the same.)
> And, wanting where its spight to try,
> Has made me live to let me dye.
> A Body that could never rest,
> Since this ill Spirit it possest.

This witty dilemma prompted some anonymous reader of a Bodleian copy to cross out the last four lines of the poem in which Body complains,

> What but a Soul could have the wit
> To build me up for Sin so fit?
> So Architects do square and hew
> Green Trees that in the Forest grew.

In the margin he wrote, 'Desunt multa' (A great deal is missing). I assume that he was perturbed at the idea that Body should have the last word in the exchange.

In **'The Definition of Love',** his most metaphysical poem, Marvell goes a step beyond the deadlock of Soul and Body. Here Fate opposes the consummation of a perfect love. Here the contending forces of innocence and experience are deadlocked, but Marvell contrives to make of this seemingly hopeless situation a qualified victory for the forces of innocence and ideal love. The obstacle of Fate or 'Impossibility' paradoxically guarantees the continuing perfection of love: the Donnean *tour de force* makes intractable opposition the preservative of the ideal. Frustration becomes a higher virtue than fruition:

> My Love is of a birth as rare
> As 'tis for object strange and high:
> It was begotten by despair
> Upon Impossibility.

The tone in which this arcane secret is presented is austere and private. Rarely does Marvell seem to address anyone in particular. He is much more solitary than Donne. His metaphoric terms are often absolute in their abstractness, unqualified by sensuous richness or appeal. The only emotion in the poem is expressed in the contemptuous dismissal of Hope:

> Magnanimous Despair alone
> Could show me so divine a thing,
> Where feeble Hope could ne'er have flown
> But vainly flapt its Tinsel Wing.

The impotence of hope finds prosodic expression in the exhausted series of short 'i's: 'its Tinsel Wing', which is contrasted with the sonorous energy of 'Magnanimous Despair alone'. Even more effective is the process by which Hope is rendered hopeless as its feebleness is underscored by the triple rhyme of 'ne'er have flown' with 'Despair alone', while the usual associations of hope are conferred magnanimously upon despair.

Still, the poet continues, he might achieve his object without hope, were it not for Fate:

> And yet I quickly might arrive
> Where my extended Soul is fixt,
> But Fate does Iron wedges drive,
> And alwaies crouds it self betwixt.

Having met magnanimous despair and hopeless hope we are not, perhaps, too surprised to encounter a Fate characterized as an anxious, small-minded busybody and something of a spoilsport. The expansive energies of the first two lines are blocked by the obstructive operation of Fate 'croud[ing] it self betwixt', while its envious insecurity becomes explicit in the next stanza:

> For Fate with jealous Eye does see
> Two perfect Loves; nor lets them close;
> Their union would her ruine be,
> And her Tyrannick pow'r depose.

Limitations of vision may be implicit in Fate's single 'Eye'. She has, none the less, good reason to be anxious. Even when held apart by her opposition the polar lovers define the world of love:

> And therefore her Decrees of Steel
> Us as the distant Poles have plac'd
> (Though Loves whole World on us doth wheel)
> Not by themselves to be embrac'd.

I don't think it is over-ingenious to see the parentheses bracketing the line 'Though Loves whole World on us doth wheel' as representing the two hemispheres of that world of love which a union of the lovers would destroy. In this magnanimous and self-denying recognition there also seems to be an allusion to Donne's famous observation that

> Dull sublunary lovers' love
> Whose soul is sense, cannot admit
> Absence, 'cause it doth remove
> Those things which elemented it.

[In *The Art of Marvell's Poetry,* 1966] J. B. Leishman makes the comparison with Donne's poem to show that Marvell's poem is essentially an ingenious series of conceits on the time-honoured theme of impossibility in love. I am inclined to prefer the idea that, having once postulated a perfect love, Marvell then takes the metaphorical commonplaces of the genre, the poles that link and separate the lovers, the microcosm of love, the opposition of fate, and so on, to construct a model that represents so precisely the existential and emotional dilemma of the lover. Innocent aspirations, blocked by Fate, lead to a more sublime innocence tested by experience:

> As Lines so Loves *oblique* may well
> Themselves in every Angle greet:
> But ours so truly *Paralel,*
> Though infinite can never meet.

The definition ends with a concluding statement as precise and satisfying as the completion of a proposition in geometry:

> Therefore the Love which us doth bind,
> But Fate so enviously debarrs,
> Is the Conjunction of the Mind,
> And Opposition of the Stars.

The sublimity of this conclusion is, of course, qualified by the underlying ironic awareness that Fate's power does not depend on her keeping the lovers apart. Like Donne, Marvell dramatizes the boundless egotism of the lover by hyperbole, but, once we grant him the sublime innocence of his love and the hostility of Fate, the rigorous precision of his definition leads inevitably and satisfyingly to such a conclusion.

Somewhat the same antagonism between innocence and experience, between reality and the ideal, is at the heart of the famous **'Horatian Ode upon Cromwell's Return from Ireland'.** Like most of Marvell's poems, the **'Ode'** was not published during his lifetime, and he wrote it, I believe, in order to come to grips with an extremely difficult political situation. Here was a dilemma which demanded a decision for or against Cromwell. A practical solution to the dilemma must be achieved without sacrificing principle. In his meteoric career seen from the perspective of the summer of 1650 Cromwell had seized the leadership of the Parliamentary forces, captured and executed the king, defeated the Irish, and was about to invade Scotland. The issue, as Marvell defines it, is whether or not a loyal Englishman can support Cromwell, and it turns on the opposition between the 'helpless Right' represented by the dead Charles I and the overwhelming might of Cromwell:

> Though Justice against Fate complain,
> And plead the antient Rights in vain:
> But those do hold or break
> As Men are strong or weak.
> Nature that hateth emptiness,
> Allows of penetration less:
> And therefore must make room

Where greater Spirits come.

'Certainly', as Professor Wallace says [in his *Destiny His Choice: The Loyalism of Andrew Marvell,* 1968], 'a doctrine of necessity is being employed to counter the cause of justice, but . . . it may be more accurate to emphasize Marvell's own appeal to a higher justice, embodied not in a constitution but in natural and revealed law.' What is Horatian about Marvell's poem is its scrupulous awareness of what must be said on either side of the question. As in Horace's ode on the defeat of Cleopatra at Actium ('nunc est bibendum'), where the celebration of a Roman victory is qualified by a panegyric of the vanquished queen, Marvell's celebration of Cromwell is heavily qualified by his panegyric on the dead Charles I:

> *He* nothing common did, or mean,
> Upon the memorable Scene:
> But with his keener Eye
> The Axes edge did try:
> Nor call'd the *Gods* with vulgar spight
> To vindicate his helpless Right,
> But bow'd his comely Head
> Down, as upon a Bed.

Yet, the praise of Charles is qualified in turn by the suggestion that his submission, however dignified and courageous, to some extent validated the force to which he submitted, for

> This was that memorable Hour
> Which first assur'd the forced Pow'r.

Marvell makes this 'memorable Scene' crucial. Before it Cromwell is presented chiefly in terms of power; afterwards he is praised for his justice, knowledge, moderation, and obedience: 'How fit he is to sway / That can so well obey'. But even this commendation is qualified by the lines that lead up to it: 'Nor yet grown stiffer with Command, / But still in the *Republick's* hand'. After such a tentative and conditional approval of Cromwell as *de facto* head of state, the remainder of the ode limits itself to anticipating his future victories in foreign wars, an area in which approval need not be qualified. In the concluding apostrophe, however, qualification is implicit:

> But thou the Wars and Fortunes Son
> March indefatigably on,
> And for the last effect
> Still keep thy Sword erect:
> Besides the force it has to fright
> The Spirits of the shady Night;
> The same *Arts* that did *gain*
> A *Pow'r* must it *maintain*.

Power won by arts, lacking the endorsement of rights, can only be maintained by ceaseless and indefatigable exertion. Our final view of Cromwell puts him among those pursuers of worldly ambition derided in **'The Garden'**:

> How vainly men themselves amaze
> To win the Palm, the Oke, or Bayes;
> And their uncessant Labours see
> Crown'd from some single Herb or Tree,
> Whose short and narrow verged Shade
> Does prudently their Toyles upbraid;

Although the word liberal has now lost its meaning on both sides of the Atlantic and was not a significant term in Marvell's time, I am inclined to attribute some of his great strength and abiding influence to a liberal imagination and a liberal conscience. His ode on Cromwell always reminds me of E. M. Forster's *Two Cheers for Democracy.* His career as poet and public servant was marked by independent judgement and a talent for making responsible discriminations. It is not surprising, then, that shortly after writing the **'Horatian Ode'** he took a position at Appleton House with the Lord General Fairfax who had retired from the leadership of the Parliamentary army because he disapproved of Cromwell's projected invasion of Scotland. In his sojourn with the Fairfaxes in Yorkshire, tutoring the girl who was so unfortunately to marry Dryden's Zimri, the dissolute Duke of Buckingham, Marvell probably wrote **'The Garden'** and other poems on life in the country in addition to a poem in Latin and two in English in honour of his master. **'Upon Appleton House'** is, among other things, a meditative or contemplative poem of ninety-seven four-square octasyllabic octet stanzas which explores the contending values of the retired life versus the active life. As I have mentioned, Marvell appears to have felt at its conclusion that he had an obligation to emerge from retirement and serve his country. At the end of 1652, with the help of Milton, he applied for the post of assistant Latin Secretary. Instead he became governor of Cromwell's protégé and prospective son-in-law, William Dutton. The awe and qualified admiration for Cromwell expressed in the **'Horatian Ode'** seem through this association to have deepened into an affection matched only by his warm relationship to his nephew, Will Popple. Early in 1655 Marvell published **'The First Anniversary of the Government under His Highness The Lord Protector'**, outstanding among poems on affairs of state for its special blend of political realism and piety. It explores the proposition that Cromwell may be a Heaven-sent ruler and that the power maintained so indefatigably at the end of the **'Horatian Ode'** might now, God willing, be endorsed by Cromwell's coronation, a step which the Lord Protector refused to take. In any event, Marvell's wisdom in the ways of innocence and experience appears brilliantly in his figurative representation of the ways in which the political opposition may help to sustain the Protectorate. He sees in Cromwell another Amphion, using *his* instrument (the Instrument of Government, 1653, which established the Protectorate) to produce political harmony:

> Such was that wondrous Order and Consent,
> When *Cromwell* tun'd the ruling Instrument;

The response is truly sublime:

> None to be sunk in the Foundation bends,
> Each in the House the highest Place contends,
> And each the Hand that lays him will direct,
> And some fall back upon the Architect;
> Yet all compos'd by his attractive Song,
> Into the Animated City throng.

The magic of this leads to the engineering genius which underlies Marvell's magnificent and accurate representation of the dynamics of the mixed state:

The Common-wealth does through their Cen-
    ters all
Draw the Circumf'rence of the publique Wall;
The crossest Spirits here do take their part,
Fast'ning the Contignation which they thwart;
And they, whose Nature leads them to divide,
Uphold, this one, and that the other Side;
But the most Equall still sustein the Height,
And they as Pillars keep the Work upright;
While the resistance of opposed Minds,
The Fabrique as with Arches stronger binds,
Which on the Basis of a Senate free,
Knit by the Roofs Protecting weight agree.

This has the brilliance and precision of **'The Definition of Love'** with the addition of gravity. The Protectorate, as Marvell contemplates it, can employ the least erected and most hostile spirits in creating something as close to the heavenly city as can be found on earth.

Phoebe S. Spinrad   (essay date 1982)

SOURCE: "Death, Loss, and Marvell's Nymph," in *PMLA*, Vol. 97, No. 1, January, 1982, pp. 50-9.

[*In the following essay, Spinrad interprets "The Nymph Complaining for the Death of Her Faun" as a statement on the mutability of life.*]

It may not be so simplistic as it sounds to say that Marvell's **"The Nymph Complaining for the Death of Her Faun"** is a traditional poem. Indeed, so many strands of tradition are woven into the poem that the reader may easily overlook the completed fabric in following the various threads of convention. And thus critics have interpreted the poem as a political, religious, or romantic allegory; as a metaphoric lament for innocence, an old order, Christ, or love; and as a literal lament for a pet or—in one reading that borders on self-parody [Evan Jones, " 'The Nymph Complaining for the Death of Her Faun,' " *Explicator* 26 (1967)]—for a child.

Paradoxically enough, all these interpretations are both true and false. That is, none can be taken alone; each must be combined with seemingly contradictory patterns to form one larger pattern that includes them all. Therefore, in tracing the development of these theories, I raise objections only to the sole validity of a particular subpattern, not to its validity within the overall pattern.

One theory arises from the very first lines of the poem: "The wanton Troopers riding by / Have shot my Faun and it will die." This image is a markedly contemporary one; the fawn has been "shot" rather than slain with an arrow, and the "troopers," as both Nicholas Guild and Earl Miner have pointed out, are most likely Cromwellian soldiers, of whom the word "trooper" was first used [Guild, "Marvell's 'The Nymph Complaining for the Death of Her Faun,' " *Modern Language Quarterly* 29 (1968); Miner, "The Death of Innocence in Marvell's 'The Nymph Complaining for the Death of Her Faun,' " *Modern Philology* 65 (1967)]. Although Miner incorporates the political overtones of "Troopers" into a more generalized lament for innocence and the pastoral order, Guild sees the entire poem as topical: a thinly disguised elegy for the

old order in England, coupled with a grateful recognition that the old will indeed yield place to new. Both critics base a good deal of their argument on a passage in Book VII of the *Aeneid*, in which the slaying of Sylvia's deer by Iulus leads to war between the Trojans and the Latins and to the subsequent establishment of Rome in Italy.

But if Marvell had wished to affirm the implacable destiny of Cromwell's new Rome, he would hardly allow his nymph, a sympathetic figure in the poem, to state so definitively that the troopers are "wanton," "guilty," and incapable of salvation or forgiveness. Of course, Marvell may be creating a naive persona in the nymph, one whose political innocence about the coming of the new order will evoke the more sophisticated reader's enlightened pity. But it may be helpful to look more closely at the *Aeneid* itself before accepting this reading.

Sylvia's deer (not a fawn, but a *cervus*, a grown deer) is both tame and wild. Its antlers are decorated and it returns home when it is wounded ("nota intra tecta refugit" 'he returns in flight to his familiar dwelling'), but it is in the habit of ranging the countryside for food and sport. When it does return wounded, it clamors for attention, and Sylvia, taking up the clamor, shouts for help until all her rough kin gather and prepare for war: "palmis percussat lacertos, / auxilium vocat, et duros conclamat agrestes" 'she beats her arms with her hands, cries for help, and calls her countrymen together' (VII.503–04).

The tone of this passage is singularly unlike that of Marvell's poem. Although both contain a dying animal and a young girl, and although Sylvia's cry for help seems to be echoed in the nymph's "O help! O help! I see it faint" (1. 93), the similarities end there. Vergil's poem emphasizes the noise and uproar that surround the death of the deer and echoes the tumult in a series of clanging spondees within the verse. Marvell's poem follows the nymph's cry with an insistence on the calm demeanor of the dying fawn and a static display of its slowly dropping tears—a deliberate slowing down and softening of the action. Even the calls for help are dissimilar. Sylvia fully expects a response to her outcry, as well as rapid action to avenge both her personal injury and the affront to her people, and the Latins fulfill her expectations on a grand Vergilian scale. The nymph, however, is crying out in a solitary desperation that knows it will receive no answer, and she has specifically waived any demand for vengeance in the first twenty-four lines of the poem. Sylvia's is a cry of anger; the nymph's, of helpless grief.

While the political upheaval in England may have moved Marvell to write a lament, the political allegory alone is insufficient to account for this difference in tone, for Sylvio's behavior, and for the specifically Christian symbolism surrounding the fawn in parts of the poem. The various religious interpretations may come closer. But even here, the amorous exchange between Sylvio and the nymph in lines 25–36 partakes too much of the often trivial wordplay of the love sonneteers to be applicable to such a subject; the deliberate toying with the emotions in this passage is out of place in a discussion of conceptual matters such as churches and doctrines.

To account for such amorous conceits and for the erotic imagery in general, some religious allegorists identify the fawn with Christ rather than with the Church, relying for their exegesis primarily on the Song of Songs just as the political allegorists rely on the *Aeneid*. This is perhaps fitting, since it is a standard theological exercise to interpret the Song of Songs as an exemplum of Christ's love for his Church, but there may be some problems in trying to use a metaphor of a metaphor as a literal text.

There is certainly no lack of Christian symbolism in the poem. And [in *Marvell's Pastoral Art,* 1970] Donald M. Friedman, who sees the religious parallel almost to the exclusion of all others, even attempts to deal with the blood imagery in lines 83–84 ("Upon the Roses it would feed / until its Lips ev'n seem'd to bleed") that some of his colleagues ignore. The bloody lip prints, he says, connect the fawn and the nymph by a "serious metaphor" distinctly Christian in its foreshadowing of the fawn's "martyrdom," which the nymph, or Christian, must share with Christ. This is a good attempt to deal with a rather disconcerting image, but Friedman's insistence on limiting the "serious metaphor" to a Christian one causes further problems in his delineation of the garden. He remarks, for example, that the colors of the flowers are "the commonplace visual signs of carnal beauty in the female"; then, by a sort of free association, he declares that the flowers can therefore "only be reminiscent of liturgical imagery of Christ and, most particularly, of the 'beloved' in the Song of Songs." This non sequitur is difficult to understand.

Furthermore, if the "wanton Troopers" are to be taken as killers of Christ—in either the literal sense of Roman soldiers or the metaphorical sense of sinners—then the blood imagery becomes confused. The nymph's words appear to deny the traditional Christian image of the soul's cleansing by the blood of Christ:

> Though they should wash their guilty hands
> In this warm life blood, which doth part
> From thine, and wound me to the Heart,
> Yet could they not be clean: their Stain
> Is dy'd in such a Purple Grain. (ll. 18–22)

The lack of cleansing efficacy in this blood hints of a sin beyond redemption, a suggestion that is alien to the Christian concept, particularly if the fawn is taken as a specifically Anglican Christ. In fact, if the next two lines did not reintroduce the image of the Lamb (or fawn) of God, the ineffectual washing of the hands would be more reminiscent of Lady Macbeth or the assassins in *Julius Caesar*.

It is interesting to note other ways in which Marvell undercuts his Christian imagery by juxtaposing it with more secular imagery. One of the most obvious, of course, is the nymph's rapid transition, in lines 24–25, from the Lamb of God to "unconstant Sylvio." Again, the contrast between the fawn's love and that of "false and cruel men" (ll. 53–54) is brought back to a secular level—one that is almost as poetically fashionable as Sylvio's puns—in lines 57–62, where the fawn's physical attributes are compared with those of the nymph and "any Ladies of the Land." What might have been a consideration of the degrees of divine and earthly love has here been reduced to a Petrarchan convention.

During the actual death of the fawn, too, Marvell alternates Christian and classical images. To be sure, pagan symbolism was often Christianized in the period, but seldom is the contrast between the two traditions as deliberately pointed as it is here. And the animal in an afterworld is pagan not only in imagery but in doctrine. It may be argued that if the fawn is a symbol of Christ, the Holy Spirit, or the Anglican church, then it would very likely go to an "Elizium," along with the saints who are poetically metamorphosed into swans, doves, lambs, and ermines; that in fact the "vanish'd" of line 105 may suggest the rising from the tomb, or the Ascension. But the design of the nymph's tomb, focusing not on the fawn but on the weeping statue of the nymph, denies any linking of the fawn with Christ crucified or risen. The fawn, lying at her feet like a faithful dog on a tombstone or a symbolic animal at the feet of a goddess in a classical frieze, is, by the end of the poem, perhaps still an extrawordly creature but certainly not Christ.

Geoffrey H. Hartman, in dealing with the Christian allegory [in " 'The Nymph Complaining for the Death of Her Faun': A Brief Allegory," *Essays in Criticism* 18 (1968)], takes a tentative step toward a more comprehensive understanding of the poem, recognizing some of the psychological stages through which the nymph goes: the substitution of one love object for another in a series of losses that can never be quite compensated for. But he places this sequence only in the religious context of the progress of the soul, thereby postulating the fawn as the Comforter, or Holy Spirit. Unfortunately, this reading forces him into the unlikely position of further postulating Sylvio as Christ, since Sylvio is the giver of the Comforter. No matter how much Hartman then tries to skew the unfavorable description of Sylvio into theologically acceptable terms (Sylvio-Christ only *seems* "unconstant" and "wild" because the earthbound soul cannot grasp his divine nature), the analogy remains incongruous.

As for the religious symbolism of the fawn and the garden in the Song of Songs, one can only agree that the imagery is similar to Marvell's, although Marvell's use of it may raise certain questions about real differences between the nymph's garden and the biblical one; for instance, the "beloved" in the Song "feedeth among lilies," whereas the fawn feeds, as will be seen, among some rather ambiguous roses. But the imagery in the Song of Songs is also common to a certain type of love literature, and to claim religious significance for it wherever it occurs is to reason backward. (One might just as easily claim that after John Donne all references to fleas must imply a love union.)

Still, attempting to produce a love allegory by interpreting the Song of Songs analogue secularly does not seem to suffice either, and within the allegory of lost love the critical view of the nymph herself sometimes becomes rather disapproving. [In *Marvell's Ironic Vision,* 1965] Harold E. Toliver, for example, decries the nymph because the world she tries to create is false and thus vulnerable to any intrusion on her fantasy. She herself is partially to blame for the death of the fawn, he suggests, as well as for the departure of Sylvio, because she will not mix any warmth with her "cold passivity." Even Rosalie Colie, who sees the nymph more as a pastoral artist than as a jilted young woman, regards her as "myopically self-regarding," adding that "her garden and her pet are, in the end, projections of herself and her own strongly aesthetic needs" [*"My Ecchoing Song": Andrew Marvell's Poetry of Criticism,* 1970]. And Lawrence W. Hyman, who does attempt to incorporate some of the religious imagery into his dichotomy between "innocent love" and "adult passion," still sees the nymph as somehow insufficient, in that she has tried to create a Garden of Eden that is no longer accessible to humankind [Hyman, *Andrew Marvell,* 1964].

One of the dangers in dealing with the love allegory is the temptation to base too much of one's argument on the question of sexuality. Hyman in particular appears to see sexuality in everything surrounding the nymph: her play with the fawn, the flowers in her garden, the troopers, and even her tears. For such critics, whether Sylvio has seduced the nymph becomes an important matter of speculation, as though a woman could not have her heart broken unless she had first had her maidenhead broken. Therefore, although these love allegorists begin to approach the major pattern of the poem, they are hampered by a different sort of exclusionary vision.

Leo Spitzer and Earl Miner seem to come closest to the whole pattern. Spitzer in particular sees that something about the nymph and her fawn is doomed within the context of the poem, but instead of placing his emphasis on the nymph's physical purity, he refers to "the superhuman that is present in the physical," the quintessential purity of beauty itself. Such a view helps to explain the juxtaposition of syntactic simplicity and metaphysical wit in the poem; it reflects, he says, "the contrast of sadness and beauty" ["Marvell's 'Nymph Complaining for the Death of Her Faun': Sources versus Meaning," *Modern Language Quarterly* 19 (1958)].

Earl Miner takes a step further in this approach. The political, the religious, and the romantic interpretations of this poem are all possible simultaneously, he says, because what is lost or dying is innocence itself—not sexual purity, not the old world order, not pure religion, not even Sylvio or the fawn or the nymph herself, but all of these. Things must naturally progress from simplicity to complexity and in doing so must necessarily draw other things after them. Hence the fawn must eventually die, either physically or symbolically; as the girl becomes a woman, the fawn becomes a deer, and existence itself necessitates change. What Miner calls "the death of innocence," then, begins to emerge as the age-old theme of mutability and the transience of all things.

Because of the universality of this pattern, I want to develop it in a somewhat unorthodox manner: by citing analogues not only in the classics, Renaissance literature, and folklore but also in the literature of later centuries. It is always dangerous, of course, to compare the productions of one period with those of a later one (as in the standard joke about the critic who demonstrated T. S. Eliot's influence on Spenser); but since I contend that the overall pattern is timeless, I must use these later writers—some of whom deliberately returned to the Renaissance for their imagery—if only as interpreters or elaborators of Marvell's

theme. And surely the critical understanding of these poets should be given at least as much weight as that of twentieth-century scholars.

But before I pursue the important point about mutability, I should like to examine the poem not as an allegory but as a psychological journey through the nymph's mind. And here another pattern becomes recognizable: a depiction of the human response to death—the death of a loved one or of oneself. Again, this depiction is not to be taken as the sole pattern, only as one of many, though perhaps, like the missing piece of a jigsaw puzzle, the one that will bring all the other pieces together.

In brief, the nymph's mind goes through a series of responses. At the first confrontation with death or loss, the mind goes into an initial and transitory shock as it states the situation to itself (ll. 1–2). This response is followed quickly by the secondary shock, or disbelief, in which the mind refuses to accept what it has stated (ll. 3–6), and then by bewilderment and a sense of injustice (ll. 7–12), which in turn lead to anger and protest at the injustice (ll. 12–24). The first movement toward philosophical acceptance (ll. 25–54) begins with a forced remembrance of the thing lost, along with an attempt at sardonicism about *all* loss (ll. 25–36). This sardonicism leads to the next stage, a focusing on the self as just in contrast with a world that is unjust (ll. 37–46). But the tone is wrong for comfort; unnaturally brittle in the first stage, it becomes cynical in the last stage, a speculation on what might have been and the possible unworthiness of the thing mourned (ll. 47–54). Since this answer is both untrue and unacceptable, it is rejected (ll. 53–54).

Once realism has turned for support to cynicism or to syllogisms that will not hold, the mind then allows itself to dwell on the merits of the thing lost and to idealize it, perhaps in apology for having maligned it (ll. 55–92). This reminiscence, which is less forced than the initial one, takes three stages: first the thing lost is seen as a static display in relation to the self (ll. 55–62); next the thing lost is seen in motion as it lived, with the beginning of recognition that its nature is to move away from the self (ll. 63–70); and finally the thing lost is elevated to an emblem of life itself (ll. 71–90). This final reminiscence, like the first one, culminates in another speculation on what might have been, this time in an idealized version that is as faulty as the cynical one (ll. 91–92).

Idealism and cynicism both having failed, the mind returns with a shock to the reality of loss (ll. 93–94), seeing with a magnifying vision the small physical details of the thing that is slipping away (ll. 95–100). The search for comfort now begins in earnest (ll. 101–22), first in attempting to fix permanently relics of the thing lost (ll. 101–04), next in seeking immortality in an afterlife (ll. 105–10), and finally in seeking an earthly immortality in monuments, often in art (ll. 111–22). But a recognition that the monuments themselves hold a potential for loss runs concurrently with this last search for immortality (ll. 117–22), and so the mind returns full circle, having been comforted only partially, and then primarily through catharsis.

That this pattern of mind is ageless and universal is evident in the way the poem's imagery and turns of phrase show up in all literary genres, from the earliest to the most recent. The very opening of the nymph's complaint echoes a child's nursery rhyme. Her bewilderment already beginning to surface in her first statement of fact—if the troopers are "wanton" and only "riding by," there is no purpose to their act—she blurts out her distress (". . . Thou ne'er dids't alive / them any harm") in the phraseology of "Ding Dong Bell":

> What a wicked boy was that
> To drown poor little pussycat
> Who never did him any harm
> But chased the rats from his father's barn.

It is interesting to note how the nymph rephrases this elementary response in her first, cynical reminiscence:

> How could I less
> Than love it? O I cannot be
> Unkind, t'a Beast that loveth me.
>
> (ll. 44–46)

She has progressed here from the nursery rhyme to the Book of Job: from the concern for another to the concern for self (Job, after all, never spared much sympathy for his stricken family and livestock), from sorrow to self-justification. These lines, significantly, form a bridge between her attempt to speak like Sylvio and her less successful attempt to indulge in "sour grapes" about the fawn. Having mentally linked Sylvio with the troopers, both of whom have destroyed something beautiful, she unconsciously becomes one of them; she begins to be "unkind," if only verbally, "t'a Beast that loveth" her.

Paradoxically enough, this disparaging of the loved one is a necessary stage in the acceptance of loss. The forced remembrance that precedes it reflects the natural tendency of the mind to link the present loss with all losses; to see death and pain as part of the human condition, something that the child's rhyme cannot do. But the nymph's self-justification, an attempt to place herself outside the human condition of *giving* pain, works just opposite to her intent and increases her own pain.

It is a sign of her discomfort with this line of reasoning that she has begun to speak in the conditional mood and to qualify her statements with such phrases as "I do not know / Whether" (ll. 47–48) and "I am sure, for ought that I / Could . . . espie" (ll. 51–52). She is learning, if only subconsciously, that there is no comfort in denying the need for comfort and that, given the universal nature of grief for loss, any attempts to magnify the self and diminish the thing lost not only fail to explain the real pain that she is feeling but add to the universal store of pain.

Since the pain cannot be reasoned away, the nymph gives in to it and dwells on the beauty of the thing lost so that she can analyze her grief into something logical enough to be dealt with. Her description of the fawn's beauty has proved the richest hunting ground for critics seeking allegories and for later poets searching for images with which to describe their own grief at the transience of beauty.

In these lines, when divorced from the more blatant politi-

cal and religious overtones of the trooper passage, the fawn itself begins to take on a more folkloric quality than before. Its speed, grace, and whiteness and its capering on "little silver feet" (l. 64) suggest the evanescence of the unicorn, that mythic symbol of innocence. (The conjunction of "silver" with "fleet" may also suggest quicksilver, another emblem of evanescence and, as I show later, of poison.) Certainly the recurrent emphasis on the fawn's whiteness strengthens the suggestion of innocence, since whiteness has always been a Western symbol of purity. But since purity in this sense is an absolute, any diminution of it necessarily destroys it; hence purity becomes so vulnerable that it is almost dangerous to itself. It is this feeling of danger, of beauty poised on the edge of destruction, that Yeats captures perfectly in a passage from *Coole Park and Ballylee, 1931* that might be an illustration of Marvell's poem:

> Another emblem there! That stormy white
> But seems a concentration of the sky;
> And, like the soul, it sails into the sight
> And in the morning's gone, no man knows why;
> And is so lovely that it sets to right
> What knowledge or its lack had set awry,
> So arrogantly pure, a child might think
> It can be murdered with a spot of ink.

This is the "Tarry, thou art so fair!" of Goethe's Faust; but it must be remembered that at the moment of trying to fix beauty in place Faust calls down destruction upon himself.

Folktales are filled with this dangerous beauty. One tale after another speaks of magic castles and gardens that will vanish if the hero tries to speak, touch them, or look too closely at them. To be inviolate, the beautiful thing must remain external to the self and must be allowed to move at will, whether away from or toward the watcher. It is the sad face of this paradox that the beauty *will* in fact be lost, whether it moves away of its own volition or vanishes at the "spot of ink," the touch of the incautious hero. An interesting variation on this theme occurs in *Through the Looking Glass,* where the fawn runs away as soon as he and Alice have emerged from the wood where things have no names. The act of naming is in itself an attempt to fix the nature of beauty.

The fleetness of the fawn is itself a traditional image. Any of Marvell's readers who have even a passing acquaintance with the classics are immediately struck by the echoes of those fleeting years in perhaps the most famous of Horace's odes: "Eheu fugaces, Postume, Postume, / labuntur anni" 'Ah, Postumus, Postumus, how the fleeting years slip by.' And this fawn, like the years, is always in a state of slipping by, of running from the nymph and remaining uncontrollable and external to her. Only when it stands and touches her does the dangerous "spot of ink" appear.

Much critical attention has been given to the nymph's garden, and indeed almost any interpretation of it is possible. It is both tame and wild, echoing the antithesis of tameness and wildness in the nymph's discourse on Sylvio (l. 34). Its lilies are formally bedded (l. 77), but the garden is also "over grown" into "a little Wilderness" with them and with those puzzling roses (ll. 72–74). Critics who decry the artificiality and insularity of the garden may find it helpful to recall that, though pastoral poets of the time sometimes admire a natural state of growth, in Renaissance drama the "wilderness" or untended garden is often a symbol of corruption. The unweeded garden in *Hamlet* has certainly become famous, and equally famous is the Duchess of Malfi's "I am going into a wilderness" [John Webster, *The Duchess of Malfi*]. But something else has begun to appear in these unweeded gardens and wildernesses, an image of that spot of ink which is present in both the nymph's garden and the gardens of later poets.

Shortly before the Duchess of Malfi speaks of going into her wilderness, her brother Ferdinand cautions her: "You live in a rank pasture here, i' th' court; / There is a kind of honey-dew that's deadly: / 'T will poison your fame . . ." (I.i.306–08). This image of the poisoned flower, usually a flower associated with love, is virtually inseparable from the roses that make the fawn's lips seem to "bleed" (ll. 83–84). Although Leo Spitzer assumes this bleeding to be merely a manifestation of the traditional lover's "bleeding heart," the rose being an emblem of love in the language of the flowers, there is surely more to the image than this. The only other blood imagery in the poem is associated with the fawn's death in the passage about the troopers: the fawn there is bleeding to death; its blood will not cleanse the troopers' guilty hands; and those hands are stained "in such a Purple Grain" with blood, blood, blood. The connection of blood with death is too firmly made to allow it to take on an entirely different meaning in the later passage.

There is something poisonous about these roses, something that Keats recognizes in his "Ode on Melancholy":

> She dwells with Beauty—Beauty that must die;
> And Joy, whose hand is ever at his lips
> Bidding adieu; and aching Pleasure nigh,
> Turning to poison while the bee-mouth
>   sips. . . .

Something, too, that Hawthorne develops in "Rappaccini's Daughter," where the "print" of those beautiful, bloodstained lips is the kiss of mortality. And something, as well, that Tennyson sees in *Maud*. His young man, whose motivation is as ambiguous as that of Hawthorne's hero, unquestionably seems to be thinking both of the "honey-dew that's deadly" and of the nymph's fawn. Speaking of Maud in what he later discovers to be an erroneous metaphor, since he himself is the destructive force in the garden, he says:

> And most of all would I flee from the cruel mad-
>   ness
> of love,
> The honey of poison-flowers and all the mea-
>   sureless
> ill.
> Ah Maud, you milkwhite fawn, you are all un-
>   meet
> for a wife. . . .
> You have but fed on the roses, and lain in the lil-
>   ies
> of life.

Later in the poem, when the young man (like the troopers

or Sylvio) has destroyed the innocence and integrity of the garden, he makes the same connection between roses and blood:

> But I know where a garden grows,
> Fairer than aught in the world beside,
> All made up of the lily and rose . . .
> It is only flowers, they had no fruits,
> And I almost fear they are not roses but
>   blood. . . .

Roses and lilies, as any critic will be quick to point out, are traditionally used together to represent the Petrarchan ideal of feminine beauty; the roses, separately, carry overtones of youth; the lilies, of purity. Even in folktales, Rose Red and Snow White are often inseparable sisters. But, associated with blood, the roses may perhaps be glancing at another literary convention: the flower as an emblem of the shortness and futility of life, as in countless seventeenth-century carpe diem poems and this sixteenth-century "May Song":

> The life of man is but a span;
> It blossoms as the flower.
> It makes no stay: is here today
> And vanish'd in the hour.

In this regard, the roses make even the lilies seem ominous, and the fawn's delight in folding "its pure virgin Limbs . . . / In whitest sheets of Lillies cold" (ll. 89–90) after eating the roses may suggest that the cold sheets of lilies are winding-sheets.

"Lillies without, Roses within" (l. 92) is probably one of the most exquisitely beautiful images in English poetry. But one of the things that make the line so beautiful is its poignancy: it cannot exist. The nymph has returned here to her contrary-to-fact conditionals: "Had it liv'd long" (l. 91), it would have come to this, but it will not live long. This is the same phrasing that the nymph uses in her earlier, cynical reflection (l. 47), and neither speculation is valid.

That the lilies and roses are almost like matter and anti-matter, self-doomed from the start, is apparent in almost all the imagery surrounding the nymph, her fawn, and their garden. The nymph cannot remain childlike; the fawn, "had it liv'd long," must have become a grown deer; and the "Spring time of the year" (l. 75) must turn to winter and the flowers die. The bleeding lips of the fawn are a symbol of mortality, and the "Lillies without" carry their own death within; they "dwell with Beauty—Beauty that must die."

This realization, too, is a necessary stage through which the mind must pass in learning to deal with death and loss: to understand their universal necessity and to develop a unity with all pain. The thing lost is a symbol of all loss—and paradoxically, mourning for the individual loss soothes the hurt of all the losses that have gone before. In this respect, seeing the fawn as a surrogate love, the love allegorists approach the larger pattern, but the image of the dying fawn absorbs into itself more than the death of a lover; it epitomizes the passing of all "quick bright things [that] come to confusion." [*A Midsummer Night's Dream* I.i.149].

Seeing the nymph as self-centered and as exaggerating her loss, Rosalie Colie appears to miss the point in decrying the nymph's ensuing grief ritual: "Niobe after all lost *all* her children; this girl has lost a single white deer." Samuel Johnson is more perceptive about the matter:

> We always make a secret comparison between a part and the whole; the termination of any period of life reminds us that life itself has likewise its termination; when we have done any thing for the last time, we involuntarily reflect that a part of the days allotted us is past, and that as more is past there is less remaining. . . . [B]y vicissitude of fortune, or alteration of employment, by change of place, or loss of friendship, we are forced to say of something, *this is the last.*

What Colie sees as the nymph's unnecessary pother over her own and her fawn's tears is actually a valuable lesson that the nymph must learn and that the poet is leading the reader to learn: by universalizing the idea of pain, she will be able to transcend the thoughtless cruelty of the troopers and Sylvio—not by imitating it, as she tried to do in her cynical stage, but by understanding the pain of things outside the self. Like any other human creature, the nymph does attempt to salvage physical relics of the thing lost in a last effort to fix the transient beauty, but it is interesting to observe what she does with her vial of tears, her own pain and the fawn's mingled in the Vergilian tears of things.

In all the controversy over "*Diana's* Shrine" (1. 104), two relatively important points seem to have been overlooked. Diana may represent the chastity or purity violated in the killing of the fawn, or Innocence, and Diana is the goddess of the hunt, a point that has caused some critical bemusement. But the two objects scared to Diana are the deer and the cypress tree, and in discussing the deer Cyparissus accidentally slays in Ovid's *Metamorphoses,* most critics seem to have overlooked the significance of the cypress tree: that Cyparissus' transformation became sacred to Diana, not because he had killed a deer, but because he felt grief for its unnecessary death. In the same way, critics who mention Diana's revenge against Actaeon—her turning him into a deer who is killed by his own hunting dogs—find unanswerable the question this allusion raises; they fail to see the implications in the legend that Actaeon is not only punished but taught a lesson about the sanctity of things connected with Diana, including her sacred deer. In some versions of the legend, Actaeon-turned-deer is even described as weeping while he dies, like the nymph's fawn.

Diana's shrine, then, is a perfectly logical place for the nymph's vial of tears; the offering attempts to rectify the injustice complained of earlier in the lament and bears out the nymph's first instinctive cry: "ev'n Beasts must be with justice slain" (1. 16).

Once the relics are obtained and the offering made, the mind, by a natural human instinct, grasps at the possibility of immortality, whether in a divine afterlife or in earthly monuments. Don Cameron Allen notes the prevalence of laments for pets in the seventh book of the Greek Anthology, in which they are described as roving the Elysian Fields, but in adding that "Marvell's readers would be more likely to remember Catullus' lament on the death of Lesbia's sparrow," he quotes only the description of the sparrow's domesticity, omitting the following lines on its passage to the afterworld:

> Qui nunc it per iter tenebricosum
> Illuc unde negant redire quemquam.
> At vobis male sit, malae tenebrae
> Orci, quae omnia bella devoratis;
> Tam bellum mihi passerem abstulistis.
> O factum male! io miselle passer!
> Tua nunc opera meae puellae
> Flendo turgiduli rubent ocelli.

> . . . who now travels through the shadowy way to that place from which none may return. But woe to you, grim shades of Orcus, that devour all lovely things; for you have torn from me my lovely sparrow. Oh, wicked deed! Oh, oh, unhappy sparrow! Because of you, my love's dear little eyes are red and swollen with weeping. [Catullus]

This passage is interesting in that it compresses into eight lines the grief, the railing at injustice, the universality of pain, the transience of beauty, and the image of almost excessive weeping that occur repeatedly in laments of this sort, including the nymph's. Also interesting is Catullus' use of the double diminutive in line 18 ("turgiduli . . . ocelli"), in which both the noun and its modifying adjective have diminutive suffixes, a device that Catullus uses in only two other places.

Such pathetic diminution occurs regularly in the Greek Anthology and all the "dapper little elegiac verses" (in Louis MacNeice's phrase) that were patterned on the Anthology, including those of the twentieth century. It is a way of translating the bewilderment and sense of injustice into unequivocal terms by making the thing lost utterly blameless and pathetically insignificant in the grand scale of things. MacNeice himself, in his poem "The Death of a Cat," perhaps comes closest of all the critics to explaining why the nymph is so distraught and why Marvell gave her a fawn to mourn:

> Sentimentality? Yes, it is possible;
> You and I, darling, are not above knowing
> The tears of the semi-, less precious things,
> A pathetic fallacy perhaps, as the man
> Who gave his marble victory wings
> Was the dupe—who knows—of sentimentality,

> Not really classic. The Greek Anthology
> Laments its pets (like you and me, darling),
> Even its grasshoppers; dead dogs bark
> On the roads of Hades where poets hung
> Their tiny lanterns to ease the dark.
> Those poets were late though. Not really classical.

> *(Collected Poems)*

The same impulse that makes poets hang "tiny lanterns" in commemoration of loss makes the nymph and all her human kin build monuments to their sorrow. Erecting a monument is not only a way to "ease the dark" but an attempt to convince the self that the thing lost is still alive in some way. From the makers of the earliest grave markers to the builders of the most elaborate statue-adorned tombs, human creatures have taken a certain comfort in viewing poor reproductions of the dead; from John Donne to Clarissa Harlowe, they have gained some satisfaction in planning their own tombs; and from the writer of the first classic "go, little book" to the subjects of the clippings in the modern newspaper morgue, they have hoped that their art or accomplishments would gain them some sort of immortality in this world.

Planning one's own or another's funeral is certainly a literary commonplace of the sixteenth and seventeenth centuries, from Juliet's "when he shall die, / Take him and cut him out in little stars" (*Romeo and Juliet* III.ii.21–22) to such popular songs as this anonymous poem that John Dowland set to music in *A Musical Banquet* (1610):

> In darknesse let mee dwell, the ground shall sorrow be,
> The roofe Dispaire to barre all cheerful light from mee,
> The wals of marble blacke that moistned still shall weepe,
> My musicke hellish jarring sounds to banish friendly sleepe.
> Thus wedded to my woes, and bedded to my Tombe,
> O let me living die, till death doe come.

Othello's and Hamlet's dying instructions about their reputations are part of this tradition, as is Aspatia's famous and somewhat soggy funeral plan for herself in Beaumont and Fletcher's *The Maid's Tragedy*:

> As soon as I am dead,
> Come all and watch one night about my hearse;
> Bring each a mournful story and a tear,
> To offer at it when I go to earth;
> With flattering ivy clasp my coffin round;
> Write on my brow my fortune; let my bier
> Be borne by virgins, that shall sing by course
> The truth of maids and perjuries of men.
>
>   (II.i.101–08)

Sentimentality? Yes, it is possible. But in the face of death and loss, when human life seems insignificant, there is a need to reaffirm one's own reality—if not importance—by building such pitiful monuments. Even folk ballads are filled with characters ordering their deathbeds to be prepared, from Lord Randall to the dying lovers in the Sweet William songs, including one whose opening stanza makes a connection between a "milkwhite sheet" and death:

> O mother, go and make my bed;
> Spread me that milkwhite sheet,
> That I may go and lie down on the clothes
> To see if I can sleep.
>   ["O Mother Go and Make My Bed"]

Or the stricken lover may order a grave for the beloved:

> My love shall have a coffin
> And the nails shall shine yellow,
> And my love she shall be buried
> On the banks of Green Willow.
>   ["The Banks of Green Willow"]

The nymph's tomb partakes, too, of the classic tradition of metamorphosis hinted at in the reference to the Heliades and of the religious and folkloric legends of weeping (or bleeding) statues. And of course the monument is also a symbol of the artist's work, which is expected to live on when he or she is gone. But even here, as in the garden, there is a spot of ink: the first stirrings of suspicion that such immortality is itself insufficient. The alabaster statue cannot capture the white essence of the fawn, and the very tears that flow from the monument will erode the marble itself.

So the poem comes full circle, and it would seem that mutability has won. All things must pass—the fawn, the old world order, pastoral simplicity, love, innocence, and all the surrogates that humanity seizes on in compensation for the latest loss. But, as in the Mutabilitie Cantos of *The Faerie Queene,* mutability does not have the last word after all. By coming to see the inevitability and universality of change and loss, the nymph and her reader have attained, if not comfort, at least catharsis; if not relief, at least a sort of marble repose; if not a defense against future loss, at least an enlarged understanding of it.

"The Nymph Complaining for the Death of Her Faun," then, is a traditional poem. Like all art, it confronts the questions of time, death, loss, and mutability—and finds no answers, only a new and more beautiful way to state the questions, always in terms of the questions that have gone before.

FURTHER READING

Bibliography

Collins, Dan S. *Andrew Marvell: A Reference Guide*. Boston: G. K. Hall & Co., 1981, 449 p.
    Annotated index of writings about Marvell arranged chronologically by date of publication.

Dees, Jerome S. "Recent Studies in Andrew Marvell (1973-1990)." *English Literary Renaissance* 22, No. 2 (Spring 1992): 273-95.
    Lists criticism on Marvell published from 1973 to 1990. Dees orders the criticism by subject and title.

Biography

Hunt, John Dixon. *Andrew Marvell: His Life and Writings*. Ithaca, N.Y.: Cornell University Press, 1978, 206 p.
    Attempts to "relate . . . Marvell's poetry to his experience of life in seventeenth-century Europe."

Legouis, Pierre. *Andrew Marvell: Poet, Puritan, Patriot*. Oxford: Clarendon Press, 1965, 252 p.
    Combines critical study of Marvell's work with biographical information. The book, an abridged translation of Legouis's original 1928 French edition, includes chapters entitled "Marvell's Poetical Masters," "The Lyrical Poet," "Cromwell's Poet," and "The Satirist in Verse."

Criticism

Anderson, Linda. "The Nature of Marvell's Mower." *Studies*

in English Literature 1500-1900 31, No. 1 (Winter 1991): 131-46.

Contends that in the four "mower" poems "the Mower defines himself as a demigodlike figure in an unfallen Eden" while "Marvell presents him as a childlike figure, unable or unwilling to distinguish between his own desires and reality."

Berthoff, Ann E. *The Resolved Soul: A Study of Marvell's Major Poems.* Princeton, N.J.: Princeton University Press, 1970, 243 p.

An analysis organized around two critical objectives: "to define the thematic unity of Marvell's poetry" and "to define the limits by which interpretations of his metaphors should be guided."

Bradbrook, M. C., and Thomas, M. G. Lloyd. *Andrew Marvell.* Cambridge: Cambridge University Press, 1940, 161 p.

Study of Marvell "as a representative of his age and as individually remarkable." Bradbrook and Thomas assert that "Marvell's writings illuminate the development of the English language during one of its most crucial periods, when the emergence of modern prose style resulted in rapid changes both in structure and vocabulary."

Brett, R. L., ed. *Andrew Marvell: Essays on the Tercentenary of His Death.* Oxford: Oxford University Press, 1979, 128 p.

Comprised of essays on Marvell by John Kenyon, William Empson, Barbara Everett, and Muriel Bradbrook.

Calhoun, Thomas O., and Potter, John M., eds. *Andrew Marvell: The Garden.* Columbus, Ohio: Charles E. Merrill, 1970, 146 p.

Includes eight essays on Marvell's poem "The Garden" by various notable critics.

Carey, John, ed. *Andrew Marvell: A Critical Anthology.* Harmondsworth, England: Penguin Books, 1969, 351 p.

Reprints commentaries on Marvell dating from his lifetime through the early 1960s, presenting an historical perspective on the development of his critical reputation.

Chernaik, Warren L. *The Poets Time: Politics and Religion in the Work of Andrew Marvell.* Cambridge: Cambridge University Press, 1983, 249 p.

Contains discussion of the relationships between Marvell's poetry and the English Revolution, his career in politics, and his Christianity.

Condren, Conal, and Cousins, A. D., eds. *The Political Identity of Andrew Marvell.* Aldershot, England: Scolar Press, 1990, 221 p.

Includes three essays that respectively focus on "Upon Appleton House," "The Last Instructions to an Artist," and Marvell's major poems on the subject of Oliver Cromwell.

Cullen, Patrick. "Andrew Marvell." In his *Spenser, Marvell, and Renaissance Pastoral*, pp. 151-202. Cambridge, Mass.: Harvard University Press, 1970.

Analyzes Marvell's poetry in the context of the pastoral literary tradition. Cullen subdivides Marvell's pastoral verse into Christian and amorous lyrics.

Donno, Elizabeth Story, ed. *Andrew Marvell: The Critical Heritage.* London: Routledge & Kegan Paul, 1978, 385 p.

Reprints commentary on Marvell from 1673 through 1923. In an introduction, Donno summarizes the evolution of Marvell's literary reputation.

Friedenreich, Kenneth, ed. *Tercentenary Essays in Honor of Andrew Marvell.* Hamden, Conn.: Archon Books, 1977, 314 p.

Contains several essays on Marvell's poetry, including commentaries by Harold Toliver, Joseph H. Summers, and Muriel C. Bradbrook.

Greene, Thomas M. "The Balance of Power in Marvell's 'Horatian Ode.' " *ELH* 60, No. 2 (Summer 1993): 379-96.

Avers that the historical episode depicted in "An Horatian Ode upon Cromwel's Return from Ireland" "is represented not only as inherently mysterious but arcane. The true subject of the poem . . . seems to be the intrusion of the uncanny into history."

Griffin, Patsy. "Structural Allegory in Andrew Marvell's Poetry." *Journal of English and Germanic Philology* 91, No. 3 (July 1992): 325-43.

Finds that the structure of Marvell's poetry allegorically parallels the "fortunate fall"—a providential fall from divine grace followed by redemption.

Kegl, Rosemary. " 'Joyning My Labour to My Pain': The Politics of Labor in Marvell's Mower Poems." In *Soliciting Interpretation: Literary Theory and Seventeenth-Century English Poetry*, edited by Elizabeth D. Harvey and Katharine Eisaman Maus, pp. 89-118. Chicago: University of Chicago Press, 1990.

Analyzes "the ways in which Andrew Marvell's mower poems emphasize labor and, in so doing, participate in seventeenth-century struggles both over class and over gender."

Klause, John. *The Unfortunate Fall: Theodicy and the Moral Imagination of Andrew Marvell.* Hamden, Conn.: Archon Books, 1983, 208 p.

Attempts to demonstrate that Marvell's guiding intellectual and spiritual principles "are embodied with such consistency in certain themes and images that we can conceive of a strongly characterized 'moral imagination' which informs his work, dictating subject and manner of treatment." Furthermore, Klause states that Marvell's "moral imagination" is most fully revealed in the poet's search for comprehensibility in the divine plan.

Leishman, J. B. *The Art of Marvell's Poetry.* London: Hutchinson & Co. Ltd., 1966, 328 p.

Argues that Marvell's poetry—specifically his nonsatiric verse—could have been produced neither in another historical period nor by another person. Leishman also demonstrates the affinity of Marvell's work to that of other poets of his era.

Lord, George deF., ed. *Andrew Marvell: A Collection of Critical Essays.* Englewood Cliffs, N.J.: Prentice-Hall, Inc., 1968, 180 p.

Essays on Marvell's poetry by Lord, T. S. Eliot, Earl Miner, and seven other critics.

Lynch, Denise E. "Politics, Nature, and Structure in Marvell's 'The Last Instructions to a Painter.' " *Restoration: Studies in English Literary Culture, 1660-1700* 16, No. 2 (Fall 1992): 82-92.

Examines the structure and political content of "The Last Instructions to a Painter," contending that Marvell's intent in the poem was to "provoke as a 'natural force' within the body politic a direct challenge to the royal prerogative."

Patrides, C. A., ed. *Approaches to Marvell: The York Tercentenary Lectures.* London: Routledge & Kegan Paul, 1978, 354 p.

Collection of fifteen essays that include discussions of "Bermudas," "Upon Appleton House," Marvell's occasional poetry, and the religious dimension of his verse. Other essays are entitled " 'Till Prepared for Longer Flight': The Sublunar Poetry of Andrew Marvell" and "Sight and Insight in Marvell's Poetry."

Patterson, Annabel M. *Marvell and the Civic Crown.* Princeton, N.J.: Princeton University Press, 1978, 264 p.

Studies the relationship of Marvell's politics to his verse, specifically as evinced in the Oliver Cromwell poems, the Lord Fairfax poems, the "painter" poems, and the "statue" poems.

Sokol, B. J. "Logic and Illogic in Marvell's 'To His Coy Mistress.' " *English Studies* 71, No. 3 (June 1990): 244-52.

Contends that "To His Coy Mistress" "closely imitates the form of a logical argument by the rule of inference known as 'indirect proof' or *reductio ad absurdum*. The identification of its form helps reveal a very witty play of logic and illogic in the poem, an interplay which heightens feeling and also indicates a subtle critique of certain modes of feeling."

Summers, Claude J., and Pebworth, Ted-Larry, eds. *On the Celebrated and Neglected Poems of Andrew Marvell.* Columbia: University of Missouri Press, 1992, 256 p.

Essays that "explore the range and variety of Marvell's art, not only in his celebrated lyrics, Cromwell poems, and 'Upon Appleton House,' but also in the neglected poems of his canon."

Toliver, Harold E. *Marvell's Ironic Vision.* New Haven, Conn.: Yale University Press, 1965, 232 p.

Aims "to explicate particular poems [by Marvell] and to look at the times in a perspective sufficiently deep to give some sense of the context of those poems."

Wallace, John M. *Destiny His Choice: The Loyalism of Andrew Marvell.* Cambridge: Cambridge University Press, 1968, 266 p.

Interprets political verse by Marvell in relation to its contemporary historical context. Wallace devotes chapters to such poems as "An Horatian Ode upon Cromwel's Return from Ireland," "The Last Instructions to a Painter," and "Upon Appleton House."

Wilding, Michael, ed. *Marvell: Modern Judgements.* London: Macmillan, 1969, 302 p.

Collection of essays on Marvell's poetry by numerous critics, including T. S. Eliot, William Empson, Cleanth Brooks, Frank Kermode, F. R. Leavis, and A. Alvarez.

Wiltenburg, Robert. "Translating All That's Made: Poetry and History in 'Tom May's Death.' " *Studies in English Literature* 31, No. 1 (Winter 1991): 117-30.

Comments on "Tom May's Death" with the aim of elucidating "three features bearing on the interrelation of poetry and history: Jonson's authority in the poem; the condemnation not only of May but of May's 'author' Lucan; and the extraordinary vehemence of the whole."

Additional coverage of Marvell's life and career is contained in the following sources published by Gale Research: *Concise Dictionary of British Literary Biography, 1660-1789*; *Dictionary of Literary Biography,* **Vol. 131;** *DISCovering Authors*; *Literature Criticism from 1400 to 1800,* **Vol. 4; and** *World Literature Criticism.*

Thomas Merton

1915-1968

French-born American philosopher, essayist, poet, play-wright, editor, and translator.

INTRODUCTION

Merton was a Trappist monk who became a prolific poet and prose writer and an influential social activist despite his vows of silence. His poetry was informed by his con-templative life, his compassion for the victims of exploita-tion, and his objection to the materialistic values of mod-ern Western culture. Although he was regarded strictly as a Catholic poet during the early years of his career, his later collections established him as a highly innovative and experimental artist whose works encompass a broad range of political and personal themes.

Biographical Information

Merton was born in Prades, France, the son of two artists, both of whom died by the time Merton reached the age of sixteen. He was educated at the Lycée de Montauban in France and the Oakham School in England; he then spent a year at Clare College, Cambridge, before entering Columbia University in New York, where he studied En-glish literature, earning a B.A. in 1938 and an M.A. in 1939. At Columbia he was strongly influenced by what be-came a lifelong friendship with the noted literary critic Mark Van Doren. Merton converted to Catholicism dur-ing the late 1930s and entered the Trappist monastery Our Lady of Gethsemani in Kentucky in 1941. Because the Trappists require their members to take a vow of silence which includes strict limitations on writing, Merton's lit-erary output was initially severely circumscribed by his monastic duties. However, he was soon given numerous writing assignments by his superiors, and although he fre-quently came into conflict with Trappist censors, by the 1950s he was virtually free to publish whatever he wished. In 1944 he published his first poetry collection, *Thirty Poems*, and in 1948 he published his autobiography *The Seven Storey Mountain*, which became a best-seller and made him a reluctant celebrity. He continued to receive expanded responsibilities in the monastery, and in 1955 he achieved the esteemed position of Master of Novices. Dur-ing the 1950s and 1960s Merton became increasingly con-cerned with political events occurring in the outside world, and he began advocating awareness and activism rather than isolation as the proper response to the world's problems. At the same time, he became increasingly inter-ested in the study of other religions, particularly Zen Bud-dhism. Merton died as a result of accidental electrocution in 1968 in Bangkok, Thailand, where he had been attend-ing an ecumenical conference.

Major Works

Many of the poems in Merton's early collections *Thirty Poems*, *A Man in the Divided Sea* (1946), and *Figures for an Apocalypse* (1948) focus specifically on Old and New Testament imagery and events. During the 1950s, howev-er, Merton turned from doctrinal religious subjects to vivid descriptions of daily life in a monastery as evidenced in such poems as "Trappists, Working," and "Three Post-cards from the Monastery," which are included in *Select-ed Poems of Thomas Merton* (1950). His concern with worldly, as well as religious, topics became increasingly apparent in *Emblems of a Season of Fury* (1963), which addresses political subjects including racism and the American egotism surrounding space travel. Notable among Merton's most experimental works are *Cables to the Ace; or, Familiar Liturgies of Misunderstanding* (1968) and *The Geography of Lograire* (1969), both of which com-bine prose with poetry and satirize the abuse of language and imagery that pervades modern culture. In addition to poetry, Merton's oeuvre includes numerous works of au-tobiography, social criticism, and theology.

Critical Reception

Assessments of Merton's poetry are varied—some critics find the majority of his verse flawed while others consider him among the most important poets of his generation. Some reviewers have objected to his frequently moralistic and sentimental tone and to the political aim of many of his poems, which they judge inferior to his prose. Others, however, praise the integrity of his message and find his poetic voice refreshingly direct, vital, and sincere, often noting that his poetic vocation was inextricably linked with his contemplative life and his religious purpose. Commenting on the significance of poetry in Merton's oeuvre, Anthony Padovano observed: "His prose never registered the changes [in his life] as radically as did his poetry. His poetry was often the barometer of his soul. In the younger days, it was lyrical and free; in the middle years, passionate and angry; at the end, cosmic and visionary."

PRINCIPAL WORKS

Poetry

Thirty Poems   1944
A Man in the Divided Sea   1946
Figures for an Apocalypse   1948
The Tears of Blind Lions   1949
Selected Poems of Thomas Merton   1950
The Strange Islands: Poems   1957
Emblems of a Season of Fury   1963
Cables to the Ace; or, Familiar Liturgies of Misunderstanding   1968
Landscape, Prophet and Wild-Dog   1968
The Geography of Lograire   1969
Early Poems: 1940-42   1972
He Is Risen: Selections from Thomas Merton   1975

Other Major Works

The Seven Storey Mountain   (autobiography)   1948; also published as *Elected Silence: The Autobiography of Thomas Merton* [revised edition], 1949
What Is Contemplation?   (essays)   1948; also published as *New Seeds of Contemplation* [revised edition], 1962
Seeds of Contemplation   (essays)   1949; also published as *New Seeds of Contemplation* [revised edition], 1962
The Ascent to the Truth   (essays)   1951
Bread in the Wilderness   (essays)   1953
The Sign of Jonas   (journal)   1953
No Man Is an Island   (essays)   1955
The Living Bread   (essays)   1956
Praying the Psalms   (essays)   1956; also published as *The Psalms Are Our Prayer*, 1957; also published as *Thomas Merton on the Psalms*, 1970
The Silent Life   (essays)   1957
Thoughts in Solitude   (essays)   1958
The Secular Journal of Thomas Merton   (journal)   1959
Disputed Questions   (essays)   1960
Spiritual Direction and Meditation   (essays)   1960

The New Man   (essays)   1962
Life and Holiness   (essays)   1963
Seeds of Destruction   (essays)   1964; also published as *Redeeming the Time* [abridged edition], 1966
Seasons of Celebration   (essays)   1965; also published as *Meditations on Liturgy*, 1976
Conjectures of a Guilty Bystander   (journal)   1966
Mystics and Zen Masters   (essays)   1967
Faith and Violence: Christian Teaching and Christian Practice   (essays)   1968
Zen and the Birds of Appetite   (essays)   1968
The Climate of Monastic Prayer   (essays)   1969; also published as *Contemplative Prayer*, 1969
Three Essays   (essays)   1969
Opening the Bible   (essays)   1970
Contemplation in a World of Action   (essays)   1971
Thomas Merton on Peace   (essays)   1971; also published as *The Nonviolent Alternative* [revised edition], 1980
The Zen Revival   (essays)   1971
The Asian Journal of Thomas Merton   (journal)   1973
Ishi Means Man: Essays on Native Americans   (essays)   1976
Thomas Merton on Zen   (essays)   1976
The Monastic Journey   (essays)   1977
Love and Living   (essays)   1979
Thomas Merton on St. Bernard   (essays)   1980
The Literary Essays of Thomas Merton   (essays)   1981
Woods, Shore, Desert: A Notebook, May, 1968   (journal)   1982

CRITICISM

Robert Lowell   (review date 1945)

SOURCE: "The Verses of Thomas Merton," in *The Commonweal*, Vol. XLII, No. 10, 22 June 1945, pp. 240-42.

[*Winner of two Pulitzer Prizes and a National Book Award, Lowell was among the most highly respected American poets of his generation as well as an acclaimed translator, playwright, and critic. Below, he presents a mixed assessment of Merton's verse.*]

Thomas Merton's career has been varied and spectacular: Cambridge University, the *New Yorker* and the Trappist monastery of Our Lady of Gethsemani. One can understand only too easily why the Protean Mr. Laughlin of the New Directions Press would be fascinated. I am sure that Catholics altogether like the idea of an "experimental" Trappist. But American Catholic culture is in a relatively receptive state of transition; in the arts, as in other things, we are taking our cue from France. Unfortunately, Merton's work has attracted almost no attentive criticism; the poet would appear to be more phenomenal than the poetry.

There is some justice in this neglect. Merton is a modest, not altogether satisfactory minor writer. But he is also, as far as my experience goes, easily the most promising of our American Catholic poets and, possibly, the most consequential Catholic poet to write in English since the death of Francis Thompson. Why the last forty years of the Catholic literary revival, which have seen the prose of Chesterton, Dawson and Waugh, have produced nothing as lasting as the light verses of Belloc is no doubt due to complex, partially intangible, causes. We must take what comes. What Merton writes is his own, subtle and intense. So small and genuine an achievement is worth consideration.

The purpose of this review is to point up what Merton has done; this involves an analysis of his limitations and faults. I shall quote to the extent of making a short anthology and hope that each quotation will be read over until it is understood. My comments are more or less footnotes.

"The Flight into Egypt"

Through every precinct of the wintry city
Squadroned iron resounds upon the streets;
Herod's police
Make shudder the dark steps of the tenements
At the business about to be done.

Neither look back upon Thy starry country
Nor hear what rumors crowd across the dark
While blood runs down those holy walls,
Nor frame a childish blessing with Thy hand
Towards that fiery spiral of exulting souls!

Go, Child of God, upon the singing desert,
Where, with eyes of flame,
The roaming lion keeps Thy road from harm.

This is modern and traditional, graceful and quietly powerful. The first ten lines are probably the finest in the entire book. Note especially the stern imagery and rhetorical éclat of the first stanza; the subtle shift of rhythm in the second stanza, and the unity of symbol, meaning and sound in line 10. About the last three lines I am less certain. Too much depends on the word *singing* (presumably, the poet means that the desert is simple and alive, in contrast to the tortured, twisted fury of the town) which prepares for the sinless flame of the lion.

"The Blessed Virgin Mary Compared to a Window"

Because my will is simple as a window
And knows no pride of original earth,
It is my life to die, like glass, by light;
Slain in the strong rays of the bridegroom
    son. . . .

For light, my lover, steals my life in secret.
I vanish into day, and leave no shadow
But the geometry of my cross,
Whose frame and structure are the strength
By which I die. . . .

Because I die by brightness and the Holy Spirit
The Sun rejoices in your jail, my kneeling Christian . . .

At first glance this is merely a tour-de-force, in imitation of Donne's "Of My Name in the Window." Then one realizes how persistently and honestly the conceit has been elaborated, how right the tone is for Our Lady. The figure of the window-frame and its shadow is almost as good as

its original. Donne's and Crashaw's contributions to the poem detract nothing from its sincerity and freshness. The extracts that I have quoted should have been the entire poem, for the rest, in spite of much incidental brilliance, is repetitive, loose, wordy.

One of Merton's faults is a contrivance that he may have learned from some of the less successful poems of Crashaw (e. g., "The Weeper"), the atomic conceit: each conceit is an entity and the whole poem is seldom much more than the sum of its parts, often it is considerably less. My quotations should have made it plain that Merton is not writing a seventeenth century pastiche; he is using the old devices as an artist, not as an antiquarian. At the same time he follows so closely on the heals of his predecessors that the capacity of his vision is narrowed. Much of the old immediacy, power and mass are lost. In fact, Merton's poems, like Christina Rosetti's, are precariously unlocated in time or place. Nor is this much helped by a trick that he may have gotten from Edith Sitwell or Cummings, that is, using a sound word where one would expect a *light* word. Occasionally this yields most effective lines, as in a Crucifixion poem which opens with: "When Romans gambled in the clash of lancelight." (*Lancelight* is an alliterative, Hopkinsian compound that works; however, the last line of the same poem is ruined by Hopkins: "Reeks of the death-thirst man-life found in the forbidden apple.") Elsewhere, as in the *singing desert* of my first quotation, a mannerism is made to bear the burden of inspiration.

"Flight Into Egypt" is in Merton's most original style; **"A Window"** is more derivative but hardly inferior. There is a third Merton who is glib, sentimental and romantic.

"The Holy Child's Song"

When My kind Father, kinder than the sun,
With looks and smiles bends down
And utters my bodily life,
My flesh obeying, praises Heaven like a smiling
    cloud.
Then I am the gay wheatfields, the serious hills:
I fill the sky with words of light, and My incarnate songs
Fly in and out the branches of My childish voice
Like thrushes in a tree.

These lines are clearly superior to Kilmer's unwittingly obscene "Tree," but thinness is not disguised by one or two apt words and an ordered irregularity of meter. A lofty subject and enthusiastic imagery are often imaginative narcotics.

A variation on the style of **"The Flight Into Egypt"** appears in the nature poems:

When cold November sits among the reeds like
    an unlucky fisher
And ducks drum up as sudden as the wind
Out of the rushy river,
We slowly come, robbed of our rod and gun,
Walking amid the stricken cages of the trees.

This is charming and the details are solid as the details of **"The Holy Child's Song"** should have been solid. Unfortunately here, as in most of the other nature poems, the fine opening is undeveloped. Instead the cages flounder on into an impossible devotional metaphor, upholstered with *keys, jails* and *jailers.*

"For My Brother Reported Missing in Action, 1943"

Sweet brother, if I do not sleep
My eyes are flowers for your tomb;
And if I cannot eat my bread,
My fasts shall live like willows where you died.
If in the heat I find no water for my thirst,
My thirst shall turn to springs for you, poor
    traveller.

Where, in what desolate and smoky country
Lies your poor body, lost and dead?
And in what landscape of disaster
Has your unhappy spirit lost its road?

Come, in my labor find a resting place
And in my sorrows lay your head;
Or rather take my life and blood
And buy yourself a better bed—
Or take my breath and take my death
And buy yourself a better rest.

When all the men of war are shot
And flags are fallen into dust,
Your cross and mine shall tell men still
Christ died on each, for both of us.

For in the wreckage of your April Christ lies
    slain
And Christ weeps in the ruins of my spring:
The money of whose tears shall fall
Into your weak and friendless hand,
And buy you back to your own land:
The silence of Whose tears shall fall
Like bells upon your alien tomb.
Hear them and come: they call you home.

To appreciate how this string of commonplace figures constantly keeps shifting and moving and never becomes insincere, extravagant or dead, the reader should have tried his luck with epitaphs and have failed—have failed and thought he succeeded. Comparison should be made with Crashaw's verses on "A Man and His Wife Who Were Buried Together." There the metaphors are worked out with logic and care and the meter is much firmer; but Merton's poem has its own virtues and is not overshadowed.

Mark Van Doren   (essay date 1959)

SOURCE: An introduction, in *Selected Poems of Thomas Merton,* revised edition, New Directions Publishing Corporation, 1967, pp. xi-xvii.

[*The winner of the Pulitzer Prize for poetry in 1940, Van Doren was a highly respected American poet, playwright, novelist, short story writer, critic, and historian. Merton was strongly influenced by Van Doren's lectures while he was a student at Columbia University, and the two maintained a strong friendship throughout Merton's life. In the following introduction to the* Selected Poems of Thomas Merton, *first published in 1959, Van Doren focuses on the dual roles of contemplation and sensory perception in Merton's poetry.*]

In the summer of 1953 Thomas Merton wrote to me from Gethsemani: "Our cow barn burned down in little over twenty minutes or half an hour—like a pile of brush. We could do nothing to put it out. Everybody thought it was a really beautiful fire, and it was. I am sending you a poem about it." The poem was **"Elegy for the Monastery Barn,"** and I liked it so much that six years later, when I knew I was going to write this preface, I wrote Merton saying I hoped it would be among the poems he had selected. He replied: "I forget whether or not I included the Barn on the original list, perhaps I was shy about it. As a matter of fact it is for me subjectively an important poem, because when I was a kid on a farm in Maryland (yes, even that, for a while) a barn burned down in the middle of the night and it is one of the earliest things I can remember. So burning barns are for me great mysteries that are important. They turn out to be the whole world, and it is the Last Judgement."

Well, the poem is here, and it is as good a place as any to start looking at and listening to the poet in Thomas Merton. But one further document has a bearing on the subject. The preface to *The Strange Islands,* 1957, ends with these sentences: "'**Elegy for the Monastery Barn**' was written after the cowbarn at Gethsemani burned down, one August evening in 1953, during the evening meditation. The monks left the meditation to fight a very hot fire and the poem arrived about the same time as the fire truck from the nearest town." The bearing is in the humor, which Merton never is without, and in the knowledge he keeps of the way things go in this world. The slowness of the truck, the swiftness of the poem, the childhood memory: all of these are somehow there, illuminating if not explaining the happy power awakened in Merton's mind as it races through the realities of his theme. For the burning barn is really an old lady dressed for her last hour in unaccountable finery, nor is any distinction to be made between her proud cries and the crackling of the flames. And she leaves us when she is gone with delicate memories of what she had been during the years when we ignored her: of her solitude, her peace, her patience as she waited for this end. The fifty invisible cattle, the fifty past years, are just as real; and so at the close is Merton's flight into another dimension where the Holy One sits in the presence of disaster. All is real; nothing is made up; this, we instantly believe, is the true content of the subject, which like any other subject starts on earth and gets in its own natural way to heaven.

Such, I take it, is what Merton means in the note on "Poetry and Contemplation" which he appends to the present volume. He says there, better he thinks than he did ten years ago, and in this I believe him to be right, that poetry at its best is contemplation—of things, and of what they signify. Not what they can be made to signify, but what they actually do signify, even when nobody knows it. The better the poet, the more we are convinced that he has knowledge of this kind, and has it humbly. "The earliest fathers," Merton wrote me in 1954, "knew that all things, as such, are symbolic by their very being and nature, and all talk of something beyond themselves. Their meaning is not something we impose upon them, but a mystery which we can discover in them, if we have the eyes to look with." The right eyes for the purpose are keen and honest, and there had better be some humor in them too. At least that is where poetry begins, whether its aim is religious or not. And certainly, if its aim is religious, it must begin there if it is ever to move us deeply. Religious poetry is rooted in things as much as any other kind of poetry is. Without that root it is merely pious, as its secular counterpart is merely poetical.

The sight and sound and feel of things is everywhere in Merton's poetry. Consider the first line of **"Trappists, Working"**:

> Now all our saws sing holy sonnets in this world
> of timber.

The sound, so sudden and robust, brings with it a sense of the joy with which it is made, and the context of that joy. Perhaps there is no sound at all in the beginning lines of **"The Trappist Cemetery—Gethsemani"**:

> Brothers, the curving grasses and their daughters
> Will never print your praises.

But no sound was intended; the prim alliteration in the second line is like a finger laid upon the lips, forbidding speech where no speech would be proper. The silence asked for here is nothing like the heavier sort that states itself in the first of **"Three Postcards from the Monastery"**:

> The pilgrim passes swiftly.
> All the strange towns,
> Wrapped in their double cloaks
> (Of rain and of non-entity)
> Veil their elusive faces.

The wit of the parenthesis is no less deadly for being all but voiceless, as befits the faceless towns behind their veils of rain. What a plenitude of sound, however, comes to us out of eleven words in **"The Trappist Abbey: Matins,"**

> where some train runs, lost,
> Baying in eastward mysteries of distance.

And again it is true that the thing we hear speaks of more than itself; its skilful music is in the service of a thought so wide that all the world at dawn, near by and far away, is sleepily included. Elsewhere we read:

> But sound is never half so fair
> As when that music turns to air
> And the universe dies of excellence.

Those lines from **"A Psalm"** bring sound to a dead stop, drowned as it were in itself, and signifying by its very extinction the universe beyond sense.

Sight and sound and feeling. I have spoken so far only of sound, and indeed that may be enough, for in the poetry of Thomas Merton all the senses work together to one end, the letting of things declare themselves. Which of the senses is dominant, for instance, in this passage from **"The Sowing of Meanings"**?

> For, like a grain of fire
> Smouldering in the heart of every living essence
> God plants His undivided power—

> Buries His thought too vast for worlds
> In seed and root and blade and flower,
> Until, in the amazing light of April,
> Surcharging the religious silence of the spring,
> Creation finds the pressure of his everlasting secret
> Too terrible to bear.
> Then everywhere we look, lo! rocks and trees
> Pastures and hills and streams and birds and firmament
> And our own souls within us flash.

It is something to be seen and heard and felt in one miraculous moment; also, to be wondered at and contemplated, thought about and blissfully forgotten. Yet sound is somehow for Merton the carrying sense, the medium through which experience of any magnitude makes itself seen and felt. Of any magnitude—a reminder that Merton is a noticer of little things as well as huge ones. Of children, for instance, and their

> little voices, light as stems of lilies.

Are these voices heard or seen? Or felt? It does not matter, in view of the unearthly sweetness they signify, any more than it matters how we decide to explain the magic by which St. Agnes, with no thought of us in her small head, steals all our love as we behold her.

> Hear with what joy this child of God
> Plays in the perfect garden of her
> martyrdom, . . .
> Spending the silver of her little life
> To bring her Bridegroom these bright flowers
> Of which her arms are full. . . .
> Her virtues, with their simple strings,
> Play to the Lover hidden in the universe.

The foregoing would suggest that the special reputation of Merton's poem **"For My Brother: Reported Missing in Action, 1943"** is not an accident. No poem in the book is better known, and the reason may lie in the music it makes. It is the kind of music that only poetry can make: not pure sound, of course, but something buried in the words and (in this case) mourning there. *The Seven-Storey Mountain* tells the story of the brother's death in prose that moves the reader too; without, however, assembling the sounds that are climaxed here in two paradoxical verses:

> The silence of Whose tears shall fall
> Like bells upon your alien tomb.

The poem, having created its own silence in preparation for these lines, drops them into our imagination where it is possible for tears that make no noise to sound nevertheless like delicate, distinct bronze, hopelessly far away. The figures of the poem are justly celebrated: the sleepless eyes as flowers, the fasts as willows, the thirst as springs, and the money of breath and death and weeping. Yet figures alone do not make a great poem. There must be a music that absorbs them and relates them, and gives them in the end a power for which we cannot assign the cause. We can say that the very intensity of the poet's fear that he will fail is somehow the reason for his success; we can guess that inarticulate grief manages here, simply because it must, to become articulate after all; but it is truer to say that in such a poem sadness sings—a low note, in perfect pitch, that carries around the world.

For Merton there is another world beyond this one where his brother died, and where he himself writes poetry. But the poetry is a way to that world. Indeed, given his endowment, is may well be the way, so that mystic and poet, seer and singer, in his case are one.

Carol Johnson   (review date 1960)

SOURCE: "The Vision and the Poem," in *Poetry*, Vol. XCVI, April-September, 1960, pp. 387-91.

[*Below, Johnson offers a mixed review of* Selected Poems, *faulting Merton's occasional "romantic excesses."*]

Thomas Merton's **Selected Poems** is a book in which the appendix demands to be read first. Merton has revised "Poetry and Contemplation", an early effort of his to resolve a dilemma which he now realizes to have been an illusion, and includes it here. Really a sermon rehearsing from the authority of the Church Fathers the modes of the contemplative life, its interest for anyone reading the poems is in emphasizing unmistakably the fascination for its writer of the *psychology* of such experiences. On the other hand, what is ventured about poetry is so negligible, off hand, and trite as to account for the casually dionysian quantity of unrealized possibilities for poems which fill this collection.

He allows that contemplation does not of itself make poetry: "One must not be a 'seer' but also [sic] and especially a 'creator'." He understands that the practical intellect has work to do in making a poem, but wants instantly to pass over this to assume that "a man already has this natural gift", and presumably some executive sense of how to use it.

Santayana in a graceful error once called scepticism the chastity of the intellect. A bit of this exercised by the poet upon his verses would help as a corrective for the romantic excesses wrought in his eagerness to be excused from uninfused "objectivized human reasoning". It should have prevented him from ever committing to paper the ludicrous **"An Elegy for Five Old Ladies"** in Smart's manner: "Old companions are sitting silent in the home. Five of their number have suddenly gone too far . . . / Their ride was not lucky. It took them very far out of bounds. / Mrs. Watson said she saw them all go at three forty five . . . / It was a season when water is too cold for anyone, and is especially icy for an old person. / The brazen sedan was not to be trusted." And it should have assisted him to build true poems from the occasionally creditable fragments. In the **"Aubade: Lake Erie"** for example, the original figure is unpretentious and palatable; we are glad to see the metaphor.

> When sun, light handed, sows this Indian water
> With a crop of cockles,
> The vines arrange their tender shadows
> In the sweet leafage of an artificial France.

We can accept the conceit of the children, and perhaps forgive the illogic of the sentiment partially redeemed by the baroque felicity of the third line of the following stanza:

> Awake, in the frames of windows, innocent children,
> Loving the blue, sprayed leaves of childish life,
> Applaud the bearded corn, the bleeding grape,

We may enjoy their being made to cry:

> "Here is the hay-colored sun, our marvelous cousin,
> Walking in the barley,
> Turning the harrowed earth to growing bread,
> And splicing the sweet, wounded vine . . ."

But Merton does not know how to stop them. They have to go on ("Lift up your hitch-hiking heads") for another stanza. There has got to be not one, but a hundred "unheeding" Luthers rising inexplicably from the dead to search the horizon for gap-toothed factories. Though somehow he gets them in hand at the end to "grope in the green wheat, / Toward the wood winds of the western freight", the poem can offer no real resolution, only the auditory moment, the nicely turned slant rhyme.

There is a respectable number of such moments. From **"The Trappist Cemetery—Gethsemane"**:

> Brothers, the curving grasses and their daughters
> Will never print your praises . . .
> How like the swallows and the chimney swifts . . .
> How like these children of the summer evening
> Do your rejoicing spirits
> Deride the dry earth with their aviation!

In **"Trappists, Working"** the felled oaks ". . . fall like cataracts, / Pouring their roar into the wood's green well." In the Blakean **"A Responsory, 1948"**:

> Suppose the dead could crown their wit
> With some intemperate exercise,
> Spring wine from their ivory
> Or roses from their eyes?

Near the close of a poem for his brother, reported missing in action, are the lines:

> The silence of Whose tears shall fall
> Like bells upon your alien tomb

about which Mr. Van Doren suggests that "the very intensity of the poet's fear that he will fail is somehow the reason for his success". This seems so just and enlightened a comment that one is impelled to wish the poet had been reduced to such fear with each poem he tried to write. Altogether too often he has let his high spirits dictate an easy way out. There are too many intemperate cries, shouts, weepings, and leapings here to bear feasibly the burden of the poems they are set to sustain; they demean the noble sentiments Merton records in his essay.

Anybody's private vision is apt to sound pretty silly to others unless a tolerable metaphor can be found to interpret it. If we must question the ungoverned excesses that flaw these efforts, we should commend the equilibrium of the humor which obtains in such better instances as **"A Practical Program for Monks"**:

> The monastery, being owner of a communal
>   rowboat, is the antechamber of heaven.
> Surely that ought to be enough.
>   . . . . .
>
> Yes, I have taken care of the lamp. *Miserere.*
> Have you a patron saint, and an angel?
> Thank you. Even though the nights are never
>   dangerous, I have one of everything.

This is in the spirit of Apollinaire with whose extravagance no one would quibble.

Sister Mary Gilbert   (review date 1964)

SOURCE: "Fusion and Fission: Two by Merton," in *The Sewanee Review,* Vol. LXXII, No. 4, October-December, 1964, pp. 715-18.

[*In the following review, Gilbert comments on how the diverse themes in* Emblems of a Season of Fury *are unified by "the universality of Merton's brotherhood."*]

What is likely to strike the general reader first is the heterogeneity of [***Emblems of a Season of Fury***]. It consists largely of poems dealing with what the jacket copy terms "nuclear-age pathology," but it also includes three elegies, a group of metaphysical poems, a long prose letter on the Cold War, and a section of translations from five Latin American poets and from Raissa Maritain.

But this apparent scattering will not mislead the reader who knows how the capacity of the cultivated mind to discover relation is intensified in the contemplative, for whom the most diverse elements are reduced to the unity of simplicity, a step beyond their complexity fully realized.

Traces of the earlier Merton are still in evidence: a predilection for the striking image ("The dog smiles, his foreleg curled, his eye like an aster"); and the perennial attraction to silence, which appears and reappears in poems like **"A Messenger from the Horizon," "Love Winter When the Plant Says Nothing,"** and **"Night-Flowering Cactus"**:

> When I open once for all my impeccable bell
> No one questions my silence:
> The all-knowing bird of night flies out of my
>   mouth.

In fact, all of the poems ought to be read with a generous measure of silence around them in order to approximate the conditions from which they spring. One of the most beautiful is a long prose poem, **"Hagia Sophia,"** built on the hours of the Divine Office.

The reader who demands his Merton calcified like Lot's wife will frequently be put off by a cultivated flatness of line, the intrusion of rhythms traditionally more congenial to prose than to verse, and a calculated ironic understatement that raises the recurrent question of poetry and propaganda. When, for example, in **"Chant To Be Used in Processions Around a Site with Furnaces,"** the poet brings the grisly re-enactment to a climax with

> Do not think yourself better because you burn
>   up
> friends and enemies with long-range missiles
>   without
> ever meeting what you have done

one wonders whether the primary impulse of the poem may not be moralistic.

A similar irony is at work in **"And the Children of Birmingham," "And So Goodbye to Cities,"** and **"Why Some Look Up to Planets and Heroes,"** the last of which satirizes superficial attitudes toward space flight:

> What next device will fill the air with burning
>   dollars
> Or else lay out the low down number of some
>   Day
> What day? May we consent?
> Consent to what? Nobody knows.
> Yet the computers are convinced
> Fed full of numbers by the True Believers.

The unifying principle in this collection seems to be the universality of Merton's brotherhood: to it, we owe the fury against all that is ignoble and inhuman; to it, the compassion for the refugee, the jailed ladies, the victims of power politics and exploitation; and to it, the sense of personal responsibility and the tremendous receptivity to all that is most vital in other cultures.

This vitality is demonstrated in translations from César Vallejo and Pablo Antonio Cuadra, along with such lesser-known poets as Alfonso Cortes, the mad Nicaraguan.

The same understanding that can transcend geography is able to make leaps in time, to consider the recondite and the antiquarian in a relevant way. And so we have, besides, several poems dealing with somewhat esoteric monastic subjects and others of an archaic or primitive cast. Allusive always, Merton gathers his imaginative materials from Red Riding Hood through E. E. Cummings and John of the Cross; from the Beats to Rufinus, the *New York Times,* and Greek mythology.

Hayden Carruth   (review date 1970)

SOURCE: A review of *The Geography of Lograire,* in *The Hudson Review,* Vol. XXIII, No. 1, Spring, 1970, p. 187.

[*Carruth is an American poet, novelist, critic, and editor. Below, he offers a positive review of* The Geography of Lograire, *commenting that "it falls among [Merton's] best works."*]

The Geography of Lograire, by Thomas Merton, [is a] book-length poem in four books, part of a longer work "in progress," left by Merton at his death. However, what we have here is complete in itself. The most curious part is a section of twenty pages called "Queens Tunnel," autobiographical, confessional, cryptic. Much play on the word *aquilon* with its associations, north wind, noses, eagles, Roman (and U. S.) imperialism, Eliot. "Famous John is inventing you a trap with his agents. Old effigy with Anglican sabres. That turning stair goes up to a stone tiger. Tiger burns with his own secret fright. Sinners are betting on a walking kettle of eyes. Tiger tiger burning in the bay

Merton (center) with a group of fraternity brothers at Columbia University.

escapes double vision. Lettertrap for old Posthumus." The reference to Eliot (Posthumus [sic] = Possum) is obvious; the contrast, not flattering, between *Ash Wednesday* and Blake's Tyger also. I suspect that "Famous John" is John the Evangelist, and that "Queens Tunnel" is a new Revelations, and that *Lograire* itself, which Merton told a friend was taken from Francois Villon, is actually an anagram for something I have not discovered yet (probably in Latin?), and that much of the material in this section of the poem is, if not heretical (which would be unlikely), at least undoctrinal. (I have searched all Villon's work and what is known of his life without finding any *sufficient* justification for ascribing "Lograire" to this source, though it is true that according to the less probable of two stories Villon was born at a place of that name.) Other parts of Merton's poem deal with 17th-century English radicalism, the Amerindian and Melanesian revolutionary religious cults, airplane trips, criticism of Malinowsky—plenty of fascinating material. The writing is gutty, artistically forthright (no compromise with poetic expediency), and shows Merton at a pitch of invention. It falls among his best works, I think, as good a conclusion to his poetic life as anyone could hope for. (Though I'm told there are masses of his writing still stored away.) It will keep the exegetes busy for years at any rate, which ought to please them, though some, the churchly orthodox, will probably be chagrined by what they find. (Yet not all the bandwagon softheads will be comforted either by Tom Merton's fortitude.)

Jascha Kessler (review date 1970)

SOURCE: "Keys to Ourselves," in *The Saturday Review*, New York, Vol. LIII, No. 18, 2 May 1970, pp. 34-6.

[*Kessler is an American short story writer, poet, critic, novelist, and playwright. Below, she presents a positive review of* The Geography of Lograire.]

Thomas Merton's *The Geography of Lograire* may be the past year's most important book of poems. Merton died in 1968, so we shall not have the additions he planned for this "work in progress"; still, taking it as it is suffices. What the work in effect seems to be is a squaring of the sphere we call the Earth. The poem has four sections—"South," "North," "East," "West"—whose aim is "to play out . . . the same struggle of love and death, [to] enact the common participation of the living and the dead in the work of constructing a world and a viable culture." Now, we have had plenty of stuff since 1910 that is based on the "universal and primitive myth-dream," but *The Geography of Lograire* is not merely modernist—not at all. If one approaches the universal and primitive from the structuralist and linguistic angle, that mine of myth seems again both inexhaustible and novel—but one has to be a poet who can exert the enormous and controlled verbal power that Merton had available to him here, a power that at once stuns and exhilarates.

"Lograire" is the map of his imagination, and its scale is ambiguous, indefinable, and indefinite because it is in his mind and yet is a four-dimensioned chart of the world the poet has constructed, partly by constant observation of objective reality—the brute physical facts—and by study of books and memories, and partly also by means of the sheer transformational pressure of his gift. What emerges is a new language that projects his vision of life and death-in-life, and holy love: death known as it is built into our society in the form of police, undertakers, and guilt, and love as it comes through in the poet's abiding tender, wondrous, and, above all, intelligent voice: the language is never, even in prayer, sentimental or soft. It is, however, quite difficult to say in so many words what the poem is doing, which I take to be the first sign that we are in the presence of an important achievement in poetry.

To make a gross remark, one is struck by Merton's consummate ease in handling free, or open, forms, poetic prose, and even a sort of blank blank verse. As one reads it becomes clearer that the forms of American poetry, or verse per se, are being used as part of a larger method by a virtuoso, with the aim of representing, in terms of "geography," the things that have happened to men in different eras—that is, to ourselves and to other societies and civilizations—as if he were translating them all into our own American lingo. The effect is to digest their experience into ours, or even ours into theirs, which is what translation is.

In Lograire Merton finds pre-Columbian Indians, Africans, Muslim Arabs, Hindus, anarchist English ultra-Protestants (the Ranters), Stone Age men of the South Seas, and American Indians. The commonalty is not simply man, or humanity, but our religious impulse, aspiring and fluid with all the protean strengths of the spirit, for which Merton's neo-surreal mode of the mind's wakeful dreaming is but the vehicle of expression. Like Joyce, Merton is forced, because he uses language, to speak, and speaking seems conscious, as though consciousness is made of words, or words create consciousness. But also the id, the subconscious, the secretive and lonely ego, the superego, even a super-superego become the substance of the poem, and are made to speak in words even while they invisibly inform the poetry that underlies its mere words.

How so? Merton presents, for example, a long "Mafia Id" section; he shows the subconscious in the rendering of the cargo cult mythos (funny and poignant at once); he offers liturgies of the superego, and conveys what I've called the super-superego, or God's mad and/or maddening grace, by means of his own lyric voice, which he melds with that of the world's voice in what he terms an "endless inscription." The poem is devastatingly absurdist, lit by gleams of truth, our truths, offered as logical insanities. All this is part of its mysterious strength, as witness the following excerpts:

> "I now General Overseer Concession Registrar
> Of Rains and Weather Committeeman
> For Pepsi-Cola all over the veldt
> Flail of incontinent clergy
> Wave my highstrung certificate in times of change
> Don't you need a Defender with a medical guarantee?"

> . . . . .

> The sacred books are confiscated by police to keep eyes under sightless dome. Study famous text in court. Sacred words kept shut in horny room. They keep my novels in a box of candy. Shine continental glad warm being in Law. Witness defies sentence structure. Chatterly wins sightless connection in timeworn nickle viewer: hierarchic spectacle. Eyes down everyone. Fold hands, walk aisles, composures, make up for Lawrence in Church. Save famous continental dome from Reds. Extort glad news from Receiver. Famous John will live in hiding with "Roses of Life." Latest sacred arrested books saved up in jealous Senates of memory for more fun until better business. Keep eyes ahead gone dead dome: a shiny bald Church with a hole in the head a veritable pantheon. Fulltime overwork for Monsignori canonizing randy films. . . .

> Dear Togs. I have chosen electric life with spades. The lines here are almost new. Home is underwater now. Conscience is a bronco well busted. Memory secured by electronic tape. Gunshots on the glassy swamps of night. Uniforms wade under willows calling to the dead.

> . . . . .

> So Christ went down to stay with them Niggers and took his place with them at table. He said to them, "It is very simple much simpler than

you imagine." They replied, "You have become a white man and it is not so simple at all."

> . . . . .

> Comes a big slow fish with tailfins erect in light smog
> And one other leaves earth
> Go trains of insect machines
> Thirtynine generals signal eight
> Contact barrier four

> A United leaves earth
> Square silver bug moves into shade under wing building
> Standby train three black bugs indifferent
> A week after he got sick
> A long beetle called Shell
> On a firm United basis
> Long heavy-assed American dolphin touches earth
> Please come to the counter
> Where we have your camera
> Eastern Airlines has your camera
> And two others drink coffee
> Out of yellow paper cups

> Big Salvador not cooled off yet
> From sky silver but
> Hotel Fenway takes off at once
> To become Charles' Wain
> **("Day Six O'Hare Telephone")**

Excerpts cannot, of course, show their full complexity without the resonating structure of the whole book. Merton seems to have opened his mind like a gigantic radio network to map the geography of man. Whatever his personal form of belief, the chart he draws of the human world has mutually significant reference points that hardly need transformation formulas to express our own family's language: we all begin—perhaps almost all end—our lives as members of one cult, the rites of which vary only as our histories do, and, from the perspective of Lograire, histories fan out and fold again. Merton has not reduced us, however, to the level of the merely primitive cultus in his syncretic (and high-order) religious geography; he has instead entered us, our technologies, feathers and printed papers and plastic charms and all, into its larger life by means of wit, compassion, and a most profoundly disinterested understanding of what we are. **Lograire** is simply an astonishing work.

Richard Kostelanetz (review date 1978)

SOURCE: "The Sounds of Silence," in *The New York Times Book Review,* 5 February 1978, p. 20.

[*An American poet, essayist, short story writer, and novelist, Kostelanetz is noted in particular as a writer and supporter of contemporary avante-garde literature. In the following negative review of* The Collected Poems of Thomas Merton, *he faults the stylistic aspects of Merton's verse, concluding that "what remains most interesting about Merton is not his art or his thought but his life."*]

A labor of publishing love, over a thousand pages in length, **The Collected Poems of Thomas Merton** is a disappointing volume. Bad lines abound from the book's beginning, whose opening poem, **"The Philosophers,"** begins: "As I lay sleeping in the park, / Buried in the earth, / Waiting for the Easter rains / To drench me in their mirth / And crown my seedtime with some sap and growth." A more conscientious craftsman would have cleaned such doggerel up, or out.

It was commonly joked that Merton, having taken the vow of silence, then wrote tons of garrulous prose. His poems are similarly verbose, generally more prosy than poetic, and undistinguished in both language and idea. Indicatively, Merton's poems are scarcely anthologized, and his name rarely appears in histories of American literature, his general eminence notwithstanding.

One trouble with the poems is that they are incorrigibly derivative, in a variety of styles. Little here has sufficient personal signature to be instantly attributable to Merton; even less is memorable. His religious poems, which one might expect to be extraordinary, pale beside T. S. Eliot's or those of either St. John of the Cross or, more recently, Brother Antoninus, and Merton's later poems are not much better than his earlier ones. There is nothing here as singularly inventive as, say, the "macaronic" language that enhances his novel, *My Argument With the Gestapo* (1969; written 1941).

The Collected Poems suggests to me that Merton's true medium was not poetry at all, but *prose*. The best passages here are such prose aphorisms as, "The way of man has no wisdom, but the way of God has." Or, "An age in which politicians talk about peace is an age in which everybody expects war." The best individual "poems" are those composed of curt prose paragraphs—not only the **"Original Child Bomb"** (1962), which has been widely reprinted for its political content, but my own favorites, **"Chant to Be Used in Processions Around a Site With Furnaces"** and **"Cables to the Ace."** (The latter is dedicated to his college classmate Robert Lax, whom I regard among America's greatest experimental poets, a true minimalist who can weave awesome poems from remarkably few words. Though a survivor, Lax remains the last unacknowledged—and, alas, uncollected—major poet of his post-60's generation.)

The Collected Poems also includes a section of "Humorous Verse" (which is rarely funny), **"A French Poem"** and translations, along with several "concrete poems" that Merton wrote in the final year of his life. (Only one of the last, **"Awful Music,"** is passable.) The vain attempts at "songs" particularly indicate that poetic music was not Merton's forte, and his poems suffer from both a general remoteness that perhaps reflects the monastic life and the facile indulgences that are more typical of a literary recluse immune to professional criticism.

The strongest theme of *The Collected Poems* is neither religious nor political but autobiographical, suggesting that what remains most interesting about Merton is not his art or his thought but his life. Quite simply, his example made credible an extreme religious option that would strike most of us as unthinkable. His example also earned the devotion of several loyal publishers and thousands of readers, who eagerly consumed whatever he wrote. For them too, however, the man loomed larger than his work.

Robert McDowell   (review date 1978)

SOURCE: A review of the *Collected Poems of Thomas Merton* in *The Hudson Review,* Vol. XXXI, No. 2, Summer 1978, pp. 381-82.

[*McDowell is an American poet, critic, essayist, and screenwriter. Below, he offers a positive review of Merton's* Collected Poems.]

It is difficult, in the space of this article, to examine adequately the exceptional qualities of Thomas Merton—because they are so many. If you tried to come up with the components that go into the making of a first-rate poet, your prototype might bear an uncanny resemblance to him. Put simply, Merton is one of our great poetic talents of this century. If anybody has doubts, the **Collected Poems** should quickly dispel them. Reading the work entire is like entering a unique world created just for the occasion. It is no hasty construction, but a self-sustaining environment in which the landscape has been filled out, in which the living and the dead are real. It is as if the poet had tasted and understood every essence that makes up the world we live in, and out of the banquet proceeded to remake it and shape his own. Isn't this the ultimate aim of poetry?

Merton's life was strangely suited to the attainment of this end. Though he lived his last twenty-seven years in the Monastery of Our Lady of Gethsemane where he enjoyed the rare and constant solitude so many poets dream of, Merton never withdrew from Man in a spiritual sense. It is true that he felt revulsion from the world outside—sometimes with compassion, and sometimes without it—but he always somehow *saw* the world.

> Everywhere there is optimism without love
> And pessimism without understanding,
> They who have new clothes, and smell of hair-
>   cuts
> Cannot agree to be at peace
> With their own images, shadowing them in win-
>   dows
> From store to store.
>   (**"How to Enter a Big City"** Part III)

If what he saw was profound, he was a reluctant prophet. He never exaggerated his individual worth, though his vision was uncompromising and often tinged with an almost late Yeatsian rage.

> Go, stubborn talker,
> Find you a station on the loud world's corners,
> And try there, (if your hand be clean) your
>   length of patience:
> Use there the rhythms that upset my silences,
> And spend your pennyworth of prayer
> There in the clamor of the Christless avenues;
>
> And try to ransom some one prisoner
> Out of those walls of traffic, out of the wheels of
>   that unhappiness!
>   (**"The Poet, to His Book"**)

Also, Merton resembles Yeats in that he continued to grow as a writer. From his formal early poems to his late experiments in Surrealism, the voice remains vital and believable. It is seldom too religious, too metaphysical, too much the social critic; it is a combination of all of these, a large voice emerging to embody a large country. If the voice is not wholly American (it sometimes has the international flavor of Howes) it is, first and last, erudite and convincing. But it is American often enough for us to call it our own, to point to it as an example to young poets who should stay at home and begin to observe their language and their land. It is the modern American voice in which the corporate and the spiritual Man become one.

Merton's language never sacrifices beauty for shock value nor truth for the secure and unimaginative ring of an opinion that is either too personal or too popular. No matter how odd the style, or how tentative the subject, he always *makes sense* in the poem. One comes to this book and quickly forgets criticism.

One comes to this book . . . one should. It contains all of the published books; it includes two collections of unpublished poems, translations from several languages, a forgettable section of concrete poetry, and humorous verse. . . .

There is a great need anywhere for a poet like Thomas Merton. "Though we may run / in the dark, our destiny is full of glory." This is what poetry is all about. Call it nobility if you must; call it anything you like. We can use it.

Sister Thérèse Lentfoehr   (essay date 1979)

SOURCE: *Words and Silence: On the Poetry of Thomas Merton,* New Directions, 1979, 166 p.

[*An American poet who maintained a friendship with Merton, Lentfoehr is considered an authority on Merton's works. In the following excerpt from her study* Words and Silence: On the Poetry of Thomas Merton, *she discusses recurring social and religious themes in the poet's work.*]

After considering in some detail the several collections of poetry in the Thomas Merton canon (excepting the two last works published in his lifetime, *Cables to the Ace,* and *The Geography of Lograire*), it would seem pertinent at this point to cross chronological barriers in order to focus on poems dealing with specific subject matters that occur with a certain frequency.

It is unarguable that, whether overt or not, the ultimate referral point and matrix of all his writings—prose as well as poetry—is basically religious: the binding of man to God. Still, when considering the complete poetry canon, only about a third of the poems might be viewed as having specific religious themes. Among these a goodly number derive their inspiration from the Incarnation, with such events as proliferate from it—the Annunciation, Visitation, Nativity, Passion, and the Eucharist. In the first three the Virgin Mary's role is paramount, and since so many poems cluster around her, or are addressed to her, it seems important to isolate some of them for comment.

"The Blessed Virgin Compared to a Window" appears in Merton's first collection, *Thirty Poems* (1944), and at once conjures up Gerard Manley Hopkins's "The Blessed Virgin Compared to the Air We Breathe." Both poems elaborate a "metaphysical conceit": Merton's, the metaphor of a window representing the docile, pure soul of Mary through which God can transmit Himself unobstructedly as light through glass, and Hopkins's, the trope comparing her to air surrounding and pervading us by her influence, since she has but "one work to do / Let all God's glory through." Curiously, though Merton had read extensively in Hopkins, and while at Columbia had seriously considered writing a doctoral dissertation on his poetry, he never seems to have been influenced by Hopkins's sprung-rhythm prosody. It is also of interest to note that some ten years later, in a conference given the young monks at the abbey in his capacity of novice-master, Merton gave a careful analysis of the Hopkins poem.

The metaphor of the window is not original with Merton nor with Hopkins. The latter speaks of "glass-blue days" and of "This blue heaven" (Mary) transmitting "The hued sunbeam [Christ] perfect, not altering it." But the metaphor had earlier sources. While Merton was still at Columbia he became familiar with the sixteenth-century Spanish mystic, St. John of the Cross, and purchased a copy of *The Ascent of Mount Carmel,* which he read assiduously in his Greenwich Village apartment. The book is an extended commentary on a poem concerning the union of the human and divine wills, in which St. John used the comparison of a ray of sunlight striking a window.

> Although obviously the nature of the window is distinct from that of the sun's ray (even if the two seem identical), we can assert that the window is the ray of light of the sun by participation.

But the metaphor was in turn borrowed by St. John of the Cross from the Pseudo Areopagite's *De Mystica Theologia* (Bk. II, Ch. 5).

Merton's poem begins:

> Because my will is simple as a window
> And knows no pride of original earth,
> It is my life to die, like glass, by light:
> Slain in the strong rays of the bridegroom sun.

The word "simple" must be taken in its scholastic precisions, as having "no parts outside of parts" (St. Thomas). Merton uses it again in this same specific sense in a poem on St. Thomas Aquinas in which "the black-friar breaks the Truth, his Host, / Among his friends the simple Substances" [*A Man in the Divided Sea*]. The metaphor of the "bridegroom sun" is obviously from the Canticle of Canticles, a symbolism that appears frequently in spiritual theology. The poem continues:

> Because my love is simple as a window
> And knows no shame of original dust,
> I longed all night, (when I was visible) for dawn
>   my death:
> When I would marry day, my Holy Spirit:
> And die by transubstantiation into light.

The reference to transubstantiation and to the lover must again be given their full theological resonances.

Another Marian poem, and one of Merton's finest, is **"The Messenger,"** a pre-Trappist poem first published in *Spirit,* then reprinted in *Thirty Poems,* and later in the poetry column of *The New York Times Book Review.* With Lady-day in its context of spring, the "annunciation imagery" is striking, as the "tongue of March's bugle" warns of "the coming of the warrior sun."

> When spring has garrisoned up her army of
>   water,
> A million grasses leave their tents, and stand in
>   rows
> To see their invincible brother.
> Mending the winter's ruins with their laughter,
> The flowers go out to their undestructive wars.

Then, counseling the flowers to "Walk in the woods and be witnesses, / You, the best of these poor children," Merton moves into the final stanza, which begins the swiftness of Gabriel's descent:

> When Gabriel hit the bright shore of the world,
> Yours were the eyes saw some
> Star-sandalled stranger walk like lightning down
>   the air,
> The morning the Mother of God
> Loved and dreaded the message of the angel.

In the poem **"The Oracle,"** on a quite different theme, its final stanza alludes to Gabriel's swift movement of descent when

> . . . already, down the far, fast ladders of light
> The stern, astounding angel
> Starts with a truer message,
> Carrying a lily.

And once again in **"Aubade—The Annunciation"**

> Desires glitter in her mind
> Like morning stars:
>
> Until her name is suddenly spoken
> Like a meteor falling.

A related theme is that of the visitation of Mary to Elizabeth, on which Merton wrote two poems: **"The Evening of the Visitation"** and **"The Quickening of St. John Baptist."** In the former he asks nature to participate:

> Still bend your heads like kind and humble kings
> The way you did this golden morning when you
>   saw
> God's Mother passing.

Manuscript versions of **"The Quickening of St. John Baptist"** present an interesting study in development: the beginnings—two columns of pencil jottings (twenty-four lines) on a folded sheet, in which some of the key lines of the poem already appear, as for instance:

> Her salutation
> Sings in the stone valley like a Charterhouse bell.

Most of the poem is a questioning of St. John Baptist, and is couched in hermit imagery:

> . . . small anchorite!

How did you see her in the eyeless dark?
> . . . . .
> You need no eloquence, wild bairn,
> Exulting in your hermitage,
> Your ecstasy is your apostolate,
> For whom to kick is *contemplata tradere.*

His vocation is with the Church's "hidden children":

> The speechless Trappist, or the grey, granite
>   Carthusian,
> The quiet Carmelite, the barefoot Clare,
> Planted in the night of contemplation,
> Sealed in the dark and waiting to be born.
> Night is our diocese and silence is our ministry
> Poverty our charity and helplessness our
>   tongue-tied sermon.
> Beyond the scope of sight or sound we dwell
>   upon the air
> Seeking the world's gain in an unthinkable expe-
>   rience.

In the second version of this poem (thirty-five lines), already the first line of the final version appears, "Why do you fly from the drowned shores of Galilee?" In the manuscript of the final version (seventy-one lines) the original title, **"A Quickening: A Song for the Visitation,"** has been given its present title, **"The Quickening of St. John Baptist,"** and dated Feast of St. John Baptist, 1947.

Another poem in the same collection, *The Tears of the Blind Lions,* **"To the Immaculate Virgin, on a Winter Night,"** though written over twenty years ago, has a special contemporary significance, as Merton speaks of "a day of blood and many beatings"—

> I see the governments rise up, behind the steel
>   horizon,
> And take their weapons and begin to kill.

There is also an allusion to the proximity of Fort Knox: "Out where the soldiers camp the guns begin to thump / And another winter time comes down / To seal your years in ice." The last lines of the poems are especially poignant:

> Lady, the night has got us by the heart
> And the whole world is tumbling down.
> Words turn to ice in my dry throat
> Praying for a land without prayer,
>
> Walking to you on water all winter
> In a year that wants more war.

Another poem, the last with the Virgin Mary as theme, **"The Annunciation,"** was written as a billet for the nuns of the New York Carmel and is in Merton's new manner, more free of elaboration, and in this instance somewhat reminiscent of a pre-Raphaelite painting:

> The girl prays by the bare wall
> Between the lamp and the chair.
> (Framed with an angel in our galleries
> She has a richer painted room, sometimes a
>   crown.
>
> But seven pillars of obscurity
> Build her to Wisdom's house, and Ark, and
>   Tower.
> She owns their manna in her jar.)
>
> Fifteen years old—

The flowers printed on her dress
Cease moving in the middle of her prayer
When God, Who sends the messenger,
Meets his messenger in her heart.
Her answer, between breath and breath,
Wrings from her innocence our Sacrament!
In her white body God becomes our Bread.

These poems form an easy transition to the theme of the
Nativity, in which one is aware of the sensitivity, gentleness, and joy of their author's spirit in presence of this
mystery, as in **"The Holy Child's Song"**:

When midnight occupied the porches of the
Poet's reason
Sweeter than any bird
He heard the Holy Child.

In a type of envelope style, rarely used by Merton, the
above three lines are used again as a refrain at the poem's
end, enclosing the child's songs as they "Fly in and out the
branches of my childish voice / Like thrushes in a tree."

And when my Mother, pretty as a church,
Takes me upon her lap, I laugh with love,
Loving to live in her flesh, which is my
house. . . .

In these poems nature is frequently used as setting—the
winter season, and the animals, as the child continues his
song:

In winter when the birds put down their flutes
And wind plays sharper than a fife upon the icy
rain,
I sit in this crib,
And iaugh like fire, and clap My golden hands:
To view my friends the timid beasts—
Their great brown flanks, muzzles and milky
breath!

In the poem **"Advent,"** in metaphor we find the animals
again: "minds, meek as beasts, / Stay close at home in the
sweet hay; / And intellects are quieter than the flocks that
feed by starlight." The moon and skies are invoked to
"pour down your darkness and your brightness over all
our solemn valleys." In **"Carol"**:

God's glory, now, is kindled gentler than low
candlelight
Under the rafters of a barn:
Eternal Peace is sleeping in the hay,
And Wisdom's born in secret in a straw-roofed
stable.

In **"The Fall of Night,"** the farmers coming home from
the fields sing:

We bring these heavy wagons full of hay to make
your bed,
O Mercy, born between the animals.

Finally, in the poem **"A Christmas Card,"** Merton paints
a winter canvas as

. . . one by one the shepherds, with their snowy
feet,
Stamp and shake out their hats upon the stable
dirt,
And one by one kneel down to look upon their
Life.

Another frequent theme is that of children, to whom Merton often alludes, especially in his early poems. It has been
said that in every poet there is a child, since in some fashion he invariably retains a child's vision. Merton is no exception, and with this vision has come an empathy with
children that characterizes some of his most sensitive
poems. In **"The Winter's Night,"** when "the frost cracks
on the window,"

One says the moonlight grated like a skate
Across the freezing winter.
Another hears the starlight breaking like a knife-
blade
Upon the silent, steelbright pond. . . .
Yet it is far from Christmas, when a star
Sang in the pane, as brittle as their inno-
cence. . . .
The moonlight rings upon the ice as sudden as
a footstep;
Starlight clinks upon the dooryard stone, too
like a latch,
And the children are, again, awake,
And all call out in whispers to their guardian an-
gels.

In **"Aubade: Lake Erie,"** after the sun "light handed" has
sown "this Indian water / With a crop of cockles," Merton calls to the children:

Awake, in the frames of windows, innocent chil-
dren,
Loving the blue, sprayed leaves of childish life,
Applaud the bearded corn, the bleeding grape,
And cry:
"Here is the hay-colored sun, our marvelous
cousin,
Walking in the barley."

Again in **"Evening"** is the children's interpretation of nature:

They say the sky is made of glass,
They say the smiling moon's a bride.

. . . . .

They name the new come planets
With words that flower
On little voices, light as stems of lilies.

As Merton celebrated the candor and innocence of children, so too he was most vulnerable to their suffering. In
an early poem, **"Aubade: Harlem,"** "in the sterile jungles
of waterpipes and ladders," he pictures a typical scene,
one known to him firsthand, since before he entered the
monastery he had spent many hours working in Harlem
at Friendship House. The beginning and final stanza of the
poem are the same, as we see.

Across the cages of the keyless aviaries,
The lines and wires, the gallows of the broken
kites,
Crucify, against the fearful light,
The ragged dresses of the little children.

One of the most interesting of Merton's poems on children
is **"Grace's House,"** written in 1962 and inspired by a
four-year-old child's pencil drawing of a house on a hill.
With meticulous exactitude Merton details each object of
the sketch—"No blade of grass is not counted, / No blade

of grass forgotten on this hill." He details the house on the summit; a snow cloud rolling from the chimney; flowers; curtains, "Not for hiding, but for seeing out"; trees, from which animals peek out; a dog, "his foreleg curled, his eye like an aster"; a mailbox "full of Valentines for Grace".

> There is a name on the box, name of a family
> Not yet ready to be written in language.

In the second stanza appears the theme around which all resonances cluster, as Merton fastens on an apparently insignificant detail which nonetheless provides the leitmotif of the poem, namely:

> There is no path to the summit—
> No path drawn
> To Grace's house.

—which provides the contrast between our world and hers, "our Coney Island," and her "green sun-hill",

> Between our world and hers
> Runs a sweet river
> (No, it is not the road
> It is the uncrossed crystal
> Water between our ignorance and her truth.)

The poem's last line re-introduces the theme, as Merton casually mentions "a rabbit / And two birds"—

> . . . bathing in the stream
> which is no road, because
>
> Alas, there is no road to Grace's house!

Interestingly, the German edition of Merton's *Selected Poems* is titled *Gracias Haus* and the poem is first of the thirty-eight which comprise the selection. On sending a copy of this edition to a friend he remarked, "I think they did a very nice job. Glad my little Grace made the title!"

At about the same time **"Grace's House"** was written, a newspaper photograph of a young Chinese refugee, stopped in her flight to Hong Kong and kneeling in tears as she begged to be admitted to the city, loosed in Merton a bitterly ironic poem, **"A Picture of Lee Ying,"** written in a free, almost documentary style, as he mocks the platitudinal excuses offered by the authorities.

> *Point of no return* is the caption, but this is meaningless she must return that is the story
>
> She would not weep if she had reached a point of no return what she wants is not to return

Merton's irony cuts deep:

> When the authorities are alarmed what can you
> do
>
> You can return to China
>
> Their alarm is worse than your sorrow

But he tells her not to look at the dark side, for "You have the sympathy of millions." Then the devastatingly paradoxical conclusion:

> As a tribute to your sorrow we resolve to spend
> more money on
> nuclear weapons there is always a bright side

Merton's mounting concern over the racial question found its expression in another children's poem, one of deep compassion, addressed to Carole Denise McNair, one of the children killed that tragic September of 1963 in Birmingham. The poem is titled **"Picture of a Black Child with a White Doll"** and is an implicit indictment of a society in which such a crime could happen.

> Your dark eyes will never need to understand
> Our sadness who see you
> Hold that plastic glass-eyed
> Merchandise as if our empty-headed race
> Worthless full of fury
> Twanging and drooling in the southern night
> With guns and phantoms
> Needed to know love.

This is in contrast to the irony that marked another poem, **"And the Children of Birmingham,"** its sharp, objective, matter-of-fact statement set in the framework of a children's story, as it parodies "Little Red Riding Hood," "Grandma's pointed teeth / ('Better to love you with')." The present poem, even as it contrasts the dark child with "That senseless platinum head / Of a hot city cupid," is pervaded by a tenderness that distinguishes its author:

> Next to your live and lovely shade
> Your smile and your person
> Yet that silly manufactured head
> Would soon kill you if it could think. . . .
>
> So without a thought
> Of death or fear
> Of night
> You glow full of dark red August
> Risen and Christian
> Africa purchased
> For the one lovable Father alone.

And when all was done, "They found you and made you a winner"—

> Even in most senseless cruelty
> Your darkness and childhood
> Became fortune yes became
> Irreversible luck and halo.

Not only to the suffering of children did Merton extend his concern but also to such as were caught up in some tragic circumstance or were victims of the judgment of an unhappy society. One of the most poignant poems Merton wrote, **"There Has to Be a Jail for Ladies,"** is one in which he genuinely compassionates and pleads for the "ladies of the street," when "their beauty is taken from them, when their hearts are broken," while the government wants a jail for them "when they are ugly because they are wrong." He tells them:

> I love you, unhappy ones. . . .
> Tell me, darlings, can God be in Hell?
> You may curse; but he makes your dry voice
> turn to butter. . . .
> He will laugh at judges.
> He will laugh at the jail.
> He will make me write this song.

And the last stanza carries an unforgettable image:

> God will come to your window with skylarks

Merton (far left) during ordination rites.

And pluck each year like a white rose.

Like the seventeenth-century metaphysical poets whom Merton during his early student years much admired, he too wrote a number of elegies. The first, written for his brother, is well known and often quoted—**"For My Brother: Reported Missing in Action, 1943"**. A longer poem, **"The Trappist Cemetery—Gethsemani,"** is addressed to his brother monks who lie in the burial ground circling the apse of the abbey church. Paradoxically, the poem is a song of joy rather than of mourning as Merton tells them not to fear that "The birds that bicker in the lonely belfry / Will ever give away your legends," but exhorts them to look and "See, the kind universe / Wheeling in love above the abbey steeple / Lights up your sleepy nursery with stars." In a somewhat effusive metaphor he recounts their lives, then asks that they teach us "how to wear / Silence, our humble armor. . . . / Because your work is not yet done," and at the last day, when "your graves, Gethsemani, give up their angels,"

> Return them to their souls to learn
> The songs and attitudes of glory.
> Then will creation rise again like gold
> Clean, from the furnace of your litanies:

> The beasts and trees shall share your resurrection,
> And a new world be born from these green tombs.

This poem was recorded for the Harvard Vocarium Series by the British playwright Robert Speaight, and also included in the *Selected Poems* edited by him in England in 1950.

For **"Elegy for the Monastery Barn,"** which first appeared in *The Strange Islands,* and later in Mark Van Doren's edition of Merton's *Selected Poems* (1959 and 1967), Merton furnished us the "poetic occasion," saying [in the preface to *The Strange Islands*] that it "was written after the cowbarn at Gethsemani burned down, one August evening in 1953, during the evening meditation. The monks left the meditation to fight a very hot fire and the poem arrived about the same time as the fire truck from the nearest town." It received comment by Mark Van Doren in his introduction to *Selected Poems,* as he had requested to include this poem about which he knew Merton to be somewhat shy. Merton remarked:

> As a matter of fact it is for me subjectively an important poem, because when I was a kid in

Maryland (yes, even that, for a while) a barn burned down in the middle of the night and it is one of the earliest things I can remember. So burning barns are for me great mysteries that are important. They turn out to be the whole world, and it is the Last Judgement.

In the poem the barn is presented under the image of an old lady who, for her last hour, had dressed herself in "Too gay a dress" and calls to the countryside, "Look, how fast I dress myself in fire!" But for those who worked in her she leaves vivid memories:

> She, in whose airless heart
> We burst our veins to fill her full of hay,
> Now stands apart.
> She will not have us near her. Terribly,
> Sweet Christ, how terribly her beauty burns us
> now!

But as legacy she has left them her solitude, her peace, her silence. Clustered around the metaphor of the barn is the monks' ignorance of her vanity, hence their surprise at seeing her "So loved, and so attended, and so feared." The "Fifty invisible cattle" return, and the past years as well "Assume their solemn places one by one" for this little minute of their destiny and meaning, as

> Laved in the flame as in a Sacrament
> The brilliant walls are holy
> In their first-last hour of joy.

The last two stanzas of the poem are reminiscent of the liturgy of Easter night relevant to the blessing of the new fire, Lumen Christi, which is later thrice plunged into the baptismal water. In both text and imagery the first line of the final stanza alludes to Luke 21:21, in which, foretelling the destruction of Jerusalem, Christ warns those in Judea to flee to the mountains and those in the city to depart.

> Flee from within the barn! Fly from the silence
> Of this creature sanctified by fire.

The second line touches on the petition "Sanctify this new fire," from the Exultet of the Easter night vigil. Merton continues:

> Let no man stay inside to look upon the Lord!
> Let no man wait within and see the Holy
> One sitting in the presence of disaster
> Thinking upon this barn His gentle doom!

Again there is an allusion to Luke (21:27), where "they will see the Son of Man coming in a cloud." The event of the barn fire is still kept in its spiritual dimension as it presents "the Holy / One . . . / Thinking upon this barn His gentle doom!" It is *His* barn, since all things are His and He is all things, which recalls a moving passage in William J. Lynch's *Christ and Apollo,* speaking of the Christic imagination which

> begins to assume the order of creation and to lift it into its own vitality. Thus Christ is water, gold, butter, food, a harp, a dove, the day, a house, merchant, fig, gate, stone, book, wood, light, medicine, oil, bread, arrow, salt, turtle, risen sun, way, and many things besides.

With its theological resonances and significances this elegy stands out among Merton's finest, as his poetic imagination lifts a simple event—the burning barn—through the zone of the Teilhardian cosmic Christ to that of apocalyptic vision.

Emblems of a Season of Fury contains four elegies. **"Song for the Death of Averroes,"** is a simple narrative in verse-prose style, a form Merton was beginning to use in a number of poems, and is adapted from Ibn Al Arabi, after the Spanish version of Asin Palacios. The young man was sent by his father on an errand to his friend Averroës at the latter's request "to learn if it were true that God had spoken to [him] in solitude." Though at first troubled, Averroës afterward rejoiced and praised God,

> . . . who has made us live in this time when there exists one of those endowed with mystical gifts, one able to unlock His door, and praised be He for granting me, in addition, the favor of seeing one such person with my own eyes.

Ibn Al Arabi never saw Averroës again, but attended his funeral in Cordova, and saw his coffin carried on one side of the beast of burden and the books he had written on the other. To a remark of the scholar Benchobair, "No need to point it out, my son, for it is clearly evident! Blessed be thy tongue that has spoken it!" Ibn Al Arabi set the words apart for meditation:

> I planted the seed within myself thus, in two verses:

> "On one side the Master rides: on the other side, his books.
> Tell me: his desires, were they at last fulfilled?"

In the same collection there are two occasional elegies, one for Ernest Hemingway, another for James Thurber. Merton speaks affectionately of Hemingway, who passes "briefly through our midst. Your books and writings have not been consulted. Our prayers are *pro defuncto N.*"

> How slowly this bell tolls in a monastery tower
> for a whole age, and for the quick death of an unready dynasty, and for that brave illusion: the adventurous self!

> For with one shot the whole hunt is ended!

That for James Thurber is written in a tighter structure as Merton entreats him.

> Leave us, good friend, Leave our awful celebration
> With pity and relief.
> You are not called to solemnize with us
> Our final madness.

> You have not been invited to hear
> The last words of everybody.

Still another elegiac poem in the same collection, **"An Elegy for Five Old Ladies,"** had its beginning in a *New York Times* report of their deaths, "ranging in age from 80 to 96," in a driverless car which, rolling across the lawn of a rest home, plunged into a lake.

> Let the perversity of a machine become our common

study, while I name loudly five loyal spouses of
death!

One of Merton's late poems, **"Elegy for Father Stephen,"**
first published in *Commonweal,* is for a fellow monk, one
of whose duties was to tend a flower garden and prepare
bouquets for the altars of the abbey church. Merton calls
him "Confessor of exotic roses / Martyr of unbelievable
gardens"—

> Whom we will always remember
> As a tender-hearted careworn
> Generous unsteady cliff
> Lurching in the cloister
> Like a friendly freight train
> To some uncertain station.

The metaphors are strong fibered, yet the poem carries no
sadness as Merton recalls chance meetings with the monk.

> Sometimes a little dangerous at corners
> Vainly trying to smuggle
> Some enormous and perfect bouquet
> To a side altar
> In the sleeves of your cowl.

But on the day of the burial,

> A big truck with lights
> Moved like a battle cruiser
> Toward the gate
> Past your abandoned garden. . . .

The closing lines of the elegy are tender and joyous:

> As if Leviathan
> Hot on the scent of some other blood
> Had passed you by
> And never saw you hiding among the flowers.

Though at the time this poem was written, October 1966,
Merton was already experimenting with surrealistic techniques, this elegy moves through clusters of simple yet
strong imagery.

Another theme that runs through the fabric of much of
Merton's poetry, if not explicitly then implicitly, is that of
a denunciation of the so-called "world," though it is well
to recall that in an entry in an early Journal, dated December 18, 1941, four days after his entering the monastery,
he wrote: "I never hated less the world, scorned it less, or
understood it better." Thus, he writes of the "city" because it is a symbol of much that dehumanizes man; even
the titles of certain of his poems indicate this, such as the
early **"Hymn of Not Much Praise for New York City":**

> . . . never let us look about us long enough to
>   wonder
> Which of the rich men, shivering in the over-
>   heated office,
> And which of the poor men, sleeping face-down
>   on the *Daily Mirror*
> Are still alive, and which are dead.

"In the Ruins of New York":

> This was a city
> That dressed herself in paper money.
> She lived four hundred years
> With nickels running in her veins.

"And So Goodbye to Cities":

> For cities have grown old in war and fun
> The sick idea runs riot.

And in **"How to Enter a Big City":**

> Everywhere there is optimism without love
> And pessimism without understanding.

The city as a symbol of "modern society" and the emptiness of technological man who, in conforming himself to
its dictates, tends to lose all spiritual orientation was a frequent Merton theme. He had said of technology that it
"alienates those who depend on it and live by it. It deadens
their human qualities and their moral perceptiveness."
Yet at the same time he realized that it was a fact and a
necessity of modern life. Yet there is a danger—

> of technology becoming an end in itself and arro-
> gating to itself all that is best and most vital in
> human effort: thus man comes to serve his ma-
> chines instead of being served by them. This is
> completely irrational. One whom I have always
> admired as a great social critic—Charlie Chap-
> lin—made this clear long ago in "Modern
> Times" and other films.

In a poem, **"First Lesson About Man,"** he ironically describes this condition:

> Man begins in zoology
> He is the saddest animal
>
> He drives a big red car
> Called anxiety
> He dreams at night
> Of riding all the elevators
> Lost in the halls
> He never finds the right door.

In brief, flat statements Merton continues his description:
"Whenever he goes to the phone / To call joy / He gets
the wrong number / He knows all guns. . . . / He flies
his worries / All around Venus. . . . / He drives a big
white globe / Called death." The "lesson" is logically followed by an interrogation:

> Now dear children you have learned
> The first lesson about man
> Answer your text
>
> "Man is the saddest animal
> He begins in zoology
> And gets lost
> In his own bad news."

An earlier version of this last stanza read (two last lines):
"And that is where he generally / Ends."

But Merton's vision of what an ideal world, an ideal city
should be, he made explicit in his morality play, ***The
Tower of Babel.*** As set in Augustinian context, he contrasts the city of man with the city of God—the former as
symbol is destroyed "to give place to the light which it
might have contained."

> . . . This new city will not be the tower of sin,
> but the City of God. Not the wisdom of men
> shall build this city, nor their machines, not their
> power. But the great city shall be built without

hands, without labor, without money and without plans. It will be a perfect city, built on eternal foundations, and it shall stand forever, because it is built by the thought and the silence and the wisdom and the power of God. But you, my brothers, and I are stones in the wall of this city. Let us run to find our places. Though we may run in the dark, our destiny is full of glory.

Victor A. Kramer   (essay date 1984)

SOURCE: *Thomas Merton,* Twayne Publishers, 1984, 164 p.

[*Kramer is an American educator and critic. In the following excerpt from his study* Thomas Merton, *he focuses on Merton's portrayal of contemporary humankind in* Collected Poems.]

Collected Poems, a thousand-page volume, [includes new poems that were unpublished at the time of Merton's death.] These new poems do not exhibit startling changes in technique, yet there are several points to be noted; interesting is the fact that Merton continued to experiment with various techniques. Thus, while many of his final shorter poems are conventional, others, especially the prose-poems, are unusual. Two characteristics stand out about the lyrics in this final collection. Merton includes many personal pieces in which he seems almost horrified at what he sees reflected about contemporary man, who remains unaware of his need for contemplation; but Merton is also able to attain distance, and even to laugh. This is so because he sees many connections between his life and others, while he also seems to realize that his poetry means much more to him than it ever can for others. Both **"The Originators"** and **"With the World in My Bloodstream"** bring this point home (these are the first two poems in the collection). There is a kind of lightness in many of these poems, even though Merton's view of the contemporary world (and history) is sometimes almost frightening. His title poem **"A Song: Sensation Time at the Home"** also exemplifies this. This poet certainly realizes that poetry will have little immediate effect—especially upon readers who are caught up *only* in their own sensations. This is the world of *Cables* where

Experts control
Spasms
Fight ennui
While giant smiles and minds
Relax limits
Save $ $ $ $ $.

It is a world which seems to be in large part lost, yet more important it is one about which the poet speaks kindly, with wit and irony, even though man seems to have given up by giving in. **"A Tune for Festive Dances in the Nineteen Sixties,"** about man's loss of identity, is a related poem. **"Man the Master"** amplifies the same themes, but again in a humorous way. Man seems so busy that he has forgotten about himself, *as self*:

Here he comes
Bursting with individuals
All his beliefs fat and clean. . . .
With innumerable wits and plans

Nations and names problems and resolutions.

In some of these poems there exists a consistent note close to disgust. Poems such as **"Picture of a Black Child with a White Doll"** and **"Man the Master"** illustrate this. Yet it is important to realize that while there is such a somber quality, even close to bitterness, there is as well a lightness to balance it. Thus, on the one hand, Merton can provide a gaiety, yet on the other he will not bring himself to stop thinking about the distortions of contemporary man. The poet smiles, but he cannot forget his **"First Lessons About Man"** which are that

Man begins in zoology
He is the saddest animal
He drives a big red car
Called anxiety. . . .

Somewhat the same must be observed about the three prose-poems which close this collection. All treat man's misuse of language, the twisting of language to his selfish benefit, not for the benefit of others, yet all of these prose-poems are also presented with distance and humor which makes it possible for Merton's compassion to shine through. These three prose-poems which conclude **"Sensation Time"** are further indications of the writer's interests toward the very end of his career. **"Plessy vs Ferguson: Theme and Variations"** might be compared to the noise of *Cables* since in both language seems often to be used to obscure rather than to clarify. This is a study, above all, in the abuse of language. **"Rites for the Extrusion of a Leper"** implies that the Church itself can be guilty of language abuse. Merton's point is that civil government and the church continue to find ways to arrange meaning for their own benefit.

The last prose-poem, **"Ben's Last Fight"** apparently means many things. It seems to be an autobiographical poem, and it also is a statement by Merton about poetic technique. Father Louis is saying that he has learned that he can now relax. Fights with rules, with language, with the changing concerns of the world of man, are interesting, but ultimately of little lasting import; yet words can help man to remember such facts, too.

Scott Nelson   (essay date 1986)

SOURCE: "Three Decades of Poetry: Merton's Spiritual Maturation," in *Toward an Integrated Humanity: Thomas Merton's Journey,* edited by M. Basil Pennington, Cistercian Publications, 1988, pp. 240-50.

[*In the following essay, originally presented at a Merton Conference held in 1986, Nelson examines several of Merton's poems and suggests that despite his varied roles, the poet was primarily a mystic.*]

Diversity marked the life of Thomas Merton. He was a virtual chameleon as he shared different aspects of himself with the many he came to know throughout his lifetime. As Michael Mott observes [in *The Seven Mountains of Thomas Merton*], Merton had the rare gift of making a person feel that for a time he was on the most intimate and open terms with Merton; but such a rapport could create the problem of having 'many people thinking that they alone knew what Merton thought or planned'. Some of these people insist to this day that they knew Merton better than anyone, and then they launch into a description of the man they knew, emphasizing the elements of political activist, peacenik, writer, artist, radical Catholic, disillusioned Christian, poet, Zenman, contemplative, young father, middle-aged lover, and whatever else, perhaps highlighting one or two primarily and paying a lip service to the other facets. Merton was indeed all of these things; but the most neglected side of the man is central to all of his endeavors. For as varied and wide ranging as he was, Merton was continually and consistently sourced from the center of the mystical realm (sometimes called God) throughout his entire life. This concept, while hardly new, is what this short paper will attempt to clarify through the examination of some randomly selected poems written by Merton at ten year spans thus comprising his monastic life. [The poems quoted in this essay were published in Merton's **Collected Poems**.]

'A Letter to My Friends' was published in *A Man in the Divided Sea,* but as the subtitle suggests, was written in 1941 upon 'entering the Monastery of Our Lady of Gethsemani'. Full of pious romanticism and naiveté, this poem is a didactic representation of *contemptio mundi* and the reaching out of man towards the divine (*kopos*). On the former pole the young novice Merton seeks haven from the world, his past (his future), and his guilt by entering,

> This holy House of God,
> Nazareth, where Christ lived as a boy,
> These sheds and cloisters,
> The very stones and beams are all befriended
> By cleaner sun, by rarer birds, by lovelier flow-
> ers.

Such an idyllic setting is misleading in the sense that the monastery threshhold does not serve to keep out the grime and dirt of humanity. The sun, birds and flowers are the same on both sides of the abbey wall; but greater acuity is afforded to the cloistered monk. Yet it is not the peaceful appearances or the false hope of simple security that leads men inward,

> Lost in the tigers' and the lions' wilderness,
> More than we fear, we love these holy stones,
> These thorns, the phoenix's sweet and spikey
> tree.
> More than we fear, we love the holy desert,
> Where separate strangers, hid in their disguises,
> Have come to meet, by night, the quiet Christ.

In his tradition of the earliest Desert Fathers, Merton paints a scene of entering the untamed regions, where aridity and hence certain death exist, and where man alone would perish without the divine assistance. Fear is natural in such a portrait, yet the 'holy stones' are 'loved' as are the 'thorns'. In this love is the acceptance of the same suffering of Christ which is to share simultaneously in his resurrection; for as the mythical phoenix sacrificed itself on a funeral pyre in the desert only to assume a new life, so too is the desire of the monk. This desire is not born out of the perverse grasping for nonexistence. It is the hope that, like the phoenix, like Christ, the monk will arise to a new life. It is in this beloved desert that individuals,

hidden in their cowls, are brought together on an intrinsic level to await in silent expectation and darkness (as at the Office of Vigils) for Christ. These stanzas expose the often neglected side of monastic life and, at times, of Christian life in general. Yet the seeming sense of escapism and piteous contempt creeps back into the poem as Merton continues,

> We who have some time wandered in those
> crowded ruins,
> (Farewell, you woebegone, sad towns)
> We who have wandered like (the one I hear) the
> moaning trains,
> (Begone, sad towns!)
> We'll live it over for you here.
>
> Here all your ruins are rebuilt as fast as you de-
> stroy yourselves,
> In your unlucky wisdom,
> Here in the House of God
> And on the holy hill,
> Where fields are the friends of plenteous heaven,
> While starlight, as bright as mana,
> All our rough earth with wakeful grace.

As they too are men, monks have all once lived among the world's and their own failings; but the monk takes the radical stance and assumes responsibility for his life by sacrificing it, by renouncing his past, and laying his future on the highest altar. Inseparable from this offering is the elemental commitment to all people as Christ's sacrifice is for all generations even though the historical event occurred some time in the past. In this sense, the monastic vocation becomes a living sacrifice that is not merely a metaphor, or simply a reminder of a perfect way of life. It is a life in which the suffering and rising of Jesus Christ is embodied for all, so that the monk can state that he will 'live it over for you here'. Even in a world where self destruction and ignorance marry, where the towns have become sad, this sacrificial action of the monastic community serves to bolster and shore up the earth, or if you will, the mystical body of Christ (*koinonia*); for the 'ruins are rebuilt as fast

Merton, shortly after he was ordained into the priesthood.

as you destroy yourselves.' While this notion could have a broader meaning in terms of the instrumental position of the monastery versus the entire Church, it is clear that at the time of his writing this poem Merton was thinking strictly in the light of his vocation. He most readily identifies the physical domain of the monastery as he alludes to the trains he hears in the distance (which one could in fact hear from Gethsemani at that time), the expanse of farmland (the match mates of 'plenteous' skies), and like many novices who find novelty in the early morning rising, he remembers the starlight of the Office of Vigils.

The 'desert's' hope materializes and is fostered by the monastery as Merton sketches further the grounds and architecture of Gethsemani in the final stanza:

> And look, the ruins have become Jerusalems,
> And the sick cities re-arise, like shining Sions!
> Jerusalems, these walls and rooves,
> These bowers and fragrant sheds,
> Our desert's wooden door,
> The arches, and the windows, and the tower!

This early poem reflects Merton's total immersion within the novitiate. His consistent referral to the stillness of the night serves to 'record the poet's love of nature, of solitude, and the contemplative vocation' as do many of the other pieces included in *A Man in the Divided Sea.* **'A Letter To My Friends'** is Merton consciously identifying with his contemplative vocation and it simultaneously exhibits his deep association with the world and its inhabitants. Yet both of these elements await clearer definition through the goal of his calling, and consequently the crux of this poem, which is God, Christ, the Sublime.

Nearly ten years later Merton was still writing as a contemplative, a monk; however there is no longer the robust romanticism through superfluous words. *The Strange Islands* (1957) found him writing about the initial sense of his calling in a greatly matured fashion as exhibited by **'In Silence'**.

> Be still
> Listen to the stones of the wall.
> Be silent, they try
> To speak your
> Name.
> Listen
> To the living walls.
> Who are you?
> Who
> Are you? Whose
> Silence are you?

In this unusual syncretism of animism and quietude, the 'poet's rare vision is toward a profound experience and the reader must be prepared to extend himself to meet it' [according to Thérèse Lentfoehr in *Words and Silence*]. That the stones are alive represents his intuitive experience of all the world as being infused with the spirit of God. One must be still, however, to listen, to feel the earth's pulse asking the angst sustaining, 'Who are you?' A step further is the question, 'Whose silence are you?' In another way, one might ask when all is still, when the mind is silent, when the heart is calm, and hence the ego quieted to the point where it seems that there is no room for the self, then

what are you? More acutely, since 'you' are no longer and silence pervades, whose essence, 'whose silence' have you become?

> Who (be quiet)
> Are you (as these stones
> Are quiet). Do not
> Think of what you are
> Still less of
> What you may one day be.
> Rather
> Be what you are (but who?) be
> The unthinkable one
> You do not know.

Amidst the longing, almost painful desire to confront and push through the 'Who are you?' of the mind, the heart reveals the advice to be quiet, still. It is the same heart that reiterates the fundamental question of the mind further into the poem—and it is at this deeper, more intrinsic level that the self is compelled to a leap of consciousness and of faith. Merton recognizes here that to be still is to fall from time into timelessness through transcending, even suspending, one's thoughts of what the ego is and may become in the future. It is in this void (this desert) that the self unites with God, 'the unthinkable one', who is unknowable outside of this condition.

> O be still, while
> You are still alive,
> And all things around you
> Speaking (I do not hear)
> To your own being,
> Speaking by the Unknown
> That is in you and in themselves.

Exemplified here is Duns Scotus' influence upon Merton, as God, the 'Unknown,' is recognized, if not always acknowledged ('I do not hear'), as permeating all that exists. The pleading voice which opens the stanza is rooted in the fleeting reality of life. At this point the poem is less dispersed in its thrust so that now it verges upon the passionate and ceases to be a purely cognitive function of man. Rather, having fed upon the spiritual desperation of inner blindness wrought by empiricism, it has become a paean to truly live.

> I will try, like them
> To be my own silence:
> And this is difficult. The whole
> World is secretly on fire. The stones
> Burn, even the stones
> They burn me. How can a man be still or
> Listen to all things burning? How can he dare
> To sit with them when All their silence
> Is on fire?

Man, Merton, accepts the challenge to live. More particularly, he assumes the task in the same way as the stones are their own silence. The irony and difficulty lie in the fact that one cannot be silent alone, by oneself, when all things burn. Yet one must become still to be a part of life at this level. This silence is not a simple quietude expressed through a nihilistic violation of life. It is the affirmation of existence on the most vibrant plane, that of the Creator himself. In this realm of silence, the acceptance of one's life is at the same time to be consumed totally, as by fire, in the experience of tapping into this sublime mystery of God. Yet, both the doubt and confusion of rational man surfaces naturally at the contrary state of these affairs; for 'How can a man be still or listen to all things burning?' With the further realization of the magnitude of this dilemma it becomes inconceivable and audacious for man to know God when even 'silence is on fire'; but it is in the flames of all things burning that one sacrifices everything (foremostly the ego) to the Unknown, to God, and then becomes silently alive or, as the poem suggests, 'secretly on fire'.

Finally, in **"Sensation Time at the Home,"** written in the last years of his life but not published until 1977 in the *Collected Poems*, 'the old quiet Merton of the desert' [George Woodcock, in *Thomas Merton: Monk and Poet*] reemerges after partially disappearing in *The Geography of Lograire* and *Cables to the Ace*. 'The Secret' is an unusual piece in that it lacks both the piety and levity of the other examples examined in this paper. It is almost childlike, yet there are contained in its simple lines qualities of the shamanistically arcane. Written in the early hours of the morning, the poem 'occurred all of a sudden' [according to Lentfoehr] and its magic springs forth in like manner.

> Since I am
> Somebody's dream,
> I have a good life.
>
> Sometimes I go away in my sailboat on a cloud
> and take a quiet little trip.
>
> I have a secret
> which I have learned how to read inside myself;
> if I told it to you,
> it would make you laugh.

Life is good for the poet. It is not a dream, nor he merely part of one either. He is a dream belonging to 'Someone' other than himself. As a dream, it is his nature to go on 'quiet little' trips. Who owns this dream? Where does it go when partaking of its gentle excursions? Alas, it is a secret understandable within poet's spirit—the dream. It is a secret that could elicit derisive laughter; but would most likely encourage a loving smile. It depends not upon the dream, or the dreamer (God); but upon the sharer of this secret as to how it is received.

> My heart is naked
> and no one can put clothes on it,
> and nothing can be put on
> that will not immediately fall off.
>
> My secret is ignorant,
> it doesn't sing songs,
> no lie,
> it has nothing to tell you.

Boldly the dream is so pure that it stands as Adam stood, innocent in the light of the Creator. This dream's innocence cannot be lost and nothing can alter its intrinsic quality of goodness as it is indivisible from the Creator. It is here that the dream's secret is revealed as it stands unhidden in its nakedness. Paradoxically, this obvious state 'has nothing to tell anyone', it is 'no lie', and it is dumbly 'ignorant', yet by its elemental purity it doesn't need to 'sing songs' to be heard.

> My two eyes
> are maps of the planet—
> I see everything
> and nothing upsets me.
>
> Just now
> I was in China
> and saw there a great peace of happiness
> that belonged to one man.
>
> And I have been to the center of the earth,
> where there is no suffering.

Eyes have become mirrors, calm topographical settings, upon which is reflected and observed the life throes of creation. The sight penetrates into the deepest finality, seeing 'everything' in its wholeness through the purity of the dream so that nothing 'upsets' the viewer. It is the power of the dream, or rather its nature, that allows it to travel the distances to China (in a 'sailboat on a cloud'), and certainly beyond in order to see so much happiness in one man. This vision is in part a continuation of the dream's secret: that suchness abides in the world if one could but become the dream of the dreamer. As dream is inseparable from the dreamer, so man is inseparable from God and in this realization is the secret's other part: that man need not strive on his own, indeed he cannot, in order to live in bliss. Further defining and affirming this revelation is the poet's journey where there is found no suffering at the center or *axis mundi*.

> If on your loneliest nights,
> I visit other planets
> and the most secret stars of all,
> besides being no one,
> know that I am you
> everybody.

Merton reminds his reader: Even in his solitary escapades to the soul's furthest reaches, he is not to despair though he becomes dissolved in the dreamer's dream. For it is here that man becomes wholly one through God.

> But if I go away
> without giving you a name to remember me
> with,
> how will I find
> the right dream to return to?
>
> You won't have to mark down
> on your calendar that I am coming back;
> don't bother to write me into your notebooks.
> I will be around
> when you aren't thinking about me,
> without hair or a neck,
> without a nose and cheeks
> no reputation—
> there won't be anything.

The body is not lasting, names are not for remembering, and there is no right dream. For there is only 'Somebody's dream' in which there is no departure and no returning and hence where one's travels are timeless. Consequently, there is no need to mark and set aside days for ourselves in this reality as God is always, and what is and was oneself that was and is not God 'won't be anything.' What then was Thomas Merton, this dream of the divine dreamer?

I am a bird
which God made.

George Kilcourse　(essay date 1987)

SOURCE: " 'The Paradise Ear': Thomas Merton, Poet,"
in *The Kentucky Review,* Vol. VII, No. 2, Summer, 1987,
pp. 98-121.

[*In the following excerpt, Kilcourse examines the evolution
of Merton's poetic sensibility by analyzing examples of his
verse from the 1940s through the 1960s.*]

One can effortlessly trace discontinuities of style and poetic maturity between the Merton of the 1940s and the Merton of the 1960s. Most evident are his dependence in the
early poems on similes and an elegant, florid diction. The
writing labors as self-consciously poetic, even imitative of
Donne, Eliot, and others whose metaphysical conceits
Merton envied. Here is an example, from an early verse
entitled **"Poem"**:

　　Light plays like a radio in the iron tree;
　　Green farms fear the night behind me
　　Where lightenings race across the western
　　　world.

　　Life, like a woman in the moving wheat,
　　Runs from the staring sky
　　That bends upon the earth like a reflector.

Or, another selection, from **"The Greek Women"**:

　　The ladies in red capes and gold bracelets
　　Walk like reeds and talk like rivers,
　　And sigh, like Vichy water, in the doorways;

　　　　　. . . . .

　　And, opening their eyes wide as horizons,
　　Seem to await the navy home from Troy.

Rather than personify, Merton's images and symbols collapse into abstractions in the early poems. He frequents
the theme of the world's wickedness, pyrotechnic images
contrasting starkly with the halcyon monastic refuge. Ur-
banscapes grate and force violent images of decay and
moral torpor. **"In the Ruins of New York"** portrays such
a simplistic contrast in this passage:

　　Oh how quiet it is after the black night
　　When flames out of the clouds burned down
　　　your cariated teeth,
　　And when those lightenings,
　　Lancing the black boils of Harlem and the
　　　Bronx,
　　Spilled the remaining prisoners,
　　(The tens and twenties of the living)
　　Into the trees of Jersey,
　　To the green farms, to find their liberty.

Antitheses remain taut in the imagery: black-white, dark-
ness-light, prisoner-freedom, urban-pastoral, earth-sky;
Merton sometimes successfully cultivates the tension of
these and other pairings as in the haunting "black girls"-
"white girls" imagery from **"Song for Our Lady of
Cobre,"** written spontaneously during his Cuban trip; or
the moving starkness of tense images of transformation in
the poem, less self-conscious and spontaneous, occasioned

by his brother's death in World War II, **"For My Brother,
Reported Missing in Action, 1943"**:

　　Sweet brother, if I do not sleep
　　My eyes are flowers for your tomb;
　　And if I cannot eat my bread,
　　My fasts shall live like willows where you died.
　　If in the heat I find no water for my thirst,
　　My thirst shall turn to springs for you, poor
　　　traveller.

Here Merton trusts the direct metaphor. And a natural
rhythm reinforces the poet's hope, through the density of
an apocalyptic evil: "In the wreckage of your April Christ
lies slain." Once again, Merton's poetic gifts thrived under
the pressure of autobiography and the poet's interpretive
rendering of experience.

Themes of alienation, exile, solitude, freedom, and the
identity/illusion quandary characterize Merton's poetry
of the 1940s. There is no decided breakthrough or season-
ing of the young poet—though his obvious gift with metaphor and imagery and diction auditions, as Eliot well
dubbed it, "hit or miss." At his worst, the early poet Merton writes sentimental, romantic poems, stylistically
clumsy and burdened with an ideology of monasticism
that spurns the world and hurls invectives in his wake.

Anthony Padovano's careful and literate interpretation of
Merton, *The Human Journey,* incorporates analyses of the
poetry to an extent unrivalled by the studies of any other
scholar. Padovano outlines a key critical insight into Merton:

　　His prose never registered the changes [in his
　　life] as radically as did his poetry. His poetry was
　　often the barometer of his soul. In the younger
　　days, it was lyrical and free; in the middle years,
　　passionate and angry; at the end, cosmic and vi-
　　sionary.

The sole volume of verse in the 1950s, *The Strange Islands*
(1957), found a lengthy morality play, *The Tower of
Babel,* crowding its pages. However, indications of a
leaner, more pruned and direct style, concrete images, and
even new irony are evident in Merton's imagination.
"Landscape," "In Silence," "Stranger," and **"Elegy for
the Monastery Barn"** stand welcome if awkwardly beside
the stale Merton style of the 1940s. By the time of *Emblems of a Season of Fury* (1963), the discontinuity in
style and theme proved irreversible for Merton. There ra-
diates a Zen-like concreteness and sense of paradox in the
poem, **"Song for Nobody"** that remains vintage Merton.

　　A yellow flower
　　(Light and Spirit)
　　Sings by itself
　　For nobody
　　A golden spirit
　　(Light and emptiness)
　　Sings without a word
　　By itself.

　　Let no one touch this gentle sun
　　In whose dark eye
　　Someone is awake.

　　(No light, no gold, no name, no color

And no thought:
O, wide awake!)

A golden heaven
Sings by itself
A song to nobody.

George Woodcock's earlier study, *Thomas Merton: Monk and Poet,* has employed a useful distinction in dividing Merton's poems into "choir" and "desert" poetry. In the main, this division serves to characterize the poetry of the two periods we are considering. It also reflects the two discontinuous monastic stances Merton adopted. What Woodcock's dichotomy suggests, however, is a lack of continuity throughout Merton's poetry that overlooks a deeper coherence. I do not wish to overstate this argument, nor do I intend to neglect it. Several illustrations will suffice.

In both his prose and poetry Merton clusters a complex of images symbolizing true contemplation. In the 1949 classic volume, *Seeds of Contemplation,* he quickly volunteers, "hell is perpetual alienation from the true self." Spiritual awakening and maturity involves the loss of a false self, the ego or empirical self, the illusion, the mask, or superficial consciousness. In turn, the true self or authentic identity of the person breathes freely after the spiritual ordeal, or ongoing process, has been engaged. In the concluding pages of the 1961 revision of that same volume, *New Seeds of Contemplation,* Merton offers an antidote to the narcotic of life without contemplative depth. He calls it the innocence of "paradise consciousness":

> When we are alone on a starlit night; when by chance we see the migrating birds in autumn descending on a grove of junipers to rest and eat; when we see children in a moment when they are really children; when we know love in our own hearts; or when, like the Japanese poet Basho, we hear an old frog land in a quiet pond with a solitary splash—at such times the awakening, the turning inside out of all values, the "newness," the emptiness and the purity of vision that make themselves evident, provide a glimpse of the cosmic dance.

Three poems spanning the canon of Merton's poetry evidence his use of the child's innocence to symbolize this awakening and spiritual integrity. The first, **"Aubade: Lake Erie"** (*Thirty Poems*), reminisces autobiographically about the vineyards on Lake Erie, "an artificial France":

> Awake, in the frames of the windows, innocent
>   children
> Loving the blue, sprayed leaves of childish life,
> Applaud the ˙ bearded corn, the bleeding
>   grape. . . .

Their dawn rising, "when their shining voices, clean as summer, / Play, like church bells over the field," summons the "hitchhiking" hoboes who fail to heed or see the morning sun as "our marvelous cousin." These aliens, homeless vagabonds, "grope, in the green wheat, / Toward the wood winds of the western freight." Unlike the children, they fail to celebrate or even to imagine the eu-

charistic images Merton discretely weaves through the imagery.

Merton's identification of the child's imaginative life as more real than adult exile appears again in **"Dirge for a Town in France"** (*A Man in the Divided Sea*). Here he constructs a stronger metaphor for childhood, the carousel:

> O, it is not those first, faint stars
> Whose fair light, falling, whispers in the river;
> And it is not the dusty wind,
> Waving the waterskirts of the shy-talking fountain,
>
> That wakes the wooden horses' orchestra,
> The fifing goldfinch, and the phony flutes,
> And the steam robins and electric nightingales
> That blurred the ding of cymbals,
> That other time when childhood turned and
>   turned
> As grave as sculpture in a zodiac.

The image of "wakeful" childhood innocence, the imaginative response as a more real response than the adult capitulation, finds a successful, stark contrast.

> But the men die, down in the shadowy doors,
> The way their thoughts die in their eyes,
> To see those sad and funny children
> Run down the colonnade of trees
> Where the carnival doesn't exist:
>
> Those children, who are lost too soon,
> With fading laughter, on the road along the
>   river:
> Gone, like the slowing cavalcade, the homeward
>   horses.

Interestingly, the poet identifies the women (mothers) of the town, perched on the "one-time finery of iron, suburban balconies," akin to the child's innocent response to reality and the sacramental flowers: "The roses and mimosas in the windows / Adore the night they breathe, not understanding."

In **"Grace's House"** (*Emblems of a Season of Fury*) Merton achieves his most symbolic treatment of the consciousness of paradise. The poem was occasioned by a child's (a real Grace) sending him a drawing of her home. It is archetypal:

> On the summit: it stands on a fair summit
> Prepared by winds: and solid smoke
> Rolls from the chimney like a snow cloud.
> Grace's house is secure.
> No blade of grass is not counted,
> No blade of grass forgotten on this hill.
> Twelve flowers make a token garden.
> There is no path to the summit—
> No path drawn
> To Grace's house.

There is now a Zen-like wakefulness in the child's vantage at the window:

> All the curtains are arranged
> Not for hiding but for seeing out.
> In one window someone looks out and winks.
> Two gnarled short

Fortified trees have knotholes
From which to look out.
From behind a corner of Grace's house
Another creature peeks out.

And the poem ends reiterating that, "Alas, there is no road to Grace's house."

Other examples, often with the vantage from a window, of this unself-conscious spiritual wakefulness imaged through the child—but distorted by the adult—can be found in poems such as **"The Winter's Night"** (***Thirty Poems***), **"Birdcage Walk"** (***The Strange Islands***), and **"Macarius and the Pony"** (***Emblems of a Season of Fury***).

Before turning to a necessarily cursory glance at Merton's antipoetry of 1967 and 1968, I call attention to an observation made by John Eudes Bamberger, a Cistercian abbot in New York state and a Gethsemani companion and former student of Merton. It pertains directly to the explication of these poems.

> I think that for Thomas Merton the experience of being forgiven by God was one of his deepest experiences. It wouldn't appear normally because usually he gave the impression of being a rather carefree, happy-go-lucky, freewheeling type of person. But, when you knew him well, there always was this awareness that he had been very bad off at one time. . . . It is a fact that quite early he was all but homeless for all practical purposes and that prior to entering the monastery he felt he had lost what was best in his life, his human innocence. . . . And somehow he was able, because of the experience of God, to believe that God had recreated his innocence.

[In "The Crossroads of Myth and Irony: Thomas Merton's 'Change of Address,'" *Cithara* 20 (1981):15-23] I have proposed that Merton's final, sustained poems, *Cables to the Ace* and *The Geography of Lograire,* demonstrate the mature range of his imagination by irony and the forms of antipoetry. These mosaics, as he called both collections, were invented to achieve the marginal monk's task of saving the post-Christian world from its spiritual inertia. Their satire and parody achieve the "wakefulness" of Merton's earlier poems, although now the poet shakes us from the nightmare of our contemporary world's depersonalizing anesthesia.

Again and again the poetic process summons an authentic communication with the deepest self and other solitudes. "Decode your own scrambled message," Merton prescribes in **"Miami You Are About to be Surprised"** (***Geography of Lograire***). In a universal structure of south, north, east, and west cantos, Merton moves from autobiographical self-interpretation through the irony of Cargo cults and Ghost Dances of Third World cultures desperate for myth and ritual, to interpret meaning out of their disintegrating cultures. Unfinished and rough as Merton's transformation of diverse sources proves to be, the real geography he explores is the inner self and the seduction of the false, superficial, illusory self. It marks the apex of his poetic power to recreate our innocence, interpersonally and as a global culture.

While Merton referred to ***The Geography of Lograire*** as "my summa of offbeat anthropology," his ***Cables to the Ace*** collection achieves a significant effect in its own right as spiritual wakefulness and innocence. It is only the marginal monk who can recognize communication gone amok in the advertising age's images—images that neutralize and seduce us. Thus, Merton's parody of the Marlboro pages of a magazine provides a devastating invitation to look again:

> I will get up and go to Marble country
> Where deadly smokes grow out of moderate heat
> And all the cowboys look for fortunate slogans
> Among horses asses.
>
> (*Collected Poems*)

But hope strides through the closing ruins of the poem. Here is one of the several prayers and epiphanies that punctuate the poem which Merton ironically subtitles, **"Familiar Liturgies of Misunderstanding."**

> Slowly, slowly
> Comes Christ through the garden
> Speaking to the sacred trees
> Their branches bear his light
> Without harm.
>
> (*Collected Poems*)

The abusers of language, from Caliban, the cursing antihero borrowed from Shakespeare, to the newscaster whose cadenced babble Merton brilliantly parodies in a breathless nonsense staccato symbolizing our immunity to communication, all mistake the Advent of the Word in history. The Edenic garden recalls the innocence of paradise, the spiritual wakefulness again compromised. In n. 78 [of ***Collected Poems***] Merton has mirrored and recollected his own imaginative persona in an irrepressible hope. The poem was written in 1966, during his affair with a young nurse.

> Love's wreckage is then left to lie
> All around the breathless shores
> Of my voice
> Which on the coasts of larking meadows
> Invented all these and their mischievous noises
>
> So those lovers teach April stars
> To riot rebel and follow faithless courses
> And it doesn't matter
> The seed is not afraid
> Of winter or the terrible sweetness
> Of spring's convivial nightmare
> Or the hot surprise and dizzy spark
> Of their electric promise
>
> For the lovers in the sleeping nerve
> Are the hope and the address
> Where I send you this burning garden
> My talkative morning-glory
> My climbing germ of poems.
>
> (*Collected Poems*)

The biographer Michael Mott has remarked of Thomas Merton's progress in the arena of literary criticism that "he changed from an occasional reviewer to a critic. . . ." At one point Merton openly named his method "sapiential," a sophianic or wisdom approach germane to monastic culture. This heightened critical power coincided with the hermitage years, years in which he read with-

out interruption and wrote porous essays on the hidden levels of truth in the fictional models of Faulkner, Camus,
and Flannery O'Connor, and explored the writing of
Walker Percy. His weekly conferences with the novices
and other monks dating from All Hallow's Eve 1964
through late November 1966 are preoccupied with poetry
and literary theory and expositions of the work of favorites: Eliot, Peguy, Auden, Blake, Hopkins, Rilke, and
Edwin Muir.

While it would be mistaken to portray Merton as a *systematic* literary theorist or critic, one can trace an inchoate
theory in the later period. In the context of his entire career, this development affords an additional perspective to
appreciate and critically assess his own poetry. During the
voluntary embargo on his writing of poetry in the 1950s,
Merton ventured to survey the Psalms in a volume of
1953, *Bread in the Wilderness.* One of his earliest and most
promising essays on poetic theory, it suggests an interest
in the Psalms as poetry and in poetic form as a part of the
Revelation communicated by the Psalmist. Of immediate
interest is an image Merton employs to typify the poet's
vision of the objective, "given" world. The parallels between the original person in Creation (paradise) and the
poet are characteristic of Merton. Created nature, he says,
has been given to man as a clean "window." The Fall symbolically renders it opaque so that we no longer view the
transparency or, more strictly, translucency, of all things
to the light of God. Human persons suffer an inability to
penetrate the meaning of the world in which we live.
Myths and symbols degenerate.

Merton renders this "corruption of cosmic symbolism"
analogous to the dilemma of the poet in a room with his
window the dominant medium of vision. As daylight prevails he sees through the window pane, clearly perceiving
the objective, symbolic world, and through it, God. With
nightfall, however, he maintains an ability to see through
the window to the outside only as long as there is no light
in the room. The problem begins when our lights go on,
"Then we see only ourselves and our own room reflected
in the pane." An immense part of reality, Merton warns,
is lost, abandoned in the process. The poet loses the rich,
symbolic character of the world outside his window. The
poet is no longer able to image the "world beyond." The
poet becomes absorbed in the self's reflections in the window. "They began to worship what they themselves were
doing," Merton announces, and it was "too often an
abomination." Nature was no longer symbol but illusion.
These coordinates of Merton's own poetics—the window
as symbol, paradise consciousness, and an objective theory
of art—map the geography of Merton's poetry.

His abilities and talents as a teacher equipped Merton to
initiate the younger monks at the abbey into the subtleties
of poetry. Fortunately, tape recordings of these enthused
classes survive to complement the fragments of critical
theory scattered throughout his loosely collected essays,
published in various books.

Like his sometime mentor, Jacques Maritain, Merton
would affirm that "Nature is all the more beautiful as it
is laden with emotion. Emotion is essential in the perception of beauty." However, there is an appropriate mode

for poetry to communicate emotion. A poet is successful
to the degree that he offers his readers objective correla-
tives (images, symbols) that specify his emotions. In recreating that perception of reality, the reader has no other
medium than the poem itself. "A great poet gives you a
poem," Merton says, "which stands on its own right and
which is real; a reality that speaks of this encounter with
life." Conversely, "A less great poet tells you how he feels
about it."

Merton would turn repeatedly to Rilke throughout these
lectures. He described him as the poet of *innerlichkeit,* in-
wardness or interiority. He reports on the "poetic phenomenology of the innocent 'out-gazing' proper to the
child, against which the child is systematically educated."
In his zoo poems (e. g., "The Panther," a particular Merton favorite) Rilke, Merton points out, reports that "the
animal simply 'gazes out' without any consciousness of a
center which gazes." He turns to the *Duino Elegies* and
comments on the child being taught "to 'be opposite,' to
stand against objects, and to be never anything else but a
subject confronting object." We have a unique published
Merton comment on Rilke in a few pages of *Mystics and
Zen Masters* that develops Rilke's poetic sensibility in a
contrast of the Western mystical tradition and Zen:

Merton in his late forties.

The pure consciousness (as also the apophatic mystical intuition) does not look *at* things, and does not ignore them, annihilate them, negate them. It accepts them fully, in complete oneness with them. It looks "out of them," as though fulfilling the role of consciousness not for itself only but *for them also*. This is certainly a deep spiritual insight on the part of Rilke. The "outgazing" of this *Duino Elegy* throws important light on the characteristic Rilkean "inseeing" (*Einsehen*). In-seeing implies identification, in which, according to Rilke's normal poetic consciousness, the subject is aware of itself as having penetrated by poetic empathy into the heart of the object and being united with it.

While translating South American poets Merton discovered the work of Cesar Vallejo. It was evident that here he contacted another "solitude," another "marginal existence" kindred to himself. Beneath the superlatives (a characteristic fault of Merton's enthusiasm) he directed an encomium to Vallejo's identity as the "universal, Catholic . . . poet of this time."

> So what I mean is that Vallejo is totally human as opposed to our zombie poets and our little girl poets and our incontinents. I have never really thought out all that must begin to be said about Vallejo, but he is tremendous and extraordinary, a huge phenomenon, so much more magnificent (in the classical sense) than Neruda, precisely because he is in every way poorer. No matter what they do with Vallejo, they can never get him into anybody's establishment.

No surprise that Merton had immersed himself in the Spanish and Portuguese-speaking poets of Latin America. Two essays in *Raids on the Unspeakable* record his solidarity with and debt to their work. In part, these discussions are attempts to reformulate a theory of poetry. They refine and make emphatic Merton's own poetics. The second of the two essays, first published in 1965, is "Answers on Art and Freedom." In it, the autonomy of the artist, the "useless"-ness of the poet's work, Merton insists, must never be compromised. He protests both censorship and propaganda (even didactic or moral theories) in art, particularly poetry. Merton here reclaims his objective theory of art.

The better-known first essay, seven pages of vintage Merton, is "Message to Poets." "We who are poets know the reason for a poem is not discovered until the poem itself exists," he opens. He applauds the hope and "new fire" exhibited by the young Latin American poets, whose solidarity is "not in tutelage to established political systems or cultural structures." The spontaneity of their meeting (February 1964 in Mexico City) Merton attributes to an innocence on which the artist depends; it is a matter of "interior personal conviction 'in the spirit,' " a "belief" that roots "in fidelity to life rather than to artificial systems."

The prophetic and poetic functions merge once again for Merton in forwarding a spirit of hopefulness. Prophecy he recommends above derision, for "to prophesy is not to predict but to seize upon reality in its moment of highest expectation and tension toward the new." The poet's dis-

covery of this in ordinary existence gives birth to a lyric definition of poetry:

> Poetry is the flowering of ordinary possibilities.
> It is the fruit of ordinary and natural choice.
> This is its innocence and dignity.
>
> . . . . .
>
> Let us obey life, and the Spirit of Life that calls us to be poets, and we shall harvest many new fruits for which the world hungers—fruits of hope that have never been seen before. With these fruits we shall calm the resentments and the rage of man.

Merton's related description of the poets as dervishes suggests the ecstasy they bring into the form and structure of words, the "poem itself" that comes into existence. Merton goes on to describe the poets' "Heraclitean river which is never crossed twice":

> When the poet puts his foot in that ever-moving river, poetry itself is born out of the flashing water. In that very instant, the truth is manifest to all who are able to receive it.
>
> No one can come near the river unless he walks on his own feet. He cannot come there carried in a vehicle.
>
> No one can enter the river wearing the garments of public and collective ideas. He must feel the water on his skin. He must know that immediacy is for naked minds only and for the innocent.

This bears an unmistakable echo of "the uncrossed crystal / Water between our ignorance and her truth" in the poem **"Grace's House."**

Finally, in 1966 Merton sketched some enduring vectors for his poetics when he wrote a salient critical review of Louis Zukofsky's *Collected Short Poems, 1956-64.* In Zukofsky, Merton remarks the "chaste and sparing" use of language. The sound of the music actually leads him to structure "the ideas musically instead of logically"—which communicates more meaning than mere words; "so much so that it cannot be broken down easily into concepts and the poem has to be respected, left alone, only to be read over and over." The fully mature, sophisticated, and difficult poetry of Zukofsky, Merton points out, is made up of the "language of children"—"the language of everyday becomes charged with expectations—the language of paradise."

It is this complete acceptance of the *"whole thing"* that one must hear with "the paradise ear," Merton insists. Zukofsky's childlike attitude he analyzes as "the unlimited curious senses of confused anticipation which is the stuff of ordinary life." And, likewise, this anticipation is "aware of itself as a question that does not provoke an answer to dispose of it." In effect, "each poem is very much the same question but brand new." Zukofsky had understood uniquely the reality of the question, Merton surmises, "because here is a poet who has the patience and the good sense to listen." Merton centers the critical commentary on an imaginative summary of "the paradise ear":

All really valid poetry (poetry that is fully alive, and asserts its reality by its power to generate imaginative life) is a kind of recovery of paradise. Not that the poet comes up with a report that he, an unusual man, has found his own way back into Eden; but the living line and the generative association, the new sound, the music, the structure, are somehow grounded in a renewal of vision and hearing so that he who reads and understands recognizes that here is a new start, a new creation.

A brief appreciation of Thomas Merton, poet, cannot presume to explore all the dimensions of this multifaceted, talented person; but it can invite both Merton scholars and readers to include more thoughtfully this dimension of the integral Merton in their study. I dare to envision Merton studies venturing beyond the plateau of these nearly twenty years of significant and valuable theological and spiritual investigations. A truly interdisciplinary scrutiny of his mature writings awaits. The poetry offers, Merton would have said, with precious veins of metaphor and symbol, the "wrought passion" of his artist's gifts. To possess them, we must follow his advice:

> To go down alone
> Into the night sky
> Hand over hand
> And dig it like a mine.

> *(Cables to the Ace)*

FURTHER READING

Bibliography

Breit, Marquita, ed. *Thomas Merton: A Bibliography*. Metuchen, N.J.: The Scarecrow Press, 1974, 180 p.
    A comprehensive bibliography of primary and secondary materials on Merton's life and works.

Biography

Furlong, Monica. *Merton: A Biography*. San Francisco: Harper & Row, 1980, 342 p.
    Attempts to reconcile conflicting impressions of Merton's life. Furlong asserts: "I have avoided the reverential approach, have tried to see him as the normal man he was."

Lawlor, Patrick T. "Poet to Teacher: Thomas Merton's Letters to Mark Van Doren." *Columbia Library Columns* XXXIX, No. 1 (November 1989): 18-30.

Discusses Merton's friendship and correspondence with poet and educator Mark Van Doren.

McInerny, Dennis Q. *Thomas Merton: The Man and His Work*. Washington, D.C.: Consortium Press, 1974, 128 p.
    Biographical introduction to Merton's life and writings.

Mott, Michael. *The Seven Mountains of Thomas Merton*. Boston: Houghton Mifflin Company, 1984, 690 p.
    Widely considered the most complete biography of Merton.

Wilkes, Paul, ed. *Merton: By Those Who Knew Him Best*. San Francisco: Harper & Row, 1984, 171 p.
    Presents biographical commentary by Merton's closest friends and acquaintances including Ernesto Cardenal, Joan Baez, and Robert Lax.

Criticism

Glimm, James York. "Thomas Merton's Last Poem: 'The Geography of Lograire'." *Renascence* (Winter 1974): 95-104.
    Discusses Merton's criticism of Western culture in *The Geography of Lograire*.

Irwin, John T. Review of *The Geography of Lograire*, by Thomas Merton. *Sewanee Review* LXXXI, No. 1 (Winter 1973): 164-66.
    Argues that "*The Geography of Lograire* should not be judged as a single long poem or even as a collection of poems. It is best appreciated as an imaginative commonplace book."

The Kentucky Review: A Thomas Merton Symposium VII, No. 2 (Summer 1987).
    Special issue featuring biographical and critical commentary on Merton.

McDowell, Robert. Review of *Collected Poems*, by Thomas Merton. *The Hudson Review* XXXI, No. 2 (Summer 1978) 381-82.
    Positive review of *Collected Poems*.

Sutton, Walter. "Thomas Merton and the American Epic Tradition: The Last Poems." *Contemporary Literature* 14, No. 1 (Winter 1973): 49-57.
    Discusses Merton's use of satire in *Cables to the Ace* and *The Geography of Lograire*.

Woodcock, George. *Thomas Merton, Monk and Poet: A Critical Study*. Vancouver: Douglas & McIntyre, 200 p.
    Examines Merton's writings in the context of the diverse roles he assumed during his life.

Alexander Pushkin

1799-1837

(Full name Alexander Sergeyevich Pushkin; also transliterated as Pushchkin, Púshkin, Pouchkin, Poushkin, Púskin, Pùshkin, Puškin) Russian poet, dramatist, short story writer, novelist, essayist, and critic.

INTRODUCTION

Pushkin is as significant to Russian culture as William Shakespeare is to English. Emphasizing the simplicity and beauty of his native tongue, Pushkin transformed Russian literary language and helped Russian literature to escape the domination of eighteenth-century European classicism. Known primarily for his narrative poems, particularly *Yevgeny Onegin* (1833; *Eugene Onegin*) and *Medny vsadnik* (1837; *The Bronze Horseman*), Pushkin absorbed many of the structural and stylistic characteristics of European writers—notably François Voltaire, Lord Byron, Shakespeare, and Sir Walter Scott—and recast them in a uniquely Russian mold. Pushkin's works exhibit a universality of theme and human emotion which Fyodor Dostoevsky proclaimed as the essence of the Russian people and Russian art.

Biographical Information

Pushkin was born in Moscow in 1799. An aristocrat by birth, he was proud of his ancestors, particularly his maternal great-grandfather, Abram Petrovich Hannibal, a Moorish noble who had been kidnapped from Africa, taken to Russia, and later made a ward of Peter the Great. Pushkin grew up in a social setting heavily influenced by French culture, and he became familiar at an early age with the classic works of French literature from the seventeenth and eighteenth centuries. As a child, he developed a close relationship to his nurse Arina, who told him fairy tales and folk legends, which he later incorporated into such works as *Ruslan i Lyudmila* (1820; *Ruslan and Lyudmila*) and *Skazki* (1834). In 1811 he was sent to the government lycée at Tsarskoe Selo, where he excelled in the study of French and Russian literature and wrote prolifically. At an examination in 1815 he recited his poem "Vospominanie v Tsarskom Sele" ("Remembrance in Tsarskoe Selo") before Gavril Derzhavin, one of the leading Russian poets of the day, who was greatly impressed with Pushkin's work. After graduating in 1817, Pushkin was appointed to the Ministry of Foreign Affairs and assigned to St. Petersburg. There he alternated between periods of reckless dissipation and intense writing, finishing his first full-length work, *Ruslan and Lyudmila*, in 1820. Just prior to its publication, however, Czar Alexander I exiled Pushkin to southern Russia for the allegedly revolutionary political sentiments expressed in his poetry. (Censorship would remain a lifelong problem; even after Nicholas I appointed himself the poet's personal censor, Push-

kin remained under strict observation, forbidden to travel freely or leave Russia.) During the first four years of his six-year exile, he retained his civil service position and lived in various towns in the Caucasus and Crimea. Despite bouts of gambling and drinking, he was productive during his years in southern Russia, writing, among other works, *Kavkazski plennik* (1822; *The Captive of the Caucasus*), *Bakhchisaraiski fontan* (1824; *The Bak-chesarian Fountain*), and much of *Tsygany* (1827; *The Gypsies*). On the recommendation of his superior, with whose wife he had been having an affair, Pushkin was dismissed from the civil service in 1824 and placed under the direct supervision of his father at the family estate of Mikhailovskoye. Two years later, Nicholas I pardoned Pushkin, formally ending his exile. For the remainder of his life Pushkin resided primarily in St. Petersburg. He married Natalia Nikolaevna Goncharova in 1831 and also completed *Eugene Onegin*, which was not published in its entirety until 1833. During the later part of his career, he wrote substantially less poetry, devoting his efforts instead to short stories and novellas. In 1837 he was mortally wounded in a duel with George d'Anthès, an Alsatian nobleman who was openly courting Pushkin's wife. The poet died two days later.

Major Works

Considered chronologically, Pushkin's poetry, which diverges widely in style and subject matter, reflects the evolution of his artistic maturity as well as the development of his personal philosophy. However, despite the varied nature of his works, several recurring themes, namely those of personal freedom, power, and religion, lend his poetical oeuvre a sense of unity. Critics generally divide Pushkin's works into three periods. His early works, those written before his exile, include the narrative poem *Ruslan and Lyudmila*—a comic epic which celebrates freedom and love as it addresses the theme of youth coming to maturity—and numerous shorter poems, most of which were never published because of the bold attitudes he expressed concerning erotic love, politics, and religion. His "Vol'nost': Oda" ("Ode to Liberty"), for example, suggests that monarchs do not possess divine right and that tyrannical abuses of power will lead to retribution from one's subjects. The second period in Pushkin's career roughly parallels his exile in southern Russia and at Mikhailovskoye. Two of his narrative poems from this period, *The Captive of the Caucasus*—which contrasts civilized and primitive cultures as it addresses themes of the individual versus society—and *The Bak-chesarian Fountain*—which treats envy and jealousy—reveal the extensive influence of Lord Byron in terms of technique, character, and structure. With *The Gypsies*, however, Pushkin's work exhibits a distinct break with the Byronic method of his earlier efforts, and many critics consider it the principal forerunner of his mature work. Concerned with problems of freedom, fate, and destiny, the poem is structurally sound, unlike his earlier poems, and forces the reader to make a moral judgment on dilemmas inherent in the narrative rather than simply sharing in the emotions of the protagonist. Of Pushkin's poems on religious themes *Gavriiliada* (1821; *Gavriliada*) is the most infamous for its treatment of the Immaculate Conception as a love intrigue involving Mary, Satan, the angel Gabriel, and God. Pushkin's religious philosophies, however, underwent radical transformation during the 1820s, as evidenced by such poems as "Zhil na svete rytsar' bednyi" ("There Was a Poor Knight"), which presents a wholly opposite view of Mary, and "Demon" ("The Demon"), which indicts the atheistic, cynical, and skeptical worldview of French Rationalism. The principle poems from the last period of his career are his most enduring works, *Eugene Onegin* and *The Bronze Horseman*. Described as a novel in verse, *Eugene Onegin* was written over an eight year period (1823-31) and is a story of twice-rejected love set against a detailed picture of Russian life in the early nineteenth century. Though the plot of *Eugene Onegin* is relatively simple, its style and narrative method are considered exceedingly complex, and the work has elicited a variety of interpretations, with critics describing it variously as a brilliant lyrical poem, an autobiography, or a parody of the creative process. *The Bronze Horseman* contrasts the omnipotence of Peter the Great with the helplessness of the protagonist, who is symbolic of the masses sacrificed for the construction of St. Petersburg—the capital city built on the site of a swamp at Peter's command—and the glory of imperial Russia. The poem also addresses several other themes through juxtaposition, including: Slavophilism versus Westernization, paganism versus Christianity, and humankind versus nature.

Critical Reception

Pushkin is considered by many critics the greatest and most influential Russian writer. Despite such claims, however, his works are rarely read in foreign countries because his superlative style virtually defies translation. His influence, though, is evident in the more widely known works of such Russians as Dostoevsky, Leo Tolstoy, Ivan Turgenev, and Nikolai Gogol, each of whom acknowledged his debt to Pushkin. As many commentators have noted, *Eugene Onegin*'s realistic presentation of scene and character provided the model for the modern Russian novel. In assessing Pushkin's works, commentators have generally lamented the early influence of Byron but have praised Pushkin's imaginative understanding of human character and his ability to maintain the universality of his themes despite the distinctly Russian context of his work. Scholars have also remarked on Pushkin's immense impact on Russian culture. Noted nineteenth-century Russian philosopher and writer Alexander Herzen said of him: "As soon as he appeared he became necessary, as though Russian literature could never again dispense with him. The other Russian poets are read and admired; Pushkin is in the hands of every civilized Russian, who reads him again and again all his life long."

PRINCIPAL WORKS

Poetry

Ruslan i Lyudmila [*Ruslan and Lyudmila*] 1820
*Gavriiliada [*Gavriliada*] 1821
Kavkazski plennik [*The Captive of the Caucasus*] 1822
Bakhchisaraiski fontan [*The Bak-chesarian Fountain*] 1824
Stansy 1826
Bratya razboiniki [*The Robber Brothers*] 1827
Graf Nulin [*Count Nulin*] 1827
Tsygany [*The Gypsies*] 1827
Poltava [*Poltava*] 1829
Domik v Kolomne [*The Little House in Kolomna*] 1833
Yevgeny Onegin [*Eugene Onegin*] 1833
Skazki 1834
Medny vsadnik [*The Bronze Horseman*] 1837
Pushkin's Poems 1945

Other Major Works

Boris Godunov [*Boris Godunoff*] [first publication] (drama) 1831
†*Motsart i Sal'eri* [*Mozart and Salieri*] [first publication] (drama) 1831
Povesti Belkina [*The Tales of Belkin*] (short stories) 1831
†*Pir vo vremya chumy* [*A Feast during the Plague*] [first publication] (drama) 1832

Pikovaya dama [*The Queen of Spades*] (novella) 1834

Istoriya Pugacheva (history) 1835

Kapitanskaya dochka [*The Captain's Daughter*] (novella) 1836

Puteshestvie v Arzrum [*A Journey to Arzrum*] (travel essay) 1836

†*Skupoi rytsar* [*The Covetous Knight*] [first publication] (drama) 1836

Arap Petra Velikogo [*The Negro of Peter the Great*] (unfinished novel) 1837

Istoriya sela Goryukhina [*History of the Village of Goryukhina*] (unfinished novel) 1837

†*Kammeny gost* [*The Stone Guest*] [first publication] (drama) 1839

Dubrovski [*Dubrovsky*] (unfinished novel) 1841

Rusalka [*The Water Nymph*] [first publication] (unfinished drama) 1841

Table Talk (essays) 1857

The Letters of Alexander Pushkin. 2 vols. (letters) 1963

The Critical Prose of Alexander Pushkin (criticism) 1969

Pushkin on Literature (letters, journals, and essays) 1971

*This work was circulated widely in manuscript form but never published by Pushkin.

†These works are collectively referred to as "The Little Tragedies."

CRITICISM

Ivan Kireevsky (essay date 1828)

SOURCE: "On the Nature of Pushkin's Poetry," in *Literature and National Identity: Nineteenth-Century Russian Critical Essays,* edited and translated by Paul Debreczeny and Jesse Zeldin, University of Nebraska Press, 1970, pp. 3-16.

[*In the following excerpt from an essay that was originally published as "Nechto o kharaktere poezii Pushkina" in the journal* Moskovsky vestnik, *Kireevsky remarks on Pushkin's development as a poet and the influence of Lord Byron's works on Pushkin's poetry.*]

Accounting for the pleasure works of art give us is both an indispensable requirement of, and one of the highest gratifications for, the educated mind: why then has so little been said about Pushkin? Why have his best works been left unexamined, and why do we hear, instead of analysis and judgment, only fatuous exclamations: "Pushkin is a poet! Pushkin is a real poet! *Onegin* is a superb poem! *The Gypsies* is a masterly work," and so forth? Why has no one so far ventured to define the over-all nature of his poetry, to appraise its merits and faults, and to determine what rank our poet has succeeded in acquiring among the leading poets of his time? . . .

When speaking about Pushkin . . . it is difficult to express

one's opinion resolutely; it is difficult to bring the diversity of his works into focus and to find a general criterion for the nature of his poetry, which has taken on so many different shapes. For, excepting the beauty and originality of their poetic language, what traces of common origin do we find in *Ruslan and Liudmila, The Prisoner of the Caucasus, Onegin, The Gypsies,* and so forth? Not only is each of these narrative poems different from the others in its plot development and in its manner of narration (*la manière*), but some of them differ in their very nature, reflecting diverse views of the world by the poet, so much so that in translation it would be easy to take them for works, not of one, but of several authors. The light humor—a child of gaiety and wit—which in *Ruslan and Liudmila* dresses all objects in sparkling colors, is no longer to be encountered in the poet's other works. In *Onegin,* its place is taken by scathing mockery—an echo of a skepticism of the heart. Good-natured gaiety has here changed into a dismal coldness which regards all objects through the dark veil of doubt, conveys its observations through caricature, and creates only in order to revel in the imminent destruction of its creature. In *The Prisoner of the Caucasus,* on the other hand, we find neither the trust in fate which vivified *Ruslan,* nor the contempt for human beings that we remark in *Onegin.* Here we see a soul embittered by treason and loss, yet one that has still not betrayed itself, nor lost the freshness of its former sensations; one still faithful to its sacred inclinations. It is a soul maimed but not conquered by fate; the outcome of the struggle is still a question of the future. In the narrative poem *The Gypsies,* the nature of the poetry is again unique, different from Pushkin's other narrative poems, and the same can be said about almost every one of his major works.

Yet after a careful perusal of Pushkin's works, from *Ruslan and Liudmila* to chapter five of *Onegin,* [In a footnote the translator states: "Only five chapters had been published at the time Kireevsky was writing his review."] we find that his poetry—with all its meandering course—has had three periods of development, each of which differs sharply from the others. We shall attempt to define the distinctive feature and content of each of these, and then draw broad conclusions about Pushkin's poetry in general. . . .

I would call the first period of Pushkin's poetry, that including *Ruslan* and some minor lyrics, the period of the *Italian-French School.* The sweetness of Parny, the ingenuous, light wit, the delicacy, the purity of form, which are all characteristic of French poetry in general, have here been united with the splendor, lively exuberance, and freedom of Ariosto. . . .

While in his subsequent works Pushkin was to endow almost all the creatures of his imagination with the individuality of his own character and way of thinking, here he often appears a *poet inventor.* He does not seek to convey to us his own special view of the world, of fate, life, and man; he simply creates for us a new fate, a new life, a new individual world, and populates it with beings that are new and disparate, belonging exclusively to his creative imagination. This is the reason why no other poem of his has the same completeness and congruity which we remark in **Ruslan.** This is why each canto, each scene, each digression has its own distinctive, full existence; why each part is woven into the pattern of the whole creation so indispensably that nothing could be added or subtracted without utter loss of harmony . . . This is why the author, correlating the parts with the whole, carefully avoids anything pathetic which might stir up the reader's soul. For strong feelings are incompatible with the comically miraculous; they agree only with the majestically marvelous. Charm alone can lure us into the realm of magic; and if in the midst of enchanting impossibility something affects us in all seriousness, making us revert to ourselves, then good-bye to our faith in the improbable! Miraculous specters are scattered to the winds and the whole world of the fantastic collapses, disappears, the way a motley dream is interrupted when something among its concoctions reminds us of reality. The Finn's story, if it had a different ending, would destroy the effect of the whole poem. . . . In general one can say that even if an exacting criticism should find weak, uneven passages in **Ruslan and Liudmila,** still it will detect nothing superfluous or irrelevant in it. Chivalry, love, sorcery, feasts, war, mermaids—all the poetry of an enchanted world—were here combined in one creation, and despite the motley parts, everything is well-proportioned, harmonious, *congruous.* . . .

If in **Ruslan and Liudmila** Pushkin was exclusively a *poet* faithfully and unfalteringly transmitting the impulses of his fancy, in **The Prisoner of the Caucasus** he appears as a *poet-philosopher* who in his poetry tries to depict the doubts of his reason and thus gives all objects the general color of his individual views, often forsaking the objects in order to dwell in the realm of abstract thinking. What he presents, in **The Prisoner, Onegin,** and other works, are no longer sorcerers with their miracles, nor unconquerable heroes or enchanted gardens; rather, his subject is real life and the human being of our time, with his emptiness, insignificance, and dullness. Unlike Goethe, however, he does not seek to elevate his object by revealing both the poetry in ordinary life and a full reflection of all mankind in contemporary man; rather, like Byron, he sees only contradiction in the whole world, only betrayed hope, so that one could call almost every one of his heroes *disillusioned.*

It is not only in his view of life and man that Pushkin concurs with Byron, the bard of *The Giaour*: he also resembles him in other aspects of his poetry. The manner of presentation is the same; so is the tone and the form of his poems; there is the same vagueness with regard to the whole and the same detailed explicitness in the parts; the structure is the same; and even the characters in most cases are so similar that at first glance one would take them for immigrant aliens who have journeyed from Byron's world into Pushkin's creations.

Nevertheless, despite such similarity to the British poet, we find in **Onegin,** in **The Gypsies,** in **The Prisoner,** and in other works so much original beauty belonging exclusively to our poet, such guileless freshness of feeling, such veracity of description, such subtlety in observation and naturalness in presentation, such originality in language, and, finally so much that is purely Russian that even in this period of his poetry he cannot be called a mere imitator. . . . It is evident to those who have looked into the souls of both poets that Pushkin did not meet Byron accidentally, but borrowed from him, or more accurately, unwittingly submitted to his influence. Byron's lyre had to reverberate in his epoch, for it was itself the voice of its epoch. One of two antagonistic tendencies of our time gained expression in it. Is it surprising that it did not sound for Pushkin in vain? Only perhaps he yielded too much to its influence. Had he retained more originality, at least in the exterior form of his poems, he would have invested them with even greater excellence.

Byron's influence was manifested first of all in **The Prisoner of the Caucasus.** Here the marks of similarity mentioned above are particularly evident. The structure of the poem demonstrates, however, that this was Pushkin's first attempt in this particular manner: for the descriptions of the Circassians, their way of life, customs, games, and so forth—which fill the first canto—arrest the action to no end, snap the thread of interest, and do not accord with the tone of the poem as a whole. It is one's impression that the poem has not one, but two unblended subject matters, each appearing separately and diverting attention and feeling in two different directions. But by what merits is this important fault redeemed! What poesy pervades all the episodes! What freshness, what power of feeling! What veracity of lively descriptions! No other work by Pushkin offers so many faults and so many beauties.

Just as great—or perhaps an even greater—similarity to Byron appears in **The Fountain at Bakhchisarai,** but here a more skillful execution reveals the greater maturity of the poet. . . . All the digressions and interruptions are tied together by one prevalent feeling; everything strives to produce one principal impression. An apparent irregularity in narration is an invariable criterion of the Byronic manner; but this irregularity is only seeming, for the dissonant presentation of objects reverberates in the soul as a harmonious train of sensations. . . .

How naturally and harmoniously are eastern voluptuousness and sensuality here blended with the strongest outbursts of southern passion! The contrast between the luxurious description of the harem and the gravity of the principal action betrays the author of **Ruslan.** He has descended to earth from the immortal world of enchantment, but he has not lost his sense of enthralling sensuality even in the midst of conflicting passions and misfortunes. His art of poetry in **The Fountain** could be compared with the Oriental peri who, although bereft of paradise, has retained her unearthly beauty: her aspect is thoughtful and grave, but through the affected coldness a strong agitation of her spirit is perceptible. . . .

The poem of Pushkin's which is furthest from Byron is **The Robber Brothers,** despite the fact that by its subject matter, episodes, descriptions, and all other elements it must be called a replica of *The Prisoner of Chillon.* It is more a caricature than an imitation of Byron. Bonnivard and his brothers suffered "For the God their foes denied"; and however cruel their torment may be, there is an element of poetry in it which commands our sympathy. On the other hand, Pushkin's detailed description of the sufferings of the captured robbers engenders only revulsion—a feeling similar to what we experience at the sight of the torment of a criminal justly sentenced to death. It can be asserted that there is nothing poetic in this poem beyond the introductory stanzas and the charming versification—which latter is always and everywhere a mark of Pushkin.

This charming versification is seen above all in **The Gypsies,** where the mastery of versecraft has reached its highest degree of perfection and art has assumed the appearance of free casualness. Here it seems that each sound has poured forth from the soul unconstrained, and everything is pure, complete, and free, despite the fact that each line—except perhaps two or three in the whole poem—has received the ultimate in polish.

Does the content, however, have the same merit as the form? We see a nomadic, semibarbaric people which knows no laws, despises luxury and civilization, and loves freedom above all. Yet this people is familiar with sentiments characteristic of the most refined community: the memory of a former love and a nostalgia for the inconstant Mariula fill the old gypsy's whole life. But, while the gypsies experience exclusive, lasting love, they do not recognize jealousy; Aleko's feelings are incomprehensible to them. One might assume that the author wished to represent a golden age, in which people were just without laws, in which passions never trespassed beyond proper limits, in which all was free but nothing disturbed the general harmony, and inner perfection was the result, not of an arduous education, but of the happy innocence of a natural integrity. Such an idea could have great poetic merit. But here, unfortunately, the fair sex destroys all the enchantment, and while the gypsies' love is *"drudgery and anguish,"* their wives are like the moon which "serenely strays, / On all creation gently pouring / Her undiscriminating rays." Is this feminine imperfection compatible with the perfection of the tribe? The gypsies either do not form permanent, exclusive attachments, or if they do they are jealous of their inconstant wives; in the latter case revenge and other passions cannot be alien to them. If such is the case, then Aleko cannot seem strange and incomprehensible to them, then European manners differ from theirs only by the advantages of education, and then they represent, not a golden age, but simply a semibarbaric people which is not bound by laws and is poor and wretched, just like the actual gypsies of Bessarabia. And then the whole poem contradicts itself. . . .

But there is a quality in **The Gypsies** which redeems in a way the disorder of the subject matter. This quality is the poet's greater originality. The author of "A Review of Literature in 1827" correctly observed that this poem reveals a struggle between Byron's idealism and the Russian poet's nationally oriented paintings. Indeed, take the description of gypsy life separately, regard Zemfira's father, not as a gypsy, but simply as an old man with no reference to his nationality, consider the passage about Ovid: the completeness of creation, developed in all details and inspired by an originality, will prove to you that Pushkin had already sensed the power of his independent talent, free of foreign influences.

All the faults of **The Gypsies** are functions of these two discordant tendencies: one original and one Byronic. Therefore the very imperfection of the poem is a guarantee of the poet's future progress.

A striving for an independent brand of poetry is even more manifest in **Eugene Onegin,** although not in its first chapters where Byron's influence is obvious, nor in the manner of narration which derives from *Don Juan* and *Beppo,* nor even in the character of Onegin himself, which is of the same kind as that of Childe Harold. But the further the poet moves from his main hero, abandoning himself to collateral descriptions, the more independent and national he becomes.

The time of Childe Harolds, thank God, has not yet come for our fatherland: young Russia has not partaken of the life of western states and our people, as a personality, is not getting old under the weight of others' experiences. A brilliant career is still open to Russian activity; all kinds of art, all branches of knowledge still remain to be mastered by our fatherland. Hope is still given to us: what is the disillusioned Childe Harold's business among us?

Let us examine which qualities the British flower transplanted into Russian soil has retained and which it has lost.

The British poet's most cherished vision is an extraordinary, lofty creature. Not a paucity, but a superabundance of inner strength makes this creature unsympathetic to his environment. An immortal idea dwells in his heart day and night, consuming all his being and poisoning all his pleasures. Whatever shape it takes—haughty contempt for mankind, nagging sense of guilt, gloomy despair, or insatiable yearning for oblivion—this idea is all-embracing and everlasting. What is it if not an instinctive, constant striving for the better, a nostalgia for an unattainable perfection? . . .

On the other hand, Onegin is an entirely ordinary and insignificant being. He is also indifferent to his environment; not despair, however, but an inability to love made him cold. His youth also passed in a whirlpool of amusement and dissipation, but he was not carried away by turbulent passion and an insatiable soul; rather he led a fashionable fop's empty, indifferent life on the parquet floor of the salon. He also quit the world and people; not, however, in order to seek scope for his agitated thoughts in solitude, but because he was equally bored everywhere,

> Because he yawned with equal gloom
> In any style of drawing room.

He does not lead a special inner life which rises above the lives of other people, and he despises mankind merely because he is unable to respect it. There is nothing more common than this breed of people, and there could not be less poetry in such a character.

This is, then, the Childe Harold of our fatherland: praise be to the poet that he did not present us with the real one. For, as we have already said, the time for Childe Harolds has not come to Russia, and we pray to God that it never will.

It seems that Pushkin himself felt the emptiness of his hero and for this reason did not anywhere in the novel try to bring him close to his readers. He gave him no definite physiognomy; he represented, not one person, but a whole class of people in his portrait: Onegin's description may fit a thousand different characters. . . .

As far as *Eugene Onegin* in general is concerned, we have no right to judge the plot by its beginning, although we can hardly imagine the possibility of a well-composed, complete, fertile plan emerging after such a beginning. Still, who can discern the limits of possibility for such poets as Pushkin? It is their prerogative to amaze their critics at all times.

The faults of *Onegin* are in essence the last homage Pushkin paid to the British poet. The narrative's innumerable merits—Lensky, Tatiana, Olga, St. Petersburg, the countryside, the dream, the winter, the letter, and so forth—are our poet's inalienable property. It is in these that he clearly reveals the innate tendency of his genius. These signs of original creation in *The Gypsies* and in *Onegin,* coupled with the one scene we know from *Boris Godunov,* [In a footnote the translator states: Kireevsky is referring to the monastery scene which had been "published in *Moskovsky restnik* 1 (1827)."] constitute, though they do not exhaust, the third period in the development of his poetry, which could be called the *period of Russo-Pushkinian poetry.* Its essential features are: a pictorial vividness, a certain abandon, a singular pensiveness, and, finally, an ineffable quality, comprehensible only to the Russian heart: for what can you call the feeling with which the melodies of Russian songs are imbued, to which the Russian people most frequently resort, and which can be regarded as the center of its spiritual life?

In this period of Pushkin's development one particularly notices an ability to be absorbed in the environment and in the passing moment. This same ability is the foundation of the Russian character: it is at the very inception of all the virtues and failings of the Russian people. From this ability emanate courage, lightness of heart, intractability of momentary impulses, generosity, intemperance, vehemence, perspicuity, geniality, and so on and so forth. . . .

The above-mentioned scene from *Boris Godunov* particularly manifests Pushkin's maturity. The art which is such a narrow frame represents the spirit of the epoch, monastic life, Pimen's character, the state of contemporary affairs, and the beginning of the dramatic action; the special, tragically serene atmosphere that involves the chronicler's life and presence for us; the new, striking manner in which the poet acquaints us with Grishka; and finally the inimitable, poetic, precise language: all this taken together makes us expect of this tragedy—let us say it boldly—something *magnificent.*

Pushkin was born to be a dramatist. He is too many-sided, too objective to be a lyric poet. One can observe in each of his poetic tales an instinctive urge to endow each separate part with individual life—an urge injurious to the whole in epic creations but necessary and invaluable to the dramatist. . . .

Few are selected by fate to enjoy the affection of their con-

temporaries during their lifetime. Pushkin belongs to their number, which reveals to us still another important quality in the nature of his poetry: a *congruence with his time.*

It is not enough to be a poet in order to be a national poet: it is also necessary to have been raised, as it were, in the midst of the nation's life and to have shared in the fatherland's hopes, aspirations, and passions—in short to live its life and to express it spontaneously while expressing oneself. Such a lucky attainment may be a rare accident: but are beauty, intelligence, insight—all the qualities with which man captivates man—not just as accidental? And are these latter qualities any more substantial than the capacity to reflect a nation's life in oneself?

Fyodor Dostoevsky   (essay date 1880)

SOURCE: "On the Unveiling of the Pushkin Memorial," in *Pages from the Journal of an Author,* translated by S. S. Koteliansky and J. Middleton Murry, George Allen and Unwin, Ltd., 1916, pp. 47-68.

[*Among Russia's best-known novelists, Dostoevsky is considered one of the most outstanding and influential writers of modern literature and is best known for his novels* Prestuplenye i nakazanye (*1866;* Crime and Punishment) *and* Brat'ya Karamozovy (*1880;* The Brothers Karamazov). *In the following excerpt from a speech that he delivered before the Society of Lovers of Russian Literature in June, 1880, he remarks on Pushkin's importance to Russian literature and culture.*]

Pushkin is an extraordinary phenomenon, and, perhaps, the "unique phenomenon of the Russian spirit," said Gogol. I will add, "and a prophetic phenomenon." Yes, in his appearing there is contained for all us Russians something incontestably prophetic. Pushkin arrives exactly at the beginning of our true self-consciousness, which had only just begun to exist a whole century after Peter's reforms, and Pushkin's coming mightily aids us in our dark way by a new guiding light. In this sense Pushkin is a presage and a prophecy.

I divide the activity of our great poet into three periods. I speak now not as a literary critic. I dwell on Pushkin's creative activity only to elucidate my conception of his prophetic significance to us, and the meaning I give the word prophecy. I would, however, observe in passing that the periods of Pushkin's activity do not seem to me to be marked off from each other by firm boundaries. The beginning of *Eugène Onyegin,* for instance, in my opinion belongs still to the first period, while *Onyegin* ends in the second period when Pushkin had already found his ideals in his native land, had taken them to his heart, and cherished them in his loving and clairvoyant soul. It is said that in his first period Pushkin imitated European poets, Parny and André Chénier, and above all, Byron. Without doubt the poets of Europe had a great influence upon the development of his genius, and they maintained their influence all through his life. Nevertheless, even the very earliest poems of Pushkin were not mere imitations, and in them the extraordinary independence of his genius was expressed. In an imitation there never appears such individual suffering and such depths of self-consciousness as

Pushkin displayed, for instance, in **The Gipsies,** a poem which I ascribe in its entirety to his first period; not to mention the creative force and impetuosity which would never have been so evident had his work been only imitation. Already, in the character of Aleko, the hero of **The Gipsies,** is exhibited a powerful, profound, and purely Russian idea, later to be expressed in harmonious perfection in Onyegin, where almost the same Aleko appears not in a fantastic light, but as tangible, real, and comprehensible. In Aleko Pushkin had already discovered, and portrayed with genius, the unhappy wanderer in his native land, the Russian sufferer of history, whose appearance in our society, uprooted from among the people, was a historic necessity. The type is true and perfectly rendered, it is an eternal type, long since settled in our Russian land. These homeless Russian wanderers are wandering still, and the time will be long before they disappear. If they in our day no longer go to gipsy camps to seek their universal ideals in the wild life of the Gipsies and their consolation away from the confused and pointless life of our Russian intellectuals, in the bosom of nature, they launch into Socialism, which did not exist in Aleko's day, they march with a new faith into another field, and they work zealously, believing, like Aleko, that they will by their fantastic occupations obtain their aims and happiness, not for themselves alone, but for all mankind. For the Russian wanderer can find his own peace only in the happiness of all men; he will not be more cheaply satisfied, at least while it is still a matter of theory. It is the same Russian man who appears at a different time. . . .

[In **The Gipsies**] already is whispered the Russian solution of the question, "the accursed question," in accordance with the faith and justice of the people. "Humble yourself, proud man, and first of all break down your pride. Humble yourself, idle man, and first of all labour on your native land"—that is the solution according to the wisdom and justice of the people.

"Truth is not outside thee, but *in* thyself. Find thyself in thyself, subdue thyself to thyself, be master of thyself and thou wilt see the truth. Not in things is this truth, not outside thee or abroad, but first of all in thine own labour upon thyself. If thou conquer and subdue thyself, then thou wilt be freer than thou hast ever dreamed, and thou wilt begin a great work and make others free, and thou wilt see happiness, for thy life will be fulfilled and thou wilt at the last understand thy people and its sacred truth. Not with the Gipsies nor elsewhere is universal harmony, if thou thyself art first unworthy of her, malicious and proud, and thou dost demand life as a gift, not even thinking, that man must pay for her." This solution of the question is strongly foreshadowed in Pushkin's poem. Still more clearly is it expressed in **Eugène Onyegin,** which is not a fantastic, but a tangible and realistic poem, in which the real Russian life is embodied with a creative power and a perfection such as had not been before Pushkin and perhaps never after him. . . .

[At the beginning of the poem, Eugène] is still half a coxcomb and a man of the world; he had lived too little to be utterly disappointed in life. But he is already visited and disturbed by

The demon lord of hidden weariness.

In a remote place, in the heart of his mother country, he is of course an exile in a foreign land. He does not know what to do and is somehow conscious of his own quest. Afterwards, wandering over his native country and over foreign lands, he, beyond doubt clever and sincere, feels himself among strangers, still more a stranger to himself. . . .

Tatiana is different. She is a strong character, strongly standing on her own ground. She is deeper than Onyegin and certainly wiser than he. With a noble instinct she divines where and what is truth, and her thought finds expression in the finale of the poem. Perhaps Pushkin would even have done better to call his poem *Tatiana,* and not **Onyegin,** for she is indubitably the chief character. She is positive and not negative, a type of positive beauty, the apotheosis of the Russian woman, and the poet destined her to express the idea of his poem in the famous scene of the final meeting of Tatiana with Onyegin. One may even say that so beautiful or positive a type of the Russian woman has never been created since in our literature, save perhaps the figure of Liza in Turgeniev's *A Nest of Gentlefolk.* But because of his way of looking down upon people, Onyegin did not even understand Tatiana when he met her for the first time, in a remote place, under the guise of a pure, innocent girl, who was at first so shy of him. He could not see the completeness and perfection of the poor girl, and perhaps he really took her for a "moral embryo." She, the embryo! She, after her letter to Onyegin! If there is a moral embryo in the poem, it is he himself, Onyegin, beyond all debate. . . .

In the immortal lines of the romance the poet represented [Tatiana] coming to see the house of the man who is so wonderful and still so incomprehensible to her. I do not speak of the unattainable artistic beauty and profundity of the lines. She is in his study; she looks at his books and possessions; she tries through them to understand his soul, to solve her enigma, and "the moral embryo" at last pauses thoughtfully, with a foreboding that her riddle is solved, and gently whispers:

Perhaps he is only a parody?

Yes, she had to whisper this; she had divined him. Later long afterwards in Petersburg, when they meet again, she knows him perfectly. . . .

[Onegin] has no root at all, he is a blade of grass, borne on the wind. She is otherwise: even in her despair, in the painful consciousness that her life has been ruined, she still has something solid and unshakable upon which her soul may bear. There are the memories of her childhood, the reminiscences of her country, her remote village, in which her pure and humble life had begun: it is

the woven shade,
Of branches that o'erhang her nurse's grave.

Oh, these memories and the pictures of the past are most precious to her now; these alone are left to her, but they do save her soul from final despair. And this is not a little but rather much, for there is here a whole foundation, unshakable and indestructible. Here is contact with her own land, with her own people, and with their sanctities. And he—what has he and what is he? Nothing, that she should follow him out of compassion, to amuse him, to give him a moment's gift of a mirage of happiness out of the infinite pity of her love, knowing well beforehand that to-morrow he would look on his happiness with mockery. No, these are deep, firm souls, which cannot deliberately give their sanctities to dishonour, even from infinite compassion. No, Tatiana could not follow Onyegin.

Thus in **Onyegin,** that immortal and unequalled poem, Pushkin was revealed as a great national writer, unlike any before him. In one stroke, with the extreme of exactness and insight, he defined the very inmost essence of our high society that stands above the people. He defined the type of the Russian wanderer before our day and in our day; he was the first to divine him, with the flair of genius, to divine his destiny in history and his enormous significance in our destiny to be. Side by side he placed a type of positive and indubitable beauty in the person of a Russian woman. Besides, of course, he was the first Russian writer to show us, in his other works of that period, a whole gallery of positively beautiful Russian types, finding them in the Russian people. The paramount beauty of these lies in their truth, their tangible and indubitable truth. It is impossible to deny them, they stand as though sculptured. I would remind you again. I speak not as a literary critic, and therefore do not intend to elucidate my idea by a particular and detailed literary discussion of these works of the poet's genius. Concerning the type of the Russian monkish chronicler, for instance, a whole book might be written to show the importance and meaning for us of this lofty Russian figure, discovered by Pushkin in the Russian land, portrayed and sculptured by him, and now eternally set before us in its humble, exalted, indubitable spiritual beauty, as the evidence of that mighty spirit of national life which can send forth from itself figures of such certain loveliness. This type is now given; he exists, he cannot be disputed; it cannot be said that he is only the poet's fancy and ideal. You yourself see and agree: Yes, he exists, therefore the spirit of the nation which created him exists also, therefore the vital power of this spirit exists and is mighty and vast. Throughout Pushkin sounds a belief in the Russian character, in its spiritual might; and if there is belief, there is hope also, the great hope for the man of Russia. . . . [No] single Russian writer, before or after him, did ever associate himself so intimately and fraternally with his people as Pushkin. . . .

> **Throughout Pushkin sounds a belief in the Russian character, in its spiritual might; and if there is belief, there is hope also, the great hope for the man of Russia. No single Russian writer, before or after him, did ever associate himself so intimately and fraternally with his people as Pushkin.**
>
> **—*Fyodor Dostoevsky***

All these treasures of art and artistic insight are left by our great poet as it were a landmark for the writers who should come after him, for future labourers in the same field. One may say positively that if Pushkin had not existed, there would not have been the gifted writers who came after him. At least they would not have displayed themselves with such power and clarity, in spite of the great gifts with which they have succeeded in expressing themselves in our day. But not in poetry alone, not in artistic creation alone: if Pushkin had not existed, there would not have been expressed with the irresistible force with which it appeared after him (not in all writers, but in a chosen few), our belief in our Russian individuality, our now conscious faith in the people's powers, and finally the belief in our future individual destiny among the family of European nations. This achievement of Pushkin's is particularly displayed if one examines what I call the third period of his activity.

I repeat, there are no fixed divisions between the periods. Some of the works of even the third period might have been written at the very beginning of the poet's artistic activity, for Pushkin was always a complete whole, as it were a perfect organism carrying within itself at once every one of its principles, not receiving them from beyond. The beyond only awakened in him that which was already in the depths of his soul. But this organism developed and the phases of this development could really be marked and defined, each of them by its peculiar character and the regular generation of one phase from another. Thus to the third period can be assigned those of his works in which universal ideas were pre-eminently reflected, in which the poetic conceptions of other nations were mirrored and their genius re-embodied. Some of these appeared after Pushkin's death. And in this period the poet reveals something almost miraculous, never seen or heard at any time or in any nation before. There had been in the literatures of Europe men of colossal artistic genius—a Shakespeare, a Cervantes, a Schiller. But show me one of these great geniuses who possessed such a capacity for universal sympathy as our Pushkin. This capacity, the pre-eminent capacity of our nation, he shares with our nation, and by that above all he is our national poet. The greatest of European poets could never so powerfully embody in themselves the genius of a foreign, even a neighbouring, people, its spirit in all its hidden depth, and all its yearning after its appointed end, as Pushkin could. On the contrary, when they turned to foreign nations European poets most often made them one with their own people, and understood them after their own fashion. Even Shakespeare's Italians, for instance, are almost always Englishmen. Pushkin alone of all world poets possessed the capacity of fully identifying himself with another nationality. . . . How profound and fantastic is the imagination in the poem *A Feast in Time of Plague.* But in this fantastic imagination is the genius of England; and in the hero's wonderful song about the plague, and in Mary's song,

> Our children's voices in the noisy school
> Were heard. . . .

These are English songs; this is the yearning of the British genius, its lament, its painful presentiment of its future. Remember the strange lines:

Once as I wandered through the valley
wild. . . .

It is almost a literal transposition of the first three pages
of a strange mystical book written in prose by an old English sectarian—but is it only a transposition? In the sad
and rapturous, music of these verses is the very soul of
Northern Protestantism, of the English heresiarch, of the
illimitable mystic with his dull, sombre, invincible aspiration, and the impetuous power of his mystical dreaming. . . . [Pushkin is] in my opinion a prophetic phenomenon, because . . . because herein was expressed the national spirit of his poetry, the national spirit in its future
development, the national spirit of our future, which is already implicit in the present, and it was expressed pro-
phetically. For what is the power of the spirit of Russian
nationality if not its aspiration after the final goal of universality and omni-humanity? No sooner had he become
a completely national poet, no sooner had he come into
contact with the national power, than he already anticipated the great future of that power. In this he was a seer,
in this a prophet. . . .

[Beyond] all doubt, the destiny of a Russian is pan-
European and universal. To become a true Russian, to become a Russian fully, (in the end of all, I repeat) means
only to become the brother of all men, to become, if you
will, a universal man. All our slavophilism and Western-
ism is only a great misunderstanding, even though historically necessary. To a true Russian, Europe and the destiny
of all the mighty Aryan family is as dear as Russia herself,
as the destiny of his own native country, because our destiny is universality, won not by the sword, but by the
strength of brotherhood and our fraternal aspiration to re-
unite mankind. . . .

I say that to this universal, omni-human union the heart
of Russia, perhaps more than all other nations, is chiefly
predestined; I see its traces in our history, our men of genius, in the artistic genius of Pushkin. . . . He surely
could contain the genius of foreign lands in his soul as his
own. In art at least, in artistic creation, he undeniably revealed this universality of the aspiration of the Russian
spirit, and therein is a great promise. If our thought is a
dream, then in Pushkin at least this dream has solid foundation. Had he lived longer, he would perhaps have revealed great and immortal embodiments of the Russian
soul, which would then have been intelligible to our European brethren; he would have attracted them much more
and closer than they are attracted now, perhaps he would
have succeeded in explaining to them all the truth of our
aspirations; and they would understand us more than they
do now, they would have begun to have insight into us,
and would have ceased to look at us so suspiciously and
presumptuously as they still do. Had Pushkin lived longer,
then among us too there would perhaps be fewer misunderstandings and quarrels than we see now. But God saw
otherwise. Pushkin died in the full maturity of his powers,
and undeniably bore away with him a great secret into the
grave. And now we, without him, are seeking to divine his
secret.

M. Khrapchenko   (essay date 1939)

SOURCE: "Pushkin's Epic Poems," in *Pushkin: A Collec-
tion of Articles and Essays on the Great Russian Poet A. S.
Pushkin,* The U.S.S.R. Society for Cultural Relations with
Foreign Countries, 1939, pp. 93-105.

[*In the essay below, Khrapchenko surveys Pushkin's narrative poetry, focusing on the poet's concern with humanistic
themes.*]

Pushkin, the literary master, the man of great sentiment
and ideas, with his striking emotional and lyrical perception of life, showed a bent for works involving a broad
comprehension of the world. An incomparable lyrical
poet, he was at the same time author of remarkable epic
works. In Pushkin's view lyrical poetry was not incompatible with epos. In his epic works he wished to remain a
poet who expressed much in little, striving to attain the
maximum of tenseness and pointedness. These distinguishing features of Pushkin's literary genius made the
epic poem his favourite genre, and he wrote epic poems
at the various stages of his literary path.

Ruslan and Ludmila was Pushkin's first important work
that appeared in print (1817–1820). It was written with
youthful fervour and played an important part in the history of Russian literature.

In this poem Pushkin discarded the principles of classicism, the dominant literary tendency of the days, and
broke with the exuberance and pomposity of the classical
style; the poet could no longer be satisfied with the an-
aemic pallor and dryness of "elevated" poetry, and the
conventionality and narrowness of the gallant court literature was foreign to him. The easy flow of poetical narration, concreteness and full-bloodedness in manner of portrayal are the dominating elements in *Ruslan and Ludmila.*

Ruslan and Ludmila takes the reader into ancient Russia.
Prince Vladimir gives his daughter in marriage to a knight
called Ruslan. On the wedding night the beautiful bride
Ludmila is abducted by the sorcerer Chernomor. Four
knights set out in search of the vanished princess. The description of the "heroic" adventure of the knights is imbued with fine humour and is rendered in a merry, playful
tone. The "grand" knights are treated by Pushkin with derision; there is very little "chivalrous" magnanimity and
nobility in their manner and neither is valour among their
virtues.

Ruslan and Ludmila is full of comical descriptions of the
world of magic. The poetry of mystery was being grafted
on Russian literature at that period. Zhukovsky had done
a great deal to develop magic and mystery literature in
Russia. In his poem Pushkin parodied Zhukovsky's ballad
"The Twelve Sleeping Maidens" with its tales of horror.
The sorcerer Chernomor is a comical personage. The
"horrors" call forth nothing but a smile. The idea of two
worlds so typical of the reactionary romanticists is severely condemned by Pushkin. Both heroics and mystery recede to the background before the worldly experiences of
man, before the charm of human emotions. The humorous

narration is very often interrupted by scenes of riotous enjoyment of the good things of life.

In **Ruslan and Ludmila** there are strong notes of the hymn of life:

> A merry host of youthful maidens
> Are clustering around the khan.
> With young sweet smelling birch-tree branches
> One of the maidens fans the knight,
> And fragrance on the air is wafted.
> Another one his tired limbs
> Soothes with essence of spring roses
> And lavishly his curls dark
> With aromatic scents perfumes.
> Enveloped in his blissful raptures
> The knight forgot the captive princess
> But yesterday so dear to him.
> Tormented by the sweetest yearnings,
> His wand'ring eye is all aglow;
> Tense with voluptuous expectation
> His heart is melting, he's on fire.

Both the manner of narration and the poetical language of the poem were marked by their daring and novelty. In this poem Pushkin made ample use of common popular language and of popular tales and legends. The popular style of the poem and the new path struck by it gave rise to sharp controversies and served even as a cause of severe attacks on the part of the followers of the old school. The poem was the first weighty blow struck by the young poet at the beginning of a literary demarcation between the writers of the pseudo-classical school and the followers of the new tendency in literature.

Pushkin called for assertion of life and sang its joys. In his *Gavriliada* Pushkin makes even the denizens of heaven partake of the feast of earthly enjoyment. Pushkin relates of the love which the lord of heaven, the archangel Gabriel and Satan feel for the virgin Mary, of their rivalry, struggle and love intrigues. The influence of Voltaire's "Maid of Orleans" is here clearly in evidence. However, the peculiar feature of Pushkin's *Gavriliada* is that its "heroes" are the lords of heaven; hence the great expressiveness and keeness of the poem. The poet relates with charming humour how the denizens of heaven fall a prey to mortal feelings, emotions and passions.

> Let's speak about the strange affairs of love.
> . . . . .
> You too, o lord, hast known its palpitation,
> You too, o lord, like man, hast known its flame.
> God, the creator's tired of creation,
> He's bored with heaven's services and prayers—
> He psalms of tender love begins to chant
> And sing aloud: "I love you, Mary,
> My immortality in weariness I drag . . .
> Where are my wings? To Mary shall I fly
> And on her breast shall find my relaxation . . ."
> Et caetera . . . all that he could contrive . . .
> . . . Noticing the angel's gifts and wit
> The lord of hosts had lavished on him praise,
> Appointed him as confidential envoy
> And after dusk to Mary sent in haste.

The actions of the gods are in no way distinguishable from those of men. Rivalry, struggle and deceit thrive in heaven as they do on earth. Pushkin in his *Gavriliada* was preaching atheistical ideas and demolishing heavenly idols.

The publication of Pushkin's *Gavriliada* could not even be thought of. In 1828, when manuscript copies of the poem began to be circulated, the tsarist government rightly presuming that the author of this poem could be no other than Pushkin, subjected the poet to an examination. Once more, for the third time, the poet was confronted with the menace of exile. This time it meant remote Siberia. Pushkin preferred to deny his authorship of the poem. Only after the Revolution of 1917 was *Gavriliada* published in full; hitherto only fragments of the poem appeared in print.

Pushkin was dethroning gods and storming heaven, for the sake of man and earthly life. The poet was inspired by the idea of the full development of man. By his whole nature Pushkin was a humanist in the broadest and noblest sense of the word. Having been educated according to the best standards of West-European culture and organically associated with the Decembrist movement, Pushkin strove with all his heart for new social forms of human life.

The autocracy zealously guarded the traditions of serfdom. Free thought was suppressed. The system of feudal hierarchy throttled the social life of Russia. A man was judged not by his qualities but by his birth, blood and social station. "The uniform, only the uniform" dominated everything. Asiatic inertness and stagnation reigned supreme blighting all that was best in society. And in this gloomy atmosphere of the reaction of Nicholas I Pushkin sang his hymn of Man. Man was the hero of his poems, Man, free of all hierarchic and social gradations.

In his **The Prisoner of the Caucasus** written in 1821 Pushkin draws a contrast between a proud independent individuality and a society that tolerates nothing new.

> He knew the truth of world and men,
> He knew of faithless life the value.
> Having found treason in hearts of friends
> And nightmares in the dreams of love,
> No longer willing to be a victim
> Of vanity by him so long
> Despised, of double-tongued malice
> Or simple-hearted calumny,
> World's fugitive, the friend of nature,
> Departed from his homely bounds
> And to a distant country fled
> Allured by freedom's joyful vision.
> O Freedom! It is you alone
> He looked for in the world of deserts.

The hero of **The Prisoner of the Caucasus** flees to the Caucasus where the wild freedom of primitive, natural life had been preserved. The poet endows his hero, who dared to rebel, with traits of inner greatness and peculiar power.

> His anguish, his rebellious spirit
> He buried deeply in his heart.
> . . . . .
> The captive on a mountain's summit
> Alone above a thund'ring cloud
> Would the return of sun await,
> Beyond the reach of raging storm,
> He'd to the claps and howl of tempest

Be listening with a thrill of joy.

Disappointed in people, the hero of *The Prisoner of the Caucasus* finds no peace here either. He is indifferent to all that proceeds around him; even the grandeur and beauty of the Caucasus leaves him cold.

The world of "outcasts," of people who turned their back on society, was drawn by Pushkin in his *The Brothers Highwaymen.* They are people who do not submit to authorities and law. There are many of them:

> Here you will find a fugitive
> Come from the defiant shores of Don,
> A Jew with jet-black locks of hair,
> And some wild children of the steppes,—
> A Kalmyk or Bashkir deformed,
> A red-haired Finn,
> Some idle member
> Of the nomadic Gypsy tribe.

Knocked out of their rut, cast out and persecuted, these people were thirsting for bloody vengeance. Their life is full of terrible exploits, of unusual adventures. They are hungering for freedom and are prepared to defend it desperately.

> As through the streets one day, in chains,
> We trudged along collecting alms
> To supplement the jail's resources,
> We counsel in a whisper took,
> Resolved to dash for longed-for freedom;
> Quite close to us the river ran,
> We to it turned and from the steep bank
> Splash! and were swimming in deep water.
> . . . Behind us
> A hue and cry was raised: "Catch! Catch!"
> Two guards came sailing from afar,
> But we the island reached already,
> With stones we knock our irons off
> We tear each other's rags away
> That soaking wet have weighed us down . . .
> We see the chase after our persons,
> But bravely, full of burning hope
> We sit and wait. There, one is drowning . . .
> The other passed the deeper part,
> With gun in hand he now is wading . . .
> Good aim—two stones come down upon him
> And blood came gushing on the waves:
> He sank—once more we plunged and swam,
> This time not one dared to pursue us,
> We reached the other shore in safety
> And to the woods! . . .

Pushkin saw how under the conditions prevailing in his days people were thrown on the refuse heap of life and he keenly felt the hatred burning in their hearts. Pushkin felt deep sorrow for those whom society was callously mutilating and turning into human waste.

Strong characters, people of strong passions, attracted the attention of the poet. *The Fountain of Bakhchisarai* is a poem depicting sharp conflicts and great characters. The heroes of this poem—Ghirey, Zarema and Mary have the breath of heated passion. Mary is placed in the harem. She strains all the power of her will to escape the horrible fate of a concubine. Ghirey's love for Mary excites the jealousy of the hot-tempered Zarema. In vain did she attempt to

regain her place in Ghirey's heart, the khan grew indifferent to her. Tormented by jealousy Zarema kills Mary and perishes herself. The vivid emotions of these heroes are rendered by Pushkin with great expressiveness.

The theme of the Orient, of "free" peoples, was an integral part of all romantic poems depicting extraordinary characters. The austere simplicity and naturalness of the East is contrasted with the effeminateness and falsity of upper society.

> All's scanty, wild and so discordant,
> But so alive and full of ferment,
> So alien to our lifeless joys
> And to our idle mode of living
> Just like a tedious tune of bondslaves.

In the romantic poems of Pushkin one can feel the influence of Byron. However, the poems are not imitations, and Pushkin's original talent revealed itself with great power in these poems. The boundless pessimism and despondency so typical of Byron is not to be found in Pushkin who had a much broader world outlook, and that is the reason why Byron's influence on Pushkin was not of long duration. In his *Gypsies* (1824) Pushkin dethrones Byron's heroes. In this poem Pushkin is already entering, so to speak, into a controversy with Byron.

The idea of the non-acceptance of a society founded on falsity underlies his poem *The Gypsies.*

> . . . The vileness of their stifling town!
> Where men do herd in crowds, nor breathe
> The morning fresh, or mountain free,
> Or scent of spring on meadow sweet;
> Are shamed of love, and banish thought,
> Consent to sell their freedom dear,
> To fetish idols bow their heads,
> Will sue for pelf, and hug their chains.
> What have I left? The falser's lie,
> The smirking bigot's narrow creed,
> The senseless hate of unwashed mob,
> Ranks, orders, titles, bought with shame.

Aleko, the hero of *The Gypsies,* feels oppressed by his environment and leaves it. He is attracted by the free life of the Gypsies. However, he ignores social ties and places his own will and wishes above them. The personal strivings of the individual are the all important things for him. He cared nothing for the traditions of the Gypsy camp or for the wishes and desires of other people. Zemfira, a free Gypsy girl, was in love with him. But later her love for him passed away and she fell in love with somebody else. Aleko, offended by this "self-will" of Zemfira, kills both, her and her lover. And the old Gypsy says to him:

> "Go, leave us now, thou haughty man!
> We wild folk have no law to bind,
> To torture, or to punish men;
> We need no sinner's blood, or groans,
> Nor can we with a murd'rer live.
> Thou art not born for wild free will,
> Thou wouldst thyself alone be free;
> Thy voice will strike but terror here
> Among the good and free in soul;
> Harsh thou art and rash: so, leave us!
> Farewell, and peace abide with thee!"

Pushkin sang the praises of human individuality, but he was at the same time utterly against egocentrism.

In the character of Aleko the poet had in fact laid bare the contradictions of bourgeois individualism. A man brought up in a bourgeois environment is prepared to rebel against the handicaps of society, but places his own egoistic aims in the centre of the world. This kind of hero became more and more estranged from Pushkin. From the portrayal of individualistic rebels Pushkin passed to the portrayal of society, to the creation of real characters.

This manner of creative work found its expression in his *Eugene Onegin.* Here Pushkin's realistic method fully asserted itself. The origin of this method may be traced to his narrative poems in which Pushkin never departed from reality. Underlying his romantic poems is the living sense of a real world. However, in his poems Pushkin expressed the contradictions of reality in an abstract and conventional form. The actual relations were depicted in the form of the relations between an individual and society. The romantic poems represented a stage on the road to realism or the embryonic form of the latter. The further development of Pushkin's realism demanded the inclusion in his poetry of the multiform aspects of life as a whole.

In his poem *Count Nulin* Pushkin, in a humorous vein, depicts prosaic reality.

> In th' last dates of September
> (Excuse this turn of vulgar prose)
> How boring life is in the village—
> Cold winds, thin flakes of snow, mud, rain,
> The howl of wolves. But how it gladdens
> The hunter's heart. He knows no rest,
> On horseback in the fields he prances,
> He finds his bed where'er he can,
> He curses, drenched in rain, and riots
> In th' joy of devastating raids.
> In the meantime what does his wife do
> At home alone without her husband?
> Well, has not she enough to do?
> To pickle mushrooms, feed the geese,
> To give the orders for the meals,
> To peep into the shed and pantry.
> A mistress' eye is sorely needed
> To see that nothing is amiss.

The poet depicts plain ordinary people who however have a predilection for vulgar romanticism.

In his *Count Nulin* Pushkin depicts a Lucretia of the Russian manor.

"At the end of 1825," wrote Pushkin, "I was in the country. While reading over Shakespeare's rather weak poem 'Lucrece' I thought that had it occurred to Lucretia to give Tarquinius a box on the ear, it would perhaps have cooled his spirit and forced him to retreat in disgrace. Lucretia would not have committed suicide, Publicola would not have become enraged, the caesars would not have been driven out and the world and history might have been different."

Lucretia was turned by Pushkin into a lady dying of ennui in the country and Tarquinius into count Nulin who happened to pass that country place. The "heroes" of this poem, possessing no outstanding qualities, appear before us with all their simple sentiments and actions. The tragedy is gone and there only remains a vulgar incident depicted in an artistic manner with unusual wit, lightness and brilliance.

The reactionary critics of that time wanted the poet to educate people in a "conservative" spirit. His retort in the form of avoidance of moralization is typical of both *Count Nulin* and *A Little House at Kolomna.* Pushkin achieved the needed effect in spite of the censorship. He wrote:

> And blessed is he who of his tongue is master,
> Who firmly holds his inmost thoughts in leash,
> Who in his heart becalms, subdues of stifles
> The serpent's sudden hiss that there resounds . . .
> "No moping" is my doctor's strictest order:
> So if you please, I'll rather drop this subject!

The poem *A Little House at Kolomna* is interesting because in this poem Pushkin depicts a new social environment. From the inmates of manors and outcasts Pushkin passes to the democratic sections of society. Pushkin takes his heroes from among the "poor" people who live on the outskirts of the city. The poet is attracted by the type of a plain girl who is leading a life of toil.

> Parasha (so was our bonny maiden called)
> Could scour, wash and iron, sow and plait.

The poet compares this plain girl with a countess, a beauty of vain and haughty demeanour.

> I recollect the countess often here
> Would come (her name I do not now remember).
> . . . Compared with her
> Parasha seemed a poor, poor thing indeed.

And nevertheless Pushkin gives all preference to the modest Parasha who with her simplicity of manner and her natural beauty is placed above the countess.

> But happier a hundred times was she
> With whom, my reader, you have made acquaintance
> My simple-hearted, dear good soul, Parasha.

The essential mark distinguishing *A Little House at Kolomna* from the other poems and particularly from *Count Nulin* is the representation of types of plain people, the portrayal of the life of toilers.

While working on *Eugene Onegin,* a novel in verse, and on *The Negro of Peter the Great,* a historical novel of social life, Pushkin was at the same time writing his epic *Poltava.* The pivotal idea of this poem is the contrast between the unity of the state and the mutinous attempt at dismemberment and disunion. The poem depicts one of the most interesting stages in Russian history, viz. the period of Peter I who effected the reform of the country and consolidated its power and unity. The central figure of the poem is Mazeppa, hetman of the Ukraine. Entering upon his struggle against Peter, Mazeppa concludes an alliance with the Swedes, with Charles XII. Pushkin condemns the traitor to his country. Mazeppa is stimulated in his actions by his insatiable ambition and his lust of revenge. Mazeppa is urged into the fight not by ideas of freedom or of the welfare of the people but by purely egoistical motives.

> Not many probably do know
> That he's a man of tameless will,
> That he by hook or crook prepared is
> His enemies to trap and down,
> That till his death he would bear malice
> To those who slighted him but once,
> That gratitude is not his virtue,
> That there is nothing he holds sacred,
> That in his heart there is no love,
> That human blood he'd spill like water,
> That he despises and mocks freedom,
> That "fatherland" is nought to him.

Mazeppa sacrifices the interests of the country and the life of those near to him to his personal ambition. Mary, the daughter of his friend Kochubey, secretly leaves her parents' home to share with the intrepid old man, Mazeppa, unequal love and the dangers of heroic battles. But Mazeppa was a base and treacherous man. Without any hesitation he executes Kochubey, her father, being fully aware that this act meant the doom of Mary who left her parents for his sake. Thus the figure of the traitor to his own country stands revealed before us in its disgusting nakedness.

In contrast to the type of the cunning traitor Mazeppa Pushkin depicts Peter I as the embodiment of the idea of the unity of the country.

Peter I is also depicted in Pushkin's poem *Bronze Horseman,* but here a conflict of a different nature is developed.

In his *The Bronze Horseman* Pushkin sings the praise of culture transforming human activity:

> Where once, by that low-lying shore,
> In waters never known before
> The Finnish fisherman, sole creature,
> And left forlorn by stepdame Nature,
> Cast ragged nets—today, along
> Those shores, astir with life and motion,
> Vast shapely palaces in throng
> And towers are seen: from every ocean,
> From the world's end, the ships come fast,
> To reach the loaded quays at last.

Human labour brings life where there was none. Wilderness and waste are changed by creative work. In the course of man's persevering struggle with nature wonderful objects are being created. In the poem Petersburg is taken as the symbol of all-conquering culture:

> A century—and that city young,
> Gem of the Northern world, amazing,
> From gloomy wood and swamp upsprung,
> Had risen in pride and splendor blazing.

In this connection the personality of Peter I, the founder of Petersburg, is shown in a very favourable light.

However, the culture grafted upon the country by the will of the autocrat benefited only the upper classes while the lower orders had to suffer all the privations and bear all the sacrifices. For these orders this culture was the source of incalculable suffering.

Yevgeni, the hero of *The Bronze Horseman,* is of the common people. He works in some chancery, "shunned the presence of the great" and "cared not of forebears dead and rotten, or antique matters long forgotten." Life made him no presents and "he had to win for himself independence and honour by his own labour." With bitterness in his heart Yevgeni thought of the "idle folk" who "lived easily and lightly." He was not looking for fortune but hoped to gain for himself some modicum of happiness. However, reality shattered all his hopes. During the terrible Petersburg flood the people dear to him perished and with them the girl he loved. Happiness proved impossible. The loss of all that is dear to Yevgeni is perceived as a symbol of the sacrifices which again and again are being brought for the glory of the autocrats. Shaken by the fateful events Yevgeni went mad. But his thoughts begin to clear when he happens to come across the statue of Peter I. Yevgeni recognizes the "potentate", the "lord of doom." In his soul there awakens the feeling of protest; Yevgeni is full of indignation and hatred. Yevgeni blames Peter for the miserable life man is forced to lead in the city, which bears his name and which he founded for the well-to-do. In the accusations of Yevgeni one hears plainly the voice of the lower orders, of the disinherited.

Pushkin saw the contrasts of the city; he felt the growing wrath of the common people and the coming struggle against social inequality.

> Where leapest thou? and where, on whom,
> Wilt plant thy hoof?—Ah, lord of doom
> And potentate, 'twas thus, appearing
> Above the void, and in thy hold
> A curb of iron, thou sat'st of old
> O'er Russia, on her haunches rearing!

With Yevgeni the poet introduced into Russian literature a new hero. He is of the common people, a man of toil, a representative of the democratic sections of society. His attitude to despotism, state and culture is revealed in the poem. The new democratic hero so far lacks confidence in his powers and in the justice of his protest. The greatness of Peter overwhelms Yevgeni. But when he came to his senses he began to understand the causes of the social evils. Pushkin foreshadows the inevitability of a sharp struggle.

In his *The Bronze Horseman* Pushkin takes an interest not so much in the outward life of his new hero as in his inner world, in the awakening of the spirit of protest, which is revealed by Pushkin with extreme brilliance. The description of his new, democratic hero is warmed up by deep sympathy. The upper circles of society consider the lower orders as mere building material of history. Pushkin, however, was indignant at this barbarous attitude of exploiters and displayed his own attitude of deep humanism. In *The Bronze Horseman* one can hear the echoes of Pushkin's other works such as "The Station-master" and *The Captain's Daughter* in which he denounced slavery and cruelty.

This poem is distinguished from Pushkin's other works by the exceptional depth and laconic manner in which the dramatic fate of the people on the lower rungs of the social ladder is depicted.

The Bronze Horseman has greatly influenced the subsequent development of Russian literature. The types of "poor" men with which our literature teems take their origin from the hero of *The Bronze Horseman.*

The poet's palette is exceedingly rich in colour. Pushkin possessed the remarkable art of ironic narration. Introducing lyrical elements in his poetical story and imbuing the latter with his impetuous passion, Pushkin created poems of great power. One is struck by the austere pathos and serene grandeur of his *Poltava.* In *The Bronze Horseman* it is the masterful psychological sketch, as well as the monumentality of the epic scenes that make an irresistible impression.

Throughout all his works Pushkin appears before us as a poet who was closely connected with the people. The reason for the great popularity of his works is to be found in the true picture he gives of society and its lower orders and in the great liberationist ideas with which his works are imbued. His penetrating mind of a thinker and his poetical genius have created pictures and images which will stir the emotions of man for a long time to come because they reflect the great truth of life.

C. M. Bowra (essay date 1955)

SOURCE: "Pushkin," in his *Inspiration and Poetry,* Macmillan & Co., 1955, pp. 153-73.

[*An English critic and literary historian, Bowra is known for his extensive writings on classical and modern literature. In the excerpt below, he compares Pushkin and Shakespeare, and remarks on the distinguishing characteristics and concerns of Pushkin's poetry, particularly his depiction of power.*]

[Pushkin's] genius is ultimately of the Shakespearian kind. This is not to say that he is so great a poet as Shakespeare. But he is Shakespearian in the sense that his genius worked not from any organised system of convictions but from an imaginative understanding of human beings. Of course he knew Shakespeare and imitated him up to a point in *Boris Godunov,* but he would not have imitated him so successfully if he had not had some real affinity with him. Pushkin enjoyed the living scene in the same way as Shakespeare, and had a similar gift of seeing the implicit poetry of human situations and actions and characters. It is this which enabled him to write with so fine and so easy an understanding of Gipsies and Caucasians, of old women like his nurse, of young women like Tatyana, of ruthless potentates like Peter the Great, of poor broken creatures like Evgeny in *The Bronze Horseman,* of ambitious adventurers like the False Dmitri and Marina of Poland, of rakes like Graf Nulin, and traitors like Mazepa. In a wide range of human types Pushkin discovered an essential poetry and displayed it not with any personal bias but somehow for its own sake, in its own right, with its own claims. His range of creation is much narrower than Shakespeare's, his details less rich, his imaginative reach less adventurous, but ultimately he belongs to the same class because what counts with him and sets his creative faculties to work is the poetical appeal of human beings.

A creative gift of this kind demands for its full realisation a poetry in which abstract ideas are kept in a subordinate place and introduced not for their intrinsic worth, but for the light which they throw on the characters who hold them or act in accordance with them. Whereas both Dante and Milton deal richly in ideas for their own sake, Shakespeare is interested in them because they are part of the infinite variety of human nature. His own ideas are to be found, if anywhere, not in explicit statements, but in the way in which he so constructs a plot as to elicit emotional responses from us and to guide us to conclusions more imaginative than intellectual. The same is true, up to a point, of Pushkin. In his longer poems, whether narratives or dramas, he shows how well he understands the poetry of ideas when they are expressed in emotion or action. His characters say what they think, but there is no assurance that Pushkin would agree with them. It is they who count. He asks that we should see them as they are, and respond to them. It is not for nothing that he was the father of the Russian novel, not merely in short stories like *The Queen of Spades,* but in his long poem *Evgeny Onegin,* or that his Lisa and Tatyana are the first examples of the Russian girl who makes so enchanting reappearances in Turgenev and Tolstoy. Pushkin had in him much of the novelist, in the sense that his creations live as human beings in their own strength and make us like them for their own sakes.

But though Pushkin had these Shakespearian gifts, he did not realise them on a Shakespearian scale or always in a Shakespearian way. For this an inferiority of genius is partly responsible, but this was accentuated by his time and circumstances, which were not favourable to his peculiar endowment. Shakespeare drew greatly, no doubt without realising it, on the new ideas which had come from Italy about the importance and the possibilities of man. His natural taste for human beings was strengthened and helped by the conception that man has unlimited potentialities and is a fascinating subject for his own sake, irrespective of theological or even of political doctrines. Pushkin found no such encouragement in his time. Though in youth he absorbed the liberal ideas which had filtered through to Russia from the French Revolution, the failure of the Decembrists, when he was twenty-six years old, taught him not to expect too much of politics, and his remaining years were spent in the knowledge that he and his fellow-countrymen were doomed to live in an age of increasing despotism. It may well be doubted whether in these years Russia was a land to encourage a poetry which needed for its widest fulfilment a confident belief in the worth of every man. It had certainly nothing of the Elizabethan spaciousness, the sense of vast worlds to be conquered both on the map and in the mind, the trust that no goal was impossible for anyone who had the courage to seek it. The regime of Nicholas I demanded a narrow and exacting conformity. Pushkin resisted it as best he could, but it hampered the free movement of his genius and deprived him of the encouragement which a temperament of his kind needs for its happy development.

Moreover, Pushkin's circumstances were completely unlike Shakespeare's. Shakespeare belonged to the new middle class and enjoyed all its splendid opportunities for social intercourse both in London and the country. Pushkin, like Shelley and Byron and Leopardi, was an aristocrat, and, more significantly, an impoverished aristocrat. He was distrusted and disliked by the rich nobles who gathered at the court and had the ear of the Emperor. Pushkin might despise them for their dubious lineage, but he was powerless against them. He lived in their world, but as an inferior, and in his last years almost as a lackey. The restrictions which the Tsar imposed on his movements gave him few chances to study a wide range of human types and ways of life. What chances he had, he took. He studied Gipsies in Bessarabia and primitive mountaineers in the Caucasus; he picked up folk-lore and folk-tales; he delved into the State archives to learn about rebels like Stepan Razin and Pugachev. But in the main his life was confined within narrow limits. He was never allowed to go abroad, and missed the enlargement of horizon which did so much for Byron and Shelley. Most of his life was spent in or near St. Petersburg or at his home in the country. He moved in high society, which gave him many subjects for personal poetry but did little to nurture his naturally Shakespearian gifts. In other times or in another country he might have turned his love of human beings to create a vast world of living persons. Indeed, if he had been born even twenty years later in Russia, he might have done in verse something equivalent to what the great novelists did in prose. But the time was against him and limited the play of his creative powers.

These restrictions were not without their compensations. They meant that Pushkin wrote not only narrative poems and plays about other people, but lyrical poems about himself which have a wonderful range and strength and skill. We cannot complain of him, as we can of Shakespeare, that he tells us too little about himself. He is not only delightfully frank but able to make marvellous poetry about incidents which lesser men would find trivial and uninspiring. Like Camões and Tasso, Pushkin is a master both of narrative and of lyrical poetry because his personal problems were too insistent to allow him to confine himself to the objective presentation of other men's lives. But more than Camões or Tasso, Pushkin applies to his lyrical poetry the same kind of outlook which he gives to his narratives. For him each personal situation lives for its own sake and has a dramatic appeal for him. If he saw the world as a stage, he knew that he himself was one of the actors, and he watched his own life with a mixture of insight and detachment which makes every one of his lyrical poems the record of a dramatic episode, complete in itself and stirring because of the situation which it presents. Even when he unveils his innermost thoughts, Pushkin does not philosophise or draw general conclusions. What interests him in his own life is just the same kind of thing that interests him in the lives of others. That is why his lyrical poetry is different from that of Shelley or Leopardi or Lermontov. With all its candour and sweetness and astonishing truth to the emotions it remains somehow dramatic, and that is its special strength.

With such gifts Pushkin was fundamentally unlike the Romantic poets of his age who followed Byron in developing to the utmost their personal idiosyncrasies and treating the universe as a background for magnificent gestures. Though Pushkin was deeply impressed by Byron and

learned much from him, his was not a Byronic personality, except in his discontent with his circumstances and his quarrel with the existing social scheme. He lacked Byron's capacity to make himself the centre of a world and to fit everything into it. Even when he wrote on what look like Byronic subjects in *The Gipsies* and *Poltava,* his sense of human beings and dramatic situations led him to produce an essentially different kind of poetry. Though he began *Evgeny Onegin* with the idea of making it a second *Don Juan,* he soon passed beyond this and made it an independent narrative in which his personal tastes are kept to a subordinate place. He was not interested in cutting a figure before the world, and was quite incapable of pose. Though in his poetical world he himself plays a considerable part, he is by no means the only figure in it, and when he introduces other figures, he does so, not because they resemble himself or represent some unfulfilled ambition of his own, but because they engage his fancy and sympathy and understanding.

If Pushkin differed from Byron and the Byronic poets by the special character of his outlook, he differed no less in the quality of his art. It was their misfortune that in their devotion to their special experience they were often unable to submit their unrestrained temperaments to the stiff discipline which poetry demands. Pushkin, it is true, resembled the Romantics in being able to write poetry only when the creative fit was on him. Then he would work for days and nights on end, unconscious of everything except the poem which was forming itself in his mind. At last he would reappear with the finished work of art. So, we may imagine, Shakespeare too worked. But, unlike Shakespeare, Pushkin cannot be accused of never blotting a line. His manuscripts are as crowded as Flaubert's with erasions and corrections and second and third and fourth thoughts. All these came to him helter-skelter in the bustling, crowded process of composition. He differed completely from most of the Romantics in that his critical sense was excited at the same time as his creative powers. He had so clear an idea of what poetry ought to be and so sure a judgment in writing it that he did not cease composition until his highly critical taste was satisfied that every word was as right as he could make it.

Pushkin is, in fact, a classical writer. He certainly owed something to the classical past. Though he did not know Greek, he was well grounded in Latin, preferred Apuleius to Cicero at school, and later, when he was in Bessarabia, was led by the memory of Ovid's exile at Tomi to study his poetry. But he owed more to recent writers who wrote in a classical tradition, whether French poets of the eighteenth century or his own Russian forerunner and friend, Zhukovsky. When Pushkin began to write, Russian was still largely an unexploited language. Much, indeed, had been done to establish a metric and a style, but vast untried possibilities still lay open. In this respect Pushkin again resembles Shakespeare, who had at his disposal a language which had indeed been prepared for use but had not been fully exploited, still less ravaged. But while Shakespeare's English was a wild, exuberant, colloquial growth, which drew strength from all classes of society, Pushkin's Russian was largely confined to the language of educated people and conformed almost inevitably to the standards of elegance which the eighteenth century had sanctified. Although his lyrical poems are written in a wide variety of metres, and his plays in what was for Russians a new kind of blank verse, Pushkin had to operate with stricter forms than Shakespeare and to satisfy a prevailing taste for elegance and harmony. Of course he made many innovations and greatly enriched the language of Russian poetry, but he remains a classical poet in his finish, his neatness, his balance, his restraint.

Pushkin is also a classical poet in another sense. His poetry is indeed individual in that every word does its special work and the whole result is a unique thing which only he could have written. But this poetry is based on the familiar experience of ordinary men. Pushkin takes this, refines it, and makes the most of it, but it remains profoundly and essentially human in its truth to common life. This is not what his Romantic contemporaries do. They delight in the unfamiliar and the unknown, in their own original whims and fancies, and the less close these are to the familiar world, the more they like them. Pushkin was classical in his firm hold on the essential facts of human experience, on the feelings and thoughts of ordinary people. Even when he took what look like Romantic subjects and wrote fairy-tales or stories about primitive barbarians, he tried to pierce through the unfamiliar exterior to the fundamental humanity behind it. He knew that Gipsies and Caucasians were not in the least like his own circle, but he was less attracted by their remoteness from it than by a suspicion that in some ways they were more real. He explored human nature with the insight of genius, but always with an eye to its permanent and essential qualities. To appreciate his success we must look not to his contemporaries in any European country, but to great poets of the past who are concerned with the natural movements of the human heart and not with the exotic or the esoteric or the peculiar.

This classical outlook requires a master to make use of it. It falls too easily into formality or stiffness or pomposity. The demand for harmonious versification may mean that a poet secures it at the expense of his content. But when this manner is handled by a poet who has much of importance to say and is fully aware of both the limitations and the advantages of his medium, the result is sometimes a flawless blend of manner and matter. If the poet keeps his eye on the human appeal of his subject and makes every effort to present it fully, the classical manner has an irresistible simplicity, because it preserves the essential qualities of something keenly felt and vividly realised. In his use of words Pushkin may be compared with Racine. Though Racine's vocabulary is smaller and more stylised, and though he operates with almost a single metre, he resembles Pushkin in his combination of lucidity and power. In such poetry the depth and strength of what is said lose nothing by being completely clear. Perhaps, too, we may compare Pushkin with Virgil. Virgil is indeed more elaborate, but he too is concerned with the ordinary, familiar emotions. He understands them so well and finds so much in them that he has no need to explore unusual regions of the spirit. In these poets candour and passion fall naturally into a formal pattern and give life to it. That is the secret of the classical style, and one of the reasons for its perennial appeal.

Pushkin has an extraordinary simplicity both of manner and of content. Indeed, when we first read him, with our minds full perhaps of Dostoevsky and certainly expecting something wild and strange, we may find this simplicity disconcerting. It all seems very quiet, very neat, even unadventurous. Pushkin's subjects seldom give a shock of wild surprise. He seldom lets himself go with such denunciations of the universe as we find in Leopardi, whose life was almost coterminous with his. The great poet of the most emotional and least inhibited of European peoples seems at first sight strangely self-controlled and to eschew any extravagance or excess. In translation he may even appear to be flat, since he lacks the qualities which survive most easily in translation—exciting themes, bold imagery, and violent effects. But when we read him closely and know him better, we find ourselves in the presence of a very unusual poetry, whose first quality is its effortless, direct approach to experience. Just because Pushkin understands so well the range and strength of human feelings, he is able to present them in what looks a very simple shape. This simplicity comes from inspired insight and embracing sympathy, from an understanding which knows its subject so well that it brushes aside anything which is not absolutely essential.

This simplicity is accompanied by a candour which is peculiarly Russian. Just as the great Russian novelists seem to be the only ones capable of telling what first love really is or of describing guilt and remorse, so Pushkin is able, without any protective irony or preparatory excuse, to speak of all kinds of emotion with complete frankness. A set of poems on Amalia Riznich illustrates his frankness and close observation of his own emotions. He was much in love with her, and one or two poems show the power of his passion. Then in 1825 he heard the news of her death, and, despite his love for her, he found that somehow the news did not distress him. He tells how he hears of it with indifference and is surprised that their passion, with its fire and stress and sweetness, its suffering and folly, should end like this. He looks in his heart and finds no sorrow and no regret. Only a Russian could speak like this; only Pushkin could make a truly moving poem of it. Five years later, in 1830, Pushkin found himself assailed by memories of Amalia, whose death had meant so little to him, and this time he regrets her death bitterly in three of his finest poems. In one he summons her spirit from the grave because he wishes to tell her that he still loves her. In a second he imagines that he is kissing her, but feels that he is as dead to her in one way as she is to him in another, though none the less he sends her his greeting, his farewell as a friend might say farewell to a friend before going into exile. In a third poem he reminds her of their last meeting, when they tore their lips apart and she promised to continue their embrace in her own southern land: . . .

> But there, alas! where azure gleam
> Irradiates the vaulted skies,
> Beneath the cliff where waters dream,
> You fell asleep, no more to rise.
> Your beauty in the grave's abyss
> Has vanished, and your misery—

Gone is the resurrection kiss . . .
I wait for it. It is for me.

[In a footnote, Bowra states: "The translation follows a text which is almost certainly not that which Pushkin wrote. We might, in the interests of accuracy, emend 'Beneath the cliff where waters dream' to 'By olive-trees where waters dream.' "] This is the simplicity of the heart which has no truck with poses or pretences and must speak the truth. It is presented in words no less simple, and direct, and passionate.

This simplicity in no way impoverishes Pushkin's poetry but enriches it by its concentration on what really matters. When he sought to get every word right, he was guided by a desire to secure the greatest possible richness of content, to extract from a situation all that was most exciting and most exalting in it. He was capable of most emotions from rapturous joy to black despair; he was not above pride and envy; he had moments of sharp irony and savage abuse. Whatever the occasion might be, he made the most of it. That is why he is a great poet of love. He does not try, like Shelley, to reduce all the manifestations of love to a celestial pattern, nor, like Byron, is he suspicious of even the most tender and innocent affections. Pushkin knows the whole gamut of love from his own experience, and that is why he understands it so well in others. He fell in love with many women, and on each occasion surrendered himself completely to it. With his embracing sympathy he needed someone to whom he could give his devotion, some altar on which to lay his heart. Love was the full expression of his tenderness and need for affection and worship. It brought out his noblest qualities and even awoke religious feelings of joy and sanctity. In his lines to Anna Kern he tells how her reappearance in his life wakens him to God, inspiration, life, tears, and love. In his chaste and exalted **"The Beauty"** he speaks of the impression, akin to a sense of holiness, which a beautiful woman makes on him. In an incomparable poem of eight lines, addressed to an unnamed woman who has never known of his devotion, he reveals the generous and tender nature of a love which still survives when its hopeless passion is finished: . . .

I loved you once, and in my soul, maybe,
Love is not altogether dead to-day.
But you shall not be troubled more by me;
I would not sadden you in any way.
I loved you silently and hopelessly,
Racked now by jealousy and now by shame;
I loved so truly and so tenderly—
God grant some other's love may be the same.

Pushkin displays the same strength and purity of passion when he describes love in others, from the self-sacrificing devotion of the girl in **The Prisoner of the Caucasus** to Tatyana's first love for Onegin [in **Eugene Onegin**], or Maria's wild and fatal passion for Mazepa [in **Poltava**]. It is not merely that this poetry lacks anything false or pretentious or that Pushkin never over-dramatises himself or his characters: it is rather that he sees a situation so clearly and responds to it so warmly that he goes straight to its heart and grasps its essential nature.

This poetry is firmly founded in truth. Pushkin matched his keen intelligence with a scrupulous honesty. His wide sympathy did not beguile him into misinterpreting the real elements of a situation, nor did he falsify anything in order to make it more exciting. Again and again he refuses to shirk the implications of a subject or to make it conform to some conventional idea of human behaviour. This gift may be seen abundantly in his dramas and narrative poems. It informs his portrait of Onegin, who is neither good nor bad, but an average man spoiled by idleness and boredom; of Zemfira in **The Gipsies,** a wild creature who follows her emotions so faithfully that, when she ceases to love a man, she cannot keep up any pretences; of Marina in *Boris Godunov,* who knows that Dmitri is an impostor but is fascinated by his reckless dreams of power and his shameless self-confidence; of the old traitor, Mazepa, who accepts a young girl's love and then sacrifices it to his own relentless ambition. Such characters, and others like them, are built not from abstract ideas or dreaming desires but from a keen, sometimes ruthless, examination of life. Pushkin drew much of his dramatic power from this unflinching insight. All his situations are built firmly on human nature. The result is that we understand at once what he means and do not have to make any awkward adjustments to appreciate his poetry.

> **Pushkin drew much of his dramatic power from his unflinching insight into human ambitions and desires. All his situations are built firmly on human nature. The result is that we understand at once what he means and do not have to make any awkward adjustments to appreciate his poetry.**
>
> **— C. M. Bowra**

Pushkin's sense of truth is part of his delightful sanity. Perhaps sanity on this scale is not a quality for which we usually look in Russian writers. It may be present often enough in the great novelists and the later poets, but it is not what we love them for or most admire in them. Indeed, we are so accustomed to talk of the Russian soul and its agonies and frenzies that sanity like Pushkin's may even seem alien to the most authentic manifestations of the Russian genius. We are liable to look in his poetry for what Virginia Woolf calls 'this cloudy, yeasty, precious stuff, the soul'. With Dostoevski and Blok, with Chekhov and Esenin, this is right enough. But it is not right with Pushkin. However much he did to form Russian poetry and the Russian character, he did not form the Russian notion of the soul in its more advanced and more reckless manifestations. That was perhaps the work of Nekrasov, though no doubt he merely gave expression to something already existing in many men and women. Pushkin was different. He was absorbed by human nature in many of its aspects; he examined it with sympathy and love, but not with violent apprehensions about its salvation or damnation or with searching questions about the worth of even the smallest actions before the Throne of Grace. He had a profound sense of good and evil, but his wide understanding did not allow him to condemn anyone about whom he did not know the full facts. His sanity kept him to his task of giving to men and women a wide and imaginative sympathy, but forbade him to take greater risks.

Pushkin's poetry is so rich and satisfying that we hardly feel any need to look for a consistent philosophy in it or to ask what his ultimate vision of life is. No doubt he himself would have said that he had nothing of the kind, but was content to interpret what came to him through the mood and insight of the moment. At first sight we may well think that he has no unifying outlook. He was a man of many contradictions and allowed them to appear in his poetry. Though he disliked the domineering methods of Nicholas I and suffered much from them, he once at least praised him in all honesty for his generosity. At one time he would regard the universe as governed by a merciless destiny, at another speak in the language of devout Christian faith. His liberal conception of Russia's destiny did not prevent him from outbursts of bellicose patriotism. But such inconsistencies were merely the result of his impressionable nature. When he said a thing, he believed it; and there is no possible doubt of his sincerity. Such a man might well have no final philosophy, and it would be quite understandable, if he never made up his mind on certain fundamental questions. This indeed might be argued. Though his narratives and plays have certain leading ideas which shape their course, they do not come to explicit conclusions or even force us to such emotional judgments as Shakespeare does. We might well think that the human scene was enough for Pushkin, and that he loved it so much that he did not wish to make it conform to any metaphysical scheme.

Yet if we look at the succession of Pushkin's great works, we see something developing which is, if not a guiding idea, at least a frame of mind, a way of arranging and interpreting experience, an assertion of certain contrasts and conflicts. No doubt Pushkin was largely unconscious of this line of thought because it was forced on him by circumstances in his own life. It is an ever-growing concern about the relation of the ordinary individual to powers which dominate and hamper him. Pushkin's life may well account for his persistent interest in this subject. At the Lycée of Tsarskoe Selo he had, in his inspired and marvellous boyhood, known an enchanting carelessness and irresponsibility. His schooldays were indeed the happiest of his life. He made friendships which lasted till death; he fell in love; he wrote his first poems; he made innumerable jokes about his teachers and his companions. Never did a man of genius have so full and happy a boyhood as Pushkin, or regret it so keenly ever afterwards. Until death Pushkin would have liked to regain this lost happiness, to be once again his full, unhampered, reckless, boyish self. The malice of circumstances forbade. Pushkin was frustrated by inadequate means, by a none too suitable marriage, by the rasping supervision of his work conducted by the Tsar through Count Benckendorff, by many kinds of humiliating restrictions, and by his own jealous temperament which brought him to death at the age of thirty-

seven in a duel fought over his wife's honour. Pushkin, who was capable of exultant joy and liked most kinds of pleasure, suffered miserably from the lack of liberty. He wished to be free absolutely, to be magnificently and unmistakably himself, to fulfil his nature as he knew that, if circumstances only allowed, he could. How bitterly he felt in his last years that he had failed may be seen from some lines which he wrote to his wife: . . .

> 'Tis time, my friend, 'tis time. For rest the heart is aching.
> Day follows day in flight, and every hour is taking
> Life's little pieces, while together you and I
> Make plans to live. But look how soon we both shall die.
>
> Not happiness—but rest and freedom life possesses.
> Long to an envied fate my dreaming fancy presses,
> And long, a worn-out lackey, I have plotted flight
> To some far cloister where are work and chaste delight.

When he wrote these lines, Pushkin had begun to give up the unequal struggle, but the desire for freedom was still strong in him, even if it was only for freedom from a round of wearisome and humiliating duties. The conflict between this obsessing desire and his inhibiting circumstances accounts for much in the development of his poetry and a certain pattern in his creative life.

In his longer works the issues with which Pushkin deals fall into a kind of pattern which suggests an individual, if not very articulate, metaphysic. He presents life as divided into two parts which are almost necessarily hostile to one another. On the one side is the world of ordinary men and women, creatures of emotion and passion, longing to enjoy freedom and happiness. Some of them are entirely charming and delightful; others are hard and even sinister. But all alike are human in their desire to follow their own ambitions and satisfy their own desires. Despite their efforts, they are doomed to failure or disaster, and good and bad alike are foiled by circumstances. On the other side Pushkin sets great powers, present perhaps in the government of the universe but more obviously at work in human life, whether in some men, who are unlike the rest of their kind in their prodigious energy and ruthless love of power, or in systems of society and government, which deny or ruin the happiness of their subjects, or even in ordinary human beings whose natural instincts are crossed and countered by strange, alien flashes of destructive energy. These powers, wherever they are to be found, are formidable, relentless, and inhuman, but somehow impressive and always to be treated with respect and fear. Sooner or later the one class comes into conflict with the other, and the second invariably wins. In depicting this struggle Pushkin was as impartial as a man could be. Wherever his own sympathies might lie, to whichever class he felt himself to belong, he was too scrupulous and too sensitive not to present both sides with dispassionate justice and understanding. His poetical universe is built on the struggle between the common desires of men and women and incal-

Natalie Pushkin, the poet's wife.

culable powers, within and without them, which break into their lives and defeat them.

Pushkin sometimes treats of this struggle at a human and indeed a political level. He is one of the first European poets to make political power an almost absolute element. Sophocles and Dante deal with it, but in relation to wider schemes of existence and value; Pushkin makes it live in its own right, beyond explanation or appeal. His attitude towards it is curiously ambiguous. On the one hand it fascinates him, and he finds a notable example of it in Peter the Great. Pushkin spent some time in studying the history of Peter's reign; he liked to recall that he himself was descended from Peter's Abyssinian, the ruthless and furious Hannibal; he liked almost everything about Peter and implicitly exalts him as what a Tsar ought to be. In *Poltava* Peter is the authentic hero, the superman, who gains glory through violent action. When he suddenly makes his appearance, we feel ourselves in the presence of some daemonic being: . . .

> Surrounded
> By followers, the best preferred,
> Came Peter, as he spoke the word,
> Out of his tent. His eyes shone brightly,
> His face struck terror. Swiftly, lightly,
> Moved Peter, wearing, as he trod,
> The splendour of the wrath of God.

This is what Pushkin sees in the embodiment of imperial power, and there is no doubt of his admiration for it.

On the other hand, Pushkin also saw that such power has its ruthless and even hideous side. He created his myth for this in his poem **"Anchar."** It tells of the upas-tree, which grows in the desert and oozes a poison which pollutes the air and allows no bird or beast to come near. One day a King sends his servant to gather the poison. He does so and brings it back to the King, only to die at once from it. The King then dips his arrows in it and uses them to spread death and destruction among all his neighbours. Into this poem Pushkin puts ideas and emotions which are almost antithetical to those which he puts into *Poltava.* The King, who sends for the poison, has no motives other than the exercise of power and destruction for their own sakes. In this he resembles the tree which was born on a day of wrath and feeds its leaves and roots on poison. In a world of natural things it is unnatural in that it destroys life and is shunned by everything alive. Even the winds flee from it, and its only company is the sand at its roots which receives the venomous dew from its branches. So, too, the King is an unnatural monster among men. His only motive is the lust of power, and this leads him to destroy. Such a creature has no regard for his servants and sacrifices them to his cold, abstract, unnatural purpose. This is the other side to Pushkin's complex notion of power. If Peter at Poltava shows its glory, the King shows its horror and savagery.

In this dual system Pushkin had, no doubt, his personal preferences. In his own life he suffered too much from the heartless whims of imperial power not to feel abundant sympathy for the oppressed. At times he could hardly avoid giving the impression that he thinks such power abhorrent and its results evil. In *Poltava* the girl, Maria, goes mad because her husband, Mazepa, who is himself a traitor, has her father executed on a false charge of treachery. He desires power for its own sake, and for it turns to treachery and murder. His wife's happiness is of no importance to him in comparison with his ambitions, and though in the end he fails to get what he wants, he feels no remorse for his vile doings. In *Mozart and Salieri* Salieri poisons Mozart because he cannot endure that a man so gifted should be alive. He tries to justify himself with sophistries, but he does not convince even himself, and indeed his malignity is almost without motive, the instinctive hatred of the cold and uncreative pedant for the warm and abundant genius. In these two cases the principle of destruction is closely allied to the love of power. Mazepa and Salieri cease to be human when their dominating passion is aroused, and their victims, Maria and Mozart, are human beings who have their full share of life and gaiety and suspect no evil in those who destroy them. Through such stories Pushkin shows his sense of a conflict in which the lust for power murders many delightful natural things.

Yet, despite his personal inclinations, Pushkin kept his impartiality on this central issue. He continued to feel the appeal of power and to admit its hold on him. He balanced the competing claims and gave the final expression of his view in **The Bronze Horseman,** in which the issue is raised almost to a metaphysical plane. On one side is the pathetic

Evgeny, whose life is ruined when his betrothed dies in a great flood and whose crazed wits are haunted by the statue of Peter the Great which he frequents. There is no denying that Evgeny has a profound and even tragic pathos and is a symbol of ordinary men who are broken alike by circumstances and by a social system over which they have no control. But that is only half the picture. The other half consists of Pushkin's obvious admiration for the granite city which Peter the Great, in defiance of natural conditions, built on the Neva marshes, and of his sense of awe before the great monarch whose statue becomes an emblem of incarnate power, as it haunts the insane Evgeny and makes him think that he is pursued by it: . . .

> And rushing through the empty square,
> He hears behind him as it were
> Thunders that rattle in a chorus,
> A gallop ponderous, sonorous,
> That shakes the pavement. At full height,
> Illumined by the pale moonlight,
> With arm outflung, behind him riding
> See, the bronze horseman comes, bestriding
> The charger clanging in his flight.
> All night the madman flees; no matter
> Where he may wander at his will,
> Hard on his track with heavy clatter
> There the bronze horseman gallops still.

If Evgeny appeals to us by his helpless pathos and is a fit example of all human beings whose lives are ruined by ruthless power, the Bronze Horseman has his own magnificence and awakes at least awe and fear.

Pushkin's dual system of power and pathos, of inscrutable, inhuman forces, and an all too human humanity, resembles in some ways that of the Attic tragedians. Just as he saw life dominated by relentless and awful powers, so in their gods the Greeks saw not dissimilar beings, radiant indeed and alluring but remote and merciless. If Pushkin believed that life is ultimately at the mercy of powerful forces, he knew that these are also to be found in ourselves and our systems, that they are within and without us. So, too, the Greeks might set their gods on Olympus but know that they work also in the hearts of men. Indeed, we may press the comparison farther. For, just as Pushkin's characters fail through their desire to be too fully themselves, so the Greeks attributed many disasters to the desire of men to get more than the rules of life allow. In such a system the defeated call for compassion and the victors for awe. The poet, whether Pushkin or Sophocles, sees both sides of the conflict and understands them equally.

Yet Pushkin's outlook is not ultimately like that of the Greeks. The Greeks believed that in the last analysis man is but a shadow in a dream and that all his ambitions and efforts are as nothing: let him remember this and be humble. But Pushkin loves his human creatures and never questions the ultimate worth of their happiness. He brings his opposing elements together in fierce conflicts, but in these he finds something thrilling and exciting, a challenge and an inspiration. In his *Feast at the Time of Plague* he dramatises the exaltation which men feel in the immediate presence of death. The very thought that everything will soon be finished only makes it more delightful and more worth having. In his own way Pushkin has a tragic out-

look. He holds out no hope of compensations for suffering; he does not suggest that the universe is ultimately either right or reasonable; he insists that the most delightful people are the most likely to come to disaster. But the paradox of Pushkin's tragic outlook is that it makes him a poet of joy. Though some of his assumptions are basically as pessimistic as Leopardi's, he draws exactly opposite conclusions from them. When he surveyed his own failures and defeats or was haunted by regret and remorse, his answer was not to wish for annihilation but to look forward to new moments of delight: . . .

> But oh! my friends, I do not ask to die!
> I crave more life, more dreams, more agony!
> Midmost the care, the panic, the distress,
> I know that I shall taste of happiness.
> Once more I shall be drunk on strains divine,
> Be moved to tears by musings that are mine,
> And haply when the last sad hour draws nigh,
> Love with a farewell smile may gild the sky.

This was the kind of life which Pushkin desired for himself and for others. If he had a philosophy, it was that the cruel conditions of existence can best be defied if in the time at our disposal we try to be most truly ourselves and to make the most of our natural desire for affection and joy.

Yury Lotman (essay date 1966)

SOURCE: "The Structure of *Eugene Onegin*," in *Russian Views of Pushkin's 'Eugene Onegin',* edited and translated by Sona Stephan Hoisington, Indiana University Press, 1988, pp. 91-114.

[*In the following excerpt from an essay originally published in the journal* Uchenye zapiski Tartuskogo gosudarstvennogo universiteta, *Lotman analyzes* Eugene Onegin's *structure, noting its impact on characterization and theme.*]

[In an] earlier article I attempted to show how Pushkin's ideas about what determines a man's character changed during the years he was working on the text of *Eugene Onegin,* and that, correspondingly, the literary plan of the novel underwent evolution. However, even if one assumes that I succeeded in showing that the evolution in literary principles was in accord with the evolution in Pushkin's ideas, the question still remains: Why does the novel exist in the reader's consciousness as a whole, given such a clear shift in the author's aesthetic position? To put it differently: Why didn't Pushkin, who was such a severe critic of his own work, make changes in chapters which were written from a position he no longer espoused? Or why didn't he abandon the novel? Often Pushkin did abandon unfinished sketches of stories and novels which lagged behind the tempo of his literary development, but with *Eugene Onegin* he proceeded differently. Over the years he stored up chapters, he "garnered the stanzas" of his "motley" novel and created an organic whole from heterogeneous parts. The inevitable contradictions which arose as a result of this process did not disturb him at all. To the contrary, as if fearing that the reader would not notice them, he hurried to report at the end of Chapter I:

> I have gone over it severely,
> And contradictions there are clearly

Galore, but I will let them go,

And, in fact, contradictions are evident in the characterization of the hero, even within Chapter I. From studying Pushkin's evolution as a poet it is quite easy to explain why he altered the ironic characterization of Onegin's disenchantment (cf., for example, the mocking note to I, 21, where Onegin's exclamation that the ballet leaves him cold is labeled "A trait of chilled sentiment worthy of Childe Harold"), making that disenchantment appear tragic in I, 44-46: "He who has lived and thought can never / Look on mankind without disdain" [I, 46]. It is equally easy to explain why the characterization of Tatyana changed. From "She knew our language only barely / . . . In her own language she was slow / To make her meaning clear" [III, 26], she became "Tatyana—Russian in her feeling" [V, 4]. It is considerably more difficult, however, to explain why Pushkin did not eliminate these and other contradictions when he compiled the stanzas and chapters into a single text. When we attempt to list these "contradictions," we become convinced that they occupy a very significant place in the literary fabric of the novel. This makes us wonder if what we perceive to be a "contradiction" is not really a significant structural element.

In order to resolve this question let us introduce the concept "point of view." This concept manifests itself as the relationship of a system to its subject ("system" in a given context may be realized either on the linguistic level or on some other higher level). By "subject of a system" (whether ideological, stylistic, or whatever) we mean a consciousness capable of generating such a structure and, consequently, a consciousness which can be reconstructed in the process of reading the text.

A literary system is constructed as a hierarchy of relationships. The very concept "to have meaning" implies the presence of a certain attitude, that is, of a definite orientation. But since the literary model, in its most general form, reproduces an image of the world for a given consciousness, that is, models the relationship between the individual and the world (in particular, between a cognizing individual and the cognizable world), then this orientation will be both subjective and objective in nature.

In Russian poetry before Pushkin typically all the subjective and objective relationships expressed in the text converged in a single fixed focus. In eighteenth-century literature, which we know as Classicism, this single focus transcended the author's personality and coincided with the concept of Truth, in whose name the artistic text spoke. The relationship of truth to the world represented became the artistic point of view. The fixed and monosemantic nature of these relationships, their convergence toward a single center, corresponded to the notion that Truth was eternal, indivisible, and immutable. Though indivisible and unchanging, Truth was at the same time hierarchical—that is, it revealed itself to different consciousnesses in differing degrees. Hence the corresponding hierarchy of points of view, which formed the basis of the rules governing the various genres.

In Romantic poetry the points of view also converged toward a firmly fixed center, and the relationships themselves were monosemantic and highly predictable (this explains why the Romantic style is so easy to parody). The center, which was the subject of the poetic text, coincided with the author's personality, becoming his lyrical double.

However, a text may be structured in such a way that the points of view are not focused in a single center but form a diffused subject made up of different centers. The relationships between these centers create additional meanings. For example:

> In vain I hasten on to Sion's heights; I feel
> Sin ravenously racing close upon my heel;
> The hungry lion tracks a fleeing roebuck's scent.

Clearly one cannot attribute both "dusty nostrils" and "fleeing roebuck's scent" to a single point of view. The first has as its subject the man observing the lion; the second, the lion itself, since man is incapable of perceiving the track of a roebuck as something which gives off an odor, to say nothing of a pungent scent. But "hungry lion" and "dusty nostrils" do not have a single subject center either, since one implies an observer who is not concretized in space, while the other implies the contemplation of the lion at close range, at a distance which would permit the observer to discern the dust covering the lion's nostrils. Thus, even if we restrict ourselves to the final two lines, we observe not one focal center for the points of view but a kind of diffused subject embodying a series of viewpoints. The relationships between them become an additional source of meanings. Obviously, if one is striving to create an illusion of reality, to endow certain combinations of words with the character of the reproduced object, one will find that this second structural principle opens up greater possibilities.

As we noted, in Russian literature before Pushkin typically the point of view expressed in a work was fixed. In this sense the multiplicity of viewpoints in the genre system of Classicism and the singleness of viewpoint (based on philosophical subjectivism) in the lyrics of Zhukovsky were phenomena of the same sort. The number of possible viewpoints was small, determined for the reader by his previous literary experience. Inevitably, if the reader found that a literary text diverged from some point of view, he assumed that this was a sign that the text belonged to another system with another fixed structure.

Ruslan and Lyudmila marked an important stage in the development of Pushkin's own literary system. Here the innovation was largely negative in character. Taken as a whole the poem did not fit any one of the canonical points of view. The mechanism used, which posed such difficulties for critics at the time, was relatively simple. Each of the individual fragments constituting the text easily accorded with traditional notions. However, the commingling of points of view, which would have been unthinkable in the preceding period, transformed the world of Pushkin's poem into a kingdom of relativity. The fixed nature of the relationships between the work and its subject was undermined by play, which ironically revealed the conventionality of all the viewpoints ascribed to the author.

Eugene Onegin marked a new stage in text construction.

In a well-known note, "On Prose" (1822), Pushkin explicitly opposes expression and content in purely semiotic terms. He condemns periphrastic prose (most notably the school of Karamzin) because it is not truthful. And here the criteria for truthfulness are very interesting. Pushkin rejects the notion that a text should be constructed according to conventional rules. To the structurally organized text ("glittering expressions") he opposes "simple" content, conceived of as life itself. Now "life" in a literary work is non-aestheticized speech; it is a text which is artistically unorganized and therefore true. But naturally, any text, once it is incorporated into a literary work, becomes a literary text. Thus we are confronted by the problems of constructing a literary (i. e., organized) text, which will imitate a nonliterary (unorganized) one, of creating a structure which will be perceived as the *absence* of structure.

In the course of this [essay] we will attempt to show how such a textual structure is generated in Pushkin's novel. As we will see, in order to evoke in the reader the feeling that the text is simple, its language colloquial, its plot lifelike and spontaneous, and its characters natural, a far more complex literary construct was required than any known at that time. The effect of *simplification* was achieved at the price of greatly *complicating* the structure of the text.

In the 1822 note Pushkin expresses the conviction that only by renouncing the false conventionality of existing literary styles can one achieve artistic truth. To tell the truth means to state things simply. . . .

In 1822 Pushkin thought that "simple speech" was essential for prose but that "poetry was another matter." However, subsequently his understanding of "prose" (prose conceived of as simplicity, the rejection of literary conventions, the movement of content into an extra-literary series—i. e., realia) expanded to embrace poetry as well. And here the process of prosifying poetry was viewed as a struggle for truthfulness and pithiness.

One of the most widespread devices used in *Eugene Onegin* is that of exposing the real-life content of romantic expressions when brought face to face with the "prose" of reality. This device is particularly obvious in passages where the author's style is formed in opposition to the system of conventional literary expressions. The text that emerges consists of two paired parts, where one of the parts—the "simple" one—acts as the *meaning* of the other, exposing its literary conventionality:

> He thinks: "I will be her redeemer,
> Will not permit the shameless schemer
> With sighs and praise and sultry art
> To tempt the inexperienced heart,
> That noisome gnawing worm shan't slither
> Near the young lily's tender stem
> Oozing his poison, to condemn
> The yet half-open bud to wither."
> *And all this meant was, in the end:*
> *I shall be shooting at my friend.*
>   [the italics are Lotman's]

Here the "simple" part of the text, which is constructed of extrasystemic vocabulary (extrasystemic from the standpoint of the conventional first part), is perceived to be prose or, what in this case is equivalent, content, the *meaning* of Lensky's monologue. The specific rhythmic organization of the text ceases to be relevant. It is not significant since it is characteristic of both opposing texts, and therefore it does not preclude our thinking that the final two lines lack structural organization. The rhythmically organized text becomes a recreation of colloquial prose. Everything that distinguishes the text from colloquial prose loses significance, and everything that coincides with it becomes a sign of differentiation. . . .

Since only the "false" plane has structure, the "true" plane can only be characterized negatively as the *absence* of any marked structural quality. Similarly, Tatyana shapes her own personality in correspondence with the system of expression she has assimilated:

> . . . and in herself discovers
> Another's glow, another's smart,

Her real personality is the living equivalent of the conventional romantic heroine she perceives herself to be:

> Her fancy-fed imagination
> Casts her in turn as heroine
> Of every favorite creation,
> Julie, Clarissa, or Delphine.

Here we are not talking about any concrete system of consciousness, although in this cluster of ideas one can easily detect elements of Romanticism. What we have in mind is much broader: it is the conventional bookish model of the world, encompassing the *sum total* of literary traditions present in Pushkin's time. This unified structure, wherein are joined the conventional image of the heroine and the conventional system of expression, also determines the type of hero. In this system Onegin can be perceived only when translated into Tatyana's conventional language. To her, he is "dear hero," "guardian angel," or "demon of temptation." If he is "dear hero," he will be "perfection come to earth," endowed "With soul so tender, intellect, / Abetted by attractive looks." If he is a "tempter," he will be "a brooding Vampire, / Or wandering Melmoth, dark of brow." In Tatyana's mind each of these variants of the hero will decisively determine the development of the love affair. Either vice will inevitably be punished ("by the end of the final quire") and true love triumph, or the seduced heroine will perish ("She murmurs: 'I shall be undone' "). For Tatyana, the traditional norms of plot construction in the novel become a ready-made pattern for comprehending real-life situations. In order to expose the falsity of this (romantic) model of the world, an inverted system is constructed. Instead of "art reproducing life," "life reproduces art."

Tatyana is more inclined to see Onegin as a "tempter": ". . . before her loomed / Eugene in person, glances sparkling, / Portentous like a shadow darkling." That there is no third possibility is evident from the fact that the romantic Lensky thinks in the very same categories: "redeemer—seducer." Pushkin affirms the falsity of this interpretation of the hero and, consequently, the falsity of this entire structure. However, when it comes to giving a true characterization of the hero, he can speak only in negative terms:

> But hers [our hero], whatever type you guessed,
> *Was not a Grandison, at best.*
> [the italics are Lotman's]

Thus, when a style is called for that is not simply polemically opposed to literary clichés but completely independent of them, this system is no longer satisfactory.

Let us consider the stylistic structure of two stanzas [34 and 35] from Chapter IV in the novel:

> As freedom's lover, glory's gallant,
> His mind on stormy fancies fed,
> Vladimir might have tried his talent
> On odes—which Olga never read.
> Your elegist, now, must be fearful
> To face his love and read his tearful
> Effusions [creations] to her! Yet than this,
> They say, there is no higher bliss.
> Yes—count the modest lover blessed
> Who may recite [his dreams] beneath the eyes
> Of Her for whom he sings and sighs,
> Young beauty, languorously placid!
> Though this, when all is said and done,
> May not be her idea of fun.
> My own harmonious contriving
> I bring to my old Nanny's ears,
> A crop of dreams for the surviving
> Companion of my childhood years.
> To chase a dull meal, I belabor
> A stray and unsuspecting neighbor
> By seizing hold of his lapel
> And spouting blank verse by the ell,
> Or else (and here the joke is over)
> Beset by heartache and the Muse,
> I wander by my lake and choose
> To flush a flock of ducks from cover,
> Who, hearing those sweet stanzas ring,
> Break from the shoreline and take wing.

In these stanzas one and the same situation—"the poet reading his verses to his beloved"—is repeated over and over in stylistically contrasting systems. Each of the three components in the situation—"poet," "verses," "beloved"—is transformed:

I	Vladimir	odes	Olga
II	elegist	creations	love
III	modest lover	dreams	Her for whom he sings and sighs, Young beauty, languorously placid
IV	I	crop of dreams	old Nanny
V	I	blank verse	neighbor
VI	I	sweet stanzas	flock of ducks

Correspondingly, each time the act of reading the verses is designated in a particular way: "I read," "I spout," "I flush." And the reaction of the one being read to undergoes the same sort of "transformation":

> . . . Odes—which Olga never read.

> . . . Yet than this,
> They say, there is no higher bliss.

> Blessed . . .
> Though this, when all is said and done,
> May not be her idea of fun.

> Who, hearing those sweet stanzas ring,
> Break from the shoreline and take wing.

The meaning of these lines is constructed according to a complex system. Each separate lexical unit acquires additional stylistic meaning depending on the nature of the structure into which it is incorporated. Here the immediate environment of a given word plays a particularly important role. The act of the poet in III and IV is characterized almost identically: "Who may recite [read] his dreams . . ." [III]; "Crop of dreams . . . and / My own harmonious contriving / I bring [read] . . ." [IV]. But since in III this act links "the modest lover" and his "young beauty, languorously placid," while in IV it links the "I" and his "old Nanny," identical words are endowed with profoundly different stylistic meaning. "Dreams" in III is incorporated into a conventional (in the literary sense) phraseological structure and correlates with IV according to the principle of false expression—true content. "Old Nanny" relates to "young beauty, languorously placid" in exactly the same way. But the antithesis, "conventional poetry—true prose," is complicated by the fact that the "old Nanny" is simultaneously "companion of childhood years," and this combination is presented not as an ironic juncture of different styles but as a monosemantic stylistic group.

In place of the antithesis "poetry-prose," there emerges the antithesis "false poetry-true poetry." "Freedom's lover, glory's gallant" and his "odes" acquire special meaning from the fact that "Olga never read them." (In this case the relationship works both ways: Olga's indifference reveals the bookish nature of Lensky's "stormy fancies" since the line ". . . odes—which Olga never read" sounds like the voice of sober prose, which in the structure of the novel is invariably associated with truth. But, at the same time, the indisputable poetic charm of "glory" and "freedom" and "stormy fancies" underscores Olga's mundaneness.) In the lines "Yet than this, / They say, there is no higher bliss" the combination of two units which are equated—one colloquial, the other conventional and literary—results in a "deflating" stylistic effect.

However, meaning in these stanzas is not generated simply by syntagmatic linkage. The words arranged vertically in columns are perceived as variants of single invariant meanings. And not one of them relates to another as content to expression: they are superimposed one on the other, producing complex meaning. The incorporation into a single paradigm of such remote and seemingly incompatible notions as "Her for whom he sings and sighs," "old Nanny," "neighbor," "flock of ducks" is an important means of semantic intensification. The result is a unique kind of semantic suppletion, where words which are disparate and remote are perceived at the same time to be variants of a single concept. This makes each variant of the concept difficult to predict and, consequently, particularly significant. And here it is essential to note something else. Not only do remote lexemes converge in a complex arch unit, but elements from different (often opposing) stylistic systems are incorporated into a single stylistic structure. Such an equation of different stylistic levels leads to the realization of the relativity of each separate stylistic system and to the emergence of irony. The dominant role irony plays in creating the stylistic unity of *Eugene Onegin* is obvious and has been noted by critics. . . .

The mechanism of irony constitutes one of the fundamental keys to the novel's style. Let us examine it on the basis of the following examples [Chapter II, stanzas 36 and 37]:

> So they grew old like other mortals.
> At last a final mansion drew
> Asunder its sepulchral portals
> Before the husband [spouse], wreathed anew.
> Near dinnertime he died, contented,
> By friends and neighbors much lamented,
> By children, faithful wife, and clan,
> More truly mourned than many a man.
> He was a simple, kindly *barin,*
> And where his earthly remnant rests,
> A graven headstone thus attests:
> "A humble sinner, Dmitri Larin,
> God's servitor and brigadier,
> Found peace beneath this marble here."

> To his ancestral hall returning,
> Vladimir Lensky sought the plot
> Of his old neighbor's [humble] last sojourning
> And sighed in tribute to his lot.
> And long he mourned for the departed:
> "Poor Yorick!" quoth he, heavy-hearted,

In these stanzas the stylistic breaks are produced not by a system of transformations of one and the same extrastylistic content, but by a succession of different stylistic modes, one replacing the other. The first line, "So they grew old like other mortals," is clearly neutral. What is striking here is the marked absence of any signs pointing to a particular poetic style. Stylistically speaking, this line is *without point of view.* The next three lines are characterized by a sustained lofty (in the spirit of the eighteenth century) style and by a corresponding point of view. The periphrases "a final mansion drew / Asunder its sepulchral portals" and "wreathed anew" (instead of "he died") and vocabulary like "spouse" and "wreathed" could not have evoked in Pushkin's reader any other literary associations. However, in the following line the solemn periphrases are translated into another system: ". . . he died." The style of the subsequent lines is not neutral at all because of its prosaic character, which is achieved by linking accurate prosaic expressions. In the given textual construct, these endow the style with a tinge of veracity and hence poeticality, which then combines with the elements that deflate the style. The detail "near dinnertime" in combination with "a final mansion drew / Asunder its sepulchral portals" gives a slightly comic tinge to the old-fashioned rural naiveté. The time of death is reckoned by the time of eating. Compare:

> . . . I like to tell
> The hours' advancing, like the locals.
> By luncheon, dinner, tea; we yokels
> Keep track of time without much fuss;
> Our stomachs watch the clock for us.

The same comic effect is created by combining the solemn

"much lamented" and "neighbors," since the character of the neighboring country landowner was familiar to the reader of *Eugene Onegin* and had already been sketched out earlier in the same chapter. In light of this, "children" and "faithful wife," who "much lamented" the deceased, can only be perceived as archaic and pompous stock phrases. . . . The lofty poetics of the eighteenth century is perceived as a string of clichés, behind which lies an old-fashioned and naive consciousness, provincial culture, simple-mindedly experiencing the yesteryear of the nation's intellectual development. However, the line "More truly mourned than many a man" reveals that these archaic clichés contain an element of truth. Although they remain clichés, obligatory in epitaphs of the high style, and, although they bear the imprint of clumsy provincialism, they do not prevent the text from being a bearer of truth. The line "He was a simple, kindly *barin*" introduces a completely unexpected point of view. The semantic orientation suggests that the subject of this system is a serf. For the subject of the text, the object (Larin) is a *barin* and *from this point of view* appears "simple" and "kind." In this way the contours of patriarchal relationships ruling in the Larin's household continue to be outlined. All these repeated stylistic and semantic switches are synthesized in the concluding lines of the stanza—in the text of the epitaph (which simultaneously is both solemn ["humble sinner," "found peace"] and comic ["God's servitor *and* brigadier"]), with its naive equation of earthly and heavenly powers. . . .

These examples have demonstrated . . . that the succession of semantic and stylistic breaks creates not a focused but a diffused multiple point of view, which thus becomes the center of a supersystem perceived to be an illusion of reality itself. Moreover, what is important to the realist, who seeks to transcend the subjectivism of semantic and stylistic "points of view" and to recreate objective reality, is the nature of the relationships between these multiple centers, these diverse (adjacent or superimposed) structures. None of them cancels out any of the others; they all correlate. Consequently, the text means not only what it means but something else as well. The new meaning does not cancel out the old but correlates with it. Because of this, the literary model reproduces an extremely important dimension of reality—that aspect which attests to the impossibility of giving any definitive and final interpretation.

The principle of the semantic and stylistic break is only one manifestation of the general structural design of *Onegin.* On a lower level it is manifested in the intonational diversity of the novel. Different intonations coexist and, consequently, are equated on a scale of artistic values, and all this is organically linked with the principle of "chatter"—transcending the limits of any fixed literary structure.

Since the lexical and semantic structure of the verse influences the style of recitation, the equivalence of different types of intonation is determined by the breaks analyzed above. However, there is also another aspect to the "melodics": its link with the rhythmic and syntactic texture of the verse.

On the level of intonation, the reproduction of reality is in large measure a matter of re-creating the illusion of colloquial intonations. This does not mean that constructions borrowed directly from everyday speech are simply transferred into the text of the novel. After all, the structure of the verse and the specific manner in which it is recited are given; therefore, "colloquiality" is not a rejection of them but a matter of building a superstructure over them. Thus, on this level too the aim of imitating a free and easy manner of speaking turns on the creation of a "superstructure." And here again objectivity (perceived as being "beyond structure") results from increasing both quantitatively and qualitatively the structural bonds and not from weakening them—not from destroying structures but from creating a structure of structures (systems). . . .

In my earlier article on *Eugene Onegin,* I attempted to outline the principles which shaped the construction of character in the novel. Now I would like to ascertain the means used to unite such diverse literary constructs into a single structural whole. One of the distinguishing features of character construction in the novel is the fact that the novel can very easily be divided into distinct synchronic sections (chapters). Pushkin conceived of the chapter as the natural unit of construction—moreover, a unit of considerable independence.

As a rule, the chapter initiates a new turn in the plot and, as I tried to show in my earlier article, a new type of character construction as well. The chapter, taken as a separate unit, is a synchronically organized system, in which each literary character is only one component of the function, the correlation of characters. As Grigory Vinokur noted: "The relationships between the author and his hero are fully formulated, and, in order to understand the meaning of *Eugene Onegin* as a whole, one must recognize that these relationships are no less important than the plot. . . . Pushkin's objective was not simply to portray a typical individual. Alongside the portrait of the hero there emerges a self-portrait of the narrator, so that each illuminates the other."

In each synchronic section not only the author and the hero but all the characters form a correlated system. Moreover, what is given, what is primary, is not the characters themselves but the functions (the relations between characters). Thus, for example, the plan for Chapter I assumed a relationship between a moral ideal (approximating the aims of the Union of Welfare) and a superficial young man, outwardly in contact with progressive circles (like Repetilov in Griboedov's play *Woe from Wit*). This opposition is manifested in the following antitheses:

	A	B
I	true education "lofty mind"	superficial, shallow education
II	civic-mindedness "lofty labors"	idleness empty pursuits superficial Byronism
III	true love	worldly love-making
IV	lofty art	light poetry voluptuous, base art

Outwardly the hero belongs to the author's circle. He is capable of carrying on a "learned conversation" with the ladies and "even a manly argument," just as Repetilov can talk about "Byron, as well as important matters." The real difference between the author and the hero—i. e., their true functional relationship—is revealed through the ironic tone of the narration.

However, in the second synchronic section of Chapter I, the functional correlation between characters breaks down. Onegin acquires significance; his character gains depth. He draws closer to the sphere of values esteemed by the author. Simultaneously, changes in the conceptual field take place. Disenchantment and skepticism, which were treated as signs of worldly eccentricity, move over into column A, becoming the sign of a "lofty mind" ("He who has lived and thought . . ."). Both inwardly and in terms of the plot, Onegin and the author find themselves side by side. With the function broken, the irony disappears.

> **Because the poetics of *Eugene Onegin* establishes a new paradigm of characters for each chapter and, simultaneously, makes the novel an unfinished construct, one permitting continuation, the heroes acquire the character of complex structures, which in principle can be interpreted in an infinite number of ways.**
>
> —*Yury Lotman*

In each new synchronic section it is the *relationship* established between characters that is most important. The intelligent skeptic (Onegin) versus the youthful enthusiast (Lensky); the sister Olga—ideal of the "romantic" poet, a hackneyed literary character (". . . Novels [take your choice] / All paint the type to satisfaction") who is most ordinary versus the sister Tatyana with a provincial name and original character; "contemporary man" (Onegin) versus the girl (Tatyana) who believes "in simple folkways of the past." The most complicated antitheses are found in Chapter VIII. However, within each synchronic section the antithesis does not emerge by itself but derives from a general notion of what contemporary man is like. Moreover, the traits of the hero are not presented as a list of individually named qualities but as a sum total of oppositions. In the course of working on the novel Pushkin evolved. A number of his ideological and artistic principles changed, and, correspondingly, his notion of what constitutes the essence of character changed. This is illustrated by the following diagram:

I	Intellect Education	Ignorance Superficiality
II	Intellect Skepticism Sobriety	Enthusiasm Naiveté Romanticism

III	Intellect	Naiveté
	Spiritual weariness	Capacity for pure feeling
IV	Intellect	Naiveté
	Egoism	*Narodnost'* [national character]
V	Striving for	Fulfillment of duty
	happiness	Intellect

Depending on the nature of the principal antithesis (and we are only pointing out the principal ones; in the actual fabric of the work each synchronic section is represented not by one antithesis but by a hierarchy of semantic oppositions), the hero type also changes. In each case the heroes—i. e., the intersecting functional relationships within each synchronic section—acquire distinct characteristics and different motivations. Thus, if in Chapter I superficial education, ignorance of the achievements of enlightenment, was perceived as an obstacle separating the hero from the positive ideal, then in Chapter V the very same thing (in combination with naiveté and spiritual purity) is perceived as a positive factor.

In this way, one and the same character may in different chapters be characterized in very different—at times, totally opposite—ways. Compare the assessment of Onegin in Chapter VII, 24, which is offered as the opinion of the author (and Tatyana), to that in Chapter VIII, 12, which is presented as the opinion of "sensible men." The number of such breaks in the construction of character is very large. However, while the adoption of new principles of constructing the artistic model was prompted by changes in Pushkin's literary method and inevitably led to contradictions in the text of the novel, the refusal to eliminate them immediately acquired something of a programmatic character. Moving through the text, the reader passed from one synchronic section to another, and each of them created its own particular image of the functional relationships. But, even though in the separate publications of Chapter I (1825), Chapter VII (1830), and Chapter VIII (1832), Onegin seemed to represent totally different characters belonging to different systems, when brought together in the indivisible text of the novel, all these Onegins took on a certain unity.

A paradigm of the character emerges where very different functional intersections, designated within each individual section by the name "Onegin," come together vertically to form a system of variants joined by invariant unity. Because of this, the new literary principles do not cancel out the old ones but join with them to form a functional whole. Thus, instead of affirming the idea that there is only one possible way to represent an object by literary means, it is suggested that there are many ways to re-create an object in its different states.

Because the poetics of the novel establishes a new paradigm of characters for each chapter and, simultaneously, makes the novel an unfinished construct, one permitting continuation, the heroes acquire the character of complex structures, which in principle can be interpreted in an infi-

nite number of ways. This reveals yet another structural principle of Pushkin's novel. Not only is it constructed as a system of correlated heterogeneous structures and parts, but it *has an open character.* In terms of plot it can go on; it can be extended in other respects as well. It is a literary system, a construct which is designed in principle to be extended. With this is linked the novel's special fate, for its open character makes it correlate with the *entire* subsequent tradition of Russian literature and not simply with some of its individual trends. The deliberately polemical plot construct is also linked with this. The novel—and Belinsky pointed out this peculiarity—is not finished by anything. The usual novel construct, which Pushkin sensed to be a jumping-off point, implied the presence of a plot ending. Addressing his friends, Pushkin wrote ironically:

> You are quite justified in saying
> That it is strange, in fact betraying
> Bad form, to break the novel off
> With half already set in proof;
> And that the least one ought to do
> Is get the hero duly married,
> Or if he can't do better, buried,
> And with a cordial adieu
> Deliver the supporting cast
> Out of the labyrinth at last.

"To break the novel off," to leave it unfinished, is a conscious literary principle. The novel "with an ending" (a "marriage" or a "burial") gives a finite model of infinite life. Pushkin consciously constructs his text as a recreation of the very principle of infinity. At the same time we should point out something else: the finite model relates to the infinite as *langue* to *parole* (to use the terminology of Ferdinand de Saussure). The novel "with an ending" relates to real life the same way (this, of course, does not preclude the fact that within the text of such a novel levels of language and speech can and should be distinguished). Pushkin's novel is an unfinished text which reproduces another unfinished text (reality). Consequently, the language (the finite system) is not given; it must be deduced. And the test of the truth of this language will be whether it can serve to describe the speech act (the text) accurately. But one and the same text can be described in different ways. And it is precisely this that constitutes the profound literary significance of Pushkin's novel in verse. The author gives the reader complexly structured language which the reader must take for speech (language acts as imitation of the speech of another system). The complex structural construction becomes a re-creation of extrastructural reality.

The reader himself must create a model which will be both more defined and, inevitably, more impoverished than Pushkin's text. Precisely this was the subsequent fate of Pushkin's novel. It nourished different interpretations—very often ones that distorted its meaning and were polemical. All too often the interpretations oversimplified the novel. But it was this breadth of possible interpretations that permitted the novel to exert such a long influence on subsequent literature.

Hugh McLean on character and tone in *Eugene Onegin*:

By means of a variety of techniques, both structural and stylistic, Puškin has imposed upon us a complex attitude toward his characters, including not only empathy with their emotions, sharing of their joys and sorrows, but an acute awareness of their weaknesses, their folly, their self-delusions, and even of their fictionality. This complex attitude is the intellectual counterpart, in both author and reader, of the complexity of tone, that mixture of jocularity and lyricism, that is such a striking feature of [*Eugene Onegin*] itself. . . .

[Why] does Puškin choose to tune his novel to this particular key, to give it a tone at once "jocular and passionate," lyrical and ironic? The answer, I think, is that no matter what literary conventions he may have been following and no matter what his models may have been, this combination of contradictory tonalities suited him. In some way it harmonized with his own nature, and he made it very much his own. It suited him because it expressed a vision of life, a philosophy, an attitude toward the world and toward human experience that appealed to him. It was his own existential stance, one he maintained to a remarkable degree in his own life.

Hugh McLean, in his "The Tone(s) of Evgenij Onegin," *in* California Slavic Studies, Volume VI, *University of California Press, 1971.*

John Bayley   (essay date 1971)

SOURCE: *Pushkin: A Comparative Commentary,* Cambridge at the University Press, 1971, 369 p.

[*Bayley is an English educator and critic. In the following excerpt, he examines Pushkin's* Skazki *and* The Little House in Kolomna, *focusing on their relation to works by other writers.*]

If we compare [*Ruslan and Lyudmila*] it with the *Skazki,* written ten years later, the contrast is not so much between two ways of treating the marvellous, as between poetry whose internal workings are almost insolently open for our inspection, and poetry which is sealed off from it, sheathed in the simplicity of total sophistication. We noticed the neglect in *Ruslan* of the tight interior logic of fairy-tale, a neglect sardonically justified by Pushkin in his preface to the second edition. But in the *Skazki* he makes this logic the principle which both creates and conceals their art.

Neither *Ruslan* nor the *Skazki* are in a self-conscious sense Russian poems. Pushkin knew instinctively that—as Pevsner has put it—while great art is national, national art is bad art. And yet *Ruslan* does give us the feeling . . . of a society apprehending itself, through the medium of a great poet's craft, in a sort of microcosmic idyll. The idyll is insulated: it does not raise questions or suggest issues about such a society in the way that *Evgeny Onegin* does

. . . and its kind of appeal and popularity reflects only this happy and immediate sense of self-discovery . . . .

When, in 1828, Pushkin added the famous Prologue to *Ruslan and Lyudmila,* did he perhaps enjoy the incongruity between the actual provenance of the poem and the Prologue's assertion that it would contain homely marvels 'smelling of Russia', tales like the traditional one of Tsar Kashchey or Baba Yaga and the hut on fowl's legs? The *Skazki,* too, though written at the height of Pushkin's poetic maturity, were in their way as unexpected and disconcerting to theoretically-minded contemporaries as *Ruslan* had been. Polevoy, by then an outspoken enemy of Pushkin's, chided him in the *Moscow Telegraph* for writing in a form 'lower than the model', a significant objection from a serious folklorist who wanted simultaneously to worship *narodnost* and to elevate it. Though most literary versions of folk poetry had been done in the same trochaic form, he also objected to the metre of the *Skazki*—the clipped tetrameter whose air of simplicity conceals the most assured craftsmanship—and advised Pushkin to go to school with the antiquarian versifier Danilov. The unfavourable reaction was general, except among Pushkin's closest friends. Even to Belinsky they seemed mere adaptations of popular material, too straight-forward to qualify as poetry. Turgenev thought them the slightest of all Pushkin's work, and it was not until Rimsky-Korsakov made an opera of "Tsar Saltan" that they became widely known. In the Soviet era they are of course praised highly as examples of how Pushkin drew his art from the traditions of the people.

The representative of the people, canonised in Pushkinian hagiography, is the Pushkin family nurse, Arina Rodionovna, whom the poet came to know well during his exile at Mikhailovskoye after his years in the south. She had plenty of old stories, which she probably embroidered and improved on herself when she told them to Pushkin, as an intelligent and shrewd transmitter of a verbal tradition would tend to do. Pushkin was very fond of her. He made her the model for Tatyana's nurse in *Evgeny Onegin,* and he addressed two poems to her, one a fragment. "Winter Evening," the other, has become as much a part of the consciousness of the Russian reader—from childhood onwards—as nursery rhymes are to his English equivalent; but instead of the simplicity of such rhymes the poem has the sophistication of a perfectly balanced compound, as elaborate on its miniature scale as *Ruslan and Lyudmila.* It reproduces in literary terms a homely occasion, poet and nurse sitting together with a snowstorm howling outside the 'decrepit hovel' (*vetkhaya lachuzhka*), which is appropriate to the convention of story-telling on a winter's night, and leads into the other *topoi* of drinking-song and ballad of sentiment. . . .

> Let's drink, good friend of my poor boyhood,
> let's drown our sorrow. Where's the jug? It will
> cheer our hearts. Sing me a song: how the blue
> tit lived quietly beyond the sea. Sing me a song:
> how the maiden went to fetch water in the morning.

A single word—*tikho* (quietly)—acts as catalyst for the poetic compound. It is one of Pushkin's favourite words, usually in the simplest descriptive context and in association with night, moonlight, water, the breeze, and so on. Here it jumps what F. W. Bateson would call 'the semantic gap' between the literary common-place of the poet and the naive life of the old nurse's vocabulary as narrator. We hear the story, as she tells it, through the medium of the poet's reaction: his nostalgia, part stylised, part actual—Pushkin's recurrent longing for *pokoy i volya* (peace and freedom)—to escape to the magic other land of art and tale where the blue-tit lived quietly. It is of importance that the nurse does not speak in the poem: we are aware of her matter-of-fact presence through the comfort it brings to the poet. The perspective of narrative and dialogue is accomplished in the four verses of a short lyric; not long after Pushkin had been working on the full-scale dialogue between Tatyana and her nurse in the third chapter of *Evgeny Onegin.*

From Arina Rodionovna Pushkin heard stories on which he made notes, still extant, recording not only the material itself but the way in which it had been told to him. One of these gives the narrative formula used in the opening lines of the Prologue to *Ruslan and Lyudmila* . . .

> At a curving shore of the sea stands an oak; on that oak a golden chain; and on that chain walks a cat. As it walks up it tells stories—as it walks down it sings songs.
>
> [Compare to the poem] . . . By a curving shore a green oak; a golden chain on that oak; and night and day a learned cat walks round and round on that chain: when it goes to the right it strikes up a song: to the left—it tells a tale.

The oak-tree has become green: the cat has become learned. The epithets need each other for the rhyme, but they show also *curiosa felicitas*; the plain vision of the one and the genial implication of the other (the wonder in itself, and as it is considered by the intelligence) combine to make the scene burst upon the reader with an impact far more terse and sensational than in the story formula. That, for all its effectiveness in setting the scene, suggests the leisurely tempo of a simple evening's tale. By stylising and exaggerating the syntactic economy of the scene-setting phrases (the otiose verb *stoit* [stands] is cut out), Pushkin's iambics beat the directness of folktale at its own game. We might notice, too, that the learned cat is not stylised but naturalised, so that we seem to see the beast stalking left or right at the circumference of its golden chain.

Though written much later, the *Skazki* share the same secret of exaggerating, so to speak, the folktaleness of folktale—to refine an essence which has nothing primitive or old-world about it. Inference can be as sharp, meaning as contemporary, as in the narrative poem of mixed origin. Indeed in **"The Tale of the Golden Cockerel"** a modern fantasy has almost certainly been grafted on the form of the *Skazka*. The tales of Washington Irving in a French translation were very popular in Russia around 1833, and Polevoy noted, perhaps not unmaliciously, a resemblance between his *Knicker-bocker* and Pushkin's *Tales of Belkin*. More important, the poet Anna Akhmatova has noticed that Pushkin owned a French translation of *The Alhambra,* and that a fragment of 1833, the year before **"The**

Golden Cockerel" was written, reproduced fairly exactly the details of one of these 'Haroun al Rashid' tales, mild spoofs on the manner of the *Arabian Nights.* In the Alhambra story a bronze horseman is placed on a tower to warn the ruler of approaching enemies. Inside the tower are model armies which the ruler has only to knock down in order to destroy the real armies which are advancing against him. It was this detail that Pushkin reproduced in the fragment, but it is clear that its whimsical ingenuity would not have suited the *skazka*: Pushkin used instead the much older *motif,* found everywhere in legend, of the ruler sending out a succession of armies and finally going out to battle in person. The coincidence of the bronze horseman *motif* with Pushkin's poetic masterpiece of 1833 is striking but probably not significant; though it may have prompted the substitution of the golden cockerel. Though the similarities of the fragment are not reproduced in **"The Tale of the Golden Cockerel"** there can be little doubt that the tale was modelled on Irving's oriental fantasia rather than on any folklore source, but Pushkin cared as little as Shakespeare where his stories came from: he enjoyed them without reverence and adapted them without pedantry. Source hunting is a proper Pushkinist activity and the title of Azadovsky's article, 'Arina Rodionovna or "The Brothers Grimm' ", shows how widely and inconclusively the net must be cast, for Pushkin's nurse herself had picked up many of her tales not from old traditions but from new tales and translations that had filtered through by word of mouth to a largely unlettered peasantry—but in the case of **"Tsar Saltan," "The Tale of the Parson and his Man Balda,"** and the others, it cannot do much to enhance our enjoyment or our critical appreciation. **"Balda"** is an excellent comic tale in the straight tradition of folk *fabliau,* which suffered somewhat from the emendations Zhukovsky made to get it past the censorship; **"Tsar Saltan"** is a perfect lyrical masterpiece, the most formally beautiful of them all, and the one that most sustains throughout the length of a tale the atmosphere and taste of magic in the *Ruslan* prologue. **"The Dead Princess and the Seven Heroes"** is not on the same level, and **"The Fisherman and the Fish"** is pure folklore on a slighter scale.

The origins of **"The Golden Cockerel"** and its hint of political meaning give it a special place. More remarkable than any specific reference—for popular rhymes are after all traditionally full of cryptic or subversive comment—is Pushkin's use of the *skazka* to create a grue-some little tableau of the nature, in any age, of power: its irresponsibility and its blindness. As such a 'peepshow' (to use Tolstoy's term) it would not be absurd to class it with Tolstoy's own story *Hadji Murad,* and *The Bronze Horseman.*

Tsar Dadon is a king who takes his absolute power completely for granted, and he is genuinely amazed at being held to a promise. Insensately aggressive in his prime, he now wishes for a quiet old age, but his realm is threatened from all sides and his generals are in despair. . . .

> They would be on the watch, looking to the south, but no, from the east an army approaches.

Like Chaucer in similar contexts, Pushkin imposes a

hooded irony of his own on the droll vitality of the hypothetical narrator. Dadon consults a wise man, an astrologer and eunuch, and is given a golden cockerel who stands on a spire and crows at the approach of any danger. The Tsar can sleep at last, and when he is aroused by the next alarm we hear his voice: . . .

> 'Our Tsar! Father of the people!' the general cries—'Sovereign awake! Disaster!' 'What is it, gentlemen?' says Dadon, yawning —'Eh? Who's there? What disaster?'

His sons are sent out with armies and fail to return. He sets out with a third army and finds in a narrow ravine among the mountains a silken tent; before it lie the slaughtered troops and his two sons who have killed each other. Then out of the tent appears a beautiful maiden, the Queen of Shemakha, and Dadon's lamentations come to an abrupt end. . . .

> Like a bird of night before the sun the Tsar was silent, looking into her eyes, and before her he forgot the death of his two sons.

But he has promised the eunuch anything he may ask as a reward, and he claims the Queen. In vain he is asked to choose something else: he tries to hold the exasperated Tsar to his promise and is told to clear off. . . .

> The old man wanted to argue, but with some people it is disadvantageous to pick a quarrel.

(Pushkin noted in his text his own original reading *No s tsaryami plokho uzdorit* [but it is a bad business to pick a quarrel with Tsars] and it is this which has led commentators to connect the poem with his own relations with Nicholas.) When the old man still attempts to argue Dadon strikes him dead. The maiden laughs. . . .

> The whole capital shuddered but the girl—'Hee, hee, hee!' and 'Ha, ha, ha!' Obviously she has no fear of the sin.

We hear the discordant sound in the sudden silence; it makes a curiously uncanny moment, an instant dramatic revelation like that of Dadon looking into her eyes; and its effect is not trivialised but enhanced by the pious platitude of the narrator. The cockerel flies down from the steeple and pecks the Tsar's head: he groans and dies, and the Queen vanishes.

It is not easy to describe the story without making it appear as lightweight as Pushkin's contemporaries found it, but the real achievement of the **Skazki** can only be measured by comparison with what was similar to them in the European literature of the time. Ballad, legend, and supernatural or uncanny verse tales were the stock in trade of contemporary romanticism, but nowhere—with a very few exceptions—do they rise above the mediocre when they are deliberately simple and naive: the poets of the Schillerian age strove to reproduce the naive but succeeded best when it became the starting point of reflection—ballads with a meaning, tales with moral depth. The 'meaning' and the 'depth' of **"The Golden Cockerel"** are natural aspects of its narrative function; they do not justify or implicitly patronise it; and **"Tsar Saltan,"** as a triumph of simple tale-telling, has no equivalent in European

verse—only in the prose of Grimm and Hans Andersen. . . .

. . . . .

The model [for **The Little House at Kolomna,** written in the Boldino autumn of 1830, is Byron's] *Beppo,* which bears a far closer relation to **The Little House** than does any other poem of Byron to a poem of Pushkin's. *Beppo* is a pilot poem and an artistic polemic, an exploration of the stanza and method used in *Don Juan.* **The Little House** is also polemical, but instead of being a preliminary poem it is a deliberate breakaway from the completed **Onegin.**

In the spring of 1830 Bulgarin had attacked Pushkin as a 'French versifier', who copied Byron without understanding him. Other attacks followed, both from Bulgarin in the *Northern Bee* and Polevoy in the *Moscow Telegraph,* deriding Pushkin's pride in his aristocratic origins and suggesting that as a writer he had become a back number, turning out increasingly inferior chapters of a poem already *passé.* Pushkin's immediate reply was an epigram (*Ne to beda, chto ty polyak . . .*); his real response was the extraordinary burst of creation that autumn at Boldino. All he wrote there was a new departure, and the opening stanza of **The Little House** makes—as a kind of symbol of the real and remarkable innovations of the *Little Tragedies* and the *Tales of Belkin*—a humorously defiant gesture of novelty: . . .

> The four-stress iambic line bores me: everyone writes it. It's time to leave it as an amusement for the little fellows. I have long wished to take up the octave. And in fact together with it I would make myself master of the three-rhyme ending. Off we go towards fame! Rhyme and I live together on simple terms; two come of themselves and they bring along the third.

In invoking the metre, Pushkin by implication summons Byron to his side, both as an ally against the attacks of grovelling professionals—'in foolscap uniforms turned up with ink'—and as a fellow aristocrat who wrote with negligent ease. Byron too had brushed aside the vulgar notion that trivial events were not suited to poetic narrative; he too disliked the talk of men of letters ('One hates an author that's *all author*') preferring

> Men of the world who know the world like men . . .
> Who think of something else beside the pen.

The Byron whom Pushkin had been careful to place in **Evgeny Onegin,** with amused neutrality, as an egoist and the reason for so much studied egoism in others, is now a fellow sufferer (and fellow aristocrat) with whom Pushkin is glad to carry on the fight against 'the would-be wits and can't-be gentlemen', toadies, journalists, bourgeois fashion and bourgeois hypocrisy.

But Byron can prove an embarrassing ally. Once his tone and manner have been adopted (and Byron's sniping at mere men of letters is far more vindictive than Pushkin's instinct against protesting too much could have found comfortable) it is difficult to get outside him and use him as a point of departure. Pushkin surrenders to his idiom in *The Little House* as he does on a smaller scale to that of Wordsworth in **"Vnov ya posetil"** ["I Visited Again"], but the boisterous dexterity of Byron is more easily accommodated than is Wordsworth's insidious quiet. In both poems Pushkin contrives none the less to set a distance between himself and his overpowering model: in **"Vnov ya posetil"** by changing the 'I' persona from rural wanderer to reflective landowner; and in *The Little House* by adopting a subtly different poetic stance from that of his fellow nobleman while remaining, so to speak, fraternally arm in arm with him.

The first version of *The Little House* contained several stanzas of direct polemic against Bulgarin and the offending periodicals, and this Pushkin may have intended to publish separately and anonymously in Delvig's *Literary Gazette,* an unsuccessful periodical which Pushkin had helped to launch as a rival to the *Northern Bee.* But at the end of 1830 the *Literary Gazette* was suppressed for printing a poem celebrating the change of regime in France, and when *The Little House* was published under Pushkin's name three years later in the almanac *Novoselye* the stanzas were removed, and in the absence of this localised polemic the general intention shows up clearly; a new stanza, a new kind of poem, a humorous *conte* which gentlemen—if not critics and journalists—should enjoy.

Suburban Kolomna was a long way from fashionable Venice—here is one big initial difference from *Beppo*—and yet Pushkin's poem gives no impression of deliberately selecting a scene from humble life. Tales with such a scene have by tradition a very obvious point and moral, either a lachrymose one (Karamzin's *Poor Liza*) or a bawdy. Remove such a point and moral, and the result appeared to contemporary critics nothing but a frivolous exercise in the new art of the Russian octave, though it earned the admiration of Gogol and later of Belinsky, who referred to the creation of a 'special class of poem' by Pushkin as the first hint of the new Russian school of naturalism. M. L. Gofman, who did much to establish the poem's text and who emphasised its polemical origin in the journalistic skirmish, expressed a measure of judicious agreement in his view that Pushkin was seeking a new kind of realistic style by using the octave less flamboyantly than Byron, with no grotesquerie of enjambement and dialogue. An anonymous critic in the magazine *Galatea* (1839) robustly maintained that the sole function of the piece was to naturalise the Italian octave, while at the other end of the scale there are (as always with Pushkin) no lack of speculations about its possible profound and hidden meaning. Gershenzon in *Mudrost Pushkina* finds in it a concealed revelation of the passionate love of Pushkin's youth when he lodged in Kolomna; and the poet Khodasevich thought it revealed his superstitious sense of the intervention of diabolical powers in human life (the devil, presumably, can vanish away at will, but has to shave while living among the humankind he seduces). The sensible Bryusov concentrates on the verbal parallels with *Beppo* and with another of its successors—Musset's *Namouna.* Pushkin, we remember, excepted Musset from his condemnation of modern French poetry 'because he is the first French poet who has been able to grasp the tone of Byron's facetious works, which are in reality no joking matter'.

Is *The Little House* then no joking matter? The interpretative Pushkinians certainly do not think so, but it is possible to feel that Pushkin, and Musset too, may have taken Byron too much *au pied de la lettre.* Like his scorn of the scribbling tribe, his insistence on the laughter that 'leaves us so doubly serious shortly after', is a pose that goes with the technique rather than a considered reference to the nature of the tale he tells. Yet Pushkin, who was himself contemplating the same step, must have been struck by Byron's two references to prose, for which he would keep more serious matters ('I'll keep them for my life (to come) in prose') and by the 'Beppoid' convention that here is a form as down-to-earth as prose but which can avoid its logic and disclaim its need to complete a proposition it has begun. The Beppoid poet makes a virtue of being at the mercy of his medium, as Tolstoy's Anna Scherer 'smiles at her own impetuosity' and exploits her 'charming defect' of never finishing a sentence, and it is here that Pushkin, with quiet emphasis and perhaps deliberately, dissociates himself from his model.

> This story slips forever through my fingers,
> Because, just as the stanza likes to make it,
> It needs must be, and so it rather lingers . . .

Pushkin's will not linger. When he has explained his premises he is going to get down to business—unlike Byron and Musset—and show that the poet need not adopt a comically helpless stance before the exigencies of the octave. The tail need not wag the dog, nor the dog point out how well the motion becomes him. Instead, like Napoleon or Tamerlane, Pushkin will marshal his rhymes like an army and put them through their exercise: to vary the metaphor, he will keep the pert muse of the genre in order. . . .

> Sit, muse; little hands in sleeves, little feet under the bench! Don't twirl about, giddy creature! Now, let's begin.—There was once a widow, about eight years ago, a poor old lady with one daughter. Their humble dwelling was by the church of the Intercession, just behind its gatehouse. I see, as if it were today, an attic, three windows, the porch and the door.

From now on there will be no digressions except ones that are in keeping with the dramatic *atmosphere* of the poem, in which Pushkin himself will become not a commentator but an actor, wandering round Kolomna and surveying the three-storied house (conceivably a parallel to the triple rhymes of the octave) which has replaced the *domik* in which his characters used to live. Are they still alive? His own youth has vanished as they have done. . . .

> I became sad: I looked askance at the tall building. If a fire had enveloped it utterly at that moment the flame would have been agreeable to my embittered eye. The heart is full of strange fantasies; so much nonsense goes through one's head when one strolls alone or together with a friend.

> He is in bliss then indeed who is absolute master of his words and holds his thoughts well in control, who can put to sleep or stifle the serpent who hisses by moments in his heart. But he who babbles all is at once marked down as a cad . . . I drink Lethe's waters . . . the doctor has forbid-

den me sadness: let's leave this—do me the favour.

We can see here how the Beppo poet's artlessly random utterance is ingeniously converted by Pushkin into a fictional narrative method—the narrator's inability to control his thoughts about the past, and the memories that assail him when he wanders through familiar streets like Baudelaire or Dostoevsky's underground man. Between such a narrator and the story he tells there will clearly be some undisclosed and sensitive connection. The authorial 'I' of Evgeny Onegin is by its convention a free man: his tastes, griefs, adventures may be referred to openly and neutrally. The author of **The Little House** is in terms of its convention a haunted man. Instead of being separated from the frothy tale and appearing in exclamations about former days and the seriousness that follows laughter, the idea of 'no joking matter' is now integrated into the tale's narrative perspective, its wry uncertainty. The author is both involved and detached; he has his wounding memories, and yet the characters of his story were seen by him only through a window or when he attended church. The tale's inconsequence faithfully reflects the lack of any continuous relation with them.

They have the vividness of a picture studied from well back, and the author tells us that he has seen a hundred times figures like his old widow in the portraits of Rembrandt. He is seeing them from a very different perspective from that which Evgeny in **The Bronze Horseman** desperately imagined two very similar people (the daughter's name Parasha is common to both poems) but he too is seeing them from a distance and in a kind of dream. The author's dream likes to play round the picture of Parasha and her mother leading their quiet life in Kolomna. All depends on the angle of vision, and here again we have a clue to Pushkin's comment on such a poem as 'no joking matter'. . . .

> In winter the shutters were closed early, but in summer all the house was open to the night. Pale Diana gazed long on the young girl in the window. (No novel could do without this; so it is decreed.) And so it chanced that when the mother had long been snoring the daughter still gazed at the moon and heard the mewing of tom-cats on the tiles, the indication of some shameless encounter, the distant cry of the watch, the striking of the hours—and that was all. The night is wonderfully calm in peaceful Kolomna. Occasionally two shadowy forms glimmered forth from houses. In her lassitude the girl could hear her heart nudge the yielding cloth of her bodice.

The run on between the stanzas is admirable, as are the stops in mid-line which suggest in depth the monotony of the scene as in a novel of Balzac. The moon watches the girl as the poet watches her in memory: the parenthesis shows the widening gap between the author as a brooding Jamesian *conscience* and as the facetious poetic commentator on a non-tale, a parody of an event. This commentator tells the 'Beppoid' tale which acts as a stalking horse for the real preoccupation of his colleague, which declares itself at the beginning of stanza 21, introduced by the visits of mother and daughter to church. . . .

> There, I recall, a countess always came in her carriage . . . (what her name was I really don't know). She was rich, young;

The 'I' who remembers here, sensed an intriguing melancholy behind the proud bearing of the countess to whom he never spoke; and the interest with which he studied her must only have produced, as he now realises, her mechanical reaction to yet another obvious admirer. The persona of this countess could be related to the married Tatyana, and to Donna Anna of *The Stone Guest,* while Gershenzon was no doubt right that Pushkin summons up here the memory of an actual *grande dame* whom he used to see when he lived in Kolomna. It is more important, though, that Pushkin has taken a hint from *Beppo* and used it in a very unBeppo-like fashion.

> I've seen some balls and revels in my time,
> And stayed them over for some silly reason,
> And then I looked (I hope it was no crime)
> To see what lady best stood out the season . . .
> I never saw but one (the stars withdrawn)
> Whose bloom could after dancing dare the dawn.
>
> The name of this Aurora I'll not mention,
> Although I might, for she was naught to me
> More than that patent work of God's invention,
> A charming woman whom we like to see;
> But writing names would merit reprehension . . .

The woman who was naught to Byron is a good deal to the Jamesian speculator, brooding over and shaping his memories. The idea of a Beppo tale with a lighthearted surface and a wry, unappeased undercurrent of emotion, with two distinct narrative tones instead of digressions, begins to take on a functional possibility. But unfortunately there is no more to be done with the countess. The Jamesian recollector disappears, and the Beppo commentator can only use her for a series of sententious comparisons with Parasha, comparisons where Pushkin may have intended to impress the journalists with his preference for simple, unfashionable topics and people, but which only strike the reader as new version of an old cliché.

> Our new acquaintance, the simple and good
> Parasha, was a hundred times more fortunate
> than her, reader.

We hear no more of the countess, and the rest of the tale is a brilliant exercise in *ottava rima* narration, brisk, witty, and economical. The old cook dies; Parasha sets out to engage a new one, and returns with a tall awkward girl who seems to know nothing of household matters but is modest, quiet, and cheap. At church next Sunday the widow is assailed by a sudden fear that the new servant may have stayed at home to steal: she runs home and finds her shaving in Parasha's mirror. The servant vanishes—did Parasha blush? 'I know nothing more.' 'You mean that's all? What about a moral?' 'There is none—or rather yes there is. Wait a moment.' The moral of course is that shaving is not suited to female servants who, besides, should not be engaged for nothing.

Though the adventure of the new cook is as spirited as the *Beppo* recognition scene, **The Little House** cannot be called a masterpiece by Pushkinian standards. The word is no doubt as beside the point as the complaints of the imaginary reader (and the actual critics) about the story's pointlessness, but Pushkin is the kind of artist who cannot but invoke even in a *jeu d'esprit* the logic and the shapeliness of great art. **Count Nulin,** written five years earlier, has these on its small scale as much as **Evgeny Onegin** on its wider one, and so have the **Skazki.** But **The Little House** is filled with suggestions and loose ends which it does not help to explain away as an aspect of its genre, for the fact is that neither stanza nor genre really suited Pushkin. The swinging knockabout satire that Byron commands is not his forte, and the alliance he tacitly invokes—between two gentlemen and men of the world against the scribbling tribe—proved unworkable. Haunted memories, farce, polemic chat, make uneasy bedfellows in the poem, and cannot be synergised like the equally heterogeneous elements in **Evgeny Onegin.** In modifying the *Beppo* technique Pushkin has not really transformed it, and **The Little House** is his only poem in which modification and paraphrase of a source does not yield a commensurate gain.

D. S. Mirsky on Pushkin's *Skazki*:

The charm of these tales lies in their beautiful consistency of style and fairy-tale logic, and in their absolute freedom from "meaning". They are pure creations out of a given material—things of beauty. Their peculiarity is that in making these things Pushkin did not make his personal and traditional tastes the criterion of their beauty, but subordinated their composition to the inherent laws discovered by him in the possibilities of the given folk-tales. This is why, perhaps, after all, in spite of the argument being "borrowed", they are the most purely creative of Pushkin's works. The making of these stories was the making of a world obeying its own immanent laws and independent of this world of ours. The beautiful and logical consistency of these laws may be regarded as Pushkin's highest achievement and his greatest claim to poetical pre-eminence.

D. S. Mirsky, in his Pushkin, *1926.*

John Fennell (essay date 1973)

SOURCE: "Pushkin," in *Alexander Pushkin: Modern Critical Views,* edited by Harold Bloom, Chelsea House Publishers, 1987, pp. 73-116.

[*An English educator and critic, Fennell specializes in Russian history and literature. In the following excerpt from an essay that was originally published in* Nineteenth-Century Russian Literature: Studies of Ten Russian Writers, *he examines the narrative technique, structure, and style of Pushkin's narrative poems.*]

The *poema,* or narrative poem, was the verse genre most widely practised by Pushkin. It enjoyed—especially the heroic-epic version of it—enormous popularity and pres-

tige in eighteenth-century Russia. At the beginning of the nineteenth century, however, tastes changed. The neoclassical epic, as well as other subgenres of the *poema,* ceased to thrill the reading public or to attract the professional poets. Instead the lyrical Romantic *poema* captivated imaginations. Byron's *Childe Harold* and the "Eastern Poems" swept Russia as they had swept western Europe before. The heroic epic, with its lofty subjects and matching stilted style, its conventional idealized heroes with whom the impersonal author has no emotional contact, its slow-moving episodic narrative which throws no light on the faceless characters but merely serves to illustrate the unreal, almost mediaeval, struggle between good and evil, between black and white—all this was replaced by a *poema* with a new content, a new, subjective attitude to life, a new interest in man's inner conflicts and emotions.

The lyrical Byronic epic attracted Pushkin's attention at an early stage in his career. Apart from one youthful attempt at the heroic-comic, **Ruslan and Lyudmila** (1817-20), and the witty, erotic, blasphemous parody, **Gavriliada** (1821), all Pushkin's first essays in the genre were based on the Byronic pattern. His so-called "Southern Poems"—**The Prisoner of the Caucasus (Kavkazskiy plennik)** (1820-21), **The Robber Brothers (Brat'ya-razboyniki)** (1821-22) and **The Fountain of Bakhchisaray (Bakhchisarayskiy fontan)** (1821-23)—are impregnated with the spirit and technique of the "Eastern Poems." The influence of Byron can be seen in the plot, the structure, the subjective treatment of the characters, the narrative method and other features as well. This pervasive influence was both obstructive and unproductive. It held Pushkin back, binding him to many of the cliché-ridden effusions of his schoolboy poetry and forcing him to perpetuate the tiresome habit of conveying other people's emotions by means of other people's stale commonplaces. Of course, there are flashes of realistic description and unmistakably Pushkinian phraseology, and there is plenty of mellifluous diction. For all the secondhand nature of much of the writing we cannot forget that this is after all Pushkin—bad Pushkin, perhaps, and some of it poetry which Pushkin himself later regretted having written, but still with glimpses of the mature poet. It was only in **The Gipsies (Tsygany)** (1824) that Pushkin abandoned his Byronic manner and for the first time in a sustained piece of writing showed the direction much of his mature work was to take.

When considering the subject matter of many of Pushkin's major writings one is struck by the fact that certain intellectual demands are being made on the reader and that the reader is forced willy-nilly to become involved in some problem or other inherent in the narrative. Now this does not occur to any noticeable degree in the epic *poemy* of the eighteenth century. In them one is given an ideal picture, a struggle, say, between good and evil, the outcome of which is obvious from the start. In the Byronic poem the reader merely observes and shares the hero's emotions and spiritual conflicts. We are simply invited to witness the record of anguish, ecstasy, passion, or whatever it may be, but seldom asked to pass judgement or to query motives. This is all done for us by the author who obligingly, if irritatingly, forestalls our own response by letting us share in *his* emotional approach to the situation. In Pushkin's early "Southern Poems" no intellectual demands are made. There are no problems to solve. *The Prisoner of the Caucasus* is little more than an illustration of the traditional Romantic juxtaposition of civilization and primitive society: we witness the captive's misery, boredom, disillusionment; we note the contrast with the naive native girl; we observe his callous behaviour and enjoy the lush descriptions of nature. But that is all. There is no question of passing moral judgements, condemning, approving, deciding who is right and who is wrong. Much the same applies to *The Fountain of Bakhchisaray.* We are given a glamorous picture of the harem with a psychological study of envy and jealousy thrown in. But we are not called upon to judge the posturing hero or indeed to ask ourselves any significant questions about the story.

The Gipsies, however, is a "problem piece," the first in Russian literature, and if we are to obtain satisfaction from it we must firstly decipher the problems and then find a solution to them. Pushkin does not commit himself explicitly; he remains aloof. But nevertheless he scatters clues and we find ourselves asking such questions as What is Freedom? What is the power of Fate? Is only the slave of passions defenceless against Destiny? Or are all men subject to "blind cunning Fate"?

It is precisely this implicit posing of questions and this demand made on the reader to involve himself which make *The Gipsies* so unlike any of Pushkin's previous *poemy.* But a still greater breach with the "Romantic-Byronic" past is marked by the formal elements of *The Gipsies*—the structure, the narrative technique and the style.

A distinguishing feature of the earlier *poemy* is their structural weakness. They lack symmetry and proportion. One can scarcely talk of the "structure" of *Ruslan and Lyudmila,* for example—it is little more than a collection of anecdotes loosely strung together. *The Prisoner of the Caucasus* is remarkable structurally only for its imbalance. Pushkin seems to have little control over his material: in part 2 the Captive takes fifty-eight lines to pour out his heart to the Circassian girl, while nearly 200 of the 371 lines of part 1 are used for grandiose nature descriptions or sketches of the customs of the natives. Still more uncontrolled is the structure of *The Fountain of Bakhchisaray,* a jumble of exotically garish scenes barely connected with each other and seemingly thrown together in an attempt to dazzle and to break free from the laws of classical architectonics. But in *The Gipsies* there is a considerable tightening up, an economy and compactness, a structural balance between various parts of the work: words echo words; situations mirror each other with what Blagoy calls "mathematical consistency." At times the compactness shatters any illusion of reality there may have been: at the very beginning of the action, for example, Zemfira manages to pack into eight lines (ll. 43-50) an astonishing amount of information about Aleko, excellent stuff for the swift advancement of the plot, but quite out of keeping with her highly strung, passionate nature. One must not of course imagine that in *The Gipsies* Pushkin jettisons all the structural devices of the Romantic *poema;* as Zhirmunsky has shown in his *Bayron i Pushkin,* many of the

Byronic techniques—the scene-setting overture, the abrupt entry *in medias res,* the omniscient author's reminiscence which serves as the hero's "prehistory," the dramatic scenes, to quote a few—are retained by Pushkin. But the overall impression is one of restraint, balance and clarity.

The narrative technique of Byron's "Eastern Poems" is largely conditioned by the centripetal nature of the subject matter. Concentration on the psyche of the hero demands an omnipresent and omniscient author, commenting, interrupting, questioning, exclaiming, digressing, conditioning and, above all, assimilating with the central character. Now it is true that in Pushkin's early "Southern Poems" there is a modicum of aloofness foreign to the "Eastern Poems." But neither *The Prisoner* nor *The Fountain* can be described as in any sense objective pieces of narrative.

In *The Gipsies,* on the other hand, Pushkin seems to be trying to get as far away as possible from the subjective narrative technique of his early works and to distance himself from characters, story and reader, to make himself remote and unidentifiable. By far the largest part of the poem consists of purely objective narrative—either scenery or action painting (the gipsies' camp, for example [1-30, 73-89] or the description of their way of life [225-54])—or of dramatic dialogue with stage directions. There is no involvement, no intimacy. Only the setting is given, and the words and actions of the dramatis personae have to carry the argument. However, some form of psychological explanation is essential. The author has to emerge occasionally and to inform us of certain things—of Aleko's background and prehistory (120-39), for example. But this is kept to a minimum, and a great deal of psychological motivation and interpretation is given us in what might be described as disguised narrated speech, in which the third person singular is used in place of the first person, thus making an interior monologue part and parcel of the author's uninterrupted flow of narrative. For example, in the first passage describing Aleko after he has joined the gipsies we read: "Gloomily the young man gazed at the now-empty plain, and he did not dare to explain to himself the secret cause of his sorrow. Black-eyed Zemfira is with him; now he is a free dweller of the world" (94-99). After the physical description of Aleko gazing at the plain ("gloomily" describes his features, his stance; not necessarily his emotions), the words "and he pondered": could be supplied and the remainder of the passage could be read as direct speech (i. e., in the *first* person singular)—"I dare not explain . . . Zemfira is with me." This method of disguising soliloquy as part of the narrative not only enables the author to keep up his flow without breaking off for a fragment of direct statement and thus to economize and avoid "Romantic spread," but also creates a certain degree of authorial detachment. Indeed, almost the only passage in *The Gipsies* in which Pushkin intrudes on the narrative in order *personally* to portray the innermost thoughts of a character is when he describes Aleko's sleep and awakening just before the murder (440ff.). Here he both informs us of Aleko's mental condition ("fear seizes him"; he is "oppressed by foreboding") and even gives us an inkling of what his dream was like ("in his mind a vague vision plays"), all things which of course an extrinsic recorder of speech and action could not be expected to know or relate.

Although Pushkin in *The Gipsies* cuts his role as omniscient revealer of other people's thoughts and emotions right back, he is still unable to rid himself of the equally, if not more, obtrusive role of poet-commentator. But again, these intrusions are far less numerous than in earlier works. Only on one occasion does he allow himself the luxury of an unmotivated lyrical irruption into the fairly calm narrative stream: at the end of the vivid picture of the raising of the gipsy camp in the morning after Aleko's arrival, Pushkin, as if unable to leave good alone, comments on the scene. "It is all so brisk and restless, *so foreign to our dead pleasures, so foreign to this empty life, which is as monotonous as the song of slaves*" (90-93). This personal comment, this angry, isolated relation of the poem to the poet's world, strikes a jarring note. An entirely new dimension is gratuitously added, gratuitously because Pushkin is going to make the same point anyhow in the various speeches of Aleko and the Old Man, and make it *indirectly* and all the more effectively.

Apart from this isolated personal comment there are of course other authorial interruptions. But their aim is quite different. It is not to comment on life, to reveal the *true* author behind the story (which is certainly the aim of Pushkin's remarks on "our dead pleasures"), or to make the reader compare conditions of fiction and life. The aim is functional. They serve to shift the scenery, to move from one phase to another, or to stress one particular theme. For example, the allegorical "God's little bird" song (104-19) which introduces Aleko's prehistory is preceded by two rhetorical questions: "But why does the young man's heart quake? By what care is he oppressed?" (102-3). These immediately call up the communicative author, not to give his views as was the case ten lines earlier, but to serve as a plot-pusher, a bridge between Aleko's vain ruminations on the causes of his "secret misery" and the omniscient author's description of his background. It is just as artificial a device as the *Ptichka bozhiya* allegory. The same sort of thing occurs at the end of Aleko's prehistory when Pushkin again intrudes ("But, God, how passions played with his docile soul!" 140-45). This time the purpose is perhaps slightly more personal and revelatory of the author's thoughts, or rather his designs on the reader, in that it serves to weight the Fate theme. But it is still basically a *structural* device in so far as it helps to warn the reader of the conclusion to expect. In other words, when Pushkin emerges in person in *The Gipsies* and declares his presence openly by addressing the reader or exclaiming to the world in general, he is on all occasions, with the one exception mentioned above, merely employing a variant of an artifice beloved of the eighteenth-century fiction writer. True it is slightly less crude than the question and answer technique, such as we find in say *The Corsair*:

> Who o'er his placid slumber bends?
> His foes are gone, and here he hath no friends;
> Is it some seraph sent to grant him grace?
> No, 'tis an earthly form with heavenly face!

and certainly rarer and more discreet than the rhetoric which bespatters *The Prisoner* and *The Fountain* or the euphuistic "*druz'ya moi*'s" and "*chitatel*'s" of *Ruslan and Lyudmila,* but it serves the same function.

The reason for Pushkin's striving for this type of objectivity in *The Gipsies* is to be found in the poem's purpose. The more demands a work makes on the reader, the more the author is obliged to avoid, hide or disguise any partiality he may feel. He must not give the game away. The very fact that Pushkin is here attempting a problem piece and forcing participation on his readers compels him to distance himself from his subject, his characters and, ultimately, his readers.

Now it is often true to say that the further back an author places himself the more freely he can manipulate different "voices" within his work. The Romantic writer who is always ready in the wings, stepping forward to interfere with the narrative, tends to restrict all his explanations and comments to one voice—his own, or that of his implied author (which of course may differ from his own). And Pushkin in his early works makes all other voices sound like his own authorial voice. The light bantering tone of *Ruslan and Lyudmila* hardly alters throughout, in spite of the deliberate mixture of genres. The earlier "Southern Poems" are equally monophonic, although in *The Prisoner* there are already glimpses of a descriptive style which stands in sharp contrast to, say, the hero's effusions or the banal utterances of the heroine. *The Gipsies,* on the other hand, is Pushkin's first major work in which he consistently, and successfully, attempts to differentiate between stylistic layers and to use different voices for different purposes. It is not only his most "objective" work to date; it is his first truly polyphonic work.

Four basic voices can be distinguished: those of the "objective narrator," the Old Man, Aleko and Zemfira. Of course these are not exclusive. Other minor stylistic currents are also discernible: the folkloric, for example (see the two songs) and the diverse tones of the authorial intruder, which vary according to the topic or character under scrutiny.

The objective narrator's voice—the voice with which Pushkin describes background and actions—is austere and laconic. The vocabulary is unemotional and undecorative. The aim is to present a picture which describes with precision what is visible and audible; consequently the descriptive elements—the adverbs and adjectives—are monosemantic; they have no overtones: "cold" means low in temperature and not "unemotional," "frigid" or "gloomy." All words convey exact, precise information; they give no impression of emotions felt by the author. Occasionally a picture is given greater expressiveness by the use of a "subjective" or "intellectual" adjective added to a concrete noun. The tame bear is described (245) as gnawing its "frustrating" or "irksome" (*dokuchnuyu*) chain, not its "thick," "iron" or "heavy" chain; this immediately evokes the angle of the bear's head or the glint in its eye. The descriptive elements used in the burial scene (493-97)—*robko* (shyly), *vstrevozhennoy* (alarmed), *skorbnoy* (mournful)—fulfil the same function and allow the reader's imagination more scope than the unvarnished depiction of most scenes. The syntax matches the vocabulary in austerity and simplicity. The sentence structure is startlingly bare and artless. Take for example the six lines describing the gipsy encampment (7–12): . . .

> Between the wheels of the waggons, / Half covered-over with rugs, / A fire burns; around it a family / Cooks its supper; in the open steppe / The horses graze; behind the tent / A tame bear lies in freedom.

Here, apart from the swift-flowing participial clause in the second line, the syntax is reduced to the subject + predicate combination (*sem'ya gotovit uzhin*: a family cooks its supper). The remarkably prosaic nature of the descriptive passages is increased by enjambement (note how the last four lines of the above quotation all flow into each other) and by the typically Pushkinian tendency to catalogue (see especially 14-17; 80ff.). But what stamps such passages most as prosaic is the almost total absence of metaphor. In the first thirty lines of the poem and in the description of the striking of the camp (73-89), for example, only two moribund metaphors can be found—*niskhodit sonnoe molchanie* (sleepy silence descends); *volynki govor* (the sound, lit. "talk," of pipes)—and they are virtually dead.

The Old Man's voice is close to that of the author-narrator. This is hardly surprising, for he is the one character whose views Pushkin patently shares; he can indeed be called his mouthpiece. The lexis is similar to the narrator's. Even when dealing with such abstract concepts as pride, freedom or will in his final speech to Aleko (510-20), he manages to lend his words a concrete flavour. Instead of vague adjectives ("we are lawless, unvindictive, unemotional" etc.) he uses nouns and verbs: "We have no *laws*; we do not *torture*, we do not *put men to death*; we have no need of *blood* or *groans*." The syntax of most of his speeches is again remarkable for its simplicity. The tale of Mariula (370-409), for example, which begins with a naive little jingle . . .

> Listen: I will tell you / A tale about myself.

contains in all its forty lines only one subordinate clause (372-73). The three lines describing his awakening on the morning after Mariula's departure (400-402) . . .

> I was sleeping peacefully; dawn flashed; / I woke up; my beloved was not there! / I look for her, call her—all trace has vanished.

consists of seven abrupt syntactical units in twice as many words. At times the syntax becomes unnaturally compressed, as for example in his first speech (51-62) when in a series of machine-gun-like utterances he outlines a programme of Aleko's activities, or when he drops his pearls of aphoristic folksy wisdom before Aleko (414-17). Metaphors are rare in his speech, but he has a propensity for nature similes—for instance he uses an extended comparison with the moon while explaining the nature of woman to Aleko; and in the best mediaeval folkloric tradition the moon is anthropomorphized (343-58).

Only once does Pushkin slacken his grip on the Old Man—when he has him rouse the lovers with the cliché "abandon your couch of bliss" (72). Otherwise the portrait is carefully sustained. True he makes him round off the story of Ovid with three lines of almost impenetrable

syntactic opaqueness (214-16) and has him use coy periphrasis and hackneyed metaphors to describe his own youth (379-80; 381-82; 389-90): but the complexities of the first are an imitation of Ovid's style, while the artificialities of the second represent an attempt to stress the romantic nature of youth and to contrast it with the plain realism of maturity. We are left with the picture of simplicity, natural wisdom, proximity to nature and absence of false emotionalism.

The voice of Aleko—i.e., his own speech and the words used by the narrator to describe him—is sharply contrasted with that of the objective narrator and the Old Man. As the representative of false, artificial civilization, of "stuffy towns" (*dushnye goroda*), he uses, and is described in, an artificial, borrowed language. His vocabulary is abstract, imprecise and emotional. He hardly opens his mouth without uttering such words as *volnenie* (excitement), *bezumnyy* (mad), *nezhnyy* (tender), *unynie* (gloom), *pustinnyy* (deserted), *utomitel'nyy* (exhausting), *milyy* (dear)—words which reflect the condition of his soul, its emptiness perhaps. When he wakes up on the night of the murder (443ff.) he stretches out his hand *jealously*, but his *timid* hand seizes the *cold* sheets. Pushkin goes on to describe his emotions in a series of conventional melodramatic clichés: he gets up *with trepidation*; fear *seizes him*; *hot and cold* run through his body; he is *fearful* to look at, etc., etc., and we are reminded of the astonishing brevity with which the parallel awakening of the Old Man is described. As one would expect, the syntax is far more complex than that of the objective narrator of the Old Man. Aleko's heated outburst in answer to the Old Man's string of calm simple aphorisms (414-17) is masterly in its confusion and intricacy. But the main distinguishing feature of Aleko's voice is his use of rhetorical devices. He talks in bursts of exclamations, parallelisms, oxymorons, repetitions; indeed at times his language is so artificial and abstruse that one wonders what a simple girl like Zemfira could have made of it (see particularly 168-76; 217-24). Metaphors abound, although most of them are well-worm clichés and merely stress the artificiality of his speech.

There is little to say about the language of Zemfira. It occupies only about a tenth of the poem, and Pushkin seems to have given it as little thought as he gave the delineation of her physical appearance or character. It is as simple as he can make it. The short sharp prosaic bursts of speech (e. g., the night scene, 305ff.), the uncomplicated sentence structure, the plain "concrete" vocabulary (see especially her touchingly naive description of what *she* thinks life in the cities must be like, 164-67) and the almost total absence of imagery tell us all that we need to know about this primitive, instinctive child of nature.

If so much space has been devoted to *The Gipsies* it is not so much because of its intrinsic merits as because of its importance in the history of Pushkin's development as a writer. It marks the halfway stage—the breach with the "Romantic-Byronic" past and the beginning of new literary interests, a preoccupation with new stylistic techniques. As a largely experimental work it has its faults—strident melodrama, a woodenness of character portrayal, here and there inconsistencies of style—but these do not detract from the reader's aesthetic appreciation, as does the overall impression of coldness: the more Pushkin aspires towards objectivity in his sloughing off of Byronism the remoter the work becomes from the author and the less it tells us about him. In the succeeding *poemy*—and indeed in much of his mature work—Pushkin abandons this unnatural Olympian pose; he draws close and reveals himself, or rather varying aspects of himself, to his readers. It is as though he began to realize that this self-inflicted isolation was foreign to his generous nature: he must show his thoughts, not disguise them by means of artificial distancing devices. He must give the reader a picture of himself and make him aware of his presence, whether as wit, philosopher, historian, patriot or poet.

At first glance *Count Nulin* (*Graf Nulin*) (1825) appears to be as objective a work as any. Authorial intrusion seems minimal. It looks like nothing but an exercise in the "low style," full of "prosaic ravings," "contemptible prose" and the "variegated rubbish of the Flemish School"; (expressions used by Pushkin to describe certain elements of his style in *Evgeny Onegin*); an attempt merely to paint the squalor and boredom of provincial life and to strip it of romantic glamour. But *Count Nulin* does not consist solely of prosaic descriptions of the farmyard; it has a plot centred on a faintly erotic anecdote, and fluttering behind it all is the frivolous, lighthearted, witty and highly skilled narrator, holding back information where necessary, nudging us, winking, hinting. He intrudes again and again, either to guide us through the narrative, to push on the plot, to follow the Count around and explain his motives, or to comment with sophistication and mock sententiousness and to draw his readers into the fun. The frothy, unserious, at times conventional (*druz'ya moi!* [my friends!]) authorial remarks reveal precisely that gay image of himself which Pushkin wanted his readers to receive.

For all Pushkin's joyous self-revelation in *Count Nulin,* we can hardly call him *engagé*: there is really nothing beyond say the pleasures of hunting—revealed in a few lines—to be involved in; and he is still too much the professional storyteller to drop all pretence and reveal himself as the *artist* revelling in the creative joys of painting a totally unsentimental picture of nature (the grey drab colours of the farmyard, the noises, the smells almost) or of evoking *physically* an emotional crisis (the angry frightened heroine's reaction to Nulin's sexual assault): . . .

> With all her might she gives Tarquin / A box on the ear, yes, yes! / A box on the ear and what a one!

In *Poltava* (1828), however, Pushkin involves himself up to the hilt, this time as the passionate patriot-historian.

Just as in *Count Nulin* no demands were made on the readers—we were merely *entertained* by a witty raconteur—so here we are not asked to pose or answer any questions, to judge the behaviour of Maria or Mazepa. We are simply guided through the narrative by the omnipresent Pushkin, given his appreciation or criticism, and even supplied with his explicit interpretation in an epilogue (in the passage of time the Mazepas of this world are forgotten,

the Peters survive). As we inferred from *The Gipsies* that the more demanding a work, the remoter the author tends to make himself, so here we can observe the converse: the less the reader is expected to work, the more the author-narrator is likely to intrude.

And intrude he does. True, it is an impersonal intrusion; there are no *I*'s, *my*'s or *our*'s. But we have every other form of irruption into the text. His hand is felt at every turn. He sees, knows and describes everything. He shifts from scene to scene, from character to character. He interprets his puppets' thoughts, explains their motives and reactions. As plot manipulator he emerges with the by now familiar rhetorical questions ("But where is the Hetman!" After the battle in part 3 he asks seven rhetorical questions and then proceeds to answer them); he even comments on the dramatic irony of Maria's ignorance at the end of part 1 ("O, if only she knew! . . . But the murderous secret is still hidden from her"). But it is as biased historical commentator that Pushkin makes his presence most felt. From the very first we are told what to think about Mazepa. There is nothing ambiguous about him. It is not just oblique criticism put into the thoughts and words of Kochubey (though there is plenty of this); Pushkin tells us what a villain he is, subjectively sprinkling him with such epithets as "cunning," "evil," "blood-thirsty," "criminal," etc. He even addresses him personally ("O destroyer of hold innocence!" part 3). And at the same time he tries to make us feel pity for the noble Kochubey and admiration for the glorious Peter. Nothing is left for us to do but enjoy the soft evocations of nature (*Tikha Ukrainskaya noch'* [Calm is the Ukrainian night] etc.), and admire the solemn majesty of the odelike rhetoric, to follow the love story around which the work is centred, and to be caught up with poor Maria in her awful predicament. Pushkin the hero-worshipper, the patriot, by making his presence felt continuously, has freed us of any effort. We do not even have to question his sincerity or reliability as narrator.

Although Pushkin's last *poema, The Bronze Horseman,* poses problems as vital and engaging as any in *The Gipsies,* although it seemingly gives no explicit answers but leaves a series of question marks, and although it compels the reader to collaborate if he is to receive full satisfaction, nevertheless it is impregnated with Pushkin's presence. Pushkin emerges as the *personal* author, not just the omniscient narrator dipping into the minds of his characters ("A restless care disturbs [the Count]") or the commentator putting his views across in the third person ("Mazepa is evil, treacherous, cunning, etc."). Thus paradoxically *The Bronze Horseman* is at the same time the most and the least revealing of all his *poemy*: the more we read it the more we know about Pushkin and yet the more we become confused about its ultimate meaning.

How should we interpret this simple-looking little *povest'*? What do the statue, the elements, the "hero" symbolize? From Belinsky to the present day hardly a critic has refrained from giving his own interpretation, or from confirming or rejecting his predecessors' views. There have been political, sociopolitical, religious, metaphysical, literary, historical exegeses. Ingenious "signals" have been picked up and codes deciphered. *The Bronze Horseman* has been used to demonstrate most theories concerning Pushkin's life and thought. Pushkin, it would seem, can be made to emerge from the work in any guise that suits the literary historian.

There is no purpose to be gained here by speculating on the meaning of the poem or on Pushkin's purpose in writing it. We can only address the reader to some of the voluminous literature on the subject, suggest that he follow the complex history of its genesis and its connection with other works ("Ezersky," "My Hero's Genealogy" ["Rodoslovnaya moego geroya"] and *My Genealogy* [*Moya rodoslovnaya*]) traced by the Soviet scholar O. S. Solov'eva, and limit ourselves once again to a discussion of some of the work's formal aspects in the hope that such an investigation may help the reader to find his own "solution" to *The Bronze Horseman.*

The Bronze Horseman is a *povest'*, a short story in verse told by an omnipresent and omniscient narrator. This is made quite explicit in the succinct "frame" passage at the end of the introduction: . . .

> There was a dread time, / The memory of it is
> still fresh. . . / About it, my friends, for you /
> I will begin my narrative. / My tale will be sad.

The author has of course already established his presence. Having started the *poema* disguised as a courtly ode writer, aloof, but nonetheless communicating Peter's thoughts and omnisciently sweeping over the traditional "hundred years" (*Proshlo sto let*) between the foundation of the city and the present day, he emerges at last as the undisguised authorial *I.* From the start of the great lyrical confession of love for the city (*Lyublyu tebya, Petra tvoren'e* [I love you, city of Peter's creation], 43) to the sombre beginning of the narrative proper in part 1, Pushkin thrusts himself upon our imagination. The evocations of the city are shown through his eyes and his eyes alone. After seven lines crammed with rich musical and rhetorical devices (chiasma, repetition, hypallage, oxymoron) Pushkin lowers the tone to the utmost simplicity of prosaic utterance—almost to understatement—to portray himself as the focal point of the whole poem, reading, writing, lampless in his room: . . .

> When in my room / I write or read without a
> lamp

Vision follows vision, each enriching not only our image of the city but also our knowledge of the poet: with every line the picture of Pushkin grows vivider in our eyes, until by the end of the last majestic outburst—the final passionate apostrophe to Petropolis—we have experienced the whole gamut of his poetic emotions. He has established himself in our minds as the poet capable of experiencing delight at the humble pleasures of the city (*beg sanok* [the sledges coursing], 61; *devich'i litsa* [the faces of girls], 62; etc.) and rapture at its majestic aspects (67-83). From now on we know that the *I,* whether stated or implied, is Pushkin.

For the rest of the poem Pushkin, whether interpreting the agony of the populace (*Osada! pristup!* [Siege! Assault!], 190ff.), allowing Evgeny's feelings to pour out in interior monologue or narrated speech, or even explaining the anthropomorphized Neva's motives (*I sporit' stalo ey nevmoch'* [She could no longer endure the struggle] 170), has immediate access to and contact with his reader. Only on one occasion are we given momentarily to mistrust him, when he indulges in faint irony at the expense of the hack Khvostov (344-46). Otherwise we know where we are. There is no ambiguity. *Bednyy, bednyy moy Evgeniy* (My poor, poor Evgeny!) is not just a cliché. It means what it says: Evgeny is the object of Pushkin's profound compassion. And of course when it comes to the grand authorial comments there is no mistaking Pushkin's voice. He no longer needs to comment with the authority of his own voice. Instead he smoothly glides from the thoughts of his hero into his own. At the end of part 1, for example, he rounds off Evgeny's despairing monologue, dramatically rendered in narrated speech (*Bozhe, Bozhe! tam—Uvy!* [O God, O God! There, alas!] 241-48), with a rhetorical question asked by Evgeny (*Ili vo sne / On eto vide?* [Or is he dreaming this?] —i.e., *Ili vo sne ya eto vizhu?* [Or am I dreaming this?]) and follows it with the great despairing question, uttered in true Pushkinian tones: . . .

> Or is all our / Life nothing but an empty dream,
> / Heaven's mockery at earth?

The same thing occurs in part 2 when mad Evgeny approaches the statue (404-23): the author shows us his thoughts—Evgeny recognizes the scene of the tragedy "and the [marble] lions and the square" (409)—and then launches into a rhetorical monologue which in its sheer majesty of expression is clearly Pushkin's own (*i togo, / Kto . . .* [and him who . . .], 409-10, down to . . . *podnyal na dyby* [. . . reared up], 423). Again, there is no *I;* indeed Pushkin, by mentioning Evgeny's sudden lucidity (*Proyasnilis' / V nem strashno mysli* [His thoughts became terribly clear], 404-5), almost deludes us into believing that these are the madman's thoughts. But only for a moment. There can be no mistaking the lofty intonations. Only Pushkin could exclaim . . .

> O mighty master of Fate!

If the masterly narrative skill with which Pushkin establishes his own impression and image on the work distinguishes *The Bronze Horseman* from the other *poemy,* so too does the interweaving of stylistic patterns. We have remarked above that in *The Gipsies* Pushkin's chilly remotenss helped him to manipulate several voices; such polyphony and contrapuntal style is far less noticeable in all succeeding *poemy* except *The Bronze Horseman. Count Nulin* and *The Little House in Kolomna* (*Domik v Kolomne*) (1830) are both basically monophonic works, not only because the subject dealt with in both is restricted to a particular milieu which it scarcely leaves, but also because a particular, somewhat narrow, "Pushkin" is always making himself felt. Even in *Poltava,* which embraces a variety of scenes, milieus and social strata, and where, it is true, one can pick out two or three separate linguistic strains, there is still no striking stylistic differentiation between the various themes; there are no characteristic "voices."

In *The Bronze Horseman,* however, Pushkin for the first time achieves what might be called a synthesis of authorial intimacy and stylistic polyphony. Now much has been written about the contrasting and blending of stylistic patterns in **The Bronze Horseman.** In particular Pushkin's sharply contrasting treatment of what are called the "Petrine style" and the "Evgeny style" has been dealt with in detail: the lofty descriptions of Peter and his bronze image, with their archaisms, rhetoric and alliteration reminiscent of the courtly odes of the eighteenth century and the naked prosaic descriptions of Evgeny and his thoughts and actions have been more than once studied by the Pushkin specialists and need no further comment here. But what might be called the "third manner"—the style used to describe the elements and certain aspects of St. Petersburg—has received considerably less attention from the critics. It is of course not always easy to say where the boundary between this and the other two styles runs. At times this third manner looks like a fusion of the Petrine style and the Evgeny style: the second half of the introduction (43ff.), for example, modulates from the jingle of . . .

> When in my room / I write or read without a lamp

to the majestic alliterative rumble of . . .

> The smoke and thunder of your fortress,

at the same time containing lines reminiscent of the cosy townscapes of **Evgeny Onegin** (see especially 63-66). Those passages, however, which have as their central "character" the river, the rain, the wind or even the time of year are on the whole distinguishable from the rest of the poem.

It has often been remarked that **The Bronze Horseman** is the most "atmospheric" of Pushkin's works, and there can be little doubt that this is largely due to the intensity of these "elemental" passages. How is the effect achieved? The vocabulary is modern—archaisms such as *khladom* (cold) (98), *bregami* (banks) (171) or *peni* (foam) (382) are exceptional; it is simple—so simple that at times one can attach the intonations of popular speech (*duri* [madness], *nevmoch'* [unable], *poutru* [in the morning], 169-71); it is unemotional and concrete; and it is precise—words tend to be semantically unambiguous. Even if a polysemantic word appears at first reading ambiguous because of its position in the sentence, the ambiguity is soon dissolved by the context. An attribute such as *mrachnyy* when qualifying *val* (wave) at the beginning of a sentence could have several connotations apart from its purely denotary sense of "dark": "fearful," "gloomy" or "sullen," for instance; and in . . .

> The sullen wave / Splashed against the embankment

it could mean any of these, until the wave is metaphorically personified by *ropshcha peni* (reproachfully grumbling) and by the graphic simile of the unsuccessful petitioner, and "sullen" becomes the appropriate epithet. The syntax matches the vocabulary in simplicity (e. g., *Uzh bylo posdno i temno* [Already it was late and dark], 103), almost the only form of subordination being gerundial clauses (*pechal'no voya* [sadly howling]). It is the richness of the imagery combined with the subtlety of the "orchestration" that gives the work its evocative atmospheric power.

The imagery is remarkably bold and often startlingly original. It is based exclusively on the pathetic fallacy. Nature is personified throughout either by metaphors or by similes. In the nine lines at the beginning of part 1, for example, the inanimate is animated in a series of vivid images: November breathes; the Neva tosses like a sick man in his restless bed; the rain beats angrily; the wind howls gloomily. In the first five lines of the introduction to part 2 the Neva is personified by metaphor, this time as an evil-doer returning from some cataclysmic act of destruction (earlier, in the description of the flood, the waves "climb into windows like thieves," 191, cf. 341): the animation is intensified by an extended simile (265-73) in which a band of marauders are pictured bursting into a village and returning home laden with loot, each of the four lines describing their retreat syntactically and lexically balancing the Neva's metaphorical withdrawal. A few lines further on the scene of the crime is converted to a battlefield: the waves are now "full of the triumph of victory" (279) and the Neva now "breathes heavily" (echoing the breathing of November in line 98) "like a horse galloping home from battle" (forestalling the image of the battlefield to come in line 305). We are never allowed to forget that Nature is as alive and active as Evgeny. Verbs, adjectives and adverbs continually bring the elements to life or keep them alive, the effectiveness of the metamorphosis being frequently heightened by the addition of a subjective-emotional epithet—to say that the wind howled *gloomily* or *sadly* implies an *additional* element of personification: the wind is not just a person howling, but a gloomy or a sad one; or again, the "violence" by which the Neva is exhausted (261) is described as "insolent" (*naglym*), an adjective which properly qualifies a human being—an imaginary bandit—and brings "violence" to life.

Again and again the effectiveness of the imagery and the intensity of the mood are heightened by the virtuosity of the "sound-painting"—the astonishing arrangement of syllables, vowels and consonants to convey various effects. In no *poema,* indeed in no long work of Pushkin was such ambitious orchestration attempted as in **The Bronze Horseman.** It is not just a question of simple *sound imitation* by means of onomatopaeic effects (e. g., *Shipen'e penistykh bokalov* [The hiss of foaming goblets]) or words devoid of onomatopoeic effects (e. g., *Serdito bilsya dozhd' v okno* [Angrily the rain beat against the window]) where the words taken separately have no peculiarly sonorous qualities but when taken together produce the desired acoustic effect by virtue of the peculiar combination of consonants and vowels. This technique is indeed frequently used to illustrate the sounds conveyed by the words: the boom of the cannons (*Tvoey tverdyni dym i grom* [The smoke and thunder of your fortress]—*dyn, dym, grom*), the howling of the wind (*vly . . . unylo,* 161), the gurgling of the water (*Kotlom klokocha i klubyas'* [Bubbling like a cauldron and swirling], 181). But Pushkin also manipulates his sounds simply in order to achieve certain sound patterns and thus to heighten the effect of a line or a passage. At times he does this in order to imprint a phrase upon the reader's mind, in the same way as he uses variation of metre to lend lustre or weight to a line of particular significance. We have only to compare . . .

Heaven's mockery at earth

with the variant forced upon Pushkin by the censor . . .

Fate's mockery at earth

to see how effective and memorable the original alliteration is. But mostly it is applied to whole passages, as for example the second half of the description of the flood (*Pogoda pushche svirepela* [The weather raged more fiercely], 179ff.).

The pattern is often extraordinarily complex, and it is not proposed to examine the technique or to attempt to improve on Bryusov's analysis. Suffice it to stress that the more one examines the text of ***The Bronze Horseman,*** the more intricate the pattern appears. At a first reading of the "hymn" to St. Petersburg, for example, . . .

> I love you, [city of] Peter's creation, / I love your stern, harmonious aspect, / The majestic flow of the Neva, / Her granite banks, / The iron tracery of your railings, / Your pensive nights' / Transparent twilight and moonless gleam

one might notice the alliteration of *strogiy / stroynyy,* or the combination of liquid consonants in p*r*oz*r*achnyy sum-*r*ak, b*l*esk bez*l*unnyy. But a deeper study would reveal such effects as the insistent play on *t* (*t-tr-tvr*) in *Lyublyu tebya Petra tvoren'e,* the parallel alternations of the dentals and their palatalized consonants (*d→zh: t→ch*) in *derzhavnoe techen'e,* and the interplay of *r* and *g* in be*re*govoy-*g*ranit-o*g*rad-uzo*r* chu*g*unnyy.

It is of course virtually impossible to say what makes Pushkin's sound-painting devices so aesthetically effective and distinguishes them from the distressing vulgarity of say Bal'mont or mere cleverness. But undoubtedly a large part of their effectiveness is due to this "hidden" quality, to the unobtrusive tact with which Pushkin exploits them and to the subtle interplay of meaning and sound.

Perhaps a further study of these formal aspects of ***The Bronze Horseman*** will help the reader to understand why its impact on generations of critics has been so powerful and why it is so often called the "greatest" of all his works. To summarize, we can provide a few superlatives of our own which may prove more helpful than "greatest." Of all Pushkin's *poemy,* ***The Bronze Horseman*** is the most intimate and personal. It is the most successful experiment with contrasting, blending and interplay of stylistic layers. It contains the most developed and the most evocative imagery; and its texture is enlivened by the richest "orchestration" and sound-painting. Of course many more superlatives could be added to the list and the second term of comparison of many of them could be extended. "Of all Pushkin's *poemy*" could read "of all Pushkin's works."

A. D. P. Briggs   (essay date 1983)

SOURCE: *Alexander Pushkin: A Critical Study,* Croom Helm, 1983, 257 p.

[*In the following excerpt, Briggs analyzes the style, structure, and themes of* The Bronze Horseman.]

One of the finest of Leningrad's tourist attractions is the

> Ever since childhood we have kept in memory a cheerful name: Pushkin. It is a name, a sound which has filled many days of our lives. Somber names of emperors, generals, inventors of instruments of murder, names of torturers and martyrs of life; and together with them, this radiant name: Pushkin.
>
> —*Alexander Blok, in his "On the Mission of the Poet," in* Modern Russian Poets on Poetry, *edited by Carl R. Proffer, 1976.*

two-hundred-year-old equestrian statue of Peter the Great (1672-1725) commissioned by Catherine II and executed by a French sculptor, E.M. Falconet. For all its splendour this statue, known universally as 'The Bronze Horseman' after Pushkin's narrative poem in which it appears, is a curious work of art. It was intended as a tribute to Peter, and in particular to his almost superhuman achievement in building a new city on the inhospitable swamps of northern Russia. A spirit of dynamism and domination, consciously infused into the scheme from the earliest sketches, was perpetuated through the enormous difficulties which Falconet himself overcame during the twelve years of design and construction, and it survives in the resulting monument. Nevertheless, a closer look at the statue cannot fail to reduce the sense of admiration with which it is at first approached. To begin with, three incompatible visual metaphors are mixed together. Peter is depicted, astride his massive Orlov charger, riding uphill and about to surmount the crest. This hardly corresponds to the base of the statue, a 1,500-ton granite block called 'The Thunder Stone' which has been hacked into the shape of a breaking wave. Neither of these images squares with the swamp serpent which the horse is trampling in mid-gallop with its hind hoofs. This necessary constructional device was introduced at a late stage to provide an extra anchorpoint and it looks like what it is, an irreconcilable afterthought. Besides this, the tsar himself has been given some less than regal attributes, a squat figure, a puffy face, a quizzical gaze and a puzzling right-hand gesture about which there has been much speculation. How far is Peter really in control of his mount? Is he about to fall back, recover himself, even soar up into space? Is he urging the steed on or restraining it in the face of some catastrophic hazard?

Whether by accident or design Falconet has created an ambiguous monument which qualifies its praise of the addressee even as it is bestowed by calling attention as much to the tsar's human deficiencies as to his transcendent qualities. This ambiguity evidently held a special appeal for Pushkin for he has used the selfsame property as a source of enrichment for his poem ***The Bronze Horseman.*** Pushkin's ambiguity owes nothing to vagueness, indecision or *force majeure*; it is a deliberately chosen policy based upon a desire to set out a series of antitheses in such a way that their ultimate irreconcilability should be disguised. The idea worked so well that the poem exactly matches the statue in its ironical combination of conflicting interests into an appealing and harmonious whole. The reconciliation of opposing forces on a number of different levels is the greatest claim to fame of *The Bronze Horseman.*

So high is this pinnacle of fame that there is now nothing controversial about the greatness of the poem. Critics, when they pronounce upon it, find that their main task is to avoid repeating already used superlatives. The least that is normally said of the poem is that it is Pushkin's finest; it is commonly rated the leading poem in the Russian language and John Bayley has overtopped all his predecessors by describing it [in his *Pushkin,* 1971] as 'the most remarkable of nineteenth-century poems', presumably in any language. The praise may seem extravagant to non-Russian speakers and Walter Arndt, perhaps with that remark in mind, describes *The Bronze Horseman* [in his *Pushkin Threefold,* 1971] as 'overpraised by some' and then only as 'perhaps the most significant of Pushkin's narrative poems'. The warning against an excess of enthusiasm is useful, but the limitations implied here by the word 'perhaps' seem as excessive in the opposite direction. There is no real case for reducing *The Bronze Horseman* in rank. From all points of view and by any standards this is an exceptional piece of poetry deservedly occupying a distinguished place in Russian literature and outstanding in the context of Pushkin's own work.

Much energy has been spent determining the sources of this masterpiece. This kind of research will not show how, or by what distance, the poem outclasses its rivals but the multiple sources are important for a full understanding and they call for a brief rehearsal. *The Bronze Horseman* was a long time maturing in Pushkin's mind and there were one or two false starts, fragments of which have been preserved, in particular **'The Genealogy of my Hero'** (1836) and **'Yezersky'** (1833). His preoccupation with Russian history and specifically with Peter the Great was of long duration; *The Bronze Horseman* clearly relates to *The Negro of Peter the Great* (1827), *Poltava* (1828) and the unfinished *History of Peter I* (1831-6). The animation of the statue in the Don Juan legend, as recreated by Pushkin in *The Stone Guest* (1830), might have suggested the similar event in his greatest narrative poem, especially since the statue in each case communicates first by a movement of the head. It is also true that the names Yevgeniy and Parasha are not unique to this poem. Thus there are many reflections elsewhere in Pushkin of some of the features of *The Bronze Horseman.* It has also been demonstrated that further ideas, great and small, as well as certain phrases and even whole lines were borrowed by Pushkin from other writers, including Batyushkov, Vyazemsky, Gnedich and Shevirev. Ryleyev's name may be added to the list for there are a number of borrowings from his poem *Voynarovsky* (1824-5). Certain contemporary anecdotes concerning incidents during the St Petersburg floods of 1826 and the historical account of these catastrophes by V.N. Berkh (wrongly described by Pushkin as V.I. Berkh in his foreword) were also in the poet's mind as he wrote. Much the most important of the external sources,

however, was a long work by the Polish poet Adam Mickiewicz entitled *Forefathers' Eve.* Mickiewicz was well known to Pushkin and they are reported to have held a long conversation one day beneath the monument itself. Parts of Mickiewicz's poem, especially that section of Part Three known as the 'Digression', contain overt criticism not only of Peter but also of the city and empire he created. At one point, for instance, Mickiewicz suggests that while Rome was built by men and Venice by the gods St Petersburg was the product of Satan. It goes without saying that this work was banned in Russia but Pushkin certainly knew it well. Although he agreed with some of the sentiments he retained the right to refute such criticism when it was voiced by a foreigner. His apotheosis of Peter and St Petersburg in the Introduction to *The Bronze Horseman* is obviously some kind of reply to Mickiewicz.

These are some of the main sources which have been identified. However, the accurate pinpointing of them does not even begin to explain why the resulting work should be so highly esteemed. What happens in the poem? What meanings does it possess which make it so important? What formal qualities distinguish it from its predecessors and rivals?

There are three sections to *The Bronze Horseman,* an introduction and two numbered parts. The introduction describes Peter the Great's conception and then creation of a city on the northern swamps which became so grand that it outshone even the capital. Pushkin extols the city and its activities for about 80 lines, congratulating Peter on his domination of the harsh elements. Part One reintroduces the city in an ugly situation amid worsening winter weather and presents another hero, Yevgeniy somebody-or-other, a poor clerk upon whom most of our attention will be focussed from now on. (Half the total lines of the poem are devoted to Yevgeniy.) We learn of his simple dreams for domestic happiness with his fiancée Parasha. A high point of this section is Pushkin's furious description of the flooding of the city which even the tsar can do nothing to resist. In Part Two, once the waters have begun to recede, Yevgeniy, helped by a chance encounter with a ferryman, makes his way over to Parasha's house but everything there has been destroyed and washed away. Yevgeniy's mind cannot stand the strain. He loses his reason and begins to roam the city. One night he comes across Falconet's statue. Blaming Peter for having created the city in the first place he threatens him. The huge idol seems to look round at him. Yevgeniy runs away and keeps on running; all night he seems to hear the clanging steed thundering behind him. After this experience he always slinks unobtrusively past whenever he has to cross that same square. But he doesn't last much longer. His dead body is washed up on a little island, discovered on the threshold of Parasha's wrecked home itself and buried.

This simple but tragic story is tightly packed with a number of competing themes, some Russian, some universal. One of the first secrets of its success is the sheer density of *The Bronze Horseman.* As well as being the last of Pushkin's narrative poems it is also the shortest of the serious ones; none of the various versions exceeds five hundred lines which makes it one third the length of *Poltava* and only just over half as long as *The Captive of the Caucasus.* It is the only one (excluding the less serious *Count Nulin* and *The Little House in Kolomna*) with a contemporary, recognisable situation and it possesses even a brief foreword emphasising the reality of the events described. Thus, at a stroke, Pushkin has updated, intensified and authenticated his material.

The meanings of *The Bronze Horseman,* overt and inferential, can scarcely be pinned down; they add to themselves and contradict each other, run off into new directions and find constant renewal, prompted by all manner of references. These range from straightforward statements and questions about human affairs to a quite new system of symbolism, itself covering a broad range with the immediately obvious (like the symbolic horseman himself) at one end and minute half-hints of other worlds and deeper issues at the other. The ideas are grouped in a way traditionally beloved by the Russians, in polarities. Most of the main antithetical preoccupations of Russian history and culture are included in *The Bronze Horseman,* either as stark confrontations or merely as embryonic comparisons. The age-old, still unresolved Westernising/Slavophile question is represented in Peter's whole concept of St Petersburg as a window into Europe; Russia's westward movement is shown to bring about both good and evil consequences. This controversy sharpens its focus if it is narrowed to the local, but also long-lasting problems of Russia versus Poland. The hidden polemic with Mickiewicz shows that Pushkin had Russo-Polish relations in mind (perhaps the Polish uprising of 1830 in particular) though he is more concerned with aggressive defence of his homeland than with the more awkward international issues involved. Other political events alluded to surely include the Decembrist uprising of 1825 which had taken place under the very eyes of the Bronze Horseman in Senate Square (now Decembrists' Square) and during which shots were fired into the crowd from alongside the very ornamental lions which crop up twice in Pushkin's poem. A further Russian question raised in passing is that of the competition between Moscow and St Petersburg for pre-eminence as the capital city.

A French scholar has suggested that the whole poem is an allegory of the relationship between Pushkin and Nicholas I. A better known American one, Edmund Wilson, emphasises the poem's long-lasting relevance to Russian politics by drawing a parallel between Peter the Great and Joseph Stalin. In this context it seems preferable to set personalities aside. Pushkin's poem invites consideration of a general political issue which has bedevilled his countrymen for centuries, that of the autocracy *vis-à-vis* the common people. The problem here is that Russia seemed to need a strong, decisive leader. Such a man could make things happen and direct the destiny of Russia into greatness. On the other hand, what about the rights of ordinary people under a dictatorship? Pushkin leads us first into admiration for Peter and his grandiose achievements, then, like Falconet, makes us wonder how certain and secure things are by undermining the tribute with hidden ambiguity.

> Fearsome in all the darkness now!
> What contemplation in that brow!

> What strength and sinew in him hidden!
> And in that horse what fiery speed!
> Where do you gallop, haughty steed?
> Where will those falling hoofs be ridden?
> O mighty overlord of Fate!
> With iron curb, on high, like this
> Did you not raise on the abyss
> Our Russia to her rampant state?

At the same time we are persuaded into ever deeper sympathy for Yevgeniy and are forced to weigh the interests of the petty individual against those of the great overlord. There can be no facile resolution of such a fundamental political problem and Pushkin is not simple-minded enough to suggest one. We are left with the two opposing principles, autocracy and democracy, attempting to fill the same space.

This is the point where the significance of *The Bronze Horseman* begins to extend outwards into universality. Yevgeniy may be seen as a Russian victim protesting against his maltreatment at the hands of the autocracy. So vast is the background of the poem and so anonymous is Yevgeniy that he may also be taken to represent any ordinary man caught up in the great movements of history. His destiny is controlled for him and his simple dreams are destroyed like those of any common citizen drafted into an army, or those of any refugee or war widow. One of the great questions posed inferentially by the poem is this: how do you assess the contrary claims of whole countries, states and political systems on the one hand and of ordinary, innocent, peace-loving subjects on the other? The state must grow and prosper—Pushkin does not doubt that—but many innocents will be ground to pieces in the wheels of progress and it is impossible to withhold sympathy from them. Pushkin's contribution to their cause, lest they be forgotten, is to record the pitiful, meaningless protest of one such victim.

These are some of the social, historical and moral questions raised by *The Bronze Horseman.* Even judged on this level, taking into account also the excitement and pathos of the story itself, it stands out as an important Russian poem. The true distinguishing feature of the work, however, is that it incorporates a further theme of such sublimity that these lesser questions are made to appear trivial, local and short-lived. Pushkin recalls for us at the opening of the poem, at its end and at several points during the story, that before societies of any kind came into existence there were at work the great forces of nature. *The Bronze Horseman* is a reminder of those elemental powers which operate all round us. What is man's position in relation to nature? Has he the right to confront her with his own interventionary schemes? How successful will these be if he does? Here we see Peter turned inside out, which is one of the miracles of such a short narrative poem. To Yevgeniy, as to Pushkin, he appears as a looming, menacing figure invested with maximum power. To Mother Nature he, and his pitiful successor Alexander I, look quite different. Peter and Alexander are mere humans. They may win the occasional battle against the elements but nature is not to be subdued for long. She will claim her own. That message is clear throughout the poem but it is pointed up with peculiar irony at the end of the introduction when the narrator states his confident wish that the defeated elements will make their peace with Peter and discontinue their futile enmity. Almost without pausing for breath he goes on to recall a very recent disastrous occasion when the elements showed beyond any doubt that they were not defeated, nor was their enmity futile, nor had they the slightest intention of leaving Peter to his everlasting sleep. This is one of the most telling juxtapositions of contrary ideas in the whole poem. Moreover, nothing in the course of the story will suggest that this is the last fling of a vanquished enemy. Everything speaks of the temporary subjugation of the seas; nature will come again.

The issue raised here is a very large one, nothing less than a consideration of man's ability to dominate his environment. This enables *The Bronze Horseman* to take rank alongside some of the great myths and legends of the past. Peter's outrageous, superhuman act, the construction of a city where climate and topography said it was not possible, renders him a worthy comparison with Icarus, Prometheus and Canute. The saddest incident in this poem is neither Yevgeniy's tragic discovery that his sweetheart is dead, nor his persecution, nor his death; it is, if we can bring ourselves to think in broader terms about the true capabilities and limitations of men, that pathetic moment when Tsar Alexander I puts in his appearance at the height of the flood, the people having turned to him in their panic.

> Then out came he,
> Sad, stricken, on the balcony.
> 'The Tsars,' he said, 'may not contest
> God's elements.'

If not the tsars, then who?

Such are the chief preoccupations of this magnificent poem. Beginning with the sad tale of Yevgeniy they take the mind in an upward and outward spiral from the local to the eternal. All manner of other ideas are, incidentally, tossed off in passing, bits of food for the intellect or spirit. Is there such a thing as destiny? Peter invokes that force himself and is related to it more than once by the narrator. Yevgeniy seems destined for tragedy throughout, his Fate is said to await him as he approaches Parasha's annihilated home, and it can only be as a result of some malevolent kismet that his corpse and the wreckage of her house are washed up together on the same tiny island. There are interesting hints at the contradistinctions between paganism and Christianity borne out in the subtle juxtaposition of non-religious and religious images. (These latter two points will shortly be considered in more detail.) Finally, the poem includes a clear suggestion that to distinguish between reality and unreality (in one of its several forms: sleep, dreams and madness) is not so easy as it might seem. Perhaps Pushkin is sending us back to Calderon and Plato; perhaps Cervantes is also in his mind, since it is as a madman that Yevgeniy finds sudden understanding.

The Bronze Horseman is the most mature, the most serious, the most speculatory of all Pushkin's works. It is at the same time a *tour de force* of compactness and harmonisation, introducing and uniting so many disparate notions

in such a short space. The next task is to discover some of the ways by which all this is achieved.

Despite its thematic saturation *The Bronze Horseman,* by playing upon diversity and relying upon hints and symbols, manages not to appear overcharged. The same is true of the poetic contrivances employed; although numerous and multicoloured they are not permitted to cloy. The safeguards in this case are brevity and an instinct for modulation. Consider, for example, Pushkin's use of simile, metaphor and sound effects, which are hard to separate because they so often come together. The poem is crammed with similes and metaphors, sometimes swirling along in an eddying current not unlike the river itself. In fact, the river and the flood use up most of them, and some extend over several lines. The river is like a sick man tossing and turning in his bed, a spitting cauldron, a wild beast, an attacking army, a villainous gang scurrying out of a sacked village and strewing plunder down the streets, a hostile simmering liquid over a hot fire, a panting warhorse retreating from the field. These unpleasant images, used in the purple patches of *The Bronze Horseman,* are usually accompanied by other devices; a scudding run of couplets takes over from the *andante* movement of quatrain rhyme-groups, violent enjambement wrenches the tetrameters into a kind of rhythmic prose and a torrent of acoustic effects is let loose. This might mark the downfall of a lesser poet. The vital things to know are when to turn off the whole machine and what to say afterwards; Pushkin does know. The flood scene provides a good example. The rise of the river is traced from the previous night, onomatopoeia and alliteration are employed to depict the fury of the flood, an exclamatory climax comes in the breathless recitation of all the objects seen swimming down the streets (twenty-one words without a single verb, long and sonorous ones fitted three and four to a line in a way that English would be hard put to match), a wail of panic from the people creates the briefest possible transition and then—silence. Out comes the solitary tsar in the sad moment described above. The whole business has taken thirty-five lines.

Another instance occurs at the start of Part One. Nine lines are devoted to a description of the menacing river, the clouds, the cold, the wind and rain. Without warning and with only the words 'At that time . . .' as a hinge Pushkin swings into a quite different tone with the casual introduction of Yevgeniy. He soon proceeds into out-and-out flippancy when considering with the reader what parts of Yevgeniy's biography should be included and what left out. Shortly after this will come Yevgeniy's reflections and then the storm and the flood. These examples are not exceptional. The whole poem subdivides into thirty or so short paragraphs—the grand paean addressed to St Petersburg is the longest of them all and it occupies only forty lines of the introduction—but the changes in tempo and tone occurring both within and between them are innumerable. Crises and climaxes multiply in a mercurial procession and all the time the Russian language oscillates between different poles, the archaic and the modern, the poetic and the realistic, the grandiloquent and the down-to-earth, the dignified and the colloquial, conforming with exact appropriateness to each momentary need. It is this

The sculpture of Peter the Great by E.-M. Falconet on which Push-kin based The Bronze Horseman.

kind of easy modulation from subject to subject and mood to mood, engineered with fluidity and perfect timing, based upon the flimsiest of transitional remarks, which is the saving grace of this dense work with its serried sections.

With Pushkin clearly at the height of his powers we are impelled to look for further merits in his finest poem. There are some interesting surprises in his rhyming. Apart from a couple of agreeable, but accidental-looking, half-rhymes (*neyu* with *svirepela/revela* and *sledov* with *zlo/voshlo*), there seems to be little unusual about the rhymes of **The Bronze Horseman.** Pushkin had no interest in the obvious poetical pyrotechnics achievable by revolutionary departures from canonised metres or rhymes. That goes for the rhymes themselves but the disposition of them is something different. . . . The changes are rung mainly in the interests of diversity and they are part of what is often loosely described as Pushkin's 'flexibility' or 'plasticity' of form. On rare occasions the variation bears a clear relationship with the surface meaning of the poem so that it is possible to reveal a subtly hidden and exciting device by which the form of the poem reinforces the story-line. A suspicion that this poem of so many other unusual

qualities will prove exceptional in this regard is vindicated by an examination of the rhymes.

One outstanding feature of the rhyme-scheme is the extent to which that staple unit, the quatrain, is subordinated. Groups other than quatrains have a field day, especially couplets and the asymmetrical five-line groups. Virtually half of this reduced proportion of quatrains, moreover, belongs to the envelope type (abba). This makes for an inordinately high incidence of couplets and an increasingly high expectation of them in the reader's mind. From that flow both the speedy movement of **The Bronze Horseman** and the sense of shock and disturbance when, at key points and on several occasions, the poetic fabric is apparently torn apart and the narrative leaps forward rapidly and jerkily, performing wild tricks with enjambement, rhyme-patterns and everything else that comes to hand. The flood, Yevgeniy's descent into madness and the chase scene provide the best examples of this.

There is one startling occasion when the rhymes simply refuse to settle into any small, complete pattern. They go on repeating and falling over themselves in a section which is irreducible to anything less than nineteen lines. It is the description of Yevgeniy half way through Part Two, beginning 'But my poor, poor Yevgeniy . . .' which contains this unadvertised and protracted disruption. The nineteen lines are constructed upon seven rhymes (three feminine, four masculine) which are intermingled with only a loose background of logical order to begin with and chaos at the end. The scheme reads: AbAbCbCddCeeFgFgCgg. It sets out with all the appearance of normality, AbAb . . . but the reappearance of that 'b' rhyme in line six (*um, shum* and now *dum*) sounds the first false note. The scheme now proceeds into increasing derangement, ending with an almost nonsensical (for Pushkin) six-line unit which introduces a new masculine rhyme 'g' (*dobrom*), repeats the preceding feminine one 'F', repeats the 'g', harks absurdly back to the thrice-used 'C' last heard from seven lines previously and then thumps down two more 'g's, making four in all. Only now can this rhyming group be said to be complete.

Pushkin is neither a capricious nor a self-indulgent rhymster. Such a jumble is therefore unimaginable without some underlying cause. Not that the phenomenon, let alone the reason for it, is directly noticeable on the level of consciousness. Remarkable though this passage is there is no evidence that it has attracted any attention; even the few verse translators, who must have seen it when following the rhyme-scheme, have disregarded Pushkin at this point, lengthened the section and superimposed their own, better organised, groups of rhymes. Despite the absence of any blatant signals, however, this departure from normality is an important one. At some subconscious level of appreciation the eye darts about in an attempt to make sense of that large group, to establish at least a hypothetical norm against which the deviations might be sensed as enjoyable eccentricities. There is no such sense of order. This simply could not happen in Pushkin if all were well up on the surface of the story. What is happening there at this stage is that Yevgeniy loses his reason and we are told (in that very section) of the first demented wanderings of his body and mind. As he rambles around in increasing bewilderment and alienation so does the rhyme-scheme which is used in the telling of his story. There are a few further instances of this kind of parallelism in other narratives. . . . [One of them occurs] in the abduction scene at the beginning of **Ruslan and Lyudmila**; another long group of twenty lines occurs in **The Gipsies** immediately following the murder (lines 487-506) but this is the best example of the story-line finding supporting expression in the formal deeps beneath that level.

Nor is that the only unusual trick of form. Take, for instance, the opening ten and a half lines of **The Bronze Horseman** which are as well known as any in Russian.

> Na beregu pustynnykh voln
> Stoyal on, dum velikikh poln
> I vdal' glyadel. Pred nim shiroko
> Reka neslasya; bednyy cheln
> Po ney stremilsya odinoko.
> Po mshistym, topkim beregam
> Cherneli izby zdes' i tam,
> Priyut ubogogo chukhontsa;
> I les, nevedomyy lucham
> V tumane spryatannogo solntsa
> Krugom shumel.

> On a shore beside the desolate waves
> *He* stood, filled with lofty thoughts,
> And gazed into the distance. Before him
> The broad river coursed along; a poor skiff
> Moved down it all alone.
> Here and there along the mossy, swampy banks
> Black huts could be seen,
> The homes of wretched Finns;
> And the forest, unknown to the rays
> Of the sun hidden in the mist,
> Made its murmur all around.

No one seems to have noticed how strange they are, these celebrated lines describing Peter standing silently on the northern swamps and what he sees. The odd thing here is that those ten lines fall into a clear, repeated rhyming pattern which is not only not repeated again in **The Bronze Horseman** but which does not appear anywhere else in Pushkin. Why should it be so? There are at the famous head of this famous poem two identical five-line groups rhyming aaBaB. This is some sort of catch. At first sight it looks almost as if the poem might be in couplets. That theory holds good until the end of line four which fails to produce the expected 'B' rhyme (with *shiroko*). By the end of line five we think we have it; there is a complete five-line unit aaBaB. How satisfying when that same unit repeats itself. And yet, seen in context, this phenomenon is a strange one. In Pushkin's poems five-line groups rarely accompany each other and virtually never start the narrative off even singly. When they do follow each other they are usually different five-line groups. And here are two of these groups right at the start of the poem. By line ten the subconsciously seeking eye distinctly expects a third such group. Perhaps this will be a whole poem written in strange, unseparated and disguised stanzas? This theory is quickly demolished. The second line of the next group fails to fit the pattern. A group of aBaB is formed and we are then off into the usual stream of quatrains with occasional variations. How can we explain this anomalous be

ginning? Is it merely a question of formal frivolity? This seems unlikely in view of the seriousness of the poem and the absence of similar examples elsewhere in Pushkin. Indecisiveness or a change of mind? Certainly not in a Pushkin at the peak of his powers when his sureness of touch is at its least questionable. Some kind of trickery? There seems no point in that. There has to be a more sensible explanation.

The real clue lies in the fact that the short opening section is markedly offset in formal terms from what follows. If it can be shown that the sense of that section is also somehow offset then we shall have established a meaningful parallelism. There is indeed such a distinction. At first Peter surveys an almost primeval world, an alien element, incomprehensible to him in its naturalness, its wastage and its poverty. He will see it almost immediately through the prism of its potential but before that he must be allowed to glimpse and take in the pristine scene, to assess it as it now is before he changes it. That pristine scene is what occupies the first ten lines of the poem the form of which is equally alien and mystifying. Line eleven changes everything. Peter snaps out of it, begins to think clearly and lays his plans for the future. The tenor of this and the next nine lines is quite different from the opening. Peter is already beginning to impose his order on the alien scene. Naturally as he does so the opening 'stanza' effect disappears and Pushkin imposes his own familiar order on an alien-seeming rhyme-scheme. Thus as Peter assumes control of the wasteland he takes charge of everything at once, both in the natural scene being described and in the devices used to describe it. Once again it is possible to indicate a subtle and unusual formal property working to good purpose in **The Bronze Horseman.** One of the remarkable aspects of this one is that for once the true mode of chaining together the rhymes is postponed for ten lines and the exception to that rule is given first. The variation thus precedes the theme, the syncopation comes before the standard rhythm, which adds poignancy and emphasis to the opening of the poem.

There is in addition a slight taste of irony behind the whole method used here. The exactitude of that opening pattern aaBaB, so carefully chopped off at line five for emphasis, so meticulously repeated up to line ten, suggests an underlying sense of meaningful order which belongs to the natural world as described therein. Peter cannot see it. He must change it, imposing his own rhythms and constructions upon the apparent chaos before him. How wrong he was, both in failing to comprehend the self-enclosed logic of that natural scene and in attempting to destroy it—this is the burden of the whole subsequent story, or a large part of it. If it is not being too fanciful, one might claim that those opening 'stanzas' help reinforce the message that nature has her own ways upon which she will insist and to which she will return despite the best efforts of men to change them. Incidentally the end of the poem has a rhyme scheme of four quatrains with one interpolated couplet. There is no attempt to suggest nature's return by recreating the opening five-line groups, for which we may be thankful. Whatever else one may decide about these tricks of rhyming it is certain that Pushkin did not preconceive them mechanically. Had he been of the mentality to organise the ending deliberately into a formal reflection of the unusual opening he would have lacked the very spontaneity which created the whole poem in the first place.

The varied themes and moods of **The Bronze Horseman** are integrated and harmonised in several ways, Pushkin modulating from one to the next with inimitable fluency. The shortness of the poem helps too; there is no time for it to run out of control. Another unifying force is the rather complicated system of interrelated references within the poem. The darkness, the wind, the rain, the proud Idol with its outstretched hand, the house in Senate Square with its two lions standing on sentry guard, all these, and other details too, are mentioned on more than one occasion. Such cross-references within the poem help stitch the thing together tightly. However, this system is seen at its most effective not in such random instances but in the way that the beginning of the poem relates to its ending and the way that the ending looks back not merely to the beginning but elsewhere within the poem as well.

First the beginning and the end. They share a close association, which is a force for good, encircling the poem in a cyclic structure significant for both form and meaning. We are finally returned to a place remarkably similar to where we began, removed from Peter's city, another deserted shore. It is surprising how many images and even specific words are common to both scenes, not merely the plentiful obvious parallels—water, the river, the bank, the waves, the beach—but more unusual ones too; 'uninhabited', 'poor', 'black', 'dilapidated', 'fisherman', 'shack' are all words which, with some slight shifts in meaning, reappear at the end to remind us of the beginning. (Some of them appear elsewhere in the poem too.) Both scenes are alike in their stillness and remoteness. Individually and together they suggest the eternal presence of nature which we have argued to be the most serious theme of the poem. Man, in so far as he appears at all, seems like an insignificant, anonymous intruder. The murmuring forest and sportive waters have a more dynamic role in these moments than Peter or Yevgeniy or either of the fishermen.

As well as providing a back reference to the point of departure, this special ending seems to have another function. Its air of finality, of true deathliness, comes not only from the barrenness of the little island but also from a strange intermixture of pagan and Christian images which together suggest a remote after-life into which dead souls may proceed. The crossing of water before the body can come to rest, together with the mention of a boat and its coming to moor on the island, appear vaguely to recall Charon's ferrying of souls across the Styx. Perhaps this would be too vague if that was everything, but it is not. A sharper focus is achieved if we recall Yevgeniy's earlier crossing of the waters just after the storm. It was an absurdly unreal occurrence in the midst of events taken from cruel actuality. A boat suddenly appeared out of nowhere ('like a godsend') and he was transported across by a carefree ferryman who charged him a *grivennik* (ten kopecks, only a small sum) despite the great difficulties, hardships and dangers of the journey. At that time it is most unlikely that Yevgeniy would have met any ferryman still plying his trade, let alone doing it with good cheer, and one who

would 'willingly' take grave risks for a derisory fee without waiting for other passengers. This figure is beyond doubt a reminder of Charon, even down to the low-value obol which his clients had to pay. His appearance in the story is otherwise unwarranted. So, incidentally, are the coffins which float down the street washed out of their cemetery by the floods. It is possible that these coffins are, and probable that this latter-day Charon is nothing other than a gratuitous *memento mori,* a grisly prophecy of Yevgeniy's inevitable tragedy. The grotesque arrival and behaviour of the untimely ferryman is a solemn prediction of his death. That death almost comes immediately when the boat all but capsizes. There is a moment of anguish and 'finally . . .' (the word *nakonets* comes at a line-end and we hasten forward to find out what happened)—'it reached the shore'. Yevgeniy is apparently safe, but there is the irony of it. He might as well have perished. In fact, even in surviving he does still perish, for all that awaits him now is a slow decline, after a terrible shock and the sadness of bereavement, through madness, wandering and persecution to death itself. This first crossing is the true one. Charon, having received his nominal fee, completes his task by delivering Yevgeniy into hell. All of this is gently recalled by the closing scene of the poem which involves another crossing of the water.

And yet the ending is actually a Christian one. In that closing scene the word *Voskresen'ye* is mentioned. Not only does this word evoke that holy day Sunday, reminding us of churchgoing, but it also carries with it still some vestige of its original meaning, 'Resurrection'.

> Or else a civil servant comes
> Boating on a Sunday,
> To this deserted island.

Yevgeniy was just such a civil servant and here he is transported at the end of the story across the waters to the remote island. His cold corpse was buried there *radi Boga,* a phrase which means loosely 'out of charity' though its literal meaning is 'for the sake of God', a Christian or semi-Christian, touch with which the poem ends. Greek and Christian mythologies work here in double harness to draw out the little island into a symbol of the after-life. This is not, as it happens, the only occasion when Greek and Christian references occur in close juxtaposition. Towards the end of Part One at the height of the flood St Petersburg (elsewhere Petrograd and Grad Petrov) is suddenly rechristened Petropolis and compared to Triton, a Greek merman-god. Only a few lines later the people are shown to be in dread of the wrath of the Christian God and the tsar himself refers to his own impotence in the face of God's elements.

There is, however, even more than this in the ending of **The Bronze Horseman.** Working away at the same time is a convolution of irony which is at once sadly amusing and profoundly disturbing. In the first place Yevgeniy was washed up on to the island with a ruined little house. Whether they arrived together or separately does not matter; either way their arrival here is remarkable. What does matter is that this is clearly Parasha's house. Earlier this was described as 'a ramshackle little house' (*vetkhiy domik*); now it is virtually the same (*domishko vetkhiy*).

Yevgeniy's corpse is found not just anywhere but lying on the very threshold, with all the connotations that the phrase has, in any language, of an impending stride into new and exciting experiences—if you are allowed across. So near and yet so far. The inference is not merely that Nature (or Peter or Fate) has demolished Yevgeniy, but that she (or he or it) has first been cruel enough to allow him tantalisingly near to the realisation of his modest ambitions, to the very threshold of a new life, before destroying him. This sad and cruel irony is confirmed if we look back to the ruminative soliloquy of Yevgeniy in Part One which is sometimes omitted because it was struck out in the manuscript but is often reinstated nowadays because editors and public like it so much. This twenty-one line passage, beginning, 'Me, get married? Well, why not . . .', is well worthy of inclusion both *per se* and as a key piece in the system of cross-references. It is introduced by the words, 'What was he thinking about, then?' which recall the solemn, 'And he was thinking . . .' introduction to Peter's grand schemes; how ordinary and modest Yevgeniy's plans appear by comparison. It also contains a reference to trips out on a Sunday, which identifies Yevgeniy again with the Sunday/Resurrection reference at the end. More importantly still, it predicts a happy life coming to a serene end in a domestic burial scene with the grandchildren seeing them off lovingly into the grave. There is a painfully ironic distinction between this day-dreamed idyll, ending 'And our grandchildren shall bury us', and the actuality 'His cold corpse / Was buried out of charity'. The warmth and love of a hoped for family burial is brutally replaced by a bleak anonymous interment.

All these thoughts, symbols and back references come together, packed tightly into the last eighteen lines. The ending thus provides a moving summation of some of the main themes of **The Bronze Horseman** and it certainly emphasises the ironic smallness, insignificance and importance of human endeavour when set against the great movements of nature. Isn't this what life is like? —the poem seems to ask at the end. You dream, you act, you build, but it is all without meaning and value. If you happen to be born a tsar your grandiose schemes may take on an air of deep purpose and permanence but they are swept aside by the destructive forces of nature as easily and as soon as she chooses. If you are less lucky and are of low birth even the most modest of plans are liable to instant demolition from any of several quarters. Not only that, but nature seems to take a cruel pleasure in dangling before us the ironical promise of success, achievement, happiness, significance and permanence before atomising our schemes. Pushkin makes an accusation similar to that of Gloucester in Act IV Scene I of *King Lear*,

> As flies to wanton boys, are we to the gods;
> They kill us for their sport.

As an object lesson in building on past successes and simultaneously learning from past mistakes, **The Bronze Horseman** would be difficult to surpass. This narrative poem succeeds in recreating what was of value, disparately spread, in all Pushkin's earlier serious narratives—an exciting tale, convincing evocation of place and character, a sense of the dramatic, an instinct for variety, an awareness of history, the incorporation of a moving personal

story, the posing of moral questions—and adds to all that a new dimension of serious political and philosophical speculation. At the same time every one of the earlier defects is discarded, the vagueness, lack of verisimilitude, the constrictions provided by the Romantic hero and his plight, the tendency to go on too long, the inner fragmentation which works against unity. The meanings are many and profound, the form is a blend of spontaneity and authority perfected to a degree unusual even for such an instinctively disciplined master as Pushkin. So great is the distance between this poem and its confrères within the [narrative poem] genre that one scarcely wonders that it has been so lavishly praised.

Kyril FitzLyon   (essay date 1983)

SOURCE: An introduction to *Narrative Poems by Alexander Pushkin and by Mikhail Lermontov,* translated by Charles Johnston, Vintage Books, 1983, pp. vii-xix.

[*FitzLyon is a Russian-born British economist, translator, nonfiction writer, and critic. In the excerpt below, he remarks on* Onegin's Journey *and* Count Nulin.]

Onegin's Journey . . . has had a curious history. Pushkin originally intended it to follow Chapter Seven of **Eugene Onegin,** in which Tatyana is taken to Moscow and meets "that fat general," Prince N., whom she eventually marries. The present Chapter Eight would then have become Chapter Nine. However, for reasons which he said were "important to him, but not to the public," Pushkin decided to omit **Onegin's Journey.** But when a friendly critic pointed out that this made "the transition from Tatyana, the provincial young girl, to Tatyana, the grand lady," too abrupt and unexplained, Pushkin compromised by publishing some of the **Journey** stanzas as a kind of appendix to Chapter Eight. These are the stanzas that Charles Johnston translated and published some two years after his translation of **Eugene Onegin.** . . . (Additional stanzas were published after Pushkin's death.)

It is not possible to guess with any degree of confidence at the reasons that prompted Pushkin to discard **Onegin's Journey,** and which he found so "important." He may have thought it broke the poem's mold either stylistically or by straying too far from the subject, or both these things at once. For its subject matter and perhaps for inspiration, he had drawn on his memories of visits he himself had made to the Crimea and the Caucasus, and he was able to include some stanzas he had written five years previously describing his own stay in Odessa.

Eugene Onegin's final chapter (now renumbered Chapter Eight) and "fragments"—Pushkin's expression—of **Onegin's Journey** were published in 1832. The year 1827 (five years before) saw the publication of **Graf Nulin,** which introduces a new genre into Russian poetry—the anecdotal. It was a genre Pushkin was to repeat (on a different theme and in a different metre) in **The Little House in Kolomna** and which was to find imitators in Lermontov and Turgenev.

Graf Nulin is based on Shakespeare's *The Rape of Lucrece.* As much, that is, as a joke can be based on a tragedy.

In December 1825, says Pushkin in a note discovered among his papers, he was rereading Shakespeare's poem (which he found "pretty feeble," partly, no doubt, because he was reading it in a French translation) when it occurred to him that world history would have been different if only Lucrece had slapped Tarquin's face as he was about to rape her. It would probably have cooled his ardour, she would not have committed suicide, and Rome would not have become a republic. "The idea came to me," says Pushkin, "of parodying history and Shakespeare. I couldn't resist the double temptation and wrote this story in a couple of mornings." Later he admitted to a further English literary influence. Byron's *Beppo,* he wrote, was another source of his inspiration for **Graf Nulin.** For his "parody" he chose not world history, kings, captains, and beautiful high-born ladies, all in classical antiquity, but the modest contemporary background of a Russian country house, a bored young woman whose husband is absent not on affairs of state or war, but merely on a hunting expedition, and a fashionable fop (his name means "zero") delighted at the prospect of an easy lay.

A number of small details in *Lucrece* and **Graf Nulin** resemble one another, but often the resemblances are seen as in a distorting mirror. Tarquin, on his way from his own bed to Lucrece's, throws "his mantle rudely o'er his arm" and creeps stealthily from room to room, nervously mindful of "grating" doors. Nulin, in a similar situation, grabs his "bright silk dressing gown" and is "in mortal terror" of creaking floorboards as he sets out on his escapade. Both these unworthy heroes are compared to a tomcat, yet Tarquin, unlike poor Nulin, is also a "grim lion [who] fawneth o'er his prey." Both wives inform their husbands after the event, though not quite in the same spirit, but then the events differ too. Tarquin achieves his goal—with momentous consequences for himself, Lucrece, and the world; Nulin achieves nothing except a slap in the face.

Pushkin's poem had a mixed reception on publication. The more serious critics found it immoral as well as too flippant for a great national poet (aged twenty-six). But a few reviewers praised it, and the public loved it. So, fortunately for Pushkin, did the emperor Nicholas I. He had constituted himself Pushkin's personal censor and had seen the poem in manuscript, thought it "delightful," and asked Benckendorff, his formidable chief of police, to inform Pushkin that he had read it "with great pleasure." His verdict has been echoed by every reader of Pushkin ever since.

Donald Fanger (essay date 1983)

SOURCE: "Influence and Tradition in the Russian Novel," in *The Russian Novel from Pushkin to Pasternak,* edited by John Garrard, Yale University Press, 1983, pp. 29-50.

[An American educator and critic, Fanger has written extensively on nineteenth-century Russian literature. In the following excerpt, he addresses Pushkin's handling of character, plot, narrative persona, and theme in Eugene Onegin.]

Pushkin's demonstratively subtitled "novel in verse," **Eugene Onegin,** was hailed by Belinsky as the first such "na-

---

Melchior D. de Wolff on *Eugene Onegin* and romantic literature:

To the rule that the important literary works of the world do not fit into clear-cut categories of genre or style, Puškin's novel in verse forms no exception. Although Dmitry Čiževsky in the early 1950s could still argue that *Evgenij Onegin* "belongs to the age of romanticism and bears clear marks of that period, perhaps clearer than in any other of Puškin's works," more recent studies . . . have convincingly pointed out that the novel represents a turning-point in the history of Russian literature. In this connection, it is important to refer to Donald Fanger's idea that *Evgenij Onegin* contains a "dual emphasis—on presentation and on creation." If Fanger is right, and I believe he is, these emphases should be regarded as the signs of Puškin's awareness of the conventional character of the stylistic and thematic elements of romantic literature, especially the wastage these conventions were subject to, and of the author's judgment *vis à vis* the necessity of innovative endeavors. Simultaneously, *Evgenij Onegin* is to be conceived of as a fictional work originating from the romantic tradition of the long poem (*poema*), and as a programmatic discussion of what a novel, or any epic narrative, should look like. In this respect, the importance of the continuous flux of authorial asides and references to the process of writing . . . can hardly be overestimated.

Melchior D. de Wolff, in his "Romanticism Unmasked: Lexical Irony in Aleksandr Puškin's Evgenij Onegin, " *in* Convention and Innovation in Literature, *1989.*

---

tional" work, filling a void at once qualitative and quantitative. Not only, as Belinsky claims, had there been "not a single decent [Russian] novel in prose"; one Soviet scholar has reckoned that with the exception of Narezhny's neglected fictions, not a single Russian novel of *any* kind had appeared between 1802 and 1823! Hence Belinsky's interest in playing down the hybrid nature of **Onegin** and viewing it as primarily narrative. It was, in his view, at once a study in contemporary character, an affecting story, and an encyclopedia of Russian life. As for the poetic form, he and most of his followers in the nineteenth century tended to treat that as no more than an effective, if eccentric, means—ignoring the fact, as Eikhenbaum later put it, that an **Onegin** in prose would require "much more complex motivation, a far greater number of events and characters, and would have excluded the possibility of introducing into the narration a whole volume of lyrics."

It remained for the twentieth century to explore what many readers must have sensed: that this radically "free novel," as its author called it, achieves its freedom by consistently playing off the conventions of prose against those of poetry. For present purposes, the nature of this freedom may be located in three key features: the nature of character, the handling of plot, and the role of the narrative persona. All raise conventional expectations in the reader, only to baffle them.

In the traditional novel, as Ian Watt has suggested, either
plot or character may be dominant, but always at the expense of the other term. A complex plot (as in a mystery
story) requires a certain *disponibilité* of character; the
complex patterning of episodes demands a particular consistency from the principal characters, who must in no
case be problematic enough to rival the situational prob-
lematics in which they are involved. Conversely, novels
whose main purpose is to explore the complexities of character must simplify and reduce the patterns of event, since
their logic arises from the characters and relationships in
question. **Onegin** would seem, if only from its title, to belong to the latter category. And in fact, as Lotman has observed, it is their relations with *him* (and not with each
other) that provide a rationale for the presence of virtually
all the significant characters in the novel—with the partial
exception of Tatiana, who threatens increasingly to usurp
Onegin's centrality, because her suggestive presence depends equally on a series of juxtapositions with others.

In both cases, those others are presented sketchily (if in
varying degree), as familiar *givens*: Lensky takes such
form as he has from the motif of mistiness (misty Germany, cloudy romanticism), Olga from the stereotyped novels of the day; and Tatiana's husband—whose appearance
in the final chapter would call for a great deal more description and explanation in a prose novel—amounts as
presented to no more than "a personified circumstance,"
not mainly of plot, as Lotman claims, but of the central
theme (which, as I shall try to show, might be identified
as biography).

For Pushkin demonstrably mocks plot by making it minimal and schematic. Slonimsky has noted that its central
line—the Onegin-Tatiana love story—rests before the denouement in chapter 8 on three meetings, at each of which
one partner speaks while the other is silent. Gukovsky
confines it more strictly to two mechanically symmetrical
situations:

FIRST PART

1. They meet.
2. At first glance, she falls in love with him.
3. She writes him a letter.
4. There is no reply. She suffers.
5. They meet tête-à-tête; no one is around. She
   trembles and is silent. He makes a didactic and
   unfair speech, though one marked by honesty
   and warmth. At this point the line breaks off.

SECOND PART

1. They meet.
2. At first glance, he falls in love with her.
3. He writes her a letter.
4. There is no reply. He suffers.
5. They meet; no one is around. He trembles and
   is silent. She makes a speech, of the kind he had
   made earlier. Here the line breaks off: the novel
   is over.

The novel, however, is not over; plot is merely abandoned
in favor of what has been the main thing all along. Here
are the concluding four stanzas (the translation is Nabokov's):

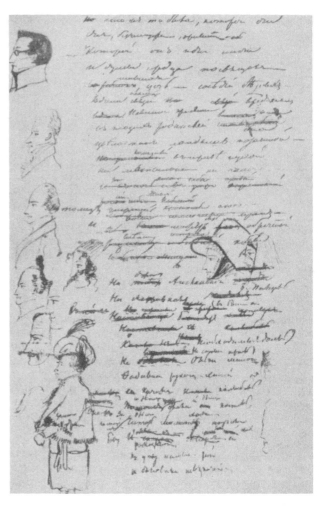

Manuscript page of Eugene Onegin.

XLVIII

She has gone. Eugene stands
as if by thunder struck.
In what a tempest of sensations
his heart is now immersed!
But there resounds a sudden clink of spurs,
and there appears Tatiana's husband,
and here my hero,
at an unfortunate minute for him,
reader, we now shall leave
for long . . . forever . . . After him
sufficiently along one path
we've roamed the world. Let us congratulate
each other on attaining land. Hurrah!
It long (is it not true?) was time.

XLIX

Whoever, O my reader,
you be—friend, foe—I wish to part
with you at present as a pal.
Farewell. Whatever in these careless strophes
you might have looked for as you followed me—
tumultuous recollections,
relief from labors,
live images or witticisms,
or faults of grammar—

God grant that in this book, for recreation,
for dreaming, for the heart,
for jousts in journals,
you find at least a crumb.
Upon which, let us part, farewell!

L

You, too, farewell, my strange traveling
companion, and you, my true ideal,
and you, my live and constant,
though small, work. I have known with you
all that a poet covets:
obliviousness of life in the world's tempests,
the sweet discourse of friends.
Rushed by have many, many days
since young Tatiana, and with her
Onegin, in a blurry dream
appeared to me for the first time—
and the far stretch of a free novel
I through a magic crystal
still did not make out clearly.

LI

But those to whom at amicable meetings
its first strophes I read—
"Some are no more, others are distant,"
as erstwhiles Sadi said.
Without them was Onegin's picture finished.
And she from whom was fashioned
the dear ideal of "Tatiana" . . .
Ah, much, much has fate snatched away!
Blest who left life's feast early,
not having to the bottom drained
the goblet full of wine;
who never read life's novel to the end
and all at once could part with it
as I with my Onegin.

What these lines demonstrate is the way the elements of a novel are, in **Onegin,** embedded in a kind of poetic discourse that uses them for larger, non-novelistic purposes, and from which they take their sense. The narrative persona presents, evaluates, and dismisses his characters; his concerns in the passages usually labeled digressions dovetail with the novelistic elements but finally subsume them through his insistence on having created the narrative in the first place. There is thus a dual emphasis—on presentation and on creation: **Eugene Onegin** must be read at the same time as a fiction and as a meditation on the writing of fiction, its expressive possibilities and its limits. But even the second element bifurcates: all the attention to literary stereotypes and conventions (which led Leon Stilman to claim that **Onegin,** which Varnhagen von Enze called an encyclopedia of Russian life, should rather be regarded as a *literary* encyclopedia) makes it a disquisition about writing, its means and ends—and about its reciprocal relations with active experience ("life's novel").

The constant literary discussions and demonstrations in **Onegin** have a strategic function which, as Lotman shrewdly observes, is to overcome not particular forms of literariness—that is, identifiable styles or conventions—but "literariness as such," by devising an artistic structure (something organized) that would imitate nonartistic (unorganized) reality: "to create a structure that would be apprehended as the *absence* of structure." This is essentially a variation on the principle of the *Quixote,* with the difference that here the creator participates openly as such. The ending of chapter 6, no less than the ending of chapter 8 just quoted, shows this with a complexity too rich to do justice to here:

In due time I shall give you an account
in detail about everything.

XLIII

But not now. Though with all my heart
I love my hero;
though I'll return to him, of course;
but now I am not in the mood for him.
The years to austere prose incline,
the years chase pranksome rhyme away,
and I—with a sigh I confess—
more indolently dangle after her.
My pen has not its ancient disposition
to mar with scribblings fleeting leaves;
other chill dreams,
other stern cares,
both in the social hum and in the still
disturb my soul's sleep.

XLIV

I have learned the voice of other desires.
I've come to know new sadness.
I have no expectations for the first,
and the old sadness I regret.
Dreams, dreams! Where is your dulcitude?
Where is its stock rhyme juventude?
Can it be really true
that withered, withered is at last its garland?
Can it be true that really and indeed,
without elegiac conceits,
the springtime of my days is fled
as I in jest kept saying hitherto,
and has it truly no return?
Can it be true that I'll be thirty soon?

XLV

So! My noontide is come, and this
I must, I see, admit.
But anyway, as friends let's part,
O my light youth!
My thanks for the delights,
the melancholy, the dear torments,
the hum, the storms, the feasts,
for all, for all your gifts
my thanks to you. In you
amidst turmoils and in the stillness
I have delighted . . . and in full.
Enough! With a clear soul
I now set out on a new course
to rest from my old life.

XLVI

Let me glance back. Farewell now, coverts
where in the backwoods flowed my days,
fulfilled with passions and with indolence
and with the dreamings of a pensive soul.
And you, young inspiration,
stir my imagination,
the slumber of the heart enliven,
into my nook more often fly,
let not a poet's soul grow cold,

callous, crust-dry,
and finally be turned to stone
in the World's deadening intoxication
in that slough where with you
I bathe, dear friends!

Here, too, one notes the dropping of the narrative thread in favor of a meditation on the seasons of life ("Can it be true that I'll be thirty soon?") and on the corresponding stages of *poetic* life ("The years to austere prose incline"). These are the reciprocating themes that unify the work; and they come together in the notion of biography—the picture of life, which subsumes the biographies of the characters in the meditations of a creator-narrator who keeps them company; that is, treats them as instruments of self-expression and at the same time as independent beings. The lyrical burden of *Onegin* is carried only in part by the story; much of it arises from the poetic discourse (asides and personal references) that subsumes the story. Both emphasize the work of time, the passing of youth and passionate illusion, and the overt insistence on art adds a transcendence even as it registers their limitation in a real world that offers no other transcendence. So one might say that the ultimate "hero" of *Onegin* is Youth, whose fate is to become the constitutive factor of adult biography.

This is the implication of the ending (a non-ending in terms of plot)—and a rationale for abandoning Onegin at a critical point in his fortunes. Eugene's baffled love, like Tatiana's faithful love, is dropped (along with the theme of love itself) in favor of a closing emphasis on the larger themes of creation, youth, time—with specific stress on the fact that this text was written and published over a period of eight years, in the course of which the author, the reader, and the very age changed. The work itself embodies these changes, in its evolution from an improvisational exercise in the free generation of a text to the glorification of a verbal medium—which, without ever ceasing to proclaim itself as such, at length takes on a moral value alongside the aesthetic, the narrative, the cognitive.

Eugene Onegin, in other words, is not only major fiction but a poetic meditation on the creation and the sense of fictions. Thus Pushkin terms it a "free novel."

Leslie O'Bell   (essay date 1985)

SOURCE: "Young Pushkin: *Ruslan and Liudmila* in its Lyric Context," in *The Russian Review,* Vol. 44, No. 2, April, 1985, pp. 139-55.

[*In the following excerpt, O'Bell discusses* Ruslan and Lyudmila *within the context of Pushkin's early lyrics and social poetry.*]

Present-day readers will find that the current critical literature has little to say about *Ruslan and Liudmila.* To a large extent the critics have explained it through its sources instead of trying to reveal it on its own terms as one of the creative milestones of Pushkin's work. Literary history has taken the place of appreciation instead of serving it. It has been all too easy to lose touch with the young Pushkin, that Proteus in the making.

Ruslan and Liudmila is the natural culmination of early Pushkin. Of course, the work of his school years at the Lycée can be read for its own sake. As Tynianov put it, Pushkin at eighteen was already a fully formed poet of a certain kind. Yet after he became a poet of another, more romantic kind in the 1820's, Pushkin grew ever more selective in his assaying of the early verse. Of the many poems written between 1815 and the summer of 1819 he had published a handful. After many attempts at revision, his first collection, the 1826 edition, presents still fewer. So we may take a narrow, retrospective view of Pushkin's accomplishments at the Lycée.

In retrospect, the Lycée period is summed up in its heir, **Ruslan and Liudmila,** the masterpiece of Pushkin's youth. The work epitomizes a spirit of play which is natural in a precocious talent but which remained with Pushkin all his life and was the attribute of his enviable inner freedom. Among his narrative poems only **Onegin** would be longer. But size is just an indication of scope. **Ruslan and Liudmila** brings together everything that Pushkin had learned to that point in a captivating mix of shifting tones and planes. Using Russian material, but following Voltaire's *Maid of Orleans* and Ariosto's *Orlando Furioso,* the young Pushkin reproduces the typical beginning of all modern literature by presenting traditional plot as seen through the skeptical eye of the lyrical subject. **Ruslan and Liudmila** is not epic; it is not even romance. It is conscious of its fallen nature but delights in its new perceptions, already full of psychological observations, already lamenting that in the present age of iron, art must speak the unflattering truth. In a real sense **Ruslan and Liudmila** paves the way for **Onegin.** As many critics have noted, **Onegin** is addressed to "the friends of Ruslan and Liudmila." Voltaire had praised Ariosto's narrator in the following terms:

> What especially delighted me in this prodigious work was that its author, always in command of his material, treats it with gay badinage. He effortlessly gives voice to the sublimest things only to finish with a twist of pleasantry which is neither out of place nor recherchée.

When Pushkin wrote in 1825 of **Onegin,** "What a novel needs is *chattiness,*" he was surely remembering such tributes as well as Sterne and company. The lyrical presence in Pushkin's tale incorporates something of Ariosto's worldly courtier and also of Voltaire's enlightened *philosophe,* but he is still the "chatter-box in love" whom Pushkin had discovered in himself as early as 1813 in **"To Natal'ia."** Pushkin put into **Ruslan and Liudmila** his sensitivity to all the stylistic currents swirling around him and associated with so many social and intellectual formations. He also brought to the work the readiness to test poetry for truth against personal perception, a personal perception confident of being the yardstick of human nature.

These artistic values are beautifully embodied in the work, which was truly epoch-making, but why is it the perfect vehicle for their realization? What is the story all about? Measured by the yardstick of human nature, the theme of **Ruslan and Liudmila** could be defined as "doing what comes naturally." First of all, this is an erotic poem. It revolves around the quest of Ruslan for his bride Liudmila, kidnapped by a hideous old wizard on her wedding night from her wedding bed, a quest which pits him against three rivals, who are sometimes waylaid in interesting circumstances, and so forth. It specializes in the erotic travesty of epic motifs. Thus, the hero must do battle for the wizard's beard, less a symbol of wisdom than of his general prowess. Of enormous length, it is borne on cushions by a procession of black slaves. . . . The great oath which Ruslan swears before taking on the wizard is, "I'll unbeard you!" He boasts, "Where is now your beauty, your strength!" But Pushkin later wrote that no one had ever criticized the main defect of the poem, that it was "cold." *Ruslan and Liudmila* is a work of imagination, not of passion. Its purely imaginative eroticism is perhaps best typified in the scene where the hero thrills at last to bear the heroine in his arms, but she sleeps an enchanted sleep, only an image of herself as she dreams with flushed cheeks of the very man who carries her. *Ruslan and Liudmila* appeals first to the senses, then to the imagination, but finally to reason. It dwells on love, but for ulterior motives: because love is young, because love is free, because love should be natural. That is what it celebrates in doing what comes naturally. All the literary artifice so ingeniously spoofed in the poem, from Russian heroic song through the romantic Gothic, only throws the natural into stronger relief.

The "chattiness" that surrounds *Ruslan and Liudmila* does not contain its entire artistic value. The fairy-tale plot, too, has a contribution to make when read after the manner of the philosophical tale. The plot may appear to be pure fluff, a pretext for laughter, but on further reflection the laughter has its point. To generalize its comic message: the evil magic in this world emanates from the graybeards and hags who connive to imprison the heroine, frustrate the hero, and impose their perverted will. But since they go counter to the order of things they are merely grotesque. A happy ending is assured to youth, which has nature and thus good magic on its side. Chernomor cannot prevail because "his learning is not strong against the law of time."

The reader would be right to suspect something quasi-allegorical in the way that the plot manipulates those implausibly detached attributes, the beard, the head and the hat. The first critics of *Ruslan and Liudmila* said that no mother would permit her daughter to read that immoral work. This objection hardly deserves rebuttal. Newer critics do not take the poem seriously at all, except possibly as literary artifice. They are equally wrong, for behind each brilliant invention lies a thought, and the reader who does not catch on misses half the joke. *Ruslan and Liudmila* invites us to draw the witty morals from its fable, for the mock epic also has the makings of a true comic epic where all is well that ends well.

The evil powers in *Ruslan and Liudmila* are not truly dangerous. Still, they issue challenges against which it is well to be armed in order to come through the trials victorious. The first challenge to youth and love comes from the graybeards and elicits the mock-epic side of the poem. The second comes from youth's false friends, yielding melancholy, ennui and treachery, the mock-sentimental, mock-romantic side (these are especially prominent on the re-

turn journey, when the first challenge has been dealt with). In parallel sequences we see hero and heroine separately meeting the two challenges, for each has to display the right qualities if they are to be reunited. Coincidentally, the poem presents the contrasting fates of Ruslan's unsuccessful rivals who are either overarmed for the fight (where lightness is strength) or disarmed before the encounter. Finally, there is the poet, who both assimilates himself to Ruslan and distinguishes himself from him, celebrating his own, at least temporary, victory over fortune.

First let us follow this plot and these characters. After Chernomor's thunderbolt hits, Ruslan is plunged into despair, and the narrator sympathizes with him at this moment of romantic crisis when "hope and faith slowly perish in your soul." But Ruslan recovers, instructed by the old Finn as to who his enemy is and enlightened about love and the laws of time. The hermit's own story, encapsulated at this point, serves as a comic warning that love cannot be compelled and that romance out of season will bring its own punishment. The reader laughs as the Finn flees from his Naina, whom he has conquered too late, from the old crone stirred into incongruous girlish raptures, a parody of love. Ruslan is now in a position to eliminate his first rival and pursuer, the envious Rogdai, Liudmila's gloomy admirer, for the romantic gloom must give way. Meanwhile, Liudmila, cast as the languishing beauty, wanders through a symbolic garden of artificial, enchanted spring surrounded by bleak, dead winter. However, with delightful frivolity she omits to drown herself. After summoning a desperate resolve, she thinks better of it and decides to eat. When the decisive confrontation comes and the graybeard is paraded before her, she snatches off his nightcap, shows her fist, and frightens off the enemy horde with her screams. She is funny, but winning, too—not in the prose of the languid beauty but as herself, a naturally lively, spirited young girl. These qualities will see her through. The little coquette playfully tries on the wizard's nightcap and finds the means to become his tormentor as a will-o'-the-wisp. Her curiosity has armed her. The best defense is to know your enemy and laugh at him. This wise laughter is Liudmila's discovery, much as the law of time was Ruslan's. It, too, merits an aphorism from the author: "All night in tears she marvelled at her fate—and laughed. The beard frightened her, but Chernomor she now knew. He was ridiculous, and terror is never compatible with laughter." . . .

Can the villain who has been so deftly relieved of his nightcap by such a heroine wait long to lose his beard to the hero?

Ruslan must now arm for the fight. He nearly succumbs again psychologically as he strays over the old battlefield-graveyard with its reminders of mortality, the vanity of all efforts, oblivion. . . . But, like Liudmila, he soon gets his bearings and plucks his weapons from amongst the very piles of bones. Next in the progress toward the Beard comes the classic Enlightenment motif, the struggle against the empty Head, from whom he wins the magic sword. Ruslan, it turns out, will avenge this empty Head against his brother the Beard and bring to an end their long feud: first the vainglorious giant, then the malicious dwarf. The whole intellectual and psychological sequence of Ruslan's progress is well thought out and thoroughly satisfying.

Predictably, in a comic-cosmic battle, Ruslan cuts off the beard and tames the old wizard, but in an effective anti-climax Liudmila cannot be awakened from her enchanted sleep, sequel to Chernomor's last stratagem. Thus, Liudmila is still as "rapt" as on the night of her abduction. The way back turns out to be as hard as the way there. Its presiding evil genius is Naina, who supports the deceiver Farlaf who treacherously plunges his sword into Ruslan's heart and performs the second abduction of Liudmila. The narrator allows us to think for a moment that this quintessential piece of romantic villainy can succeed as the impostor tries, but in vain, to claim Liudmila as his prize. The Finn is then produced once more to heal Ruslan's wounds with the magic waters of life and death and bestow on him the magic ring: the sword for the way out, the ring for the way back.

Ruslan's story of sword and ring is a psychological parable lightly but firmly sketched. Its hero is the brave youth of Russian fairy tale brought up to date, whose states of mind are projected and criticized through various epic, sentimental and romantic conventions. Though many motifs have a folkloric provenance, they are used by a young writer who presents them in the context of the latest literary fashions; we are far from a stylization of the genuine folk manner. Naturally, each of Ruslan's unsuccessful rivals in the story has his own literary sphere, but a limited one. Rogdai is the furious gloomy romantic, the archaic warrior-knight, and the easiest for Ruslan to dispose of. Farlaf, first known as a *krikun,* or boisterous table-companion, turns traitor and impostor, filling another and much more dangerous romantic *emploi.* But Rogdai and Farlaf hardly figure beside Ratmir, who is developed in two outstanding passages, the famous parody of Zhukovskii's *Twelve Sleeping Maidens* and the idyll which Ruslan visits on his way back to Kiev with the sleep-enchanted Liudmila. Ratmir's romantic passion is contemplative; therefore, he is easily disarmed as he listens to the first song of the maidens. But his eventual not-too-austere epicurean retirement has its share of wisdom. Fisherman and hero, he and Ruslan complement each other, embodying heroism and the straightforward "love and friendship of olden times." The "modern" treachery of Farlaf which follows, with its threat of romantic disillusionment, shows the more black against this background. Thus Pushkin manages the three rivals so that they set off Ruslan, defining him as the true hero of the tale. He also uses them to delimit a whole psychological world proper to youth coming into maturity against the background of old values falling to "modern" ones. And all this is imparted as if in jest through the medium of a fairy tale.

To refer *Ruslan and Liudmila* to its most primitive substratum in folklore, the story of youth against age is also the story of life over death. Liudmila is transported to a garden perversely flourishing in the middle of a moribund plain and eventually falls into the deep sleep from which the magic ring awakens her as if from death. Ruslan, as good as slain by the treacherous Farlaf, revives when the

Finn sprinkles him first with the water of death, then with the water of life gotten from the secret spot guarded from time immemorial by "a pair of spirits." Liudmila flirts with suicide and Ruslan encounters his mortality on the battlefield-boneyard. The style of *Ruslan and Liudmila* is a continual refreshment to the spirit dulled by epic pretensions and sickened with sentimental-romantic melancholies. The plot, treated with considerable psychological finesse, deals essentially with a deliverance and a renewal. Perhaps a happy escape would be the term for it.

In some ways *Ruslan* turns out to be not so much mock-romantic as proto-romantic. Here Pushkin plays with the motifs of the robber-bridegroom, the demonic double, the captive, and so on, pretending that none of this is serious. But this is only a first encounter. The fairy tale allows Pushkin to conjure away realities that manifest themselves again almost immediately. What the laughter of *Ruslan and Liudmila* denies proves itself strong in the exotic Southern poems, the new, more impassioned elegies and the crisis of the lyrics surrounding the poem "The Demon" (1823): "In the days when all the impressions of existence were new to me . . . then some kind of malicious spirit began secretly to visit me." . . .

From the inspired play of *Ruslan and Liudmila,* Pushkin moves on to satire and to a bitter irony in the middle period that covers the creation of *Onegin.* But the gaiety and even frivolity which made *Ruslan* possible help bring him through to a true and not a premature maturity. *Ruslan and Liudmila* is Pushkin's *Magic Flute* where he is both Tamino charming the beasts and Papageno with his glockenspiel.

Much is carried forward from *Ruslan and Liudmila,* most of all the bantering narrator, who is already more than a little detached from the comic plot. He intrudes with comparisons, professes nostalgia for the days of yore, and paints himself certainly a baser creature than Ruslan. He juxtaposes to the plot discourses on art and digressions about his own life. He both distinguishes himself from Ruslan and assimilates himself to him. In the Epilogue, he hints at a parallel between the hero and himself: he, too, would have perished had not friendship restored his freedom. But what threatens him is not so easily dealt with. The final lines of the poem find him lamenting his losses and the disappearance of poetry in sight of the Caucasus.

Ideally, an interpretation of *Ruslan and Liudmila* as the summation of Pushkin's early achievement should also show how the poem is integrated with the whole of his early creation. In fact, *Ruslan* was one of those works into which a writer puts everything that he knows at a given moment, everything that he is capable of. In a sense *Ruslan* was contemporaneous with all of Pushkin's early poetry. While he composed it he was putting the Lycée verse through several revisions and also writing the new lyrics of 1818-1820. *Ruslan and Liudmila* could be said to have witnessed everything up to Pushkin's abrupt departure for the Caucasus, where he penned the poem's Epilogue.

Rereading the early poetry one understands how Pushkin peopled his tale and whence he drew its contrasting tones. Here we meet the hermit in his cell and the Ossianic bard recounting the passions of youth from a distance and think of the Finn (**"Osgar"**). We meet the dreamer, the "youthful philosopher" who refuses strife and fame, and think of Ratmir's idyll (**"The Dreamer"**). We meet the lusty hussar equipped with an enormous moustache and sense a boy's admiration for warriors (**"Whiskers, A Philosophical Ode"**), but sense even more his sly humor. Pushkin tries on the epaulets and discards them; in his Lycée cell he is closer to the dreamer and the monk (**"To Galich"**). He searches for the philosophical attitude (the phrase "happy the man" recurring in different contexts) but without entirely losing a sage detachment from all parties. He is already everywhere and nowhere. The treatment of the rivals in **Ruslan** derives from the friendly epistles with their adumbration of the different paths in life that lay before the small band at school. Pushkin learned the group portrait in pieces like **"Carousing Students"** where he rang the changes on an assortment of characters. Only Ruslan himself seems to come from nowhere. Actually, he is an abstraction of naive youth seen in retrospect. Liudmila is the girlish image of the same and also the inspiring spirit or Muse. Pushkin first found something like her in the **"Beauty Who Took Snuff,"** too pert to be sentimental, and something else in a poem to his sister which presents the first of many evocations of the languid heroine, peruser of novels. The Finn's origin has been mentioned. When he expounds on love and nature's laws as Ruslan's mentor, he anticipates the narrator's plan for the hero. The Finn, in fact, is a comic interpretation of the wise maturity with which the author likes to think that he views the action.

The mentality of the narrator, the most interesting study of all, is composed of shifting tones incorporated from the various spheres of the lyrics. There, from the first, he was embarrassed at the role of serious poet. At the beginning he knows only the poetry of love and friendship. He applauds the natural, as when he discerns the appealing reality of a pretty girl through her bad acting (**"To a Young Actress"**). He is the Satyr who skeptically listens to the shepherd's laments (**"Bliss"**). But soon he is surprised by melancholy, by mutability, and the *poésie fugitive* enters his repertory. He embraces the Anacreontic where praise of pleasure and rejection of heroics often end on a note of chilling *memento mori*. A young-old man like Anacreon, he writes with youthful gaiety but already about youthful gaiety: the "wise man of pleasure" confronting the dream of life. He practices his modulations of tone to do justice to the combination of high spirits and melancholy. The elegiac becomes philosophical; the imagination is its creator, as well as memory brooding on the play of time. Thoughts of death assail him: "tomorrow I would die," "I saw Death, she sat down in silence," "still I burned and with indifferent sorrow gazed on the games of youth from far away."

No longer naive, he becomes in Schiller's terms the sentimental or self-conscious poet, producing in the idyllic and elegiac mode, on the one hand, and in the satirical on the other. He knows himself to be a dreamer and marvels at the power of fancy. But he is still the Satyr who laughed at the shepherd, and a more wicked Satyr now. He turns to classical Bacchanals, finding romantic melancholy too cool for his madness (**"The Triumphs of Bacchus," "To a**

Dreamer"**). He addresses the dreamy Zhukovskii with the slyly balanced phrase: . . . "Happy the man who knows the voluptuous pleasure / Of elevated thoughts and poetry." He needs to mock. But even mockery takes practice, and Pushkin rehearsed for **Ruslan and Liudmila** in very early pieces like **"The Monk,"** an erotic subject where nature, aided by the detached apparition, the Skirt, has its way with the old cleric. For mock narrative we must add the abandoned **"Bova,"** the *conte*/fairy tale with a rambling story-teller and Russian trappings. New possibilities opened in the Ossianic poems with their bard and their natural cyclization around heroes embattled for love. For mock balladic material we have **"The Cossack"** with its surprise cynical ending. Mock elegy is represented subtly by the smiling melancholy of the Anacreontic poems and overtly in pieces like **"The Tear,"** lamented as it falls into the cup. As for self-mockery, that is most wittily begun in **"My Portrait"** where Pushkin characterizes himself (in French) as a young pleasure-seeking scamp, a chatter-box, a devil for pranks and a monkey-face.

All these poems constitute the preparation for **Ruslan** in its separate psychological and artistic elements. There is also a history to the art of their combination. To take just one example, there is **"Sleep,"** the mock-ode of 1816. The poet invokes sleep and idleness, not fame or even love: "Happy the man who can lose himself in sleep." But this brings on a reaction; the poet prescribes exercise in moderation. An evocation of falling asleep forms the bridge to the final section, a lyrical digression where the sleep theme widens into the theme of dreams and the poetic imagination. This is Pushkin's first dramatization of inspiration, as the speaker summons up the memory of his bed-time stories, fairy tales which followed him into his dreams. Under the spell, his young mind flew in fancy, creating its own inventions. The final note, however, jars: he has "tasted the dream of young love" only to awaken to the silence of day. Now the satirist, now the epicurean, now the boy-dreamer, the speaker ends as the disillusioned youth. **Ruslan and Liudmila,** too, was born of the fairy tales and of the awakening.

If the poem follows bodily from the Lycée verse, it seems harder to square with the political satire and the epigrammatic salvoes of 1817-1820 which resulted in Pushkin's southern exile. On emerging from the cloistered isolation of the Lycée, Pushkin threw himself into the whirl of life in the capital: the theater and its bohemian escapades, balls, cards, infatuations, "orgies," literary salons and political coteries; in short, a liberation, a free field for experimentation of all kinds. Some of Pushkin's new friends with high-minded political ideals reproached him for his frivolity and tried to point him in a more worthwhile direction, enlisting him in the service of liberty against tyranny. This was the first of many attempts to direct his pen and above all to elevate his subjects. Pushkin came to take this friendly shaming seriously, the more so because he was often dissatisfied with his life. But his temperament accepted their advice on its own terms. He sometimes taunted them: "a poem is never worth more than a smile upon voluptuous lips." He could turn a tirade upon his homeland into a compliment intended for a certain lady (**"But yesterday I saw Golitsyna and am reconciled with my native land"**).

When he at last reverses the Anacreontic pose and calls for the Muse of liberty to smash his pampered lyre there is an audible grinding of gears. Pushkin is supposed to have planned an underground satirical collection to complement his first volume of published verse. But this was much later, and the separation of two branches was the product of external circumstances. There is no real split between art for art's sake and civic aims: all Pushkin's early production represents freethinking in various forms. Familiarity and irreverence saturate *Ruslan and Liudmila* whose parodic style might be characterized in Pushkin's words as "a fortunate heresy of taste and doctrine." Parody frequently goes hand in hand with satire, and in Arzamas circles the stylistic fight against the Slavo-Russian barbarians was often portrayed as part of the struggle for true enlightenment. Pushkin practiced literary satire, as distinct from parody, in the **"Shade of Fonvizin,"** a survey of the contemporary scene where he accompanies the greatest Russian eighteenth-century satirist on an imaginary journey from Hades. After a long and fruitless search for new talent, Fonvizin discovers it at last in Batiushkov, the modern Anacreon whom he vainly tries to waken from his slumbers. Here we see the old satirist recognizing the young sybarite—both Fonvizin and Batiushkov are genuine poets, and each is an alter ego for Pushkin.

The epigrams have the same deftness and jauntiness as *Ruslan and Liudmila.* They are wit and play, though they can be sharp enough, as for example in **"Fairy tales,"** where Alexander I graciously bestows on humanity its human rights. It is the few serious satires, like the oft-analyzed **"Liberty"** or **"The Village,"** which seem to disharmonize. Yet, again as Schiller taught, for the sentimental or reflective poet satire is but the other side of elegy, revolt instead of lament. Indeed, the serious satires are not pure satire. They contain laments, elegiac passages followed by a moral awakening, a pattern found in many developed elegies. Alternatively, Pushkin exploits the other available contrast, idyll.

Freedom is always the central theme. **"To Licinius"** bemoans the servile times and proposes a retreat to the tranquil countryside while prophesying the fall of a Rome corrupted by slavery. **"Liberty"** is the title of the ode which finally resulted in Pushkin's exile. It might as well have been called "Equality before the Law." In the best liberal tradition, its theme is the sovereignty of law, which alone guarantees liberty against the arbitrary excesses of tyrants and the mob alike. Conversely, the poem concludes that a people's "liberty and peace," that is, its freedom and security from mistreatment, are the true guardians of the throne. The poem thus presents a resounding lesson to princes, the tone broken now and again with exclamations of Alas! and Woe, woe! The dangerous thing about it was the juxtaposition of the death of Louis XVI with the murder of Paul I, an unmentionable subject during the reign of Alexander I, his son and one of the conspirators. The poem could not fail to be influential when it drew its power from the violation of a fundamental taboo with its tableaux of regicide and patricide. These dramatized scenes were too suggestive, though they had little to do with the purported message of the poem that kings should bow before the law. Did it not call on the fallen slaves to rise up?

This loftiest and heaviest of freedom poems speaks of "sacred liberty." The phrase recurs in **"To Chaadaev."** This poem is the first of several milestones in the history of Pushkin's relations with the most important of his new mentors, a man who would become one of the most original political minds in Russia. Though they often differed, Chaadaev was Pushkin's intellectual companion to the end. "The star of enthralling happiness will rise," say the famous lines, "and on the ruins of despotism our names will be inscribed.". . .

The poem is more personal and thus more revealing of the inner springs of Pushkin's new passion. For that is exactly what it is: "we await in hope and longing the moment of sacred liberty, as a young lover awaits the moment of a sure assignation.". . .

This is the simile that he finds; if it seems to intrude into the political context, that is because Pushkin assimilates the two passions as two experiences of romantic renewal. *Ruslan and Liudmila* pictures a youth rescued from melancholy and revived after a passage through death. Several love poems of the period also present the drama of emptiness, anomie, followed by a sudden rekindling of love (**"To Her"**). Another such moment is enshrined as a vision in **"The Recovery,"** a significant title. Soon Pushkin was to jest about his recuperation from a serious illness. A bit later, reflections on the reemergence of a Raphael from under the daubings of an ignorant hand gave rise to the simile, "thus error vanishes from my tormented soul and visions of my first, pure days arise within." . . .

The poem is called **"Rebirth."** The "unlawful sketch" of the painter-vandal senselessly besmirches the work of the true artist. This is a deeper self-criticism than the rhetoric of **"Liberty"** ("Break my self-indulgent lyre") because the judgment appeals to the larger regularities of life, its laws, its meaning. **"To Chaadaev"** speaks of the passing of illusions and first hopes, be they political or simply those of lost youth, but then, using the vocabulary of love, Pushkin reaffirms the vitality of the "noble impulses of the soul": "Desire still burns within you . . . we burn with freedom." Now it is Russia that will awaken from sleep with her vigorous youth as her champions. The final exhortation of the poem is to faith: "The star of enthralling happiness will rise, comrade, believe it!"

The final poem in this brief series is **"The Village"** of 1819. Here the modulation is from idyll to elegy with satirical undertones. It is an idyll interrupted and reenvisaged. The free country life turns out to be not so free or so wholesome as it appears, or as convention would make it. The poem is Pushkin's protest against serfdom. Alexander is said to have acquired it through Chaadaev, read it and transmitted his thanks to the author for the good sentiments that it inspired. In the last year of his life, when composing the famous **"Monument"** in imitation of the Horatian ode, Pushkin adduced as a pledge of his immortality that he had roused kind feelings and glorified freedom in his cruel age, an undoubted reference to the poem of 1819. There, the emphasis is on feeling, not analysis or political program. The poem is very much in the sentimentalist tradition begun in Russia by Radishchev. His banned *Journey from Petersburg to Moscow* had taken him into the Russian countryside where he was alternately charmed and horrified. In **"The Village"** the mood changes abruptly; the whole power of the poem inheres in the sudden shift away from the pastoral where the dreamer enjoys "untrammeled idleness, the friend of reflection," enjoys *his* liberation from the fetters of society, studies how to worship law with a free heart (a reference to **"Liberty"**) and asserts his independence of judgment. He feels himself reawakening to noble ambition. So far, this repeats a familiar pattern of rededication. [In a footnote, O'Bell adds: "An apt commentary is this passage from 'To Her': 'All bloomed anew! I thrilled with life once more the enraptured witness of nature. I felt more keenly, breathed more free, sensed virtue's hold more strongly.' "] But then the speaker is struck by the disharmony of social conditions with the smiling landscape before him. The other, unspoken disharmony is the contrast between his liberty and the people's bondage. . . . [He] can only hope for a better future, evoking "slavery fallen at the tsar's command." If he has revived under the beneficent influence of the country, it must in turn be renewed through his efforts; such is the argument of the poem.

The lament is proper, since the poem is not able to rise to the heights of somber eloquence. The much-mocked rhetoric would not serve, and **"The Village"** remains a poisoned idyll. In **"The Prophet"** Pushkin would find the biblical imperative to silence the sentimentalist's lament. Not: "O, if only my verse could stir hearts; why does a fruitless fire burn in my breast and why has fate not given me the fearsome gift of oratory?" Rather: "Arise, prophet, see and hearken and . . . sear the word into the hearts of men." However, this was only after the catastrophe of 1825.

These few poems comprise Pushkin's entire early body of social commentary. He had very real flashes of political enthusiasm which he greeted as a form of inspiration, but the free spirit is more pervasive in his early poetry than the freedom-loving one. Blok, writing after the 1917 revolution, defined the poet's very vocation as dwelling in a "secret freedom." The phrase is drawn from Pushkin's youthful poetry. It refers to freedom cherished secretly and sung in the celebrated odes (**"To Pliuskova," "To Orlov"**). However, since the general freedom has been withheld, it also refers to the poet's independence, his liberty as an inner possession "till then." "Love and secret freedom inspired a simple hymn in my heart." "I will withdraw with my secret freedom, my shepherd's pipe, pleasure and nature, beneath the shelter of my ancestral woods . . . I will wait."

Ruslan and Liudmila, Pushkin's early lyrics, his first social poetry-all testify, not to a first awakening, but a first reawakening. The intervening discovery was that of elegy; the elegiac becomes the constant sounding board. The pattern is set as early as **"Reminiscences at Tsarskoe Selo"** with its introductory melancholy landscape. Or **"Napoleon on Elba"**: the moon hanging over the cliff where the hero, in the dead quiet, reflects gloomily on mutability and his past before making one last effort to regain his freedom. "I am here alone, full of mutinous thought." What had preceded came to seem like paradise. All the poems

which return to Tsarskoe Selo do so with a penetrating nostalgia. "Memory, picture before me those magical places where I live in spirit." If it is true that Pushkin symbolizes eternity in landscapes where light shines on peaceful waters, then the lake at Tsarskoe Selo was his first eternity. Later came the "mad youth," the wildness for experience, the search for the "science of happiness" and the shock of social evils. The moving spirit of elegy is a sense of the mutability of life and the inevitability of death, the acknowledgement of a fundamental insecurity verging on unreality. Thus, the romantic elegy fixes on the inconstancy or infidelity of the beloved or of the affections themselves. The crisis of faith is not intellectual, and religious skepticism is, so to speak, only a practical application of this attitude. Thus, in his farewell to the Lycée, **"Unbelief,"** Pushkin appeals for the compassion of his listeners. He cannot help it if the "mind seeks for a Deity, but the heart cannot find it." The formulation is unusual: not the ardent heart contradicted by analytic reason or science; rather, a willing mind confronted by the emptiness of the heart. There may be some unshakeable first principle, but the sensibility is not in touch with it. The crisis was to deepen before it could be resolved. Pushkin has often amazed his readers with his verve, his natural resilience, the sheer range of his inner resources, with his famed inner freedom. He, however, tended to see himself as one of the unlucky.

Pushkin came to a hard-won maturity, though he did not live to a ripe old age. But he never ceased to identify with the young. The later poetry finds him typically in a setting among "mad youth." Repeatedly, his plots return to the predicaments of youth, as witnessed by the young pretenders in *Boris Godunov* and *Poltava,* all the protagonists of *Onegin* and the eighteenth-century youth of *The Captain's Daughter.* Sketches for a broad contemporary novel, "A Russian Pelham," show Pushkin preoccupied with his own coming out, sorting reminiscences of 1819-20 in 1834-35. When, in the crisis of mid-life attested in **"The Wanderer,"** the Evangelist crossed his path, he appeared in the image of a "youth reading a book."

The law of Pushkin's creation is a continuous conservation of experience. There is an economy to the development of his psychological profiles. There is a cumulative, or rolling, wavelike progression whereby each is carried forward into the new phase. *Ruslan and Liudmila* tells the story of the youth that was, accompanied by Pushkin's current self as commentator and companion. Later, *Onegin* creates a veritable fugue of the ages of man: the youth becomes Lenskii, the next self emerges, stylized as the new hero, and a new commentator and companion accompanies both of them—and Tat'iana—up to the threshold of maturity. "Can I really soon be thirty?" But if *Onegin* is a novel where time is out of joint, *Ruslan,* good fairy tale that it is, embodies the lawful, time in joint, obeying the dictum of the early verse "be young in your youth" (**"Stanzas to Tolstoi"**). It is the masterpiece of youth.

Germann Andreew   (essay date 1986)

SOURCE: "Pushkin: Bard of Harmony," translated by Albert Leong, in *Proceedings: Summer 1986 Intensive*

*A self-portrait that Pushkin sketched in the album of E.N. Ush-
kova. The poet depicts himself wearing the nightcap of a monk.
The other figure is a devil making fun of him.*

Workshop in Chinese and Russian, edited by Albert
Leong, University of Oregon Books, 1987, pp. 122-35.

[*A German educator and critic, Andreew specializes in
nineteenth- and twentieth-century Russian literature. In
the following excerpt, he traces Pushkin's philosophical development from atheism to Christianity as expressed in his
poetry.*]

The proximity of a Russian intellectual to national consciousness is defined by his attitude towards Christianity.
Atheism is a phenomenon alien to the Russian spirit. A
Russian can criticize the church, unmask it (as Tolstoi
did), or regard this or that religious postulate sceptically.
But pure atheism, unconditionally excluding the existence
of a Will beyond man's and affirming the omnipotence of
scientific knowledge, is a phenomenon introduced into
Russia from the West. Nikolai Berdiaev was absolutely
correct when he asserted: "The themes of Russian literature will be Christian even when Russian writers consciously repudiate Christianity." And this is true not only
of Russian literature, but also, more broadly, of the Russian intelligentsia and Russian thought in general. . . .

Aleksandr Pushkin would not be an expression of Russian
national consciousness, as he is acknowledged to be, if he
had remained a cynic in the manner of Voltaire, whose
thought was close to him in his lyceum years, or had continued to affirm "the lessons of pure atheism" that he
learned from an Englishman traveling in Odessa. Since
personalism is considered the core of Russian social con-

sciousness, and Pushkin the poetic expression of that personalistic world view, one cannot say—without contradicting ourselves—that Pushkin was an atheist, since personalism is based on the Christian concept of personality.

And, indeed, Pushkin's creative work was developed
under a most powerful conflict in himself between atheistic cynicism and lofty Christian spirituality, and the latter
ultimately won out in his work.

While much has been said of Pushkin's theme of flight
from society, we do not find the theme of secluding oneself
in order to speak with God or about God. And, indeed,
until a certain period, the theme of God was not stated
clearly in Pushkin's works. But, in 1834, Pushkin wrote
his poem **"It's time, my friend, it's time"** (**"Pora, moi
drug, pora"**). Pushkin projected a continuation of this
poem, but did not do so for some reason. But an outline
for its continuation can be found in his manuscripts and
reads as follows: "Oh, will I soon move my home to the
country—the fields, garden, peasants, books, works of poetry, family, love, religion, death. . ."

Pushkin had become a religious artist about ten years before writing these lines, but only now did he become aware
of the religious basis of his individualism. He had come to
understand the necessity of flight that was religiously motivated, so that this flight would not merely express an
egotistical dissatisfaction with society, as it had been with
his heroes Aleko (**The Gypsies**) and Evgenii Onegin.

In his lyceum and early post-lyceum years Pushkin was
powerfully infected by Voltaire's cynicism. Voltaire at
that time was the young poet's idol. However, as it turned
out later, this infatuation with Voltaire was not enough to
shape Pushkin's consciousness. For young Pushkin, Voltaire was simply the most entertaining writer: "The best
read, the least tiresome" ("Vsekh bolee prochitan, vsekh
menee tomit") [**"The Town"** (**"Gorodok"**) 1815]. Voltaire's unbridled cynicism corresponded more with Pushkin's "African temperament" than with his spiritual
makeup. In the lyceum Pushkin had two nicknames:
"Monkey" and "The Frenchman." By calling him "Monkey," Pushkin's fellow students did not have in mind his
habit of mimicry or his external appearance: Pushkin was
extremely active and liked to climb trees—hence his resemblance to a monkey. And Pushkin was called "Frenchman" because he affected Voltaire's cynicism and irony.
This imitation of Voltaire made Pushkin non-Russian, for
whatever faith a Russian holds, he treats this faith seriously. Moreover, it is not at all in the Russian spirit to mock
the Virgin Mary.

The most powerful expression of Voltaire's influence on
Pushkin is seen in his narrative poem, **Gavriiliada.** The
theme of the Virgin Mary is resolved here in the style of
French courtesan poetry filled with playful and extremely
risqué passages. The great moment of Christianity—the
miracle of Christ's birth—is treated in the **Gavriiliada** as
a love intrigue at court: "Pogovorim o strannostiakh liub-
vi (drugogo ia ne mysliu razgovora)" ["Let us speak of
perverse love (I have no other discourse in mind)"]. Mary,
like a society lady, chooses a lover: "No Gavriil kazalsia
ei milei . . . / Tak inogda suprugu generala / Zatianutyi

prel'shchaet ad"iutant." ("But Gabriel seemed handsomer to her . . . / As an adjutant in uniform sometimes enchants a general's wife.")

There are many elements in the *Gavriiliada* echoing Classical poems that expressed the ancient Greek concept of Olympus, notions that entered Russia through French neo-Classical literature. Here, the Christian God comes to an earthly woman for love, as the Homeric gods did. The expulsion of Adam and Eve from the Garden of Eden is explained in the poem by God's jealousy. After all, God created Eve for Himself, and not for Adam! And when Adam and Eve came together, a jealous God took vengeance upon them. Superficially, cynicism appears to be one of the central elements of the poem: whose son Christ was is unknown, since Mary had three lovers in one day—the Devil, the angel Gabriel, and God Himself.

Berdiaev noted that the Virgin Mary was dearer to the Russian people than Christ. Thus, Pushkin's portrayal of Mary as a dissolute woman most decisively separated him from Russian national roots.

Nor was it accidental that Pushkin categorically denied writing the *Gavriiliada* when the government decided to punish Pushkin for this poem. As he wrote to P. A. Viazemskii: "The government finally got hold of the *Gavriiliada.* They attribute it to me and denounced me, and I will probably have to answer for someone else's prank unless Prince Dmitrii Gorchakov doesn't show up from the other world to claim his property." (Letter of September 1, 1828)

However, Pushkin did not need to put the blame on Gorchakov. Pushkin had every right to say in 1828 that the *Gavriiliada* was not his, since Pushkin that year was about to write the poem, **"There Was a Poor Knight" ("Zhil na svete rytsar' bednyi"),** in which his image of the Virgin Mary has nothing in common with the image of Mary in the *Gavriiliada.* In fact, there was no work of his he disliked more than the *Gavriiliada.* A rather tolerant man, Pushkin would become enraged when people would start to talk about it. He gathered up and destroyed all copies of the *Gavriiliada,* so that Pushkin's original manuscript and most copies have not come down to us.

It would be incorrect to think that Pushkin repudiated this poem simply from fear of punishment. He did not wish to answer for a work whose spirit did not reflect his true, deep convictions in any way. The same thing happened with his inscription in a notebook containing his *Poltava*—"And I could laugh at . . ."—next to a drawing of five hanged Decembrists. A. Belinkov interprets this inscription as a sign of Pushkin's cowardice or even betrayal. But Pushkin's refusal to share the fate of the Decembrists was not out of cowardice, nor was it cowardice that made him repudiate the *Gavriiliada:* he did not wish to bear responsibility for ideas that he no longer shared in essence. Pushkin, for instance, firmly stood up for *Boris Godunov,* a work no less dangerous than the *Gavriiliada.* Nor did Pushkin repudiate the *Bronze Horseman.* Despite the Tsar's insistence that he make changes in both works, Pushkin did not modify a single line. For that reason, the *Bronze Horseman* was not published during Pushkin's lifetime.

At the beginning of the 1820's Pushkin was totally indifferent to religion. And, regardless of the artistic merit of his works from this period, they cannot be considered unconditionally as expressions of Russian national consciousness. Nor did Pushkin single out Christianity for mockery: he made fun of religion in general. It is sufficient to recall his verses, **"Christ has arisen" ("Khristos voskres,"** 1821), in which Pushkin jokingly expresses a willingness to convert from Christianity to any other faith if that was necessary to possess a woman, to understand how far Pushkin departed from the core of the Russian spirit while under the influence of French materialism and revolutionary ideas.

By the second half of the 1820's, Pushkin was fully formed as a poet and as a representative of Russian social thought. This was possible because Pushkin by that time had outgrown and overcome the superficial influence of French culture and had come to accept the world as a harmonious whole illuminated by a Divine plan. With such an attitude towards the world, religious problems acquired a serious meaning for Pushkin that totally excluded cynical mockery of religion.

Pushkin's serious attitude towards religion did not arise at any particular moment. The striving for faith and a pure attitude towards God always resided in the depths of his soul. Not long after the *Gavriiliada* was written, Pushkin included lines in *The Fountains of Bakhchisarai* that a man without faith could not have written. His Mariia, a captive in the harem of ruthless Khan Girei, preserves her purity, and her salvation is the divine power of the Virgin Mary:

> She is allowed to live alone
> In a remote part of the harem:
> And, it seems, in this solitude
> *Someone unearthly was concealed.*
> There, day and night burns a lamp
> *Before the visage of the most sacred Virgin;*
>
> · · · · ·
>
> And, meanwhile, as all around
> Sinks in mindless languor,
> The nook, saved by a miracle,
> Conceals the *strict sanctuary.*
> Like a heart, given up to vice,
> Amid sinful ecstasies
> Keeps a *sacred* pledge,
> A single *divine* feeling . . .

Pushkin's oblique repentance for the *Gavriiliada* can be seen both in the bright visage of the Virgin and in acknowledging that a heart given up to vice nonetheless preserves religious feelings "amid sinful ecstasies."

Doubts about the truth of atheism began to torment Pushkin by the end of his stay at the Lyceum. It is no accident that he wrote a poem, **"Lack of Faith" ("Bezverie,"** 1817), for his exit examination in Russian literature. This poem, while not truly Christian, bears witness to Pushkin's agonizing doubts about the truth of atheism, to which he was devoted with all his heart and soul. In any case, the need for religion was clear to Pushkin. He was aware how solitary a person is without faith: "Deprived of all support, a son fallen from faith / Already sees with horror, that he is alone in the world, / And a mighty hand with the world's gifts / Is not extended to him from beyond this world's bounds."

Here, the main thing is the young poet's attraction to the world as a unified whole and his conviction that this world can be unified only by a world beyond man. Moreover, from this poem it is clear that Pushkin then already wished to believe, so that reason would not contradict the heart, for he was looking for a monolithic faith. As long as "the mind seeks God, but the heart does not find Him," the poet refuses to acknowledge the existence of God. But one thing Pushkin knew for certain: until he found God, he was doomed to emotional and spiritual agonies. Pushkin envies those who have found God: " 'Lucky ones!' he thinks, 'Why can't I. .,' / Forgetting stern and impotent reason, / 'Bow down before God with a single faith!' "

The world of the church is depicted in this poem as a world of salvation, while the world lacking faith is cold and joyless: on the one hand, "sweet choral singing," "resplendent ceremony of sacred altars," and "the pastor's voice"; on the other, "a darkened soul," "mute tedium," "the soul's melancholy," and "coldness towards everyone." This poem, therefore, expresses the purely Russian conviction that *whether I believe or not, I know that my salvation is in faith.* This disbelief in another world and, at the same time, a longing for it determined Pushkin's profound moods at the beginning of the 1820's, moods contradicting the mocking tone of the *Gavriiliada,* the epistle **"To V. L. Davydov,"** and the epigrammatic **"Christ Has Arisen."** In 1823 Pushkin wrote the poem **"Sweet Hopes"** (**"Nadezhdoi sladostnoi"**), in which once again is heard the poet's agonized desire to believe in infinity, in another world. This desire resembles the purest, child-like thoughts: "Childishly breathing sweet hopes, / When would I believe, that the soul once, / Fleeing from decay, carried off eternal thoughts, / Memory, and love for infinite depths."

But Pushkin still does not believe in infinity, in God. This does not gladden him, does not affirm human reason in the universe, but frightens him instead: "I am terrified . . . And sadly look upon life once again . . ." At the conclusion of **"Monument"** (**"Pamiatnik"**), a poem in which Pushkin sums up his spiritual quest and expresses firm faith in eternity: "No, all of me shall not die—the soul in the sacred lyre / Will outlive my ashes and *avoid decay . . ."*.

Between his desire to believe in that which keeps the soul from decaying and the tranquil assurance of **"Monument"** lies the agonizing spiritual path of the Russian poet. But as early as 1823 Pushkin already knew that disbelief in the harmony of the world, in eternity, is a temptation by the Devil that brings "only suffering, the fruits of an empty heart," as Pushkin wrote in his poem, **"I Have Outlived My Desires"** (**"Ia perezhil svoi zhelan'ia"**).

Pushkin scholars are prone to connect this or that poem with concrete facts of his life and to discern specific people

alluded to in his verses. This approach brushes aside the more substantive philosophical content of Pushkin's works. In **"The Demon"** (**"Demon,"** 1823), critics were stirred by the question—Who was Pushkin's demon? —and came to the correct conclusion that it was A. N. Raevskii. Pushkin, anticipating the possibility of a simplistic understanding of **"The Demon,"** intended to explicate in prose the content of this work, something he did very rarely. In a draft of his article, "On the Poem 'The Demon,' " he wrote: "Many people have indicated the person whom Pushkin intended to portray in this strange poem. But it appears they are incorrect; at least I see in **'The Demon'** a greater moral purpose." Further on, Pushkin underscores the philosophical meaning of the poem: "The great Goethe calls the eternal enemy of humanity the *spirit of negation* (emphasis by Pushkin). And did Pushkin not wish to personify this spirit of *negation and doubt* (emphasis by Pushkin) in his demon, and—in a compressed picture—to outline its distinctive features and *sorrowful influence* on the morality of our age?" Pushkin was not completely just: at that time there were already people (especially V. F. Odoevskii) who understood the meaning of that poem more broadly than simply depicting a specific person.

"The Demon" was written the same year Pushkin began *Evgenii Onegin,* the year when Pushkin turned to a religious perception of the world. It was precisely the period when Pushkin became disenchanted with the Decembrists and with the world view connected with this movement.

"The Demon" is not an indictment of any one person or group of people. It is an invective directed against an entire world view that exerted "a ruinous influence" on the development of European consciousness, an atheistic, sceptical, and cynical world view. Pushkin regarded himself as one of the sacrifices of a negation "tempting Providence" and sundering the spirit of hope and faith. In **"The Demon"** the organic essence of Pushkin's nature is revealed. Here standing before us is not the author of the *Gavriiliada* and other cynical verses, but Pushkin, to whom "all impressions of existence—maidens' glances, the rustling of an oak grove, and the noctural song of a nightingale"—are precious, the Pushkin stirred by "lofty feelings, freedom, glory, love, and inspired art."

However, the poem should be understood not only as poetic self-revelation, for it contains the "confession of a child of the age," the age of French rationalism and the French Revolution that was inspired, in part, by that rationalism, by that spirit of negation and disbelief. The Demon embodies the destructive, diabolical principle: the poet describes that system with words such as "spiteful genius" and "inexhaustible slander"; his speeches bear "cold venom" and disseminate a mood of "melancholy." The conclusion of the poem defines the future program of Pushkin's creative work. Pushkin says of the demon: "He did not believe in love or freedom; / He looked upon life with irony—/ And he did not wish to bless anything in all of nature."

From this point on, Pushkin's creative work becomes the antithesis of this demonic principle and becomes an affirmation. In **"The Demon"** Pushkin parts with the destructive, sceptical European world view or, more precisely, with the French Enlightenment and proclaims his positive position by negating diabolical delusions. And Pushkin would carry out this program to the end of his days, and would only on two or three occasions pay tribute to these demonic views once held by him, but which were neither organic to him nor to Russian national consciousness.

The mistrust of the French Enlightenment that arose in Pushkin and the awareness of a new form of slavery inherent in it were generally known to discerning Russians of the time. Disenchantment with French ideas among the Russian intelligentsia occurred earlier than among the intellectuals of Western Europe.

Reflecting upon the fate of freedom in Europe, Pushkin in his poem **"To the Sea"** compares the tyranny of the French Enlightenment—which was perceived in the West as a new stage of human liberation—with the usual, ancient forms of tyranny. He sees no moral difference between "enlightened" countries and "tyrannies": "The fate of the land is everywhere the same: / Where there is a drop of good, there either enlightenment or a tyrant stands on guard."

Twenty-five years before these lines were penned, Antonovskii's speech had resounded within the walls of the university's boarding school of which he was director. Fresh on the heels of the French Revolution, he said: "Oh, it is time to sense that enlightenment without pure morality, and intellectual refinement without enriching the heart, are vile sores that exterminate virtue not only among whole families, but also among entire peoples." Antonovskii and Pushkin were not direct witnesses of the French Revolution, but the characteristic Russian approach to political events from the standpoint of their moral content, and not from reflections about the rationality of this or that system abstracted from the welfare of individual human beings, determined the Russians's assessment of the French Enlightenment. And it is not surprising that Russians who lived in Paris and witnessed the revolution recoiled from it with horror. . . .

It is possible that Russian messianism was born from this concept of the significance of morality in assessing political and social changes and from the conviction that only Russian consciousness holds these notions of morality.

Pushkin's contemporary, V. F. Odoevskii, had written: "The Russian conquest of Europe will take place, but it will be a spiritual conquest, since only the Russian mind can unify the chaos of European learning." These words remain true today. In any case, a large part of the Russian emigration headed by Solzhenitsyn is convinced that only Russian thought can bring spiritual salvation to the West. Without knowing it, however, they are repeating the views of Pushkin's contemporary, I. V. Kireevskii, that not only the fate of Russia, but also the fate of all of Europe depends on *"Our enlightenment,"* meaning by "our" enlightenment its religious and moral content. This moral content lies at the root of Pushkin's creative work and, consequently, of all Russian literature. . . .

The rupture of Pushkin and, generally, all of Russian social thought with the French Enlightenment coincided with a growing interest in German idealistic philosophy on the part of the Russian intelligentsia. And, to a certain degree, this rupture took place under the influence of German idealistic philosophy.

Fichte's and Schelling's concentration on problems of freedom of personality brought Pushkin close to German philosophy. Not only his hero Lenskii, but even Pushkin himself, received "freedom-loving dreams" from "misty Germany." Moving towards an awareness of a personalistic way of thinking, Pushkin could find an ally neither in the circle of French philosophers nor among official Russian ideologists, but only in one of the representatives of a brilliant pleiade of German philosophers of the time—Schelling. In his *Philosophical Investigations on the Essence of Human Freedom,* Schelling wrote: "The idea of reducing the entire content of philosophy to the concept of freedom has liberated the human spirit in all its manifestations (and not only in the sphere of its inner life) and has caused a mightier upsurge in all branches of science than any preceding revolution."

And, indeed, Pushkin can be called a revolutionary precisely in this sense: the struggle for freedom of human personality under the conditions of an autocratic Russian state was bound to have greater consequences than the Decembrist uprising on Senate Square in 1825.

The struggle to crush one social class in the name of another is, in essence, the task of both revolutionaries and governments (they only have different classes in mind). But a person struggling for freedom of personality has nothing in common with the rulers of a state. The state (and revolutionaries as well) requires servants ready to carry out their commands, not free men and women. Therefore, states consider dubious what the former progressive, A. Perovskii-Pogorel'skii, formulated in the 1830s: "that the appearance of Russian Kants and Fichtes in our fatherland would be useful.". . .

If Schelling and Kant were akin to Pushkin in their focus on the idea of personality, Hegel eliminated the revolutionary idea of arbitrary transformation of the world from Pushkin's world view. Hegel's notion that "all that is real is rational" compelled Pushkin to seek a rational explanation for human vices, rather than justify them. Believing in a Higher power (which Hegel called the Absolute Spirit), Pushkin became an artist of lofty objectivity from the end of the 1820's. To Pushkin, the flow of history no longer seemed chaotic nor to require the interference of revolutionary agents. On the contrary, these revolutionaries now appeared to him in the form of devils who cause people to stray from the spiritual path in the turbid night of atheism (see his poem **"The Devils"** [**"Besy"**]).

In his creative work Pushkin became possessed by the idea that reality was a natural form of the development of some Higher power. "I accept everything and bless everything" henceforth became the core of Pushkin's attitude towards reality. . . .

Immediately after **"The Devils,"** Pushkin wrote his **"Elegy."** In this poem a radiant and harmonious picture of human life is opposed to diabolical disharmony. Devils whirling around weaken man ("We have no strength to go any further"), but understanding the world as divine harmony strengthens man: "At times I *revel in harmony* again." The world as a harmonious unity of suffering and happiness, of joy and grief, is the realization of a radiant plan: "I wish to live, in order to think and suffer; / And I know there will be pleasures among sorrows, cares, and troubles."

In this picture of human life, suffering as the source of thought—in place of the atheistic attempt to avoid suffering—bears witness to Pushkin's penetration into the essence of Christian faith. The impact of Hegelian logic—which treats harmony as the expression of the transition from thesis to antithesis, and synthesis emerging from thesis and antithesis—can be seen in the structure of the **"Elegy."** While thesis and antithesis are not absolute, synthesis is.

The poem opens with a thesis about the bitterness of life: "My path is sorrowful." Then follows the antithesis: "But, friends, I do not wish to die; / I wish to live in order to think and suffer." And, finally, comes the synthesis: ". . . and, perhaps, love will flash a parting smile at my sad sunset." Moreover, the thesis and antithesis in the elegy are not totally contradictory. They are antonyms rather than antithetical: the antithesis is contained in the thesis, and the synthesis already grows out of this interpenetration: "The extinguished merriment of mindless years / Is as oppressive to me as vague tipsiness. / But, like wine, the sadness of bygone days / In my heart is stronger when aged."

Suffering, as the thesis, also contains happiness—the power of feeling. And the finale juxtaposes the same two disparate principles: "And, perhaps, love will flash a parting smile at my sad sunset." The sad sunset—life's end—is brought to life by love's smile, which blesses the acceptance of death as the natural finale of man's path.

This structure is inherent in Pushkin's most important works of the 1830's: Dunia and Vyrin in "The Station Master," Mozart and Salieri in his little tragedy, Grinev and Pugachev in *The Captain's Daughter,* the prince and the miller's daughter in *Rusalka,* Peter the Great and Evgenii in *The Bronze Horseman*—all these distinctive theses and antitheses merge in the reader's consciousness into a single *harmonious* whole, into synthesis as a manifestation of divine intent.

Metropolitan Anastasii, investigating Pushkin's relation to religion and the Russian Orthodox Church, opposes Pushkin to Dostoevskii: "While Dostoevskii, in his at times genuinely 'cruel' talent, reveals before our eyes the abyss of evil and suspends us over it for a long time, Pushkin's muse of harmony cannot endure contact with profound evil. Pushkin ultimately endeavors to transform into radiant accord any disharmony he encounters in life." Such a world view is fundamentally opposed to a revolutionary one. A revolutionary condemns the thesis, extols the antithesis, and takes action to destroy synthesis and harmony. State power is incapable of accepting the antithesis and also distorts harmony. In this sense both revolutionaries and State power are equally godless. A truly religious consciousness demands not the destruction of the world, but faith in the justice of the Divine plan.

Recalling his revolutionary youth, Pushkin wrote in his poem, **"Again I visited"** ("Vnov' ia posetil"): "I saw a foe in the dispassionate judge." These lines were not included in the final version and are preserved only in earlier manuscript variants.

Beginning approximately in 1825, Pushkin himself became that dispassionate (or, rather, impartial) judge. The ability to listen to and understand both sides of a question began to determine the representation of conflicts in the poet's works. Two contradictory, profoundly antonymical phenomena—life and death, good and evil, cruelty and mercy, love and hate, nobility and baseness of character, autocrat and subject, extravagance and miserliness, fidelity and betrayal—all found a place in Pushkin's creative work and were presented as essential elements of harmony.

On the surface, however, such an approach to life might seem to confirm the indifference and even amorality of the poet. Was it not Pushkin's Grishka Otrep'ev in *Boris Godunov* who asserted that Pimen "takes note of good and evil with indifference." After becoming the chronicler of human life in general and Russia in particular, Pushkin repudiated all political positions that viewed the world as an object for transformation and began to write religious, humanistic poetry. He did not flatter some people or "unmask" others but, instead, exposed sins: hatred, greed, cruelty, servility, betrayal. Pushkin poeticized beauty, love, fidelity, nobility of character, and mercy. In Pushkin's creative work, man is shown in the grip of passions and either overcomes them or becomes their slave. In this respect, Pushkin's work is connected with medieval Russian literature, which affirms the same concept of man, as the scholar D. S. Likhachev has shown.

Pushkin is by no means indifferent to this choice. Reflecting on his creative work, he writes in **"The Elegy"**: "I shed tears over my inventions." Pushkin perceives the principle of good and evil in man, rejoices when good triumphs, and suffers when man surrenders to evil. Boris Godunov, Peter the Great, Pugachev, Dunia, and Sil'vio (in **"The Shot"**) perform acts of good and evil. . . .

[Pushkin] arrived at faith in the harmony of the world after the temptation of the revolutionary Decembrist movement. It was poetry, according to Pushkin, that saved him from disharmonious notions of the world. Beginning with **"The Prophet"** ("Prorok"), Pushkin became the representative of a view of art in which the artist is an intermediary between Heaven and Earth, between God (or Absolute Spirit, in Hegel's terminology) and people.

In the same unfinished fragment of the poem, **"Again I visited,"** Pushkin writes: "My inexperienced youth was / Wasted in fruitless ordeals, / In my heart seethed turbulent feelings / And hatred, and dreams of pale vengeance. / But sacred *providence* dawned on me / Like a *mysterious* shield, / Poetry like a *consoling angel* / Saved me, and my soul *was resurrected.*"

This concept of the poet as the agent of Divine will is extremely characteristic of Russian consciousness in general. In no other country of the world is there such a lofty attitude towards the poet, at times expressing itself even in the form of exaggerated aspirations for authority and power, or interfering with the poet's everyday life. Seeing the injustice of Russian social conditions, unhappy people in Russia believed, and still believe, that the omnipotent poet has the last word. When Pushkin died in 1837, an enormous number of people came to bid him farewell. Only a few of them had read his work: they had come to say farewell to a prophet, to a priest, to a defender, to someone who was free from human authority and who was faithful only to God.

Pushkin himself wrote in his poem, **"Monument"** (**"Pamiatnik"**): "O muse, be obedient to God's decree . . . / Only God's . . ." The world exists only by God's decree. In this world there are certain natural laws, in particular, the natural cycle of good and evil, of life and death, of generations. Pushkin believed that the artist's mission was to reconstitute these natural laws in poetic form. And so he proclaimed these laws without allowing evil and injustice to manifest themselves in this state of general harmony.

Pushkin's poem, **"Again I visited,"** is the clearest expression of his mature world view. Here he presents a picture of movement, the colors of which encompass grief, joy, triumph, sadness, light, and darkness: the old nanny *died*; the fisherman brings in a "*meager* catch"; "the mill is *rundown*"; the road is "*rutted* by rain"; a tired old tree stands alone; "a *sullen* comrade" of my youth. But a "*young grove*" is already replacing the old generation; the new generation will enter into its "*mighty* late stage" and "*outgrow* my acquaintances." New "*merry* and *pleasant* thoughts" will engage the attention of new generations of people.

The lyric hero of this poem is the connecting link between the past and the future. This hero embodies the past, which "keenly embraces" him, the present ("here's the little house fallen from favor"; "here's the hill"; "here's the young grove"), and the future: "But let my grandson hear your welcome sound when, returning from friendly discourse, full of merry and pleasant thoughts, he passes you in the dark of night and remembers me."

Understanding the fate of a single person as a link in the endless development of humanity makes human existence profoundly meaningful and, moreover, requires a person to accept responsibility for his own life, as well as the lives of others, a responsibility crucial for the self-disclosure of Absolute Spirit.

Stephanie Sandler   (essay date 1989)

SOURCE: *Distant Pleasures: Alexander Pushkin and the Writing of Exile*, Stanford University Press, 1989, 253 p.

[*In the following excerpt, Sandler examines themes of pleasure, domination, gender, and nationalism in* The Captive of the Caucasus.]

Judging from readers' immediate enthusiasm (which even Pushkin acknowledged) and from Pushkin's careless endorsements in letters to friends, *The Prisoner of the Caucasus* was conceived and received as a poem with which one could have a great deal of fun. The judgment that *The*

Vladimir Nabokov on the influence of French literature on Pushkin:
I shall now make a statement for which I am ready to incur the wrath of Russian patriots: Alexandr Sergeyevich Pushkin (1799-1837), the national poet of Russia, was as much a product of French literature as of Russian culture; and what happened to be added to this mixture, was individual genius which is neither Russian nor French, but universal and divine. In regard to Russian influence, Zhukovski and Batyushkov were the immediate predecessors of Pushkin: harmony and precision—this was what he learned from both, though even his boyish verses were more vivid and vigorous than those of his young teachers. Pushkin's French was as fluent as that of any highly cultured gentleman of his day. Gallicisms in various stages of assimilation populate his poetry with the gay hardiness of lucern and dandelion invading a trail in the Rocky Mountains. *Coeur flétri, essaim de désirs, transports, alarmes, attraits, attendrissement, fol amour, amer regret* are only a few—my list comprises about ninety expressions that Pushkin as well as his predecessors and contemporaries transposed from French into melodious Russian. . . . Pushkin was acquainted with English poets only through their French models or French versions; the English translator of *Onegin,* while seeking an idiom in the Gallic diction of Pope and Byron, or in the romantic vocabulary of Keats, must constantly refer to the French poets.
Vladimir Nabokov, in his "Problems of Translation: 'Onegin' in English," in Partisan Review, *Fall 1955.*

Prisoner of the Caucasus is not a particularly serious work has extended down to our own day, evidenced in the relative neglect of the poem by twentieth-century critics, except for those concerned with Byron's impact on Pushkin (something Pushkin quite acknowledged) or with entertainments based on Pushkinian themes (the ease with which *The Prisoner of the Caucasus* has become a ballet once again suggests that the poem is properly an amusement). In this response of readers two things about *The Prisoner of the Caucasus* are highlighted: either the poem is an instance of foreign cultural conquest or it is an evening's pleasure. But the tale is itself an investigation into the relationship between passing pleasures and foreign conquest. The pleasure is that of sexual involvement, but the conquests are several. Not only is Russia's military domination of the Caucasus at issue in *The Prisoner of the Caucasus,* but also the epistemological superiority of the Russian hero is brought sharply into relief.

By juxtaposing two radically different human experiences, play (or pleasure) and domination (or pain), Pushkin's tale also separates quite aggressively those who speak and those who are silenced. My task will be to read the pain hidden in *The Prisoner of the Caucasus*'s textual pleasures: the plot of captivity hides an untempered presentation of the white male captive's unique status in the poem as a discerning human subject. My concern is how his position entails the subjection of others and what that relationship of domination means for the joy this poem is thought to bear.

The hero is an unnamed Russian soldier, captured by a group of Caucasian tribespeople, the Circassians (in Russian, the Cherkesy). In his fetters the captive can do little except watch the people and land around him, and his descriptions are as authoritative as those of the narrator. What is striking is how, for the Russian captive, these people are almost universally male and invincibly militant. Nearly every person mentioned is a man, and battle is practically the only activity that engages these men. The first lines show us Circassian men, sitting before their houses, recollecting battles, horses, and women—but it is the battles to which their attention returns: . . .

> In the *aul,* on their doorsteps,
> The idle Circassians sit.
> The sons of the Caucasus talk
> Of martial, deadly strife,
> Of the beauty of their steeds,
> Of the pleasures of wild languor;
> They remember former days'
> Successful incursions,
> The deceits of clever *Uzdens,*
> The blows of their cruel *shashki,*
> And the accuracy of unavoidable arrows,
> And the ashes of destroyed villages,
> And the caresses of black-eyed captive women.

An arriving horseman announces that he has captured a Russian, from whose perspective the poem now proceeds. The Russian describes many aspects of Circassian life in abstract terms ("Their faith, customs, upbringing, . . . hospitality, thirst for battle"), but there is also a single, typical man imaged in, again, military terms: . . .

> . . . sometimes a swift Circassian,
> . . . would fly freely
> Across the wide steppe, across mountain,
> Trained beforehand for battle.
> . . . . .
> The Circassian is covered with arms;
> He is proud of them, comforted by them:
> On him there is armor, gun, quiver,
> Kuban saddle, dagger, lasso
> And *shashka,* his eternal companion
> For all labors and leisure.
> . . . . .
> He is always the same; the same visage
> Unconquerable, unyielding.

And on the description goes, at three times again the length of what I have cited here, serving not only to interpolate in the static description a narrative of battle, but also to impress on us that the essence of these Circassian men is in their readiness and superiority in battle. Even a later description of the men at play devolves into a war game, where their spirits are described as "born for war." The Circassian men are knowable only in their aggressivity, and since they hold a Russian as their prisoner, these descriptions leave the impression that the Circassians are successfully dominant in the Caucasus. I will return to this false impression, as Pushkin does, in considering the epilogue praising Russia's military superiority.

A Circassian woman, also unnamed, falls in love with the Russian and eventually sets him free. She is the tale's only woman character. She is anticipated in the opening description of *The Prisoner of the Caucasus,* where the male pleasures include a "wild languor," more specifically, the "caresses of black-eyed captive women." That women enter the narrative as captured cannot be unimportant in this tale about a Russian captive. Indeed, it is clear that the Circassian woman is as circumscribed by the conventions of her culture as the literally captured man: she is someone whose value is in her "caress." Thus, in a review of *The Prisoner of the Caucasus* praised by Pushkin, Prince Viazemsky commented that the only thing known about the Circassian woman was that she was capable of love—and, for him, this was enough.

The Circassian woman is immediately a wonderfully nurturing figure. She returns to health a man several times described as dead: in the first words about him, the Russian captive is "mute," "motionless," and "like a corpse"; he suffers a "mortal sleep" and "putrid chill"; he neither sees nor hears. He comes to life from the sight of the Circassian woman and only then takes the fermented mare's milk (*kumys*) that she offers: . . .

> . . . her touching glance, the heat of her cheeks,
> Her gentle voice all say:
> Live! and the captive comes to life.
> And, with his last bit of strength,
> Submissive to her tender request,
> He leaned up and the salutary drink
> Soothed his weary thirst.

She lingers "as if she wanted / To comfort the captive by her mute presence." An ideal source of comfort, the Circassian woman is initially portrayed well within the most universal of all feminine stereotypes, the provider of life, the mother figure who herself says nothing, indeed, "is" nothing except what she gives to others.

In addition, and no less stereotypically, the Circassian woman is sexual. *The Prisoner of the Caucasus* narrates her admission of love for the Russian captive. Lavish attention is paid her entreaty. She has felt his "mute kisses" in the "night's darkness," his "burning with languor and desire." The Circassian woman is represented as a creature of sexual passion, and that alone. She asks the Russian to "love her," for no one else has so "kissed her eyes"; no one else has stolen into her bed, she adds. The assurance of previous chastity proves not that she is uninterested in sex, but that she has always thought of herself as defined by some deferred sexual involvement. Spurned, she later frees the captive and refuses his impulsive offer to flee with him. The Circassian woman drowns herself in the end, as though to confirm that once she can no longer give herself in love, she has no reason to live. Indeed, her response to the Russian's words of rejection is to lose all her former life-affirming energies; now *she* is deathlike, her gaze "unmoving," "pale as a ghost," her hand turned "cold."

The process by which the Circassian woman absorbs the Russian man's deadness still requires some explanation, but perhaps first one should ask whether the sexual stereotypes I have outlined are legitimately objectionable. One Pushkin scholar has seen in *The Prisoner of the Caucasus* a kind of ethnographic realism. Perhaps there is validity in reproducing cultural norms in which men defend territory, and women nurture and comfort in ways that include sexual gratification. Moreover, the poem's almost exclusive reliance on the Russian captive's powers of observation might indicate a more properly epistemological realism, wherein the asymmetries described are simply those an outsider would arguably perceive.

These are important points to notice, lest we charge Pushkin with a sexism based on the standards of our own very different culture and historical moment. Still, the desire to see realism in this quintessentially romantic poem is itself suspect: one of the poem's themes, and hence part of its epistemological attitude, is the consequences of extreme subjectivity. The Russian captive sees nothing except in its relation to his sense of himself. On what grounds can he acknowledge and act upon the personhood of the Circassian tribespeople?

If the Russian captive is as psychologically consistent as Byron's heroes, on whom he is modeled, there can be little doubt about the answer. Though the tale encourages us to see the Circassian woman as tragically sacrificed in the liberation of a captive, her fate has all along been determined by his egoism. She does emerge, because of her self-sacrifice, as an admired heroine, though we might want to qualify our admiration for her heroism because she completely conforms to nineteenth-century European conventions of self-effacing and thus debased womanhood. But there is a more serious criticism to be offered here: the Circassian woman is represented as having traveled a path of suspiciously Byronic emotions. When the Russian captive describes this woman he is still describing himself. The exchange of life and death imagery, noted above, contributes to a sense that there is an exchange of attributes between the captive and the Circassian woman; yet the more one considers their relationship the less appropriate "exchange" seems as a descriptive structure. More precisely, the Russian man confers upon all that he sees characteristics that accord with his sense of himself.

I will describe, then, how the Russian man's perspective is so controlling and then turn to a description of the Circassian woman. At the end of the first part of *The Prisoner of the Caucasus,* the narrator pauses to ask if the captive looks into himself (in search of a sense of his past) or at the world around him: . . .

> Did he regret days gone by,
> Days of disappointed hopes,
> Or, curious, did he contemplate
> Amusements of bleak simplicity?
> Did he read in this faithful mirror
> The habits of a wild people?—
> He hid the movements of his heart
> In deepest silence,
> And on his high brow
> Nothing was betrayed.

The irony is that it makes no difference where the captive looks in the end. The image of the mirror (one that will recur in *The Fountain of Bakhchisarai*) signals the Russian's glance as one that returns what he himself projects. Hence the lines just quoted that begin by asking what the

Russian "contemplates" in the "wild people" around him conclude with the observation that these people can discern nothing in him: . . .

> His careless courage
> Caused the terrible Circassians to marvel,
> They had mercy on his youth
> And in whispers among themselves
> They were proud of their acquisition.

The Circassians find him incomprehensible, but he has no such difficulty in describing them. The Russian's emotions may be unnamable, but they control the poetry: his proud silence precedes and seems to determine the Circassian pride in "their acquisition," as if this were another reflected perception.

Another passage, the description of the Circassian warrior quoted earlier, also shows the Russian's powers of projecting his mental state. The Circassian warrior is notably singular, his solitude a simulation of the captive's willed isolation. For both the captive and the mythic rider, there is only the companionship of animals, as if the accepting animals were a replacement for the demanding social life both have escaped. Flight from society, however, accurately describes the Russian captive; it is one of his more Byronic traits ("He knew people and society, / Knew the value of life's disloyalty, / . . . A fugitive from society, friend of nature, / He abandoned his native land"). But nothing that we know about Circassian society logically motivates the alienation of a local man. When the Russian captive turns from describing Circassian social life to envisioning a lone warrior in martial adventures, he has again imposed on the world around him his ways of imagining himself.

One can make a similar case about his presentation of the Circassian woman who saves him at the price of her life. As though to prepare us for her transformation into a semblance of the Russian captive, she is described at the moment she frees him in newly masculine, and military, terms. A dagger and a metal file are gleaming at her side (as requisite reflecting surfaces and as symbols of martial power); she "seems to be going off into secret battle, or military exploit." To the Russian's sudden invitation to flee with him, the Circassian woman responds with words that, while standard for the love elegies of the period, are striking in *The Prisoner of the Caucasus* because they repeat the emotions expressed by the Russian captive. . . .

> No, Russian, no!
> The sweetness of life is gone;
> I knew everything, I knew joy,
> And it is all over, even the traces are lost.
> Is it possible? you loved another!. .
> Find her, love her;
> For what do I still yearn?
> What causes my despair?. .
> Farewell! the blessings of love
> Be with you at all times.
> Farewell—forget my pain,
> Give me your hand . . . for the last time.

The bitterness that it is now too late to love is typical of the Byronic male hero and precisely the tale this Russian captive told of himself. His speech is quite long (significantly, much longer than hers), but a few lines suffice to make the point. He had advised: . . .

> Unlucky friend, why didn't you
> Appear before me earlier,
> In those days when I believed in hope
> And the ecstasy of dreams!
> But it is late: I am dead to joy, . . .

Pushkin masks the similarity between these two moments by a vivid contrast in the two characters' emotional tenor. The Russian speaks with a cruelty that we never see in the Circassian woman (only in *The Gypsies* do we see such a transfer), the worst moments of which are his confession that he has always been thinking of another woman while in her arms and his twice-repeated prediction that she will soon find someone else to love. When the Circassian woman's kindness and lack of self-pity are contrasted to the Russian's arrogance and self-absorption, the difference between the two is so striking that we overlook how she has taken on the outlines of Byronic characterization, particularly in her ability to say "no" to love.

Throughout *The Prisoner of the Caucasus* there is a massive externalization of the captive's values: while he is a captive in the physical sense that he is not free to go, the Russian maintains an inner sense of psychological freedom. Perhaps the most startling instance of this power to compel the Caucasian culture to conform to his expectations occurs when the Circassian woman inexplicably changes from a silent conveyor of her emotions to a fluent speaker of a language the Russian understands. Her first appearance had been marked by a nonverbal exchange occasioned by their ignorance of each other's language: . . .

> His greedy soul catches
> The enchanting sound of pleasing speech
> And the glances of a young maiden.
> He does not understand the foreign words,
> But her touching glance, the heat of her cheeks,
> Her gentle voice says:
> Live!

This acknowledgment of the Circassian woman's otherness is, as I have suggested, perhaps insufficient grounds for us to conclude that she is a person in the eyes of the Russian, but it is a step in that direction, which is canceled once she begins to speak (and to speak, one should add, in the passionate and loving tones that are familiar from the conventions of European Romantic writing). The very fact of having her speak, though necessary for the action of *The Prisoner of the Caucasus,* conquers the integrity and dignity with which the Circassian woman is first presented. The poem shows how she becomes something the Russian understands completely, particularly when she takes her own life: "he understood everything" ("vse ponial on") is his famous response to her suicide.

A circle closes around this poem in a way that is not immediately apparent, certainly not to readers who have exalted the Circassian woman for her fine ethical act. The question that remains is whether the Circassian woman is dominated because she is a woman or because she is a "native," or both. To see how gender and nationalism have conspired in the poem, I want to consider its format: a dedication to Nikolai Raevsky and an epilogue about the

Russian colonization of the Caucasus enfold the tale about a Russian man and a Circassian woman so that the masculine values of friendship and war are exalted with great intensity.

Nikolai Raevsky was a close friend of Pushkin's. He was a son of General Nikolai Raevsky, brother of Alexander Raevsky, a Byronic figure in his own right and the presumed subject of Pushkin's lyric **"The Demon"** ("Demon," 1823). Raevsky's three sisters include Maria Volkonskaya and Ekaterina Orlova, both of whom Pushkin seems to have romanced before their marriages (and, with Ekaterina Orlova, perhaps after). Pushkin met and traveled with the Raevsky family during the first months of his exile; he recalled their trip to the Crimea and the Caucasus fondly and he maintained a long-standing connection to the entire family.

It is clear from the dedication of *The Prisoner of the Caucasus* that the friendship with Nikolai Raevsky was intense and mutual. It begins:

> Accept with a smile, my friend,
> This offering of my free muse:
> To you I have dedicated a banished lyre's song
> And the inspiration of my leisure.
> When I was languishing, innocent and joyless,
> And could hear the whispered gossip from every
> side,
> When the cold dagger of betrayal
> And torpid dreams of love
> Tormented and numbed me,
> Still I could find tranquility in your presence;
> I could breathe easier in my soul—we loved each
> other:
> And the storms around me no longer raged,
> I blessed the gods for this peaceful refuge.

These tender poetic lines can be read as expressing the high value placed on friendship in Pushkin's age. The expectation that the lines will be completely understood by their addressee shows well the intimacy of Pushkin's friendship with Raevsky.

Pushkin had several reasons for invoking his closeness with Raevsky. First, the dedication serves to introduce *The Prisoner of the Caucasus* to its wider audience of readers. The emotional states described in the poem are prepared in the introducing dedication: Raevsky "saves" Pushkin from slander and a kind of life-threatening torrent of emotion in a way that foreshadows the salvation of the Russian captive. Raevsky's act of liberating and protecting Pushkin has a less complicated aftermath than one finds in the end of *The Prisoner of the Caucasus*: his loyalty produced the poem, or so the dedication says; the Circassian woman's loyalty ends the Russian's captivity but in a way that also ends any relationship between them and the narrative that has brought them to readers. Among other distinctions, the fact that it is a friendship between two men makes the Pushkin-Raevsky bond simpler and more durable. There are important reasons for the advantages of male friendship, not least of which is the possibility of a relationship between equals and the presumption of shared values and cultural codes. Anyone who studies Pushkin's life and works will quickly sense how much his was an age in which, among men of Pushkin's class and intellectual and political predispositions, the bond that most powerfully organized social relations was that of male friendship.

What this means for *The Prisoner of the Caucasus* is that a tale about a repudiated sexual relationship is located in the context of a more satisfying and productive friendship between men. The Circassian woman's place in the exchanges that occur in the text is a way to locate her value more precisely. Her suicide indicates that she has nothing left for herself once her potential sexual connection with the Russian captive has proved impossible; thus we might say that whatever value she has in the text is not hers to determine. She is exchangeable among men, as she herself laments at the moment that she worries that she will be given in marriage: . . .

> I know the sacrifice readied for me:
> My father and stern brother
> Want to sell me to someone I do not love
> In a strange aul for a price of gold; . . .

The Circassian woman wants to implore her father and brother not to do this, but she quickly admits that this would be useless—and she names the dagger or poison as her alternatives. Her worth in gold is tenable only so long as one man can give her to another man. The suicide translates into event the sad fact that in and of herself she is represented as nothing. The Circassian woman is an entity that the men in her culture can exchange, but when she tries to give herself away, to the Russian captive, the result is her destruction.

The work of modern anthropologists in studying the cultural meaning of gift-giving is quite useful in understanding the status that is being conferred on the Circassian woman. Building on now classic texts by Claude Lévi-Strauss and Marcel Mauss, Gayle Rubin has stressed [in "The Traffic in Women: Notes on the 'Political Economy' of Sex," in *Toward an Anthropology of Women,* 1975] that when men bestow gifts on one another, women are frequently the gift:

> If it is women who are being transacted, then it is the men who give and take them who are linked, the woman being a conduit of a relationship rather than a partner to it. . . . And it is the partners, not the presents, upon whom reciprocal exchange confers its quasimystical power of social linkage. The relations of such a system are such that women are in no position to realize the benefits of their own circulation.

Rubin's observation that "women are in no position to realize the benefits of their own circulation" reiterates the sense that, in *The Prisoner of the Caucasus,* the structures that make the Circassian woman a potential gift prevent her from being fully alive to and for herself. Of her nothing is told that is not an element of her value to men.

In 1825 Pushkin wrote that "women have no character, they have passions in their youth: that is why it is so easy to portray them." The immediate context for this extraordinary remark is a criticism of Byron's male heroes, so that Pushkin's claim about women's characterlessness is grounded in assumptions about the Byronic hero's ex-

treme subjectivity. *The Prisoner of the Caucasus* is Pushkin's most Byronic poem and perhaps his only poem in which a woman of passion, rather than of character, appears. If there was ever a female character who did not resist literary portrayal, it is the Circassian woman, so fully does she embody submissiveness even when she strays outside the boundaries of what her culture expects of her.

Pushkin's comments about the ease with which women can be portrayed were offered, as it turns out, in a letter to Raevsky. Were there more documentation of their friendship, disdain for women might prove to have been a recurring feature of the relationship. Even without other material, the 1825 letter can return us to the dedication of *The Prisoner of the Caucasus* and its implicit use in strengthening the friendship between the two men. To use Rubin's terms the Circassian woman and her tale were a gift Pushkin gave Raevsky. The poem testifies to, and is the result of, their closeness. Pushkin often used poems in letters to friends as tokens of his attachment: one particularly sees this during the years of exile. In a letter to his closest friend, Pushkin told Prince viazemsky, "my verses are searching for you all over Russia." Most of the men in Pushkin's circle wrote verse, and their exchange of new poems as well as the habit of writing epistolary verse meant that poetry drew friends together and often symbolized their closeness. That the sharing of work strengthened friendship is not something one need criticize: what is questionable is the imposition of gendered social arrangements on the epistolary exchange. Letters were written by and for men. Women might be written about, but always positioned so as to facilitate an exchange between men. The dedication creates such a triangle in *The Prisoner of the Caucasus,* one that will be repeated in *The Fountain of Bakhchisarai.*

There is a second problem raised by the dedication: what is it about Raevsky that makes *him* the man to whom Pushkin dedicates *The Prisoner of the Caucasus*? Here one has to consider the ways in which Pushkin draws himself in Raevsky's image. By the time Pushkin dedicated *The Prisoner of the Caucasus* to him, Raevsky was far away. The poem is a memento of their closeness, a verse that memorializes intimacy no longer possible, and that evidences the lasting bond between them even when they were so far apart. . . .

> Here you will find memories
> Of days that were, perhaps, dear to the
>   heart,
> The contradictions of passions,
> Familiar dreams, familiar sufferings
>   And the secret voice of my soul.

The dedication claims that the text will tell a shared experience, that its dreams and sufferings are already known (*znakomye*) to Raevsky, as if they were his own feelings. The uncertainty most central to the dedication, though, has to do with how much Pushkin and Raevsky can have shared. While Pushkin speaks of "the contradictions of passions," what one feels more crucially is a contradiction that seems necessary for the dedication to occur at all: . . .

> We have parted ways in life: barely, just barely

Had you bloomed, enfolded by calm, when, like
   your heroic father,
You, a chosen youth, proudly flew
Into fields of blood, beneath clouds of enemy arrows.
The fatherland has treated you with kind tenderness,
Like a precious sacrifice, like the truest gleam of
   its hopes.
I early experienced grief, I was stricken by persecution;
I am the sacrifice of slander and vengeful ignorance;
But, my heart strengthened by freedom and
   steadfastness,
     I waited calmly for better days;
     And the happiness of my friends
     Was my sweet consolation.

Pushkin tells us that he and Raevsky are now geographi-
cally separate, and he goes on to demonstrate that their
fates have also been quite opposite. Raevsky follows his father's example in pursuing military service. He is a "chosen youth" and a "precious sacrifice," someone the "fatherland" protects as a vessel for its future hopes. Pushkin
describes himself as persecuted by these same forces: rather than a valued soldier, he has been the target of slander
and ignorance. Raevsky's military life puts him at risk
"beneath clouds of enemy arrows," but he has the "kind
tenderness" of the state as a comfort. Pushkin's "persecution" also makes him into a "sacrifice," but he is not
prized enough for anyone to protect. Pushkin is consoled
by knowing that his friends are happy, he says, a fine twist
on the possibility that these same friends would themselves be his protection.

Pushkin suggests, then, in the parallelisms and differences
of these lines, that some resemblances will make Raevsky
an ideal listener to his poem, but a few distinctions, chiefly
how Pushkin has suffered, cannot be ignored. We might
say that in these lines, Pushkin articulates a sense of difference from Raevsky that does not undermine more important similarities; nor, conversely, does Pushkin's need for
these similarities (a need that I will consider in a moment)
cause him to overlook or to minimize crucial differences.
I stress this point because it will otherwise be lost when
I turn from dedication to epilogue, that is, from the
poem's opening to its conclusion.

Before turning to the epilogue, I want to make one final
point about the dedication by referring to the ways that
dedications function textually and to the specifics of this
act of dedication. The premise of most dedicatory lines is
that of connection between speaker and addressee. To say
to someone "I write these lines for you" is to say that a
prior relationship exists to make the addressee an especially knowledgeable or valuable reader; it is also to say that
he or she has in some way made it possible for the lines
to be written in the first place. Pushkin works these two
implications so that the relationship between dedication
and poem feels reversible: his intimacy with Raevsky has
made the tale possible, and the familiar tale makes the affirmation of closeness in the dedication plausible.

Pushkin is not unique for his age in writing dedications for

his longer works, though he does so more readily and
more unusually. . . .

Pushkin . . . appears to seek a particular inclination from
his readers on the basis of his friendship with Nikolai
Raevsky, son of a great military hero and himself on the
way to heroic status. I turn now to the epilogue of *The
Prisoner of the Caucasus,* which glorifies Russia's expanding military might so fervently that one can see how this
association with Raevsky works in the dedication. I will
not cite here the entire page-and-a-half epilogue (from an
invocation to a muse who has allowed poetry about the exotic Caucasus to flow it moves to a song of celebration that
the poet might one day sing). Here, though, are some excerpts, along with the end of the epilogue in full: . . .

    Thus the muse, carefree friend of dreams,
    Flew to the lands of Asia
    And plucked for herself a wreath
    Of wild Caucasian flowers.
    . . . . .
    Perhaps, she will repeat
    The legends of the terrible Caucasus;
    She will tell the tale of far-off lands
    . . . . .
    And I will sing of that glorious hour
    When, sensing a bloody battle,
    Our two-headed eagle rose
    Over the indignant Caucasus;
    . . . . .
    The ferocious battle cry has died down:
    Everything is subjugated to the Russian sword.
    Proud sons of the Caucasus,
    You gave battle and died in horrible numbers;
    But our blood did not save you,
    Nor did enchanted armor,
    Nor mountains, nor swift steeds,
    Nor your love for wild freedom!
    Like the tribes of Batyi,
    The Caucasus will betray its forefathers,
    It will forget the voice that thirsts for battle,
    It will forsake the arrows of battle.
    A fearless traveler will now approach
    Those ravines where you have banded together,
    And your punishment will be trumpeted forth
    By the darkened tones of tales to be told.

By the end of the epilogue, Pushkin is moved to praise
Russia's conquest of the Caucasus. Rather than echoing
the descriptions of Circassian courage and steadfastness
that mark the poem proper, these lines describe the Caucasian peoples as abandoning the traits that have made
them who they are (abandoning their ancestors, in the
poem's metaphors) in order to become a conquered people, subjects of an invincible imperial presence. The conquest of the Caucasus, which was to endure another thirty
years and be marked by fierce resistance from native peoples, is here transformed into a quick victory for Russia.

Pushkin's wish to celebrate Russia's victory, while not
strong enough to erase all lament for the conquered people's "love for wild freedom," leads him to align himself
with the conquerors and to promise to write poetry praising their victory. He speaks as Russian citizen and as poet,
recalling the images of Raevsky son (and father) invoked
in the dedication, but now with none of the tempering self-
consciousness of someone who has been persecuted. Push-

kin's patriotism is untroubled by any sense of the unjustice done to people whose lives are destroyed by colonial invasion, which is to say that he takes no opportunity to see oppression in thi historical event. There is only satisfied victory: "Everything is subjugated to the Russian sword." As Walter Vickery has put it, [in "Pushkin: Russia and Europe," *Review of National Literatures* (1972)], with reference to the ending of *The Prisoner of the Caucasus,* "Where Russian foreign policy interests were involved, Pushkin was not about to be sidetracked by thoughts of the virtues of primitive peoples."

How has Pushkin, the poet who casts himself as a voice for oppressed serfs in **"The Countryside,"** and the one who so resonantly and so often during his exile speaks of himself as an outsider, come to such a juncture in this, his first Southern poem? Readers of Pushkin will know that it is not unheard of for him to praise Russia's military might, either in the victory over Napoleon (e. g., **"Napoleon na El'be"** / **"Napoleon on the Elba,"** 1815; **"Aleksandru"** / **"To Alexander,"** 1815) or in the empire's ascendancy to world power under Catherine the Great (**"Vospominanie v Tsarskom Sele"** / **"Remembrance in Tsarskoe Selo,"** 1814). That these are poems from Pushkin's youth, when naïve enthusiasm for military conquest might be temporary, is not a sufficient explanation, for there is another "Napoleon" poem written once Pushkin was in exile (1821). Here the poem mostly allies itself with battle-weary people who have every reason to oppose Napoleon's tyranny, but there is also the following, exclamatory apostrophe: . . .

> Russia, martial queen,
> Remember your ancient rights!
> Darken, sun of Austerlitz!
> Burst into flame, great Moscow!
> A different age has dawned:
> Vanish, brief moment of our shame!
> Bless Moscow, Russia!
> War: this is our vow until death!

Pushkin's patriotism in this 1821 poem is of a piece with that expressed in the epilogue to *The Prisoner of the Caucasus,* written the same year, and though we might want to distinguish his mercilessness toward French invaders from his indifference to the sufferings of invaded Caucasian tribespeople, both derive from expressions of unqualified support for the military actions of the Russian government, a government of which Pushkin could be quite critical on issues of serfdom, censorship, bureaucracy, and Court whimsy.

The visible militancy of the epilogue of *The Prisoner of the Caucasus* is not, then, an aberration in Pushkin's oeuvre, which means that it is not occasioned by conventions of the Byronic tale, for example, or by the particularities of Pushkin's friendship with Raevsky. Nor were these attitudes so unconsciously embedded in men of Pushkin's class that they ought to strike us as undistinctive: Pushkin's close friend Prince Viazemsky wrote to Alexander Turgenev in 1822 that he regretted Pushkin's decision to "bloody" the last lines of his poem. Viazemsky saw that poetry "should never be a glorification of butchery."

The praise for imperial Russia that closes *The Prisoner of*

the Caucasus needs to be accounted for in reading the poem, particularly since it sounds a note of indifferent mastery that resonates elsewhere in the tale. The will to domination heard in *The Prisoner of the Caucasus* complements the poem's readiness to use a Circassian woman to liberate a Russian man—and to use her tale to draw closer two male friends. The politics of this Southern tale are not lodged in equality across boundaries of gender or nationality, nor is there much sympathy here for the oppressed. The politics are aggressively expansionist, where strength means military might, and where life and liberty can be acquired at the price of people whose limitations or death are not felt to mean much at all. Pushkin turns Byron's Orientalism, then, into a narrative of conquest in his first try at the genre. By his next effort, he is already using the Oriental tale's violence less exploitatively— which is to say that the murdered "others" in *The Fountain of Bakhchisarai* will be not so very "other" after all.

FURTHER READING

Bibliography

Wreath, Patrick J., and Wreath, April I. "Alexander Pushkin: A Bibliography of Criticism in English." *Canadian-American Slavic Studies* 10, No. 2 (Summer 1976): 279-304.
> Lists essays and books published in English between 1920 and 1975 as well as selected reviews of books about Pushkin.

Biography

Magarshack, David. *Pushkin: A Biography.* New York: Grove Press, 1967, 320 p.
> Comprehensive and well-received biography of Pushkin.

Vickery, Walter N. *Pushkin: Death of a Poet.* Bloomington: Indiana University Press, 1968, 146 p.
> Covers Pushkin's fatal duel with Georges d'Anthes and the events which led to it.

Criticism

Berman, Marshall. "Pushkin's *Bronze Horseman*: The Clerk and the Tsar." In his *All That Is Solid Melts into Air: The Experience of Modernity*, pp. 181-89. New York: Simon and Schuster, 1982.
> Discusses *The Bronze Horseman* in relation to its St. Petersburg setting.

Bethea, David M., ed. *Puškin Today.* Bloomington: Indiana University Press, 1993, 258 p.
> Collection of essays covering various topics in Pushkin's writings as well as commentary on his life and its context.

Bloom, Harold, ed. *Alexander Pushkin.* Modern Critical Views. New York: Chelsea House Publishers, 1987, 231 p.
> Collects essays by American, English, and Russian critics on various aspects of Pushkin's writings.

Clayton, J. Douglas. *Ice and Flame: Aleksandr Pushkin's "Eugene Onegin."* Toronto: University of Toronto Press, 1985, 224 p.

Detailed analysis of the characters, genre, style, structure, and meaning of Pushkin's novel in verse..

Cross, Samuel H., and Simmons, Ernest J., eds. *Centennial Essays for Pushkin*. 1937. Reprint. New York: Russell & Russell, 1967, 226 p.

Essays addressing various aspects of Pushkin's life and writings.

Jensen, Peter Albert, and others, eds. *Text and Context: Essays to Honor Nils Ake Nilsson*. Stockholm, Sweden: Almqvist & Wiksell International, 1987, 202 p.

Contains two essays on Pushkin, with one addressing theme in *Count Nulin* and the other covering Pushkin's reaction to liturgical poetry.

Katz, Michael R. "Pushkin's Literary Ballads." In his *The Literary Ballad in Early Nineteenth-Century Russian Literature*, pp. 139-65. London: Oxford University Press, 1976.

Analyzes Pushkin's poems written in the ballad form and assesses his contribution to the ballad genre.

Kodjak, Andrej, and Taranovsky, Kiril, eds. *Alexander Puškin: A Symposium on the 175th Anniversary of His Birth*. New York: New York University Press, 1976, 220 p.

Collection of essays divided into three sections covering Pushkin's poetry, prose, and narrative poetry and drama.

Lavrin, Janko. *Pushkin and Russian Literature*. 1947. Reprint. New York: Russell & Russell, 1969, 226 p.

Overview of Pushkin's life and works. Lavrin considers Pushkin "the most vital link between Russian and English literature."

Lednicki, Wacław. *Pushkin's "Bronze Horseman": The Story of a Masterpiece*. Berkeley: University of California Press, 1955, 163 p.

Interprets *The Bronze Horseman*, focusing on its "autonomy of aesthetic motifs," its unity of aesthetic purpose, and the theme of the state versus the individual. Lednicki also argues that the poem should be considered in the context of Pushkin's interest in the political problems of Poland and his friendship with the Polish poet Adam Mickiewicz.

Mandelker, Amy, and Reeder, Roberta, eds. *The Supernatural in Slavic and Baltic Literature: Essays in Honor of Victor Terras*. Colombus, Ohio: Slavica Publishers, 1988, 402 p.

Contains two essays addressing the supernatural in *The Bronze Horseman* and two other studies that cover Pushkin's poetry in general.

Muchnic, Helen. "Pushkin's Unwritten Poetics." *Transactions of the Association of Russian-American Scholars in the U.S.A.* XX (1987): 3-32.

Overview of Pushkin's career focusing on the dominant themes and tone of his works.

Shaw, J. Thomas. "Parts of Speech in Puškin's Rhymewords and Nonrhymed Endwords." *The Slavic and East European Journal* 37, No. 1 (Spring 1993): 1-22.

Statistical analysis of Pushkin's choice of rhymewords throughout his career.

Vickery, Walter N. *Alexander Pushkin*. New York: Twayne Publishers, 1970, 211 p.

Critical overview of Pushkin's life and works.

Additional coverage of Pushkin's life and career is contained in the following sources published by Gale Research: *DISCovering Authors*; *Nineteenth-Century Literature Criticism*, Vols. 3, 27; *Something about the Author*, Vol. 61; and *World Literature Criticism*.

Poetry Criticism
INDEXES

Literary Criticism Series
Cumulative Author Index

Cumulative Nationality Index

Cumulative Title Index

How to Use This Index

The main references

> Calvino, Italo
> 1923-1985.....CLC 5, 8, 11, 22, 33, 39,
>   73; SSC 3

list all author entries in the following Gale Literary Criticism series:

BLC = *Black Literature Criticism*
CLC = *Contemporary Literary Criticism*
CLR = *Children's Literature Review*
CMLC = *Classical and Medieval Literature Criticism*
DA = *DISCovering Authors*
DC = *Drama Criticism*
HLC = *Hispanic Literature Criticism*
LC = *Literature Criticism from 1400 to 1800*
NCLC = *Nineteenth-Century Literature Criticism*
PC = *Poetry Criticism*
SSC = *Short Story Criticism*
TCLC = *Twentieth-Century Literary Criticism*
WLC = *World Literature Criticism, 1500 to the Present*

The cross-references

> See also CANR 23; CA 85-88;
>   obituary CA 116

list all author entries in the following Gale biographical and literary sources:

AAYA = *Authors & Artists for Young Adults*
AITN = *Authors in the News*
BEST = *Bestsellers*
BW = *Black Writers*
CA = *Contemporary Authors*
CAAS = *Contemporary Authors Autobiography Series*
CABS = *Contemporary Authors Bibliographical Series*
CANR = *Contemporary Authors New Revision Series*
CAP = *Contemporary Authors Permanent Series*
CDALB = *Concise Dictionary of American Literary Biography*
CDBLB = *Concise Dictionary of British Literary Biography*
DLB = *Dictionary of Literary Biography*
DLBD = *Dictionary of Literary Biography Documentary Series*
DLBY = *Dictionary of Literary Biography Yearbook*
HW = *Hispanic Writers*
JRDA = *Junior DISCovering Authors*
MAICYA = *Major Authors and Illustrators for Children and Young Adults*
MTCW = *Major 20th-Century Writers*
NNAL = *Native North American Literature*
SAAS = *Something about the Author Autobiography Series*
SATA = *Something about the Author*
YABC = *Yesterday's Authors of Books for Children*

Literary Criticism Series
Cumulative Author Index

A.
See Arnold, Matthew

A. E. . . . . **TCLC 3, 10**
See also Russell, George William
See also DLB 19

A. M.
See Megged, Aharon

A. R. P-C
See Galsworthy, John

Abasiyanik, Sait Faik 1906-1954
See Sait Faik
See also CA 123

Abbey, Edward 1927-1989 . . . . . . **CLC 36, 59**
See also CA 45-48; 128; CANR 2, 41

Abbott, Lee K(ittredge) 1947- . . . . . . **CLC 48**
See also CA 124; DLB 130

Abe, Kobo 1924-1993 . . . . . **CLC 8, 22, 53, 81**
See also CA 65-68; 140; CANR 24; MTCW

Abelard, Peter c. 1079-c. 1142 . . . **CMLC 11**
See also DLB 115

Abell, Kjeld 1901-1961 . . . . **CLC 15**
See also CA 111

Abish, Walter 1931- . . . . **CLC 22**
See also CA 101; CANR 37; DLB 130

Abrahams, Peter (Henry) 1919- . . . . . **CLC 4**
See also BW 1; CA 57-60; CANR 26;
DLB 117; MTCW

Abrams, M(eyer) H(oward) 1912-... **CLC 24**
See also CA 57-60; CANR 13, 33; DLB 67

Abse, Dannie 1923-. . . . . **CLC 7, 29**
See also CA 53-56; CAAS 1; CANR 4;
DLB 27

Achebe, (Albert) Chinua(lumogu)
1930- . . . . . **CLC 1, 3, 5, 7, 11, 26, 51, 75;**
BLC; DA; WLC
See also BW 2; CA 1-4R; CANR 6, 26;
CLR 20; DLB 117; MAICYA; MTCW;
SATA 38, 40

Acker, Kathy 1948- . . . . **CLC 45**
See also CA 117; 122

Ackroyd, Peter 1949- . . . . **CLC 34, 52**
See also CA 123; 127

Acorn, Milton 1923-. . . . . **CLC 15**
See also CA 103; DLB 53

Adamov, Arthur 1908-1970 . . . . . . **CLC 4, 25**
See also CA 17-18; 25-28R; CAP 2; MTCW

Adams, Alice (Boyd) 1926- ... **CLC 6, 13, 46**
See also CA 81-84; CANR 26; DLBY 86;
MTCW

Adams, Andy 1859-1935. . . . . **TCLC 56**
See also YABC 1

Adams, Douglas (Noel) 1952- ... **CLC 27, 60**
See also AAYA 4; BEST 89:3; CA 106;
CANR 34; DLBY 83; JRDA

Adams, Francis 1862-1893. . . . . . . **NCLC 33**

Adams, Henry (Brooks)
1838-1918 . . . . **TCLC 4, 52; DA**
See also CA 104; 133; DLB 12, 47

Adams, Richard (George)
1920- . . . . **CLC 4, 5, 18**
See also AITN 1, 2; CA 49-52; CANR 3,
35; CLR 20; JRDA; MAICYA; MTCW;
SATA 7, 69

Adamson, Joy(-Friederike Victoria)
1910-1980 . . . . **CLC 17**
See also CA 69-72; 93-96; CANR 22;
MTCW; SATA 11, 22

Adcock, Fleur 1934-. . . . . **CLC 41**
See also CA 25-28R; CANR 11, 34;
DLB 40

Addams, Charles (Samuel)
1912-1988 . . . . **CLC 30**
See also CA 61-64; 126; CANR 12

Addison, Joseph 1672-1719 . . . . **LC 18**
See also CDBLB 1660-1789; DLB 101

Adler, C(arole) S(chwerdtfeger)
1932-. . . . . **CLC 35**
See also AAYA 4; CA 89-92; CANR 19,
40; JRDA; MAICYA; SAAS 15;
SATA 26, 63

Adler, Renata 1938-. . . . . **CLC 8, 31**
See also CA 49-52; CANR 5, 22; MTCW

Ady, Endre 1877-1919 . . . . **TCLC 11**
See also CA 107

Aeschylus
525B.C.-456B.C. . . . . **CMLC 11; DA**

Afton, Effie
See Harper, Frances Ellen Watkins

Agapida, Fray Antonio
See Irving, Washington

Agee, James (Rufus)
1909-1955 . . . . **TCLC 1, 19**
See also AITN 1; CA 108;
CDALB 1941-1968; DLB 2, 26

Aghill, Gordon
See Silverberg, Robert

Agnon, S(hmuel) Y(osef Halevi)
1888-1970 . . . . **CLC 4, 8, 14**
See also CA 17-18; 25-28R; CAP 2; MTCW

Aherne, Owen
See Cassill, R(onald) V(erlin)

Ai 1947-. . . . . **CLC 4, 14, 69**
See also CA 85-88; CAAS 13; DLB 120

Aickman, Robert (Fordyce)
1914-1981 . . . . **CLC 57**
See also CA 5-8R; CANR 3

Aiken, Conrad (Potter)
1889-1973 . . . **CLC 1, 3, 5, 10, 52; SSC 9**
See also CA 5-8R; 45-48; CANR 4;
CDALB 1929-1941; DLB 9, 45, 102;
MTCW; SATA 3, 30

Aiken, Joan (Delano) 1924-. . . . . **CLC 35**
See also AAYA 1; CA 9-12R; CANR 4, 23,
34; CLR 1, 19; JRDA; MAICYA;
MTCW; SAAS 1; SATA 2, 30, 73

Ainsworth, William Harrison
1805-1882 . . . . **NCLC 13**
See also DLB 21; SATA 24

Aitmatov, Chingiz (Torekulovich)
1928- . . . . **CLC 71**
See also CA 103; CANR 38; MTCW;
SATA 56

Akers, Floyd
See Baum, L(yman) Frank

Akhmadulina, Bella Akhatovna
1937- . . . . **CLC 53**
See also CA 65-68

Akhmatova, Anna
1888-1966 . . . . **CLC 11, 25, 64; PC 2**
See also CA 19-20; 25-28R; CANR 35;
CAP 1; MTCW

Aksakov, Sergei Timofeyvich
1791-1859 . . . . **NCLC 2**

Aksenov, Vassily . . . . **CLC 22**
See also Aksyonov, Vassily (Pavlovich)

Aksyonov, Vassily (Pavlovich)
1932- . . . . **CLC 37**
See also Aksenov, Vassily
See also CA 53-56; CANR 12

Akutagawa Ryunosuke
1892-1927 . . . . **TCLC 16**
See also CA 117

Alain 1868-1951 . . . . **TCLC 41**

Alain-Fournier . . . . **TCLC 6**
See also Fournier, Henri Alban
See also DLB 65

Alarcon, Pedro Antonio de
1833-1891 . . . . **NCLC 1**

Alas (y Urena), Leopoldo (Enrique Garcia)
1852-1901 . . . . **TCLC 29**
See also CA 113; 131; HW

Albee, Edward (Franklin III)
1928- . . . . . . **CLC 1, 2, 3, 5, 9, 11, 13, 25,**
53; DA; WLC
See also AITN 1; CA 5-8R; CABS 3;
CANR 8; CDALB 1941-1968; DLB 7;
MTCW

Alberti, Rafael 1902-. . . . . **CLC 7**
See also CA 85-88; DLB 108

Alcala-Galiano, Juan Valera y
See Valera y Alcala-Galiano, Juan

Alcott, Amos Bronson 1799-1888 . . **NCLC 1**
See also DLB 1

Alcott, Louisa May
1832-1888 . . . . **NCLC 6; DA; WLC**
See also CDALB 1865-1917; CLR 1;
DLB 1, 42, 79; JRDA; MAICYA;
YABC 1

Anthony, Florence
  See Ai

Anthony, John
  See Ciardi, John (Anthony)

Anthony, Peter
  See Shaffer, Anthony (Joshua); Shaffer,
    Peter (Levin)

Anthony, Piers 1934- . . . . **CLC 35**
  See also AAYA 11; CA 21-24R; CANR 28;
    DLB 8; MTCW

Antoine, Marc
  See Proust, (Valentin-Louis-George-Eugene-)
    Marcel

Antoninus, Brother
  See Everson, William (Oliver)

Antonioni, Michelangelo 1912- . . . . . **CLC 20**
  See also CA 73-76; CANR 45

Antschel, Paul 1920-1970. . . . . . **CLC 10, 19**
  See also Celan, Paul
  See also CA 85-88; CANR 33; MTCW

Anwar, Chairil 1922-1949 . . . . **TCLC 22**
  See also CA 121

Apollinaire, Guillaume . . **TCLC 3, 8, 51; PC 7**
  See also Kostrowitzki, Wilhelm Apollinaris
    de

Appelfeld, Aharon 1932- . . . . **CLC 23, 47**
  See also CA 112; 133

Apple, Max (Isaac) 1941-. . . . . . . **CLC 9, 33**
  See also CA 81-84; CANR 19; DLB 130

Appleman, Philip (Dean) 1926- . . . . . **CLC 51**
  See also CA 13-16R; CAAS 18; CANR 6,
    29

Appleton, Lawrence
  See Lovecraft, H(oward) P(hillips)

Apteryx
  See Eliot, T(homas) S(tearns)

Apuleius, (Lucius Madaurensis)
  125(?)-175(?) . . . . **CMLC 1**

Aquin, Hubert 1929-1977. . . . . **CLC 15**
  See also CA 105; DLB 53

Aragon, Louis 1897-1982 . . . . **CLC 3, 22**
  See also CA 69-72; 108; CANR 28;
    DLB 72; MTCW

Arany, Janos 1817-1882. . . . . **NCLC 34**

Arbuthnot, John 1667-1735 . . . . **LC 1**
  See also DLB 101

Archer, Herbert Winslow
  See Mencken, H(enry) L(ouis)

Archer, Jeffrey (Howard) 1940- . . . . **CLC 28**
  See also BEST 89:3; CA 77-80; CANR 22

Archer, Jules 1915- . . . . **CLC 12**
  See also CA 9-12R; CANR 6; SAAS 5;
    SATA 4

Archer, Lee
  See Ellison, Harlan

Arden, John 1930- . . . . **CLC 6, 13, 15**
  See also CA 13-16R; CAAS 4; CANR 31;
    DLB 13; MTCW

Arenas, Reinaldo
  1943-1990 . . . . **CLC 41; HLC**
  See also CA 124; 128; 133; HW

Arendt, Hannah 1906-1975 . . . . **CLC 66**
  See also CA 17-20R; 61-64; CANR 26;
    MTCW

Aretino, Pietro 1492-1556 . . . . **LC 12**

Arghezi, Tudor. . . . . **CLC 80**
  See also Theodorescu, Ion N.

Arguedas, Jose Maria
  1911-1969 . . . . **CLC 10, 18**
  See also CA 89-92; DLB 113; HW

Argueta, Manlio 1936-. . . . . **CLC 31**
  See also CA 131; HW

Ariosto, Ludovico 1474-1533. . . . . **LC 6**

Aristides
  See Epstein, Joseph

Aristophanes
  450B.C.-385B.C. . . . **CMLC 4; DA; DC 2**

Arlt, Roberto (Godofredo Christophersen)
  1900-1942 . . . . **TCLC 29; HLC**
  See also CA 123; 131; HW

Armah, Ayi Kwei 1939- . . . . **CLC 5, 33; BLC**
  See also BW 1; CA 61-64; CANR 21;
    DLB 117; MTCW

Armatrading, Joan 1950- . . . . **CLC 17**
  See also CA 114

Arnette, Robert
  See Silverberg, Robert

Arnim, Achim von (Ludwig Joachim von
    Arnim) 1781-1831 . . . . **NCLC 5**
  See also DLB 90

Arnim, Bettina von 1785-1859. . . . **NCLC 38**
  See also DLB 90

Arnold, Matthew
  1822-1888 . . . . . **NCLC 6, 29; DA; PC 5;
                                                     WLC**
  See also CDBLB 1832-1890; DLB 32, 57

Arnold, Thomas 1795-1842 . . . . . **NCLC 18**
  See also DLB 55

Arnow, Harriette (Louisa) Simpson
  1908-1986 . . . . **CLC 2, 7, 18**
  See also CA 9-12R; 118; CANR 14; DLB 6;
    MTCW; SATA 42, 47

Arp, Hans
  See Arp, Jean

Arp, Jean 1887-1966. . . . . **CLC 5**
  See also CA 81-84; 25-28R; CANR 42

Arrabal
  See Arrabal, Fernando

Arrabal, Fernando 1932- . . . **CLC 2, 9, 18, 58**
  See also CA 9-12R; CANR 15

Arrick, Fran. . . . . **CLC 30**

Artaud, Antonin 1896-1948 . . . . . **TCLC 3, 36**
  See also CA 104

Arthur, Ruth M(abel) 1905-1979. . . . **CLC 12**
  See also CA 9-12R; 85-88; CANR 4;
    SATA 7, 26

Artsybashev, Mikhail (Petrovich)
  1878-1927 . . . . **TCLC 31**

Arundel, Honor (Morfydd)
  1919-1973 . . . . **CLC 17**
  See also CA 21-22; 41-44R; CAP 2;
    SATA 4, 24

Asch, Sholem 1880-1957 . . . . **TCLC 3**
  See also CA 105

Ash, Shalom
  See Asch, Sholem

Ashbery, John (Lawrence)
  1927- . . . . . . **CLC 2, 3, 4, 6, 9, 13, 15, 25,
                                                   41, 77**
  See also CA 5-8R; CANR 9, 37; DLB 5;
    DLBY 81; MTCW

Ashdown, Clifford
  See Freeman, R(ichard) Austin

Ashe, Gordon
  See Creasey, John

Ashton-Warner, Sylvia (Constance)
  1908-1984 . . . . **CLC 19**
  See also CA 69-72; 112; CANR 29; MTCW

Asimov, Isaac
  1920-1992 . . . . . . **CLC 1, 3, 9, 19, 26, 76**
  See also BEST 90:2; CA 1-4R; 137;
    CANR 2, 19, 36; CLR 12; DLB 8;
    DLBY 92; JRDA; MAICYA; MTCW;
    SATA 1, 26, 74

Astley, Thea (Beatrice May)
  1925- . . . . **CLC 41**
  See also CA 65-68; CANR 11, 43

Aston, James
  See White, T(erence) H(anbury)

Asturias, Miguel Angel
  1899-1974 . . . . **CLC 3, 8, 13; HLC**
  See also CA 25-28; 49-52; CANR 32;
    CAP 2; DLB 113; HW; MTCW

Atares, Carlos Saura
  See Saura (Atares), Carlos

Atheling, William
  See Pound, Ezra (Weston Loomis)

Atheling, William, Jr.
  See Blish, James (Benjamin)

Atherton, Gertrude (Franklin Horn)
  1857-1948 . . . . **TCLC 2**
  See also CA 104; DLB 9, 78

Atherton, Lucius
  See Masters, Edgar Lee

Atkins, Jack
  See Harris, Mark

Atticus
  See Fleming, Ian (Lancaster)

Atwood, Margaret (Eleanor)
  1939- . . . . . **CLC 2, 3, 4, 8, 13, 15, 25, 44,
                                        84; DA; PC 8; SSC 2; WLC**
  See also AAYA 12; BEST 89:2; CA 49-52;
    CANR 3, 24, 33; DLB 53; MTCW;
    SATA 50

Aubigny, Pierre d'
  See Mencken, H(enry) L(ouis)

Aubin, Penelope 1685-1731(?) . . . . **LC 9**
  See also DLB 39

Auchincloss, Louis (Stanton)
  1917- . . . . **CLC 4, 6, 9, 18, 45**
  See also CA 1-4R; CANR 6, 29; DLB 2;
    DLBY 80; MTCW

Auden, W(ystan) H(ugh)
  1907-1973 . . . . . . **CLC 1, 2, 3, 4, 6, 9, 11,
                                                   14, 43; DA; PC 1; WLC**
  See also CA 9-12R; 45-48; CANR 5;
    CDBLB 1914-1945; DLB 10, 20; MTCW

Audiberti, Jacques 1900-1965 . . . . . . **CLC 38**
  See also CA 25-28R

Behrman, S(amuel) N(athaniel)
  1893-1973 .... **CLC 40**
  See also CA 13-16; 45-48; CAP 1; DLB 7,
  44

Belasco, David 1853-1931 .... **TCLC 3**
  See also CA 104; DLB 7

Belcheva, Elisaveta 1893- .... **CLC 10**

Beldone, Phil "Cheech"
  See Ellison, Harlan

Beleno
  See Azuela, Mariano

Belinski, Vissarion Grigoryevich
  1811-1848 .... **NCLC 5**

Belitt, Ben 1911-................. **CLC 22**
  See also CA 13-16R; CAAS 4; CANR 7;
  DLB 5

Bell, James Madison
  1826-1902 .... **TCLC 43; BLC**
  See also BW 1; CA 122; 124; DLB 50

Bell, Madison (Smartt) 1957- ...... **CLC 41**
  See also CA 111; CANR 28

Bell, Marvin (Hartley) 1937-..... **CLC 8, 31**
  See also CA 21-24R; CAAS 14; DLB 5;
  MTCW

Bell, W. L. D.
  See Mencken, H(enry) L(ouis)

Bellamy, Atwood C.
  See Mencken, H(enry) L(ouis)

Bellamy, Edward 1850-1898 ...... **NCLC 4**
  See also DLB 12

Bellin, Edward J.
  See Kuttner, Henry

Belloc, (Joseph) Hilaire (Pierre)
  1870-1953 .... **TCLC 7, 18**
  See also CA 106; DLB 19, 100, 141;
  YABC 1

Belloc, Joseph Peter Rene Hilaire
  See Belloc, (Joseph) Hilaire (Pierre)

Belloc, Joseph Pierre Hilaire
  See Belloc, (Joseph) Hilaire (Pierre)

Belloc, M. A.
  See Lowndes, Marie Adelaide (Belloc)

Bellow, Saul
  1915- ...... **CLC 1, 2, 3, 6, 8, 10, 13, 15,
  25, 33, 34, 63, 79; DA; SSC 14; WLC**
  See also AITN 2; BEST 89:3; CA 5-8R;
  CABS 1; CANR 29; CDALB 1941-1968;
  DLB 2, 28; DLBD 3; DLBY 82; MTCW

Belser, Reimond Karel Maria de
  1929- .... **CLC 14**

Bely, Andrey .... **TCLC 7**
  See also Bugayev, Boris Nikolayevich

Benary, Margot
  See Benary-Isbert, Margot

Benary-Isbert, Margot 1889-1979... **CLC 12**
  See also CA 5-8R; 89-92; CANR 4;
  CLR 12; MAICYA; SATA 2, 21

Benavente (y Martinez), Jacinto
  1866-1954 .... **TCLC 3**
  See also CA 106; 131; HW; MTCW

Benchley, Peter (Bradford)
  1940- .... **CLC 4, 8**
  See also AITN 2; CA 17-20R; CANR 12,
  35; MTCW; SATA 3

Benchley, Robert (Charles)
  1889-1945 .... **TCLC 1, 55**
  See also CA 105; DLB 11

Benedikt, Michael 1935- .... **CLC 4, 14**
  See also CA 13-16R; CANR 7; DLB 5

Benet, Juan 1927-................ **CLC 28**
  See also CA 143

Benet, Stephen Vincent
  1898-1943 .... **TCLC 7; SSC 10**
  See also CA 104; DLB 4, 48, 102; YABC 1

Benet, William Rose 1886-1950 ... **TCLC 28**
  See also CA 118; DLB 45

Benford, Gregory (Albert) 1941-.... **CLC 52**
  See also CA 69-72; CANR 12, 24;
  DLBY 82

Bengtsson, Frans (Gunnar)
  1894-1954 .... **TCLC 48**

Benjamin, David
  See Slavitt, David R(ytman)

Benjamin, Lois
  See Gould, Lois

Benjamin, Walter 1892-1940 ..... **TCLC 39**

Benn, Gottfried 1886-1956........ **TCLC 3**
  See also CA 106; DLB 56

Bennett, Alan 1934- .... **CLC 45, 77**
  See also CA 103; CANR 35; MTCW

Bennett, (Enoch) Arnold
  1867-1931 .... **TCLC 5, 20**
  See also CA 106; CDBLB 1890-1914;
  DLB 10, 34, 98

Bennett, Elizabeth
  See Mitchell, Margaret (Munnerlyn)

Bennett, George Harold 1930-
  See Bennett, Hal
  See also BW 1; CA 97-100

Bennett, Hal .... **CLC 5**
  See also Bennett, George Harold
  See also DLB 33

Bennett, Jay 1912-............... **CLC 35**
  See also AAYA 10; CA 69-72; CANR 11,
  42; JRDA; SAAS 4; SATA 27, 41

Bennett, Louise (Simone)
  1919- .... **CLC 28; BLC**
  See also BW 2; DLB 117

Benson, E(dward) F(rederic)
  1867-1940 .... **TCLC 27**
  See also CA 114; DLB 135

Benson, Jackson J. 1930-.......... **CLC 34**
  See also CA 25-28R; DLB 111

Benson, Sally 1900-1972 .... **CLC 17**
  See also CA 19-20; 37-40R; CAP 1;
  SATA 1, 27, 35

Benson, Stella 1892-1933........ **TCLC 17**
  See also CA 117; DLB 36

Bentham, Jeremy 1748-1832 ..... **NCLC 38**
  See also DLB 107

Bentley, E(dmund) C(lerihew)
  1875-1956 .... **TCLC 12**
  See also CA 108; DLB 70

Bentley, Eric (Russell) 1916-....... **CLC 24**
  See also CA 5-8R; CANR 6

Beranger, Pierre Jean de
  1780-1857 .... **NCLC 34**

Berger, Colonel
  See Malraux, (Georges-)Andre

Berger, John (Peter) 1926- ...... **CLC 2, 19**
  See also CA 81-84; DLB 14

Berger, Melvin H. 1927- .... **CLC 12**
  See also CA 5-8R; CANR 4; CLR 32;
  SAAS 2; SATA 5

Berger, Thomas (Louis)
  1924- .... **CLC 3, 5, 8, 11, 18, 38**
  See also CA 1-4R; CANR 5, 28; DLB 2;
  DLBY 80; MTCW

Bergman, (Ernst) Ingmar
  1918- .... **CLC 16, 72**
  See also CA 81-84; CANR 33

Bergson, Henri 1859-1941 .... **TCLC 32**

Bergstein, Eleanor 1938- .... **CLC 4**
  See also CA 53-56; CANR 5

Berkoff, Steven 1937-............. **CLC 56**
  See also CA 104

Bermant, Chaim (Icyk) 1929- ...... **CLC 40**
  See also CA 57-60; CANR 6, 31

Bern, Victoria
  See Fisher, M(ary) F(rances) K(ennedy)

Bernanos, (Paul Louis) Georges
  1888-1948 .... **TCLC 3**
  See also CA 104; 130; DLB 72

Bernard, April 1956- .... **CLC 59**
  See also CA 131

Berne, Victoria
  See Fisher, M(ary) F(rances) K(ennedy)

Bernhard, Thomas
  1931-1989 .... **CLC 3, 32, 61**
  See also CA 85-88; 127; CANR 32;
  DLB 85, 124; MTCW

Berrigan, Daniel 1921-............. **CLC 4**
  See also CA 33-36R; CAAS 1; CANR 11,
  43; DLB 5

Berrigan, Edmund Joseph Michael, Jr.
  1934-1983
  See Berrigan, Ted
  See also CA 61-64; 110; CANR 14

Berrigan, Ted.................... **CLC 37**
  See also Berrigan, Edmund Joseph Michael,
  Jr.
  See also DLB 5

Berry, Charles Edward Anderson 1931-
  See Berry, Chuck
  See also CA 115

Berry, Chuck.................... **CLC 17**
  See also Berry, Charles Edward Anderson

Berry, Jonas
  See Ashbery, John (Lawrence)

Berry, Wendell (Erdman)
  1934- .... **CLC 4, 6, 8, 27, 46**
  See also AITN 1; CA 73-76; DLB 5, 6

Berryman, John
  1914-1972 ...... **CLC 1, 2, 3, 4, 6, 8, 10,
  13, 25, 62**
  See also CA 13-16; 33-36R; CABS 2;
  CANR 35; CAP 1; CDALB 1941-1968;
  DLB 48; MTCW

Bertolucci, Bernardo 1940- .... **CLC 16**
  See also CA 106

Bertrand, Aloysius 1807-1841 .... **NCLC 31**

Bertran de Born   c. 1140-1215 . . . . . **CMLC 5**

Besant, Annie (Wood)   1847-1933 . . . **TCLC 9**
See also CA 105

Bessie, Alvah   1904-1985. . . . . **CLC 23**
See also CA 5-8R; 116; CANR 2; DLB 26

Bethlen, T. D.
See Silverberg, Robert

Beti, Mongo. . . . . **CLC 27; BLC**
See also Biyidi, Alexandre

Betjeman, John
1906-1984 . . . . **CLC 2, 6, 10, 34, 43**
See also CA 9-12R; 112; CANR 33;
CDBLB 1945-1960; DLB 20; DLBY 84;
MTCW

Bettelheim, Bruno   1903-1990 . . . . . . **CLC 79**
See also CA 81-84; 131; CANR 23; MTCW

Betti, Ugo   1892-1953 . . . . **TCLC 5**
See also CA 104

Betts, Doris (Waugh)   1932- . . . . **CLC 3, 6, 28**
See also CA 13-16R; CANR 9; DLBY 82

Bevan, Alistair
See Roberts, Keith (John Kingston)

Beynon, John
See Harris, John (Wyndham Parkes Lucas)
Beynon

Bialik, Chaim Nachman
1873-1934 . . . . **TCLC 25**

Bickerstaff, Isaac
See Swift, Jonathan

Bidart, Frank   1939- . . . . **CLC 33**
See also CA 140

Bienek, Horst   1930- . . . . **CLC 7, 11**
See also CA 73-76; DLB 75

Bierce, Ambrose (Gwinett)
1842-1914(?) . . . . **TCLC 1, 7, 44; DA;
SSC 9; WLC**
See also CA 104; 139; CDALB 1865-1917;
DLB 11, 12, 23, 71, 74

Billings, Josh
See Shaw, Henry Wheeler

Billington, (Lady) Rachel (Mary)
1942- . . . . **CLC 43**
See also AITN 2; CA 33-36R; CANR 44

Binyon, T(imothy) J(ohn)   1936- . . . . **CLC 34**
See also CA 111; CANR 28

Bioy Casares, Adolfo
1914- . . . . **CLC 4, 8, 13; HLC**
See also CA 29-32R; CANR 19, 43;
DLB 113; HW; MTCW

Bird, C.
See Ellison, Harlan

Bird, Cordwainer
See Ellison, Harlan

Bird, Robert Montgomery
1806-1854 . . . . **NCLC 1**

Birney, (Alfred) Earle
1904- . . . . **CLC 1, 4, 6, 11**
See also CA 1-4R; CANR 5, 20; DLB 88;
MTCW

Bishop, Elizabeth
1911-1979 . . . . . . **CLC 1, 4, 9, 13, 15, 32;
DA; PC 3**
See also CA 5-8R; 89-92; CABS 2;
CANR 26; CDALB 1968-1988; DLB 5;
MTCW; SATA 24

Bishop, John   1935- . . . . **CLC 10**
See also CA 105

Bissett, Bill   1939- . . . . **CLC 18**
See also CA 69-72; CAAS 19; CANR 15;
DLB 53; MTCW

Bitov, Andrei (Georgievich)   1937- . . . **CLC 57**
See also CA 142

Biyidi, Alexandre   1932-
See Beti, Mongo
See also BW 1; CA 114; 124; MTCW

Bjarme, Brynjolf
See Ibsen, Henrik (Johan)

Bjornson, Bjornstjerne (Martinius)
1832-1910 . . . . **TCLC 7, 37**
See also CA 104

Black, Robert
See Holdstock, Robert P.

Blackburn, Paul   1926-1971 . . . . . . **CLC 9, 43**
See also CA 81-84; 33-36R; CANR 34;
DLB 16; DLBY 81

Black Elk   1863-1950 . . . . **TCLC 33**
See also CA 144

Black Hobart
See Sanders, (James) Ed(ward)

Blacklin, Malcolm
See Chambers, Aidan

Blackmore, R(ichard) D(oddridge)
1825-1900 . . . . **TCLC 27**
See also CA 120; DLB 18

Blackmur, R(ichard) P(almer)
1904-1965 . . . . **CLC 2, 24**
See also CA 11-12; 25-28R; CAP 1; DLB 63

Black Tarantula, The
See Acker, Kathy

Blackwood, Algernon (Henry)
1869-1951 . . . . **TCLC 5**
See also CA 105

Blackwood, Caroline   1931- . . . . **CLC 6, 9**
See also CA 85-88; CANR 32; DLB 14;
MTCW

Blade, Alexander
See Hamilton, Edmond; Silverberg, Robert

Blaga, Lucian   1895-1961 . . . . **CLC 75**

Blair, Eric (Arthur)   1903-1950
See Orwell, George
See also CA 104; 132; DA; MTCW;
SATA 29

Blais, Marie-Claire
1939- . . . . **CLC 2, 4, 6, 13, 22**
See also CA 21-24R; CAAS 4; CANR 38;
DLB 53; MTCW

Blaise, Clark   1940- . . . . **CLC 29**
See also AITN 2; CA 53-56; CAAS 3;
CANR 5; DLB 53

Blake, Nicholas
See Day Lewis, C(ecil)
See also DLB 77

Blake, William
1757-1827 . . . . . **NCLC 13, 37; DA; WLC**
See also CDBLB 1789-1832; DLB 93;
MAICYA; SATA 30

Blasco Ibanez, Vicente
1867-1928 . . . . **TCLC 12**
See also CA 110; 131; HW; MTCW

Blatty, William Peter   1928- . . . . **CLC 2**
See also CA 5-8R; CANR 9

Bleeck, Oliver
See Thomas, Ross (Elmore)

Blessing, Lee   1949- . . . . **CLC 54**

Blish, James (Benjamin)
1921-1975 . . . . **CLC 14**
See also CA 1-4R; 57-60; CANR 3; DLB 8;
MTCW; SATA 66

Bliss, Reginald
See Wells, H(erbert) G(eorge)

Blixen, Karen (Christentze Dinesen)
1885-1962
See Dinesen, Isak
See also CA 25-28; CANR 22; CAP 2;
MTCW; SATA 44

Bloch, Robert (Albert)   1917- . . . . **CLC 33**
See also CA 5-8R; CANR 5; DLB 44;
SATA 12

Blok, Alexander (Alexandrovich)
1880-1921 . . . . **TCLC 5**
See also CA 104

Blom, Jan
See Breytenbach, Breyten

Bloom, Harold   1930- . . . . **CLC 24**
See also CA 13-16R; CANR 39; DLB 67

Bloomfield, Aurelius
See Bourne, Randolph S(illiman)

Blount, Roy (Alton), Jr.   1941- . . . . . **CLC 38**
See also CA 53-56; CANR 10, 28; MTCW

Bloy, Leon   1846-1917. . . . . **TCLC 22**
See also CA 121; DLB 123

Blume, Judy (Sussman)   1938- . . . **CLC 12, 30**
See also AAYA 3; CA 29-32R; CANR 13,
37; CLR 2, 15; DLB 52; JRDA;
MAICYA; MTCW; SATA 2, 31

Blunden, Edmund (Charles)
1896-1974 . . . . **CLC 2, 56**
See also CA 17-18; 45-48; CAP 2; DLB 20,
100; MTCW

Bly, Robert (Elwood)
1926- . . . . **CLC 1, 2, 5, 10, 15, 38**
See also CA 5-8R; CANR 41; DLB 5;
MTCW

Boas, Franz   1858-1942. . . . . **TCLC 56**
See also CA 115

Bobette
See Simenon, Georges (Jacques Christian)

Boccaccio, Giovanni
1313-1375 . . . . **CMLC 13; SSC 10**

Bochco, Steven   1943- . . . . **CLC 35**
See also AAYA 11; CA 124; 138

Bodenheim, Maxwell   1892-1954 . . . **TCLC 44**
See also CA 110; DLB 9, 45

Bodker, Cecil   1927- . . . . **CLC 21**
See also CA 73-76; CANR 13, 44; CLR 23;
MAICYA; SATA 14

Boell, Heinrich (Theodor) 1917-1985
See Boll, Heinrich (Theodor)
See also CA 21-24R; 116; CANR 24; DA;
DLB 69; DLBY 85; MTCW

Boerne, Alfred
See Doeblin, Alfred

Bogan, Louise 1897-1970..... **CLC 4, 39, 46**
See also CA 73-76; 25-28R; CANR 33;
DLB 45; MTCW

Bogarde, Dirk .... **CLC 19**
See also Van Den Bogarde, Derek Jules
Gaspard Ulric Niven
See also DLB 14

Bogosian, Eric 1953- .... **CLC 45**
See also CA 138

Bograd, Larry 1953-............. **CLC 35**
See also CA 93-96; SATA 33

Boiardo, Matteo Maria 1441-1494 .... **LC 6**

Boileau-Despreaux, Nicolas
1636-1711 .... **LC 3**

Boland, Eavan (Aisling) 1944-... **CLC 40, 67**
See also CA 143; DLB 40

Boll, Heinrich (Theodor)
1917-1985 .... **CLC 2, 3, 6, 9, 11, 15, 27,
39, 72; WLC**
See also Boell, Heinrich (Theodor)
See also DLB 69; DLBY 85

Bolt, Lee
See Faust, Frederick (Schiller)

Bolt, Robert (Oxton) 1924-........ **CLC 14**
See also CA 17-20R; CANR 35; DLB 13;
MTCW

Bombet, Louis-Alexandre-Cesar
See Stendhal

Bomkauf
See Kaufman, Bob (Garnell)

Bonaventura.................... **NCLC 35**
See also DLB 90

Bond, Edward 1934-....... **CLC 4, 6, 13, 23**
See also CA 25-28R; CANR 38; DLB 13;
MTCW

Bonham, Frank 1914-1989........ **CLC 12**
See also AAYA 1; CA 9-12R; CANR 4, 36;
JRDA; MAICYA; SAAS 3; SATA 1, 49,
62

Bonnefoy, Yves 1923-........ **CLC 9, 15, 58**
See also CA 85-88; CANR 33; MTCW

Bontemps, Arna(ud Wendell)
1902-1973 .... **CLC 1, 18; BLC**
See also BW 1; CA 1-4R; 41-44R; CANR 4,
35; CLR 6; DLB 48, 51; JRDA;
MAICYA; MTCW; SATA 2, 24, 44

Booth, Martin 1944-.............. **CLC 13**
See also CA 93-96; CAAS 2

Booth, Philip 1925-.............. **CLC 23**
See also CA 5-8R; CANR 5; DLBY 82

Booth, Wayne C(layson) 1921- ..... **CLC 24**
See also CA 1-4R; CAAS 5; CANR 3, 43;
DLB 67

Borchert, Wolfgang 1921-1947 ..... **TCLC 5**
See also CA 104; DLB 69, 124

Borel, Petrus 1809-1859........ **NCLC 41**

Borges, Jorge Luis
1899-1986 ... **CLC 1, 2, 3, 4, 6, 8, 9, 10,
13, 19, 44, 48, 83; DA; HLC; SSC 4;
WLC**
See also CA 21-24R; CANR 19, 33;
DLB 113; DLBY 86; HW; MTCW

Borowski, Tadeusz 1922-1951...... **TCLC 9**
See also CA 106

Borrow, George (Henry)
1803-1881 .... **NCLC 9**
See also DLB 21, 55

Bosman, Herman Charles
1905-1951 .... **TCLC 49**

Bosschere, Jean de 1878(?)-1953... **TCLC 19**
See also CA 115

Boswell, James
1740-1795 .... **LC 4; DA; WLC**
See also CDBLB 1660-1789; DLB 104, 142

Bottoms, David 1949-............ **CLC 53**
See also CA 105; CANR 22; DLB 120;
DLBY 83

Boucicault, Dion 1820-1890...... **NCLC 41**

Boucolon, Maryse 1937-
See Conde, Maryse
See also CA 110; CANR 30

Bourget, Paul (Charles Joseph)
1852-1935 .... **TCLC 12**
See also CA 107; DLB 123

Bourjaily, Vance (Nye) 1922-... **CLC 8, 62**
See also CA 1-4R; CAAS 1; CANR 2;
DLB 2, 143

Bourne, Randolph S(illiman)
1886-1918 .... **TCLC 16**
See also CA 117; DLB 63

Bova, Ben(jamin William) 1932-.... **CLC 45**
See also CA 5-8R; CAAS 18; CANR 11;
CLR 3; DLBY 81; MAICYA; MTCW;
SATA 6, 68

Bowen, Elizabeth (Dorothea Cole)
1899-1973 ...... **CLC 1, 3, 6, 11, 15, 22;
SSC 3**
See also CA 17-18; 41-44R; CANR 35;
CAP 2; CDBLB 1945-1960; DLB 15;
MTCW

Bowering, George 1935-........ **CLC 15, 47**
See also CA 21-24R; CAAS 16; CANR 10;
DLB 53

Bowering, Marilyn R(uthe) 1949-... **CLC 32**
See also CA 101

Bowers, Edgar 1924- .... **CLC 9**
See also CA 5-8R; CANR 24; DLB 5

Bowie, David .... **CLC 17**
See also Jones, David Robert

Bowles, Jane (Sydney)
1917-1973 .... **CLC 3, 68**
See also CA 19-20; 41-44R; CAP 2

Bowles, Paul (Frederick)
1910- .... **CLC 1, 2, 19, 53; SSC 3**
See also CA 1-4R; CAAS 1; CANR 1, 19;
DLB 5, 6; MTCW

Box, Edgar
See Vidal, Gore

Boyd, Nancy
See Millay, Edna St. Vincent

Boyd, William 1952-........ **CLC 28, 53, 70**
See also CA 114; 120

Boyle, Kay
1902-1992 ..... **CLC 1, 5, 19, 58; SSC 5**
See also CA 13-16R; 140; CAAS 1;
CANR 29; DLB 4, 9, 48, 86; DLBY 93;
MTCW

Boyle, Mark
See Kienzle, William X(avier)

Boyle, Patrick 1905-1982......... **CLC 19**
See also CA 127

Boyle, T. C.
See Boyle, T(homas) Coraghessan

Boyle, T(homas) Coraghessan
1948-........ **CLC 36, 55; SSC 16**
See also BEST 90:4; CA 120; CANR 44;
DLBY 86

Boz
See Dickens, Charles (John Huffam)

Brackenridge, Hugh Henry
1748-1816 .... **NCLC 7**
See also DLB 11, 37

Bradbury, Edward P.
See Moorcock, Michael (John)

Bradbury, Malcolm (Stanley)
1932- .... **CLC 32, 61**
See also CA 1-4R; CANR 1, 33; DLB 14;
MTCW

Bradbury, Ray (Douglas)
1920- ... **CLC 1, 3, 10, 15, 42; DA; WLC**
See also AITN 1, 2; CA 1-4R; CANR 2, 30;
CDALB 1968-1988; DLB 2, 8; MTCW;
SATA 11, 64

Bradford, Gamaliel 1863-1932..... **TCLC 36**
See also DLB 17

Bradley, David (Henry, Jr.)
1950- .... **CLC 23; BLC**
See also BW 1; CA 104; CANR 26; DLB 33

Bradley, John Ed(mund, Jr.)
1958- .... **CLC 55**
See also CA 139

Bradley, Marion Zimmer 1930-..... **CLC 30**
See also AAYA 9; CA 57-60; CAAS 10;
CANR 7, 31; DLB 8; MTCW

Bradstreet, Anne
1612(?)-1672 .... **LC 4; DA; PC 10**
See also CDALB 1640-1865; DLB 24

Bragg, Melvyn 1939- .... **CLC 10**
See also BEST 89:3; CA 57-60; CANR 10;
DLB 14

Braine, John (Gerard)
1922-1986 .... **CLC 1, 3, 41**
See also CA 1-4R; 120; CANR 1, 33;
CDBLB 1945-1960; DLB 15; DLBY 86;
MTCW

Brammer, William 1930(?)-1978 .... **CLC 31**
See also CA 77-80

Brancati, Vitaliano 1907-1954..... **TCLC 12**
See also CA 109

Brancato, Robin F(idler) 1936-..... **CLC 35**
See also AAYA 9; CA 69-72; CANR 11,
45; CLR 32; JRDA; SAAS 9; SATA 23

Brand, Max
See Faust, Frederick (Schiller)

Copeland, Stewart (Armstrong)
  1952- .... **CLC 26**
  See also Police, The

Coppard, A(lfred) E(dgar)
  1878-1957 .... **TCLC 5**
  See also CA 114; YABC 1

Coppee, Francois 1842-1908 ...... **TCLC 25**

Coppola, Francis Ford 1939- .... **CLC 16**
  See also CA 77-80; CANR 40; DLB 44

Corbiere, Tristan 1845-1875 ..... **NCLC 43**

Corcoran, Barbara 1911- .... **CLC 17**
  See also CA 21-24R; CAAS 2; CANR 11,
  28; DLB 52; JRDA; SATA 3, 77

Cordelier, Maurice
  See Giraudoux, (Hippolyte) Jean

Corelli, Marie 1855-1924........ **TCLC 51**
  See also Mackay, Mary
  See also DLB 34

Corman, Cid................... **CLC 9**
  See also Corman, Sidney
  See also CAAS 2; DLB 5

Corman, Sidney 1924-
  See Corman, Cid
  See also CA 85-88; CANR 44

Cormier, Robert (Edmund)
  1925- .... **CLC 12, 30; DA**
  See also AAYA 3; CA 1-4R; CANR 5, 23;
  CDALB 1968-1988; CLR 12; DLB 52;
  JRDA; MAICYA; MTCW; SATA 10, 45

Corn, Alfred (DeWitt III) 1943- .... **CLC 33**
  See also CA 104; CANR 44; DLB 120;
  DLBY 80

Cornwell, David (John Moore)
  1931- .... **CLC 9, 15**
  See also le Carre, John
  See also CA 5-8R; CANR 13, 33; MTCW

Corrigan, Kevin.................. **CLC 55**

Corso, (Nunzio) Gregory 1930- ... **CLC 1, 11**
  See also CA 5-8R; CANR 41; DLB 5, 16;
  MTCW

Cortazar, Julio
  1914-1984 ...... **CLC 2, 3, 5, 10, 13, 15,**
  33, 34; HLC; SSC 7
  See also CA 21-24R; CANR 12, 32;
  DLB 113; HW; MTCW

Corwin, Cecil
  See Kornbluth, C(yril) M.

Cosic, Dobrica 1921- .... **CLC 14**
  See also CA 122; 138

Costain, Thomas B(ertram)
  1885-1965 .... **CLC 30**
  See also CA 5-8R; 25-28R; DLB 9

Costantini, Humberto
  1924(?)-1987 .... **CLC 49**
  See also CA 131; 122; HW

Costello, Elvis 1955-............. **CLC 21**

Cotter, Joseph Seamon Sr.
  1861-1949 .... **TCLC 28; BLC**
  See also BW 1; CA 124; DLB 50

Couch, Arthur Thomas Quiller
  See Quiller-Couch, Arthur Thomas

Coulton, James
  See Hansen, Joseph

Couperus, Louis (Marie Anne)
  1863-1923 .... **TCLC 15**
  See also CA 115

Court, Wesli
  See Turco, Lewis (Putnam)

Courtenay, Bryce 1933- .... **CLC 59**
  See also CA 138

Courtney, Robert
  See Ellison, Harlan

Cousteau, Jacques-Yves 1910- ...... **CLC 30**
  See also CA 65-68; CANR 15; MTCW;
  SATA 38

Coward, Noel (Peirce)
  1899-1973 .... **CLC 1, 9, 29, 51**
  See also AITN 1; CA 17-18; 41-44R;
  CANR 35; CAP 2; CDBLB 1914-1945;
  DLB 10; MTCW

Cowley, Malcolm 1898-1989 .... **CLC 39**
  See also CA 5-8R; 128; CANR 3; DLB 4,
  48; DLBY 81, 89; MTCW

Cowper, William 1731-1800....... **NCLC 8**
  See also DLB 104, 109

Cox, William Trevor 1928- ... **CLC 9, 14, 71**
  See also Trevor, William
  See also CA 9-12R; CANR 4, 37; DLB 14;
  MTCW

Cozzens, James Gould
  1903-1978 .... **CLC 1, 4, 11**
  See also CA 9-12R; 81-84; CANR 19;
  CDALB 1941-1968; DLB 9; DLBD 2;
  DLBY 84; MTCW

Crabbe, George 1754-1832....... **NCLC 26**
  See also DLB 93

Craig, A. A.
  See Anderson, Poul (William)

Craik, Dinah Maria (Mulock)
  1826-1887 .... **NCLC 38**
  See also DLB 35; MAICYA; SATA 34

Cram, Ralph Adams 1863-1942.... **TCLC 45**

Crane, (Harold) Hart
  1899-1932 .... **TCLC 2, 5; DA; PC 3;**
  WLC
  See also CA 104; 127; CDALB 1917-1929;
  DLB 4, 48; MTCW

Crane, R(onald) S(almon)
  1886-1967 .... **CLC 27**
  See also CA 85-88; DLB 63

Crane, Stephen (Townley)
  1871-1900 .... **TCLC 11, 17, 32; DA;**
  SSC 7; WLC
  See also CA 109; 140; CDALB 1865-1917;
  DLB 12, 54, 78; YABC 2

Crase, Douglas 1944- .... **CLC 58**
  See also CA 106

Crashaw, Richard 1612(?)-1649...... **LC 24**
  See also DLB 126

Craven, Margaret 1901-1980....... **CLC 17**
  See also CA 103

Crawford, F(rancis) Marion
  1854-1909 .... **TCLC 10**
  See also CA 107; DLB 71

Crawford, Isabella Valancy
  1850-1887 .... **NCLC 12**
  See also DLB 92

Crayon, Geoffrey
  See Irving, Washington

Creasey, John 1908-1973.......... **CLC 11**
  See also CA 5-8R; 41-44R; CANR 8;
  DLB 77; MTCW

Crebillon, Claude Prosper Jolyot de (fils)
  1707-1777 .... **LC 1**

Credo
  See Creasey, John

Creeley, Robert (White)
  1926- ..... **CLC 1, 2, 4, 8, 11, 15, 36, 78**
  See also CA 1-4R; CAAS 10; CANR 23, 43;
  DLB 5, 16; MTCW

Crews, Harry (Eugene)
  1935- .... **CLC 6, 23, 49**
  See also AITN 1; CA 25-28R; CANR 20;
  DLB 6, 143; MTCW

Crichton, (John) Michael
  1942- .... **CLC 2, 6, 54**
  See also AAYA 10; AITN 2; CA 25-28R;
  CANR 13, 40; DLBY 81; JRDA;
  MTCW; SATA 9

Crispin, Edmund .... **CLC 22**
  See also Montgomery, (Robert) Bruce
  See also DLB 87

Cristofer, Michael 1945(?)- .... **CLC 28**
  See also CA 110; DLB 7

Croce, Benedetto 1866-1952 ...... **TCLC 37**
  See also CA 120

Crockett, David 1786-1836 .... **NCLC 8**
  See also DLB 3, 11

Crockett, Davy
  See Crockett, David

Crofts, Freeman Wills
  1879-1957 .... **TCLC 55**
  See also CA 115; DLB 77

Croker, John Wilson 1780-1857 .. **NCLC 10**
  See also DLB 110

Crommelynck, Fernand 1885-1970 .. **CLC 75**
  See also CA 89-92

Cronin, A(rchibald) J(oseph)
  1896-1981 .... **CLC 32**
  See also CA 1-4R; 102; CANR 5; SATA 25,
  47

Cross, Amanda
  See Heilbrun, Carolyn G(old)

Crothers, Rachel 1878(?)-1958..... **TCLC 19**
  See also CA 113; DLB 7

Croves, Hal
  See Traven, B.

Crowfield, Christopher
  See Stowe, Harriet (Elizabeth) Beecher

Crowley, Aleister................. **TCLC 7**
  See also Crowley, Edward Alexander

Crowley, Edward Alexander 1875-1947
  See Crowley, Aleister
  See also CA 104

Crowley, John 1942-.............. **CLC 57**
  See also CA 61-64; CANR 43; DLBY 82;
  SATA 65

Crud
  See Crumb, R(obert)

Crumarums
  See Crumb, R(obert)

Day Lewis, C(ecil)
  1904-1972 .... **CLC 1, 6, 10**
  See also Blake, Nicholas
  See also CA 13-16; 33-36R; CANR 34;
    CAP 1; DLB 15, 20; MTCW

Dazai, Osamu .... **TCLC 11**
  See also Tsushima, Shuji

de Andrade, Carlos Drummond
  See Drummond de Andrade, Carlos

Deane, Norman
  See Creasey, John

de Beauvoir, Simone (Lucie Ernestine Marie
    Bertrand)
  See Beauvoir, Simone (Lucie Ernestine
    Marie Bertrand) de

de Brissac, Malcolm
  See Dickinson, Peter (Malcolm)

de Chardin, Pierre Teilhard
  See Teilhard de Chardin, (Marie Joseph)
    Pierre

Dee, John 1527-1608 .... **LC 20**

Deer, Sandra 1940- .... **CLC 45**

De Ferrari, Gabriella .... **CLC 65**

Defoe, Daniel
  1660(?)-1731 .... **LC 1; DA; WLC**
  See also CDBLB 1660-1789; DLB 39, 95,
    101; JRDA; MAICYA; SATA 22

de Gourmont, Remy
  See Gourmont, Remy de

de Hartog, Jan 1914- .... **CLC 19**
  See also CA 1-4R; CANR 1

de Hostos, E. M.
  See Hostos (y Bonilla), Eugenio Maria de

de Hostos, Eugenio M.
  See Hostos (y Bonilla), Eugenio Maria de

Deighton, Len .... **CLC 4, 7, 22, 46**
  See also Deighton, Leonard Cyril
  See also AAYA 6; BEST 89:2;
    CDBLB 1960 to Present; DLB 87

Deighton, Leonard Cyril 1929-
  See Deighton, Len
  See also CA 9-12R; CANR 19, 33; MTCW

Dekker, Thomas 1572(?)-1632 .... **LC 22**
  See also CDBLB Before 1660; DLB 62

de la Mare, Walter (John)
  1873-1956 .. **TCLC 4, 53; SSC 14; WLC**
  See also CDBLB 1914-1945; CLR 23;
    DLB 19; SATA 16

Delaney, Franey
  See O'Hara, John (Henry)

Delaney, Shelagh 1939- .... **CLC 29**
  See also CA 17-20R; CANR 30;
    CDBLB 1960 to Present; DLB 13;
    MTCW

Delany, Mary (Granville Pendarves)
  1700-1788 .... **LC 12**

Delany, Samuel R(ay, Jr.)
  1942- .... **CLC 8, 14, 38; BLC**
  See also BW 2; CA 81-84; CANR 27, 43;
    DLB 8, 33; MTCW

De La Ramee, (Marie) Louise 1839-1908
  See Ouida
  See also SATA 20

de la Roche, Mazo 1879-1961 ...... **CLC 14**
  See also CA 85-88; CANR 30; DLB 68;
    SATA 64

Delbanco, Nicholas (Franklin)
  1942- .... **CLC 6, 13**
  See also CA 17-20R; CAAS 2; CANR 29;
    DLB 6

del Castillo, Michel 1933- .... **CLC 38**
  See also CA 109

Deledda, Grazia (Cosima)
  1875(?)-1936 .... **TCLC 23**
  See also CA 123

Delibes, Miguel .... **CLC 8, 18**
  See also Delibes Setien, Miguel

Delibes Setien, Miguel 1920-
  See Delibes, Miguel
  See also CA 45-48; CANR 1, 32; HW;
    MTCW

DeLillo, Don
  1936- ..... **CLC 8, 10, 13, 27, 39, 54, 76**
  See also BEST 89:1; CA 81-84; CANR 21;
    DLB 6; MTCW

de Lisser, H. G.
  See De Lisser, Herbert George
  See also DLB 117

De Lisser, Herbert George
  1878-1944 .... **TCLC 12**
  See also de Lisser, H. G.
  See also BW 2; CA 109

Deloria, Vine (Victor), Jr. 1933- .... **CLC 21**
  See also CA 53-56; CANR 5, 20; MTCW;
    SATA 21

Del Vecchio, John M(ichael)
  1947- .... **CLC 29**
  See also CA 110; DLBD 9

de Man, Paul (Adolph Michel)
  1919-1983 .... **CLC 55**
  See also CA 128; 111; DLB 67; MTCW

De Marinis, Rick 1934- .... **CLC 54**
  See also CA 57-60; CANR 9, 25

Demby, William 1922- .... **CLC 53; BLC**
  See also BW 1; CA 81-84; DLB 33

Demijohn, Thom
  See Disch, Thomas M(ichael)

de Montherlant, Henry (Milon)
  See Montherlant, Henry (Milon) de

Demosthenes 384B.C.-322B.C. .... **CMLC 13**

de Natale, Francine
  See Malzberg, Barry N(athaniel)

Denby, Edwin (Orr) 1903-1983 ..... **CLC 48**
  See also CA 138; 110

Denis, Julio
  See Cortazar, Julio

Denmark, Harrison
  See Zelazny, Roger (Joseph)

Dennis, John 1658-1734 .... **LC 11**
  See also DLB 101

Dennis, Nigel (Forbes) 1912-1989 .... **CLC 8**
  See also CA 25-28R; 129; DLB 13, 15;
    MTCW

De Palma, Brian (Russell) 1940- .... **CLC 20**
  See also CA 109

De Quincey, Thomas 1785-1859 ... **NCLC 4**
  See also CDBLB 1789-1832; DLB 110; 144

Deren, Eleanora 1908(?)-1961
  See Deren, Maya
  See also CA 111

Deren, Maya .... **CLC 16**
  See also Deren, Eleanora

Derleth, August (William)
  1909-1971 .... **CLC 31**
  See also CA 1-4R; 29-32R; CANR 4;
    DLB 9; SATA 5

Der Nister .... **TCLC 56**

de Routisie, Albert
  See Aragon, Louis

Derrida, Jacques 1930- .... **CLC 24**
  See also CA 124; 127

Derry Down Derry
  See Lear, Edward

Dersonnes, Jacques
  See Simenon, Georges (Jacques Christian)

Desai, Anita 1937- .... **CLC 19, 37**
  See also CA 81-84; CANR 33; MTCW;
    SATA 63

de Saint-Luc, Jean
  See Glassco, John

de Saint Roman, Arnaud
  See Aragon, Louis

Descartes, Rene 1596-1650 .... **LC 20**

De Sica, Vittorio 1901(?)-1974 ..... **CLC 20**
  See also CA 117

Desnos, Robert 1900-1945 .... **TCLC 22**
  See also CA 121

Destouches, Louis-Ferdinand
  1894-1961 .... **CLC 9, 15**
  See also Celine, Louis-Ferdinand
  See also CA 85-88; CANR 28; MTCW

Deutsch, Babette 1895-1982 .... **CLC 18**
  See also CA 1-4R; 108; CANR 4; DLB 45;
    SATA 1, 33

Devenant, William 1606-1649 .... **LC 13**

Devkota, Laxmiprasad
  1909-1959 .... **TCLC 23**
  See also CA 123

De Voto, Bernard (Augustine)
  1897-1955 .... **TCLC 29**
  See also CA 113; DLB 9

De Vries, Peter
  1910-1993 .... **CLC 1, 2, 3, 7, 10, 28, 46**
  See also CA 17-20R; 142; CANR 41;
    DLB 6; DLBY 82; MTCW

Dexter, Martin
  See Faust, Frederick (Schiller)

Dexter, Pete 1943- .... **CLC 34, 55**
  See also BEST 89:2; CA 127; 131; MTCW

Diamano, Silmang
  See Senghor, Leopold Sedar

Diamond, Neil 1941- .... **CLC 30**
  See also CA 108

di Bassetto, Corno
  See Shaw, George Bernard

Dick, Philip K(indred)
  1928-1982 .... **CLC 10, 30, 72**
  See also CA 49-52; 106; CANR 2, 16;
    DLB 8; MTCW

Doyle, Sir A. Conan
　See Doyle, Arthur Conan

Doyle, Sir Arthur Conan
　See Doyle, Arthur Conan

Dr. A
　See Asimov, Isaac; Silverstein, Alvin

Drabble, Margaret
　　1939- .... **CLC 2, 3, 5, 8, 10, 22, 53**
　See also CA 13-16R; CANR 18, 35;
　　CDBLB 1960 to Present; DLB 14;
　　MTCW; SATA 48

Drapier, M. B.
　See Swift, Jonathan

Drayham, James
　See Mencken, H(enry) L(ouis)

Drayton, Michael　1563-1631 .... **LC 8**

Dreadstone, Carl
　See Campbell, (John) Ramsey

Dreiser, Theodore (Herman Albert)
　　1871-1945 .... **TCLC 10, 18, 35; DA;
　　　　　　　　　　　　　　　WLC**
　See also CA 106; 132; CDALB 1865-1917;
　　DLB 9, 12, 102, 137; DLBD 1; MTCW

Drexler, Rosalyn　1926- .... **CLC 2, 6**
　See also CA 81-84

Dreyer, Carl Theodor　1889-1968.... **CLC 16**
　See also CA 116

Drieu la Rochelle, Pierre(-Eugene)
　　1893-1945 .... **TCLC 21**
　See also CA 117; DLB 72

Drop Shot
　See Cable, George Washington

Droste-Hulshoff, Annette Freiin von
　　1797-1848 .... **NCLC 3**
　See also DLB 133

Drummond, Walter
　See Silverberg, Robert

Drummond, William Henry
　　1854-1907 .... **TCLC 25**
　See also DLB 92

Drummond de Andrade, Carlos
　　1902-1987 .... **CLC 18**
　See also Andrade, Carlos Drummond de
　See also CA 132; 123

Drury, Allen (Stuart)　1918- .... **CLC 37**
　See also CA 57-60; CANR 18

Dryden, John
　　1631-1700 ... **LC 3, 21; DA; DC 3; WLC**
　See also CDBLB 1660-1789; DLB 80, 101,
　　131

Duberman, Martin　1930- .... **CLC 8**
　See also CA 1-4R; CANR 2

Dubie, Norman (Evans)　1945- ...... **CLC 36**
　See also CA 69-72; CANR 12; DLB 120

Du Bois, W(illiam) E(dward) B(urghardt)
　　1868-1963 ...... **CLC 1, 2, 13, 64; BLC;
　　　　　　　　　　　　　　DA; WLC**
　See also BW 1; CA 85-88; CANR 34;
　　CDALB 1865-1917; DLB 47, 50, 91;
　　MTCW; SATA 42

Dubus, Andre　1936- ... **CLC 13, 36; SSC 15**
　See also CA 21-24R; CANR 17; DLB 130

Duca Minimo
　See D'Annunzio, Gabriele

Ducharme, Rejean　1941- .... **CLC 74**
　See also DLB 60

Duclos, Charles Pinot　1704-1772 ..... **LC 1**

Dudek, Louis　1918- .... **CLC 11, 19**
　See also CA 45-48; CAAS 14; CANR 1;
　　DLB 88

Duerrenmatt, Friedrich
　　.............. **CLC 1, 4, 8, 11, 15, 43**
　See also Duerrenmatt, Friedrich
　See also DLB 69, 124

Duerrenmatt, Friedrich
　　1921-1990 ..... **CLC 1, 4, 8, 11, 15, 43**
　See also Duerrenmatt, Friedrich
　See also CA 17-20R; CANR 33; DLB 69,
　　124; MTCW

Duffy, Bruce　(?)- .... **CLC 50**

Duffy, Maureen　1933- .... **CLC 37**
　See also CA 25-28R; CANR 33; DLB 14;
　　MTCW

Dugan, Alan　1923- .... **CLC 2, 6**
　See also CA 81-84; DLB 5

du Gard, Roger Martin
　See Martin du Gard, Roger

Duhamel, Georges　1884-1966 .... **CLC 8**
　See also CA 81-84; 25-28R; CANR 35;
　　DLB 65; MTCW

Dujardin, Edouard (Emile Louis)
　　1861-1949 .... **TCLC 13**
　See also CA 109; DLB 123

Dumas, Alexandre (Davy de la Pailleterie)
　　1802-1870 .... **NCLC 11; DA; WLC**
　See also DLB 119; SATA 18

Dumas, Alexandre
　　1824-1895 .... **NCLC 9; DC 1**

Dumas, Claudine
　See Malzberg, Barry N(athaniel)

Dumas, Henry L.　1934-1968 ..... **CLC 6, 62**
　See also BW 1; CA 85-88; DLB 41

du Maurier, Daphne
　　1907-1989 .... **CLC 6, 11, 59**
　See also CA 5-8R; 128; CANR 6; MTCW;
　　SATA 27, 60

Dunbar, Paul Laurence
　　1872-1906 ...... **TCLC 2, 12; BLC; DA;
　　　　　　　　　　　　　PC 5; SSC 8; WLC**
　See also BW 1; CA 104; 124;
　　CDALB 1865-1917; DLB 50, 54, 78;
　　SATA 34

Dunbar, William　1460(?)-1530(?) .... **LC 20**

Duncan, Lois　1934- .... **CLC 26**
　See also AAYA 4; CA 1-4R; CANR 2, 23,
　　36; CLR 29; JRDA; MAICYA; SAAS 2;
　　SATA 1, 36, 75

Duncan, Robert (Edward)
　　1919-1988 .... **CLC 1, 2, 4, 7, 15, 41, 55;
　　　　　　　　　　　　　　　　PC 2**
　See also CA 9-12R; 124; CANR 28; DLB 5,
　　16; MTCW

Dunlap, William　1766-1839 .... **NCLC 2**
　See also DLB 30, 37, 59

Dunn, Douglas (Eaglesham)
　　1942- .... **CLC 6, 40**
　See also CA 45-48; CANR 2, 33; DLB 40;
　　MTCW

Dunn, Katherine (Karen)　1945- ..... **CLC 71**
　See also CA 33-36R

Dunn, Stephen　1939- .... **CLC 36**
　See also CA 33-36R; CANR 12; DLB 105

Dunne, Finley Peter　1867-1936.... **TCLC 28**
　See also CA 108; DLB 11, 23

Dunne, John Gregory　1932-........ **CLC 28**
　See also CA 25-28R; CANR 14; DLBY 80

Dunsany, Edward John Moreton Drax
　　Plunkett　1878-1957
　See Dunsany, Lord
　See also CA 104; DLB 10

Dunsany, Lord.................... **TCLC 2**
　See also Dunsany, Edward John Moreton
　　Drax Plunkett
　See also DLB 77

du Perry, Jean
　See Simenon, Georges (Jacques Christian)

Durang, Christopher (Ferdinand)
　　1949- .... **CLC 27, 38**
　See also CA 105

Duras, Marguerite
　　1914- ...... **CLC 3, 6, 11, 20, 34, 40, 68**
　See also CA 25-28R; DLB 83; MTCW

Durban, (Rosa) Pam　1947-........ **CLC 39**
　See also CA 123

Durcan, Paul　1944-............ **CLC 43, 70**
　See also CA 134

Durkheim, Emile　1858-1917 ...... **TCLC 55**

Durrell, Lawrence (George)
　　1912-1990 .... **CLC 1, 4, 6, 8, 13, 27, 41**
　See also CA 9-12R; 132; CANR 40;
　　CDBLB 1945-1960; DLB 15, 27;
　　DLBY 90; MTCW

Dutt, Toru　1856-1877........... **NCLC 29**

Dwight, Timothy　1752-1817...... **NCLC 13**
　See also DLB 37

Dworkin, Andrea　1946- .... **CLC 43**
　See also CA 77-80; CANR 16, 39; MTCW

Dwyer, Deanna
　See Koontz, Dean R(ay)

Dwyer, K. R.
　See Koontz, Dean R(ay)

Dylan, Bob　1941- ...... **CLC 3, 4, 6, 12, 77**
　See also CA 41-44R; DLB 16

Eagleton, Terence (Francis)　1943-
　See Eagleton, Terry
　See also CA 57-60; CANR 7, 23; MTCW

Eagleton, Terry .... **CLC 63**
　See also Eagleton, Terence (Francis)

Early, Jack
　See Scoppettone, Sandra

East, Michael
　See West, Morris L(anglo)

Eastaway, Edward
　See Thomas, (Philip) Edward

Eastlake, William (Derry)　1917-.... **CLC 8**
　See also CA 5-8R; CAAS 1; CANR 5;
　　DLB 6

Eastman, Charles A(lexander)
　　1858-1939 .... **TCLC 55**
　See also YABC 1

Engel, Marian 1933-1985. . . . . **CLC 36**
See also CA 25-28R; CANR 12; DLB 53

Engelhardt, Frederick
See Hubbard, L(afayette) Ron(ald)

Enright, D(ennis) J(oseph)
1920- . . . . **CLC 4, 8, 31**
See also CA 1-4R; CANR 1, 42; DLB 27;
SATA 25

Enzensberger, Hans Magnus
1929- . . . . **CLC 43**
See also CA 116; 119

Ephron, Nora 1941- . . . . **CLC 17, 31**
See also AITN 2; CA 65-68; CANR 12, 39

Epsilon
See Betjeman, John

Epstein, Daniel Mark 1948- . . . . **CLC 7**
See also CA 49-52; CANR 2

Epstein, Jacob 1956- . . . . **CLC 19**
See also CA 114

Epstein, Joseph 1937- . . . . **CLC 39**
See also CA 112; 119

Epstein, Leslie 1938- . . . . **CLC 27**
See also CA 73-76; CAAS 12; CANR 23

Equiano, Olaudah
1745(?)-1797 . . . . **LC 16; BLC**
See also DLB 37, 50

Erasmus, Desiderius 1469(?)-1536. . . . **LC 16**

Erdman, Paul E(mil) 1932- . . . . **CLC 25**
See also AITN 1; CA 61-64; CANR 13, 43

Erdrich, Louise 1954- . . . . **CLC 39, 54**
See also AAYA 10; BEST 89:1; CA 114;
CANR 41; MTCW

Erenburg, Ilya (Grigoryevich)
See Ehrenburg, Ilya (Grigoryevich)

Erickson, Stephen Michael 1950-
See Erickson, Steve
See also CA 129

Erickson, Steve . . . . **CLC 64**
See also Erickson, Stephen Michael

Ericson, Walter
See Fast, Howard (Melvin)

Eriksson, Buntel
See Bergman, (Ernst) Ingmar

Eschenbach, Wolfram von
See Wolfram von Eschenbach

Eseki, Bruno
See Mphahlele, Ezekiel

Esenin, Sergei (Alexandrovich)
1895-1925 . . . . **TCLC 4**
See also CA 104

Eshleman, Clayton 1935- . . . . **CLC 7**
See also CA 33-36R; CAAS 6; DLB 5

Espriella, Don Manuel Alvarez
See Southey, Robert

Espriu, Salvador 1913-1985. . . . . **CLC 9**
See also CA 115; DLB 134

Espronceda, Jose de 1808-1842 . . . **NCLC 39**

Esse, James
See Stephens, James

Esterbrook, Tom
See Hubbard, L(afayette) Ron(ald)

Estleman, Loren D. 1952- . . . . **CLC 48**
See also CA 85-88; CANR 27; MTCW

Eugenides, Jeffrey 1960(?)- . . . . **CLC 81**
See also CA 144

Euripides c. 485B.C.-406B.C. . . . . **DC 4**
See also DA

Evan, Evin
See Faust, Frederick (Schiller)

Evans, Evan
See Faust, Frederick (Schiller)

Evans, Marian
See Eliot, George

Evans, Mary Ann
See Eliot, George

Evarts, Esther
See Benson, Sally

Everett, Percival L. 1956- . . . . **CLC 57**
See also BW 2; CA 129

Everson, R(onald) G(ilmour)
1903- . . . . **CLC 27**
See also CA 17-20R; DLB 88

Everson, William (Oliver)
1912- . . . . **CLC 1, 5, 14**
See also CA 9-12R; CANR 20; DLB 5, 16;
MTCW

Evtushenko, Evgenii Aleksandrovich
See Yevtushenko, Yevgeny (Alexandrovich)

Ewart, Gavin (Buchanan)
1916- . . . . **CLC 13, 46**
See also CA 89-92; CANR 17; DLB 40;
MTCW

Ewers, Hanns Heinz 1871-1943 . . . **TCLC 12**
See also CA 109

Ewing, Frederick R.
See Sturgeon, Theodore (Hamilton)

Exley, Frederick (Earl)
1929-1992 . . . . **CLC 6, 11**
See also AITN 2; CA 81-84; 138; DLB 143;
DLBY 81

Eynhardt, Guillermo
See Quiroga, Horacio (Sylvestre)

Ezekiel, Nissim 1924- . . . . **CLC 61**
See also CA 61-64

Ezekiel, Tish O'Dowd 1943- . . . . **CLC 34**
See also CA 129

Fadeyev, A.
See Bulgya, Alexander Alexandrovich

Fadeyev, Alexander . . . . **TCLC 53**
See also Bulgya, Alexander Alexandrovich

Fagen, Donald 1948- . . . . **CLC 26**

Fainzilberg, Ilya Arnoldovich 1897-1937
See Ilf, Ilya
See also CA 120

Fair, Ronald L. 1932- . . . . **CLC 18**
See also BW 1; CA 69-72; CANR 25;
DLB 33

Fairbairns, Zoe (Ann) 1948- . . . . **CLC 32**
See also CA 103; CANR 21

Falco, Gian
See Papini, Giovanni

Falconer, James
See Kirkup, James

Falconer, Kenneth
See Kornbluth, C(yril) M.

Falkland, Samuel
See Heijermans, Herman

Fallaci, Oriana 1930- . . . . **CLC 11**
See also CA 77-80; CANR 15; MTCW

Faludy, George 1913- . . . . **CLC 42**
See also CA 21-24R

Faludy, Gyoergy
See Faludy, George

Fanon, Frantz 1925-1961 . . . . . **CLC 74; BLC**
See also BW 1; CA 116; 89-92

Fanshawe, Ann . . . . **LC 11**

Fante, John (Thomas) 1911-1983 . . . **CLC 60**
See also CA 69-72; 109; CANR 23;
DLB 130; DLBY 83

Farah, Nuruddin 1945- . . . . **CLC 53; BLC**
See also BW 2; CA 106; DLB 125

Fargue, Leon-Paul 1876(?)-1947 . . . **TCLC 11**
See also CA 109

Farigoule, Louis
See Romains, Jules

Farina, Richard 1936(?)-1966 . . . . **CLC 9**
See also CA 81-84; 25-28R

Farley, Walter (Lorimer)
1915-1989 . . . . **CLC 17**
See also CA 17-20R; CANR 8, 29; DLB 22;
JRDA; MAICYA; SATA 2, 43

Farmer, Philip Jose 1918- . . . . **CLC 1, 19**
See also CA 1-4R; CANR 4, 35; DLB 8;
MTCW

Farquhar, George 1677-1707 . . . . **LC 21**
See also DLB 84

Farrell, J(ames) G(ordon)
1935-1979 . . . . **CLC 6**
See also CA 73-76; 89-92; CANR 36;
DLB 14; MTCW

Farrell, James T(homas)
1904-1979 . . . . **CLC 1, 4, 8, 11, 66**
See also CA 5-8R; 89-92; CANR 9; DLB 4,
9, 86; DLBD 2; MTCW

Farren, Richard J.
See Betjeman, John

Farren, Richard M.
See Betjeman, John

Fassbinder, Rainer Werner
1946-1982 . . . . **CLC 20**
See also CA 93-96; 106; CANR 31

Fast, Howard (Melvin) 1914- . . . . . . **CLC 23**
See also CA 1-4R; CAAS 18; CANR 1, 33;
DLB 9; SATA 7

Faulcon, Robert
See Holdstock, Robert P.

Faulkner, William (Cuthbert)
1897-1962 . . . . . **CLC 1, 3, 6, 8, 9, 11, 14,
18, 28, 52, 68; DA; SSC 1; WLC**
See also AAYA 7; CA 81-84; CANR 33;
CDALB 1929-1941; DLB 9, 11, 44, 102;
DLBD 2; DLBY 86; MTCW

Fauset, Jessie Redmon
1884(?)-1961 . . . . **CLC 19, 54; BLC**
See also BW 1; CA 109; DLB 51

Faust, Frederick (Schiller)
1892-1944(?) . . . . **TCLC 49**
See also CA 108

Ford, Elbur
See Hibbert, Eleanor Alice Burford

Ford, Ford Madox
1873-1939 .... **TCLC 1, 15, 39**
See also CA 104; 132; CDBLB 1914-1945;
DLB 34, 98; MTCW

Ford, John 1895-1973............ **CLC 16**
See also CA 45-48

Ford, Richard 1944-.............. **CLC 46**
See also CA 69-72; CANR 11

Ford, Webster
See Masters, Edgar Lee

Foreman, Richard 1937-.......... **CLC 50**
See also CA 65-68; CANR 32

Forester, C(ecil) S(cott)
1899-1966 .... **CLC 35**
See also CA 73-76; 25-28R; SATA 13

Forez
See Mauriac, Francois (Charles)

Forman, James Douglas 1932-...... **CLC 21**
See also CA 9-12R; CANR 4, 19, 42;
JRDA; MAICYA; SATA 8, 70

Fornes, Maria Irene 1930-...... **CLC 39, 61**
See also CA 25-28R; CANR 28; DLB 7;
HW; MTCW

Forrest, Leon 1937- .... **CLC 4**
See also BW 2; CA 89-92; CAAS 7;
CANR 25; DLB 33

Forster, E(dward) M(organ)
1879-1970 ..... **CLC 1, 2, 3, 4, 9, 10, 13,**
15, 22, 45, 77; DA; WLC
See also AAYA 2; CA 13-14; 25-28R;
CANR 45; CAP 1; CDBLB 1914-1945;
DLB 34, 98; DLBD 10; MTCW;
SATA 57

Forster, John 1812-1876 .... **NCLC 11**
See also DLB 144

Forsyth, Frederick 1938-...... **CLC 2, 5, 36**
See also BEST 89:4; CA 85-88; CANR 38;
DLB 87; MTCW

Forten, Charlotte L. .... **TCLC 16; BLC**
See also Grimke, Charlotte L(ottie) Forten
See also DLB 50

Foscolo, Ugo 1778-1827 .... **NCLC 8**

Fosse, Bob .... **CLC 20**
See also Fosse, Robert Louis

Fosse, Robert Louis 1927-1987
See Fosse, Bob
See also CA 110; 123

Foster, Stephen Collins
1826-1864 .... **NCLC 26**

Foucault, Michel
1926-1984 .... **CLC 31, 34, 69**
See also CA 105; 113; CANR 34; MTCW

Fouque, Friedrich (Heinrich Karl) de la Motte
1777-1843 .... **NCLC 2**
See also DLB 90

Fournier, Henri Alban 1886-1914
See Alain-Fournier
See also CA 104

Fournier, Pierre 1916-............ **CLC 11**
See also Gascar, Pierre
See also CA 89-92; CANR 16, 40

Fowles, John
1926- .... **CLC 1, 2, 3, 4, 6, 9, 10, 15, 33**
See also CA 5-8R; CANR 25; CDBLB 1960
to Present; DLB 14, 139; MTCW;
SATA 22

Fox, Paula 1923-................ **CLC 2, 8**
See also AAYA 3; CA 73-76; CANR 20,
36; CLR 1; DLB 52; JRDA; MAICYA;
MTCW; SATA 17, 60

Fox, William Price (Jr.) 1926- ..... **CLC 22**
See also CA 17-20R; CAAS 19; CANR 11;
DLB 2; DLBY 81

Foxe, John 1516(?)-1587 .... **LC 14**

Frame, Janet .... **CLC 2, 3, 6, 22, 66**
See also Clutha, Janet Paterson Frame

France, Anatole .... **TCLC 9**
See also Thibault, Jacques Anatole Francois
See also DLB 123

Francis, Claude 19(?)- .... **CLC 50**

Francis, Dick 1920- .... **CLC 2, 22, 42**
See also AAYA 5; BEST 89:3; CA 5-8R;
CANR 9, 42; CDBLB 1960 to Present;
DLB 87; MTCW

Francis, Robert (Churchill)
1901-1987 .... **CLC 15**
See also CA 1-4R; 123; CANR 1

Frank, Anne(lies Marie)
1929-1945 .... **TCLC 17; DA; WLC**
See also AAYA 12; CA 113; 133; MTCW;
SATA 42

Frank, Elizabeth 1945-............ **CLC 39**
See also CA 121; 126

Franklin, Benjamin
See Hasek, Jaroslav (Matej Frantisek)

Franklin, Benjamin 1706-1790... **LC 25; DA**
See also CDALB 1640-1865; DLB 24, 43,
73

Franklin, (Stella Maraia Sarah) Miles
1879-1954 .... **TCLC 7**
See also CA 104

Fraser, (Lady) Antonia (Pakenham)
1932- .... **CLC 32**
See also CA 85-88; CANR 44; MTCW;
SATA 32

Fraser, George MacDonald 1925-.... **CLC 7**
See also CA 45-48; CANR 2

Fraser, Sylvia 1935-.............. **CLC 64**
See also CA 45-48; CANR 1, 16

Frayn, Michael 1933-...... **CLC 3, 7, 31, 47**
See also CA 5-8R; CANR 30; DLB 13, 14;
MTCW

Fraze, Candida (Merrill) 1945-..... **CLC 50**
See also CA 126

Frazer, J(ames) G(eorge)
1854-1941 .... **TCLC 32**
See also CA 118

Frazer, Robert Caine
See Creasey, John

Frazer, Sir James George
See Frazer, J(ames) G(eorge)

Frazier, Ian 1951-................ **CLC 46**
See also CA 130

Frederic, Harold 1856-1898...... **NCLC 10**
See also DLB 12, 23

Frederick, John
See Faust, Frederick (Schiller)

Frederick the Great 1712-1786 ...... **LC 14**

Fredro, Aleksander 1793-1876..... **NCLC 8**

Freeling, Nicolas 1927- .... **CLC 38**
See also CA 49-52; CAAS 12; CANR 1, 17;
DLB 87

Freeman, Douglas Southall
1886-1953 .... **TCLC 11**
See also CA 109; DLB 17

Freeman, Judith 1946-........... **CLC 55**

Freeman, Mary Eleanor Wilkins
1852-1930 .... **TCLC 9; SSC 1**
See also CA 106; DLB 12, 78

Freeman, R(ichard) Austin
1862-1943 .... **TCLC 21**
See also CA 113; DLB 70

French, Marilyn 1929-...... **CLC 10, 18, 60**
See also CA 69-72; CANR 3, 31; MTCW

French, Paul
See Asimov, Isaac

Freneau, Philip Morin 1752-1832 .. **NCLC 1**
See also DLB 37, 43

Freud, Sigmund 1856-1939 .... **TCLC 52**
See also CA 115; 133; MTCW

Friedan, Betty (Naomi) 1921- ...... **CLC 74**
See also CA 65-68; CANR 18, 45; MTCW

Friedman, B(ernard) H(arper)
1926- .... **CLC 7**
See also CA 1-4R; CANR 3

Friedman, Bruce Jay 1930-.... **CLC 3, 5, 56**
See also CA 9-12R; CANR 25; DLB 2, 28

Friel, Brian 1929-........... **CLC 5, 42, 59**
See also CA 21-24R; CANR 33; DLB 13;
MTCW

Friis-Baastad, Babbis Ellinor
1921-1970 .... **CLC 12**
See also CA 17-20R; 134; SATA 7

Frisch, Max (Rudolf)
1911-1991 ..... **CLC 3, 9, 14, 18, 32, 44**
See also CA 85-88; 134; CANR 32;
DLB 69, 124; MTCW

Fromentin, Eugene (Samuel Auguste)
1820-1876 .... **NCLC 10**
See also DLB 123

Frost, Frederick
See Faust, Frederick (Schiller)

Frost, Robert (Lee)
1874-1963 .... **CLC 1, 3, 4, 9, 10, 13, 15,**
26, 34, 44; DA; PC 1; WLC
See also CA 89-92; CANR 33;
CDALB 1917-1929; DLB 54; DLBD 7;
MTCW; SATA 14

Froude, James Anthony
1818-1894 .... **NCLC 43**
See also DLB 18, 57, 144

Froy, Herald
See Waterhouse, Keith (Spencer)

Fry, Christopher 1907-........ **CLC 2, 10, 14**
See also CA 17-20R; CANR 9, 30; DLB 13;
MTCW; SATA 66

Gelbart, Larry (Simon) 1923- . . . **CLC 21, 61**
See also CA 73-76; CANR 45

Gelber, Jack 1932- . . . . **CLC 1, 6, 14, 79**
See also CA 1-4R; CANR 2; DLB 7

Gellhorn, Martha (Ellis) 1908- . . **CLC 14, 60**
See also CA 77-80; CANR 44; DLBY 82

Genet, Jean
1910-1986 . . . **CLC 1, 2, 5, 10, 14, 44, 46**
See also CA 13-16R; CANR 18; DLB 72;
DLBY 86; MTCW

Gent, Peter 1942- . . . . **CLC 29**
See also AITN 1; CA 89-92; DLBY 82

Gentlewoman in New England, A
See Bradstreet, Anne

Gentlewoman in Those Parts, A
See Bradstreet, Anne

George, Jean Craighead 1919- . . . . . . **CLC 35**
See also AAYA 8; CA 5-8R; CANR 25;
CLR 1; DLB 52; JRDA; MAICYA;
SATA 2, 68

George, Stefan (Anton)
1868-1933 . . . . **TCLC 2, 14**
See also CA 104

Georges, Georges Martin
See Simenon, Georges (Jacques Christian)

Gerhardi, William Alexander
See Gerhardie, William Alexander

Gerhardie, William Alexander
1895-1977 . . . . **CLC 5**
See also CA 25-28R; 73-76; CANR 18;
DLB 36

Gerstler, Amy 1956- . . . . **CLC 70**

Gertler, T. . . . . **CLC 34**
See also CA 116; 121

Ghalib 1797-1869 . . . . **NCLC 39**

Ghelderode, Michel de
1898-1962 . . . . **CLC 6, 11**
See also CA 85-88; CANR 40

Ghiselin, Brewster 1903- . . . . **CLC 23**
See also CA 13-16R; CAAS 10; CANR 13

Ghose, Zulfikar 1935- . . . . **CLC 42**
See also CA 65-68

Ghosh, Amitav 1956- . . . . **CLC 44**

Giacosa, Giuseppe 1847-1906 . . . . . . **TCLC 7**
See also CA 104

Gibb, Lee
See Waterhouse, Keith (Spencer)

Gibbon, Lewis Grassic . . . . **TCLC 4**
See also Mitchell, James Leslie

Gibbons, Kaye 1960- . . . . **CLC 50**

Gibran, Kahlil
1883-1931 . . . . **TCLC 1, 9; PC 9**
See also CA 104

Gibson, William 1914- . . . . **CLC 23; DA**
See also CA 9-12R; CANR 9, 42; DLB 7;
SATA 66

Gibson, William (Ford) 1948- . . . **CLC 39, 63**
See also AAYA 12; CA 126; 133

Gide, Andre (Paul Guillaume)
1869-1951 . . . . **TCLC 5, 12, 36; DA;
SSC 13; WLC**
See also CA 104; 124; DLB 65; MTCW

Gifford, Barry (Colby) 1946- . . . . **CLC 34**
See also CA 65-68; CANR 9, 30, 40

Gilbert, W(illiam) S(chwenck)
1836-1911 . . . . **TCLC 3**
See also CA 104; SATA 36

Gilbreth, Frank B., Jr. 1911- . . . . **CLC 17**
See also CA 9-12R; SATA 2

Gilchrist, Ellen 1935- . . **CLC 34, 48; SSC 14**
See also CA 113; 116; CANR 41; DLB 130;
MTCW

Giles, Molly 1942- . . . . **CLC 39**
See also CA 126

Gill, Patrick
See Creasey, John

Gilliam, Terry (Vance) 1940- . . . . **CLC 21**
See also Monty Python
See also CA 108; 113; CANR 35

Gillian, Jerry
See Gilliam, Terry (Vance)

Gilliatt, Penelope (Ann Douglass)
1932-1993 . . . . **CLC 2, 10, 13, 53**
See also AITN 2; CA 13-16R; 141; DLB 14

Gilman, Charlotte (Anna) Perkins (Stetson)
1860-1935 . . . . **TCLC 9, 37; SSC 13**
See also CA 106

Gilmour, David 1949- . . . . **CLC 35**
See also Pink Floyd
See also CA 138

Gilpin, William 1724-1804 . . . . **NCLC 30**

Gilray, J. D.
See Mencken, H(enry) L(ouis)

Gilroy, Frank D(aniel) 1925- . . . . **CLC 2**
See also CA 81-84; CANR 32; DLB 7

Ginsberg, Allen
1926- . . . . . . **CLC 1, 2, 3, 4, 6, 13, 36, 69;
DA; PC 4; WLC 3**
See also AITN 1; CA 1-4R; CANR 2, 41;
CDALB 1941-1968; DLB 5, 16; MTCW

Ginzburg, Natalia
1916-1991 . . . . **CLC 5, 11, 54, 70**
See also CA 85-88; 135; CANR 33; MTCW

Giono, Jean 1895-1970 . . . . **CLC 4, 11**
See also CA 45-48; 29-32R; CANR 2, 35;
DLB 72; MTCW

Giovanni, Nikki
1943- . . . . . . **CLC 2, 4, 19, 64; BLC; DA**
See also AITN 1; BW 2; CA 29-32R;
CAAS 6; CANR 18, 41; CLR 6; DLB 5,
41; MAICYA; MTCW; SATA 24

Giovene, Andrea 1904- . . . . **CLC 7**
See also CA 85-88

Gippius, Zinaida (Nikolayevna) 1869-1945
See Hippius, Zinaida
See also CA 106

Giraudoux, (Hippolyte) Jean
1882-1944 . . . . **TCLC 2, 7**
See also CA 104; DLB 65

Gironella, Jose Maria 1917- . . . . **CLC 11**
See also CA 101

Gissing, George (Robert)
1857-1903 . . . . **TCLC 3, 24, 47**
See also CA 105; DLB 18, 135

Giurlani, Aldo
See Palazzeschi, Aldo

Gladkov, Fyodor (Vasilyevich)
1883-1958 . . . . **TCLC 27**

Glanville, Brian (Lester) 1931- . . . . . . **CLC 6**
See also CA 5-8R; CAAS 9; CANR 3;
DLB 15, 139; SATA 42

Glasgow, Ellen (Anderson Gholson)
1873(?)-1945 . . . . **TCLC 2, 7**
See also CA 104; DLB 9, 12

Glaspell, Susan (Keating)
1882(?)-1948 . . . . **TCLC 55**
See also CA 110; DLB 7, 9, 78; YABC 2

Glassco, John 1909-1981 . . . . **CLC 9**
See also CA 13-16R; 102; CANR 15;
DLB 68

Glasscock, Amnesia
See Steinbeck, John (Ernst)

Glasser, Ronald J. 1940(?)- . . . . **CLC 37**

Glassman, Joyce
See Johnson, Joyce

Glendinning, Victoria 1937- . . . . **CLC 50**
See also CA 120; 127

Glissant, Edouard 1928- . . . . **CLC 10, 68**

Gloag, Julian 1930- . . . . **CLC 40**
See also AITN 1; CA 65-68; CANR 10

Glowacki, Aleksander 1845-1912
See Prus, Boleslaw

Gluck, Louise (Elisabeth)
1943- . . . . **CLC 7, 22, 44, 81**
See also Glueck, Louise
See also CA 33-36R; CANR 40; DLB 5

Glueck, Louise . . . . **CLC 7, 22**
See also Gluck, Louise (Elisabeth)
See also DLB 5

Gobineau, Joseph Arthur (Comte) de
1816-1882 . . . . **NCLC 17**
See also DLB 123

Godard, Jean-Luc 1930- . . . . **CLC 20**
See also CA 93-96

Godden, (Margaret) Rumer 1907- . . . **CLC 53**
See also AAYA 6; CA 5-8R; CANR 4, 27,
36; CLR 20; MAICYA; SAAS 12;
SATA 3, 36

Godoy Alcayaga, Lucila 1889-1957
See Mistral, Gabriela
See also BW 2; CA 104; 131; HW; MTCW

Godwin, Gail (Kathleen)
1937- . . . . **CLC 5, 8, 22, 31, 69**
See also CA 29-32R; CANR 15, 43; DLB 6;
MTCW

Godwin, William 1756-1836 . . . . . . **NCLC 14**
See also CDBLB 1789-1832; DLB 39, 104,
142

Goethe, Johann Wolfgang von
1749-1832 . . . . **NCLC 4, 22, 34; DA;
PC 5; WLC 3**
See also DLB 94

Gogarty, Oliver St. John
1878-1957 . . . . **TCLC 15**
See also CA 109; DLB 15, 19

Gogol, Nikolai (Vasilyevich)
1809-1852 . . . . **NCLC 5, 15, 31; DA;
DC 1; SSC 4; WLC**

Grayson, Richard (A.) 1951- .... **CLC 38**
See also CA 85-88; CANR 14, 31

Greeley, Andrew M(oran) 1928- .... **CLC 28**
See also CA 5-8R; CAAS 7; CANR 7, 43;
MTCW

Green, Brian
See Card, Orson Scott

Green, Hannah .... **CLC 3**
See also CA 73-76

Green, Hannah
See Greenberg, Joanne (Goldenberg)

Green, Henry.................... **CLC 2, 13**
See also Yorke, Henry Vincent
See also DLB 15

Green, Julian (Hartridge) 1900-
See Green, Julien
See also CA 21-24R; CANR 33; DLB 4, 72;
MTCW

Green, Julien................ **CLC 3, 11, 77**
See also Green, Julian (Hartridge)

Green, Paul (Eliot) 1894-1981...... **CLC 25**
See also AITN 1; CA 5-8R; 103; CANR 3;
DLB 7, 9; DLBY 81

Greenberg, Ivan 1908-1973
See Rahv, Philip
See also CA 85-88

Greenberg, Joanne (Goldenberg)
1932- .... **CLC 7, 30**
See also AAYA 12; CA 5-8R; CANR 14,
32; SATA 25

Greenberg, Richard 1959(?)- .... **CLC 57**
See also CA 138

Greene, Bette 1934- .... **CLC 30**
See also AAYA 7; CA 53-56; CANR 4;
CLR 2; JRDA; MAICYA; SAAS 16;
SATA 8

Greene, Gael .... **CLC 8**
See also CA 13-16R; CANR 10

Greene, Graham
1904-1991 .... **CLC 1, 3, 6, 9, 14, 18, 27,
37, 70, 72; DA; WLC**
See also AITN 2; CA 13-16R; 133;
CANR 35; CDBLB 1945-1960; DLB 13,
15, 77, 100; DLBY 91; MTCW; SATA 20

Greer, Richard
See Silverberg, Robert

Greer, Richard
See Silverberg, Robert

Gregor, Arthur 1923- .... **CLC 9**
See also CA 25-28R; CAAS 10; CANR 11;
SATA 36

Gregor, Lee
See Pohl, Frederik

Gregory, Isabella Augusta (Persse)
1852-1932 .... **TCLC 1**
See also CA 104; DLB 10

Gregory, J. Dennis
See Williams, John A(lfred)

Grendon, Stephen
See Derleth, August (William)

Grenville, Kate 1950- .... **CLC 61**
See also CA 118

Grenville, Pelham
See Wodehouse, P(elham) G(renville)

Greve, Felix Paul (Berthold Friedrich)
1879-1948
See Grove, Frederick Philip
See also CA 104; 141

Grey, Zane 1872-1939 .... **TCLC 6**
See also CA 104; 132; DLB 9; MTCW

Grieg, (Johan) Nordahl (Brun)
1902-1943 .... **TCLC 10**
See also CA 107

Grieve, C(hristopher) M(urray)
1892-1978 .... **CLC 11, 19**
See also MacDiarmid, Hugh
See also CA 5-8R; 85-88; CANR 33;
MTCW

Griffin, Gerald 1803-1840 .... **NCLC 7**

Griffin, John Howard 1920-1980.... **CLC 68**
See also AITN 1; CA 1-4R; 101; CANR 2

Griffin, Peter .... **CLC 39**

Griffiths, Trevor 1935- .... **CLC 13, 52**
See also CA 97-100; CANR 45; DLB 13

Grigson, Geoffrey (Edward Harvey)
1905-1985 .... **CLC 7, 39**
See also CA 25-28R; 118; CANR 20, 33;
DLB 27; MTCW

Grillparzer, Franz 1791-1872...... **NCLC 1**
See also DLB 133

Grimble, Reverend Charles James
See Eliot, T(homas) S(tearns)

Grimke, Charlotte L(ottie) Forten
1837(?)-1914
See Forten, Charlotte L.
See also BW 1; CA 117; 124

Grimm, Jacob Ludwig Karl
1785-1863 .... **NCLC 3**
See also DLB 90; MAICYA; SATA 22

Grimm, Wilhelm Karl 1786-1859 .. **NCLC 3**
See also DLB 90; MAICYA; SATA 22

Grimmelshausen, Johann Jakob Christoffel
von 1621-1676 .... **LC 6**

Grindel, Eugene 1895-1952
See Eluard, Paul
See also CA 104

Grisham, John 1955(?)- .... **CLC 84**
See also CA 138

Grossman, David 1954- .... **CLC 67**
See also CA 138

Grossman, Vasily (Semenovich)
1905-1964 .... **CLC 41**
See also CA 124; 130; MTCW

Grove, Frederick Philip .... **TCLC 4**
See also Greve, Felix Paul (Berthold
Friedrich)
See also DLB 92

Grubb
See Crumb, R(obert)

Grumbach, Doris (Isaac)
1918- .... **CLC 13, 22, 64**
See also CA 5-8R; CAAS 2; CANR 9, 42

Grundtvig, Nicolai Frederik Severin
1783-1872 .... **NCLC 1**

Grunge
See Crumb, R(obert)

Grunwald, Lisa 1959- .... **CLC 44**
See also CA 120

Guare, John 1938- .... **CLC 8, 14, 29, 67**
See also CA 73-76; CANR 21; DLB 7;
MTCW

Gudjonsson, Halldor Kiljan 1902-
See Laxness, Halldor
See also CA 103

Guenter, Erich
See Eich, Guenter

Guest, Barbara 1920- .... **CLC 34**
See also CA 25-28R; CANR 11, 44; DLB 5

Guest, Judith (Ann) 1936- .... **CLC 8, 30**
See also AAYA 7; CA 77-80; CANR 15;
MTCW

Guild, Nicholas M. 1944-......... **CLC 33**
See also CA 93-96

Guillemin, Jacques
See Sartre, Jean-Paul

Guillen, Jorge 1893-1984......... **CLC 11**
See also CA 89-92; 112; DLB 108; HW

Guillen (y Batista), Nicolas (Cristobal)
1902-1989 ..... **CLC 48, 79; BLC; HLC**
See also BW 2; CA 116; 125; 129; HW

Guillevic, (Eugene) 1907-......... **CLC 33**
See also CA 93-96

Guillois
See Desnos, Robert

Guiney, Louise Imogen
1861-1920 .... **TCLC 41**
See also DLB 54

Guiraldes, Ricardo (Guillermo)
1886-1927 .... **TCLC 39**
See also CA 131; HW; MTCW

Gunn, Bill .... **CLC 5**
See also Gunn, William Harrison
See also DLB 38

Gunn, Thom(son William)
1929- .... **CLC 3, 6, 18, 32, 81**
See also CA 17-20R; CANR 9, 33;
CDBLB 1960 to Present; DLB 27;
MTCW

Gunn, William Harrison 1934(?)-1989
See Gunn, Bill
See also AITN 1; BW 1; CA 13-16R; 128;
CANR 12, 25

Gunnars, Kristjana 1948-......... **CLC 69**
See also CA 113; DLB 60

Gurganus, Allan 1947-............ **CLC 70**
See also BEST 90:1; CA 135

Gurney, A(lbert) R(amsdell), Jr.
1930- .... **CLC 32, 50, 54**
See also CA 77-80; CANR 32

Gurney, Ivor (Bertie) 1890-1937 ... **TCLC 33**

Gurney, Peter
See Gurney, A(lbert) R(amsdell), Jr.

Guro, Elena .... **TCLC 56**

Gustafson, Ralph (Barker) 1909-.... **CLC 36**
See also CA 21-24R; CANR 8, 45; DLB 88

Gut, Gom
See Simenon, Georges (Jacques Christian)

Guthrie, A(lfred) B(ertram), Jr.
1901-1991 .... **CLC 23**
See also CA 57-60; 134; CANR 24; DLB 6;
SATA 62; SATA-Obit 67

Harrison, Elizabeth Cavanna 1909-
See Cavanna, Betty
See also CA 9-12R; CANR 6, 27

Harrison, Harry (Max) 1925-...... **CLC 42**
See also CA 1-4R; CANR 5, 21; DLB 8;
SATA 4

Harrison, James (Thomas)
1937-............ **CLC 6, 14, 33, 66**
See also CA 13-16R; CANR 8; DLBY 82

Harrison, Kathryn 1961-......... **CLC 70**
See also CA 144

Harrison, Tony 1937-............. **CLC 43**
See also CA 65-68; CANR 44; DLB 40;
MTCW

Harriss, Will(ard Irvin) 1922-...... **CLC 34**
See also CA 111

Harson, Sley
See Ellison, Harlan

Hart, Ellis
See Ellison, Harlan

Hart, Josephine 1942(?)-.......... **CLC 70**
See also CA 138

Hart, Moss 1904-1961............ **CLC 66**
See also CA 109; 89-92; DLB 7

Harte, (Francis) Bret(t)
1836(?)-1902........ **TCLC 1, 25; DA;**
SSC 8; WLC
See also CA 104; 140; CDALB 1865-1917;
DLB 12, 64, 74, 79; SATA 26

Hartley, L(eslie) P(oles)
1895-1972................ **CLC 2, 22**
See also CA 45-48; 37-40R; CANR 33;
DLB 15, 139; MTCW

Hartman, Geoffrey H. 1929-....... **CLC 27**
See also CA 117; 125; DLB 67

Haruf, Kent 19(?)-.............. **CLC 34**

Harwood, Ronald 1934-........... **CLC 32**
See also CA 1-4R; CANR 4; DLB 13

Hasek, Jaroslav (Matej Frantisek)
1883-1923................... **TCLC 4**
See also CA 104; 129; MTCW

Hass, Robert 1941-............. **CLC 18, 39**
See also CA 111; CANR 30; DLB 105

Hastings, Hudson
See Kuttner, Henry

Hastings, Selina.................. **CLC 44**

Hatteras, Amelia
See Mencken, H(enry) L(ouis)

Hatteras, Owen................. **TCLC 18**
See also Mencken, H(enry) L(ouis); Nathan,
George Jean

Hauptmann, Gerhart (Johann Robert)
1862-1946................... **TCLC 4**
See also CA 104; DLB 66, 118

Havel, Vaclav 1936-........ **CLC 25, 58, 65**
See also CA 104; CANR 36; MTCW

Haviaras, Stratis................. **CLC 33**
See also Chaviaras, Strates

Hawes, Stephen 1475(?)-1523(?)..... **LC 17**

Hawkes, John (Clendennin Burne, Jr.)
1925-...... **CLC 1, 2, 3, 4, 7, 9, 14, 15,**
27, 49
See also CA 1-4R; CANR 2; DLB 2, 7;
DLBY 80; MTCW

Hawking, S. W.
See Hawking, Stephen W(illiam)

Hawking, Stephen W(illiam)
1942-...................... **CLC 63**
See also BEST 89:1; CA 126; 129

Hawthorne, Julian 1846-1934..... **TCLC 25**

Hawthorne, Nathaniel
1804-1864...... **NCLC 39; DA; SSC 3;**
WLC
See also CDALB 1640-1865; DLB 1, 74;
YABC 2

Haxton, Josephine Ayres 1921-.... **CLC 73**
See also CA 115; CANR 41

Hayaseca y Eizaguirre, Jorge
See Echegaray (y Eizaguirre), Jose (Maria
Waldo)

Hayashi Fumiko 1904-1951....... **TCLC 27**

Haycraft, Anna
See Ellis, Alice Thomas
See also CA 122

Hayden, Robert E(arl)
1913-1980...... **CLC 5, 9, 14, 37; BLC;**
DA; PC 6
See also BW 1; CA 69-72; 97-100; CABS 2;
CANR 24; CDALB 1941-1968; DLB 5,
76; MTCW; SATA 19, 26

Hayford, J(oseph) E(phraim) Casely
See Casely-Hayford, J(oseph) E(phraim)

Hayman, Ronald 1932-........... **CLC 44**
See also CA 25-28R; CANR 18

Haywood, Eliza (Fowler)
1693(?)-1756................... **LC 1**

Hazlitt, William 1778-1830...... **NCLC 29**
See also DLB 110

Hazzard, Shirley 1931-........... **CLC 18**
See also CA 9-12R; CANR 4; DLBY 82;
MTCW

Head, Bessie 1937-1986... **CLC 25, 67; BLC**
See also BW 2; CA 29-32R; 119; CANR 25;
DLB 117; MTCW

Headon, (Nicky) Topper 1956(?)-... **CLC 30**
See also Clash, The

Heaney, Seamus (Justin)
1939-......... **CLC 5, 7, 14, 25, 37, 74**
See also CA 85-88; CANR 25;
CDBLB 1960 to Present; DLB 40;
MTCW

Hearn, (Patricio) Lafcadio (Tessima Carlos)
1850-1904................... **TCLC 9**
See also CA 105; DLB 12, 78

Hearne, Vicki 1946-.............. **CLC 56**
See also CA 139

Hearon, Shelby 1931-............ **CLC 63**
See also AITN 2; CA 25-28R; CANR 18

Heat-Moon, William Least........ **CLC 29**
See also Trogdon, William (Lewis)
See also AAYA 9

Hebbel, Friedrich 1813-1863..... **NCLC 43**
See also DLB 129

Hebert, Anne 1916-........ **CLC 4, 13, 29**
See also CA 85-88; DLB 68; MTCW

Hecht, Anthony (Evan)
1923-................. **CLC 8, 13, 19**
See also CA 9-12R; CANR 6; DLB 5

Hecht, Ben 1894-1964............. **CLC 8**
See also CA 85-88; DLB 7, 9, 25, 26, 28, 86

Hedayat, Sadeq 1903-1951....... **TCLC 21**
See also CA 120

Hegel, Georg Wilhelm Friedrich
1770-1831................. **NCLC 46**
See also DLB 90

Heidegger, Martin 1889-1976...... **CLC 24**
See also CA 81-84; 65-68; CANR 34;
MTCW

Heidenstam, (Carl Gustaf) Verner von
1859-1940................... **TCLC 5**
See also CA 104

Heifner, Jack 1946-.............. **CLC 11**
See also CA 105

Heijermans, Herman 1864-1924... **TCLC 24**
See also CA 123

Heilbrun, Carolyn G(old) 1926-..... **CLC 25**
See also CA 45-48; CANR 1, 28

Heine, Heinrich 1797-1856....... **NCLC 4**
See also DLB 90

Heinemann, Larry (Curtiss) 1944-.. **CLC 50**
See also CA 110; CANR 31; DLBD 9

Heiney, Donald (William)
1921-1993................... **CLC 9**
See also CA 1-4R; 142; CANR 3

Heinlein, Robert A(nson)
1907-1988...... **CLC 1, 3, 8, 14, 26, 55**
See also CA 1-4R; 125; CANR 1, 20;
DLB 8; JRDA; MAICYA; MTCW;
SATA 9, 56, 69

Helforth, John
See Doolittle, Hilda

Hellenhofferu, Vojtech Kapristian z
See Hasek, Jaroslav (Matej Frantisek)

Heller, Joseph
1923-.... **CLC 1, 3, 5, 8, 11, 36, 63; DA;**
WLC
See also AITN 1; CA 5-8R; CABS 1;
CANR 8, 42; DLB 2, 28; DLBY 80;
MTCW

Hellman, Lillian (Florence)
1906-1984...... **CLC 2, 4, 8, 14, 18, 34,**
44, 52; DC 1
See also AITN 1, 2; CA 13-16R; 112;
CANR 33; DLB 7; DLBY 84; MTCW

Helprin, Mark 1947-..... **CLC 7, 10, 22, 32**
See also CA 81-84; DLBY 85; MTCW

Helvetius, Claude-Adrien
1715-1771................... **LC 26**

Helyar, Jane Penelope Josephine 1933-
See Poole, Josephine
See also CA 21-24R; CANR 10, 26

Hemans, Felicia 1793-1835...... **NCLC 29**
See also DLB 96

Hemingway, Ernest (Miller)
1899-1961.... **CLC 1, 3, 6, 8, 10, 13, 19,**
30, 34, 39, 41, 44, 50, 61, 80; DA; SSC 1;
WLC
See also CA 77-80; CANR 34;
CDALB 1917-1929; DLB 4, 9, 102;
DLBD 1; DLBY 81, 87; MTCW

Hempel, Amy 1951-............. **CLC 39**
See also CA 118; 137

Henderson, F. C.
See Mencken, H(enry) L(ouis)

Henderson, Sylvia
See Ashton-Warner, Sylvia (Constance)

Henley, Beth . . . . **CLC 23**
See also Henley, Elizabeth Becker
See also CABS 3; DLBY 86

Henley, Elizabeth Becker 1952-
See Henley, Beth
See also CA 107; CANR 32; MTCW

Henley, William Ernest
1849-1903 . . . . **TCLC 8**
See also CA 105; DLB 19

Hennissart, Martha
See Lathen, Emma
See also CA 85-88

Henry, O. . . . . **TCLC 1, 19; SSC 5; WLC**
See also Porter, William Sydney

Henry, Patrick 1736-1799 . . . . **LC 25**

Henryson, Robert 1430(?)-1506(?). . . . **LC 20**

Henry VIII 1491-1547 . . . . **LC 10**

Henschke, Alfred
See Klabund

Hentoff, Nat(han Irving) 1925- . . . . . **CLC 26**
See also AAYA 4; CA 1-4R; CAAS 6;
CANR 5, 25; CLR 1; JRDA; MAICYA;
SATA 27, 42, 69

Heppenstall, (John) Rayner
1911-1981 . . . . **CLC 10**
See also CA 1-4R; 103; CANR 29

Herbert, Frank (Patrick)
1920-1986 . . . . **CLC 12, 23, 35, 44**
See also CA 53-56; 118; CANR 5, 43;
DLB 8; MTCW; SATA 9, 37, 47

Herbert, George 1593-1633 . . . . **LC 24; PC 4**
See also CDBLB Before 1660; DLB 126

Herbert, Zbigniew 1924- . . . . **CLC 9, 43**
See also CA 89-92; CANR 36; MTCW

Herbst, Josephine (Frey)
1897-1969 . . . . **CLC 34**
See also CA 5-8R; 25-28R; DLB 9

Hergesheimer, Joseph
1880-1954 . . . . **TCLC 11**
See also CA 109; DLB 102, 9

Herlihy, James Leo 1927-1993 . . . . . . **CLC 6**
See also CA 1-4R; 143; CANR 2

Hermogenes fl. c. 175- . . . . **CMLC 6**

Hernandez, Jose 1834-1886 . . . . . . **NCLC 17**

Herrick, Robert
1591-1674 . . . . **LC 13; DA; PC 9**
See also DLB 126

Herring, Guilles
See Somerville, Edith

Herriot, James 1916- . . . . **CLC 12**
See also Wight, James Alfred
See also AAYA 1; CANR 40

Herrmann, Dorothy 1941- . . . . **CLC 44**
See also CA 107

Herrmann, Taffy
See Herrmann, Dorothy

Hersey, John (Richard)
1914-1993 . . . . **CLC 1, 2, 7, 9, 40, 81**
See also CA 17-20R; 140; CANR 33;
DLB 6; MTCW; SATA 25;
SATA-Obit 76

Herzen, Aleksandr Ivanovich
1812-1870 . . . . **NCLC 10**

Herzl, Theodor 1860-1904 . . . . **TCLC 36**

Herzog, Werner 1942- . . . . **CLC 16**
See also CA 89-92

Hesiod c. 8th cent. B.C.- . . . . **CMLC 5**

Hesse, Hermann
1877-1962 . . . . **CLC 1, 2, 3, 6, 11, 17, 25,
69; DA; SSC 9; WLC**
See also CA 17-18; CAP 2; DLB 66;
MTCW; SATA 50

Hewes, Cady
See De Voto, Bernard (Augustine)

Heyen, William 1940- . . . . **CLC 13, 18**
See also CA 33-36R; CAAS 9; DLB 5

Heyerdahl, Thor 1914- . . . . **CLC 26**
See also CA 5-8R; CANR 5, 22; MTCW;
SATA 2, 52

Heym, Georg (Theodor Franz Arthur)
1887-1912 . . . . **TCLC 9**
See also CA 106

Heym, Stefan 1913- . . . . **CLC 41**
See also CA 9-12R; CANR 4; DLB 69

Heyse, Paul (Johann Ludwig von)
1830-1914 . . . . **TCLC 8**
See also CA 104; DLB 129

Hibbert, Eleanor Alice Burford
1906-1993 . . . . **CLC 7**
See also BEST 90:4; CA 17-20R; 140;
CANR 9, 28; SATA 2; SATA-Obit 74

Higgins, George V(incent)
1939- . . . . **CLC 4, 7, 10, 18**
See also CA 77-80; CAAS 5; CANR 17;
DLB 2; DLBY 81; MTCW

Higginson, Thomas Wentworth
1823-1911 . . . . **TCLC 36**
See also DLB 1, 64

Highet, Helen
See MacInnes, Helen (Clark)

Highsmith, (Mary) Patricia
1921- . . . . **CLC 2, 4, 14, 42**
See also CA 1-4R; CANR 1, 20; MTCW

Highwater, Jamake (Mamake)
1942(?)- . . . . **CLC 12**
See also AAYA 7; CA 65-68; CAAS 7;
CANR 10, 34; CLR 17; DLB 52;
DLBY 85; JRDA; MAICYA; SATA 30,
32, 69

Hijuelos, Oscar 1951- . . . . . . **CLC 65; HLC**
See also BEST 90:1; CA 123; HW

Hikmet, Nazim 1902(?)-1963 . . . . **CLC 40**
See also CA 141; 93-96

Hildesheimer, Wolfgang
1916-1991 . . . . **CLC 49**
See also CA 101; 135; DLB 69, 124

Hill, Geoffrey (William)
1932- . . . . **CLC 5, 8, 18, 45**
See also CA 81-84; CANR 21;
CDBLB 1960 to Present; DLB 40;
MTCW

Hill, George Roy 1921- . . . . **CLC 26**
See also CA 110; 122

Hill, John
See Koontz, Dean R(ay)

Hill, Susan (Elizabeth) 1942- . . . . **CLC 4**
See also CA 33-36R; CANR 29; DLB 14,
139; MTCW

Hillerman, Tony 1925- . . . . **CLC 62**
See also AAYA 6; BEST 89:1; CA 29-32R;
CANR 21, 42; SATA 6

Hillesum, Etty 1914-1943 . . . . **TCLC 49**
See also CA 137

Hilliard, Noel (Harvey) 1929- . . . . . . **CLC 15**
See also CA 9-12R; CANR 7

Hillis, Rick 1956- . . . . **CLC 66**
See also CA 134

Hilton, James 1900-1954 . . . . **TCLC 21**
See also CA 108; DLB 34, 77; SATA 34

Himes, Chester (Bomar)
1909-1984 . . . . **CLC 2, 4, 7, 18, 58; BLC**
See also BW 2; CA 25-28R; 114; CANR 22;
DLB 2, 76, 143; MTCW

Hinde, Thomas . . . . **CLC 6, 11**
See also Chitty, Thomas Willes

Hindin, Nathan
See Bloch, Robert (Albert)

Hine, (William) Daryl 1936- . . . . **CLC 15**
See also CA 1-4R; CAAS 15; CANR 1, 20;
DLB 60

Hinkson, Katharine Tynan
See Tynan, Katharine

Hinton, S(usan) E(loise)
1950- . . . . **CLC 30; DA**
See also AAYA 2; CA 81-84; CANR 32;
CLR 3, 23; JRDA; MAICYA; MTCW;
SATA 19, 58

Hippius, Zinaida . . . . **TCLC 9**
See also Gippius, Zinaida (Nikolayevna)

Hiraoka, Kimitake 1925-1970
See Mishima, Yukio
See also CA 97-100; 29-32R; MTCW

Hirsch, E(ric) D(onald), Jr. 1928- . . . **CLC 79**
See also CA 25-28R; CANR 27; DLB 67;
MTCW

Hirsch, Edward 1950- . . . . **CLC 31, 50**
See also CA 104; CANR 20, 42; DLB 120

Hitchcock, Alfred (Joseph)
1899-1980 . . . . **CLC 16**
See also CA 97-100; SATA 24, 27

Hitler, Adolf 1889-1945 . . . . **TCLC 53**
See also CA 117

Hoagland, Edward 1932- . . . . **CLC 28**
See also CA 1-4R; CANR 2, 31; DLB 6;
SATA 51

Hoban, Russell (Conwell) 1925- . . **CLC 7, 25**
See also CA 5-8R; CANR 23, 37; CLR 3;
DLB 52; MAICYA; MTCW; SATA 1,
40, 78

Hobbs, Perry
See Blackmur, R(ichard) P(almer)

Hobson, Laura Z(ametkin)
1900-1986 . . . . **CLC 7, 25**
See also CA 17-20R; 118; DLB 28;
SATA 52

Hochhuth, Rolf   1931-........ **CLC 4, 11, 18**
See also CA 5-8R; CANR 33; DLB 124;
MTCW

Hochman, Sandra   1936-......... **CLC 3, 8**
See also CA 5-8R; DLB 5

Hochwaelder, Fritz   1911-1986...... **CLC 36**
See also CA 29-32R; 120; CANR 42;
MTCW

Hochwalder, Fritz
See Hochwaelder, Fritz

Hocking, Mary (Eunice)   1921-..... **CLC 13**
See also CA 101; CANR 18, 40

Hodgins, Jack   1938-.............. **CLC 23**
See also CA 93-96; DLB 60

Hodgson, William Hope
1877(?)-1918 .... **TCLC 13**
See also CA 111; DLB 70

Hoffman, Alice   1952-............. **CLC 51**
See also CA 77-80; CANR 34; MTCW

Hoffman, Daniel (Gerard)
1923-.................. **CLC 6, 13, 23**
See also CA 1-4R; CANR 4; DLB 5

Hoffman, Stanley   1944-........... **CLC 5**
See also CA 77-80

Hoffman, William M(oses)   1939-... **CLC 40**
See also CA 57-60; CANR 11

Hoffmann, E(rnst) T(heodor) A(madeus)
1776-1822 .... **NCLC 2; SSC 13**
See also DLB 90; SATA 27

Hofmann, Gert   1931-............. **CLC 54**
See also CA 128

Hofmannsthal, Hugo von
1874-1929 .... **TCLC 11; DC 4**
See also CA 106; DLB 81, 118

Hogan, Linda   1947-............. **CLC 73**
See also CA 120; CANR 45

Hogarth, Charles
See Creasey, John

Hogg, James   1770-1835.......... **NCLC 4**
See also DLB 93, 116

Holbach, Paul Henri Thiry Baron
1723-1789 .... **LC 14**

Holberg, Ludvig   1684-1754 .... **LC 6**

Holden, Ursula   1921-............. **CLC 18**
See also CA 101; CAAS 8; CANR 22

Holderlin, (Johann Christian) Friedrich
1770-1843 .... **NCLC 16; PC 4**

Holdstock, Robert
See Holdstock, Robert P.

Holdstock, Robert P.   1948-........ **CLC 39**
See also CA 131

Holland, Isabelle   1920- .... **CLC 21**
See also AAYA 11; CA 21-24R; CANR 10,
25; JRDA; MAICYA; SATA 8, 70

Holland, Marcus
See Caldwell, (Janet Miriam) Taylor
(Holland)

Hollander, John   1929-...... **CLC 2, 5, 8, 14**
See also CA 1-4R; CANR 1; DLB 5;
SATA 13

Hollander, Paul
See Silverberg, Robert

Holleran, Andrew   1943(?)-......... **CLC 38**
See also CA 144

Hollinghurst, Alan   1954-.......... **CLC 55**
See also CA 114

Hollis, Jim
See Summers, Hollis (Spurgeon, Jr.)

Holmes, John
See Souster, (Holmes) Raymond

Holmes, John Clellon   1926-1988.... **CLC 56**
See also CA 9-12R; 125; CANR 4; DLB 16

Holmes, Oliver Wendell
1809-1894 .... **NCLC 14**
See also CDALB 1640-1865; DLB 1;
SATA 34

Holmes, Raymond
See Souster, (Holmes) Raymond

Holt, Victoria
See Hibbert, Eleanor Alice Burford

Holub, Miroslav   1923-............ **CLC 4**
See also CA 21-24R; CANR 10

Homer   c. 8th cent. B.C.-..... **CMLC 1; DA**

Honig, Edwin   1919-.............. **CLC 33**
See also CA 5-8R; CAAS 8; CANR 4, 45;
DLB 5

Hood, Hugh (John Blagdon)
1928-.................... **CLC 15, 28**
See also CA 49-52; CAAS 17; CANR 1, 33;
DLB 53

Hood, Thomas   1799-1845........ **NCLC 16**
See also DLB 96

Hooker, (Peter) Jeremy   1941-...... **CLC 43**
See also CA 77-80; CANR 22; DLB 40

Hope, A(lec) D(erwent)   1907-.... **CLC 3, 51**
See also CA 21-24R; CANR 33; MTCW

Hope, Brian
See Creasey, John

Hope, Christopher (David Tully)
1944-...................... **CLC 52**
See also CA 106; SATA 62

Hopkins, Gerard Manley
1844-1889 .... **NCLC 17; DA; WLC**
See also CDBLB 1890-1914; DLB 35, 57

Hopkins, John (Richard)   1931-...... **CLC 4**
See also CA 85-88

Hopkins, Pauline Elizabeth
1859-1930 .... **TCLC 28; BLC**
See also BW 2; CA 141; DLB 50

Hopkinson, Francis   1737-1791 ...... **LC 25**
See also DLB 31

Hopley-Woolrich, Cornell George   1903-1968
See Woolrich, Cornell
See also CA 13-14; CAP 1

Horatio
See Proust, (Valentin-Louis-George-Eugene-)
Marcel

Horgan, Paul   1903- .... **CLC 9, 53**
See also CA 13-16R; CANR 9, 35;
DLB 102; DLBY 85; MTCW; SATA 13

Horn, Peter
See Kuttner, Henry

Hornem, Horace Esq.
See Byron, George Gordon (Noel)

Horovitz, Israel   1939-............ **CLC 56**
See also CA 33-36R; DLB 7

Horvath, Odon von
See Horvath, Oedoen von
See also DLB 85, 124

Horvath, Oedoen von   1901-1938... **TCLC 45**
See also Horvath, Odon von
See also CA 118

Horwitz, Julius   1920-1986......... **CLC 14**
See also CA 9-12R; 119; CANR 12

Hospital, Janette Turner   1942-..... **CLC 42**
See also CA 108

Hostos, E. M. de
See Hostos (y Bonilla), Eugenio Maria de

Hostos, Eugenio M. de
See Hostos (y Bonilla), Eugenio Maria de

Hostos, Eugenio Maria
See Hostos (y Bonilla), Eugenio Maria de

Hostos (y Bonilla), Eugenio Maria de
1839-1903 .... **TCLC 24**
See also CA 123; 131; HW

Houdini
See Lovecraft, H(oward) P(hillips)

Hougan, Carolyn   1943- .... **CLC 34**
See also CA 139

Household, Geoffrey (Edward West)
1900-1988 .... **CLC 11**
See also CA 77-80; 126; DLB 87; SATA 14,
59

Housman, A(lfred) E(dward)
1859-1936 ...... **TCLC 1, 10; DA; PC 2**
See also CA 104; 125; DLB 19; MTCW

Housman, Laurence   1865-1959 ..... **TCLC 7**
See also CA 106; DLB 10; SATA 25

Howard, Elizabeth Jane   1923- ... **CLC 7, 29**
See also CA 5-8R; CANR 8

Howard, Maureen   1930- ..... **CLC 5, 14, 46**
See also CA 53-56; CANR 31; DLBY 83;
MTCW

Howard, Richard   1929- ...... **CLC 7, 10, 47**
See also AITN 1; CA 85-88; CANR 25;
DLB 5

Howard, Robert Ervin   1906-1936... **TCLC 8**
See also CA 105

Howard, Warren F.
See Pohl, Frederik

Howe, Fanny   1940- .... **CLC 47**
See also CA 117; SATA 52

Howe, Julia Ward   1819-1910 ..... **TCLC 21**
See also CA 117; DLB 1

Howe, Susan   1937-............... **CLC 72**
See also DLB 120

Howe, Tina   1937-................ **CLC 48**
See also CA 109

Howell, James   1594(?)-1666 .... **LC 13**

Howells, W. D.
See Howells, William Dean

Howells, William D.
See Howells, William Dean

Howells, William Dean
1837-1920 .... **TCLC 7, 17, 41**
See also CA 104; 134; CDALB 1865-1917;
DLB 12, 64, 74, 79

Howes, Barbara   1914-............. **CLC 15**
See also CA 9-12R; CAAS 3; SATA 5

Johnson, J. R.
See James, C(yril) L(ionel) R(obert)

Johnson, James Weldon
1871-1938 . . . . **TCLC 3, 19; BLC**
See also BW 1; CA 104; 125;
CDALB 1917-1929; CLR 32; DLB 51;
MTCW; SATA 31

Johnson, Joyce 1935- . . . . **CLC 58**
See also CA 125; 129

Johnson, Lionel (Pigot)
1867-1902 . . . . **TCLC 19**
See also CA 117; DLB 19

Johnson, Mel
See Malzberg, Barry N(athaniel)

Johnson, Pamela Hansford
1912-1981 . . . . **CLC 1, 7, 27**
See also CA 1-4R; 104; CANR 2, 28;
DLB 15; MTCW

Johnson, Samuel
1709-1784 . . . . **LC 15; DA; WLC**
See also CDBLB 1660-1789; DLB 39, 95,
104, 142

Johnson, Uwe
1934-1984 . . . . **CLC 5, 10, 15, 40**
See also CA 1-4R; 112; CANR 1, 39;
DLB 75; MTCW

Johnston, George (Benson) 1913- . . . **CLC 51**
See also CA 1-4R; CANR 5, 20; DLB 88

Johnston, Jennifer 1930- . . . . **CLC 7**
See also CA 85-88; DLB 14

Jolley, (Monica) Elizabeth 1923- . . . **CLC 46**
See also CA 127; CAAS 13

Jones, Arthur Llewellyn 1863-1947
See Machen, Arthur
See also CA 104

Jones, D(ouglas) G(ordon) 1929- . . . . **CLC 10**
See also CA 29-32R; CANR 13; DLB 53

Jones, David (Michael)
1895-1974 . . . . **CLC 2, 4, 7, 13, 42**
See also CA 9-12R; 53-56; CANR 28;
CDBLB 1945-1960; DLB 20, 100; MTCW

Jones, David Robert 1947-
See Bowie, David
See also CA 103

Jones, Diana Wynne 1934- . . . . **CLC 26**
See also AAYA 12; CA 49-52; CANR 4,
26; CLR 23; JRDA; MAICYA; SAAS 7;
SATA 9, 70

Jones, Edward P. 1950- . . . . **CLC 76**
See also BW 2; CA 142

Jones, Gayl 1949- . . . . **CLC 6, 9; BLC**
See also BW 2; CA 77-80; CANR 27;
DLB 33; MTCW

Jones, James 1921-1977 . . . . **CLC 1, 3, 10, 39**
See also AITN 1, 2; CA 1-4R; 69-72;
CANR 6; DLB 2, 143; MTCW

Jones, John J.
See Lovecraft, H(oward) P(hillips)

Jones, LeRoi . . . . **CLC 1, 2, 3, 5, 10, 14**
See also Baraka, Amiri

Jones, Louis B. . . . . **CLC 65**
See also CA 141

Jones, Madison (Percy, Jr.) 1925- . . . **CLC 4**
See also CA 13-16R; CAAS 11; CANR 7

Jones, Mervyn 1922- . . . . **CLC 10, 52**
See also CA 45-48; CAAS 5; CANR 1;
MTCW

Jones, Mick 1956(?)- . . . . **CLC 30**
See also Clash, The

Jones, Nettie (Pearl) 1941- . . . . **CLC 34**
See also BW 2; CA 137

Jones, Preston 1936-1979 . . . . **CLC 10**
See also CA 73-76; 89-92; DLB 7

Jones, Robert F(rancis) 1934- . . . . **CLC 7**
See also CA 49-52; CANR 2

Jones, Rod 1953- . . . . **CLC 50**
See also CA 128

Jones, Terence Graham Parry
1942- . . . . **CLC 21**
See also Jones, Terry; Monty Python
See also CA 112; 116; CANR 35; SATA 51

Jones, Terry
See Jones, Terence Graham Parry
See also SATA 67

Jones, Thom 1945(?)- . . . . **CLC 81**

Jong, Erica 1942- . . . . . . **CLC 4, 6, 8, 18, 83**
See also AITN 1; BEST 90:2; CA 73-76;
CANR 26; DLB 2, 5, 28; MTCW

Jonson, Ben(jamin)
1572(?)-1637 . . . . **LC 6; DA; DC 4; WLC**
See also CDBLB Before 1660; DLB 62, 121

Jordan, June 1936- . . . . **CLC 5, 11, 23**
See also AAYA 2; BW 2; CA 33-36R;
CANR 25; CLR 10; DLB 38; MAICYA;
MTCW; SATA 4

Jordan, Pat(rick M.) 1941- . . . . **CLC 37**
See also CA 33-36R

Jorgensen, Ivar
See Ellison, Harlan

Jorgenson, Ivar
See Silverberg, Robert

Josephus, Flavius c. 37-100 . . . . . . **CMLC 13**

Josipovici, Gabriel 1940- . . . . **CLC 6, 43**
See also CA 37-40R; CAAS 8; DLB 14

Joubert, Joseph 1754-1824 . . . . **NCLC 9**

Jouve, Pierre Jean 1887-1976 . . . . . . **CLC 47**
See also CA 65-68

Joyce, James (Augustine Aloysius)
1882-1941 . . . . . . **TCLC 3, 8, 16, 35; DA;**
SSC 3; WLC
See also CA 104; 126; CDBLB 1914-1945;
DLB 10, 19, 36; MTCW

Jozsef, Attila 1905-1937 . . . . **TCLC 22**
See also CA 116

Juana Ines de la Cruz 1651(?)-1695 . . . **LC 5**

Judd, Cyril
See Kornbluth, C(yril) M.; Pohl, Frederik

Julian of Norwich 1342(?)-1416(?) . . . . **LC 6**

Just, Ward (Swift) 1935- . . . . **CLC 4, 27**
See also CA 25-28R; CANR 32

Justice, Donald (Rodney) 1925- . . **CLC 6, 19**
See also CA 5-8R; CANR 26; DLBY 83

Juvenal c. 55-c. 127 . . . . **CMLC 8**

Juvenis
See Bourne, Randolph S(illiman)

Kacew, Romain 1914-1980
See Gary, Romain
See also CA 108; 102

Kadare, Ismail 1936- . . . . **CLC 52**

Kadohata, Cynthia . . . . **CLC 59**
See also CA 140

Kafka, Franz
1883-1924 . . . . **TCLC 2, 6, 13, 29, 47, 53;**
DA; SSC 5; WLC
See also CA 105; 126; DLB 81; MTCW

Kahanovitsch, Pinkhes 1884-1950
See Der Nister

Kahn, Roger 1927- . . . . **CLC 30**
See also CA 25-28R; CANR 44; SATA 37

Kain, Saul
See Sassoon, Siegfried (Lorraine)

Kaiser, Georg 1878-1945 . . . . **TCLC 9**
See also CA 106; DLB 124

Kaletski, Alexander 1946- . . . . **CLC 39**
See also CA 118; 143

Kalidasa fl. c. 400- . . . . **CMLC 9**

Kallman, Chester (Simon)
1921-1975 . . . . **CLC 2**
See also CA 45-48; 53-56; CANR 3

Kaminsky, Melvin 1926-
See Brooks, Mel
See also CA 65-68; CANR 16

Kaminsky, Stuart M(elvin) 1934- . . . **CLC 59**
See also CA 73-76; CANR 29

Kane, Paul
See Simon, Paul

Kane, Wilson
See Bloch, Robert (Albert)

Kanin, Garson 1912- . . . . **CLC 22**
See also AITN 1; CA 5-8R; CANR 7;
DLB 7

Kaniuk, Yoram 1930- . . . . **CLC 19**
See also CA 134

Kant, Immanuel 1724-1804 . . . . **NCLC 27**
See also DLB 94

Kantor, MacKinlay 1904-1977 . . . . **CLC 7**
See also CA 61-64; 73-76; DLB 9, 102

Kaplan, David Michael 1946- . . . . . . **CLC 50**

Kaplan, James 1951- . . . . **CLC 59**
See also CA 135

Karageorge, Michael
See Anderson, Poul (William)

Karamzin, Nikolai Mikhailovich
1766-1826 . . . . **NCLC 3**

Karapanou, Margarita 1946- . . . . **CLC 13**
See also CA 101

Karinthy, Frigyes 1887-1938 . . . . . . **TCLC 47**

Karl, Frederick R(obert) 1927- . . . . . **CLC 34**
See also CA 5-8R; CANR 3, 44

Kastel, Warren
See Silverberg, Robert

Kataev, Evgeny Petrovich 1903-1942
See Petrov, Evgeny
See also CA 120

Kataphusin
See Ruskin, John

Lelchuk, Alan 1938-.............. **CLC 5**
See also CA 45-48; CANR 1

Lem, Stanislaw 1921-....... **CLC 8, 15, 40**
See also CA 105; CAAS 1; CANR 32;
MTCW

Lemann, Nancy 1956-............ **CLC 39**
See also CA 118; 136

Lemonnier, (Antoine Louis) Camille
1844-1913 .... **TCLC 22**
See also CA 121

Lenau, Nikolaus 1802-1850 ..... **NCLC 16**

L'Engle, Madeleine (Camp Franklin)
1918- .... **CLC 12**
See also AAYA 1; AITN 2; CA 1-4R;
CANR 3, 21, 39; CLR 1, 14; DLB 52;
JRDA; MAICYA; MTCW; SAAS 15;
SATA 1, 27, 75

Lengyel, Jozsef 1896-1975......... **CLC 7**
See also CA 85-88; 57-60

Lennon, John (Ono)
1940-1980 .... **CLC 12, 35**
See also CA 102

Lennox, Charlotte Ramsay
1729(?)-1804 .... **NCLC 23**
See also DLB 39

Lentricchia, Frank (Jr.) 1940-...... **CLC 34**
See also CA 25-28R; CANR 19

Lenz, Siegfried 1926-............ **CLC 27**
See also CA 89-92; DLB 75

Leonard, Elmore (John, Jr.)
1925- .... **CLC 28, 34, 71**
See also AITN 1; BEST 89:1, 90:4;
CA 81-84; CANR 12, 28; MTCW

Leonard, Hugh
See Byrne, John Keyes
See also DLB 13

Leopardi, (Conte) Giacomo (Talegardo
Francesco di Sales Save
1798-1837 .... **NCLC 22**

Le Reveler
See Artaud, Antonin

Lerman, Eleanor 1952-............ **CLC 9**
See also CA 85-88

Lerman, Rhoda 1936-............ **CLC 56**
See also CA 49-52

Lermontov, Mikhail Yuryevich
1814-1841 .... **NCLC 5**

Leroux, Gaston 1868-1927....... **TCLC 25**
See also CA 108; 136; SATA 65

Lesage, Alain-Rene 1668-1747....... **LC 2**

Leskov, Nikolai (Semyonovich)
1831-1895 .... **NCLC 25**

Lessing, Doris (May)
1919- ..... **CLC 1, 2, 3, 6, 10, 15, 22, 40;**
DA; SSC 6
See also CA 9-12R; CAAS 14; CANR 33;
CDBLB 1960 to Present; DLB 15, 139;
DLBY 85; MTCW

Lessing, Gotthold Ephraim
1729-1781 .... **LC 8**
See also DLB 97

Lester, Richard 1932-............ **CLC 20**

Lever, Charles (James)
1806-1872 .... **NCLC 23**
See also DLB 21

Leverson, Ada 1865(?)-1936(?) .... **TCLC 18**
See also Elaine
See also CA 117

Levertov, Denise
1923- ...... **CLC 1, 2, 3, 5, 8, 15, 28, 66**
See also CA 1-4R; CAAS 19; CANR 3, 29;
DLB 5; MTCW

Levi, Jonathan.................... **CLC 76**

Levi, Peter (Chad Tigar) 1931-..... **CLC 41**
See also CA 5-8R; CANR 34; DLB 40

Levi, Primo
1919-1987 .... **CLC 37, 50; SSC 12**
See also CA 13-16R; 122; CANR 12, 33;
MTCW

Levin, Ira 1929- .... **CLC 3, 6**
See also CA 21-24R; CANR 17, 44;
MTCW; SATA 66

Levin, Meyer 1905-1981 .... **CLC 7**
See also AITN 1; CA 9-12R; 104;
CANR 15; DLB 9, 28; DLBY 81;
SATA 21, 27

Levine, Norman 1924-............ **CLC 54**
See also CA 73-76; CANR 14; DLB 88

Levine, Philip 1928-.. **CLC 2, 4, 5, 9, 14, 33**
See also CA 9-12R; CANR 9, 37; DLB 5

Levinson, Deirdre 1931-.......... **CLC 49**
See also CA 73-76

Levi-Strauss, Claude 1908- .... **CLC 38**
See also CA 1-4R; CANR 6, 32; MTCW

Levitin, Sonia (Wolff) 1934- .... **CLC 17**
See also CA 29-32R; CANR 14, 32; JRDA;
MAICYA; SAAS 2; SATA 4, 68

Levon, O. U.
See Kesey, Ken (Elton)

Lewes, George Henry
1817-1878 .... **NCLC 25**
See also DLB 55, 144

Lewis, Alun 1915-1944........... **TCLC 3**
See also CA 104; DLB 20

Lewis, C. Day
See Day Lewis, C(ecil)

Lewis, C(live) S(taples)
1898-1963 ..... **CLC 1, 3, 6, 14, 27; DA;**
WLC
See also AAYA 3; CA 81-84; CANR 33;
CDBLB 1945-1960; CLR 3, 27; DLB 15,
100; JRDA; MAICYA; MTCW;
SATA 13

Lewis, Janet 1899-.............. **CLC 41**
See also Winters, Janet Lewis
See also CA 9-12R; CANR 29; CAP 1;
DLBY 87

Lewis, Matthew Gregory
1775-1818 .... **NCLC 11**
See also DLB 39

Lewis, (Harry) Sinclair
1885-1951 ..... **TCLC 4, 13, 23, 39; DA;**
WLC
See also CA 104; 133; CDALB 1917-1929;
DLB 9, 102; DLBD 1; MTCW

Lewis, (Percy) Wyndham
1884(?)-1957 .... **TCLC 2, 9**
See also CA 104; DLB 15

Lewisohn, Ludwig 1883-1955...... **TCLC 19**
See also CA 107; DLB 4, 9, 28, 102

Lezama Lima, Jose 1910-1976 ... **CLC 4, 10**
See also CA 77-80; DLB 113; HW

L'Heureux, John (Clarke) 1934-.... **CLC 52**
See also CA 13-16R; CANR 23, 45

Liddell, C. H.
See Kuttner, Henry

Lie, Jonas (Lauritz Idemil)
1833-1908(?) .... **TCLC 5**
See also CA 115

Lieber, Joel 1937-1971............ **CLC 6**
See also CA 73-76; 29-32R

Lieber, Stanley Martin
See Lee, Stan

Lieberman, Laurence (James)
1935- .... **CLC 4, 36**
See also CA 17-20R; CANR 8, 36

Lieksman, Anders
See Haavikko, Paavo Juhani

Li Fei-kan 1904-................ **CLC 18**
See also CA 105

Lifton, Robert Jay 1926-.......... **CLC 67**
See also CA 17-20R; CANR 27; SATA 66

Lightfoot, Gordon 1938-........... **CLC 26**
See also CA 109

Lightman, Alan P. 1948-.......... **CLC 81**
See also CA 141

Ligotti, Thomas 1953- .... **CLC 44; SSC 16**
See also CA 123

Liliencron, (Friedrich Adolf Axel) Detlev von
1844-1909 .... **TCLC 18**
See also CA 117

Lima, Jose Lezama
See Lezama Lima, Jose

Lima Barreto, Afonso Henrique de
1881-1922 .... **TCLC 23**
See also CA 117

Limonov, Eduard.................. **CLC 67**

Lin, Frank
See Atherton, Gertrude (Franklin Horn)

Lincoln, Abraham 1809-1865..... **NCLC 18**

Lind, Jakov .... **CLC 1, 2, 4, 27, 82**
See also Landwirth, Heinz
See also CAAS 4

Lindbergh, Anne (Spencer) Morrow
1906- .... **CLC 82**
See also CA 17-20R; CANR 16; MTCW;
SATA 33

Lindsay, David 1878-1945 .... **TCLC 15**
See also CA 113

Lindsay, (Nicholas) Vachel
1879-1931 .... **TCLC 17; DA; WLC**
See also CA 114; 135; CDALB 1865-1917;
DLB 54; SATA 40

Linke-Poot
See Doeblin, Alfred

Linney, Romulus 1930- .... **CLC 51**
See also CA 1-4R; CANR 40, 44

Lukacs, Gyorgy (Szegeny von) 1885-1971
  See Lukacs, George
  See also CA 101; 29-32R

Luke, Peter (Ambrose Cyprian)
  1919- .... **CLC 38**
  See also CA 81-84; DLB 13

Lunar, Dennis
  See Mungo, Raymond

Lurie, Alison 1926- .... **CLC 4, 5, 18, 39**
  See also CA 1-4R; CANR 2, 17; DLB 2;
  MTCW; SATA 46

Lustig, Arnost 1926- .... **CLC 56**
  See also AAYA 3; CA 69-72; SATA 56

Luther, Martin 1483-1546 .... **LC 9**

Luzi, Mario 1914- .... **CLC 13**
  See also CA 61-64; CANR 9; DLB 128

Lynch, B. Suarez
  See Bioy Casares, Adolfo; Borges, Jorge
  Luis

Lynch, David (K.) 1946- .... **CLC 66**
  See also CA 124; 129

Lynch, James
  See Andreyev, Leonid (Nikolaevich)

Lynch Davis, B.
  See Bioy Casares, Adolfo; Borges, Jorge
  Luis

Lyndsay, Sir David 1490-1555 ...... **LC 20**

Lynn, Kenneth S(chuyler) 1923- .... **CLC 50**
  See also CA 1-4R; CANR 3, 27

Lynx
  See West, Rebecca

Lyons, Marcus
  See Blish, James (Benjamin)

Lyre, Pinchbeck
  See Sassoon, Siegfried (Lorraine)

Lytle, Andrew (Nelson) 1902- ...... **CLC 22**
  See also CA 9-12R; DLB 6

Lyttelton, George 1709-1773 .... **LC 10**

Maas, Peter 1929- .... **CLC 29**
  See also CA 93-96

Macaulay, Rose 1881-1958 ..... **TCLC 7, 44**
  See also CA 104; DLB 36

Macaulay, Thomas Babington
  1800-1859 .... **NCLC 42**
  See also CDBLB 1832-1890; DLB 32, 55

MacBeth, George (Mann)
  1932-1992 .... **CLC 2, 5, 9**
  See also CA 25-28R; 136; DLB 40; MTCW;
  SATA 4; SATA-Obit 70

MacCaig, Norman (Alexander)
  1910- .... **CLC 36**
  See also CA 9-12R; CANR 3, 34; DLB 27

MacCarthy, (Sir Charles Otto) Desmond
  1877-1952 .... **TCLC 36**

MacDiarmid, Hugh
  .... **CLC 2, 4, 11, 19, 63; PC 9**
  See also Grieve, C(hristopher) M(urray)
  See also CDBLB 1945-1960; DLB 20

MacDonald, Anson
  See Heinlein, Robert A(nson)

Macdonald, Cynthia 1928- ...... **CLC 13, 19**
  See also CA 49-52; CANR 4, 44; DLB 105

MacDonald, George 1824-1905 ..... **TCLC 9**
  See also CA 106; 137; DLB 18; MAICYA;
  SATA 33

Macdonald, John
  See Millar, Kenneth

MacDonald, John D(ann)
  1916-1986 .... **CLC 3, 27, 44**
  See also CA 1-4R; 121; CANR 1, 19;
  DLB 8; DLBY 86; MTCW

Macdonald, John Ross
  See Millar, Kenneth

Macdonald, Ross ..... **CLC 1, 2, 3, 14, 34, 41**
  See also Millar, Kenneth
  See also DLBD 6

MacDougal, John
  See Blish, James (Benjamin)

MacEwen, Gwendolyn (Margaret)
  1941-1987 .... **CLC 13, 55**
  See also CA 9-12R; 124; CANR 7, 22;
  DLB 53; SATA 50, 55

Macha, Karen Hynek
  1810-1846 .... **NCLC 46**

Machado (y Ruiz), Antonio
  1875-1939 .... **TCLC 3**
  See also CA 104; DLB 108

Machado de Assis, Joaquim Maria
  1839-1908 .... **TCLC 10; BLC**
  See also CA 107

Machen, Arthur .... **TCLC 4**
  See also Jones, Arthur Llewellyn
  See also DLB 36

Machiavelli, Niccolo 1469-1527 .. **LC 8; DA**

MacInnes, Colin 1914-1976 ...... **CLC 4, 23**
  See also CA 69-72; 65-68; CANR 21;
  DLB 14; MTCW

MacInnes, Helen (Clark)
  1907-1985 .... **CLC 27, 39**
  See also CA 1-4R; 117; CANR 1, 28;
  DLB 87; MTCW; SATA 22, 44

Mackay, Mary 1855-1924
  See Corelli, Marie
  See also CA 118

Mackenzie, Compton (Edward Montague)
  1883-1972 .... **CLC 18**
  See also CA 21-22; 37-40R; CAP 2;
  DLB 34, 100

Mackenzie, Henry 1745-1831 .... **NCLC 41**
  See also DLB 39

Mackintosh, Elizabeth 1896(?)-1952
  See Tey, Josephine
  See also CA 110

MacLaren, James
  See Grieve, C(hristopher) M(urray)

Mac Laverty, Bernard 1942- .... **CLC 31**
  See also CA 116; 118; CANR 43

MacLean, Alistair (Stuart)
  1922-1987 .... **CLC 3, 13, 50, 63**
  See also CA 57-60; 121; CANR 28; MTCW;
  SATA 23, 50

Maclean, Norman (Fitzroy)
  1902-1990 .... **CLC 78; SSC 13**
  See also CA 102; 132

MacLeish, Archibald
  1892-1982 .... **CLC 3, 8, 14, 68**
  See also CA 9-12R; 106; CANR 33; DLB 4,
  7, 45; DLBY 82; MTCW

MacLennan, (John) Hugh
  1907-1990 .... **CLC 2, 14**
  See also CA 5-8R; 142; CANR 33; DLB 68;
  MTCW

MacLeod, Alistair 1936- .... **CLC 56**
  See also CA 123; DLB 60

MacNeice, (Frederick) Louis
  1907-1963 .... **CLC 1, 4, 10, 53**
  See also CA 85-88; DLB 10, 20; MTCW

MacNeill, Dand
  See Fraser, George MacDonald

Macpherson, (Jean) Jay 1931- ...... **CLC 14**
  See also CA 5-8R; DLB 53

MacShane, Frank 1927- .... **CLC 39**
  See also CA 9-12R; CANR 3, 33; DLB 111

Macumber, Mari
  See Sandoz, Mari(e Susette)

Madach, Imre 1823-1864 .... **NCLC 19**

Madden, (Jerry) David 1933- ... **CLC 5, 15**
  See also CA 1-4R; CAAS 3; CANR 4, 45;
  DLB 6; MTCW

Maddern, Al(an)
  See Ellison, Harlan

Madhubuti, Haki R.
  1942- .... **CLC 6, 73; BLC; PC 5**
  See also Lee, Don L.
  See also BW 2; CA 73-76; CANR 24;
  DLB 5, 41; DLBD 8

Madow, Pauline (Reichberg) .... **CLC 1**
  See also CA 9-12R

Maepenn, Hugh
  See Kuttner, Henry

Maepenn, K. H.
  See Kuttner, Henry

Maeterlinck, Maurice 1862-1949 ... **TCLC 3**
  See also CA 104; 136; SATA 66

Maginn, William 1794-1842 .... **NCLC 8**
  See also DLB 110

Mahapatra, Jayanta 1928- .... **CLC 33**
  See also CA 73-76; CAAS 9; CANR 15, 33

Mahfouz, Naguib (Abdel Aziz Al-Sabilgi)
  1911(?)-
  See Mahfuz, Najib
  See also BEST 89:2; CA 128; MTCW

Mahfuz, Najib .... **CLC 52, 55**
  See also Mahfouz, Naguib (Abdel Aziz
  Al-Sabilgi)
  See also DLBY 88

Mahon, Derek 1941- .... **CLC 27**
  See also CA 113; 128; DLB 40

Mailer, Norman
  1923- ...... **CLC 1, 2, 3, 4, 5, 8, 11, 14,
  28, 39, 74; DA**
  See also AITN 2; CA 9-12R; CABS 1;
  CANR 28; CDALB 1968-1988; DLB 2,
  16, 28; DLBD 3; DLBY 80, 83; MTCW

Maillet, Antonine 1929- .... **CLC 54**
  See also CA 115; 120; DLB 60

Mais, Roger 1905-1955 .... **TCLC 8**
  See also BW 1; CA 105; 124; DLB 125;
  MTCW

Maistre, Joseph de   1753-1821.... **NCLC 37**

Maitland, Sara (Louise)   1950-...... **CLC 49**
See also CA 69-72; CANR 13

Major, Clarence
1936- .... **CLC 3, 19, 48; BLC**
See also BW 2; CA 21-24R; CAAS 6;
CANR 13, 25; DLB 33

Major, Kevin (Gerald)   1949-....... **CLC 26**
See also CA 97-100; CANR 21, 38;
CLR 11; DLB 60; JRDA; MAICYA;
SATA 32

Maki, James
See Ozu, Yasujiro

Malabaila, Damiano
See Levi, Primo

Malamud, Bernard
1914-1986 ...... **CLC 1, 2, 3, 5, 8, 9, 11,**
18, 27, 44, 78; DA; SSC 15; WLC
See also CA 5-8R; 118; CABS 1; CANR 28;
CDALB 1941-1968; DLB 2, 28;
DLBY 80, 86; MTCW

Malaparte, Curzio   1898-1957 ..... **TCLC 52**

Malcolm, Dan
See Silverberg, Robert

Malcolm X.................. **CLC 82; BLC**
See also Little, Malcolm

Malherbe, Francois de   1555-1628..... **LC 5**

Mallarme, Stephane
1842-1898 .... **NCLC 4, 41; PC 4**

Mallet-Joris, Francoise   1930-...... **CLC 11**
See also CA 65-68; CANR 17; DLB 83

Malley, Ern
See McAuley, James Phillip

Mallowan, Agatha Christie
See Christie, Agatha (Mary Clarissa)

Maloff, Saul   1922-................ **CLC 5**
See also CA 33-36R

Malone, Louis
See MacNeice, (Frederick) Louis

Malone, Michael (Christopher)
1942-...................... **CLC 43**
See also CA 77-80; CANR 14, 32

Malory, (Sir) Thomas
1410(?)-1471(?) .... **LC 11; DA**
See also CDBLB Before 1660; SATA 33, 59

Malouf, (George Joseph) David
1934-...................... **CLC 28**
See also CA 124

Malraux, (Georges-)Andre
1901-1976 ...... **CLC 1, 4, 9, 13, 15, 57**
See also CA 21-22; 69-72; CANR 34;
CAP 2; DLB 72; MTCW

Malzberg, Barry N(athaniel)   1939-... **CLC 7**
See also CA 61-64; CAAS 4; CANR 16;
DLB 8

Mamet, David (Alan)
1947-........ **CLC 9, 15, 34, 46; DC 4**
See also AAYA 3; CA 81-84; CABS 3;
CANR 15, 41; DLB 7; MTCW

Mamoulian, Rouben (Zachary)
1897-1987 .... **CLC 16**
See also CA 25-28R; 124

Mandelstam, Osip (Emilievich)
1891(?)-1938(?) .... **TCLC 2, 6**
See also CA 104

Mander, (Mary) Jane   1877-1949... **TCLC 31**

Mandiargues, Andre Pieyre de...... **CLC 41**
See also Pieyre de Mandiargues, Andre
See also DLB 83

Mandrake, Ethel Belle
See Thurman, Wallace (Henry)

Mangan, James Clarence
1803-1849 .... **NCLC 27**

Maniere, J.-E.
See Giraudoux, (Hippolyte) Jean

Manley, (Mary) Delariviere
1672(?)-1724 .... **LC 1**
See also DLB 39, 80

Mann, Abel
See Creasey, John

Mann, (Luiz) Heinrich   1871-1950... **TCLC 9**
See also CA 106; DLB 66

Mann, (Paul) Thomas
1875-1955 .... **TCLC 2, 8, 14, 21, 35, 44;**
DA; SSC 5; WLC
See also CA 104; 128; DLB 66; MTCW

Manning, David
See Faust, Frederick (Schiller)

Manning, Frederic   1887(?)-1935... **TCLC 25**
See also CA 124

Manning, Olivia   1915-1980...... **CLC 5, 19**
See also CA 5-8R; 101; CANR 29; MTCW

Mano, D. Keith   1942-.......... **CLC 2, 10**
See also CA 25-28R; CAAS 6; CANR 26;
DLB 6

Mansfield, Katherine
.... **TCLC 2, 8, 39; SSC 9; WLC**
See also Beauchamp, Kathleen Mansfield

Manso, Peter   1940-............ **CLC 39**
See also CA 29-32R; CANR 44

Mantecon, Juan Jimenez
See Jimenez (Mantecon), Juan Ramon

Manton, Peter
See Creasey, John

Man Without a Spleen, A
See Chekhov, Anton (Pavlovich)

Manzoni, Alessandro   1785-1873.. **NCLC 29**

Mapu, Abraham (ben Jekutiel)
1808-1867 .... **NCLC 18**

Mara, Sally
See Queneau, Raymond

Marat, Jean Paul   1743-1793....... **LC 10**

Marcel, Gabriel Honore
1889-1973 .... **CLC 15**
See also CA 102; 45-48; MTCW

Marchbanks, Samuel
See Davies, (William) Robertson

Marchi, Giacomo
See Bassani, Giorgio

Margulies, Donald................. **CLC 76**

Marie de France   c. 12th cent. -.... **CMLC 8**

Marie de l'Incarnation   1599-1672.... **LC 10**

Mariner, Scott
See Pohl, Frederik

Marinetti, Filippo Tommaso
1876-1944 .... **TCLC 10**
See also CA 107; DLB 114

Marivaux, Pierre Carlet de Chamblain de
1688-1763 .... **LC 4**

Markandaya, Kamala .... **CLC 8, 38**
See also Taylor, Kamala (Purnaiya)

Markfield, Wallace   1926-.......... **CLC 8**
See also CA 69-72; CAAS 3; DLB 2, 28

Markham, Edwin   1852-1940...... **TCLC 47**
See also DLB 54

Markham, Robert
See Amis, Kingsley (William)

Marks, J
See Highwater, Jamake (Mamake)

Marks-Highwater, J
See Highwater, Jamake (Mamake)

Markson, David M(errill)   1927-.... **CLC 67**
See also CA 49-52; CANR 1

Marley, Bob...................... **CLC 17**
See also Marley, Robert Nesta

Marley, Robert Nesta   1945-1981
See Marley, Bob
See also CA 107; 103

Marlowe, Christopher
1564-1593 ..... **LC 22; DA; DC 1; WLC**
See also CDBLB Before 1660; DLB 62

Marmontel, Jean-Francois
1723-1799 .... **LC 2**

Marquand, John P(hillips)
1893-1960 .... **CLC 2, 10**
See also CA 85-88; DLB 9, 102

Marquez, Gabriel (Jose) Garcia...... **CLC 68**
See also Garcia Marquez, Gabriel (Jose)

Marquis, Don(ald Robert Perry)
1878-1937 .... **TCLC 7**
See also CA 104; DLB 11, 25

Marric, J. J.
See Creasey, John

Marrow, Bernard
See Moore, Brian

Marryat, Frederick   1792-1848.... **NCLC 3**
See also DLB 21

Marsden, James
See Creasey, John

Marsh, (Edith) Ngaio
1899-1982 .... **CLC 7, 53**
See also CA 9-12R; CANR 6; DLB 77;
MTCW

Marshall, Garry   1934-............ **CLC 17**
See also AAYA 3; CA 111; SATA 60

Marshall, Paule
1929-........ **CLC 27, 72; BLC; SSC 3**
See also BW 2; CA 77-80; CANR 25;
DLB 33; MTCW

Marsten, Richard
See Hunter, Evan

Martha, Henry
See Harris, Mark

Martial   40-104 .... **PC 10**

Martin, Ken
See Hubbard, L(afayette) Ron(ald)

Meyer, June
See Jordan, June

Meyer, Lynn
See Slavitt, David R(ytman)

Meyer-Meyrink, Gustav   1868-1932
See Meyrink, Gustav
See also CA 117

Meyers, Jeffrey   1939- . . . . **CLC 39**
See also CA 73-76; DLB 111

Meynell, Alice (Christina Gertrude Thompson)
1847-1922 . . . . **TCLC 6**
See also CA 104; DLB 19, 98

Meyrink, Gustav . . . . **TCLC 21**
See also Meyer-Meyrink, Gustav
See also DLB 81

Michaels, Leonard
1933- . . . . **CLC 6, 25; SSC 16**
See also CA 61-64; CANR 21; DLB 130;
MTCW

Michaux, Henri   1899-1984 . . . . . . **CLC 8, 19**
See also CA 85-88; 114

Michelangelo   1475-1564. . . . . **LC 12**

Michelet, Jules   1798-1874 . . . . . . **NCLC 31**

Michener, James A(lbert)
1907(?)- . . . . **CLC 1, 5, 11, 29, 60**
See also AITN 1; BEST 90:1; CA 5-8R;
CANR 21, 45; DLB 6; MTCW

Mickiewicz, Adam   1798-1855 . . . . . **NCLC 3**

Middleton, Christopher   1926- . . . . . . **CLC 13**
See also CA 13-16R; CANR 29; DLB 40

Middleton, Richard (Barham)
1882-1911 . . . . **TCLC 56**

Middleton, Stanley   1919- . . . . **CLC 7, 38**
See also CA 25-28R; CANR 21; DLB 14

Migueis, Jose Rodrigues   1901- . . . . . **CLC 10**

Mikszath, Kalman   1847-1910 . . . . . **TCLC 31**

Miles, Josephine
1911-1985 . . . . **CLC 1, 2, 14, 34, 39**
See also CA 1-4R; 116; CANR 2; DLB 48

Militant
See Sandburg, Carl (August)

Mill, John Stuart   1806-1873 . . . . . **NCLC 11**
See also CDBLB 1832-1890; DLB 55

Millar, Kenneth   1915-1983 . . . . **CLC 14**
See also Macdonald, Ross
See also CA 9-12R; 110; CANR 16; DLB 2;
DLBD 6; DLBY 83; MTCW

Millay, E. Vincent
See Millay, Edna St. Vincent

Millay, Edna St. Vincent
1892-1950 . . . . . . **TCLC 4, 49; DA; PC 6**
See also CA 104; 130; CDALB 1917-1929;
DLB 45; MTCW

Miller, Arthur
1915- . . . . **CLC 1, 2, 6, 10, 15, 26, 47, 78;
DA; DC 1; WLC**
See also AITN 1; CA 1-4R; CABS 3;
CANR 2, 30; CDALB 1941-1968; DLB 7;
MTCW

Miller, Henry (Valentine)
1891-1980 . . . . **CLC 1, 2, 4, 9, 14, 43, 84;
DA; WLC**
See also CA 9-12R; 97-100; CANR 33;
CDALB 1929-1941; DLB 4, 9; DLBY 80;
MTCW

Miller, Jason   1939(?)- . . . . **CLC 2**
See also AITN 1; CA 73-76; DLB 7

Miller, Sue   1943- . . . . **CLC 44**
See also BEST 90:3; CA 139; DLB 143

Miller, Walter M(ichael, Jr.)
1923- . . . . **CLC 4, 30**
See also CA 85-88; DLB 8

Millett, Kate   1934- . . . . **CLC 67**
See also AITN 1; CA 73-76; CANR 32;
MTCW

Millhauser, Steven   1943- . . . . **CLC 21, 54**
See also CA 110; 111; DLB 2

Millin, Sarah Gertrude   1889-1968 . . **CLC 49**
See also CA 102; 93-96

Milne, A(lan) A(lexander)
1882-1956 . . . . **TCLC 6**
See also CA 104; 133; CLR 1, 26; DLB 10,
77, 100; MAICYA; MTCW; YABC 1

Milner, Ron(ald)   1938- . . . . **CLC 56; BLC**
See also AITN 1; BW 1; CA 73-76;
CANR 24; DLB 38; MTCW

Milosz, Czeslaw
1911- . . . **CLC 5, 11, 22, 31, 56, 82; PC 8**
See also CA 81-84; CANR 23; MTCW

Milton, John   1608-1674 . . . **LC 9; DA; WLC**
See also CDBLB 1660-1789; DLB 131

Minehaha, Cornelius
See Wedekind, (Benjamin) Frank(lin)

Miner, Valerie   1947- . . . . **CLC 40**
See also CA 97-100

Minimo, Duca
See D'Annunzio, Gabriele

Minot, Susan   1956- . . . . **CLC 44**
See also CA 134

Minus, Ed   1938- . . . . **CLC 39**

Miranda, Javier
See Bioy Casares, Adolfo

Mirbeau, Octave   1848-1917 . . . . . . **TCLC 55**
See also DLB 123

Miro (Ferrer), Gabriel (Francisco Victor)
1879-1930 . . . . **TCLC 5**
See also CA 104

Mishima, Yukio
. . . . . . **CLC 2, 4, 6, 9, 27; DC 1; SSC 4**
See also Hiraoka, Kimitake

Mistral, Frederic   1830-1914 . . . . . **TCLC 51**
See also CA 122

Mistral, Gabriela. . . . . **TCLC 2; HLC**
See also Godoy Alcayaga, Lucila

Mistry, Rohinton   1952- . . . . **CLC 71**
See also CA 141

Mitchell, Clyde
See Ellison, Harlan; Silverberg, Robert

Mitchell, James Leslie   1901-1935
See Gibbon, Lewis Grassic
See also CA 104; DLB 15

Mitchell, Joni   1943- . . . . **CLC 12**
See also CA 112

Mitchell, Margaret (Munnerlyn)
1900-1949 . . . . **TCLC 11**
See also CA 109; 125; DLB 9; MTCW

Mitchell, Peggy
See Mitchell, Margaret (Munnerlyn)

Mitchell, S(ilas) Weir   1829-1914 . . **TCLC 36**

Mitchell, W(illiam) O(rmond)
1914- . . . . **CLC 25**
See also CA 77-80; CANR 15, 43; DLB 88

Mitford, Mary Russell   1787-1855. . **NCLC 4**
See also DLB 110, 116

Mitford, Nancy   1904-1973. . . . . . . **CLC 44**
See also CA 9-12R

Miyamoto, Yuriko   1899-1951 . . . . . **TCLC 37**

Mo, Timothy (Peter)   1950(?)- . . . . . . **CLC 46**
See also CA 117; MTCW

Modarressi, Taghi (M.)   1931- . . . . . . **CLC 44**
See also CA 121; 134

Modiano, Patrick (Jean)   1945- . . . . . **CLC 18**
See also CA 85-88; CANR 17, 40; DLB 83

Moerck, Paal
See Roelvaag, O(le) E(dvart)

Mofolo, Thomas (Mokopu)
1875(?)-1948 . . . . **TCLC 22; BLC**
See also CA 121

Mohr, Nicholasa   1935- . . . . . . **CLC 12; HLC**
See also AAYA 8; CA 49-52; CANR 1, 32;
CLR 22; HW; JRDA; SAAS 8; SATA 8

Mojtabai, A(nn) G(race)
1938- . . . . **CLC 5, 9, 15, 29**
See also CA 85-88

Moliere   1622-1673 . . . . **LC 10; DA; WLC**

Molin, Charles
See Mayne, William (James Carter)

Molnar, Ferenc   1878-1952. . . . . . . **TCLC 20**
See also CA 109

Momaday, N(avarre) Scott
1934- . . . . **CLC 2, 19; DA**
See also AAYA 11; CA 25-28R; CANR 14,
34; DLB 143; MTCW; NNAL; SATA 30,
48

Monette, Paul   1945- . . . . **CLC 82**
See also CA 139

Monroe, Harriet   1860-1936. . . . . . . **TCLC 12**
See also CA 109; DLB 54, 91

Monroe, Lyle
See Heinlein, Robert A(nson)

Montagu, Elizabeth   1917- . . . . **NCLC 7**
See also CA 9-12R

Montagu, Mary (Pierrepont) Wortley
1689-1762 . . . . **LC 9**
See also DLB 95, 101

Montagu, W. H.
See Coleridge, Samuel Taylor

Montague, John (Patrick)
1929- . . . . **CLC 13, 46**
See also CA 9-12R; CANR 9; DLB 40;
MTCW

Montaigne, Michel (Eyquem) de
1533-1592 . . . . **LC 8; DA; WLC**

Montale, Eugenio   1896-1981 . . . **CLC 7, 9, 18**
See also CA 17-20R; 104; CANR 30;
DLB 114; MTCW

Mueller, Lisel 1924-.......... **CLC 13, 51**
See also CA 93-96; DLB 105

Muir, Edwin 1887-1959.......... **TCLC 2**
See also CA 104; DLB 20, 100

Muir, John 1838-1914.......... **TCLC 28**

Mujica Lainez, Manuel
1910-1984.................. **CLC 31**
See also Lainez, Manuel Mujica
See also CA 81-84; 112; CANR 32; HW

Mukherjee, Bharati 1940-......... **CLC 53**
See also BEST 89:2; CA 107; CANR 45;
DLB 60; MTCW

Muldoon, Paul 1951-.......... **CLC 32, 72**
See also CA 113; 129; DLB 40

Mulisch, Harry 1927-............. **CLC 42**
See also CA 9-12R; CANR 6, 26

Mull, Martin 1943-.............. **CLC 17**
See also CA 105

Mulock, Dinah Maria
See Craik, Dinah Maria (Mulock)

Munford, Robert 1737(?)-1783....... **LC 5**
See also DLB 31

Mungo, Raymond 1946-.......... **CLC 72**
See also CA 49-52; CANR 2

Munro, Alice
1931-........ **CLC 6, 10, 19, 50; SSC 3**
See also AITN 2; CA 33-36R; CANR 33;
DLB 53; MTCW; SATA 29

Munro, H(ector) H(ugh) 1870-1916
See Saki
See also CA 104; 130; CDBLB 1890-1914;
DA; DLB 34; MTCW; WLC

Murasaki, Lady................. **CMLC 1**

Murdoch, (Jean) Iris
1919-...... **CLC 1, 2, 3, 4, 6, 8, 11, 15,**
22, 31, 51
See also CA 13-16R; CANR 8, 43;
CDBLB 1960 to Present; DLB 14;
MTCW

Murnau, Friedrich Wilhelm
See Plumpe, Friedrich Wilhelm

Murphy, Richard 1927-........... **CLC 41**
See also CA 29-32R; DLB 40

Murphy, Sylvia 1937-............. **CLC 34**
See also CA 121

Murphy, Thomas (Bernard) 1935-... **CLC 51**
See also CA 101

Murray, Albert L. 1916-......... **CLC 73**
See also BW 2; CA 49-52; CANR 26;
DLB 38

Murray, Les(lie) A(llan) 1938-..... **CLC 40**
See also CA 21-24R; CANR 11, 27

Murry, J. Middleton
See Murry, John Middleton

Murry, John Middleton
1889-1957.................. **TCLC 16**
See also CA 118

Musgrave, Susan 1951-........ **CLC 13, 54**
See also CA 69-72; CANR 45

Musil, Robert (Edler von)
1880-1942.................. **TCLC 12**
See also CA 109; DLB 81, 124

Musset, (Louis Charles) Alfred de
1810-1857................... **NCLC 7**

My Brother's Brother
See Chekhov, Anton (Pavlovich)

Myers, Walter Dean 1937-... **CLC 35; BLC**
See also AAYA 4; BW 2; CA 33-36R;
CANR 20, 42; CLR 4, 16; DLB 33;
JRDA; MAICYA; SAAS 2; SATA 27, 41,
71

Myers, Walter M.
See Myers, Walter Dean

Myles, Symon
See Follett, Ken(neth Martin)

Nabokov, Vladimir (Vladimirovich)
1899-1977..... **CLC 1, 2, 3, 6, 8, 11, 15,**
23, 44, 46, 64; DA; SSC 11; WLC
See also CA 5-8R; 69-72; CANR 20;
CDALB 1941-1968; DLB 2; DLBD 3;
DLBY 80, 91; MTCW

Nagai Kafu.................... **TCLC 51**
See also Nagai Sokichi

Nagai Sokichi 1879-1959
See Nagai Kafu
See also CA 117

Nagy, Laszlo 1925-1978........... **CLC 7**
See also CA 129; 112

Naipaul, Shiva(dhar Srinivasa)
1945-1985................. **CLC 32, 39**
See also CA 110; 112; 116; CANR 33;
DLBY 85; MTCW

Naipaul, V(idiadhar) S(urajprasad)
1932-.......... **CLC 4, 7, 9, 13, 18, 37**
See also CA 1-4R; CANR 1, 33;
CDBLB 1960 to Present; DLB 125;
DLBY 85; MTCW

Nakos, Lilika 1899(?)-........... **CLC 29**

Narayan, R(asipuram) K(rishnaswami)
1906-................. **CLC 7, 28, 47**
See also CA 81-84; CANR 33; MTCW;
SATA 62

Nash, (Fredric) Ogden 1902-1971.. **CLC 23**
See also CA 13-14; 29-32R; CANR 34;
CAP 1; DLB 11; MAICYA; MTCW;
SATA 2, 46

Nathan, Daniel
See Dannay, Frederic

Nathan, George Jean 1882-1958... **TCLC 18**
See also Hatteras, Owen
See also CA 114; DLB 137

Natsume, Kinnosuke 1867-1916
See Natsume, Soseki
See also CA 104

Natsume, Soseki .... **TCLC 2, 10**
See also Natsume, Kinnosuke

Natti, (Mary) Lee 1919-
See Kingman, Lee
See also CA 5-8R; CANR 2

Naylor, Gloria
1950-.......... **CLC 28, 52; BLC; DA**
See also AAYA 6; BW 2; CA 107;
CANR 27; MTCW

Neihardt, John Gneisenau
1881-1973................. **CLC 32**
See also CA 13-14; CAP 1; DLB 9, 54

Nekrasov, Nikolai Alekseevich
1821-1878................. **NCLC 11**

Nelligan, Emile 1879-1941....... **TCLC 14**
See also CA 114; DLB 92

Nelson, Willie 1933-.............. **CLC 17**
See also CA 107

Nemerov, Howard (Stanley)
1920-1991.............. **CLC 2, 6, 9, 36**
See also CA 1-4R; 134; CABS 2; CANR 1,
27; DLB 6; DLBY 83; MTCW

Neruda, Pablo
1904-1973..... **CLC 1, 2, 5, 7, 9, 28, 62;**
DA; HLC; PC 4; WLC
See also CA 19-20; 45-48; CAP 2; HW;
MTCW

Nerval, Gerard de 1808-1855...... **NCLC 1**

Nervo, (Jose) Amado (Ruiz de)
1870-1919................. **TCLC 11**
See also CA 109; 131; HW

Nessi, Pio Baroja y
See Baroja (y Nessi), Pio

Nestroy, Johann 1801-1862...... **NCLC 42**
See also DLB 133

Neufeld, John (Arthur) 1938-...... **CLC 17**
See also AAYA 11; CA 25-28R; CANR 11,
37; MAICYA; SAAS 3; SATA 6

Neville, Emily Cheney 1919-....... **CLC 12**
See also CA 5-8R; CANR 3, 37; JRDA;
MAICYA; SAAS 2; SATA 1

Newbound, Bernard Slade 1930-
See Slade, Bernard
See also CA 81-84

Newby, P(ercy) H(oward)
1918-................... **CLC 2, 13**
See also CA 5-8R; CANR 32; DLB 15;
MTCW

Newlove, Donald 1928-............ **CLC 6**
See also CA 29-32R; CANR 25

Newlove, John (Herbert) 1938-..... **CLC 14**
See also CA 21-24R; CANR 9, 25

Newman, Charles 1938-........... **CLC 2, 8**
See also CA 21-24R

Newman, Edwin (Harold) 1919-.... **CLC 14**
See also AITN 1; CA 69-72; CANR 5

Newman, John Henry
1801-1890................. **NCLC 38**
See also DLB 18, 32, 55

Newton, Suzanne 1936-........... **CLC 35**
See also CA 41-44R; CANR 14; JRDA;
SATA 5, 77

Nexo, Martin Andersen
1869-1954................. **TCLC 43**

Nezval, Vitezslav 1900-1958...... **TCLC 44**
See also CA 123

Ng, Fae Myenne 1957(?)-......... **CLC 81**

Ngema, Mbongeni 1955-.......... **CLC 57**
See also BW 2; CA 143

Ngugi, James T(hiong'o)........ **CLC 3, 7, 13**
See also Ngugi wa Thiong'o

Ngugi wa Thiong'o 1938-..... **CLC 36; BLC**
See also Ngugi, James T(hiong'o)
See also BW 2; CA 81-84; CANR 27;
DLB 125; MTCW

Nichol, B(arrie) P(hillip)
1944-1988.................. **CLC 18**
See also CA 53-56; DLB 53; SATA 66

O'Grady, Timothy 1951-. . . . . **CLC 59**
See also CA 138

O'Hara, Frank
1926-1966 . . . . **CLC 2, 5, 13, 78**
See also CA 9-12R; 25-28R; CANR 33;
DLB 5, 16; MTCW

O'Hara, John (Henry)
1905-1970 . . . . . . **CLC 1, 2, 3, 6, 11, 42;
SSC 15**
See also CA 5-8R; 25-28R; CANR 31;
CDALB 1929-1941; DLB 9, 86; DLBD 2;
MTCW

O Hehir, Diana 1922- . . . . **CLC 41**
See also CA 93-96

Okigbo, Christopher (Ifenayichukwu)
1932-1967 . . . . . **CLC 25, 84; BLC; PC 7**
See also BW 1; CA 77-80; DLB 125;
MTCW

Olds, Sharon 1942-. . . . . **CLC 32, 39**
See also CA 101; CANR 18, 41; DLB 120

Oldstyle, Jonathan
See Irving, Washington

Olesha, Yuri (Karlovich)
1899-1960 . . . . **CLC 8**
See also CA 85-88

Oliphant, Margaret (Oliphant Wilson)
1828-1897 . . . . **NCLC 11**
See also DLB 18

Oliver, Mary 1935-. . . . . **CLC 19, 34**
See also CA 21-24R; CANR 9, 43; DLB 5

Olivier, Laurence (Kerr)
1907-1989 . . . . **CLC 20**
See also CA 111; 129

Olsen, Tillie
1913- . . . . **CLC 4, 13; DA; SSC 11**
See also CA 1-4R; CANR 1, 43; DLB 28;
DLBY 80; MTCW

Olson, Charles (John)
1910-1970 . . . . . **CLC 1, 2, 5, 6, 9, 11, 29**
See also CA 13-16; 25-28R; CABS 2;
CANR 35; CAP 1; DLB 5, 16; MTCW

Olson, Toby 1937- . . . . **CLC 28**
See also CA 65-68; CANR 9, 31

Olyesha, Yuri
See Olesha, Yuri (Karlovich)

Ondaatje, (Philip) Michael
1943- . . . . **CLC 14, 29, 51, 76**
See also CA 77-80; CANR 42; DLB 60

Oneal, Elizabeth 1934-
See Oneal, Zibby
See also CA 106; CANR 28; MAICYA;
SATA 30

Oneal, Zibby . . . . **CLC 30**
See also Oneal, Elizabeth
See also AAYA 5; CLR 13; JRDA

O'Neill, Eugene (Gladstone)
1888-1953 . . . . . . **TCLC 1, 6, 27, 49; DA;
WLC**
See also AITN 1; CA 110; 132;
CDALB 1929-1941; DLB 7; MTCW

Onetti, Juan Carlos 1909-. . . . . . . **CLC 7, 10**
See also CA 85-88; CANR 32; DLB 113;
HW; MTCW

O Nuallain, Brian 1911-1966
See O'Brien, Flann
See also CA 21-22; 25-28R; CAP 2

Oppen, George 1908-1984 . . . . **CLC 7, 13, 34**
See also CA 13-16R; 113; CANR 8; DLB 5

Oppenheim, E(dward) Phillips
1866-1946 . . . . **TCLC 45**
See also CA 111; DLB 70

Orlovitz, Gil 1918-1973 . . . . **CLC 22**
See also CA 77-80; 45-48; DLB 2, 5

Orris
See Ingelow, Jean

Ortega y Gasset, Jose
1883-1955 . . . . **TCLC 9; HLC**
See also CA 106; 130; HW; MTCW

Ortiz, Simon J(oseph) 1941-. . . . . . . **CLC 45**
See also CA 134; DLB 120

Orton, Joe . . . . **CLC 4, 13, 43; DC 3**
See also Orton, John Kingsley
See also CDBLB 1960 to Present; DLB 13

Orton, John Kingsley 1933-1967
See Orton, Joe
See also CA 85-88; CANR 35; MTCW

Orwell, George
. . . . **TCLC 2, 6, 15, 31, 51; WLC**
See also Blair, Eric (Arthur)
See also CDBLB 1945-1960; DLB 15, 98

Osborne, David
See Silverberg, Robert

Osborne, George
See Silverberg, Robert

Osborne, John (James)
1929- . . . . **CLC 1, 2, 5, 11, 45; DA; WLC**
See also CA 13-16R; CANR 21;
CDBLB 1945-1960; DLB 13; MTCW

Osborne, Lawrence 1958- . . . . **CLC 50**

Oshima, Nagisa 1932- . . . . **CLC 20**
See also CA 116; 121

Oskison, John Milton
1874-1947 . . . . **TCLC 35**
See also CA 144

Ossoli, Sarah Margaret (Fuller marchesa d')
1810-1850
See Fuller, Margaret
See also SATA 25

Ostrovsky, Alexander
1823-1886 . . . . **NCLC 30**

Otero, Blas de 1916-1979. . . . . **CLC 11**
See also CA 89-92; DLB 134

Otto, Whitney 1955-. . . . . **CLC 70**
See also CA 140

Ouida . . . . **TCLC 43**
See also De La Ramee, (Marie) Louise
See also DLB 18

Ousmane, Sembene 1923- . . . . **CLC 66; BLC**
See also BW 1; CA 117; 125; MTCW

Ovid 43B.C.-18th cent. (?). . . **CMLC 7; PC 2**

Owen, Hugh
See Faust, Frederick (Schiller)

Owen, Wilfred (Edward Salter)
1893-1918 . . . . . . **TCLC 5, 27; DA; WLC**
See also CA 104; 141; CDBLB 1914-1945;
DLB 20

Owens, Rochelle 1936-. . . . . **CLC 8**
See also CA 17-20R; CAAS 2; CANR 39

Oz, Amos 1939- . . . **CLC 5, 8, 11, 27, 33, 54**
See also CA 53-56; CANR 27; MTCW

Ozick, Cynthia
1928-. . . . . **CLC 3, 7, 28, 62; SSC 15**
See also BEST 90:1; CA 17-20R; CANR 23;
DLB 28; DLBY 82; MTCW

Ozu, Yasujiro 1903-1963 . . . . **CLC 16**
See also CA 112

Pacheco, C.
See Pessoa, Fernando (Antonio Nogueira)

Pa Chin
See Li Fei-kan

Pack, Robert 1929-. . . . . **CLC 13**
See also CA 1-4R; CANR 3, 44; DLB 5

Padgett, Lewis
See Kuttner, Henry

Padilla (Lorenzo), Heberto 1932-. . . **CLC 38**
See also AITN 1; CA 123; 131; HW

Page, Jimmy 1944-. . . . . **CLC 12**

Page, Louise 1955-. . . . . **CLC 40**
See also CA 140

Page, P(atricia) K(athleen)
1916- . . . . **CLC 7, 18**
See also CA 53-56; CANR 4, 22; DLB 68;
MTCW

Paget, Violet 1856-1935
See Lee, Vernon
See also CA 104

Paget-Lowe, Henry
See Lovecraft, H(oward) P(hillips)

Paglia, Camille (Anna) 1947-. . . . . . . **CLC 68**
See also CA 140

Paige, Richard
See Koontz, Dean R(ay)

Pakenham, Antonia
See Fraser, (Lady) Antonia (Pakenham)

Palamas, Kostes 1859-1943 . . . . **TCLC 5**
See also CA 105

Palazzeschi, Aldo 1885-1974. . . . . . . **CLC 11**
See also CA 89-92; 53-56; DLB 114

Paley, Grace 1922-. . . . **CLC 4, 6, 37; SSC 8**
See also CA 25-28R; CANR 13; DLB 28;
MTCW

Palin, Michael (Edward) 1943-. . . . . **CLC 21**
See also Monty Python
See also CA 107; CANR 35; SATA 67

Palliser, Charles 1947-. . . . . **CLC 65**
See also CA 136

Palma, Ricardo 1833-1919. . . . . **TCLC 29**

Pancake, Breece Dexter 1952-1979
See Pancake, Breece D'J
See also CA 123; 109

Pancake, Breece D'J . . . . **CLC 29**
See also Pancake, Breece Dexter
See also DLB 130

Panko, Rudy
See Gogol, Nikolai (Vasilyevich)

Papadiamantis, Alexandros
1851-1911 . . . . **TCLC 29**

Papadiamantopoulos, Johannes 1856-1910
See Moreas, Jean
See also CA 117

Papini, Giovanni 1881-1956. . . . . . . **TCLC 22**
See also CA 121

Paracelsus 1493-1541. . . . . **LC 14**

Pessoa, Fernando (Antonio Nogueira)
    1888-1935 .... **TCLC 27; HLC**
    See also CA 125

Peterkin, Julia Mood 1880-1961.... **CLC 31**
    See also CA 102; DLB 9

Peters, Joan K. 1945- .... **CLC 39**

Peters, Robert L(ouis) 1924- .... **CLC 7**
    See also CA 13-16R; CAAS 8; DLB 105

Petofi, Sandor 1823-1849....... **NCLC 21**

Petrakis, Harry Mark 1923- .... **CLC 3**
    See also CA 9-12R; CANR 4, 30

Petrarch 1304-1374. .... **PC 8**

Petrov, Evgeny .... **TCLC 21**
    See also Kataev, Evgeny Petrovich

Petry, Ann (Lane) 1908- ...... **CLC 1, 7, 18**
    See also BW 1; CA 5-8R; CAAS 6;
    CANR 4; CLR 12; DLB 76; JRDA;
    MAICYA; MTCW; SATA 5

Petursson, Halligrimur 1614-1674 .... **LC 8**

Philipson, Morris H. 1926- .... **CLC 53**
    See also CA 1-4R; CANR 4

Phillips, David Graham
    1867-1911 .... **TCLC 44**
    See also CA 108; DLB 9, 12

Phillips, Jack
    See Sandburg, Carl (August)

Phillips, Jayne Anne
    1952- .... **CLC 15, 33; SSC 16**
    See also CA 101; CANR 24; DLBY 80;
    MTCW

Phillips, Richard
    See Dick, Philip K(indred)

Phillips, Robert (Schaeffer) 1938-... **CLC 28**
    See also CA 17-20R; CAAS 13; CANR 8;
    DLB 105

Phillips, Ward
    See Lovecraft, H(oward) P(hillips)

Piccolo, Lucio 1901-1969......... **CLC 13**
    See also CA 97-100; DLB 114

Pickthall, Marjorie L(owry) C(hristie)
    1883-1922 .... **TCLC 21**
    See also CA 107; DLB 92

Pico della Mirandola, Giovanni
    1463-1494 .... **LC 15**

Piercy, Marge
    1936- ...... **CLC 3, 6, 14, 18, 27, 62**
    See also CA 21-24R; CAAS 1; CANR 13,
    43; DLB 120; MTCW

Piers, Robert
    See Anthony, Piers

Pieyre de Mandiargues, Andre 1909-1991
    See Mandiargues, Andre Pieyre de
    See also CA 103; 136; CANR 22

Pilnyak, Boris .... **TCLC 23**
    See also Vogau, Boris Andreyevich

Pincherle, Alberto 1907-1990 ... **CLC 11, 18**
    See also Moravia, Alberto
    See also CA 25-28R; 132; CANR 33;
    MTCW

Pinckney, Darryl 1953- .... **CLC 76**
    See also BW 2; CA 143

Pindar 518B.C.-446B.C......... **CMLC 12**

Pineda, Cecile 1942-............. **CLC 39**
    See also CA 118

Pinero, Arthur Wing 1855-1934 ... **TCLC 32**
    See also CA 110; DLB 10

Pinero, Miguel (Antonio Gomez)
    1946-1988 .... **CLC 4, 55**
    See also CA 61-64; 125; CANR 29; HW

Pinget, Robert 1919- .... **CLC 7, 13, 37**
    See also CA 85-88; DLB 83

Pink Floyd...................... **CLC 35**
    See also Barrett, (Roger) Syd; Gilmour,
    David; Mason, Nick; Waters, Roger;
    Wright, Rick

Pinkney, Edward 1802-1828 ..... **NCLC 31**

Pinkwater, Daniel Manus 1941-.... **CLC 35**
    See also Pinkwater, Manus
    See also AAYA 1; CA 29-32R; CANR 12,
    38; CLR 4; JRDA; MAICYA; SAAS 3;
    SATA 46, 76

Pinkwater, Manus
    See Pinkwater, Daniel Manus
    See also SATA 8

Pinsky, Robert 1940-........ **CLC 9, 19, 38**
    See also CA 29-32R; CAAS 4; DLBY 82

Pinta, Harold
    See Pinter, Harold

Pinter, Harold
    1930- ..... **CLC 1, 3, 6, 9, 11, 15, 27, 58,
                                73; DA; WLC**
    See also CA 5-8R; CANR 33; CDBLB 1960
    to Present; DLB 13; MTCW

Pirandello, Luigi
    1867-1936 ...... **TCLC 4, 29; DA; WLC**
    See also CA 104

Pirsig, Robert M(aynard)
    1928-................... **CLC 4, 6, 73**
    See also CA 53-56; CANR 42; MTCW;
    SATA 39

Pisarev, Dmitry Ivanovich
    1840-1868 .... **NCLC 25**

Pix, Mary (Griffith) 1666-1709....... **LC 8**
    See also DLB 80

Pixerecourt, Guilbert de
    1773-1844 .... **NCLC 39**

Plaidy, Jean
    See Hibbert, Eleanor Alice Burford

Planche, James Robinson
    1796-1880 .... **NCLC 42**

Plant, Robert 1948- .... **CLC 12**

Plante, David (Robert)
    1940-................... **CLC 7, 23, 38**
    See also CA 37-40R; CANR 12, 36;
    DLBY 83; MTCW

Plath, Sylvia
    1932-1963 ..... **CLC 1, 2, 3, 5, 9, 11, 14,
             17, 50, 51, 62; DA; PC 1; WLC**
    See also CA 19-20; CANR 34; CAP 2;
    CDALB 1941-1968; DLB 5, 6; MTCW

Plato 428(?)B.C.-348(?)B.C.... **CMLC 8; DA**

Platonov, Andrei .... **TCLC 14**
    See also Klimentov, Andrei Platonovich

Platt, Kin 1911- .... **CLC 26**
    See also AAYA 11; CA 17-20R; CANR 11;
    JRDA; SAAS 17; SATA 21

Plick et Plock
    See Simenon, Georges (Jacques Christian)

Plimpton, George (Ames) 1927-..... **CLC 36**
    See also AITN 1; CA 21-24R; CANR 32;
    MTCW; SATA 10

Plomer, William Charles Franklin
    1903-1973 .... **CLC 4, 8**
    See also CA 21-22; CANR 34; CAP 2;
    DLB 20; MTCW; SATA 24

Plowman, Piers
    See Kavanagh, Patrick (Joseph)

Plum, J.
    See Wodehouse, P(elham) G(renville)

Plumly, Stanley (Ross) 1939- ...... **CLC 33**
    See also CA 108; 110; DLB 5

Plumpe, Friedrich Wilhelm
    1888-1931 .... **TCLC 53**
    See also CA 112

Poe, Edgar Allan
    1809-1849 ..... **NCLC 1, 16; DA; PC 1;
                                SSC 1; WLC**
    See also CDALB 1640-1865; DLB 3, 59, 73,
    74; SATA 23

Poet of Titchfield Street, The
    See Pound, Ezra (Weston Loomis)

Pohl, Frederik 1919- .... **CLC 18**
    See also CA 61-64; CAAS 1; CANR 11, 37;
    DLB 8; MTCW; SATA 24

Poirier, Louis 1910-
    See Gracq, Julien
    See also CA 122; 126

Poitier, Sidney 1927-............. **CLC 26**
    See also BW 1; CA 117

Polanski, Roman 1933- .... **CLC 16**
    See also CA 77-80

Poliakoff, Stephen 1952- .... **CLC 38**
    See also CA 106; DLB 13

Police, The...................... **CLC 26**
    See also Copeland, Stewart (Armstrong);
    Summers, Andrew James; Sumner,
    Gordon Matthew

Pollitt, Katha 1949- .... **CLC 28**
    See also CA 120; 122; MTCW

Pollock, (Mary) Sharon 1936-..... **CLC 50**
    See also CA 141; DLB 60

Pomerance, Bernard 1940-........ **CLC 13**
    See also CA 101

Ponge, Francis (Jean Gaston Alfred)
    1899-1988 .... **CLC 6, 18**
    See also CA 85-88; 126; CANR 40

Pontoppidan, Henrik 1857-1943 ... **TCLC 29**

Poole, Josephine .... **CLC 17**
    See also Helyar, Jane Penelope Josephine
    See also SAAS 2; SATA 5

Popa, Vasko 1922-............... **CLC 19**
    See also CA 112

Pope, Alexander
    1688-1744 .... **LC 3; DA; WLC**
    See also CDBLB 1660-1789; DLB 95, 101

Porter, Connie (Rose) 1959(?)- ..... **CLC 70**
    See also BW 2; CA 142

Porter, Gene(va Grace) Stratton
    1863(?)-1924 .... **TCLC 21**
    See also CA 112

Robinson, William, Jr. 1940-
See Robinson, Smokey
See also CA 116

Robison, Mary 1949- . . . . CLC 42
See also CA 113; 116; DLB 130

Rod, Edouard 1857-1910 . . . . TCLC 52

Roddenberry, Eugene Wesley 1921-1991
See Roddenberry, Gene
See also CA 110; 135; CANR 37; SATA 45

Roddenberry, Gene . . . . CLC 17
See also Roddenberry, Eugene Wesley
See also AAYA 5; SATA-Obit 69

Rodgers, Mary 1931- . . . . CLC 12
See also CA 49-52; CANR 8; CLR 20;
JRDA; MAICYA; SATA 8

Rodgers, W(illiam) R(obert)
1909-1969 . . . . CLC 7
See also CA 85-88; DLB 20

Rodman, Eric
See Silverberg, Robert

Rodman, Howard 1920(?)-1985 . . . . . CLC 65
See also CA 118

Rodman, Maia
See Wojciechowska, Maia (Teresa)

Rodriguez, Claudio 1934- . . . . CLC 10
See also DLB 134

Roelvaag, O(le) E(dvart)
1876-1931 . . . . TCLC 17
See also CA 117; DLB 9

Roethke, Theodore (Huebner)
1908-1963 . . . . . . CLC 1, 3, 8, 11, 19, 46
See also CA 81-84; CABS 2;
CDALB 1941-1968; DLB 5; MTCW

Rogers, Thomas Hunton 1927- . . . . . CLC 57
See also CA 89-92

Rogers, Will(iam Penn Adair)
1879-1935 . . . . TCLC 8
See also CA 105; 144; DLB 11

Rogin, Gilbert 1929- . . . . CLC 18
See also CA 65-68; CANR 15

Rohan, Koda . . . . TCLC 22
See also Koda Shigeyuki

Rohmer, Eric . . . . CLC 16
See also Scherer, Jean-Marie Maurice

Rohmer, Sax . . . . TCLC 28
See also Ward, Arthur Henry Sarsfield
See also DLB 70

Roiphe, Anne (Richardson)
1935- . . . . CLC 3, 9
See also CA 89-92; CANR 45; DLBY 80

Rojas, Fernando de 1465-1541 . . . . . . LC 23

Rolfe, Frederick (William Serafino Austin
Lewis Mary) 1860-1913 . . . . . . TCLC 12
See also CA 107; DLB 34

Rolland, Romain 1866-1944 . . . . TCLC 23
See also CA 118; DLB 65

Rolvaag, O(le) E(dvart)
See Roelvaag, O(le) E(dvart)

Romain Arnaud, Saint
See Aragon, Louis

Romains, Jules 1885-1972 . . . . CLC 7
See also CA 85-88; CANR 34; DLB 65;
MTCW

Romero, Jose Ruben 1890-1952 . . . TCLC 14
See also CA 114; 131; HW

Ronsard, Pierre de 1524-1585 . . . . LC 6

Rooke, Leon 1934- . . . . CLC 25, 34
See also CA 25-28R; CANR 23

Roper, William 1498-1578 . . . . LC 10

Roquelaure, A. N.
See Rice, Anne

Rosa, Joao Guimaraes 1908-1967 . . . CLC 23
See also CA 89-92; DLB 113

Rosen, Richard (Dean) 1949- . . . . . . CLC 39
See also CA 77-80

Rosenberg, Isaac 1890-1918 . . . . . . TCLC 12
See also CA 107; DLB 20

Rosenblatt, Joe . . . . CLC 15
See also Rosenblatt, Joseph

Rosenblatt, Joseph 1933-
See Rosenblatt, Joe
See also CA 89-92

Rosenfeld, Samuel 1896-1963
See Tzara, Tristan
See also CA 89-92

Rosenthal, M(acha) L(ouis) 1917- . . . CLC 28
See also CA 1-4R; CAAS 6; CANR 4;
DLB 5; SATA 59

Ross, Barnaby
See Dannay, Frederic

Ross, Bernard L.
See Follett, Ken(neth Martin)

Ross, J. H.
See Lawrence, T(homas) E(dward)

Ross, Martin
See Martin, Violet Florence
See also DLB 135

Ross, (James) Sinclair 1908- . . . . . . CLC 13
See also CA 73-76; DLB 88

Rossetti, Christina (Georgina)
1830-1894 . . . NCLC 2; DA; PC 7; WLC
See also DLB 35; MAICYA; SATA 20

Rossetti, Dante Gabriel
1828-1882 . . . . NCLC 4; DA; WLC
See also CDBLB 1832-1890; DLB 35

Rossner, Judith (Perelman)
1935- . . . . CLC 6, 9, 29
See also AITN 2; BEST 90:3; CA 17-20R;
CANR 18; DLB 6; MTCW

Rostand, Edmond (Eugene Alexis)
1868-1918 . . . . TCLC 6, 37; DA
See also CA 104; 126; MTCW

Roth, Henry 1906- . . . . CLC 2, 6, 11
See also CA 11-12; CANR 38; CAP 1;
DLB 28; MTCW

Roth, Joseph 1894-1939 . . . . TCLC 33
See also DLB 85

Roth, Philip (Milton)
1933- . . . . . . CLC 1, 2, 3, 4, 6, 9, 15, 22,
31, 47, 66; DA; WLC
See also BEST 90:3; CA 1-4R; CANR 1, 22,
36; CDALB 1968-1988; DLB 2, 28;
DLBY 82; MTCW

Rothenberg, Jerome 1931- . . . . CLC 6, 57
See also CA 45-48; CANR 1; DLB 5

Roumain, Jacques (Jean Baptiste)
1907-1944 . . . . TCLC 19; BLC
See also BW 1; CA 117; 125

Rourke, Constance (Mayfield)
1885-1941 . . . . TCLC 12
See also CA 107; YABC 1

Rousseau, Jean-Baptiste 1671-1741 . . . LC 9

Rousseau, Jean-Jacques
1712-1778 . . . . LC 14; DA; WLC

Roussel, Raymond 1877-1933 . . . . . TCLC 20
See also CA 117

Rovit, Earl (Herbert) 1927- . . . . CLC 7
See also CA 5-8R; CANR 12

Rowe, Nicholas 1674-1718 . . . . LC 8
See also DLB 84

Rowley, Ames Dorrance
See Lovecraft, H(oward) P(hillips)

Rowson, Susanna Haswell
1762(?)-1824 . . . . NCLC 5
See also DLB 37

Roy, Gabrielle 1909-1983 . . . . CLC 10, 14
See also CA 53-56; 110; CANR 5; DLB 68;
MTCW

Rozewicz, Tadeusz 1921- . . . . CLC 9, 23
See also CA 108; CANR 36; MTCW

Ruark, Gibbons 1941- . . . . CLC 3
See also CA 33-36R; CANR 14, 31;
DLB 120

Rubens, Bernice (Ruth) 1923- . . . CLC 19, 31
See also CA 25-28R; CANR 33; DLB 14;
MTCW

Rudkin, (James) David 1936- . . . . . . CLC 14
See also CA 89-92; DLB 13

Rudnik, Raphael 1933- . . . . CLC 7
See also CA 29-32R

Ruffian, M.
See Hasek, Jaroslav (Matej Frantisek)

Ruiz, Jose Martinez . . . . CLC 11
See also Martinez Ruiz, Jose

Rukeyser, Muriel
1913-1980 . . . . CLC 6, 10, 15, 27
See also CA 5-8R; 93-96; CANR 26;
DLB 48; MTCW; SATA 22

Rule, Jane (Vance) 1931- . . . . CLC 27
See also CA 25-28R; CAAS 18; CANR 12;
DLB 60

Rulfo, Juan 1918-1986 . . . . . CLC 8, 80; HLC
See also CA 85-88; 118; CANR 26;
DLB 113; HW; MTCW

Runeberg, Johan 1804-1877 . . . . . . NCLC 41

Runyon, (Alfred) Damon
1884(?)-1946 . . . . TCLC 10
See also CA 107; DLB 11, 86

Rush, Norman 1933- . . . . CLC 44
See also CA 121; 126

Rushdie, (Ahmed) Salman
1947- . . . . CLC 23, 31, 55
See also BEST 89:3; CA 108; 111;
CANR 33; MTCW

Rushforth, Peter (Scott) 1945- . . . . . CLC 19
See also CA 101

Ruskin, John 1819-1900 . . . . TCLC 20
See also CA 114; 129; CDBLB 1832-1890;
DLB 55; SATA 24

Sarton, (Eleanor) May
        1912- . . . . CLC 4, 14, 49
    See also CA 1-4R; CANR 1, 34; DLB 48;
        DLBY 81; MTCW; SATA 36

Sartre, Jean-Paul
        1905-1980 . . . . CLC 1, 4, 7, 9, 13, 18, 24,
            44, 50, 52; DA; DC 3; WLC
    See also CA 9-12R; 97-100; CANR 21;
        DLB 72; MTCW

Sassoon, Siegfried (Lorraine)
        1886-1967 . . . . CLC 36
    See also CA 104; 25-28R; CANR 36;
        DLB 20; MTCW

Satterfield, Charles
    See Pohl, Frederik

Saul, John (W. III) 1942- . . . . CLC 46
    See also AAYA 10; BEST 90:4; CA 81-84;
        CANR 16, 40

Saunders, Caleb
    See Heinlein, Robert A(nson)

Saura (Atares), Carlos 1932- . . . . CLC 20
    See also CA 114; 131; HW

Sauser-Hall, Frederic 1887-1961. . . . CLC 18
    See also CA 102; 93-96; CANR 36; MTCW

Saussure, Ferdinand de
        1857-1913 . . . . TCLC 49

Savage, Catharine
    See Brosman, Catharine Savage

Savage, Thomas 1915- . . . . CLC 40
    See also CA 126; 132; CAAS 15

Savan, Glenn . . . . CLC 50

Saven, Glenn 19(?)- . . . . CLC 50

Sayers, Dorothy L(eigh)
        1893-1957 . . . . TCLC 2, 15
    See also CA 104; 119; CDBLB 1914-1945;
        DLB 10, 36, 77, 100; MTCW

Sayers, Valerie 1952- . . . . CLC 50
    See also CA 134

Sayles, John (Thomas)
        1950- . . . . CLC 7, 10, 14
    See also CA 57-60; CANR 41; DLB 44

Scammell, Michael . . . . CLC 34

Scannell, Vernon 1922- . . . . CLC 49
    See also CA 5-8R; CANR 8, 24; DLB 27;
        SATA 59

Scarlett, Susan
    See Streatfeild, (Mary) Noel

Schaeffer, Susan Fromberg
        1941- . . . . CLC 6, 11, 22
    See also CA 49-52; CANR 18; DLB 28;
        MTCW; SATA 22

Schary, Jill
    See Robinson, Jill

Schell, Jonathan 1943- . . . . CLC 35
    See also CA 73-76; CANR 12

Schelling, Friedrich Wilhelm Joseph von
        1775-1854 . . . . NCLC 30
    See also DLB 90

Schendel, Arthur van 1874-1946 . . . TCLC 56

Scherer, Jean-Marie Maurice 1920-
    See Rohmer, Eric
    See also CA 110

Schevill, James (Erwin) 1920- . . . . CLC 7
    See also CA 5-8R; CAAS 12

Schiller, Friedrich 1759-1805 . . . . NCLC 39
    See also DLB 94

Schisgal, Murray (Joseph) 1926- . . . . . CLC 6
    See also CA 21-24R

Schlee, Ann 1934- . . . . CLC 35
    See also CA 101; CANR 29; SATA 36, 44

Schlegel, August Wilhelm von
        1767-1845 . . . . NCLC 15
    See also DLB 94

Schlegel, Friedrich 1772-1829 . . . . NCLC 45
    See also DLB 90

Schlegel, Johann Elias (von)
        1719(?)-1749 . . . . LC 5

Schlesinger, Arthur M(eier), Jr.
        1917- . . . . CLC 84
    See also AITN 1; CA 1-4R; CANR 1, 28;
        DLB 17; MTCW; SATA 61

Schmidt, Arno (Otto) 1914-1979. . . . CLC 56
    See also CA 128; 109; DLB 69

Schmitz, Aron Hector 1861-1928
    See Svevo, Italo
    See also CA 104; 122; MTCW

Schnackenberg, Gjertrud 1953- . . . . . CLC 40
    See also CA 116; DLB 120

Schneider, Leonard Alfred 1925-1966
    See Bruce, Lenny
    See also CA 89-92

Schnitzler, Arthur
        1862-1931 . . . . TCLC 4; SSC 15
    See also CA 104; DLB 81, 118

Schor, Sandra (M.) 1932(?)-1990 . . . CLC 65
    See also CA 132

Schorer, Mark 1908-1977 . . . . CLC 9
    See also CA 5-8R; 73-76; CANR 7;
        DLB 103

Schrader, Paul (Joseph) 1946- . . . . . . CLC 26
    See also CA 37-40R; CANR 41; DLB 44

Schreiner, Olive (Emilie Albertina)
        1855-1920 . . . . TCLC 9
    See also CA 105; DLB 18

Schulberg, Budd (Wilson)
        1914- . . . . CLC 7, 48
    See also CA 25-28R; CANR 19; DLB 6, 26,
        28; DLBY 81

Schulz, Bruno
        1892-1942 . . . . TCLC 5, 51; SSC 13
    See also CA 115; 123

Schulz, Charles M(onroe) 1922- . . . . CLC 12
    See also CA 9-12R; CANR 6; SATA 10

Schumacher, E(rnst) F(riedrich)
        1911-1977 . . . . CLC 80
    See also CA 81-84; 73-76; CANR 34

Schuyler, James Marcus
        1923-1991 . . . . CLC 5, 23
    See also CA 101; 134; DLB 5

Schwartz, Delmore (David)
        1913-1966 . . . . . . CLC 2, 4, 10, 45; PC 8
    See also CA 17-18; 25-28R; CANR 35;
        CAP 2; DLB 28, 48; MTCW

Schwartz, Ernst
    See Ozu, Yasujiro

Schwartz, John Burnham 1965- . . . . CLC 59
    See also CA 132

Schwartz, Lynne Sharon 1939- . . . . . CLC 31
    See also CA 103; CANR 44

Schwartz, Muriel A.
    See Eliot, T(homas) S(tearns)

Schwarz-Bart, Andre 1928- . . . . CLC 2, 4
    See also CA 89-92

Schwarz-Bart, Simone 1938- . . . . CLC 7
    See also BW 2; CA 97-100

Schwob, (Mayer Andre) Marcel
        1867-1905 . . . . TCLC 20
    See also CA 117; DLB 123

Sciascia, Leonardo
        1921-1989 . . . . CLC 8, 9, 41
    See also CA 85-88; 130; CANR 35; MTCW

Scoppettone, Sandra 1936- . . . . CLC 26
    See also AAYA 11; CA 5-8R; CANR 41;
        SATA 9

Scorsese, Martin 1942- . . . . CLC 20
    See also CA 110; 114

Scotland, Jay
    See Jakes, John (William)

Scott, Duncan Campbell
        1862-1947 . . . . TCLC 6
    See also CA 104; DLB 92

Scott, Evelyn 1893-1963. . . . . CLC 43
    See also CA 104; 112; DLB 9, 48

Scott, F(rancis) R(eginald)
        1899-1985 . . . . CLC 22
    See also CA 101; 114; DLB 88

Scott, Frank
    See Scott, F(rancis) R(eginald)

Scott, Joanna 1960- . . . . CLC 50
    See also CA 126

Scott, Paul (Mark) 1920-1978. . . . CLC 9, 60
    See also CA 81-84; 77-80; CANR 33;
        DLB 14; MTCW

Scott, Walter
        1771-1832 . . . . NCLC 15; DA; WLC
    See also CDBLB 1789-1832; DLB 93, 107,
        116, 144; YABC 2

Scribe, (Augustin) Eugene
        1791-1861 . . . . NCLC 16

Scrum, R.
    See Crumb, R(obert)

Scudery, Madeleine de 1607-1701. . . . . LC 2

Scum
    See Crumb, R(obert)

Scumbag, Little Bobby
    See Crumb, R(obert)

Seabrook, John
    See Hubbard, L(afayette) Ron(ald)

Sealy, I. Allan 1951- . . . . CLC 55

Search, Alexander
    See Pessoa, Fernando (Antonio Nogueira)

Sebastian, Lee
    See Silverberg, Robert

Sebastian Owl
    See Thompson, Hunter S(tockton)

Sebestyen, Ouida 1924- . . . . CLC 30
    See also AAYA 8; CA 107; CANR 40;
        CLR 17; JRDA; MAICYA; SAAS 10;
        SATA 39

Shestov, Lev 1866-1938 .... TCLC 56

Shiel, M(atthew) P(hipps)
1865-1947 .... TCLC 8
See also CA 106

Shiga, Naoya 1883-1971.......... CLC 33
See also CA 101; 33-36R

Shimazaki Haruki 1872-1943
See Shimazaki Toson
See also CA 105; 134

Shimazaki Toson................. TCLC 5
See also Shimazaki Haruki

Sholokhov, Mikhail (Aleksandrovich)
1905-1984 .... CLC 7, 15
See also CA 101; 112; MTCW; SATA 36

Shone, Patric
See Hanley, James

Shreve, Susan Richards 1939-...... CLC 23
See also CA 49-52; CAAS 5; CANR 5, 38;
MAICYA; SATA 41, 46

Shue, Larry 1946-1985........... CLC 52
See also CA 117

Shu-Jen, Chou 1881-1936
See Hsun, Lu
See also CA 104

Shulman, Alix Kates 1932-...... CLC 2, 10
See also CA 29-32R; CANR 43; SATA 7

Shuster, Joe 1914- .... CLC 21

Shute, Nevil.................... CLC 30
See also Norway, Nevil Shute

Shuttle, Penelope (Diane) 1947-..... CLC 7
See also CA 93-96; CANR 39; DLB 14, 40

Sidney, Mary 1561-1621 .... LC 19

Sidney, Sir Philip 1554-1586.... LC 19; DA
See also CDBLB Before 1660

Siegel, Jerome 1914- .... CLC 21
See also CA 116

Siegel, Jerry
See Siegel, Jerome

Sienkiewicz, Henryk (Adam Alexander Pius)
1846-1916 .... TCLC 3
See also CA 104; 134

Sierra, Gregorio Martinez
See Martinez Sierra, Gregorio

Sierra, Maria (de la O'LeJarraga) Martinez
See Martinez Sierra, Maria (de la
O'LeJarraga)

Sigal, Clancy 1926-............. CLC 7
See also CA 1-4R

Sigourney, Lydia Howard (Huntley)
1791-1865 .... NCLC 21
See also DLB 1, 42, 73

Siguenza y Gongora, Carlos de
1645-1700 .... LC 8

Sigurjonsson, Johann 1880-1919... TCLC 27

Sikelianos, Angelos 1884-1951 .... TCLC 39

Silkin, Jon 1930-........... CLC 2, 6, 43
See also CA 5-8R; CAAS 5; DLB 27

Silko, Leslie (Marmon)
1948-................. CLC 23, 74; DA
See also CA 115; 122; CANR 45; DLB 143

Sillanpaa, Frans Eemil 1888-1964... CLC 19
See also CA 129; 93-96; MTCW

Sillitoe, Alan
1928- .... CLC 1, 3, 6, 10, 19, 57
See also AITN 1; CA 9-12R; CAAS 2;
CANR 8, 26; CDBLB 1960 to Present;
DLB 14, 139; MTCW; SATA 61

Silone, Ignazio 1900-1978 .... CLC 4
See also CA 25-28; 81-84; CANR 34;
CAP 2; MTCW

Silver, Joan Micklin 1935- .... CLC 20
See also CA 114; 121

Silver, Nicholas
See Faust, Frederick (Schiller)

Silverberg, Robert 1935- .... CLC 7
See also CA 1-4R; CAAS 3; CANR 1, 20,
36; DLB 8; MAICYA; MTCW; SATA 13

Silverstein, Alvin 1933- .... CLC 17
See also CA 49-52; CANR 2; CLR 25;
JRDA; MAICYA; SATA 8, 69

Silverstein, Virginia B(arbara Opshelor)
1937- .... CLC 17
See also CA 49-52; CANR 2; CLR 25;
JRDA; MAICYA; SATA 8, 69

Sim, Georges
See Simenon, Georges (Jacques Christian)

Simak, Clifford D(onald)
1904-1988 .... CLC 1, 55
See also CA 1-4R; 125; CANR 1, 35;
DLB 8; MTCW; SATA 56

Simenon, Georges (Jacques Christian)
1903-1989 .... CLC 1, 2, 3, 8, 18, 47
See also CA 85-88; 129; CANR 35;
DLB 72; DLBY 89; MTCW

Simic, Charles 1938-... CLC 6, 9, 22, 49, 68
See also CA 29-32R; CAAS 4; CANR 12,
33; DLB 105

Simmons, Charles (Paul) 1924-..... CLC 57
See also CA 89-92

Simmons, Dan 1948-............. CLC 44
See also CA 138

Simmons, James (Stewart Alexander)
1933- .... CLC 43
See also CA 105; DLB 40

Simms, William Gilmore
1806-1870 .... NCLC 3
See also DLB 3, 30, 59, 73

Simon, Carly 1945-.............. CLC 26
See also CA 105

Simon, Claude 1913-....... CLC 4, 9, 15, 39
See also CA 89-92; CANR 33; DLB 83;
MTCW

Simon, (Marvin) Neil
1927-.......... CLC 6, 11, 31, 39, 70
See also AITN 1; CA 21-24R; CANR 26;
DLB 7; MTCW

Simon, Paul 1942(?)- .... CLC 17
See also CA 116

Simonon, Paul 1956(?)- .... CLC 30
See also Clash, The

Simpson, Harriette
See Arnow, Harriette (Louisa) Simpson

Simpson, Louis (Aston Marantz)
1923- .... CLC 4, 7, 9, 32
See also CA 1-4R; CAAS 4; CANR 1;
DLB 5; MTCW

Simpson, Mona (Elizabeth) 1957-... CLC 44
See also CA 122; 135

Simpson, N(orman) F(rederick)
1919- .... CLC 29
See also CA 13-16R; DLB 13

Sinclair, Andrew (Annandale)
1935-................... CLC 2, 14
See also CA 9-12R; CAAS 5; CANR 14, 38;
DLB 14; MTCW

Sinclair, Emil
See Hesse, Hermann

Sinclair, Iain 1943-.............. CLC 76
See also CA 132

Sinclair, Iain MacGregor
See Sinclair, Iain

Sinclair, Mary Amelia St. Clair 1865(?)-1946
See Sinclair, May
See also CA 104

Sinclair, May................. TCLC 3, 11
See also Sinclair, Mary Amelia St. Clair
See also DLB 36, 135

Sinclair, Upton (Beall)
1878-1968 ...... CLC 1, 11, 15, 63; DA;
WLC
See also CA 5-8R; 25-28R; CANR 7;
CDALB 1929-1941; DLB 9; MTCW;
SATA 9

Singer, Isaac
See Singer, Isaac Bashevis

Singer, Isaac Bashevis
1904-1991 .... CLC 1, 3, 6, 9, 11, 15, 23,
38, 69; DA; SSC 3; WLC
See also AITN 1, 2; CA 1-4R; 134;
CANR 1, 39; CDALB 1941-1968; CLR 1;
DLB 6, 28, 52; DLBY 91; JRDA;
MAICYA; MTCW; SATA 3, 27;
SATA-Obit 68

Singer, Israel Joshua 1893-1944 ... TCLC 33

Singh, Khushwant 1915-........... CLC 11
See also CA 9-12R; CAAS 9; CANR 6

Sinjohn, John
See Galsworthy, John

Sinyavsky, Andrei (Donatevich)
1925- .... CLC 8
See also CA 85-88

Sirin, V.
See Nabokov, Vladimir (Vladimirovich)

Sissman, L(ouis) E(dward)
1928-1976 .... CLC 9, 18
See also CA 21-24R; 65-68; CANR 13;
DLB 5

Sisson, C(harles) H(ubert) 1914-..... CLC 8
See also CA 1-4R; CAAS 3; CANR 3;
DLB 27

Sitwell, Dame Edith
1887-1964 .... CLC 2, 9, 67; PC 3
See also CA 9-12R; CANR 35;
CDBLB 1945-1960; DLB 20; MTCW

Sjoewall, Maj 1935-.............. CLC 7
See also CA 65-68

Sjowall, Maj
See Sjoewall, Maj

Skelton, Robin 1925- .... CLC 13
See also AITN 2; CA 5-8R; CAAS 5;
CANR 28; DLB 27, 53

Skolimowski, Jerzy 1938-......... **CLC 20**
See also CA 128

Skram, Amalie (Bertha)
1847-1905 .... **TCLC 25**

Skvorecky, Josef (Vaclav)
1924-.................. **CLC 15, 39, 69**
See also CA 61-64; CAAS 1; CANR 10, 34;
MTCW

Slade, Bernard................ **CLC 11, 46**
See also Newbound, Bernard Slade
See also CAAS 9; DLB 53

Slaughter, Carolyn 1946-.......... **CLC 56**
See also CA 85-88

Slaughter, Frank G(ill) 1908- ...... **CLC 29**
See also AITN 2; CA 5-8R; CANR 5

Slavitt, David R(ytman) 1935-.... **CLC 5, 14**
See also CA 21-24R; CAAS 3; CANR 41;
DLB 5, 6

Slesinger, Tess 1905-1945 .... **TCLC 10**
See also CA 107; DLB 102

Slessor, Kenneth 1901-1971........ **CLC 14**
See also CA 102; 89-92

Slowacki, Juliusz 1809-1849 ..... **NCLC 15**

Smart, Christopher 1722-1771........ **LC 3**
See also DLB 109

Smart, Elizabeth 1913-1986........ **CLC 54**
See also CA 81-84; 118; DLB 88

Smiley, Jane (Graves) 1949-.... **CLC 53, 76**
See also CA 104; CANR 30

Smith, A(rthur) J(ames) M(arshall)
1902-1980 .... **CLC 15**
See also CA 1-4R; 102; CANR 4; DLB 88

Smith, Betty (Wehner) 1896-1972... **CLC 19**
See also CA 5-8R; 33-36R; DLBY 82;
SATA 6

Smith, Charlotte (Turner)
1749-1806 .... **NCLC 23**
See also DLB 39, 109

Smith, Clark Ashton 1893-1961 .... **CLC 43**
See also CA 143

Smith, Dave.................. **CLC 22, 42**
See also Smith, David (Jeddie)
See also CAAS 7; DLB 5

Smith, David (Jeddie) 1942-
See Smith, Dave
See also CA 49-52; CANR 1

Smith, Florence Margaret
1902-1971 .... **CLC 8**
See also Smith, Stevie
See also CA 17-18; 29-32R; CANR 35;
CAP 2; MTCW

Smith, Iain Crichton 1928- .... **CLC 64**
See also CA 21-24R; DLB 40, 139

Smith, John 1580(?)-1631 .... **LC 9**

Smith, Johnston
See Crane, Stephen (Townley)

Smith, Lee 1944-.............. **CLC 25, 73**
See also CA 114; 119; DLB 143; DLBY 83

Smith, Martin
See Smith, Martin Cruz

Smith, Martin Cruz 1942-......... **CLC 25**
See also BEST 89:4; CA 85-88; CANR 6,
23, 43

Smith, Mary-Ann Tirone 1944-..... **CLC 39**
See also CA 118; 136

Smith, Patti 1946- .... **CLC 12**
See also CA 93-96

Smith, Pauline (Urmson)
1882-1959 .... **TCLC 25**

Smith, Rosamond
See Oates, Joyce Carol

Smith, Sheila Kaye
See Kaye-Smith, Sheila

Smith, Stevie .... **CLC 3, 8, 25, 44**
See also Smith, Florence Margaret
See also DLB 20

Smith, Wilbur A(ddison) 1933-..... **CLC 33**
See also CA 13-16R; CANR 7; MTCW

Smith, William Jay 1918- .... **CLC 6**
See also CA 5-8R; CANR 44; DLB 5;
MAICYA; SATA 2, 68

Smith, Woodrow Wilson
See Kuttner, Henry

Smolenskin, Peretz 1842-1885.... **NCLC 30**

Smollett, Tobias (George) 1721-1771 .. **LC 2**
See also CDBLB 1660-1789; DLB 39, 104

Snodgrass, W(illiam) D(e Witt)
1926-............. **CLC 2, 6, 10, 18, 68**
See also CA 1-4R; CANR 6, 36; DLB 5;
MTCW

Snow, C(harles) P(ercy)
1905-1980 .... **CLC 1, 4, 6, 9, 13, 19**
See also CA 5-8R; 101; CANR 28;
CDBLB 1945-1960; DLB 15, 77; MTCW

Snow, Frances Compton
See Adams, Henry (Brooks)

Snyder, Gary (Sherman)
1930-............. **CLC 1, 2, 5, 9, 32**
See also CA 17-20R; CANR 30; DLB 5, 16

Snyder, Zilpha Keatley 1927-...... **CLC 17**
See also CA 9-12R; CANR 38; CLR 31;
JRDA; MAICYA; SAAS 2; SATA 1, 28,
75

Soares, Bernardo
See Pessoa, Fernando (Antonio Nogueira)

Sobh, A.
See Shamlu, Ahmad

Sobol, Joshua.................... **CLC 60**

Soderberg, Hjalmar 1869-1941 .... **TCLC 39**

Sodergran, Edith (Irene)
See Soedergran, Edith (Irene)

Soedergran, Edith (Irene)
1892-1923 .... **TCLC 31**

Softly, Edgar
See Lovecraft, H(oward) P(hillips)

Softly, Edward
See Lovecraft, H(oward) P(hillips)

Sokolov, Raymond 1941-.......... **CLC 7**
See also CA 85-88

Solo, Jay
See Ellison, Harlan

Sologub, Fyodor .... **TCLC 9**
See also Teternikov, Fyodor Kuzmich

Solomons, Ikey Esquir
See Thackeray, William Makepeace

Solomos, Dionysios 1798-1857 ... **NCLC 15**

Solwoska, Mara
See French, Marilyn

Solzhenitsyn, Aleksandr I(sayevich)
1918-...... **CLC 1, 2, 4, 7, 9, 10, 18, 26,
34, 78; DA; WLC**
See also AITN 1; CA 69-72; CANR 40;
MTCW

Somers, Jane
See Lessing, Doris (May)

Somerville, Edith 1858-1949 ..... **TCLC 51**
See also DLB 135

Somerville & Ross
See Martin, Violet Florence; Somerville,
Edith

Sommer, Scott 1951-............. **CLC 25**
See also CA 106

Sondheim, Stephen (Joshua)
1930-............... **CLC 30, 39**
See also AAYA 11; CA 103

Sontag, Susan 1933-... **CLC 1, 2, 10, 13, 31**
See also CA 17-20R; CANR 25; DLB 2, 67;
MTCW

Sophocles
496(?)B.C.-406(?)B.C..... **CMLC 2; DA;
DC 1**

Sorel, Julia
See Drexler, Rosalyn

Sorrentino, Gilbert
1929-............ **CLC 3, 7, 14, 22, 40**
See also CA 77-80; CANR 14, 33; DLB 5;
DLBY 80

Soto, Gary 1952-........ **CLC 32, 80; HLC**
See also AAYA 10; CA 119; 125; DLB 82;
HW; JRDA

Soupault, Philippe 1897-1990 ...... **CLC 68**
See also CA 116; 131

Souster, (Holmes) Raymond
1921-.................... **CLC 5, 14**
See also CA 13-16R; CAAS 14; CANR 13,
29; DLB 88; SATA 63

Southern, Terry 1926-............. **CLC 7**
See also CA 1-4R; CANR 1; DLB 2

Southey, Robert 1774-1843 .... **NCLC 8**
See also DLB 93, 107, 142; SATA 54

Southworth, Emma Dorothy Eliza Nevitte
1819-1899 .... **NCLC 26**

Souza, Ernest
See Scott, Evelyn

Soyinka, Wole
1934-....... **CLC 3, 5, 14, 36, 44; BLC;
DA; DC 2; WLC**
See also BW 2; CA 13-16R; CANR 27, 39;
DLB 125; MTCW

Spackman, W(illiam) M(ode)
1905-1990 .... **CLC 46**
See also CA 81-84; 132

Spacks, Barry 1931-............. **CLC 14**
See also CA 29-32R; CANR 33; DLB 105

Spanidou, Irini 1946-............. **CLC 44**

Spark, Muriel (Sarah)
1918-........ **CLC 2, 3, 5, 8, 13, 18, 40;
SSC 10**
See also CA 5-8R; CANR 12, 36;
CDBLB 1945-1960; DLB 15, 139; MTCW

Spaulding, Douglas
See Bradbury, Ray (Douglas)

Spaulding, Leonard
See Bradbury, Ray (Douglas)

Spence, J. A. D.
See Eliot, T(homas) S(tearns)

Spencer, Elizabeth 1921- . . . . **CLC 22**
See also CA 13-16R; CANR 32; DLB 6;
MTCW; SATA 14

Spencer, Leonard G.
See Silverberg, Robert

Spencer, Scott 1945- . . . . **CLC 30**
See also CA 113; DLBY 86

Spender, Stephen (Harold)
1909- . . . . **CLC 1, 2, 5, 10, 41**
See also CA 9-12R; CANR 31;
CDBLB 1945-1960; DLB 20; MTCW

Spengler, Oswald (Arnold Gottfried)
1880-1936 . . . . **TCLC 25**
See also CA 118

Spenser, Edmund
1552(?)-1599 . . . . **LC 5; DA; PC 8; WLC**
See also CDBLB Before 1660

Spicer, Jack 1925-1965 . . . . . . **CLC 8, 18, 72**
See also CA 85-88; DLB 5, 16

Spiegelman, Art 1948- . . . . **CLC 76**
See also AAYA 10; CA 125; CANR 41

Spielberg, Peter 1929- . . . . **CLC 6**
See also CA 5-8R; CANR 4; DLBY 81

Spielberg, Steven 1947- . . . . **CLC 20**
See also AAYA 8; CA 77-80; CANR 32;
SATA 32

Spillane, Frank Morrison 1918-
See Spillane, Mickey
See also CA 25-28R; CANR 28; MTCW;
SATA 66

Spillane, Mickey . . . . **CLC 3, 13**
See also Spillane, Frank Morrison

Spinoza, Benedictus de 1632-1677 . . . . **LC 9**

Spinrad, Norman (Richard) 1940- . . . **CLC 46**
See also CA 37-40R; CAAS 19; CANR 20;
DLB 8

Spitteler, Carl (Friedrich Georg)
1845-1924 . . . . **TCLC 12**
See also CA 109; DLB 129

Spivack, Kathleen (Romola Drucker)
1938- . . . . **CLC 6**
See also CA 49-52

Spoto, Donald 1941- . . . . **CLC 39**
See also CA 65-68; CANR 11

Springsteen, Bruce (F.) 1949- . . . . . . **CLC 17**
See also CA 111

Spurling, Hilary 1940- . . . . **CLC 34**
See also CA 104; CANR 25

Squires, (James) Radcliffe
1917-1993 . . . . **CLC 51**
See also CA 1-4R; 140; CANR 6, 21

Srivastava, Dhanpat Rai 1880(?)-1936
See Premchand
See also CA 118

Stacy, Donald
See Pohl, Frederik

Stael, Germaine de
See Stael-Holstein, Anne Louise Germaine
Necker Baronn
See also DLB 119

Stael-Holstein, Anne Louise Germaine Necker
Baronn 1766-1817 . . . . **NCLC 3**
See also Stael, Germaine de

Stafford, Jean 1915-1979 . . . **CLC 4, 7, 19, 68**
See also CA 1-4R; 85-88; CANR 3; DLB 2;
MTCW; SATA 22

Stafford, William (Edgar)
1914-1993 . . . . **CLC 4, 7, 29**
See also CA 5-8R; 142; CAAS 3; CANR 5,
22; DLB 5

Staines, Trevor
See Brunner, John (Kilian Houston)

Stairs, Gordon
See Austin, Mary (Hunter)

Stannard, Martin 1947- . . . . **CLC 44**
See also CA 142

Stanton, Maura 1946- . . . . **CLC 9**
See also CA 89-92; CANR 15; DLB 120

Stanton, Schuyler
See Baum, L(yman) Frank

Stapledon, (William) Olaf
1886-1950 . . . . **TCLC 22**
See also CA 111; DLB 15

Starbuck, George (Edwin) 1931- . . . . **CLC 53**
See also CA 21-24R; CANR 23

Stark, Richard
See Westlake, Donald E(dwin)

Staunton, Schuyler
See Baum, L(yman) Frank

Stead, Christina (Ellen)
1902-1983 . . . . **CLC 2, 5, 8, 32, 80**
See also CA 13-16R; 109; CANR 33, 40;
MTCW

Stead, William Thomas
1849-1912 . . . . **TCLC 48**

Steele, Richard 1672-1729 . . . . . . **LC 18**
See also CDBLB 1660-1789; DLB 84, 101

Steele, Timothy (Reid) 1948- . . . . . . **CLC 45**
See also CA 93-96; CANR 16; DLB 120

Steffens, (Joseph) Lincoln
1866-1936 . . . . **TCLC 20**
See also CA 117

Stegner, Wallace (Earle)
1909-1993 . . . . **CLC 9, 49, 81**
See also AITN 1; BEST 90:3; CA 1-4R;
141; CAAS 9; CANR 1, 21; DLB 9;
DLBY 93; MTCW

Stein, Gertrude
1874-1946 . . . . . . **TCLC 1, 6, 28, 48; DA;**
WLC
See also CA 104; 132; CDALB 1917-1929;
DLB 4, 54, 86; MTCW

Steinbeck, John (Ernst)
1902-1968 . . . . . . **CLC 1, 5, 9, 13, 21, 34,**
45, 75; DA; SSC 11; WLC
See also AAYA 12; CA 1-4R; 25-28R;
CANR 1, 35; CDALB 1929-1941; DLB 7,
9; DLBD 2; MTCW; SATA 9

Steinem, Gloria 1934- . . . . **CLC 63**
See also CA 53-56; CANR 28; MTCW

Steiner, George 1929- . . . . **CLC 24**
See also CA 73-76; CANR 31; DLB 67;
MTCW; SATA 62

Steiner, K. Leslie
See Delany, Samuel R(ay, Jr.)

Steiner, Rudolf 1861-1925 . . . . **TCLC 13**
See also CA 107

Stendhal
1783-1842 . . . . . **NCLC 23, 46; DA; WLC**
See also DLB 119

Stephen, Leslie 1832-1904 . . . . **TCLC 23**
See also CA 123; DLB 57, 144

Stephen, Sir Leslie
See Stephen, Leslie

Stephen, Virginia
See Woolf, (Adeline) Virginia

Stephens, James 1882(?)-1950 . . . . . . **TCLC 4**
See also CA 104; DLB 19

Stephens, Reed
See Donaldson, Stephen R.

Steptoe, Lydia
See Barnes, Djuna

Sterchi, Beat 1949- . . . . **CLC 65**

Sterling, Brett
See Bradbury, Ray (Douglas); Hamilton,
Edmond

Sterling, Bruce 1954- . . . . **CLC 72**
See also CA 119; CANR 44

Sterling, George 1869-1926 . . . . **TCLC 20**
See also CA 117; DLB 54

Stern, Gerald 1925- . . . . **CLC 40**
See also CA 81-84; CANR 28; DLB 105

Stern, Richard (Gustave) 1928- . . . **CLC 4, 39**
See also CA 1-4R; CANR 1, 25; DLBY 87

Sternberg, Josef von 1894-1969 . . . . . **CLC 20**
See also CA 81-84

Sterne, Laurence
1713-1768 . . . . **LC 2; DA; WLC**
See also CDBLB 1660-1789; DLB 39

Sternheim, (William Adolf) Carl
1878-1942 . . . . **TCLC 8**
See also CA 105; DLB 56, 118

Stevens, Mark 1951- . . . . **CLC 34**
See also CA 122

Stevens, Wallace
1879-1955 . . . . **TCLC 3, 12, 45; DA;**
PC 6; WLC
See also CA 104; 124; CDALB 1929-1941;
DLB 54; MTCW

Stevenson, Anne (Katharine)
1933- . . . . **CLC 7, 33**
See also CA 17-20R; CAAS 9; CANR 9, 33;
DLB 40; MTCW

Stevenson, Robert Louis (Balfour)
1850-1894 . . . . **NCLC 5, 14; DA;**
SSC 11; WLC
See also CDBLB 1890-1914; CLR 10, 11;
DLB 18, 57, 141; JRDA; MAICYA;
YABC 2

Stewart, J(ohn) I(nnes) M(ackintosh)
1906- . . . . **CLC 7, 14, 32**
See also CA 85-88; CAAS 3; MTCW

Swenson, May
1919-1989 .... **CLC 4, 14, 61; DA**
See also CA 5-8R; 130; CANR 36; DLB 5;
MTCW; SATA 15

Swift, Augustus
See Lovecraft, H(oward) P(hillips)

Swift, Graham 1949- .... **CLC 41**
See also CA 117; 122

Swift, Jonathan
1667-1745 ...... **LC 1; DA; PC 9; WLC**
See also CDBLB 1660-1789; DLB 39, 95,
101; SATA 19

Swinburne, Algernon Charles
1837-1909 ...... **TCLC 8, 36; DA; WLC**
See also CA 105; 140; CDBLB 1832-1890;
DLB 35, 57

Swinfen, Ann .... **CLC 34**

Swinnerton, Frank Arthur
1884-1982 .... **CLC 31**
See also CA 108; DLB 34

Swithen, John
See King, Stephen (Edwin)

Sylvia
See Ashton-Warner, Sylvia (Constance)

Symmes, Robert Edward
See Duncan, Robert (Edward)

Symonds, John Addington
1840-1893 .... **NCLC 34**
See also DLB 57, 144

Symons, Arthur 1865-1945 ...... **TCLC 11**
See also CA 107; DLB 19, 57

Symons, Julian (Gustave)
1912- .... **CLC 2, 14, 32**
See also CA 49-52; CAAS 3; CANR 3, 33;
DLB 87; DLBY 92; MTCW

Synge, (Edmund) J(ohn) M(illington)
1871-1909 .... **TCLC 6, 37; DC 2**
See also CA 104; 141; CDBLB 1890-1914;
DLB 10, 19

Syruc, J.
See Milosz, Czeslaw

Szirtes, George 1948- .... **CLC 46**
See also CA 109; CANR 27

Tabori, George 1914- .... **CLC 19**
See also CA 49-52; CANR 4

Tagore, Rabindranath
1861-1941 ...... **TCLC 3, 53; PC 8**
See also CA 104; 120; MTCW

Taine, Hippolyte Adolphe
1828-1893 .... **NCLC 15**

Talese, Gay 1932- .... **CLC 37**
See also AITN 1; CA 1-4R; CANR 9;
MTCW

Tallent, Elizabeth (Ann) 1954- ..... **CLC 45**
See also CA 117; DLB 130

Tally, Ted 1952- .... **CLC 42**
See also CA 120; 124

Tamayo y Baus, Manuel
1829-1898 .... **NCLC 1**

Tammsaare, A(nton) H(ansen)
1878-1940 .... **TCLC 27**

Tan, Amy 1952- .... **CLC 59**
See also AAYA 9; BEST 89:3; CA 136;
SATA 75

Tandem, Felix
See Spitteler, Carl (Friedrich Georg)

Tanizaki, Jun'ichiro
1886-1965 .... **CLC 8, 14, 28**
See also CA 93-96; 25-28R

Tanner, William
See Amis, Kingsley (William)

Tao Lao
See Storni, Alfonsina

Tarassoff, Lev
See Troyat, Henri

Tarbell, Ida M(inerva)
1857-1944 .... **TCLC 40**
See also CA 122; DLB 47

Tarkington, (Newton) Booth
1869-1946 .... **TCLC 9**
See also CA 110; 143; DLB 9, 102;
SATA 17

Tarkovsky, Andrei (Arsenyevich)
1932-1986 .... **CLC 75**
See also CA 127

Tartt, Donna 1964(?)- .... **CLC 76**
See also CA 142

Tasso, Torquato 1544-1595 .... **LC 5**

Tate, (John Orley) Allen
1899-1979 .... **CLC 2, 4, 6, 9, 11, 14, 24**
See also CA 5-8R; 85-88; CANR 32;
DLB 4, 45, 63; MTCW

Tate, Ellalice
See Hibbert, Eleanor Alice Burford

Tate, James (Vincent) 1943- ... **CLC 2, 6, 25**
See also CA 21-24R; CANR 29; DLB 5

Tavel, Ronald 1940- .... **CLC 6**
See also CA 21-24R; CANR 33

Taylor, Cecil Philip 1929-1981 ..... **CLC 27**
See also CA 25-28R; 105

Taylor, Edward 1642(?)-1729.... **LC 11; DA**
See also DLB 24

Taylor, Eleanor Ross 1920- .... **CLC 5**
See also CA 81-84

Taylor, Elizabeth 1912-1975 ... **CLC 2, 4, 29**
See also CA 13-16R; CANR 9; DLB 139;
MTCW; SATA 13

Taylor, Henry (Splawn) 1942- ...... **CLC 44**
See also CA 33-36R; CAAS 7; CANR 31;
DLB 5

Taylor, Kamala (Purnaiya) 1924-
See Markandaya, Kamala
See also CA 77-80

Taylor, Mildred D. .... **CLC 21**
See also AAYA 10; BW 1; CA 85-88;
CANR 25; CLR 9; DLB 52; JRDA;
MAICYA; SAAS 5; SATA 15, 70

Taylor, Peter (Hillsman)
1917- ...... **CLC 1, 4, 18, 37, 44, 50, 71;
SSC 10**
See also CA 13-16R; CANR 9; DLBY 81;
MTCW

Taylor, Robert Lewis 1912- .... **CLC 14**
See also CA 1-4R; CANR 3; SATA 10

Tchekhov, Anton
See Chekhov, Anton (Pavlovich)

Teasdale, Sara 1884-1933.......... **TCLC 4**
See also CA 104; DLB 45; SATA 32

Tegner, Esaias 1782-1846........ **NCLC 2**

Teilhard de Chardin, (Marie Joseph) Pierre
1881-1955 .... **TCLC 9**
See also CA 105

Temple, Ann
See Mortimer, Penelope (Ruth)

Tennant, Emma (Christina)
1937- .... **CLC 13, 52**
See also CA 65-68; CAAS 9; CANR 10, 38;
DLB 14

Tenneshaw, S. M.
See Silverberg, Robert

Tennyson, Alfred
1809-1892 .. **NCLC 30; DA; PC 6; WLC**
See also CDBLB 1832-1890; DLB 32

Teran, Lisa St. Aubin de .... **CLC 36**
See also St. Aubin de Teran, Lisa

Teresa de Jesus, St. 1515-1582 ...... **LC 18**

Terkel, Louis 1912-
See Terkel, Studs
See also CA 57-60; CANR 18, 45; MTCW

Terkel, Studs .... **CLC 38**
See also Terkel, Louis
See also AITN 1

Terry, C. V.
See Slaughter, Frank G(ill)

Terry, Megan 1932- .... **CLC 19**
See also CA 77-80; CABS 3; CANR 43;
DLB 7

Tertz, Abram
See Sinyavsky, Andrei (Donatevich)

Tesich, Steve 1943(?)-.......... **CLC 40, 69**
See also CA 105; DLBY 83

Teternikov, Fyodor Kuzmich 1863-1927
See Sologub, Fyodor
See also CA 104

Tevis, Walter 1928-1984 .... **CLC 42**
See also CA 113

Tey, Josephine.................. **TCLC 14**
See also Mackintosh, Elizabeth
See also DLB 77

Thackeray, William Makepeace
1811-1863 .... **NCLC 5, 14, 22, 43; DA;
WLC**
See also CDBLB 1832-1890; DLB 21, 55;
SATA 23

Thakura, Ravindranatha
See Tagore, Rabindranath

Tharoor, Shashi 1956- .... **CLC 70**
See also CA 141

Thelwell, Michael Miles 1939- ..... **CLC 22**
See also BW 2; CA 101

Theobald, Lewis, Jr.
See Lovecraft, H(oward) P(hillips)

Theodorescu, Ion N. 1880-1967
See Arghezi, Tudor
See also CA 116

Theriault, Yves 1915-1983........ **CLC 79**
See also CA 102; DLB 88

Theroux, Alexander (Louis)
1939- .... **CLC 2, 25**
See also CA 85-88; CANR 20

Vonnegut, Kurt, Jr.
    1922- . . . . . . **CLC 1, 2, 3, 4, 5, 8, 12, 22,**
        40, 60; DA; SSC 8; WLC
    See also AAYA 6; AITN 1; BEST 90:4;
        CA 1-4R; CANR 1, 25;
        CDALB 1968-1988; DLB 2, 8; DLBD 3;
        DLBY 80; MTCW

Von Rachen, Kurt
    See Hubbard, L(afayette) Ron(ald)

von Rezzori (d'Arezzo), Gregor
    See Rezzori (d'Arezzo), Gregor von

von Sternberg, Josef
    See Sternberg, Josef von

Vorster, Gordon 1924- . . . . **CLC 34**
    See also CA 133

Vosce, Trudie
    See Ozick, Cynthia

Voznesensky, Andrei (Andreievich)
    1933- . . . . **CLC 1, 15, 57**
    See also CA 89-92; CANR 37; MTCW

Waddington, Miriam 1917- . . . . **CLC 28**
    See also CA 21-24R; CANR 12, 30;
        DLB 68

Wagman, Fredrica 1937- . . . . **CLC 7**
    See also CA 97-100

Wagner, Richard 1813-1883 . . . . . . **NCLC 9**
    See also DLB 129

Wagner-Martin, Linda 1936- . . . . . . **CLC 50**

Wagoner, David (Russell)
    1926- . . . . **CLC 3, 5, 15**
    See also CA 1-4R; CAAS 3; CANR 2;
        DLB 5; SATA 14

Wah, Fred(erick James) 1939- . . . . . . **CLC 44**
    See also CA 107; 141; DLB 60

Wahloo, Per 1926-1975 . . . . **CLC 7**
    See also CA 61-64

Wahloo, Peter
    See Wahloo, Per

Wain, John (Barrington)
    1925- . . . . **CLC 2, 11, 15, 46**
    See also CA 5-8R; CAAS 4; CANR 23;
        CDBLB 1960 to Present; DLB 15, 27,
        139; MTCW

Wajda, Andrzej 1926- . . . . **CLC 16**
    See also CA 102

Wakefield, Dan 1932- . . . . **CLC 7**
    See also CA 21-24R; CAAS 7

Wakoski, Diane
    1937- . . . . **CLC 2, 4, 7, 9, 11, 40**
    See also CA 13-16R; CAAS 1; CANR 9;
        DLB 5

Wakoski-Sherbell, Diane
    See Wakoski, Diane

Walcott, Derek (Alton)
    1930- . . . . **CLC 2, 4, 9, 14, 25, 42, 67, 76;**
        BLC
    See also BW 2; CA 89-92; CANR 26;
        DLB 117; DLBY 81; MTCW

Waldman, Anne 1945- . . . . **CLC 7**
    See also CA 37-40R; CAAS 17; CANR 34;
        DLB 16

Waldo, E. Hunter
    See Sturgeon, Theodore (Hamilton)

Waldo, Edward Hamilton
    See Sturgeon, Theodore (Hamilton)

Walker, Alice (Malsenior)
    1944- . . . . **CLC 5, 6, 9, 19, 27, 46, 58;**
        BLC; DA; SSC 5
    See also AAYA 3; BEST 89:4; BW 2;
        CA 37-40R; CANR 9, 27;
        CDALB 1968-1988; DLB 6, 33, 143;
        MTCW; SATA 31

Walker, David Harry 1911-1992 . . . . **CLC 14**
    See also CA 1-4R; 137; CANR 1; SATA 8;
        SATA-Obit 71

Walker, Edward Joseph 1934-
    See Walker, Ted
    See also CA 21-24R; CANR 12, 28

Walker, George F. 1947- . . . . **CLC 44, 61**
    See also CA 103; CANR 21, 43; DLB 60

Walker, Joseph A. 1935- . . . . **CLC 19**
    See also BW 1; CA 89-92; CANR 26;
        DLB 38

Walker, Margaret (Abigail)
    1915- . . . . **CLC 1, 6; BLC**
    See also BW 2; CA 73-76; CANR 26;
        DLB 76; MTCW

Walker, Ted . . . . **CLC 13**
    See also Walker, Edward Joseph
    See also DLB 40

Wallace, David Foster 1962- . . . . **CLC 50**
    See also CA 132

Wallace, Dexter
    See Masters, Edgar Lee

Wallace, Irving 1916-1990 . . . . **CLC 7, 13**
    See also AITN 1; CA 1-4R; 132; CAAS 1;
        CANR 1, 27; MTCW

Wallant, Edward Lewis
    1926-1962 . . . . **CLC 5, 10**
    See also CA 1-4R; CANR 22; DLB 2, 28,
        143; MTCW

Walpole, Horace 1717-1797 . . . . **LC 2**
    See also DLB 39, 104

Walpole, Hugh (Seymour)
    1884-1941 . . . . **TCLC 5**
    See also CA 104; DLB 34

Walser, Martin 1927- . . . . **CLC 27**
    See also CA 57-60; CANR 8; DLB 75, 124

Walser, Robert 1878-1956 . . . . **TCLC 18**
    See also CA 118; DLB 66

Walsh, Jill Paton . . . . **CLC 35**
    See also Paton Walsh, Gillian
    See also AAYA 11; CLR 2; SAAS 3

Walter, Villiam Christian
    See Andersen, Hans Christian

Wambaugh, Joseph (Aloysius, Jr.)
    1937- . . . . **CLC 3, 18**
    See also AITN 1; BEST 89:3; CA 33-36R;
        CANR 42; DLB 6; DLBY 83; MTCW

Ward, Arthur Henry Sarsfield 1883-1959
    See Rohmer, Sax
    See also CA 108

Ward, Douglas Turner 1930- . . . . **CLC 19**
    See also BW 1; CA 81-84; CANR 27;
        DLB 7, 38

Ward, Mary Augusta
    See Ward, Mrs. Humphry

Ward, Mrs. Humphry
    1851-1920 . . . . **TCLC 55**
    See also DLB 18

Ward, Peter
    See Faust, Frederick (Schiller)

Warhol, Andy 1928(?)-1987 . . . . **CLC 20**
    See also AAYA 12; BEST 89:4; CA 89-92;
        121; CANR 34

Warner, Francis (Robert le Plastrier)
    1937- . . . . **CLC 14**
    See also CA 53-56; CANR 11

Warner, Marina 1946- . . . . **CLC 59**
    See also CA 65-68; CANR 21

Warner, Rex (Ernest) 1905-1986 . . . . **CLC 45**
    See also CA 89-92; 119; DLB 15

Warner, Susan (Bogert)
    1819-1885 . . . . **NCLC 31**
    See also DLB 3, 42

Warner, Sylvia (Constance) Ashton
    See Ashton-Warner, Sylvia (Constance)

Warner, Sylvia Townsend
    1893-1978 . . . . **CLC 7, 19**
    See also CA 61-64; 77-80; CANR 16;
        DLB 34, 139; MTCW

Warren, Mercy Otis 1728-1814 . . . **NCLC 13**
    See also DLB 31

Warren, Robert Penn
    1905-1989 . . . . **CLC 1, 4, 6, 8, 10, 13, 18,**
        39, 53, 59; DA; SSC 4; WLC
    See also AITN 1; CA 13-16R; 129;
        CANR 10; CDALB 1968-1988; DLB 2,
        48; DLBY 80, 89; MTCW; SATA 46, 63

Warshofsky, Isaac
    See Singer, Isaac Bashevis

Warton, Thomas 1728-1790 . . . . **LC 15**
    See also DLB 104, 109

Waruk, Kona
    See Harris, (Theodore) Wilson

Warung, Price 1855-1911 . . . . **TCLC 45**

Warwick, Jarvis
    See Garner, Hugh

Washington, Alex
    See Harris, Mark

Washington, Booker T(aliaferro)
    1856-1915 . . . . **TCLC 10; BLC**
    See also BW 1; CA 114; 125; SATA 28

Washington, George 1732-1799 . . . . . . **LC 25**
    See also DLB 31

Wassermann, (Karl) Jakob
    1873-1934 . . . . **TCLC 6**
    See also CA 104; DLB 66

Wasserstein, Wendy
    1950- . . . . **CLC 32, 59; DC 4**
    See also CA 121; 129; CABS 3

Waterhouse, Keith (Spencer)
    1929- . . . . **CLC 47**
    See also CA 5-8R; CANR 38; DLB 13, 15;
        MTCW

Waters, Roger 1944- . . . . **CLC 35**
    See also Pink Floyd

Watkins, Frances Ellen
    See Harper, Frances Ellen Watkins

Watkins, Gerrold
    See Malzberg, Barry N(athaniel)

Watkins, Paul 1964- . . . . **CLC 55**
    See also CA 132

Watkins, Vernon Phillips
1906-1967 . . . . **CLC 43**
See also CA 9-10; 25-28R; CAP 1; DLB 20

Watson, Irving S.
See Mencken, H(enry) L(ouis)

Watson, John H.
See Farmer, Philip Jose

Watson, Richard F.
See Silverberg, Robert

Waugh, Auberon (Alexander) 1939- . . **CLC 7**
See also CA 45-48; CANR 6, 22; DLB 14

Waugh, Evelyn (Arthur St. John)
1903-1966 . . . . . . **CLC 1, 3, 8, 13, 19, 27,
44; DA; WLC**
See also CA 85-88; 25-28R; CANR 22;
CDBLB 1914-1945; DLB 15; MTCW

Waugh, Harriet 1944- . . . . **CLC 6**
See also CA 85-88; CANR 22

Ways, C. R.
See Blount, Roy (Alton), Jr.

Waystaff, Simon
See Swift, Jonathan

Webb, (Martha) Beatrice (Potter)
1858-1943 . . . . **TCLC 22**
See also Potter, Beatrice
See also CA 117

Webb, Charles (Richard) 1939- . . . . . . **CLC 7**
See also CA 25-28R

Webb, James H(enry), Jr. 1946- . . . . **CLC 22**
See also CA 81-84

Webb, Mary (Gladys Meredith)
1881-1927 . . . . **TCLC 24**
See also CA 123; DLB 34

Webb, Mrs. Sidney
See Webb, (Martha) Beatrice (Potter)

Webb, Phyllis 1927- . . . . **CLC 18**
See also CA 104; CANR 23; DLB 53

Webb, Sidney (James)
1859-1947 . . . . **TCLC 22**
See also CA 117

Webber, Andrew Lloyd . . . . **CLC 21**
See also Lloyd Webber, Andrew

Weber, Lenora Mattingly
1895-1971 . . . . **CLC 12**
See also CA 19-20; 29-32R; CAP 1;
SATA 2, 26

Webster, John 1579(?)-1634(?) . . . . **DC 2**
See also CDBLB Before 1660; DA; DLB 58;
WLC

Webster, Noah 1758-1843 . . . . **NCLC 30**

Wedekind, (Benjamin) Frank(lin)
1864-1918 . . . . **TCLC 7**
See also CA 104; DLB 118

Weidman, Jerome 1913- . . . . **CLC 7**
See also AITN 2; CA 1-4R; CANR 1;
DLB 28

Weil, Simone (Adolphine)
1909-1943 . . . . **TCLC 23**
See also CA 117

Weinstein, Nathan
See West, Nathanael

Weinstein, Nathan von Wallenstein
See West, Nathanael

Weir, Peter (Lindsay) 1944- . . . . **CLC 20**
See also CA 113; 123

Weiss, Peter (Ulrich)
1916-1982 . . . . **CLC 3, 15, 51**
See also CA 45-48; 106; CANR 3; DLB 69,
124

Weiss, Theodore (Russell)
1916- . . . . **CLC 3, 8, 14**
See also CA 9-12R; CAAS 2; DLB 5

Welch, (Maurice) Denton
1915-1948 . . . . **TCLC 22**
See also CA 121

Welch, James 1940- . . . . **CLC 6, 14, 52**
See also CA 85-88; CANR 42

Weldon, Fay
1933(?)- . . . . . . **CLC 6, 9, 11, 19, 36, 59**
See also CA 21-24R; CANR 16;
CDBLB 1960 to Present; DLB 14;
MTCW

Wellek, Rene 1903- . . . . **CLC 28**
See also CA 5-8R; CAAS 7; CANR 8;
DLB 63

Weller, Michael 1942- . . . . **CLC 10, 53**
See also CA 85-88

Weller, Paul 1958- . . . . **CLC 26**

Wellershoff, Dieter 1925- . . . . **CLC 46**
See also CA 89-92; CANR 16, 37

Welles, (George) Orson
1915-1985 . . . . **CLC 20, 80**
See also CA 93-96; 117

Wellman, Mac 1945- . . . . **CLC 65**

Wellman, Manly Wade 1903-1986 . . **CLC 49**
See also CA 1-4R; 118; CANR 6, 16, 44;
SATA 6, 47

Wells, Carolyn 1869(?)-1942 . . . . . . **TCLC 35**
See also CA 113; DLB 11

Wells, H(erbert) G(eorge)
1866-1946 . . . . **TCLC 6, 12, 19; DA;
SSC 6; WLC**
See also CA 110; 121; CDBLB 1914-1945;
DLB 34, 70; MTCW; SATA 20

Wells, Rosemary 1943- . . . . **CLC 12**
See also CA 85-88; CLR 16; MAICYA;
SAAS 1; SATA 18, 69

Welty, Eudora
1909- . . . . . . **CLC 1, 2, 5, 14, 22, 33; DA;
SSC 1; WLC**
See also CA 9-12R; CABS 1; CANR 32;
CDALB 1941-1968; DLB 2, 102, 143;
DLBY 87; MTCW

Wen I-to 1899-1946 . . . . **TCLC 28**

Wentworth, Robert
See Hamilton, Edmond

Werfel, Franz (V.) 1890-1945 . . . . . . **TCLC 8**
See also CA 104; DLB 81, 124

Wergeland, Henrik Arnold
1808-1845 . . . . **NCLC 5**

Wersba, Barbara 1932- . . . . **CLC 30**
See also AAYA 2; CA 29-32R; CANR 16,
38; CLR 3; DLB 52; JRDA; MAICYA;
SAAS 2; SATA 1, 58

Wertmueller, Lina 1928- . . . . **CLC 16**
See also CA 97-100; CANR 39

Wescott, Glenway 1901-1987 . . . . **CLC 13**
See also CA 13-16R; 121; CANR 23;
DLB 4, 9, 102

Wesker, Arnold 1932- . . . . **CLC 3, 5, 42**
See also CA 1-4R; CAAS 7; CANR 1, 33;
CDBLB 1960 to Present; DLB 13;
MTCW

Wesley, Richard (Errol) 1945- . . . . . . **CLC 7**
See also BW 1; CA 57-60; CANR 27;
DLB 38

Wessel, Johan Herman 1742-1785 . . . . **LC 7**

West, Anthony (Panther)
1914-1987 . . . . **CLC 50**
See also CA 45-48; 124; CANR 3, 19;
DLB 15

West, C. P.
See Wodehouse, P(elham) G(renville)

West, (Mary) Jessamyn
1902-1984 . . . . **CLC 7, 17**
See also CA 9-12R; 112; CANR 27; DLB 6;
DLBY 84; MTCW; SATA 37

West, Morris L(anglo) 1916- . . . . . **CLC 6, 33**
See also CA 5-8R; CANR 24; MTCW

West, Nathanael
1903-1940 . . . . . **TCLC 1, 14, 44; SSC 16**
See also CA 104; 125; CDALB 1929-1941;
DLB 4, 9, 28; MTCW

West, Owen
See Koontz, Dean R(ay)

West, Paul 1930- . . . . **CLC 7, 14**
See also CA 13-16R; CAAS 7; CANR 22;
DLB 14

West, Rebecca 1892-1983 . . **CLC 7, 9, 31, 50**
See also CA 5-8R; 109; CANR 19; DLB 36;
DLBY 83; MTCW

Westall, Robert (Atkinson)
1929-1993 . . . . **CLC 17**
See also AAYA 12; CA 69-72; 141;
CANR 18; CLR 13; JRDA; MAICYA;
SAAS 2; SATA 23, 69; SATA-Obit 75

Westlake, Donald E(dwin)
1933- . . . . **CLC 7, 33**
See also CA 17-20R; CAAS 13; CANR 16,
44

Westmacott, Mary
See Christie, Agatha (Mary Clarissa)

Weston, Allen
See Norton, Andre

Wetcheek, J. L.
See Feuchtwanger, Lion

Wetering, Janwillem van de
See van de Wetering, Janwillem

Wetherell, Elizabeth
See Warner, Susan (Bogert)

Whalen, Philip 1923- . . . . **CLC 6, 29**
See also CA 9-12R; CANR 5, 39; DLB 16

Wharton, Edith (Newbold Jones)
1862-1937 . . . . . . **TCLC 3, 9, 27, 53; DA;
SSC 6; WLC**
See also CA 104; 132; CDALB 1865-1917;
DLB 4, 9, 12, 78; MTCW

Wharton, James
See Mencken, H(enry) L(ouis)

Wharton, William (a pseudonym)
.... CLC 18, 37
See also CA 93-96; DLBY 80

Wheatley (Peters), Phillis
1754(?)-1784 .... LC 3; BLC; DA; PC 3;
WLC
See also CDALB 1640-1865; DLB 31, 50

Wheelock, John Hall 1886-1978 .... CLC 14
See also CA 13-16R; 77-80; CANR 14;
DLB 45

White, E(lwyn) B(rooks)
1899-1985 .... CLC 10, 34, 39
See also AITN 2; CA 13-16R; 116;
CANR 16, 37; CLR 1, 21; DLB 11, 22;
MAICYA; MTCW; SATA 2, 29, 44

White, Edmund (Valentine III)
1940- .... CLC 27
See also AAYA 7; CA 45-48; CANR 3, 19,
36; MTCW

White, Patrick (Victor Martindale)
1912-1990 .. CLC 3, 4, 5, 7, 9, 18, 65, 69
See also CA 81-84; 132; CANR 43; MTCW

White, Phyllis Dorothy James 1920-
See James, P. D.
See also CA 21-24R; CANR 17, 43; MTCW

White, T(erence) H(anbury)
1906-1964 .... CLC 30
See also CA 73-76; CANR 37; JRDA;
MAICYA; SATA 12

White, Terence de Vere 1912- ...... CLC 49
See also CA 49-52; CANR 3

White, Walter F(rancis)
1893-1955 .... TCLC 15
See also White, Walter
See also BW 1; CA 115; 124; DLB 51

White, William Hale 1831-1913
See Rutherford, Mark
See also CA 121

Whitehead, E(dward) A(nthony)
1933- .... CLC 5
See also CA 65-68

Whitemore, Hugh (John) 1936- ..... CLC 37
See also CA 132

Whitman, Sarah Helen (Power)
1803-1878 .... NCLC 19
See also DLB 1

Whitman, Walt(er)
1819-1892 ..... NCLC 4, 31; DA; PC 3;
WLC
See also CDALB 1640-1865; DLB 3, 64;
SATA 20

Whitney, Phyllis A(yame) 1903- .... CLC 42
See also AITN 2; BEST 90:3; CA 1-4R;
CANR 3, 25, 38; JRDA; MAICYA;
SATA 1, 30

Whittemore, (Edward) Reed (Jr.)
1919- .... CLC 4
See also CA 9-12R; CAAS 8; CANR 4;
DLB 5

Whittier, John Greenleaf
1807-1892 .... NCLC 8
See also CDALB 1640-1865; DLB 1

Whittlebot, Hernia
See Coward, Noel (Peirce)

Wicker, Thomas Grey 1926-
See Wicker, Tom
See also CA 65-68; CANR 21

Wicker, Tom .... CLC 7
See also Wicker, Thomas Grey

Wideman, John Edgar
1941- .... CLC 5, 34, 36, 67; BLC
See also BW 2; CA 85-88; CANR 14, 42;
DLB 33, 143

Wiebe, Rudy (Henry) 1934-... CLC 6, 11, 14
See also CA 37-40R; CANR 42; DLB 60

Wieland, Christoph Martin
1733-1813 .... NCLC 17
See also DLB 97

Wiene, Robert 1881-1938 .... TCLC 56

Wieners, John 1934- .... CLC 7
See also CA 13-16R; DLB 16

Wiesel, Elie(zer)
1928- .... CLC 3, 5, 11, 37; DA
See also AAYA 7; AITN 1; CA 5-8R;
CAAS 4; CANR 8, 40; DLB 83;
DLBY 87; MTCW; SATA 56

Wiggins, Marianne 1947- .... CLC 57
See also BEST 89:3; CA 130

Wight, James Alfred 1916-
See Herriot, James
See also CA 77-80; SATA 44, 55

Wilbur, Richard (Purdy)
1921- .... CLC 3, 6, 9, 14, 53; DA
See also CA 1-4R; CABS 2; CANR 2, 29;
DLB 5; MTCW; SATA 9

Wild, Peter 1940- .... CLC 14
See also CA 37-40R; DLB 5

Wilde, Oscar (Fingal O'Flahertie Wills)
1854(?)-1900 .... TCLC 1, 8, 23, 41; DA;
SSC 11; WLC
See also CA 104; 119; CDBLB 1890-1914;
DLB 10, 19, 34, 57, 141; SATA 24

Wilder, Billy .... CLC 20
See also Wilder, Samuel
See also DLB 26

Wilder, Samuel 1906-
See Wilder, Billy
See also CA 89-92

Wilder, Thornton (Niven)
1897-1975 ...... CLC 1, 5, 6, 10, 15, 35,
82; DA; DC 1; WLC
See also AITN 2; CA 13-16R; 61-64;
CANR 40; DLB 4, 7, 9; MTCW

Wilding, Michael 1942- .... CLC 73
See also CA 104; CANR 24

Wiley, Richard 1944- .... CLC 44
See also CA 121; 129

Wilhelm, Kate .... CLC 7
See also Wilhelm, Katie Gertrude
See also CAAS 5; DLB 8

Wilhelm, Katie Gertrude 1928-
See Wilhelm, Kate
See also CA 37-40R; CANR 17, 36; MTCW

Wilkins, Mary
See Freeman, Mary Eleanor Wilkins

Willard, Nancy 1936- .... CLC 7, 37
See also CA 89-92; CANR 10, 39; CLR 5;
DLB 5, 52; MAICYA; MTCW;
SATA 30, 37, 71

Williams, C(harles) K(enneth)
1936- .... CLC 33, 56
See also CA 37-40R; DLB 5

Williams, Charles
See Collier, James L(incoln)

Williams, Charles (Walter Stansby)
1886-1945 .... TCLC 1, 11
See also CA 104; DLB 100

Williams, (George) Emlyn
1905-1987 .... CLC 15
See also CA 104; 123; CANR 36; DLB 10,
77; MTCW

Williams, Hugo 1942- .... CLC 42
See also CA 17-20R; CANR 45; DLB 40

Williams, J. Walker
See Wodehouse, P(elham) G(renville)

Williams, John A(lfred)
1925- .... CLC 5, 13; BLC
See also BW 2; CA 53-56; CAAS 3;
CANR 6, 26; DLB 2, 33

Williams, Jonathan (Chamberlain)
1929- .... CLC 13
See also CA 9-12R; CAAS 12; CANR 8;
DLB 5

Williams, Joy 1944- .... CLC 31
See also CA 41-44R; CANR 22

Williams, Norman 1952- .... CLC 39
See also CA 118

Williams, Tennessee
1911-1983 ..... CLC 1, 2, 5, 7, 8, 11, 15,
19, 30, 39, 45, 71; DA; DC 4; WLC
See also AITN 1, 2; CA 5-8R; 108;
CABS 3; CANR 31; CDALB 1941-1968;
DLB 7; DLBD 4; DLBY 83; MTCW

Williams, Thomas (Alonzo)
1926-1990 .... CLC 14
See also CA 1-4R; 132; CANR 2

Williams, William C.
See Williams, William Carlos

Williams, William Carlos
1883-1963 .... CLC 1, 2, 5, 9, 13, 22, 42,
67; DA; PC 7
See also CA 89-92; CANR 34;
CDALB 1917-1929; DLB 4, 16, 54, 86;
MTCW

Williamson, David (Keith) 1942-.... CLC 56
See also CA 103; CANR 41

Williamson, Jack.................. CLC 29
See also Williamson, John Stewart
See also CAAS 8; DLB 8

Williamson, John Stewart 1908-
See Williamson, Jack
See also CA 17-20R; CANR 23

Willie, Frederick
See Lovecraft, H(oward) P(hillips)

Willingham, Calder (Baynard, Jr.)
1922- .... CLC 5, 51
See also CA 5-8R; CANR 3; DLB 2, 44;
MTCW

Willis, Charles
See Clarke, Arthur C(harles)

Willy
See Colette, (Sidonie-Gabrielle)

Willy, Colette
See Colette, (Sidonie-Gabrielle)

Wyss, Johann David Von
 1743-1818 .... **NCLC 10**
 See also JRDA; MAICYA; SATA 27, 29

Yakumo Koizumi
 See Hearn, (Patricio) Lafcadio (Tessima
 Carlos)

Yanez, Jose Donoso
 See Donoso (Yanez), Jose

Yanovsky, Basile S.
 See Yanovsky, V(assily) S(emenovich)

Yanovsky, V(assily) S(emenovich)
 1906-1989 .... **CLC 2, 18**
 See also CA 97-100; 129

Yates, Richard 1926-1992 ..... **CLC 7, 8, 23**
 See also CA 5-8R; 139; CANR 10, 43;
 DLB 2; DLBY 81, 92

Yeats, W. B.
 See Yeats, William Butler

Yeats, William Butler
 1865-1939 ..... **TCLC 1, 11, 18, 31; DA;
 WLC**
 See also CA 104; 127; CANR 45;
 CDBLB 1890-1914; DLB 10, 19, 98;
 MTCW

Yehoshua, A(braham) B.
 1936- .... **CLC 13, 31**
 See also CA 33-36R; CANR 43

Yep, Laurence Michael 1948- ...... **CLC 35**
 See also AAYA 5; CA 49-52; CANR 1;
 CLR 3, 17; DLB 52; JRDA; MAICYA;
 SATA 7, 69

Yerby, Frank G(arvin)
 1916-1991 .... **CLC 1, 7, 22; BLC**
 See also BW 1; CA 9-12R; 136; CANR 16;
 DLB 76; MTCW

Yesenin, Sergei Alexandrovich
 See Esenin, Sergei (Alexandrovich)

Yevtushenko, Yevgeny (Alexandrovich)
 1933- .... **CLC 1, 3, 13, 26, 51**
 See also CA 81-84; CANR 33; MTCW

Yezierska, Anzia 1885(?)-1970 ..... **CLC 46**
 See also CA 126; 89-92; DLB 28; MTCW

Yglesias, Helen 1915- .... **CLC 7, 22**
 See also CA 37-40R; CANR 15; MTCW

Yokomitsu Riichi 1898-1947 ...... **TCLC 47**

Yonge, Charlotte (Mary)
 1823-1901 .... **TCLC 48**
 See also CA 109; DLB 18; SATA 17

York, Jeremy
 See Creasey, John

York, Simon
 See Heinlein, Robert A(nson)

Yorke, Henry Vincent 1905-1974 ... **CLC 13**
 See also Green, Henry
 See also CA 85-88; 49-52

Yoshimoto, Banana .... **CLC 84**
 See also Yoshimoto, Mahoko

Yoshimoto, Mahoko 1964-
 See Yoshimoto, Banana
 See also CA 144

Young, Al(bert James)
 1939- .... **CLC 19; BLC**
 See also BW 2; CA 29-32R; CANR 26;
 DLB 33

Young, Andrew (John) 1885-1971 .... **CLC 5**
 See also CA 5-8R; CANR 7, 29

Young, Collier
 See Bloch, Robert (Albert)

Young, Edward 1683-1765 .... **LC 3**
 See also DLB 95

Young, Marguerite 1909- .... **CLC 82**
 See also CA 13-16; CAP 1

Young, Neil 1945- .... **CLC 17**
 See also CA 110

Yourcenar, Marguerite
 1903-1987 .... **CLC 19, 38, 50**
 See also CA 69-72; CANR 23; DLB 72;
 DLBY 88; MTCW

Yurick, Sol 1925- .... **CLC 6**
 See also CA 13-16R; CANR 25

Zabolotskii, Nikolai Alekseevich
 1903-1958 .... **TCLC 52**
 See also CA 116

Zamiatin, Yevgenii
 See Zamyatin, Evgeny Ivanovich

Zamyatin, Evgeny Ivanovich
 1884-1937 .... **TCLC 8, 37**
 See also CA 105

Zangwill, Israel 1864-1926 .... **TCLC 16**
 See also CA 109; DLB 10, 135

Zappa, Francis Vincent, Jr. 1940-1993
 See Zappa, Frank
 See also CA 108; 143

Zappa, Frank .... **CLC 17**
 See also Zappa, Francis Vincent, Jr.

Zaturenska, Marya 1902-1982 .... **CLC 6, 11**
 See also CA 13-16R; 105; CANR 22

Zelazny, Roger (Joseph) 1937- ..... **CLC 21**
 See also AAYA 7; CA 21-24R; CANR 26;
 DLB 8; MTCW; SATA 39, 57

Zhdanov, Andrei A(lexandrovich)
 1896-1948 .... **TCLC 18**
 See also CA 117

Zhukovsky, Vasily 1783-1852 .... **NCLC 35**

Ziegenhagen, Eric .... **CLC 55**

Zimmer, Jill Schary
 See Robinson, Jill

Zimmerman, Robert
 See Dylan, Bob

Zindel, Paul 1936- .... **CLC 6, 26; DA**
 See also AAYA 2; CA 73-76; CANR 31;
 CLR 3; DLB 7, 52; JRDA; MAICYA;
 MTCW; SATA 16, 58

Zinov'Ev, A. A.
 See Zinoviev, Alexander (Aleksandrovich)

Zinoviev, Alexander (Aleksandrovich)
 1922- .... **CLC 19**
 See also CA 116; 133; CAAS 10

Zoilus
 See Lovecraft, H(oward) P(hillips)

Zola, Emile (Edouard Charles Antoine)
 1840-1902 ...... **TCLC 1, 6, 21, 41; DA;
 WLC**
 See also CA 104; 138; DLB 123

Zoline, Pamela 1941- .... **CLC 62**

Zorrilla y Moral, Jose 1817-1893 .. **NCLC 6**

Zoshchenko, Mikhail (Mikhailovich)
 1895-1958 .... **TCLC 15; SSC 15**
 See also CA 115

Zuckmayer, Carl 1896-1977 .... **CLC 18**
 See also CA 69-72; DLB 56, 124

Zuk, Georges
 See Skelton, Robin

Zukofsky, Louis
 1904-1978 .... **CLC 1, 2, 4, 7, 11, 18**
 See also CA 9-12R; 77-80; CANR 39;
 DLB 5; MTCW

Zweig, Paul 1935-1984 .... **CLC 34, 42**
 See also CA 85-88; 113

Zweig, Stefan 1881-1942 .... **TCLC 17**
 See also CA 112; DLB 81, 118

PC Cumulative Nationality Index

PC Cumulative Title Index